PHILIP ROTH

ALSO BY BLAKE BAILEY

The Splendid Things We Planned:
A Family Portrait

Farther and Wilder:
The Lost Weekends and Literary Dreams
of Charles Jackson

Cheever:
A Life

A Tragic Honesty:
The Life and Work of Richard Yates

PHILIP ROTH

The Biography

Blake Bailey

JONATHAN CAPE
LONDON

1 3 5 7 9 10 8 6 4 2

Jonathan Cape, an imprint of Vintage, is part of the Penguin Random House group
of companies whose addresses can be found at global.penguinrandomhouse.com.

Penguin
Random House
UK

First published by Jonathan Cape in 2021

penguin.co.uk/vintage

A CIP catalogue record for this book is available from the British Library

ISBN 9780224098175

Printed and bound in Great Britain by Clays Ltd, Elcograf S.p.A.

The authorised representative in the EEA is Penguin Random House Ireland,
Morrison Chambers, 32 Nassau Street, Dublin DO2 YH68

Penguin Random House is committed to a sustainable future
for our business, our readers and our planet. This book is made
from Forest Stewardship Council® certified paper.

For Mary and Amelia

I don't want you to rehabilitate me.
Just make me interesting.

—Philip Roth to his biographer

CONTENTS

PHILIP ROTH

PROLOGUE

On October 23, 2005, Philip Roth Day was cele-brated in Newark. Two busloads of fans went on the Philip Roth Tour, stopping at evocative locations—Washington Park, the public library, Weequahic High—where passengers took turns reading perti-nent passages from Roth's work. Finally the crowd disembarked outside Roth's childhood home at 81 Summit Avenue, cheering wildly when Roth himself arrived in a limousine. "Now you just step up here and give me a kiss!" said Mrs. Roberta Harrington, the present owner of the house, and Roth kept her at his side the rest of the day. Mayor Sharpe James, whom Roth adored ("a big-city mayor with all the bluster and chicanery"), said a few words before Roth pulled away the black cloth covering the historical plaque on his house: "This was the first childhood home of Philip Roth, one of America's greatest writers of the 20th and 21st centuries. . . ." Next, Roth and the crowd moved across the street to the corner of Summit and Keer, which a white-on-green street sign now proclaimed to be Philip Roth Plaza.

Afterward a reception was held at Roth's childhood library branch, Osborne Terrace, where the mayor rose to the lectern: "Now, you Weequahic boys don't think that us South Side boys know how to read," he said to Roth, referring to the mostly black high school he'd attended around the time Roth had been at Weequahic. Then the mayor read ("wonderfully") a passage from *The Counterlife*:

> "If you're from New Jersey," Nathan had said, "and you write thirty books, and you win the Nobel Prize, and you live to be white-haired and ninety-five, it's highly unlikely but not impossible that after your death they'll decide to name a rest stop for you on the Jersey Turnpike. And so, long after you're gone, you may indeed be remembered, but mostly by small

children, in the backs of cars, when they lean forward and tell their parents, 'Stop, please, stop at Zuckerman—I have to pee.' For a New Jersey novelist that's as much immortality as it's realistic to hope for."

Finally it was Roth's turn to speak: "Today, Newark is my Stockholm, and that plaque is my prize. I couldn't be any more thrilled by any recognition accorded to me anywhere on earth. That's all there is to say." A few days earlier, his friend Harold Pinter had won the Nobel.

"Mr. Roth is a writer whose skill and power are greater than his admittedly great reputation," wrote the eminent critic Frank Kermode, eight years before, after reading *American Pastoral*—Roth's novel about the fall of Newark, and the larger loss of American innocence in the sixties, which would go on to win the Pulitzer. Kermode may have been thinking of an earlier novel, also set in Newark, on which much of Roth's reputation continued to rest: *Portnoy's Complaint*, his 1969 best seller about a mother-haunted, shiksa-chasing Jewish boy who masturbates with a piece of liver ("I fucked my own family's dinner"). Much of what Roth later wrote was in reaction to the mortifying fame of this book—the widespread perception that Roth had written a confession instead of a novel, and never mind the perception among elements of the Jewish establishment that Roth was a propagandist on a par with Goebbels and Streicher. The great Israeli philosopher Gershom Scholem went so far as to suggest that *Portnoy* would trigger something akin to a second Holocaust.

Given his whole magisterial oeuvre—thirty-one books—Roth would earnestly come to wish he'd never published *Portnoy*. "I could have had a serious enough career without it and I would have sidestepped a barrage of insulting shit"—charges of Jewish self-hatred, misogyny, and general unseriousness. "I'd written this book about sex and jerking off and whatever, so I was a kind of clown or fuck artist. But then I finally beat them down. Fuckers."

■　■　■　■

ROTH WAS AMONG the last of a generation of heroically ambitious novelists that included such friends and occasional rivals as John Updike, Don DeLillo, and William Styron (a neighbor in Litchfield County, Connecticut), and arguably Roth's work stands the best chance of enduring. In 2006, *The New York Times Book Review* canvassed some two hundred "writers, critics, editors, and other literary sages," asking them to identify the "single best work of American fiction published in the last twenty-five years." Six of the twenty-two books selected for the final list were written by Roth: *The Counterlife, Operation Shylock, Sabbath's Theater, American Pastoral, The Human Stain,* and *The Plot Against America.* "If we had asked for the single best writer of fiction of the past twenty-five years," A. O. Scott wrote in the accompanying essay, "[Roth] would have won."

But of course Roth's career extended well beyond the prescribed twenty-five years, beginning with *Goodbye, Columbus,* in 1959, for which he won the National Book Award at age twenty-six. His third novel, *Portnoy's Complaint,* was on the 1998 Modern Library list of the 100 best English-language novels of the twentieth century, while *American Pastoral* was, with *Portnoy,* subsequently included on *Time* magazine's 100-best list of 2005. During the fifty-five years of his career, Roth's evolution as a writer was astounding in its versatility: after the deft satire of his early stories in *Goodbye, Columbus,* he went on to write two somber realistic novels (*Letting Go, When She Was Good*) whose main influences were Henry James and Flaubert respectively—an odd apprenticeship, given the outlandish farce of the *Portnoy* era that followed (*Our Gang, The Great American Novel*), the Kafkaesque surrealism of *The Breast,* the comic virtuosity of the Zuckerman sequence (*The Ghost Writer, Zuckerman Unbound, The Anatomy Lesson, The Prague Orgy*), the elaborate metafictional artifice of *The Counterlife* and *Operation Shylock,* and finally a synthesis of all his gifts in the masterly, essentially tragic American Trilogy: *American Pastoral, I Married a Communist,* and *The Human Stain.* In the final decade of his career, Roth continued to produce novels—almost one a year—exploring profound aspects of mortality and fate. Altogether his work forms "the truest picture we have of the way we live now," as the poet Mark Strand put it in his remarks for Roth's Gold Medal at the 2001 American Academy of Arts and Letters ceremonial.

Roth deplored the misconception that he was essentially an autobiographical writer, while making aesthetic hay of the matter with lookalike alter egos that include a recurring character named Philip Roth. Some novels were more autobiographical than others, to be sure, but Roth himself was too protean a figure to be pinned to any particular character, and relatively little is known about the actual life on which so vast an oeuvre was supposedly based. Some of the confusion on this point was deeply embarrassing to the author. "I am not 'Alexander Portnoy' any more than I am the 'Philip Roth' of Claire [Bloom]'s book," he brooded over the actress's scurrilous 1996 memoir, *Leaving a Doll's House*. Were it not for Portnoy, Roth believed, his former wife "would never have dared to perpetrate" a version of himself so blatantly at odds with the "disciplined, steady, and responsible" person he always considered himself to be.

Certainly this is how Roth was portrayed in Janet Hobhouse's posthumous roman à clef, *The Furies*, whose characters include a famous writer named Jack modeled on Roth. He and Hobhouse had had an affair in the mid-1970s—they'd lived in the same building near the Metropolitan Museum—and her portrait remains perhaps the most rounded of a man who, though a household name, stayed largely out of the public eye. While her narrator accounts for the more conventional aspects of Jack/Roth's charm ("not just the speed of his mind, but the playfulness, the willingness to leap, dive, flick the wrist, keep the game going"), she is seduced foremost by his "monkish habits," the way "he organized his existence around the two pages a day he set himself to write": "I thought yearningly of the contained, near-ascetic life going on two floors below me: the sober twilight perusals of literary journals, the rustle of foreign correspondence in a Jamesian high silence."

For what it's worth, Roth perceived himself as the opposite of anti-Semitic or misogynistic, and indeed had little patience for reductive categories one way or the other. His "monkish" lifestyle, for instance: "My reputation as a 'recluse,'" he wrote a friend, "was always idiotic." What it meant, essentially, was that he liked to be "blissfully" occupied with his work in rural surroundings, as opposed to "gossip[ing] about [him]self to people in New York or appear[ing] on late-night TV." In fact he was often intensely engaged with the world, repeatedly traveling to Prague in the seventies and befriending dissident writers such as Milan Kundera and Ludvík Vaculík, whose books he promoted in the West with the Writers from the Other Europe series he edited at Penguin for many years. Also, during his relationship with Bloom, he divided his time among London, New York, and Connecticut, while spending weeks in Israel to research aspects of *The Counterlife* and *Operation Shylock*—or, in the years after, traveling wherever else he wanted to go to learn about glove making or taxidermy or grave digging; he even undertook, once, a reading tour for *Patrimony*, so at least he'd know what that was like, too. But the better part of his career was quite as Hobhouse described it: the daylight hours doggedly spent at his desk, and nights in the company of a woman—both of them reading, if Roth had his way. "What should I have been doing instead so as not to be labeled a recluse," he remarked, "passing my nights at Elaine's?"

It's true Roth managed to have a florid love life, which he was apt to discuss "in a sort of kindly reverie," the way Dr. Johnson bethought himself of Hodge, his favorite cat. An essential side of Roth remained the cherished son of Herman and Bess—"a pleasing, analytic, lovingly manipulative good boy," as his alter ego Zuckerman chidingly describes him in *The Facts*—whose probity was such that he married two disastrously ill-suited women, not least because they desperately wanted him to. (This while refusing any number of more compatible partners.) And meanwhile he steadily rebelled against his own rectitude, quite as the clinical definition of "Portnoy's Complaint" would have it: "A disorder in which strongly-felt ethical and altruistic impulses are perpetually warring with extreme sexual longings, often of a perverse nature." Portnoy, again, is among the least autobiographical of a gallery including Zuckerman, Kepesh, and Tarnopol, but in each character is a kindred duality. As for Roth himself, his greatest urge was always to serve his own genius—amid the keen distractions, albeit, of an ardently carnal nature. "Philip once said something about Colette's husband Willy," said his friend Judith Thurman. "He was talking about the fin de siècle, this world of eroticism, and he said, 'It was so wonderful! They walked around with a buzz twenty-four hours a day.' Meaning a sexual buzz. Think if you have a musical ear, so that you're out in the street and the taxi is C minor and the bus is G major and you're hearing *all* these things, and translate that as a sexual vibe."

■ ■ ■ ■

ALONG WITH THE LIKES OF Willa Cather, William Faulkner, and Saul Bellow, Roth was awarded the Academy of Arts and Letters' highest honor, the Gold Medal in fiction, a year after the completion of his American Trilogy. The following year, 2002, at the National Book

Awards ceremony, Roth received the Medal for Distinguished Contribution to American Letters and used the occasion to correct "a pertinent little misunderstanding": "I have never thought of myself, for the length of a single sentence, as an American Jewish or a Jewish American writer," he wrote in his highly prepared remarks, "anymore than I imagine Theodore Dreiser or Ernest Hemingway or John Cheever thought of themselves as American Christian or Christian American writers." Susan Rogers, his main companion at the time, remembered that Roth worked on the speech for two or three months prior to the ceremony, and read it aloud to her "at least six times."

After his American Trilogy—what some called his "Letter to Stockholm" series—a consensus formed that Roth stood alone among contemporary novelists. Stockholm, however, remained unmoved. "The child in me is delighted," Bellow had said about awards in general and the Nobel in particular; "the adult in me is skeptical." Roth appropriated the remark for his own boilerplate, and meanwhile he couldn't help thinking about the most conspicuous difference in his and Bellow's respective careers—especially after Bellow's widow gave Roth the top hat her husband had worn in Stockholm, which Roth displayed ever after on a stereo speaker in his apartment. (Roth was asked whether it fit his own head: "No, I can't fill Saul's hat," he said. "He's a much better writer.") Toward the end of his life, Roth would walk (very slowly) from his Upper West Side apartment to the Museum of Natural History and back, stopping on almost every bench along the way—including the bench on the museum grounds near a pink pillar listing American winners of the Nobel Prize. "It's actually quite ugly, isn't it?" a friend observed one day. "Yes," Roth replied, "and it's getting uglier by the year." "Why did they put it there anyway?" Roth laughed: "To aggravate me."

PART ONE

LAND HO!

1933–1956

Bess with her adored second-born at Belmar Beach.
"He who is loved by his parents is a conquistador,"
Roth liked to say, amid later glory.

Dᴜʀɪɴɢ ᴀ ᴛʀɪᴘ ᴛᴏ Iꜱʀᴀᴇʟ, ɪɴ 1984, Rᴏᴛʜ ᴛᴏᴏᴋ ʜɪꜱ friend David Plante—a gay, gentile writer—to the Orthodox Quarter of Jerusalem, Mea She'arim, where the two stood on a corner watching Hasidim milling about in their black coats and hats, the boys with their heads shorn except for long side curls. Almost everyone, young and old, wore thick eyeglasses. "You could be in a shtetl in Poland in the eighteenth century," said Roth, whose grandparents had grown up in such a place. One Hasid passed by with a towel over his shoulder, and the writers followed to where the man met other Hasidim for their afternoon bath. "Wait till I get this around," Roth chuckled to his companion, "—Plante standing outside a bathhouse trying to pick up a Hasid."

For Roth, levity was better than nostalgia in the face of this living reminder of his family origins. He could hardly remember his grandparents ever speaking of the old country, of the people they'd left behind, and was left to surmise that the shtetls of Galicia weren't really like the Broadway version of Sholem Aleichem, what with winsome Jews "singing show tunes that brought tears to your eyes," as Roth put it. His father's parents came from an especially bleak corner of that bygone world—Kozłów, near the city of Tarnopol, which is perhaps best remembered (among Jews anyway) as the site of the Khmelnytsky Uprising in the seventeenth century. Throughout the Middle Ages, Polish landowners had employed Jewish agents to collect rents and taxes from the peasantry, who meanwhile were reminded every Sunday, in church, that the Jews had killed Christ. "Pole, Yid, and hound—each to the same faith bound," read the legend commonly nailed to trees where a Pole, Jew, and dog had been hanged. Almost every Jew in Tarnopol was killed or expelled in the massacre, and the city itself was burned to the ground.

By the nineteenth century, Galicia was the northernmost province of the Austro-Hungarian Empire, whose 1867 constitution allowed freedom of religion and equal rights for all subjects. Such liberality did little to improve the lot of Galician Jews, however, whose population exploded with refugees fleeing pogroms in neighboring Russia. Some fifty thousand a year died of starvation, and by the 1880s Galicia had both the highest birth and death rates among the old Polish territories, with only half its children living to the age of five. "Often the relations between the social strata of the shtetl came to little more than a difference between the poor and the hopelessly poor," wrote Irving Howe. Galician Jews usually lived amid a welter of grim huts and cobbled streets winding every which way to a crowded marketplace—a dreary insular world menaced by disorderly gentiles. Solace was found in ritual and piety. A good Jew's life was finely regulated by 613 *mitzvoh*, commandments, everything from reciting blessings for one's homely pleasures to lighting candles and slaughtering chickens just so. Children were cowed with tales of dybbuks and golems, their marriages were arranged, their baser impulses rigorously suppressed. No wonder the more intelligent among them learned to laugh at the wretched way God's chosen people saw fit to live.

The law was embodied by rabbis, and one of these in Kozłów was Roth's great-grandfather, Akiva, who also had a reputation as a storyteller. His son Alexander, called Sender, was studying to be a rabbi when he married, in 1886, Bertha Zahnstecher, whose Flaschner connections on her mother's side would stand the family in good stead once they came to America. Over the course of twenty-five years, Bertha bore nine children with Sender—two of whom, Freide and Pesie, died in infancy; of the surviving seven, Philip Roth's father, Herman, was the first to be born in the New World.

Roth knew even less about his mother's side of the family, and virtually nothing about their origins in the old country. What may be gleaned from basic genealogical data is that Roth's maternal grandfather and namesake, Philip (Farvish) Finkel, was also born near Tarnopol in the town of Bialy Kamien (White Stone), the second of five brothers. As for Roth's maternal grandmother, Dora Eisenberg, she grew up roughly 250 miles away near czarist Kiev, and was almost certainly moved to emigrate, with three sisters and two brothers, to escape the vicious anti-Semitism that prevailed throughout the empire after the assassination of Alexander II, in 1881, by a revolutionary group that czarists claimed (falsely) to be dominated by Jews.

The worst of these pogroms took place in Kiev, where gentile mobs ran amok through Jewish neighborhoods, ransacking shops and the Brodsky vodka warehouse. As if constant terror weren't enough, the May Laws of 1882 effectively prohibited Jews from owning property or pursuing higher professions such as law, government, teaching, or the officer corps. Konstantin Pobedonostsev, the czar's reactionary adviser, proposed a formula for purging the Jews: "One-third conversion, one-third emigration, and one-third starvation." Such was the nightmare some 2.5 million Russian Jews would flee, many seeking refuge in America, between 1881 and 1920.

What Philip Roth heard, growing up, was that both his grandfathers had emigrated to escape conscription. Military service wasn't as punitive for Jewish subjects of the benign Austrian emperor, Franz Joseph, as it was under the czars, but even the relatively lenient three-year period of active duty was longer than most Galician Jews were willing to be parted from family and religion. Nor was the society of gentiles any more comfortable in the army as elsewhere; in Joseph Roth's novel about the decline of the Austro-Hungarian Empire, *The Radetzky March*, a drunken gentile officer insults a Jewish army surgeon, Max Demant—"Yid, Yid, Yid!"—leading to a duel and the doctor's death.

It was common for husbands to emigrate alone and bring their families over later. Sender Roth departed aboard the S.S. *Westernland* on March 5, 1898, more than two years in advance of Bertha and their three boys. One of Bertha's Flaschner uncles had prospered as a shoe merchant in Brockton, Massachusetts, and offered to sponsor Sender's plan to set up as a rabbi in Boston. Aboard the boat, however, Sender apparently had misgivings—rabbis were hardly as revered in America as in Europe, never mind the question of livelihood—and decided to debark at Ellis Island. A landsman aboard the boat had assured Sender that he could get them jobs at a hat factory in East Orange, New Jersey; moreover, Sender's sister Fannie and her husband, Nathan Cohen (later Kuvin), lived in nearby Newark and agreed to let Sender stay with them until he saved enough money to pay his family's passage.

When Philip Finkel received his draft notice, he changed his name to Bara and arranged to follow his older brother, another Nathan, to

Elizabeth, New Jersey. The ruse was also adopted by other Finkel brothers; the last to emigrate, Marcus, was listed as "Barer" when he finally departed from Rotterdam aboard the S.S. *Rijndam* on September 4, 1920.* His last permanent address was given as Zloczow, near Tarnopol, where Jewish refugees from Bialy Kamien had settled after the shtetl was destroyed by fire in 1902.

As for the remaining Jews of Galicia, almost every one of them would perish in the Holocaust—a catastrophe predicted as early as 1923 by the poet Uri Zvi Greenberg, a Bialy Kamien–born Zionist who considered mass extermination the "tragic but almost inevitable outcome of Jewish indifference to their destiny." What became of the remaining eighteen thousand Jews in Tarnopol was typical: five thousand were slaughtered within a month of the Nazi occupation in June 1941, and another thousand were shot in a nearby forest the following March; the rest were packed into a ghetto—Galicia's first—whence they were transported to the Bełżec death camp, among others, before final liquidation on June 20, 1943.

■ ■ ■ ■

BERTHA ROTH LEFT her mother and sisters behind when she emigrated on November 3, 1900—also aboard the *Westernland*—with her sons Kiwe, Mojsche, and Abraham, aged twelve, nine, and three, respectively, and renamed Charlie, Morris, and Ed when they arrived in Newark. Like most Eastern European Jews, they settled amid the slums of the Third Ward, on Broome Street, one block parallel to the sprawling commerce of Prince Street. This re-creation of a shtetl market in America—nicknamed "Baghdad on the Passaic"—was a jumble of pushcarts and stalls hawking everything from live carp, pastrami, and pickles to all sorts of clothing and gadgets, the vendors roughly grabbing at pedestrians to come over and have a look at their wares.

"Do you remember the story you told me about Grandpa?" the nineteen-year-old Philip Roth wrote a dying Bertha in 1952. "It was a

---

* Anne Valentine—one of Roth's first cousins on his mother's side—remembers this as Bara and thinks Barer was probably a misspelling based on a mispronunciation. Her and Philip's maiden aunt, Anita/Honey, used the name professionally and spelled it Bara.

sad and wonderful story about some men that were going to sell Grandpa some property on Baldwin Avenue. And you told me that when Grandpa came to them with the money—and it was a Sunday too—when Grandpa came with the money, which was all he had ever saved, they took the money from him." Despite getting fleeced by goyim in his first attempt to escape the seedy rental flat on Broome, Sender was soon able to buy a house on nearby Rutgers Street. Four more children were born during their fourteen years there—Herman in 1901, Rebecca (Betty) in 1903, Bernard in 1905, and Milton in 1912—while any number of penniless relatives just off the boat, as many as twelve at a time, also came and went. Bertha dutifully cooked and cleaned for them. A stolid *balabusta* (good homemaker) who spoke hardly a word of English, Bertha was given to scrubbing the outside wooden stairs on her knees when otherwise at a loss.

Sender was hardly one to discourage her diligence, and at least one of his children—Philip's kindly Uncle Bernie—despised the old man for the way he treated their saintly mother. But then, Sender himself was no idler: over the years he'd steamed so many hats that one arthritic hand was frozen in a kind of four-finger victory salute. At least he wasn't alone in his labors. Four sons would leave school at an early age to join him in the hat factory, like most children of immigrants in the Newark of that era. Charlie, Morris, and Ed were all working by the age of twelve, whereas Philip Roth's father, Herman ("Little Hymie"), was allowed to remain in school until the statutory age of fourteen. Herman's eighth-grade education was manifest in his erratic spelling and punctuation, as well as a lifelong tendency to capitalize at random ("Why does your father capitalize all these letters?" Neil Klugman asks Brenda, an immigrant's daughter, in *Goodbye, Columbus*). "What's interesting," Roth observed of his father, "is that not in all his years in a responsible managerial position with an important American corporation—nor in all his years of reading the newspaper from cover to cover every single day—did anything about writing English, anything large or small, sink in. Strange, no?" And yet this too was a goad to Roth's literary vocation: "You are *the family voice*," he wrote in a hectoring memo to himself. "Not pushing these men aside, but giving *voice* to their inarticulateness."

"The Newark scramblers" was how Philip described Herman and

his brothers, three of whom—Charlie, Morris, and Milton—he never knew except as family legends. The prodigious Morris left home early and started his own businesses: a movie theater and a shoe-store-cum-factory where tips were put on laces as per his own patent. Morris owned one of the first automobiles in the city and hired a live-in nanny to take care of his four children while his pretty, spendthrift wife, Ella, pursued a hectic social life. His older brother, Charlie, also opened a successful shoe store in another part of town (the better to avoid direct competition with Morris), and also married young and had four children.

At the age of twenty-nine, in 1920, Morris's appendix burst and he died of peritonitis; his wife remarried a bounder named Block, who helped her spend the rest of her late husband's money before deserting her. The four children were raised by various relatives, with Bertha claiming Morris's only son, Gilbert. Sixteen years later, Charlie died of pneumonia in the arms of his brother Herman, who idolized him. Herman's older son, Sandy, eight at the time, never forgot the warm spring day he saw his father shambling back to their house on Summit Avenue, where he collapsed against a porch banister and burst into tears. The boy had never seen his father cry.

Charlie's death, in 1936, was all the more unbearable given that it followed, by four years, perhaps the greatest tragedy of all—the death of the family wunderkind, Milton, at age nineteen. Milton was born twenty-five years after his oldest brother and already had a number of nieces and nephews, roughly his age, who regarded him as a brilliant, lovable brother figure. Milton had graduated high school at the age of sixteen (as would his nephew Philip) and was a senior at the Newark College of Engineering—the first Roth to go to college—when he complained one day of a terrible stomachache and was given an enema by his well-meaning mother. His niece Florence—who'd played violin with Milton and considered his death "the worst tragedy of [her] entire life"—used to say he died of stupidity, given that an enema was hardly the best way to treat what would prove another case of peritonitis.

It was the scourge of the Roth men, whose appendixes tended to be retrocecal—that is, located behind their large intestines, where swelling went undetected until it was too late. Herman was another victim, in 1944, but was saved, barely, by the new sulfa powder. That was the first time Philip would see his father cry: Herman had been given less than a fifty-fifty chance, and returned from the hospital traumatized and thirty pounds lighter ("his shrunken face disclosed itself to us as a replica of my elderly grandmother's"). The next generation would be likewise afflicted.

■ ■ ■ ■

As a CHILD Philip never knew his many Finkel cousins in nearby Elizabeth. Eventually he met a few of them, and thereby cultivated a vague idea of Finkel prosperity—at least in comparison with the "*farsh-tunken*" (stinking) Roths in Newark—but was never quite sure why his sweet-natured maternal grandmother, Dora, had broken all connection with her late husband's family.

On the dining room sideboard, in Philip's childhood home, were portraits of his two namesakes, both dead before he was born: his revered Uncle Milton, of course, who looked a bit like George Gershwin, and his Finkel grandfather, Philip, a dapper, stoutish, dark-haired fellow with a little mustache. Philip and Dora had met and married a few years after immigration, and both spoke a fair amount of English; otherwise Philip was every inch the forbidding, Old World, Orthodox patriarch. His third daughter, Mildred, would forever cringe at the memory of her father grimly swinging a live chicken over their heads on the eve of Yom Kippur, and even the more obscure holidays were observed to a nicety. Many years later, Philip Roth sought out an older Finkel cousin, Ann Maltzman, who surprised him by remarking how much she'd adored his "gentle" grandfather as a little girl.

Philip Roth's mother, Bess (Batya), was born in 1904, the second of five children. At the time, her father owned a grocery and meat market and was flush enough to employ a Russian immigrant named Anna as a live-in servant. By all accounts the extended families on both sides were close, at least for a while, an impression borne out by the startling repetition of names among the offspring: Dora and her two Eisenberg sisters all had daughters named Bess, and the Finkel brothers sired a variety of Mildreds, Ethels, and Emanuels. Elizabeth was mostly an Irish Catholic town, and the cousins confined their socializing almost entirely within the family. The oldest Finkel, Nathan, was likely the most successful: Listed as a "peddler" in the 1903 city directory, he soon had his own real estate business and owned what a grandson described as a "mansion" (since razed) at 1350 North Avenue. He also helped his brothers emigrate, whereupon each did his part to help the others get started. A younger brother, Joseph, began as a butcher in Philip's shop before opening his own grocery on the same street.* The youngest, Michael, was a wholesale butter and egg man, and Marcus, the last to arrive from Europe, owned a flourishing service station and was said to go around in a chauffeur-driven Rolls.

Philip Finkel's career took a curious turn in 1909, when he was suddenly listed as a dealer of "coal, hay, masons' material" at 250 Second Street. His new venture was short-lived, however, and by 1915 he was back on First Street as a grocer—this around the time an advertisement appeared in the October 1 issue of the *New York Lumber Trade Journal*: "Nathan Finkel & Son are conducting a retail lumber yard business at Elizabeth, N. J. Mr. Finkel is well known in Elizabeth, having been engaged in real estate there for more than a score of years. The yard is at Second Street and Port Avenue"—i.e., 250 Second Street, where Philip's yard had been. The nature of this appropriation—whether benevolent, hostile, or a little of both—is unknown. The Finkel "Son" in question was Nathan's oldest, Julius, who was all of nineteen at the time, and had already been collecting rents for his father as a student at Battin High School. In the event, both Nathan and Julius soon returned to real estate full-time, while the coal/lumber business was taken over by Nathan's younger son, Emanuel, who ran it more or less successfully, as Finkel Fuel, until his early death from a heart attack.

After Philip Finkel died, his widow and children almost never mentioned the other Finkels. Philip Roth always assumed a slight class superiority on his mother's side of the family, given her high school education and the evidence of his two grandfathers' portraits: Philip Finkel appeared to be a middle-class European, whereas Sender was a seedier-looking greenhorn in his shiny, wrinkled, ill-fitting suit. Roth's imagination was fired in earnest, however, in 2012, when a Finkel cousin he'd just met (reaching out to such people, at last, in his retirement) showed him a 1927 portrait of his mother in her stunning, lace-train wedding gown, cradling a vast bouquet and standing at the bottom of a rather

---

* The Roths were plagued with appendicitis, the Finkels with heart disease, and Philip Roth would inherit both. The grocer Joseph Finkel, for his part, died of a heart attack at age fifty-four—an end hastened by a robber who locked him in his own freezer overnight.

impressive staircase. "I was dumbstruck," said Roth. "'What hall is this? They rented a hall?'" No, the cousin replied, it was his grandfather Philip's house—all of which was starkly at odds with the relative penury of his grandmother Dora's situation while Roth was a child, to say nothing of his own struggling parents. What little he knew, what little he could find out from a few Finkel cousins, was that a falling-out had taken place among the brothers, who were known to have "crazy tempers" on top of the usual patriarchal bossiness. Roth heard something, too, about Finkel Fuel on Second Street, and thus conceived an idea ("I have pieced this story together out of bits and pieces of information that have come my way over the years") that the brothers had all been coal barons together. "For some reason [Philip Finkel] said 'I'm getting out,'" Roth speculated, "and they gave him his share. He was a rich man"—the wedding gown! the grand staircase!—"so let's say his share was $100,000. . . . That was money in 1927, and he put his money in the stock market. So we know what happened."

Not exactly. What Roth didn't know until even later in life was that his Finkel grandfather dabbled in coal only briefly and was mainly a grocer of whatever means—until 1924, that is, when he belatedly got into the real estate business with Nathan. Perhaps this was the association that led to a definitive breach, but all that a few surviving Finkels can say for sure is that "the family sort of disintegrated," as Anne Valentine put it. Nor is it unreasonable to guess that the Finkel brothers failed to rally around Dora when her husband died of Crohn's disease on June 24, 1929, at age fifty-one—after which the stock market crashed, the Depression began, and Dora and her children moved into a rather shabby two-story at 830 Sheridan Avenue.

As for Finkel Fuel, such as it was: after Emanuel's death it fell into the hands of Marcus's sons, Louis and Joseph, and presently dwindled away. Louis killed himself, and the other Finkels ("miserable and nasty" people, according to one of Marcus's granddaughters) were carried off in droves by heart disease. Bess was always careful not to hurt her mother's feelings by mentioning the in-laws, though she got back in touch with many of her cousins after Dora's death in 1951, especially once she and Herman had retired to Elizabeth in the sixties. Amy Buxbaum (the grocer Joseph Finkel's granddaughter) remembered Bess and her mother, Milly (yet another Mildred), chatting on a bench together almost every day, waiting for Amy to get out of school. But Bess had been dead more than thirty years when her famous son finally cobbled together—by his own lights—the whole riches-to-rags family romance, and by then it was no use to him. "Too bad," he said. "A family of rich relatives and powerful uncles (one chauffeur-driven in a Rolls-Royce!) never to come under the scrutiny of the little budding novelist."

■ ■ ■ ■

THE HIGH STYLE OF Bess Finkel's wedding on February 20, 1927, didn't last. Four years earlier she'd graduated from Battin High and found work as a legal secretary, meanwhile living at home with her parents and older sister, Ethel, whom she helped care for the younger girls, Milly and Honey, and their adored brother, Mickey (yet another Emanuel). During these years Herman Roth had worked as a "shoe dog" in his brother Charlie's store, and after his marriage he opened his own shop on Bloomfield Avenue in Newark. The Roths' first son, Sanford (Sandy), was born December 26, 1927, and a couple of years later the shoe store folded in the Depression. By 1930 all three Roths and four Finkels (Ethel had married and moved out) were crammed into the little house on Sheridan Avenue in Elizabeth, and for a few months Herman took odd jobs such as city marshal and short-order cook.* Finally, through a friend, he was hired as an insurance salesman for Metropolitan Life.

Herman's impressive thirty-six-year career began at rock bottom, working his childhood streets in the Third Ward, nowadays populated mostly by poor black families. "He went around the *shvartzes* and got the pennies," was how his niece Florence indelicately described the task of selling burial insurance six days a week,† especially on Saturday when household heads were likely to be home. It was hard work, but Herman was a fervent believer in the Met Life philosophy—an umbrella for a rainy day—all the more so in these years before FDR's social net. Also,

---

* His expertise as a cook was reflected in the one dish he always made in his wife's rare absences: salami and eggs. "All right, boys, here we go!" he'd announce to his sons, then flip the salami—*whish*—in the pan.

† In the same interview, the eighty-five-year-old Florence decried the term *shvartze* (quite properly) as offensive, so her comment here was perhaps an unconscious generational slip.

philosophy or no, Herman was determined to do what it took to get his few-penny premiums. Philip sometimes accompanied him on Saturdays ("*This is my boy*—"), listening intently while Herman chatted with customers and inquired, by name, about this or that family member. "Well, she died three years ago," someone might say, in which case Herman (having expressed a seemly regret) would mention that the deceased's burial policy was still in effect and therefore a premium was due. "And they'd pay him," Philip recalled. "Insurance man comes round, you pay him. That's the deal." Decades later, a man named Bernard Disner—who regarded Herman as a revered mentor in the insurance game—related one of his boss's favorite mantras: "Bernie, you don't have enough larceny."

On March 19, 1933, Philip Milton Roth was born at Beth Israel Hospital, where "every boy [he] knew had been born as well and, at the age of eight days, ritually circumcised in the hospital sanctuary." By then his family was living, along with most of the city's second-generation Jews, amid the tidy tree-lined streets of the Weequahic section, built some twenty years earlier on the former Lyons Farms at the southwest edge of Newark, the old boundary between the Hackensack and Raritan Indian lands. Weequahic ("head of the cove") was so named by its main developer, Frank J. Bock, who fortuitously attracted a preponderance of Jews with advertisements for "cheap high-class building plots" and "NO SALOONS."

By the time Philip was born, the family had moved from a slightly dingier place on Dewey Street to 81 Summit Avenue, a two-and-a-half-family house whose modest façade would one day be distinguished by a historical plaque. The Roths' apartment—two bedrooms and a pleasant sun parlor on the second floor—was the nicest of the four they would occupy in Weequahic; the monthly rent was $38.50 ("I think we could get it now for the same," Roth said in 2010), and it was a quick walk to Chancellor Avenue School and Weequahic High, two of the best public schools in the state. Their block of almost identical gabled houses with little brick stoops and patches of lawn ran along a high crest of the city (hence Summit), and on snowy days the children would gather at the corner of nearby Keer Avenue and swoop two blocks downhill to Leslie Street. The only better sledding in the area was arguably at the 311-acre Weequahic Park, designed by the Olmsted brothers and featuring a lake, golf course, and harness-racing track.

Though he grew up during perhaps the most anti-Semitic decade in American history, Roth noted that his own part of Newark "was as safe and peaceful a haven . . . as his rural community would have been for an Indiana farm boy." Weequahic was bounded by gentile townships such as Irvington, once a hub of the pro-Nazi Bund and later, for Alexander Portnoy, a vaguely anxious paradise of ice-skating shiksas. Newark itself comprised a constellation of self-contained ethnic villages—Down Neck, Woodside, Vailsburg, Forest Hill—each with its own identity, its own little shops and churches, clustered around a thriving downtown business district. But none of these, not even Weequahic, was entirely homogeneous. One of the Proustian bouquets Sandy Roth would associate with childhood was the "stench of horseshit" on warm days as he passed St. Peter's, the big Catholic orphanage on Lyons Avenue where the nun-harried children grew their own vegetables and hung on the fence staring at passersby. Along with the hundred or so orphans, a few local Catholic kids also attended the grammar school at St. Peter's—including Tony Sylvester, the son of an Italian family who lived next door to the Roths on Summit, one of three gentile families on the block. Tony and Philip played together as kids, and on Christmas the Roth boys would admire the Sylvesters' tree, but there was no socializing among the parents aside from basic civility. On Jewish holidays, for instance, Tony's mother would make him wear nice clothes and admonish him to behave with special respect.

Their common aim was to work hard and make a place among the American middle class. "You give the wrong idea with that diddle-diddle music," Roth irritably wrote the BBC producer Alan Yentob, a friend, after watching the man's 2014 documentary, *Philip Roth Unleashed*. Roth pointed out that he didn't hear a klezmer band until he was almost sixty, so it hardly made sense, in the program, to evoke his childhood ambience thus—as opposed to playing tunes from the American songbook, preferably as performed by Roth's beloved Billy Eckstine and Newark's own Sarah Vaughan. "During all my growing up in the Weequahic neighborhood I never saw a skull cap on the head of anybody in the street or on the head of anyone in all the houses of friends and relatives that I drifted through almost daily as a youngster. What you fail to communicate was the triumph of secularism in a mere two generations."

Roth's later nostalgia for the place was hardly universal. Across the street on Summit was Betty Anne Bolton—"the most beautiful girl in Newark," said Roth, "our Gene Tierney"—who got out as early as she could, fleeing to France while still in her teens.* "I wanted something different from the way these people were living," she said. "Everybody interested in money; just married, children—a boring suburban life." There was a time when Roth would agree; like the literary idols of his youth, Thomas Wolfe and Sherwood Anderson, like myriad writers the world over, Roth would long to escape (as his alter ego Zuckerman put it) "the boredom, the righteousness, the bigotry, the repetitious narrow-minded types" of his hometown—then spend the rest of his life thinking about it.

---

* More than sixty years later she and her husband, Georges Borchardt, both literary agents, attended a ceremony at the French consulate, on Fifth Avenue, where Roth was named a Commander of the Legion of Honor.

Two

A MONG THE GALLING ASPECTS OF ROTH'S *PORTNOY* FAME was the general perception that the hero's archetypal Jewish mother, Sophie, was based on Bess Roth. Both Philip and Sandy remembered their home lives—at least during the later years of their growing up—as nothing if not conventional and decorous, largely thanks to their mother's example: they seldom raised their voices; the boys had nice manners and used profanity so rarely that Sandy never forgot his mortification the night he came home from the navy and excitedly said "fuck" while regaling his parents in the kitchen. As Philip icily noted (in so many words) on more than one occasion, "Bess Roth was never depicted as the overbearing, domineering Sophie Portnoy, nor was the overbearing, domineering Sophie Portnoy intended to depict Bess Roth."

The truth is complicated, and at other times Roth conceded that Sophie Portnoy was somewhat modeled on the more "suffocating" mother his older brother had known as a little boy, when Bess was younger, poorer, and under a strain. Indeed Sandy would go so far as to claim, late in life, that his "spirit [had been] broken" by his mother—who let it be known, both tacitly and not, that her love was contingent on his meeting a series of subtle, exacting demands. Offhand, he remembered the time Bess and her friend Mrs. Kaye took their boys on the number 14 bus to see a movie downtown: Sandy wanted to hold his own nickel like Mrs. Kaye's son, but his mother made him beg for it, then scolded him—"I *told* you I should have it!"—when he couldn't fetch it quickly enough from his pocket.

His mother's rare-enough lapses have "to be put in context with the loving-kindness," Philip insisted, and never mind that he himself was hardly an ideal child. Whereas his older brother had been obedient to the point of timidity, little Philip was "very stubborn and very territorial," in his own words—even given to screaming, flailing tantrums, for which he was never punished in any corporal way. Which is not to say he escaped his mother's "unthinkingly cruel" side, at least when younger, and certain episodes are indeed reimagined in *Portnoy's Complaint*. "It soon became apparent that his main problem was his castration anxiety vis-à-vis a phallic mother figure," Roth's real-life psychiatrist, Hans Kleinschmidt, wrote in a 1967 paper detailing scenes that would soon appear in the funnier, more stylish form of Roth's novel. He wrote, for example, about the time the six-year-old Philip threatened to run away from home, whereupon his mother packed a little bag and put the boy outside the back door, where he stood on a dreary interior landing lit by a single dusty bulb, at the head of a narrow stairway leading to the wide, forbidding world. "I can remember howling with fear and banging on the door, begging to be let back in," Roth wrote for his biographer. "This punishment was repeated several times."

"Castration anxiety" seems less an idle Freudian cliché when one considers the scene in *Portnoy* where Sophie sits beside her little son, who won't eat, and brandishes a bread knife with "little sawlike teeth": "Doctor, *why*, why oh why oh why oh why does a mother pull a knife on her own son? I am six, seven years old. . . . Why a *knife*, why the threat of *murder*. . . ." Why indeed? When recalling this drastic tactic, Roth had a hard time pinning down his own age at the time: Was he in a high chair, or as old as Alex in the novel? "Oh, that happened more than once," said his older brother, who was careful to point out that the knife in question wasn't really sharp enough to cause more than emotional wounding.

Alex Portnoy also remembers the time his mother took him, age eleven, to his uncle's clothing store to get a bathing suit: "'I want one with a jockstrap in it!' [Alex says] Yes, sir, this just breaks my mother up. 'For *your* little thing?' she asks, with an amused smile." Dr. Kleinschmidt somberly recorded, "He was eleven years old when he went with his mother to a store to buy a bathing suit," quoting his mother's amused dismissal as "'You have such a little one that it makes no difference.'" Given the presence of a "saleslady" in this version—versus Portnoy's jovial Uncle Nate—one may imagine the boy feeling "ashamed, angry, betrayed and utterly helpless," as Kleinschmidt wrote. Roth, however, deplored the shrink's "clumsy, tone-deaf reporting": on the man's couch he'd mentioned feeling "embarrassed," period, at this "barely consequential act of parental stupidity," and moreover pointed out that his mother's "momentary amusement, though ill-advised, was not without empirical justification."

Ribaldry of any sort was a rare indulgence for Bess Roth; her niece Florence remembered the way she used to finish her son's sentences "every time Philip would open his mouth," lest he say the wrong thing, and was in general "very controlling." As for Dr. Kleinschmidt (described as "New York's last Freudian" in a *New Yorker* piece written by another of his patients, Adam Gopnik), he tended to attribute most of Roth's problems—"compulsive masturbation" among them—to the phallic mother figure. Suffice it to say, "phallic" is a reductive category for Bess Roth; on the other hand, she was certainly engaged with the phallic well-being of her favorite baby boy, whose penis she made a point of wiping every time he urinated. ("Make a nice sis, *bubala*," says Sophie Portnoy, "make a nice little sissy for Mommy.")

Roth was the first to admit that he and his mother "had a great romance," especially during the first five years of his life, when she'd occasionally resort to extreme disciplinary measures. For the most part, though, he remembered it as "heaven": they were alone all day, talking and talking, playing the kind of games Sandy had relished in *his* early childhood. Wistfully the older son remembered how his mother used to greet him each day at the kitchen door—"May I take your hat?" (hanging up his father's straw hat)—and lead him to his own little side table, watching him lovingly while he ate. "Obviously," said Sandy, "when Philip came along those games ceased." Instead Sandy was enlisted to push the cherished *bubala* around in his carriage, up and down Summit, whenever his busy mother was distracted from the same pleasures. "He was the best-looking little fucker you ever saw," Sandy observed. "He had these black, silky-soft curls, strong little face, dark eyes." Philip was inclined to agree: apart from his winsome appearance, he had a way of saying "napnik" for "napkin," and no wonder his mother was his "slave" ("I was too adorable for words"). The passion was mutual; indeed, one may wonder whether he ever again found the "pure bliss" afforded by "the colossal bond to my mother's flesh"—as he wrote in perhaps the most lyrical passage of *The Facts*—"whose metamorphosed incarnation was a sleek black sealskin coat into which I, the younger, the privileged, the pampered papoose, blissfully wormed myself."

Later Roth would examine those dark little eyes of his in childhood photos, and infer that, from the age of two or so, he'd already known he was "superior to these people." No wonder his uncle Ed called him Sourball: in his face was a grim determination to go his own way. Kindergarten, then, was a splendid change—being in school, among other kids, confirmed him in his idea of himself and provided an outlet for his willfulness. Right away he was enchanted by the alphabet frieze above the chalkboard—the capital A, the small a; the capital B, the small b—a copy of which he always kept in his writing studio, later, thus reminding himself that books, after all, are merely words made out of letters. As for his adoring, controlling mother: One stormy day she and a dozen other mothers gathered in the foyer of Chancellor Avenue School, carrying little raincoats and rubbers so their children wouldn't get soaked on the way home. Philip spotted her and gave her "a killing look." *"Go!"* he said, venturing alone into the tempest. Tarnopol's father, at the end of *My Life as a Man*, reminds his son of a similar episode to illuminate certain grown-up predicaments: "Everything you had to do by yourself, to show what a big shot you were—and look, Peppy, look what has come of it!"

Roth's memory of his own independence—suddenly won, circa the age of five—is belied by another anecdote from Kleinschmidt, whose basic thesis was that his patient used narcissism "as a defense against anxiety engendered by separation from his mother." Such anxiety, as Kleinschmidt saw it, could be traced to the way little Philip coped with the separation that schooling imposed. Given that he "experienced his mother as both good and bad," he liked to imagine that his teachers were really his mother (the good one) in disguise, and hence "he was able to feel protected and thereby avoided any school phobias." This evocative fantasy provides the opening vignette of *Portnoy*: "She was so deeply imbedded in my consciousness that for the first few years of school I seem to have believed that each of my teachers was my mother in disguise." But whereas Kleinschmidt proposed a calming projection of the good mother, little Portnoy suspects a more sinister import to such shape-shifting: "Of course, when she asked me to tell her all about my day at kindergarten, I did so scrupulously. I didn't pretend to understand all the implications of her ubiquity, but that it had to do with finding out the kind of little boy I was when I thought she wasn't around—that was indisputable."

And yet Roth remembered his childhood as an idyll, mostly, over which his mother presided with impeccable, doting competence. "Lafayette, we are here!" he'd proclaim, returning from another triumphant school day—usually to find a slice of freshly baked cake ("under a covering of wax paper, to keep it fresh") and a cold glass of milk waiting. "He who is loved by his parents is a conquistador," he liked to say, amid later glory, and this applied to more than strictly literary endeavors. "The little Jewish boy does grow up to think of himself as all-cherishable," the critic Alfred Kazin wrote in his diary on December 14, 1968, while mulling an advance copy of *Portnoy*, "and it has taken the contemporary sexual revolution to persuade him that his obsession with fucking is by no means strange or unfulfillable." That Roth was cherished even by the standards of Jewish boyhood is beyond doubt; the degree to which this was a good thing is another matter. For his friend Jonathan Brent, the most compelling detail in *The Facts* was that rhapsodically remembered sealskin coat. About *that*, he told Roth, he'd like to find out more: "And [Philip] said, 'Well, you're not gonna find out.' And in fact you never do find out."

■ ■ ■ ■

BEFORE HIS TWELFTH BIRTHDAY, Sandy remembered campaigning hard for a new bicycle; instead he got a sleek little Olivetti typewriter. He never touched it, and when another birthday came around he repeated his request for a bicycle: "They said, 'If you give up your typewriter, we'll give you a bicycle.' And the punch line is: Little did I know that all the words in *Goodbye, Columbus* were in that typewriter." Philip was bemused by the anecdote: it was true he'd typed most of his first book on an Olivetti Lettera 22, but in fact that model hadn't been available until 1950 or so, and the typewriter his parents had given him was a beloved Royal. At any rate he was still in grade school when his mother taught him how to touch-type, thereby proving a steadier, more patient teacher than his father, whose part it was to teach him how to drive. (*"Not that! Aww for chrissake. . . ."*)

"I was clever and liked school, where I did well," Roth wrote for the 1965 edition of *Midcentury Authors*, "but the education I remember came largely out of comic books, radio programs, movies, newsreels, baseball, and the evening paper. I don't remember any of the books I read as a child." Later in his career, however, Roth would describe himself as an "avid" childhood reader, often seen riding his bicycle to the Osborne Terrace branch of the Newark Public Library and filling his basket with books. He would also remember that he particularly enjoyed the work of Howard Pease—"the Joseph Conrad of children's literature"—whose influence led him to roll a clean sheet of paper into his Royal and type "*Storm Off Hatteras*," and, beneath that, "by Eric Duncan," since he didn't think Philip Roth was a proper writer's name. Duncan's career expired on that first sheet of paper (though Roth would later wish, half seriously, that he'd resurrected the pseudonym for *Portnoy's Complaint*).

Jewish American cultural figures of the second and third generation, from Bernard Malamud to the Broadway producer Max Gordon, were apt to remember their childhood homes as devoid of books or anything else in the way of serious art, and so with Roth. Accounts vary as to the number and type of volumes in the Roth home library. Sandy claimed there was nothing but a "second-rate encyclopedia," whereas his cousin Florence, who used to babysit, definitely remembered a bowdlerized edition of Shakespeare that Herman had won as a sales prize from Met Life. "I can think of four books that were in the house while I was in grade school," Philip told an interviewer in 2011: three novels by Sir Walter Scott that a nice person had given Herman while he recuperated from peritonitis ("just what my father needed"), as well as *Berlin Diary*, by William L. Shirer. Bess's labors left her with little time for reading, but according to Philip she managed "five or six books a year" borrowed from the pharmacy's rental library—"not junk but popular novels that had acquired moral prestige, like the works of Pearl Buck, her favorite author." And Herman, of course, read newspapers: the *Newark Evening News*, regrettably Republican ("by the standards today it would be *The Daily Worker*"), and the left-wing *PM*.

Even more than Pearl Buck, Roth's mother liked reading monthly women's magazines such as *Ladies' Home Journal*, *Good Housekeeping*, and *Redbook*, the better to improve her already considerable proficiency at cooking, child-rearing, sewing, and managing the family budget. Among friends and family she was famous for keeping a preternaturally clean home. "She would dust all day long," said Sandy, "so that dirt never hit the surfaces of the room." What her niece Florence disparaged as the behavior of a "control freak" was, to Philip, a laudable "love of order" that included ironclad rules for bedtime: According to Sandy, their childhood curfew was nine o'clock—"not 9:01"—when they'd be "tucked in so tight you couldn't breathe," what with the precisely folded "hospital corners" that would someday make her boys the envy of their military barracks. For Sunya Felburg, another niece, the memory of Bess Roth unfailingly conjured the lovely fragrance of lemon oil with which she cleaned her floors; no wonder her sons would appraise their friends' houses with dubious eyes and noses, holding their water until they could use their own squeaky-clean toilet. As for neighbors on Summit who owned dogs—well, Philip would marvel at such matters his entire life: "I don't get it," he said at age seventy-two. "Why don't you have a monkey or a pig in your house?" In that respect he would always be his mother's child. Returning from mah-jongg *chez* Roth, the mother of Philip's schoolmate Dorothy Brand remarked, "You should see Philip's drawers! They're so neat!" Bess had led the ladies into her son's room and lovingly opened each drawer, so they could see for themselves the beautifully folded underwear and so forth.

When Bess died, among the few keepsakes Philip took for himself was an old recipe box that seemed to contain the genie spirit of his "uncomplaining and happy mother": in the upper-right-hand corner of each card, in her meticulous cursive, was the name of whoever had given her the recipe, to which she would always carefully refer as "So-and-so's recipe" rather than her own. Feeding her boys was perhaps her greatest joy. There was the constant cake-making—marble, banana, angel food, chocolate layer, on and on—and at least two meals a day that included lunch, for which her sons were expected to come home even in high school, when Sandy, at least, would have preferred grabbing a sandwich at the coffee shop with the other "hip" kids; Bess, however, wouldn't hear of it, and for the same reason as Mrs. Portnoy's ("how do you think Melvin Weiner gave himself colitis? . . . Because he eats *chazerai* [garbage, pig food]!"). Dinner always included a cheap but tasty cut of meat, maybe a tongue or *brust* hammered into tenderness and served with plenty of gravy and raisins or what you will. It certainly wasn't *chazerai*, though the writer Isaac Rosenfeld wondered whether the sheer volume of Jewish mothers' "forced feedings" was the foundation for later "ulcers, diabetes, and intestinal cancer" ("No wonder we had bypass surgeries," said Sandy)—the price one paid, maybe, for the sense of security a mother's food provided in a hostile world.

By 1940 Herman was making a bit less than seventy-five dollars a week before taxes, all of which he turned over to his wife. Because of her wise husbandry, Philip never suspected how poor they sometimes were; later he was "intrigued" by her bank books ("with their deposit and withdrawal numbers printed in red and black") from the Howard Savings Bank, where she usually managed to put a few dollars aside into a "Christmas Club account" for special luxuries. "Whatever your husband gives you, you take five dollars out of that and you plant it into your own bank account," she instructed her niece Florence, who was reminded of the advice when her two-year-old son smashed the Roths' glass-topped coffee table—a Christmas Club purchase Bess had particularly cherished. "She just, for a moment or two, registered her dismay," Philip recalled; Florence's face, however, became one of such baroque horror ("I broke something that belonged to Aunt Bess!") that her sturdy husband, Irv, had to run outside to collect himself.

As her children got older, Bess was able to bring her skills more and more into the public sphere. She was president of the PTA at Philip's school when he was in fourth grade, and also president of her local chapters of the Jewish women's organizations Hadassah and Deborah. (Another of Philip's keepsakes was his mother's Deborah badge, a gold four-leaf clover with a zircon in the middle: "Meritorious Award Bess Roth" is inscribed on the back.) For meetings she wore a gray pin-striped suit and silk blouse, and conducted herself with the kind of cheerful poise that came easily in the company of other Jews. "In a predominantly gentile environment, however," her son noted, "she lost her social suppleness and something too of her confidence, and her instinctive respectability came to seem more of a shield with which to safeguard herself than the natural expression of her decency."

She was, in short, "a little too comme il faut," as Philip was the first to admit. Certainly her extended family understood that Bess was a stickler for manners, and they would sooner break wind at the dinner table than neglect to write her a thank-you note. Bess herself remained the nonpareil. After she and Herman attended Dorothy Brand's first piano recital, Bess sent the girl a gift of hankies and a thoughtful note about how her husband had been so thrilled by the performance he could hardly stay put in his seat.

▪   ▪   ▪   ▪

HERMAN WAS AS EXCITABLE as his wife was decorous, and it was probably for the best that he deferred to her in matters relating to their sons' education. Bess trusted the boys to do their work and get good grades, and it was she who always signed their report cards after careful scrutiny. Herman would intercede only by accident, as it were, like the time he noticed how ten-year-old Philip signed his name: *"You call this handwriting? Write your name right!"*

Neither parent was much good at being idle. Bess would allow herself to listen to the radio after dinner, while the boys did the dishes, but it was all but impossible for her to sit still unless she were knitting a sweater or scarf. As for Herman, he worked twelve- or thirteen-hour days, six days a week, which usually meant heading out again after dinner to collect a few more premiums while less industrious men were settling down for the night. Maybe these men were Italian or Irish or German, in which case, if they failed in America, they could conceivably go back whence they came; Jews had no such option. For Herman's part he was only too aware that he lacked credentials apart from his superabundant vigor, and hence his sons' abiding image of a man throwing his coat back on and humping out the door with a fat black ledger under his arm, returning around eight or nine o'clock to sit a while longer at the table and survey his day's transactions. When the boys got up in the morning, for school, he was gone again. Years later, as a literature professor, Philip would often discuss Kafka's "Letter to His Father," whereof he once made the following note: "Family as the maker of character. Family as the primary, shaping influence. Unending relevance of childhood." For him it was consummately so, and hard to say where one parent ended and the other began in the formation of his own character. "The idea that you don't have to work all the time," he told a journalist in 1991, "that's news to me."

Herman's exuberance could be trying. The "bane of my childhood," said Philip, was shopping expeditions to his cousin Moe's haberdashery in Irvington. *"What're your school colors?"* Herman would demand of his son, in a voice loud enough to be taken as a general canvassing of the store. "Orange and brown," Philip would meekly reply, whereupon Herman would hail Moe: *"Lemme see something in orange and brown!"* Given a measure of his mother's refinement, Philip was so tortured by these outings that he was never again able to find pleasure in buying his own clothes. "It's absurd," he said in 2006. "I don't own any clothes. I own a blazer and a suit and I'm seventy-two years old and a man of great eminence."

Herman took his patriarchal role seriously, and could always be counted on as a "fixer" for the many people he considered family, whether actually related or not. His pal George Finneman's daughter taught at a school for handicapped children on Twenty-third Street in Manhattan, and desperately wanted an apartment in nearby Stuyvesant Town—a middle-class complex owned by Metropolitan Life, where Sandy would live for many years—but the waiting list was "hundreds long"; the daughter finally called Herman, who got her an apartment within twenty-four hours. "To this day," said the woman's father, "our girls respectfully speak of him as Uncle Herman." His actual nieces and nephews also knew they could count on Herman, especially for "Polonius-like advice-giving," as Philip put it. When in the midst of some financial or marital woe—even, heaven forbid, considering divorce—they knew the phone would shortly ring and they'd get "a good dose of Herman," said Sandy. Sometimes it was more welcome than others. Philip considered his father a classic *noodge* (pesterer), and gave both his endearing and difficult qualities to various fathers in his fiction: Gabe Wallach's, Swede Levov's, Marcus Messner's, to name a few. In 1970, at a time when Philip's hair was unusually long, his father wrote him: "What do I see when I look at you. 'Nachas' [pleasure, proud enjoyment]. . . . Your hair cut does not enhance your beatiful [sic] Physical or Intelligent image." A fortnight passed without tonsorial alteration, so Herman tried a different tack: "There are unfortunately roveing the streets of New York people who are looking for and inviteing trouble. Anyone with long hair could be a victim of these stuped fascists minded right wingers. . . . Yours for a new Hair Do / Dad."

Herman was a dutiful son, and every Sunday morning, without fail, he took his boys to visit their paternal grandmother, Bertha, then on to Dora Finkel in the afternoon. Later Philip would think of his father as "the man in the middle"—the middle child of seven, the first born in

America, a man whose burden it was to mediate between the traditions of his parents and "the demands of the future," as his Americanized children would have it. Unlike his brothers Ed and Bernie—who rarely bestirred themselves to attend Reform services at B'nai Jeshurun— Herman remained at least putatively Orthodox, taking his family on High Holidays to the nearby Schley Street Synagogue, where men sat downstairs and women upstairs, though the rabbi was clean-shaven and nobody wore side curls. As for the Roths' everyday observances: "Orthodox would have said too much and Conservative too little," as Philip remembered.* For as long as their parents were alive, Bess and Herman were careful to keep a kosher home, to light Shabbat candles every Friday, and to send their sons to Hebrew school (Sandy for five years, Philip for three) so they'd be prepared for their bar mitzvahs. That was as far as it went, though, and most of it was later dropped. In *Patrimony*, Philip is startled and a little crestfallen to learn that his father abandoned his tefillin—the small leather boxes containing bits of scripture that Orthodox men place on their forehead and arm while saying prayers—in a locker at the YMHA, rather than bequeath it to one of his sons ("He probably thought I would have scoffed at the very idea . . . and forty years earlier he would have been right"). "This action says more about the relation of non-observant Jews to their ancient faith in America than anything I have ever read," Alfred Kazin wrote in his review of the book. "And Philip Roth didn't even have to make this up!"

The most potent embodiment of family solidarity—key to Jewish survival at any time, all the more so in secularized America—was the Flaschner Family Association, consisting of some 150 families from Newark and Boston, where annual conventions were alternately held. The Flaschners—who considered themselves very *balabatische* (respectable, well-mannered), so noted in their written history—were connected to the Roths via Bertha's mother, and Herman was deeply proud of this thriving clan with its own quarterly newspaper, directory, and communal services such as a Happy Day Fund for the sick and an Education

---

* In *Goodbye, Columbus*, Mrs. Patimkin asks Neil whether he's Orthodox or Conservative. "I considered. 'Well, I haven't gone in a long time . . . I sort of switch . . .' I smiled. 'I'm just Jewish,' I said, well-meaningly, but that too sent Mrs. Patimkin back to her Hadassah work."

Fund to help members send their children to college. Both Herman and Bernie served terms as president in the early forties, and little Philip looked forward to conventions where he met his "exotic cousins from distant Boston"; such gatherings were a particular comfort during the war, given the many Flaschner relations in the service, all of them solemnly remembered when everyone rose to sing the family song (to the tune of "Auld Lang Syne"):

> *We are the Flaschner Family*
> *Made Up of Young and Old,*
> *To Carry On for Friendship's Sake*
> *Like Silver and Like Gold . . .*

For Herman it was especially heartening to see how many of his cousins were flourishing as Americans—their children going on to college to become doctors and lawyers and businessmen. *He's loaded*, Herman liked to say, perhaps his highest commendation.

■　■　■　■

IN THE LATE THIRTIES, Herman had been made an assistant manager at the Newark office, a position (indeed the highest possible position, with little exception) held mostly by Jews, whose families became the Roths' closest friends. The women had their mah-jongg circle, the men kibitzed over pinochle in their kitchens, and during summer holidays the families would gather for picnics at South Mountain Reservation, a park about ten miles west of Weequahic, playing softball and horseshoes and listening to ball games "on somebody's static-ridden portable radio."

On Saturday evenings the men would sometimes take their sons to the Russian *shvitz* bath on Mercer Street, in the old Jewish slum where Herman had grown up. "I was seven, eight, nine years old," Philip remembered, "and it was a great adventure to see all these naked men. . . . All this physical abandon that had nothing to do with sex. No Adonises were there." The *shvitz* was a "haven," then, from the orderly world of work and wives—a place to sit around amid a "concerto of farts" and tell bawdy jokes, all but oblivious to the variety of bellies and *tuchases* and balls hanging out. A generation before, Herman had gone with his father for the foremost purpose of cleanliness, since there was only an outhouse and no hot water at home, but nowadays it was all splendid animal indulgence—a steam bath, a good beating with oak leaves to get the blood running, a massage with wintergreen oil, a communal nap. One of the "boys" in Herman's circle was a butcher who brought steaks and chops to be cooked in the bath's kitchen and served with big platters of mashed potatoes and onions, all of it washed down with a gallon of Chianti. Around midnight, sated and braced for another hardworking week, the men dispersed.

Even more than his parents, Philip's most constant companion was his brother. Throughout boyhood they slept side by side in twin beds, walked to and from school, and kept each other company on weekend nights when Bess and Herman were out and Sandy babysat. So inseparable were they—or rather, so attached was Philip—that Sandy's friends used to say if he ever stopped short, his little brother would "disappear right up his ass." Almost every Saturday, Sandy took Philip along on a bus to the Roosevelt or Rex Theater to watch movies all day. Around Easter one year, when Philip was seven, the Rex had a contest that involved guessing the number of jelly beans in a big glass jar; the winner received a chocolate bunny. "Tell me a big number," Philip said to his brother, who'd just given his own guess, and Sandy obliged. Later they came out of the movie and Philip's name was on the marquee: "WINNER OF THE CHOCOLATE EASTER BUNNY: PHILIP ROTH!" "That was my brother's life with me," said Philip retrospectively.

At the time (perhaps later too) Sandy begrudged him nothing: "That's the way things were and it suited me fine." Philip, in turn, considered Sandy the "kindest, gentlest older brother" imaginable; he couldn't remember ever having a fight of any consequence, though Sandy would get exasperated with his brother's crazy high spirits in their parents' absence—playing indoor tag, jumping from one bed to the other—and finally fall down and play dead until Philip got scared (*"San? San—? Oh c'mon San!"*). Mostly the boys amused themselves with radio, a ubiquitous presence growing up: there was a portable in the kitchen that Bess listened to while she cleaned and cooked, a big console model in the sun parlor, and finally, blissfully, a radio on the table between the brothers' beds that they played at low volume after lights-out ("the height of my childhood transgression"). For the rest of his life Philip kept a little radio next to his bed, whereas Sandy would entertain himself, and others, by singing the pop tunes of his youth and imitating voices from his favorite programs.

"There was something of the dreamy fantast in my brother," Philip reflected a few years after Sandy's death, citing (among other things) the way he used to "tap dance like mad on the open parquet floor" when he was a boy. "But did he take lessons then? No. The fun was dreaming about it." In fact—as Sandy's third and final wife, Dorene Marcus, remembered—he'd wanted to take tap lessons as early as the age of five, but Bess had always refused: "And the reason was," said Marcus, who'd heard the woeful story many times, "he didn't have any 'stick-to-it-iveness.'" His mother's skepticism was, of course, part of a larger narrative: "She adored Philip and did not adore him," said Marcus, summing up the "thread" that ran through all her husband's memories of childhood. Philip himself allowed that the five-year difference between them had been unfortunate in some respects ("by the time he's seven, I'm two and still getting all this baby attention"), and, yes, perhaps his own connection with Bess had been stronger, but all the same she had adored *both* her boys. Why, when Sandy was away at navy boot camp, his mother would stare desolately at his empty chair in the kitchen and start crying whenever one of his favorite songs, "Mam'selle," came over the radio. Philip told this story to Sandy toward the end of his life (and later at his funeral), and Sandy looked "wonder struck."

Or maybe he just wasn't buying it. As a boy Sandy had been desperate to please both his demanding parents, and passively obedient whether he pleased them or not (*"No no! Not like that! Jesus Christ!"* Herman exploded when the eleven-year-old tried to wash the car as he'd been told), and the emotional consequences were manifold. As an adult Sandy would "drive [his] wives crazy" by always insisting on getting somewhere at least half an hour early, and he was fired from his first two advertising jobs because of "duck fever," as he called it—a fear of failure so intense that his hands shook too badly to do his work. Relatedly, perhaps, he developed a "hair-trigger temper that used to scare people"—all the more because he was so gentle otherwise. Finally, after his first bypass operation in his fifties, Sandy went to a psychologist who tried to cure his rage with hypnosis: "I remember throwing my head back and thrusting my arms to the sky theatrically," Sandy remarked of one such session, "and saying *'I beat them!*

I beat them!'"—that is (as he explained when asked about "them"), he'd managed to become something of a success despite his family's belittling.

Sandy would mellow somewhat, but a "world-class" hypochondria remained. "He subscribed to half a dozen university medical newsletters and read them cover to cover," Philip remembered. "That constituted most of his evening reading." When they spoke on the phone, Sandy would worriedly relate some ominous new symptom, and once Philip rushed home from London on the Concorde because Sandy thought a blur in his vision was a brain tumor. Above all he feared melanoma and Lyme disease—crossing streets to get out of the sun, and refusing to walk in the woods when he visited Philip in Connecticut. "He was an anxious guy," said Dorene Marcus. "He grew up not feeling safe, and I think that relates to Bess probably. . . . The saddest thing about Sandy was he thought, to her, he was the B student and Philip was the A student."

Three

I N THE EARLY YEARS OF THE TWENTIETH CENTURY, THE Orthodox population of Newark's Third Ward would occasionally celebrate life in America with a parade along Prince Street, a mass of bearded and behatted men marching proudly to "The Stars and Stripes Forever." Saul Bellow told Roth that his father used to look forward to paying taxes in such a wonderful country, and Roth replied that Herman had felt the same way, even in times of relative poverty; he also loved voting, at least during FDR's presidency.

Philip Roth was born two weeks after Roosevelt's first inauguration, and about seven weeks after Hitler became chancellor. That March of 1933, some two thousand Newark Jews gathered at the YMHA's Fuld Hall to protest the Nazi regime while, across the Hudson, ten times as many filled Madison Square Garden. Probably Roth's first inkling of Nazi persecution was news of Kristallnacht, on November 9, 1938, when ninety-one Jews were killed and thirty thousand arrested in the mayhem that destroyed thousands of synagogues and Jewish businesses in Germany. Six months later, the British House of Commons issued its White Paper of 1939, effectively closing Palestine to all but a fraction of European Jewish refugees; Cynthia Ozick wrote Roth in 2004 that her grandmother had begun "weeping and literally beating her breast" when she read the news in the Yiddish paper.

Jewish support of Roosevelt was almost unanimous. Not only did he staunchly oppose the Nazis, but he appointed a Jew to the Supreme Court, Felix Frankfurter, and surrounded himself with Jewish advisers such as Bernard Baruch and Henry Morgenthau. For Jewish immigrants and their still-struggling children, the New Deal came close to the socialism many espoused amid an often brutally capitalistic society. "The Jews have *drei veltn*," said the Tammany Hall politician Jonah

Goldstein: *"die velt, yene velt, und Roosevelt"* (three worlds: this world, the other world, and Roosevelt). Among the iconic imagery of Roth's wartime boyhood were Norman Rockwell's *Saturday Evening Post* covers illustrating FDR's Four Freedoms—Freedom of Speech and Worship, Freedom from Want and Fear. "There isn't a face in any of the four illustrations that isn't imbedded in my memory," said Roth, "right down to the man's face looking backwards out of the picture"—a Thanksgiving feast—"in the lower-right-hand corner of 'Freedom from Want.'" His mother's greatest heroine was Eleanor Roosevelt, whose column, "My Day," was her most essential reading; when Philip, in his midtwenties, spotted Mrs. Roosevelt in a Madison Avenue store, he couldn't resist telling her of his mother's admiration, then promptly phoned home to tell a tearful Bess about their meeting.

Anti-Semitic demagoguery flourished during the thirties. The German American Bund marched in New York wearing Nazi uniforms and waving swastika flags along with the Stars and Stripes. At a 1939 Bund rally in Madison Square Garden—as well attended as the Jewish anti-Nazi protest six years before—Bund leader Fritz Julius Kuhn railed against "Frank D. Rosenfeld" and his "Jew Deal," which he characterized as a Bolshevik-Jewish conspiracy. Roth remembered his father cursing only twice during his childhood, and in both cases the boy was alerted to the existence of anti-Semitism: once while they were listening to the fascist priest Father Coughlin on the radio (*"filthy bastard!"*), and once when they drove past the Bund beer garden in Union, New Jersey, a memory Roth included in *The Plot Against America*.

On December 7, 1941, a Sunday, the eight-year-old Philip was playing with friends in the alley next to his house on Summit Avenue, when his father called from the sun parlor window, asking him to come upstairs; the news of Pearl Harbor had just come over the radio. In Newark and elsewhere, Jews flocked to recruiting stations to prove their patriotism, and Philip became suddenly aware of a reality beyond Weequahic "of powerful forces, unknown, uncontrollable, unpredictable, and menacing, that could threaten our secure familiar little world at any moment." Almost daily the headlines blasted some fresh catastrophe—WAKE ISLAND FALLS; BATAAN FALLS; CORREGIDOR FALLS—and every night the Roths listened tensely to the war news given by commentators such as Gabriel Heatter, H. V. Kaltenborn, and especially Walter Winchell:

"Good evening, Mr. and Mrs. North America and all the ships at sea," Winchell announced in his stentorian nasal, a telegraph key rattling in the background, "let's go to press. . . ." On a warm day, Roth remembered, you could walk the streets of Weequahic and hardly miss a word of Winchell's broadcast as it poured out of every window.

Daily life was consumed with the war effort. Roth and his friends saved newspapers and foraged for discarded cigarette packs, from which they carefully peeled away the foil until they had a ball big enough to bring to school, the drop-off place, along with their newspapers. Everybody worked on at least two victory gardens, an individual patch in the backyard and a communal garden tended with the neighbors. Because of gas rationing, the Roths made the three-mile Sunday trip to Elizabeth on foot, skirting a cemetery and crossing a bridge over the railroad tracks. Both parents were conspicuous in their volunteerism. Herman was an air-raid warden, walking the streets at night shouting, *Turn your light out! Pull your shades down!*" Bess sold war bonds at Chancellor Avenue School with other PTA mothers—passing out collection booklets to the students and encouraging them to buy twenty-five-cent war stamps; once they filled their booklets with seventy-five stamps, a total of $18.75, they could redeem it for a bond that would mature to a value of $25 in ten years.

Philip was conscientious about writing "newsy" V-mail letters to his older cousins and uncles in the service, and would always keep a tender memory of what they'd looked like in their uniforms. Every day, walking to school, he was reminded of their absence by the "terrifying symbol" of tragic sacrifice that appeared in several windows along the streets of his neighborhood: a Gold Star flag. According to a plaque that was later mounted outside the auditorium, fifty-seven students from Weequahic High were eventually killed in the war.

■ ■ ■ ■

WHEN THE RENT WAS RAISED on the Roths' Summit Avenue apartment, they moved three blocks away, in May 1942, to a somewhat seedier place at 359 Leslie Street—another second-floor flat in a two-and-a-half-family house that Bess made clean and pleasant. Moving day was especially memorable for Philip: as he departed 81 Summit that morning, his mother reminded him to go to their new apartment for lunch. So automatic, though, was his two-minute trot from school to their old back door (and perhaps he was rushing, à la Portnoy, to catch his mother in midtransformation from her teacherly guise) that at first he didn't realize his mistake when he found the door ajar and heard men's voices; he peeked inside and everything was gone! "Instantaneously I reasoned that there had been a German invasion and my mother had been abducted—or worse." Abruptly his memory was jogged when he saw the men painting the walls, and he bolted over to Leslie, where his lunch, as ever, was waiting for him on the oilcloth cover of their kitchen table.

He was always in a rush to get to school, his speed hindered only by a traffic cop at the corner of Chancellor and Summit. Eileen Lerner remembered their class as a close-knit, promising group of kids, and Philip was "right up there"; indeed, when her mother once pointed out that she herself had gone to school with a famous person—orchestra leader Shep Fields—Eileen had a hunch that someday she'd say the same of Philip Roth. Both Chancellor Avenue School and Weequahic High were on a yearly two-term schedule that allowed some students to enter and graduate in January, and in fourth grade Philip skipped his second term ("4B") and became a fifth grader; four years later he'd skip 8B to begin high school at age twelve. ("There are still things I don't know because of those two half-years," he mused in 2012. "Lay and lie." He laughed. "I might spend my retirement . . .") Before leaving his fellow fourth graders behind, Roth gave a rousing performance that fall as Columbus, stalking downstage in his cape and pointing dramatically into the audience: "Land ho!" he declared, while the others stood mumbling "mutinously" behind him. A revelatory moment: "Knowing that my mother was in the audience," he said, "I remember feeling all the power that was in me."

When asked in later years what his son was really like as a kid, Herman Roth accurately replied, "Philip was an all-American boy who loved baseball." In that respect he was exactly like his friends. While doing homework or lying in bed, he kept his ball, bat, and glove close at hand—the standard "fetishes" of a Weequahic boyhood "that validated our own spotless credentials as American kids." Later he'd channel his old fervor into a sprawling comic novel about a hapless, itinerant ball team, the Ruppert Mundys—a tribute, in part, to afternoons spent at Ruppert Stadium watching the Triple-A Newark Bears with his father and brother.

Among major league teams he favored the Brooklyn Dodgers, and loved listening to the radio announcer Red Barber re-create the excitement of away games with the aid of ticker tape and a little stick to evoke the crack of a bat. Roth would later attribute his Dodgers fandom to the influence of John R. Tunis's baseball novels (*The Kid from Tomkinsville* et al.), but his old neighbor Tony Sylvester pointed out that practically every man jack in Weequahic was pro-Dodgers ("Ducky" Steinberg, a boy on their block, was so avid he tossed his radio out the window when they lost). Roth's most cherished memory of his team was the day he and a friend, Bob Lapidus, journeyed all the way to Ebbets Field ("we might have taken Conestoga wagons along the Oregon Trail to get there") to see the great Jackie Robinson. "I saw you go eight for nine against the Pirates in a doubleheader in 1947," said the "awestruck" Roth in 1972 (around the time he was finishing *The Great American Novel*), when he ran into Robinson at a book party for Roger Kahn's *The Boys of Summer*.

On summer days Roth would leave home first thing in the morning and walk two blocks to Chancellor Playground—"the field"—where he'd grab a softball out of the equipment box and throw it around with new arrivals, until enough boys had gathered to form teams. The playground director, Louis "Bucky" Harris, was a kindly middle-aged man who coached football at Weequahic High during the school year; usually he'd play third base and coordinate five-inning round-robin games that went on all day (with an hour off for lunch), until five or five thirty.* On Sundays, after dinner, the boys would rush back to the field to watch a colorful group of men play for teams sponsored by Newark manufacturing companies—and this, too, was "bliss": a lot of working Joes and the odd sports celebrity like Allie Stolz ("the local pug") laughing and bantering in the evening twilight. In *The Facts* Roth eulogized "the field," which would vanish amid construction of Untermann Field in the late

---

* Many years later, Bucky Harris's son Brian got in touch with Roth to inquire whether he'd used his father as the model for Bucky Cantor, the playground director in *Nemesis*. "That he was called 'Bucky' and that he was a playground director at Chancellor—those were two identifying facts that I did indeed borrow for the hero of *Nemesis*," Roth replied. "But beyond that I borrowed nothing in the book because I knew nothing about his life." Some years earlier, as we shall see, Roth had inadvertently turned a far more glaring spotlight on Weequahic sports legend Seymour "Swede" Masin, a retired liquor salesman at the time.

1940s: "If ever I had been called on to express my love for my neighborhood in a single reverential act, I couldn't have done better than to get down on my hands and knees and kiss the ground behind home plate."

He was less reverential on the subject of Hebrew school, which he began attending at the age of ten, three afternoons a week, for his grandparents' sake. In those days there were no fewer than seventeen little shuls in Weequahic, mostly named after their streets, and Roth's studies at the Schley Street Synagogue's Talmud Torah took him two blocks in the opposite direction from the hallowed field. It was, said Roth, the only school where he failed to excel: "I didn't know what we were reading or hearing: Abraham, Isaac—what is this stuff? Is it history? Fairy tales? . . . They lived in tents. I couldn't figure this out; Jews in the Weequahic section, they didn't live in tents." On the other hand, it would have been "unnatural" for a Weequahic boy not to attend Hebrew school, and Roth "had no interest in being abnormal and unnatural"; also, it was what one did to become a man, and that he coveted dearly.

Talmud Torah was also the only school where Roth was a discipline problem, though he was hardly exceptional in that respect. The class bristled against the boredom of reciting the *aleph-bet* by making fun of their hapless refugee *melamed*, Mr. Rosenblum, whose effigy was hanged "more than once" from a lamppost outside the classroom window. Even for a *heder*, the grungy little yellow-brick building was "a shit school," as Roth unrepentantly remembered—a place reeking of the boys' uproarious farts, the pickled herring gobbled by an old sexton, and cat piss in the basement where the man kept his pets ("in fact his name was Katz").

One boon of Talmud Torah, so Roth claimed, was that he "learned to be funny" there; he was also guided by the Borscht Belt shtick of Henny Youngman, by Jewish radio comedians such as Eddie Cantor and his beloved Jack Benny. Roth was, in fact, widely regarded as a smart aleck—"drawn to the rhetoric and postures of ridicule," as he later put it. Marty Castelbaum described Roth's style as "giving you the shiv"; a terrible athlete, Castelbaum was usually exiled to right field during softball games, and one day he made a weak throw that dribbled its way to second base. Trotting back to the bench once the inning was over, he was met by Roth and their friends. "Well, here comes Carl Furillo Castelbaum!" said Roth, referring to the golden-armed right fielder for the Dodgers. "How does it feel, Carl, to be able to throw to second in only three bounces?"—etc. Forever after, the boy was known as Carl Furillo Castelbaum.

■ ■ ■ ■

DURING THE WORST of the summer heat, much of Weequahic removed itself to Bradley Beach, an outpost of the neighborhood on the Jersey Shore. The Roths usually went for a couple of weeks, at least, and sometimes Bess and the boys would take a place on Lareine Avenue for the whole summer, while Herman visited on weekends. The same two families usually shared a rental cottage with the Roths: Bill and Lena Weber and their son Herbie, who was Sandy's age, and Joe and Selma Green, whose pretty daughter, Ruth, was three years older than Philip. As a matter of ritual, the parents would stop on the way down in Asbury Park, two miles to the north, and weigh their children on the big scale; at the end of the summer, returning, they'd do the same and "squabble over whose kid had gained the most," said Sandy.

On Lareine the three families became one, the mothers cooking breakfast in a communal kitchen and then letting their kids run loose on the beach all day. The first year, when he was four or five, Philip stayed with his mother while Sandy and Herbie Weber went swimming or, on rainy days, to the local theater, watching Tarzan movies that left them bellowing like the Jungle King every time they barreled into the water. Later Philip was allowed to tag along, and Sandy was conscientious as ever about teaching him how to ride the waves, or taking him fishing along the Shark River Inlet between Belmar and Avon. At night, too ("as if he hadn't had enough of a kid brother all day long"), Sandy would include Philip when the older boys ventured onto the boardwalk to play pinball and talk about girls. According to Sandy, Herbie Weber was a "veritable Scheherazade" when it came to telling fanciful stories about his make-out exploits, and once, when the three were lined up at a urinal, he made little Philip laugh so hard that he wheeled around and soaked Herbie's white flannel trousers.

When he was sixteen, Sandy got a job running the Pokerino concession at the arcade ("sort of the peak of my career as a human teenager"), and at night he and his Weequahic pals would gather at a pavilion off the boardwalk and dance the jitterbug. After the war it would be Philip's turn to dance and canoodle, inhaling the heady bouquet of sea salt in a girl's hair: "I think I kissed more kisses between the ages of thirteen and seventeen than I will kiss the rest of my life," he wrote in a 1959 paean to Bradley Beach, "Beyond the Last Rope." As a boy, meanwhile, he pined for their lovely housemate, Ruth, albeit fruitlessly given the age difference; besides, Bess Roth seemed to hope she could interest Ruth in her older son. Already the girl called Bess "Mom" and confided in a way she couldn't with her actual mother, while Bess gently warned her not to eat Hostess Cup Cakes once she began to fill out as a woman. "She was always cuddling me and making sure I grew up right," Ruth Green Stamler remembered. "She didn't have a daughter—it was me." As much as she might have liked to have Bess as a mother-in-law, though, she simply couldn't get excited about Sandy—a nice enough playmate when they were little, and later a skinny, quiet fellow bent over his drawing pad, quite unlike the burly *shagitz* (gentile) football player she began dating in high school (to Bess's dismay).

Eventually Ruth fell out of touch with the Roths, though her children knew she'd been friends with a boy who went on to become a world-famous writer. One day, in 2009, her daughter read a newspaper piece about Roth, who said he wished he could see more of his childhood friends; without telling her mother, the woman wrote a letter care of his agent, and a few weeks later Ruth Stamler got a phone call at her home in San Diego: "Hi, Ruthie!" After a pleasant chat—Roth asked her to write down memories of his mother—the two agreed to meet for lunch the next time she was in New York with her son, an entertainment lawyer who had clients there. "Bess and Herman, are you looking down on this?" she said, sitting opposite Roth that October, at Nice Matin, a café down the block from his Upper West Side apartment. For two hours they pored over photos from their days on the beach, and finally just sat clutching hands. "I keep looking for 'Ruthie,'" Roth wrote afterward. "Want her to transform herself into Ruthie." As for Stamler's impression, she remembered having a "lovely afternoon" but wondered why her childhood friend had looked so sad the whole time, for all his sweetness, and decided it had something to do with his lifelong obsession—"all these thoughts that he had to get out and put on paper." "Lonely after she left," Roth wrote. "The little girl who shared our childhood summers at the shore. . . . The two survivors. Frightening. The last two left who lived in that summer house from 1938 on. A man and a woman beyond sex."

■ ■ ■ ■

THE "LONGEST, SADDEST DAY of my young American life," said
Roth, was April 12, 1945, when FDR died of a cerebral hemorrhage just
as the war in Europe was coming to an end. Roth was among the crowd
in downtown Newark who stood, bereft, as the funeral train "passed
with lumbering solemnity" during its trip from Washington to Hyde
Park. When V-E Day came less than a month later, the Roth family sat
around the radio listening to Norman Corwin's long demotic masterwork, *On a Note of Triumph*, whose opening lines were fixed in Roth's
mind for all time:

> *So they've given up.*
> *They're finally done in, and the rat is dead in an alley*
>   *back of the Wilhelmstrasse. . . .*

It went on like that for sixty-two pages, as Roth learned when he bought
the book—the first he ever owned—and endeavored to memorize it.
Corwin was his "first writing idol": the author of an American epic that a
patriotic young man, formed by the war, craved; he was the precursor to
Roth's next idol, Thomas Wolfe, and Wolfe in turn would lead to his all-
time hero, Saul Bellow. But he never forgot Corwin, and the two became
friends some fifty years later, when Roth got in touch while writing *I
Married a Communist*. The novel was nominated for a *Los Angeles Times*
Book Prize, and Corwin, almost ninety years old, happily attended the
ceremony on Roth's behalf in case his novel won (it didn't).

    The Roth family stopped going to Bradley Beach in the early years of
the war, when the little towns along the Jersey Shore were blacked out,
the beaches littered with detritus from torpedo warfare and patrolled by
Coast Guard dogs sniffing the air for Nazi saboteurs. The Roths' first
summer back was 1944, and they were there again in August 1945, when
atomic bombs were dropped on Hiroshima and Nagasaki. Japan surrendered a few days later, and that night people poured into the streets
of Bradley Beach banging pots and pans and honking their horns. Kids
formed a conga line along the boardwalk, and Philip was among them,
his jubilation tempered somewhat by the sight of older people sobbing
on benches—"probably the parents of boys who had been killed," he

thought. "The war was over and it was a wonderful thing, but not for them. They would have this grief forever."

For years he and his schoolmates had been indoctrinated in the principles for which the country fought: justice, equality, freedom for all. Once a week they spent an hour singing hymns for every branch of the armed forces, and occasionally the anthem of the Chinese Communists ("which tells you something about the politics of the teachers in that school"), with its stirring rebuke of Japanese imperialism that so delighted Roth: "In*dignation fills the hearts of all of our country*men! *A*-rise*! A*-rise*! A*-RISE*!* . . ." The prewar ways of racial and religious prejudice, it seemed, would evaporate in view of this great collective struggle. And yet: that first summer back in Bradley Beach had been blighted by the incursion of "*lumpen* kids" from Neptune, a nearby gentile town, who swarmed over the boardwalk yelling "Kikes!" and beating up any Jewish kids they could get their hands on. Such hatred was learned at home, burnished for generations, and perhaps impervious to history.

A gang of violent urchins was one thing, and the more subtle anti-Semitism practiced by the gentile executives at Metropolitan Life was another, but the latter was just as unfair and destructive in its insidious way. Herman Roth was under pressure not only to work harder at his everyday duties but also to appear "a nice and regular guy," as Philip noticed, a man who knew his place and followed the rules. For this he'd been rewarded with a promotion by his district manager, Sam Peterfreund, perhaps the only Jew (other than the treasurer) who'd managed to penetrate the company's august leadership. Herman was painfully respectful toward the man he always called Boss, a big dapper bald fellow with "a slightly mysterious German accent" whose occasional appearance at the Roths' dinner table was "like the Second Coming," Sandy recalled: "Everybody hung on his every word, and it was all bombast." As for Philip, he might have shared a measure of his father's awe, but the rule to which Peterfreund was a rare exception was rank injustice (*"Indignation!"*), and by the age of twelve Philip was determined to become "a lawyer for the underdog," an ambition echoed by the motto he'd written in his eighth-grade autograph book: "Don't step on the underdog."*

---

* "There's the title of your book," Roth told me with a smile. (He said the same of "Land Ho!")

And he was affronted by more than just the plight of his fellow Jews. Along with Newark's first and only Jewish mayor, Meyer Ellenstein— whose two terms began the year of Roth's birth—the boy was adamantly opposed to goyish bigotry against black people. Reform-minded blacks and Jews, to be sure, enjoyed considerably better rapport than in subsequent decades: black newspapers vigorously editorialized against Nazi persecution, and the Jews of Newark joined forces with black citizens on the local Interracial Council, the Socialist Party, and the Congress of Racial Equality. Mayor Ellenstein had placed advertisements in Southern newspapers alerting blacks to the availability of jobs in his thriving industrial city and supported their efforts to desegregate City Hospital. In Weequahic, however (where Ellenstein also lived), blacks were all but invisible; indeed, the only place Roth ever saw his family's sweet-natured maid, Viola Johnson, was either in their house or on the corner, waiting for a bus back to the Third Ward. Viola came once a week, and Roth remembered that his mother went out of her way to treat the woman kindly, even preparing food for Viola's family when she was sick and couldn't work. Sandy took a somewhat less idealized view: Viola, like all the maids in Weequahic, was grossly underpaid and invariably called "the *shvartze*" in her absence. According to their cousin Florence— whose family shared Viola—Aunt Bess was "very democratic" about sitting down in the kitchen and eating lunch with Viola, after which she'd wash the woman's plate and silverware with scalding water ("Oh, you know how hard it is to get mayonnaise off silverware these days," Sophie Portnoy explains to her maid, when caught in the act of her furious scrubbing).

As an instance of his prodigious altruism, Alex Portnoy remembers the time he "led [his] entire eighth-grade class in refusing to participate in the annual patriotic-essay contest sponsored by the D. A. R."—this because the Daughters of the American Revolution had barred black contralto Marian Anderson from performing at "Convention Hall" in Washington, D.C. Many years later, the president of Roth's eighth-grade class at Chancellor Avenue School, Edward Sable, wrote a letter gently correcting Roth on a few points: "In Portnoy's Complaint, Portnoy was the class president and Marian Anderson the performer. Marian Anderson's situation mirrored the one of [black pianist] Hazel Scott seven years later"—i.e., in late 1945, when the actual boycott took place.

"She also was not allowed to perform at Constitution [not "Convention"] Hall." As for the student who led the boycott in Hazel Scott's behalf, it was Edward Sable himself. "Eddie tells me in *Portnoy's Complaint* that I organized it," Roth remarked, "but I didn't say I did it, I said Portnoy did it. I wasn't going to have it in *Portnoy's Complaint* that Eddie Sable did it." But in earlier interviews Roth had, in fact, claimed that the boycott had been his idea (also that the performer in question was Anderson): "I had a friend named Eddie Sable who was class president," he said in 2004, "and I said [to Sable], 'We can't participate in this essay contest.'"

Roth was disabused during a long phone chat with Sable in 2010. Sable explained that the letter proposing a boycott had been drafted by him and his older brother, then shown to their eighth-grade teacher, Sophia McCaffery, who wanted nothing to do with it; Principal Albin Frey, however, approved it without hesitation, and the thirty-six members of the eighth-grade class voted unanimously in favor of sending it to the newspaper. CHILDREN SHUN DAR CONTEST, read the headline in the *Newark Star-Ledger*: "Essays on 'Why the DAR is Undemocratic and un-American' will shortly bombard DAR headquarters." The *Star-Ledger* mentioned four students who had met at Sable's house to work out the details: Richard Sobel, Leon Ninburg, Ronald Traum, and Sable himself, the last of whom received threatening letters and phone calls after the article appeared, but also a heartening endorsement from Mrs. James Otto Hill, president of the Interracial Council: "We highly commend your actions taken in regards to the un-American 'lily-white' policy of the National Daughters of the American Revolution." Roth, like Portnoy, also remembered that he and five other classmates had been honored at the CIO Political Action Committee convention that December, when the celebrated left-wing columnist Dr. Frank Kingdon approached the children onstage and said, "Boys and girls, you are going to see democracy in action here this morning."* Whatever his vagueness

---

* So Roth remembered it in various interviews. In *Portnoy*, Dr. Kingdon addresses Alex directly as the clear leader of the group: "*Young man* [italics added], you are going to see democracy in action here this morning." Roth was perhaps chosen to attend the convention, with his five classmates, because he was eighth-grade vice president. It's worth mentioning that Roth was apt to concede the fallibility of his own memory, especially vis-à-vis episodes he'd transmuted into fiction. He himself sent me the various newspaper clips corroborating Sable's account.

about other details, Roth was fairly certain his fellow classmates on the dais included a Russian immigrant named Anita Zurav, who had "wonderful breasts" and carried a copy of *The Daily Worker*.

On January 30, 1946, Roth graduated from Chancellor Avenue School,* and for the morning ceremony he and Dorothy Brand ("the smartest girl in the class") had written a morality play titled *Let Freedom Ring!* The two main characters were Tolerance and Prejudice, and a surviving fragment of the script includes the latter's opening monologue, in which he traces his villainous role in American history and concludes, *"I am going to try to make pre[judice]. part of your ideal as it was part of the Nazi ideal."* The rest of the play is lost, but its authors remember that it involved Prejudice (Roth) and Tolerance (Brand) visiting the homes of various minority families, whom Prejudice naturally disparages in advance, only to be enlightened by Tolerance, who points out, say, that Italians don't all smell of garlic and indeed aspire to get good educations and so forth. At last Prejudice slinks off in defeat, while Tolerance leads the class in singing Frank Sinatra's popular tune about racial and religious harmony, "The House I Live In." At Roth's seventy-fifth birthday tribute at Columbia University, he referred to the play as his true "beginning" as a writer: "It isn't perhaps entirely far-fetched to suggest to you that the twelve-year-old boy who coauthored *Let Freedom Ring!* was father to the author who wrote *The Plot Against America.*"

---

* On his final report card, Roth received As and (mostly) Bs in his academic subjects; his "personality" grades included As in Initiative and Industry, and Bs in Cooperation, Dependability, Emotional Stability, and Health Habits. He was a five-foot-four, 108-pound twelve-year-old at the time of his graduation.

Four

O N March 30, 1969, a month after *Portnoy* was published, Roth's father drolly warned him that his old rabbi, Herman L. Kahan, was asking around for his "telephone Number [sic] or address. . . . He probably did not cherish the Bar Mitzvah bit [in *Portnoy*] and wants to lay it on." The "bit" had to do with "Rabbi Warshaw"—a.k.a. "Rabbi Syllable"—a "fat, pompous, impatient fraud" who stinks of Pall Mall cigarettes and ponderously commends Alex on his "one hunder-ed and-a fif-a-ty eight-a" IQ at the boy's bar mitzvah. It was true Rabbi Kahan was a chain smoker, apt to send Philip to the corner store with a quarter for cigarettes (Old Golds, not Pall Malls), and Roth thinks the rabbi might have mentioned that the bar mitzvah boy was about to enter high school at the tender age of twelve (without actually specifying IQ), but otherwise he was "an unpretentious man" who tended to use the usual number of syllables when he spoke.

Roth acquitted himself at his bar mitzvah, at pains to impress family and friends, reading from the Torah "at breakneck speed (if not with full comprehension)." Afterward, though, he was done forever with the religious side of Judaism, telling his parents as much the next morning. Herman showed a little disappointment but was mollified by his levelheaded wife. Years later Roth would describe his personal religion, on a Post-it, as "polyamorous humorist."

■ ■ ■ ■

At Weequahic High the student population jumped after the war, so freshmen had to be bused to an annex at Hawthorne Avenue School, about fifteen minutes away. The first teacher Roth saw each morning, in homeroom, was Dr. Robert Lowenstein—Doc Lowenstein to his students—who'd recently been discharged from the Army Air Corps, for which he'd served in North Africa, Italy, and Yugoslavia. Lowenstein wore both his valor and his erudition (a Ph.D. in French literature from Johns Hopkins) lightly, and this "combination of braininess and masculinity" made a great impression on Roth; he gave such qualities to Murray Ringold in *I Married a Communist*, along with Lowenstein's pronounced reluctance to suffer fools, which often took the form of hurling blackboard erasers at their heads. Roth never forgot the way he'd handled a couple of tough Italian kids, Albie and Duke, whose indifference to being "lovable, dutiful boys" (unlike the school's Jewish majority) had aroused Roth's curiosity. "How far can you guys spit?" Lowenstein asked the pair one day, when erasers had failed to do the trick. "Roth, open the windows." While the others scrambled out of the way, Lowenstein told the Italians to stand across the room and try spitting all the way out the window; both fell short, whereupon Lowenstein sent a loogie sailing easily outdoors. "Now sit down and shut up," he said.

In 1947, the Roths moved a few houses up the block to a first-floor flat at 385 Leslie, and Philip resumed walking to school—Weequahic High's main building, next door to his old grade school on Chancellor Avenue. The high school had opened the year of Roth's birth, designed in a handsome art deco style by the same architectural firm that had designed the swanky Robert Treat Hotel in downtown Newark; in 1939 a WPA mural was added to the school lobby, "History of the Enlightenment of Man," a work of social realism that Sandy disparaged as the painterly equivalent of Norman Corwin: "stylized, heavy-handed—'This Is America!' *Clank clank clank*." The basic effect, however, was elevating, a tone upheld by the school's principal during those first two decades, Max J. Herzberg, a prolific book reviewer for the *Newark Evening News* and author of the Latin primer used by his freshmen. Roth remembered Herzberg as "a very academic, very serious man" and considered himself well served by the principal's insistence that students memorize a list of poems including "Annabelle Lee," "Invictus," "When Lilacs Last in the Dooryard Bloom'd," and the Prologue to *The Canterbury Tales* ("Whan that aprill with his shoures soote . . ."), which in later years Roth would "slowly recite over and over" every time he had to endure an invasive medical procedure with only a local anesthetic.

Weequahic High embodied the postimmigrant ardor for education, if not quite for culture per se—as Roth put it, "It wasn't a culture of books;

it was a culture with a tremendous *respect* for books." The main aspiration, though, was professional success and the dignity that attended it (*"Help, help, my son the doctor is drowning!"*), and at Weequahic High the gravity of that pursuit was palpable. In its first three decades, the school was reputed to have produced more doctors, lawyers, dentists, and CPAs than practically any high school in the country, certainly in New Jersey, and the flip side of the coin was an almost giddy disdain for the pointless, goyish violence of contact sports—a spirit captured by the school's unofficial fight song, a portion of which Roth included in *Portnoy*:

> *Give a yell, give a yell*
> *A good, substantial yell*
> *And when we yell, we yell like hell*
> *And this is what we yell*
> *Ikey, Mikey, Jake, and Sam*
> *We're the boys who eat no ham**
> *We play football, we play soccer*
> *We keep matzohs in our locker*
> *Aye, aye, aye, Weequahic High!*
> *White bread, rye bread*
> *Pumpernickel, challah,*
> *All those for Weequahic,*
> *Stand up and hollah!*

So famously bad was the football team that its only victory, Roth's sophomore year, sparked a riot of sorts. Indeed, until fullback Fred Rosenberg plunged two yards into the end zone for the 6–0 margin, the Weequahic Indians had never beaten Barringer High in their fourteen-year history; as time expired, the Barringer side of City Stadium began streaming ominously toward the Jewish seats. Roth remembered making it out to the parking lot and onto a bus, which was surrounded by "ten or fifteen of the enemy . . . hammering their fists against its sides." The driver

---

* A fellow Weequahic graduate, Charles Marcus, wrote a letter to Roth reminding him that the cafeteria at their almost all-Jewish high school had, oddly enough, "served delicious ham sandwiches."

pulled away just as Roth slammed his window down on some viciously prying fingers.

Before Untermann Field was completed in 1949, a football game was about the only reason for leaving a neighborhood where everything was a few steps away and almost every face was familiar. Roth lived right around the corner from his favorite hangout, Halem's candy store, where he could always find friends around the pinball machine indulging in "wise guy talk and sex talk"; another candy store, George's, was right across the street, and doubled as a bookie joint. A little farther along Chancellor was a "Hot Dog and *Chazerai* Palace" (as Mrs. Portnoy would have it), Syd's, where Sandy and Philip worked part-time filling paper bags with greasy delicious fries, served with a wooden fork. As Sandy remembered, *all* the mothers—not just his—had misgivings about Syd's, and Philip would pay a final tribute to the place in *Nemesis*, wherein Mrs. Beckerman laments the polio death of a boy who "wanted to be another Louis Pasteur" but instead "had to go to eat in a place *crawling* with germs."

Roth's best friend, Marty Weich, lived at 287 Leslie, about a block away on the other side of Lyons Avenue. Tall, handsome, polite—"every mother's dream of the Jewish prince," said their friend Bob Heyman—Weich was a good student and a dutiful son, rushing to his parents' kosher butcher shop after school (in college too) so he could help make deliveries. He was even a good athlete, the only one of Roth's circle who made a varsity team, basketball, a sport that was nonviolent and hence respectable. The two boys had met in Lowenstein's homeroom at a time when Roth was enamored of the Sweet Science—a legacy of wartime boxing nights at Laurel Garden, where he and Sandy had blown their allowances betting a nickel on each fight ("one of us taking the black guy and the other the white guy or if both fighters were of the same race we bet the light trunks versus the dark trunks"). Challenging the larger, gentle-looking Weich, Roth promptly flung off his gloves (elasticized but unlaced) when Weich began to "flail the shit out of [him]."

Many years later, while writing *Indignation*, Roth consulted Weich about the niceties of kosher butchery ("Flick two chickens, Markie"). And in the previous decade, the two had discussed a far more somber aspect of Weich's history, one that they'd skirted back in their school days. As everybody in the neighborhood had known, though, Marty's older brother Bertram ("Chubby") had been shot down and killed during an air raid over the Philippines in 1944. His parents were destroyed by the news: his mother took to bed and wept for months ("stupefied, finished"), and his father, a genial man who used to love kibitzing with customers, fell silent and rarely spoke again except to family. This was the basis for the tragedy in *Sabbath's Theater*—the death of Sabbath's brother, Morty—and, fifty years later, when Roth asked for details, Weich still couldn't discuss it without crying. ("The crying was a lesson," said Roth. "I bet my money on Sabbath's grief . . . that's what propels his philosophy, his attitude: everything you love disappears.") Weich remembered the terrible day he came home from school, age twelve, and saw the rabbi's car and immediately knew the worst. When his friend Bernie Swerdlow came around to the back stairs for a visit, Marty burst into tears and shut the door on him.

Swerdlow was another member of Lowenstein's homeroom at the Hawthorne annex, and it was he who told Roth about Chubby's death when they first met. Swerdlow lived between Roth and Weich on Lyons, behind a tailor shop owned by his Russian immigrant parents—a family even more beset by tragedy than Weich's: an older brother, Charles, had died two years before Bernie was born, while another brother, Sol, was schizophrenic and eventually lobotomized. As for Bernie himself, he suffered from colitis so severe that he had to leave school for two years and wear a colostomy bag. Unlike Weich (but very like Mickey Sabbath), Swerdlow rebelled against his misfortunes with an almost antic perversity—"a little devilish guy," said Bob Heyman, who would "talk, talk, talk, talk." Once, when Doc Lowenstein couldn't get him to shut up, he yanked Swerdlow to his feet and slammed him against the lockers outside his classroom. The boy expected a "right hook," but instead Lowenstein asked him what grammar school he'd attended, and thereby discovered that Swerdlow had come from a school for the handicapped, Branch Brook.

With Lowenstein, at least, Swerdlow probably didn't touch on his precocious erotic career at the school, among disabled girls, and never mind the girl who lived upstairs from his parents' shop and gave hand jobs! Such were the tales he told his pals with relish, and Roth paid close attention, later writing about Portnoy's "lascivious classmate, Smolka, the tailor's son," to say nothing of the colitis-stricken, french-fry-eating

Melvin Weiner. When Swerdlow miraculously went on to finish medical school ("he tried to screw female orderlies in the stairwell," said Heyman) and become a psychiatrist—just like Marty Weich—he copped to being the model for Melvin Weiner (but not Smolka) in an interview with the *Star-Ledger*: "I am using the book [*Portnoy*] as an RX," he told the newspaper. "I have patients—all males—with problems concerning their mothers and a relationship with guilt, and an inability to function as they should. . . . [Roth] used me so why shouldn't I use him?"

Stuart Lehman was another friend with a blighted childhood—a matter too fraught to discuss at the time, though Roth would eventually canvass him as well, while writing *Nemesis*. Like Bucky Cantor's mother, Lehman's had died when he was a small child, and his father (for reasons unknown) had declined to raise him, leaving him in the care of his grandparents. Lehman's friends called him "the Tiger" because he was so consummately the opposite: sweet and unassuming, he loved spending time at the Roth house, where he had a pair of de facto siblings and parents, too, since Herman and Bess doted on him and were forever encouraging him to stay for dinner (*"Eat up! Eat what's on your plate!"*). When his grandfather died in 1954, just after Stu and the others had finished college, Bess wrote him a condolence note: "If, in a small way, we can make up to you for this loss, you know you have only to ask it of us. From the time you came to our home, as a friend of Philip's, you have always seemed a part of the family."

Somewhere toward the temperamental center of things was the puckish Bob Heyman, who lived in a one-family house on the more affluent part of Keer, below Maple Avenue; his prosperous father owned a necktie company, Beau Brummell Ties, and their next-door neighbor was the Apple King of Newark. Heyman's parents and maternal grandparents were all born in America—his mother was a first cousin of Milton Berle, who would attend Bob's wedding and meet Philip and the others—and they comported themselves, said Roth, with "no taint of Jewishness." The family attended the grand Conservative temple on High Street, Oheb Shalom, and belonged to a suburban swimming club that Roth would use in the opening scene of *Goodbye, Columbus*. Perhaps the most potent status symbol was the finished basement *chez* Heyman: a spacious, pine-paneled rec room with its own bar, hi-fi, and bathroom. One day the exuberant Roth was there, singing along with the Four Aces, when he thrust his fist upward on the last word of *"Tell! Me! WHY!"* and put a hole in the ceiling. Alarmed, the boys ran to the hardware store for a bag of plaster and tried to patch it up, but Mr. Heyman was bleakly unimpressed by their work. "He's a wise guy," the man observed of the culprit.

Perhaps he was aware of Roth's spot-on imitation of his Brooklynese *hocking* (nagging, berating) of his son, Robert, or "Robbit!" (For a time Heyman had a Japanese girlfriend who thought Roth and the others were saying "Rabbit"; thus she and her friends took to calling him Usagi— or even Usagi-san—rabbit in Japanese.) But the boys themselves were delighted by Roth's shtick: "He was like a spark plug," said Heyman, "a dynamo, and he made us funny." For Roth's part, the most cherished times of adolescence were the long bull sessions with his male friends, in somebody's car late at night, when they'd laugh about their sexual frustration and plan the illustrious conquests to come—"something like the folk narrative of a tribe passing from one stage of human development to the next." In 1982, Roth sat on the edge of a card game in Miami Beach, chatting with his widowed father and their old friends from the neighborhood; one of his playmates' mothers took his hand and said, "Phil, the feeling there was among you boys—I've never seen anything like it again." Roth replied ("altogether truthfully") that he hadn't either.

■　■　■　■

WHILE ROTH WAS IN HIGH SCHOOL, his father went deeply into debt after the failure of a frozen-food distributorship he'd started with friends. By then Herman had despaired of advancing further at Metropolitan Life, and the roughly $125 a week he made as an assistant manager seemed more meager than ever with two sons heading to college. The money he borrowed for the new business* went mostly toward the purchase of a big refrigerated truck, which he took out at night to make deliveries and hustle business; on weekends he drove to Philadelphia and attended to paperwork at the company's office. But it was no use: by then Birds Eye had been marketing frozen food for more than fifteen years, and Herman's enterprise foundered among the 140 or so competitors that had sprung up in the meantime.

---

* In *The Facts*, Roth estimates "some $8,000" was borrowed; in various interviews and notes, he gives figures ranging from $18,000 to $30,000.

As luck would have it, Metropolitan Life was finally feeling pressure brought to bear by FDR's Fair Employment Act, and Herman was belatedly promoted to manager of the Union City district, about twenty minutes northeast of Newark. As Philip recalled, it was "the worst office in New Jersey," full of "goyish drunks," but if anyone could rout these miscreants out of bars and back to work, it was Herman. ("Big-shot goyim," says Levov's hard-driving father in *American Pastoral*, "the presidents of companies, and they're like Indians with firewater.") "Every nickel will be paid back" was the mantra with which Herman goaded himself over the next few years, becoming "a figure of considerable pathos and heroism in my eyes," said Philip in 1974, "a cross of a kind between Captain Ahab and Willy Loman." It was a hard time for both parents, and Sandy remembered a series of "mild but distressing" arguments arising from the constant niggling over money—even the odd quarter for ice cream after the movies. Because Herman was a renter with no collateral to speak of (and because the Met would have fired him if they'd caught wind of a second job), he'd had to borrow most of the money from his brothers, Ed and Bernie, to whom he hated being beholden.

Certainly it didn't help, at the time, that Herman's brothers were more successful than he. The owner of a cardboard box company, Ed had bought a one-family house in Irvington that his daughter, Florence, touted as "very elegant" by Roth standards, what with its fireplace flanked by built-in bookcases ("my father enrolled me in Book-of-the-Month Club when I was thirteen") and fancy Victrola ("there was no Victrola at Bess and Herman's"). Philip admitted that ownership of a one-family house put Ed "one step up" on the socioeconomic ladder, but the implication that his eldest uncle was a reader or otherwise refined was "over the top," given the man's sixth-grade education and slum-street manners. "He had a big voice and small brain," said Sandy, and even Ed's daughter conceded his foul temper and tendency to snipe: "When I went to high school, if I got a B, [he'd say] 'Why didn't you get a B+?' If I got a B+, [he'd say] 'Why didn't you get an A?'" He was, in short, a less benevolent version of Herman; their niece Marilyn (Betty's younger daughter) always regarded the latter as a kind man, whereas her most salient memory of Ed was the time she'd slugged him for being mean to her mother ("I was a tough Newark girl").

Philip found his uncle entertaining in small doses, and Ed seemed to have a soft spot for his promising nephew. The highlight of their relationship was a 1948 trip to Princeton for a football game against Rutgers. Before kickoff, Ed took Philip to see the white clapboard cottage of a family hero, Albert Einstein, on Mercer Street. Ed made a point of warning Philip about Princeton's anti-Semitic elitism, and both cheered for the state university, Rutgers, and its great Jewish All-American, Leon Root.* At Ed's funeral in 1973, his nephew professed to be "stunned" when Aunt Irene, the widow, flung her arms around Philip and said of her "rough, aggressive, temper-ridden" husband, "Philip, nobody understood him." "It wasn't just writers who felt misunderstood!" Roth wrote a friend. "As a Kafka reader I oughtn't to have had to be reminded."

Uncle Bernie was the most successful of all, and easily the most worldly. Though he owned a small insurance company and lived in an elegant one-family house in upper-middle-class Maplewood, he was hardly a complacent Jewish bourgeois—on the contrary, he'd been an actual Communist in his youth, and was careful to point out to his nieces and nephews that they must never refer to his live-in maid as a *shvartze*. Bernie's relations with the men in his family were bound to be problematic, going back to his decision to marry a portly young woman with prematurely gray hair, Byrdine Block, who came from a relatively affluent family of German Jews. "She's not really Jewish," Sender reportedly observed, while Herman indelicately wondered why his little brother wanted to marry a woman who "looks old enough to be your mother." Eventually the brothers reconciled, but things fell apart again twenty years later, when Bernie declared that he was divorcing the mother of his two daughters and marrying a younger woman. Bess and Herman "were as stunned as if they'd heard that he'd killed somebody," and naturally gave their support to Byrdine, a warm and gracious woman who was one of Bess's knitting pals besides. When Bernie compounded the scandal by

---

* The Scarlet Knights prevailed that day, 22–6, for their first-ever victory at Princeton. Roth later met Leon Root at the playwright Arthur Miller's memorial service in Roxbury, Connecticut, where Root lived during the warmer months. Roth mentioned the 1948 Princeton game, and the two became friendly; since Roth lived in nearby Warren, he'd occasionally consult Root, an eminent orthopedic surgeon, about his back problems.

leaving his second wife a week or so after the honeymoon, Herman again saw fit to console the wronged woman.

"Bernie was on a different plane than Herman," said his son-in-law, Don Aronson, who was persuaded to wear Paul Stuart clothing by the stylish Bernie (as was Bernie's nephew Philip). For a while Bernie went through a Reichian phase and would sit in an orgone box—which, however, left him feeling enervated rather than revitalized, until it transpired that he'd placed the box above a doctor's office and was being bombarded by X-ray radiation. At Duke University he underwent periodic fasting cleanses, and one night he phoned his daughter from Princeton and reported in a strange, halting voice that he'd joined an LSD experimentation group. "He was a man ahead of his time," said his granddaughter Nancy Chilton, who noted that Bernie had collected Nakashima furniture well before it began appearing at the Metropolitan Museum; he took her to Nakashima's woodworking studio in New Hope, Pennsylvania, when she was ten, and also on shopping expeditions for antique clocks.

As for that scandalous first divorce: Bernie and Byrdine remained such good friends that she was sometimes introduced as his "other wife"—this in light of his taking a third wife, Ruth, whom Byrdine and their daughter Margery had both insisted he marry, overcoming his reluctance after the fiasco of his second marriage. Meanwhile he kept his exasperation in check vis-à-vis the moralizing Bess and Herman, not least because he was fond of their children. "Sandy was his usual charming self," he observed in passing after a 1966 visit with his brother's family, though the main subject of his letter was the already rather famous Philip, a person of "dignity, refinement and beauty" whom Bernie had come to regard as a kindred soul. ("They're all celebrity fuckers," Sandy remarked of this common preference among the family.) "In my own way," Bernie continued, "my feelings reached out towards Phillip [sic], and I found in him a rare human being. I can now understand a quality that must stem from the very marrow of his bones, that makes him the obvious genius that he is, and I just feel that his writings in the future will be even greater than that of the past because of this rare quality that I sense is within him." One assumes Bernie felt vindicated three years later, with the worldwide success of *Portnoy*, which incidentally gave him and Byrdine a piquant new moniker for Herman's wife: "Mrs. Portnoy."

. . . .

ACCORDING TO ROTH'S 1965 *Midcentury Authors* entry, the first book that made a momentous impact on him was *Citizen Tom Paine*, by Howard Fast—"a gifted mediocre writer" (as he later put it) who appealed to his youthful patriotism and burgeoning sense of social injustice. Still enthralled by Corwin, too, young Philip was writing radio plays that were apprentice exercises, said Sandy, akin to his own "drawing of Li'l Abner's collar." In *I Married a Communist*, the young Nathan Zuckerman hopes to impress a hard-boiled University of Chicago professor, Leo Glucksman, with his Corwin- and Fast-inspired play *The Stooge of Torquemada*. "Who taught you art is slogans?" Glucksman berates him. "This play of yours is crap. It's awful. It's infuriating. It is crude, primitive, simple-minded, propagandistic crap." Mentors like Glucksman would come later for Roth; at the time he had Irv Cohen, a radical ex-GI who'd married his cousin Florence in 1946. The rangy, argumentative redhead had more in common with Philip than just a high-minded affinity for the common man; both were crazy about baseball, for one thing, and Cohen would fungo balls to the boy on Sunday afternoons and take him to Dodgers games at Ebbets Field. Cohen worked as a truck driver for his father-in-law's box company, and sometimes he'd take Philip on delivery runs; best of all was stopping at a roadside diner after a long morning of unloading the truck, sweatily disembarking like a couple of real working stiffs.

Cohen had grown up poor in Newark and dropped out of high school, harboring the resentments of a bright, self-educated young man from a deprived background. Roth seemed to recall he'd read a few key books at Cohen's behest—*Looking Backward*, *The Jungle*, Arthur Miller's *Focus*—but mostly Cohen worked on him with "didactic hocking." Unlike his fictional counterpart, Ira Ringold, Cohen was never a card-carrying Communist, but rather associated with the loose confederacy of left-wing causes known as the Popular Front; as such, he was an enthusiastic supporter of Henry Wallace, the 1948 presidential candidate for the Progressive Party, whose virtues he doggedly impressed on Philip. Cohen served as one of Wallace's bodyguards during campaign appearances in New Jersey, and once Philip helped him set up chairs at a meeting of the pro-Wallace American Veterans Committee. Both Herman Roth and his older brother Ed took a dim view of Cohen's politics. "Don't give me that Commie crap!" was a frequent refrain when they engaged with the young man, who seemed especially determined to prevail in the presence of his protégé, Philip, who in turn was deeply torn: Strom Thurmond's Dixiecrats were also draining votes away from Truman, and a vote for Wallace could help swing the election to the Republican Thomas Dewey. In the end Philip was relieved he couldn't vote yet, and nothing but thrilled when Truman won. Soon enough, too, he became disenchanted with Cohen's "simpleminded ideology," though he thought of the man tenderly and attended his funeral in 2003. At the cemetery he asked Florence where her parents were buried, and lo, they were close at hand—right beside their obstreperous son-in-law. "Okay, Pop," said Florence. "Irv is here. You've got someone to argue with now."

For Sandy—and perhaps Philip more indirectly—the most important family mentor was Bess's little brother, Mickey, a bachelor artist of humble means. Mickey kept a little photography studio in Philadelphia, coloring his black-and-white portraits by hand and sleeping on a couch in the back room. Summers he closed shop and traveled abroad to the great museums of Europe, reproducing the old masters with an impressive degree of technical skill.* Sandy was rarely without a drawing pad from the age of thirteen or so, and his facility for dashing off likenesses was amazing to Philip and his friends. For high school Sandy had wanted to attend the vocational Arts High, which would have entailed a thirty-minute bus ride, but his parents preferred he stay close to home. It was Mickey who suggested a compromise, and so the boy began taking Saturday classes at his uncle's alma mater, the Art Students League in Manhattan. Philip was astonished to learn that his teenage brother got to sit in the same room with a naked woman once a week, and there were even more naked bodies in the various art books Mickey gave him, including the classic work on anatomy drawing by Mickey's old teacher George Bridgman.

After high school Sandy enlisted in the navy for two years, and when he was discharged in 1948 he enrolled as a commercial art student at

---

* Or so I surmise based on the one Mickey Finkel painting I ever saw—not a copy of the old masters, but rather an accomplished portrait of his nephew Philip Greiss as a rose-lipped infant.

Pratt Institute in Brooklyn, with all fees paid by the G.I. Bill. Almost every Friday night he'd come home to Newark, spread newspapers over the dining room table, set up his easel and other materials, and sit there doing his homework until his departure Sunday evening. By then the Roth house had become a social hub for the brothers' friends, and, while Sandy worked, the "second- and third-hand Buicks" would pull up and the place would get noisy with kibitzing and laughter. Bess loved feeding so many nice Jewish boys, and Herman would join the card game and tell his jokes. Sandy's circle of twenty-year-old pre-professionals were "raucous but not obscene" around Bess and Herman; when it was only the boys, though, the conversation quickly turned to sex. "What'd you get?" they'd ask one another about their Friday night dates. This was when Sandy's jokester navy buddy Arnie Gottlieb would shine, dazzling the "hypnotized" Philip with his inspired lewdness: "He was the first stand-up comic I ever saw live," he remembered. "I had talents in that direction myself, and Arnie was an unforgettable model."

For the last year of high school, Philip and Marty Weich double-dated with a pair of pretty cousins, Betty Rogow and Joan Gelfman, and so it went for senior prom. After the dance their friends were planning to gather at Billy Rose's Diamond Horseshoe in Times Square, and Philip—who'd never drunk anything alcoholic except Passover Manischewitz—asked his mother to name a drink he could order. Scarcely more bibulous than her son, Bess suggested he try asking for a "Canasta Collins," and this he did. The waiter looked briefly puzzled ("probably there was no such thing"), then scribbled it down and canvassed the others. One by one, they all ordered Canasta Collinses.

According to his yearbook, Roth was on the Prom Committee and seemed to live up to the character summary under his senior photo: "A boy of real intelligence, / Combined with wit and common sense." The wit part was reflected in such items as his "dream" of being appointed "Ambassador to Lower Slobbovia" (both he and Sandy were *Li'l Abner* fans) or even elected "5B President"—an allusion perhaps to his actual standing as 4A vice president. Common sense and solidity were further suggested by his other offices: he sat on student councils for both his 4A class and the school at large, and served as a so-called Sagamore ("a hall patrol jerk," he explained, "who sat in a chair in one of the halls during a free hour to be sure that whoever was walking in the hall had a pass").

Otherwise the flashy, grade-skipping wunderkind of grammar school (*"Land ho!"*) had settled into a passably diligent regular guy. The towering author who would someday appear on the cover of *Le Nouvel Observateur* as "Philippe Roth / Le roi" was a mediocre French student whose cutting up in class, with Dorothy Brand, was once conspicuously punished by their martinet teacher, Mademoiselle Cummings, who clapped her hands and made them stand in silence for "fifteen minutes *by the clock.*" He was a somewhat better Spanish student, but both languages dissipated over time and he was monoglot as an adult. Overall Roth was a B student who got occasional As in subjects such as English and history, Cs in math and PE, and even a D in physics ("I learned what it was to be dumb in physics"). Such a record seems mediocre amid the rampant grade inflation of a later era, but at Weequahic High, in 1950, it was good enough to rank Roth a respectable 15th out of a bright, industrious class of 173. Still, nobody envisaged him as a future Commandeur de la Légion d'Honneur. When *The New York Times* sent a reporter to Weequahic in the wake of Roth's *Portnoy* notoriety, the consensus among his teachers was "intelligent but unimpressive," and his pal Stu Lehman couldn't help boasting that he (a pre-med student!) had outscored Roth in *English* on their college placement test.

■ ■ ■ ■

ROTH GRADUATED ON January 25, 1950, and wouldn't begin college until the fall; meanwhile he and his family endured a tragedy that would haunt them forever. Philip's kindly aunt Ethel ("Ettie"), Bess's oldest sister, had been the brains of the family, working as her father's bookkeeper in her early teens. She and Bess adored each other, and looked alike, but Ethel lived in Pelham, New York, and toll calls were a luxury. The wife of a dry cleaner, Max Greiss, Ethel remained "a terribly nice woman" despite some pretty daunting sorrows: her son, Philip, suffered from ulcerative colitis, and her daughter, Helene, was mentally disabled. During their occasional visits to Weequahic, the two Philips (both named after their grandfather) would walk to the ball field at school, waiting every so often for Helene to catch up in her wandering way.

That spring Ethel was terminally ill with cancer of the tongue that had spread to the throat and lymph nodes. She needed round-the-clock care, but her husband was busy tending his shop, and their children had special needs of their own. Bess offered to take care of Ethel as long as it took. With Sandy at Pratt, she proposed to let her sister have his bed, giving Philip the option of sharing a room with the dying woman, or else sleeping on a couch in the parlor. "I wanted to prove I was strong," Roth remembered, and of course he was fond of Ettie and loath to shirk his duty in caring for her. The woman was all too lucid and in agonizing pain, and would often have bad nights when she couldn't hide her suffering; also, half her tongue had been cut away, and her speech was "spooky" at the best of times. "This was not usual," Roth remembered. "Most kids didn't have to endure that unless they were in a war zone." Still, he was deeply impressed by his parents' compassion. Bess was flawlessly loving and attentive, and Herman made a point of pretending that Ethel was on the mend, helping her to her feet each night and taking her on a "constitutional" around the parlor: "That's a girl, Ethel, you can do it," he'd say, while he led her tottering from one piece of furniture to the next, barely able to keep her feet.

Finally she was admitted to Mount Vernon Hospital, near Pelham, where she died in June. Nobody had told Dora that her oldest daughter was slowly succumbing to a terrible form of cancer; instead they said Ethel had had a sudden stroke and never revived. It didn't matter: Dora went into decline and died the following February. As for Philip: though he'd often claim he was "glad" for the experience ("a tremendous education"), his brother thought it was "terribly traumatic" for such an impressionable young man. Curiously Philip was later convinced his aunt had died in 1946, when he was even younger and more vulnerable; he was startled to be reminded, late in life, that the episode had actually occurred shortly after high school. Remembering Ethel during a taped interview in 2004, he broke down and couldn't speak for long intervals. "I learned too much," he said in a choked and strangely childish voice. "I saw it, and remember seeing it. . . . Without my brother. My brother was gone." He was also affected by his mother's grief, which never went away. Ethel's daughter, Helene, was sent to a group home in upstate New York about a year after her mother's death, and one night, many years later, Bess was watching a news feature about that very institution when the adult Helene appeared on the screen—a "dead ringer" for her mother, and hence for Bess, who burst into tears. The nearest Roth ever got to converting the ordeal into fiction was in *The Plot Against America*, where little Philip's amputee cousin, Alvin, shares a room with him. In real life he was sometimes irresistibly reminded of Ethel's torment when he himself was suffering—as he was, many years later, from ghastly back pain that had intensified while he was trying to withdraw from Vicodin. "That poor woman," he began to sob, "that poor woman."

W ITH EIGHT MONTHS TO KILL BEFORE COLLEGE IN
the fall, Roth and a couple of his fellow 4A graduates, Bob Heyman
and Gerry Lechter, got jobs as stock clerks at the bargain-priced department store S. Klein, which was soon to open a new location on Broad Street
in Newark. For a month the boys took the PATH train into Manhattan
to receive training at the mother store on Union Square; then, in Newark,
they lasted six weeks or so before getting collectively sacked. *"Watch the
rack, or you'll be watching it from underneath!"* they'd shout, scampering
through the crowded store to return items to the floor from the Refund
Department, pausing only to ogle the Italian salesgirls. Sometimes, when
the return items included ladies' undergarments, Heyman would challenge
Roth to see how quickly he could unhook a bra with his eyes shut.

During lunch breaks on Union Square, Roth had wandered over to the
used bookstores along Fourth Avenue, and bought a number of Modern
Library editions for twenty-five cents apiece (a third of his hourly pay).
His first real exposure to serious literature had come two years before,
when Sandy brought home a summer reading list from Pratt that included
Anderson's *Winesburg, Ohio*. In later years Roth liked to describe his
younger self as "exogamous" ("I wanted to go *out*"), and he discovered the
world beyond Newark largely through Anderson and other gentile writers with provincial origins in the South and Midwest—Faulkner, Dreiser, Lardner, Lewis, Caldwell—an aesthetic education he remembered
on receiving his lifetime achievement medal at the 2002 National Book
Awards: "through the ruthless intimacy of literature, its concreteness, its
unabashed focus on all the particulars—through the passion for the singular and the aversion to generality that is fiction's lifeblood—I would try
to come to know their American places as specifically as I knew my own."
While still a teenager, Roth was captivated above all by the gargantuan

lyricism of Thomas Wolfe, the lonely wandering epic novelist who sought to "set down America as far as it can belong to the experience of one man." Wolfe was the catalyst for Roth's ambition to become an artist of titanic appetites—geographic, intellectual, sexual—and he even succeeded in pressing Wolfe's sprawling tomes on his friends. Heyman, in his retirement, would remember his old wistful longing to lead a Wolfean life, and try to revisit *Look Homeward, Angel* ("insufferable!").

After he was fired from Klein's, Roth lasted a single day working at a garage door factory in Irvington, sitting in a dark cubbyhole with a keg of nails he was supposed to sort by size. That done, his remaining five months of freedom were given over to softball games and flirting with girls who came around to watch. He also lifted weights, he said, so he could become strong enough to get a girl "to put her hand on [his] cock." As he evoked the era sixty-two years later, "The erections of 1950 were exactly the same as the erections of 2012, but the erections of 1950 had nowhere to go." Reflecting on the bygone phenomenon of blue balls ("no kid knows what they are anymore"), he described nights on a porch glider with the petite Elaine Goldberg, toward whom he exerted a "monumental" tenacity, to little avail. "Bent over like a cripple" afterward, he'd limp as far as a clump of bushes near the high school, "savagely beating off" to ease the pain, then proceed to Syd's and sit down with Stu Lehman or one of the others. (*"You got the blue balls?" "Yeah."*) Another erotic milestone for the boys was the time they lied about their age to get into the Little Theatre, on Broad Street, and see Hedy Lamarr run naked through the woods in *Ecstasy* (*"This is it!"* they whispered, jostling one another as the scene approached). There was also the Empire Burlesque, where Roth would sometimes claim to have been a virtual regular ("I spent many Sunday afternoons there," he said in 1958), though later he recalled a single anticlimactic visit around the age of fifteen, when he ruefully learned that seedy comedians outnumbered the women in G-strings.*

---

* That one visit (or many) to the Empire did afford Roth with his all-time favorite joke ("as every woman I've ever been with knows"), which he recounted as follows: "Two guys in these dirty mangy tuxedos are on the stage and they're walking toward each other as if it's on the street. And suddenly one guy says to the other guy, 'How do you pronounce it: Hawaii or Havaii?' And the guy says, 'Havaii.' He says, 'Thank you,' and [the other guy] says 'You're velcome.'" Roth exploded with laughter. "It's still the best joke I've ever heard."

Perhaps the closest Roth and his friends came to sex were necking parties in Heyman's finished basement—"the most beautiful word in the English language," as Roth liked to say (he also insisted it *was* one word: "finishedbasement"). Daytime they'd while away the hours playing Ping-Pong and telling jokes; at night they'd bring dates and dance to Billy Eckstine records ("while pressing your groin as hard as possible into the groin of your sweet young partner"). Roth's main date that first year out of high school was Joan Bressler, who'd been two years above him at Weequahic and now attended teachers' college in New York. A relatively sophisticated young woman, Bressler introduced him to contemporary fiction in the form of her favorite author, Truman Capote, whose work he read with a certain deference at the time. Six decades later, though, Joan Bressler Greenspan (by then a widow living in River Edge, New Jersey) received a letter from her old boyfriend setting her straight on that point: "Capote and I got to know and dislike each other in the sixties, and I liked seeing him skewered in that movie about him.* An unpleasant and a limited writer."

■ ■ ■ ■

DURING HIS LAST YEAR at Weequahic High, Roth had toyed with the idea of pursuing journalism rather than law, and an adviser suggested he consider applying to the University of Missouri. "You're not going to Missouri," said his father. "It's too far away and we can't afford it." Roth had hoped to get at least as far afield as Rutgers' main campus in New Brunswick, but he was turned down for scholarships both there and at the local campus in downtown Newark, almost certainly because he had to report his father's income—a decent figure now that Herman was a district manager—but couldn't mention the man's even more impressive debts, lest the information get back to Metropolitan Life. Fortunately the fees were negligible at Newark Rutgers, where he'd be joined by his

---

* Almost certainly *Capote* (2005), with Philip Seymour Hoffman, rather than the similar *Infamous* (2006), with Toby Jones, since Hoffman gave a public reading from Roth's *Everyman*, in 2007, and it would have been natural for Roth (who otherwise watched very few movies pre-retirement) to research the actor via his best work.

friends Weich, Lehman, and Swerdlow, but not Heyman, who went away to Lafayette College in Easton, Pennsylvania.

Every weekday morning Roth rode the number 14 bus for twenty minutes to Raymond Boulevard, whence he walked another ten minutes to one of the two buildings that composed the physical plant of his then four-year-old college: a refurbished brewery on Rector Street, where he had his biology class and lab, and a refurbished bank building about five blocks away, near the Newark Museum, where he took Composition and Literature, Intermediate Spanish, and History of Western Civilization. The only greenery was a wedge of Washington Park ("drunks and all"), so named as the site where George Washington "had trained his scrappy army," as Neil Klugman points out in *Goodbye, Columbus*. Roth loved his classes and got straight As, and at one time or another considered majoring in every subject, including biology. His zeal was fed by a number of first-rate professors who'd been purged from more prestigious academies in New York, casualties of the pre-McCarthy blacklist, a fact that naturally resonated with the future "lawyer for the underdog," as Roth still fancied himself. Also he was now surrounded by books on a daily basis at the Newark Public Library, where he spent hours between classes roaming amid the open stacks—a once novel concept promoted by its legendary librarian, John Cotton Dana, who'd also provided the city's growing immigrant population with collections of books in French, German, Polish, Lithuanian, and Italian. "What took place here was a robust engagement with all the new society had to offer," Roth said of the palazzo-style building that embodied, for him, the best of Newark, and served as an abiding reminder of his own intellectual flowering.

Around noon Roth would take his brown-bag lunch out of his briefcase and sit with classmates in the park—sometimes old friends, but also new Italian and Irish acquaintances from high schools (Barringer, South Side) that had once seemed strange and hostile to a sheltered Weequahic boy. For Roth this was perhaps the best part of college, the very meaning of adulthood—"a great emancipation from Jewish xenophobia," as he put it, from a ghetto-bred paranoia toward goyim that scarcely distinguished between Polish peasantry and Thomas Jefferson. Even at home he couldn't escape it—as when Herman didactically reminded him of the time Sender had beaten his twenty-three-year-old son Ed "to prevent him from marrying a worldly woman": "They don't have that kind of discipline anymore," Herman concluded, whereupon his sixteen-year-old son bolted from the dinner table in a rage. Not for nothing would Roth, in *Portnoy*, give the name Hymie to the brutal uncle who manhandles his son Heshie for even considering marriage to a shiksa—the "key moment" of the novel, as far as its author was concerned.

And this was only one aspect of the "poignant abyss" widening between him and his father, his education deepening in direct relation to his disdain for Herman's coarseness. In *The Anatomy Lesson*, Zuckerman remembers the comfort he found, as a young man, rereading an old *Partisan Review* essay by Milton Appel, reminiscent of a 1946 essay by Appel's model, Irving Howe, "The Lost Young Intellectual," which touches on the vastly different ideas a Jewish father and son, in America, tend to have about the uses of higher education: "The father desires in his son the fulfillment of his own undeveloped and frustrated ambitions.

> "My son shouldn't have to work in a shop" . . . he will literally work himself to death so that his son can go to college. But—and here is where the tragic conflict erupts—to the father intellectual achievement has become wedded to professional success—this he learned in America. . . . But our intellectual who has rebelled against the standards of bourgeois capitalist society cares little about professional success; he wishes to be a great novelist or immerse himself in a great cause, neither of which are particularly remunerative occupations. What is the good, asks the father, of my son's education, his intelligence, his *edelkeit* [refinement]—if he can't make a living? And what is the good, asks the son, of being a success if it means succumbing to philistine standards of values?

Such a conflict would particularly arise (*He'll starve to death!*) when Roth began losing interest in a legal career. Meanwhile, Herman's anxiety mounted as his promising boy became more independent—more "worldly," for better and for worse—until the father's surveillance seemed to border on the obsessive: *Where are you going? . . . Where is he? What time is it? . . .*

Roth longed to go away—to live on a proper campus, where, not incidentally, he could pursue a less furtive love life. Around Thanksgiving he encountered the once hapless Marty ("Carl Furillo") Castelbaum, chatting with friends on the corner outside Halem's candy store. The young man was transformed: poised and dapper in his white bucks and Bucknell sweater, chatting easily about his pre-med courses and life on campus. Many years later, an elderly Dr. Castelbaum laughed when reminded of Roth's impression of him as newly mature circa 1950: "That's not what happened. I had a picture of the shiksa—*that's* what happened." But then, arguably, a tall blonde shiksa was the essence of what Roth had meant by "maturity" and "campus" (in a letter to John Updike, in 1988, he mentioned his appreciation for the actress Kim Basinger and added, "She was what I was looking for at Bucknell"). "*This?*" he said outside Halem's that day, gazing at the photo Castelbaum had produced from his wallet. "You're going out with *this?*" The young man assured him it was so, and Roth decided then and there that Bucknell was for him.

In March 1951, he and his parents drove to Lewisburg for an interview with Dean Mary Jane Stevenson. Right away Roth was favorably impressed by the five-and-a-half-hour drive through bleak Pennsylvania coal towns, reassured that the college wasn't easily reached via public transportation. Then they hit the lush Susquehanna Valley, the cupolas and spires and chiming clock on campus: the whole ambience of small-town gentile America, Republican and middle-class, but otherwise unpretentious and welcoming. Castelbaum was there, too, showing them around, and he didn't fail to point out Larison Hall, where his shiksa girlfriend lived.

That spring Roth got a job selling *Collier's* subscriptions door to door, determined to pay his way through college as much as possible. Every morning a crew chief drove him and five others to a different neighborhood in some nearby town. Underage when he was first hired, Roth later claimed to have applied for a Social Security card under the name Jack Phillips, and thus he introduced himself to various housewives. As he demonstrated his spiel in 2006: "'Hi, I'm Jack Phillips, from Crowell-Collier. You folks get *Collier's?*' I'm behind the screen door. '*No!*' [mimicking a customer's nasty voice]. 'Well, it's been revamped and revitalized! . . . I got a copy here if you'd like to see it. . . .'" A suave, good-looking eighteen-year-old, Roth was sometimes invited inside by lonely matrons, albeit with no better result than the odd sale or glass of lemonade, to his lasting chagrin. ("One of the guys used to say 'Keep your dick in your pants. You can ruin your life.' I *wanted* to ruin it.") Still, he got four dollars per subscription, and managed to sell two or three a day—"a fortune to me"—and loved all the Wolfean wandering around strange neighborhoods, wondering about all the singular little lives behind every door.*

■ ■ ■ ■

WHEN THE TIME CAME to leave, Roth felt as excited as George Willard at the end of *Winesburg, Ohio* ("Hey, you George. How does it feel to be going away?")—though of course their destinations were inverted, given that George was escaping to "the city" and Roth to a place very like Winesburg. For the first leg of the journey he took his first-ever plane trip, on a little prop plane with "a sloping cabin floor," to Williamsport, where he caught a bus for the last twenty-five miles to Lewisburg. If he wanted a different world than Weequahic, here it was: "The campus was entirely white," he remembered. "I don't think there were any Jews on the faculty." As for other marginal groups: he would later learn that his foremost mentor, Mildred Martin, was paid roughly half what her male counterparts made, and while homosexuals were certainly somewhere on campus, they were decidedly closeted. Of the three gay men Roth thinks he encountered at Bucknell, one was the art teacher and the other two were among his first three roommates, all Jews. One would become a friend of Roth through their participation in the drama society, Cap and Dagger; Roth later heard this man had come out of the closet after some thirty years of marriage with children. Another shared a bunk with Roth, a boy named Dick who would serve as the model for the insufferable Flusser in *Indignation*. "Why? Afraid you won't get your beauty sleep?" he taunted the others, when they asked him to turn off his phonograph in the middle of the night. After a few days, Roth went knocking on doors and found an empty bed among quieter roommates: Gordon Mogerley and Don Fagin, engineering and C&F (commerce and finance) majors respectively, who stuck to their studies except when Fagin discreetly played jazz records at a seemly hour.

While Roth (still pre-law) spent almost every night in the library until it closed, the goyim of Bucknell were "getting drunk, getting pinned,

---

* Forty-seven years later, Roth went to the Social Security office in Torrington, Connecticut, to inquire why he wasn't receiving his checks, and so discovered his money had hitherto gone into Jack Phillips's account.

[and] not studying"; also they liked cooling their heels at the movies, whereas Roth figured he saw maybe two movies during his entire time in Lewisburg. Ten years later, as one of the country's leading young Jewish intellectuals, Roth would opine for a *Commentary* symposium that Jews of his generation were united *not* by "a complex of values or aspirations or beliefs" but rather by a "powerful disbelief"—to wit, "the rejection of the myth of Jesus as Christ." Thus, an especially hateful requirement, at Bucknell, had been weekly chapel attendance during which Roth would sit dourly reading Schopenhauer. "I felt like a Houyhnhnm who had strayed on to campus from *Gulliver's Travels*."

While home for Thanksgiving, he was all the more eager to catch up with Marty Weich, Bob Heyman, and Stu Lehman. They went to New York that Friday and hung around the Biltmore Hotel, hoping to meet college girls, and finally parked in front of Roth's house on Leslie Street, where they hilariously rehashed their failures until sometime after midnight. What Roth would later describe as the "worst domestic disaster in our life as a family" began when he tried the back door of his first-floor flat and found it had been double-locked. "Shhh, quiet," his mother whispered, after he'd pounded the door, "your father's furious." *"How the hell do I know where you are!"* Herman shouted from his bedroom, and his son shouted back: "It's none of your business where I am!" *"You could be in a whorehouse!"* Amid Herman's ranting, Bess urged Philip to go to bed, and Sandy, home from Pratt, whispered "Take it easy, forget it." The next morning, however, Philip heard his father in the parlor going on about whorehouses again and sprang out of bed to confront him: "Goddamn it, leave me alone! Don't you know what I am? Look what I do!"—meaning the grades, the nice friends, and a decent measure of filial piety besides. But his father insisted he'd end up throwing it all down the drain, and kept repeating, in tears, "You're a plum! You're a plum!" Finally both men ended up in their rooms, at opposite ends of the apartment, while Sandy tried calming his brother and Bess worked on her husband. In retrospect, Philip would trace his father's crazy, baseless worry to the trauma of losing his brothers Morris, Charlie, and Milton—but then, too, in light of certain events, he would come to view it as not so baseless: "The worries of parents are legitimate," he said. "Things are gonna befall their children. So their hearts break for their children before they even fuck up because they *are* gonna fuck up."

■ ■ ■ ■

THAT FALL Roth joined the all-Jewish fraternity, Sigma Alpha Mu, though he'd also been rushed by a nondenominational local house, Phi Lambda Theta, and even the gentile Theta Chi, whose only Jewish member had a gentile name and happened to be president; the latter tried hard to persuade Roth to join, but Herman had lectured his son about the advantage of being with Jewish boys, and besides Philip worried his role as "an honorary WASP" might sap his natural exuberance. Indeed, he admired the way his SAM brethren managed to assimilate at Bucknell without sacrificing a certain flamboyance inherent in being Sammies, as they were called, which always reminded Roth of "the pushiest of pushy Jews, Sammy Glick."

During his brief association with the Sammies, Roth befriended a colorful C&F major named Dick Denholtz, and the two wrote, directed, and starred in a "wildly uninhibited" burlesque of *Guys and Dolls* ("a musical I knew note by note and word by word"), set at Bucknell, which was the hit of the interfraternity Mid-Term Jubilee. Less rewarding, but no less madcap, was the Sammy "Sand Blast": an indoor beach party, in February, that involved removing all rugs and furniture from the downstairs dining hall and two living rooms, so the entire first floor could be flooded with three inches of sand. Roth thought risking a collapsed floor was a bit much for the would-be bacchanal, which in fact wasn't all that memorable: the coeds' bikinis exposed barely an inch of midriff, and Roth's own spunky blonde date—a young woman nicknamed the Bos (for Bosom)—proved every bit as virtuous as the others. For months afterward, the food had bits of sand in it, and the greasy fare at the SAM house—prepared by an alcoholic ex-sailor naturally called Cookie—had been none too savory to begin with. Given that the house was "a pigpen" smelling of sweat socks, and that it was three times farther from the library, where Roth longed to be, than the men's dorm, his departure after a single year was almost inevitable.

At first his passion for learning was more promiscuous than ever. He'd found his constitutional law class so engrossing that he'd accepted an invitation to spend a semester at American University in Washington, D.C.—but then became enthralled with his world literature class and decided to double-major in English and political science, and finally dropped pre-law altogether. One of the teachers who influenced his decision was C. Willard Smith—"Willard" to students in Cap and Dagger, with whom he liked to take small parts in campus plays. A Princeton man of cheerful, tweedy demeanor, Willard invited Roth to take over Literary Criticism one day and read his paper on Thomas Mann's *Mario and the Magician*, a novella everyone in the class had been assigned to critique. While Willard twinkled in the back of the room, Roth assumed the lectern and read with calm authority—a "Land ho!" moment that made him decide, on the spot, to be a literature professor.

Roth's class in American drama was taught by a tall, bespectacled, balding young man named Bob Maurer, the son of a butcher from Roselle Park, New Jersey, right next to Elizabeth and Newark. One evening the two bumped into each other on campus, and Roth explained he was coming from a meeting of the yearbook staff. Maurer inquired why he was interested in the yearbook, and Roth replied, "Because I think I ought to learn to get along with people." Maurer's response was a revelation to the young man whose father had pressed on him, at age fourteen, Dale Carnegie's *How to Win Friends and Influence People*: "Why would you want to learn a thing like that?" Maurer, a gentile, loved chatting with Roth about their nonintersecting New Jerseys, and soon he invited him and his friend, Pete Tasch—by far the best and funniest students in Maurer's class—to have dinner with him and his wife, Charlotte, who for three years had been William Shawn's secretary at *The New Yorker*.*

The couple struck Roth as nearly ideal human beings—"smart, humorous, deeply tolerant"—and their "dinky" redbrick house became a favorite hangout for the rest of his time at Bucknell. On Saturday nights they'd sit around drinking Gallo wine and listening to E. E. Cummings, the subject of Bob's ongoing dissertation. During the Army–McCarthy hearings Roth would rush down the hill from his morning class and watch a tiny-screened TV with Bob—both of them pacing the floor, raging, while Charlotte made them sandwiches. Most compelling of all, perhaps, was the stylish way the couple dealt with poverty: "it seemed to confer an admirable independence from convention without having

---

* Shawn was nonfiction editor at the time, and Charlotte Maurer remained friendly neighbors in Maine with one of his writers, E. B. White. Shawn was named chief editor after founding editor Harold Ross's death in 1951.

turned them, tiresomely, into fifties bohemians," Roth wrote in *The Facts*. This—along with the pedagogical authority he'd discovered in Willard's class—helped confirm him in his choice to live austerely as a scholar and/or "a serious writer who was so good that his books made no money."

Among fellow students, Roth's best friends were Tasch and Dick Minton. The three had resigned together from Sigma Alpha Mu during the fall semester of Roth's second year in Lewisburg; afterward they filled time working on the campus humor magazine, *Et Cetera*—founded the previous year under the stewardship of one Anne Schoonmaker, who'd primly declared in her first editorial, "Material which depends on filth for laughs is not humorous." Roth, however, was inspired by Cummings's gleeful lines about starting a magazine "fearlessly obscene," and, taking over as editor that fall, he purged the old staff in favor of Tasch, Minton, and a few like-minded others. Essential to the tone of the thing were the urbane Maurers—especially Charlotte, given all she'd gleaned from her time at *The New Yorker*. "One of our friends, a sociology major if you're interested, told us an amusing story the other afternoon," began a typical item from *Et Cetera*'s "Transit Lines," a "two-page miscellany of putatively witty reportage," as Roth put it, that owed much to *The New Yorker*'s "Talk of the Town," including its arch deployment of the royal we.

The larger mission of Roth's *Et Cetera* was to provide a smart, witty alternative to the inane campus newspaper, *The Bucknellian*—all the more after the presidential election that year, as Roth asserted his solidarity with the "civilized minority" who'd supported Adlai Stevenson versus "the philistine majority who had overwhelmingly elected Eisenhower President." In uber-Republican Lewisburg, Roth had made a point of wearing a Stevenson button and even campaigning door to door for "the poor benighted egghead," as he later wrote a friend. He also tried raising the public's consciousness about the evils of McCarthyism with a Browningesque monologue in *Et Cetera*, "I'd Like to Be More Definite but You Know the Times," in which a well-meaning coward gives hesitant voice to his indignation: "some people from a certain state in a certain country have as their spokesman a certain senator / . . . unfair and sort of vile and sour / Sort of has just—well, just—well, for crying out loud, just too damn much power!" And certainly, in a better world, *The Bucknellian* would have felt scooped when Roth assigned a long piece on the

Lewisburg Penitentiary to Tasch, who even wangled an advertisement from the place that "made you want to commit a crime and go there," said Roth.

Roth and Tasch learned the hard way about the trickier aspects of putting out a magazine. Roth had wanted to solicit articles from faculty, and that fall his crusty but lovable history professor, J. Orin Oliphant, obliged him with a facetious piece about the misuse of English. After a long night with Tasch at the printer in Milton, across the Susquehanna River, Roth rushed to Oliphant's office with a copy hot off the press: "Thank you, Philip!" said Oliphant, opening the magazine to his piece. "Oh my god! Oh Christ! It's not in order!" Indeed, the sleepy lads had put an earlier part of the man's article after what was supposed to be the end, and so on. "All right!" Oliphant sighed at last. "You tried and it didn't work!"

■ ■ ■ ■

FOR ROTH, the promise embodied by Castelbaum's shiksa was slow to bear fruit, and indeed Bucknell seemed puritanical even by the standards of Eisenhower's America. Men outnumbered women four to one, and the women were sequestered in the old "Girl Seminary" buildings, Larison, Harris, and Hunt, down the hill from the men. Grim housemothers guarded the virtue of their charges, who were expected to be back in their rooms no later than eleven at night (eight for freshmen). "No men could go anywhere near the dorms unless he was meeting one of the girls," Roth remembered, "and then he could wait with his coat on in the downstairs common room (while being administered a dose of saltpeter . . . some believed that it was liberally sprinkled onto the food prepared for unknowing males at the university dining hall)." For the amusement of a few close friends, Roth composed a ditty he liked to declaim "in stentorian tones": "Larison, Harris, and Hunt, / that's where they keep all the cunt." During his first year, Roth had pursued cheerleaders such as Pat McColl and Annette Littlefield, who drew a hard line at any form of petting, and no wonder: When Roth's friend Jane Brown was admonished by the Waspy Honor Council for "inappropriate kissing," she suspected it had more to do with her boyfriend Eddie's Jewishness than her behavior per se. As her big sister in Kappa Delta remarked, "They think we're crazy for dating Jewish boys, because we can't marry them."*

At the beginning of junior year, Roth had presided over a meeting to recruit new staff for *Et Cetera,* and one of the girls in attendance was Ann Sides, who became art editor and began dating Roth. "I was highly susceptible to slight, pretty blondes with brains," Roth wrote her in 2009, shortly after he'd sent her a copy of his latest novel, *Indignation,* which contained certain key details derived from their affair. At Bucknell, Sides had been a member of the sorority most known for its pulchritude, Tri Delt, though she considered herself an "odd girl out" there: her first two years had been spent at Kutztown State Teachers College ("an overgrown high school") in her hometown of Williamsport, until she dropped out and spent a year working as a chambermaid at a nearby resort. "We kicked dead leaves and talked about Thomas Wolfe," she replied to Roth in 2009, when he asked her to remind him how they'd spent time together. They also went to a football game and, more notably, a "drunken brawl" at the Sammy house, after which, in the backseat of somebody's car, they engaged in heavy petting; Sides returned to her sorority suite drunk and "delirious" ("I was pretty sure I was in love"), singing and dancing, and, like Jane Brown, was hauled up before the Honor Council for ambiguous reasons.

The episode that ended things took place at the local cemetery, a traditional trysting spot, where Roth had driven Sides in his roommate Ned Miller's car: "to my astonishment and hers," Roth remembered, "she performed fellatio." Roth claimed this was nothing he wanted or expected (though he thought he might have taken his penis out, in hope of a hand job)—indeed, all he knew about such an act, he said, was that "whores did it"; in the moment he remembered thinking the girl's parents must be divorced. Sides remembered things differently. "It wasn't the least bit romantic," she said, claiming Roth had put a hand on the back of her head: "I think it was more of an encouragement, not coercive, but I didn't know how to politely withdraw." It may have been so, given that Roth

---

* One night, in 2011, Roth was walking his old classmate Jane Brown Maas back to her apartment on the Upper East Side, when he regaled her with his old "Larison, Harris, and Hunt" ditty. "My god," she thought, "suppose Philip Roth were to be hit by a car and die right here. The media would ask me what were his last words."

would concede more than once, in all apparent innocence, that one had to "have an aggressive side" in those days to get anything in the way of sex: "I don't mean nasty aggressive; I mean a forceful nature."

Roth was seventy-six when he got back in touch with Sides, post-*Indignation*, inquiring with sincere curiosity what she'd made of the incident at the cemetery (a linchpin scene in the book). "I was surprised," she wrote back, "—no, I was appalled. . . . I didn't have any resources for dealing with it so I just cut you out of my life." That was another thing they remembered differently: how it ended. Like Marcus in the novel, Roth recalled being unable to make sense of things and moreover suspecting there was "something a little broken" in Sides, so he kept his distance. Sides, in turn, had had similar feelings of remorse and confusion, but was quite certain she was the one who broke it off, when Roth called a couple of nights later to ask her out for another date. In fact she was so upset she phoned her father immediately afterward and told him about the breakup (though not what had led up to it). "Well, you don't need to be dating a Jewish boy," he said, betraying an anti-Semitism whereof she'd had no previous inkling.

"I feel very tenderly toward her," Roth said, a few years before he was moved to contact Ann Sides Bishop. "If there were any reason to go to the reunion, it would be to see this seventy-two-year-old woman." As it happened, Bishop had been "dining out on Philip Roth for years," as she put it: her granddaughter had been a Ph.D. candidate at Penn a few years after Roth's time as a celebrated faculty member, and the young woman was "lionized" when her colleagues learned that her grandmother had dated Roth. As for Bishop's impression of *Indignation*, she differed with certain of the objective details but was struck by her affinity with the character she'd inspired, Olivia Hutton: both were intelligent and more than a little tormented; while at the dreary college in Williamsport, Bishop had also considered (without actually attempting) suicide. For a few years after *Indignation*, she and Roth wrote occasional letters until it "saltpetered out," said Roth, who meanwhile had typed up notes for a new story he never got around to writing, "The Elderly": "I send copy of Indignation. Get letters. Hers terrifically intelligent. Begin to phone. Pretend it had been different. . . . Tell me about your alcoholism. . . ."

■ ■ ■ ■

THE MAURERS AND OTHERS loved to hear Roth hold forth about his old Jewish neighborhood—the sexual misadventures of the Seltzer King, the ravenous appetites of "the 300-pound bon vivant Apple King"—but no such exuberance, or any Jews even, made their way into his apprentice fiction. Roth, in *The Facts,* was candid about his main influences: "In those first undergraduate stories I managed to extract from Salinger a very cloying come-on and from the young Capote his gossamer vulnerability, and to imitate badly my titan, Thomas Wolfe, at the extremes of self-pitying self-importance." His first published story (in the May 1952 *Et Cetera*), "Philosophy, or Something Like That," owes its diction and whimsy almost entirely to Salinger. As the ten-year-old narrator observes of another kid, "He was a pretty good catcher, but, boy, he was fat—like a cigar. That's funny. I'm funny, you know?" There's also a bit of evocative scab-picking ("The kind of scab you get when you fall down from skating") that was surely borrowed from "Just Before the War with the Eskimos," whereas the final quip ("I'm not allowed to play with Pantheists") seems more or less the original product of a sophomore mind. Capote would prove a more congenial master, as Roth's strongest *Et Cetera* story by far, "The Fence" (May 1953), was a virtual homage to the author of *Other Voices, Other Rooms* ("I wanted to have a picture taken, like Capote, on the couch," said Roth). "The Fence" features another ten-year-old narrator (indeed the story takes place on his tenth birthday), who the reader infers is privileged, given the "winey carpet" his toes brush "faintly," though the rest of the setting is vague except for an orphanage next door—transplanted, horses and all, from Weequahic. The titular fence separates the narrator from some frolicking orphans, to whom he guiltily tosses one of his birthday gifts, then a ball, but the orphans have wandered away. "I had held so tightly to the orphanage fence that the pattern of the wire was printed upon my palm," the story ends, with nice understatement.

After resigning from the Sammies, Roth's social life was divided between *Et Cetera* and the "oddball members of Cap and Dagger," with whom he gathered for nightly rehearsals in Bucknell Hall, an elegant little nineteenth-century building with a cathedral ceiling. Roth's roles included Happy Loman in *Death of a Salesman* ("*MA*-awm!" he'd later mimic his aggrieved response to being called a "philandering bum") and the Shepherd in *Oedipus Rex,* but he made his most lasting impression as the raffish Ragpicker in *The Madwoman of Chaillot*. Jack Wheatcroft, a young instructor who went on to become a lifelong friend, first met Roth in his Ragpicker makeup and commended his performance—a moment Wheatcroft would remember while presenting Roth with Bucknell's highest honor, the Stephen Taylor Medal, in 2008:

> Fifty-six years later still I can see the slight nod and controlled smile of acknowledgment I received. Since he was in costume and makeup, I had no idea what Philip Roth looked like. But I did recognize his poise, dignity, graciousness, qualities that the Ragpicker had not exhibited. And I sensed that such a difference meant that Philip Roth had to have an understanding of the complex relationship that exists between a fictional character and what we call the real self. Well, the Ragpicker and Philip Roth have gone on to live together for fifty-six years.

That spring of 1953, a transfer student from Endicott Junior College in Massachusetts, Elizabeth "Betty" Powell, began coming around to Cap and Dagger rehearsals to prompt from the script or otherwise help the director. Like her predecessor, Ann Sides, Powell was a slight, pretty blonde with brains—an honor student (in psychology) who rather intimidated Roth with her worldliness, the way she chain-smoked and drank martinis. "Stop *mooning*!" she'd chide him, whenever he tried wooing her. As it happened, her sophistication was cultivated, and her pensive expression bespoke a troubled past: her parents were divorced, and she lived with her mother in Teaneck, New Jersey; her father ("a goy drunk") was a commander in the navy, and both he and her brother were on the roughneck side. During visits to campus, the brother would always insist on drinking too much with Betty and Philip, and the latter would invariably vomit.

"She wouldn't give me a tumble in the beginning," said Roth, who pressed his cause until finally he persuaded her to have "clumsy" and eventually "less clumsy" sex. The couple liked eating dinner in town, and afterward would stop at the Wheatcrofts' on Third Street for coffee and dessert. Jack adored Betty, and took to calling her the Booper after Betty Boop; much of her and Roth's hasty coupling took place on the Wheatcrofts' bed during joint babysitting jobs ("I got more ass on Jack's bed than he ever did," Roth observed, before adding in an explanatory way: "He and his wife slept there"), or else on the laundry room floor in one of the (men's) dormitories. A sense of boon companionship was born of such furtive exertions, and the two became inseparable. The previous summer Roth had happily worked as a counselor at Pocono Highland Camp in East Stroudsburg, Pennsylvania, and toward the end of junior year he phoned the director and got him to hire Betty, too. Like Bucky and his girlfriend in *Nemesis*, the two would slip away from campfires and row a boat out to a little lake island to make love.

For that year's Thanksgiving, Roth took Betty home to meet his parents, and was gratified by how easily she "shed the wryness" and became sweet and gracious. If there was any strain, it was all between Philip and his father—or rather it was all on Philip's part, as he was more appalled than ever by what he considered the man's vulgarity. ("He didn't know about *Sir Gawain and the Green Knight*, the Pearl Poet. . . .") Even then Philip knew he was being unfair, that Herman was doing his best, but still he couldn't bear it; he felt like Emma Bovary hating the sight of her husband's back.

CHAPTER

Six

Roth's favorite professor at Bucknell was Mildred Martin, a wry, middle-aged Midwesterner who earned his respect with a gravitas that was often mistaken for severity. "She scared nine-tenths of the student body," said her student Jesse Bier, "mostly by false reputation, but she was essentially the kindest of human beings, however skeptical her mind." A lifelong spinster who "rather shrank from physical contact" (Bier), Martin lived in an eighteenth-century clapboard house on South Front Street with a faculty couple, Harold and Gladys Cook, and together they drank nightly martinis for most of their adult lives. Possessed of "solid learning" she was keen to impart, albeit with no desire to seem impressive about it, Martin provided a crucial service for Roth: "She valued me. This is what I needed and what I got. . . . Look, somebody has to tell you that you're smart and that you're doing the right thing." His friendship with Miss Martin would continue to evolve until her death more than forty years later.

The highlight of Roth's undergraduate career was "The Seminar"—Martin's two-semester, invitation-only honors course that covered the entirety of English literature "from its beginnings to the present," or from Beowulf to Stephen Spender, as things stood then. For nine credit hours per semester (the equivalent of three regular courses) the workload was immense: Students had to read one or two books a week, as well as fifty pages in Albert Baugh's *Literary History of England*, an underlined copy of which Roth would forever keep on the library table of his Connecticut living room. Because of Baugh, he liked to say, "I still know who Barnaby Goodge is and what *Tottle's Miscellany* is and am the only person on West Seventy-ninth who has read *Ralph Roister Doister*." Some of his other reading included Marlowe's *Doctor Faustus*, a lot of Shakespeare (four plays, the sonnets, "The Phoenix and the Turtle"), *Tom Jones*,

Tristram Shandy, the major Romantics, at least one novel from Trollope's *Barchester* series, Thomas Huxley, selected passages from *Ulysses*, and more. Students wrote a lot, too: at least one weekly critical paper and a summary of the assigned Baugh pages, all of it "scrutinized for accuracy and for common sense by Miss Martin."

The class of eight students met for three hours every Thursday afternoon, either in the Vaughan Literature Building library, or in Miss Martin's living room on South Front Street. Sitting beside the fireplace in the latter, Roth would admire the old rugs and floorboards, the vast shelves of books, and look forward to his own "life of reading books and writing about them"—and, of course, talking about them. Discussions often got heated, as students sought to impress Miss Martin with their superperceptive sniping at "unsubstantiated" opinions, or criticism that was merely "subjective." As Roth recalled, "She herself had no more animus than a radar screen locating objects in space: what Mildred Martin located were our weaknesses of observation and expression. Nothing imperfect flew by her unnoted. She was the first of my scrupulous editors—the sternest, the most relentless, the best." In 1991, during a videotaped chat with Roth, Martin still remembered the excitement of that particular seminar class—her best ever, she thought, along with the 1948–49 group that included Wheatcroft—and laughed about the time Roth and Minton had become so exercised over a line in Yeats's "Sailing to Byzantium" that they stood shouting at each other while "Tasch was egging you on."

> ROTH: I remember! Dick was wrong and I was right. . . .
> MARTIN: . . . I never had people so excited about the meaning of a line. Do your students ever get that excited in New York?

Martin also remembered the "four frightened girls" in class, daunted by the brilliance of Roth, Minton, and a TA named John Tilton ("smart in an academic way," Roth said of the last, "but no flair"). On December 2, 1953, Martin wrote a reminder in her diary that Roth had agreed to teach her world lit class in her absence ("I did," said Roth, "and loved it"), and on December 15, she reflected, "When I was 21, in comparison with Roth and Minton, I was a child." In the same entry she noted that Susie Kiess had stopped coming to class, and "Mrs. Bender" had dropped, too, after bursting into tears while Roth read his paper on "The Fight at Finnsburg"; fleeing to the kitchen, Mrs. Bender returned at last to say "I know the answer to that question," gave it, and disappeared forever. Martin did not seem disconcerted, and indeed looked forward to the remaining two girls' departures after every Thursday class, while the boys went on bickering and the five of them would "[begin] to have a really good time."

Along with his cherished Baugh, another old college book Roth would retain to the end was an anthology of essays, *Toward Liberal Education*, wherein he'd discovered the satire of Philip Wylie, the now all-but-forgotten author of *Opus 21, Generation of Vipers,* and *Finnley Wren.* To the young Roth, Wylie's mandarin railing against "Momism," advertising, and popular culture in toto was a bracing revelation. Later Roth would revisit his idol and find his work "pompous, mannered, superior, arrogant . . . everything I must have loved then"; indeed, at the time, Wylie was a crucial step toward framing certain grievances against the crasser bumpkins on campus and his own upbringing.*

The quintessence of local vulgarity was still *The Bucknellian,* especially as it existed in 1953, under the editorial hand of Barbara (Bobby) Roemer, a popular girl on campus who also served as vice president of Tri Delt and captain of the cheerleading squad. It occurred to Roth, in retrospect, that his infamous attacks on her newspaper were a little aroused by jealousy—students actually read the thing in droves, which could hardly be said of *Et Cetera*—but then, too, it was just a ghastly rag: "If you're a satirist you're being thrown a slow curve with *The Bucknellian,*" he said, "and you just time yourself and just smack it out of the fucking ballpark."

"There is a theory that if a thousand monkeys were chained to a thousand typewriters for an unspecified number of years," Roth's editorial for the Spring 1953 issue began,† "they would have written all of the great literature that has been set down in the world by human beings. If

---

* Roth's girlfriend during much of the sixties, Ann Mudge, turned out to be related to Wylie—a "jolly" man whom Roth was thrilled to meet over dinner one night in 1964.

† *Et Cetera* was published quarterly, but the dating of its issues was erratic. Sometimes they were dated by season ("Spring"), sometimes by month ("May"), and sometimes neither ("Mid-Year").

such is the case, what is holding up production of *The Bucknellian*? We do not expect Miss Roemer and her cohorts to turn out great literature, for, after all, they are not monkeys, but we do expect them to publish a newspaper." Thus Roth explained his motive for including, as that issue's centerfold, a satirical facsimile of *The Bucknellian* that mimicked, among other things, Miss Roemer's own well-known editorial voice: "Gee whiz, why can't we have some school spirit here at ivy-covered B. U.! Huh, why not? Boy, at other schools they yell their heads off at athletic contests; they go hog wild, at other schools!" Another typical item in Roth's *Bucknellian* came with the headline TRI DELTI [sic] AND PIPHI TIE FOR FIRST IN ANNUAL CAKE BAKE; PHI MU TAKES THIRD SPOT WITH MARBLE CAKE and went on soberly to record that the Phi Mu's entry had been relegated to third place because of a lack of "fluffiness" and "texture" in their product. CHEERS TO CONTINUE read another headline—and so on.

The parody was a hit among the campus smart set, and one of the letters published in the subsequent (May) issue of *Et Cetera* was jointly signed by Mildred Martin, Bob Maurer, Jack Wheatcroft, and one Ruth Lavare: "We wish to commend you and your staff for having absorbed one of the lessons for which students come to college—that criticism intelligently used is one of the best instruments for directing inevitable change." Another of Roth's admirers, C. Willard Smith, wrote to congratulate him on the "good humor" and "satirical wit" of the facsimile per se, allowing that it made its point "if the shoe fits." Willard continued, "But in the editorial, you virtually presented Miss Roemer a pair of *I. Miller* super specials of exact size. . . . I might even add that your editorial seemed to me almost unchivalrous." Willard was far from alone in thinking so. Bobby Roemer was reduced to tears and (some say) scarred for life, and her managing editor, Red Macauley, came knocking on Roth's door and seemed ready to deck the "little Jewish Swift," as Roth called his younger self—"Swiftberg."

And Swiftberg wasn't done. A year later Roth introduced his second *Bucknellian* parody with an editorial titled "A Physician's Apologia," from this epigraph by Dryden (no less): "he who writes honestly is no more an enemy to the offender, than the physician to the patient, when he prescribes harsh remedies to an inveterate disease." Reminding the reader that he'd previously addressed the condition of Bucknell's "diseased newspaper," Roth reported that his mockery had struck some as "cruel and callous, and others (more perceptive) as immoral and/or immature; a few were struck by the unfortunate truth of the remarks. If *The Bucknellian* was struck at all, I fear its granite skin was not pierced." Once more unto the breach, then, with another satire composed mostly of banal spoofing of Roemer's fondness for frat gossip and school spirit. One item, however—based on an actual weekly feature in the newspaper—made the campus community take startled notice. "Girl of the Weak [sic]" was illustrated by Matisse's *Odalisque Seated with Arms Raised*, a nude with hairy armpits, and purported to be about Honor Goodgirl: "Since Honor is an Education Major, she is on the Dean's List. She is from her local state, and is also a sea-shell collector of sorts, an amateur horticulturist, and a virgin. When asked to comment upon this wide variety of interests, she said, 'I really am a virgin.'"

The dean of men in 1954 was a former Bucknell football star named Mal Musser; lanky, bald, and affable, the man was a foremost proponent of what the college liked to call its Hello Spirit—a spirit Musser thought Swiftberg had roundly abused. Answering Musser's summons, Roth found the man grimly surveying his portrait of Honor Goodgirl. "Young man," said Musser, once Roth had seated himself, "this is *not* in the Bucknell spirit. *The Bucknellian* is a fine"—etc. Roth was also censured by the Board of Publications, and while no one demanded that *Et Cetera* shutter its offices, Roth (like Marcus Messner in *Indignation*) was all but certain he'd "fucked [him]self." Soon he'd be expelled and drafted, if not sent to Korea; at the very least he'd lost his chance at a decent graduate school scholarship. Nor did it help (he suspected) that his name was Roth, that his associates were Tasch, Minton, and a Sammy business manager named Pincus—"a little nest of Jews," as he later put it.

All but broken for the time being, he was "nearly in tears" when he appeared on Miss Martin's doorstep. "'Well,'" she remembered saying, "'if you're going to be a satirist you're going to be misunderstood all your life.' And he kind of gazed at me and said, 'Is that true?'" In Roth's case it was eminently true, and he would come to view Honor Goodgirl as an emblem of his future greatness—"the work of an incipient Mickey Sabbath" who'd left his "quivering sensitivity" behind. For Bobby Roemer, the parodies were perhaps the first dark clouds swarming along her horizon. Some fifteen years later she came to the office of Dr. Martin Castelbaum and noticed his Bucknell diploma while he took her history. She asked him when he'd graduated, and he told her. "Don't you *know* me?" she inquired, a little frantically. Dr. Castelbaum—who'd rarely stepped outside the library in college, and whose romance with the shiksa was, truth be known, as chaste as it was short-lived—confessed that he didn't. The woman burst into tears: "Those were the happiest days of my life! I was editor of *The Bucknellian*, I was a cheerleader, I was *everything* at Bucknell!" And she rushed out of his office, never to return.*

"How richly it fulfills the promise of Honor Goodgirl!" Charlotte Maurer congratulated Roth in 1971, on the publication of *Our Gang*, a tasteless satire of the Nixon administration. "I imagine that only Bob and I, and possibly Mildred Martin, remember how long you've been a master satirist," she said, naming the novel's co-dedicatees.

■　■　■　■

THOUGH MORE STUDIOUS than ever, Roth would court disaster in a way that his father, for one, might have foreseen. Seniors were allowed to live off campus, and that year Roth and Tasch took rooms at a boardinghouse belonging to a pious white-haired widow, Mrs. Purnell, who informed them forthwith that women (that is, one's fiancée) were allowed to visit only on Sunday, for tea, and only then if the door was left open. One Sunday evening, a few weeks into his final semester, Roth was lying in bed with Betty Powell when he heard his landlady return from what he thought would be a longer family visit in nearby Mifflinburg; waving Betty under the bed, Roth hastily got dressed, grabbed a book, and smiled at the bleak-faced widow on his way out. He planned to go around and open a window for Betty, but the old lady was in his room like a shot, prodding the girl with her foot: "Get out of there, you hussy!" Roth spotted Betty fleeing the house, and walked her back to her room before returning to confront Mrs. Purnell. He found the woman dialing (presumably) the dean of men. "You had no right to scare that girl that way!" Roth blustered, foreseeing his "life in a shambles," especially given his relations with Musser.

He found refuge at the Maurers, asking to speak alone with Bob.

* When Roth received the Taylor Medal in 2008, *The Bucknellian* tracked down its old editor, Barbara Roemer Gibb, for a comment: "There never was and there won't be a response," she replied, calling the attack "unprovoked."

"Have you paid your rent?" Bob asked the haggard Roth, who replied he'd only paid half. Bob assured him that the mean old widow wouldn't dare risk forfeiting half her rent money, now that it was too late in the semester to find another lodger, and meanwhile laughter exploded from the kitchen where Charlotte had been listening. Roth slept at his friends' house for a couple of nights while awaiting a last, fatal summons from Dean Musser. When nothing happened, he returned to his room *chez* Purnell, and sure enough his landlady never mentioned the incident again, nor did Roth invite Betty to visit, even for tea.

Within weeks another disaster loomed: Betty's period was late. Both she and Roth had applied for prestigious graduate school scholarships, but if Betty was pregnant they'd have little choice but to marry and stay in Lewisburg—living amid the quonset huts of Bucknell Village, supporting themselves as TAs while earning their homely Bucknell master's degrees. For a couple of weeks Roth waited for Betty each night outside the student commons, and each night she'd greet him with a fraught little shake of her head; one night, however, she arrived beaming. Roth was likely the more ecstatic of the two: "Having narrowly escaped premature domesticity and its encumbering responsibilities," he wrote in *The Facts*, "I abandoned myself to dreams of erotic adventures that I couldn't hope to encounter other than on my own."

On April 15, 1954, Dean Musser informed Roth ("Hearty congratulations") that he was one of a handful of seniors elected to Phi Beta Kappa, and a week later Miss Martin noted in her diary that Roth had come around to discuss the speech he'd been chosen to give at the induction ceremony. He was also one of eight magna cum laude graduates (plus a single summa), having received mostly As and the odd B in ROTC and C in PE. As for Betty Powell, she was the recipient (cum laude) of the Wainwright D. Blake Award for Outstanding Senior in Psychology.

Back in New Jersey that June, Roth faced a dilemma: after three months on a waiting list, he'd finally been offered a full scholarship to the University of Pennsylvania, where a brilliant older cousin, Sandy Kuvin (then pursuing his medical studies at Cambridge in England), had attended both college and graduate school; Kuvin had nothing but good things to say about the place. Meanwhile the University of Chicago had immediately offered Roth a scholarship, but a few alumni had "given [him] reports not entirely satisfactory," as Roth wrote to Miss

Martin in the "Lord Chesterfield" diction (as he later put it) that he adopted in his early letters to that formidable woman. One factor tipping him toward Chicago was his admiration for the university's former (until 1951) president, Robert Maynard Hutchins, whose classic essay opposing college football, "Gate Receipts and Glory," had also appeared in Roth's beloved anthology, *Toward Liberal Education*. In an early draft of *Zuckerman Unbound*, a young Nathan imagines himself quoting the essay in a speech, amid the kind of fastidious little cues Roth himself was apt to scribble into the scripts of his every public utterance:

> "The substitute for athleticism," as Robert M. Hutchins had written in "Gate Receipts and Glory," "is light and learning. (*Pause for alliteration to sink in*) The colleges and universities which (*Sarcastically*) taught the country football, can teach the country that the effort to discover truth (*Significant pause*), to transmit the wisdom of the race (*Significant pause*), and to preserve civilization (*Significant pause*) is exciting and (*Bitter irony*) perhaps important too."

What would prove the decisive consideration, however, was that Betty Powell had accepted a scholarship to Penn. That summer the couple met for lunch at the Biltmore, and Roth calmly announced he was going to Chicago, in light of which he didn't see the point of continuing their affair. "I didn't do it with relish," he remembered. "I did it with dispatch. I had no finesse. . . . That was the first blow I ever dealt a woman." Saying goodbye at the Port Authority Bus Terminal, Roth watched his old girlfriend leave on an escalator, where she began to sob; with some little surprise he realized she must have loved him after all.

She was, in fact, already replaced or soon to be. On June 28, Roth began work as a counselor at a YMHA day camp, Forest Lodge, a fifteen-mile bus trip from Newark. "I took my twelve ten year olds into the forest for a hike," he wrote Miss Martin at the end of that first day; "moccasined Arctic trapper that I am, I proceeded to lose myself and the group; it took us two hours to find our way out; we walked about eight miles; for a moment—I must admit—when it looked as though they were going to have to send a helicopter out to find us, a tiny stab of panic rose in my gallant breast." Nowhere in this account was any mention of a fellow counselor named Maxine Groffsky—a stunning eighteen-year-old who caught Roth's eye while diving gracefully into the pool. A willowy girl with hair "the color of an Irish setter," Groffsky had a kind of blasé athleticism that Roth evoked in his letters by calling her Jordan Baker, the jaunty golfing socialite in *Gatsby*. The model for Brenda Patimkin in *Goodbye, Columbus*, Groffsky was from suburban Maplewood rather than Short Hills (in the novella), though both places were on either side of South Mountain Reservation—an uphill trip from Newark "that brought one closer to heaven," as Neil Klugman would have it, what with the sweeter breezes and grander houses at that elevation.

The couple began seeing each other day and night; on weekends they played tennis in South Orange, and Roth was a regular guest at the Groffsky dinner table. Roth would tweak a few facts, but otherwise the family mirrored the Patimkins at every salient point: Maxine's older brother, Paul, was a basketball star at the University of Michigan, and their younger sister, Irene, was an assertive kid who attended kosher summer camp and later moved to Israel. What the children had in common was the doting solicitude of their father, Herman, a rough-hewn Polish immigrant who'd made a killing as a wholesale glass distributor.* Maxine's attractive mother, Belle, was old friends with Uncle Bernie's first wife, Byrdine, whose daughter Margery had been friends with Maxine at Columbia High School—another reason Philip was so readily accepted by the family, though the proper Belle kept an eye on things. When Maxine proposed visiting her boyfriend in Chicago that fall, her mother quashed the idea: a girl who pursues a boy so obviously is not "conventional," she explained, with some little severity.

"I was never a wise guy with parents," Roth said of his younger self, whose perfect manners vis-à-vis the Groffskys were belied by his tendency—once he began sleeping over at their big five-bedroom house on Richmond Avenue—to skulk the halls after hours and have sex with Maxine. Still, he was careful not to betray certain Philip Wylie–esque

---

* When I asked Stu Lehman to describe Herman Groffsky, he said the man bore an "incredible" resemblance to the actor who played Mr. Patimkin in the movie, Jack Klugman. I doubt Roth would have disagreed: by far his favorite scene (perhaps from *any* movie based on his books) was between Mr. Patimkin/Klugman and his beloved daughter, at the wedding, where he tells her she can have anything in the world she wants.

perceptions of their garish prosperity and the way it shaped their souls; for Bob Heyman's benefit, though, he tried to explain what he would later dramatize far better: "They are crude and solid and as happy as God will let them be, they are gluttonous and warm and fearful and sometimes loving and selfish and generous too; and that is their problem." Certainly Paul Groffsky suspected none of this; that fall, Roth made a point of cheering on his potential future brother-in-law at the Northwestern game, in Evanston, and really he didn't consider Paul a "lunkhead"—à la Ron in the novel—so much as "boring," whereas Paul was at pains to point out, later, that he didn't really own the Ann Arbor equivalent of a "Columbus record"—"E. E. Cummings reading to students (verse, silence, applause)"—though he did have a record of Big Ten fight songs that he played "more than once."

The big point of the affair, for Roth, was sex—a rather prosaic business with Betty Powell, and anything but with Maxine, or Mackie as he called her. Nor was there any controversy about getting a diaphragm, since both were eager to enhance their pleasure, and indeed about the only detail Roth recalled of that transaction was Mackie's breezy announcement afterward: "I'm wearing it." At the beginning of September—a few days before he left for Chicago and she left for her freshman year at Cornell—the couple joined Stu Lehman and his fiancée at a rental house in Loch Arbour on the Jersey Shore. Lehman remembered thinking that Roth and his new girlfriend seemed "made for each other. . . . They were both very attractive people—tall, good-looking—and she seemed to be able to handle his acerbic sense of humor and his sexual appetites, at least as far as we knew." At the time Roth professed to have low expectations for the teenager's suitability as an intellectual companion, conceding to Heyman that "she has her charming moments, which it is often worth waiting for"; however, with respect to her way of slipping into his cabana, say, and blowing him before he changed into his trunks, he was considerably less ambivalent. "No doubt [Betty Powell] is far more understanding and clever than Mackie," he wrote Heyman, "but I wonder what is more important. I was beginning to doubt my masculinity until Mackie responded so healthily and beautifully. It's paradoxical, I think, that Betty, who is certainly more feminine than Maxine, should be the cold one, and that Maxine, the girl-boy, should play the role of the woman so much better."

CHAPTER

Seven

Roth would often refer to his first year in Chicago (1954–55) as the best of his life—a time when he'd pursued his "Byronic dream" of "bibliography by day, women by night." It began with his second-ever plane trip, followed by a cab from Midway to the Windermere Hotel in Hyde Park (where he'd stay that first night only), during which he excitedly asked his old black cabbie where he might find Robie House and Oak Park (Hemingway) and so on. Finally the man glanced over his shoulder and said, "Son, if you can't get laid in Chicago, you can't get laid anywhere." Guided by the novels of Nelson Algren, Roth dropped his bags at the hotel and headed to a strip bar on the corner of Dearborn and Division, where a young dancer named Pepper put a hand on his thigh and sat chatting with him while he bought her overpriced drinks out of his tiny student budget.

For the first week or two Roth took a cramped room at the International House, befriending a former ballet dancer from Panama who was fun to "pal around with," at first, until one night he made a pass at Roth. "I wouldn't hurt you, baby," the man laughed at Roth's utter astonishment. Finally, after a frantic four-day search, Roth found more suitable quarters at the Disciples Divinity House on East Fifty-seventh—a "magnificent" room, he wrote Heyman, "big, light, and full of character (Gothic as all get-out)." Most of Roth's twenty or so housemates were Protestant divinity students, though soon enough Roth struck up friendships with a couple of Jewish boys in the English department, Barry Targan and Herb Haber, who also took rooms at the Divinity House. Haber remembered a certain amount of raillery among their Christian housemates, who debated whether Jews were heathen or pagan, properly speaking, and did they have any real chance of attaining heaven?

An excitable fourth was added to their circle in the person of Arthur

Geffen, a Brooklyn prodigy who'd left high school early to enroll in Hutchins's three-year master's program. Geffen supported himself as a part-time bartender at the University Tavern, where he and Roth would compete to see who could make Haber and Targan fall off their stools laughing. Roth's routines included an impersonation of Bobby Kennedy talking in a Bugs Bunny voice, as well as a more or less constant flow of improvisation with Geffen ("Alongside him I'm John Wayne," said Roth)—long tipsy evenings when they'd play Iago and a jive-talking Othello, or speak entirely in Hemingway locutions. The university was, in short, a kind of demi-paradise for Roth: "like some highly evolved, uto-pian extension of the Jewish world of my origins, as though the solidarity and intimate intensity of my old neighborhood life had been infused with a lifesaving appetite for intellectual amusement and experimentation." In the classroom, too, the friends from Brooklyn and Newark could better grapple with "the intimidating power of Henry James and literary good taste generally" by remembering that Isabel Archer was, after all, a typ-ical shiksa.

And yet: the main thing about being an ambitious Jewish boy was keeping your nose clean. John Condor—an "arch and a bit splendid" (Roth) Wasp at the Divinity House—suddenly lit out for New Orleans in the middle of the term, and a few days later returned with a head-ful of happy memories. Roth, Targan, and Haber brooded about this at Jimmy's Bar one night and abruptly decided, by god, they'd do the same thing! Piling into Targan's '41 Chevy, they got as far as Attica, Indiana, where they exchanged a look "and turned back into the people we really were," said Targan. They were back in Chicago by sunrise.

Roth became closest of all to an older graduate student in English, Bob Baker, a short man with a mustache who'd met his wife, Ida, while traveling in Venice with the merchant marine. Roth doted on their little boy, Geoffrey, and loved listening to the couple chatter in Italian while Ida, an excellent cook, made dinner for everyone. Baker, a gentile from Oregon, deserves much of the credit for sending Roth to the work of Saul Bellow, and when Roth himself began writing seriously, he referred to Baker as his "Chicago Maxwell Perkins"—the first and best reader of his manuscripts.

One day Roth lay sunning himself on the Divinity House roof with Haber and Targan. "You know," he said, rather solemnly, "this may be as good as it gets for us." Many years later—after marriage and children and a mostly happy life—Haber remembered that moment on the roof and grasped its profundity: When indeed were they ever again so free, among good people who read books and loved to laugh? "Phil was the only one I ever knew who could see and understand that," he said. "Talk about wisdom—I thought he had enough of it. And talent and drive to become who he was."

■ ■ ■ ■

BRIGHT AND EARLY, Roth would head to the commons for the same daily breakfast—two pieces of toast spread thick with marmalade and topped by three strips of bacon on each—then off to the library or an early class. That first quarter his three courses included ("hold your breath," he wrote Heyman) Bibliography and "a dainty little thing entitled 'History and Culture,'" the utility of which he accepted grudgingly at best; his other course, on Mark Twain, was more engaging. At the time the English Department was divided between young Turks like Elder Olson ("I loved his name," said Roth) who called themselves Neo-Aristotelians—they considered New Criticism to be marred by its supposedly "subjective" emphasis on irony, metaphor, and ambiguity somewhat in general—and the old guard who approached literature in a then more traditional cultural-historical context. Walter Blair, the department chair and Roth's Twain professor, embodied the old guard. Blair's manner was what one might have expected from a foremost authority on American humor and the tall tale; wryly he forbade Roth to write a paper "on the structure of *Tom Sawyer*" because (a) "he'd rather we didn't write 'critical papers,'" so Roth noted, and (b) in 1939 Blair himself had published a paper titled "On the Structure of *Tom Sawyer*." What Roth liked about Blair was his "down-to-earth appreciation of what made Twain funny. . . . He didn't make *Huckleberry Finn* into what Trilling made it into," Roth observed; "he made it into *Huckleberry Finn*. And I thought, God, this stuff is literature!" A leading Roth scholar, Bernard Rodgers, would someday write a paper about Walter Blair's conception of Southwestern humor and its influence on Roth's *The Great American Novel*.

Roth found much to like in the Neo-Aristotelians, too, reading *Ulysses* in Olson's Form and Structure in Contemporary British Literature ("the course isn't as pompous as all that") and admiring the approach taken by a visiting British scholar, Joan Bennett ("a most delightful, exciting, and clear-thinking woman"), who explained that her course on the Victorian novel was also, really, on the form of the novel per se. As Roth wrote the Maurers, "For the first time in months (since the best sessions of last year's seminar), the wheels are beginning to turn, and I'm getting that gigantic boost that comes every so often, with me, from thinking." He was less impressed by another celebrated faculty member, Morton Dauwen Zabel, a former editor of *Poetry* magazine, who by 1954 was "sleepwalking . . . toward a decent retirement," as the poet George Starbuck put it—or, as Roth informed the Maurers, "Zabel is out of his mind." Despite the man's tendency to lose his train of thought and stare disconcertingly into space for minutes at a time, his confidential review of Roth's Yaddo application, three years later, was lucid enough: "[Roth] is a very decent fellow, not vivacious or notably lively in his personality, but sober, steady, well-conducted, very well-mannered and considerate." Clearly Zabel had never observed Roth at the University Tavern with Art Geffen, riffing on Zabel's performance in an imaginary football game played by loony academics.

The professor who would prove most important to Roth, both pedagogically and professionally, was the dean of humanities, Napier Wilt. Ted Solotaroff—who would have reasons to envy Roth, one of which was Roth's favored status with Wilt—dismissed the dean as a lightweight ("not a scholar or a critic"): "His field was nineteenth-century American drama, whose slight significance had left him free to exercise his formidable congeniality and cunning in advancing his career. A heavy, florid man, he was a traveler, a bon vivant, discreetly gay, and every year or two he would bring a graduate student under his warm, powerful wing." Roth was a notable instance of the latter, and he never imagined that the gruff-mannered Wilt—who drove a secondhand Rolls and lived with his mother and longtime partner, Bill—was any more gay than Roth's own bachelor uncle, Mickey: "I just thought he was a bon vivant of the kind Henry James wrote about. He knew everybody all over Chicago."

Wilt himself was something of a James scholar, and Roth's first impression of his mentor was that he possessed a good deal of "Jamesian superciliousness and pomposity": Wilt treated his second-quarter graduate students "like so much offal," announcing in Introduction to Literary Methods ("pre-criticism," he called the course) that he'd try to keep things as "simpleminded" as possible: "Half the class is petrified, and the other half angry," Roth wrote. "I, Hercules-like, span the two—pissed-off in a frightened way." Once Wilt began to thaw, though, he turned out to be a witty, unpretentious reader of the classics, which he discussed in almost personal terms, as if he were acquainted with the authors and even their characters. Roth's favorite course that year was Wilt's American Literature (1919–1929)—essentially a study of the Lost Generation, among whom Wilt numbered himself, having been gassed in World War I: "he's always lecturing in terms of 'we,'" Roth wrote. "—'We all were reading Cummings in those years,' 'We all were excited over *This Side of Paradise*,' etc." Each student was assigned to give a cultural overview of a particular year in the twenties, and Roth got "the most terrific year"—1925—encompassing *Gatsby*, *Manhattan Transfer*, and *The New Yorker*'s first issue.

Since leaving Bucknell, Roth had been working hard at his own fiction—so hard, in fact, that he'd given Wilt and other professors pause. "It was felt his interest was too much in the writing of fiction, too little in graduate work," Wilt would observe in a recommendation letter a few years later, en route to concluding that Roth had proved adept at both fiction writing and scholarship. At the time, fired by Wilt's interest, Roth dusted off a couple of stories he'd written that summer—still oscillating between the styles of Capote and Salinger, albeit with ever more accomplished mimicry. Indeed, one might even say "The Day It Snowed" is more Capote than Capote—or, as Roth later put it, "I make Capote look like a longshoreman." Once again the hero is a winsome, sensitive boy, Sydney, whose dawning awareness of death is treated with a kind of Southern Gothic surrealism. "Suddenly people began to disappear," the story opens. "First it was his Aunt Wilma who looked like his mother except that her eyes were soft and pale blue, like two pieces of sky lifted from the morning horizon." When Sydney's stepfather also "disappears," the boy goes worriedly looking for him and encounters a mysterious old man, who leads him to the cemetery where his family is gathered. Sydney is counterintuitively elated to learn that his stepfather and Aunt Wilma didn't, after all, "do it on purpose," but panics when the old man begins to depart: "'Mister, Mister Man, please come back—' but before he could reach the sidewalk, the big black hearse, like an angry whale, came charging down the left side of the road to be first in the funeral line, and it crushed the boy to the ground, like feet crush acorns, and it shattered forever his thin glass voice." *Mademoiselle* had already returned the story when Roth showed it to Wilt, who laconically approved ("It's good, Roth") and advised him to try the prestigious campus literary magazine, the *Chicago Review*, where it appeared in the Fall 1954 issue, along with critical studies by Kenneth Burke and Elder Olson.

Roth was launched. "The Day It Snowed" caused a splash on campus, and the author became "a star" (Haber) among his classmates. Within a week of the story's appearance, Dean Wilt got in touch with an editor at E. P. Dutton, William Doerflinger, who wrote Roth a note inquiring whether he was working on a novel "we could have the privilege of seeing"; Roth replied that he was happy to give Dutton first consideration on any longer work in progress, declining to mention that such a work didn't exist. Another boon of his first *Chicago Review* publication would prove to be his friendship with one of the student-editors, George Starbuck, who would go on to become a distinguished poet and the editor (at Houghton Mifflin) of Roth's first book. Urbane and good-natured, Starbuck once spotted Roth trotting up the steps of Disciples Divinity House and shouted, deploringly, "I'd rather see you entering a brothel!"

"I'm still an apprentice, and so I have a right to keep shopping around, trying things on, if only for size," Roth wrote the Maurers that December, frankly admitting he was "currently addicted with [sic] a kind of New Yorker–J. D. Salinger prose style" and that his latest story, "The Contest for Aaron Gold," seemed well suited for such an approach. What Roth would later describe as "the last of my 'sensitive' stories" began to give its author qualms ("I felt twinges at some of the cute passages") within two months of writing it. Still, "Aaron Gold" was easily the best rendering of his (and Salinger's) favorite subject: a sensitive and often gifted person bruised by a cruel world. Here the protagonist is an Austrian war refugee, Werner Samuelson, who takes a job teaching ceramics at a summer camp, where he's opposed by a bullying camp director and a swimming instructor named Lefty Shulberg, a brawny philistine who once had a cameo in a Tarzan movie, fighting Johnny Weissmuller underwater. "It took hundreds of years until men saw how much happier they could be if they surrounded themselves with beautiful—beautiful objects of art," Werner shyly tells his students, only one of whom, Aaron Gold, is receptive: While the other boys sculpt pancakes and baseballs, flying away at the first blast of Lefty's whistle, little Aaron lingers over a "small clay figure, a knight apparently, whose chest was covered with armor and whose spindly legs wouldn't have done him much service against a good, fast dragon." As with that charming, resonant dragon, Salinger's voice is heard in the frequent goddam-ing of the camp director, who suspects something improper about the potter's relationship with the boy: "Wait'll Lefty hears about this goddam thing," he berates Werner. "Look at this goddam thing! . . . What kind of game are you and that little queer trying to play anyhow!" It all ends badly, but Roth himself was richly rewarded for what was, withal, a well-made story. Less than a year after his *Chicago Review* breakthrough, "Aaron Gold" was accepted by a little magazine at Cornell, *Epoch*, and later chosen by Martha Foley for her *Best American Short Stories of 1956*. "I feel skyrocketed into fame," Roth exulted over the Foley triumph, "like a Nobel Prize winner."

■ ■ ■ ■

DURING THAT FIRST QUARTER at Chicago, the "bibliography by day" part of Roth's "Byronic dream" was fulfilled in spades, although there was little in the way of "women by night." "Frankly, I have seen no mermaids as yet with whom I should desire conversation, copulation, or co-habitation," he wrote Heyman at the end of September; "even the girls who aren't intelligent look it—intense, pale, a little neurotic, a little self-pitying." Meanwhile he missed Mackie terribly—all the more, perhaps, given that she had plenty of dates at Cornell, and blithely told him as much during their biweekly phone chats.

Roth's celibacy was hardly for lack of trying. He and Haber were even willing to dance to Hebrew folk songs at a Hillel mixer in hope of enticing some hearty Zionist to bed, but dancing was as far as things went. Finally, one night at Jimmy's, Roth "picked up [his] one and only black girl" (ever)—a light-skinned Roosevelt College student whose name enchanted him: Arizona McGill. Women were no more welcome at the Divinity House than at Mrs. Purnell's, and Roth had to smuggle her into the basement. The two dated for a short while, and Roth never forgot his meeting with Arizona's even lighter-skinned mother, who told him that certain relatives of hers were "lost to all their people"—that is, had decided to pass as white, "never to return," a detail that would occur to Roth forty-four years later, while writing *The Human Stain.*

The closest Roth came to having a steady girlfriend that year was a skittish graduate student named Pat McEnerney, who'd recently given up ballet and decided to become a teacher. Haber described her as a kind of female "mascot" for their group, a slender woman with a lovely face and slick-backed hair—rather like a prettier Olive Oyl, or the histrionic interpretive dancer in Jules Feiffer's cartoons. Roth would sometimes evoke McEnerney's "sweet spontaneous sensibility" by telling about the time she was secretary at *Poetry* magazine and met her hero, E. E. Cummings, at a party. She'd "memorized a little speech beforehand" but found herself tongue-tied in the poet's presence, staring at him with mute adoration; finally, as he was about to depart, he suddenly returned to give her a fervent kiss on the forehead. "Thank you for your poetry," she managed to say.

Roth was fascinated by the morbidities of her Irish Catholic background: she went to mass every Sunday (Roth "loved to watch her kneel") despite having been molested by a priest, while her father, who objected to her ballet dancing, had once tied her ankles together and put her in the closet when he learned she was taking lessons on the sly. In her basement apartment, on the corner of Fifty-seventh and Kimbark, she would dance for Roth in her underwear ("enchantment itself"), but her inhibitions otherwise included vaginismus, a constricted vagina, which made intercourse impossible. In later years Roth was touched by the memory of her vulnerability and sweetness, and whenever he'd go to Chicago— to visit Sandy, Bellow, others—he'd try to find her name in the phone book. "I'd give anything to speak to her," he said in 2013 (unaware that she'd died four years earlier).

■ ■ ■ ■

By way of an honor's thesis, Roth was required to write two long essays—one, as he recalled, on Donne's poem, "At the Round Earth's Imagin'd Corners, Blow," and the other on a play, perhaps *Juno and the Paycock* by Sean O'Casey. For his final exam he was sent home for the summer of 1955 to read and ponder Montaigne's "An Apology for Raymond Sebond," then returned in August to write twenty-five pages on the subject. He was awarded his M.A. with honors, and was "almost anxious" to get on with his Ph.D.—two years hence: the war in Korea was over but the draft was still in effect, and Roth had decided to enlist in the fall and get it over with.

Earlier that year, his father had been promoted to manager of a big Metropolitan Life office in the South Jersey town of Maple Shade; he and Bess bought a house (their first) in nearby Moorestown—"a small, 'nice,' Quaker town ten miles from Philadelphia," Philip wrote the Maurers; "the neighborhood, of course, is Jewish, so please don't become disturbed." The neighborhood might have been Jewish but it was no Weequahic—rather a raw, nondescript subdivision, its rows of tract houses forlornly exposed on treeless streets. Bess missed her old friends, and soon they bought a pied-à-terre on Elizabeth Avenue in Weequahic and made the two-hour trip almost every weekend and holiday. Philip, meanwhile, would occasionally squat at Aunt Milly's place in Elizabeth (an arrangement he used "very loosely" in *Goodbye, Columbus* as Neil's extended stay with Aunt Gladys), where he sang for his supper by telling dialect stories that made his thirteen-year-old cousin, Anne, laugh so hard her "face and stomach" would hurt.

He also stayed at the Groffskys' in Maplewood. He and Mackie had been reunited at Thanksgiving and Christmas that year, after which they wrote almost daily "sex letters" and Mackie decided to transfer to Barnard to be closer to New Jersey and Roth. The two were becoming more compatible in other ways, too; as Heyman remembered, the young Maxine aspired to an intellectual camaraderie with Roth, eager to read books he recommended and indulge in sophisticated banter about, say, his former hero Cummings. "I mean, for christ [sic] sake," Roth wrote of his disenchantment with the poet, "love is love and roses are roses and how long can he keep poking George F. Babbitt in the mouth? . . . A friend and I (the friend is Jordan [i.e., Maxine]) have a little game: every once in a while we write e. e. cummings type poems (usually walking the street), like 'dung is to cow / as stars to the moon / and I / love you.'"

She also kept him company while he ran around a high school track— and did sit-ups, push-ups, and chin-ups on the inner grass field—part of his intensive fitness routine prior to basic training, lest he end up getting injured or even contracting spinal meningitis from the filthy barracks like an old boyhood friend, Larry Klinghoffer. With or without such exercise, though, the couple's strenuous sex games might have kept their minds and bodies in good working order. It was generally in the air between them. Chatting with Mr. and Mrs. Groffsky one night, Roth glanced over their heads and caught sight of their daughter mischievously touching herself at the top of the stairs. "I am young, drunk (on sex), and can never die!" was Roth's mantra that summer, echoing his beloved Wolfe. "I thought I was invincible."

T HE BETTER TO GET ON WITH HIS MILITARY SERVICE, Roth had turned down teaching jobs at the University of Nebraska ("Willa Cather I'm not") and Concordia, a small college near Fargo. Sweating out his final term at Chicago, Roth prayed "the slaphappy Congress" would finally end the draft now that the war was over; then he hoped a bum knee (injured in a softball game when he was eleven) might render him 4F, but an army doctor on Governors Island officially declared him 1A that August. A fellow New Jersey boy and University of Chicago alumnus, Joe Josephson, had been told by a recruitment sergeant in Trenton that he could get away with a two-year service if he enlisted (versus the usual three or four years for volunteers), so he and Roth enlisted together on the same day, September 19, 1955. Roth was a little rueful over his decision, at Bucknell, to quit ROTC after a single semester because he was opposed to compulsory military training; if he'd taken advanced ROTC, he would have entered as a lieutenant instead of a private: "The first, though not the last, of the naive 'principles' with which I subverted myself," he later reflected.

His first weeks, at Fort Dix, were even grimmer than expected. "They shall/or will never make a soldier out of me," he wrote the Maurers on October 15; "and I shall never make literati (or whatever the hell it is) out of them. I shall grit my teeth for two years." Roth's barracks was a "hell-hole" that had been, as recently as a week before, a stockade for African American prisoners. On arrival every two soldiers were given a bucket of hot soapy water and told to scrub every square inch of the walls, floors, and bed frames, as well as the row of twelve filthy toilets opposite twelve filthy sinks, and a "scummy, open communal shower (open to the toilets) at the far end." This went on for two weeks, until basic training officially began on October 3, and still they hardly made "a dent in the filth": "Everything smelled of shit all the time."

Roth made friends with "a small contingent of the company who'd been to college"—a remarkably diverse group that included Barrington Boardman, Martin Garbus, and Matthew Andresino. The affable Boardman was an archetypal Wasp from Bridgeport, Connecticut: tall and square jawed, he'd come from ten generations of Yale and would later author a book titled *From Harding to Hiroshima: An Anecdotal History of the United States from 1923 to 1945*. Garbus, a Bronx Jew, would become a distinguished civil rights lawyer and occasional friend and jogging companion to Roth when both lived in Woodstock and Manhattan. As for Andresino, he was enduringly bemused by Roth's fondness for a self-described "grubby Italian kid from Buffalo," whom Roth called Wolly from the Italian *guaglione* (boy, urchin).

Roth's time in the army would, if nothing else, afford material for one of his best stories, "Defender of the Faith," about an unscrupulous Jewish soldier named Grossbart, who uses his religion (and whatever else) to get out of unpleasant duties. Marty Garbus claimed that Grossbart was based on "a wise-ass Jew" they'd known at Fort Dix named Sherry, "who was endlessly playing every single conceivable angle"; indeed, Roth remembered Sherry as one of three buddies who snuck off the base with him that fall, driving eighteen miles to his parents' house in Moorestown, where everyone took hot showers and ate one of Bess's home-cooked meals before dashing back in time to avoid detection.

When Andresino was told (in 2013) the basic plot of "Defender of the Faith," he opined that Grossbart resembled no one so much as the author himself, remembering Roth's ingenuity in evading the grubbier aspects of basic training. "Actually, though," Roth had written Bob Heyman after his first week at Fort Dix, "I do not have too much to complain about, because, when upon the night of arrival the Sergeant asked who could type, my right arm went up faster then [sic] the world's fastest erection. Since then I've gotten out of every indecent, undignified detail, and have been squatting before my weapon in the orderly room, typing out mess cards, morning reports, sick call crap, etc. I have found a home." Even before Roth's typing boondoggle—according to Andresino—he'd also gotten out of cleaning the barracks that first Friday night by excusing himself ("with great glee") for religious services, and gave the same excuse every Friday thereafter. Nor was this just one man's impression: Roth's friend Joe Josephson remembered a time-test drill for which every soldier in the company had to assemble his rifle and report outside for inspection; Josephson was still struggling when Roth breezed past him en route to the parade ground, and would have gotten in trouble were it not for "a kind of crude character" who stayed behind to help him. "So the moral of the story is," said Josephson, "you never know in an emergency who's gonna come through for you."

To be fair, there were many indecent, undignified details that Roth did not or could not evade. Every ten days he drew twenty hours of KP: peeling potatoes, ladling soup in the chow line, cleaning the grease trap, and so on. On the last day of basic, around midnight, he and another guy were wearily hefting a kettle of potatoes when Roth's partner dropped his end and Roth yanked up so the kettle wouldn't come down on the man's toes. He felt a searing pain in his lower back, and when he woke up the next morning he could hardly walk—"the beginning of a lifetime's back trouble," he noted. During his two-week post-basic leave, Roth went to an osteopath in Moorestown who diagnosed the injury as a sprained sacroiliac, advising Roth to rest on a heating pad and not make any sudden, jerky movements.

Perhaps he bore that in mind with Maxine, though it doesn't seem to have diminished the pleasure they continued to take in each other's company. After basic, she came down from New York to visit him at his parents' house, and on a couple of previous occasions she'd picked him up at Fort Dix for weekend leaves. "I would ride along in the backseat and when they got to New York they would dump me," said Andresino, remembering with awe "the most beautiful woman you could imagine" spiriting his friend away. For his part Roth would later reminisce about the passionate way he and Groffsky "tore each other's clothes off" at the door of their hotel room: "I haven't done that in a while," he mused at age seventy-nine. "I take them off nicely, I hang them up, I get in bed and I read. And I enjoy it just as much as I enjoyed tearing the clothes off."

■　■　■　■

WHEN HE RETURNED to Fort Dix in December, Roth was assigned to clerk-typist school, where his mother's touch-type lessons stood him in good stead. The "brutally boring" course—eight hours a day for eight weeks—involved learning how to process reports and type up duty rosters, sick slips, etc., but as the best typist in class Roth would be given first dibs on his next assignment: "As it works out, the slow typists have all been going to Greenland and points even norther," he wrote Heyman; "the fast boys (I am a fast boy) get the stateside assignments if they want them, or Europe." At first Roth thought he'd plump for the free trip to Europe ("in my mind's eye I am sleeping with a fetching Nazi-type blond, vigorous and catlike and washing my underwear and socks"), but when it came to a point he couldn't leave Mackie, whom he thought, in certain moods, he might like to marry someday. By the time he graduated in February—and was presented with a silver identification bracelet for finishing first in his class ("You should be damn proud of this, Roth," said the presiding major)—he'd chosen an assignment at Walter Reed Army Medical Center in Washington.

The personnel officer at the hospital was impressed by Roth's academic credentials and gave him a plum job in the Public Information Office, where his main task was interviewing new patients and writing press releases for their hometown newspapers. It was easy but tedious work, leavened only a little by the tumult surrounding Eisenhower's admission as a patient, in June 1956, for an acute inflammation of the small intestine; Roth later claimed to have shaken the president's hand, though mostly he interacted with a young man from the White House press office who'd commandeered his desk and "whose un-Daedalian Republican outlook on life it was my youthful duty to skewer heartlessly in sardonic letters to a girlfriend back in New Jersey."

Roth's fiction, meanwhile, had stalled amid the distractions of army life, as well as a sense that his apprenticeship had led him into a dead end. He didn't want to write about sensitive children anymore, and when he tried writing about Jews—as in a novel, aborted after some thirty pages, "about an old Jew who can't make up his mind between money and god"—the results were just as lugubrious. Given that he couldn't seem to make compelling fiction out of his own experience, Roth found himself all too susceptible, still, to the influence of whatever writer he happened to be reading most intensively at the time. While in Chicago the previous March, Roth had reported to the Maurers that he'd written a story with "a little too much Hemingway in it," and otherwise most of his effort was spent "vulcanizing [his] old stuff." Finally he swore "not to write a goddam word for at least a year," or at least until his critical and imaginative faculties were no longer at such fatal odds. So matters stood prior to his arrival at Walter Reed, where at last he had the means "to be a strict schedule abiding writer" again. "I've got to begin to work or else I'm sure I'll give up on myself," he wrote, "and I'm too—well, not good; but full of the rumor of promise to not give myself and writing a big decent chance. Well, I will."

Perhaps the most important aesthetic lesson of Roth's youth, via readings of *The Catcher in the Rye* and *Huckleberry Finn*, was "the power of a voice"—now if only he could find a voice that sounded more like his own. Crucially, around the time he worried about giving up on himself, he discovered *The Adventures of Augie March* (1953) and was struck by a "kind of high-faluting [sic] conversational tone I like," and also by Saul Bellow's willingness to indulge in sprawling narrative abundance, not at all constrained by Neo-Aristotelian concerns with form and structure. Interviewed for a 1993 BBC documentary on Roth, Bellow pointed out that he and his younger colleague were both "book-intoxicated street kids from American cities" and particularly applauded the quality in Roth's work that was arguably most derived from his own—"a combination of street language and literary sophistication"—or, as Roth said of Bellow, "he has managed brilliantly to close the gap between Thomas Mann and Damon Runyon." While reading *Augie March* in 1956, it occurred to Roth that he himself had "ideas galore for stories"—stories with actual Jews in them, and Newark too.

That year he was further inspired by Bellow's *Seize the Day*, with its vivid evocation of Jewish life on the Upper West Side—devoid of the sentimentality that marked the work of the "apologists, nostalgists, publicists, and propagandists" who had dominated Jewish American fiction prior to Bellow. And Bernard Malamud's *The Assistant* was "the next clump on the head," as Roth put it, "which is you can write about the Jewish poor, you can write about the Jewish inarticulate, you can describe things near at hand, like a grocery store. . . . And that had a terrific impact on me." Though it would take decades for Roth to render Newark with the kind of painstaking, reportorial detail characteristic of his American Trilogy, the sketchy beginnings of such a project were inspired by Malamud's Brooklyn and Bellow's Chicago and Upper West Side. By the time *The Assistant* was published, in 1957, Roth had taken his first real steps toward an awesome maturity, and so was moved to write the Maurers with a hubris only somewhat tongue-in-cheek: "[Malamud] and Bellow are the only two people, outside of me, that are writing things worth reading." And Roth was reading everything they published—the Malamud stories soon to be collected in *The Magic Barrel*, for instance, which he snapped up "the day they appeared" in *Partisan Review* and *Commentary*. Far from the Runyonesque eloquence of Augie March and company, the Yiddish-inflected immigrant speech found in Malamud was "a heap of broken verbal bones that looked, until he came along and made them dance to his sad tune, to be of use no longer to anyone other than a Borscht Belt comic or a professional nostalgist." And Malamud's people were something of both, and this too was a revelation: you could feel sorry for his Jewish failures but also laugh at them; their wry acceptance of every kind of misery reminded Roth of the "eerie clowning" of Beckett's Molloy and Malone.

Of these two masters, and rivals, Bellow would prove the more congenial—a matter of temperament as much as style. A great admirer of Bellow's second novel, *The Victim*, Roth was in awe—but a little skeptical too—of what would ultimately seem the "revolutionary" exuberance of *Augie March*: a rejection of the alienated, conscience-haunted ethos of Bellow's first two novels, of Kafka and Dostoyevsky, of formal niceties altogether, a doffing of the "Flaubertian corset" (as their friend Richard Stern put it) that bristled against everything Roth had soberly accepted at the University of Chicago. "As for Augie March," Roth noted in 1956, "I can't bring myself to say good things of it, though one sort of feels obliged to in its huge presence." Its presence would only grow huger as Roth advanced in his own work—a little awkwardly at first, with the meandering set pieces of his first novel, *Letting Go*, and thence to the ranting flamboyance of *Portnoy* and other novels, an effect that would become so typically Rothian that Alfred Kazin dubbed it "the aria bit." Finally, having attained a like eminence, Roth was ideally receptive to Bellow's reminiscence (for Roth's benefit) of his "triumphant feeling," after a long creative malaise, when he wrote the first paragraph of *Augie March*: "In the next two years I seldom looked into Fowler's *Modern English Usage*." Roth would often quote Augie's first six words as a declaration of independence: "I am an American, Chicago born." An *American*— not a Jew, not a Jewish American, but a fully immersed participant in the commotion of American life. Indeed, like Roth's previous literary idol, Wolfe, Bellow had discovered America as a grand subject—but, as Roth liked to say, "where Wolfe was merely a half-genius with the limitations of a half-genius, Bellow was a complete genius without any limitations I could see." For Roth, the only twentieth-century American writer of comparable stature was Faulkner.

After dinner each night at Walter Reed, Roth would return to his typewriter in the Public Information Office and work on his fiction until ten o'clock, and it was here he wrote his first Philip Roth story, so to speak. The previous August, he and his Chicago friends—Haber, Targan, and Geffen—had gathered in Greenwich Village to celebrate their master's degrees, and a tipsy Geffen had told them about a kid in his Brooklyn Hebrew school who'd once threatened to jump off the synagogue roof. As Roth was leaving (early, sober) he took Geffen aside and asked whether he planned to use the anecdote in his fiction; Roth agreed to give him five years before he, Roth, appropriated the story, though in fact he waited all of seven months. "I've never been so in control in my life," he remarked after finishing "The Conversion of the Jews." "I junked stuff, re-wrote, thought long and deeply (as I can, anyway), paced, bitched, wrote heatedly. All the things writers are supposed to do. It all worked, I think (and hope). I have never felt more like a writer in my life."

In Geffen's anecdote the boy went up to the roof as a random prank, but Roth makes it a matter of heated debate, between Oscar (Ozzie) Freedman and his fellow Hebrew students, about the Immaculate Conception. "'To have a baby you gotta get laid,' Itzie theologized. 'Mary hadda get laid.'" But Ozzie insists that a God who can make heaven and earth in six days can also "let a woman have a baby without having intercourse," and when he puts the question to their teacher, Rabbi Binder, the exasperated man ends up smacking him in the nose. Fleeing to the roof, Ozzie threatens to jump before a growing audience that includes his mother, the Fire Department, his ecstatic classmates, and of course the mortified rabbi, who's forced to kneel with the others and recant his position that Jesus was merely "historical." Both he and Ozzie's mother have struck the boy because of his doctrinal impudence, and so Ozzie ends the public shaming with a moral—"You shouldn't hit me about God"— before jumping into a firemen's net "like an overgrown halo." The resolution is a little pat, but the story's considerable virtues include characters who speak ("And what do you gotta open your mouth!") and look exactly as they should—"a round, tired, gray-haired penguin of a woman" in the case of Ozzie's mother, who "didn't look like a chosen person" even when she dressed up. A nice illustration, in short, of the "combination of street language and literary sophistication" noted by Bellow.*

■ ■ ■ ■

BEFORE HE LEFT for Walter Reed and they for Europe, Roth had assured his friends Andresino and Boardman that he would get out of the army in six months because of his bad back; a few months later, overseas, the two received a postcard—"I'm out"—and laughed, assuming their wily pal had pulled another fast one. In fact he was in agony, and while working at Walter Reed he'd seemed to get worse by the day. In April, an army doctor gave Roth a back brace for what he said was a lumbosacral strain—"what they used to call a touch of lumbago," as Roth put it in his 1962 story based on the ordeal, "Novotny's Pain." Roth tried toughing it out for a month or so, until he could no longer bend over to pull his socks on and tie his shoelaces—an office performed each morning by a kindly barracks mate, Nelson Goldberg, a biochemist who worked in the hospital laboratories.†

Finally Roth went on sick call and was admitted to Walter Reed as a patient; now diagnosed with a herniated disk, he refused surgery because he didn't want to be operated on by army doctors—whereupon a skeptical psychiatrist-colonel accused him of malingering and sent him to a dreary rehabilitation hospital in the Maryland woods, Forest Glen, where he was surrounded by amputees who moaned and cried out in

---

* Years later, as an English professor at the University of Minnesota, Arthur Geffen liked to teach his old friend's widely anthologized story: "I used to read it to my class and tell them, 'I'm gonna tell you a true story, and you can decide which is the better story, and you can decide what makes the better story the better story.'" Almost invariably they preferred Roth's version to Geffen's (also quite colorful) recounting of the actual event, whereupon they'd discuss "the intellectual freight of the story and the absence of intellectual freight in the event."

† Goldberg went on to an illustrious career that would end up benefiting Roth and countless others via his discovery of the substance cyclic GMP, a cellular messenger whose effect on hormones would lead to other discoveries, most notably the drug Viagra.

their sleep. Roth was stunned by the injustice of it: "I was learning how things happen independently of one's own massive exertions," he wrote forty years later, "how all one's planning, tenacity, ingenuity and forcefulness can mean nothing and come to nothing. I was getting a tiny whiff of how unsweet life can smell." When Roth refused to accept that he was "passive-aggressive"—that his pain was a "somatic" manifestation of his resentment toward the army ("Somatic my ass," he wrote the Maurers)—the psychiatrist threatened to classify him as "unfit" and recommend him for an undesirable discharge. As an army psychiatrist explains to Novotny, "It's what we use to get the crackpots out—bedwetters, homos, petty thieves, malingerers, and so on."

Roth languished at Forest Glen for a month, until it occurred to him to phone his Democratic congressman, Frank Thompson, and tell his story to an assistant. A week later, in mid-July, he was returned to Walter Reed for a meeting with the Medical Discharge Board, which awarded him ("to my astonishment") an honorary discharge with a 20 percent disability pension, or about thirty dollars a month. The pension was overturned less than a year later, however, when it was determined that Roth's "injury existed prior to service"; outraged, he solicited testimonials to the contrary from Haber and others, but the decision stood.

Suddenly at loose ends, Roth returned to his parents' house in Moorestown and tried to find a job before his separation pay ran out. By then he was a rather attractive prospect—what with his master's degree and a story in that year's Foley anthology—and received a number of modest but interesting offers. "Thanks for sending me that nice young man," William Shawn wrote his former secretary, Charlotte Maurer, after interviewing Roth at *The New Yorker.* Roth, in turn, found Shawn to be "very kind, in his gnome-like way," though he was thrown by Shawn's diffident observation that perhaps Roth considered his own work "too avant-garde" for the magazine. "I stammered for a moment," Roth wrote the editor afterward, "but what I wanted to say, I think, is that I like to think of myself as not avant-garde, or rear-guard, or New Yorker, or Partisan Review, but as Myself." By way of evidence he submitted "The Conversion of the Jews," and a month later ("We are constitutionally slow") was offered a fact-checking job. He also met with one of his brother Sandy's colleagues at J. Walter Thompson, Charles Jackson, author of *The Lost Weekend,* who was then working as a script editor for

Kraft Television Theatre. Jackson—who struck Roth as nice but "rather sheepish"—offered him a job synopsizing scripts at seventy-five dollars a week, and also arranged for him to meet with Jackson's publisher, Roger Straus, who wore a yachting cap and offered Roth a copy-editing job. Roth declined, though the two would meet again some twenty years later, when Straus became his publisher.

Roth was mulling his options when he received a telegram from Napier Wilt in Chicago: an instructorship on the freshman composition faculty had opened up at the last minute; it paid four thousand a year and would give Roth the freedom to write, especially during long academic holidays, and also pursue his Ph.D. "I was flabbergasted," he noted at the time, "and wrote back yes, yes, yes, I would." He was about to leave in mid-September when he was felled by an attack of back pain so severe he was unable to walk for nearly a week. Spooked, he went to Philadelphia with Maxine and was examined by two different doctors. The first, at the University of Pennsylvania Medical School, told him he had two herniated disks that would require immediate surgery; Roth almost fainted at the news—likely the end of his once-in-a-lifetime chance to become one of the youngest faculty members at the University of Chicago. Fortunately, the second doctor found only a single herniated disk and recommended that Roth wear an ungainly steel brace for six months, followed by physical therapy. "In the meantime," Roth wrote the Maurers, "I am to do without swimming, tennis, and violent sexual encounters, not to mention casual, peaceful ones. It will be a long six months."

In 1998, the writer Ben Yagoda was combing old *New Yorker* files in the course of researching his book about the magazine, and noticed Roth had been offered a fact-checking job forty-two years before. He dropped Roth a note, asking what had happened, and Roth explained that he'd decided to take the job in Chicago, "and proceeded almost immediately to fuck up my life for the next ten years."

PART TWO

DON'T STEP ON THE UNDERDOG

1956–1968

*Maggie ("petite, attractive and 30ish") as she
appeared on page 3 of the April 14, 1964,* Daily News.
(Copyright © Getty Images)

AT THE END OF SEPTEMBER 1956, ROTH RETURNED TO Chicago, his back brace rather splendidly concealed beneath a pale brown glen plaid suit he'd bought at Brooks Brothers with his separation pay. This, he thought, was where his adult life would truly begin—as a nicely attired teacher with the army behind him. As he'd written Heyman a year before, at the beginning of that ordeal, "All I know, Bob, is that life is very short, and freedom is very precious, and that when I get out I'm going to live right up to the hilt, and make these brief years extravagant as hell. I'm going to go where I want and do what I want to do—if I can ever figure out what that is—and BE, thoroughly BE."

One of his first forays as a free man wishing to BE would end very badly indeed. After a party for new faculty at the Quadrangle Club, where he'd allowed himself a few shots of bourbon, Roth and friends were heading to dinner when he spotted a short, attractive blonde who used to wait tables at a sandwich joint, Gordon's. Barry Targan remembered her as "somebody we would kibitz with," but always with a sense that she and they "were in two different worlds"; he was shocked when his friend Philip—"the golden boy"—began dating her steadily. That night in October, however, Roth was simply determined to pick up a pretty shiksa. Waving his friends on, he stopped her on the street and insisted he knew all about her—that she'd been a waitress at Gordon's, that she was from Michigan, that she was the mother of a little boy and a girl he'd once seen at the restaurant. Remembering the encounter fifty years later, Roth said, "I couldn't have been more fluent, more charming, funnier. I couldn't have shown off more of my wares." She agreed to join him for a cup of coffee at Steinway's Drugstore, and so it began.

Her name was Margaret (Maggie) Martinson, the granddaughter of Norwegian immigrants—"a direct descendant of the Vikings," as her son, Ronald,* pointed out—who came from a small resort town on Lake Michigan, South Haven, a kind of Midwestern Catskills for Chicago Jews.† The native population was largely gentile, and Maggie's father, Glenn "Red" Martinson, was the town drunk. Maggie grew up in the home of her maternal grandfather, Herb Mitchell—known as Daddy Herb to the family—a kindhearted butcher who'd employed Red for a time in his meat market. Later Red worked as a carpenter, and later still as an electrician for Vaughan Aluminum; in the latter capacity, said Maggie's first husband, Burt Miller, Red was knocked off a ladder more than once when he grabbed live wires while in his cups. Despite such mishaps, Red was well liked in the town: A handsome man's man, he "loved everybody he ever met," said Miller; "he drank a lot, so he met a lot of people." But Red deteriorated as his disappointments mounted, and by the time Roth had entered the picture, he was in prison for petty theft.

"The great dark event of Maggie's youth," said Roth, was the time she called the police on her father when he came home, drunk, and caused a ruckus. Roth remembered this as happening around the time Maggie was fifteen or sixteen—the same age as Lucy Nelson, the heroine of Roth's 1967 novel, *When She Was Good*, who coldly orders the cops to take her father, Whitey (one of the cops' drinking buddies), away so she can get on with her homework. "With that act of jailing her father," Roth reflected many years later, "there came to the fore a capacity to go to terrible extremes to achieve what she wanted. She had proved at sixteen that she was tougher than anyone she knew and simultaneously unhappier." Certainly it was the end of Red, who disappeared from South Haven and his daughter's life forever. "I deeply regret the pain and sorrow I have caused you and Margaret," he wrote his wife from prison, and in a separate letter one finds these cryptic remarks: "As far as Margaret is concerned you don't know all of it. In fact probably a very small half. So there is no need to go into that." "Then go back to period of college, impregnation, suggestion of abortion," Maggie wrote in her notes for an autobiographical novel she was trying to write when she met

---

* A pseudonym; I've also changed the names of Maggie's first husband and their daughter.

† Including the young Saul Bellow, whose family used to vacation at a local kosher resort, Yashenovsky's.

Roth. "At this point show family, father and his attempt to fuck." Only
once would Maggie intimate to Roth that her father had molested her;
in any case Red finally killed himself, said Burt Miller, by walking in
front of a semitrailer.

Maggie liked to romanticize herself as "a scholar and a bohemian,"
at least by the standards of South Haven. As she wrote of her fictional
counterpart, Nancy Morrow:

> The dulness [sic] of the town of her parents had made her a cynical, sar-
> donic young lady and if her parents, her teachers were tolerant, her class-
> mates found her unapproachable. The young men weren't sure what she
> was about any way and it was simpler to pursue girls they could court
> without danger of having the absurdity they suspected was present in
> their manners pointed out, analyzed, [and] forgiven in one witty sentence.

Perhaps because more callow youths feared her gimlet eye, the eighteen-
year-old Maggie began "running with" (as he put it) Burt Miller, recently
discharged from the navy and working as a tuner in a piano factory; he
also played trombone at occasional jazz gigs.

Later, Maggie would tell Roth that she'd spent a year at the University of Chicago before getting pregnant and having to drop out and
marry Burt. Roth was rightly impressed that a girl from such a benighted
little town had gotten into the university at the height of the Hutchins
era, though in fact she'd lasted only a single quarter in the fall of 1947,
auditing two courses and earning a P (Pass) in English and a D in math.
Her passing grade in English was a highlight she meant to emphasize
in her novel about Nancy, a brilliant, stoically pregnant coed at the University of Chicago who charms her married English professor, Charles:
"Nancy was one of those who remained after class or cornered Charles
in the coffee shop to talk on about the relation of the didactic action to
the thesis in English drama. Gradually she became aware of the intensity
with which Charles bestowed his attention to her remarks and with great
delight and incredulity she realized it was her developing womanliness
he attended."

Her marriage to Burt gave her little to romanticize. As she would often
remind their first-born, Ronald, his father had wanted him aborted but
Maggie had insisted the man do his duty and marry her. Unlike Nancy

Morrow, she was not such a scholar and a bohemian as to be willing to carry on as an unwed mother in college, though she might have reconsidered had she an inkling of what life with Burt would be like. While attending commercial art classes at night, he worked packing lamps at Marshall Field's and lived, with wife and child, in a one-room, seven-dollar-a-week walk-up on the South Side. A prostitute lived above them, said Burt, "and brought her work home," while Ronald remembered once trying to entice a rat with a piece of food, until his father appeared and booted the hungry rodent away. For whatever hard-to-fathom reasons, they had a second child, Helen, in 1950; Maggie would later tell Roth that Burt had impregnated her "by force," though Burt insisted he was at least as miserable in the marriage as she: "She complained constantly about how hard she had to work—take care of the kids and what have you—and why wasn't I making more money? In other words, she turned into a bitch."

Maggie and Burt would tell different versions of what led to their divorce, neither of which appears to be entirely untrue. "I divorced my first husband on grounds of physical cruelty," Maggie later claimed in court documents, and both children attest to their father's occasional violence. At six foot two, Burt was fully a foot taller than Maggie, and perhaps a hundred pounds heavier, and, according to his daughter, he was "an aggressive, paranoid, intrusive person" who yelled and pushed Maggie around a lot. Both children remembered what Helen called "the beginning of the end"—the night Burt put his fist through a window because Maggie had tried locking him out. As for Burt, he elided such discord when telling of how he caught his wife cheating on him with an auto mechanic—a man named Bob who'd been an anthropology student before opening a garage on Fifty-fifth Street, and who indeed was involved with Maggie at one time or another, as both Roth and a mutual friend confirmed. "That's on record," Burt asserted for his part. "My lawyer was Stephen Love—well-known cat. He's the one who put the detectives on her . . . and this is how I got custody of my children."

Burt had the means to hire "the biggest-gun attorney in Chicago," said Helen, because of well-heeled relatives, and certainly this had something to do with how Maggie lost custody. She would often tell Roth that her first husband had "stolen" her children, whatever that meant, and later Roth was justly skeptical: "Despite her avowal of gruesome victimization at the hands of yet another merciless *shagitz*," he wrote in *The Facts*, "my grandparents"—i.e., who understood the dark ways of the goyim all too well—"might even have surmised that the woman, having discovered that she was emotionally incapable of mothering anyone, had herself effectively let the two children go." In fact there was a consensus view, among Burt and the children both, that Maggie's parenting style was on the laissez-faire side. Burt once came to pick up his toddler daughter and found her wandering alone on the Midway, and Ronald fondly recalled his long childhood days skipping school and hanging out at the Museum of Science and Industry, "doing," he said, "what the fuck I wanted."

Paying Burt's legal bills were his uncle and aunt in Kenosha, Wisconsin, Wilbur and Beatrice Walton, the models for the Sowerbys in *When She Was Good*. Wilbur ("Uncle Walt") had made a fortune teaming with Emmet Culligan to found the Culligan Soft Water Company ("Hey, Culligan man!"), and the couple also rallied around their nephew when custody arrangements were being worked out. "We never had much of a home life with Maggie and [Burt]," said Ronald. "They were divorced in 1955, and I was asked with which parent I wanted to live. I said 'neither' and so we were shipped down to our second cousins in San Antonio, Gilbert and Janet Boerner." "Gib" Boerner had married the Waltons' daughter, Janet, and subsequently made a success opening up soft-water markets in Texas at his father-in-law's behest. It would later transpire that Janet had been suffering from early-onset Alzheimer's, which might have explained why, almost daily, she broke off a willow branch and savagely beat the back of Helen's legs. Her husband wore a big college ring that he'd thump on Ronald's pate when the boy got fresh, and Gib also had a playful way of picking up both kids by their heads. The arrangement lasted about a year, until Burt remarried and bought a house in Country Club Hills, south of Chicago, and was therefore able to resume guardianship; the Boerners, meanwhile, had begun to adopt children of their own.

■　■　■　■

In the beginning Roth was simply fascinated by all the "goyish chaos" Maggie evoked: divorce from a monstrous husband, who "stole" her children and farmed them out to dubious cousins in Texas, etc. It was like leafing through the pages of a Dreiser novel, and when the luridness gave him pause, Roth reminded himself that this, after all, was what Flaubert had meant by "*le vrai*" (real life), and moreover Roth longed to be a *man*, serious and reliable, perhaps in guilty response to his even greater longing to be free and extravagant. Besides, he admired Maggie as a diamond in the rough, and his friends agreed that she had a kind of likable spunk. "I was impressed by her," said Herb Haber. "Very bright, very funny, good sense of humor. And I remember Phil telling me he depended on her wisdom." This was certainly a persona Maggie wistfully cultivated, though she was also capable of an impressively self-deflating objectivity, as in an analysis she wrote for her psychotherapist in the summer of 1958:

> I think I'm quite medium in total affect. I'm attractive in an average way and I have a moderately compelling personality. At best, I can be quite witty and bright and I think at best I can be a winning person. I have always been able to verbalize my ideas so that I think I appear more intelligent than I am, though in truth, I would say I am a reasonably bright person. . . . I'm not sweet and although I suspect some people would say I was lovely and gracious I think my friends would say I'm also crabby and exacting.

Those who were less invested in perceiving Maggie as a peer of sorts, though they might concede her better qualities (cleverness among them), knew "she was not an intellectual in any sense"—as the writer Richard Stern pointed out—"but she cared about what intellectuals did and their position." Indeed, she cared more than ever, now that she was a secretary in the Division of Social Sciences, working under the assistant dean, Ruth Denney, wife of Reuel, himself a poet-scholar and coauthor of the sociological classic *The Lonely Crowd*, whose primary author, David Riesman, taught a course at the university that Roth was auditing that year. And Roth was impressed, understandably, by how far the former waitress had come in so short a time. Early in their courtship she invited him to have drinks at the faculty club with her and the German philosopher Max Horkheimer, who'd clearly taken a shine to the engaging young secretary.

In those days Roth's main repugnance was toward Maggie's physical person, though he took pains to dissemble this. Later he'd cruelly dub her the Monkey because of her short, heavy legs,* but that wasn't the worst of it, as Lydia Ketterer—a saner, sweeter, fictional version of the "real" Maureen (the Maggie character) in *My Life as a Man*—candidly enumerates for Zuckerman in the novel's prefatory "Courting Disaster": "I'm five years older than you. My breasts sag, not that they ever amounted to much to begin with. Look, I have stretch marks. My behind's too big, I'm hamstrung. . . . I don't have orgasms." And still her drab recitation omits the most unspeakable, alarming thing—namely the "withered and discolored" vagina that has borne two children and that Zuckerman forces himself to kiss: "I took no pleasure in the act, she gave no sign that she did; but at least I had done what I had been frightened of doing, put my tongue to where she had been brutalized, as though—it was tempting to put it this way—that would redeem us both." Asked if this was an aspect of the real Maggie, Roth wanly nodded and invoked the Brothers Grimm: "This was like some mythological nemesis. The underdog isn't so pretty."

Meanwhile he was still seeing something of his brainy, gorgeous, young and wealthy girlfriend at Barnard, Maxine, though his relations with the Groffskys had soured over the past year, perhaps because the parents had found their daughter's diaphragm—the immediate cause of the rift between Neil and Brenda in *Goodbye, Columbus*, though in later years Roth wasn't sure whether he'd based the episode on fact. Some such calamity is suggested, however, in his letter to Heyman of January 1956, shortly before he departed for Walter Reed: "I have been dispossessed, rightfully and wrongfully I think, from 449 Richmond Avenue. . . . Poor Mackie has been dispossessed too, I fear." Here Roth went on a heavy satirical rant against Paul Groffsky's "wishy-washy gutless" new wife, Elaine, who'd usurped Mackie's place (such as it was) in her mother's affections, especially in light of the recent unnamed catastrophe. "All of which adds up: Mackie becomes black sheep; I, black shepherd; I care not a jot; Mackie is crushed, for they are her family; result: you can imag-

---

* Interesting given the moniker's later fame in *Portnoy*, which actually had its beginnings as yet another attempt to fictionalize the Maggie disaster; Roth would insist, however, and somewhat persuasively, that the ultimate form the Monkey took in his novel bore little or no resemblance to Maggie.

ine. . . . So Elaine comes, Mackie goes, I with her . . . perhaps some day to marry her, to live with her a rocky spasmodically impassioned life; a short one as long as it may be in years; a life enriched perhaps by sleeping next to a beautiful woman. . . . I wonder." Almost a year later, on November 26 (six or seven weeks after their first meeting), Roth referred to Maggie as his "newest, closest friend" in a letter to the Maurers; then, after an "unsuccessful" visit with Maxine that Christmas, he declared their affair over for the "messy, usual, uninteresting-to-others" reasons.

A few months later, in May 1957, Roth reported that his old Bucknell girlfriend, Betty Powell, had recently been in touch with big news—she was marrying a geology instructor at Penn ("John Whateverthehellhisnameis"), and they were coming to Chicago for the man's postdoctoral fellowship: "Next Maxine will marry and bring her husband here. They're after me." At least twice Roth and Maggie had coffee with the couple in Chicago, whereupon Roth wondered whether he'd "want to be [Betty's] friend" if he met her again for the first time. And yet he was unnerved, twenty-two years later, when he came across her obituary in *The New York Times*; that night he managed to get her widower on the phone, and the man told him the whole "grisly" tale about how Betty, age forty-seven, a psychology professor at Long Island University, had been reduced by throat cancer to "squealing and squeaking" whenever she tried to speak. From the *Times* Roth learned that Betty had become a prominent researcher in her field, to wit: "the relation between accident-proneness and distorted vision."

"I wanted a harder test," Roth wrote in *The Facts*, explaining why he'd chosen a bitter, impoverished, sexually undesirable divorcée over Groffsky, whose later life as Paris editor of *The Paris Review* was untouched by the dull mores of Maplewood. Her colorful career would include an affair with the bisexual artist Larry Rivers, who liked to mention that she was the model for Brenda Patimkin in the course of boasting (erroneously) that he'd taken her away from Roth, drawing cartoons of the latter with a long, dunce-cap-shaped head.

■ ■ ■ ■

WEEKDAY MORNINGS Roth put on his glen plaid suit and taught three sections of freshman comp; at mid-year he reported to Miss Martin that he found his freshmen to be "wise, sophisticated, anxious students, which, by the way doesn't make their writing any the less barbarous." Easily the most hateful part of the job was grading sixty or so weekly essays, which Roth divided by seven so he could spread the pain evenly over his days. And yet he was zealous, always, about exposing "clichéd expression or mindless argument" with plentiful marginal comment; as Zuckerman puts it in "Courting Disaster," "I was waging a kind of guerrilla war against the army of slobs, philistines, and barbarians who seemed to me to control the national mind, either through the media or the government. The presidential press conference provided me with material for any number of classroom sessions." After some early nerves, Roth loved the actual teaching part, almost losing control of one class when he became a little too "gay" with them ("that is, joyous," he clarified for the Maurers), though mostly he managed to curb his urge to entertain; he made a point of calling his students Miss and Mister and responded with stolid propriety when girls tried to flirt with him.

Roth had spent his first month back in Chicago at the Divinity House, then found a "tiny" apartment at the corner of Fifty-seventh and Ellis, near Stagg Field. After lunch he'd change into old clothes and try to write at his kitchen table, where he kept his Olivetti Lettera 22, another separation-pay purchase. During that first term he wrestled with a story "about a Jewish guy who marries a Gentile girl (who happens to be, in many ways, Betty Powell)." On their wedding night the groom is seized with resentment for his bride's "blond hair and her dead Gatsby-like father, and her brother (a sad imitation of her father) and her mother, and the fact that she knows the names of her great-grandparents and where they lived, etc etc." Nothing appears to have come of this—nothing, that is, until similar threads were woven into Portnoy's attitude toward shiksas like the Pumpkin and Sarah Abbott Maulsby ("I don't seem to stick my dick up these girls, as much as I stick it up their backgrounds"). Roth, at any rate, would work at his Olivetti until five o'clock or so, then get dinner at the commons and allow himself a beer at Jimmy's or the University Tavern if he'd managed to grade the requisite number of essays.

A low point of each week was the staff meeting, where Roth would vie with other egos in trying to spice up the syllabus with a little Orwell, or tweak the weekly lesson plan in otherwise interesting ways. The head of the composition faculty was a Tolstoy scholar named Ed Wasiolek, whom Roth would skewer in Letting Go as the pompous Spigliano: "As it were, my ass," the narrator reflects, apropos of Spigliano's remark that they should point out to students "how Gibbon impresses upon the reader the geography of the event with the geography, as it were, of the prose." Wasiolek further endeared himself to Roth by reminding him, solemnly and often, that he'd better complete his Ph.D. if he wanted to stay on the faculty—the kind of helpful advice Roth was apt to mimic for the amusement of his new friends, Tom and Jacqueline Rogers, to whose home he'd repair for après-meeting drinks.

Tom was a tall, burly, bearded fellow, the son of a Standard Oil executive, who attended the University of Chicago Lab Schools before going to Harvard and the Iowa Writers' Workshop, where he met his French-born wife, Jacqueline Ragner. Roth had pegged Tom as a kindred soul at that first meeting in Cobb Hall, and when he spotted him again at the commons with his wife, Roth asked if he could join them. Tom said yes, but sensed his wife was annoyed. As he wrote Roth in 2006, "We were newly married, she wanted me for herself. . . . Then within minutes you had her in your hand and kept her there for the rest of her life. Your charm was such that no one could even want to resist it and Jacquie never even tried." When Roth pressed her, Jacquie said she came from a part of France that had nothing to recommend it except they raised a lot of geese; Roth, delighted, referred to her thereafter as his "friend from the goose district of France." He considered the Rogerses his "second married couple"—after Bob and Ida Baker—and took an avuncular interest in their daughters, Becky and Susie.

Roth's equally enduring, but far more problematic, friendship with Ted Solotaroff would not begin until the following academic year, when Roth started taking classes for his Ph.D. "On the first day of a course on Henry James in the fall of 1957," Solotaroff remembered,

I found myself sitting next to two newcomers: a small intense guy in an army field jacket who laughed a lot, and a dark debonair fellow in a jacket and tie who kept him laughing but who looked like he had strayed into class from the business school. The first introduced himself as Art Geffen, the second as Phil Roth. . . . They were talking about Leslie Fiedler, who had recently published his notorious outing essay, "Come Back to the Raft [Ag'in], Huck Honey." What did I think of it. "Fiedler is an intellectual kike," I announced.

The remark, Solotaroff admitted, was "intended to shock" and appeared to have that effect. Later in class, however, when another student began to expound "symbolic religious interpretations" in a discussion of *Daisy Miller*, the professor—Napier Wilt—asked Solotaroff what he thought; the latter dismissed the reading as "idiotic," an argument "immediately seconded" by Roth. "Like two strangers in a pickup basketball game who discover they can work together, we passed the argument back and forth for a minute or two, running up the score of common sense."

It might have been the beginning of a beautiful friendship—certainly their common background seemed to bode well: Solotaroff was a Jew from Elizabeth, and both had spent idyllic days at the Empire Burlesque and on the boardwalks of Belmar and Bradley Beach. By 1957, however, Roth was by far the more favored of the two, a comparison that was apt to make Solotaroff all the more bitter about his own grinding circumstances. While Roth, four and a half years younger, was already an instructor at one of the nation's great universities, Solotaroff was supporting a wife and two sons on the three thousand a year he made teaching four courses at Indiana University's Calumet Center, amid the sooty industrial outskirts of Gary—this while taking three courses at Chicago toward his own belated Ph.D.

And that was hardly the worst of it. Solotaroff—who went on to become one of the best editor-critics of his time—longed to write fiction, and Roth was as "responsibly frank" about his friend's work then as later. The first time they exchanged short stories, Solotaroff gave Roth his latest, three-year-old story about two waiters, old and young, who chat about their jobs in the locker room of the Oyster Bar; Roth described it as "exhausted Hemingway stuff," and Solotaroff wished he could retaliate in kind about "Aaron Gold," despite its inherent merit as a Foley story and, he had to admit, its vast superiority period. "How come you know so much about being a potter?" Solotaroff asked, and Roth said he didn't: "I read something about it and made the rest up." This offhand remark was "like the Last Judgment" to Solotaroff: his years of working in restaurants availed him nothing when he tried to make fiction out of it, whereas Roth had made a potter's vocation "not just credible, but the significant center of the story." Compared with Roth, Solotaroff seemed to embody what Brendan Behan meant when he likened critics to eunuchs in a harem—he knew how it was done, but was unable to do it himself—and yet he was far more determined than most eunuchs. "I read Ted's story," Roth wrote Tom Rogers twenty years later. "Ashes mostly, I thought, with just a little ember or two. I don't know why he wants to write fiction when he is probably one of the two or three readable and intelligent fiction critics in the country. Oh, I do know why, but it seems to me he has better and bigger things to be doing with his writing hours than writing about two Jews over a pastrami sandwich. That's what I do!"

And finally there was Solotaroff's domestic predicament. He never forgot the one time Roth suffered to visit his seedy apartment in a poor black neighborhood, perching himself "like a social worker on the edge of a couch over which I had nailed an old shag rug to cover the holes." Dostoyevsky was in the air—because of the squalor, of course, but also as an abiding passion of Solotaroff's wife, a raven-haired Russian scholar who did her melancholy best to care for two asthmatic children. And there on the ragged couch was Roth, the debonair bachelor resplendent in glen plaid. Still, Solotaroff wondered a little at the uses to which Roth put his freedom: Maggie had recently dated a friend of his, Jay Aronson, who'd sniffed trouble and "split fairly quickly"; Roth, however, seemed to relish the challenge. "So we had that to talk about," Solotaroff remembered, "two saviors of troubled young women comparing notes."

Maggie's railroad flat was on the second floor of an apartment house at the corner of Fifty-seventh and Dorchester, a few blocks east of Roth's place, and when his back was hurting he'd go over and lie in a hot bath. Often, too, he'd return for dinner and grade essays afterward, while Maggie worked on laying new linoleum in the kitchen or chipping away paint to expose the original pine mantel of her fireplace—projects that impressed Roth as "game," along with the way she made ends meet by renting a back room to a free spirit named Joanne, the model for Sissy in *Letting Go*, who (like Sissy) dated black guys and was often too broke to pay rent. Maggie shared a back porch with another divorcée, Jane Kome, a big blonde who was "attractive in a kind of blowzy Blythe Danner way," as Roth put it; both her looks and her feisty good humor in the face of single motherhood would be given to Martha Reganhart in Roth's first full-length novel, though Martha's savage arguments with Gabe were inspired by Maggie, as was Martha's chaotic medicine cabinet and messiness generally.

Early that spring Maggie discovered she was pregnant, professing amazement given her diligent use of a diaphragm. The anxious couple consulted a friendly GP, who suggested they try a drug that might induce heavy bleeding and lead to a legal D&C in the hospital. To their great relief it worked, and, while Maggie was recovering, Roth visited her room with flowers and Champagne. He found her chatting with a middle-aged man who proved to be the hospital rabbi. After the chaplain had excused himself, Maggie responded to Roth's bewildered question with the information that she'd registered at the hospital as a Jew. "I had my first sense that she was crazy," Roth remembered, "but it was fleeting." Rather than pursue the matter then and there, Roth let it go with a chuckle. "What the hell you do that for?" he asked. "I wouldn't let one of those guys near me."

Ten

Tom Rogers introduced Roth to his friend Dick Stern, a fellow Iowa Workshop graduate who taught creative writing at Chicago. Stern was five years older than Roth and married (unhappily) with two children; he'd published a few stories in little magazines and was working on his first novel. That spring of 1957, Dean Wilt gave Stern two thousand dollars to invite four writers to campus at five hundred apiece—a distinguished roster that comprised Bellow, Robert Lowell, Flannery O'Connor, and Ralph Ellison. Bellow came on May 1 and agreed to preside over two classes: one for discussing his own work, the other for discussing a student's.

Bellow's visit was especially momentous. In recent years his reputation had been bolstered by the first of three National Book Awards, for *Augie March*, and the subsequent publication of his acclaimed novella *Seize the Day*. Casting about for a manuscript worthy of their guest, Stern asked to mimeograph "The Conversion of the Jews," though Roth wasn't one of his students, and—Stern's admiration notwithstanding—the story had been briskly refused by *The New Yorker* and various quarterlies. While the anonymous author sat in back of the class, discreetly silent, the twenty or so students discussed the story a little severely until Bellow took his turn—a cherished moment preserved in *The Ghost Writer*, where Bellow appears in the thin disguise of Felix Abravanel, who defends Nathan Zuckerman's story ("largely with his laugh") against the "orthodox Forsterites" who think its characters lack the "round" quality prescribed by *Aspects of the Novel*. After class Roth was thrilled when he was invited to join Bellow and Stern for coffee at the Reynolds Club—though he sensed Bellow's breezy charm was a species of aloofness, and in fact Bellow "left [Roth] where he found [him]" rather than help place his admirable story. Still, Roth had made a definite impression on the great man, who would remember "Conversion" as "the real thing": "When I was a little kid, there were still blacksmiths around," he wrote Roth twelve years later, "and I've never forgotten the ring of a real hammer on a real anvil."

Because of his appearance in the Foley anthology, Roth had returned to campus as a minor celebrity, and editors at the *Chicago Review* were eager to publish more of his work. That spring Roth gave them a little satire, "Positive Thinking on Pennsylvania Avenue," making fun of a folksy bedtime prayer the president liked to say, according to the positive-thinking guru Norman Vincent Peale. As Roth wrote, "'Lord,' the President's prayer begins, 'I want to thank You for helping me today. You really stuck by me. . . .' The Lord is not so much his shepherd, Mr. Eisenhower indicates, as his helper, his *aide-de-camp*." The author goes on like that, swinging a heavy rubber mallet at some pretty broad targets; the intelligentsia's rabid distaste for Ike seems a bit much these days, given certain of his successors, but the editor of *The New Republic*, Gilbert Harrison, was happy to reprint the piece for his June 3, 1957, issue, and the author was reviled in a subsequent letters column. "[T]he most distasteful article I have ever read in *The New Republic*," one reader wrote. "[A] fatuous piece of boorishness," said another, "and in wretched taste."

By then Harrison had already asked the young wag if he'd like a gig reviewing TV shows for the magazine; Roth replied that he'd prefer to review movies, even though he rarely went to the movies and, by his own admission, had "never read a movie review in [his] life." Later he'd dismiss his work in the genre as "unreadable, rich with snide condescension and little more," but at the time he was simply delighted by the chance to ridicule popular culture for a wide audience and make easy money doing it (twenty-five bucks a review). Because of Roth's determination to enjoy himself—versus any serious attempt to grapple with aesthetics, since he viewed almost all movies as *ipso facto* crap—certain of his pieces have worn well regardless of their nominal subjects. "Miss [Audrey] Hepburn brings to the role her usual elfishness," he wrote of *Love in the Afternoon*; "she is certainly a handsome young woman, but there continues to be something a bit wearing about an elf that knows it's an elf." Perhaps inspired by his shtick with the ineffable Geffen, Roth wrote his "review" of *The Sun Also Rises* (starring an ill, sallow-faced Tyrone Power as the impotent Jake Barnes) in the form of a Hemingway dialogue between the critic and a *poule* he meets outside the movie theater:

"But Jake has this wound—" the *poule* began.

"That's tough all right," I said, "but not seedy."

She took it for a pun. "You are a hard man."

"What the hell," I said, "what the hell."

As it happened, Roth also wrote the odd piece about TV; indeed, his favorite contribution to *The New Republic* was a definitive take on the Miss America pageant as it then existed, "Coronation on Channel Two," in which he described lovely young contestants having to "extricate" themselves "from the gleeful ooze secreted by the master of ceremonies, Bert Parks."

After a few months, though, the weekly chore began to pall, and besides Roth was sick of the magazine's "butchers" who chopped his prose to "smithereens." The sinecure had provided enough money to buy a ten-year-old Plymouth from his cousin Kenny in Newark, and meanwhile Roth was replaced at *The New Republic* by Stanley Kauffmann, a less funny but more responsible critic who would hold the post for forty-five years, until his death in 2013.

■ ■ ■ ■

AFTER THAT FIRST pregnancy scare, Roth entertained thoughts of keeping his distance from Maggie; by then, however, their friends perceived them as a couple and tended to invite them over as such. Also Maggie was eager to prove her usefulness, as when Roth had "a bad siege with [his] back" in May, and "Maggie cared for [him], kindly, sweetly," as he wrote the Maurers. She was willing to be of use in less conventional ways, too. Roth admired the charms of a certain graduate assistant for the Committee on Social Thought, Diane, who made a point of attending weekly Social Sciences teas—arranged by the secretary, Maggie—because she was poor and hungry and the food was free. At some point Maggie became "inordinately interested" in her, as Diane recalled, suggesting a threesome with her boyfriend, Philip Roth, a campus wunderkind the woman was eager to meet. In retrospect Diane had "no doubt" Maggie was the instigator, and Roth also said that Maggie was the one who "pushed for it" ("'Let's fuck Diane'"). For her part Maggie noted a "Story idea" about two lovers who are both "imaginative" and "intelligent": "He one day suggests it would be exciting to introduce a 3rd person. She is shocked by the idea."

As Roth remembered the logistics of the occasion (*chez* Maggie), Diane and Maggie went into the bedroom first, followed by Diane and Roth, and finally the three went in together. Since Diane was essentially a lesbian, Roth "felt terribly left out" ("If I start crying, you'll have to understand"); waiting for the two women to emerge, he said, was like "waiting for a haircut." In fact, it was hardly a red-letter evening for either Roth or their guest; afterward the two met for coffee and agreed the whole thing had been peculiarly uncomfortable, perhaps because Maggie seemed so keen on controlling things. Diane made a point of avoiding the Social Sciences secretary thereafter, but was left with "the distinct impression that Maggie was determined to marry Philip Roth. . . . She wasn't good-looking, she didn't strike one as intellectually ambitious, but she certainly was one of the most determined people I ever met."

Roth had hoped to spend the summer of 1957 working on his fiction at the Yaddo or MacDowell art colonies, but both turned him down. Instead he drove to Falmouth, Cape Cod, at the end of June, agreeing to pick up Maggie in Boston a week or so later, when her own vacation was due. Alone with his thoughts, Roth had dire misgivings. Since the pregnancy, especially, his arguments with Maggie had become fierce, and he was unsettled by the novelty of her rage; it occurred to him that the only time he'd ever "seen anybody in the flesh enraged" was during that terrible argument with his father six years before. (*"How the hell do I know where you are! You could be in a whorehouse!"*) Now it was an almost daily occurrence. A weeklong tryst on Cape Cod with "a quiet, easygoing, plainish girl"—an education major at Boston University who was waiting tables at a local restaurant—made the prospect of Maggie's turbulence all the more disheartening. Sure enough, she arrived in Boston with her guns loaded, furious that Roth hadn't stayed with her in Chicago that summer. For three days they wrangled about this and related matters, until Roth threw in the sponge: he would drive her to New York, he proposed, while he caught up with his parents in Moorestown. In the car Maggie weepily harangued him: she had only *two weeks* of vacation a year, and he'd ruined it! The least he could do was take her along to meet his parents, the way he'd taken Maxine and Betty, or wasn't she *good* enough . . . ? "When she wouldn't stop I wanted to kill her," said Roth. "Instead I took her home with me."

The visit went poorly, and not because Maggie wasn't Jewish. His parents had gotten along fine with Betty Powell, after all, and were even a little disappointed when Philip hadn't married her. (Of course, being a shiksa was hardly an asset. Joan Roth, a cousin, remembered how Bess and Herman had routinely warned her away from the goyim: "*You're a Jew, of course you date a Jew. You marry a Jew! . . . You can't trust a goy. He'll love you and leave you!*' The irony," said Joan, "was that I *did* marry a gentile and the first words he learned was *shiker shagitz*"—drunk gentile.) As for Maggie, she was a perfect package of folly, the gist of which Roth conveyed in *The Facts*: "No, what they saw to frighten them wasn't the shiksa but a hard-up loser four years my senior, a penniless secretary and divorced mother of two small children, who, as she was quick to explain at dinner the first night, had been 'stolen' from her by her ex-husband." Somehow Bess made it through breakfast the next morning, and when she asked Philip and the woman whether they had any laundry from their trip, Maggie gladly surrendered her dirty underwear. "I cannot do this woman's laundry," Bess told her son in the kitchen an hour later (in *The Facts*, Roth has her walking three miles to Maple Shade, weeping, to complain to Herman of this final indignity). "She will have to go." In the car Maggie asked to say goodbye to Philip's father, in whose office she complained bitterly about how rudely she'd been treated. Herman listened with an air of managerial sympathy, careful however to call the woman Mrs. Miller. Finally Philip drove her on to New York, where she presently caught a plane back to Chicago, whither he himself was due to return a month later.

■ ■ ■ ■

FOR VARIOUS REASONS Roth had hoped for a change of venue once he got started on his Ph.D. From Harvard he anticipated a fellowship worth at least $1,500, and at the last moment he also applied to Columbia "just in case Harvard falls through. . . . Trilling and Barzun and Eric Bentley *sound* more exciting than a return to Walter Blair and Company." Both programs accepted Roth but without stipends, whereas Chicago offered $1,000 and Dean Wilt sweetened the deal with another $1,500 if Roth would agree to teach a section of composition. Thus Roth found himself back in Chicago, again as a graduate student, that fall. Along with Wilt's class on Henry James ("Just now I put down Portrait of A Lady, and wonder what my writing efforts will ever amount to next to *that*"), he took Contemporary Criticism and Anglo-Saxon, the last of which he particularly loathed.

Somehow Roth managed to evolve as a fiction writer while keeping up with the demands of a doctoral program and grinding out weekly pieces for *The New Republic*.* Another milestone was tagged that fall, when he sold "You Can't Tell a Man by the Song He Sings"—his story about Albie and Duke, the tough Italian kids in his freshman homeroom at Weequahic—to *Commentary*, which he'd been reading devotedly since he first discovered it in the periodical room at Bucknell. Though the magazine would someday launch a number of scathing attacks on his work and person, at the time Roth found it a liberating guide for intellectual American Jews of his generation, who "wanted to leave [their] narrow backgrounds, but maintain [them]selves as Jewish men." In *Commentary* he encountered the work of not only Bellow and Malamud, but other favorites such as Isaac Rosenfeld's ribald analysis of the kosher laws, "Adam and Eve on Delancey Street," and Wallace Markfield's sardonic look at Jewish family life in Brooklyn, "The Country of the Crazy Horse." ("The novelist, what's his name, Markfield," muses Portnoy, "has written in a story somewhere that until he was fourteen he believed 'aggravation' to be a Jewish word.") "I thought, 'Boy I'm in it, it's great,'" Roth remembered, thinking of the first time he visited the New York offices of *Commentary* and met its then editor, Martin Greenberg (brother of the art critic Clement), who quickly became a friend: "He'd read everything, but he talked like a guy from the neighborhood." It's noteworthy, however, that the actual person who plucked Roth's first story out of the slush pile was a recently hired assistant editor, Norman Podhoretz, who would become one of Roth's most bitter enemies once he took over as editor in chief, in 1960, and eventually led the magazine in a gallingly different direction.

Back in January 1957, Roth had finished the first draft of a sixty-two-page novella, *Expect the Vandals*, inspired by a news story about Japanese

---

* Roth was still reviewing movies during the Fall 1957 semester; his final piece for *The New Republic* was published in the February 17, 1958, issue.

soldiers in the Philippines who didn't know the emperor had surrendered and so remained hidden away on one of the islands. "You'll be especially happy to know that there is not a Jew or a child (or an adolescent for that matter) in the entire thing," Roth wrote the Maurers, pleased that he'd managed to "barrel through" such an extended piece of work, though he realized it would need "a radical rewriting" (involving, among other things, his turning one of the main characters into at least a nominal Jew, Moe Malamud). Five months later, Roth sent a revised version to Ballantine for consideration as part of their New Short Novels series, and by the time they returned it, in September, Roth had received an intriguing invitation from the new assistant fiction editor at *Esquire*, Gene Lichtenstein, who recalled:

> Philip sent in a satire of ornithologists and it was terrible, really terrible. I'm not sure why, but instead of sending a rejection slip back, I wrote a note on the back of the slip saying, "This is terrible. You should be ashamed of yourself. You obviously know how to write, so why don't you send me the best short story you have?" And by return mail I got a seventy-five-page manuscript, *Expect the Vandals*. I read it and sent back a letter saying "This is flawed but I'm really interested. Do you want to work on it?" . . . So we went back and forth, and he kept changing it.

By the time "Expect the Vandals" was accepted for the December 1958 issue, it had been trimmed down from novella length and polished to a high shine, and was probably better than its author would later remember (always with a shudder). Moe and Ken are the only survivors of an attempted landing on a Japanese-occupied atoll; the story's original germ is touched on, provocatively, in its opening pages, when Moe observes from a ledge as the Japanese stragglers learn of their defeat: "Thirty-nine Japs had lined up, rifles in mouth. At the command, the triggers were pulled, and the tops of heads sailed into the air like confetti." Jewishness is not a salient issue in the story, unless one associates Jewishness with the kind of sensitivity and discernment that Moe possesses and his buddy, Ken, does not, hence the poignancy of their interdependence. Queer studies scholars (who would come to show a remarkable degree of interest in Roth's work) may one day rediscover the all-but-forgotten "Expect the Vandals," with its startlingly overt homoeroticism: Moe's nursing of the crippled Ken entails brushing a fly away from his naked groin, and kissing his forehead in a burst of tenderness.

Perhaps the main importance of "Vandals" was the paycheck—$850—almost as much as Roth's entire fellowship from the university. "I laughed all the way to the bank," he said, when Solotaroff gloomily observed that the story wasn't as funny as Roth's pieces in *The New Republic*. And that wasn't all: a year later, Columbia Pictures bought the dramatic rights for $2,000 plus a 10 percent cut of the profits—a meager sum by movie standards, but the production was low budget and anyway it was all gravy to Roth.*

By then he'd already decided to quit school after a single quarter and devote his time to writing and teaching. "I strangled on Anglo-Saxon," he wrote Miss Martin, "and kept thinking about stories I wanted to write while talking about stories Henry James *did* write." Roth had other reasons to settle for an incomplete in Anglo-Saxon. After "The Conversion of the Jews" had been rejected for the third and fourth times—by *Kenyon Review* and *Botteghe Oscure* ("Those guineas'll take anything," Roth had mistakenly predicted of the latter)—the author "hopelessly" sent it off to *The Paris Review*, where it languished in a slush pile for five months before falling into the hands of a reader, Rose Styron, whose famous husband, William, was among Roth's most admired near contemporaries. A few years later she'd have occasion to tell Roth in person about her role in publishing one of his best-known stories—the beginning of a lifelong friendship with the couple. For now she considered the story "marvelous," but would have to wait for final approval from the editor, George Plimpton, who was then in Cuba. "Why the hell did he go, is what I want to know," Roth complained to the Maurers. As he would shortly learn, Plimpton had gone to Cuba to conduct his famous interview with Hemingway, and that interview would appear, with "Conversion," in the Spring 1958 issue. Roth's story would receive further exposure in *The Best American Short Stories of 1959*.

Hemingway was on his mind when he decided to depart that summer

---

* The movie, *Battle of Blood Island*, was shot in Puerto Rico in the summer of 1959, on a budget of $51,579 mostly put up by the legendary B-movie director Roger Corman, who appears in a cameo as an American soldier. Roth's windfall would not include a profit percentage, since the movie grossed only $28,828.

for an indefinite stay in Europe ("Hemingway didn't get his Ph.D.," he
remarked to Cousin Florence). Meanwhile Wilt gave him two sections
of composition in the spring, and Roth also agreed to teach a weekly
night class in creative writing at the university's Downtown College,
an extension mostly attended by adults with day jobs. For his introductory lecture, "The Strategies and Intentions of Fiction," Roth conscien-
tiously recited twenty-five pages replete with the wisdom of Flaubert,
Dostoyevsky, Henry James, et al., then asked for questions; there was
only one—from a neatly dressed, middle-aged black woman: "Professor,
I know that if you're writing a friendly letter to a little boy, you write
on the envelope 'Master.' But what if you're writing a friendly letter to a
little girl? Do you still say 'Miss'—or just what *do* you say?"

■ ■ ■ ■

Since finishing "Vandals," Roth had lost no time embarking on
a full-blown novel, alternately titled *The Interpreter* and *The Go-Between*,
about a Jewish American businessman who travels to Frankfurt to shoot
a German, any German, as revenge for their crimes against the Jews.
Roth was a little stymied by the fact that he'd never been to Germany—
or had any experiences at all, really, similar to those of his characters—
and yet he was certain the idea itself would sustain the writing of what
was sure to be "a powerful moral document. . . . All I can say is that I
think the book suggests that by 1957 the crimes have become so gross, so
complex, the guilt so impossible to pin down, forgiveness impossible to
portion out . . . that morality, as always, takes a God to understand." Five
months later Roth was still convinced his novel was "exciting and crucial
(the story and the issues I mean)," though he'd managed to eke out fewer
than a hundred pages despite interest from an editor at Random House,
who wanted to see a manuscript when Roth came to New York for his
spring vacation.

Around this time Roth was also considering a long, comic story about
the Groffskys—this after a lunch at the University Tavern with Dick
Stern, an avid laughing audience for Roth's adventures "in Jewish sub-
urbia with the dazzling daughter of a prosperous dealer in plate glass."
"Write *that*, for God's sake!" said Stern, as they walked back to campus.
At first Roth was skeptical: "I wanted to be morally serious like Joseph

Conrad. I wanted to exhibit my dark knowledge like Faulkner. I wanted to be deep like Dostoyevsky. I wanted to write *literature*. Instead I took Dick's advice and wrote *Goodbye, Columbus*." Such advice was based on what Stern (and others) had observed as "a discrepancy between Philip as he told stories and Philip as he wrote stories"; Stern thought Wilt's "heaping Henry James" on Roth was helpful only up to a point, whereas Stern was pushing him toward a reckoning akin to Bellow's abrupt rejection of *literature*, or literary good manners, when it came to writing *Augie March*—a novel about life as he really knew it, evoked in a voice inimitably his own.

As for big ideas, they were already baked into the Patimkin saga: an encounter between a striving young intellectual—steeped (no doubt) in the highbrow class attitudes of Riesman, Paul Goodman, C. Wright Mills, and the like—and the "pig heaven" (Bellow's term) of newly assimilated Jews learning how to adapt to the country-club culture of midcentury America. Later Roth would faintly deplore his Chicago-bred intellectual smugness, which he was at pains to spell out in his preface to the thirtieth-anniversary edition of *Goodbye, Columbus*, referring to himself in the third-person: "His cultural ambitions were formulated in direct opposition to the triumphant, suffocating American philistinism of that time: he despised *Time, Life*, Hollywood, television, the best-seller list, advertising copy, McCarthyism, Rotary Clubs, racial prejudice, and the American booster mentality." And yet his genial and even nostalgic condescension vis-à-vis the Patimkins would prove an ideal vantage point, and, relieved of the burden to animate ideas per se, Roth learned he "could hit long fungos," as he later put it—a baseball trope echoed in an unpublished fragment about Zuckerman's ecstatic discovery of his powers: "He would pound his fists on the walls of the little apartment in an expression of delight, of wonder with himself. And cry out loud, 'C'mon baby, c'mon baby,' like an infielder talking-up his pitcher. . . . A thousand perfect words a day: the wit! the tone! the mean asides! The conversations he simply seemed to take off some spool in his head! His head—could it be?—the head of a genius?"

Since he was dealing directly with raw, recent experience—and finding a slyly ironic voice in the process—Roth would later deny there were any "literary antecedents" for *Goodbye, Columbus*. In many respects, though, it stands as a kind of Jewish *Gatsby*, given the charm of its prose and humor, its concision, and its theme of meretricious American-style success. Fitzgerald was on Roth's mind when he referred to the jaunty, athletic Maxine as Jordan Baker, but the equivalent of Brenda, in terms of the story, is pure Daisy Buchanan—the golden girl with "two wet triangles" on the back of her polo shirt (after strenuous tennis with "Simp" Stolowitch), "where her wings would have been if she'd had a pair. . . . The smallness of the wings did not bother me—it would not take an eagle to carry me up those lousy hundred and eighty feet that make summer nights so much cooler in Short Hills than they are in Newark." Neil is both Nick Carraway and a bookish, manqué Gatsby, never less than skeptical about the Patimkins and their prizes ("Gold dinnerware, sporting-good trees, nectarines, garbage disposals, bumpless noses"), and yet lyrical about the larger Jewish success story they embody—"a story of the West" tracing the progress of postimmigrant generations "towards the edge of Newark, then out of it, and up the slope of the Orange Mountains, until they had reached the crest and started down the other side, pouring into Gentile territory as the Scotch-Irish had poured through the Cumberland Gap."

For Roth, the main advantage of writing a book such as *Goodbye, Columbus*, instead of his Conradian Frankfurt opus, was that he discovered how funny and shrewd he could be, on paper, given a peripheral narrator whose main function is to find Jewish correlatives for Gatsby's "gorgeous pink rag of a suit"—the whole zany fantasia of American gentility. The playlet of Neil's first dinner with the Patimkins does in fact read like a conversation "he simply seemed to take off some spool in his head," yet every line highlights, wittily, some fundamental aspect of the speaker, and in a single brief exchange we comprehend the family tout court:

MR. P.: He eats like a bird.

JULIE: Certain birds eat a lot.

BRENDA: Which ones?

MRS. P.: Let's not talk about animals at the dinner table. Brenda, why
 do you encourage her? . . .

Mrs. Patimkin's prim, wistful admonition is also reflected (obliquely) in her lunkhead son's affected fondness for "semi-classical" music such as Kostelanetz and Mantovani, though given his druthers he'd listen to his Columbus record for the umpteenth time, mooning over his bygone glory on the basketball court,* and meanwhile Mrs. Patimkin's twin sisters, Rose and Pearl, appear at Ron's wedding with white hair "the color of Lincoln convertibles."

Writing "a thousand perfect words a day" (or thereabouts), as if he were simply taking it off a spool, Roth finished his comic novella in roughly a month and declared it "positively the best thing I've done." Suddenly he felt "in league with Malamud," and his friend Solotaroff agreed that both Roth and Malamud, with Bellow, were engaged in a similar project of "adapting [Yiddishkeit] to modernism." One evening—after a long day poring over antique issues of the *Boston Evening Transcript* for his dissertation on James's sources for *The Bostonians*—Solotaroff stopped at Roth's apartment to drink a beer and listen to his friend read this early passage from his work in progress:

> Though I am very fond of desserts, especially fruit, I chose not to have any. I wanted, this hot night, to avoid the conversation that revolved around my choosing fresh fruit over canned fruit, or canned fruit over fresh fruit; whichever I preferred, Aunt Gladys always had an abundance of the other jamming her refrigerator like stolen diamonds. "He wants canned peaches, I have a refrigerator full of grapes I have to get rid of . . ." Life was a throwing off for poor Aunt Gladys, her greatest joys were taking out the garbage, emptying her pantry, and making threadbare bundles for what she still referred to as the Poor Jews in Palestine. I only hope she dies with an empty refrigerator, otherwise she'll ruin eternity for everyone else, what with her Velveeta turning green, and her navel oranges growing fuzzy jackets down below.

Solotaroff recognized the shtick as the kind of thing bandied about with Geffen at University Tavern ("The fruit routine was in fact a variation

---

* Ron Patimkin's model, Paul Groffsky—every bit as nice and obliging as Roth had led me to expect—claimed he never read *Goodbye, Columbus* (or even watched the movie), explaining that he preferred "mainly nineteenth-century authors, particularly Dickens and George Eliot."

of the two-neckties joke"*)—but then, too, this deft sketch of famil-
ial bemusement was "something new" in American fiction: "Roth was
making public . . . the mentality of many of us who were trying now
to liberate ourselves from twenty centuries, or so it felt, of communal
solidarity, moral authoritarianism, and adaptive hypocrisy." At any rate,
Roth didn't so much as look at his Frankfurt novel during the month or
so he spent working on *Goodbye, Columbus*.

■ ■ ■ ■

AFTER THEIR NIGHTMARE summer vacation in Massachusetts and
Moorestown, Roth and Maggie somehow managed to reconcile during
the fall; by late January 1958, however, the affair seemed over for good,
or so Roth reported a little apologetically to the Maurers: "I am always
telling you that so and so and I are no longer seeing each other, and I
guess the reason is always the same—marriage." He assured his friends
he was very sad about things, but really it couldn't be helped. As for
Maggie, she dealt with heartbreak by deciding to keep a journal ("under
the influence of Virginia Woolf"), and her first entry recorded a "moving
experience" with a delicatessen owner, who wondered why such a "good
looking girl" didn't have a boyfriend on Saturday night: "I replied there
were some but not the one I wanted. He then got me frozen bagels."

Perhaps the most notable outcome of Roth's Anglo-Saxon course was
that he briefly dated one of his classmates, Susan Glassman, a soignée
Radcliffe graduate who lived on Lake Shore Drive, the daughter of an
orthopedic surgeon who'd been team doctor for the Chicago Bears and
the Blackhawks. Remembering the experience, Roth would invariably
describe the woman as "a pain in the ass": she was forever expecting him
to drop everything and take her to the hairdresser or some such, and
he would do it, and still she "resisted [his] advances." On February 10,
she accompanied Roth to a lecture at the Hillel House given by Bellow,
who, it so happened, had met Glassman on a previous occasion at Bard
College. "I'm just going to go up and say hello to him," she told Roth

---

* To wit: For his birthday, a husband gets two ties from his mother-in-law. Wishing to
seem a good son-in-law, he wears one of them to the next family dinner. Upon seeing
her, he tries a friendly smile, but is met with a disappointed look. "So, you didn't like the
other one?"

afterward, and that was pretty much the last he saw of Glassman, who would become the third Mrs. Bellow in 1961. "Turned out to be the best thing that ever happened to me," said Roth, "and the worst thing that ever happened to Saul."

Also in attendance at Hillel House was Maggie, who gave a brittle laugh when Roth came over to say hello. "Well," she said, "if *that's* what you like—!" When Roth went home that night he found a terse note in his mailbox "to the effect that a rich and spoiled Jewish clotheshorse was exactly what I deserved." Maggie meant it, too. That night, in full Nancy Morrow mode, she wrote in her journal: "Philip appeared at the lecture with Susan and it was a relief for I *couldn't* be jealous of her—She's a petulant self-concerned girl of a type I find at best boring and at worst a nuisance. Instead, I was able to feel emancipated from him for if he really wants this sort of girl then I see him as a different person that I don't really recognize and that I certainly don't want." For a time Roth also dated an editorial assistant at the *Bulletin of the Atomic Scientists*, whose impression on Maggie, if any, went unrecorded. All such matters became moot when Dick Stern played "a disastrous Cupid role," as he later put it, by inviting his friend Philip and his former babysitter Maggie to his thirtieth birthday party on February 25. Before Roth quite knew what was happening, he and Maggie "began to see each other again," as he wrote the Maurers, "for company's sake, and then, and then, etc."

Perhaps he figured he'd soon be a free man in Europe—a prospect, naturally, that made Maggie "very distraught," according to a mutual friend, and was bound to cause more and more friction as his departure date approached. Already Roth was contriving to make a more permanent escape. Unknown to Maggie, he'd applied for a creative-writing fellowship at Stanford for the fall; if that fell through, he hoped to sell *Goodbye, Columbus* to *Esquire* and thus have enough money to stay in Europe until February 1959 or so, whereupon he'd return to Chicago and teach. And what of Maggie? As Roth recalled, he'd made her "furious" by floating an idea to live in New York once he returned from Europe; then, a week or so later, Maggie decided to follow him there: "What was bizarre was that her children had just moved to [the suburbs of] Chicago from Texas," said Roth. "She would be able to see them regularly now—and so she was going to go to New York." At the time, however, Roth's own New York plans appear to have been a smoke screen; as he confided to Gene Lichtenstein, he himself had suggested that Maggie move to the city and "pave the way" for him, when in fact he was hoping to end up in Palo Alto or stay in Europe (and eventually return to a Maggie-less Chicago). He implored Lichtenstein to arrange some kind of editorial job for Maggie at *Esquire*, and meanwhile, too, he set up interviews for her at *Commentary*, *The New Yorker*, and elsewhere. "Maggie saw a lot of people and was well received in all quarters, though she got no promise of work," Roth reported after they returned from New York in late March, while Maggie confided to her journal that the city had inspired "a strange kind of terror. . . . I wanted to take refuge with someone and, of course, the someone is Philip. How terrible this longing for a mate is."

For Roth, the trip was an unequivocal triumph. Since "Aaron Gold" had appeared in the Foley book, he'd had an agent of sorts, a genteel Princeton man named Joe McCrindle who liked taking long trips abroad. Roth wanted an agent who stayed in New York and focused on her clients, and Lichtenstein sent him to a friend, Candida Donadio, a hungry new employee of the Herb Jaffe Agency; within a few years the motherly, chain-smoking Donadio would command a stellar client list including John Cheever, Joseph Heller, Mario Puzo, Thomas Pynchon, and Roth, whom she promised, that spring, to find better-paying commercial markets for his short work and get him a good advance for a novel. Best of all, he had a festive lunch with George Plimpton at the latter's East Seventy-second Street town house, where Roth also met Plimpton's *Paris Review* colleagues Bob Silvers, Blair Fuller, and their friend Joan Dillon (daughter of Douglas Dillon, later secretary of the treasury under John F. Kennedy), who lived mostly in Paris and asked Roth to look her up when he came over. Roth hit it off all around: Silvers and Fuller became longtime friends, and Roth would always be smitten by the "worldly and glamorous and gracious" Plimpton. "Oh boy! How're ya, boy?" he greeted Roth, wringing the young man's hand and applauding his work in that ebullient mid-Atlantic accent ("I think from George you might have known how Henry James talked"). Roth felt like Augie March—"Look at me, going everywhere!"—and that night he phoned Tom and Jacquie Rogers and said as much.

Practically the day he returned to Chicago he got a letter from Fuller, who spoke for everyone when he said how sorry he was Roth hadn't submitted a manuscript for their Aga Khan Prize (five hundred dollars), given to the best *Paris Review* story of the year; he'd missed the dead-line, March 1, but if he was interested . . . ? Three weeks later Fuller acknowledged receipt of "Epstein," which was now among "six or seven" finalists for the prize. Roth had written a draft of the story back in June 1957, but it had taken a long time to get the tone right. "It is the first time I've written a story with sex scenes,* and it was a delight, but I don't know if a success," he wrote the Maurers. Solotaroff, for one, was "put off by all the ugly physical detail"—the *shmutz* (dirt, filth), in short. "The *shmutz* is the story!" Roth snapped.

Indeed, Roth had decided (for the first but hardly last time) that shmutz, the franker the better, was the funniest and truest way to account for certain basic human failings, such as an aging, hardworking Jewish man's wish to enjoy the pleasures of the flesh at least once more—that is, with a woman other than his wife, Goldie, whom he "watched as she dropped her white nightdress over her head, over the breasts which had funneled down to her middle, over the behind like a bellows, the thighs and calves veined blue like a roadmap. . . . The nipples were dragged down like a cow's, long as his little finger. He rolled back to his own side [of the bed]." That was the sort of thing that bothered Solotaroff, but the ravages of time are to the point: Epstein remembers when his twenty-three-year-old daughter was a "little pink-skinned baby" instead of a pimply woman with ankles "thick as logs," romantically entangled with a "chinless, lazy smart aleck whose living was earned singing folk songs in a saloon"—hardly a suitable heir for Epstein Paper Bag Company, which the poor man has built from the ground. In any case, the consequences of Epstein's unchivalrous thoughts are not lightly punished; after a three-week lark on the beach with a merry widow, he notices a telltale sore that he prays is a sand rash or something he got "from the toilet seat," until he finally breaks down and delivers a marvelous cri de coeur: "When they start taking things away from you, you reach out, you *grab*—maybe like a pig even, but you grab. And right, wrong, who knows! With tears in your eyes, who can see the difference!" Finally his heart bursts with remorse, and as he's loaded into an ambulance a doctor glances under the blanket and assures Goldie that the sore, at least, is simply an "irri-

---

* Roth didn't write *Goodbye, Columbus*—which also has sex scenes—until the following February.

tation." (The nature of that sore, as Plimpton remembered, was "the only editorial help" he ever gave Roth—this while preparing the Aga Khan Prize–winning story for publication in the Summer 1958 issue: "It was clear Philip didn't know the first thing about what syphilis looked like. I had to call him up and straighten him out on his venereal symptoms.")

"Maggie and I must confuse hell out of you—or I must," Roth wrote the Maurers on April 10. "But we are back being Friends Again, or we are the most enjoyable people we know, and the inevitable end we're just ignoring, etc etc." Norman Mailer was coming to campus that month as the latest writer to visit Stern's class, and Maggie and Roth decided to give a party "for just about everybody we knew in Hyde Park" and asked Stern to invite his celebrated guest. Once again Roth made a point of sitting quietly in back of the class while Mailer held forth, and Stern told him afterward that Mailer had particularly inquired about him and remarked, "It's those silent guys you have to watch out for." At the party, however, Mailer showed up with a glamorous local painter, June Leaf, and he and Roth had "a brief easygoing conversation" about how much Roth admired *The Naked and the Dead*. The party was a big success in every way—"all of bohemian Chicago was there"—and Roth was impressed by how well Maggie acquitted herself as hostess.

It would prove the latest Last Hurrah for the two. Roth was leaving Chicago in May, and Maggie was even more relentless than expected in letting him know her displeasure. Always—and rather shrewdly, from a tactical perspective—she made a point of impugning his moral and emotional stability. His abandonment of her was "wicked" and "irresponsible," and again (as before when he'd tried to end things) she declared him "unable to love" and urged him to see a psychiatrist. "She also told me that the reason I couldn't stay with one woman was not because I was an exuberant, libidinous young man in his twenties but because I was 'a latent homosexual,'" Roth recalled. "That pseudo-Freudian label was used very freely in those years about young men who . . . might not want to marry the women who might want to marry them." "It makes me angry to think I had so much to give and it actually was so satisfying to us both and still Philip rejects," Maggie wrote in her journal. "How stupid he is."

Not without cause, Roth felt sheepish about enticing her to move to New York and did his best to make sure she at least had gainful employment once she got there. As luck would have it, Lichtenstein was taking a sabbatical from *Esquire* that created a temporary opening for a slush-pile reader, and at Roth's urging he got his boss, Rust Hills, to hire Maggie. "A very dear friend of mine has just come to New York," Roth presently wrote Bob Silvers and others. "Her name is Margaret [Miller] and she is a totally charming woman. I suspect she's going to be lonely for a while and anxious to meet people." By then he and Maggie had parted on ostensibly friendly terms; she'd asked for his itinerary in Europe so she could write him, and hoped he would write her back. Roth was left with an impression of Maggie at her best and was far from alone, later, in wondering at the unusual duality of her nature. "I really feel like one born without one of the senses but it's really that I have no conscience," she'd written in her journal that April. "I have the mind to reason what is right and wrong but I have no moral repugnance to keep me from any-thing but I have [a] huge amount of self pity where my wickedness keeps me from having the good things that life gives to good girls."

R OTH DEPARTED ON JUNE 6, 1958, ABOARD THE *STAA-tendam*, occupying himself either with Ping-Pong or reading in a deck chair. From Southampton he took a train to London and found a bed-and-breakfast around the corner from the British Museum. That first day (on Miss Martin's recommendation) he saw the Rosetta Stone and the Elgin Marbles, then after dinner he "stumbled on Soho" and found the sidewalks crowded with prostitutes. "I made a circuit of Soho Square and then chose one," he remembered, "who led me up a steep flight of stairs to a small room where our business was quickly transacted." The rest of that rainy week he dutifully visited every site he knew in London of literary significance, from Donne's church to Carlyle's house and various other places relevant to writers he'd encountered in Baugh's *Literary History of England*.

In Paris he stayed at a little Left Bank hotel that Jacquie Rogers had recommended and lost no time looking up the local editor of *The Paris Review*, Nelson Aldrich—"a handsome young man of qualities," as Roth put it, whose background could scarcely have been more different than his own. The great-grandson and namesake of a Republican senator, Aldrich was a product of St. Paul's and Harvard; he'd read a couple of Roth's stories and knew the author was roughly his own age, but whatever he expected fell short of the actuality: "I don't think I've ever so quickly been attracted to a man," said Aldrich. "I felt that we were boys together talking about girls. We didn't talk about books or writers—we talked about Paris and its delights." The young men drifted from one café to the next, and after Roth had met Aldrich's girlfriend, Jill, she remarked to Aldrich, "Very funny man but I felt he was always looking up my skirt."

On a Tuesday night in early July, Roth was presented with the Aga

Khan Prize at the splendid Bois de Boulogne residence of Prince Aly Khan, the son of Aga Khan III ("the staggeringly rich leader of the Ismaili Muslims") and third husband of Rita Hayworth. As Roth reported, a little high-mindedly, to Miss Martin: "There were all kinds of elegant people with titles there, and a *Match* photographer took my picture, and all of it had absolutely so little to do with writing, and even with me, that it was in the end rather more pathetic than comic." Roth refrained from mentioning the ruckus caused at one point when the butler detained his date, a young woman on a motorbike whom he'd picked up at the Café Odeon; she loudly insisted she was invited until Roth went downstairs to sort things out. After the party, a group repaired to the Left Bank for dinner, and Roth found himself sitting next to the writer Irwin Shaw, who every so often would remind him, over the years, that he still had an open invitation to visit the Shaws in Paris or Switzerland.

Since getting out of the army two years before, Roth's life had been a heavy (if mostly fruitful) grind of writing and teaching and coping with Maggie; that summer he allowed himself "to do absolutely nothing," or anyway he didn't bother to write. With a friend from Chicago, he met two Swedish girls and paired off with one of them, Monica—"a wonderful interlude" that lasted two or three weeks before Roth decided to head south to Italy at the end of July. (Monica invited him to visit her in Sweden, and soon enough Roth would sorely regret not having taken her up on it.) At the American Express Roth hitched a ride with two countrymen, stopping along the way at Carcassonne, Arles, Avignon, and Nice; he was felled by a sudden attack of back pain in Livorno, and had to lie down in a hotel for a few days. Finally he strapped himself into his steel brace and caught a train to Florence.

"I'm fond of looking at Paris, but it was Florence that really charmed me thoroughly," he wrote Miss Martin. "I was there five days and left foolishly for Venice, where I lasted about 36 hours. I had the feeling that if I wrote out a big enough check there, someone would sell me San Marco." In Florence Roth had been struck by the piquant incongruity of vulgar Americans and gorgeous, abiding art ("Every surface in the city, the bastards painted"), but he soon returned to Paris to spend a few weeks "calmly alone," reflecting on his latest good fortune.

Back in February he'd heard from his old Chicago friend George Starbuck, who'd also quit graduate school and taken a job as editor at

Houghton Mifflin in Boston; Starbuck had been following Roth's career
with interest and wondered whether he was working on a novel. Roth
replied that he was indeed working on something set in Frankfurt,
The Go-Between, but was particularly excited about a long story he was
just then completing, *Goodbye, Columbus;* he wondered whether it was
hefty enough to submit (perhaps as part of a larger collection?) for their
Houghton Mifflin Fellowship ($2,500), the oldest publisher-sponsored
award of its kind: "I shall be twenty-five next week and stouter," Roth
wrote, "and feel a tiny knife in my side as I race to be a boy wonder."
Such was his hurry that he held fast when Starbuck pressed him only
for the unfinished novel; Roth understood "the prejudice against books
of stories from novelless writers," but felt certain that *Goodbye, Columbus* "could have a very wide appeal, perhaps to that same group who
buy Salinger by the thousands." Finally, when Roth threatened to take
his work elsewhere, Starbuck agreed to consider both the novella and a
fragment of *The Go-Between*. *The New Yorker* and *Esquire*, meanwhile,
had both passed on the long and problematic *Goodbye, Columbus*, but
Roth's friends at *The Paris Review* were willing to publish every word of
it ("It looks as though it's going to take up the whole magazine," he wrote
the Maurers, "tra la"), as early as their Autumn–Winter 1958 issue—
meaning that three consecutive issues would feature work by the young
and still rather unknown Philip Roth.

That left the editor in chief of Houghton Mifflin, Paul Brooks, with
a "knotty publishing problem" as he wrote in an internal memo. Given
that *Goodbye, Columbus* was to be published in full by *The Paris Review*,
it made sense for Houghton to combine it with other stories ("on the
pattern of Carson McCullers' BALLAD OF SAD CAFE"): "One difficulty, perhaps, is that the denouement hinges on an incident involving a
contraceptive apparatus—and it is hard to see how this could be changed
without rewriting the whole story." As for Roth's other manuscript—"57
pages and a synopsis of a novel set in Frankfurt"—it had been received
with "the greatest enthusiasm" by Starbuck, but Brooks and two of their
colleagues (both of whom knew Frankfurt) were not "nearly so enthusiastic," Brooks noted. "It seems to me that the difference between this
and his American writing is the difference between a story that starts
with an intellectual idea and a story that embodies the life that the
author has lived." Such was the astute reasoning that led, five days later,

to their offering Roth a $1,000 advance to publish *Goodbye, Columbus and Other Stories*, whereas the novel would remain "under consideration for a Fellowship" pending submission of a more complete manuscript. Roth got the news on August 4 in Paris and was "thrilled"—but then his agent, Donadio, negotiated a counteroffer of $2,500 from Viking, which Houghton promptly agreed to match *and* publish the collection as a prestigious Houghton Mifflin Fellowship Book. Whereupon Roth wired Napier Wilt, requesting a yearlong leave of absence.

■ ■ ■ ■

Roth boarded the *Hanseatic* on August 21, 1958, in Hamburg, and spent much of the crossing in the company of a young English architect, Vernon Gibberd. One evening they stood on deck watching the sun go down, and the moment it slipped behind the horizon, Roth broke into raucous applause that caused a few of his fellow passengers to chuckle nervously and others to edge away with offended looks. The cumulative effect of such antics was charming: "In the right mood," said Gibberd, "he was the greatest company in the world." Roth divided the two-volume Olympia Press edition of *Lolita* between them, to be smuggled into the States as contraband, only to find the Putnam edition had been published in America that very month. Also Roth managed to have an affair on the boat and worried, in passing, that the woman might get pregnant. "He was pretty laissez-faire about these things," Gibberd observed.

Roth and Maggie had corresponded steadily over the summer, and (outward behavior to the contrary) Roth's heart had grown a bit fonder in her absence. "She is a rare person," he wrote Solotaroff, "and if I were a little rarer I'd have not screwed things up so often." He made it clear he wanted her to stay in New York rather than return to Chicago after her *Esquire* job ended, and when his ship came in she was standing on the pier, waving radiantly in a white dress that made her look like a summer bride ("Maybe that was the idea").

Gene Lichtenstein had also gone to Europe for the summer, while his wife, Cynthia, a second-year law student at Yale, stayed behind to clerk for a firm in New York; as it happened she was house-sitting for the poet W. H. Auden and his partner, Chester Kallman, who liked to spend half the year in Ischia, off the coast of Italy. Cynthia, a Philadelphia debutante and Radcliffe graduate, didn't like the dirty Bowery or

Auden's dirty apartment, though the worst part by far was her room-mate: Maggie. "*I don't want a strange man coming here overnight! How dare he!*" the latter railed in one case, when Cynthia proposed letting an old friend, Tony Bailey, sleep over while in town from Connecticut. Though Cynthia was formidable in her own right, she was so taken aback by the older woman's fury that she allowed herself to be browbeaten. The whole summer was like that. Meanwhile Roth and her husband bumped into each other in Paris and whiled away the afternoon in a café. "Too bad there's not a war on," Roth laughed. "We could send the girls letters about how hard life is here in Europe." "All I care to say is that the portrait Philip painted of Maggie in his later novel [*My Life as a Man*] was quite an accurate one," Cynthia noted. She remembered Roth asking her—at a time when he and Maggie were freshly estranged—"Why didn't you *warn* me?" Said Cynthia in 2015, bitter still: "I didn't because neither man" (Roth or her ex-husband) "paid any attention to me or cared what I thought and never thought to inquire how my summer had gone."

Soon after his return, Roth finally cracked *The New Yorker*. Fiction editor Rachel MacKenzie had been cultivating him ever since read-ing "You Can't Tell a Man by the Song He Sings" in the November 1957 *Commentary*, struck by its congenial blend of "humor and serious-ness." Roth reminded her that his then agent McCrindle had already sent the magazine a version of "Epstein"—which, not surprisingly, was found to have too much shmutz, whereas *Goodbye, Columbus* was too long (and dirty enough in its own right). The first piece they bought was a brief "casual" for the back of the magazine, "The Kind of Person I Am," inspired by partygoers in Hyde Park who presume to pigeonhole the author—"Oh *that's* the kind of person you are"—based on the books he reads and so forth ("They're so goddamned infuriating," Roth wrote the Maurers, "not to mention boring, that I wrote this piece"). Around this time Roth also finished "Defender of the Faith" and was certain it was "the best thing I've done."* On October 6, 1958, MacKenzie wrote Roth: "I shall be grieved and distressed if it doesn't go through—I felt, reading it, that special excitement you feel when you come on a first-rate, perfectly controlled story—but it may offer problems for us." There would,

---

* An estimate that would hold up over the years—"the first good thing I ever wrote"—even as his previous "best thing," *Goodbye, Columbus*, fell and fell in its author's favor.

in fact, be problems galore, but for now the story had found its way into Mr. Shawn's briefcase and was finally bought, on October 27, for a staggering $2,200.

The story is neither "sensitive" nor leavened much with humor, and hence Roth's enduring satisfaction with it; the notion of Jewish solidarity has rarely been so pitilessly tested in the nuanced light of human nature. "Let the goyim clean the floors!" Private Grossbart cackles, overheard by his sergeant, Nathan Marx, a decent man who has released Grossbart and two other Jews from barracks-cleaning duty so they can attend shul. So convincing is Grossbart's piety, at other times, that Marx can hardly believe his ears, and soon his tribal fellow-feeling is tested again when Grossbart complains about the *trafe* (non-kosher food) the army makes them eat: "'That's what happened in Germany,' Grossbart was saying, loud enough for me [Marx] to hear. 'They didn't stick together. They let themselves get pushed around.'" It's the summer of 1945, at a training camp in Missouri; both Marx and his gentile captain, Barrett, have survived terrible combat in Europe, and the captain, at least, is astonished by Grossbart's audacity about the *trafe*.

> "Do you hear [Marx] peeping about the food? Do you? I want an answer, Grossbart. Yes or no."
>
> "No, sir."
>
> "And why not? He's a Jewish fella."
>
> "Some things are more important to some Jews than other things to other Jews."
>
> Barrett blew up. "Look, Grossbart. Marx, here, is a good man—a goddam hero. When you were in high school, Sergeant Marx was killing Germans. . . ."

But Marx himself is all too susceptible to what seems, at least, a sincere sense of entitlement. And Grossbart doesn't hesitate to impugn his character, in the most galling way imaginable, to get what he wants:* "I've

---

* Not unlike Maggie vis-à-vis Roth, though it would be years before he'd learn the extent of her hypocrisy, and more years still before he would come to terms with it (if he ever did). The affinity between Maggie and Grossbart suggests a vast unconscious wisdom on Roth's part—often evident when considering his art versus his life.

run into this before . . . but never from my own!" he says, when Marx
hesitates to give him a pass ("No passes during basic") so he can have a
proper Seder meal with relatives in St. Louis. "They say that Hitler himself was half a Jew," Grossbart persists, before bursting into tears. Lest
he seem Hitlerian even to himself, Marx goes so far as to sign passes
(in the captain's name) not only for Grossbart but his two buddies, and
is rewarded with an egg roll rather than the gefilte fish he requested.
There was, in fact, no Seder; the whole ruse—Hitler and tears—was for
the sake of a day's escape to a Chinese restaurant. In the end, however,
Grossbart is left weeping in earnest, when Marx thwarts his ploy to get
out of being sent to the Pacific with the rest of his company. "There's no
limit to your anti-Semitism, is there?" Grossbart rages. "You really want
me dead!" "*You'll* be all right," Marx says, repressing an urge to seek
pardon for his not inconsiderable vindictiveness.

While waiting for a verdict from *The New Yorker*, Roth had immediately started work on another long story about a conscience-stricken Jew,
"Eli, the Fanatic." "It may be great," he wrote Solotaroff after finishing a
fifty-two-page draft. "Then again, no." Roth's ambivalence would later
curdle into loathing for a story that, arguably, became his most popular:
widely anthologized and taught, especially in Israel, as a fable portraying the failings of the Diaspora. The idea had come to him in a curious
way: Maggie's mother was the advertising manager for the South Haven
newspaper, and a friend of hers—a young Jewish reporter who'd since
moved to New York—had told Roth about a Hasidic group that started
a yeshivah in a local suburb, unsettling its more assimilated Jewish residents. By way of research Roth visited a yeshivah in the Williamsburg
section of Brooklyn with his old Chicago friend, Herb Haber, who'd
grown up there; Maggie went along but had to wait outside, so the boys
wouldn't see her.

In Roth's fictional Woodenton, New York, three years after the war,
a yeshivah has been established by some refugees including the director, Tzuref, and a silent young man ("a regular greenhorn") in a black
suit and hat. Eli Peck, a harassed young lawyer, is sent to the yeshivah
as an emissary. "The stores along Coach House Road tossed up a burst
of yellow—it came to Eli as a secret signal from his townsmen: 'Tell
this Tzuref where we stand, Eli. This is a modern community, Eli, we
have our families, we pay taxes.'" The main problem is the greenhorn's

grungy, Old World outfit; the Jews of Woodenton have been allowed to buy property there only since the war, and are afraid that any hint of "extreme practices" will offend their Protestant neighbors. "Certainly such amity is to be desired," Eli writes Tzuref. "Perhaps if such conditions had existed in prewar Europe, the persecution of the Jewish people, of which you and those 18 children have been victims, could not have been carried out with such success—in fact might not have been carried out at all." Tzuref's reply is brief: "The suit the gentleman wears is all he's got." *All he's got* means exactly that: the man escaped the tragedy of Europe with nothing but the clothes on his back, and the disparity between his desolate condition and the prosperity of Eli and his neighbors—between European and American Jews generally—suggests an almost unbearable absurdity; the man in the black suit, whose face is "no older than Eli's," piques a part of the latter's conscience that suspects he doesn't "*deserve* to be happy," as his wife puts it. The better to remind his Jewish neighbors, then, that they *are* Jews, just like the myriad dead of Europe, Eli appropriates the greenhorn's suit and walks from one side of Coach House Road to the other, saying "Sholom" to the president of the Lions while his friends murmur about previous nervous breakdowns.

Roth would often describe the creative process as a kind of dialectic—a given book or story is conceived in reaction to the one that preceded it—and "Eli" seems to have been written somewhat in penance for "Defender of the Faith": instead of a pathologically selfish Jew who exploits the tragedy of his people for personal gain, we are given, in Eli, an anti-Grossbart burdened by a mad (or seemly) sense of guilt. From the beginning, though, Roth worried he'd swung the dialectic too far in the opposite direction, beyond the point of mawkishness, and for hours a day he "bang[ed] away" at his typewriter, torturing a story that "should be brilliant, but isn't." "There's a point at which banging becomes tiring, malicious, and immoral, and I just about reached it today," he wrote the Rogerses, fully a week before he relinquished the thing to Starbuck. "Eli *moved* the people who read it here," his editor reassured him, "and when I mention that you may still be working on it, they give me the worried look I'd give Hemingway if he told me he had decided to beef up *The Killers* a little and deepen the characterization." MacKenzie, however, rejected "Eli" for *The New Yorker*: "We all agree that there are remarkable things in the story, but we feel that it keeps sliding off into caricature and farce and that in the end it falls between realism and didactic modern fable, the emotional thread breaking and the lesson taking over." Such a critique conveyed something of what Roth would ultimately say in more damning terms; however, when *Commentary* accepted it for their April 1959 issue—only a month before publication of *Goodbye, Columbus*, the book, for which it served as the final story—he decided, at least for a while, that he liked the thing after all.

■　■　■　■

WHILE IN EUROPE Roth got word that he'd been turned down for the Stanford Fellowship ("which is stupid on their part, but fuck em")—another reason to spend the year in New York. For the first two months he stayed with his parents in Moorestown during the week, which soon palled for the usual reasons, now including Herman's chagrin over his son's decision to leave teaching and make a living as a writer (*"He'll starve!"*). After a few weekends of searching, Roth found a "delightful" two-room basement apartment on East Tenth between Third and Second Avenue, catercorner to St. Mark's Church and a few blocks away from the famous kosher dairy restaurant, Ratner's, in the heart of Little Ukraine. The rent was only eighty a month, and after whitewashing the rooms and buying some Salvation Army furniture, he moved in on November 1.

As Roth pointed out in *The Facts*, "these were the most triumphant months of my life." In early October he'd been put up for a week at the Parker House, in Boston, while he met Paul Brooks and company at Houghton and went over his book ("page by page") with Starbuck, who proved an excellent editor. Back in August, when Roth had written Starbuck to accept Houghton's offer, he mentioned that he had a new story he was eager to show him, "Defender of the Faith." Starbuck was so impressed he decided to cut "Vandals" and "Aaron Gold" in favor of stories with a more explicitly Jewish focus. As Roth later remarked, "George, in a way, determined my future, because *I* didn't think that was my subject. I didn't know what my subject was."

At the age of twenty-five, Roth was on the brink of considerable literary fame and had made friends with some of the most prominent editors in Manhattan: Marty Greenberg, Bob Silvers, Gene Lichtenstein, and of course Plimpton, who promptly phoned to inquire how things had gone in Paris (*"How'd it go, boy?"*) and invite him to a big party. As Roth wrote the Rogerses a few days before moving to East Tenth, "Pass on to Brother Stern—subtly, of course—the party Maggie and I attended at George Plimpton's last night: guest list: Joshua Logan, Irwin Shaw, Allen Ginsburg [sic] (and lover), Harold Brodkey, John Marquand, Jr." The last became a friend: a regular of *The Paris Review* crowd, Marquand wrote under the name John Phillips to avoid confusion with his then famous father; he and Roth took to meeting a couple of times a week to walk through Greenwich Village to a Bleecker Street café, where they "mesmerized each other with descriptions of our wildly disparate social backgrounds." Marquand was trying to follow up his moderately successful first novel, *The Second Happiest Day*, published five years before; when he died in 1995, at age seventy-one, Roth went to his funeral and wondered over the ."great anguish" of a talented man who, try as he might, could produce only one more published book, *Dear Parrot: Pertaining to the Care, Nurture, and Befriending of Man's Oldest Pet.*

Amid the deepening turbulence of his Maggie attachment, Roth would often fear that Marquand's fate would prove his own, but in the early fall of 1958 he simply wished she'd go back to Chicago. More impressive even than the literary luminaries at Plimpton's party, to Roth, were the gorgeous young women he longed to flirt with, if not for Maggie's hawkish eye. Making matters worse, her *Esquire* job had ended without any prospect of another, and she was having trouble making rent on her "awfully small, awfully over priced apartment" on West Thirteenth. Roth's stature in the literary world—soon to explode with *Goodbye, Columbus*—seemed especially to threaten her. As an unemployed, thirty-year-old (as of September 29) former secretary and waitress, she seemed an unlikely consort for such a handsome, promising young man, and, when put on the spot, she had a way of overplaying her bravado. At a party that fall, Roth found himself talking to one of his favorite critics, Leslie Fiedler, a fellow Newarker who remarked at one point that he had "five or six children," as Roth wrote Solotaroff, whereupon Maggie earnestly inquired whether he was Catholic:

What a golden mouth she is. So Fiedler said no, and Maggie, unable to drop a scalding potato, says well a Protestant can have em too, and smiled. And shmuck that I am I come forth with a deathless two words:

"He's Jewish." If you want to know what a conversation murderer it was try saying it aloud, with some volume, because others are screaming all around. So much for LF. He confided to Maggie later that EM. Forster was or is a homosexual novelist. Maggie, a rugged girl, pushed him on it, and said in effect he was full of crap. I turned at this point and talked to a pretty girl. She was stupid but straight.

Always it came back to the women. One night when Roth was impotent with her, Maggie flew into a rage about "all the girls [he] screwed in Europe," and Roth was disinclined to deny it. Soon he began openly dating other people, and her demands for his attention took more and more bizarre forms, as when she'd end up in the hinterlands after taking the wrong subway and call him from a phone booth, "panting and incoherent, begging [him] to come get her." He wanted desperately to be rid of her, but the possibility that she'd kill herself—as she threatened often enough—gave him pause. "It isn't fair!" she said. "You have everything and I have nothing, and now you think you can dump me!"

Twelve

I**N A** *N**EWARK** E**VENING** N**EWS** **PROFILE OF THE YOUNG** author ("Newark Boyhood Fiction Material") that appeared on December 7, 1958, Roth made the curious claim that he wanted to live in the New Jersey suburbs ("preferably Glen Ridge") "when he gives up bachelorhood." Perhaps it was a sop to Maggie or his parents or both; meanwhile he wrote a "funny piece" intended for *The New Yorker*, "Why to Stay Single, Though Harried," that neither the magazine nor Maggie liked very much. Thirty years later, a *New York Times* reporter would wonder (apropos of *The Facts*) how Roth of all people had blundered into "such a lurid, pathological" relationship, and Roth replied (smiling), "I made a mistake."

One problem was that Roth was nothing if not independent minded— an aspect of his character that was good for his writing and occasionally disastrous for his personal life. Though he dropped hints in letters to his closest friends, for the most part he was loath to confide, always, just how frighteningly dismal things had become between Maggie and him, and in New York he had only his new architect friend from the *Hanseatic*, Vernon Gibberd, and a few pleasant acquaintances in the literary world. That left his brother, Sandy, who was now a married thirty-year-old art director at Batten, Barton, Dustin & Osborn, living in nearby Stuyvesant Town, the father of two adopted children—a totality of facts that had more or less estranged him (benignly) from Philip, the intellectual writer. "Philip was very stiff-necked," Sandy observed in 2007. "He thinks he can solve all his problems and he doesn't need anybody."

Philip's brief against his brother began with Sandy's marriage, in August 1954, to Trudy Schanker, a kindhearted but plain young woman who excited a sort of pitying tenderness in Sandy that wasn't quite love, and certainly had nothing to do with sex. Before Sandy came along—

they liked to jitterbug together—Trudy's circumstances had been a little poignant. Her parents died when she was a child and she'd been raised by her older sister, a singer in the Metropolitan Opera chorus; the sisters lived together while Trudy helped support the household as a secretary at Mount Sinai Hospital. At Philip's college graduation in May 1954, Sandy was visibly rattled, though years would pass before he admitted that he'd been trying to figure out what to do about Trudy, who'd staked all her hopes on marrying him, and was quite openly desperate about things. In 2006, Sandy told an interviewer that he'd actually banged his head against the wall on his wedding day: "I realized I'd never be an artist if I got married," he said; nor would he have a freewheeling sex life, at least not without considerable guilt. Philip was appalled at his brother's docility, casting back to the little Sandy in a white suit who used to sit all day on a hot porch because he'd been told to stay put. That, Philip thought, would never be him.

Because Trudy had only a single defective kidney, she couldn't bear children, and they adopted two boys, in 1957 and 1958. Both times Philip acted as intermediary, experiences he used in *Letting Go* for Gabe's disastrous role in the Herzes' adoption. For Philip things went smoothly enough. The first time, he was asked to meet the mother at the hospital, after she gave birth, and pretend to be the husband while walking her outside to a taxi; then he took the baby around the corner to where Sandy and Trudy waited in a car. In that case the mother was a "very sweet and very pretty" teenager, so ashamed that she never once looked at Philip during the half hour or so they were together. The second time, just over a year later, the mother was a fetching Icelandic woman who had a civilian job at Fort Dix; Roth's job was to drive her to a Manhattan courthouse so she could sign a form consenting to an out-of-faith adoption, and during the long day in a car together the woman was lively and even flirtatious toward her son's future uncle.

Among the many discarded draft pages of Roth's 1974 novel, *My Life as a Man*, there's this: "[Zuckerman] had a tendency to inflate himself before his older brother, particularly to boast (subtly, of course) of his adventurous spirit—and what after all could be more adventurous than living with a divorcée, five years his senior, whose husband had stolen her child from her? An incest victim, no less." Perhaps this was one way he had of suggesting to Sandy that marriage to such a "dull and uninteresting" person as Trudy was the opposite of adventurous, whereas Trudy considered her brother-in-law to be (so he wrote the Rogerses at the time) "very selfish." As for the divorcée and alleged incest victim in question, she and Trudy had despised each other ever since Maggie and Philip's visit to Woodstock, Connecticut, where Sandy and Trudy had vacationed during the late summer of 1958; reminiscent of her behavior with Bess the previous summer, Maggie had acted like "a pig," said Sandy, dumping her dirty underwear on Trudy, among other demands, while Trudy was busy coping with a toddler. As for Philip, when he wasn't boasting about his adventurous spirit, he would come to Stuy Town and, Sandy recalled, "literally hide out in my apartment." However, if either Sandy or their parents ventured to suggest that Maggie was trouble, Philip would revert to the five-year-old who once ordered his mother to *"Go!"* when she brought his raincoat to school—insisting, by god, he'd go out with whomsoever he liked, etc.

■　■　■　■

ROTH WOULD LATER attribute his hospitalization at the beginning of January 1959 to anal fissures, caused by inferior French toilet paper; close, but in fact he'd had a rectal polyp removed, and for this reason he was told to give himself an enema the night before the operation. In an episode that would serve as the donnée for one of Maggie's few finished short stories ("From such revelatory moments does great art grow," Roth later reflected), he was unable to find his "wounded little aperture," as he put it, and finally asked Maggie to do the honors. Indeed, she was with him before, during, and after the procedure, the better to be of use caring for him. "In the hospital I just enjoyed the attention of all my nurses," Roth wrote the Rogerses on January 18, a week after his release, "especially one with an out-of-this-continent Irish accent who Maggie glared into submission." By then Maggie had lost her most recent job and "sublet" her apartment, as Roth wrote the Rogerses ("Old Maggie quit her job"*), and at that time she seems to have been ensconced on East Tenth for quite a while. Later, Roth would claim he hadn't seen her in weeks or even months before the "rainy February Sunday" she

---

* I was unable to determine the nature of the short-lived job Maggie got sometime late that fall, after her *Esquire* job ended in August.

knocked on his door, weeping, and accused him of being as bad as her father ("You and Rust Hills and my father!"), whereupon he endeavored yet again to "prove [him]self otherwise." She could sleep on a sofa in his living room for "a week," he remembered telling her, but the sofa ("more like a loveseat") proved too small, and after the first night they agreed to share his double bed—chastely, more or less. "This was a friend I was doing a good deed for," he said in 2012.

On January 18, they seemed a happy couple, at least in letters. Roth also wrote the Maurers that day, mentioning that Maggie ("dear girl") had given him a kitten named Allegra as a "post-hospital present," and Maggie herself wrote the couple and explained that the kitten was named "after Allegra Kent whom we saw dance with the N.Y. Ballet and with whom Philip has been enamored ever since. Philip never had pets in his clean, clean New Jersey home and is a bit worried about it but taking it pretty well. His love for the cat confirms an inkling I have about how he'll be with his children, a very loving and concerned papa." One can unpack that sentence in a number of interesting ways, but the main impression is one of walls closing in, whatever Roth might have thought at the time. Among Maggie's motives for setting her trap, however, money seems to have had low priority, contrary to another of Roth's later animadversions: "She was a battler and she was going to save herself, though not by looking for a new job to replace the one she'd lost," he wrote in 2011. "If things panned out, she'd never have to work again." In fact, though she'd recently quit her job ("the first time I've ever gotten angry and quit a job," she assured the Maurers), she had plenty of freelance work—having just revised an index for the Anchor paperback of Kierkegaard's *Either/Or*, no less—and on January 30 she was hired full-time as a production editor for Harper & Brothers. "Well, Philip has time for his writing and I don't," a friend remembered her complaining.

In *The Facts*, Roth would paint a far bleaker picture of his cohabitation with Maggie than their respective 1959 accounts of the kitten Allegra and Maggie's careful postoperative nursing would suggest: "I'm as surprised today as I was then that we didn't wind up—one or both of us—maimed or dead. . . . By the beginning of the year in which *Goodbye, Columbus* was to be published, I was nearly as ripe for hospitalization as she was, my basement apartment having all but become a psychiatric ward with café curtains." Before Maggie had lost (or sublet) her apartment on West Thirteenth, it had been burglarized, she claimed, and among the stolen items was the old Royal typewriter Roth's parents had given him as a boy—a "sacred relic" that had stood him in good stead through high school, college, and graduate school: "It was my plow," he said. "It was my sewing machine. It was my rifle and my fishing rod." But Maggie had wanted to work on her own fiction, and after all Roth was using the Olivetti by then. On or about February 18—a full five weeks after he'd departed the hospital in Maggie's care and constant company, during which they'd barely managed not to maim or kill each other—Roth noticed Maggie's winter coat hanging in the hallway and "on an impulse" searched the pockets and found a pawn ticket for his old Royal. When he confronted her with it, Maggie burst into tears and said she'd been broke and had no choice, but Roth finally put his foot down: it was time for her to go. "I can't go," she said. "I'm pregnant."

Roth was stunned. "It was true that in the middle of the night there had been two, three, even perhaps four fantasy-ridden, entangled couplings," he wrote in *The Facts* ("I'm also quite bored with only having intercourse when he awakes partially in the middle of the night," Maggie wrote in her journal), but he was certain that for a long time he'd been "erotically too mummified" even to dream about sex. "So I am a good Jewish boy and she is an hysterical schizophrenic Gentile girl," he would later write Bob Baker. "I am covered with guilt and trying to figure a way out, and she begins to weep endlessly and tell me that if I don't marry her she is going to kill herself." She also threatened that—before (or in lieu of) killing herself—she would carry the baby to term and then "leave it on [his] parents' doorstep." Affecting lightheartedness, Roth said she had to get a rabbit test, at least, and rinsed out a herring jar for her to pee into and take to Estroff's Pharmacy around the corner.

As Maggie would eventually confess, she hadn't gone directly to Estroff's but had taken a detour east to Tompkins Square Park, where she found an obviously pregnant black woman and explained to her that she, Maggie, was involved with "a scientific experiment" and would pay three dollars (the sum varied over the years) for a jar of the woman's urine. This was the urine Maggie collected at the woman's "grisly apartment" (as Roth wrote Baker) and brought to Estroff's, whereupon it was analyzed at Mirkin Laboratories on East Twelfth. The rabbit test was supposed to take three days. "I had never lived through three such days before in my life," Roth wrote in *My Life as a Man*,* "though I was to know a hundred more just as grim and frightening in the years to come." He'd been afraid to leave the apartment those first two days, lest she kill herself in his absence, but suspense got the better of him on the second night and he went for a little walk, popping in at the pharmacy on Second Avenue just in case the results were in. "Does 'positive' mean 'Yes, she's not pregnant'?" he remembered asking Mr. Estroff.

That night he walked roughly 225 city blocks—from the East Village to Columbia and back—trying to figure out what to do next. In this connection he would often think of the last act of Chekhov's *Three Sisters*, when the cuckolded Andrey, pushing his baby Bóbik around in a carriage, gets a piece of advice from old Chebutykin: "Put on your hat, take your walking stick in your hand, and clear off . . . clear off and keep going, keep going without looking back. And the farther away you get the better it will be." Roth was considering Oregon, where Bob and Ida Baker lived nowadays; Maggie could have whatever was left behind in the apartment. Almost surely he would have done that, were it not for his parents; but who knew what such a loose cannon would do? Also, she might actually commit suicide, for which Roth would feel more than a little responsible. The main thing, he decided, was to persuade her to have an abortion; after the fetus was gone he could reconsider his options, maybe, but meanwhile he'd have to promise to marry her. And try to seem happy about it. What transpired when he returned from his long walk was, to the best of his recollection, recorded more or less exactly in *My Life as a Man*, wherein Tarnopol assures Maureen (the Maggie character) that he wants to marry her "whether [she's] pregnant or not." "Oh, darling," Maureen replies, "we'll be happy as kings!" Roth missed the allusion to *A Child's Garden of Verses* and was puzzled by the androgynous implications of her response to a marriage proposal "so obviously delivered without heart or hope," but anyway he pressed on with the rest of his bargain: a baby at this point would almost certainly mean the end of his writing career, he said, and therefore he'd appreciate

---

* The novel about Maggie's urine ruse that "more precisely duplicated the autobiographical facts," said Roth, than anything else in his fiction, for the simple reason (learned at agonizing length) that to "reshape even its smallest facet would have been an aesthetic blunder, a defacement of her life's single great imaginative feat."

her agreeing to an abortion; this she readily did, since of course there was no baby to abort.

The next day Roth phoned his old friend Marty Weich, who was then in the midst of his internship at Flower Fifth Avenue Hospital; two hours later, Weich called back and gave him the name of an abortionist on Park Avenue. The cost, as Roth recalled, was roughly equal to his bank balance at the time: three hundred dollars. When he offered to accompany her to the doctor's office, Maggie brusquely declined (a relief, since he worried he could be arrested), then pocketed the money and spent the afternoon in a Times Square movie theater, watching and rewatching Susan Hayward in *I Want to Live!* (about a cocktail waitress who dies in the gas chamber for a crime she didn't commit: "right up Maureen's alley," Tarnopol reflects). This, anyway, was the version Roth told in his novel and in *The Facts*, and elsewhere, for a long time; in 1966, however, around the time of the actual event—four and a half years after Maggie's confession—Roth wrote his friend Baker: "But it turns out that instead of going to the doctor she told me she went to, who produced a period in her by means of 'a shot,' she went to the Turkish bath and sat there for three hours before coming home to tell me that the baby was gone, somehow. Pure bullshit, not even good bullshit, but in my madness, I believed it all."

In *My Life as a Man*, Maureen returns from her "abortion" looking "pale and wan (the strain of sitting six hours at the movies)," and claims the doctor had plied a knife and given her nothing for the pain "but a tennis ball to squeeze"—the same story Roth would recycle fifty-plus years later for his biographer, a false memory that was nothing less than the main reason he usually gave for deciding to marry her after all: "I had married her because I believed I had seriously wounded her in a horrible abortion."

Near the end of his life, Roth conceded that he must have misremembered aspects of Maggie's tale and later confession—the result of endlessly trying to fictionalize the episode—most crucially (a) that she hadn't actually claimed to be "seriously wounded," much less without anesthetic, and (b) that she'd whiled away the afternoon in a Turkish bath rather than a movie theater. That she was "weeping and enraged" on her return from the miscarriage/abortion, however, he remembered vividly: "it may well have been that she was berating me, if not for the horrors of the abortion, for the terrible indignity I had caused her, but wildly berate me she did. A second subject for which she berated me was her certainty that now that she had done as I asked, I was going to run out on her." In the latter respect she had, of course, simply guessed the truth, and in reaching for her old refrain—*"You're worse than my father!"*— she was taking precisely the right tack. In any case Roth caved—just as his brother had caved, albeit under a less frantic brand of pressure. "To whom was I preaching my probity?" Roth would wonder and wonder. "Was all this taking place in a Conrad novel? *'You miserable sonofabitch you're worse than my father!'* Why couldn't I have said: *'Ten* times worse. And if you don't get your ass outta here in five minutes I'll *show* you how much worse.'* . . . Why couldn't I have said that!"

Roth wanted to believe that Maggie had mentioned a knife *and no anesthetic*—that it had taken at least that much to force his hand—but really all she had to do was tell him he wasn't being Good. "That's the hook you get him on," said a later (nicer) girlfriend, laughing. *Why couldn't I have said that?* It was the sort of question Roth endeavored to answer again and again in his early fiction—in "Defender of the Faith," "Eli, the Fanatic," and *Letting Go.* "The drama of adult responsibility," as he put it, "the promptings of conscience, moral striving, the demands of manliness." In his case—and Sandy's too—he was goaded to do the right thing not only by certain midcentury norms of male propriety, but by an eons-long tradition of *menschlichkeit*.

"Seven years ago this month," Roth wrote a friend in February 1966, "I tried hard as I could to earn the award for the Nicest Jewish Boy of the Century." Another aspect of the whole nightmare that Roth would come to rue ("my collapse is pathetic") was the way Maggie forced him to follow through on his promise *the very next day*—Sunday, February 22—Washington's Birthday—when they had to take a train all the way to Yonkers to find a person who could legally wed them. "It was a farce," said Vernon Gibberd, one of two witnesses with his girlfriend, Diana. The wedding took place in the suburban home of a Justice of the Peace named Hinchcliffe, whose gouty foot was elevated during the proceedings, and who half-listened to the murmur of spring-training baseball scores on the radio. That night Roth and Maggie took a room at the Algonquin ("because of the literary associations"), where Roth was impotent, though Maggie was too happy to care. As for Roth, he felt "broken, like an animal is broken."

He wasn't alone. "The pain Maggie inflicted on me was equaled if not exceeded by the pain I inflicted on my parents," he remembered. The day after his wedding, Philip informed Bess and Herman with a carefully worded letter, and the day it arrived Uncle Bernie phoned Sandy and said they had to go to Moorestown right away or else Herman might "do something drastic." They were there for some three hours before Herman began to calm down, and Sandy never mentioned the ordeal to his brother.* Within a week or two, anyway, their parents had decided to make the best of it—what else could they do?—and for Herman that meant *hocking* his son to behave a little more like a proper husband. The first item on his agenda was for Philip to give up his slummy apartment in the East Village and live in Stuy Town near his brother's family, and also to replace his wife's "piece of shit" coat.

"I have just about had as much as I can bear," Roth wrote Solotaroff on March 11, "and I regret that you must be the first outside ear to have to listen. My brother and sister-in-law have also nettled, wherever they could, though my brother's instincts are good; he succumbs, unfortunately, to his wife's stupidity and selfishness." (Sandy: "I had this Boy Scout attitude that if my brother wanted to marry her she was a good person. It was crazy.") For a wedding present, Roth's parents had given the couple an expensive set of Spode china, which ended up in Maggie's possession along with just about everything else after their separation, when Roth implored the judge to bear in mind that it was "not an accident" his father had also given him—"in my name alone"—some rainy-day AT&T stock that his estranged wife was now eager to get her hands on too. Meanwhile, during the marriage, she made a point of calling her parents-in-law Mr. and Mrs. Roth.

---

* He did, however, discuss it during a taped 2007 interview, to which Philip listened after his brother's death two years later. "For as long as he lived Sandy never told me about this horrible event," Philip confirmed in 2013.

Thirteen

R OTH WAS GRATEFUL TO *ESQUIRE*'S FICTION EDITORS, Rust Hills and Gene Lichtenstein, for giving him his first big commercial sale with "Expect the Vandals" (never mind their part in trying to take Maggie off his hands), and made a point of giving them first crack at the stories that would end up in *Goodbye, Columbus*. "Epstein" and the title novella were declined for understandable reasons (shmutz and length), but Roth was startled when "Defender of the Faith" was also declined in spite of the enthusiastic support of both Hills and Lichtenstein. Still, he expected a positive result when "Eli, the Fanatic" was "being bickered about at Esquire," as he reported to the Rogerses: "All the editors supposedly have read and liked it, and now they're wondering if it's safe for them to do it." Though he didn't know it yet, and would never quite get the story straight, Roth had been effectively banned from the magazine by its executive director, Fritz Bamberger, an émigré from Hitler's Germany who finally called Lichtenstein onto the carpet. "This is a self-loathing Jew," he said. Lichtenstein, taken aback, began to remonstrate but was angrily cut off: "Do you know about *Ken?*" Bamberger asked. "Read about it." What Lichtenstein learned about *Ken*—a short-lived magazine of the thirties founded by *Esquire*'s editor in chief, Arnold Gingrich—was that its editors had defied the Catholic Church by running a story about the church's support of Franco in Spain, whereupon advertisers had abandoned the magazine and it was shut down after little more than a year. "We will never publish this man's stories," Bamberger declared of Roth.*

The New Yorker, of course, had no such compunction about "Defender

---

* Roth's fiction did not reappear in *Esquire* until 1962, the year Bamberger resigned.

of the Faith," which would go on to win second prize in the 1960 *O. Henry Awards* volume and earn its author a third appearance in the *Best American Short Stories* series. Roth never forgot the excitement of waiting for the March 14, 1959, issue of the magazine to arrive at his local news-stand, across from Klein's on Fourteenth Street; on his third visit that morning he was finally able to buy two copies (one for his parents), and the rest of that day he read his story while eating, walking through the park, sitting on the toilet—again and again. "It was thrilling," he said. "I had begun."

"I just received a letter this morning from a New Yorker reader accus-ing me of being an anti-semite," he wrote the Maurers a few days later. "I'm arranging a party to go up to the Bronx, where he lives, and burn a cross on his lawn, so he can see the real thing." If Roth had considered this an aberration, he was soon disabused; within a day or two Rachel MacKenzie, his editor, phoned to say that a number of Jewish readers had already canceled their subscriptions, and the magazine had drafted a letter for such people, as follows:

> We found Philip Roth's "Defender of the Faith" an honest and moving study of an individual who used his religion for selfish ends, thus involv-ing another person in a tragic conflict of loyalties, and we are astonished that you should find it distasteful in any way. It was far from the author's intentions to write anything anti-Semitic, and the editors would not allow anything they felt was derogatory of any religion to be published in the magazine.

But the letters kept coming. At first Roth was rather excited by the con-troversy; he hadn't really been pilloried since his infamous send-up of *The Bucknellian* (save the odd crank who'd objected to his Eisenhower piece in *The New Republic*). He was curious about who these people were and what exactly was on their minds, and insisted *The New Yorker* forward every letter, "adverse or not." "Your one story makes people—the gen-eral public—forget all the great Jews who have lived," a typical detractor wrote, "all the Jewish boys who served well in the armed services, all the Jews who live honest hard lives the world over." By "general public," it occurred to Roth, his correspondent meant *gentiles*—the main reader-ship for *The New Yorker*, after all, which had hitherto published stories only about "cute Jews," as Roth put it, à la Leo Rosten's *The Education of H*Y*M*A*N K*A*P*L*A*N*. Just as the Jews of Woodenton had feared goyish reprisal for the greenhorn's eccentricity in "Eli, the Fanatic," Jewish readers of the magazine were accusing Roth of shaming them—*a shanda fur die goyim.*

It was a sensitive time for postwar American Jewry. The events of the Holocaust were more and more openly discussed; an American edition of Elie Wiesel's *Night* would be published the following year, and even non-reading Jews were aware of the Broadway production of *The Diary of Anne Frank*, whose movie version was released the same week as "Defender of the Faith" appeared in *The New Yorker*. Many Jews wanted their heroes to be saintly victims such as Frank, or better still the kind of warriors found in Leon Uris's *Exodus*, the biggest best seller of 1958 (indeed, the biggest best seller in the United States since *Gone with the Wind*). As Alfred Kazin would point out on the occasion of Roth's sixtieth birthday, the writing of fiction was a relatively novel aspect of Yiddish letters, which valued so-called wisdom literature over the purely aesthetic: "any Jewish American novelist is in for trouble if he retraces Mark Twain on the subject—'Jews are members of the human race; worse than that I cannot say of them.'"

MacKenzie asked Roth for permission to give his phone number to the Anti-Defamation League of B'nai B'rith, and on April 10 they got in touch ("Oh to be a liberal now that spring is here," said Roth), inviting him to meet with two ADL representatives for lunch. When the day came, Roth was relieved to find himself with sympathetic fellows who only wanted to make him aware of certain complaints and answer whatever questions he might have. Roth told them how bewildering it was to be accused of anti-Semitism, all the more given his youthful ambition to study law and defend the rights of Jews, possibly on behalf of B'nai B'rith. When he asked what kind of complaints they'd received, he was shown a letter from the current president of the Rabbinical Council of America, Emanuel Rackman: "What is being done to silence this man?" the rabbi had written. "Medieval Jews would have known what to do with him."

Perhaps the worst part, for Roth, was explaining to his parents—so soon after the Maggie debacle—the "outcry" over his *New Yorker* story that had led to his meeting with the ADL. "What outcry?" said Herman. "Everybody loved it. What is the outcry? I don't get it." Herman, especially, had been apt to pluck issues of *Commentary* and *The Paris Review* from where they were proudly displayed on a side table, reading passages aloud to guests; he was gobsmacked that actual rabbis had seen fit to brand his son a self-hating Jew. As for Bess, she would get an earful over the years from her Hadassah and Deborah friends who were "only too happy" to mention the latest outcry. "Philip, *are* you an anti-Semite?" she finally asked him one day, over coffee. "Ma," he said. "What d'you think?" "No!" "Well, there's your answer."

What with one thing and another, then, Roth was in no mood to mince words when Rabbi Rackman wrote him directly and—without mentioning his letter to the ADL about medieval justice—suggested he'd done Roth a favor by forbearing to go over his head and explain things to *The New Yorker* ("I do not want to compound the sin of informing"). "I am indeed sorry that you are outraged at my story, 'Defender of the Faith,'" Roth replied on April 30. "Grossbart no more stands for all Jews than Hamlet stands for all Danes, Othello for all Negroes and/or Moors, Raskolnikov for all students or all Russians. Nor does Marx, the hero, stand for all Jews." Roth wondered why Rackman and certain other detractors hadn't bothered to mention Sergeant Marx, "a man of stern moral conscience . . . I suggest it doesn't serve their purpose"—a purpose similar, Roth wrote, to that of "the late Senator McCarthy":

> He who criticizes must be silenced—that is a terrible tenet to have to live by, Rabbi, and I should imagine even more terrible to a spiritual leader, a person who as a helper and friend is apt to be engaged by men's problems of conscience even more than the rest of us. . . .
>
> I resent deeply and cannot forgive you your insulting letter which demands of me a kind of Jewish patriotism which is akin to the kind of American patriotism demanded by Senator McCarthy a while back. I resent and cannot forgive you the charge you make that my story was conceived and written out of an "anxiousness to receive better fees." . . . I am willing to be morally responsible for every word I write, and I will take whatever action seems to me necessary to defend my integrity. That, after all, Rabbi, was what my story was about. . . .

It was presumptuous of you, Rabbi Rackman, to speak of yourself to me as "a leader of his people." You are not my leader, and I can only thank God for it.

■ ■ ■ ■

ON MARCH 23, 1959—six weeks before publication of *Goodbye, Columbus*—Roth mentioned to his advertising contact at Houghton, Anne Ford, that it might be "profitable to pour a little gas on the fire" by running an ad in *The New Yorker*: "I am a little interested in selling this old book, my bride having expensive and delectable taste." Ford understood this to mean that the young first-time author wanted to emphasize, explicitly, that he'd been attacked as a self-hating Jew, and wondered whether such an approach might "boomerang" to their common disadvantage. The next day Starbuck dashed off a note assuring Roth that nobody "thought you meant anything so crude as to advertise the controversy" and regretted that the book's ad budget ($1,500) was, in any case, committed elsewhere. Roth was indeed exasperated by the misunderstanding but pushed Starbuck to "keep [his] hand in with the [*New Yorker*] ad"—that is, a conventional quote ad that didn't refer to his alleged anti-Semitism per se. Starbuck, as ever, did as he was told, but Roth was "flabbergasted" when the ad in question failed to attribute its main quotation to Alfred Kazin ("his name carries immense weight"), whose glowing review in *The Reporter* was headlined TOUGH-MINDED MR. ROTH: "Several weeks ago I was awakened," Kazin wrote, "while reading *The New Yorker*, by Philip Roth's 'Defender of the Faith,' a story with such extraordinary guts to it that I went around for days exhilarated by the change of the literary weather." Kazin had been a hero ever since Roth had read *On Native Grounds*, and the most thrilling part of Roth's prepublication cocktail party on May 6—at the East Thirty-fifth Street penthouse of Barbara Krohn, a Houghton editor, and her husband, David (later Roth's ophthalmologist)—was Kazin's presence. His parents and Sandy also came, and Maggie managed to behave herself ("Of course she did—all this was exactly what she had hoped to obtain with the urine fraud").

As Saul Bellow would acknowledge in his *Commentary* review, *Goodbye, Columbus* was a milestone of sorts ("the hero of Jewish fiction two decades ago knew nothing of Jewish suburbs, country clubs, organized cancer fund drives, large sums of money, cars, mink, or jewelry"), and he and Kazin were joined by a host of other critics in weighing its impact. Roth read and reread every syllable of these reviews, no matter how provincial, but of course it was Bellow's notice that meant more, perhaps, than any of the thousands that would follow during Roth's long career: "*Goodbye, Columbus* is a first book but it is not the book of a beginner," Bellow began. "Unlike those of us who came howling into the world, blind and bare, Mr. Roth appears with nails, hair, and teeth, speaking coherently. At twenty-six he is skillful, witty, and energetic and performs like a virtuoso." No wonder the piece helped mitigate the impression of coldness Bellow had made on Roth when they'd met, most recently, at the Hillel House in Chicago ("I think he suspects me of wanting to usurp his position," said Roth, "in which he is entirely correct"). Fortunately—given a friendship that would take decades to find its feet—Roth never saw the unexpurgated version. As the "outraged" Bellow wrote Dick Stern, the review had gotten "some of its teeth drawn" by the magazine's editors just prior to publication, so that his actual opinion of the book was considerably at odds with the printed version.

Leslie Fiedler's review in *Midstream* was almost pure rhapsody: "Newark, *our* Newark," he announced, had finally produced a laureate ("how can he be only twenty-six?") who was, perforce, "as vulgar, comical, subtle, pathetic and dirty as itself." Moreover this had happened in the nick of time, since the Newark that Fiedler had known in his youth was already passing into history. Fiedler could hardly have known just how forsaken Newark would become in the years ahead, or how vividly Roth would portray its glory and decline, but the final paragraph of his review heralds something of this: "Newark! A Florence it will never be in the minds of men, nor a Baghdad nor a Paris; but after Roth, we can hope that perhaps it will survive on library shelves ravaged by ambitious boys as another Yonville or Winesburg, Ohio."

Irving Howe, the consummate New York intellectual, gave a somewhat more grudging appraisal in *The New Republic*: "Mr. Roth's stories do not yield pleasure as much as produce a squirm of recognition: surely, one feels, not all of American Jewish life is like this, but all too much of it is becoming so." Howe commended the author's "deadpan malicious accuracy" in sketching the Patimkins, which, he conceded, was "ferociously exact"—indeed, "too exact, too close to surface realities, there is not enough imaginative transformation. Mr. Roth is dedicated to a kind of mimetic revenge." Roth was affronted by the "slippery" ambivalence of the review (albeit not as affronted as thirteen years later, when Howe would retract almost everything positive from these early impressions): "I figure fuck Howe anyway," he wrote the Bakers. "It isn't my fault that people aren't eating as much chopped liver as they used to."

As a first-time author, Roth took himself even more seriously than his impressive roster of critics—admitting to friends that he was in the habit of phoning bookstores and asking if they carried *Goodbye, Columbus*, then hanging up; also, he and Maggie made a point of taking their nightly strolls along bookstore-heavy streets so she could ask the same question in person. The book was on the brink of a third printing (4,312 copies sold in the first three weeks), and would ultimately sell almost 13,000 in hardback—"phenomenal for a book of stories by a jackoff from the woods," as Roth noted. That August he got a fan letter from Kirk Douglas, and in *Charm* magazine the rugged young author was featured in a photo spread—along with two first novelists (Nora Johnson and Sylvia Ashton-Warner)—solemnly playing with Allegra the cat: "[Roth] has a handsomely remote manner that seems to belie his writing," the caption read: "a lusty, often comic and frequently terrifying portrayal of bourgeois Jewish life in America." In *The Ghost Writer*, Zuckerman mentions his appearance in a *Saturday Review* piece on America's "young, unknown writers," for which he'd been photographed with his cat, Nijinsky; sensing (correctly) that his revered mentor, E. I. Lonoff, considers such publicity unseemly, he explains: "'The girl who came around to take the pictures'—and whom I had tried unsuccessfully to throw onto the floor—'said she'd just take the picture of the cat for Betsy and me.'"

In later years Roth would all but disown his first book ("a very, very weak piece of writing") and, groping to explain its appeal to the august likes of Bellow, Kazin, and Fiedler, would suggest that "they didn't know there were people like that." In a belated "hatchet piece" that appeared in the Fall 1960 *Partisan Review*, a young Jeremy Larner*

---

* Larner went on to win the 1973 Best Original Screenplay Oscar for *The Candidate*, starring Robert Redford.

had made rather the same point: "Each of these knowledgeable men [Bellow et al.] verifies Roth's portrait of the Jewish upper-middle class and sets forth qualified but positive claims for his merits as a novelist"—however, Larner added, such "non-bourgeois intellectuals" as Bellow were "mistaken on both counts" because of their "basic ignorance of the people Roth writes about." Larner, with cocky aplomb, proceeded to enumerate the various ways Roth had mischaracterized his social types. At the time Roth was rightly astonished ("Jee-sus") by the "jerkiness" of Larner's review, though again it anticipated certain of his own misgivings. "Neil [Klugman] is nothing more than the allegorical Poor Boy . . . he does not seem to exist outside of his frustration with the Patimkins," said Larner, and in 2004 Roth agreed: "There's no character there; he's just an attitude." In almost every respect Roth was harder on his title novella than even his most savage critics, and he'd forever nurse particular chagrin over the Gauguin-loving black child at the library ("mawkish Mr. Roth at his most lovable") and the winsomely kvetching Aunt Gladys ("facile and a cliché"). Yet for many years he would often be informed, wistfully, by critics and everyday readers alike, that he'd never quite "fulfilled the promise" of his first book.

This was all the more galling given that a substantial part of the book was the despised "Eli, the Fanatic." Already, in December 1959, Roth suspected (as he wrote Miss Martin) that the story lacked "depth," and in the apparent hope of correcting this defect, he rewrote its ending for the paperback and Literary Guild editions—thus making it, if not deeper, at least more touching. In the original version (the one that would survive for posterity via the Library of America) we are given Eli's third-person thoughts, briefly, as he visits his newborn son in the maternity ward while wearing the greenhorn's suit and hat: "He'd make the kid wear it! Sure! . . . A smelly hand-me-down, whether the kid liked it or not!" In the revised version, however, Eli delivers a first-person speech to the baby: "'I'm your father . . . I'm wearing a black hat and a black suit . . . and special underwear. In a little while Dr. Eckman'll make me take off the whole business . . . But I'll keep the suit at home . . . and I'll wear it again. I promise. Every year on the nineteenth of May, I'll wear it. I promise.'" Eli goes on like that, telling his infant son that he too will wear a black suit and hat, and they'll walk together that way:

"'And you'll make your son wear it. . . . And your son's son's son . . . and we'll never forget . . . *Remember!*'"* In due course Roth would dreadfully repent of this ending, and for the rest of his life he remained aghast at the story's enduring appeal—even among such estimable people as the chancellor of the Jewish Theological Seminary, Arnold Eisen, who volunteered to Roth that he "loved" the story and had taught it for years; as Eisen remarked to an interviewer: "Roth was way ahead of anyone else in recognizing that [the Holocaust was] the shadow in the closet of American Jewish life."

Another notable aspect of "Eli" is the potent way its hero embodies a theme reflected in the other stories, too, and throughout the work that would follow: the individual in revolt against the community, the I against the They—the refractory author's persistent mulling of Kafka's pensée "In man's struggle against the world, bet on the world." Because of the world and its expectations, Roth had cultivated "a certain insidious softness" (as he put it) in his work and person—hence the Capote-like apprentice who'd wished to be admired for his sensitivity and "powdery prose," hence "the Nice Accommodating Jewish Boy" who'd married Maggie and whom Roth would endeavor to squeeze out of himself "drop by drop" à la Chekhov and his serfdom. Roth persisted, in short, to refine his own values independent of those the world was apt to impose. As he remarked in 2016, "You might say that right down through *Sabbath's Theater* and *American Pastoral* to *Indignation* and *Nemesis* the implications and ambiguities and contradictions inherent to goodness—and badness—has been the master obsession."

The more hard-nosed he became, the less he liked *Goodbye, Columbus*. "I wish this kid's book would disappear," he sighed in 2004—nine years before the Library of Congress designated it as one of the "Books That Shaped America," a distinguished list of American works chosen "for their impact on millions of individual lives and on the course of the nation."

■   ■   ■

---

* During one of our first-ever chats, Roth mentioned how much he hated the story, and I asked him about this alternative ending (which I'd encountered, shortly after college, in an anthology). A look of horror flashed over his face when reminded of this version.

A CODA: Three weeks before publication of *Goodbye, Columbus*, Roth received a letter from Samuel S. Goldberg of Goldberg & Hatterer: "Our client, Miss Maxine Groffsky, informs us that you have written a work of fiction in which she is not only recognizably portrayed as are members of her family but, in addition, she claims you have traduced and maligned her." Goldberg suggested that his client be allowed to inspect the manuscript prior to publication "so that matters complained of may be considered and removed"; he'd also alerted *The Paris Review* of Groffsky's complaint, even though the novella had already appeared there, as Groffsky was surely aware. Indeed, it seemed likely she was acting at the behest of her family, whose reputation in Maplewood—so rumor went— had been as blackened as that of Thomas Wolfe's family and friends in Asheville, North Carolina.*

A quarter century later, Roth attended a speech given at the Jerusalem YMHA by Abba Eban, the Israeli foreign affairs minister, calling for peaceful negotiation with the PLO. Afterward Roth was accosted by a woman who introduced herself as Irene Groffsky, Maxine's younger sister, who wanted to tell him to his face, at long last, just how much she hated him for ruining her family's life—etc. On she went. When she was finally done, Roth replied, "Irene, if you can find it in your heart to forgive Yasser Arafat, surely you can find it in your heart to forgive me." But apparently not; the woman stormed off without a further word.

---

* Maxine Groffsky was cordial but firm when she declined my request for an interview. To the best of Roth's recollection, he submitted Samuel Goldberg's letter of April 13, 1959, to the Houghton legal department and heard nothing further.

Fourteen

A T THE END OF JUNE—JUST BEFORE MOVING TO AMA-gansett, Long Island, for the summer—Roth and Maggie took a road trip (in Herman's Cadillac) to visit friends in Chicago and Maggie's family in South Haven, a town that seemed as exotic to Roth as Bombay: "what made me so curious was that it was the backdrop for the grim saga of gentile family suffering that was hers." They stayed at the home of Daddy Herb, Maggie's grandfather, and his second wife ("Aunt Hervey"), and indeed slept in the very room Maggie had occupied for most of her childhood, after Red Martinson had proved incapable of keeping a roof over their heads. Roth liked the easygoing Herb, and the two sat out on the porch at night chatting about one thing and another ("never had no desire to visit no furrin country," said Herb, when Roth mentioned their plans to live in Europe). Maggie's mother, Evelyn, lived in a basement apartment close to her job at the *South Haven Tribune*; she neatly hoarded piles and piles of newspapers on every surface of her smoke-filled apartment, where two nicotine-addicted dogs (forever gob-bling up her cigarette butts) kept her company in lieu of her long-gone husband. Roth liked Evelyn, too, and hardly recognized the chastened "victim" her daughter had described.

"Roth is the son-in-law of Mrs. Evelyn Martinson, TRIBUNE advertising manager," the newspaper announced after their departure ("Author Married to Local Woman"), identifying Roth as "the son of Mr. and Mrs. Simon [sic] Roth of Newark, N. J." and the recent recipient of an award given to him by "the Paris Review editor [sic], the Agha Kahn [sic]." Maggie's marriage was well received by all, not only because her husband was such a promising young writer, but a Cadillac-driving Jew to boot, not unlike the other well-heeled Jews who descended on the town every summer. As Aunt Hervey liked to point out, "They're dark ugly little fellas, Margaret, but they're good to their wives and children."

As a married man, Roth worried all the more about making a living as a writer and had been considering a return to the University of Chicago in the fall, or else trying for a job in New York so Maggie could stay on at Harper & Brothers. All that changed on April 9, when he was informed that he'd been awarded a Guggenheim Fellowship to work on his Frankfurt novel, *The Go-Between*. Requesting a grant of $4,100, Roth mentioned that Houghton thought his work in progress "lacks milieu and specificity," so Roth thought a stay in Germany would be helpful; when the foundation gave him as much as $4,500, Roth decided on a more congenial venue, Rome, whither he and Maggie planned to travel aboard the *Liberté* after spending the summer in Amagansett, a safe distance (110 miles) from the distractions of Manhattan. Soon they found a charming plum-colored house on Montauk Highway, a duplex divided inside by a staircase and wall, for even less (seventy-five a month) than Roth's little apartment in the East Village. Their landlord, Bill, lived in the other half of the house, and welcomed them to the neighborhood by walking them to the nearest bar—Roth's "first experience of a gay bar."

If anything, their social life was livelier and more literary than ever. Down the road toward the beach was the Irish Canadian writer Brian Moore, whose novel *The Lonely Passion of Judith Hearne* Roth had read and admired; Moore was twelve years older but "never pulled rank," and Roth was equally fond of his wife, Jackie. A bonus was the odd visit from their best Canadian friend, Mordecai Richler, a young Jewish writer, like Roth, with an acclaimed book that year, *The Apprenticeship of Duddy Kravitz*; both men were given to a kind of antic *spritzing* (joking), albeit more boozily in Richler's case. Another young writer who became part of the circle was Josh Greenfeld, a lonely bachelor who had a way of showing up at the Roths' around dinnertime, or joining them and the Moores when they drove to Gosman's fish store in Montauk, a few tables on a dock where the day's catch was served. Finally, too, there was the writer Wallace Markfield: "The Country of the Crazy Horse" would rate an allusion in *Portnoy* and the author's wife, Anna, would provide the beguiling Brooklyn accent of Paul Herz's old girlfriend Doris in *Letting Go*. Markfield was working on a first novel, eventually published as *To an Early Grave*—about the late writer Leslie Braverman (based on Isaac Rosenfeld), "a secondary talent of the highest order"—which established whatever reputation Markfield would enjoy before fading away. As Roth recalled, "Wally was crazily intelligent, sardonic, wry, comic in the classic mordant Jewish way and, to my mind, a wonderful writer but one who never could marshal all his strength in one strong book."

In Amagansett as in Manhattan, Maggie was intimidated by the high-powered literary company and would occasionally overcompensate by announcing that she was her husband's "editor," or pontificating about some aspect of Henry James; at other times, though, she seemed to run out of steam and become "extraordinarily mundane and flat," as their friend Blair Fuller remembered. "Curiously, Philip is constantly pushing me, to read, to write, to study," she wrote in her journal on October 6, 1959 (still in Amagansett):

> In truth, out here I know I want most to keep house, cook, garden, read for pleasure and follow that proverbial life we both sneer at so. At the same time, more and more, among our friends I feel defensive about accomplishment. . . . There is no doubt that I'm filled with great anger still which is irritated by the demands made on me. . . . Obviously my therapy only quieted the storm and didn't eradicate it. However, after meeting all those analysts this summer out here I feel even analysis is closed to me as a solution. I must keep treading water I know that but I feel such a strong desire to stop and that I'm drowning anyway.

The main psychoanalyst in their midst was an affable Canadian friend of the Moores, Bruce Ruddick, who practiced in Manhattan and spent summer weekends on Long Island with his artist wife, Dorothy, and their three children. Toward the end of that summer Roth's parents had come for a visit, and one evening the Ruddicks stopped by for drinks, the six of them sitting outside on lawn chairs watching the sun go down. For about ten minutes everything seemed fine, but then Maggie began arguing with Bruce Ruddick—about psychoanalysis. As Roth remembered, his wife wouldn't give an inch and finally "became so fierce and slighting" that Herman couldn't bear it (Ruddick, after all, was not only a guest but a *doctor*). "Margaret," he gently ventured, "as far as I can tell, you and the doctor aren't really—" *"Shut up!"* Maggie snapped. An astonished silence, then Philip jumped to his feet: "That's it! That's enough! Go!"—and, uncharacteristically abashed, Maggie retreated to their bedroom.

Eager to assert some semblance of compatibility, Maggie had announced after the wedding that she wanted to convert to Judaism, to which end she'd taken her husband along to meet with a Reconstructionist rabbi, Jack Cohen, at the Society for the Advancement of Judaism on the Upper West Side. Cohen had given her a number of books to read, and Roth would point these out to visitors in Amagansett and make fun of his studious shiksa wife. "Maggie is hot into the Bible," he wrote Solotaroff, "taking deuteronomy seriously, about how you can't eat the pelican or any of the good things, and you should be nice to widows and divorced ladies, and you should have an altar 6X3X41/2 [sic]. Nothing like a nice authoritarian faith, if you have to have one." All this culminated in a second wedding ceremony at Cohen's synagogue that December, a "vulgar and ludicrous" business, as Roth would have it, that his parents attended with the usual bewildered politeness. Until her own Jewish funeral, Maggie would never again take part in any Jewish ritual or holiday or refer to Judaism, period, at least in Roth's hearing.

Because Roth had gotten busy on a television script, they'd decided to stay in Amagansett through the end of the year, and after the other vacationers had departed, they were much alone together. Roth was at pains, as ever, to convey an impression of normalcy to their friends: "Maggie does a good deal of reading—she's still studying to be a Jew—and exotic cooking," he wrote in late October. "There's a fine aroma of garlic in all quarters. There's also TV, our first experience with it, and we have sat gloomy and frozen before some horrors." Mostly, though, they fought. Roth remembered tossing a plate of sunny-side-up eggs at her head one morning ("You clean it up," she said, after ducking), and in her journal Maggie wrote about trying to kiss him one night while he lay reading on the sofa: "Oh Maggie you bore me," he said, pushing her away. Roth tried to make it up the next morning—squeezing orange juice and "kissing around"—but Maggie remained furious, until Roth accused her of being like Marty Greenberg's wife,* who'd promised to leave him penniless when he asked for a divorce. "This again makes me feel that Philip's affection and consideration come not from his heart but from his fear that I will divorce him and make claims that will tie him up for life," Maggie noted.

Roth was preparing for Rome by studying *Italiano Ultrarapido* for an hour each night after dinner, whereupon he'd join his wife in the living room and they'd resume whatever quarrel they'd been having with their food. More and more, Roth would end up fleeing to the beach, where he'd walk for miles along the cold, black, crashing waves, feeling doomed. "One night around midnight," he remembered, "I was so crazed by her unceasing opposition on every last issue that had arisen that day that instead of going to bed, I went out to the car and this time, rather than driving to the beach, I headed for Montauk." Flooring the gas pedal, Roth had a vague idea of flying off the easternmost tip of Long Island into the sea: "I was not only indifferent to death," he said, "I welcomed it." On that point, at least, he and his wife were en rapport. "I do think more often about suicide," she wrote that fall, "it seems to grow as a possibility although I really wouldn't do it now I'm certain. That sounds contradictory but it's just that suicide has an increasing fascination and I see it as finally my fate like something you want to do for a long time and won't let yourself but you know in your heart that sometime you'll have the opportunity and everything will be right and you'll give into it."

■　■　■　■

ALMOST TWO YEARS AFTER his first "flashy idea," *The Go-Between* continued to give Roth fits. The more he plugged away, the more it occurred to him that he was at sea with the whole concept of what a novel was, or what he himself was supposed to be as a writer. "Every once in a while I write a line and think what Kazin said, then another line and think what Howe said, and then on the next say go screw them all," he wrote Solotaroff. He'd begun to wonder if he'd ever be a novelist

---

* That is, his *first* wife. Greenberg's second wife was the writer Paula Fox.

("What patience you need, what faith"), when around midsummer he resumed writing about a place he actually knew: Chicago. Within two months he'd written more pages, two hundred, than he'd ever managed on the Frankfurt manuscript. His first Chicago novel, *Distracted and Unblessed*, was about a young man from a prosperous Jewish family who pursues an idealistic shiksa by volunteering for Henry Wallace during the 1948 presidential campaign. By September he'd put this aside to work on a second Chicago novel even closer to his own experience, *Debts and Sorrows*, and within a few weeks he had almost a hundred pages ("I'm flying"). Roth had been rereading *The Portrait of a Lady*, and was trying to cultivate a narrative voice more orotund than the near vernacular of *Goodbye, Columbus* ("I was writing a big novel and I wanted, as it were, a big and impressive voice"), as well as to approximate something of James's gravitas ("the intricacy of motive; the gap between intention and consequence"). Starbuck visited Amagansett in November and subsequently wrote a memo to Paul Brooks, at Houghton, describing a manuscript that was already quite like the final version of *Letting Go*, with the climactic sequence about a botched adoption clearly envisaged by the author. "This is the expectable young autobiographical novel," Starbuck reported, "but Roth is making it into something funny, touching, and quite original."

But this, too, had to be deferred for a potentially lucrative project resulting from a meeting that summer with two TV producers. Fred Coe had discussed the possibility of Roth's adapting "Defender of the Faith" for *Playhouse 90*, but reconsidered when he discovered how controversial the story was. Meanwhile Robert Alan Aurthur was trying to drum up scripts for a new dramatic anthology on NBC, *Sunday Showcase*, that ran opposite *The Ed Sullivan Show* (perhaps the main reason it lasted a single season). Roth soon had a first draft he was "crazy about," though he worried it would prove "to[o] gutsy for the network." Indeed, it seems fair to imagine that Roth's teleplay, *A Coffin in Egypt*, might have been gutsy enough to end his career, especially in the wake of "Defender of the Faith." He'd derived the idea from a recent article in *Commentary* about Jacob Gens, the Jewish head of the Vilna ghetto in Lithuania, who'd been responsible for rounding up a thousand Jews a month for the extermination camps. Roth was fascinated by the story's moral complexity, though he could scarcely ignore its incendiary potential as a prime-time

TV program. "I realize completely that the decision to help exterminate a thousand people a month is a big hot potato for the audience to swallow about a character in the first act," he wrote Aurthur. "Well, it's a big hot potato for the character to swallow about himself! For the Jews to swallow!" As the world would shortly learn from Hannah Arendt, Jews in Gens's position felt tortured, of course, but also considered themselves to be like captains "whose ships were about to sink and who succeeded in bringing them safe to port by casting overboard a great part of their precious cargo." In Hungary, for example, Dr. Rudolf Kastner was able to save exactly 1,684 people—the wealthier Jews who'd bribed their way onto the so-called Kastner train to Switzerland—among the nearly half million deported to Auschwitz.

Roth didn't stint on the moral complexity. The Gens character, Solomon Kessler, is naturally aghast when he's given his mandate by a Nazi officer, Holtz, a decent fellow who likes Kessler (Roth wasn't interested, he wrote Aurthur, in writing about another evil Nazi). As leader of the ghetto, Holtz explains, Kessler will be expected to round up a thousand Jews from "time to time" for the camps. "The Jew is the enemy, the Jew must die—those are Hitler's words, not mine," says Holtz. "You choose them, whatever way seems fair. The aged, the idiotic, the unemployed, vagabonds." Kessler goes about his work, sick at heart, but when the first group of doomed, elderly Jews begins to rebel and shout *"Murderer!,"* Kessler steels himself:

> KESSLER: Do you want a thousand, or *ten* thousand! . . . You! On the train! . . .
>
> OLD MAN: What did I do? Why—
>
> KESSLER: I don't know what you did! You lived a life—come on! Come on! . . .
>
> OLD MAN: I'm seventy-eight. Rabbi, who can be buried in a strange place? . . .
>
> SMOLENSKIN [the rabbi] (*in great pain, and with some confusion*): "So Joseph died, being an hundred and ten years old, and they embalmed him, and he was put in a coffin in Egypt." You remember? Joseph himself. Joseph himself had to wait for his sons to carry his bones to the homeland.
>
> OLD MAN: I'm not Joseph, Rabbi. I'm me.

There's little in the way of heroism among the Jews of Vilna—indeed most want only to save their own skins. When the sixty-four-year-old sexton is chosen for deportation, after surviving two years of winnowing, he reminds Kessler that the Russians are coming ("why should *anyone* go?"), and, when Kessler is unmoved, he points out that Rabbi Smolenskin is older than he: "You play favorites!" By then Kessler's only friend is the Nazi, Holtz, who tries to persuade him to flee the retribution of his own people: "There's a theory of Freud's, Solomon, that the Jews themselves killed Moses. Well, you have been their Moses, their deliverer."

It's unknown what actor Roth had in mind for the sympathetic, Freud-reading Nazi, but he liked the idea of Montgomery Clift for Kessler—what with his "quality of nervousness, uncertainty, shlemie-liness"—whereas Aurthur was thinking about Eli Wallach. That Aurthur was still soberly considering the project, after reading three drafts of Roth's script, attests to its power; for quite a while, in fact, the man temporized—claiming that NBC would fly Roth back from Europe sometime that spring for production—but in the end wiser heads prevailed, and Roth was paid off ($4,000) for his trouble. "They were correct to turn it down," Roth said fifty-one years later. "The fury it would have aroused in Jewish viewers would have been enormous. . . . But it was just that moral horror that excited my imagination." By then Roth had a better idea of the backlash he would have faced, based on his own experience and that of Arendt, whose *Eichmann in Jerusalem* began appearing in *The New Yorker* three years after Roth had dramatized, in his teleplay, one of Arendt's most inflammatory points: that leaders of Nazi-imposed Jewish councils (*Judenräte*) had been complicit in the genocide of their own people. Given also her theory that Eichmann himself was "a mediocre bureaucrat"—versus a monster whose evil beggars the imagination—Arendt became the focus of what Irving Howe described as "a civil war" among Upper West Side intellectuals, and (like Roth) was roundly reviled from pulpits all over the world as a self-hating Jew.

■ ■ ■ ■

ON DECEMBER 22, 1959, Roth and Maggie belatedly departed for Italy aboard the *Vulcania*. Maggie wrote in her journal that "cabin class is shabby . . . and most of our fellow passengers are middle-income, middle-aged and middlebrow," but, on docking in Cannes, she was delighted with their big elegant room at the St. Yves Hotel. They bought a car on arrival, a Renault, and spent the afternoon driving around the mountains overlooking the city. "Now we will rest and fuck ["fuck" crossed out; "make love" inserted]," Maggie wrote. "Last night we saw a movie with Bridgette [sic] Bardot, the first we've seen in which a breast and a man kissing it was revealed. It was very arousing." The next day they drove on to Florence, where they stayed near the Uffizi at a shabby-genteel pensione "out of Henry James," as Roth remembered ("eccentric elderly professors . . . spinster women"); Roth was happy to be back, even with Maggie, who seemed content to wander everywhere with him, despite freezing weather.

In Rome they found a "marvelous" four-room apartment on a little street, Via di Sant'Eligio, across the Tiber from Trastevere. As Roth wrote Solotaroff, "Our apartment has huge rooms and a marvelous view from my study—and our dining room—of the little dome of an old Raphael church [Sant'Eligio degli Orefici] and then the river, and above and beyond that, the Janiculum hill, green, with umbrella pines and elegant cypresses and even a lighthouse which flashes red, green, and white at night, and is supposed to light the way home for those guineas who have migrated to the Argentine." Life, indeed, seemed a little too good to be true; even the tension between husband and wife—all but unceasing since that terrible episode with Bruce Ruddick in Amagansett—had dissipated somewhat.

Then Maggie announced she was pregnant again, the third (really the second) time in three years, despite her professed use of a diaphragm. This time Roth brooked no discussion; he found the name of an English-speaking doctor in the *Rome American*, and the man promptly arranged a D&C and even gave them a lift to the furtive location: "The following night we drove across black Rome with him," Roth recalled, "past the steps of Santa Maria Maggiore—which I wanted to crawl all the way up straight into the arms of Jesus, certain that we were going to be busted and in Catholic Italia I would wind up in chains and serving on a road gang under the Sicilian sun for the rest of my life." While a nice woman performed the procedure and their driver administered anesthetic, Roth sat in an outer office sweatily perusing *Hudson River*

Bracketed, by Edith Wharton. Maggie was a little dazed afterward but regained her old strength by the time they returned to their apartment. "You monster," she berated Roth, "you made me go through this! I'm bleeding now because of this! I know all you want to do is fuck other women and leave me."

Fifteen

THE PACE OF ROMAN LIFE SUITED ROTH. HE WORKED
in the morning, and while everything was closed in the afternoon he
took long walks or read; for about two dollars he and Maggie could eat a big
restaurant dinner, and nobody tried to hustle them out the door while they
lingered with friends getting "quietly high" on *vino*. Among the many congenial people they met in Rome were the Styrons, Bill and Rose: the two
men knew and admired each other's work, and Rose informed Roth that it
was she who'd found "Conversion of the Jews" in *The Paris Review* slush pile.
Bill had recently finished his second novel, *Set This House on Fire*, and until
publication in May he had nothing to do but spend money and sit around
the Caffè Doney "looking at the tarts." After a few months of long, rollick-
ing dinners and picnics in the Roman countryside, Roth reported to Bob
Baker that his new friend Styron "was one of the first guys in a long time
who I could talk to, and bullshit with, and feel easy about the whole thing."
Above all Roth could make Styron laugh, and one of his more intricate jokes
would be recited at length in *Sophie's Choice* by the title heroine's flamboyant,
schizophrenic boyfriend, Nathan Landau (partly inspired by Roth).*

---

* In the joke, a country-club member, Shapiro, is trying to persuade others to invite his
friend Tannenbaum to be a member, while one of the latter's violent detractors, Ginsberg,
dozes nearby. From the novel: "Nathan's voice grows incomparably oleaginous, gross with
fatuity and edged with just the perfect trace of Yiddish as he limns Shapiro's quaveringly
hopeful apostrophe to Max Tannenbaum. 'To tell what a great human being Max Tannenbaum is I must use the entire English alphabet! From A to Z I will tell you about
this beautiful man! . . . A he is Admirable. B he is Beneficial. C he is Charming. D he is
Delightful. . . .'" Around the letter "I," Ginsberg wakes up and says, "'J oost a minute!
(Majestic pause) K he's a Kike! L he's a Lummox! M he's a Moron! N he's a Nayfish! O
he's an Ox! P he's a Prick! Q he's a Queer! R he's a Red! S he's a Shlemiel! T he's a Tochis!
U you can have him! V ve don't want him! W X Y Z—I blackball the *shmuck!*'"

Roth's closest friend, however, was a writer—now utterly forgotten—named Robert V. Williams, who'd published one novel in 1952, *The Hard Way*, and was soon to publish his second (and last), *Shake This Town*. "Hot rod stuff," wrote an unusually dour *Kirkus* reviewer about the first, "which is stepped up with sex and a certain surface suspense, for a questionable and certainly not quality market. P. L.'s [public librarians]—watchout." *Shake This Town* would rate a slightly more polite notice from *The New York Times Book Review*, which mentioned its "stereotyped hoods" and tagged it "a fight novel." Williams was ten years older than Roth and loved to regale him about his delinquent youth in New Jersey, with a drunken thief of a father who reminded Roth of Pap Finn. Williams's wife, Harriet ("Hatch"), was a librarian from a more genteel background in Falmouth, Massachusetts; she would take a job at the University of Iowa library in the fall, when the Roths left Rome for Iowa City. "If you're gonna live there, *we're* gonna live there," said Bob Williams, whom Roth described as "a responsible vagabond."

At the American Academy, on the Janiculum, was that year's winner of the Prix de Rome, Harold Brodkey, as well as the head of the Stanford writing program, Wallace Stegner. Roth's loathing for Brodkey (and vice versa) was likely inevitable, though it didn't help that Brodkey had sat behind him, mumbling derisively, during a lecture given by Bellow at an auditorium on the Via Veneto; Roth had turned around and asked Brodkey to be quiet, but the latter's mockery had become, if anything, more gleeful. Afterward Roth wrote Starbuck:

> He's the first young man I have almost punched in the mouth since I was ten years old. But the season in Rome is young and he may yet go back to America toothless. . . . He said to me one night at a restaurant things like: "Well, of course I've read a good deal more than you have . . ." And then when I finally told him I thought he better be still he said, "I will not take instructions from you and certainly not until you're a good deal better than you are."

Stegner, by contrast, was solid and unpretentious; he let Roth know there was a job waiting for him at Stanford if he wanted it, and Roth was more than a little receptive. In the midst of his Roman idyll he was leery of returning to New York, and besides he'd never been to California and thought the change of climate would be good for his wife, whose sinuses had been killing her for more than a year. "See, you marry out of the faith, hoping to find a decent nose," Roth wrote Solotaroff, "and they're really no better than our own."

Maggie's sinuses were, of course, the least of their problems. Even at the best of times she couldn't resist interrupting his work on the thinnest of pretexts ("Could you go out and get half a pound of Parmesan cheese?"), and Roth was ecstatic when a friend at the Academy offered him a studio to use while working on *Letting Go*. Outside that sanctuary, however, his marital rows became more and more ferocious ("even the Italians were in awe"), until Roth confided to Bob Williams that he was approaching the end of his rope. Bob and Harriet were about to leave for a weeklong trip to Sorrento, and invited Maggie along in the hope that things would simmer down a bit. "The next week alone in Rome was bliss," Roth remembered, "though I did nothing but the most ordinary things." "One forgets the pains of single life," he wrote Starbuck on March 5, at the end of that halcyon week, "but one forgets some of the joys too." In the same letter he thought to add: "Hey, who was nominated for the National Book Award? Not me?"

On Friday, March 18, 1960, a day before Roth's twenty-seventh birthday, Starbuck satisfied his curiosity with an exuberant telegram: "DEAR GREAT WHOOP PHIL," it began, and proceeded to quote the citation for that year's fiction winner: "A novella and five short stories which depict with exhilarating freshness various aspects of American Jewish life in transition. This first book by a young writer is notable for its assurance, its rare high spirits, and its clarity of vision." Starbuck ended with another "WHOOP" and asked Roth to cable some acceptance remarks for the ceremony on Wednesday.

Roth was the youngest writer ever to win, in any category, beating a strong field of fiction finalists that included Bellow's *Henderson the Rain King*, Faulkner's *The Mansion*, and John Updike's first novel, *The Poorhouse Fair* (but not Allen Drury's best-selling *Advise and Consent*, which would win that year's Pulitzer). "Brendan Gill made my career," Roth liked to say of the fiction judge who, in Roth's certain opinion, had pushed hardest for *Goodbye, Columbus*.* Among the various women Roth had picked

---

* The other fiction judges that year were Kay Boyle, Alexander Laing, William Peden (who'd reviewed Roth's collection for the *Times Book Review*), and Charles J. Rolo.

up in Europe during the summer of 1958, one, in Italy, had mentioned she was a former girlfriend of Gill; she urged Roth to get in touch with the *New Yorker* writer when he went back to the States, and sure enough the two hit it off over drinks at the Algonquin and a subsequent dinner on East Tenth. "It was the imp of the perverse that he chose this book for the NBA," said Roth. "And that was when it began for me."

His jubilation was short-lived. After cabling his parents the happy news ("HAVE WEAK BOWEL AS RESULT"), a second telegram from Starbuck directed him to buy a round-trip ticket (economy rate) for a Tuesday arrival in New York—thus his publisher had decided its handsome young star should collect his award in person, even if it meant flying him all the way over from Italy. "Between [telegram] #2 and #3," Roth recalled, "all hell broke loose in my house." "*How can you* dare *go without me?*" Maggie erupted. "*You'll fuck all those girls!*" Roth tried to remonstrate: it was only an overnight trip, practically, and they simply couldn't afford to go out of pocket on a second ticket. Et cetera. Nothing availed. Finally he sent a civil, despondent telegram to Starbuck: he couldn't come after all; he'd composed a brief statement for the ceremony and hoped Starbuck would be the one to read it and accept the award for him. Starbuck, amazed, managed to get Roth on the telephone at two o'clock Monday afternoon: "*Testy*," he noted of Roth's tone. "Holding out for Maggie too." In fact, Roth was enduringly furious that Houghton wouldn't do its part to assuage his wife's rage ("Gentlemen Wasps," he later glossed), and meanwhile Starbuck was trying desperately to make things right: "Various calls to Candida Donadio," he jotted for the record. "4:10 PM Monday Called Asher at Meridian, who called back at 5:05"—whereupon the haggard man sent a triumphant telegram (#3) to Roth, noting that Meridian had agreed to cover Maggie's ticket.

Meridian Books was bringing out a quality paperback of *Goodbye, Columbus* ($1.45) with a classic cover design by Paul Rand: a red lipstick kiss with the title in white cursive below, amid blue stars. Aaron Asher—who would go on to edit Saul Bellow, Milan Kundera, and many others, including Roth at two different publishers—had joined a fellow University of Chicago graduate, Arthur Cohen, at Meridian when he first came to New York in the midfifties. As very few people would know until his death in 2008, Asher had lived his first eight years in Klaipèda, Lithuania, until a maternal uncle in Chicago, a doctor, persuaded the family to emigrate in 1937. Asher's wife, Linda, knew nothing of this until she saw his birth certificate prior to their marriage; Asher quipped that he'd wanted her to love him for more than just his exotic background. Another person he told was his roommate at the University of Chicago, the future film director Mike Nichols, who'd also fled Hitler as a child. The trauma of Asher's early years was evident in certain lifelong aversions: he was incensed by entertainments such as *The Producers* that found humor in Nazis, and considered *Schindler's List* a ghastly piece of kitsch because it celebrated a "good German" as an emblematic hero of the Holocaust. As for his acquaintance with Roth, it had preceded the paperback deal for *Goodbye, Columbus* by a year or so, when Asher's sister sublet a Chicago apartment from "a guy named Philip Roth," as she wrote her brother in New York. "He says he's a writer." Shortly after Roth's return from Europe that summer, the Ashers had come to dinner at his basement apartment on East Tenth, where they also met Maggie. "What the hell's he doing with *her?*" they both said, in effect, on departing that night.

On Tuesday, the day before the ceremony, the Roths flew to New York aboard "one of those transatlantic murder birds," as Roth put it; he'd become jittery about flying since his marriage to Maggie. ("National Book Award!" she hooted, when they finally emerged from a bad spell of turbulence. "Big deal!") The other two winners that year were Robert Lowell (poetry) for *Life Studies*, and Richard Ellmann (nonfiction) for his biography of James Joyce, and the three were enjoined to give a press conference before the ceremony at the Astor Hotel; "they treated their questioners like well-intentioned, ignorant children," noted a "Talk of the Town" item in *The New Yorker*, "and gave satisfaction to all." Roth ("who had flown in from Rome a few hours before and looked as if he'd like a nice long nap") was asked whether he was a product of the short story "renaissance" and replied with bemused courtesy that, as a young writer, he'd "naturally started with short stories, and now, at twenty-seven, he was working on a novel." And no, he knew nothing about Ezra Pound's recent return to Italy. Then a lot of photos were taken, including a few where the three men are holding a copy of *Goodbye, Columbus* between them, and another where Maggie is holding the book, smiling tensely, and Roth has a look of blank-faced exasperation.

"I'm bustin' my buttons!" Herman said in the Astor ballroom, where he and Bess, Sandy and Trudy, and Aunt Milly were among an audience of more than a thousand ("the largest turnout the National Book Awards ever has known"), including a number of "non-prize-winning" authors who were introduced to the book-industry crowd by a "large female semi-literate," according to Leslie Fiedler: "Even Ayn Rand's mad glare could scare up no more than a ripple of recognition, while poor Allen Drury, doomed to win nothing better than a Pulitzer Prize, could not even muster a respectable hand to console him." In those days the winners, announced in advance, were asked to prepare acceptance speeches, and at first Roth was stumped; then it occurred to him that he wanted to explain "why [he] didn't want to say anything," and this he did at length. As he would later recall the occasion—his first public utterance as a writer—"I burst onto the stage and I told them, 'I am honored and delighted, and I accept your award with the highest of spirits.'" On the plane from Italy, he continued, he'd been reading about a recent *Esquire* magazine symposium at the Iowa Writers' Workshop, where Ralph Ellison, Mark Harris, Dwight Macdonald, and Norman Mailer had been canvassed about "The Condition and Function of the Writer in Contemporary American Society." Roth observed:

> The concern is with *writers* instead of *writing*; the concern is with poses and postures, with etiquette, as if the manners of the writer ultimately determined the manner of the writing. . . . "Should the writer?" "Can the writers?" "Is the function of the writer in contemporary . . . ?" Baloney! What questions! What a lightweight novelistic approach to human character! Imagine—should Jane Austen? Can Thomas Hardy? Is it the function of Sir Walter Scott . . . ?

What would prove a rather characteristic diatribe "drew sustained applause from the audience," so the *Newark Evening News* reported.

That night he and Maggie were invited to a party at the publicist Ben Sonnenberg's Gramercy Park mansion, where Roth was approached by an attractive young woman, Jean Stein, who conversationally inquired, "Who's your editor?" "George Starbuck," he replied, whereupon Maggie yanked him aside and announced it was time to leave. But they'd only just arrived, said Roth, and there were a hundred or so people he wanted to meet. "Why did you tell that silly bitch that George Starbuck is your editor?" she snapped. "*I'm* your editor!" This was hardly the first time Maggie had made the claim, and it wasn't entirely baseless. "She's the only person alive for whom I change whole sentences in stories," Roth had commended her in a letter to Bob Silvers (the point of which was to introduce her to an important "publishing" contact in New York and, he hoped, get her out of his life), and of course she did have a fair amount of experience as a reader and editor (textbooks mostly) at Harper & Brothers. As it happened, though, that wasn't the main issue in the present case. "*You wanted to fuck her!*" she burst out, once they were back at the hotel. "*If I hadn't come with you to New York, you would have fucked everybody!*" Roth—furious that she'd managed to ruin even this, the greatest triumph of his young life—declared that he wanted to leave her. "*Try it,*" she said, "and you'll end up penniless just like Marty Greenberg" ("he said the thought of what Mrs. Greenberg is doing frightens him," she'd noted in her journal); now that he'd won his big award he thought he could "run off with any stupid girl who fawned over [him] at a party." Well, he *couldn't.* He was married.

By the time Roth was slated to appear on "The Mike Wallace Interview," he was notably poor company—"pugnacious," as he described his mood at the time; and yet (given Wallace's own reputation for pugnacity) he was determined to be "firm and thoughtful" and hoped both he and Wallace would emerge from the show with a measure of self-respect. It was not to be, though Roth could hardly have foreseen anything amiss given, say, Wallace's assistant, a nice young man who had come to his hotel room the day before and diffidently asked a lot of questions that Roth considered seemly and decent for the most part. "Maybe we can get his back up," the young man wrote in his memo to Wallace. Among his suggested interview questions (typed in caps) was this representative specimen, aimed at Roth's contention that he wasn't an "essentially Jewish writer": "CRITICS HAVE SAID THAT YOUR HUMOR IS 'TYPICALLY JEWISH HUMOR', THAT YOUR RANGE IS 'NARROW.' COULD IT BE THAT THE THINGS WHICH GET YOU ANGRY ARE LIMITED, AND THAT YOUR SOCIAL CRITICISMS ARE LIMITED, SIMPLY BECAUSE YOU'RE TOO INVOLVED WITH THE THEME OF THE JEWS?" On the air, Wallace was sensitive enough to elide personal matters ("he doesn't want to talk about fact that he married a shicksa" [sic]), and rather tried to be as offensive as possible on the subject of Roth's work. "Reading your book," he said, "I got the impression you don't care for the Jews." Roth, his back up instantly, replied that he "was under no obligation to care for them or not care for them," and proceeded to rattle off the names of Jewish characters in his book that he happened to like. Wallace stopped him: none of their viewers would know the actual names, so maybe they should just move on. . . . "Hey, Mike," said Roth, during a break, "you want to go after me or you want to talk to me?" The former, apparently; when it was over, though, Wallace gave Roth an amiable smile and complimented him on "being [his] own man."

That morning Roth had met "a very sweet woman" from the *New York Post* at the Astor Bar. She mentioned a piece by Charles Angoff that had been widely printed in the Jewish press, suggesting that Roth's work was "an exhibition of Jewish self-hate." Roth gave the woman what he thought was a nuanced and politic response: Angoff, he said, was from an older generation of Jewish writers, and Roth thought the man's time might be better spent writing "a piece of fiction about snot-noses like [Roth], and how they relate to his generation," instead of "bilious articles" for Jewish community newspapers. A few weeks later, back in Italy, Roth received the woman's piece ("The NBA Winner Talks Back") from his clipping service: "My advice to [Angoff] is to write a book about why he hates me," he was quoted as saying. "It might give insights into me and him, too." As Roth reflected at the time, "I decided then and there to give up a public career."

■ ■ ■ ■

As the Roman weather turned hot ("when you pass the whores on the street you can smell their underarms," he wrote Baker), he and Maggie planned to leave toward the end of June, driving north through France and spending the summer in London. Roth jauntily informed friends that they'd stayed at the Eden Roc in Cap d'Antibes "like Dick and Nicole Diver," perhaps remembering what had happened on a mountain road just outside Siena, where Maggie had suddenly announced, *"I'm going to kill both of us!"* and—à la the schizophrenic Nicole in *Tender Is the Night*—tried to steer the little Renault over a precipice. Roth managed to wrest the wheel away in time, but he had to stop the car and collect himself before warily resuming their long northward journey. "We drove up through the Rhône Valley in France," he remembered. "It was spectacularly beautiful and I felt trapped with a woman who was mad."

On arriving in the British Isles they were joined by the Styrons, with whom they hired a cab and toured Wales and Ireland. By then *Set This House on Fire* had been published to scathing reviews, though at least one had been quite positive, and this Styron kept in an inside jacket pocket and would furtively peruse (as Roth noticed in the rearview mirror) from time to time. While their wives went shopping in Dublin, the men embarked on a "Joycean trek" around the city that was supposed to wind up at the Guinness brewery, where they'd been promised a fascinating guided tour. On the way Roth remarked that the Irish were a terribly repressed people; if you looked directly at the women, he said, they automatically hid their bosoms ("he was right," Styron noted). The brewery was closed, Trinity Library was covered in "hideous scaffolding," the River Liffey was "full of mud and garbage," and finally the two writers escaped a dreary drizzle by ducking into a shooting gallery and whiling away the afternoon playing pinball and mugging in photo booths. Later Styron would remember Roth's "ability to convert these ghastly dead ends and moments of existential insult into an episode of both genuine gravity and high hilarity. It was one of the truly memorable days of my life, and among the most richly enjoyed."

In London, the Roths were again fortunate in their lodgings, subletting a top-floor flat at 89 Redington Road, in Hampstead, from the rector of St. Mary-le-Bow. Their dining room afforded a splendid view of the city, and Roth was able to immure himself in a book-lined study. On nearby Flask Walk was the poet and critic Al Alvarez, then poetry editor for *The Observer*, a champion of contemporary American poets such as Plath, Berryman, and Lowell. "He's in the same shit I am," Alvarez observed of Roth, when he and his wife, Ursula, went to dinner that first time on Redington Road. As he later wrote, "We became friends from the start because both of us, back then, were edgy young men with failing marriages and a nose for trouble, who believed, as literary folk did back in the high-minded '50s, that literature was the most honorable of all callings and were baffled when life didn't work out as books had led us to expect." The seeds of friendship would flower more fully in 1977—long after their "nightmare wives" (Alvarez) had vanished—when Roth began spending half-years in London only to find his domestic life as problematic as ever.

Meanwhile things were relatively tranquil in Hampstead until mid-

July, when Maggie got word from Daddy Herb that a throat culture had revealed her mother's lungs "were full of cancer," and that she had "two weeks possibly three" to live. On July 17, Roth wrote Baker that Maggie had phoned South Haven "and decided finally not to go back on the advice of her grandfather, who says her mother recognizes no one, etc." However, as Roth later remembered the episode, Daddy Herb had actually "pleaded with her to come back and be with her mother during the few weeks she was expected to live." Roth offered to pay her way, but he couldn't afford to go himself; they were on a strict budget and had already booked passage back to the States for September 1. "I'm not leaving you alone," said Maggie. "You'll fuck everybody in London!" "I was very sad to recieve [sic] your letter this morning," she wrote Daddy Herb and Aunt Hervey on August 2. "Although I didn't really believe the new medicine would do miricles [sic], I had selfishly perhaps, hoped it would keep Mother alive until I got there." Amid furious bouts of weeping, she berated Roth for keeping her away from her mother's side as she lay dying.

Truth be known, Roth hadn't wanted to return to the States at all, much less to take another teaching job. "I want *no* part of the academic community, meetings, chickenshit, nonsense, politicking, etc.," he wrote the Maurers from Rome on April 11. "Had enough at Chicago in two years to last me and mine for ever." In a better world, he would have stayed in Rome indefinitely and had a string of Italian girlfriends; he was confident he'd get at least a $15,000 advance for *Letting Go*, and since he thought he could easily live in Rome for a thousand a year. . . . But reality was something else, and by April 18—a mere week after his exultant manifesto to the Maurers—Maggie wrote to inform Paul Brooks, at Houghton, that her husband would be taking a job at either Stanford or Iowa in the fall. That spring Maggie had learned that her first husband, Burt Miller, and his second wife were divorcing after only a year of marriage, and Maggie insisted that she and Roth had to get back to the States as soon as possible to save her "babies" from the sole guardianship of that "wicked simpleton."

If Roth couldn't have Rome, he'd at least hoped for the sunny climes of Palo Alto, but no: Iowa City was a few hours away from Maggie's children in the Chicago area, so Iowa City it was. Explaining their choice to friends, Roth mentioned the advantage of proximity ("I think that'll be good for everyone"), and also claimed the money was better at Iowa. In fact, the director of the Iowa Writers' Workshop, Paul Engle—"a *gonif*" (thief), as Roth would forever describe him—had offered him a mere $5,500 a year, "perhaps the sorriest salary in the history" of the Workshop, as Roth would learn soon enough; he even had to cover moving expenses and reimburse Engle for $125 the man had put down on a rental house for his new faculty member. To be sure, as the youngest-ever winner of the National Book Award, Roth was a hot property—but, after all, he'd approached Engle, not vice versa, and somewhat at the last moment too, so Engle figured he was doing Roth a favor.

H OUGHTON MIFFLIN HAD AN OPTION ON ROTH'S NEXT two books, but on June 22, 1960, Starbuck got a call from Candida Donadio, whose sad duty it was to explain her client's "prolonged and intense dissatisfaction" with Houghton's handling of *Goodbye, Columbus*. As Starbuck reported to Brooks, Roth's discontents included Houghton's "tight-fistedness" (the plane ticket, etc.), a shoddy production job on the book itself ("minute printing"), and their "gross mishandling of his brother's design for the jacket." In the last case: Roth had originally requested the designer Milton Glaser, whose jacket for Malamud's *The Magic Barrel* he'd admired (and who would go on to design a lion's share of Roth's later books), but Glaser "screwed it up"; Sandy was happy to do the work for free, and "came up with a pretty good, gay jacket," as Philip thought—a naked woman standing at a window, her back to the viewer, with a prominent bowl of fruit in the foreground. Sandy's version was brightly colored, with a lot of yellow sunlight that Houghton, for whatever reason, changed to gray; the mild-mannered Sandy had been angry enough to phone the publisher and denounce them as "a bunch of pricks." "Received the book," Roth wrote Starbuck on March 29, 1959; "am happy, really. Except about that m-f cover."

Roth had exempted Starbuck from his general indictment of Houghton, and indeed would later claim his main reason for changing publishers was Starbuck's departure (though Starbuck didn't actually leave until the following year, and had no immediate plans to leave at the time). Meanwhile Roth had complained to friends that "the people are sweet, but it's like being published by Ginn and Company, who aren't even in business anymore; no, Funk and Wagnalls"—until Styron arranged a lunch, in Rome, between Roth and Donald Klopfer of Random House. "I think that the whole Philip Roth business is deplorable," noted the gentlemanly Brooks, when he caught wind that Klopfer had offered Roth a minimum $20,000 advance on his novel and a guaranteed advertising budget of $5,000, and had promised moreover to top any offer Houghton was willing to make, option or no. Roth hoped such daunting largesse would cause Houghton to back down and release him outright, but Starbuck ("in fairness to Phil, since we felt we could do a superior job of promoting his next book") gently insisted that they be allowed at least to consider a partial manuscript of *Debts and Sorrows* (as it was still called).

"FIVE OF US INCLUDING MYSELF HAVE NOW READ FIRST THREE HUN-DRED PAGES OF DEBTS AND SORROWS WITH ENORMOUS ENTHUSIASM AND INCREASED RESPECT," Brooks cabled Roth on July 22. "WE ALL FEEL THAT THIS WILL BE ONE OF THE MOST IMPORTANT BOOKS WE HAVE BEEN PRIVILEGED TO PUBLISH AND WE INTEND TO BACK IT TO THE LIMIT." Houghton matched Random's $20,000 and guaranteed an even higher advertising budget—but the implications of the plane ticket still rankled. By early fall, Donadio thought it a "propitious time" for a formal release, and a couple of weeks later Roth signed a contract with Random House for a $21,000 advance, payable in three installments—one of only two times he'd ever accept money before a book's completion.

■ ■ ■ ■

BY THEN the Roths had moved into a pleasant white clapboard house on verdant North Linn Street, with a faint view of the Iowa River from an upstairs window. Roth was new to small-town Midwestern life, and was taken aback by the aggressive friendliness of perfect strangers; as he wrote in "a stupid, complaining piece" about Iowa City that would appear in a 1962 *Esquire* ("Iowa: A Very Far Country Indeed"), he found himself beguiled into conversation almost every time he ventured out to buy milk or razor blades. By way of settling in, he'd subscribed for a time to the state's largest daily, *The Des Moines Register*, but amid the presidential campaign of 1960 he couldn't stomach the paper's politics. The better to convey the local ethos to Styron, he sent a postcard with an oafish joke printed on the front ("WORK IS THE CURSE OF THE DRINKING CLASS"); on the back he'd written:

Dear Styrone-

We have read youre' book BURN THIS PLACE DOWN and such filth
and smut hasn't enterd our lives in a long time, th. GOD. We can only feel
sorry for you, and warn you to keep clear of Iowa if you KNOW whats gd.
for you.

Signed CLAUDE & IDA RUNKLE

Another thing Roth would complain about in his *Esquire* piece was the
byzantine ordeal of buying liquor at the only state-licensed store in a
town of 33,000, which entailed a certain amount of paperwork and waiting. The only tipple available over the counter was beer (3.2), which he
and Maggie usually drank at Kenney's Bar, since it was right around the
corner from the one theater where they occasionally saw a movie. That
was about it for nightlife.

In fact Roth enjoyed himself; because there was so little to do in that
"rosy-cheeked town," the Workshop writers went out of their way to
entertain themselves. As he wrote Solotaroff in November, "I had forgotten, truly, that there were pleasures to be had in social contacts—after
all the ambitiousness of NY socializing, and Rome—but I am discovering it again, and it is a great source of joy." Roth relished the male
camaraderie of the place: he and Bob Williams were all but inseparable,
especially on Saturdays, when (after sleeping in from Friday night poker
parties) they made a point of attending home football games, while Saturdays in spring were given over to softball games between the poetry
and prose writers. Mark Strand was then a graduate student whose first
wife, Antonia, was in Roth's fiction class, and he often pitched for the
poets' team; forty years later—in a tribute he wrote for the presentation
of Roth's Gold Medal from the Academy of Arts and Letters—Strand
praised his old foe's hitting prowess almost as lavishly as he praised
American Pastoral.

Roth's back had stopped hurting him (for the time being) and he was
also able to play tennis with a Korean graduate student roughly his age,
Richard Kim, who'd been born Kim Eun Kook in North Korea and
served as a general's adjutant in the South Korean army during the war.

Kim had learned colloquial English from watching American movies in the army, and during his years in Iowa he worked on his novel about the Korean War, *The Martyred*—a copy of which his widow, Penelope, noticed near Roth's elbow in a 2013 PBS documentary about Roth. She promptly wrote him a letter, pointing out that her late husband's novel had recently been reissued as a Penguin Classic and thanking Roth for his part in its success ("I consider you its godfather"). Roth had read the book in drafts, and when it was finished, in 1963, he helped Kim find a publisher, George Braziller, and pressed the book on friends such as Styron (noting "the sheer fucking heroism that must have gone into the writing"). The book was nominated for the National Book Award and translated into fourteen languages.

Roth's best friend on the faculty was George P. Elliott, whose wife, Mary Emma, was editor of *The Hudson Review*. George was a big man, fond of food and drink, and both husband and wife were fun-loving but high-minded in conversation. George was about to publish his story collection, *Among the Dangs*, which included one of his first published stories, from 1949, "The NRACP"—an acronym for National Relocation Authority: Colored Persons, which, it gradually transpires, is actually a program of genocide against black Americans, who are surreptitiously turned into canned dog food. In later years, as the civil rights movement became increasingly beset by violence, such caustic satire would seem more prescient, but at the time it managed to offend readers of almost every political stripe, or anyway such readers as Elliott was ever able to attract. His relatively innocuous novels included *Parktilden Village* and *David Knudsen*, about which Roth's opinion may be inferred from a 1967 letter recommending Elliott for a Rockefeller grant: "The impact he makes on the American consciousness, as both a critic and a novelist"—a poet too—"will largely be determined by the work he is to do, and not the work he has done." Both George and Mary Emma provided vital feedback throughout Roth's progress on *Letting Go* (a title they suggested), and at one point Roth proposed George as an alternate executor of his literary estate. The Roths were bereft when the Elliotts departed Iowa in 1961 ("we're even a little leery of next year without them"), and Philip kept occasionally in touch once they landed at Syracuse University in 1963. Alas, by the time George dropped dead of a heart attack in 1980, he was forgotten by the reading public, and Roth eventually lost track of Mary Emma as well.

■ ■ ■ ■

GIVEN HIS NEGLIGIBLE SALARY, Roth was relieved that his teaching load, at least, was light. That first semester he taught a single two-hour workshop on Mondays and held individual conferences on Tuesdays, and the rest of his time was mostly his own. Six students would submit stories each week, and Roth would choose the two best (or most conducive to discussion) and mimeograph them for his other students in advance of the Monday session. Roth was dubious about the efficacy of "teaching" (a word he liked to entomb in quotes) writing as a craft, but he did find value in "educating the students in the workings of the literary imagination"—that is, in asking such questions as "Why this story in the first place? What is the necessity for your telling it and my reading it? Why is the story 'important'?"

As Paul Engle was apt to point out, the brightest people at the University of Iowa were the writers ("The most brilliant scholars go to Harvard . . . but where can the writers go except here and Stanford?"), but Roth saw little evidence of that in his own students' "atrocious" work. "Not only do you have to read the crap," he complained, "but then you have to think about it and discuss it, tenderly, with them." Among his own workshop group that first year, the only writer he considered promising was Mary Elsie Robertson, whose first collection, *Jordan's Stormy Banks*, had been accepted by Atheneum for publication in the spring. "I don't think we were a very illustrious lot," Robertson agreed many years later, remembering Roth's teaching manner as "affable" but to the point. By most accounts Roth did his best to mask his exasperation with middling work, but his reluctance to mince words resulted in hurt feelings from time to time. "Part of our function," he told an interviewer, "is to discourage those without enough talent. A lot of people come for self-expression or therapy. We try to put a stop to that."

Roth's later pronouncements on MFA programs were even more categorical: "I think it's a great waste of time," he said in 2012. "Get them the fuck out of there. They should shut all those places down." Teaching students how to *read*—versus write—was another matter. During his second semester at Iowa, Roth taught a Contemporary Fiction course, and this he enjoyed and would always enjoy. Then and later, Roth liked to teach books in tandem, the better to demonstrate the different ways authors approach similar themes in terms of craft and moral point of view: Bowen's *Death of the Heart* and Golding's *Lord of the Flies*; Bellow's *The Victim* and Malamud's *The Assistant*. At Iowa, too, he made things easier for himself by assigning each student to teach at least one novel on the syllabus (an idea he might have retained from his bravura lecture on *Mario and the Magician* for Willard Smith's class at Bucknell), which forced them to study the book intensively as well as work on their pedagogy.

But mostly it helped him preserve his sanity, which was parlously contingent on his productivity as a writer. "I know that I am a holy terror to live with if I haven't been writing steadily," he admitted, and so for the past year he'd been giving most of his waking hours, five or six days a week, to gouging out a big, impressive novel worthy of the youngest-ever winner of the National Book Award. After he'd written the first, relatively facile three hundred pages or so, the manuscript had been "slow going," since Roth had gone over and over his early pages tinkering with point of view and tone ("it's getting funny, thank god") until it was essentially a different novel, whatever the sameness of plot. Indeed, with few exceptions (the title novella of *Goodbye, Columbus* was one), Roth would always find novel writing a ghastly protracted slog, for which his mantra would always be, in effect, *I will not be defeated by this thing.* In the case of the cumbersome *Letting Go*, he was further goaded by a wistful determination to get his book out "under the wire"—that is, before his thirtieth birthday.

For this reason, mainly, he was having second thoughts about accepting Rust Hills's invitation to appear at that year's *Esquire* symposium in San Francisco—an event he'd publicly dismissed (in his NBA acceptance speech) as a silly and cynical waste of time, hence his being invited in the first place. Roth refused to commit himself until he knew the subject of that year's symposium, and Hills wrote back asking him what he'd *like* it to be. Nothing, Roth specified, about the role, function, or condition of the *writer*, but rather about the actual *writing*. Hills happily obliged: "Writing in America Today" it was. In the end Roth agreed to go because, after all, it was an expenses-paid chance to see the West

Coast—as he'd wished before being frog-marched to the Midwest—and even take a side trip to visit the Bakers in Oregon.

Also, of course, he was flattered to be asked. The featured writers at the previous two symposia had been an illustrious bunch: Bellow, Wright Morris, Leslie Fiedler, and Dorothy Parker at the first, held at Columbia, and Ralph Ellison et al. in Iowa City. As it happened Roth had been in the audience at Columbia and was abidingly charmed by Bellow's response to all the pontification "about isolation, alienation of the writer, etc.": "Let the other fellow be alienated," Bellow chuckled, when asked for his thoughts.* A certain amount of strife among the panelists was desirable, and, as *The New York Times* would report, it was hoped that young Roth would serve as a disputatious foil for his fellow panelists James Baldwin and John Cheever—but, as Roth noted, "If anything we had the unity of one of those combat details sent out on a night mission in movies about the Korean War—a Negro, a Protestant, and a Jew." Roth had met Baldwin a few years before in New York and the two men got along warmly, whereas Cheever had been so smitten with *Goodbye, Columbus* that he was moved to write a rare note to its publisher: "This is not for publication because I don't believe in setting a good book afloat on a spate of quotations but I would like to thank you for the immense pleasure I took in the Roth stories. It was my wife who said that she is very grateful to Mr. Roth for having proved to her that somebody lives in Newark."†

The program began October 20 at Berkeley, where Cheever was scheduled to speak followed by a panel discussion and questions; Roth would speak the next night at Stanford, and Baldwin the third night at San Francisco State. Roth was pleasantly startled to find that all three

---

* A line Roth saved up for Felix Abravanel in *The Ghost Writer*: "Alienation? Oh," he said, with that light laugh, "let the other guy be alienated."

† Bellow wasn't the only colleague with a bon mot in *The Ghost Writer*. After reading *The Professor of Desire*, in 1977, Cheever wrote the author as follows: "[In 1959] I first read a paragraph or two of yours and came into the house shouting to Mary [his wife] that Roth—whoever he was—had the most compelling voice I had encountered in years. I don't mean style; I mean voice—something that begins at around the back of the knees and reaches well above the head." Roth was so impressed with the compliment that he used it almost verbatim in his subsequent novel, attributing it to E. I. Lonoff.

writers had much the same thing to say—"that is, the unmanageability of much of the American social scene as material for fiction." In Roth's judgment, the "most dimwitted" questions were asked that first night at Berkeley, where Cheever was accused of "anti-Americanism" and "willful obscurity"; also someone wanted to know if writers made a decent living, and "some poor woman," reported Roth, "got up and in a quivering voice asked us some question about 'the bard of Stratford,' which I understood to be an unflattering comparison between that gentleman's talents and the combined talents of the three of us on the stage." At Stanford, the first question for Roth came from a woman seated near the front, who said she'd wanted to get a good look at him and then asked why he was so anti-Semitic (a subject Roth hadn't raised in his remarks), while another man seemed almost angry: "If you don't like it here, Mr. Roth, where else would you like to live, what other century, what other country?" Roth decided to pass on the question, and the man sat down with a vindicated look.

What Roth had said to provoke such umbrage would soon be published as "Writing American Fiction," to which he would facetiously refer in future years as the "Roth Doctrine." Its composition had been a desperate business: leaving Libby Herz of *Letting Go* sitting in an analyst's office for two weeks, Roth had become increasingly "edgy and mean and unstable" while he tried to think of something, anything, worth saying to a large and presumably literary audience at Stanford. Finally it occurred to him (apropos of the symposium's theme) that none of the serious American novels Roth had read in the past two or three years had been about the big public scene, a matter that apparently had been consigned to lesser writers such as Drury, Herman Wouk, Sloan Wilson, and "Broadway's *amor-vincit-omnia* boys"; perhaps the big public scene was simply too outlandish for first-rank writers to tackle with any confidence. By way of illustration, Roth opened with a lovingly prolix account of a notorious unsolved murder case in Chicago a few years back, when two sisters named Grimes had gone to an Elvis movie, *Love Me Tender*, and never returned; when at last a suspect was arrested, Benny Bedwell, "some good-natured soul" arranged for Benny's mother to meet the murdered sisters' mother: "Their picture is taken together," Roth wrote, "two overweight, overworked American ladies, quite befuddled but sitting up straight for the photographers."* How, Roth wondered, did an American writer at midcentury "make *credible* much of American reality. It stupefies, it sickens, it infuriates, and finally it is even a kind of embarrassment to one's own meager imagination. . . . Who, for example, could have invented Charles Van Doren? Roy Cohn and David Schine? . . . Eisenhower?" Roth went on to consider the work of various estimable fiction writers, and found all of them more or less concerned with private matters ("The only advice we seem to get from Salinger is to be charming on the way to the loony bin")—which, to Roth's mortification, would be construed by some readers to mean that he *deplored* this tendency in his peers' work.

Bernard Malamud would reach that conclusion a couple of days later when he heard Roth's speech in Monmouth, Oregon, where Bob Baker had arranged an honorarium for his friend that would cover expenses for a long-awaited visit. Since 1957 Baker had been an English professor at the Oregon College of Education (later Western Oregon University), while back in 1949 Malamud had moved from New York to Corvallis (about twenty miles to the south), where he taught at Oregon State College (later Oregon State University). One of Roth's pleasures in winning the National Book Award was that he'd succeeded Malamud, the 1959 winner for *The Magic Barrel*, to which the president of Baker's college referred as *The Pork Barrel* when he introduced Malamud (standing) to the audience prior to Roth's speech. A subsequent account in the *Times* would report that Roth, while at Stanford, had accused Malamud of "resorting to metaphors, rather than rendering society accurately," an invidious formulation of his actual remarks (or so Roth thought), as follows:

The Jews of *The Magic Barrel* and the Jews of *The Assistant* are not the Jews of New York City or Chicago. They are Malamud's invention, a metaphor of sorts to stand for certain possibilities and promises and I am further inclined to believe this when I read the statement attributed to Malamud which goes, "All men are Jews." . . . [H]is people live in a timeless depres-

---

* According to his 1957 Yaddo application (declined), one of Roth's writing projects at the time had been a play about the Grimes sisters—not the murder per se, said Roth, so much as the lurid cultural phenomena attached to it.

sion and a placeless Lower East Side; their society is not affluent, their predicament is not cultural.

Fair enough, but Malamud's demeanor *chez* Baker afterward was on the dour side, and indeed Roth would learn that his elder had been a little affronted. ("If you mention a writer's name without saying he's the greatest writer in the world," Roth remarked, "you put him down.") Mind, it was hard to tell; at the best of times Malamud was not known for high spirits, and many remarked on his startling humorlessness, among them Roth, who would hear the man tell exactly two jokes ("Jewish dialect jokes, expertly recounted") during the twenty-five years of their acquaintance.* That night in Oregon, Malamud's stolid lack of charisma reminded Roth of certain of Herman's colleagues at Metropolitan Life. Toward the end of the evening, perhaps in hope of cheering their guest up, Baker and Roth eagerly inquired how he managed to produce world-class fiction given his heavy teaching and domestic responsibilities. As Baker recalled, "Patiently, exactly, he laid out for us the details of his MWF teaching, his TThSat writing and his Sunday familying—no swerving, no cheating on any element. Heading out, jaw set, he delivered his curtain line with quiet fervor: 'I am a very disciplined man.' And then he jerked open the door of—and stepped into—the closet." Nobody laughed, least of all Malamud.

■   ■   ■   ■

RECENTLY SOLOTAROFF HAD dropped his dissertation on *The Bostonians* and taken a job as editor at *Commentary*, largely thanks to a long and well-received piece he'd written for the *Times Literary Supplement* on the Jewish role in American letters (an assignment for which Roth had recommended him, having declined to write it himself); as such he offered to publish Roth's "Writing American Fiction" in their March 1961 issue, and Roth was eager for him to do so. Though Roth had been rather pleased with himself, at first, for having raised the tone of *Esquire*'s symposium by focusing on novels versus novelists ("I didn't

---

* In his life as in his fiction, Malamud's humor (such as it was) tended to fly beneath even the most perceptive radar: "Bellow gets Nobel Prize," he noted in his diary for October 21, 1976, "I win $24.25 in poker."

talk about Bellow, but about Henderson; not about Styron but Set This House on Fire, etc."), he was infuriated by Robert Gutwillig's account in the *Times Book Review* ("Dim Views Through Fog") that seemed to suggest Roth had attacked the writers per se, instead of noticing certain tendencies in their work. "I was not, in R. G.'s phrase, 'taking them to task,'" he wrote in his letter to the *Times*, "but trying to uncover the relationship between the self and the culture in two books, namely, *Henderson the Rain King* and *Set This House on Fire*." As for the likes of Herman Wouk, Jerome Weidman, et al., he'd never said (pace Gutwillig) that they wrote "middle-class" novels: "I consider myself a member of that class. I said they wrote bad novels." Gutwillig replied, with gentle disdain, that he'd been quoting not only from Roth's prepared speech "but also from his frequent extemporaneous remarks and from his extended answers to questions from the audience"; it was possible he'd "oversimplified" or given "improper emphasis," as Roth would have it, but he seriously doubted it.

When Roth's piece about the stupefying, sickening, infuriating nature of contemporary American reality ran in *Commentary*, its readers responded in much the same way as his more indignant interrogators at Stanford. "When we get a few more [letters]," Solotaroff wrote him, "so that we can take advantage of freight rates, I'll send the whole lot to you for reply. I don't think that any literary article in *Commentary* has provoked such controversy since Dwight MacDonald's piece on Cousins [sic]."* Roth responded to the abuse with mischievous but determined clarity. "I love joy, especially sheer joy," he assured Constance H. Poster, who'd wondered why Roth partook so little of the "sheer joy of mere existence expressed by most poets." Roth continued: "My point as regards *Henderson*, however, is that the joy Bellow finds there he does not find in the world of Asa Leventhal or Tommy Wilhelm† or even Augie March, but in an Africa that makes no claim whatsoever to being *real*. That's all." Eugene Ziller took exception to Roth's "complaint" against Malamud, whereas Roth insisted there was nothing of complaint in his point that

---

* He means James Gould Cozzens, whose novel *By Love Possessed* (1957) Macdonald had savaged in "By Cozzens Possessed," which arguably cost the novelist a Pulitzer and left his reputation in tatters.

† The protagonists of Bellow's *The Victim* and *Seize the Day*, respectively.

"many contemporary writers"—himself included—seem to share a "discomfort" toward realism. "Where has [Roth] been all these millennia?" wondered Joseph Mindel of Larchmont, New York. "Hasn't he heard about Sodom and Gomorrah, or listened to Isaiah and Jeremiah? Where was he during the dreadful days in the house of Agamemnon?" To Mindel's parting shot that he suffered from "historical illiteracy," Roth had this to say: "Okay—where were *you* during the dreadful days in the house of Agamemnon? Let's stand up and be counted."

The controversy over a speech Roth had dashed off in a frenzy, after two weeks of pencil chewing, never quite went away. Two basic misreadings would continue to dog him: (a) that he'd been chiding his colleagues ("taking them to task") for failing to write realistic novels about big sociopolitical issues; and, conversely, (b) that he and they should "avert their eyes" (as Tom Wolfe would put it) from the whole stupefying, sickening scene. As for Roth's dismay over that scene as it stood in 1960 (never mind during the dreadful days in the house of Agamemnon), well, that would come to seem, by his own reckoning, naive. "Little did we know that some twenty years later the philistine ignorance on which we would have liked to turn our backs would infect the country like Camus's plague," he said in 1984; the wag who imagined a President Reagan, in 1960, would have been reviled for "perpetrating a crude, contemptible, adolescent, anti-American wickedness," as opposed to brilliantly prophesying the rise of "a terrifyingly powerful world leader with the soul of an amiable, soap-opera grandmother . . . and intellectual equipment of a high school senior in a June Allyson musical"—the apotheosis of "American-style philistinism run amok." And indignation over Reagan would itself seem very quaint indeed with the advent of President Trump, a multiple-bankrupt-casino-mogul-turned-reality-TV-star who would become, toward the end of Roth's life, the terrifyingly powerful leader of the free world.

Meanwhile the Roth Doctrine was memorably invoked in Tom Wolfe's 1989 essay "Stalking the Billion-Footed Beast," in which the author jovially reproached Roth for discouraging "a generation of serious young writers" from even attempting "a realistic novel with the scope of Balzac, Zola, or Lewis"—that is to say, the kind of novel Wolfe himself had written, *The Bonfire of the Vanities*, in which the "beast" had been wrestled to the ground by virtue of Wolfe's strenuous legwork and sheer vaulting ambition. Roth had recently published a pretty ambitious novel in its own right, *The Counterlife*, while his friend Updike had just finished the last volume of his Rabbit Angstrom Tetralogy, but Roth didn't specify these matters in his reply to Wolfe, who, he noted, had once ("albeit a bit drolly") referred to him, Roth, as "the American Dickens": "Maybe he doesn't think much of my work now that he's become a novelist himself. That's okay, too. But that he should want to cast me, at this late date, in the role of the American Mallarmé who, with a single flourish of the pen, turned a whole generation against realism strikes me, frankly, as nuts." To a subsequent interviewer Roth mildly remarked, "Tom's strengths don't lie in literary analysis." Reminded that Wolfe now called Roth the best novelist of his generation, Roth clarified: "Tom Wolfe is sometimes right and sometimes wrong."

M AGGIE'S CHILDREN, RONALD AND HELEN, RODE THE train to Iowa every month or so. Roth and Bob Williams took them to football games, and over Christmas Roth and his faculty friend Vance Bourjaily went rabbit hunting with the twelve-year-old Ronald. At the time both kids seemed nice enough—especially the eager-to-please Helen—but Roth was still hoping to return to Europe after a single year in Iowa, all the more now that he was flush with Random House money. "So long as we are unencumbered with kids, I think we'll try to keep on the move," he wrote Solotaroff in October; "that is, live abroad someplace for a long stretch of time."

Maggie had other plans. Leaving her children alone with that "monster" Burt Miller was out of the question; it was their duty as parents to make sure Ronald and Helen had a proper home. For the twenty-seven-year-old Roth, "duty" was as potent a word as ever, having much to do with "manliness," an even more prestigious value; thus he "compounded [his] entrapment preposterously," as he later put it, "assuming responsibility for two bewilderingly raised, love-deprived, parent-bereft, ill-educated children, ten and twelve, slates no longer clean and badly shattered, who were not mine and whom I barely knew." That pretty much covered it. As for the man he would badger for custody rights, Roth portrayed him as the well-meaning rube Roy Bassart in *When She Was Good*, and would increasingly come to believe that Miller was a mostly innocuous dolt ("He bought that book *How to Be a Dummy for Dummies*") who, like himself, had had the bad luck of getting in Maggie's way. Certainly Miller blamed Maggie for Roth's adverse opinion circa 1961: "Because of what Maggie told him, he thought I was an unfit father. . . . But he didn't have the faintest idea what was going on."

This is true, though not in the way Miller intended. Rather, it would have been hard even for Maggie to conjure just how badly things had deteriorated in Country Club Hills. On weekdays Miller commuted to his day job, in Chicago, as an art director for Libby, McNeill and Libby, where he specialized in mechanical drawings (lawn mowers, electric razors, and the like); then one day a subdivision neighbor—married to the niece of jazz guitarist Eddie Condon—invited Miller to play trombone at a nightclub in Chicago Heights, whereupon Miller began spending entire weeks, Monday to Saturday, away from Country Club Hills. "I had a great life," he reminisced. "I would do it over again."

For a while he left his children in the care of his young wife, Denise*— "a piece of work," as her former stepdaughter Helen recalled:

> [Burt] was going to do what he's always done, which was to disappear and leave her with these two kids. I fared better than [Ronald]; I learned how to duck. . . . [Ronald] became a different person. He got angrier, and when he would talk back to her . . . she used to take metal rulers to him from my father's art easel and hit him and hit him and hit him. It was terrifying. . . . I think she stuck it out for a year.

Country Club Hills was a recent development of mostly identical tract houses on otherwise featureless farmland; during the day a housekeeper would sometimes watch the children, who had to walk miles to school and back, but most nights they were alone together, or so they both remember. "I took care of my children," their father insisted in 2013, twenty-five years or so after the last time he'd spoken to either of them. "They would tell you, if you ever met one, that I fed them pretty good and they loved the casseroles I used to make." "Let me give you some hard facts," said Helen (also in 2013). "When [Denise] left, the good news was that [Ronald] wasn't getting beaten anymore, and I stopped shitting in my bed out of absolute anxiety." Her brother made them brown-bag lunches each day, and when Helen came home from school she'd stay at a neighbor's house across the street and play with their baby boy, who soon died of intestinal cancer. "It was a nightmare," she said. "I did not see or have a parent in my life during the week at all. People go to jail for

---

* A pseudonym.

this. So I don't know what kind of fucking casseroles [Burt] is referring to. We ate TV dinners every single night—and [Burt] didn't make them; my brother did." Finally the children got a surprise visit from Burt's kindly aunt, Bea Walton, who looked around and "went nuts," as Helen remembered.

Thereafter the Waltons paid to have someone pick up the children from school and watch them in their father's absence, but still they were much alone together, and before long—when he was about eleven and she nine—Ronald, according to his sister, began molesting her. Things had begun innocently enough. Ronald explained to his little sister how babies were made, and for a while ("just being silly") they would some-times pretend to have sex. One night, though, he began choking her while trying to pull her pants down, until she squirmed loose and locked herself in her bedroom, then crawled out the window and ended up at the hospital after people had spotted her wandering around, coughing. Ronald said he "never had affection toward [his] sister" after she put the cops on him that night, and bitterly denied her allegations.

So things stood when Roth (scarcely guessing the worst) retained a lawyer in Chicago and worked to gain the children's trust and persuade them, by degrees, that Maggie was *not* an unfit mother despite what their father had been telling them for years. "His torturing of Maggie has been without relief," Roth wrote a friend; "at least, so long as she was single. My torturing of him is carried on at a higher plane—that is, I simply don't get off his ass." Miller corroborated this: Roth was "a real pain in the ass," he said, always forcing him to answer some new plead-ing in court, until the two met face-to-face on the twenty-sixth floor of a Chicago skyscraper. "I took an immediate dislike to him because of his smart-ass demeanor: 'Look at me, I'm a big shot!'" said Miller, who "came damn close" to throwing Roth out the window.

Finally it was decided—"after much expense and anguish"—that it was in neither child's interest to remain in Country Club Hills with (or, most of the time, without) Burt Miller. Roth and Maggie wanted Helen to come live with them in Iowa City, and Helen desperately wanted the same: "She's a sweet, lovely-looking little girl," Roth wrote the Bakers, "who really needs at this point in her life to be rescued." As for Ronald, a moody and often intractable twelve-year-old, he would continue his education that fall at a good boarding school in Chicago, Morgan Park

Philip Roth's paternal grandfather,
Sender, a rabbinical student in Galicia
and a hat steamer in America.

Philip Finkel, Roth's maternal
grandfather and namesake.

Philip Roth's father, Herman ("Little Hymie")—the first among nine siblings to be born in America— with his older brother Ed.

Philip Roth's mother, Bess, on her wedding day—February 20, 1927—a photograph Roth discovered late in life, after his mother's death. The lace-train wedding gown and impressive staircase gave him an inflated idea of the Finkels' pre-Depression prosperity.

Another of Philip's namesakes, his uncle Milton, who was a senior at the Newark College of Engineering (the first Roth to go to college) when he died of peritonitis at age nineteen.
(COURTESY OF PHILIP ROTH ESTATE)

Bess Roth's beloved brother, Mickey, a struggling artist.
(COURTESY OF PHILIP ROTH ESTATE)

The Roth men—Herman, Sandy, and Philip—
at Bradley Beach on the Jersey Shore, circa 1937.

From left: Bess, Philip, Herman, and Sandy.

Philip and Sandy at Bradley Beach, circa 1941.
(Courtesy of Philip Roth Estate)

"Philip was an all-American boy who loved baseball," Herman Roth would say, accurately enough, when asked what his famous son had been like as a kid.
(Courtesy of Philip Roth Estate)

LEFT: *Philip Roth, about to enter high school at age twelve.*
(Courtesy of Philip Roth Estate)

BELOW: *Roth (back row, fourth from right) with his eighth-grade graduating class at Chancellor Avenue School.*
(Courtesy of Philip Roth Estate)

*Roth and friends at Billy Rose's Diamond Horseshoe after the Weequahic
High School prom. Everybody ordered "Canasta Collinses." Men, left to right: Roth,
Marty Weich, two unidentified friends, Bob Heyman.*

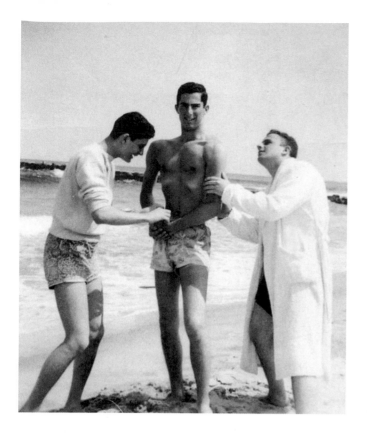

POCONO HIGHLAND CAMPS
SUMMER 1952   BUNK # 18

Roth as the Ragpicker and Jane Brown as the Madwoman in the fall 1952
Bucknell production of The Madwoman of Chaillot.

(COURTESY OF PHILIP ROTH ESTATE)

LEFT: *Roth's senior portrait at Bucknell, 1954.*

BELOW: *Roth (right) with his friends and fellow graduate students at the University of Chicago, Barry Targan (center) and Herb Haber (left).*

RIGHT: *Private Roth at Fort Dix, New Jersey, 1955. An injury on the last day of basic training led to a lifetime of back pain.*
(COURTESY OF PHILIP ROTH ESTATE)

BELOW: *Maxine Groffsky—the model for Brenda Patimkin in* Goodbye, Columbus—*during a visit to Roth's parents' home in Moorestown, New Jersey.*
(COURTESY OF PHILIP ROTH ESTATE)

The young author with Allegra the cat, Manhattan, 1959.

Maggie Martinson and Roth during a special day in Yonkers, 1959.

Roth with the eight-year-old Helen.

Winners of the 1960 National Book Award: Robert Lowell (poetry),
Richard Ellmann (nonfiction), and Roth, the youngest-ever winner at age twenty-six.

Maggie, circa 1960.

Academy; Roth agreed to contribute to his tuition, but the Waltons would pay the bulk of it. Meanwhile both children spent the summer of 1961 in Amagansett, where Roth had rented a big house and arranged for them to receive tutoring.

Raised amid the hothouse parenting of ultrastudious Weequahic, Roth was unprepared for the almost total ignorance of his long-neglected charges: Ronald was barely literate and Helen not even that. "It was quite pathetic, and we were in a state of shock for a while because of it," he wrote Solotaroff. "It just seemed a bottomless pit that we couldn't even begin to fill. Neither of these kids has done an hour's homework in the three years they have lived with their father! Can you imagine?" In Ronald's case the need was urgent, since Morgan Park had insisted on intensive tutoring as a condition of admittance. Five days a week he met with Cora Zelinka, a schoolteacher friend of the Roths (married to Sid, a TV comedy writer), who tutored him in English and math; Roth supplemented their lessons with one-on-one talks about books and writing mechanics. In 1975, Ronald would remember these sessions in an interview with a Jewish community newspaper ("Papa Portnoy: Philip Roth as a Stepfather"): "I've got to say that if it were not for the positive influence Philip had on my life at that time, I might be in jail today." The first book Roth had assigned to him was *The Red Badge of Courage*, which they discussed over a snack at the kitchen table; Roth explained basic concepts such as metaphor and foreshadowing, and asked the boy why Stephen Crane had written the book in the first place. "No, I wasn't really into having a parent," Ronald told his 1975 interviewer, who'd wondered whether Roth's manner had been fatherly, "and Philip was perceptive enough not to try to force this kind of relationship on me." Roth readily admitted he'd never felt much in the way of affection for the boy ("he was emotionally goofy, far from quick-witted, didn't like being touched"), but he was unfailingly patient even toward Ronald's more repellent lapses—as when the boy affected a swastika, until Roth made him read Uris's *Exodus* and also took pains to describe certain Nazi atrocities as they'd transpired at the Nuremberg trials. Withal he was touched by Ronald's "sad air of an outsider" despite his efforts, and was fatherly enough to explain a few key facts about sex. "Philip was the first person to tell me that people had intercourse for fun, not just to have babies," Ronald remembered. "On masturbation, Philip quoted this

Harvard dude who said that 98 percent of everyone masturbates and the other 2 percent lie."

"Maggie's rapport with [her children] was just about nil," Roth later claimed, though Helen disputed this in her own case. After the dread odyssey of San Antonio and Country Club Hills, her mother and she were "strangers in some ways," said Helen, though Maggie tried to make up for lost time; almost every day in Amagansett the two would sit under a tree, the little girl's head in her mother's lap, while Maggie read to her from *The Secret Garden* and *Charlotte's Web*. Ronald was another matter. "His father has made special use of him," Roth noted at the time, "and did such a fantastic and ugly job of turning him against Maggie, that it made a good deal of our summer a nightmare." Ronald would later insist that Burt had never said a bad word against his first wife,* and indeed had a way of "wistfully look[ing] at the ceiling" whenever he spoke of her. Maggie "tried to destroy everyone in her path," Ronald said in 1975. Both he and Burt remembered a time in Chicago when she'd slapped the boy so hard she bloodied his nose (Burt responded, he said, by shoving her against a tree and threatening to "break her goddamn neck" if she ever did it again), whereas in Amagansett Maggie struck her son with a bicycle pump. "I had to stop her from hitting him a second time," Roth remembered.

That fall the Roths moved to another rental house in Iowa City (sublet from the philosopher Gustav Bergmann), and Philip got a more vivid sense of the challenges posed by his stepdaughter. The night before Helen's first day of school, he went to kiss her good night and remind her to set her alarm clock, and the girl diffidently informed him that she couldn't tell time. He already knew she couldn't read, add, or subtract. "She was drowning," he said. "I thought it was my job to save her. . . . She was so sweet, so willing, she'd been *so* fucked over." It didn't help that Maggie was ashamed of her daughter's incompetence and would berate her whenever they sat at a table trying to do homework ("the last thing a kid needs who is struggling with reading and writing," said Helen, "is having a parent disappointed and pissed at them"). Maggie was pleased, however, when she learned that her daughter had a very

---

* Hardly my own experience vis-à-vis Burt Miller, never mind what Roth perceived at the time.

high IQ ("Your IQ is higher than Philip's!" she announced), and Roth in turn proudly wrote friends about the girl's "whopping I.Q." despite what he'd previously reported of her illiteracy. Because Maggie wasn't up to it, Roth took over the job of helping Helen with homework after dinner and would also read bedtime stories with her. "He did take on the task of teaching me how to read, and he was incredibly patient," said Helen, still emotional about things in late middle age. As a girl she'd particularly loved a book of Russian fairy tales that she and Roth read many times ("with a blue cover, and a bird on this cover"); after every sentence Roth would pause and help her break it down. "Each little pebble of success that I had," she said, "warmed me to him and he to me."

"It was my husband's opinion that the child was mental retarded [sic]," Maggie testified in a 1963 affidavit, "and he wanted to put her in a special school when we came East. I resisted this proposal, however, and Helen was sent to a reading clinic five days a week as well as to the public school. She has improved greatly and many of our friends were astonished that Philip was so ready to see her as a moron." "He was very devoted to that youngster, and he wanted to help her like crazy," said Howard Stein, an Iowa drama professor and Roth's best friend (next to the Williamses) that second year. "It was terribly painful for him. . . . And her mother wasn't too responsive." After that first semester, Roth reported to the Maurers that Helen had been attending the Reading Clinic—a program connected with the university's School of Education—for an hour each day before school, and "now likes to read books—amazing!" Later Helen would agree the program had been "a godsend," and pointed out that Roth, not her mother ("Maggie would not do it," Stein affirmed), was the one who got up at five thirty every morning to drive her.

Quite apart from what he figured to be his duty, Roth enjoyed the girl's company. As she began to overcome her shyness, she smiled and laughed easily and was a genial companion to his friends and their children. Not only would Roth take her to school in the morning but he also liked meeting her afterward and walking her home, and it was he who took her trick-or-treating and even drove her friends home from Brownie meetings and so forth. "I began to thrive," she said, on "finding out what it was to have a good father." Next to her bed was a tchotchke shelf with little animal toys and other treasures Roth had given her every so often ("Pick a hand"), and soon the girl felt secure enough to tell him she loved him. "[Helen]'s presence has really taught the two of us (Maggie and I) so much," Roth wrote the Maurers, "that I could go on for fifty pages about it,—and maybe someday I will." Maggie, in her journal, recorded that her daughter was "getting prettier by the moment," and Maggie also noticed the easy affection between her husband and Helen—the way they snuggled in a chair while reading, or held hands while walking together. "Driving back alone with me from the beach one hot afternoon," Roth remembered in 2014, "squeezed up against me in her wet bathing suit after the two of us had rolled for several hours through the heavy surf with [Helen] safely clutched to my chest, she lifted her child's face like a little leaf all juiced up on photosynthesis. 'Kiss me, Philip,' she said, 'the way you kiss Mother.'"* Unlike Swede Levov in *American Pastoral*, Roth did not oblige her, and he would have been wise, too, not to mention the episode to his wife. One day he and Helen spent a raucous afternoon raking leaves and singing nonsense songs ("*Oh Lydia, oh Lydia, my encyclopydea, oh Lydia the tattooed lady*"), while Maggie watched balefully from the kitchen; later, after Helen had gone to bed, she turned on Roth: "If you ever fuck my daughter," she snarled, "I'll drive a knife right down into your heart."

■ ■ ■ ■

GIVEN HIS FRAUGHT HOME LIFE, Roth would always be a little amazed that he'd managed to write a long (950 pages in typescript) novel of which he remained more or less unashamed. "I had managed to write a full-length novel full of strongly drawn portraits of men and women, told from multiple perspectives, and grounded in serious moral themes," he retrospectively assessed. "I had set out to demonstrate my maturity as a writer." On October 8, 1961, Roth announced that the book was finished after two years and two months of almost incessant labor— then immediately began to panic ("sure I'd never put down another word again") and returned to the manuscript for another two months, rewriting an ending that Random House had considered a little too bleak. Finally, when that was done, he wrote the story about injuring his back in the army, "Novotny's Pain," and promptly sold it to *The New Yorker*.

---

* Helen doesn't remember this incident, though she certainly concedes that she was flirtatious toward her stepfather.

"Philip is such a seer," Maggie wrote in her journal on December 28, noting this latest triumph. "I suppose this is a sort of pinnacle in our lives too for everything P. does seems to succeed and we're making more and more money and even getting happier I think. I seem to feel happier with him and he behaves as though he's happy too. I'm always melancholy though, it's in the blood." Roth was only too aware of his wife's melancholia and its various harrowing forms, but he was about to embark on a "gala week" in the East and was feeling his oats, all the more given that Maggie, for once, had to stay home and care for her daughter. Amid delivering lectures at Princeton and NYU, and dropping his novel off at Random House, Roth ran into a former *Playboy* Playmate, Alice Denham, whom he'd met once at a literary party (Maggie in tow). This time he promptly arranged a tryst at her apartment the next day, and, after a long afternoon of sex, mentioned he'd be in town for another week and would certainly call again. On sober second thought, however, he decided to leave well enough alone.

Alice Denham (Miss July of 1956) enjoyed the distinction of being the only Playmate ever to publish a story in the same issue as her centerfold, and her roster of sexual conquests—Norman Mailer, William Styron, Nelson Algren, Joseph Heller, William Gaddis, et al.—is a veritable who's who of postwar American literature. When she later published a memoir about this aspect of her career, *Sleeping with Bad Boys*, Roth couldn't bear to read it "for fear of how [he] measured up (or down) in bed against these drunken literary mastodons." But he needn't have worried: "Philip Roth was a sex fiend," she wrote. "He moved from tits to—aaaah!—so fast I was breathless. Speeded up like his talk and his head. But once he got there, he hung in long and steamy. Tepid men never move me. Philip was on fire."

Meanwhile, at Princeton, Roth met the head of the writing program, R. P. Blackmur, who subsequently offered him a job as writer in residence for the 1962–63 academic year. He also met his new celebrity publisher, Bennett Cerf, a regular panelist on TV's *What's My Line?* Finally Roth bought sweaters for Maggie and Helen before returning to Iowa City.

About two weeks later, on a sunny snow-laden day, Roth came home from campus after lunch to find his wife waiting for him in a rage. *"You son of a bitch! You filthy cheating dog! You're worse than my fucking father!"*

When she paused for breath, Roth asked what it was all about, where-upon she showed him a card (later Exhibit A in *Roth v. Roth*) that she'd opened from Alice Denham, on which was printed a Dürer woodcut of a man leading away a downcast woman (caption: "The twelve months have gone. Come on, Gredt, we'll start again"); Denham's note was brief: "Chicken! /—Alice." In 1966, Roth wrote Baker that Maggie's grand remonstrance went on "for three days running," an ineffable ordeal that he would later abridge to a mere ten or fifteen minutes—until, that is, he'd "had it with the fucking assault, which was at the same pitch of crazy intensity whether I'd said the wrong thing to the waiter at a restaurant or stuck up a bank." Yes, he confessed, *yes*, he had indeed fucked Alice Denham in New York; then he went upstairs, packed his toilet articles and some underwear, announced "I've had enough of you," and walked out the door.

He'd gone maybe two or three blocks when it occurred to him that Maggie would try to kill herself and Helen would come home from school and find her mother's body. Sure enough, when he returned, she was sitting on the floor in her underwear; a whiskey bottle and empty pill vials were nearby. "I'm going to die," she said, "I want to tell you something." Roth dragged her to her feet and upstairs to a bathroom, where he put his finger down her throat and made her throw up. Then he put her in bed. "I'm going to die," she repeated, and proceeded to tell him that she hadn't really been pregnant just before their marriage; she described her transaction with the pregnant black woman in Tompkins Square Park, and so on. "I was completely stunned on learning of her deception," Roth observed in his own affidavit for the divorce case. "Our marriage had been three years of constant nagging and irritation, and now I learned that the marriage itself was based on a grotesque lie." Roth sat in the corner of the bedroom, calmly taking it in; a two-word phrase he sometimes liked to tell himself ("when confronted by great surprises of an unhappy nature") seemed to apply: "This, too."

Roth phoned Bob Williams and asked him to pick up Helen from school and give her dinner. Then he returned to his chair in the bedroom. Soon Maggie fell asleep, and didn't die. At last he retrieved Helen and gave some excuse to the Williamses for the snafu. "I couldn't tell anyone," he remembered, "—it was all too lurid."

That spring Maggie and he slept in separate bedrooms, and Roth began having an affair with one of his students—an attractive, talented twenty-two-year-old, Lucy Warner. The young woman had caught Roth's eye before, but in light of Maggie's revelation he gave himself permission to pursue her.* Lucy was an undergraduate who'd been promoted to Roth's graduate workshop that spring because, as she recalled, one of her stories had been accepted by *The Atlantic*. Like Roth, she was rather at emotional loose ends. The previous year she'd eloped, disastrously, with another writer at the Workshop, and spent the rest of that school year as well as the fall semester in New York, disentangling herself. Both she and Roth vaguely remember his writing "See me after class" at the top of one of her papers; then he took her for a wary walk or for coffee ("he was very terrified of our being seen together") that eventuated, either that day or soon after, in their sleeping together at Warner's apartment.

Roth was in love. Amid the tense atmosphere at home, he'd sometimes spring to his feet and announce he was taking a walk, then flee across the river and up a long hill to Warner's second-floor apartment on East Burlington, where he'd skittishly hang sheets over the windows (no curtains) before getting into bed: "Cheever used to swim across Westchester County," he said; "I used to run across Iowa City." Roth's feelings were mostly reciprocated; Warner's friends at Iowa had been her short-lived husband's friends, and now she was alone. She remembered the young Roth as "skinny and nervous and funny" and of course "*very* smart" (the only person with whom she could ever discuss Italo Svevo): "I didn't feel any rough edges," she said. "I did later, but not then." Though he was careful not to burden her with any but the most salient grotesqueries about his marriage, she saw how desperate he was and liked the idea of giving him a haven. "I was always so overjoyed to see him, and felt kind of cherished."

By then Roth had already arranged to rent a house in Princeton the following year for Maggie, Helen, and himself, and had also rented a summer place in Wellfleet, on Cape Cod, near some Iowa friends, the painter Jim Lechay and his wife, Rose. That spring, however, he decided he couldn't live without Lucy Warner. On her desk was a picture of her

---

* Roth reverses things in *My Life as a Man*—that is, Maureen Tarnopol's discovery of her husband's affair with Karen Oakes (the Lucy character) precipitates Maureen's suicide attempt and confession, rather than vice versa.

family home on an island in Maine, and thither Roth hoped to escape with her, sending Maggie to Wellfleet alone. Then he would devote the summer to getting out of his nightmare marriage and starting over.

■ ■ ■ ■

GOODBYE, COLUMBUS HAD ALSO won the Harry and Ethel Daroff Memorial Award for "the year's best fiction work of Jewish interest" from the Jewish Book Council,* whose jury tended to be professors and critics, albeit professors and critics who'd given the previous year's award to *Exodus*. Roth's strongest supporter on the jury was David Boroff, who later confirmed what Roth had been told by his friend Bob Silvers (who'd accepted the award on his behalf while Roth was in Rome)—namely, that the book was an unpopular choice among sponsors and others at the ceremony. BOOK AWARD TO ROTH "TRAVESTY" AND "INSULT," read the headline of an editorial by the Jewish writer Nathan Ziprin: "It was a grave mistake for the Jewish Book Council to extend 'Jewish interest' recognition to a book that shows no understanding whatever of basic Jewish values or proper appreciation of the sensitive American Jew's relationship to his heritage."

It was Boroff who'd invited Roth to give a talk at NYU during his fateful trip east in January 1962. As Boroff would explain to an Israeli audience eighteen months later, only a few Jewish students had shown up for the occasion, though there were plenty of suburban matrons who "were very well groomed, formidably girdled, and eager for the attack":

> Indeed, Philip Roth has become a kind of shibboleth for American Jews; they define themselves and other people in terms of how they react to Philip Roth. In the suburbs, for example, there are always little cells, little revolutionary movements, of people who have read *Goodbye, Columbus* and are admirers of Philip Roth; and this sets them apart from the great mass of suburban people to whom Mr. Roth is anathema. . . ."[I]t is a kind of an issue, a way of dividing the sophisticated from the non-sophisticated. You are given a choice: Leon Uris or Philip Roth.

---

* Later known as the National Jewish Book Award for Fiction, which Roth won a total of four times.

As for gentiles, said Boroff, they regarded Roth as a "Baedeker, the guidebook to Jewish life"—which, of course, was the main rub among Roth's detractors. "Why don't you leave us alone?" they'd assail him after his talks. "Why don't you write about the Gentiles?" David Seligson—a celebrated Reform rabbi at Central Synagogue in Manhattan, whose memorial service for JFK would be nationally televised—made headlines in June 1963 when he denounced Roth from the pulpit as a veritable paradigm of the "alienated Jewish intellectual," whose "prize-winning novel [sic] *Goodbye, Columbus*, written about a Jewish adulterer"—he meant "Epstein"—"and a host of other lop-sided schizophrenic personalities, could hardly be said to be a balanced portrayal of Jews as we know them." Given his concern with balance, Seligson (and others) might have mentioned the more admirable likes of Sergeant Marx, Eli Peck, and Leo Tzuref; as for Grossbart, Epstein, and Brenda Patimkin's diaphragm, one is reminded of Isaac Singer's reply to his critics: "'Why do you write about Jewish thieves and Jewish prostitutes?' [they asked me], and I said, 'Shall I write about Spanish thieves and Spanish prostitutes? I wrote about the thieves and prostitutes that I know."

While privately "bemused" by the vehemence of his attackers, Roth was determined not to back down in public. In March 1961 he and Alfred Kazin were invited to appear at a symposium at Loyola University in Chicago, "The Needs and Images of Man," devoted to exploring the state of Catholic-Jewish relations (four years, that is, before the Vatican Council finally absolved Jews for their part in killing Christ). The gist of what Roth had said would be published in *American Judaism* as "Some New Jewish Stereotypes": "I find that I am suddenly living in a country in which the Jew has come to be . . . a cultural hero," Roth began, for the benefit of Catholics who congratulated themselves on reading Leon Uris, whose portrayal of the Jew, said Roth, as a kind of patriotic "warrior" was so silly that it was "not even worth disputing," though he invoked the testimony of Captain Yehiel Aranowicz, the master of an Israeli refugee ship, in disputing it: "The types that are described in [*Exodus*] never existed in Israel," said Aranowicz. Roth also said hard things about Harry Golden, whose maudlin comedies about virtuous immigrants on the Lower East Side (*Only in America; For 2¢ Plain*) were still popular at the time. Roth declined to show "Some New Jewish Stereotypes" to his mother, who was still trying to process the rumor that

Morton Wishengrad, a playwright, had told the Newark YMHA that her son was a better writer than Uris: "much as she loves me," Roth wrote a friend, "she just couldn't give up her cool reasonableness. I was her son, but Leon Uris—after all!"

A far sterner test awaited Roth a year later at Yeshiva University in New York, where he'd been invited to appear on a panel, with Ralph Ellison and James T. Farrell, on "Conflict of Loyalties in Minority Writers of Fiction."* "I accepted the job," Roth noted three weeks in advance, "partly because I wanted to, partly out of defiance; I think it is a purposely provocative title, and it seems to me that somebody ought to take the smug bastards on." Roth was piqued by the implication that minority literature was often controversial because of the moral failings of the writers themselves, versus certain insecurities on the part of their minority audience, who, he expected, would turn out in bloodthirsty force at Yeshiva. As it happened Farrell was replaced by a lesser-known proletarian writer of the thirties, Pietro di Donato, author of *Christ in Concrete*, who, like Ellison, mostly improvised his twenty-minute opening remarks; Roth, however, read from a carefully prepared script lest his remarks be misquoted or otherwise distorted as in San Francisco. Bearing in mind his status as a kind of "Baedeker" among gentiles, Roth alluded to "a rabbi and educator in New York City"—i.e., Emanuel Rackman, a political science professor at Yeshiva who'd wished for "medieval" justice in Roth's case—who had charged him with the "sin of informing":

> [W]hat he is suggesting is that some subjects must not be written about, or brought to public attention, because it is possible for them to be misunderstood by people with weak minds or malicious instincts. Thus he consents to put the malicious and weak-minded in a position of determining the level at which open communication on these subjects will take place. This is not fighting anti-Semitism but submitting to it: that is, submitting to a restriction of consciousness as well as communication, because being conscious and being candid are too risky.

---

* Misremembered in *The Facts* as "The Crisis of Conscience in Minority Writers of Fiction."

"Mr. Roth," the moderator inquired, after the introductory statements had been given, "would you write the same stories you've written if you were living in Nazi Germany?" Which was pretty much the tenor of the barrage that followed. Roth's interrogators seemed heedless of the fact that he'd already addressed the question in his prepared remarks, more or less, by pointing out that—contrary to Rackman's assertion that his "informing" might endanger Jews—the United States wasn't remotely analogous to Nazi Germany: The Holocaust "has taught [Rackman] nothing other than how to remain a victim in a country where he does not have to live like one if he chooses. How pathetic. And what an insult to the dead. Imagine: sitting in New York in the 1960's and piously summoning up the 'six million' to justify one's own timidity."

"I was, in a way, surprised by the colossal brutality of the argument from the other side, and finally overwhelmed," he wrote Solotaroff a week after his Yeshiva appearance. "[A]ll the strength just ran out of me, and I felt as limp as a rag." Roth had considered getting up and leaving the platform, but that would be construed as defeat, and besides he hardly had the strength by then. "What's going on here?" said Ellison, when he saw how battered Roth looked. Ellison pointed out that his own depiction of incest between a black sharecropper and his daughter—to name only one provocative aspect of *Invisible Man*—had infuriated black readers, but, after all, he wasn't a propagandist. The Yeshiva students received this information politely, then resumed attacking Roth. When it was over, the dazed man was surrounded by a scrum of shouting detractors as he tried to leave. "You were brought up on anti-Semitic literature!" said one. "Yes?" Roth replied. "And what is that?" "English literature! English literature is anti-Semitic literature!" Afterward Roth sat with Maggie and his Random House editor, Joe Fox, at the Stage Delicatessen in Midtown, wanly consuming a pastrami sandwich. "I'll never write about Jews again," he said.

And yet he still hoped to be understood, after a fashion, or at any rate to forestall some of the usual "inanities" in the Jewish press by publishing his Yeshiva remarks as "Writing about Jews" in a subsequent issue of *Commentary*. "Roth attempts to defend himself in an article, which he has the audacity to call 'Writing about Jews,'" remarked Rabbi Theodore Lewis of the Progressive Synagogue in Brooklyn in a letter to his congregation. "Roth *never* writes about Jews . . . Roth writes about more exciting and lucrative themes—adultery, sexual licentiousness, marital infidelity, lechery, and human depravity in general." Meanwhile the letters to *Commentary* again came pouring in—notably from two of his most prominent antagonists, eager to return fire. "'Look, folks, no hands,'" Harry Golden imagined Roth saying to his many gentile admirers; "'I'm one of you; look how uninhibitedly I can write of Jewish bums, just like you would like to do but haven't the guts.'" The redoubtable Rackman, too, reminded Roth, not unfamiliarly, that he'd "earned the gratitude of all who sustain their anti-Semitism on such conceptions of Jews as ultimately led to the murder of six million in our time."

Eighteen

L OOKING BACK, LUCY WARNER FOUND IT HARD TO believe that she'd ever seriously considered Roth's proposal to run away to her family house in Maine. Her mother was there, for one thing, and the woman had taken a very dim view of Lucy's hasty marriage and divorce the year before. Still, despite an almost abject wish to regain her mother's approval, Warner might have run away with Roth to *somewhere* if he hadn't expressed a curious concern about becoming too attracted to his stepdaughter as "she got a little older." "That was an alarm bell for me," Warner remembered.

Roth was devastated when she told him, toward the end of May, that she couldn't go to Maine (or wherever) with him after all. In her affidavit the following year, Maggie would claim that their separation around this time had been temporary—he'd planned to rejoin her later that summer on Cape Cod—and attributed their problems to "his emotional state prior to the publication of *Letting Go.*" This, of course, was a distortion, but plausible up to a point. "Phil, I know you are going through a bad time now," his editor, Joe Fox, had written him on April 24. "I don't need to tell you that every author goes through this torture in the month or two months before publication; you know that anyway and it doesn't help." Fox quipped that he should work on his backhand and "listen closely to whatever Maggie says," but of course Roth could hardly bear the thought of his wife, still less now that Lucy was fading from the picture. "He snarls and glowers," Maggie wrote in her journal, "I 'drive him crazy.' It seems hopeless."

As the summer holiday began, they put Helen on a train to Chicago without discussing the separation with her; Maggie figured they'd be reunited in time for Helen's arrival in Wellfleet on July 19, but for now Roth was staying in Iowa while Maggie drove east on June 7. Alone in the big rental house on Cape Cod, she puzzled over their estrangement in her journal. Though not imperceptive in other respects, she seemed blind to the main cause of her husband's dark mood: "[Philip] understands and discerns so much and really feels so little. . . . I never feel really really loved, only 'given to,' and I'm never allowed to love Philip in the emotional, physical way that I feel most naturally. It's quite terrible. *Somehow* [italics added] Philip has a deep hostile feeling for me and when face to face the emotion I sense is hatred." Meanwhile Bob Baker was startled by the news that his friends' marriage was effectively over ("I don't see that I can go back to Maggie," Roth wrote him on June 9, "without, finally, our really destroying one another"); so fond were Bob and Ida of the Roths—Maggie too—that they'd named their second and third children Philip and Margaret. Their primary loyalty was to Philip, however, and they urged him to come to Oregon and stay as long as he liked, the way he'd almost done three years ago, when he considered fleeing Maggie rather than marrying her.

In the end, though, he couldn't bring himself to board the airplane in Cedar Rapids. His fear of flying flared up amid general anxiety, and he phoned his brother instead and asked if he could stay awhile in Stuy Town; Sandy told him to come ahead—Trudy and the boys were summering on Fire Island, so Philip would have the place to himself much of the time. Finally he made his excuses to Bob Baker, who didn't like the way his friend sounded. "The black fact is that we are concerned about his mental health," Baker wrote Solotaroff afterward, begging him to keep an eye on Roth in New York and let them know how he was doing. "We love the big lug and this is pretty important to us . . . we haven't had anyone to turn to for information and—as you'll understand—we haven't wanted to press Phil."

The train trip to New York was an unpromising start to single life, as Roth stopped at a newsstand in Chicago to read the first major reviews of *Letting Go* in *Time* and *Newsweek*. He remembered staggering back to a bench as the words sank in. Two months before, he'd noted his growing dread that the novel to which he'd given so much would be dismissed as "a sad book," among other things, and here it was in black and white. "Melancholy Journey" was the title of the *Newsweek* review, whose author described Gabe Wallach as "a selfish, irresolute *kvetch*," and likened Roth's "carefully brilliant set-pieces" to "gaudy depots on the Trans-Siberian Railway." The *Time* review ("The Grey Plague") was a little more sympathetic, suggesting that writers should "solve the second-book problem the way architects solve the 13th-floor problem"— that is, by skipping from the first book to the third.

Sandy was getting ready for a party when Philip arrived that evening; noticing his brother's frayed nerves, Sandy gave him a phone number where he could be reached. Philip had taken a shower and made a sandwich when the phone rang: Maggie. Though he hadn't told her his whereabouts, she'd speculated in her journal that he wouldn't be able to board a plane to Oregon (a likely destination, as she well knew), and hence she was "betting on New York" where, she wrote, he could "have a talk with Maxine to see if his old passion is recreated. He'll also be able to see people and talk about his book." She moreover recorded the fact that she was very drunk by the time she finally got hold of the fugitive. Shouting, she told him that if he didn't stop this nonsense and come to Wellfleet she'd ruin his life, soaking him for alimony just like Marty Greenberg's first wife and denouncing him as a cheating philanderer to whosoever would listen. Afterward Roth tried calming himself with a walk, but when he returned to the apartment he began to shake and was wracked by fits of vomiting and diarrhea; finally he phoned Sandy, who came home immediately. That night Philip belatedly told his brother the whole lurid saga—from the urine ruse to the suicide-attempt-cum-confession back in January—whereupon Sandy insisted on phoning his old psychiatrist, Hans Kleinschmidt, who agreed to pencil in Sandy's celebrated brother the very next day.

Sandy had given the analyst an earful over the years about how manipulative—alternately suffocating and severe—his mother had been when he was a boy, before she'd effectively jilted him in favor of Philip. "Does your wife remind you of your mother?" was Kleinschmidt's first question for the latter, who remembered thinking, "Oh god, not the clichés right off." *No,* Philip replied—again and again, over the years— the two women could hardly be more dissimilar . . . yet Kleinschmidt would never really waver in his conviction that Bess Roth was the virtual embodiment of the "phallic mother figure."

Kleinschmidt was a fascinating figure in his own right. An expert in abstract expressionism (Kandinsky in particular), he'd actually met Philip a few years earlier in Amagansett, where he too liked to summer along with his fellow analysts and their painter-patients. A direct disciple of Freud, Kleinschmidt had grown up in Berlin and attended medical school at the University of Freiburg, finishing in Italy after fleeing the Nazis in 1933, and finally immigrating to the States. As Adam Gopnik would memorably describe him ("Max Grosskurth") in a *New Yorker* piece published eighteen months after Kleinschmidt's death in 1997—a portrait Roth considered "perfect"—Kleinschmidt was "tall, commanding, humorless," something of a dandy who affected "large, blooming shirts, dark suits, heavy handmade shoes, club ties." His specialty was creative people ("I sometimes half expected him to put up autographed glossies around the office," Gopnik wrote, "like the ones on the wall at the Stage Deli"), whom he invariably determined were narcissistic to some greater or lesser degree, a verdict he asserted with an authoritative baritone "uncannily like Henry Kissinger's."

During their first session, Roth discussed what would become "the master theme" of his first year of analysis: his almost homicidal rage over Maggie's urine fraud, not to say bafflement at how easily she'd bamboozled him. For Kleinschmidt, the young novelist (or "successful Southern playwright," as he'd style Roth in his 1967 paper, "The Angry Act") was an intriguing instance of "the interplay of narcissism and aggression" in an oedipally conflicted patient. "There's your narcissism again!" was Kleinschmidt's favorite catch-phrase vis-à-vis Roth, along with "You have to stand up for yourself!" "But when I do it," Roth would reply, "you say it's my narcissism." Nevertheless Roth stuck with the analyst, on and off, for the next three decades; Kleinschmidt was a cultured and intelligent man of the world, after all, and his advice sometimes savored of wisdom, at least when he dispensed with "the psychoanalytic shit," as Roth always considered it. Then, too, Roth needed to confide in *somebody*, and he figured Kleinschmidt's hourly rates were worth it if he could speak freely without fear of gossip—a mistaken assumption, or so Gopnik learned "after a couple of disconcerting weeks of telling [his] troubles to a sleeping therapist"; gossip, it turned out, was the only surefire way of reviving the man.

> "And so my mother's relationship with my father reminds me [says Gopnik to "Grosskurth"]—well, in certain ways it reminds me of what people have been saying about Philip Roth's divorce from Claire Bloom" . . .

Instantly, his head would jerk straight up, his eyes open, and he would shake himself all over like a Lab coming out of the water. "Yes, what are they saying about this divorce?" he would demand.

■   ■   ■   ■

About a week after his arrival in New York, Roth visited the Styrons at their home in Roxbury, Connecticut, in rustic Litchfield County. Roth informed the couple of his separation from Maggie and asked if he could rent Bill's two-room studio while they spent the summer, as ever, on Martha's Vineyard; they insisted he take the studio for free, and even let him use an extra car. Roth had never lived in the countryside and was enchanted by the nearby swimming pond, the long vistas of farmland and wooded ridges, the little general store, and even a famous playwright, Arthur Miller, who stopped by with his wife, the photographer Inge Morath, to introduce themselves at the Styrons' urging.

By then Lucy Warner had also returned to the East and was visiting her brother in Newport, Rhode Island, where he was stationed with the navy—this after an unhappy meeting with Roth at his brother's apartment in New York, the day after the drunken Maggie had threatened to leave him as destitute as Marty Greenberg. Hardly a model of solidity herself at the time, Warner was spooked by Roth's panicky behavior and bolted on the pretext of having a doctor's appointment. A couple of weeks later Roth phoned her from Connecticut, and, wishing to make amends, she agreed to take a bus to nearby Southbury. For a few days they had a pleasant visit, going on long walks and sleeping together, until one night Maggie called while they were broiling steaks. For the next hour or more, Roth and his wife yelled at each other with mounting hysteria while Warner waited outside and the steaks turned to shoe leather. The next day she left for Maine, though not before saying (or so she vaguely remembered), à la Karen Oakes in *My Life as a Man*, "I can't save you, Philip. I'm only twenty-two years old."

Pinned over Styron's desk was a Flaubert maxim that would become important to Roth too: "Be orderly and regular in your life like a bourgeois, so that you may be wild and original in your work." Settling down to the most orderly routine he could manage, Roth began writing a play, *1957: The Taming of the Id*. The setting is the Upper West Side basement apartment of an up-and-coming actor, Lawrence ("Mendy") Mendel, whose sharp-tongued and rather plain girlfriend, Ann, has just arrived by train bearing most of her worldly possessions. "'Oh, Mr. Mendel,'" she mimics a girl at the station, "'I go to Bryn Mawr and I saw you in *The Seagull.*'" Despite a wistful manqué streak ("I ought to take up a musical instrument"), Ann is all too aware of her deficiencies next to her tall, talented, good-looking boyfriend, and when he seems on the verge of leaving her—as he has once before, albeit guiltily, after she agreed to get an abortion—she claims to be pregnant a second time, and proves it by furtively obtaining urine from an "obviously pregnant" Puerto Rican woman. After much righteous haranguing from Ann, Mendy admits his hopeless sexual inconstancy and general unworthiness: "I stink. I'm a monster of me. Greedy! Selfish. Me me me me. Do you think I'm blind to myself? I should be crawling on my belly for things you don't even know about." In the end he agrees to marry her, despite every manifest inclination to the contrary.

Roth sent the script to his friend Howard Stein, the drama professor, who also happened to be aware of the underlying facts. Stein had admired *A Coffin in Egypt*, Roth's teleplay, but was unsparing about this far more personal effort, which he described as "terribly dull, bad drama, bad writing, dull self-obsessed analysis, and much much more." Roth would continue to struggle with the material—a mélange of Maggie-trauma that would need to marinate a lot longer before he knew what to do with it all, eventually using the righteous Ann-like girlfriend in *When She Was Good*, the young man's priapism in *Portnoy's Complaint*, and the crucial urine ruse (intended for both of these earlier novels) in *My Life as a Man.*

"This has been the worst month of my life," he wrote Baker on July 12, and it wasn't liable to get better now that he'd agreed to visit his angry wife in Wellfleet to coincide with Helen's arrival. Roth and Maggie had made up "some lie" about his having to work on a movie for much of the summer, and meanwhile they'd disposed of Ronald by signing him up for a six-week bicycle trip around New England for young teenagers; his touring group had spent a single night in Wellfleet, camping on the lawn of the Roths' rental house. Other visitors during Roth's brief stay on the Cape were his old Weequahic friend Stu Lehman and his wife, Bette, who came for a weekend and were struck by how "disturbed" Helen seemed amid the palpable strife between her mother and stepfather. The softhearted Lehmans got up early that Sunday morning and drove the girl to Provincetown, where they let her pick out a treasure for her tchotchke shelf.

In her 1963 affidavit Maggie claimed to have been in a state of "utter amazement" when Roth saw fit to leave Wellfleet after only a few days; more amazing still, he'd canceled their rental house in Princeton, as she learned when she called the owner a few days prior to their scheduled arrival. She demanded an explanation from the miscreant, and Roth "replied rather vaguely" that he'd assumed she and Helen would be returning to New York, where Maggie could find a job. "Since we had had no prior discussions along these lines and since I wanted our marriage to continue despite his severe emotional problems," Maggie testified, "I can in retrospect only surmise that this was his first attempt at abandonment, which he reconsidered." "My wife's frequent statements that she could not go on without me helped me to this conclusion," Roth explained to the court of his decision to give marriage another try, "for I felt genuinely sorry for this neurotic woman"—or, as he put it a few decades later, "I had essentially collapsed in the face of her threats."

■　■　■　■

SOLOTAROFF REPORTED to Baker that he'd found their friend "upset about the reception of [*Letting Go*] in some deep, baffled way," and of course chastened by life as a whole. Roth had a long way to fall from the sky-high expectations of *Goodbye, Columbus*, though really things might have been a lot worse. Prepublication excerpts of his novel had appeared in three major magazines—*Esquire, Harper's,* and *Mademoiselle*—and the first printing of twenty thousand had sold out in a week. And yet: "None of the jack-offs who reviewed it read it," Roth complained to Baker, "or if they did, they did with blinders, and it's really, to me, a little sickening and disappointing—but why should it be? Let me tell you, you write for yourself. That comes home to me especially now. It's just a god damn shame."

In fact, the book was widely and often thoughtfully reviewed, but with a pervasive sense of disappointment to be sure. Orville Prescott, in the daily *New York Times*, deplored its unwieldy length and occasional nastiness ("Mr. Roth is still so young he wants to shock"), but came to the heartening conclusion that Roth was "probably the most talented novelist under 30 in America." The headline of the Sunday *Times* review by Arthur Mizener—Bumblers in a World of Their Own—pointed to a common complaint among critics that seemed to derive from Roth's own remarks in "Writing American Fiction," or anyway a misreading thereof. Mizener mentioned two of the writers, Bellow and Styron, whom Roth had allegedly rebuked for averting their eyes from a realistic appraisal of the big public scene, and accused Roth of the same tendency—as if all three "had spent more of their lives with the Paris Review crowd or in Iowa City or some similar 'creative writing' center than was good for them as writers." Bellow also seemed familiar with "Writing American Fiction" and had likely found something amiss in Roth's remarks about the "wholly imagined" (versus realistic) world of *Henderson the Rain King*. "A recent novel like Philip Roth's *Letting Go* is a consummate example of this," he wrote in *Encounter*, referring to a trend in fiction that reflected the "unearned bitterness" of "the young American writer," who merely "defends his sensibility" rather than attacking "power and injustice" for some greater good. "Roth's hero clings to the hope of self-knowledge and personal improvement, and he concludes that with all his faults, he loves himself still. His inner life, if it may be called that, is a rather feeble thing of a few watts."

In *Letting Go* and various works to come, Roth tried puzzling out the question of why he'd thrown away the best years of his youth for the sake of a conventional idea of goodness. "All that moral precociousness and striving had made me a success in my budding literary career and a stupid, burdened failure in my private life," he said of the quandary that would persist, in some form, throughout much of his life. For now: Why the hurry to tame the id, to relinquish one's reckless freedom and assume the dull burdens of adulthood? From the vantage point of the sixties and beyond, Roth would view himself as a product of his era, when young men were taught to value themselves in proportion to the number of crippling obligations—marriage, children, career—they were willing to assume. And yet his particular case was more bewildering than most. Growing up he'd always considered himself a decent, responsible young man with compassion for the underdog, and certainly his mentors at Bucknell and elsewhere were apt to agree; suddenly, however, in his twenties, he was beset by adversaries who accused him of being wicked and irresponsible and deceitful, eminently deserving of the keenest sense of guilt. No wonder he would become so fascinated by Kafka in his thirties.

Letting Go is rightly dedicated to Maggie, who introduced the sprightly young author of *Goodbye, Columbus* to the darkness of an adult life gone irrevocably awry. Roth confected a sympathetic surrogate in the person of Martha Reganhart, a game divorcée who supports her two children as a waitress and takes college courses while seeming to bear up with a kind of sassy good cheer ("What a dumb, silly, impossible bitch" is one of her first two utterances in Gabe Wallach's hearing). Gabe finds the woman attractive—"admirable"—in a superficial way but soon finds himself distressingly overcommitted to a life whose squalor is barely held at bay. Martha's medicine chest is a "square foot of chaos," and her maternal solicitude dissembles a longing to abolish the last few years of her life and start over with a clean, childless slate. Gabe, for all the sporadic exertions of his "Jamesian" conscience, soon realizes he doesn't care enough for this blowzy woman to stomach her medicine cabinet or her exasperating children (*"I am not his father, he is not my son,"* he decides of little Markie), while she, in turn, furiously lets him know he's forfeited her good opinion and sexual favors: "Don't ever try to get me in bed again, you!" And still Gabe longs to consider himself "an educated man, a decent man"—all the more for having failed Martha—and hence meddles high-mindedly in the lives of his friends Paul and Libby Herz, whom he helps adopt a child. The wreckage mounts as Gabe takes it upon himself to deal with the birth mother's cretinous husband, who extorts more and more money from Gabe while refusing to sign a letter giving up his parental rights, until at last Gabe almost loses both his mind and the baby. What he gains in the way of self-awareness or moral redemption is left very much in doubt.

As Roth would explain the ending of his first novel a few years later, he wanted Gabe (Paul Herz too) to come up against something "unresolvable"—something that no amount of education and decency would fix. "There's a deep innocence in these people," he said, "a deep innocence about the nature of evil. They don't expect it should really *be* there. That's what makes them think that if they hurl themselves against the wall they'll finally break it down." They would do well to learn an elusive virtue suggested by the book's title—detachment, self-preservation—lest they make the same mistake as Isabel Archer in *The*

Portrait of a Lady. Mulling the lesson of Archer's ghastly marriage to Gilbert Osmond, Gabe reflects, "Terrible struggles go on in the heart, to which the heart itself will not admit, when pity is mistaken for love." Paul Herz likewise commits himself to a miserable marriage out of pity, a leaden sense of duty, and blunders away at it despite the counsel of his raffish Uncle Asher—a bachelor artist (like Roth's Uncle Mickey) who chooses to live in a shabby loft above a Third Avenue bar in exchange for sweet freedom. "Nobody owes nobody nothing," Asher repeatedly reminds his unhappy nephew.

Minor characters such as Asher, and the funny if often digressive scenes they animate, are the most appealing parts of *Letting Go.* Asher snoozes in peaceful apathy while his mistress prattles at Paul, and later one of Paul's ex-girlfriends serves him a sophisticated cup of espresso while discussing *Marjorie Morningstar* in an expertly rendered Brooklyn accent. Gabe's father gives a lovingly evoked slideshow of his European travels for friends (including his "diabetic accountant" and "Henny Sokoloff, widower and diamond king"), while explaining his new fiancée's conspicuous tippling to his son: "She's had a lot of tragedy in her life. One sunny day she goes outside her place in South Orange and her husband is being driven all over the lawn in their power mower. He's dead in his seat. It was a horrible thing."

Otherwise we're left to the "fine amenities [and] brave decisions" for which the novel's guiding spirit, Henry James, is celebrated on a London plaque—in the case of *Letting Go*, these amount to more than six hundred pages of agonizing vacillation, renunciation, and occasional domestic tumult, blessedly mitigated by the odd bit of shtick. "Line by line the writing is fine," Granville Hicks justly remarked in the *Saturday Review*, "but that does not save long stretches from being unpardonably dull and quite superfluous."

It bears repeating, though, that the novel's reception was hardly the "god damn shame" its author would have it be. Reviewers commended its better qualities and remained hopeful that Roth would one day live up to the grand promise of *Goodbye, Columbus*; meanwhile his second book sold almost 34,000 copies in hardcover, lingering around the lower rungs of the best-seller lists throughout much of that long summer. Given his gaining acclaim, Roth was named a *Seventeen* magazine "VIP," in which capacity he composed a no-nonsense piece of advice ("They Won't Make

You Normal") about reading novels ("and the writing of them, if you are feeling game"): "Novels do not pussyfoot around," Roth wrote. "They can leave you sulky, angry, fearful and desperate."* As for his own first novel, its relative failure would leave Roth sulky for years to come—until, toward the end of a long career, his canonical status assured, he was able to describe it as "so solemn and morally in earnest that it might have been taken to be my voluminous application for a novitiate in the Society of Jesuits." That said, Roth would always look pensive whenever someone said hard words about *Letting Go*, as if the novel were a faded but beloved old girlfriend whom he hated for anyone but himself to mock.

■ ■ ■ ■

FOR A WHILE the Roths lived again as a family at 232 Bayard Lane, Princeton. As the university's twenty-nine-year-old writer in residence, Roth made exactly twice his salary at Iowa, $11,000, while teaching essentially the same two courses: a writing course that met once a week for two hours, and a fiction seminar (Form and Values in Fiction) for which Roth taught his twelve undergraduate men (before the days of coeducation at Princeton) the shorter masterpieces of Mann, Conrad, Tolstoy, and Bellow. "I tried to make them attend carefully and exactly to the surface of the work, and to try to lead them away from 'deep' reading that was only an excuse for not reading," Roth explained in 1964 (though he might have said as much at any time).

Roth was charmed by the town, though he found no soulmates among his fellow faculty members, at least during those first months when he was, in any case, conversationally depleted by his thrice-weekly sessions with Kleinschmidt in New York. The novelist and translator Edmund "Mike" Keeley had been at the American Academy during Roth's time in Rome and was a great admirer of *Goodbye, Columbus*; he'd paved the way for Roth's appointment, and the two liked each other and occasionally socialized with other couples. Perhaps Roth's favorite of their

---

* Roth recommended a list of ten novels "that are decidedly not good for you" to readers of *Seventeen*: *Winesburg, Ohio, Mrs. Bridge, The Great Gatsby, Madame Bovary, Lord of the Flies, The Assistant, The Lonely Passion of Judith Hearne, Lie Down in Darkness, Anna Karenina,* and *Look Homeward, Angel*. Interesting how he included Wolfe, the hero of his youth, but not Bellow (whose remarks about *Letting Go* he might have noticed by then).

circle was the photographer Naomi Savage, who'd studied with her uncle Man Ray in California and took Roth's author photo for the paperback edition of *Letting Go.** She also took an evocative, soft-focus portrait of Maggie that Roth dearly wished he could use, later, for the jacket of *When She Was Good*, about the doomed virago Lucy Nelson; since he and Maggie were deadly enemies by then, Roth had to settle instead for Savage's photograph of another goyish blonde, Betty Fussell, the wife of his Princeton colleague Paul. Betty remembered Roth as "aloof" and even "Puritan" by the standards of their rather louche literary set†—an impression belied by Maggie's journal entry the day after that year's New Year's Eve party: "Philip was very gay and full of tricks. He's rather attracted to Betty Fussell."

Roth agreed he was somewhat aloof at Princeton—disinclined to discuss his hellish home life, and also sensing a vague distance on the part of colleagues. "Not an easy town for a hotshot young Jew writer to tumble through in those days," he explained. Happily he soon began a lifelong friendship with one of the very few Jews—and a "Jew-y Jew" too, as Roth liked to say, a big slovenly cigar-smoking *spritzer*—on the faculty: Melvin Tumin, an eminent sociologist and expert on segregation, who'd directed the Mayor's Commission on Race Relations in Detroit before heading to Princeton in 1947. Hardly content to be the first Jew in the Social Science Department (and perhaps one of four Jewish professors period), Tumin raised a ruckus over the sacrosanct, Jew-barring eating clubs, earning the lasting enmity of his goy colleagues, including President Robert Goheen. Despite a stellar publishing record and reputation as a witty and brilliant (if eccentric and uncompromising) teacher, Tumin remained an associate professor for decades, until at last it became simply too embarrassing not to promote him.

Tumin had been delighted to learn that the young author of *Goodbye, Columbus* was coming to Princeton: another Jew, and another *Newark* Jew to boot. The two hit it off over lunch and were like brothers thereafter—

---

* Savage's well-known portrait of the young Roth appears on the first volume of his Library of America edition.

† Still somewhat under the spell of Kingsley Amis, one of Roth's recent predecessors, who (some say) got the sixties started early among the Princeton literati.

Tumin the older, more pedantic brother, but always loving and protective. As Roth remarked in his eulogy, "Mine became another life that Mel took it upon himself to assist and oversee as secretary of health, education, and welfare."

Among faculty friends, Tumin alone had an inkling of the "wild and wooly time" being had by the residents of 232 Bayard Lane. "Our menage is once more intact and all is more or less well," Maggie circumspectly reported to a friend in November. "The rub is that we are undertaking a monumental therapy program (all three of us!)." This was true. Maggie was in analysis with Samuel Guttman, editor of the standard English concordance to Freud's writings and director of the Center for Advanced Psychoanalytic Studies at Princeton. Helen was seeing Shirley Van Ferney, who decided her young charge was too distracted by domestic chaos to write a report for school, and so wrote it for her: "I had to read it in front of my class and I couldn't," Helen remembered. "There was too much leakage of [Van Ferney's] life into my life, and it left me feeling incredibly empty and lost." Roth, however, considered all that therapy to be money well spent—six hundred and fifty 1962 dollars a month for the three of them—if it helped mitigate an atmosphere that remained on the fraught side. "[W]hat the end will be I don't know," he wrote Baker. "But just recently, I've begun to feel as though the pieces had been picked up, and some of the major ones were back in place— hanging by wires and tape perhaps—and I suppose that's why I can at long last write to you."

This would prove prematurely optimistic. The court would determine, in 1964, that the defendant, Philip Roth, "abandoned the plaintiff on March 1, 1963, without cause or justification therefor"—a conclusion with which the defendant was apt to differ. In Princeton he'd lasted another six months as Maggie's husband all but entirely for the sake of Helen, who was "becoming a very special person," he wrote Baker, despite the considerable odds against her. "She is quite beautiful and adult, though she performs badly in school—not that she wants to—because she reads so badly, and her life is going to be founded on other things than books. But on beautiful and passionate things, I hope." Helen appeared to be aiming for a passionate life: she and a friend were taking ballet classes, and when Roth came home from the office of an afternoon, the two girls would favor him with a dance in the living room, which usually ended with the leotarded Helen flopping into his lap. "I thought 'Oh boy, oh boy,'" said Roth. "'I'm gonna get killed and these two kids are gonna get killed too.'"

It was no idle concern. More and more, Maggie's anger encompassed both husband and daughter; she accused Helen of having "an evil streak" and would sometimes shake and slap her, telling Roth to mind his own business when he tried to interfere. And of course her perception of the girl's flirtatiousness was hardly unwarranted. "If you ever fuck my daughter, I'll drive a knife right down into your heart" had become a favorite refrain, uttered with such conviction one night that Roth waited, one eye open, for his wife to fall asleep, then stole into the kitchen and hid all the knives. "Where's a knife?" Helen called the next morning, in a hurry for school and wanting to eat a grapefruit. Roth decided that retrieving the stepladder and removing a knife from the top of the kitchen cabinet would be too conspicuous. "I advised her to eat it with her hands," he wrote Baker the following year, "and that, more or less, is how we all survived."

If that were not sufficient "cause or justification" for Roth's final departure—as the court would determine—an argument about the pronunciation of "orange" persuaded Roth himself that it was time to go. "This is pure Ionesco," he reminisced. He'd said AH-range, Maggie said OH-range, and Roth suggested they look it up in the dictionary; rather than call the whole thing off, Maggie erupted, "Why do you say I'm *wrong* all the time?!"—then removed a sandal with a hard cork heel, walked to his side of the table, and whacked him in the triceps as hard as she could. Helen began to scream. Without a word Roth went upstairs and packed his toilet kit, then left the house and took a room at the Nassau Inn. Realizing he had nothing to read, he walked to a bookstore on Nassau Street and bought a copy of *Ushant*, by Conrad Aiken.

After a few days Roth moved to a dark room with an air-shaft view at the Warwick Hotel (reduced rates for academics) on West Fifty-fourth Street in Manhattan. By then Maggie affected to find the whole thing silly, and expected Roth to return once he got over his "temper tantrum." When almost two months had passed, she went to see Kleinschmidt and was gently disabused. As she recorded in her journal on April 29, 1963:

[Kleinschmidt] said I had made one serious mistake: In confessing to Philip. I realize this too. He said he thinks he knows what course Philip would take if we were to remain married and I understood him to mean that he would be unfaithful and deserting constantly. K. has rather settled theories about the psyche and neurosis of the artist and it's hard to know whether he's right or not. . . . K.'s feeling is that it's impossible to be married to an actor or writer happily, that in other words "they're all alike." He gave Norman Mailer and J. Baldwin as examples, but is Philip really like them?

This is the only entry in Maggie's journal that alludes to the urine fraud.

CHAPTER
Nineteen

During his summer in Amagansett two years earlier, Roth had befriended an older couple, Herman and Nina Schneider. Herman was almost the same age as the other Herman, Philip's father, and had come a long way from his childhood on the mud floor of a shtetl hut in Poland. A former science teacher in the New York public schools, he'd become a wealthy man when the Schneider Science Series had been adopted as textbooks by boards of education in New York, Texas, and elsewhere—its eighty-plus titles including *How Big Is Big? From Stars to Atoms, a Yardstick for the Universe* and *Let's Look under the City: Water, Gas, Waste, Electricity, Telephone.* Herman provided the science, and his charming, worldly wife wrote the prose. Both adored Roth, who, once he fled to New York, was given the run of their elegant West Eleventh Street town house—the model for the Ringolds' town house in *I Married a Communist*; likewise the Ringolds' high-powered parties were reminiscent of those given by Nina, a *salonnière* who entertained such diverse luminaries as Mark Rothko, Alger Hiss, and Leonard Boudin. Meanwhile Roth was delighted by Herman's goatishness despite his considerable seniority. The older man liked to tell Roth about picking up women at the Metropolitan Museum, and Roth, for his part, made no secret of what was arguably his only hobby.

Free of Maggie that spring of 1963, he endeavored to make up for lost time. For the next two years or so, he would go to more parties than perhaps in the rest of his years combined—this for the usual reason single people go to parties. He loved, at least, the first and last part of the dating ritual that ensued: arriving early at a young woman's apartment so he could watch her getting dressed; the undressing later. His first girlfriend that spring was Susan, from a rich Jewish family on the Upper East Side; she and Roth liked to splash around in his bathtub at the Warwick.

Susan was soon replaced by another Susan, a *New Yorker* employee who was the granddaughter of a famous Jazz Age writer. The second Susan was followed by a voluptuous Yugoslav Italian (who was also dating the actor Marcello Mastroianni), until, as Roth vaguely recalled, their affair ended with a pensive conversation on the front steps of her brownstone.

Roth liked watching them dress and undress, but not so much waking up with them later, and sometimes they just made him anxious or left him cold. "Actually I find I am really in something of a deep freeze," he wrote Baker, a state of affairs Kleinschmidt evoked with an anecdote in "The Angry Act": "[H]e picked up a girl at a party and went to her apartment but suddenly felt an acute lack of desire, ushered in by a feeling of estrangement. He excused himself politely and left, worried that he might have hurt the girl's feelings by not sleeping with her." It didn't take an eminent disciple of Freud to discern the most immediate cause of Roth's malaise. Late at night, alone at the Warwick, he was often awakened by phone calls from his estranged, drunken wife. *"You're in bed with a Negress!"* she'd shout.

■ ■ ■ ■

R. P. BLACKMUR EXTENDED Roth's appointment as writer in residence for one more year, at Roth's request, despite there being a degree of hard feelings over the fact that Roth was no longer, technically speaking, "in residence" at Princeton. On Mondays he'd arrive by train for that day's class, and, since he had to teach another class Tuesday morning, he often spent the night at the Tumins' apartment on Prospect Street. This also meant sitting down for dinner with Mel, his wife, Sylvia, and their sons, Jonathan and Zachary, aged twelve and nine. "A meal with Mel was either straight-out lecture or a Socratic dialogue," Roth recalled, "for me no less than for his kids." Afterward the boys would adjourn to their rooms for homework and bed, and Mel would continue haranguing Roth about, say, the war in Vietnam (he was in favor) or the categorical rightness of Israel versus her enemies. Sometimes it got noisy but usually ended with laughter, and for many years the Tumins were the only people—aside from immediate family and Roth's girlfriend at a given time—whose birthdays he always made a point of remembering.

As seldom as possible Roth would stop by Bayard Lane to retrieve a few belongings for safekeeping at the Padded Wagon Storage Company, or to see Helen and say a few civil words to his wife, with whom he still hoped to reach an amicable settlement despite her brutally threatening phone calls. Meanwhile, at Princeton, Maggie was gaining a reputation as a "loose cannon," according to Betty Fussell. "She was less restrained, repressed, or undamaged than the rest of us, and in her language as in her actions she called a spade a spade. 'Come on, I've seen the way you dance with Dave'"—McFarlane, a writer friend of the Fussells—"'why don't you fuck him, for chrissake?'" Maggie's elaborate boldness about sex, Betty thought, was a matter of insecurity to some extent: it made her seem sophisticated among people who intellectually intimidated her, all the more now that her brilliant husband was out of the picture. Her friend Betty, for one, was mostly entertained by it, though she admonished Maggie not to screw her husband, Paul—though Maggie did anyway, repeatedly, each time affecting to be vaguely sorry. And really it was just a question of whoever happened to be available. One night, when Paul was away, Maggie visited Betty and got too drunk to drive home; after a few minutes on their sofa bed, she tottered upstairs and weepily asked Betty if she could get in bed with her. In a maternal spirit her hostess consented, whereupon Maggie put the woman's hand between her legs. Betty demurred and Maggie finished on her own, then wobbled to her feet and paused in the lighted doorway before returning downstairs. "For a long time," said Fussell, "that was my image of Maggie, a long, thick torso on short but sturdy legs, silhouetted against a backlight of trouble."

When the semester ended, Roth endeavored to put as many miles as possible between himself and trouble. Happily he'd been invited by the Israeli government to participate, all expenses paid, in a four-day symposium on Jewish literary and cultural issues; the other three Americans attending were the journalist Max Lerner, Leslie Fiedler, and Roth's supporter for the Daroff Award, David Boroff. "I will go anywhere people are nice to me," said Roth, who planned to linger in Israel for a few weeks after the symposium (as the government had urged him to do), then spend the rest of the summer "someplace pleasant in Europe."

The four Americans warmed up for their first public discussion— re the alienation of the Jewish American intellectual—in the office of David Ben-Gurion, who'd tendered his resignation as prime minister the day before (June 16). Sitting with his guests around a conference table, Ben-Gurion affably remarked that alienation wasn't a problem in Israel, and suggested the others immigrate en masse. "Why should we, Mr. Prime Minister?" Roth respectfully inquired, and Ben-Gurion rose to his feet and pointed out the window: "You see that street? It's a Jewish street. See that tree? It's a Jewish tree. See that bird? It's a Jewish bird." Roth would attribute the gist of these remarks to Mr. Elchanan, a Haifa welder in *The Counterlife*, and would quote Ben-Gurion *qua* himself in the same novel: "Remember, this isn't yours," the latter whispers to Zuckerman when the two shake hands for a photographer, "—it's for your parents, to give them a reason to be proud of you." Needless to say, Bess and Herman kept the framed photo of their much maligned son and the founder of Israel on a side table in their living room for the rest of their days.

The symposium rotated among auditoriums in Jerusalem, Tel Aviv, and Haifa; in later years, Roth could only remember two of his four Israeli counterparts on the panel: the Megged brothers, Aharon and Mattityahu, the second of whom never made good on his promise to take Roth to a Tel Aviv brothel. At any rate, it was the Americans—especially Roth and his fellow Newarkian, Fiedler—who were making headlines with their heterodox views. "Judging from the accounts of the reception of your gang in Israel that were appearing in the New York Times," Solotaroff wrote, "I began to wonder whether all of you would be kidnapped and put on trial under a special new provision of the Law of Return." Apropos of his soi-disant alienation as a Jewish American intellectual, Roth pointed out that he felt the same intense feelings about "the Negro problem" as less alienated Jews, who, however, didn't seem to be taking the lead in offering any kind of concerted aid ("which is not just twenty rabbis going to Birmingham"). When an Israeli professor countered that "you American Jews have lost the impetus of Jewish values," Roth confessed that he was "often confused" by such remarks: "I would very much like to hear what values of a moral nature are exclusively Jewish?" he wondered rhetorically.

2 Jewish Writers Oppose Restraint was the *Times* headline concerning the final session in Tel Aviv, where Roth and Fiedler joined forces in refusing to apologize for writers—preeminently Roth himself—who insisted on creating unsympathetic Jewish characters in their fiction. "I can't let ignorance and prejudice set the framework for my expression,"

said Roth, recapitulating his argument from the Yeshiva University disaster, when he could have used Fiedler as a wingman: "A good honest piece of literature," the critic rallied round, "cannot sustain totalitarianism or abet ignorance because a good piece of literature is in itself a microcosmic utopian state." During the Q&A, an indignant fellow wondered how Roth could contribute to Jewish thought in America without some "knowledge of Jewish history, and of the Hebrew language?" Forbearing to mention his three years at Talmud Torah, Roth replied (as he often would over the course of his career), "I am not a Jewish writer; I am a writer who is a Jew." The audience's response, according to the *Times*, was "disapproving." Another questioner wanted to know whether Roth was enough of a Jew ("even the empty psychological shell") to come to Israel for a prolonged stay: "You could then learn about what is going on here and even create fiction from the experience." Roth said that such research was for the likes of James Michener, whereas "the writer who is serious does not seem to me to pursue subjects or places, but is pursued by them"; twenty years later, however, Roth would be positively Michenerian in his dogged travel to Israel, the better to research aspects of *The Counterlife* and *Operation Shylock*.

Armed with letters of introduction from his Israeli copanelists, Roth spent the next three weeks looking up writers, professors, and kibbutzniks around the country, then proceeded to London for the rest of the summer. A day or two after his arrival, Roth met the ABC radio journalist Rod MacLeish, who offered Roth his apartment on Chelsea Embankment, free of charge, when Roth admitted he'd yet to find permanent lodgings. At loose ends—unable to write, yet cheerful withal given the absence of Maggie—Roth picked up a Chinese prostitute on Curzon Street one morning.* WHEN WRITERS AREN'T WRITING THEY BEHAVE LIKE PEOPLE was a *New York Times Book Review* headline, in August, that seemed to fit such an episode in Roth's life, but instead the roving *Times* photographer had snapped Roth in the act of buying plums and cherries at a London market (reminiscent of Neil Klugman's relish for the Patimkins' fruit), and also captured Bellow erecting a scarecrow in Tivoli, New York, and Capote checking under the hood of his

---

* By his own account, Roth misremembered this encounter in *The Facts* as having occurred during a subsequent trip to London, in 1968.

Jaguar. "Not only am I buying cherries in the New York Times photograph," Roth wrote the Rogerses, "I am also going bald." During that visit to London he'd noticed this unhappy development (after getting an especially short haircut) for the first time; thereafter, whenever he performed cunnilingus, he was "always aware of them looking down on [his] bald head."

Roth had a jolly time in London. His old friend from that first summer in Amagansett, Mordecai Richler, was living there with his wife, Florence, and introduced Roth to their bibulous social circle. He also forged an enduring friendship with the writer Julian Mitchell, who drove Roth all over England—to Bath, Stonehenge, and Gloucestershire to have dinner with Mitchell's parents—while Roth regaled him with a furious rant about his ghastly marriage. Mitchell would never again see his friend so vexed, though he noted that Roth, when young, remained hilarious and lovable even in anger ("a shining clever man"). By the end of the summer, indeed, Roth was in "recovery," he wrote Solotaroff. "With goose flesh, and trepidation, I say I'm healing!"

■ ■ ■ ■

HE SHOULD HAVE STAYED in England. On September 18, he returned to New York and was welcomed home with a party given by Random House for their celebrated young author. Things went precipitously downhill from there. In Israel, Roth had made friends with the actor Michael "Mendy" Wager—married to Henry Fonda's ex-wife, Susan, though mainly gay and even (as he confessed one night over the phone) in love with Roth—who arranged for Roth to sublet a friend's third-floor walk-up on West Sixty-eighth Street near the park. The apartment's owner was another gay actor whose walls were covered with autographed glossies; almost every night strangers would ring the doorbell downstairs, and Roth would wearily inform them via intercom that the owner was out of town. ("What about you, sweetheart?" one man inquired. "You sound kind of cute.") It was in this two-room apartment that Roth heard the news that President Kennedy had been shot. After assuring his father that he himself was fine, Roth took a long walk around "spookily quiet" Manhattan, chatting now and then with other stunned pedestrians.

While Roth had been abroad, his wife had boiled. "Where have I been?"

she wrote in her journal. "Why haven't I realized this? Philip doesn't *care* for *me*—he's *sorry* for me. It's the plight of the poor grass widow and her children that has reached him—not *me* personally—my god! It seems so plain now, how have I mistaken this before? Is this a product of analysis? I wish I could go away. It's so denigrating, I feel as though I haven't been *here* for six years." Galvanized by this bitter epiphany, Maggie brought action against Roth on June 4, charging him with abandonment and non-support, even though he'd been sending her the considerable sum of $100 a week plus monthly rent ($212.50) since his departure in March. In fact, against every conceivable sign to the contrary, Roth still hoped they could be reasonable about things—a view his first lawyer didn't share. A "reality instructor" à la Himmelstein in *Herzog* ("Sonofabitch. They'll put a meter on your nose, and charge you for breathing"), this man was represented as "Mr. Fuck Her Up the Ass Before She Fucks You" in a therapeutic playlet Roth wrote.* "Take all the money out of the bank," the lawyer advises, "because if you don't she will."

> THE GUILTY DESERTER [*crossed out; "Husband" scribbled above*]: But I can't. I promised her I would take care of her. She is hysterical. Maybe if I am nice to her now she will be nice to me later.
>
> MR. FUCK HER UP THE ASS: She'll cut your balls off. She'll rip them from your bleeding carcass and then jump on them with high-heeled shoes.
>
> ME [*crossed out; "Mr. Blank" scribbled above*]: No. She won't. She isn't that kind of woman. . . .
>
> MR. FUCK HER UP THE ASS: Horseshit. If I were her lawyer I would say, "Him? He must be worth a fortune. Pardon me Mrs. Blank, but my suggestion to you is take every penny the son of a bitch has got."

This man's advice would prove prescient; nonetheless Roth sought more temperate counsel at Weil, Gotshal & Manges (recommended by Bennett Cerf), who charged him $1,500 within the first month or so.

---

* In an interview with his biographer, Roth suggested the playlet was highly autobiographical.

That summer he'd also shelled out $312.50 to send Helen to Camp Chateaugay—in the Adirondacks near the Canadian border—owned by a Smith College sociologist, Peter Rose, a friend of the Tumins. The day after Helen's departure, Maggie traveled to another rental house in Wellfleet, even though its owner had been informed by Weil, Gotshal & Manges that the Roths had separated, and therefore the house should be rerented to another party. While the owner retained Roth's $475 deposit, Maggie stayed the rest of the summer, entertaining the Styrons and sundry others, while reminding her husband's Random House editor, Joe Fox, that she'd soon be submitting an outline for a satirical anthology they'd discussed, edited by her and including her husband's work; Fox was also looking into the possibility of getting her a Random House job that would allow her to work from home—this in accord, Fox thought, with Roth's own wishes.

To Fox she didn't mention that she'd alerted the sheriff, in Princeton, of her husband's intentions to flee to Israel, Meyer Lansky–like, and thus evade his obligations to wife and daughter; hoping to detain him at the airport, she'd interrogated Kleinschmidt and others as to his itinerary, until the drama became part of the "Princeton scuttlebutt," as Roth recalled, and the Tumins were able to warn him in time. "[T]his cunning Jew left three days before announced," he wrote Solotaroff from London, "and saved his life, I suppose. I might have killed her [in the States]. Here I say loudly Fuck Her." Maggie continued to take a wily approach with Joe Fox, advising the editor to spare Philip's feelings—despite Fox's misgivings about being less than "aboveboard"—and refrain from revealing that it was Fox himself who'd put her in touch with the top-gun matrimonial lawyer Vincent J. Malone, who was then representing Dr. James Murphy in his divorce from the future Happy Rockefeller. "The first error was to ask you about an attorney in the first place," Maggie wrote Fox, quasi-contritely, "and I had no intention of speaking to you about it when I called; it was just that I was so upset and out of control, and how the hell does one find those guys anyway?"

As Mr. Fuck Her Up the Ass had predicted, Maggie immediately moved to sequester Roth's property in the State of New York, including their joint account at the Greenwich Savings Bank with a balance of $6,806.89. Mel Tumin invited Roth to hide his money by opening an account under Tumin's name, and meanwhile Roth had managed to abscond with the balance of another joint account at the Bank of New York, which he deposited at the Israel Discount Bank (Tel Aviv branch). Thus he could go on paying for Helen's psychotherapy, which he'd recommended in the first place, while also contributing to Ronald's tuition at Morgan Park Academy. Around this time Maggie estimated for the court that she would henceforth require a monthly budget of $1,500— that is, $18,000 a year, or roughly $151,000 in 2020 dollars.

Shortly after moving to the Warwick, Roth had informed his parents of the separation and arranged to meet Herman for lunch in New York. Though usually distressed by news of domestic discord, and certainly by the prospect of divorce, Herman seemed at peace with this particular case; he offered to loan his son money (refused) and bucked him up generally. Nor did he say a word, later, about a disturbing visit from Maggie at his Maple Shade office that summer, while Philip was in Israel. "That's between you and my son," said Herman, when she appeared unannounced and began berating him about Philip's alleged failure to support her. "The little shakedown artist was here," Herman remarked afterward to Sandy, who waited until Herman was dead to relate the episode to Philip. That summer, too, Maggie forged a letter on Philip's Princeton stationery to gain access to his storage compartment at the Padded Wagon and remove some of the furniture. As for Roth's collection of books and records, she steadily refused to return them until, a year or two later, she claimed they'd been destroyed in a fire.[*]

In August, an agitated Maggie phoned Roth in London. Without a word Helen had flown directly from camp (out of Montreal) to Chicago; now she was with her father and refused to return. Roth was also upset by the news and subsequently phoned Helen and calmly discussed the matter, thereby learning that Maggie hadn't once visited her daughter at camp that summer, though Helen had repeatedly asked and Maggie was hardly burdened with responsibility otherwise. Meanwhile the girl's great-aunt, Bea Walton, had offered to pay tuition at a boarding school in Kenosha, Kemper Hall, where the Waltons lived right across the

---

[*] At this point it goes without saying, perhaps, that she either appropriated or sold whatever she could of her husband's belongings. For $500 in 2020 one could buy a copy of Starbuck's *Bone Thoughts* (1960), via Amazon, inscribed "To Phil and Maggie, who said just the best thing about it. / George."

street from campus. In her subsequent affidavit, Maggie represented her daughter's abandonment as being the result of a surreptitious plot concocted by Roth and the girl's therapist, Shirley Van Ferney.

That winter Maggie moved to New York, where the divorce laws were congenial to her cause and she could supplement her alimony with a publishing job; soon she was working fifteen hours a week for her old employer, Harper & Row, and living on Sixtieth Street between Park and Lexington. Roth, in turn, parted company with Weil, Gotshal & Manges and hired the more affordable Shirley Fingerhood, whom he'd met a few years earlier when she was dating a friend of his, the cartoonist Jules Feiffer. With no-nonsense aplomb, Fingerhood dealt with the many creditors Maggie had left behind in Princeton, among them her psychiatrist, Dr. Guttman ($1,575), the Nassau-Conover Motor Company ($294.45), and the Cousins Liquor Company (unspecified), whose attorney Fingerhood reminded that "a husband is responsible only for debts incurred by his wife for necessaries and then only where he has not given her sufficient monies to pay for her own necessaries. . . . Accordingly, we do not have to come to the question as to whether or not liquor is a necessary."

While the court considered Maggie's request for $18,000 a year plus $6,000 in counsel fees,* Roth submitted an affidavit in which he revealed that his wife had not only tricked him into marriage, but had engaged in at least one well-known adulterous affair with a friend of theirs (who might have been Paul Fussell or various others, though Roth didn't name names).

> Her recourse to falsehood and deceit as a means of having her way, regardless of the interests or integrity of others; her violent rages of a sort that finally so frightened her child that the child sought refuge elsewhere; her demanding and unrealistic attitudes of the very kind that lead her now to suggest $18,000 as a minimum amount with which she must be

---

* A total amount almost equal to Roth's gross 1963 income of $25,064.99—one of his best earning years ever, given the confluence of royalty earnings for *Letting Go* with Princeton income. Over the next three years (until he signed his next book contract), his earnings would steadily decline until they were almost half his early-1960s peak.

supported—all of these characteristics of hers made married life with her a nightmare.

"My husband, Philip Roth, has attempted to portray himself as a simple naive soul who was tricked into a marriage which he did not seek and which I, portrayed as a woman of the world, desired," Maggie replied, blithely scornful and unconstrained by the truth where it didn't suit her. She flatly denied that she'd resorted to "subterfuge" in forcing Roth to marry her, alleging (falsely) that they'd been "engaged for two years"; as for his claim that she'd been unfaithful, she denied it "without equivocation" and pointed out that he himself had "shocked" their friends with his philandering, "even going so far as to make the abhorrent boast that as a result of his excesses"—that is, in London—"he suffered from prostatitis." She appended the card from Alice Denham ("Chicken!") as Exhibit A, along with Helen's recent note to her from Kemper Hall ("My first week of school has gone very smoothly althouth [sic] we have had a lot of school work"), by way of belying Roth's claim that she and Helen were estranged. After due consideration, the court awarded Maggie $150 a week in temporary alimony and set a trial date for April 13, 1964, when Roth hoped to get that figure reduced, amid the "foul and filthy" business of airing malfeasances both real and fabricated.

WALKED OUT ON THE PLATINUM! blared the headline on page 3 of the New York *Daily News*, accompanied by a photograph of the grim-faced blonde plaintiff, decked out in black. "Under questioning by her lawyer, Vincent J. Malone, the petite, attractive and 30ish Margaret estimated that her husband makes between $30,000 and $40,000 a year from his salary as English prof at Princeton, royalties from his two books, *Goodby, Columbus* [sic] and *Getting On* [sic!], and magazine writing." Such testimony echoed Maggie's earlier contention that Roth had had "two best-selling novels published by Random House," although (as Roth subsequently countered) *Goodbye, Columbus* was in fact a story collection that hadn't been published by Random House and was hardly a best seller. With such claims of Uris-like wealth, however, Maggie had enticed the high-powered Malone to take her on in the first place, and Roth remembered the man's interest visibly waning when Roth, the defendant ("tall, dark and handsome as well as talented," noted the

Daily News), testified that his earning potential was never as great as advertised, and nowadays was decidedly on the downtick. The presiding judge, Samuel Coleman—a small, twinkly man of seventy or so, who seemed to be enjoying himself—asked Roth how much he got for a film script, since his wife had mentioned that Play Pix Productions wanted to make a movie of *Letting Go* for an exorbitant fee. Roth replied that Play Pix had offered an *option* in the amount of five thousand dollars but nothing had come of it; as for his own script writing, well, he didn't actually write for the movies, so it was hard to say. "Tell me, Mr. Roth," Coleman pursued, "how much *would* they pay you to write a film script?" "I don't know, Your Honor." "Guess." "I suppose about twenty-five thousand dollars." "And how much do you get paid by those magazines you write stories for?" "It depends on the magazine. If I publish a story in the *Partisan Review*, I make twenty-five dollars." Here the judge's playfulness was replaced by indignation: "You're an intelligent young man. You teach at Princeton University. You're a writer—don't you want to succeed? Somebody offers you twenty-five dollars for what you write, somebody offers you twenty-five thousand dollars? Which do you choose?" Fingerhood gave her client a monitory look, but instead of staying calm and indulging the judge, Roth embarked on "a high-minded lecture on high art"—with the result that alimony remained fixed at $150 for the foreseeable future.

■　■　■　■

By then Roth was seeing Kleinschmidt four times a week at $27.50 a session; asked in later years how he'd benefited from analysis, Roth would reply, "It kept me from killing my first wife." Lovingly, on Kleinschmidt's couch, he would reprise his plan to buy a hunting knife at Hoffritz, on Madison Avenue, then wait in the shadows outside her apartment and stab her to death when she came out. Kleinschmidt would sigh: "Philip, you didn't like the army that much. How will you enjoy prison?"

One day, Roth was teaching *Death in Venice* to the twelve young men in his Princeton seminar when the door swung open and there was Maggie. "I have to talk to you," she said. Roth joined her in the hallway and led her over to the third-floor stairwell. "You ever pull a trick like this again," he said, "I'll throw you down the fucking stairs." Turning away, Roth noticed he'd failed to secure the door behind him; his students were staring down at their books. Roth returned to class and shut the door. "Death in Princeton," he said.

His old friend George Elliott from the Iowa Workshop, for one, implored Roth never again to speak to Maggie outside the presence of lawyers. "Poor lost soul, she needs, now, nothing so much as to be confirmed in her secret opinion of herself," he wrote. "She forces everyone close to repudiate her, betray her, destroy her. . . . I fear there is only one possible relief for her torment now, death." Meanwhile Maggie persisted in trying to arrange a private meeting with Roth. Shortly after the Princeton incident, she phoned to say she was willing to divorce him but needed to discuss it in person. Roth suggested she take it up with his lawyer, but she insisted: "Do you or don't you want a divorce?" "Of course I do." "Then let's sit down together and talk about it." Tantalized in spite of himself, Roth invited her over; a few minutes later she arrived, sat down, and calmly announced, "I'll never divorce you." Roth told her to get out, but she only kept repeating "I'll never divorce you." Finally he tried dragging her to the door, but she clung to the legs of the chair and began screaming "Let me go! Let me go!" He dropped her near the fireplace and grabbed a poker: "I'm going to bring this fucking thing down on your head," he said—or so he told it in one version. Unlike a similar scene in *My Life as a Man*, however, he didn't proceed to beat her with a poker or his hands, and she didn't foul herself in the process. She either phoned her lawyer from Roth's apartment ("Philip tried to beat me"), or simply threatened to and began weeping until, at last, she left. About an hour later Fingerhood called to say that Maggie's lawyer was going to file an assault charge; she advised Roth to leave town for a few days.

Further in keeping with how George Elliott had envisaged things, Maggie promptly tried to kill herself again, or at least to take enough pills to make it seem that way. (She later told a friend and coworker that she'd "made sure somebody would find her.") Roth was lying low in Bradley Beach when he got the news from Fingerhood, whereupon he packed his things and paid his wife a visit at Roosevelt Hospital ("I cannot fathom my motive for doing so"). To the best of his recollection, when she came to, he actually said to her à la Peter Tarnopol, "You are in Hell," and she faintly replied, "Oh, delicious, if you're here too."

She wanted a few toilet articles from her apartment, and Roth volunteered to get them. A cop was posted at the door, which had been broken in the act of forcing it open; Roth identified himself and was allowed to enter. Again like Tarnopol, he found two intriguing items in the bedside table: a long-handled can opener he presumed was used for masturbation, and a light blue spiral notebook, her journal, that he hoped would contain evidence of the urine fraud. However, he found only the one allusion about "confessing to Philip" (mentioned above); as for the rest of it, he would reproduce several entries almost verbatim in *My Life as a Man*; in life as in art, he was puzzled and even a little stung by the journal's banality: "about as interesting on the subject of a woman's life as *Dixie Dugan*. . . . In one so cunning, how bizarre!"* As for the can opener, Roth kept it for a long time and later claimed (facetiously) to have considered giving it to his archive at the Library of Congress.

---

* In most cases I've tried to cull only the most telling, pertinent, and perceptive passages in Maggie's journal, and hence may have inadvertently misrepresented the basic tenor of what is, indeed, a pretty insipid piece of writing.

S HORTLY AFTER HE RETURNED FROM LONDON, ROTH struck up a friendship with the theater critic and Columbia professor Robert (Bob) Brustein and his wife, Norma, an actress, and soon fell into a routine of eating dinner almost weekly at their stately apartment on East Eighty-fifth. "You two bailed me out of a lot of loneliness," he wrote Bob many years later, remembering how the couple would patiently listen into the wee hours while Roth fulminated over his wife's iniquities. Roth was a few years younger than the couple—a "loony" little brother, said Bob, who could be counted on for laughs whatever his mood otherwise. Roth, in turn, was so dependent on sanctuary *chez* Brustein that he even showed up for a dinner party that had been scheduled—and tacitly canceled—on the night of the great blackout of 1965: "He arrived just on time," Brustein recalled, "having solved the dead subway problem by walking up two miles of dark streets and the dead elevator problem by walking up eight flights of stairs."

Through Brustein he met another funny Jewish guy, Albert Goldman, one of Brustein's Columbia colleagues, who'd recently begun reviewing pop music for *Life*. Brustein had met Goldman in a graduate seminar taught by Lionel Trilling; a besuited dandy with carefully oiled hair, Goldman delivered a paper on Beethoven's last quartets that left Trilling and the others rather stunned by its brilliant-seeming abstruseness. Outside of class, however, Goldman "turned into this completely other guy," said Brustein. Cackling, Goldman told his fellow grad students that he supported himself by selling shingling jobs door to door—that is, by absconding with his customers' down payments for purely speculative services. He and Roth had come from the kind of Jewish families that nurture neuroses and comic brio, and would shout over each other at the Brustein dinner table while other guests poured onto the floor laughing.

Explaining a hand tremor, Goldman said his mother used to make him pick his father's pocket. Sometimes, too, he would seem to hear this same woman's voice (though she lived in Santa Monica) while eating his morning egg at Mayhew's, a diner in the East Sixties: "Albert, your father and I have been worried sick about you!" Goldman would look up and see Roth "glaring at [him] maniacally": "Two weeks and not a word. How is it a writer, a person who sits all day behind a typewriter, can't put two words together to send to a mother who lives three thousand miles away?"

Ten years later Goldman would make his reputation with a brilliant biography, *Ladies and Gentlemen—Lenny Bruce!!,** and meanwhile he also shared his interest in rock 'n' roll with Roth, taking him along for concerts by the likes of Jimi Hendrix, Janis Joplin, and the Fugs. One night, soon after *Portnoy* was published, he took Roth backstage at Madison Square Garden for an interview with B. B. King; Roth chatted a while before leaving to claim their seats, and, as Goldman told him afterward, King looked around at his entourage, rubbed Roth's seat, and said, "That guy just made a million dollars from *writin' a book.*"

Through his friendships with like-minded Jews, Roth rediscovered something that the scourge of Maggie had almost made him forget: he was a funny guy. With Goldman he discussed a Genet-like play he wanted to write, *The Terrace*, about a brothel for nice Jewish boys: a motherly whore would bathe and powder you, then put you in Dr. Denton kiddie pajamas and tuck you into bed, where you'd fall asleep listening to "a little radio with an orange dial." The next morning a soft voice would call, "Wake up, dear, it's time to get up." For that, said Roth, he'd gladly pay fifty bucks a night. Another venue for such monologues was the Hotel des Artistes apartment of the Epsteins, Jason and Barbara—he an editor at Random House, she an editor at *The New York Review of Books.* Either solo or in tandem with the equally zany Jules Feiffer, Roth would sing and sing for his supper, riffing on Shakespeare and/or the dangers of answering a doorbell in New York. More and more, too, Roth was indulging in the pleasures of "reckless narrative disclosure" that he'd discovered on Kleinschmidt's couch. One day, with Brustein and Feiffer, he

---

* A reputation that was unmade, to some extent, by the less creditable biographies of Elvis Presley and John Lennon that followed.

was standing in the water at Lambert's Cove Beach on Martha's Vineyard, when, apropos of nothing, he began holding forth on the subject of masturbation. "It was truly gut-breaking, funny and shocking," recalled Feiffer, who almost drowned laughing. As for Brustein and his wife, their copy of *Portnoy* would be aptly inscribed, "To Bob and Norma, who encourage me in this madness."

Roth began tentatively mining this vein in his work, despite his post-Yeshiva vow never to write about Jews again. In early 1963 he started work on a madcap fantasy titled *The Last Jew* or *The Jewboy*, which he described to Bob Baker as "very promising, and very funny, and highly invented, and therein—the invention—lies the problem. How much is too much, etc?" That indeed was the question. The titular Jewboy is an orphan named Heshie who's left in a shoe box at a Jewish old-age home, where he's summarily circumcised by an ancient mohel. Over the next two hundred pages or so, Heshie is adopted by every manner of Jewish parent, including various mothers, a milkman, and a rich gangster, Taback, who teaches him that good rye bread is better than cake, and startles the boy by offering him shrimp. "What am I, Chinese?" says Taback, when Heshie mentions that he is, after all, a Jew. "Don't you have a good time with me?"

> "Life," said Heshie, "life—"
> "What about life?"
> "It isn't just good times," the boy finally got out.
> "Oh no? What else is it?"

By the end, the boy seems about to embrace Taback's philosophy, lighting out on skates across a frozen Newark lake in pursuit of a shiksa called Thereal McCoy. "Don't!" one of his stepfathers calls after him. "You're skating on thin ice!" Heedlessly speeding ahead, Heshie replies, "Oh, you dope, Daddy, that's only an expression," as the ice begins cracking around him.

"You are a very funny Jew," Joe Fox wrote Roth of *The Jewboy*, confessing however that he found the surrealism puzzling in parts. "Why Jesus and Mary?" he inquired of a digressive bit of shtick updating the Christmas story; in Roth's version, the innkeeper calls the cops on Joseph, who's startled when the police captain challenges him to compare testicles: "I'll bet you anything you want that for sheer hang and weight, the average Gentile has got balls on him that run from one and a half to two times larger than the average Jew." Roth marked this section with a folding tab of paper labeled "BALLS" (he would, in fact, find use for it later), and put the rest of the manuscript aside forever, give or take the odd detail. As he later explained, *The Jewboy* "tended to cover with a patina of wacky inventiveness material quite interesting in itself and, as in certain types of dreams and folktales, intimated much more than I knew how to confront head-on in a fiction."

In the two-plus years since *Letting Go*, he'd managed to complete a total of three stories for publication, and the most recent two were neither funny nor inventive. Moreover he wasn't writing about Jews, at least publicly, unless you count the offstage analyst Spielvogel, about whom Roth was considering a series of stories: "Like the York cycle of mystery plays," he said, "a lot of people would have this doctor, but you'd never see him." Spielvogel would, of course, emerge as the silent auditor of Alex Portnoy, but meanwhile he was mercifully dropped after a single bad story—"real shit," said Roth—that appeared in the November 1963 *Esquire*, "The Psychoanalytic Special." Inspired by Roth's mooning over the loss of Lucy Warner while riding a thrice-weekly train from Princeton to see Kleinschmidt, the story gives us the maundering thoughts of Ella Wittig, as she too mourns the loss of a lover, Perry, while stuck with a merely dull husband, Michael. That adultery can make a bad marriage bearable was a theme Roth would revisit more memorably throughout his life and work; as for "The Psychoanalytic Special," it deserves a decent burial amid the microfilm holdings.

The same may be said more emphatically of "An Actor's Life for Me," about another unhappy married couple, Juliet and Walter Appel, who comfort themselves with delusions of artistic talent. *Playboy*, perhaps, was paying Roth by the word—certainly he needed the money—which might explain why this static idea is belabored at such eerie length: eleven fine-print, multicolumn pages. Juliet despairs of acting and tries her hand at playwriting, whereas Walter despairs of playwriting and takes a job "in the business end of the theater"; thus Juliet affects to work on her play each night, while Walter notices (and notices and notices) a naked man peeping at her from an opposite window. "He should have forced her to have a child long ago," Walter reflects, but doesn't act until an umpteenth sighting of the naked man causes both of them to realize, at long last, that they might as well resign themselves to a more mundane, nonartistic domesticity: "he mounted Juliet," the story ends, "[and] proceeded to reproduce himself."

The witty prodigy who wrote the stories in *Goodbye, Columbus* had lost his way, and was himself pondering an alternative career as a playwright. Encouraged by Brustein and Howard Stein, Roth applied for a one-year Ford Foundation program intended to bring "established writers in nondramatic forms into formal association with the theater and . . . ultimately to improve the quality of plays and scripts available to American directors, actors and producers." Winning the fellowship was a foregone conclusion for one of the best fiction writers of his generation, though Roth was disgruntled when the foundation saw fit to reduce his grant to $7,500 because of his separation from Maggie, cutting the $1,500 spouse allowance that would have covered all of ten weeks of alimony. Nor was he thrilled at the prospect of being "in residence" at the American Place Theatre on West Forty-sixth, as the fellowship required, the better for him to learn "stage problems and the requirements of dramatic writing" by watching other people's plays. "It don't sound like fun," Roth morosely wrote Baker; "and if something else turns up I may wind up telling them to shove it."

But nothing much did, so Roth again turned to playwriting. His first efforts were one-act farces in the fanciful mode of *The Jewboy*. *The Fishwife* takes place in "the near future," and reflects Roth's obsessive skepticism toward marriage. The middle-aged Howard is dismayed when his young wife, Gloria, announces she is taking a second husband in keeping with their brave new world of legalized polygamy. Because neither spouse can entirely requite the needs of the other, Gloria is affianced to a tango instructor while Howard admits he's been secretly seeing a slatternly woman who shares his love of fish (Howard abhors tango dancing, Gloria fish). "Enough guilt," he proclaims in the end. "Enough hating of our own authentic selves. . . . I see life stripped of the sham and the sanctimony, of the deceit and the hypocrisy, of all the poison and the ugliness—the smallness." When Gloria takes him at his word, however, and mentions the prospect of a third husband, Howard is shocked and dismayed all over again.

Roth's other farce, *Buried Again*, was "longer and more interesting" than

The Fishwife, or so Roth thought at the time. A dead Jewish man, Weingast, appears before a reincarnation panel—four vaguely sinister types,
including a woman with "a heavy Germanic accent" (Roth had Hannah
Arendt in mind) and a bland goyish "Chairman" (Eisenhower)—who
offer to return Weingast to earth as a gentile. Amid steadily increasing
rancor on both sides, Weingast insists he wants nothing better than to
resume his quiet life as a New Jersey Jew, until the panel flatly asserts
that "mankind has had enough of Jews." "Goys!" Weingast erupts. "You
goy bastards!"—whereupon the panelists rise and begin banging gongs
behind them, a gathering clamor that culminates in "a long horrible loud
unmusical sound, a little longer than is bearable." The end. Looking
back over the decades at such efforts as *Buried Again* and *The Fishwife*,
Roth decided that "nobody has ever written worse plays than me." Pause.
"Maybe Henry James."

■ ■ ■ ■

CHEEVER AND ROTH had kept occasionally in touch since the *Esquire*
symposium a few years back, and in February 1964 Roth took a train to
Ossining to spend a weekend with Cheever's family. Cheever recorded
some impressions in his journal:

> Young, supple, gifted, intelligent, he has the young man's air of regard-
> ing most things as if they generated an intolerable heat. I don't mean
> fastidiousness, but he holds his head back from his plate of roast beef as
> if it were a conflagration. He is divorced from a girl I thought delectable.
> "She won't even give me back my ice skates." The conversation hews to a
> sexual line—cock and balls, Genet, Rechy—but he speaks, I think, with
> grace, subtlety, wit.

A month or so later, after the National Book Award ceremony, the
Cheevers invited Roth to join them for dinner at Sardi's, where they
also brought an attractive young woman who was herself a promising
writer. The two young people liked each other and slept together once
or twice—then Roth, as was his wont, disappeared. "Mr. Philip Roth /
Institute for Unpredictable Behavior / Next to Edward Albie [sic]" the
woman subsequently addressed a letter written in the form of a research
questionnaire: "1) What happened? 2) Where are we? . . ." She was more

bewildered than offended: Roth had seemed sweet-natured and funny, hardly a cad, but he reared away from romantic attachment as if it were a conflagration (as Cheever would have it).

A more sustained effort would follow with Ann Mudge, a socialite from Pittsburgh who'd been featured that January in the fashion section of the *Times* as one of four Junior Committee members who would model Van Cleef & Arpels jewelry at the Plaza's annual Diamond Ball; the other women included the late Gary Cooper's daughter, Maria, and the former Princess Elizabeth of Yugoslavia, Mrs. Howard Oxenberg, who was furious that the *Times* had used Mudge for "the Bitch of the Week picture," as Mudge put it in 2012 (remarking that Mrs. Oxenberg's royal title "and a couple of bucks will get you a cup of coffee"). That spring Mudge and Roth became acquainted at a dinner party given by Bennett Cerf and his wife, where Roth had kept the table amused with his well-polished patter about the spouse who wouldn't give him back his ice skates. In fact he and Mudge had met in passing some five years before, when Roth and Maggie had been among a group of partygoers *chez* Plimpton who'd adjourned to the Vietnamese Lantern for dinner. Mudge had sat next to Bob Silvers, who told her in a low voice who the others were: "That's Philip Roth. He's going to be a very good writer, but he's with that woman and she's going to ruin his life. She's crazy."

Appearing as "May Aldridge" in *The Facts*, the elegant Mudge had attracted Roth in part because she, like Maggie, had seemed "intriguingly estranged from the very strata of American society of which they were each such distinctively emblazoned offspring." Mudge's father was a Pittsburgh steel executive who drank and didn't like Jews, while the mother often reminded Ann and her sisters that men were only interested in their looks. Ann, whose debutante party was featured in *Town & Country*, had a horror of marrying a man like her father and spending the rest of her life at the Pittsburgh Golf Club. After drinking her way out of Bryn Mawr, she ended up at Silver Hill psychiatric hospital in Connecticut. Finally she moved to New York and took occasional work (mainly favors for friends) as an interior decorator; she was also in analysis, which is what she and Roth tended to discuss in the early days of their affair. On and off they'd be together almost five years, during which Roth never once went to Pittsburgh to meet her parents: "He was

Jewish and he wrote dirty books," said Mudge. "I don't think it bothered him too much."

The couple had barely started when Roth blew town to spend most of that summer and part of the fall at Yaddo, in Saratoga Springs—this on the recommendation of Cheever, to whom he'd explained he was about to be broke, what with the end of his Princeton job and nothing else in sight until his Ford Fellowship began on January 1, 1965. Also he desperately needed to be somewhere beyond Maggie's reach, so work could again become the center of his life.* Yaddo would prove Roth's salvation as a writer—a place of placid routine in a sylvan setting, among (mostly) congenial people. After a good night's sleep in the Trask Mansion (no vicious drunken phone calls or any prospect thereof), followed by a quiet communal breakfast, Roth would grab his lunch pail and walk through the woods to his little studio, Hillside Cottage, whence other colonists would hear typing well after most of them had stopped for the day. Roth would break for lunch (his carrot, celery, and half his sandwich long gone) and join the Armenian musician Richard Hagopian at the swimming pool. Hagopian had recently been divorced by a woman who "shoved a red hot poker up his ass," said Roth, "and let it cool there a while," so they had plenty to talk about. Then Roth would work until four or so, take a walk into Saratoga and back, swim laps, play croquet, eat dinner, and return to his lonely but inviolate bed.

There was plenty of swimming, croquet, tennis, and Ping-Pong, but Roth suspected the main sport (for him anyway) was masturbation. "Yaddo is a good place to work, not a bad place to live, and no place at all to carry with you your male part," he reported to Mendy Wager. "But too much really is made of that thing anyway." After a mostly celibate month or so, Roth and the others were joined by a new guest, Gladys Brooks, the seventy-seven-year-old widow of critic Van Wyck Brooks. "There is a very strong likelihood that I will try to go down on her at dinner," Roth wrote Styron. And yet he rather begrudged the odd visit from his own beautiful girlfriend, Mudge, who spent a few weekends at a bed-and-breakfast in town and waited for Roth to phone her. They did all the things one does during summers in Saratoga: the strawberries

---

* Roth was dejected to learn that the Ford Foundation couldn't accommodate his request for a residency as far afield as the Alley Theatre in Houston.

and cream breakfast at the racetrack; the yearling sales in the big barn at night; a drink at the Spuyten Duyvil bar afterward. By Sunday afternoons, though, Roth would be almost beside himself: "You have to leave now! I have to work!" He compensated by writing her letters at least once a week, and for her birthday he sent a singing telegram.

That first summer at Yaddo, Roth befriended Julius Goldstein, a bachelor painter fifteen years his senior, who taught part-time at Hunter College and lived most of the year in a cramped garret in the Village. Goldstein was a witty fellow who shared Roth's enthusiasm for women and baseball. He'd had an affair with the poet Delmore Schwartz's first wife, Gertrude Buckman (whom Roth would later hire as a London tour guide for Bess and Herman), and liked to reminisce about his days on a Manhattan sandlot team, the Yorkville Arrows. He called the southpaw Roth "Lefty," and after reading one of Roth's new books, he'd always preface his remarks with "Well, you put another one over on the public, Lefty." Goldstein was, in fact, a deeply melancholy man whose talk often reverted to the tragedy of his father's death while he was still in utero, and even his lighter moods were tinged with a kind of quibbling sarcasm. One of Roth's later girlfriends, who loved Goldstein, dubbed him Uncle Julio Negativo, and made a point of inviting the lonely man to their house as often as the couple could reasonably bear it.

Another important friendship that summer was with the novelist Alison Lurie, who was married to the critic Jonathan Bishop;* she and Roth formed an attachment based on mutual literary encouragement. Both had published a single novel and wondered whether they would ever publish another. Roth admired Lurie's work and told her she could be the "next mean female novelist after Mary McCarthy," whereas Lurie was so vital to Roth's progress on his second novel that she'd be numbered among the diverse group of post-Maggie supporters to whom *When She Was Good* is dedicated.† Over the next two years Lurie would critique draft after draft of the book Roth had begun soon after finishing

---

* Son of the poet John Peale Bishop, who was perhaps best known for his friendships with F. Scott Fitzgerald and Edmund Wilson.

† The book's dedication: "To my brother Sandy; to my friends Alison Bishop, Bob Brustein, George Elliott, Mary Emma Elliott, Howard Stein, and Mel Tumin; and to Ann Mudge: For words spoken and deeds done."

Letting Go—that is, around the time he'd committed his imagination to exploring non-Jewish themes and hence was trying to make fiction out of Maggie's stories about her desperate youth in South Haven, the daughter of the town drunk. "[Philip] has begun a new story about me," Maggie wrote in her journal on December 28, 1961 (a couple of weeks before Alice Denham's card arrived and Maggie confessed to the urine fraud). "That is, a woman like me with a terrified boy like [Ronald] married to a monster like [Burt]. He's very involved and excited about it. And I am excited too to see how it will work out." The original title was *The Goyim*, no less, with an epigraph supplied by Helen: "When a Jew says *goy*, what is he thinking?" The novel about the grim world of Liberty Center was meant to give an answer to that question, or rather to expose certain truths underlying the usual Jewish stereotypes of gentile life, but Roth had given up on the manuscript "after 200 pages and much sweat."

For a decade or so—beginning with that awful day in January 1962 ("Chicken!")—Roth would be fixated on finding the right narrative vehicle for the urine episode; during the summer of 1962, while separated from Maggie that first time, he'd tried using it in his play *1957: The Taming of the Id*, and also had it in mind for *The Goyim*—but when he revisited the latter, after letting some marital smoke clear, it read "like the work of a lunatic." At Yaddo, then, he'd dismally resigned himself to working on his one-act farces as well as a new version of *Taming of the Id*, but "on a chance" he'd also packed his discarded novel about Liberty Center, now titled *Time Away*. "Suddenly I saw where it was wrong and where it was right," he wrote Baker at the end of 1964, "and late in June started in on it again, working almost every day until the middle of October when I had six chapters of a new draft—that is, the whole book—and four of those chapters rewritten into a nearly final draft." All this in the quiet woods of Saratoga, where he was able to rediscover "good habits of patience" and even something of his old self-confidence.

"Philip, there will always be a bed for you here," said the seventy-nine-year-old director of Yaddo, Elizabeth Ames, when Roth departed in October. A genteel person averse to suffering fools (with whom she was apt to exaggerate her already well-advanced deafness), Ames regarded the handsome, industrious Roth as an "ideal guest," and often made a point of inviting him to tea and sitting beside him at the dinner table. "She was one of those strong, independent, highly competent, intelligent, somewhat reserved, childless women on the order of Mildred Martin who I'd always liked," said Roth, who dedicated *The Breast* as follows: "To ELIZABETH AMES, executive director of Yaddo from 1924 to 1970 and to THE CORPORATION OF YADDO, Saratoga Springs, New York, the best friends a writer could have."

■ ■ ■ ■

PHONE CALLS AT YADDO were fielded by a secretary in the Trask Mansion, and messages were left on a hall table at the end of the day, whereupon they could be returned or ignored as a guest saw fit. Perhaps the last call Roth ever returned to Maggie was sometime in July, during which he mentioned that he needed her to sign a joint tax return that would save him a thousand dollars. "The fucking cocksucking bitch" (as he described her in a subsequent letter to Baker) refused to do so unless Roth agreed to pay the thousand directly to her; rather than comply, Roth decided to "steadily and patiently go broke" between then and January, when he'd return to court and request a reduction of alimony.

Meanwhile he continued to phone Helen in Kenosha every other week, and also sent her a set of monogrammed stationery to encourage her to write. "I want to tank you [sic] so much for the check it will and has gawn to good use," she obliged him, signing her letters, "I miss you and love you very much." That summer Roth had driven her to Camp Chateaugay before heading down to Yaddo—a trip Helen remembered as a little nervous-making given her driver's tendency to lapse into long brooding silences. "You're only boring when you ask me if you're boring me," he assured her, sweetly, and a month later he paid her a visit and was delighted to find her thriving: "Too much to go into here," he wrote Baker afterward, "except to say that she is (for all her fucked-up grades in school) in love with the most intelligent boy in the camp, and reading Kafka, and very intense Joan Baez, and understands Maggie very very well; it took me years to get where she is now, and she's thirteen."

On September 2—a few days before Helen returned to school—Roth drove to the city and took her to a Broadway play (her first), an Actors' Studio production of *Three Sisters*, preceded by dinner at Sardi's. Helen remembered how her mother had lent her a pretty blue dress for the evening, and asked a lot of questions beforehand about where they were going and so forth. At the theater Helen and Roth had just settled into their seats—down front on the aisle (Mendy Wager had gotten them the tickets)—when Roth noticed a genial man with a mustache standing over them: "Mr. Philip Roth?" he inquired, and when Roth nodded the man produced a summons from his inside coat pocket. During intermission Roth left Helen in the lobby with an orange drink and pored over the papers in a toilet stall. "I am really sorry about the upset with the summons," Fingerhood wrote him a week later. "However, that is evidently our friend's way of saying that the offer of settlement which was discussed is unacceptable." Fingerhood made it clear that Maggie's lawyer could as easily have sent the papers directly to her—"but then," Roth noted, "of course the drama and the harassment would have gone out of it."

Roth's final weeks at Yaddo were blighted by two unanswered phone calls from Maggie ("both angry, I am told"), followed by a letter in which she bitterly informed him that her father had been killed the previous weekend but she couldn't go to the funeral because Roth was six weeks behind in alimony. "It happens I am one week ahead," he wrote Lurie, "but the pattern of accusation was so familiar, and the hallucinations, etc. . . . that I haven't been able to come up from under. My head has been pounding for a week; it feels stuffed; and my neck is like stone." Work, as ever, was the sovereign anodyne. Another artifact from his recent visit to Maggie's apartment (after her latest suicide attempt) was a packet of ten-year-old prison letters from Maggie's father to her mother. Roth appropriated a "collage" of quotes for Whitey's sorrowful Valentine's Day letter at the end of *When She Was Good*—the letter found frozen to the cheek of Lucy Nelson's corpse. "To put it bluntly," he wrote of Lucy's real-life model, "I wish she were dead."

A FTER RETURNING FROM YADDO, ROTH MOVED INTO A pleasant second-floor apartment at 9 East Tenth Street, between Fifth and University. Mudge fixed the place up with secondhand furniture she bought at auctions and flea markets on Roth's "pathetic budget," and Roth put off getting a phone as long as possible (he finally allowed himself one with an unlisted number). Determined to avoid the distractions of a busy social life, he was nonetheless within a couple of blocks of his good friends the Schneiders and Julius Goldstein. Roth found a homey, inexpensive Italian restaurant on Houston, Ballato's, where he ate two or three times a week either alone or with Goldstein and one or two others. As Goldstein grumbled to a mutual friend, he always ordered the cheapest thing on the menu and Roth the most expensive; then, when the check arrived, Roth would say, "Let's split it."

In January, Roth reluctantly deferred work on his novel to write plays and watch rehearsals at St. Clement's Church, where the American Place Theatre was located. That year's best production by far was Robert Lowell's *The Old Glory*, a trilogy of one-act adaptations of two Hawthorne stories as well as ("the stellar piece") Melville's "Benito Cereno," with Frank Langella as Cereno and Roscoe Lee Browne as Babo, the leader of the slave rebellion. Lowell was more than a little manic during rehearsals, and Roth distanced himself when the poet obsessively insisted on showing him snapshots of a young Indian woman he was smitten with.

While Roth moonlighted as a playwright, his friend Bob Silvers made him the *New York Review of Books'* "hatchet man in the theater," as Roth put it—at any rate he wrote two long reviews in nine months that were memorable for their provocative disregard of whatever passed for political correctness in those days. Roth's pleasant acquaintance with James Baldwin may have suffered as a result of his assessment of *Blues for Mister Charlie*:

It is soap opera designed to illustrate the superiority of black over whites. . . . They dance better. And they cook better. And their penises are longer, or stiffer. Indeed, so much that comprises the Southern stereotype of the Negro comes back through Negro mouths as testimony to their human superiority, that finally one is about ready to hear that the eating of watermelon increases one's word power.

The other play under review in Roth's first piece ("Channel X: Two Plays on the Race Conflict") was LeRoi Jones's *Dutchman*, about a white woman, Lula, who tauntingly flirts with a black man, Clay, on the subway, and finally stabs him in the heart. In the course of suggesting that the ending is gratuitous—not to say illogical, given the characters' behavior elsewhere in the play—Roth asserted that Clay "is really not Negro enough for us to be told that it is for his being a Negro that he is murdered," and also said hard things about the play's "literary pretension" and "false profundity."

For a white reviewer (a "writer-in-residence at Princeton," no less, as Roth still identified himself when the piece ran) to suggest that an educated, well-mannered black character conceived by a militant black playwright is "not Negro enough" was rash, even in May 1964, whatever the cogency of Roth's argument otherwise. "Sir, it is not my fault that you are so feebleminded you refuse to see any Negro as a man, but rather as the narrow product of your own sterile response," LeRoi Jones's indignant letter to the *New York Review* began.

You can not *categorize* men. If my character is, as you say, "not Negro enough . . .", then that would mean you have a "definition" of what Negroes are.

The main rot in the minds of "academic" liberals like yourself, is that you take your own distortion of the world to be somehow more profound than the cracker's. There is little difference except you guys have hipper cover stories . . . A writer-in-residence, indeed!

Roth's reply was unlikely to lead to cordial feelings between the two Newark writers. He reiterated that Clay ("the Negro character whom I discussed in more than the three words you choose to quote") was inconsistent as written—modest and polite in the first scene, "violently disposed" in the second. He continued:

Though charity might lead me to suggest that some clumsiness in my review caused you to misconstrue my meaning, the rhetoric and reasoning of your letter are sufficient to overwhelm any great flow of generous feelings in me. But then you would make it especially hard for anyone, I think, to trust very far your powers of analysis, literary or otherwise, when you warn emphatically in the first paragraph, "You can not *categorize* men," only to rush on in a second to speak of "the main rot in the minds of 'academic' liberals like yourself."

"I hope to do for the fags this time what I did for the colored last," Roth quipped about his second review, in February 1965, of Albee's *Tiny Alice*. Despite his close friendships with gay men (especially later), Roth could be amazingly tasteless even by the norms of the era; with respect to *Tiny Alice*, however, he couldn't abide the "galling sophistication" and "ghastly pansy rhetoric" of what was evidently meant to be an all but impenetrable allegory of gay life. "How long before a play is produced on Broadway in which the homosexual hero is presented as a homosexual," Roth wrote, "and not disguised as an angst-ridden priest, or an angry Negro"—another dig at LeRoi Jones—"or an aging actress; or worst of all, Everyman?" One reader, Morris Belsnick, subsequently wrote to the editor wondering why Roth had assumed the play's homosexual meaning was "a dirty little secret which Albee cannot face" since, after all, the very title of the play was a well-known gay expression for "a masculine derriere." Roth replied: "If Mr. Belsnick is right about the homosexual argot, and if the pun was intentional, then the play is even worse than I thought it was."

Roth's main writing project for the first six months of his Ford grant—that is, until he resigned—was a revamping of *1957: The Taming of the Id*, now titled *The Nice Jewish Boy*. The main difference is the Maggie character, renamed Lucy* and so much like her real-life counterpart that Lurie warned Roth not to make her so "unrelievedly evil": "She must also be pathetic, desperate, etc.—probably telling herself that the ends justify the means, and that marrying her will be good for Mendy and even save

---

* Instead of Ann, which at the time happened to be the name of the Maggie-like heroine in *When She Was Good*. Once he abandoned *The Nice Jewish Boy* (and *its* Lucy), the heroine of Roth's novel became Lucy.

him, from whatever she thinks he needs saving from." This, of course, could serve as an astute summation of Maggie's own rationale, though it only went so far to mitigate Roth's drastically prejudiced view of things at the time. In one of his later unpublished novels about Maggie and the urine fraud (or rather a novel about trying to write a novel about Maggie, etc.), Zuckerman remembers a failed, *Nice Jewish Boy*–like play featuring his wife "Roberta": "the wicked heroine (wearing Roberta's fierce helmet of blond hair) viciously tricks the unsuspecting hero (wearing my soulful eyes) into their marriage." That was it in a nutshell, and, to be sure, in this second version of the play, Mendy is more guileless and, yes, soulful. "Your love touches me, but I can't return it, that's all," he breaks it to Lucy, quoting Masha's words to Medvedenko in *The Seagull*. Lucy, however, is not one to be mollified by gentle rhetoric, and vows to bear his "illegitimate child" and show the world how "rotten and wicked" he is. In art as in life, the young man collapses, asking only that Lucy tell him he's "good" as the curtain falls: "Oh you are," she says, embracing his head. "You are. You're very very very very good."

The Nice Jewish Boy was sound enough to rate a reading at the American Place Theatre on June 23, 1965; Roth wanted to hear it performed in front of an invited audience, so he'd have a better sense of how to proceed toward a final draft. The director was Gene Saks, and the two lead parts were read by promising off-Broadway actors, Dustin Hoffman and Melinda Dillon. But it was no good. Roth hectored Hoffman to be more "forceful"—his usual desideratum for dramatic portrayals of characters based on himself—but neither man could make the play or its eponymous hero very original or interesting. Roth withdrew it after the reading, and spent a year or so vaguely considering another rewrite before deciding that he disliked the whole collaborative aspect of theater; meanwhile the Ford grant wasn't enough to live on, so he resigned after six months and took a teaching job for the fall.

■ ■ ■ ■

MAGGIE HAD WAITED until after the original separation and alimony decree, in April 1964, to accept a full-time job as a production editor in the College Department at Harper & Row, where she earned $100 a week before taxes. Roth, in turn, had stayed the course toward going broke except for his Ford grant and dwindling royalties from *Let-*

ting Go, and a referee was slated to consider his request for an alimony reduction on June 11, 1965. Maggie had girded herself by firing two lawyers and hiring a third on the basis of his proven ferocity. "I seem to have made an enemy," Roth observed, only a little gratified by the referee's reduction of $40 a week. Fingerhood had given him reason to hope for more, what with Maggie's earnings at Harper; even with reduced alimony, her annual income was now roughly $1,500 more than his, and meanwhile he was forced to borrow $4,000 (at 5¼ percent interest) from Joe Fox, a thousand of which went to pay back a loan to Mel Tumin.

For two years Tumin had been urging Roth to "make a clean, formal break," not only with Maggie but with her entire ménage—even or especially his beloved stepdaughter, Helen, from whom Roth had begun to distance himself after the *Three Sisters* fiasco. "I haven't had a letter from you in quiet [sic] a while," she wrote him early that spring.

> What has happened? Do you dislike me now for being Mrs. Philip Roths [sic] daughter? I am her daughter, but I'm myself also. Philip I love you for what you are and for what you did. If you hadn't it would have been the Fall of My Empire, you know that as well as I do. I know it has been hell for you and maybe still. But we have both wonderful and terrible memories. I have made the wonderful standout from the others and I hope you have too.

Roth's heart was certainly wrung, but he also knew it was a matter of time before Maggie made false claims of sexual impropriety—all the more plausible as the girl continued to bloom. Walking in the park with her mother that previous summer, Helen had innocently related a recent dream in which she married Philip and proved a more compatible wife than Maggie had.

A few days before leaving Kenosha, in June 1965, she wrote asking Roth to see her that summer ("Philip please don't avoid me"), and he knew he couldn't wait any longer. "I'm not going to be able to see you while you are in New York," he replied.

> This is difficult to write, and will be difficult for you to read, I know; but it is necessary. You are a marvelous girl and I want you to have a future full of personal accomplishment and happiness and love. I will always value the

feeling we have had for one another. I have learned a lot about courage and sweetness from watching you grow up. You have both qualities in abundance. There are few people I admire as much as I admire you.

But the time has come in my own life to give up the last connections to what has been for me a very trying experience. I am not going to explain anymore than that. If you are unable to understand why I think this is necessary, maybe in the years to come the situation will be clearer to you, and more easily understood. . . .

With love, Philip

Helen was devastated, and couldn't resist riding her bicycle to the Village and waiting for Roth on his stoop. When he came out, he sat down and sadly reiterated that he simply couldn't see her anymore and hoped she would understand someday. "I was *bereft*," she said, sobbing to remember it almost fifty years later.

■ ■ ■ ■

THAT FALL Roth began his long, happy, sporadic association with the University of Pennsylvania. From the beginning he loved the weekly ritual of taking a morning train out of Penn Station; he'd find a seat in the old-fashioned dining car and eat a good breakfast off proper crockery. He found his students bright and attractive, and made a number of lasting friendships among his colleagues—including the man who recruited him, Jerre Mangione, whom he'd first met at Yaddo and who would come to Roth's apartment on May 27, 1966, to interview him for WNET, the New York public television station. It had been six years since Roth's fractious encounter with Mike Wallace, and another twenty-seven would pass before he consented to appear on TV again. In 1966, however, the show went without a hitch, except for an item in that day's mail and the boiling heat; while elaborate cables were laid around the apartment, Roth and Mangione tried cooling off by drinking beer and are seen suppressing belches throughout the interview. The thirty-three-year-old Roth's hair is thinning around the temples but still covers most of his crown, and he seems at ease on camera, chatting lucidly with elegant little hand gestures. Thanks to Ann Mudge, the apartment is nicely appointed, with a trim little couch under an open window, a handsome old mirror over the fireplace, and a floor-to-ceiling built-in bookcase to the left of it; opposite Roth and his tidily cluttered desk is a wing chair containing his staring, bespectacled interviewer.

Around that time Maggie was occasionally in the neighborhood to attend writing classes at the New School; Roth figured she hoped to publish a book exposing him to the world as a scoundrel, and one day he spotted her approaching him on the sidewalk and gave her such a menacing glare that she almost stumbled into the gutter to avoid him. Her attitude toward his current novel was hard to pin down. Shortly after Roth had left her in the spring of 1963, she wrote Fox that she'd read a draft of "the Ann Barnes"—as the Maggie-like heroine was then called—"Time Away ms." and was "very moved by much of it"; once the book was published, however, she wrote a more cryptic response to their wedding witnesses, the Gibberds. "We had a curious letter from Maggie not long ago," Vernon wrote Roth, "in which she assumed an air of detached indifference to your recent work, and followed a vitriolic attack on it with a remark that one didn't feel bitter about it one bit, because it wasn't worth it." That day in 1966, anyway, while the WNET production crew was setting up in Roth's apartment, he thought to check his mail and found a manila envelope stuffed full of pages. Roth stood reading them in the foyer. It was a story by Maggie about a kinky fellow named Ross Phillips who derives sexual gratification from enemas, as administered by his obedient wife, rather the way Maggie had obliged Roth the night before his polyp operation in 1959. "Wouldn't it be nice if she wrote a best-seller exposing me and made so much money she got fucked out of the alimony?" Roth wrote Fingerhood a few days later, signing himself "The Dreamer."

His favorite bedtime reading was *The Complete Guide to Divorce*, by Samuel G. Kling, from which he learned that a separation lasting anywhere from eighteen months to three years—"without cohabitation and without reasonable expectation of reconciliation"—was grounds for divorce in eleven states, including Arkansas, where a former Iowa student of his, Bill Harrison (*Rollerball Murder*), was on the faculty at the state university. Thus he'd phoned Harrison in early 1965, and was offered a job in Fayetteville beginning in 1966.

Perhaps with this long-term absence somewhat in mind, he'd decided to break up with Mudge, whose meek gentility had begun to bore him a little. That meant going back on the party circuit ("I go to parties only when I am looking for a new girl"), a program that helped earn him mention among *The New York Times Magazine*'s "In Crowd" of 1965: "100 of America's wealthiest, most famous, and most creative people," including William Paley, Greta Garbo, and Truman Capote (Roth himself was ranked 79, between Richard Rodgers and Mrs. Louise Liberman Savitt; the more sociable Styron was a lowly 96). "As for being 'in,'" Roth wrote his parents, "if I could find the office where you hand in your resignation, I would. I think there must have been some mistake anyway, since I can't watusi." There was no mistake, and probably his being the youngest-ever winner of the National Book Award had less to do with it than his frequent appearances, that spring, at Bennett Cerf's apartment, where he hobnobbed with the likes of Sinatra, Claudette Colbert, and— perhaps most thrilling of all—Martin Gabel, the man who'd narrated Norman Corwin's *On a Note of Triumph* twenty years before.

It's also likely the *Times* had caught wind of Roth's fleeting involvement with Jackie Kennedy, arguably the most famous woman in the world at the time, a mere fifteen months after her husband's assassination. "Every morning a stock-market report on reputations comes out in New York," Norman Podhoretz would soon write in *Making It*. "It is invisible, but those who have eyes to see can read it. Did so-and-so have dinner at Jacqueline Kennedy's apartment last night? Up five points. . . . Did so-and-so's book get nominated for the National Book Award? Up two and five-eighths." Roth was one of the few people on the planet who came close to meeting these two diverse criteria, and it was *chez* Podhoretz where the more enviable of the two had germinated. That night Roth found himself seated on one side of Mrs. Kennedy, while the guest of honor, civil rights leader Bayard Rustin, was on the other; to Roth she vouchsafed her awe that Edmund Wilson was also in the room. "Mrs. Kennedy was beautiful, alert, alive, and very sad," an unwontedly solemn Roth reported to Lurie. "I don't think she knows what to do with herself. I was very taken with her, to be frank."

And vice versa. Perhaps a week later, Joe Fox was contacted by Kitty Carlisle Hart's social secretary, who charged him with asking Roth whether he'd be willing to serve as Mrs. Kennedy's dinner partner a few nights hence. The only immediate impediment, for Roth, was his wardrobe: he owned a total of two suits (a blue three-piece and the stalwart glen plaid) and three pairs of shoes, none of them black; the day of the party, then, he bought black shoes at Brooks Brothers and walked all over town in them (lest he cross his legs and reveal a pristinely unscuffed sole and hence the fact that he'd bought them expressly for the occasion). The party was all right: the theater critic Walter Kerr was there with his wife, Jean (author of *Please Don't Eat the Daisies*), while their hostess was partnered with the actor Tom Poston ("a poor man's Jack Lemmon"). On the sidewalk afterward, Roth offered to hail a cab for Mrs. Kennedy, but she wanted to walk a bit; when Roth worried about her heels, she raised a hand and her black limousine materialized beside them. "Do you want to come upstairs?" she asked outside her apartment building on Fifth Avenue. "Oh, of course you do." She assured him the children were sleeping (You mean the little boy who salutes like this, Roth thought, and the little girl who calls her pony Macaroni?), and they sat chatting for an hour or so. There was one lingering kiss, and a little later they said good night—though not before she gave Roth a card with her private phone number and asked him to call her.

"I wasn't up to it," he said, many years later. What business did he have dating the widow Kennedy, with only two suits and four pairs of shoes? The last time they met was 1983, at a New York Public Library gala, where he was named a Literary Lion. Then, in March 1994, he heard she was sick with cancer and gave her a call; afterward he sent her (a famous Francophile after all) the French edition of *Deception*: "Thank you for *Tromperie*," she wrote. "I can't wait." Two months later she died.

■　■　■　■

A FEW DAYS AFTER resigning his Ford Fellowship at the end of June 1965, Roth took a train to East Hampton to spend a weekend with Joe Fox, and also on that train was his estranged girlfriend, Ann Mudge. They sat together in the mostly empty car and began to flirt; at one point she dropped something on the floor between them, and when Roth ducked to retrieve it, he caught a glimpse of her fragrant leg, neatly crossed and jiggling slightly: "That was it."

They were a steady couple after that, as Roth became more and more partial to a proper domestic routine. Mudge had a trust fund and lived in a comfortable Sutton Place apartment; almost every evening Roth would go there after finishing work (often walking down from his six o'clock appointment with Kleinschmidt on East Sixty-eighth), and Mudge would have dinner waiting, served with a half bottle of wine, since she herself drank nothing stronger than Ovaltine because of her past problems with alcohol. Perhaps the best part, for Roth, was the way she would leave around six thirty in the morning to see her own analyst, then return an hour later and crawl back in bed with him. His friend Julius Goldstein would later remark that Roth had an "old-fashioned" need for a woman to take care of him, and Roth would not have disagreed: he found a mate's loving-kindness "very stabilizing"—reminiscent of coming home to his mother's tomato soup or slice of cake covered with wax paper, an essential part of his favorite Flaubert dictum, "Be orderly and regular in your life like a bourgeois . . ."

Roth had little patience for Mudge's rich friends, much less the way they wangled free decorating jobs out of her. She was highly intelligent; why didn't she do something worthwhile, he wondered, like finish her college degree? When he pressed her about it, she burst into tears and said the whole idea frightened her. What if she failed, or, worse ("in my family circle women who were accomplished were considered very strange ducks indeed"), what if she succeeded? But Roth insisted, and together they pored over the NYU catalogue and picked out courses for her. Over the next couple of years she made the dean's list and got her degree, then went on to law school. "None of that would have happened if it hadn't been for Philip," she said, and it worked both ways. After a few months with Mudge he felt "confident and strong again," and decided to cancel his plans for expediting a divorce in Arkansas.

The summer of their reunion, 1965, was also the summer he discovered Martha's Vineyard, where he'd gone in late August to visit the Brusteins. Roth was "overwhelmed": within walking distance of their house near Lambert's Cove was a lovely freshwater swimming hole, Seth's Pond, as well as a colony of writers including Styron, Lillian Hellman, Philip Rahv, and many others Roth would meet for the first time there. That summer, too, Bellow was staying on the island with his third wife, Susan Glassman, who hadn't changed much in the seven years since she and Roth had briefly dated in Chicago. "Susan looks handsome but complains a bit," Lurie had written him a few weeks before his arrival. "I was there when [Bellow] brought in the mail, a great pile of it. 'Anything for me!' Susan said. 'Not today, honey.'" The previous year Bellow had published *Herzog*, which Roth would come to consider, along with *Augie March*, "the most splendid of the splendid"; his first response, however (as with *Augie*), was quite a bit more ambivalent. "Roth is sitting by the side of the pool *smelling* in every side of *Herzog*," Kazin noted in his diary on July 7, 1965, when both were at Yaddo. A few days later Roth delivered his verdict to Lurie: "There is something morally obtuse about the book. And really too much pleading for the soul. Somewhere back of it all is that Jewish family hysteria about love." "You might not like me to say this," Lurie replied from the Vineyard, "but [Bellow] is rather like you, he made remarks you might have made." Jules Feiffer got rather the same impression a month later, when he and Roth came across Bellow sitting in his car outside a bakery in Vineyard Haven. Roth stood at the car window exchanging wisecracks with the driver, who pulled forward ever so slowly until his tires almost rolled over his younger colleague's toes. "Watch it!" Roth laughed, staggering back. "No," said Bellow, "*you* watch it."

The following summer Roth and Mudge rented a little house in the woods near the Brusteins, with a screened porch in back looking out on the bay. Roth had finished *When She Was Good* at the end of June ("Philip Roth SURPRISES US with completed ms of novel," Cerf excitedly wrote in his diary) and was looking forward to a rare summer of leisure. Mudge stayed in the city until August to keep up with her analysis, flying to the island on weekends; one day the two stopped for lunch in Edgartown on the way back from the airport, and an anti-Semitic lady loudly informed Roth that the island *used* to be Irish and English. "What century was that, you miserable cunt," he replied.

Other than that the Vineyard was "perfect," as Roth reported to Lurie. In the afternoon he and Mudge would gather with friends at Lambert's Cove Beach, or, if they wanted more privacy, they'd go a few miles down the coast to Menemsha, where they'd screw in the dunes and harvest mussels, which Mudge would cook with wine. They also saw a fair amount of the Kennedys: the Styrons were old friends, and it so happened Mudge and Teddy had been in school together at Graham-Eckes in Palm Beach ("for rich people who didn't want their social lives and travels interrupted by the nuisance of children," Mudge explained). One day Jackie invited Roth and Mudge, the Styrons, and Lillian Hellman onto her yacht for a picnic lunch on the beach; the only hard feelings she betrayed were in her somewhat austere treatment of Roth's consort. "Where are you from?" she inquired as Mudge climbed aboard; "Pittsburgh," said Mudge, whereupon their hostess looked away and that was that.

The couple also attended a festive dinner party hosted by Dick Goodwin, a former Kennedy speechwriter, whose guests included the Styrons and the junior senator from New York, Robert Kennedy. The last was in particularly good fettle, puffing a cigar and chatting with Mudge. "Is Mr. Roth going to marry you, or what?" he said, loud enough for the others to hear. "That remains to be seen," said Mudge. Kennedy turned to Roth and asked what his intentions were. "It depends, Senator, if I can ever get a divorce in your state from the wife I'm already married to." Kennedy puffed his cigar and turned to a legislative aide. "See what we can do for Mr. Roth," he said, "so he can marry Miss Mudge as soon as possible."

■ ■ ■ ■

THE GREAT DRAWBACK of living on East Tenth was noise: Greenwich Village blared outside Roth's window, especially on weekends, and an upstairs neighbor was forever blasting his hi-fi. By the fall of 1966 Roth had had enough, and he rented a top-floor apartment in the north building of Kips Bay Plaza, the new 1,118-unit complex designed by I. M. Pei and S. J. Kessler between East Thirtieth and Thirty-third Streets. From Roth's window he could see all the way from the gold-domed New York Life building to the Brooklyn Bridge; unfortunately there was a slight incline on Second Avenue, twenty-one floors below, and the clamorous grinding of gears went on at all hours. On the other hand the sixties were in full swing at Kips Bay, where Roth would proposition his female neighbors in the lobby and elevators ("easy as pie").

Toward the close of that auspicious year, on November 28, Roth and Mudge attended Capote's legendary Black and White Ball at the Plaza. He and Capote shared an editor, Fox, and of course they'd met at Cerf's. "We don't want to go to this thing, do we?" said Roth when he received an invitation. Their pre-ball dinner was at the Dakota apartment of Amanda and Carter Burden, where Roth sat next to the twenty-year-old Candice Bergen, who'd recently departed Penn because of poor grades. At the Plaza, according to the *Times*, Roth "whirled" Mudge and Mrs.

Joseph Fox and Mrs. Norman Mailer around the dance floor, as well as (he recalled) a masked stranger who proved to be President Johnson's daughter Lynda Bird. While whirling Beverly Mailer, the latter's husband lumbered in their wake muttering, cheerfully enough, "We've got to watch out for these shiksas, Roth. Never trust a gentile girl." "Now he tells me," Roth wrote Lurie the next day. "Ann and Bob Silvers and myself were sitting in a box above the dance floor when I suddenly had this grotesquely Nabokovian vision of my former mate charging across the ballroom floor with a revolver and slaying me in my evening clothes at the EVENT of the century, and in my box. It sounds like a good last scene for a comic novel."

Twenty-Two

RANDOM HOUSE EXPRESSED ITS CONFIDENCE IN *WHEN She Was Good* with a lucrative advance: $102,000, to be doled out to Roth in $17,000 yearly increments lest his wife get ideas about raising her alimony. Roth, too, was satisfied with his work, and indeed would always consider it the best among his early novels. As he wrote the Gibberds, "It took me close to four years to write it, much of the time spent howling with pain—but I'm pleased with it now, and Random House is doing a first printing of 25,000. Which is a lot."

Roth prided himself on his objective—"pitiless," as Flaubert would have it—characterization of Lucy Nelson: "There is no venom in the portrait," he said, "even though it was based on my worst enemy." Which is not to say Lucy is sympathetic so much as comprehensible—the result of much sober reflection on Roth's part as to the source of his wife's rage toward the men in her life, beginning with her father. That even a person like Maggie is born innocent and well meaning is nicely suggested in the novel's early pages, as Lucy's grandfather, Daddy Will, visits her grave and remembers "the tiny, spirited, golden-haired child that Lucy had been—how lively, bright, and sweet." The teenage Lucy vows to follow "Saint Teresa's little way of spiritual childhood," until the day her drunken father upends a pan of water in which her long-suffering mother is "soaking her beautiful, frail feet"; Lucy calls on Saint Teresa to intervene but her prayer is unanswered, whereupon she decides she can't stand Teresa's "suffering little guts" and calls the police instead. All she wants is an ordinary life without the torments of a drunken father, but her mother is too weak and her grandfather too kindhearted, so it falls to Lucy to put the man in jail. Henceforth she won't let men get away with shirking their duty (as she sees it), and her rage grows as they fail her time and again. "Goodbye, protectors and defenders, heroes and saviors," she thinks at last, utterly alone in the world. "You are no longer needed, you are no longer wanted—alas, you have been revealed for what you are. Farewell, farewell, philanderers and frauds, cowards and weaklings, cheaters and liars. Fathers and husbands, farewell!"

To be sure, Lucy's father and husband are scarcely permitted to be other than cowards and weaklings in her righteous estimation. (*Saint Lucy* was one of Roth's discarded titles, the better to highlight a sanctimony that doesn't even spare a fellow saint.) "Stone!" her father shouts, as she stands unflinching (her finger still marking her place in a schoolbook) despite the armful of snow he heaves at her before the police take him away. Nor does she "favor him with a reply" when, later, he tries to make amends by urging her to pursue her "dream" of college rather than have Roy Bassart's child. "I thought Roy a good name for this unkinglike boy who Lucy would do all she could to turn into a king," said Roth of Lucy's determination to spite her father, to reject the freedom she might have known outside Liberty Center (no less), by marrying "someone she secretly despised." "If only they'd say *no*," she wistfully rages. "NO, LUCY, YOU CANNOT. NO, LUCY, WE FORBID IT. But it seemed that none of them had the conviction any longer, or the endurance, to go against a choice of hers." Far from turning Roy into a king, Lucy reduces him to an even worse booby, barely able to open his mouth except to placate her. "Twenty-two," she thinks, "and this will be my whole life. This. This. This. This."

Roth had meant to capture Lucy's "desperate and heartbroken" quality, while also doing justice to the toll she takes on those "in the immediate orbit of her outrage"; suffice it to say, the latter part of this formulation receives his more zestful treatment. Toward the end of the novel Lucy is a castrating, self-pitying monster and little else. Having driven Roy away with an anathema even he won't tolerate—"pansy"—she assures herself of his "heartless cruelty" and doubles down on her denunciations when Roy's mother accuses her of tricking him into marriage. "But he tricked *me*, Alice! Tricked me to think he was a man, when he's a mouse, a monster! A moron! He's a pansy, that's what your son is, the worst and weakest pansy there ever was!" This is certainly out of proportion to Roy's shortcomings, and the reader is bound to feel an overdue sense of catharsis when Lucy is finally opposed by Roy's Uncle Sowerby—"my idol," as Roth admitted of the man who calls Lucy a "little ball-breaker of a bitch" to her face ("He's not a Jew, you see," Roth explained).

Malamud commended Roth's narrative skill, but also noted, "Since Lucy is rendered monolithic, relentless, half-insane, impossible to like . . . I can't include her within the compass of my feeling for the people in the book. That leaves me with pity for Whitey and his wife . . . and I felt left a little in the cold." Fair enough. Lucy's violent moralizing is exciting for a while, but finally becomes tiresome—Maggie without the nuances of wit or hypocrisy ("I have no conscience"). And Roth's comedic gift is constrained by a pitiless (Flaubert) determination "to be dull with the dull"—a scheme he carries off a little too successfully. "At the age of twenty," Roy reflects in oafish third person, "nobody had to tell him that it was high time to begin thinking about becoming a man. Because he was thinking about it, and plenty, don't worry." But it was precisely this aspect of his achievement that pleased Roth most—his evocation of Liberty Center in all "the terrible ordinariness of its ordinariness"—a naturalistic tour de force that palls well before the last of the book's three hundred or so pages.

Still, Roth had worked so long and hard on his "novel without Jews" that he could scarcely bear hearing a bad word about it, and for this reason avoided a Random House sales conference that Fox had urged him to attend. Publication had been postponed from March 1967 because the Literary Guild wanted to offer the book as a selection in June, but the news hadn't reached *Vogue* in time to stop an early mugging by Jean Stafford: "One feels that one has spent a long Thanksgiving day with a hinterland family whose interests, ambitions, politics, houses, automobiles, food, and tragedies are so studiously average that they should be subjects for a statistician rather than a novelist." "I see the handwriting and I see the wall," Roth wrote Bob Baker of this "devastatingly negative" review, "but then I've been seeing both for some time now, and learned I think how to take this stuff last time round. Or so it says here."

As it happened, the stuff he'd taken last time round would in fact be very like what was coming at him this time too; how well he'd take it was another matter. Early readers among his peers, such as Malamud, had been impressed by his craftsmanship—whatever their reservations otherwise—and Roth wondered whether it was his fate to be "a writer's writer" rather than popular ("Can't I have both, he asked"). And certainly reviewers tended to stress, once again, Roth's great promise and serious-ness. "*When She Was Good* may be another disappointment, another fail-ure," Eliot Fremont-Smith wrote in the daily *New York Times*, "—but, like *Letting Go*, a failure in terms of the tough, admirable standards that Mr. Roth's acute observation and solid, unadorned prose call forth and by which all his work, disappointing and not, should be judged. Which is to say that the failure was interesting—and the disappointment keen." The key words were "failure" and "disappointment," and while the Sunday *Times* reviewer, Wilfrid Sheed, was somewhat more appreciative, book buyers were unlikely to flock at the prospect of Lutheran characters who are "just like Jews only duller (a sociological insight which might just stand up)." Perhaps the only review that satisfied Roth was Raymond Rosenthal's in *The New Leader*, which made the point that Roth's deci-sion to let his characters "talk and act for themselves" was a modernist tendency harking back to Flaubert: "With a simplicity and modesty that are in the end lethal, Roth has written the most violently satiric book about American life since . . . Evelyn Waugh's *The Loved One.*"

"The history of my discontent," began a ten-point letter Roth wrote to his agent, Candida Donadio, seven weeks after publication—a scathing appraisal of Random House's work on *When She Was Good*, with most of the opprobrium laid on the head of Joe Fox, whose lapses included a suggestion they lower the first printing (to ten or fifteen thousand) and also refrain from sending advance galleys, a practice Fox allegedly found both expensive and "pushy." In short, he was cheap. When Roth com-plained about the absence of a *Times* ad on publication day, Fox replied that "advertising doesn't sell books"; when Roth mentioned that he was seeing a fair number of ads for the Random House novel *Fathers*, by Her-bert Gold—a writer for whom Roth had very little love—Fox pointed out that *Fathers* had sold forty thousand copies. "Well, you can tell them this, sweetie," Roth wrote his agent, "—they can have Herb Gold and his 40,000 copies and I'll go where I am advertised commensurate to my reputation. This book is going to read long after *Fathers*, and if they are too stupid to understand that, then fuck em."

Actually Fox was arguing for more advertising as late as September 8—three months after publication—reminding Cerf that the book was still selling over a thousand copies a week for a total, to date, of 27,589. That said, Fox added that his dinner with Roth the night before had gone "very pleasantly. . . . Neither of us discussed the fuss around advertising." Perhaps he'd assumed that all was well; he would learn otherwise in due course.

■ ■ ■ ■

THAT SUMMER OF 1967 Roth and Mudge were back on Martha's Vineyard, this time renting a ramshackle cottage a short walk away from the general store in West Tisbury. The days were marred by foul weather ("rain, fog, and damp"), though the couple found pleasure in watching a family of swans gliding around the pond in their backyard. Among literary friends the talk was mainly about the Vietnam War. Both Roth and Mudge were passionately opposed—all the more since Mudge's younger brother had recently been drafted and would soon be sent to Vietnam. Mudge got rid of her Dow Chemical stock because the company manufactured napalm and Agent Orange, and a little later she began working as a draft counselor at a Quaker peace center in the Village, where she befriended the writer and activist Grace Paley. Earlier that spring, she and Roth had gathered in Central Park for a peace march down Fifth Avenue, and afterward Roth was furious when the media grossly underestimated (as he saw it) the size of the crowd. Back at Mudge's apartment he impulsively phoned NBC: "Put me through to the president!" he ordered the NBC operator, who doubtfully asked for the president's name. "He's my friend," Roth replied. "I don't know his name. Put me through." Mudge laughed in the other room and Roth, abashed, hung up.

In August the Styrons gave a party for Robert Kennedy, and Jules Feiffer was approached by Under Secretary of State Nicholas Katzenbach, who proclaimed himself a fan of the left-wing cartoonist. "How can you be in an administration that's fighting this war in Vietnam and say you are a fan of mine?" Feiffer replied, but Katzenbach insisted that he too was opposed to the war. A week later, Katzenbach gave "shit-eating testimony" (as Roth put it) before the Senate Foreign Relations Committee, expressing unequivocal support of Johnson's war policy. Feiffer called a meeting among their friends on the island. Some wanted to picket Katzenbach's house, but finally they decided to take out a full-page ad in the *Vineyard Gazette*, for which Roth drafted a letter. "The Gut Issue" ran on

August 25, headed by an italicized quote from Katzenbach's testimony: "*. . . the 'gut issue here is whether or not the Congress supports the President in what he does . . .'*"; the shaming letter that followed—signed by Roth, Feiffer, Styron, Hellmann, John Hersey, and other summer neighbors of Katzenbach—rejoined that the "gut issue" was whether "a civilized and humane man" such as he would "stop playing the functionary and speak out against President Johnson's indefensible diplomacy of violence."

And Katzenbach, it turned out, wasn't the only civilized and humane man on the island who supported the war. In later years, John Updike would remember his first meeting with Roth as having taken place that summer on the porch of a *New Yorker* colleague, Bernie Taper, where he and Roth had a heated argument about Vietnam; in fact (as Roth reminded him) they'd met some eight years earlier, at the home of a Houghton editor, Jack Leggett, who lived near Updike in Ipswich, Massachusetts. The two young writers—Updike was born a year and a day before Roth—were then at the beginning of their brilliant, much compared careers, and Roth came away from Ipswich with a pleasant memory of Updike as "a kind of engaging, elongated leprechaun." That night on Taper's porch, however, Updike was strident in defending a man he considered a beleaguered "underdog": LBJ. As he wrote in his memoir, *Self-Consciousness*, "At one point Roth, in the calm and courteous tone of one who had been through many psychiatric sessions, pointed out to me that I was the most aggressive person in the room." That may have been so, though Roth remembered a civil degree of animation on both sides: "Because no one else I knew had John's view of the war, it wasn't often that I had a chance to so flagrantly exhibit my righteousness." Updike, who wasted nothing, wrote to inform Roth in 1973 that he'd given Roth's part of their argument to Skeeter, the black Vietnam vet in *Rabbit Redux*.*

Energized by his summer among (mostly) radical writers, Roth had an idea that he was eager to share with Bob Silvers, who was well con-

---

* Roth didn't recognize his argument in Skeeter's, though he was reading a lot of Kafka at the time and might have alluded to *The Metamorphosis*, thus: "Uncle Sam wakes up one morning, looks down at his belly, sees he's some cockroach, what can he do? Just keep bein' his cockroach self, is all. Till he gets stepped on. . . ."

nected with Noam Chomsky and other intellectuals on the left: namely, an indefinite general strike among antiwar academics that was aimed at shutting down as many universities as possible. Silvers was skeptical. He thought academics might be persuaded to strike for a week or two, but after all they were hardly in a position to risk their scant financial security; still, he agreed to run it by Chomsky et al. and get back to Roth. By December, however, Roth was turning down Mailer's invitation to participate in a "Writers and Editors War Tax" protest, and soon his position on activism of any kind became categorical: "I'm a writer, and whatever my political concerns are they are expressed in writing."

And so it went. Sitting around a poker table with Updike that summer—before the talk turned to Vietnam—Roth had remarked that he was "speaking up for masturbators" in his work, as indeed he'd been doing for a while now in giddy conversation with Jewish friends. The license to write about self-abuse was facilitated by other products of the zeitgeist he'd enjoyed, such as the provocateur rock group the Fugs and the LBJ-bashing satire *MacBird!* Then, too, as a writer, Roth was simply fed up with all the critics who went on about his unfulfilled promise: "nervous well-wishers may try to head Mr. Roth back to Newark at this point," Wilfrid Sheed had written of his latest novel; "certainly he handicaps himself, ties up one good hand, when he tries to go it all the way without comedy." Roth, by then, had gotten the message loud and clear: "I had written two proper books and I didn't want to write a third."

His original pages about masturbation had been part of a "longish monologue" he'd written shortly after finishing *When She Was Good*; this was meant to accompany a pornographic slide show ("full-color enlargements of the private parts"), but the finger exercise stalled after sixty or seventy pages, and only the bits about masturbation seemed salvageable. Next Roth tried again to write a novel about his wife's urine ruse, and even used a variation of the title he'd given to his play on the same theme: *The Nice Jewish Boy, or A Masochistic Extravaganza*. This was to be an extended colloquy between an urbane psychoanalyst—Spielvogel naturally—and his hysterically aggrieved patient, Abravanel, who inveighs against his vindictive shiksa wife, Erika, whom Spielvogel (à la Kleinschmidt) likes to compare with the patient's mother. "Lay off about my mother, damn it!" Abravanel explodes. He continues:

Nothing is true that's so boring—when it's boring it stops being true!
  I'm talking about my misery! I'm blowing off hate, all right! That
  nightmare! That prions [prison] of a marriage! . . . I'm lucky I'm even
  alive—the filthy little suicidal, homicidal bitch!
[SPIELVOGEL:] Let's say your marriage was a masochistic extravaganza, how's that?
[ABRAVANEL:] True! Understated, but perfectly true! . . . why, why,
  why—why did I take such ridiculous shit from such a hopeless specimen! What was I trying to be?
[SPIELVOGEL:] You tell me.
[ABRAVANEL:] A nice Jewish boy!

The psychoanalytic dynamic—the raving patient, the suave (and ultimately silent) analyst—was a crucial breakthrough. As Roth wrote in
1974, "Not until I found, in the person of a troubled analysand, the voice
that could speak in behalf of both the 'Jewboy' (with all that word signi-
fies to Jew and Gentile alike about aggression, appetite, and marginality)
and the 'nice Jewish boy' (and what that epithet implies about repression,
respectability, and social acceptance) was I able to complete a fiction that
was expressive . . . of that character's dilemma."

The Nice Jewish Boy ends, and *Portnoy's Complaint* begins, when our
protagonist leaves off talking about his wife and gets to the source of his
crippling guilt—the guilt that led him into his ghastly marriage in the
first place—his mother. When asked whether *Portnoy* was influenced by
certain foulmouthed stand-up Jewish comics of the era, Roth denied it:
"I would say I was more strongly influenced by a sit-down comic named
Franz Kafka and a very funny bit he does called *The Metamorphosis*." That
year at Penn, Roth had taught a Kafka-dominated course that he realized might have been titled "Studies in Guilt and Persecution." At the
age of thirty-three—Roth's own age at the time—Kafka had written his
famous "Letter to His Father," which begins, "Dear Father, You ask why
I am afraid of you." One of Roth's favorite assignments, beginning with
that year, was to ask his Penn students to write a similar letter to one of
their own parents. And so, with *Portnoy*, Roth took the assignment upon
himself—"a novel about yet another family-obsessed Jewish bachelor in
his thirties, which might have begun, 'Dear Mother, You ask why I am
obsessed with you. . . .'" Or, as it actually began after the long false start

of *The Nice Jewish Boy*, "So let me tell you about my mother, a vivacious, seductive, competent, energetic, childish, arbitrary, iron-willed, hysterical woman, who loved and punished with great severity, and filled my childhood with crisis and high drama." The many modifiers in that sentence would be abundantly borne out in the work that followed, so the *next* sentence (give or take a few words) became the actual opening of *Portnoy's Complaint*: "So deeply was she imbedded in my consciousness that for the first few years of school I believed that my teachers were actually my mother in disguise. . . ." Roth often spoke of the brutal business of starting a novel—the many pages he had to write before the coin rang, as it rang limpidly, at last, here. He would proceed with the *mother*, then, and put aside the Maggie-like Erika for the time being.

As for the other Portnoys: among Roth's students at Iowa had been five Jewish men who seemed always to write about the same folkloric family—the silent father who stoically stows his food away at the dinner table while a mother and sister (always) "hover over this little flame"—the son—"beating it and beating it and beating it." This, Roth realized, was an archetype going back to the shtetl, where women sewed or kept shop so their men could be free to ponder the Talmud and cultivate an inner life. Later, in America, the father worked to support the family while the mother's labors were often confined to a smaller household, and hence she poured her heart into caring for her children—her son(s) especially—who were expected to reward her love by becoming dentists, doctors, and lawyers, and bringing lots of grandchildren home. Kazin later explained the shock of recognition among second- and third-generation Jewish men who read *Portnoy* for the first time and were hauntingly reminded of what it had been like to be smothered by "the fantastic obsessive care, care, care" of the Jewish family—an obsessive care that, in Roth's case, was all but equally divided among both parents (*"You're a plum!"*).

Perhaps it bears repeating, then, that the Portnoys were not simply a folkloric paradigm—as Roth often took pains to suggest—but rather *quite* derived from his own experience growing up in an oppressively loving home. "Whew," he wrote Lurie, after a visit with his parents in October 1964 (a time when he was intensively reading Flaubert):

It is so rough, and I always think the same thing: they brought me up, how come I made it? This is not to say that they don't have their qualities

of strength and lovableness, but they are actually geniuses of the bour-
geousie [sic]—that is, they are so perfect at it. I suppose that when I have
my violent physical ailments, or fears, it is the bourgeois in me trying to
do harm to the sweet uncertain artist. Little does the bourgeois-in-me
or the B-I-M know that the S-U-A just loves physical ailments, and fear
too, for that matter. I suppose the two halves of me are in love without
knowing it.

Kleinschmidt also made much of the division in Roth's personality—
and that of the narcissistic artist generally—though he would have been
disinclined to characterize one part or the other as "bourgeois" (Flaubert's trope): rather he thought of Roth, on the one hand, as the little boy
who couldn't bear being parted from a doting (but often severe) mother
and so imagined his teachers were actually his mother in disguise—but
also the budding narcissist who considered himself "superior to these
people" and so ordered his smothering mother to "*Go!*" when she tried to
bring his raincoat and galoshes to school. "As [Spielvogel] saw it," Tarnopol explains in *My Life as a Man*, "it was my vulnerability as a sensitive
little child to the pain such a mother might easily inflict that accounted
for 'the dominance of my narcissism' as my 'primary defense.'"

And what better way to air painful, shaming memories than in the
form of a psychoanalytic monologue, which not only gave his fictional
narrator a compelling voice—that of the brittle, uncensored analysand—
but also served as an ingenious structural platform proceeding by mental
association ("blocks of consciousness") instead of chronology. It would
be a while, though, before Roth realized these various "blocks" could
be assembled into a single cohesive novel. "I have written my first short
story in four years," he wrote Lurie in late 1966 (eliding the ghastly short
fiction he'd written circa 1963–64). "It is called 'A Jewish Patient Begins
His Analysis.' I believe the story is as good as the title." What would
become the first section of *Portnoy* appeared in the April 1967 issue of
Esquire, occasioning a fracas between Roth and the magazine's editor
in chief, Harold Hayes. Roth had made an irritated phone call to the
in-house copy editor, "Miss McBride," when he discovered—too late—
that she'd taken it upon herself to tweak the wording in three of his
sentences and break two paragraphs into eight. "Miss McBride, as it

turns out, takes Roth's fiction probably more seriously than anyone else here," Hayes angrily replied to Donadio, whom Roth had charged with relaying his complaint; "and her innumerable problems of trying to get this rickety magazine into print do not include the chore of taking abuse from the outside—again, from Roth or anyone else." Hayes closed by inviting the agent to send Roth's stories elsewhere in the future: "Frankly I don't care."

Esquire, then, was out of the running when Roth finished a story he considered a continuation of "A Jewish Patient" and was thinking of titling, simply, "Fear"; it was Brustein who suggested the less abstract "Whacking Off"—a "takeoff" on *Letting Go*, and also a nod to the narrator's favorite pastime: "doubled over my flying fist, eyes pressed closed but mouth wide open, to take that sticky sauce of buttermilk and Clorox on my own tongue and teeth—though not infrequently, in my blindness and ecstasy, I got it all in the pompadour, like a blast of Wildroot Cream Oil." For various reasons, it pleased Roth to sell his dirty story for all of $125 to the very "temple of highbrowism," *Partisan Review*, explaining himself to the editor, Philip Rahv, as follows: "A masturbator yes, a capitalist no."

"I knew that all those hours I spent locked behind the bathroom door just couldn't come to nothing," Roth wrote Goldstein, noting that the Eighth Street Bookstore kept selling out of the Summer 1967 issue of *Partisan Review*. Joe Fox related a night at the Epsteins' where his colleague Jason had begun reading the story out loud to his guests, until Fox had to take over because their host was incapacitated with laughter. It was Fox who insisted that Roth was writing a novel: "it seems to me that hardly any transitional material is needed, that the material is rich and funny and sad, that the characters are all there, etc." Certainly the demand was high for more short stories about the mother-haunted, onanistic Alex Portnoy. Roth's old friend Solotaroff had recently departed *Commentary*—where memoirs about Jewish boyhood had been "coming out of [his] ears"—to start the quarterly paperback anthology *New American Review*; reading Roth's third installment, "The Jewish Blues," Solotaroff forgot his jadedness toward the genre and snapped up the piece for his inaugural issue in the fall. He also put dibs on all 110 typescript pages of Roth's fourth and final installment, which the author proposed to call "Cunt Crazy"; Portnoy's meditation on (among other things) his yen for gentile women would be published in April 1968 under the compromise title "Civilization and Its Discontents."*

That same month—just over a year since Harold Hayes had advised Roth (via Donadio) to send his work elsewhere—an associate editor at *Esquire* invited "one of the most important writers of our time" to contribute to the magazine's thirty-fifth anniversary issue. "'One of the most important writers of our time?'" Roth gleefully replied. "Oh, you must be putting me on." He pointed out that the only person who took him seriously at *Esquire* was the copy editor, according to Harold Hayes, whose sheepish apology Roth was kind enough to accept.

■   ■   ■   ■

COINCIDING WITH Alex Portnoy's first appearance in *Esquire* was a paper by Hans J. Kleinschmidt in the Spring 1967 issue of the psychoanalytical journal *American Imago*, "The Angry Act: The Role of Aggression in Creativity," which (after a lengthy explication of the narcissistic vagaries of Kandinsky, Thomas Mann, and Giacometti) presents the case of "a successful Southern playwright" whose life seems uncannily similar to Portnoy's. Both had an overbearing mother who used to pack a little bag for them when they were bad and turn them out of the house; both imagined their teachers were really their mother in disguise, a woman who "in some very clever magic way" would somehow beat them home from school before the ruse could be exposed. There were other striking parallels, perhaps the most clinching of which was "the angry act" itself. "His rebellion was sexualized," Kleinschmidt wrote of his playwright, "leading to compulsive masturbation which provided an outlet for a myriad of hostile fantasies. These same masturbatory fantasies he both acted out and channeled into his writing."

Roth recalled that he'd first spotted (on Kleinschmidt's desk) a copy of the Spring 1967 *American Imago* a year or so after it first appeared—

---

* Roth had tried yet again to write about the urine fraud in this section, and "for the first time" found himself becoming bored with his material. Prior to deferring that episode for another time/novel, he considered titling this fourth piece "The Shiksa Rag"—a pun. "I do not like 'The Shiksa Rag,'" Lurie sternly informed him.

that is, shortly after he'd finished *Portnoy*, from which Kleinschmidt had lifted supposedly autobiographical incidents, Roth claimed, and thereby "mischaracterize[d]" him. In fact, nobody had been more chagrined than Kleinschmidt himself when he discovered that his "Southern playwright" was a dead ringer for the hero of Roth's most famous novel—a novel the psychiatrist had declined to read in advance, while its author was still in analysis. "*Mr. Tarnopol is considered by Dr. Spielvogel to be among the nation's top young narcissists in the arts*," notes the italicized author bio in *My Life as a Man*, wherein Roth fictionalized (barely) the contretemps that followed once he discovered his own portrait in Kleinschmidt's paper. "Good Christ, Spielvogel, from whose example did I come to associate virility with hard work and self-discipline, if not from my father's?" So Tarnopol argues re the "ineffectual" father of a "successful Italian-American poet" in Spielvogel's "Creativity: The Narcissism of the Artist." As for his compulsive "act[ing] out sexually with other women" (as Spielvogel would have it) by way of dealing with "anger and dependency" vis-à-vis a castrating wife and mother, Tarnopol tots up his actual infidelities—"Two street whores in Italy, a friend in a car in Madison . . . and Karen"—and declares them "practically *monkish*, given the fact of my marriage." Roth himself remembered spending three or four sessions just berating Kleinschmidt for his "psychoanalytic cartoon," until finally the man put his foot down and threatened to end their relationship. Whereupon Roth backed down—"By then," he said, "I needed him"—hardly the first or last time Roth remained dependent (however angrily) on a dubious caretaker, male or female, despite his usual protestations of autonomy.

Thirteen years later, an academic named Jeffrey Berman discovered the *Imago* paper and connected it with Spielvogel's almost verbatim text in *My Life as a Man*—a finding he incorporated into a book he was writing, sending the chapter in question to Kleinschmidt for confirmation. "Since in my article I introduce the brief case history of a Southern playwright," the psychiatrist replied, "I in no way allude to or reveal the identity of the patient." He concluded by threatening Berman with an "onerous lawsuit" unless he deleted the offending passages from his otherwise "excellent and extremely well-written chapter." Berman brought a revised version of his paper to the "menacing and overbearing" Kleinschmidt's office and presently persuaded him that the evidence was all but irrefutable and any lawsuit would be idle. "As I was leaving the office," Berman reminisced, "he exclaimed, in a tone that struck me as unapologetically defiant and proud, 'Incidentally, I'm Klinger too!'"—Kepesh's psychiatrist in *The Breast*.

Twenty-Three

I N September 1967, Roth attended a publication party at "21" for Bill Styron's *The Confessions of Nat Turner;* despite his otherwise excellent physical condition after a vigorous summer on Martha's Vineyard, Roth experienced an ominous malaise that, Kleinschmidt explained, was a psychosomatic manifestation of envy for his friend. Roth denied it: he loved Styron's novel and was delighted by its success, but Kleinschmidt stood by his diagnosis "right down to the day I nearly died from a burst appendix and peritonitis," as Roth recalled.*

A couple of weeks after the party at "21"—on Wednesday, October 11—Roth felt so terrible that he finally phoned his doctor, Arthur Seligman, who sent him to Doctor's Hospital, across from Gracie Mansion. Roth was lying on a gurney when a tuxedo-attired surgeon, Ed Goodman, stopped on his way to a gala to examine him; he pressed hard on Roth's right side and the patient almost fainted with pain. Goodman shed his tuxedo and operated almost immediately, discovering that Roth's appendix had ruptured as long as a week ago, spreading deadly bacteria throughout his abdominal cavity. When Roth woke up the next day, his parents and Mudge were huddled at the foot of his bed; draining tubes protruded from his abdomen and he was heavily dosed with antibiotics, his survival in doubt for at least a day or two.

He was in the hospital for seventeen days that first time, and every night Mudge brought dinner (the hospital food was inedible) and lovingly kept him company. For a few weeks after his discharge he seemed

---

* Roth's delight over his friend's success was tempered a little, maybe, given the relative failure of *When She Was Good.* The ten-point remonstrance of Random House he'd written to Donadio that summer included "Tell Bennett [Cerf] that I am going to watch carefully the advertising of Styron's book."

to recover nicely, but then nausea returned and he resumed losing weight. Readmitted on December 6, Roth was again opened up by Dr. Goodman, who found that the stump of Roth's appendix was badly infected and also needed to be removed. "When am I going to get out of here?" Roth complained, after another sixteen days in bed. "I'm missing the fall of 1967." "Don't you get it yet?" said Dr. Goodman. "You almost missed everything."*

"Amazingly," Roth wrote in *The Facts*, "I didn't see my burst appendix as [Maggie's] handiwork, probably because the poisons of peritonitis spread through my system without her accompanying barrage of moral indictment. . . . What had killed two of my uncles, and very nearly, in 1944, killed my father, had tried and failed to kill me." Which is not to say Maggie had abandoned her efforts to bring him low. Almost five years after leaving her for good, Roth was still paying $110 a week in alimony—"court-ordered robbery" that galled him all the more when he remembered how he'd come to be married in the first place—while counting the days until September 1968, two years after their formal separation agreement, when a recently passed New York law would allow him, at last, to obtain a divorce. Meanwhile their 1966 agreement had cost him an additional $5,000 for "support and maintenance" (plus $750 in attorney fees) which "Mag" (as her attorney, Leo Boylan, fondly referred to her) had demanded two months early to cover her trip to Europe that summer.

By late 1967 it was rumored that Roth's notorious Portnoy stories were part of what would prove "the Novel of the Century (or at least of 1968)"—so Lurie had gleaned from the Epsteins—and nobody was more eager for him to finish than Maggie, who'd heard plenty about it from her colleagues in publishing. Pamela Forcey, a fellow production editor at Harper & Row, working in the cubicle adjoining Maggie's, remembered overhearing her long daily phone chats with her lawyer Boylan and others. By then Maggie was obsessed with getting "that fucker" who'd been so eager to divorce her and had unforgivably (she liked to say) cut Helen out of his life. On February 21, 1968, she fired the first cannon blast in her final campaign—an affidavit in support of almost tripling her

---

* The medical part of this episode is precisely described in *Everyman*, ending with this exchange between doctor and patient.

alimony, from $110 to $300, and also requesting another $2,000 in coun-
sel fees. This, of course, was only the beginning, based on the alleged success of his latest novel, *When She Was Good*, which had briefly appeared
near the bottom of the *Times* best-seller list; also Bantam had reput-
edly acquired paperback rights "for a price of at least $120,000.00"—
chicken feed (Maggie likely surmised, given the scuttlebutt) next to what
he stood to get, all told, for *Portnoy*. "She would have ruined me," said
Roth, remembering. He laughed: "She would have gotten my Nobel
Prize money!"

Forcey and Maggie were two of eight production editors, all women,
in the College Department, and for a time the two were friendly, meeting after work for drinks and "weekend excursions." Before that, Maggie
had been close to their supervisor—a prim, somewhat awkward woman
named Ginny, who Forcey suspected was gay or bisexual, which (she
thought) had something to do with her "tempestuous" attachment to
Maggie. At one point Maggie became president of the employees union,
and when Forcey came to her apartment one night for a drink, she found
the other six production editors all on hand: Maggie had devised a list of
grievances to submit to her boss and former friend, Ginny, and wanted
everyone to sign.* Forcey's own bond with Maggie was mostly based on
alcohol: her ex-husband had custody of their children and Forcey was
sad and tipsy much of the time; Maggie had mentioned that she had
two children of her own, but otherwise "never talked about them too
much." ("My mother was really beginning to drink a lot," Helen remembered, remarking that Maggie remained "furious" about her defection to
Kemper Hall and for a long time refused to let her return to New York
except for summer visits.) One night she and Forcey ended up in bed
together, drunk, and the next day Maggie said, "I have no morals. My
only regret is that I didn't come."

Alcohol and sex were the main anodynes in Maggie's life, and one
was more reliably available than the other. During the summer of 1966,
she divided a month in Europe between her old Princeton friends, the

---

* It's according to Forcey that Maggie was briefly president of their union, the Association
of Harper & Row Employees, but Roth remembered his first wife's title as "chairman of
the union grievances committee." "Nice?" he said to me, chuckling. "Nice touch? If you
wrote this, people would say, 'A little heavy-handed, huh?'"

Fussells and the Keeleys. For the first trip, to Nice, she had her host's assurance that she'd be well taken care of ("Paul's letter, written in his usual tumescent spirit, suggests such orgiastic revels I'm half afraid to show up"), whereas the more monogamous Mike Keeley had to inquire among his Greek friends to find a willing partner for Maggie. When he explained to her that a certain friend hadn't, in fact, been making eyes at her one night, but rather had been sleepy and merely trying to stay awake, she was so enraged that she kicked a dent in Keeley's car ("You're no help at all! What good are you?").

She took off for Antigua at the beginning of February 1967, a few days before she started a new job at the Free Press, then an imprint of Macmillan. She was fired that December, and two months later submitted the affidavit requesting an almost treble increase in alimony: her income was now reduced, she claimed, to the defendant's $110 a week plus $55 in unemployment benefits; meanwhile she'd become the sole support of her seventeen-year-old daughter. "Given the history of the plaintiff's relationship with her daughter," Roth replied in opposition, "it would seem premature to predict that [Helen Miller] will be living with the plaintiff many months more"; at any rate, he continued, the plaintiff was *not* the "sole support" of her daughter and never had been, since there was a court order requiring her first husband, Burt, to help support the girl, and moreover Roth thought some provision had been made in the will of Burt's late uncle, Wilbur Walton of Kenosha, Wisconsin.

"Defendant states that I am not the sole support of my daughter," Maggie replied on March 12, 1968. "I must disagree." The previous summer, shortly before her seventeenth birthday, Helen had gone to Europe under the auspices of American Youth Hostels; while abroad she'd "unfortunately contracted hepatitis," according to Maggie, and was subsequently expelled from Kemper Hall. She now lived in her mother's one-bedroom apartment on East Fifteenth overlooking Stuyvesant Park, and was a third-year student at the nearby Washington Irving High School. As for Burt's alleged support, Maggie claimed he hadn't made a single payment since Roth's desertion in 1963—a claim Miller predictably denied: "I don't owe her a nickel," he said in 2013. "I was the one guy in this whole mess who did the right thing." Actually, as both he and his daughter attest, he was indeed helpful in at least one respect: when Helen had gotten pregnant in Europe during the summer of 1967—what Maggie called "hepatitis" in her affidavit—Burt took her to St. Louis for an abortion.

Maggie explained to the court that her unemployment insurance was due to expire in mid-May unless she attempted to find another job, but she was impeded "because of [her] mental health." Her daughter, for one, would not have denied it: "I remember her being so rageful," she said. "I also remember enduring months and months and months of her weeping." Both mother and daughter were seeing psychiatrists—another expense—though in Maggie's case her "depression and acute anxiety," not to say intransigence, seemed little mitigated by therapy. That spring Art Geffen—Philip and Maggie's old Chicago friend—spotted her outside the Cherry Lane Theatre in the Village, and made a special effort to be friendly ("I was not gonna take Philip's side or hers"); Maggie was "stony-faced" until he finally gave up and said goodbye. Around that time, too, her friendship with Forcey abruptly ended when Maggie phoned her former coworker and asked her to dinner, whereupon the woman admitted she was already having dinner with Ginny, the supervisor. *"My enemy!"* Maggie snarled, and slammed the phone down.

"I never see shithead [Maggie], and my lawyer has given up making offers of money to get me free, since no matter what is offered she wants more," Roth reported to their wedding witnesses, the Gibberds, adding however that two years of formal separation were now grounds for divorce under the new law—all the more reason (he subsequently implored the court) *not* to proceed with an alimony hearing in the spring of 1968, as Maggie requested, since the question would naturally arise during their divorce hearing that September: "<u>If this Court requires a hearing now, I will have to pay the expense of two trials in one year.</u>" Not so fast, Maggie replied: "[Defendant] did not make current alimony payments to me for a long period in 1965 and therefore breached the terms of the separation decree, the faithful performance of which is a requisite for a divorce under the new law."* So there was that to consider.

The man who'd fired Maggie from her job at the Free Press was a

---

* A debatable point. For a few weeks in 1965, in lieu of alimony checks, Roth had sent Maggie signed withdrawal slips for their sequestered joint account at the Greenwich Savings Bank. Maggie refused to co-sign the slips, as that would have been tantamount to admitting that Roth was entitled to the funds in that account.

"gorgeous, charming, very small" editor named Carter Hunter, according to Helen, who further described him as "bright, articulate, and a major bullshitter." (Helen would presently have an affair with him.) The thirty-three-year-old Hunter and Maggie had been drinking buddies outside of work, and continued as such when they were no longer colleagues. "Oh god, Maggie," Betty Fussell thought when her friend brought Hunter along for a visit to Princeton and both got so drunk Fussell had begged them to spend the night. Helen wondered in retrospect whether *both* her mother and Hunter had been fired around that time, given their heavy drinking, but a *Times* item about a "May Wine" party at the Museum of Modern Art on May 8, 1968, suggests that Hunter, at least, was still employed: "'It's so cold out here I'm drinking January gin,' said Mr. Hunter, the slight, mustached managing editor of the Free Press, which publishes books on sociology."

On Friday, May 10, two days after the MoMA event, and a few days before Maggie's unemployment insurance was due to lapse, she and Hunter attended a party on the Upper West Side with a third friend, who urged them to take a taxi home afterward. But Hunter wanted to show off his snazzy new Jaguar convertible, and while racing along the Sixty-sixth Street transverse in Central Park, at around five in the morning, he lost control and slammed into a tree on the passenger side. Maggie was killed instantly. Helen remembered that the police had "beat the shit" out of Hunter, who was black, when they detected his condition and noticed the dead white woman in his car.

Things had been improving lately between Maggie and her daughter. Maggie was drinking less and was therefore better company, and Helen had just gotten a pleasant summer job at a shop around the corner while also volunteering for an antiwar organization (she would soon earn the nickname "Hanoi [Helen]"). Maggie was killed the day before Mother's Day; she'd known Helen had bought a gift for her, and they'd parted on loving terms. That night, however, Helen felt "extremely anxious" and couldn't sleep; she stayed up watching TV until four in the morning, and was woken around eight thirty by the phone. It was the police: Was she the daughter of Margaret Roth? "Why are you asking me these questions?" said Helen, panicking, but they only told her to sit tight and wait. A few minutes later, the doorman rang to say two policemen were coming up to see her. After she got the news, she phoned Ronald at

Morgan Academy: "My sister was very distraught," he recalled. "I felt nothing." (Burt Miller corroborated his son's bland affect: Ronald "said 'Good.' One happy family, right?")

Roth had just arrived at Kips Bay to start his morning's work when the phone rang. "Philip," said Helen, "Mother's been killed." At first he thought it was a trick—a ghoulish enticement for him "to say something self-incriminating that could be recorded and used to sway the judge to increase the alimony in our next court go-round." "And where is she now?" he asked skeptically. "In the morgue," the girl replied, bursting into tears. Roth came down to the apartment on East Fifteenth, where Helen was being comforted by a family friend; he found himself staring at the shelves of books—all the Modern Library novels he'd bought at bookstores along Fourth Avenue, and later in Hyde Park as a graduate student. Helen begged him to go identify the body, but Roth didn't think it was his place: "there were plenty of people to do that other than her or me," he wrote in *The Facts*; "if she wished, however, I would make the funeral arrangements." (As it happened Helen did have to identify her mother's remains: one side of the head was badly disfigured, while the other looked as though she were "peacefully sleeping.")

Before proceeding to the Frank E. Campbell funeral home on Madison and Eighty-first, Roth stopped back at his apartment and made a few phone calls. "Yes," Fingerhood assured him, when he asked whether this meant he was divorced in the state of New York. "Good," said Sandy, echoing the dead woman's son. Roth was walking to the subway when it occurred to him that he no longer had to divide his income; the taxi he took to Campbell's "was the first tangible result" of his liberation. "Got the good news early, huh?" the cabbie remarked as he pulled to the curb, and Roth realized he'd been whistling the entire ride.

Maggie had wanted a Jewish funeral service, and Roth was oddly gratified to find himself in the director's office with David Seligson, one of the prominent New York rabbis who'd denounced his work as a bane to the Jews. "I didn't go so far as to wear a yarmulke at the service," Roth wrote, "but had the rabbi asked me to, I would have forsworn my secular convictions out of respect for the beliefs of the deceased. When I saw the casket, I said to [Maggie], 'You're dead and I didn't have to do it.' Whereupon the late Jew replied, 'Mazel tov.'" The funeral was well attended— perhaps a hundred of Maggie's family, coworkers, fellow New School students, and members of her various therapy groups ("did they get an earful about my enemas!"), for whose sake the widower kept a seemly aspect of grief afloat. "What relief he must be feeling," Pamela Forcey remembered thinking when she spotted Roth sitting with the family. Burt Miller and Bea Walton had come for the children's sake, and other mourners included Maggie's vilified supervisor Ginny ("extremely well-mannered," Roth recalled, "perhaps a lesbian") and Carter Hunter, who still looked "dazed and shaken" but appeared uninjured except for a bandage over one eye. Roth shook hands with him but didn't inquire as to the wherefores of the accident, lest a member of Maggie's therapy groups figure him as an accomplice. "I never saw, or heard of, my emancipator again," Roth noted of the editor.*

Betty Fussell thought Helen looked like a woebegone "orphan child" at the funeral and wondered what would become of her. Helen, for her part, remembered the particular kindness of their old Princeton friend Naomi Savage, who spoke to her tenderly and later sent a "beautiful package" of photographs she'd taken of her mother and stepfather; also, for a while, Savage made a point of keeping in touch with the girl ("the *only* adult who reached out that way"). As for Roth, he was startled when Helen murmured to him, once the funeral was over, "Now we can run away together." "I wanted to be rescued," she later explained.

On May 17, Roth boarded the Adirondack bus at Port Authority and traveled to Yaddo, where he holed up in Hillside Cottage for twelve days finishing his novel. The famous last lines—Spielvogel's only utterance—had "a secondary, more personal irony" for the author, "as both hopeful instruction and congratulatory message: 'So [said the doctor], now vee may perhaps to begin. Yes?'"

---

* Helen had seen Hunter "a day or two after the accident" and attested to how battered he was on other parts of his body. He'd assured Helen that he had maximum liability insurance and encouraged her to sue him—a position he later recanted. Meanwhile, Fingerhood assured Roth that he'd be reimbursed for the $853 funeral bill as soon as Burt Miller's wrongful death action against Hunter was settled, but, as Roth remembered, Hunter "skipped town" after the funeral and "was never seen around these parts again." Roth didn't seem to grudge him the expense.

PART THREE

THE MORONIC INFERNO

1968–1975

*Roth celebrates his imminent fame and fortune about a month before
the publication of* Portnoy's Complaint *in February 1969.*

(COPYRIGHT © BOB PETERSON)

*P*ORTNOY'S COMPLAINT, PUBLISHED IN FEBRUARY 1969, would become the best-selling novel in the illustrious history of Random House; by the year's end it had been number 1 for a total of seventeen weeks and sold almost 420,000 copies in hardcover, while the Bantam edition went on to sell 3.5 million copies in the first five years. In Australia, the novel was banned and its merits raucously debated for almost two years, at the end of which literary censorship was effectively abolished in the country. As for the author: shortly after his wife was cremated, and before the publication of his most notorious novel, he said he might write a book that would "stand Kafka on his head. . . . Instead of having a guy who is more and more pursued and trapped and finally destroyed by his tormentors, I want to start with a guy tormented and then the opposite happens. They come to the jail and they open the door and they say to you, 'A terrible mistake has been made.' And they give you your suit back, with your glasses and your wallet and your address book, and they apologize to you."

On May 29, 1968, Joe Fox had excitedly informed his colleagues that Roth was a week away from delivering his new novel, for which Random House would be expected to pony up an advance that was "probably astronomical and worth every penny of it." By then the four early excerpts had made Roth a celebrity: *Time* had already called his latest work "the most brilliant piece of radical humor in years," and two months later *The New York Times* predicted *Portnoy* would "be one of the most talked about books of the winter." When Roth returned from Yaddo at the end of May, Donadio phoned Cerf and briskly negotiated an advance of $250,000, followed that summer by another $250,000 for movie rights, $350,000 from Bantam for paperback rights (Roth got half), and $60,000 from the Literary Guild. Also a sizable portion of

Roth's advance for *When She Was Good* was still unpaid, along with various foreign monies, so that Roth predicted his total income for 1968 would come to roughly $827,000.* And it was all his!

Roth prepared for wealth and fame by looking for a new car, a new apartment, and (as he mentioned to *New York* magazine) a new editor at Random House. Almost two years earlier—three days after Roth had composed his ten-point grievance letter against his publisher, dated July 28, 1967—Donadio had sat down with Fox and Cerf to talk things over. "I think it was fruitful and cleared the air," Fox wrote Roth afterward, admitting he'd been "hurt" at first, but had since seen the justice of Roth's complaints and was "heartily sorry": "For your possible interest, amusement and/or derision," Fox concluded, "what I have learned from all this has pushed me over the brink into going into therapy. If I am so insensitive to the anguishes of someone I have thought of as a close friend, as well as a treasured author to whose work and aspirations I feel very close, I am obviously in big trouble." In fact Fox got in touch with none other than Kleinschmidt, lest Roth doubt the sincerity of his remorse, which was all the more extraordinary given Fox's well-known reluctance to become attached to people he worked with. His friend and colleague Jason Epstein—who would replace him as Roth's editor—remembered a "bright line [of privacy] you didn't want to cross" vis-à-vis Fox, who told another of his authors, Edward Hoagland, that he wasn't available to him as a friend ("I have my personal life and you are not a part of it").

The first thing Roth did with his *Portnoy* windfall was write a check to Fox for the $8,000 (plus interest) he'd borrowed over the years; then he had his agent break the news that Epstein would be Roth's editor going forward. "I'm sorry, for both our sakes, that you did not feel able to tell me yourself," Fox wrote him, austerely, doubtless bearing in mind all the weekends Roth had been a guest at Fox's houses in Bedford and East Hampton—all the hilarious touch football games with Plimpton, Nelson Aldrich, and so on. "I asked Candida to sever a professional relationship for me," Roth replied. "I was 'able' to do it myself, but frankly I didn't want to. I am as fond of [you] as I've ever been, though if your engine doesn't throb any longer at the sound of my name, I can under-

---

* About $6,115,000 in 2020 dollars.

stand." Roth confessed he'd been unpleasantly reminded of the problems they'd had over *When She Was Good* when Fox had recently warned him—"in Bedford and again in your office"—not to demand so much money for *Portnoy* ("I didn't like it when rich guys were offended that I asked for a lot of money," said Roth in 2012). "You *have* been a good and devoted friend," Roth continued, "—another reason (not that I expect you'll think it a good one) why I asked my agent to do the dirty work." Fox was decidedly unpersuaded. After a gruesome encounter at a party that August of 1968, he wrote a final note to Roth clarifying his position:

> Despite our differences in the past, I considered you one of my closest friends, and if you had come in to see me Monday morning and said—sheepishly, defensively, angrily, coolly, or whatever—that for various reasons, rational or not, you wanted to change editors, we could have survived the awkwardness and remained friends. But you couldn't bring yourself to do that, and this indicates to me, rightly or wrongly, that our relationship meant far less to you than it did to me.

■ ■ ■ ■

THE NEXT BIG CHECK Roth wrote, after paying off Fox, was for two first-class tickets on the luxury liner *France*. Somewhat impulsively he'd decided to take Mudge to England for a couple of months, staying a few days in a nice hotel before renting a car and driving "the length and breadth of the British Isles"; then, during August, he planned to rent a posh flat back in London where he could work on *Portnoy* galleys. Mudge told him he'd need a proper tuxedo for dinners aboard the *France* and helped him pick one out at Barney's. "I could take you back to Pittsburgh in that," she said, admiring the result. "Sure," said Roth, "we'd wow 'em at the country club. Especially after my little book comes out." She never mentioned Pittsburgh again.

The crossing was "a delight, the food perfect," Roth wrote friends; he'd been especially pleased by a photograph in the ship's magazine of Mudge and him, splendid in their evening attire, identified as "Mr. and Mrs. Philip Roth." In fact, the prospect of connubial respectability seemed to grow more distant by the day. Shortly after arriving in London, Roth was interviewed by an attractive young journalist, who politely declined his invitation to pass the afternoon in a hotel room. Indeed, the whole trip began to pall. Roth was bothered by noisy Piccadilly traffic outside their window at the Ritz, so they moved to the Connaught; then, the night before they were to depart for the long road trip to Edinburgh, Roth became sick at Jonathan and Rachel Miller's house. Jonathan had directed *The Old Glory* at the American Place Theatre, and also, as luck would have it, had studied medicine before starting the comedy troupe Beyond the Fringe with Peter Cook, Dudley Moore, and Alan Bennett (also a guest that night). Roth had been holding forth after dinner about his near death experience the year before, then admitted he was feeling pretty queasy even as he spoke. Miller had him lie down on the butcher-block table where they'd just eaten, and after a brief examination decided to get him to University College Hospital, where he was diagnosed with adhesions beneath his appendectomy scar.

Roth was ordered to rest, eat lightly, and stay close to London; instead of Scotland, then, they traveled fifty miles to Buckinghamshire, where the Gibberds lived in a small converted pub on the Grand Union Canal (the setting for Roth's author photo on the *Portnoy* jacket). At the Gibberds', Roth reported, they slept "in a pissy-smelling (cat piss) attic room" before returning to London and renting a "barny underfurnished flat" on Glebe Place, just off the King's Road. At loose ends, Roth decided he might as well spend some money, and so embarked on a series of fittings at Kilgour, French & Stanbury on Savile Row, where he ended up buying four suits. He was also fitted for trendier duds at celebrity tailor Dougie Hayward's shop in Mayfair; the bell-bottom trousers were tight in the crotch, and a friend remarked that they looked "like an ad for the Mattachine Society." It hardly mattered, since Roth would hang all five suits in his closet at home and rarely look at them again.

"I've been a perfect crab," Roth noted, "—I keep thinking, How can this be happening to me, with all my money!" They drove through picturesque hamlets and toured old Anglo-Saxon churches, but the only thing that really engaged him was English TV—namely, the spectacle of Mayor Daley's police bludgeoning yippies on the streets of Chicago during the 1968 Democratic Convention: "[I] wondered what the hell I was doing trying vainly to have a good time abroad while the turbulence of the American sixties, which had enlivened both my fiction and my life, looked finally to be boiling over." By August he'd had enough, booking passage on the *Queen Elizabeth* and arriving in New York the morning after Labor Day. "Delighted to be back in this madhouse," he wrote a friend.

■ ■ ■ ■

MUDGE WOULD PROVE another casualty of his post-Maggie restlessness. In recent years Roth had found equilibrium in the quiet pleasure of Mudge's company; otherwise he kept more and more to himself—working all day and reading at night. Now, however, rich and free and soon to be world-famous, he had to face facts: he adored Mudge but was sexually bored with her; as a rule he thought there was a "two-year limit" to sexual interest, and marriage was deadly in any case. Also, he never again wanted to give the state power to punish his private behavior, which would inevitably include adultery if he were to marry again. "You're never coming back, lamb chop," Mudge said sadly, when he proposed a six-month separation after their return from England, and of course she was right.

Mudge remained devastated by her breakup with Roth. A mutual friend, Barbara Jakobson, mentioned to him how she and Mudge had packed up his things in her apartment, and both women had wept when Mudge remembered how much he'd loved an old pair of suede slippers. "Pure Chekhov," Roth quipped at the time, though in later years—after many women and another marriage that went disastrously awry—he would sometimes wish he'd married Mudge after all: he would have been unfaithful, and the marriage would have ended, but he might have come out of it (à la the hero of *Everyman* after marriage to the Mudge-like Phoebe) with a loving daughter who'd care for him in his dotage.

During the fall of 1968, anyway, he wasn't single for long. The year before, while gathering in Central Park for the antiwar march along Fifth Avenue, he'd bumped into his old army buddy Marty Garbus, now a leading civil rights lawyer in New York. Back in touch, Garbus had recently invited him and Mudge to a small dinner party on November 8; the two were already broken up but decided to attend. Among the six guests was a beautiful twenty-three-year-old doctoral candidate at the Union Theological Seminary, Barbara Sproul, who'd murmured of Roth and his elegant companion, "What a lovely couple"—then was startled when Roth phoned the next day asking for a date.

But not terribly startled. At the time she herself was seeing two men named Peter: a young publisher, Peter Mayer (her date *chez* Garbus), who had a cabin near hers at the Byrdcliffe Colony in Woodstock, New York, and a young newscaster from Canada, Peter Jennings, whom she'd met at the Byrdcliffe swimming pool. Otherwise she lived alone with her cat in a family apartment on East Thirty-fifth, between Park and Lexington, where her father had killed himself two years before. Her demeanor in the face of tragedy (there were others) was stoically matter-of-fact, which Roth admired: "She'd been through a lot of shit and she was solid," he said. At a tender age she maintained two homes, shuttling between them in a little MG, and worked hard on her studies while doing what she liked with her free time. That year she spent Christmas with Jennings while seeing more and more of Roth, whom she took to Woodstock one snowy weekend and showed around town and the mountains beyond. Not a great reader of fiction, Sproul asked for recommendations and Roth gave her several marked-up books from his own library. "Why did you underline that?" she asked, pointing to a particular passage, and he quietly replied "Because it's beautiful." Later explaining Roth's appeal to her twenty-three-year-old self, Sproul wrote, "In his writing, his humor, his interests, his commitment to the work and the subjects it considers, he was/is *serious—morally serious.* And that appealed to me enormously."

"The fucking was extraordinary," said Roth, whom Sproul remembered as a little abashed by their intricate sex play ("Kink would scare him"), citing a time he'd plied a vibrator and then "mous[ed] around" the next day, as if expecting a Maggie-like tirade about his wickedness. "Well, that was fun," said Sproul, proposing they get a couple of vibrators for friends and then openly asking for same at the drugstore. Others were struck by Sproul's assertiveness, at least relative to Mudge, though Kleinschmidt (for one) wasn't having any: "A mature woman wouldn't take your shit," he commented on Roth's new romance.

■ ■ ■ ■

Roth's lease at Kips Bay expired that winter, and he found more sumptuous quarters at 18 East Eighty-first Street, a stone's throw from Central Park and the Metropolitan Museum and incidentally across the street from Campbell's funeral home, where he'd said goodbye to Maggie. Roth rented one of two parlor-floor apartments in the four-story building. His spacious living room was connected via a book-lined corridor to his study, also lined with bookcases and big windows giving a view of the backyard and its single plane tree. The small, nondescript bedroom was tucked away in the rear. Roth finished moving in at the end of January 1969 and summed up the month of February as "*Awful . . .* New apartment unfurnished. No Ann." From his tall front windows he could see caskets going in and out of Campbell's, and that June he would observe thousands of heartbroken fans lining up to see Judy Garland, lying in state.

Desperate to cheer things up, Roth hired a professional decorator who arranged his living room, said Lurie, in the style of a "formal women's club" with what appeared to be a "frieze of penises around the top of the walls"; Roth also splurged on a couple of gorgeous Persian rugs, and enlisted his discerning friend Nina Schneider to help pick out a handsome leather sofa and wing chair for the study, as well as a big sturdy worktable and bamboo ladder for his bookshelves. The little beige-walled bedroom remained almost grimly bare, perhaps because of Roth's penitence for all the "fashionable decorating shit," as he wrote Kleinschmidt: "WHY DIDN'T YOU STOP ME? As our poor pal Portnoy might put it."

Portnoy's stridency was much on his mind, given the clamor arising from his hero's increasing notoriety. Jason Epstein had predicted the year before that *Portnoy* would be "the biggest book in history"—a statement that seemed less hyperbolic as time went by. On January 11, the *Times* declared Roth's novel "a certain best-seller six weeks before publication," and gave a concrete reason why, to wit, "the prevalence of masturbation."

Amid the headiness of autumn Roth had agreed to any number of interviews for what was shaping up as "a new record for publicity over-kill"—as his friend Albert Goldman would presently write in *Life*—but as the air chilled Roth felt a growing dread, and fled to Yaddo for the month of December. He returned in time for Howard Junker's pro-file in the January 13 *New York* magazine, which got the ball rolling in earnest toward persuading the public that Roth and Portnoy were one and the same: "Roth kicked the nice Jewish boy bit," Junker wrote, "the stance of the Jamesian moral intelligence, and unleashed his comic, foul-mouthed, sex-obsessed demon. His true self." Very like Alex Portnoy, Junker observed, Roth "notices every girl that passes on the street," and moreover is given to "exultant self-revelation" ever since he was "freed" by psychoanalysis and "the death of his estranged wife last May." "He got so much wrong," Roth wrote Susan Sontag (to whom he'd allegedly referred as Suzy Q. Sontag in Junker's presence), "and made so much up (and probably more out of ineptness than malice) that I can't hope to begin to straighten things out in this letter, or anywhere."

As for Goldman's feature in *Life* ("'Portnoy's Complaint' by Philip Roth Looms as a Wild Blue Shocker and the American Novel of the Sixties"), it began, at least, as a lark: the photographer Bob Peterson had accompanied the friends as they explored Roth's old haunts in Newark and spent a day at Yaddo. The piece that followed, however, went a little far in characterizing the novel as the cultural equivalent of the Second Coming: "A savior and scapegoat of the '60s, Portnoy is destined at the Christological age of 33 to take upon himself all the sins of sexually obsessed modern man and expiate them in a tragicomic crucifixion." Various Jewish luminaries—Bellow, Joseph Heller, Lenny Bruce, Mort Sahl, the Marx Brothers, et al.—were invoked as relatively minor forerunners to Roth, who "has explored the Jewish family myth more profoundly than any of his predecessors, shining his light into all corners and realizing its ultimate potentiality is an archetype of contemporary life."

Random House, meanwhile—the firm that had brought *Ulysses* to American readers in 1934—was careful to have *Portnoy* vetted for obscene and defamatory content by Arthur F. Abelman of Weil, Gotshal & Manges, who concluded that the novel, as a whole, "contains elements of redeeming social value, such as humor," but advised that a reference to Mayor Lindsay's genitals on pages 272–73 might be construed as "an invasion of privacy. . . . Furthermore, since he controls the police in this City, such reference is an unwise provocation." Given, too, that Alex Portnoy is employed in the Lindsay administration, Abelman thought it a good idea to find out whether some actual person held a similar job and otherwise resembled Roth's hero; Irving Goldhaber, assistant director of the Commission of Human Relations, worried that some such confusion might indeed ensue, so Portnoy's title was changed to "Assistant Commissioner of Human Opportunity."

Random House celebrated publication day, February 21, with a dinner at the swanky Raffles club; on the menu were "Mousse de Homard à la Sophie, Fine Champagne (Château Weequahic 1949), Monkey soupe à la Tortue aux Xérès, and Dessert à votre choix (Cordon Klienschmidt [sic])." But the fun had already begun to curdle for Roth, and the reviewers were even more exasperating than usual, what with their persistent tendency to regard his novel as a confession: "Roth's past life resembles Alex Portnoy's," said *Time*, giving examples, and even the sympathetic Brendan Gill, in *The New Yorker*, described Portnoy as Roth's "hero and counterpart." Gill was mostly enthusiastic, though, whereas the novel excited a degree of generational testiness in Alfred Kazin: "I admire it, but love it I don't," he wrote Jason Epstein. "The Jewish family torture, even for those who have gone through the mill, has in the past not been so purely psychological, has certainly in the past gone along with a certain moral and even spiritual insight. But Roth is essentially a savage writer: no nuances, and above all, no love." Kazin glossed over the worst of this verdict in his critique for *The New York Review of Books*, conceding Roth's gifts as a "mimic and fantasist" but remarking that "he can write of Jews only as hysterics" and also taking him to task for what Irving Howe would later characterize as "thin personal culture"—as Kazin put it, "he writes without the aid of general ideas (Herzog suffered twice as much as Portnoy does, but Herzog also lived in history; Portnoy lives only through his mother)." Over the years Kazin would sometimes try explaining as much to Roth, whose idea of "Jewish identity," said Kazin, was a callow secularization of a subject that "began in the desert, not in Newark." "You don't understand," he'd say, poking the younger man in the chest. "You don't even understand when I tell you you don't understand."

Less exacting or touchy critics tended to applaud the novel as not only refreshing in its gleeful obscenity, but also (contra Kazin) "painfully and playfully moving," as Roth's old Amagansett pal Josh Greenfeld wrote in his front-page rave for the *Times Book Review*, "a work that is certainly catholic in appeal, potentially monumental in effect—and, perhaps more important, a deliciously funny book, absurd and exuberant, wild and uproarious." In the daily *Times*, Christopher Lehmann-Haupt kicked off his ultimately unhappy career as a reviewer of Roth's books by declaring *Portnoy* "a technical masterpiece" that brought "the genre of the so-called Jewish novel . . . to an end and a new point of departure." For the most part, though, critics were rather evenly divided between those who admired the book and those who were offended by it—sometimes grievously—a division best represented in *The Saturday Review*: Roth appeared on the cover of an issue featuring both an endorsement by

Granville Hicks ("very much like a masterpiece") and "A Dissent" by Marya Mannes, a former *Vogue* editor, who bleakly predicted that "the mixture of bile, sperm, and self-indulgence that infuses most of *Portnoy's Complaint* should put it on the best-seller lists." She was not mistaken in that respect, nor would Roth have argued much with her reasoning; he later noted that his book's pioneering treatment of a certain "shameful, solitary addiction" had served to attract "an audience that previously had shown little interest in my writing" (an indifference to which they would return).

The main dialectic of the novel—Jewish repression versus goyish license—was somewhat inspired by Isaac Rosenfeld's "Adam and Eve on Delancey Street," which equates the consumption of *trafe* with "the whole world of forbidden sexuality, the sexuality of the *goyim*, and there all the delights are imagined to lie, with the *shiksas* and *shkotzim** who are unrestrained and not made kosher." Growing up, Portnoy comes to associate the kosher laws with the relentless strictures imposed by his family, especially his mother, who evokes the specters of polio and colitis to frighten him away from hamburgers and french fries, lest he become like the "imbecilic eaters of the execrable" who gorge on "pigs and crabs and lobsters" and enjoy the kind of squalid sex that Alex longs to have with a dream shiksa, Thereal McCoy: "Her favorite line of English prose is a masterpiece: 'Fuck my pussy, Fuckface, till I faint.' When I fart in the bathtub, she kneels naked on the tile floor, leans all the way over, and kisses the bubbles. She sits on my cock while I take a shit, plunging into my mouth a nipple the size of a tollhouse cookie. . . ." In a house where drinking a glass of milk is frowned on, Alex's longing for such degradation is all the keener, and hence the more guilt-inducing: "My wang was all I really had that I could call my own," he remarks of his main form of rebellion, most memorably with a piece of liver his mother then cooks for the family meal.

Roth's treatment of Portnoy's Uncle Hymie, the novel's most vivid embodiment of small-minded Jewish insularity, was doubtless the sort of thing Kazin considered narrowly "psychological"—that is, lacking in "moral and even spiritual insight." When Hymie's son, Heshie, wants to

* An offensive term for male gentiles.

marry a shiksa (a "Polack" at that), Hymie throws him to the floor and holds him there until "tears of surrender at last appeared on Heshie's long dark Hollywood lashes. We are not a family that takes defection lightly." Leaving nothing to chance, Hymie has already convinced his son's fiancée that Heshie has an "incurable blood disease"—this before producing five twenty-dollar bills that the "dumb, frightened" girl accepts: "Thus proving something that everybody but Heshie (and I) had surmised about the Polack from the beginning: that her plan was to take Heshie for all his father's money, and then ruin his life." The pitiless—or even "savage," as Kazin would have it—punch line comes when Heshie is killed in the war, whereupon Uncle Hymie and his wife are invariably consoled with the words "At least he didn't leave you with a *shikse* wife." When Herman (Hymie!) Roth used to tell the story of how Sender beat his son Ed to keep him from marrying "a worldly woman," the young Philip was furious at his father's vague approval (*"They don't have that kind of discipline anymore"*) of a xenophobic brutality that had no place in American life. Like Herman, though, Kazin was the son of unassimilated Yiddish-speaking immigrants; whatever his own yearnings as an American intellectual, Kazin was sentimental about the tragic history of the Jews—going back to the shtetl and even "the desert"—in a way Roth was not.

"Doctor, what should I rid myself of, tell me, the hatred . . . or the love?" Portnoy asks, and Roth himself pointed out that "the book derives such emotional force as it has from its seesawing" between lyricism and farce. "[Portnoy's] perspective is that of a wounded farceur, who takes delight in his own grievances—in that way (and only in that way) he is a distant relative of Mr. Sabbath." The difference: Roth's later hero Mickey Sabbath delights in his transgressions without a whit of Portnoy's guilt— the guilt endemic to Nice Jewish Boys whose parents treated them "as unique as unicorns on the one hand," and "selfish, evil little shits, little *ingrates,* on the other!" Portnoy remembers his mother's friend Mrs. Nimkin, who could only think of her own sacrifice ("All the [piano] lessons we gave him") when she finds her fifteen-year-old son Ronald hanging from the showerhead with a note pinned to his shirt: *"Mrs. Blumenthal called. Please bring your mah-jongg rules to the game tonight. / Ronald."* But then, too, there was the whole tragic history to consider, and hence Kazin and the like were less impressed by Portnoy's lyrical moments ("I fall asleep with my face against my mother's black sealskin coat") than by an outburst like "Do me a favor, my people, and stick your suffering heritage up your suffering ass—*I happen to be a human being!*" A few years later, Kazin was still musing in print over Portnoy's awesome solipsism ("Whom do *you* suffer for, Alex P.? I suffer for me"), weighing the irony of all the "emancipated" Jews who relate to him: " 'Your book has so many readers!' I once heard an admirer say to Roth. 'Why,' she continued enthusiastically, 'you must have at least six million readers!' "

It was Bennett Cerf's impression, when he addressed more than a thousand women at a Pittsburgh temple, that Roth's detractors were outnumbered "10 to 1"—at any rate, the book was so successful that Random House could afford to take an almost jaunty tone toward readers who wrote in protest: "Difference of opinion . . . is what makes life interesting," publicist Jean Ennis replied to Mrs. Peter J. Weiss, who'd expressed her wonder that such a respectable publisher had sullied its reputation with "this example of pornography, group defamation, exercise in a man's abnormality," and so on. Still, a suburban matron was one thing, and a stern Zionist intellectual like Marie Syrkin another; it's pleasant to imagine how the affable Cerf, for one, would have parried such points as Syrkin raised in her *Midstream* review ("The Fun of Self-Abuse"), which treated Roth's novel as a species of propaganda that would have gladdened the hearts of Goebbels and Streicher: "In both views the Jewish male is not drawn to a particular girl who is gentile, but by a gentile 'background' which he must violate sexually."

Hard words, but hardest of all came from an even more eminent personage—the great scholar of Jewish mysticism Gershom Scholem, then president of the Israel Academy of Sciences and Humanities and one of three recipients that year of the Yakir Yerushalayim (Worthy Citizen of Jerusalem) award. "This is the book for which all anti-Semites have been praying," Scholem wrote in the Hebrew-language daily *Haaretz*.

We [Jews] will pay the price, not the author who revels in obscenities. . . . I daresay that with the next turn of history, not long to be delayed, this book will make all of us defendants at court. . . . This book will be quoted to us—and how it will be quoted! They will say to us: Here you have the testimony from one of your own artists . . . I wonder what price *k'lal yis-rael* [the world Jewish community]—and there is such an entity in the eyes of the Gentiles—is going to pay for this book. Woe to us on that day of reckoning!

Roth didn't learn of Scholem's review until a visit to Israel in 1984, when a Tel Aviv professor gave him the gist of it and asked what he thought: "I said that history had obviously proved Scholem wrong: more than fifteen years had passed since the publication of *Portnoy's Complaint* and not a single Jew had paid anything for the book, other than the few dollars it cost in the bookstore." "Not yet," the professor replied; "but the Gentiles will make use of it when the time is right."*

In 2013, when the politician Anthony Weiner was busted a second time for "sexting" in the midst of his comeback mayoral campaign in New York, the *Times* published a piece—"When Politics Catches Up with 'Portnoy'"—about how such scandals were exploding "outdated cultural assumptions" about the decency of Jewish men. Eliot Spitzer—whose governorship of New York had ended five years earlier, when his fondness for high-priced prostitutes was discovered—was quoted in the article as follows: "I haven't read a novel in thirty years, I've lived one." "It's bad for the Jews," said Erica Jong, "and it makes the anti-Semites say, 'See, I told you they're animals.'" Claudia Roth Pierpont remembered that Roth was "convulsed" by the Spitzer affair, calling her up and insisting they meet for lunch to pore over newspapers together. "I was trying to establish some hifalutin complex theory about why [Spitzer] would want to destroy himself," said Pierpont, "why a man would act so stupidly when he had so much to lose. Is there something self-destructive inherent? And Philip just looked at me and said: 'No, honey. It's just cock.'"

---

* In his book about the *Portnoy* phenomenon, *Promiscuous*, Roth's friend Bernard Avishai provided this intriguing bit of trivia: "Item: The Israeli journalist Danny Rubinstein told me that his childhood friend in Jerusalem imported pornographic films in the 1960s, and one of his biggest clients was—wait for it!—Gershom Scholem."

CHAPTER

Twenty-Five

Later in his career, Roth liked to quote Czesław Miłosz: "When a writer is born into a family, the family is finished." While sitting at his typewriter Roth would follow his muse wherever she led, and the impact on family and friends was something he worried about later, if at all. And so far so good, at least where his parents were concerned: "I'm bustin' my buttons!" Herman had told everyone within earshot at the Astor ballroom when Philip won the National Book Award in 1960, and for years Bess had carefully curated scrapbooks of her son's press coverage, the good, bad, and in-between.

Roth did worry, however, that *Portnoy* might expose them to a degree of undesirable scrutiny, and a few months before publication he invited them to lunch in New York. He told them the book was about a Jewish family, and, yes, he'd borrowed the odd detail from real life, but it was decidedly a work of fiction; still, there was a certain amount of obscenity and it was bound to be a big best seller, so it was likely people would want to interview Bess and Herman. "It's perfectly okay to say 'No, thank you,' and hang up," Philip told his punctilious mother, knowing how hard it was for her to hang up on even the most irksome strangers. Fourteen years after that lunch—the year after his mother's death—he was visiting Herman in Florida, and finally learned what had happened once they parted that day. Getting into a cab, Bess burst into tears: "He has delusions of grandeur! He's never been like this before. I can't bear to think of how his heart is going to be broken."

Actually, Bess handled the press with remarkable aplomb. "I think all mothers are Jewish mothers," she'd reply, when asked whether she was indeed Sophie Portnoy. Herman told *The New York Times*, and others, that both his sons were "good boys and fine men" who'd recently helped him and Mrs. Roth celebrate their forty-second wedding anniversary.

"The music goes round and round," he wrote Philip in April. "Tonight at the temple across the way from us the Rabbi is reviewing the book. . . . You pushed the war and the students riot into the background." When Herman gave a doctor friend a rubdown in the YMHA steam room, he predicted the man would someday tell his "great-great grandchildren: Portnoys [sic] father gave him a rub." As for Bess, she might have been forgiven a little mortification when, say, the actress Mae Questel (of Betty Boop and Olive Oyl fame) cut a record titled *Mrs. Portnoy's Retort*, but Bess was simply thrilled at the mark her son had made: "My Philip," she'd sigh now and then, knitting at night.

To Howard Junker of *New York*, Bess had quipped that she planned to leave the country when the book came out; Philip decided that was a good idea, paying all expenses for a monthlong trip abroad that summer. After stops at luxury hotels in London and Paris, the Roths traveled on to Israel, where Philip had arranged for a friend's family to show them around. Herman had packed a stack of *Portnoy* hardbacks for the trip, and aboard the ship he'd accost fellow passengers and work the conversation around to his illustrious son: "How would you like an autographed copy?" he'd say, then rush back to his cabin and return with a book inscribed "From Philip Roth's father, Herman Roth."

The fact was, his parents enjoyed the spotlight a lot more than Philip did, though it took a few weeks for the novelty to wear off. "It's an odd, good time," he wrote Solotaroff, "and it won't happen again, thank God, though I wouldn't have wanted to miss the once." Being famous, he said, was like being a child (or at least a child in Weequahic): "You walk down the street and everybody knows who you are, and you don't know who they are. . . . 'Aren't you Bess's boy?'" If only the questions were that benign. Roth tried to be a good sport "the first fifteen times" he was approached in restaurants and asked whether he was eating liver. "I tried going to the theater last night," he wrote Jacquie Rogers, "and as I emerged from the taxi, a cry went up (yes, my dear, a real cry, as though I had tits and was Elizabeth Taylor): 'Portnoy!' they screamed. I rushed off to a bar for a drink, and a man immediately materialized at my side from WNEW-TV asking if I would say a few words for the camera." Given the nature of his notoriety, the attention was often nasty or downright menacing, as when a man yelled from across the street, *"Philip Roth! The enemy of the Jews!"* "I am so sorry," said Roth, when a woman blocked his and Lurie's path along Fifth Avenue and accused him of being the author of "that disgusting novel." "I know I look like him," Roth went on, "and lately this sort of thing keeps happening to me all the time!" The woman gave hasty apologies and let them pass.

Also there were galling exchanges on *The Tonight Show*, hosted by Johnny Carson. "I'd be interested in meeting Philip Roth," said Jacqueline Susann, author of louche novels such as *The Love Machine* (tugging at *Portnoy*'s ankles on the best-seller list), "but I wouldn't want to shake his hand." A more serious provocation was brought to Roth's attention by a sheepish dry-goods clerk in Saratoga (whither Roth had fled by then), who reluctantly owned that Truman Capote had accused Roth, on Carson the night before, of "setting up" his reviews for *Portnoy*.* "I am most distressed about this," Roth wrote Fingerhood, "and want to find out exactly what was said; and then to proceed from there, according to how damaging and slanderous the statement was." What Capote had said was part of his ongoing rant against "the Jewish Mafia" in American letters (this largely due to his bitterness about *In Cold Blood*, which had been passed over for all the major awards). "Bernard Malamud and Saul Bellow and Philip Roth and Isaac Bashevis Singer and Norman Mailer are all fine writers," Capote told *Playboy* in 1968, "but they're not the *only* writers in the country, as the Jewish literary Mafia would have us believe."

Within four days of Roth's request, Fingerhood forwarded an NBC transcript from the April 15 show:

> CARSON: [after noting that *Portnoy* had received a number of good reviews from "respectable" outlets such as the *Times*, whereas other reviewers had said] it's a cesspool of humor. Now, how can two people look at the same thing, literary critics and such, and draw completely two opposite views?

---

* Later Roth remembered sitting on his Persian rug at 18 East Eighty-first Street, eating barbecue chicken, when Capote suddenly appeared on TV and began gleefully slandering him. When I quoted some of his own 1969 letters proving he hadn't actually watched the show, Roth admitted this was another instance of his fiction supplanting real-life memories; it was in an early draft of *Zuckerman Unbound* where he'd written about Zuckerman eating chicken and watching Cyrus Caudwell (the Capote character) slander him on a Carson-like show.

CAPOTE: Well, it depends on whether they're friends of Philip Roth or not. (laughter)

CARSON: That's it, right there.

CAPOTE: Now, I'd say—I'll explain that remark—Philip Roth is a friend of mine and I think he is very, very talented, and he's really one of the most gifted young American writers. But you see, there's this whole thing in New York—it's called the Jewish Literary Mafia, and it starts at Columbia University and it goes through all the little magazines and what-not; and I don't mean that it's conscious or unconscious—but they promote each other continuously. And they promote this little clique of which Philip Roth is the youngest, and in many ways, the most brilliant. And they started the drum going for this book—you know—a good year and a half ago, and it's just appearing in the magazines. So, it was an inevitable thing that it would turn into what it has, because they were really pushing for it, and that's what I mean by the reviews. It depends on whether or not the reviewer was a friend of Philip Roth. Mostly, they all were.

In a way, this was egregiously unfair—certain Jewish critics had been Roth's most caustic detractors; indeed, among Capote's not-so-secret sympathizers were New York Jewish intellectuals such as Irving Howe, who were irritated by what they perceived as the unseemly careerism of Roth et al. "When Truman Capote later attacked the Jewish writers on television," Howe wrote, "he had the dissolute courage to say what more careful gentlemen said quietly among themselves." After all, two of the most influential puffs for Roth's novel—Goldman's *Life* feature and Greenfeld's rave for the *Times Book Review*—had been written by Jewish friends of the author. Nor was Roth above trying to put the fix in: when the *Chicago Sun-Times* published some mean cracks about an early *Portnoy* excerpt, Roth asked Dick Stern if he'd "want to rebut this argument in passing, by reviewing the whole book when it appears." However, he didn't always approach other Jews for such favors: "May I be so bold as to suggest that if you do find yourself interested enough to review the book," he wrote Styron about *Our Gang*, "that you consider doing it for our old friend, The N. Y. Times Sunday Book Section?"

In any case, Roth decided not to sue Capote. Rather he spotted the diminutive gadfly at a subsequent party *chez* Cerf and pinned him against the bookshelves: "I didn't like what you said about me on the Carson Show, Truman." Capote smiled—"There's nothin' I can do about *thaaaaat*"—then ducked under Roth's arms and slipped away.*

■ ■ ■ ■

ROTH'S CULTURAL UBIQUITY reached critical mass at the end of March 1969, when Paramount's version of *Goodbye, Columbus* was released into theaters. Roth was still of the opinion that all movies were "dreck culture," and therefore had accepted his $25,000 and then sought to avoid what Bellow would have called (by way of Wyndham Lewis) the Moronic Inferno. Roth was irate when a paperback tie-in edition was published with a movie still on the cover, and sternly reminded Bantam that his work should never be promoted thus: "I hope that it is now understood that in the future I would prefer that my books be presented exactly for what they are, and not adjunct, by-product, or what-have-you." He declined an invitation to attend the premiere or even to meet the actress Ali MacGraw, who his father had assured him "has the cutest little tushy." Alone, incognito, Roth ventured to see the movie in a Times Square theater, and later took Herman Schneider, who remembered Roth laughing so "uproariously" that people kept turning around to shush him. He was also amused by the *Mad* magazine parody, "Hoo-Boy, Columbus!"—especially the last panel, in which Mort Drucker's caricature of Roth (with sideburns and a turtleneck) appears. "I'm marrying one of the richest Jewish men in the world today!" says "Blanda Pretendkin," to which "Philip Raw" adds, "Yes, and if you think parts of THIS movie were vulgar and obscene, wait'll you see the movie version of my newest book, 'Pitney's Complaint'! It's so raunchy we'll end up millionaires!"

---

* In that discarded draft of *Zuckerman Unbound*, Roth invests the fictional version of this encounter with considerably more drama, and gives Cyrus Caudwell some persuasive parting lines. "You're a squirt, you're a publicity hound, you're a venomous gossip, you're a repellent narcissist, and as a writer of anything and everything you're tenth-rate," says Zuckerman, whereupon Caudwell rejoins: ". . . You *must* stop guarding yourself, and caring what Lionel and Diana [Trilling] think about you and say about you to Fred and Mark and Wystan and Danny and Pearl [various literati]. You *wrote* that book, now for goodness sake, let them all fuck themselves."

By early March, Roth had already escaped to Yaddo via the Adirondack bus, where he heard a couple in the seat behind him discussing a novel ("This book isn't any good at all") that proved to be *Portnoy*. At Yaddo the main house was closed for the season, and Roth was given the "glorious" Pink Room on the second floor of West House, a huge space with a piano at one end and twenty windows looking out on tall, snow-dusted evergreens. "I'm feeling saved," he wrote Sproul on March 6. "I really don't seem up to all the attention, vulgarity, and silliness; I slipped there at the end in New York, and I do think you've seen me just about at the bottom." But he wasn't quite so publicity scalded that he could resist picking up the odd copy of the *New York Post* to keep track of his alternative life in the city, as reported in the gossip columns of Leonard Lyons and others: "Please don't hate me," he'd allegedly implored his "fellow authors" via Lyons, who also kept readers apprised of Roth's romance with another hot young Jewish celebrity: "Barbra Streisand has no complaints about her dates with Philip Roth."

For Roth it was an immense relief to be among people who knew him foremost as a writer rather than "a sex maniac and a millionaire"—such people as Yaddo's doting, genteel secretary, Polly Hanson, herself a poet, and all the housekeepers and groundskeepers and kitchen staff who regarded Roth as simply a polite fellow who spent most of his time alone in a studio, typing. There was also a (somewhat) kindred soul just over an hour away in Bennington, Bernard Malamud, who invited Roth to visit whenever he fancied a change of scenery. When Roth first arrived at Malamud's remote clapboard farmhouse, the study door was open and Roth saw a mysterious young woman sitting on the floor sorting manuscripts—an impression he saved for *The Ghost Writer*, along with aspects of Malamud's conversation: "[He] tells me nothing happens to him," Roth wrote Solotaroff. "I should be so lucky!"

Among the ten or so guests at Yaddo was the New Zealand novelist Janet Frame, who loved playing antic games of Ping-Pong—smashing balls well beyond the bounds of the table—with Roth and another guest, Alan Lelchuk, a thirty-year-old writer whom Frame described as "a lusty young buck" and "a brilliant chap." Roth would not have disagreed. The two men had met during Roth's previous visit in December; Lelchuk was an assistant professor at Brandeis who'd completed his Stanford dissertation on George Gissing a few years before. Nowadays he pursued a studious but freewheeling bachelor life in Cambridge, where he drove a jalopy with one back door secured by a rope. As the weather got warmer, the writers took to tossing a baseball back and forth on the big lawn; Lelchuk peppered Roth with questions about his flight from fame and its bounties (female), and Roth was oddly charmed by the young man's "blunt inquisitorial style . . . tinged both by a certain unworldly, slightly unearned cynicism and more than a touch of intellectual presumption."

Roth was encouraging but brutally frank about Lelchuk's own fiction. The younger man considered himself, at the time, as little better than an apprentice; he'd published all of two stories, in *New American Review* and *Transatlantic Review*, and was working on a long political novel that was pushing four hundred pages. Roth skimmed the latter but was more taken with a separate, seventy-page story about a Cambridge radical named Lenny Pincus, who is eager to prove he's willing to commit cold-blooded murder in the service of an anarchic ideology. Roth told Lelchuk to dump the novel and expand the shorter work, and Lelchuk did as he was told. "I drove him like a slave worker," said Roth, who was intrigued by the larger possibilities of what became *American Mischief,* but found the prose "unworked. . . . He would give me twenty pages and I'd put X's through five of them and say, 'Alan, it's shit and let me tell you why it's shit.' . . . And he would go back in like a coal miner and give me another five pages and I'd say 'You got it!'" Roth broke into song: "'*By George she's got it!*' . . . He was my Eliza Doolittle."

One enticement of literary fame, for Lelchuk, was the lurid profusion of letters his friend received from *Portnoy* readers. During his first month at Yaddo, Roth had asked Random House to hold his mail, until finally curiosity got the better of him: "a truck pulled up today and out it came," he wrote Charlotte Maurer, "all the invitations to talk, to give money, to get laid, to slit my throat, to have somebody slit it for me; and then some old friends, too." Roth shared the juicier specimens with Lelchuk—especially those with photos enclosed: There was "the luscious girl in her bikini" reading Updike's *Couples* while a toddler crawled near the edge of the frame, and Lelchuk himself remembered a "very pretty" woman who described herself as "a factory worker in Ohio" and wanted to be Roth's Monkey. "Every day I had ten opportunities to ruin my life," said Roth, who permitted himself to answer only those rare letters "that seem to have been written by people who had been out of Rockland [mental hospital] for at least six months."

Roth's mail was part of a larger discussion. "Our frankness about sex and sexual experience was mutual and refreshing," Lelchuk wrote in his 2003 roman à clef, *Ziff: A Life?*

> Nothing was off-limits—talking about capacity and desire, morning versus night fucking and erotic positions, dynamo women and perverse habits, attractive (or repellent) odors and growing fondness for cunnilingus, our own weaknesses and limitations (duration of erection, declining number of orgasms), unwanted boundaries. Coming to the territory from different paths, with a variety of spices, both of us were crazy about pussy—as well as very fond of females as friends—and the pleasure to talk openly about sex was exhilarating, freeing.

All this is true, and the friends' correspondence bears it out. For Roth's delectation, Lelchuk would describe a woman's sexual attributes in starkly objective terms, and it was clear they both enjoyed women intellectually as well as erotically—albeit not always at the same time. In one case (of many), Lelchuk explained to Roth the hardships he'd endured in bed with a chain-smoking older writer of no small reputation: "You know me, Phil, must be LOVED or I can't breathe," he wrote, along with certain horrific details as to why this woman was more suitable as a friend than a lover. "I wouldn't put my dick in Alice Denham if I were you," Roth wrote in kind. "You might want to apply for a Guggenheim someday, and I understand Henry Allan Moe"—the foundation's seventy-five-year-old former president—"is hot for her."

Soon Lelchuk began seeing a woman he'd met at the MacDowell Colony the year before—"one of the most unlikely couplings I've ever witnessed," Roth said of the scrappy long-haired Brooklyn Jew and his girlfriend, a Radcliffe-educated scion of an elite Wasp lineage. At the time she was working on a book that would become a classic of its kind; then and later, she felt nothing but gratitude toward Lelchuk, who put her up in his Cambridge digs and steadily encouraged her work. "Alan wanted desperately to be Philip Roth," she remembered, in a charitable spirit that Roth's own girlfriend didn't share, though she agreed with the basic premise. "He was a complete sycophant and I didn't think Philip could see it," said Barbara Sproul, who despised Lelchuk. On two points her opinion never wavered: one, that Lelchuk was enviously "using" Roth and not to be trusted, and two, that Roth himself was (then and later) peculiarly vulnerable to "sycophantic characters," since he assumed his friends were as serious as he, and therefore didn't "understand a shallow motive." But then, too, Sproul admitted she'd been jealous of Lelchuk, to whom Roth was closer in certain ways ("He wasn't used to trusting women quite yet"), especially that first year or so when Sproul was relatively unfledged. "I bought [Sproul] a harmonica out of a machine in a toilet on the Mass. Pike," Roth wrote Lelchuk that summer. "When she blows on it her face lights up, just like Harpo Marx. If only I could encourage her to become even more like that silent saint!"

■ ■ ■ ■

ROTH MISSED THE sweetly companionable Mudge, and made a point of sending her the first advance copy of *Portnoy*—a certain passage of which might have particularly caught her eye: "Doctor, they can stand on the window ledge and threaten to splatter themselves on the pavement below, they can pile the Seconal to the ceiling—I may have to live for weeks and weeks on end in terror of these marriage-bent girls throwing themselves beneath the subway train, but I simply cannot, I simply *will* not, enter into a contract to sleep with just one woman for the rest of my days." When Roth stopped returning Mudge's phone calls, she took to mooning outside his apartment; one day he reluctantly let her in and slept with her. "I was no bargain," Mudge conceded, remembering how needy she'd become, especially toward the end when she felt Roth slipping away forever.

Her psychoanalyst—actually a tropical diseases doctor—was of the opinion that Mudge herself was to blame for her breakup with Roth (because of her neediness), and to this man Roth had drafted a letter dated March 13, 1969:

> I wanted you to know that I have written Ann Mudge a letter in which I make as clear to her as possible that our affair is over and that we really must not and cannot see each other again. I've tried to be as firm as I can be, and as truthful, and there is no doubt that she will be badly shaken

up by the letter, though I have tried also to be as kindly as I can in this kind of situation.

Roth proposed to mail his letter to Mudge on Saturday, March 15, so that she'd be likely to receive it after her Monday morning session of analysis. He'd also spoken to a few close friends and family: "I do want her to be protected from her own desperation," he wrote the doctor. "I understand that Ann may be irritated afterwards to discover that I took these people into my confidence on so personal a matter, but I think that her irritation or even her momentary humiliation is a secondary consideration right now." In the end, though, Roth couldn't bring himself to mail this letter, not only because he hated embarrassing Mudge but also because he had even less faith in her "analyst" than she did.

Nor was it easy for him to decide, once and for all, that a clean break was best for both of them; she'd been his closest friend, and he needed a friend more than ever. On April 1, the *Times* atoned for its good reviews of *Portnoy* with a pious attack on the editorial page titled "Beyond the (Garbage) Pale," whose nameless author wondered why works that "revel in gutter language" should "justify the suspension of sophisticated critical judgment. . . . Yet this does seem to be just what has been suspended in the case of many recent works, viz., one current best-seller hailed as a 'masterpiece,' which, wallowing in a self-indulgent public psychoanalysis, drowns its literary merits in revolting sex excesses." Readers were all the more likely to connect the editorial with its intended target, given that a big quote-ad for *Portnoy* appeared on the preceding page ("an American masterwork").

Now that Mudge was out of his life, it occurred to Roth that the only person he really missed in the city was Kleinschmidt (and Sproul, but she came up to Saratoga for occasional visits). As he wrote Bob Baker, "Why analysis has caught on in big cities is, I think, for just that reason: it's the only kind of friendship you can sustain." Rather than jeopardize his shaky composure with a return to "Ambition Hollow" (Manhattan), Roth confided his "emotional exhaustion" to the analyst with an epistolary cri de coeur on April 15:

I really can't stand very much more of this isolation. There's been an awful lot of it. Solitude fine, isolation no. The melancholy, and the anxiety too, has a lot to do with Ann. I miss her terribly, all the while I know Barbara is a very special young woman. . . . I feel 36 and am struck again and again by her being still only 23. She is such a mix of girl, child, and young woman, and all of it right up on the surface. . . .

Also I'm afraid. Afraid of my new Position. I have not in years . . . flushed and perspired as much as I do now, when the focus of conversation turns upon me, even here [Yaddo] at the quiet dinner table. I feel like Uncle Vanya himself—since dinner here is right out of Chekhov. . . . Yesterday in Vermont I was instantly recognized in a restaurant outside Brattleboro, and asked this morning to autograph a copy of my book by a waitress in the motel here in town where I was registered under the cute Nabokovian pseudonym . . . as Milton Rose. I redden, I perspire, my stomach drops—and the thought of the National Book Award, eleven months away, which I may or may not win, has me terrified already. I really do want to retreat—for good. . . .

I know what I want: a woman I can trust and love, and who is sweet and passionate; a home of my own to live a long life in; and to write the best books I can. . . . I suppose I ache only with vanity—and yet I would relinquish all that, vanity, and pathetic social aspirations, and that ghastly stinking bastard, that son of a bitch, Shame—gladly relinquish that—but *how*? . . .

I'll phone soon. I've got to come back sometime, I know that. Though I dread the gaping people, and my own red face, and dread seeing Ann, for the love I still feel for her. There's you, there's Barbara, and sadly, there isn't much more. I go down the roll call of New York friends, and who do I see? who do I talk to? and about what?

Such was Roth's state of mind four days before Mudge attempted suicide. She'd begun drinking again once she realized he wasn't coming back. Barbara Jakobson had taken her to an "art world party" where she met the prominent color-field painter Jules Olitski, but their brief affair only reminded her of what she'd lost. One night—coming home, drunk, from a date with Olitski—she took an overdose of sleeping pills. For two days Jakobson tried reaching her on the phone, and finally called Mudge's analyst, who reported that she'd failed to show up for her last appointment. Barbara got hold of her husband, John, on the floor of the stock exchange, and insisted he drop everything and meet her at

Mudge's apartment, where he gave the superintendent a hundred dollars to let them in. They found Mudge on the floor—dazed but somewhat conscious, having thrown up most of the pills—and accompanied her in an ambulance to St. Luke's Hospital. After she got her stomach pumped and spent a few hours behind a barred window in the psychiatric ward, Mudge was moved to a private room.

Bob Brustein was at Yaddo on April 22, and remembered that Roth had the dinner table in stitches when he was suddenly called away to the phone. He returned to the table as Uncle Vanya, stricken and silent, venturing only to say that he had to leave first thing in the morning. At St. Luke's he found Mudge sitting up brightly in bed, carefully made up for the occasion. "What the hell did you do this for?" he said. "It must have been the right thing," she replied, "if it got you down here, lamb chop." Barbara Jakobson, standing outside the door, heard Roth say "I hope you don't think this is gonna get me to marry you"—or, as Mudge remembered it, "You know I'm not coming back." "I guess I hoped you would," she said.

A week later she was released into the care of her sister Polly and brother-in-law, Neil Welliver, a well-known landscape painter whom Roth had met in 1953, oddly enough, when Welliver was the arts and crafts counselor at Pocono Highland Camp; also Roth and Mudge had witnessed the couple's wedding a few years back. Mudge had been in Philadelphia with the Wellivers for about three weeks when Roth paid her a visit. "I'm *happy*," she said, her bitter tone belied by a bright yellow knitted dress. "'I'm *happy*,' the dress says, 'I'm *happy* I'm *happy* I'm *happy* . . .'" She referred to herself as the "crazy sister in the attic." "If Ann survives," Roth wrote Lelchuk afterward, "there should be a ticker-tape parade down Broadway for her."

■　■　■　■

"I WISH TO HELL I could live in a cave," Roth noted at the end of April, when even the rustic beauty of Yaddo had become a distraction, what with the buds bursting all around him ("it's like living in the company of seven thousand eleven year old girls"). The thought of returning to the city full-time was intolerable, and he asked Sproul to find a place for him to rent in Woodstock. This she promptly did, and the little white farmhouse—"Broadview"—was perfect. Secluded on the side of a hill some two miles from town, the only sound was the occasional drumming of hooves ("beats the pneumatic drill") when deer were startled while eating apples from an orchard alongside the house. Every Thursday Roth and Sproul would drive up from the city in Roth's new LTD (a *Portnoy* purchase), stopping for dinner at the Skyline Restaurant, about a half hour from Woodstock, where Roth ordered the shrimp cocktail, medium-rare steak, baked potato with sour cream and chives, and a chocolate sundae ("heaven"). Each morning Sproul would adjourn to her own cabin on the other side of town and work until midafternoon, then return to Broadview where she could hear Roth typing and talking to himself in the upstairs guest room. Around four o'clock they'd take a walk along the back roads of Byrdcliffe Mountain, and later, in the big living room with its majestic fireplace, Roth would often read aloud the page or two he'd written that day—not for comment, but to hear how it sounded. "It was lovely and we both seemed very content," Sproul remembered.

Roth felt the same way, and was even willing to say so to Lelchuk: "Happy note," he wrote in July. "The chow at Broadview has become first-rate. I have a sore on my cock, so the fucking has fallen off, but lately we have had some delicious little meals; if I train one more girl I get to retire, or so Kleinschmidt says . . . but I may really be working a gem into shape for the next guy. When will I be the next guy?" Roth had become more and more impressed by Sproul's "tremendous competence," and indeed was a little helpless without her. One day she suddenly had to return to Manhattan, where she got a call from Roth: at the butcher he'd begun to ask for a piece of liver, but caught himself in the nick of time (lest the news spread that Portnoy was at it again) and asked for lamb chops instead; but how does one cook lamb chops, he inquired ("one is tempted to add 'sheepishly,'" Sproul remarked). Not least, hers was the voice of sweet, persistent reason. "Don't be ridiculous," she said, walking along a mountain road while he complained yet again about the morbidities of fame. "No one cares, and up here no one has any idea who you are!" Just then they heard a lone car approaching, and moved to the side of the road while the car pulled up and a woman leaned out the passenger window: *"It's Portnoy!"*

Soon he made friends with a fellow artist in a similar predicament, the painter Philip Guston, who lived about a mile away at the Maverick Art

Colony. Guston had become famous as a leading member of the New York School of abstract expressionists—until the midsixties, when he'd shocked the art world by disavowing his own work. "American abstract art is a lie, a sham, a cover-up for a poverty of spirit," he wrote. Furious about the Vietnam War and other aspects of American life, Guston no longer saw the point of sublimating his anger by "adjust[ing] a red to a blue"; instead he began to paint lightbulbs, old shoes, and cartoonish Klansmen smoking fat cigars. He'd moved to Woodstock in 1967, the better to pursue his muse in relative isolation, and would become even more reclusive after a showing of his new work at the Marlborough Gallery, in 1970, was savagely panned by Hilton Kramer in the *Times*, under the headline A MANDARIN PRETENDING TO BE A STUMBLEBUM.

Roth's and Guston's parallel courses over the next few years were the result of a fascinating symbiosis—a friendship whereby two of the most eminent figures in their respective fields lived in the remote countryside, "hiding themselves away from almost everything but their work and each other," as Roth put it. Guston was a burly Canadian Jew who— quite like Roth himself—could be loud and flamboyant among friends, but was easily wounded and prone to hibernation. In Woodstock, he liked cooking big batches of pasta for Roth and the odd other, or else the two would meet for lunch at the Aim to Please Diner in nearby Kingston, where Guston liked to filch sugar canisters and other specimens of "crapola"—objective correlatives for public discourse in the age of Richard Nixon, whom both men devotedly loathed. Early chapters of Roth's *Our Gang* inspired the painter to produce a spate of Nixon cartoons in which the president's nose appears to be a phallus, elongating with each fresh lie. His Nixon series would eventually be collected in a book, *Poor Richard*, and for Roth's fortieth birthday he drew a stylized portrait ("Happy birthday to Philip Roth from Key Biscayne") of Nixon and his cronies, half submerged in the sea: Henry Kissinger is a pair of synecdochic horn-rims and Spiro Agnew an enormous nose attached to a pinhead.

Roth's main impression of Guston was one of "terrible loneliness"—a gregarious man who'd turned his back on the world. Sharing Guston's isolation was a wife, Musa, his physical and temperamental opposite: a slight, frail-seeming, silent woman, she'd been raised by Protestant missionaries in Central America and loved to walk in the woods looking for nests and fossils and such. She was outside an open window, gardening, when Guston showed Roth around their house for the first time and came to their enormous marital bed: "This bed is so big," Guston said, "I can't even find Musa in it." An acerbic voice floated through the window: "Why don't you look?" "That's where I got the idea of the sex life of the Lonoffs," said Roth, debunking the assumption that the reclusive E. I. Lonoff and his wife, in *The Ghost Writer*, were entirely based on the Malamuds.* As Roth pointed out, Hope Lonoff is a brittle Yankee like Musa, not an Italian from Brooklyn like Ann Malamud; as for Lonoff's backstory, it was mostly derived from the life of Philip Rahv, who'd left his Ukrainian mother in Palestine while he reinvented himself in New England. The person Lonoff most resembled, however, was Roth himself—or what Roth thought he might have become if he'd stayed in the country and married Sproul, who would have insisted on a family while Roth, for his part, wrote alone in his room, "day in, day out, year in, year out."

■   ■   ■

ALL THAT LONG YEAR, Roth worked frantically on what would someday become, after many mutations and thousands of pages, *My Life as a Man*. "It's as if you'd written her out of your life," said Vernon Gibberd the previous summer, in England, a couple of months after Maggie's violent death; later Gibberd would come to believe that Maggie, whatever her trespasses, had paid a high posthumous price in the form of her

---

* One resemblance between Lonoff and Malamud was that each had a young mistress. *The Ghost Writer*'s Amy Bellette might have seemed a knowing allusion to Malamud's two-year affair in the early sixties with a Bennington student, Arlene Heyman, who was herself startled by this aspect of *The Ghost Writer*: "I think [Roth] made it up," she said in 2016. "He just happened to hit on something that happened to be true." Roth claimed he had no definite knowledge of the affair until he read a 2006 memoir by Malamud's daughter, Janna—this almost thirty years after *The Ghost Writer* was published; indeed, his own experience with Malamud had given him little reason to suspect the man was capable of such a transgression. ("Is he treating you all right?" Malamud had furtively asked Sproul the first night he met her.) According to Roth, he'd imagined Lonoff's affair based on little more than the sight of that mysterious young woman sorting manuscripts on the Malamuds' floor: "I guessed right . . . you know why? I'm a very good writer. Once I begin to make the logic of the character, I find things out that—everything we write is true, as Flaubert said. Poetry is geometry."

vile characterization in Roth's 1974 novel. One may argue, however—as Roth himself did—that revenge ran very much the other way, given how obsessively, joylessly, and often hopelessly he toiled over one of his most autobiographical and least popular books. The main aesthetic difficulty was improving on the known facts. In one of his ur-versions, the narrator remembers his first attempt to grapple with the material—to wit, a "strident failure of a play" that he'd consigned to a file folder labeled "Shit" after hearing actors read it aloud: "I wasn't making a play, I was making an indictment and a cry for help—exposing Roberta's crime to the world, which would then issue its verdict: Boy Innocent, Bitch Guilty! This is writing?" And yet his attempts at making novels (versus plays) of the urine-fraud story tended to develop along precisely the same lines, and his often bizarre attempts to take a fresh approach almost always led to a dead end. "I don't know what the fuck I'm up to," he wrote Solotaroff on April 21, 1969, and the following month he confessed to his British publisher, Tom Maschler, that his work in progress was producing "a strong desire in me to slit my throat."

Poor writing made Roth poor company, and he observed that Sproul was beginning to keep her distance—retiring after dinner to sit alone and ponder her studies. "Nothing between us now but sex," he noted that October. "The very reverse of affair with A[nn]—there, had a full life, but no sex." Then in January he received an open-ended assignment from *McCall's* to write a piece about Southeast Asia ("I think I'm supposed to bring back some recipes from Cambodia and household tips from Taiwan," he wrote Jacquie Rogers). Certainly he had nothing better to do, and Sproul was happy to assist any project that would take Roth out of his head for a while. She arranged every detail including round-the-world tickets on Pan Am—this despite Roth's fear of flying, which, he found, had dissipated now that Maggie was ashes.

They departed on February 24, 1970, stopping in Athens to visit Roth's old Princeton friends Mike and Mary Keeley; the highlight of a delightful four days was a visit to the ancient theater at Delphi, where Mike declaimed Aeschylus in the original Greek, and Roth recited his lines as the Shepherd in the Bucknell production of *Oedipus Rex*. In Thailand, Roth promised an interview to the English-language *Bangkok Post* in exchange for a guided tour of the city. Their reporter ("Some self-styled Lord Jim with a tin ear," as Roth later described him with some injustice) took them to a kickboxing match attended by an unruly pack of GIs on leave. "After declining to take a bow," *Time* reported on its "People" page, "Novelist Philip Roth could not resist a dig at a bestselling rival: 'Now if I were Norman Mailer . . . I'd be up in the ring after the first bout, kicking away at the boxers in golf shoes.'" This, of course, sounds exactly like Roth in a waggish mood, though in a mortified letter to Mailer he blamed the *Post* reporter for such a "callow statement." "At least they called me your best selling rival," Mailer benignly replied.

Walking amid the temples and buzzing street life of Bangkok, Roth was tempted to use Conradian adjectives—"ineffable, mysterious, strange"—though perhaps he was most struck by the ubiquitous availability of sex. Prior to his departure he'd had lunch with Cerf, who'd mentioned his own recent trip to Thailand. While his wife, Phyllis, napped in their hotel, the seventy-year-old publisher had gone to a massage parlor where the women gave "happy ending" hand jobs; after doubtfully kneading away at Cerf's organ, his masseuse had finally smiled and said, "He sleepy." Roth, too, paid a visit to such a place, but couldn't bring himself to regale his amused girlfriend until some eight months later, when (she recalled) he related the episode in "the subjunctive pluperfect, or something like that: 'If one would have stopped off at a massage parlor, one *might* have . . .'"

Roth and Sproul went on to Cambodia to visit the ruined temples of Angkor Wat, but Roth found the subject for his *McCall's* piece when he traveled some fifteen miles south to an inland lake ("like a large tear falling across the face of Cambodia"), hiring a boat to investigate the fifty or so bamboo huts of an impoverished fishing village. Almost two months before Nixon ordered the American "incursion" of that country, Roth wrote "Cambodia: A Modest Proposal": "And sure as hell, I thought, the day is going to come when the bombers fly in over the heads of these lake dwellers in order to 'save' them. From what?" Instead, Roth proposed to drop "food, medicine, and clothing" on the villagers—cheaper than bombs and arguably more in demand. The editors of *McCall's* were appalled by the piece ("because it makes fun of the President"), which was finally published in the October 6, 1970, issue of *Look*.

Twenty-Six

ONE REASON ROTH GAVE FOR HIS FIVE-WEEK TRIP TO Southeast Asia was a wish to be out of the country because *Portnoy* "stood no chance of winning" the National Book Award, and indeed wasn't even among the finalists*—this despite Roth's having a friend among the judges, Barbara Epstein, who'd apprised him four days before his departure, "I just want you to know that you were first on my list for the NBA but that apparently wasn't enough." Cerf was so indignant he boycotted the ceremony, and presently Roth heard a rumor that another judge, Harvey Swados—a friend of Irving Howe—had been strong in his opposition to *Portnoy*. "Well, you had no friend in Swados," Pipik remarks to "Roth" in *Operation Shylock*; "he called the shots on that committee and had it in for you but good. So much animosity—I don't get it." Neither did Roth, and it rankled. Thirty-six years later, when Barbara Epstein was dying of cancer, Roth urged his then biographer, Ross Miller, to arrange an interview with her before it was too late, and wrote out a question in which Miller was to affect that he "vaguely remembers" she was a judge:

> *Were* you a judge? If so, do you remember anything about what went into the judges' meetings? Meaningless as prizes may be in the long run— even in the short run—this was an inexplicable oversight in the eyes of many and therefore something I'll [i.e., "Miller"] have to deal with in the biography . . . that a book that has survived as a centerpiece of America's comic literature into the next century should have received not even pass-

---

* The finalists were *Fat City*, by Leonard Gardner, *Going Places*, by Leonard Michaels, *The Collected Stories of Jean Stafford*, *Slaughterhouse Five*, by Kurt Vonnegut, and *Them*, by Joyce Carol Oates, the winner.

ing recognition from the NBA judges . . . well, what should I say about this in my book?

One consolation was Roth's induction, on May 26, as the youngest member of the National Institute of Arts and Letters. Six years before, Updike had been elected at the even more tender age of thirty-two, and he and Roth were sometimes mentioned as the most likely successors, among their age cohort, to Hemingway and Faulkner. Roth often made the point that major writers born roughly ten years earlier than Updike and he—Mailer, Styron, Shaw, James Jones, et al.—were particularly burdened by ideas of manliness inherited from Hemingway: "If you're just a writer you're a sissy," Roth explained, "but if you're a drinker and a boxer and whatever else, then you're not a sissy." Such writers had fought in the war and cultivated the kind of glamor associated with wealth and getting recognized at the Stork Club; but the booze, above all, hampered their productivity, whereas the abstemious children of the Depression—Roth, Updike, DeLillo, et al.—tended to avoid the limelight and keep their noses to the grindstone, hence their astounding output relative to their elders'. "We weren't idealistic about much," said Updike of his coevals, "but we were certainly idealistic about art. We went into it with the highest kind of ambition—not to get rich or to impress women, but to make our mark as Proust and Joyce had made their mark." Roth likewise longed to emulate such "saints of the imagination" as Flaubert, James, and Conrad, and pointed out that his and Updike's was "the last pre-television generation" who believed that fiction occupied a sovereign place in American culture, that a serious novelist strove to "meet the measure of one's colleagues" in claiming the attention of their best readers. "To think that I had to run alongside that remarkable stallion all my writing life," he said of Updike, whose death in 2009 would lead to Roth's becoming, a few years later, the longest-serving literary member of what was known by then as the American Academy of Arts and Letters.

Back in 1970, the two writers were already a little uneasily aware that they were running neck and neck. Both had published their first acclaimed books in 1959, whereupon Updike, a year older, anticipated *Portnoy* with his own sexually explicit best seller of 1968, *Couples*. The following year Updike made a droll reference to the most obvious difference between them when he sent Roth a copy of his long autobiographical poem, *Midpoint*, with the title crossed out and *Poor Goy's Complaint* inserted. Indeed, Updike couldn't resist reimagining himself as a somewhat more hapless writer, Bech, who is Jewish—a lampoon Roth disliked but forgave, more or less, in light of a kinship that transcended labels of whatever sort. "We're hicks," he said. "It's just because we're such hicks that we've all become so sophisticated. Look at John Updike. Shillington, Pennsylvania. John's the biggest hick of us all, and he's the best writer of us all." Certainly Roth's all-but-unstinting regard—not always reciprocated—endeared him to his rival, who made a point of cordially introducing himself to Roth's parents when their son was inducted into the Institute of Arts and Letters. The three Roths, Updike recalled, "radiated wonderful family feeling—fondness for each other and good cheer toward the world at large."

■ ■ ■ ■

THE FIRST THING Roth wrote after shelving his novel was "On the Air," a work he always considered to be part of the same basic genre as "the three grotesquely comic books that followed": *Our Gang, The Breast*, and *The Great American Novel*. "On the Air," without doubt, is the most grotesque of the four, the product of Roth's zany impulse "to be all bad manners" after the backlash against *Portnoy*. So extreme was the exuberance of "On the Air" that Roth could never bring himself to reread it, much less reprint it.

"Like Waugh—Jewish Waugh," Roth wrote in his notes for the story. "Pulverize society and stereotypes in a fun-machine." "On the Air" opens with our narrator—a talent scout named Milton Lippman—bitterly listening to radio's "Answer Man," a "know-it-all *goy*" of the Charles Van Doren sort. Afterward Lippman writes a long letter to Einstein, imploring him to go on the radio and remind the world that "THE GENIUS OF ALL TIME IS A JEW!"—then and only then, Lippman figures, can they put an end to all this anti-Semitic persecution, the pervasiveness of which is well established in the next section, "Howard Johnson's," where Lippman takes his family for ice cream. "Every flavor except *matzohs*, Moses," snaps Scully, the proprietor, when Lippman innocently remarks on the variety of flavors. Here Roth borrowed a bit of slapstick from his abortive fantasia of six years before, *The Jewboy*, in which the innkeeper calls the cops on Jesus' father, who finds himself in a testicle-weighing contest with the police captain ("for sheer hang and weight, the average Gentile . . ."). Like some fantastically obscene Keystone Kops movie, "On the Air" goes from such a contest to a chase scene in which the police chief, with Scully's arm lodged up his rectum (long story), shoots Lippman "right-between-the-eyes"—a Jew's least vulnerable spot, "because that is where his nose begins." At this cliff-hanging moment, the reader is entreated to "tune in to this same wavelength tomorrow— till then, to all those out there 'Beyond the Pale,' good night, brethren, and sweet dreams!"

One can't help wondering what a sophisticated reader would make of this performance by a reputable author in the twenty-first century, but, as Roth pointed out in 2011, "everybody was doing it" back in 1970. His friend Bob Baker disliked the story not because he found it tasteless and/or bewildering, but rather because it struck him as derivative—"an attempt to be *au courant*," as he put it, "to accommodate to the newish mode of Barthelme & Co." Roth denied he was aping the era's myriad surrealists and black humorists ("I've been as you know talking like 'On the Air' for over a decade"), and most critics—including Solotaroff, who published the story in *New American Review* and longed for a sequel— were enthusiastic. Geoffrey Wolff singled it out for special attention in *Newsweek*, applauding the forty-two-page improvisation as Roth's answer to the challenge he'd articulated ten years ago in "Writing American Fiction"—how to "make *credible* much of the American reality": "The comic imagination seems to have been cornered by that American 'reality,'" Wolff wrote. "In a world in which so much is disordered, like an insane, murderous joke, how do you recognize what is funny?"

Roth himself seemed to have doubts about the increasingly way-ward direction of his work. Shortly after publishing "On the Air" that summer, he ran into a *Times* critic, Anatole Broyard, whom he asked to sit down for coffee. After chatting an hour or so, Roth asked the man, "What do you think I ought to do now?" Broyard, puzzled at first, real-ized that Roth was referring to his writing career: "The expression on his face was expectant, interrogative, pensive. He wanted a real answer." (A decade later, Broyard phoned Roth to confirm the details of their 1970 meeting for a *Times* piece he was writing. "Yes," said Roth, "that's about how I remember it. In fact, I have only one question: What do you think I ought to do now?")

With little stomach for getting back to his novel, Roth spent more and more time nursing his revulsion toward the Nixon administration: "Reading the morning *New York Times* and the afternoon *New York Post*, watching the seven and then again the eleven o'clock TV news—all of which I did ritualistically—became for me like living on a steady diet of Dostoevsky." For the Gibberds he described the political climate in America as "mild Fascism," and while waiting "for the knock on the door" he wondered and wondered how such a manifestly fraudulent and perhaps deranged person as Nixon could have possibly won the confidence of the electorate. On April 3, 1971—a few days after Lieutenant William Calley had been convicted for his leading role in the My Lai massacre, then immediately released from Fort Leavenworth on Nixon's order so he could await appeal under house arrest—Nixon made a statement on abortion: "I can't square [it] with my personal belief in the sanctity of human life—including the life of the yet unborn." Roth proposed an op-ed piece to protest such "gross opportunism and moral stupidity," but the *Times* considered his idea in bad taste. *"Bad taste?!"* Roth exploded. "I'll show *them* bad taste!" For *The New York Review of Books*, then, he wrote a satirical interview between "Trick E. Dixon" and "A Troubled Citizen" who expresses concern that some of the women slaughtered at My Lai might have been pregnant and hence subjected to inadvertent abortions. Soon, another Tricky episode occurred to Roth, then another—until, three months later, he was ready to deliver the entirety of *Our Gang* to his publisher.

The president of Random House, Bob Bernstein, was horrified by the manuscript and begged Roth to reconsider. During a long meeting in Bernstein's office, Roth calmly explained that his work was a pretty typical specimen of political satire, and finally the two agreed that he and his friend Lelchuk would craft an interview for the *Times Book Review* in which Roth explained his purpose in terms of that long literary tradition.* Naturally he invoked Swift's "A Modest Proposal" ("You always pull out Swift when you're doing something disgusting"), imagining an updated version of Swift's classic in the form of a Pentagon Papers–like document giving statistical justification for the slaughter of Vietnamese

---

* The *Times* passed on the piece, which appeared in the December 1971 *Atlantic Monthly* to coincide with the book's publication.

children for food, including "a first-rate contingency plan on how to barbecue with napalm, sprinkle with soy sauce, and serve." Given that *Our Gang* describes the assassination of an American president—drowned in a large womblike Baggie—Roth was at pains to point out that "more people are killed in this country every year by bullets than by satires."

■ ■ ■ ■

ROTH'S RETREAT FROM public scrutiny during the worst of his *Portnoy* fame had included a break from teaching, but after two years he found he was "lonesome and wanted some students to talk to." Like the reclusive E. I. Lonoff, he considered it healthy to use a public urinal at least once a week, and besides teaching gave him an excuse to read and think about books ("My education comes from teaching, really"). Around this time, the writer Lisa Scottoline was in Roth's English 275 seminar at Penn—sometimes titled The Literature of Desire—and remembered that she and her fifteen classmates were mostly young women who adored Roth. On the first day of class (as she wrote in a 2014 piece for the *Times*), "We students arrived early, freshly showered and perfumed, already having read every book on the syllabus." Precisely on time the tall, stoop-shouldered professor would appear in the doorway headfirst "like a well-read giraffe," dressed in his usual uniform of lightly pressed oxford shirt and khakis. He would unbuckle his watch and place it on the table in front of him, whereupon class would begin. Unlike other seminar professors who were on a first-name basis "in those let-it-all-hang-out days," he asked that they call him Mr. Roth and addressed them in kind. Also, according to Scottoline, he brought a binder of notes but seemed never to consult them, noting key points one by one "as if he apprehended the entire novel, all of a piece. . . . Imagine taking physics from Einstein. But you want to be Mrs. Einstein."

"She was very observant," Roth said of Scottoline's piece, though he demurred on a few points: "I never told anyone to call me Mr. Roth—they just did, and I called them Mr. and Miss. My notes were kept on a yellow legal pad and I looked at them throughout the class." Nor was he averse to humor, as Scottoline claimed ("he never cracked a joke, though he's a brilliantly funny writer"). It was true Roth considered the teaching of literature—that is, how to read properly—a rigorous, rather somber business. Young people, after all, were given to "habitual moralizing, ingenious interpretation," and "steamrolling generalization," whereas Roth focused on the most exquisite (and usually nonerotic) concrete details, such as this sentence from *Madame Bovary*: "She was just eating a maraschino ice that she held with her left hand in a silver-gilt cup, her eyes half-closed, and the spoon between her teeth." Roth went around the table canvassing each student for her thoughts, and was respectful to any view that seemed earnestly considered; what he couldn't stand was flippancy coupled with ignorance. "How can you open your mouth and talk when you're not prepared?" Roth snapped at an instantly penitent smart aleck (male) who hadn't read the assigned book. Roth himself was never less than meticulously prepared, and reverent toward the writers he taught: Colette's *Chéri* novels were a mainstay of his Desire course, along with *Bovary*, *Lolita*, and Genet's *Our Lady of the Flowers*. One semester Roth realized he'd selected books that were all heavy with suffering— Beckett's trilogy (*Molloy*, *Malone Dies*, *The Unnamable*), Gogol's *Dead Souls*, Solzhenitsyn's *Cancer Ward*, others—and conceived the course title Life Has Claws.

Roth's other course at Penn was English 564, Writing about Fiction, for which students were enjoined to "write intelligently and without jargon" via essay prompts such as this:

> You have been asked to introduce Chekhov's fiction to a group of intelligent high school seniors. They have perhaps heard the word "Chekhovian" and read one or two anthologized stories of his, but aside from that they are unfamiliar with the work of the Russian author.
>
> Your introductory lecture will be 3000 words, or approximately ten typewritten pages. Your goal is to familiarize them with what seems to you most important about Chekhov's stories: his social and moral focus, the mood and style of his work, his recurring preoccupations, the particular difficulties that he may pose for a reader, and, if it seems pertinent to you, the kind of pleasure and wisdom that his work yields. . . .
>
> Remember: you are referring to works with which your audience is unfamiliar, and so you will have to summarize and characterize individual works with economy, and yet without sacrificing clarity or precision.

Scottoline's recollection was that papers were returned without comment, save the letter grade on the final page, inscribed with a red Flair pen. It's true Roth had a lifelong fondness for Flair pens, but otherwise this detail of hers was the one with which he took gravest exception: Far from failing to "festoon" papers with comments, he said, "I was the ace festooner. It is not in my nature, neither as a teacher or as a friend, lover, or enemy, to let pass the tiniest grammatical error or the largest intellectual gaffe without my saying something about it." Two kinds of papers rated the most profuse commentary: the very good and the very bad. One student remarked that he'd never received so many scribbled rebukes in his life: "I felt at times you were going for blood," he complained, "picking every sentence apart so that the work looked ridiculous." Roth cordially replied that he was loath to give a serious student a C without "a very clear and wholly scrutable demonstration of what I thought was weak and misdirected in his writing and thinking about books"; that said, he invited the young man to improve his grade by writing another one-thousand-word essay. As for the very good papers—such as Wendy Univer's "Comparison of Erotic Styles" in the work of Kundera, Mishima, and others—Roth's marginal glosses were like whoops of pleasure for almost every well-turned phrase, ending with, in his bold red Flair, "This is absolutely first-rate. Congratulations. You've written exquisitely about Kundera—understood precisely what makes him tick as a writer and moralist . . . A+."

One more point in Scottoline's essay requires a little amendment: the reason Roth was her "best professor," she wrote, was "not only because of his genius, but also because of his distance." In *The Professor of Desire*, David Kepesh remarks to his students that he prefers to address them as "Mr." and "Miss" but is careful to add: "All of which is not to say that I shall try to keep hidden from you the fact that I am flesh and blood—or that I understand that you are." Kepesh's fondness for "erotic desire" as a pedagogical subject, he explains, is due to its power to "locate these books in the world of experience" and so steer students away from "that manageable netherworld of narrative devices, metaphorical motifs, and mystical archetypes." Kepesh's creator felt the same way. "Write about 2000 words on three (or, if you like, four) works of fiction that seem to you to best illustrate this wide range of human experience that is associated with sexual activity"—so read another of his prompts, one of the various ways Roth liked to remind students (some more than others) that he too was flesh and blood, and indeed considered sex one of the most

desirable aspects of teaching "back in the days"—as he later put it—
"when you weren't hauled off in chains to feminist prison if you struck up
a tender friendship with the smartest, most beautiful girl in your class."
In this respect the department chair, Joel Conarroe, played the crucial
role of selecting among students who tried to register late "for [Phil-
ip's] vastly over-subscribed class, performing" (so Conarroe noted with
some retrospective rue) "as it turned out, the role of, pardon the expression, pimp."

Conarroe's warm friendship with Roth, spanning half a century, went
back to the croquet field at Yaddo but was launched in earnest when
Conarroe was nearly expelled from the Penn library for laughing help-
lessly over "Whacking Off" in *Partisan Review*. A fan letter to the author
led to frequent lunches at the campus union, where the two discussed
their similar yet vastly different origins. The sweet-natured Conarroe—
whom Bess Roth called her "other son"—was also born to a Metropolitan Life employee and grew up in New Jersey; his tiny hometown of
Mountain Lakes, however, was goyish to an almost exotic degree, at
least for Roth, who loved hearing about such bygone rituals as the way
townsfolk "skated their Christmas trees across the frozen lake in early
January for an immense bonfire on the public beach."

As for Conarroe's efforts on Roth's behalf at Penn, well, it was a different time to be sure. "Everything seems to be in good shape for your
courses next year," he wrote Roth on April 30, 1971. "We gave the illusion of being utterly democratic in choosing your students, but in fact
picked the same ones any totalitarian dictator would have picked." When
an attractive but unfamiliar young woman asked Conarroe to write her a
recommendation, he was a little bemused until Roth dropped him a note
explaining the nature of his (Roth's) relationship with the student in
question. This jogged Conarroe's memory as to his one previous encounter with her:

> One day [he wrote Roth] she walked into my office and said she needed
> another course, and having already turned scores of hysterical supplicants
> from your course I heard my mouth saying, all the while disbelieving
> what I heard, I'm sure Mr. Roth would enjoy having you (sly grin here) in
> his class. So I'm relieved to hear that my instinct worked out better than
> most of my rational decisions, and will write her a firm penetrating letter.

The young woman lived on Long Island and occasionally visited Roth at his apartment in the city. One day Barbara Sproul found a strange pair of panties dangling from the shower head, and held them up for Roth's inspection: *"Really?"* she said. "Tell me about these." Roth's face went totally blank. "I have no idea," he replied.

When the Long Island woman graduated, in 1973, Roth took up with the brilliant Laurie Geisler, who would go on to graduate summa cum laude. "I was forty and she was nineteen," Roth remembered. "Perfect. As God meant it to be." The two parted ways when she went off to graduate school at Princeton, but were reunited twenty-five years later, in Connecticut, during a period when Roth was otherwise unattached. To Roth's terrible regret, their renascent affair ended badly—with an argument on April 16, 2000, when Roth was in a rage over a "disgusting, gossipy" piece about his beloved Bellow in *The New York Times Magazine*. Geisler was less than sympathetic, and he finally asked her to leave his house. He never saw her again.*

Not all of Roth's mentoring projects had an erotic component. In the fall of 1971, he went to a party at his colleague Jerre Mangione's house and met a middle-aged suburban housewife, Fredrica (Riki) Wagman, who wrote novels in her spare time. One of these Mangione had found promising, so the next day Roth took a taxi to Germantown and rang Wagman's doorbell: "Where's the manuscript?" She got it out of a dresser drawer—to which she'd consigned it along with three or four other manuscripts—and Roth got back in the cab and disappeared. He was shocked, in a good way, by what he read: "Ricki [sic] is more Sylvia Plath with appetite," he wrote Al Alvarez, "—a middle-class primitive, literary without knowing a thing about books." The novel, *Playing House,* was about an obsessive sexual affair between juvenile siblings—the brother based, according to Roth, on Wagman's first lover and older brother, Chuck Barris, of *Gong Show* fame ("a card-carrying beast"). Roth helped her revise the book twice, and eventually wrote an introduction to the French edition: "It would appear from *Playing House* that

---

* While remembering Geisler in a note for his biographer, Roth thought to google her and was "stunned" to find her death notice. She'd died of breast cancer at age fifty-five. Bereft, he tried to find a copy of the 1974 Penn yearbook so he'd have a picture of her, but gave up after the usual websites and eBay proved unavailing.

the prohibition forbidding sibling incest is designed primarily to protect impressionable children against sex thrills so intense, and passionate unions so all-encompassing and exclusive, that life after the age of twelve can only be a frenzy of nostalgia for those who have known the bliss of such transgression."

Roth went to extraordinary lengths to launch the career of "probably the best unpublished writer in America," pressing her work on several skittish publishers before persuading his friend Aaron Asher—then at Holt, Rinehart and Winston—to offer her a two-book contract. Wagman expressed her gratitude with a handwritten Kafka manuscript for Roth's birthday: a five-page speech Kafka had composed in honor of his employer, Dr. Marschner, when the man was appointed director of the Arbeiter-Unfall-Versicherungsanstalt (Workers' Accident Insurance Company). Roth, in turn, invited his protégée to sit in on his classes, pointing to the morbidly shy woman ("Harpo!") when he wanted her to speak up. Afterward they'd repair to Germantown for dinner with the Wagman family. Her husband, Howard, was a jolly businessman who'd made a fortune buying pig bristle (for hairbrushes) from China in pre-Nixon days. "Nobody other than this huge bear of a saint could have ever been married to her," said Roth, who used the man as the model and namesake for Everyman's darling brother Howie. Indeed, the writer and the pig bristle merchant adored each other. "Only Philip," Howard replied, when his wife inquired whether he'd ever kissed another person on the lips during their marriage.

Of the Wagmans' four children, Roth became especially attached to the eleven-year-old Nela; the night they met, at a Greek restaurant on South Street, the girl made Roth a set of vampire teeth out of the big candle on the table, and henceforth called him Fang. After family dinners, the two would perform Fake Shakespeare for the others (Nela's two older brothers would bring friends home to see the show), lurching around the room like Richard III and speaking in pseudo-Elizabethan diction. Both were superlative mimics. When *Playing House* was published in France, Roth phoned Riki and (affecting a heavy French accent) identified himself as a reporter from *Paris Match*. Nela overheard her shy mother's breathy, excited voice ("Well! I just don't know how to answer that!"), until the "interview" abruptly ended when Roth barked, *"Gotcha this time!"* and hung up. A little later, Roth himself got a call from one Christina Hagan Singh, who in a floridly singsong Indian accent announced herself as head of the "Muslim Students of North America" at Bryn Mawr; they would be honored, said Singh, if Roth would consent to be their guest: "You will be met at the station by a welcoming committee of three Punjab in customary sari and four Madras citizens and a token"—here she used a Yiddishism that tipped Roth off: *"Who is this—?!"* Afterward he insisted Nela reprise her role as Christina Hagan Singh to prank-call several reviewers he disliked.

■ ■ ■ ■

ON OCTOBER 26, 1971, adaptations of three stories from *Goodbye, Columbus*—"Defender of the Faith," "Eli, the Fanatic," and "Epstein"— opened on Broadway under the title *Unlikely Heroes*. The director was Larry Arrick, one of Roth's old Amagansett friends, who also directed the Second City improvisational troupe in the Village. Roth had declined to adapt the stories himself, though he attended at least one rehearsal and had much to say about "Eli" in particular ("when you saw it on the stage you saw what was loathsome in it very quickly"). The critical consensus was that Arrick's adaptations relied too heavily on Roth's text, though Lou Jacobi's performance as Epstein was singled out for praise.

The night of the opening at Plymouth Theatre, Roth pulled up in a taxi with his parents and Sproul, and saw that Maggie's daughter, Helen, was standing outside the box office. "She looked like some Southern waitress who'd just gotten off her job at four a.m.," Roth recalled: "skinny, washed out, and had some kind of shmatte of a dress on." Roth hadn't seen the twenty-one-year-old since her mother's funeral, though he'd gotten a desperate letter from her a year and a half before; by then she'd already married and divorced the young man who'd impregnated her in Europe during the summer of '67, and was living alone in Rochester, broke, on the edge of a breakdown. "What I'm asking from you is a loan," she wrote Roth, "a long rage [sic] loan." Roth sent her a check for five hundred dollars: "Use it for whatever you need it for and then forget about it," he replied. "And I hope things start getting better for you soon."

After a few months at the Project One commune in San Francisco, Helen, deeply depressed, had returned to New York that fall to live with friends, and had bought a ticket to *Unlikely Heroes* in hope of seeing Roth. He hugged and kissed her and insisted she sit beside him in the

theater, and join them afterward in the restaurant where an opening-
night dinner party was held. Sproul and Roth's parents also went out of
their way to be nice to the waif, who soon lapsed into a gloomy silence
from which she couldn't be roused. Trying to explain her behavior forty-
two years later, Helen cited "an old joke" about a guy who drives past a
gas station in the desert and, a few miles later, gets a flat tire:

> So he has to walk back to the station and he's having this internal con-
> versation about what he needs and he's sure the gas station attendant is
> not going to help him at all. . . . When he gets to the station and the
> attendant asks, "What can I do to help you?" the guy says "Fuck you!" . . .
> I was anticipating seeing Philip and was so desperate to see him and
> anticipated him rejecting me. So when I saw him, I could [hardly] get a
> word out.

Roth never saw or heard from his former stepdaughter again. As for
Unlikely Heroes, it closed two weeks later.

■ ■ ■ ■

GIVEN THE SUCCESS of *Portnoy*, Roth was guaranteed a big payday
even for so risky a venture as *Our Gang*. Random House paid the author
$450,000 worth of stock in its parent company, RCA, and ordered
100,000 copies for the first printing. The publication date was delayed,
ironically, to avoid conflict with the release of a memoir (*The Vantage
Point*) by LBJ—or, as the thirty-sixth president was dubbed in *Our
Gang*, "Lyin' B. Johnson." "Very funny and, if cruel, deservedly so," Mary
McCarthy blurbed Roth's book, though in her note to Jason Epstein she
remarked that all the silly names seemed the work of an unfunny libel
lawyer, and Roth's old Iowa friend George P. Elliott had "serious" reservations about the whole performance and declined to endorse it.

"You'll be delighted to hear that Publishers Weekly this week reviewed
Our Gang and called it 'sick and childish,'" Roth informed his British
publisher on September 29, 1971. "Looks like we're building up a head of
steam." Proud members of the president's "silent majority" were appalled
by what they read about the book in the press—if not in the book itself
("I do not intend to read such garbage")—and Random House girded
itself with a mollifying form letter for the author's many detractors, to

be mailed along with reprints of Roth's apologia about the history of satire in *The Atlantic Monthly*: "Perhaps some of what he says here will answer the questions and comments included in your letter." Hard-core Nixon haters were transported, of course, and one such was the eminent critic Dwight Macdonald, who clamored successfully for the privilege of reviewing the book in the Sunday *Times*: "*Our Gang* is a political satire that I found far-fetched, unfair, tasteless, disturbing, logical, coarse and very funny—I laughed out loud 16 times and giggled internally a statistically unverifiable amount. In short, a masterpiece." "Tell me how masochistic you're feeling," Tom Maschler wrote Roth of the British reviews, which he proposed to withhold from the author until further notice; these were in accord—pace Macdonald—with the overall response on Roth's side of the Atlantic.

His knack for impersonation is one of the book's redeeming features, and certainly the first fifteen pages or so are still funny and readable. "Now just one minute," Tricky replies to the Troubled Citizen, who worries that a pregnant woman might have been among the twenty-two Vietnamese civilians murdered by Calley. "We have a tradition in the courts of this land that a man is innocent until he is proven guilty. There were babies in that ditch at My Lai, and we know there were women of all *ages*, but I have not seen a single document that suggests the ditch at My Lai contained a *pregnant* woman." One hears Nixon's voice in every line—the tense gravitas even when proposing, say, to extend the vote to the unborn in time for the 1972 election ("I tell you, they have really impressed me with their silent dignity and politeness"). But once the basic joke is established—namely, that Tricky will countenance genocide but not abortion—Roth has "a tendency," as his friend Brustein told him, "to get infatuated by your own schtick-loch with the result that you sometimes go on too long after you have effectively made your point." It was a tendency that would persist in various forms throughout his career, though rarely so grindingly as in *Our Gang*—a slog at half its length, especially for latter-day readers to whom the jokes have long since exceeded their sell-by date (the orotund rhetoric of Eric Sevareid, for example). And much of the humor was stale enough to begin with, not least the names that seem appropriated from a bad *Mad* magazine parody: Erect Severehead, Robert F. Charisma, the Reverend Billy Cupcake, etc. Arguably, too, Roth trivializes one of the most enigmatic figures in American history by conceiving of him as "an old fashioned villain in the Tartuffian mold"—as a *conscious* hypocrite, in other words, versus a man who fancied himself, however preposterously, as well meaning. "Well, let me say," Tricky proclaims while running for Devil in Hell, "as regards these wholly unfounded attacks upon my bad name, that I intend . . . to issue a black paper, showing that in every single instance where they claim I was 'humane' or 'benevolent,' I was in actual fact motivated solely by political self-interest, and acted with utter indifference, if not outright contempt and cynicism, for the welfare of anybody other than myself."

But of course the main fallacy of such a project is that any amount of satirical hyperbole can do justice to the real thing; as Judge Joseph Sirica would later point out, anyone contriving to describe the events of Watergate in a film scenario "would have been laughed out of Hollywood," and indeed this was the precise nature of the dilemma Roth himself had posed in "Writing American Fiction." If he thought writers had their hands full describing the likes of Roy Cohn and Eisenhower, what astonishing hubris led him to tackle Nixon?

Five days before the publication of *Our Gang*—as one learns from the White House tapes for November 3, 1971—Nixon remarked to Bob Haldeman that he'd noticed a positive review of Roth's novel in *Newsweek*,* and wondered whether the magazine "might be very much behind" a larger smear campaign. Haldeman replied that he'd been "disturbed" enough to read an advance copy of *Our Gang*, assuring Nixon that the book wasn't nearly as good as *Newsweek* claimed: "It's a ridiculous book. And it's sickening, and it's—"

NIXON: What's it about?
HALDEMAN: It's about the president of the United States.
NIXON: I know that! I know that. What's the theme?
HALDEMAN: Trick E. Dixon. And the theme is that, uh—he's tied to the abortion thing. The thing that inspired the book was your statement on abortion, and so he's decided that—and then he juxtaposes

---

* One of the *very* few: "the funniest and most complex exercise in sustained political satire since *Animal Farm*."

that with your defense of Calley, as he puts it, who shot a woman who had a child in her. A pregnant woman. And he relates that you're defending a guy who kills a woman with an unborn child in her. It's sick, you know perverted kind of thing. It ends up with you being assassinated—or with Trick E. Dixon being assassinated, and then he goes to hell and in hell he starts to politically organize down there, and uh . . .

The chief of staff then explained to Nixon that Roth was the author of *Goodbye, Columbus* ("which became a very big movie"), but "his big thing is *Portnoy's Complaint*, which is the most obscene, pornographic book of all time."

> NIXON: Roth is, of course, a Jew.
> HALDEMAN: Oh yes.
> NIXON: Roth is a very bad guy. I know who he is, and I know the
>   Supreme Court case he was involved in, and that's what it was . . .

Here Nixon confused the two Jews: *Samuel* Roth was a publisher best known for his pirated editions of *Ulysses* and *Lady Chatterley's Lover*, and also as the plaintiff in *Roth v. United States* (1957), a Supreme Court case that led to establishing "redeeming social value" as a criterion in obscenity rulings. "Nobody corrects" Nixon's mistake, Philip Roth pointed out in 2012. "That's the terrifying bit—he talks to aides who don't even know what little he knows. . . . In short, on the basis of such a mistake they are quite prepared to harass the wrong man."

> NIXON: I think the anti-Semitic thing can be, I hate to say it, but it can
>   be very helpful to us. . . .
> HALDEMAN: There are a lot more anti-Semites than there are Jews,
>   and the anti-Semites are with us generally and the Jews sure aren't.

Later that day, talking with his aide Charles Colson, Nixon wondered whether "the Kennedy bunch" was bankrolling the recent spate of anti-Nixon satire—not just *Our Gang* but the comical documentary *Millhouse* ("costs money to make a film"). Then Nixon got an idea, apropos of "a

dirty cartoon" about Ted Kennedy he'd seen in a British newspaper on
October 30:

> NIXON: I think what it is worth, though, is to send over a couple people
> to London. . . . Mail [the cartoon] from London and mail it to every
> congressman, every senator, Democratic National Committeemen and
> the state chairmen—that kind of, a list of about eight or ten thousand,
> see what I mean? And key editors. Congressmen, senators, mayors, the
> kind of people that will talk.

He and Colson mulled the dirty trick a bit more, and Nixon reasserted
his suspicion that "the Kennedy bunch" was behind *Our Gang* et al.—
then (slyly) he added, "They wouldn't dream, of course, of handing out
a dirty cartoon." Colson chuckled, and Nixon said, "That's one thing
about us. We're gonna play this game a lot tougher" and went on muttering inaudibly, except for a few words ("bastards . . . Roth . . . give 'em
nothing this time . . ."). In any event, the only known repercussion for
(Philip) Roth was noted in the diaries of Bob Haldeman, who made sure
Portnoy's Complaint was removed from the White House library on the
order of "P" (Nixon).

"Novelist Philip Roth may well be hoping that there will always be a
Richard Nixon to kick around," *Newsweek* later reported of the "Watergate" (1973) and "Pre-Impeachment" (1974) editions of *Our Gang*,
published by Bantam in paperback printings of 100,000 and 70,000
respectively, each with a gleeful new preface by the author. "I wish publicly to apologize to President Nixon," he wrote in the first.

> Only now do I realize that I had no right whatsoever to depict him back
> then, if only in fiction, as a moral hypocrite, a lawless opportunist, a shame-
> less liar, and a thorough-going totalitarian at heart. What evidence did I
> have to support such a fantasy? . . . We—alas, I—had nothing even faintly
> resembling the incriminating kind of evidence that is now to be found every
> morning in the daily newspaper and every night on the evening news. . . .
> How I could have permitted myself to go off on this bender of cynicism
> and paranoia is, I fear, something only a psychiatrist can explain. I think I
> will break into the office of one at midnight tonight, and ask for help.

For the Pre-Impeachment edition, Roth noted that Bantam had now published the White House transcripts and therefore he himself was exposed in his failure to give the public a proper idea of the president's conversation, "as indecent as the language in some of my own fiction."

Roth wrote a final Tricky sketch for Bob Brustein's *Watergate Classics*, an anthology of playlets staged by the Yale Repertory Theatre in November 1973. Among offerings by the likes of Jules Feiffer and Art Buchwald, Roth's "The President Addresses the Nation" was widely regarded as the best and/or most disturbing: Nixon (played by Brustein) announces from the Oval Office that he's decided to remain president despite the near certainty of impeachment ("I was raised to be a Quaker, not a quitter"); then, as he gives the audience his signature two-handed victory sign, actors dressed as National Guardsmen march into the theater, bayonets drawn, and take their places in the aisles and in front of the stage. During one performance, a man in the third row yelled, *"Go to Hell!"* at Nixon/Brustein, who was shaken by the success of his and Roth's dramaturgy: "I did not want to share the fate of a nineteenth-century actor in the Wild West who once played Iago so convincingly that a member of the audience shot him dead on the spot."

Twenty-Seven

BY THE END OF 1971, ROTH HAD HIS OLD MOJO BACK, or anyway was having fun again—perhaps the most important reason to write, as he reminded Riki Wagman: "because it's the closest we can come to being back in the sand box with the pail and the shovel in the good old days of YORE." A man of his relative wealth could afford to be almost perversely subversive toward (as he put it in the mandarin *Partisan Review*) "the 'serious' values of official literary culture." Casting about for a way to top the frivolity of *Our Gang*, Roth hit on the idea of a homeless baseball team, the Ruppert Mundys—"some shit occurred in my brain," as he later explained, about Jews and baseball, though he worried such shit would be mistaken for something so serious as a deliberate metaphor. The main reason Roth undertook *The Great American Novel* was that baseball was "one of the few subjects [he] knew much about," and besides any number of reputable American authors had also written well about the game—to name a few, Malamud (*The Natural*), Mark Harris (*Bang the Drum Slowly*), and even a relative layman such as Updike, whose marvelous essay "Hub Fans Bid Kid Adieu" had memorialized Ted Williams's final time at bat.

Then, too, it was an excuse to spend five days at the Baseball Hall of Fame in Cooperstown, New York, where Roth became chummy with the archivist and was given open access to old films and assorted memorabilia (Babe Ruth's glove!). He also read "loads" of books: *Percentage Baseball*, by Earnshaw Cook, taught him that the sacrifice bunt was misguided from a scientific perspective—thus the son of a Jewish baseball owner argues in Roth's novel ("Isaac, please," his father remonstrates, "if de goyim say bunt, let dem bunt!"). Roth kept a baseball glove next to his typewriter while he worked, then snapped it up at quitting time and played catch with Sproul, who was herself deeply into the spirit of things. On a postcard (addressed from "Barbara Sproul / The Kitchen / The House") she drew a six-cent stamp featuring "Felix Mundy" with the caption "Support the Patriot League" (the lost mythical league of *The Great American Novel*), and provided Roth with all the creation-myth fodder he could possibly use—and he used it all, as she remembered:

> Crucial, of course, were members of the Baal family—Big John, his father Spit and, of course, his grandfather and originator of the entire sport, Base. And Gil Gamesh is there . . . the tiny Mexican right hander Chico Mecoatl, the speedballer Jolly Cholly Tuminikar, starters Bobo Buchis, Rocky Volos and Deacon Demeter, relievers Pollux and Merzager, Luke Gofannon . . . It was huge fun at the time watching all those gods take to the field once again. Gimme an M! Gimme a U! . . . Come on Mundys!!

Perhaps needless to say, the book is dedicated to Sproul.

Roth wrote the bulk of his baseball epic that winter at Yaddo, where he was "hot as a firecracker . . . turning out fiction by the pound, *daily*." He finished the book in January, and took his friend Julius Goldstein to a celebratory dinner in Saratoga; the very next day he started *The Breast*, visiting the library at nearby Skidmore College to bone up on endocrinology.* The idea for a novel about a man who inexplicably turns into a giant breast came partly from Kafka, of course, but also from Roth's uneasy feeling that *Portnoy* readers regarded him as a "walking prick." The better to disguise himself—or maybe just a matter of general high spirits—Roth grew a Groucho mustache during his long winter stay, until one night he helped the elderly Elizabeth Ames back to her quarters along an icy path. "At her door," Roth remembered, "Elizabeth looked up at me serenely—serenity was her ace in the hole—and said, 'Philip, do you think that mustache is helping you with your writing?' I went back to West House and shaved it off."

■ ■ ■ ■

---

* During a visit to Yaddo, the novelist Jonathan Lethem was shown to the turreted Breast Room, so named (he was told) because Roth had been "inspired by dwelling within the room's contour" to write *The Breast*.

IN 1970, Roth had hired Arthur Klein of Frankfurt, Klein, and Garbus to look after his business affairs.* Since Klein handled the legal side of his book contracts—and since, as Roth put it, publishers "were ready to stuff [money] into my pockets even if no one asked"—he didn't see the need anymore to give up 10 percent of his earnings to his agent, Donadio, whom he fired over a tearful lunch on February 7, 1972. "You know that you have been as wonderful an agent as a writer could ever want," he wrote her the next day, also sending flowers. "Unlike Portnoy, I have no complaints"—though he did, a little. Donadio was known to be "very mothering," especially to favorite male clients such as Joseph Heller, who found it comforting to pass the time shmoozing with her on the phone. "Don't get me wrong about her sweetness," said Roth, "but I was not interested in that." Roth's own sweetness was mingled with a basic aloofness toward people who, whatever their affinity otherwise, were mainly useful to him as business contacts. "Unlike most young authors whose works we have published," Bennett Cerf wrote in his posthumous memoir, *At Random*, "Philip Roth is one I've never felt close to; he has always seemed withdrawn, unwilling to make close ties." At times Roth professed to feel hurt by this rather damning verdict. When Cerf died on August 27, 1971, Roth sent a heartfelt telegram to the widow and attended the funeral with Jason Epstein; he remembered how Cerf had always been "dying to please," making Roth feel at home in New York after he'd fled the conflagration of his marriage. In the end, though, people like Cerf "were management," as Roth put it; "I was labor. I didn't trust anybody."

The hard bargain Roth drove for his next two books was liable to test even the most amiable connections. Confident that his slender, quirky novella, *The Breast*, was "the best thing [he'd] ever done," Roth asked for an advance of $225,000 with an exorbitant royalty rate of 20 percent for the first 100,000 copies, 25 up to 200,000, and 30 thereafter; the same rate obtained for the even quirkier *Great American Novel*, for which Roth requested a $236,250 advance. Submitting both books on April 14, 1972,

---

* He'd chosen the firm because of his friendship with Garbus, who was mostly a litigator. Shirley Fingerhood remained a friend of sorts—she would preside at his second wedding—though she'd served primarily as his matrimonial lawyer and was no longer needed in that capacity after Maggie's death.

Roth stipulated that *The Breast* be published first ("no later than October 15, 1972"), to be followed six months later by *The Great American Novel*. Finally—what would prove the deal breaker—Roth wanted 100 percent of the paperback proceeds instead of the usual 50-50 split with the hardcover publisher. "All of us at Random House are, of course, sorry not to be publishing Philip Roth's next book," Bob Bernstein announced on May 25. "We made a substantial offer to try to retain his next work, one that gambled on its being a huge success. If Philip had left Random House for any other reason but money I would be most concerned."

"I want to put away any notion that Philip moved from Random House to another conglomerate for a big sum of money," said Aaron Asher, the new editor in chief at Holt, Rinehart and Winston, who'd signed Roth to a multibook contract. Asher was aware of how sensitive Roth was— would always be—about perceptions of mercenary motive, and indeed Roth's move in this case was at least partly a matter of friendship, as well as a firm faith in Asher's skills. Asher's last big book at Viking before leaving for Holt had been *Mr. Sammler's Planet*, which had won Bellow his third National Book Award. Also, he and Roth "were able to agree" on the knotty point of paperback rights, which yielded Roth an uncanny $400,000 for *The Breast* alone.

Ever since that first big check for *Portnoy*, Roth had wanted to buy his own Yaddo: a bucolic retreat roughly two hours from New York, where he could spend summers and long weekends with Sproul and the odd boon companion. He'd made an offer on Broadview, in Woodstock, but the owner wouldn't sell; then, at a party *chez* Epstein, he met the painter Cleve Gray and his wife, Francine du Plessix Gray, who was about to publish her second book, *Hawaii: The Sugar-Coated Fortress*. Because he and Sproul were planning to stop in Hawaii on their way back from a spring vacation to Japan, Roth had read Gray's book in galleys and liked it; the two couples subsequently arranged to have dinner in New York, and the Grays mentioned that a house was for sale a mile and a half down the road from them in tiny Warren, Connecticut. The location, at least, was ideal: Litchfield County, in the northwest corner of the state amid the Berkshire foothills, was two hours from New York and three from Boston; better still, there was no railroad in the area, which made it hard to reach via public transportation—one of the reasons its sparse population included such diverse luminaries as Jasper Johns, Henry

Kissinger, and Bill Styron, who noted (in a 1954 letter to his then friend Mailer) that it was "distant enough to give a feeling of isolation and to be removed from the dreary station-wagon community belt but close enough so that the delights, such as they are, of Manhattan are not too difficult of access." Roth was still at Yaddo in early February, so Sproul went alone with a real estate agent to inspect the house in Warren. "We'll take it," she said, while still in the driveway.

The gray two-story clapboard farmhouse, built in 1799, was "the most beautiful house I ever saw," said Sproul, and there were other reasons to love it. Among the most important, for Roth, was that the house faced away from the main road, the front door opening onto a vista of maple and ash trees and the fields beyond, crisscrossed by mossy, venerable, low stone walls. Inside the front door was an elegant spindle staircase, original to the house along with the chestnut and oak plank floors; to the left of the entrance hall was a living room with floor-to-ceiling bookcases and a big fireplace, to the right was a parlor with paneled cupboards, more bookcases, and another fireplace. But Roth's favorite part of the house was the Stone Room: a cavernous former woodshed with a high, beamed ceiling, stone floor, and french windows. Outbuildings included a barn and carport, as well as a dilapidated 17-by-32-foot cottage about fifty yards from the house. Flat Rock Farm—soon to be rechristened "The Fiction Factory"—included forty acres of land, and Roth bought it for $110,000 in cash.

They closed on April 13, and moved in after a trip to Europe (instead of Japan); that first night, May 19, they sat in the empty living room on lawn chairs they'd brought over from Woodstock, and the next morning—a happy day—the furniture began to arrive. "We operated on the 'mud principle,'" said Roth, "which established that because the house was set in acres of fields and was at the intersection of two dirty roads, you should be able to track mud into any room." Once again with Nina Schneider's guidance, they'd bought a lot of sturdy but exquisite country furniture from Pierre Deux in the Village, such as an old refectory table with little gashes along the surface where bread had been chopped. Sproul herself gave Roth a number of cherished *objets* such as a little scroll calendar on the fireplace mantel in the living room; Roth, keenly preoccupied with the passage of time, made a point of turning the little knob every morning of his life in Connecticut. Forty years later

Sproul went back to care for Roth during an illness, and everything was almost exactly the way she'd left it.

"The best thing I ever did in my life," Roth said of the move—and so began one of his happiest eras, and one of his most stable. "I'm a great sucker for domesticity," he liked to stress. "I don't want to sit in fucking Elaine's. I want to have dinner, have a drink . . . read, get in bed, fuck, and go to sleep. What else is there? Then in the morning go back to my place, work, and so on. And every day more or less the same." As ever, it helped that Sproul was an even-tempered, industrious person who loved him. They almost never argued. When Roth got on her nerves enough to make her think *fuck you*, she'd notice him all but reeling from the unspoken blow, and hence took pains to keep mean thoughts to a minimum. For their first Valentine's Day in Connecticut, Roth drew her a big heart whose arrow tip was an ejaculating penis.

Roth furnished the separate little cottage with a cot reminding him of his first studio in the woods at Yaddo, and went on from there. That first year he added a toilet, replaced what was left of the flooring, and arranged for heat and a phone that didn't take incoming calls. A few years later he added a bed-cum-exercise-room and a screened porch in back; the place became so cozy he took to sleeping there in the winter when he was alone, returning to the main house only for meals. In the early years, though, he was rarely alone except when working, but then resolutely so. "Malamud has already been at it for two hours," he'd fret around nine in the morning, departing for his studio while Sproul went about her own work. One day she bumped into him getting lunch in the kitchen, and began to ask a question. "I only *look* like I'm not working," he said, clinging to a train of thought, and thereafter she kept mum until their late-afternoon hikes along the Housatonic River or swims in Lake Waramaug.

Roth's favorite holiday, Thanksgiving,* was a sprawling festival during

---

* A lyrical passage about the holiday, in *American Pastoral*, provides the book's title: "And it was never but once a year that they were brought together anyway, and that was on the neutral, dereligionized ground of Thanksgiving, when everybody gets to eat the same thing, nobody sneaking off to eat funny stuff—no kugel, no gefilte fish, no bitter herbs, just one colossal turkey for two hundred and fifty million people—one colossal turkey feeds all. . . . It is the American pastoral par excellence and it lasts twenty-four hours."

the Sproul era: she cooked "vast turkeys and sweet potatoes" along with a big batch of her Julia Child mushroom soup, while sending Roth out for pies, paté, caviar, and the like. For that first holiday in Connecticut, they invited as many as twenty guests—Bess and Herman, Sandy* and his boys, the Gustons, Solotaroffs, Goldstein, Lelchuk and his girlfriend, various others—and played a frenzied game of touch football on the back lawn while Herman and Guston observed bemusedly ("waiting for a broken limb") from the studio porch. For the meal they all sat down at Roth's beloved refectory table, the fire crackling away. "I loved those days," he said wistfully.

Local friends included Bill Styron and Arthur Miller—both men a little problematic, each in his own way. Styron took a shine to Sproul and sometimes made lurching passes at her when drunk, whereas Miller told rambling stories about "Marilyn," while Roth—the respectful younger colleague—suffered in silence. Roth's private opinion of Miller, the man and his work, wasn't terribly high to begin with and seemed to plummet over time, as Alfred Kazin noticed when the subject of Miller's memoir, *Timebends*, came up one night in Warren: "Philip wouldn't let go," Kazin wrote in his diary, "insisted on wiping the floor with Arthur north south west and east—bad writer, no thinker . . . on and on." Not surprisingly Roth saw little of Miller in later years, when he liked to say (as Styron reported to their mutual friend Brustein), "it is only the prospect of the Nobel Prize that keeps Arthur Miller alive from October to October."

The woman who would eventually become one of Roth's bitterest foes, Francine du Plessix Gray, gave him a warm welcome when he arrived in 1972—all the more since he was about to publish *The Breast*, which (said Roth) struck her as avant-garde. During that first dinner at the Grays' in Connecticut, Roth sat next to Francine's Russian mother, Tatiana, whom he remembered introducing herself as follows: "Why do you write book called *Breast?* I hate my breasts!" When Roth and Sproul got into their car afterward for the three-minute drive home, they announced in unison, "I never want to see those people again as long as I live!" For several years, though, Roth endeavored to cultivate a pleasant "professional" friendship with Francine, offering "polite but candid" appraisals

---

* A widower as of 1970, when his first wife, Trudy, died of ovarian cancer. More about that later.

of her work. He thought she'd found her métier with the Hawaii book, and advised her to go on writing about the other forty-nine states à la the old WPA American Guide Series. "You just don't want me to write fiction," she laughed.

Roth claimed that Francine longed for a less professional friendship, and indeed he believed her frustration in that respect was a factor in her later animosity. "She fell in love with me and was dying to get laid," he said in 2012. "It was a crush." When asked whether he'd ever succumbed to temptation, Roth indignantly denied it ("How crazy do you think I am?"), though others contradicted him on that point. A later mistress, who knew them both well, said that Roth had told her repeatedly about an early seduction, a reminiscence that ended with the refrain, "*Not* one of my proudest moments." Gray, for her part, was every bit as staunch in her denial: "I'm very lucky not to have been romantically involved with him," she said, insisting she'd turned him down the one time ("between Barbara Sproul and Claire") he asked her to dinner.

As for her husband, Cleve, Roth considered him a painter of admirable skill as well as a refined, intelligent human being—the scion of a wealthy Upper East Side Jewish family who'd changed his name from Ginsberg to Gray when he went to Princeton. ("She should have been Francine du Plessix Ginsberg," said Roth, "then I would have been friends with her.") Sproul agreed that Cleve was "a sweet, dear man" and echoed the consensus that he was essentially gay. Joel Conarroe, while house-sitting for Roth in the autumn of 1977 (Roth was in London), described a dinner attended by the Grays and the writer Leonard Michaels, who was teaching that year at Bard. "Queen Francine," Conarroe wrote Roth, was "very taken" with Michaels,

> calls him Byronic, sometimes refers to him as Byron; she came 16 times during dinner Monday night. . . . [Michaels] said he had met you, wondered whether you are still funny. Francine said oh ha ha ha yes he's very funny. So funny. Cleve got nervous when Michaels went on at some length about Byron's homosexuality, but Francine kept egging him on. . . . If there are saints in this world Cleve is a fucking saint.

Roth would not have disagreed; one of his main objections to the Grays, as company, was having to witness Francine's incessant browbeating of

her husband ("Oh, you don't know what you're talking about!"—etc.).
He was glad to hear that one night, at another friend's house, Cleve had
gotten fed up enough to shy a salad plate at her.

■　■　■　■

ROTH HADN'T WANTED to risk losing the house in Connecticut, so
they canceled their six-week vacation to Japan; instead, after the closing,
they departed for an eighteen-day tour of Venice, Vienna, and Prague.
In the window of the Café Sacher, in Vienna, they were delighted to find
a marzipan arrangement of Nixon and his cabinet; a few days later they
crossed in a taxi from sunny Austria to Czechoslovakia—like entering
a "coal-mining town in West Virginia," said Sproul. When they finally
reached Prague and checked into the Hotel Jalta on Wenceslas Square,
Sproul needed to lie down and sleep off a migraine, while Roth went out
looking for landmarks associated with his beloved Kafka. "It's the most
wonderful place!" he said hours later, remarking that he'd already bought
"a sauerkraut or something on the street" when she asked whether he was
hungry: "I realized he was in love," said Sproul, since Roth would never
eat street food (what with his mother's constant haranguing about *chazerai*) unless he felt viscerally at home in a place.

For the next three days Roth walked and walked around Old Town
Square, visiting the places he'd read about in Kafka's letters and diaries
and in Max Brod's biography—Kafka's old gymnasium, his father Her-
mann's business—and also straying into the sooty medieval alleys of the
old Jewish ghetto, where he toured the synagogues Hitler had hoped to
turn into a vast museum commemorating his destruction of European
Jewry. Every day Roth returned to the forlorn, crow-ridden Old Jewish
Cemetery behind the Pinkas Synagogue, which housed a little museum
for the victims of Theresienstadt; Roth ("somewhat stunned") studied
photographs of Prague's Jewish artists and intellectuals, who'd created a
newspaper and drama society in the concentration camp, a soccer league,
and a children's theater; there was also a little boy's Mickey Mouse doll
with a yellow star pinned to its chest. At last he made his way to the
New Jewish Cemetery, adding a pebble to the pile beside Kafka's grave.
"I understood that a connection of sorts existed between myself and this
place," he later wrote; "here was one of those dense corners of Jewish
Europe which Hitler had emptied of Jews, a place which in earlier days

must have been not unlike those neighborhoods in Austro-Hungarian Lemberg and Czarist Kiev, where the two branches of my own family had lived before their emigration to America at the beginning of the century."

Czech translations of Roth's first two books had been published by Odéon Editions, and on his second morning in Prague he was warmly received there by the director and his staff, who toasted him with slivovitz. Roth wondered whether they were interested in publishing his latest books, *Portnoy* and *Our Gang*, and was told that, alas, the "authorities" had deemed the books unsuitable for translation. Afterward Roth was approached by an editor with a slight limp, Eva Kondrysova, who asked him if he'd like to have lunch with her. "All those people are swine," she informed him at the restaurant, and in perfect English (she'd spent time at the University of Florida on a Fulbright) explained that all the decent people at the firm had been sacked after the Soviet invasion that ended the Prague Spring in 1968. Books like *Portnoy* were hardly in accord with the new mandate of politicized "socrealism," but she happened to know that the esteemed translating couple Luba and Rudolf Pellar—also translators of Hemingway and Salinger—were working on a Czech version of Roth's novel.

That night he and Sproul dined with the Pellars, who, after several bottles of wine, reviewed the more idiomatically challenging obscenities in *Portnoy* "amid gales of laughter": an act of cunnilingus, for instance, had been roughly translated as "he licked her pan" ("you know, lick the pan of the roast?"). More soberly, the couple discussed the indignities visited on liberal-minded writers, artists, and scholars under the hardline regime headquartered in the Prague Castle. "I can't put out one more play about love in the cucumber factory in Siberia," said Luba, still head of the national theater but desperate to retire. Under Soviet "normalization," writers of conscience fell into three basic categories: those who'd managed to flee the country or stay abroad during the summer invasion in 1968; those who'd already been imprisoned; and those who were kept under constant surveillance, forbidden to publish and relegated to menial jobs and the lowest category of housing. As Milan Kundera explained, such systematic destruction of Czech culture "undermined the identity of the nation, enabling it to be more easily swallowed up by Russian civilization . . . [and] put a violent end to the modern era, the era in which culture still represented the realization of supreme values."

When Roth got back to New York, he asked Bob Silvers to put him in touch with any Czech intellectuals he happened to know, and so came to befriend Antonín (Tony) Liehm. As Liehm recalled of their first meeting at the Russian Tea Room, Roth said, "I've just published a pamphlet against Nixon. . . . It's selling like hotcakes, and all that can happen to me is that I'll get a little richer. While, with you, writers that do about the same thing can count on going to prison. And I have this need to understand why they do it." Liehm gave Roth a little history lesson going back to the Soviet-backed coup d'état of 1948. In 1960, Liehm himself had become editor of *Literární noviny* (*Literary Journal*), Czechoslovakia's most influential culture magazine, with a circulation of 300,000 in a country whose total population was ten million; working with the likes of Kundera, Ludvík Vaculík, and Ivan Klíma, the magazine had served as the foremost platform for liberalization leading to the Prague Spring, and hence had ceased publication once the Warsaw Pact tanks rolled into the country on August 20, 1968. Liehm had fled to Paris two days later, and within a couple of years had wangled a job at Richmond College of CUNY on Staten Island, where he taught a course in Eastern European cinema.

Every Tuesday afternoon that fall, Roth took the Staten Island ferry to watch and discuss the weekly movie in Liehm's class. Like most Americans then, Roth had no idea who Kundera was until he saw an adaptation of *The Joke*, and meanwhile he also befriended the exiled director Jiří Weiss after watching Weiss's *Ninety Degrees in the Shade*. (One of Weiss's better-known protégés, Miloš Forman, would later become one of Roth's neighbors in Warren.) When Roth returned to Prague the following year, Weiss entrusted him with a pair of American jeans to bring to his daughter. Weiss was twenty years older than Roth and had had a young wife, who left him; in *Deception* Roth imagined a Weiss-like Czech who berates him, "Philip," for sleeping with his wife: "A really good imitation," said Roth, of what would have occurred in that case.

■ ■ ■ ■

THE BREAST, published in September 1972, was not a success. "The overwhelming reaction has been negative," Roth wrote Maschler; he was especially bitter about the *New York Times* reviews, both of which were not only negative but egregious as criticism. Fully a third of Christopher

Lehmann-Haupt's review was padded with a long quote from Roth's novel ("I am a breast . . ."), and the rest was mostly taken up by a cutely sustained boxing metaphor: Roth's outrageous premise, said Lehmann-Haupt, "almost, but not quite, knocks us out" in "round one," but then the book "dithers itself away in feints at political allegory, in shadow-boxing with psychoanalytic insights," and so on. As for John Gardner's review in the Sunday *Times*, it was so pompous and bewildering that even the *Book Review*'s editor, John Leonard, admitted to Aaron Asher, Roth's editor, that it should never have been published. Gardner wrote:

> The highest value in fiction (as everyone has always known except novelty freaks and, of course, the criticism industry) is moral stability, the ability to celebrate reality without distorting or evading it. . . . Sloppiness and self-indulgence, as in such earlier Roth novels as *When She Was Good* and *Portnoy's Complaint*, debase the vision, making it seem either false or silly. Feebleness of invention, as in some of his early stories, limits the vision to, at best, the merely touching.

Having trashed Roth's oeuvre as sloppy, self-indulgent, false, silly, or merely touching, Gardner commended *The Breast* as his best book— "Technically, at least"—but hastened to clarify that it, too, was a failure: "like a hung-up schoolboy or like the trendy popular novelist he is," Roth indulges too much in gratuitous nastiness, such as the way Kepesh, in the novel, notices the discoloration of his penis that portends his turning into a breast (a marvelous passage). Gardner rested his case: "As a rule of thumb I say, if Socrates, Jesus and Tolstoy wouldn't do it, don't."

Back in July, Roth had thanked Solotaroff for his forthcoming rave in *Esquire* (Roth "is at the top of his talent and control," etc.), though he worried the overall reception "ain't gonna be clear sailing all the way," given that neither Bellow nor Philip Rahv had liked the book. "Frankly, it left me mystified," Rahv wrote the author; whereas Kafka's approach in *The Metamorphosis* made the uncanny seem believable and was in the service of a comprehensible metaphor ("guilt for displacing the father and restitution"), Roth's aims were more opaque, to put it mildly. While he seemed intent on imitating Kafka's realism—describing precisely how the breast is washed, for example—he did so selectively, ignoring a breast's primary function. "The breast is a feeding organ," Rahv pointed out, "but it is hard to imagine your particular hero as obsessed by very strong desires to feed others." Peter Prescott—in a *Newsweek* review that praised, among other things, Roth's "sure-handed craftsmanship"—put his finger on what was perhaps the main difficulty: "Roth did not decide whether it was to be a buoyant farce like Gogol's story ["The Nose"], or a dark parable like Kafka's."

Once again, Roth and Lelchuk prepared an interview (this time for *The New York Review of Books*) meant to serve as an explanatory rebuttal. "In *The Breast*," said Roth, "my approach to the outlandish seems to me to be something like a blending of the two methods"—those of Gogol and Kafka both, whose influence is made "visible" in the book when Kepesh wonders whether his repeatedly teaching their two key stories has something to do with his predicament. In *The Metamorphosis*, Gregor Samsa's awakening as a dung beetle is precisely described: "He was lying on his hard, as it were armor-plated, back and when he lifted his head a little he could see his dome-like brown belly divided into stiff arched segments on top of which the bed quilt could hardly keep in position and it was about to slide off completely."* Similarly, in *The Breast*, Roth puts his endocrinology research to good use, as Kepesh remarks on his "spongy consistency" and helps the reader visualize him as vividly as Kafka's beetle: "At one end I am rounded off like a watermelon, at the other I terminate in a nipple, cylindrical in shape, projecting five inches from my 'body' and perforated at the tip with seventeen openings, the apertures of the lactiferous ducts." Rather than go all the way, however—as Rahv would have it—and evoke Kepesh's primary function as a "feeding organ," Roth focuses on the more farcical, Gogolian possibilities of his hero's disastrously heightened erotic susceptibility: "I would like to fuck you with my nipple," Kepesh tells a nurse. *"Did you hear me, whore? Did you hear what I want?"*

As for metaphorical clarity, Roth quietly answered Rahv (via Lelchuk) by pointing out that any attempt to assign a single meaning to Kafka's work was bound to lessen its appeal, and so with *The Breast*: "To try to unravel the mystery of 'meaning' here is really to participate to some

---

* In Willa and Edwin Muir's translation, Samsa turns into a "gigantic insect" that's generally understood to be a cockroach. Vladimir Nabokov, however, in his Cornell lectures, insisted Kafka was describing a dung beetle, and he persuaded me.

degree in Kepesh's struggle—and to be defeated, as he is." In the end, Kepesh merely accepts the reality of his fate ("he is a breast, and must act accordingly"), and is left to wrestle with the kind of breast he wishes to be: whether he will degenerate into pure sensualism ("I don't want her to read to me—I don't even listen," he tells Dr. Klinger of his girlfriend; "I just want her to squeeze me and suck me and lick me") or become an organ of higher purpose—a fanciful version of "Portnoy's Complaint," in short, wherein "strongly-felt ethical and altruistic impulses are perpetually warring with extreme sexual longings, often of a perverse nature."

For the rest of his life, Roth would believe *The Breast* was particularly worthy of rediscovery, even going to the trouble of thoroughly revising it for inclusion in *The Philip Roth Reader* (1980). The main problem with the original version, he seemed to think, was its too-mannered diction, which was perhaps meant to mimic a rather floridly translated European novel. "Because I knew there was no one really to assist me, I was never able to complete the transaction other than in a haze of magical masturbatory possibilities" is a typical passage that Roth saw fit to excise, substituting simply "Who would help me?"* Six months before his death, Roth remarked that Kafka's *Metamorphosis* remained the "best trans-species story," but he insisted the best "transgender novel" was *The Breast*, "where a man is trapped not merely in a woman's body but in the universally fetishized emblem of womanhood." His parents' view, however, would appear to be more in accord with posterity. "Ma," Roth said to the flummoxed Bess, when she sheepishly returned the book to him, "you don't have to say anything." As for Herman, he sat quietly in his son's garden with *The Breast* that first summer in Connecticut. "I have a feeling," Roth wrote a friend, "that if I steal over in that direction I may find him asleep."

And yet he was more obsessed than ever with Kafka after his first trip to Czechoslovakia, and next wrote a more explicit tribute that he dedicated to his students in that fall's Kafka course at Penn: "'I Always Wanted You to Admire My Fasting'; or, Looking at Kafka" was written, he said, to correct their tendency "to read Kafka as though he had writ-

---

* For his revision Roth used a copy of the 1973 Corgi (U.K.) paperback, almost every page of which is scored heavily with his black Flair pen. The revised text is the one that appears in the Library of America.

ten his stories on Mars, or in graduate school, instead of in Prague." The opening ten pages or so consist of an essay about Kafka's last years before his death at age forty; had he lived, Roth noted, his skull would have been shoveled out of the ovens along with those of his three younger sisters—a complex irony, given his lifelong sense of persecution on the one hand, and alienation from Jews or at least his own Jewish family on the other. "What have I in common with the Jews?" Kafka wrote in his diary. "I have hardly anything in common with myself and should stand very quietly in a corner, content that I can breathe." Roth then imagines a Kafka who lives to flee the Nazis and become a Hebrew school teacher at Schley Street Synagogue in 1942, when Kafka is fifty-nine and Roth (though the first-person narrator never refers to himself by name) a child of nine. The boy—"Little borscht-belt comic that I am"—torments his teacher by dubbing him Dr. Kishka (Yiddish for "insides") because of his sour breath and mimics "his precise and finicky professorial manner, his German accent, his gloom." The narrator's father (quite in keeping with how Herman himself might have behaved) tries to play match-maker between lonely Dr. Kafka and the spinster Aunt Rhoda (inspired by Roth's Aunt Honey), but the courtship goes awry when the couple visit Atlantic City, for reasons that can be discussed only in Yiddish around the children; the narrator's brother, however, hisses an explana-tion into his ear: "Sex!"

Roth loved the hybrid piece*—a foray into alternative history that he would repeat more extensively in novels such as *The Ghost Writer* and *The Plot Against America*, and never mind his more and more elaborate muddling of fact and fiction generally. "I'll tell you the truth," he told an interviewer who wondered, in 1987, whether "Looking at Kafka" was basically autobiographical except for the one detail of Kafka's survival. "Kafka *was* my Hebrew teacher. Only my name is not Roth."

---

* The following year he chose it for inclusion in Rust Hills's anthology *This Is My Best*, for which (per the title) the authors selected their own favorite works.

Twenty-Eight

I N THE OCTOBER 1972 *ESQUIRE* (AS PART OF A FEATURE in which four older writers each contributed an essay about a colleague under the age of thirty-five), Roth wrote in praise of Lelchuk's soon-to-be-published *American Mischief*, albeit with some pretty grave reservations whereof he warned his friend in advance—in essence, he liked the first half of the 500-plus-page novel but not so much the second: "If I had to say what went wrong, it has to do with character (yours, boy) and temperament, as much as with writing talent—in your case, for good and bad, they're inseparable. . . . Lenny"—Pincus, the protagonist—"is really a whiney prick." In his *Esquire* piece, Roth duly noted the "mean, pricky streak" that mars the novel's latter part, but also singled out Pincus's murder of Norman Mailer ("firing the fatal bullet up the author's determinedly virginal anus") as among the book's "felicitous pages."

Back at Yaddo, the two friends had wondered how Mailer would respond to such an ignominious demise even in fiction, concluding he probably wouldn't like it much—but, as Roth reflected, "since he was a writer whose animating principle was to assault every constraint of conventional decency in order to bring linguistic life to the unimaginable and unknown, he would probably have no choice but to grudgingly respect the boldness of the bad taste as well as the impulse that informed it." Roth was particularly thinking of Mailer's 1957 essay "The White Negro," in which he seems to commend the courage, or existential authenticity, of two young thugs who murder a candy-store owner—a passage that inspires Pincus to murder him.

Shortly after Roth's *Esquire* piece appeared, Mailer got in touch with Lelchuk's editor at Farrar, Straus and Giroux, Henry Robbins, and proposed that Lelchuk meet him in a bar; Mailer would bring along his friend Pete Hamill as a "second," and suggested that Lelchuk bring

Roth. "Well, if you're out of your mind, you'll do it," said Roth, when Lelchuk apprised him of the idea, "but without me as your 'second,' old friend." Instead Roth suggested they meet at his lawyers' offices, since Marty Garbus often handled publishing disputes related to censorship issues, and besides Mailer would be less apt to commit some form of drunken mayhem in a law office at nine in the morning, when Roth scheduled the meeting (claiming he had to leave by eleven). Twelve years had passed since Mailer had stabbed and nearly killed his second wife, though Mailer had shown few signs of mellowing when Roth ran into him three years later, at a *Paris Review* party, where Roth and Plimpton had to pry him off the writer Harold ("Doc") Humes, whose eyes Mailer seemed intent on gouging out of his skull. Given that Roth had made a rather derisive reference to Mailer in "Writing American Fiction" (to the effect that Mailer surely had less time for writing novels now that he was "an actor in the cultural drama" and thus occupied with being "a sociologist, a journalist, or even the Mayor of New York"), and now had characterized the murder of a fictional Mailer as "felicitous," it was safe to assume Mailer was not terribly well disposed.*

The stakes could hardly be higher for Lelchuk: if Farrar, Straus and Giroux were pressured into dropping the Mailer scene, then the entire second half of the book would have to be recast, since Pincus is arrested and jailed because of the murder. Both Lelchuk and Roth spent the week poring over Mailer's pertinent writings in preparation for the Saturday meeting at Garbus's office; then, after his Friday classes, Lelchuk caught the shuttle from Boston and headed straight to Roth's apartment, where the two conducted a mock-debate in which Roth played the part of Mailer: "You're a terrible writer and your book is shit," said Roth/Mailer. "What do you have to say to that?" This would prove decorous next to the real thing.

Garbus's office was on the thirty-sixth floor of 666 Fifth Avenue, and others in attendance included Robbins, Robert Giroux (FSG's editorial director), and Georges Borchardt (Lelchuk's agent). Rather than

---

* One may also recall Roth's (alleged) quip about his "best selling rival" taking on the Thai kickboxers in his golf shoes, though it bears mentioning that—whatever his hostility otherwise—Mailer had been one of two "seconders" for Roth's nomination to the National Institute of Arts and Letters in 1969.

bring along Pete Hamill as a second, Mailer was joined by the eminent First Amendment lawyer Charles Rembar, a cousin of his who'd argued against the prohibition of *Lady Chatterley's Lover* and other novels. Roth walked into the conference room and saw that Mailer and Rembar had already arrived, the first dressed in a blue suit that looked a little rumpled, as if he'd come directly from an all-nighter. "Good morning, Norman," said Roth, and was about to offer his hand when Mailer growled at him. Garbus began to explain the purpose of the meeting but was cut off by Mailer: "I'm going to kiss you two guys! Roth, you're the pimp and Lelchuk is your whore!" As Roth wrote in his notes at the time, "I had never before been so offended—or, for that matter, so genuinely menaced—by any other person in my life."

Rembar tried to frame Mailer's grievance in more temperate legal terms. The scene in question was libelous, he said, "in that it attributes a character to a man that is not his own character and degrades him." Which is to say, the fictional Mailer seems willing to submit to sexual defilement ("You want Mailer's cherry, kid?"), kneeling in his underpants when Pincus orders him to do so. "That's Roth, not me," said the real Mailer. Roth shrugged: "It's only sex, Norman, it beats dying." "To you!" said Mailer, who slapped his cards on the table: *Roth himself had written that scene.* "I have enough trouble writing my own books without writing somebody else's as well," said Roth. "*I* wrote the book, Mr. Mailer!" said Lelchuk, furious at finding himself on the periphery of an argument over a novel he'd spent three torturous years writing. "Your quarrel is with me!" ("Why would Norman Mailer have a paranoid thought?" Roth mock-speculated re Mailer's suspicions that he was the secret author of *American Mischief.* "Why don't you ask why Lee Harvey Oswald had a paranoid thought?")

Roth was impressed by Lelchuk's methodical argument in his defense. The first time Lelchuk tried to show Mailer one of his (Mailer's) passages about "saying the unsayable," Mailer made a lurching grab for him across the conference table—whereupon Lelchuk was moved to the far end, where he continued to read Mailer to Mailer, sliding the books over whenever Mailer snarled, "I never wrote that! . . . Where did *that* come from?" For Mailer, a coherent counterargument seemed beside the point; his main idea was to terrorize the younger writer into compliance. "By the time this is over, Lelchuk," he was subsequently quoted in the *Times*

("Roth Is Present" read a subhead), "you ain't going to be nothin' but a hank of hair and some fillings."

But of course his position was untenable and he knew it, and certainly his cousin Rembar knew it, having published *The End of Obscenity* (1968) about his own celebrated anticensorship crusades. So Mailer blustered and threatened and finally left in a huff. Lelchuk professed to be "nothing less than furious" when the meeting was leaked to the *Times*; then, a couple of weeks later, FSG sold his novel's paperback rights to New American Library for a quarter million. As for Roth: in 2012 he dismissed the meeting as inconsequential to anyone but Lelchuk; Mailer, he said, figured "he'd knock this fly off in the morning . . . [then go on] to stab somebody, or get some convict out of jail [who would] kill somebody."* Truth be known, Roth was badly shaken by the episode, noting at the time that all the men in the room were serious-minded, highly accomplished Jews. "I think, in fact, that what gave that meeting with Mailer its anguished edge, and left me with the first migraine of my life, was the undercurrent of bloody rage seemed to be tearing asunder something like a tribal council—and that our conflicting aims threatened unavoidably to erupt in fratricide."

■ ■ ■ ■

BACK IN 1960, Roth's friend Marty Greenberg had quit *Commentary* after the American Jewish Committee decided to promote "this asshole Podhoretz" (as Roth invariably called him) to be editor instead of him. Norman Podhoretz's evolving neoconservatism could be descried even then via a certain humorless Jewish chauvinism that became more pronounced after the Six-Day War in 1967—shortly before *Portnoy* turned into a lightning rod for debate over matters of Jewish American identity. The novel was reviewed in *Commentary* by associate editor Peter Shaw, who accused the author of "fanaticism in the hatred of things Jewish," provoking at least one reader to write in protest: "Whatever the final merits of *Portnoy's Complaint* (and I think they are considerable), it seems to me that a reviewer should deal with Mr. Roth's novel in other than

---

* Roth is alluding to an episode in 1981, when Mailer successfully campaigned for the release of convicted murderer and thief Jack Henry Abbott, who proceeded to stab a man to death after only six weeks of freedom.

the ad hominem (re Roth) and reductionist (re Roth's supposed attitude toward Jews) manner that Mr. Shaw does."

But the worst lay ahead, and it would come at the hands of one of Roth's intellectual heroes, Irving Howe. In some ways Howe seemed an unlikely nemesis—at least in the pages of *Commentary*, an ideological rival to Howe's own left-wing *Dissent*; by the late sixties, however, the socialist Howe had become disenchanted with the unbridled radicalism of the New Left, and this had made him more than merely crypto-sympathetic with the likes of Podhoretz. As Sam Tanenhaus wrote, Howe "was at his core a dutiful immigrant son," hence his classic compendium of the Jewish American immigrant experience, *World of Our Fathers* (1976), "with its stories of tenement sorrows and Workmen's Circles and its Yiddish soundtrack." The young Roth had been a reader of *Dissent* and admired Howe's early biography of Sherwood Anderson; but (as noted earlier) he was particularly affected by Howe's 1946 essay "The Lost Young Intellectual," which had helped him realize that his own painful sense of alienation from his parents—especially Herman—was only to be expected. As Zuckerman reflects of Howe's fictional counterpart, Milton Appel, in *The Anatomy Lesson*, "The disputatious stance, the aggressively marginal sensibility, the disavowal of community ties . . . to Zuckerman this was the very mark of the intellectual Jews in their thirties and forties on whom he was modeling his own style and thought. . . . [T]o be raised as a post-immigrant Jew in America was to be given a ticket out of the ghetto into a wholly unconstrained world of thought."

One of Roth's most perceptive critics, Mark Shechner, thought Howe was especially galled by Portnoy as a parodic portrait of his own "young Jewish intellectual two decades later, libidinized, psychoanalyzed, and propelled by bursts of Vietnam-era panic and countercultural libertinism." During the decades following Howe's account of an alienated young Jew, Egyptian president Nasser had threatened to "throw Israelis into the sea," relations had frayed between black Americans and Jews (erstwhile allies in the civil rights movement), and Howe himself had been reviled by the ragged upstarts of the student movement. Portnoy and his creator—embodiments of the heretical, impious forces that seemed to threaten worldwide Jewish prestige (and reflect grotesquely on Howe's younger self)—were ripe for some definitive censure, or, as

Shechner put it, "a mugging, pure and simple, and I pegged Howe and Podhoretz for a couple of mugs."

In the December 1972 *Commentary*, Podhoretz introduced Howe's Grand Remonstrance with a hatchet job of his own, "Laureate of the New Class," in which he observed that Roth's "point," as a writer, is that "Americans are disgusting people." Roth's contempt was by no means confined to Jews but also embraced "small-town Wasps unredeemed by patrician blood," and indeed Roth would have readers think the whole country "is inhabited exclusively by vulgarians, materialists, boors, and bored." It was true Roth considered Podhoretz himself boorish; after their first encounter in 1957—when they met in Podhoretz's office to discuss Roth's "You Can't Tell a Man by the Song He Sings"—it got back to Podhoretz that Roth had complained about his foul language, a slight he never forgot. The only Americans exempted from this "prissy" young man's disgust, he said, was his own elitist "gang," whom Podhoretz dubbed the "New Class"—i.e., readers invited by Roth "to join with him in snobbishly and self-righteously celebrating their joint superiority to everyone else around them."

Howe's more nuanced and certainly more exhaustive attack, "Philip Roth Reconsidered," began with Howe's admission that he'd been among the critics who'd overpraised Roth's first book; now that Roth was taken overseriously ("until the next fashion appears"), Howe was obliged to reexamine his earlier esteem in light of Roth's total achievement, or lack thereof. In accord with Podhoretz, Howe noted that Roth's "great need is for a stance of superiority, the pleasure, as Madison Avenue puts it, of always being 'on top of it.'" Thus his "deadpan malicious accuracy" (a mostly commendatory phrase from Howe's 1959 review) vis-à-vis the Patimkins amounted to a condescending caricature of Jewish American life, a product of the author's "thin personal culture," devoid of any real sense of tradition or "historical context"—as though *Goodbye, Columbus* should reflect the values and methods of a soup-to-nuts tome like *World of Our Fathers* (following American Jews step by step from the Old World through the Lower East Side and unto the present day) versus those of the slender satirical novella it is.

"He has largely lost his sense of Jewishness," Howe had written of his "Lost Young Intellectual" in 1946, "of belonging to a people with a meaningful tradition, and he has not succeeded in finding a place for himself in the American scene or the American tradition." As a young critic Howe had found a (cosmopolitan, nonrestrictive) place for himself by writing about Sherwood Anderson, a Midwestern gentile, not unlike Roth's decision to distance himself from Jewish themes, for a time, and write a second novel that he'd once considered titling *The Goyim*. "His attitude to the Jewish cultural tradition in which he was reared is an ambiguous compound of rejection and nostalgia," Howe also wrote of his young intellectual, and in 1959 he sternly refused to "give an inch of encouragement" to Jewish philistia who would accuse Roth of "self-hatred": "in his own way [Roth] is echoing the lines: 'By the waters of Babylon we sat down / And wept when we remembered Zion.'"

With *Portnoy*, however, Howe was confronted by a young Jewish intellectual who, as he saw it, wished "to undo the fate of birth" as part of a (self-hating?) libertine's dream to "create himself as a 'human being'" unburdened by a tragic past. And so we come to the root of Howe's animus, rather similar to that of Roth's earlier detractors:

> For some Gentile readers the book seems to have played an even more important role. After the Second World War, as a consequence of certain unpleasantnesses that occurred during the war, a wave of philo-Semitism swept through our culture. This wave lasted for all of two decades, in the course of which books by Jewish writers were often praised (in truth, overpraised) and a fuss made about Jewish intellectuals, critics, etc. Some literary people found this hard to bear [e.g., Capote and Howe himself], but they did. Once *Portnoy's Complaint* arrived, however, they could almost be heard breathing a sigh of relief, for it signaled an end to philo-Semitism in American culture, one no longer had to listen to all that talk about Jewish morality, Jewish endurance, Jewish wisdom, Jewish families. Here was Philip Roth himself, a writer who even seemed to know Yiddish [but didn't really, given his "thin personal culture"], confirming what had always been suspected about those immigrant Jews but had recently not been tactful to say.

Having gotten *that* off his chest, Howe briskly dismissed Roth's most recent books—*Our Gang* was "flaccid," *The Breast* "boring" and "tame"—and pronounced his final anathema: "Flaubert once said that a writer must choose between an audience and readers. Evidently Roth has made his choice."

Subsequently, in the magazine's letter column, Marie Syrkin glee-fully reprised the main point of her *Midstream* review of *Portnoy*—to wit, that Portnoy's desire to defile gentile women (to "stick it up their backgrounds") was "straight out of the Goebbels-Streicher script." Howe replied in what he probably figured was a magnanimous vein: "Let me only say that there should be a way of distinguishing between an anti-Semite and someone who dislikes us [i.e., Roth], or between an anti-Semitic book and someone whose book 'contains plenty of contempt for Jewish life'"—a distinction Howe himself had been careful to make in his essay.

Roth forbore to respond, and for his friends' benefit affected a kind of giddy bemusement. "I don't just hate Jews," he wrote Brustein, "I HATE AMERICANS. Tomorrow the galaxy! But it inspired me; I realized that lo and *bee*-hold, I done become a monument, at which shit *will* be hurled." Guston got into the spirit of things by sketching a cartoon, forever cherished by Roth, of an artist stabbing a critic to death. In fact Roth was "infuriated" by Howe's attack, which once again mobilized the anti-Roth forces after the smoke had finally begun to clear from previous bombardments.

Ten months after "Philip Roth Reconsidered," thousands of Egyptian and Syrian tanks rolled into Israel on Yom Kippur afternoon; within three weeks, Israeli armies were on the outskirts of Cairo and Damascus, the Arab armies in smoldering ruins behind them, and "Jewish aggression" was facing censure in the U.N. Security Council and the court of world opinion. On November 7, 1973, Lelchuk forwarded a note to Roth that he'd just received from Howe ("Thought you might like to see how you disturb the Old Man"), as follows:

Why don't you ask your friend Phil Roth to write something in behalf of Israel for the Times Op Ed Page? . . . When I or Kazin or Bellow come out in support of Israel, that's not news; no one pays attention; it's expected of us. But if Roth came out with a forthright statement, that would be news of a kind, since he has prestige with segments of the public that don't care for the rest of us. . . . Or does he still feel that, as his Port-noy says, the Jews can stick their historical suffering up their ass? (And yes, I know that there's a difference between characters and authors; but I also know that grown-ups should not pretend that it's quite the difference they tell their students it is.)

Evidently unable to improve on the exquisite sanctimony of the original, Roth reproduced this note almost word for word in *The Anatomy Lesson*, wherein Milton Appel makes the same appeal via the Lelchuk character, Ivan Felt. But whereas Zuckerman responds with a splenetic telephone call to Appel, Roth put his long-seething ire into writing, thus:

Dear Irving Howe:

My friend Alan Lelchuk just sent on to me your odd request for him to ask me to write an op-ed piece in behalf of Israel. Maybe it isn't so odd: maybe you've changed your mind about me and the Jews since you distinguished for Marie Syrkin between anti-semites like Goebbels . . . and those like Roth who "just don't like us." Of course I was grateful to you for that fine distinction. . . .

For if I read correctly your letter to Alan Lelchuk asking him to ask me what apparently you'd rather not ask me yourself, you seem to suspect (privately, that is, and not in *Commentary*'s pages) that far from "disliking Jews" for being Jews, and pathologically reviling them in my work, there is a strong possibility that I might actually be troubled by their troubles and prepared to write a piece in support of a Jewish cause.

What could have given you such an idea? Certainly not my books—certainly not Portnoy's Complaint! As you say to Lelchuk, we "grown-ups" should not kid ourselves (apparently it's okay if we kid our students) about "the differences between characters and authors." . . . At any rate: all these careful distinctions behind you, you now appear to have concluded that it isn't at all unlikely that Roth—real now, not imagined—might well be expected to make "a forthright statement" in support of Israel. Though, to be sure, he would be announcing his support to that "audience" which he has "chosen" to pander to, or cater to, or to flatter, or to exploit—I could not figure out from the damning tag to your *Commentary* piece why I had chosen this "audience," but the fact is that I did it, rather than going ahead like Flaubert and choosing "readers." In your letter to Alan you refer to this audience as "segments of the public that don't care for the rest of us." That is a very tactful way of putting it and I appreciate your not rubbing my nose in my fallen condition too much. . . .

Professor Howe, how can you (and why do you) want to make what you make of Portnoy's Complaint? "Or does he still feel that, as his Portnoy says, the Jews can stick their historical suffering up their ass." Page 76 of the text in question—why don't you take a look at it? . . . You say ". . . does he still feel that . . ." meaning me, when what that chapter called "The Jewish Blues" makes perfectly clear is that Portnoy himself doesn't even feel "that." . . . I don't see how you could miss yet again the fact that Portnoy is here recalling his antagonisms and attitudes at age *fourteen*. . . . He is recalling his adolescent outcry against the constraints of his lower-middle-class Jewish upbringing. May I ask the editor of a magazine called *Dissent* and not *Orthodoxy*, is this kind of dissent so unheard of, so invalid, is this something we know nothing about? . . . [Or when young Portnoy attacks his family's bigotry against black people] do the ironies of the boy's position escape the grownup Portnoy? *"But I will not treat any human being* (outside of my family) *as inferior!"* . . . Does the character's age amount to nothing? Or his self-irony? Or is all this just so much trickery on my part, designed to enable me to foist upon the unsuspecting reader my contempt for Jewish life and my anti-semitic message? . . .

[W]hat I don't understand is how *you* can see no connection whatsoever between Portnoy's cry (page 76) "Do me a favor, my people, and stick your suffering heritage up your ass—*I happen also to be a human being!"*—no connection between that (to quote the line in full) and the lines that immediately follow and conclude the chapter, wherein the eighteen year old sister reminds the fourteen year old boy that when all is said and done, he is a Jew, and reminds him what it would mean for him to be a Jew in circumstances other than his own, namely Nazified Europe—all the while he reminds her, plaintively, that he happens presently to be living in his own circumstances, namely their house in New Jersey. And how does it end, this chapter so indicative to you of my "dislike" for the Jews, if not my anti-semitism? Page 78: ". . . and now she begins to cry too, and how monstrous I feel, for she sheds her tears for six million, or so I think, while I shed mine only for myself. Or so I think." Whatever you may think of this scene as art, to ask about it and the book it is central to, "Does Roth still feel that, as his Portnoy says, the Jews can stick their historical suffering up their ass," is, if I may say so (since to your mind it's my crime) tendentious in the extreme. I can't believe that you'd let a student get away with a reading so blatantly at odds with the text. . . .

Finally all of this may seem entirely beside the point of your request. Confirmation, if you needed any, that I am indeed what you so delicately call "an independent soul." "At such points even the most independent of souls might find it worth saying a word." In short, an invitation (indirectly made, of course) to join you guardians of the human spirit, at least on the op-ed page. And you describe *my* moral stance as "superior"! For someone so keen on distinctions, you are awfully slow to pick up on what's staring you right in the face.

Sincerely,
Philip Roth

A chagrined Howe replied that Roth had "reason to be angry"—at Lelchuk, that is, who had the bad taste to forward a private note, without Howe's permission, that "was certainly not civil and represented an eruption of personal feelings." This, said Howe, was the sort of thing Lenny Pincus might do: "I regard it as hostile, provocative, and nasty, toward both of us." But Roth wasn't having any: "I don't think Alan was ill-mannered or provocative in sending on the xeroxed paragraph, nor do I find my opinion of you changed—to the contrary, it is only confirmed—because you would have been 'more civil' in a letter written directly to me, despite the fact that you feel about me as you do."

Ten years later, *The Anatomy Lesson* appeared, as predicted back in 1973 by Mark Shechner: "We can be sure that in some Roth story, not too far hence, we will encounter a critic, a Dr. Howe or some close equivalent, saying the most foolish and funny things one has ever heard about literature." Roth would have begged to differ on at least one point: he was always proud of the fact that Milton Appel—the critic who, in *Inquiry* magazine, "had unleashed an attack upon Zuckerman's career that made Macduff's assault upon Macbeth look almost lackadaisical"—was portrayed as fair, intelligent, and even-tempered in the face of Zuckerman's furious telephone harangue ("You sententious bastard, have you ever in your life taken a mental position that isn't a moral judgment?"). At the time, however, Roth seemed pleased to be getting some of his own back: "Much boom lowering," he wrote a friend re the soon-to-be-published

Anatomy Lesson. "Fuck 'em." This while serving, with Howe, on the prize jury for the Academy of Arts and Letters' Strauss Living Awards; knowing what lay ahead, Roth was nothing but amiable toward his old enemy.

■ ■ ■ ■

ROTH HAD NEVER HAD a proper birthday party as an adult, but for his fortieth Sproul rented out a *haimish* Czech restaurant on Third Avenue, Brochetteria, and invited more than fifty of Roth's friends: "It was a little bit of *This Is Your Life*," she remembered. "We had his teachers from college and grad school, his colleagues now, the Czechs. . . ." While Roth's favorite photographer, Nancy Crampton, took pictures, he and his delighted parents mingled with the Ashers, Gustons, Liehms, Sterns, Styrons, et al. Roth's beloved American drama professor at Bucknell, Bob Maurer, was amazed to meet Lillian Hellman in the flesh ("Whom I used to teach," he noted), and the next day Roth visited the Bucknell delegation—the Maurers, Wheatcrofts, and Miss Martin— and caught up hilariously over lunch at their hotel. "It was the best birthday of my life," he wrote the Maurers, "in large part because of seeing you all again."

Roth's literary fortunes were not keeping up with his social life. "I wasn't trying to alienate the huge audience I'd won with *Portnoy*," he later remarked of the rather mystifying novels he wrote in the early seventies, "but I didn't mind if I did. And I guess I did." *Our Gang* was on the best-seller lists for a time, but afterward Roth would wander the commercial desert for more than thirty years, his books usually selling an only respectable 30,000 or so in hardcover. As for *The Great American Novel*—the last in his post-*Portnoy* trilogy of zany, alienating books— Styron assured him that he still enjoyed the approbation of the happy few: "It's a wonderfully funny and good book, be proud of it and, again, fuck the reviews."

More and more, Roth was inclined to take such advice to heart. Along with another shoddy pan from Lehmann-Haupt in the *Times* ("pretty mechanical, far-fetched and boring"), there was also, as with *The Breast*, at least one major review by a vindictive highbrow who resented Roth's success—this time William H. Gass, who noted (in *The New York Review of Books*) the recent preponderance of sports novels, whose authors are "convinced (oh my *yes*) that their chosen sport is a marvelous metaphor for life." Like Roth's previous two books, said Gass, *The Great American Novel* was compromised by the author's "exceedingly bad taste," which served to remind the reviewer that "too much American fiction has already been written by small boys." "Please advise Professor Gass that I am too old to be grown up," Roth wryly wrote the editor, and forever after would make a point of asking other writers what they thought of Gass, as a kind of litmus test for their own worthiness.*

Occasionally Roth copped to the charge that *The Great American Novel* was a tastelessly childish performance in the best sense, beginning with the "perverse pleasure" he'd taken in the title itself: "Call me Smitty," the book begins, in homage to another great American novel that the narrator's good friend, Hemingway, disparages in favor of the baseball novel we're about to read: "*Moby Dick*," says "Hem," "is a book about blubber, with a madman thrown in for excitement. Five hundred pages of blubber, one hundred pages of madman, and about twenty pages on how good niggers are with the harpoon." Thus Papa assures the narrator that he, Word Smith, is in fact the very "son of a bitch who is going to write the Great American Novel," and Smith begins to consider the possibilities of his epic about the bygone Patriot League: "Who is Moby Dick if not the terrifying Ty Cobb of his species? . . . Their remote Nantucket? Ruppert. Their crazed and vengeful Ahab? Manager Gil Gamesh. And their Ishmael? Yes, one did survive the wreck to tell the tale—an indestructible old truth-teller called me!"

It was, of course, in his more unguarded moments that Roth dismissed (or embraced) *The Great American Novel* as a jeu d'esprit and nothing but. In a self-interview (no Lelchuk this time) for *Partisan Review*, however, Roth made a case for the book's subliminal gravitas—that is, for baseball as ("oh my *yes*") a metaphor: "a means to dramatize the *struggle* between the benign national myth of itself that a great power prefers to perpetuate, and the relentlessly insidious, very nearly demonic reality (like the kind we had known in the sixties) that will not give an inch in behalf of that idealized mythology." In later years he'd sometimes characterize *The Great American Novel* as a forerunner to *American Pastoral*, insofar

---

* Roth was quite aware of his own score-keeping. His double Pipik, in *Operation Shylock*, remembers anti-Roth insults "so small that, miraculously, even I [Roth] had forgotten them."

as the former was also "about" things falling apart à la Newark's self-destruction in the sixties, and, after all, the Ruppert Mundys (Mundy = mundane) were named after Ruppert Stadium, where the once mighty Newark Bears used to play. The better to expose the paranoia and racism that underlie the myths of America, Roth loaded his book with a lot of hit-or-miss gags about anti-Semitism, the Negro Leagues, and the rise of McCarthyism, as when Big John Baal testifies before the Dies Committee: "Sure the Mundys is mostly Commies. I think some of 'em is queers, too."

But again, in his most candid moments, Roth admitted he'd simply been beguiled by the idea of a homeless baseball team, and really he "didn't know what to make of" his own book. At the end of the novel, Roth anticipated his detractors with various rejection letters to Word Smith from publishers who have considered the manuscript in question: "It is a vicious and sadistic book of the most detestable sort," reads one of these, "and your treatment of blacks, Jews, and women, . . . is offensive in the extreme; in a word, sick." Indeed, it's interesting to consider how a more politically correct era would respond to jokes about, say, the Negro League tycoon Aunt Jemima and her filial circle of black boxers ("Kid Licorice, Kid Bituminous, Kid Smoke, Kid Crow, Kid Hershey, Kid Midnight, Kid Ink and his twin Kid Quink"), not to say the breathtaking tastelessness toward women, as when Mazuma's mother steals second with her leg hiked high in the air: "I thought maybe it was a shrimp boat dockin' at the bag," says a woozy Nickname, the second baseman.

But of course this is satire, and after all Swift was *deploring* the callousness that led to his modest proposal that Irish children be eaten by the rich. A more temperate publisher's rejection of Smitty's manuscript seems about right: "Several people here found portions of it entertaining, but by and large the book seemed to most of us to strain for its effects and to simplify for the sake of facile satiric comment the complex realities of American political and cultural life." Perhaps the main thing, for Roth, was that he'd had fun writing the book ("Enough to make Flaubert spin in his grave"), and would forever insist that he—"alone in this world"—loved it.

■　■　■　■

FOR THE NEXT FEW YEARS Roth devoted his nonwriting life to helping Czechoslovak dissidents, an ideal way to distance himself from "the trivializing idiocies" that had befallen him since *Portnoy*. Before Roth returned to Prague in the spring of 1973, Tony Liehm provided him with names and phone numbers of English-speaking Czechs such as Rita Klímová, a translator who'd spent seven years of her childhood on the Upper West Side, where her émigré father, Stanislav Budín, had edited a Czech-language newspaper. Klímová had been married to Zdenek Mlynar, a member of Alexander Dubček's cabinet, who never returned from his vacation in Vienna after the Soviet occupation of 1968; his wife, meanwhile, was marooned in Prague with their children.*

Klímová introduced Roth to the writer Ivan Klíma (no relation), who lived in the Prague suburb of Nad Lesem with his wife, Helena, and their two children. A child during World War II, Klíma and his family had miraculously survived four years of internment at Theresienstadt, the camp for Czechoslovak Jews that Nazis insisted was only a ghetto with its own government—the only Nazi camp where the Red Cross was permitted to visit; however, inmates there were regularly transported to death camps, and only nine thousand or so survived from an original population of more than seventy-five thousand. Klíma (who "looked like an intellectual Ringo Starr") had been teaching at the University of Michigan during the 1968 invasion, but elected to return to his country, where he refused to recant public speeches and writings in support of the Prague Spring. Now forbidden to publish, he was routinely interrogated and allowed only menial jobs; likewise his wife, a journalist and psychotherapist, was reduced to working as a typist, while their children were not allowed to pursue higher education unless their father conceded that the Soviet intervention had been necessary and also agreed to help the government "normalize" the political situation.

While persona non grata, Klíma had worked as a hospital orderly and

---

* Not an uncommon fate, as Roth liked to point out, since many prominent and/or artistic Czech men traveled without their families. "They were locked out of the country with their girlfriends," said Roth. "It's pure Kundera story: you go to the French Riviera, you're allowed to get out, you're in St.-Tropez . . . you got this fleshy old woman at home, and the Russians come in. You say '*Thank God!* And without even alimony! God bless Brezhnev!'"

street cleaner (fictionalized in his 1986 *Love and Garbage*), and one day
he took Roth around Prague to visit other dissidents working as jani-
tors, delivery boys, or, like Karol Sidon (chief rabbi of the Czech Republic after the Velvet Revolution), as attendants at cigarette kiosks. Thus
Bolotka explains things to Zuckerman in *The Prague Orgy*:

> "The menial work is done by the writers and the teachers and the con-
> struction engineers, and the construction is run by the drunks and the
> crooks. Half a million people have been fired from their jobs. *Every-
> thing* is run by the drunks and the crooks. They get along better with the
> Russians." I imagine Styron washing glasses in a Penn Station barroom,
> Susan Sontag wrapping buns at a Broadway bakery, Gore Vidal bicycling
> salamis to school lunchrooms in Queens—I look at the filthy floor and
> see myself sweeping it.

One night at the Budíns' house, Roth met the novelist and journalist
Ludvík Vaculík, a disheveled fellow with a bushy mustache. A lifelong
reader of Karl May, the great German chronicler of the American West,
Vaculík bet Roth he could name more Indian tribes. "Veequahic?" he
said, examining Roth's list. "Vot is dis Veequahic?" "My high school,"
said Roth, who lost by a score of 45–39, and hence was obliged to send
Vaculík a copy of Josephy's *Indian Heritage of America*. Roth described
Vaculík as a "Czechoslovak Solzhenitsyn": author of the widely translated *The Guinea Pigs*, Vaculík had demanded more liberal reforms in
his "2,000-Word Manifesto," published in June 1968, a crucial factor
in persuading Soviet officialdom that something akin to "counterrev-
olution" was afoot in the midst of the Prague Spring. Stripped of his
rights to travel or publish or receive more than a token of his foreign
royalties, Vaculík defiantly started a samizdat press, Edice Petlice (Pad-
lock Editions), which distributed books in editions of a hundred type-
written copies or so, circulated on a rental basis. When the exasperated
authorities offered to return his passport and give him rail tickets to leave
the country, Vaculík refused. "Why don't *you* leave?" he asked them. "It
amounts to the same thing."

Roth's warmest rapport was with Milan Kundera, who met him and
Sproul for dinner one night; despite the presence of Vera, his wife, Kundera gave Sproul a chipper "pouncing look" that put Roth in mind of "a

cross between a panther and a prizefighter." Still, it was Vera who usually ended up looking "as though we two men together had erotically had our way with her," since it was she who had to translate their long, hectic conversations. Like Roth, Kundera was decidedly not a joiner, and only under the pressure of events had he declared his solidarity with dissidents at the 1967 Writers' Congress, which among other things had led to his expulsion from the party in 1970; previously he'd been expelled (prior to reinstatement in 1956) shortly after the coup of 1948, an episode memorialized in his novel *The Joke*. "I learned the value of humor during the time of Stalinist terror," said Kundera, who thought he could recognize kindred spirits by the way they smiled; in *The Joke*, his hero mocks an overly earnest party member by sending her a postcard reading "Optimism is the opium of the people! A healthy atmosphere stinks of stupidity! Long live Trotsky!" Similarly, in one of his stories from *Laughable Loves*, "Edward and God"—Roth's favorite—the title character's brother is expelled from university for laughing at a fellow student who grieves over Stalin's death. *The Joke* and *Laughable Loves* were naturally popular during the Prague Spring but vanished from bookstores and libraries after the invasion, when Kundera was fired from his teaching post at the Prague Film Institute.

Roth also met Vera Saudková, the daughter of Kafka's youngest and favorite sister, Ottla.* As the niece of Prague's most famous proscribed writer (whose face, after the Velvet Revolution, would appear on cocktail napkins at the Hotel International), Saudková had been fired from her publishing job at Freedom House ("Good?" Roth chuckled) and now received many writers and scholars from the West despite constant harassment by the secret police. Roth, too, was shown her uncle's spindly writing desk and other mementos, and was deeply moved: "I was seeing these things in this place of oppression, and [Kafka was] the great poet of oppression." Remembering that W. H. Auden had married Erika

---

* "Kafka Would Have Savored the Irony of Being a German Treasure" was the headline of a letter Roth wrote to *The New York Times* in 1988, on reading about the sale (for $1.98 million) of Kafka's handwritten manuscript of *The Trial* to a West German book dealer, who'd said, "This is perhaps the most important work in twentieth century German literature, and Germany had to have it." Roth reminded *Times* readers that Kafka's sisters had all been "incinerated" by the Nazis, and that Kafka himself would have shared their fate if he'd lived into the 1940s.

Mann, Thomas's daughter, to help her flee Nazi Germany, Roth offered to marry Saudková, but she declined with a smile—her two sons were in Prague, etc. ("Or else," said Roth, "she was waiting for an offer from John Updike.")

Roth also felt an affinity for the raffish Jiří Mucha, who was curiously allowed to live amid the relative luxury of the former archbishop's palazzo on the Castle Square. In 1951, the Communists had arrested Mucha as an alleged spy and sentenced him to hard labor in the uranium mines; he was released in 1954, and thereafter seemed content to occupy himself with promoting the work of his father, the late art nouveau painter Alphonse Mucha. The regime allowed Jiří to travel to the West every so often and sell his father's art, in return for which they expected a sizable cut of the proceeds and also for Mucha to keep tabs on suspicious Westerners such as Roth. An elegant roué who spoke perfect English, Mucha was nothing if not hospitable. "If there's any place you want to see in Prague," he told Roth, "anyone you want to meet in Prague, anyone you want to fuck in Prague, please let me know and I'll arrange it." Mucha assured Roth that fifteen-year-old girls from all over the country flocked to his palazzo on Saturday nights for his famous parties. Roth never saw these hordes of fifteen-year-olds per se, though certainly the parties were freewheeling affairs; once, as he picked his way upstairs amid the copulating bodies, he was bitten on the ankle.

More than a decade later, in London, Roth would see Mucha for the last time—this at the home of Barry Humphries (Dame Edna) and his wife, Lizzie Spender. If Mucha had read *The Prague Orgy* in the meantime, he gave no sign; rather he suavely remarked that he (in his midseventies then) had a fifteen-year-old girlfriend. When Roth looked unimpressed, Mucha added, "But I've known her since she was twelve."*

■   ■   ■   ■

ROTH HAD BECOME friends with the writer Jerzy Kosinski, who in 1973 was serving his term as president of the PEN American Center. With Henry Carlisle, chairman of PEN's Freedom to Speak Committee, Kosinski suggested a series of eight-page newsletters describing

---

* A line Roth gave to the decadent Roman puppeteer in *Sabbath's Theater*.

conditions in eleven countries where the freedom to write and publish was under attack. The first (and, as it happened, last) of these was about Czechoslovakia, almost every word of which Roth wrote anonymously, so he could continue his trips to Prague without hindrance from the regime.

"Money," Klíma replied, when Roth asked what dissident writers needed most. He gave Roth a list of fourteen people (Roth added Klíma himself to make it fifteen) who were impoverished because of official persecution, and Roth proposed an "Ad Hoc Fund" whereby each dissident was matched with an American counterpart—a novelist with a novelist, a historian with a historian, and so on—who would donate fifty dollars a month to the individual in question. Roth arranged for donations to be channeled through PEN so they were tax-deductible, and enlisted the cooperation of such friends as Arthur Miller (who helped playwright Milan Uhde), Bill Styron (novelist Zdenek Pochop), and various others, including Edward Albee, Saul Bellow, Alison Lurie, Joyce Carol Oates, and Gore Vidal. Some couldn't afford the entire yearly sum of six hundred dollars, so they contributed whatever they could spare—among them, Irving Howe: "By the way," he wrote Roth, "our differences apart, I admire very much and appreciate the fact that you're doing this." This alone, perhaps, was worth Roth's considerable trouble.

The trickiest part was arranging for the distribution of funds, which required a high degree of secrecy lest the Czech government discover the nature of the transaction, in which case the money would be confiscated and the recipients punished. Roth found a dingy Hungarian travel agency in Yorkville that specialized in sending gifts to people behind the Iron Curtain, and spent hours each month filling out paperwork to make it appear that the money—in the form of Tuzex Gift Certificates*—was coming from family members in New York.

After that first year, Kosinski persuaded Roth to turn things over to American PEN, whose liberal-minded executive secretary complained that they were "playing into the hands of the State Department"—in other words, they should be helping writers who were persecuted by *right-*wing totalitarian regimes. In any case the program was allowed to qui-

---

* These could be redeemed at designated Tuzex stores in Czechoslovakia, where one could purchase a wide range of Western goods.

etly die. Roth, disgusted, had nothing more to do with PEN for the next forty years—until 2013, when he received its Literary Service Award for his efforts in behalf of European writers under the Soviet yoke.

■ ■ ■ ■

DURING HIS STOP IN LONDON on the way back from another trip to Prague, in 1974, Roth met an editor at Penguin, Kay Webb, and pitched her an idea for a paperback series of Eastern and Central European fiction, Writers from the Other Europe. As he explained to Webb, such work was being suppressed in the authors' own countries, while the authors themselves were in danger of being imprisoned and even killed; hardly anyone in the West had noticed when Isaac Babel and Osip Mandelstam were murdered, which might have been prevented if their work had received the worldwide attention it deserved—the sort of fame that protected Solzhenitsyn, for instance. Webb referred Roth to her Penguin counterparts in New York, and all agreed that a basic requirement for the series was that a given book be already published in English—this so Roth could read the books himself, and also to spare Penguin the expense of translation. In most cases the original English hardcovers had been more or less ignored, but Roth hoped to remedy the problem by using his influence to promote the books and commission new introductions by first-rate writers such as Joseph Brodsky, Czesław Miłosz, and Updike. The first two books in the series, Vaculík's *The Guinea Pigs* and Kundera's *Laughable Loves*, were ready for publication the following summer, and Roth himself wrote an introduction for Kundera explaining why his stories about "the private world of erotic possibilities" put him at odds with the present regime: "'Socialist realism,' after all, is the approved artistic mode in his country, and as one Prague critic informed me when I asked for a definition, 'socialist realism consists of writing in praise of the government and the party so that even *they* understand it.'" Three more of Kundera's books would appear in the series, until he became something of a household name in the cultured English-speaking world.

Soon Roth decided to include work by dead writers, too, largely due to his discovery of two Poles, Bruno Schulz and Tadeusz Borowski, both virtually unknown in the West. The woman who introduced Roth to their work—and that of several other Polish writers besides—was Joanna Rostropowicz Clark, who'd emigrated from Warsaw in 1971 and married the editor of *The Nation*, Blair Clark, whom Roth knew from Martha's Vineyard. He first met Clark's wife in October 1975, at a dinner party the Clarks gave at their home in Princeton; Roth sat interviewing Clark about her favorite writers, and she urged him to look up a very good 1963 translation of Schulz's *The Street of Crocodiles*.

"What a book," Roth wrote a friend, describing Schulz as "a batty writer on the order of, yes, Kafka, but batty about his Jewish father in his own sinister Polish way."* Indeed, a father appears in most of Schulz's dreamlike fiction—a typical specimen of which, "Sanatorium under the Sign of the Hourglass," Roth would place in the December 14, 1977, issue of *The New Yorker*, prior to its Other Europe appearance in a collection of the same name (Schulz's second book in the series). The year before, Roth had promoted what would become a worldwide Schulz boom ("or boomlet") by interviewing Isaac Bashevis Singer—"the only writer in America other than myself," he said, "who had ever heard of him." The interview appeared in the same issue of the *Times Book Review* (February 13, 1977) as Cynthia Ozick's glowing notice of *The Street of Crocodiles*, an assignment she'd sought at Roth's request. In gratitude he sent her a self-portrait of Schulz that would serve as the frontispiece to her 1987 novel about the writer, *The Messiah of Stockholm*, which she dedicated to Roth.

Another masterpiece that Joanna Clark recommended was *This Way for the Gas, Ladies and Gentlemen*, by Borowski, an Auschwitz survivor who later killed himself at the age of twenty-nine. Along with such writers as Céline, Genet, and Witold Gombrowicz (another Clark find), Borowski inspired Roth to implicate himself in deviant behavior—as the adulterer in *Deception*, for example—by using his own name in his work. The narrator of *This Way for the Gas*, "Borowski," endeavors to explain how he managed to survive the death camps: "Tell, then, how you bought places in the hospital, easy posts, how you shoved the 'Moslems'"—prisoners

---

* Roth was especially struck by the story of Schulz's death. During the Nazi occupation of his native Drohobycz, in 1942, Schulz had been protected by a Gestapo officer named Felix Landau who admired his remarkable paintings; one day, shortly after he'd completed a mural in Landau's home, Schulz was shot dead by another Nazi, Karl Günther, whose own "personal Jew" had been killed by Landau. "He shot my Jew, so I shot his," Günther had allegedly explained, a line Roth appropriated for the death of Siskovsky's father in *The Prague Orgy*.

who lost the will to live—"into the oven, how you bought women, men, what you did in the barracks, unloading the transports, at the gypsy camp . . . write that you, you were the ones who did this. That a portion of the sad fame of Auschwitz belongs to you as well." Borowski's book, hitherto all but forgotten, would sell more than any other title in the series except for Kundera's.

Roth became deeply fond of his mentor in Polish literature, and when Blair Clark left her in the summer of 1978, because of her drinking, Roth invited her to stay with him in Connecticut and get sober. Each day the two would meet for breakfast before Roth went to his studio to work on *The Ghost Writer*; then, before dinner, they each allowed themselves a single glass of vodka from the only bottle of liquor on the premises. One day Clark's will collapsed, and she spent the morning polishing off the half bottle of vodka; when Roth joined her for lunch, Clark swept him up in her arms and gave him a big buss on the cheek. "Joanna," he said, "you're drunk." "Yes," she sighed ("and that was the end of whatever sexual could have happened"). To give her a treat—and perhaps expose her to a cautionary figure—Roth arranged a dinner with the writer Romain Gary and his alcoholic ex-wife, the actress Jean Seberg, who were staying *chez* Styron while their son attended tennis camp in nearby Kent. As a boy in Warsaw, Gary had gone to a progressive school where, as it happened, Clark's own aunts had taught, so the two chattered happily in Polish while Roth watched them in contented silence and Seberg drank. (A year later Seberg killed herself in Paris, and Gary shot himself the year after that.)

"The reason I was drinking," said Clark, "—in [Roth's] Good Jewish Boy opinion—was that I had too little to do." The better to keep such an excellent mind occupied, Roth arranged for her to be accepted into the graduate program at Penn, where she took a course in Latin American literature taught by his friend Carlos Fuentes. One evening, after his classes, Roth took a train to Princeton to have dinner with Clark, who got drunk prior to meeting his train; the last thing she recalled was Roth getting into her car with Fuentes, who'd taken the same train and needed a lift home. "At that moment I go to blackout," Clark remembered (or rather didn't). "The tape stops. I come out, we are already in my house, Philip and I, he is giving me a cup of coffee . . . And he tells me, 'Joanna, this was the most horrific car drive of my entire life!' . . . And

I said, 'Philip, you *saw* that I was drunk. Why didn't you stop me?' . . . And he said, 'Joanna, I didn't want to shame you in front of Carlos.'" A few years later Clark got sober and joined Alcoholics Anonymous, taking Roth along to meetings so he could research aspects of *Sabbath's Theater*.

As for Writers from the Other Europe, it ended in 1989—after fifteen years and seventeen volumes—with the fall of communism in Europe and the Soviet Union. One of Kundera's main English translators, Michael Henry Heim, noted a little wryly that Roth's name on the covers was often bigger than those of the authors themselves: "But maybe that wasn't so bad because people trusted his name, and that would make them trust a name they couldn't pronounce, these foreign names . . . like Kundera and Schulz, Tadeusz Borowski, and Danilo Kis, and so on."

Twenty-Nine

W HEN ROTH HAD FINISHED *THE BREAST* IN THE
spring of 1972, he returned, a little woefully, to his "novel
about trying to write that novel" about Maggie's urine ruse. Later, critics
would point out that *My Life as a Man* was Roth's first notable foray into
metafiction—"fictional writing which self-consciously and systemati-
cally draws attention to its status as an artifact in order to pose questions
about the relationship between fiction and reality," as the critic Patricia
Waugh nicely defined it. Roth himself, however, was apt to shake his
head at what he considered a specious theoretical label: with every novel
he had to grapple with whatever form suited the material, and in this
case he was trying to gain perspective on a grievance that would not
leave him in peace, as a writer or as a man. "What I'd like to do is get
it right, finally, use it up, cause it to disappear as an obsession," Zuckerman tells an "INTERVIEWER" in one of the novel's many ur-versions.
"Get it out of my way, so I can go on." After this transcript concludes,
one comes to a page in the manuscript with a single typed line: "Okay.
Now what?" Roth's ultimate solution was to begin the novel with two
"useful fictions" written by his alter ego, Peter Tarnopol—"Salad Days"
and "Courting Disaster," featuring Tarnopol's alter ego (and presently
Roth's) Nathan Zuckerman—before proceeding to tell the "True Story"
of how his ghastly wife, Maureen, tricked him into marriage, which
indeed sticks closely to the facts of his creator's life.

One of Roth's breakthroughs was a determination to "let the repellent
in"—a phrase that would assume the force of a manifesto over the years.
Portnoy had been a beginning, but Roth always viewed *My Life as a Man*
as the first time he'd written, with little recourse to humor or other evasions, about lurid personal issues no matter how painful or shaming.
With regard to Maggie, in particular, he was determined to dispense

with any trace of romantic mythology. Before, he'd used aspects of her life as a spunky divorcée for the sympathetic Martha Reganhart in *Letting Go*, or, for Lucy in *When She Was Good*, the legend Maggie had told of her origins; but in this final fiction about his bête noire, Roth would present her as "the little criminal that she was."

On the autumn afternoon in 1973 when Roth finished the novel, he took a hot shower and began to sob: "I did it. I did it. I did it"—meaning he'd "turned the shit of that marriage into a book." Against the subsequent tide of public opinion—poor reviews and poor sales both—he would persist in his pride on that point; no less than Updike, after all, had written an early note congratulating him on a "triumph": "I hope you are reposing well in Cornwall,* and have readied your greenhouse for the coming shipment of laurels." On the contrary Roth had already sniffed an ambush, and had hoped to avoid reviews altogether by timing his next trip to Eastern Europe to coincide with publication. In Budapest, however, someone handed him a *Herald Tribune* with Anatole Broyard's *New York Times* review. Roth seemed "to have a bone to pick with women," said Broyard: women *plural*, that is, versus the one woman, Maureen Tarnopol (to whom Broyard referred throughout as Lydia, after the more benign Maureen surrogate in the prefatory fiction "Courting Disaster"). Broyard also used privileged information from his coffee with Roth, four years before, to suggest it was a mistake to congratulate him on "his versatility and continuing growth," since it seemed to Broyard (in part because Roth had told him as much) that the diversity of his work actually constituted "a restless search for some fusion of art and truth that will finally satisfy him." Broyard's implication was that he should go on searching.

Roth's protean nature was underscored by a triptych of portraits on the front page of the Sunday *Times Book Review*: the young, short-haired Roth who'd written the sprightly *Goodbye, Columbus* and the earnest *Letting Go*; the mustachioed zany of the *Portnoy* era; and the clean-shaven latter-day Roth who, according to the reviewer, Morris Dickstein, "has contributed more to the confessional climate" of our culture than even the likes of Lowell and Mailer: "Never in our history have Americans

---

* Cornwall Bridge, that is, the nearest town to Warren with an actual post office, and hence the town to which Roth's mail was addressed.

been so driven to expose themselves; in our recent revaluation of all values, privacy has been one of the big losers." Dickstein seemed about to commend Roth for, at least, his departure from the "lugubrious and realistic" tone of most confessional writing, but no: his "raunchy, delirious" approach was little more than an "unseemly imitation" of Céline and Henry Miller (an imitation Tarnopol explicitly concedes in the novel: "I'll try a character like Henry Miller, or someone out-and-out bilious like Céline for my hero instead of Gustave Flaubert—and won't be such an Olympian writer as it was my ambition to be back in the days when nothing called personal experience stood between me and aesthetic detachment"). Dickstein concluded that "the canker of arrogance and resentment" had blighted Roth's work, and its increasing anguish should not be mistaken for "emotional growth."

Nor, for that matter, was Dickstein buying the alibi Roth "cook[ed] up . . . to account for the perverse, neurotic behavior of this bizarre couple"—namely, his young hero's impulse to be "Serious in the Fifties" (the alternative title of "Courting Disaster"). As Roth wrote in one of his ur-versions, "I married her to be heroic. To be a Man. . . . In politics (for us) it was the Age of Adlai Stevenson, in literature, The Age of Henry James. Moral glamour was the rage." Thus the kind of cultural determinism that Roth is careful to emphasize throughout his novel, not least in the narrator's final line: "This me who is me being me and none other!"

In fact, more benevolent readers also suggested that Roth reconsider how the real-life Maggie had so easily made a patsy of him. A month after her death, Bob Baker had written that Roth shouldn't blame himself too harshly for what was, after all, "a horrid, long-term but transient *accident*," a point that was reiterated six years later by an admiring reader and colleague, Joyce Carol Oates, shortly after she'd interviewed Roth for *The Ontario Review*. He was mistaken, she thought, in thinking that he "or [his] hero" was "working out any particularly necessary 'destiny.'" He'd ended up with Maggie "for all the 'right' reasons, just as many people step into equally hideous situations, meaning to do right. That is why (though don't quote me on this) no one should try to be better than he is: it's hubris, and always brings disaster. You can handle only a certain amount of virtue, as much as your personality can bear, and no more." This would resonate momentously with Roth, who later remarked to Bellow, "I kept being virtuous, and virtuous in ways that were destroying me. And when I let the repellent in, I found that I was alive on my own terms."

That the rain falls on the just and unjust alike would become a crucial theme in Roth's work—that life merely *happens* to people, regardless of their moral character one way or the other. He toyed, for instance, with titling his American Trilogy "Blindsided," given that tragedy befalls his heroes—Swede Levov, Ira Ringold, and Coleman Silk—regardless of their efforts to lead, by their own lights, more or less admirable lives; Roth mocked readers who thought the three were being "punished" for their incidental flaws. "No, a man's character isn't his fate," "Roth" reflects in *Operation Shylock*; "a man's fate is the joke that his life plays on his character." Of course, it was one thing for Roth to dismiss character as a factor in shameful defeats such as his first marriage, another when he considered how he'd managed withal to become one of the greatest writers of his era. "Yes, character is destiny," he synthesized, in one of his final interviews, in 2014, "and yet everything is chance"— character matters, then, when it results in thirty-one published books, but chance is foremost when it comes to personal disaster. Roth's main fictional alter ego, meanwhile, wasn't buying it, at least where Maggie was concerned: "[Maggie] isn't something that merely happened to you," Zuckerman chides Roth at the end of *The Facts*, "she's something *that you made happen*."

Another accident that ensued from *My Life as a Man* was the enduring perception, in certain quarters, that Roth was a misogynist. "There are usually two sorts of women in Roth's heroes' lives," Dickstein wrote, not altogether unjustly: "bitchy, castrating women who attract and destroy them, and doting sexual slaves who eventually bore them." Since Roth claimed to have read only the one review—Broyard's in Budapest—he had to take his friends' words for it that he'd been tagged a "woman-hater" by certain "male critics who would please the feminist-militants," as he wrote Tom Maschler, "(I don't know how else to describe the people I mean)." Of course, there had been rumblings among these so-called militants over aspects of his previous novels, too—Lucy Nelson, the Monkey, Portnoy's mother, Ty Cobb's fondness (both in real life and in *The Great American Novel*) for the term "slits"—which might explain why Roth was so phobic about reading reviews of *My Life as a Man*. That a backlash was afoot among the "militants" was manifest in the information that Oates had noticed a "distinct dis-interest" on the part of "a well-known women's magazine" when she'd offered to write a "generally 'positive'" review of Roth's latest. Oates could grasp, after all, that he was "dealing with a woman who is a criminal" and simply letting the chips fall where they may; besides, would a "male chauvinist pig" (as Roth heard himself described for the first time on an FM radio station in 1972) have created such characters as Brenda Patimkin, Libby Herz, and Martha Reganhart? For that matter, what about the Ann Mudge character in *My Life as a Man*?—"lovely Susan," as Roth would have it, or, per contra, the ultimate embodiment of Dickstein's "doting sexual slaves." "Our knowledge of and opinions about Maggie and Ann and you prevent us from seeing the characters clearly," his friends George and Mary Emma Elliott wrote after reading the novel. "For example, we just plain liked Maggie in Iowa City for all sorts of good reasons which don't get into the novel at all, and we neither one ever liked Ann much, though she seems likable enough in her fictional avatar." Which suggests Roth overdid the repellent in this version of Maggie, and definitely helps to explain why he fell out of touch with the Elliotts after 1974.

There were two types of censure that Roth was unable to forgive or at least forget: a vicious anti-Semitic slur, and any suggestion, however playful, that he didn't like women. By 1970, Bob Brustein was dean of the Yale School of Drama, and Roth's old friend from Iowa, Howard Stein, was associate dean, and both were present at a New Haven dinner party where Norma Brustein—"a woman whose very favorite public performance was in the role of the dizzy dame whose beguiling charm is her reckless and impudent 'candor,'" as Roth wrote of her fictional counterpart, Deborah Schonbrunn, in *The Professor of Desire*—described Roth as a "killer of women." Howard Stein (who owed his present position to Roth's recommendation) relayed the remark to its target, who was naturally furious, all the more given that Ann Mudge had attempted suicide the year before. According to her husband, Norma was unaware of the Mudge episode, and was referring only to Roth's hard feelings over his first marriage, which she found everywhere in his fiction and in his determination never to marry again. When Bob tried to explain as much, Roth was decidedly unappeased, and Norma—who adored Roth—wrote a rather-too-kittenish letter of apology: "I'll loan Danny [her son] to you for a year if you tell me the name of the person" who turned her in, she said, before proceeding to assure him of her undying love, etc.* Roth rejected the apology as unserious, whereupon Bob wrote (as he recalled), "Philip, short of divorcing my wife and putting my children out for adoption, I don't know what's going to satisfy you." An "armed truce" (in Brustein's words) ensued for a couple of years: Roth affected to let bygones be bygones and resumed being friendly, if a bit more distant, until Norma's sudden death in 1979. "She's just a gossip," he observed in 2012. "These gossips, these well-poisoners, these unwell-wishers. Schadenfreude friends."

■ ■ ■ ■

AFTER NEARLY SIX YEARS together, Roth professed to be happy with Barbara Sproul, if disinclined as ever to marry and have children. The closest thing they had to a child was Sproul's fat Siamese, Ying, who played a game with Roth whereby she tried running around him, her baggy nether parts fishtailing this way and that on the polished floor. "Tell 'em about Ying," Roth would say, alluding to the way Sproul sometimes liked to tell cat stories; it was his way of letting her know she'd "crossed the line into deeply boring."

One Monday morning in October 1974, Roth and Sproul were heading back to New York from Connecticut, and Roth mentioned in passing that he was thinking about going to London "for six to eight weeks" in the spring—alone, it was understood, since she had to teach her classes at Hunter (where she was now a religion professor) and he was taking the semester off at Penn. That's fine, said Sproul, but when he returned it would be time for them to get married and have a child. ("I remember [Barbara] saying to me," said Rose Styron, "'If he doesn't marry me by my thirtieth birthday, I'm leaving.'") Roth tried to remonstrate, but Sproul was firm, abruptly ending the conversation in his living room on Eighty-first Street: "This would be a really good time to split up," she announced. "Because I really want kids and you don't, and that's not going to change. So why don't you go to London and I'll stay here and this has been wonderful." And she got up and left.

---

* I've never seen this letter, parts of which Roth disgustedly read aloud to Ross Miller in 2004, during a taped interview, before slapping the letter aside and muttering, "I don't wanna talk about this."

At first Roth was mostly fine: "I'm sad," he wrote a friend, "but I'm not depressed or demoralized." That changed a few days later, when Roth awoke so paralyzed with malaise he had to drag himself out of bed and crawl to the bathroom. What he later described as a nervous breakdown left him so "focusless, fearful, bereft" that he could hardly walk the streets and was frightened by his appearance in the mirror ("Empty eyes, a pale face"). A friend invited him to come along for a weekend visit in Connecticut with Robert Penn Warren and his wife, Eleanor Clark, and Roth jumped at the distraction, especially given the presence of their Yalie daughter, Rosanna. During a walk in the woods with his hosts, however, Roth's legs froze and he had to sit down. Finally, mortified, he was able to hobble back to the house.

Sproul had planted a gorgeous array of flowers along the old stone walls that ran on either side of Roth's studio in Connecticut, and, before moving out that fall, she added tulip bulbs that would bloom in the spring. In April it came to pass, and Roth was so overcome he confided his misery to Francine Gray, of all people, brokenly commending his "lovely and generous" ex-helpmate for the gesture. ("Actually," said Sproul, "that would have been arrogance and pride on my part.") Meanwhile the phlox and foxglove and so forth hadn't bloomed yet, and a "dumb lug" of a gardener routed them as weeds. Roth wept over the loss, as he confessed to a friend, "since it seemed that life, with its heavy-handed irony, was only confirming that so much that Barbara and I had built together was being torn apart limb by limb, root by root, etc. These have been emotional times. It doesn't take much to send me tumbling."

He and Sproul continued to meet for dinner now and then, and in June 1975 he gave her a thirtieth birthday party at Ballato's. Sproul was more than willing to be tender pals, but when Roth tried coaxing her back with promises to "think about" marriage and children, she steadily refused; at least twice they had to use Kleinschmidt as a mediator. Meanwhile she gave herself two years to "fool around"—dating the likes of the activist clergyman William Sloane Coffin and Joseph Brodsky—before marrying the playwright Herb Gardner (*A Thousand Clowns*), with whom she lived happily, with children, until his death in 2003. "Give my regards to the blueberry bushes," she wrote Roth in 2002, "the wild bee balm, the mock orange bush, the Father Hugo rose which should be in bloom off the stone room just about now. . . . They are all a part of my heart as are, most dearly, you."

■ ■ ■ ■

IN 1975, Aaron Asher left Holt to become editor in chief at Farrar, Straus and Giroux, and Roth decided to follow his friend and add his name to that prestigious house's list of great Jewish writers, including Singer and Malamud. Publisher Roger Straus considered the deal a "holding operation": Roth's first book for FSG would be a collection of essays and interviews, *Reading Myself and Others*, and Straus considered it little better than a vanity project, which they were willing to subsidize while looking forward to Roth's next novel.

If anything, the book sold even more poorly than Straus expected, and was ignored by almost every major reviewer except the *Times*, which produced the usual dutiful pans. This time Broyard made explicit reference to his 1970 meeting with Roth, who, he wrote, had been coming from the dentist when the two agreed to sit down for coffee; thus, with this book, Roth was "again coming from the dentist," and wondering if fame was "a diet that rots the teeth." In any case Broyard congratulated Roth—"a talented critic," he allowed—for his courage in leaving himself "wide open" by publishing such a hodgepodge. The kind of haymaker Broyard envisaged was delivered by Roger Sale in the *Book Review*: noting how Roth had suffered, in recent years, because he (Roth) and others had come to consider him "a major talent" instead of "an excellent minor genius" (a nice distinction), Sale reported that the present book "confirms all gloomy suspicions"; its reprinted interviews were "embarrassing in their assurance that anything Roth does is worth his and our closest scrutiny," while the essays were mostly forgettable.

In his everyday life, at least, Roth was strenuously cultivating anonymity. While in New York he often ate dinner at a cheap Hungarian cafeteria in Yorkville, Eva's, where two sisters stood behind a counter serving chicken paprikash and the like. Roth loved the place: "I didn't have to make a reservation; I didn't have to spend a hundred dollars; I didn't have to change my clothes." Best of all, almost nobody knew he was the author of *Portnoy's Complaint*. One of the few exceptions was a twenty-five-year-old paralegal named Nancy, who was dining with a friend when she spotted Roth, alone, at another table. That time she only stopped for a brief chat, but the following week she went back and found him again, and this time they had dinner together.

A fling ensued that was fun while it lasted. Nancy was from "l'école de hard knocks," said Roth, who admired the long, difficult path she took to become a lawyer—that is, she was sponsored by her firm to "read the law" in lieu of attending law school, which she couldn't afford, and eventually passed the bar exam. "Your writing drives me crazy!" she told Roth in the meantime, yanking handfuls of paperbacks from under her bed in a moment of postcoital hilarity. "I'm reading every one of these goddamn books!" She found Roth easy company ("he never really hit a false note"), happy to field questions as to whether this or that scene or detail from a novel was "true." Then one day, amicably enough, he told her it was time for them to part. "I think he just lost interest," said Nancy, who "got that," despite feeling disappointed.

By then he was caught up in a far more complicated affair—"a typhoon"—with a new upstairs neighbor on Eighty-first Street, Janet Fraser, whose husband Nick had taken a job in the city with *Newsweek*. Janet was a twenty-six-year-old writer who'd recently finished her first book, *Everybody Who Was Anybody*, about Gertrude Stein, which she published under her maiden name, Hobhouse. At first Roth thought she was English because of her accent, though in fact she was born in Manhattan to an American mother and English father, attending the Spence School before going abroad to get her bachelor's degree at Oxford. "A selling point for his damn building," said Roth, when she mentioned how the landlord had pointed out his mailbox while showing the Frasers around. The next time Roth contrived to be in the downstairs foyer so he could bump into the tall, stylish young woman, he asked her to have coffee. As Hobhouse remembered in her posthumous roman à clef, *The Furies*,* Roth was "the soul of correctness" but "unnervingly scrutinizing," and she was very conscious of being sixteen years younger while trying wittily to answer questions about her life and plans in New York.

Roth was "lonely as hell" at the time, but wary about getting involved with a married young woman—no matter how fetching and clever—who was "tremendously high-strung" and living in the same building to

---

* Originally conceived as a memoir, until Hobhouse agreed to recast it as fiction, mostly for legal reasons.

boot. They'd been platonically meeting for weeks when her husband left town on a lengthy assignment, at which point Roth became flirtatious in earnest—a phenomenon memorably described in *The Furies*:

> Once Jack [Roth] set out to charm you, there was not much you could do about it. . . . He liked talk to be like Ping-Pong, but he also liked to take the stage himself and perform. He was a brilliant mimic, and he would incorporate into his descriptions of friends, the unknown and the famous, whole chunks of reincarnation, by the subtlest shifts of body position as well as speech. What he noticed about people was unnervingly sharp, merciless, they were as though caught in the beams of a pagan god, for whom acceptance, forgiveness, was soft and unnecessary stuff.

Eventually they slept together, and for many mornings thereafter, once her husband had left for the day, Hobhouse would take the elevator—their "deus ex machina"—down to Roth's apartment and lounge around his living room while he worked. Nick Fraser traveled a lot, and in his absence Roth tended to eat dinner with Hobhouse upstairs; otherwise he'd take her to the drab Hungarian/Czech joints in Yorkville where he felt most at ease because unlikely to be detected. "Where is that boredom I ran from?" he wrote a little plaintively to a friend.

He began to worry about her recklessness. She would arrive barefoot from the elevator, or greet him exuberantly on the street, and meanwhile Roth suspected (correctly) that her husband had more than an inkling of what was going on. "I don't want to be the thing that you do," he told Hobhouse, who was adrift in her work and so even more inclined to invest herself in their affair. One day, however, she put a foot irretrievably wrong, remarking that an overzealous therapist had decided she was manic-depressive and given her lithium. Roth found the diagnosis all too plausible, and wanted to think he was finished forever with unstable romantic partners. "I loved, and in the end even relied on, this old-maidish Prufrockery of his," Hobhouse wrote in *The Furies*. "He withdrew himself from my life as politely and agilely as he knew how (and he had had years of practice at such affable-seeming but rock-hard withdrawal). After a while when I saw him again, he said that he was with someone else, asked about [Nick] and advised us to think about having children before too long."

■ ■ ■ ■

ON APRIL 3, 1975, Roth returned to Prague with Mel Tumin, whom Sproul had recruited as a companion for her ex-boyfriend, a nervous traveler at the best of times. "Everything is the same, except more so," Roth reported to her. "Alas." Klíma took Roth around to visit nine of the fifteen benefactees of his Ad Hoc Fund, which had boosted morale, a little, amid "increasingly cruel and hopeless" conditions. The authorities had conspired to make menial jobs even more obnoxious, for dissidents, by forcing them to work long hours away from home, living in cramped trailers with crude plumbing and kitchen facilities. Seven years of oppression, since the invasion, had begun to have the desired (for the regime) results. At least three eminent Czech writers—Miroslav Holub, Bohumil Hrabal, and Jiří Šotola—had decided to reclaim full citizenship by publicly confessing their "mistakes."

On his return to the States, without naming sources, Roth would give a full account of such "Stalin-era methods" to *The Washington Post* ("Prague Presses Dissidents"). Meanwhile the Czech government had begun to take menacing notice of his fondness for proscribed writers. He and his friends were followed around Prague by the secret police, who sat at adjacent tables in restaurants with their ears cocked ("thereby having learned something, I hope, about contemporary American literature and old Jewish jokes," Roth noted). One day, as he returned from a risibly awful exhibition of Soviet art, two uniformed policemen stopped Roth on the street and demanded his papers (passport, visa, hotel card). After a perfunctory examination they indicated he was to come with them, but Roth refused; when one tried to grab him, he yelled in English and broken French at pedestrians waiting for a trolley: he was an American, Philip Roth, and if the police arrested him they should report it to the American embassy. One of the cops drifted up the street to confer with a plainclothesman, and Roth broke away and jumped onto a passing trolley. Crisscrossing the city for a while, he finally dismounted at a telephone kiosk and called Klíma. "Philip, they were trying to frighten you," he laughed, advising Roth to return to his hotel and "carry on normally." But Roth, quite successfully frightened, decided to cut short his trip (including five days in "muddy Poland") and return to New York immediately.

"[T]he shit hit the fan in Prague just after I left," he wrote a friend in June, "—police raids, seizures of manuscripts, confiscation of works-in-progress and 8 and 9 hour interrogations of the writers I know." A student dissident, Jan Kavan, wrote Roth on the Klímas' behalf, advising him not to return to Prague until further notice, as he might endanger the people he most wanted to help; at any rate Roth's request for a visa was henceforth denied, and he would not return for another fifteen years, after the Velvet Revolution. "What is Roth doing here in Czechoslovakia?" the police demanded of Klíma in the meantime. "Don't you read his books?" Klíma replied. "He is here for the girls."

■ ■ ■ ■

THAT SUMMER Roth asked Joel Conarroe, his Penn colleague, to keep him company in Connecticut, since he was still feeling "harried and sad" nine months after losing Sproul; Conarroe would sleep in the studio (where Roth had recently installed a "new luxury bathroom"), and they would observe "Yaddo rules," i.e., no social commerce until four in the afternoon. They divided cooking chores down the middle. When Conarroe began to produce such exotic dishes as pork chops with chutney ("I could have done without the slice of pineapple on top," said Roth, "but I stuffed myself nonetheless"), Roth raised his game, driving as far as Torrington for premium veal steaks, which he pounded thin and served with a good bottle of wine and flowers on the table. While they sat eating by candlelight, Roth's handyman—a former calvary officer in the Marines—stopped by the Stone Room and pondered the scene: "Which one of you guys wears the skirt?"

Though he certainly didn't wear a skirt, or feel "a scintilla of sexual chemistry" between himself and Roth,* Conarroe was gay but still in the closet at the time. Indeed, his proclivities had never occurred to Roth, who assumed Conarroe was mated with a Bryn Mawr professor named Emily, with whom he tended to appear at parties. "Get yourself a girl, Joel," Herman would admonish him during visits. "They're soft! They're nice!" Finally, during Roth's first year in London two years later, Conar-

---

* On the Kinsey scale of 0 to 6—0 being entirely straight and 6 entirely gay—Conarroe rated Roth as "a zero or a minus. . . . Everybody is a little bit gay maybe," he said, "but not Philip."

roe was staying at Roth's Connecticut home when he began an affair with the composer David Del Tredici. Roth knew the latter from Yaddo, and knew he was gay, so put two and two together when he came home and found a rented piano in his studio.

Also on hand that summer were the sculptor Philip Grausman and his wife, Martha Clarke, a dancer and choreographer, who lived in nearby Washington. Clarke considered Roth the funniest man she'd ever met, remembering his zany rapport with their seven-year-old son, David, whom Roth called Ralph and vice versa. Once, Conarroe was overexplaining a joke to Grausman and Clarke ("talking in gentile," as Roth would have it) when Roth let his face drop into a bowl of pasta and left it there. "It was like having a resident Santa," said Clarke, who shared her friend's antic tendencies and would sometimes compete for laughs. Both gifted impressionists, Clarke would pantomime and Roth provide aural details as they imagined, say, the morning bathroom rituals of their mutual friends. When Clarke toured with her dance company, Pilobolus, Roth made her a tape for the road: a half-hour monologue in which he purported to be a grossly obese Indian man who liked to eat children. Another time Clarke visited Roth's house, alone, knocking a long time on his door; finally, as she began to leave, he sprang out of the bushes and tackled her.

That fall of 1975, Roth took up with a former Penn student named Louise, whom Clarke described as a wholesome, goyish athletic type ("like a lacrosse player"). At loose ends after Penn, Louise had returned to live in her parents' carriage house in the town of Litchfield while waiting tables at the Coach and Seven in nearby New Milford, where Roth and Sproul had eaten dinner that first night they moved to Warren in the spring of 1972. Now, three years later, Louise and Roth met again at a party and "began to have some kind of affair," as he put it. Physically she wasn't his type ("an awful lot of tomboy"), but he enjoyed her Yankee charm and found her company somewhat like having a spunky but dutiful daughter. She, in turn, was deeply smitten by her famous former professor, and nicely attuned to his humor. One day she gave a picnic party attended by Clarke and her Pilobolus troupe, including the young Moses Pendleton. When a praying mantis landed on the table, Roth offered Pendleton a hundred dollars to eat it; he made out a check in that amount and gave it to Louise to hold. "Do I have to eat the mandible?" Pendleton asked. "You have to eat the whole thing," said Roth, "alive." Finally, after further negotiation, Pendleton soberly declined and Roth tore up the check.

Louise's services as a nurse came in handy, as Roth was all but paralyzed that fall with neck and shoulder pain. For years he'd religiously performed morning exercises on a mat, including stretches for back pain that had all but disappeared (for now), and Marine push-ups that involved clapping before landing hard on his palms; after one of these Roth felt a searing pain in his left shoulder, which lingered as a dull, steadily worsening ache over the years, despite periodic cortisone shots and physical therapy, finally spreading to his neck. Roth's condition, blandly diagnosed as "neck-shoulder-arm syndrome," was said to be exacerbated by typing on his stalwart Olivetti, so he switched to an IBM Selectric. By the summer of 1975, however, he had to stop writing altogether and dictate his letters: "I've been through ten doctors, and half a dozen therapies, but all in all I feel as though I've been under the care of Dr. Charles Bovary," he dictated to Julian Mitchell. He'd managed to get through the fall semester at Penn wearing a neck brace, but for the winter break he was directed to lie supine for a full two weeks. "I waited on him hand and foot," said Louise, vividly remembering the tableau in Roth's living room, where he lay on a rented hospital bed, reading with the aid of prism glasses that enabled him to follow the text on his stomach without bending his neck. "I am out of bed," he reported at the end of this ordeal, "a physical wreck, but at least now I know *that* doesn't work."

Louise's main job was driving Roth back and forth to the city. The better to "figure out her life" so she could move out of her parents' backyard, she was seeing a Manhattan therapist every Friday, after which she'd swing uptown to collect Roth and return to Connecticut; on Monday she'd make a special round trip for his sake. He expressed thanks by taking her shopping for clothes, including an expensive pair of knee-high leather boots he bought for her on Madison Avenue ("I won't say it was selfish of him to make me look better in his company," she said, "but I did"). Sometimes, instead of heading directly back to Connecticut, they'd have dinner in the Village with the Schneiders, who were at pains to comfort Roth while he got over his breakup with Sproul. Herman and Louise became enduringly fond of each other; while Roth talked books with Nina, the two would go upstairs and play duets on the mandolin and flute. Roth, prone as ever to sex-talk in Herman's company, gloatingly remarked that he'd taught Louise how to give a proper blow job. "What puzzles me is your need to subjugate women," the older man replied ("the only time I can recall where I in a way reprimanded him," he said).

In fact, there was little or no sex by then: Roth was depressed and in pain, and Louise's hopes for improvement were fruitless. "I didn't feel like a girlfriend anymore," she recalled; "I felt like a maid or caretaker and chauffeur." Like Jenny in *The Anatomy Lesson*, "[s]he devised a chart"—this while he lay in the rented hospital bed for two weeks—"to trace the progress of the treatment on his outlook." Roth's grades were roughly those of his hero: at first he did well enough in Elan, Humor, Sanity, Pissing and Moaning, and Appetite, though his grade for Libido was a pretty steady F.

Little wonder he was sapped. His debilities notwithstanding, Roth was seeing no fewer than three women at the time—Krystyna (a Polish friend of Joanna Clark), Laurie Geisler, and Louise ("the cast I'd remake for *Anatomy Lesson*," he admitted)—and before he cut loose the last of these, he asked her to write down whatever she could remember of their affair; she was obliging as ever, and bemused to see, a few years later, that he'd used almost all of it in his novel. He also wanted to spend that Christmas at her parents' house—another research project, basically, the better to observe how certain echt New England Wasps went about it. "I think everybody felt pretty self-conscious," Louise remembered, noting that Roth brought a whole box of *Reading Myself and Others* to distribute as gifts among her parents and siblings.

That winter she was living alone at Roth's house in Warren, while he spent most of his time in New York. His romantic interest in her, faint at the best of times, had dissipated entirely, whereas she was more desperately in love than ever. "I can be good for Philip," she told Herman Schneider, in tears, "I can be useful." Herman assured her that women were "just grist for a literary mill" to Philip—which he didn't entirely believe, though he worried the lovable young woman "was next door to suicide" and wanted to head her off. (A quarter century later, age ninety-four, Herman was happy to report that Louise had sent him a letter, a few years back, enclosing a snapshot of her six-year-old daughter and a card announcing that she'd been awarded tenure at an Ivy League university.)

The end came abruptly that spring of 1976. One day Roth returned to Connecticut, where Louise was house-sitting for him (as usual), and he mentioned that he'd begun seeing the actress Claire Bloom. Then, casually, as she was walking out to her car, he said "Oh, by the way, can I have my keys back?" Louise—"dumbfounded"—gave them back and drove away: "And that was that."

PART FOUR

ENTERING
A DOLL'S
HOUSE

1975–1995

Philip Roth and Claire Bloom, at home in Connecticut, 1983,
photographed for House and Garden.

(PHOTOGRAPH BY SHEILA METZNER)

Thirty

FROM EARLIEST CHILDHOOD ROTH HAD HAD A SOFT spot for victims of injustice—especially women who'd been victimized by the men in their lives, beginning with their fathers and proceeding among various father surrogates over the years. That was Maggie's story, and it was Claire Bloom's, too, in spades.

"I was born in the North London suburb of Finchley on February 15, 1931," her memoir *Leaving a Doll's House* (1996) begins, "the eldest of two children born to Edward Blume (originally Blumenthal) and his wife, Elizabeth (née Grew)."* This was very similar to the opening line of her first memoir, *Limelight and After* (1982), though it corrected an omission that had been querulously noted by her first cousin Hilda Fell, in a letter to Bloom's publisher: "Her family name is not BLOOM. Our grandfather's name was Chaim BLUMENTHAL later shortened to BLUME; it was her mother who changed it to BLOOM as she thought it sounded less semitic." Thus Bloom was careful to incorporate this information into her second memoir.

Bloom had a harrowing childhood. Removed to America during the first London blitz, she returned a few years later in time for the second; in *Limelight and After* she memorably described the terrifying V-1 flying bombs: "You heard the engine, a very distinctive sound—something like the engaged signal on the telephone—then it cut out, and you counted ten. If you were still alive, it had fallen elsewhere." Nor did Bloom feel the protection of a proper father; hers was "a shadowy and irresolute

---

* Though named Elizabeth, Bloom's mother was always called Alice, from the Yiddish Alische.

figure" whom she "prefer[red]" to call Eddie—versus the more dignified Edward—in both memoirs. After the war Eddie decided to try his luck in South Africa, and thereafter Claire supported her family with acting jobs. "And she did not merely survive that," said Roth, "she gloriously pulled it off, buying her mother a house and putting her brother through school." Indeed, Roth was struck foremost by the young Claire's pluck in the face of hardship, though her daughter, Anna, viewed these early circumstances from a somewhat different angle: "My grandmother," she said, during a 1997 TV appearance with Claire, "who had a bit of a martyr streak in her, never saw any fault of my mother of any kind and I don't think my mother was ever told 'No, you can't.' Partially because she was the financial breadwinner, and you can't say that to the breadwinner."

In hindsight, Claire herself came to admit that her attachment to her mother, and vice versa, "wasn't what we would call normal"; partly she attributed their common alienation to being "Jewish in an Anglo-Saxon country," and also to the general "rootlessness" engendered by the feckless, unreliable Eddie. More and more, growing up, Claire was given to rather hysterical displays of "fearfulness" and "melancholy," as when she began "twisting [her] hair in knots and trying to eat it" when a teacher accused her of stealing a pencil. The errant Eddie would feel the brunt of this tendency when he rashly tried to reinsinuate himself into his now famous daughter's life, bringing his second wife backstage during a 1952 performance of *Romeo and Juliet* at the Old Vic: "He introduced her as my stepmother," Claire remembered in *Limelight and After*, "thus opening the way for me to play my scene. Shying away from the poor woman as though I had seen a basilisk, I said that I had no stepmother—my own mother was still living." A week later Eddie died of a thrombosis at the age of forty-two, and Claire was left to wonder whether her "callous behavior" had hastened his end.

■　■　■　■

ASKED IN 1983 what had saved him from the long siege of pain that had "reduced his life to practically nothing," Roth replied "Claire did." He liked to say he'd fallen in love with her at age nineteen, in 1952, when she'd starred with Chaplin in her first major movie, *Limelight*; fifteen years later she and Roth met in person at the East Hampton home of Roth's friends John and Barbara Jakobson. Bloom was still married to her first husband, Rod Steiger, who'd appeared for a tennis date wearing a black Speedo. *"What're you staring at?"* he barked at Roth, bursting into a room where Roth was using the phone. Roth was with Sproul when he ran into the actress again, in 1973, this time at a dinner party *chez* Epstein; by then she was with her second husband, the Broadway producer Hillard (Hilly) Elkins—a "scary guy" (Sproul) with ruffled cuffs. Sproul was struck by the way Bloom invariably got a little tearful at the end of her stories. "Wasn't she wonderful?" Roth said afterward. "God she *is*," Sproul replied, "and so *sensitive* too." ("You're a fucking killer is what you are," she remembered thinking, "and you've got the henchman [Elkins] to go with.")

In 1974 Roth was alone, and lonely, when Barbara Epstein phoned him in Connecticut to invite him to a Christmas Day party; she'd also invited Bloom, whose marriage to Elkins was nearing the end of a long skid; Epstein thought she and Roth might make a good match. Roth remembered sitting opposite a sofa containing the whole moribund family: Elkins, Bloom, and her fourteen-year-old daughter, Anna Steiger, whom Roth had last seen, fleetingly, as a gloomy seven-year-old. "She obviously despised Hilly Elkins," he remembered, "and was obviously very unhappy." Still, Bloom herself seemed vivacious as ever, and besides, Roth figured, her daughter's unhappiness "had nothing to do with" him.

One day in the fall of 1975, she and Roth bumped into each other on Madison Avenue, where Roth was on his way to see Kleinschmidt. Bloom mentioned she was about to leave for Hawaii to shoot *Islands in the Stream* with George C. Scott, and remarked, "I'm sure he's a monster." "Not all men are monsters," said Roth. "And at that point," she later told an interviewer, "I just fell madly in love with him and his little round professor's glasses." When she returned to New York a few weeks later, she phoned Roth, as promised, and they spent time together before she returned to London. The flirtation had yet to become intimate, and the writer Edna O'Brien recalled that Bloom consulted her as to what tone she should take in her first letter to Roth; O'Brien advised her to be at once "inviting and not too gushing," and this Bloom managed admirably. Roth, in his own first letter, had wondered whether she'd noticed his interest during their previous meetings, and she allowed that, yes, his "dark, piercing eyes" were hard to miss, and now that Elkins was out of the picture she intended to follow her "interests."

"Very careful and correct" she wrote of the flowers and card ("Welcome, Philip") he'd sent to her hotel room when she returned to New York on February 16, 1976, a day after her forty-fifth birthday. The two had dinner together the first three nights of her stay—either at Roth's apartment or the raffish cafeterias of Yorkville—and on the fourth night they slept together for the first time. Soon Roth declared his love for her—but reluctantly, Bloom thought, his voice "suffused with pain"; still, given his love (however painfully expressed), she was startled when she overheard him chatting on the phone with his friend Philip Grausman, the sculptor, about a trip to the Caribbean they planned to take while Bloom was still in New York (albeit a month or more after her arrival, according to Roth's diary). When she inquired, Roth explained that they'd rented a house on St. Martin quite a while ago and, yes, he was sticking to his commitment. In *Doll's House* Bloom complained of her being "treated in a strange and offhand manner" by a person who'd just professed his love for her; despite her misgivings, though, she soon wrote her "very dearest friend" from London that she'd had "a happy, lovely time," and he invited her to Connecticut the following month. Meanwhile he stayed up until 4:00 a.m. watching her play Richard Burton's girlfriend in *The Spy Who Came in from the Cold*, and wrote Dick Stern that he'd found "a great emotional soul-mate."

■ ■ ■ ■

BLOOM'S FIRST VISIT to Connecticut was scheduled to begin May 10 and last three weeks; later it struck her as typical of Roth's "deep ambivalence" toward commitment that he'd specified "very clearly" the finite duration of her visit. For Roth's part it occurred to him, also later, that she hadn't expressed the slightest compunction about leaving her sixteen-year-old daughter for whatever length of time.

Bloom was nervous that she wouldn't seem intellectual enough to Roth, perhaps underestimating the extent of his awe toward the "greatly gifted actress" with whom he'd fallen in love as a teenager: "I thought

I was with a peer and a comrade," he wrote a friend in 2012. "And for the first year I was." As it happened Bloom was remarkably well read, able to recite the intricate plots of almost every major nineteenth-century English novel; also, during that first visit, she introduced Roth to Kierkegaard's *The Crisis and a Crisis in the Life of an Actress*, wherein the philosopher reflects—resonantly for Roth, as one may imagine—on "the petty persecution" of recognition, of the rabble "beating the great drum of triviality."

Oblivious to bicentennial festivities that spring, Roth had finally started a new novel after a long fallow period, and Bloom was forewarned that he'd be working on this ("What else is there to do?") throughout her visit. "I was happy and cheerful in the mornings, until Philip left to go to his studio," she wrote; "then I began to wonder how I was going to get through the day." She tried reading, planning elaborate meals, and so on, but she had no pressing work of her own and mostly she waited for Roth to emerge in the afternoon so they could take a walk together and begin the pleasant ritual of wine and dinner and reading beside the fire. For the most part they had an easy-seeming rapport, though even then Roth's occasionally abrasive shtick was apt to rub the genteel actress the wrong way. "I didn't come here to be insulted," she murmured at one point, and Roth burst out laughing. "But of course you did," he said. "We all did. That's what I want carved on my gravestone. 'Philip Roth. He came here to be insulted.'"

Roth claimed that his stipulation of a three-week visit hadn't been a matter of gun-shy ambivalence—rather he'd assumed that three weeks was the most a working actress (and mother) could spare; as he soon learned, however, Bloom's career had tapered off (à la Kierkegaard's aging actress) until she worked maybe two months out of the year. Because of problematic finances, she'd agreed to write a children's book about her early life as an actress ("Thus avoiding all lovers and husbands," she wrote Roth, "who should have been avoided in the first place"), and Roth encouraged her to occupy herself in Connecticut by expanding this into a full-length memoir. First he fed her questions that she answered on a tape recorder, and then, with Roth's help, adapted into written form. "She was a natural writer with an extensive vocabulary and could compose fluent sentences," he remembered, "but nonetheless the writing was flat and the content skimpy until I prodded her to go back into the material time and again." During those early sessions they would work as much as two or three hours a night—assistance Bloom was happy to acknowledge in later interviews: "He was very hard, and accurate, and devastatingly cruel," she remarked with a smile.

Limelight and After: The Education of an Actress would be finished in 1981; Roth gave it a final polish before handing it over to his friend Aaron Asher, then at Harper & Row, who scheduled its publication to coincide with the author's fifty-first birthday on February 15, 1982. The centerpiece of its promotion in the States was a New York screening of *Limelight*, which was attended by the likes of Lehmann-Haupt and his *Times* colleague Michiko Kakutani, who nonetheless passed on reviewing the book, as did every other major American critic.* Still, Roth was proud of it: "I think it's the most intelligent book about being an actress that's been done," he wrote a friend. Even more gratifying, to Roth, was its total absence of gossip; one was led to believe, for instance, that Bloom's friendship with Richard Burton had entailed nothing more prurient than "read[ing] poetry endlessly to each other in our digs."

■　■　■　■

"ALL IN ALL, our first foray in domesticity was a success," Bloom wrote of her time in the country, remembering how sadly she'd watched the little scroll calendar on Roth's mantel as it ticked off one day after another toward her departure. After her visit Roth also took a "reckless step forward" away from what she'd perceived to be his epistolary reticence—that is to say, his disturbingly noncommittal "Dear Claire" was replaced with "Dearest Love." Indeed, that was the least of it: "I think you are going to have cock enough to last you a lifetime," he wrote her in June; she'd left a dress behind in his closet, and a motif of his letters that summer concerned his tendency to ravish the garment in her absence. Writing from Venice, she less ribaldly mentioned

---

* The U.K. edition was relatively well reviewed and made a few best-seller lists.

how her desire for him had almost made her faint in a gondola on the Grand Canal.

From August 10 to September 2, she hosted Roth at her three-story town house on Fawcett Street, near Chelsea, a few minutes away from Fulham Road. Roth was apt to describe the place as charming. On the first floor were lace-curtained living and dining rooms, both with fireplaces, and a little terrace out back with a plane tree and garden; on the second floor was Bloom's "luxurious, slightly whorish" bedroom, said Roth, who never mentioned the stuffed animals that Barbara Jakobson swore she saw on the bed (Dick Stern's wife, Alane Rollings, recalled that Bloom liked to take these on planes to calm her nerves); and on the third floor was Anna's room and bath, as well as a little guest room where Roth set up his workshop during the weeks of his stay. Bloom was good friends with Gore Vidal and had assured Roth that her daughter was "well trained by Gore" not to be noisy while he was working; Anna, however, was in Switzerland with her former nanny for most of Roth's stay, and seems to have kept mostly to herself during the one or two days they coincided.

Bloom was starting rehearsals for *The Innocents*, an adaptation of James's *The Turn of the Screw*, and Roth was eager to see her at work, especially since the director was Harold Pinter.* Most mornings Roth would walk Bloom to rehearsals at a church not far from her house, and sometimes he'd stay and take notes on her performance ("sometimes brutally critical," Bloom wrote, "always completely accurate")—this in hope of improving what was, he feared, a "terrible (alas)" play. But usually he stayed on the third floor at Fawcett Street, where he worked on a ninety-minute screen adaptation of Chekhov's "The Name-Day Party," since Bloom had complained about a paucity of good television roles. The story, about the grueling hypocrisy of bourgeois life, had a character that Roth considered perfect for Bloom: Olga Mihalovna, who spies her husband flirting with a pretty seventeen-year-old guest at his name-day party; already vexed by the man's boorishness, she passes the day in a

---

* One of the titular innocents in the play—the little girl, Flora—was played by an eleven-year-old Sarah Jessica Parker, later of *Sex and the City* fame.

state of incipient hysteria, until finally she explodes at him in private (a passage Roth heavily underscored in his copy of the text):

> "You may as well know that all this is revolting—revolting—revolting! I've hated you all day . . ."
>   "Olya, I wish you would give me warning when you're out of sorts so I can sleep in my study."

Roth's first attempt (of several) to create a proper vehicle for Bloom's talents "made the rounds" but was never produced.

On September 4, Bloom arrived in New York for out-of-town tryouts; she'd rented an apartment on the East Side, where she planned to stay with Anna and her mother for the duration of the play's Broadway run. Meanwhile, during tryouts in Boston, she was interviewed by a *Globe* reporter who described her as "a frail, white-china faced woman with . . . a manner as tremulous as a butterfly": "'We're friends . . . have been . . . long time,'" she "murmur[ed], almost inaudibly," when asked about her appearance on Newbury Street with Roth. When *The Innocents* premiered in New York on October 21, Roth brought his "thrilled" parents, and all agreed Bloom was wonderful as the governess; the play, however, closed after only twelve performances. In *Doll's House,* Bloom pondered her decision to remain in New York, with Roth, while she sent her mother and daughter back to England in early December; the "furious" Anna had pointed out that she'd "once again chosen a man over her," and Bloom worried the girl might be right: "perhaps I was unconsciously sacrificing her in favor of Philip." To Roth, at the time, it seemed a wholly conscious sacrifice.

One afternoon the couple returned to Roth's apartment, where Bloom discovered a note on the dining room table. "I went into the kitchen and didn't see it," Roth remembered, "but suddenly Bloom was wailing and screeching and wildly running about the apartment. She was holding in her hand a two-word note from the cleaning woman. It read, 'Christa called.' She began screaming about Christa. Who is Christa? You're having an affair with Christa! How dare you invite me to America under false pretenses! How dare you make me abandon my child to come to America while you were carrying on with this Christa!" This went on for about an hour, according to Roth. Christa was a German journalist living in Berlin who'd interviewed him a couple of years back for her newspaper; they'd hit it off and become friends.* Evidently she was in New York and wanted to get together. Some twenty years later, after Roth and Bloom had divorced, Christa remarked that she'd occasionally tried to phone him in London, but whenever she gave her name Bloom hung up on her.

Bloom, it must be said, was no stranger to furtive liaisons, and in her second memoir, at least, she was refreshingly candid on that point. Richard Burton was married to another woman during his "precious and deeply spiritual" affair with Bloom, ditto Laurence Olivier and Yul Brynner, and Bloom herself was still married to Rod Steiger when she dallied with Hilly Elkins (prior to his becoming her second husband). As for Roth, he was rarely less than forthcoming (except with whoever happened to be his main female companion at the time) on the subject of straying: "God, I'm fond of adultery," he and Mickey Sabbath liked to say. "Aren't you?" Even with so staid a fellow as Malamud, Roth couldn't resist alluding to his extracurricular love life: "Claire is off in London doing *Brideshead Revisited*," he wrote his colleague from Connecticut in 1979. "It's not easy being Stage Door Johnny. But it has its compensations."

Roth's foremost compensation in Warren—during the entirety of his time with Bloom, and then some—was a Norwegian named Inga Larsen,† a physical therapist who lived a mile down the road with her husband, a contractor, and four children. Conarroe remembered her as the sort of woman who gave off "vibrations" ("even to me") the moment she entered a room, and little wonder she served as model for the insatiable Drenka in *Sabbath's Theater*, and also—"falsified beyond recognition"

---

* In 2011, Roth emphasized that Christa was only a friend ("we never slept together"), and while he made the same point during a 2005 interview with Ross Miller—"we were friends, not lovers"—he also admitted they'd gone to bed "once, maybe twice, it wasn't for me . . ."

† A pseudonym. The real-life Inga could hardly have been more candid about things, though she asked not to be named for her family's sake. My account of her affair with Roth is as accurate as I could make it, though certain details about Inga's background have been altered.

(Roth)—for the doting, submissive "Erda" in *Leaving a Doll's House.* Inga had known Roth casually since his move to Warren in 1972, but nothing carnal happened until the fall of 1976, when he summoned Inga for her professional services. As she recalled, Roth sat in the kitchen, depressed, while she worked on his neck, and after she packed up and was ready to go, he put a hand on her breast; the following spring they picked up where they'd left off, and so began an eighteen-year affair that, said Roth, "became an adjunct to my domestic life, without which I couldn't have continued my domestic life."

Inga's own domestic life was far from ideal. After work she would come home, make dinner, and put her children to bed, whereupon her husband would fall asleep and she would tipple chardonnay, though Roth was mostly unaware of her drinking until she entered rehab many years later. At the height of their affair, she and Roth would meet as often as possible at their favorite trysting spots: behind a cluster of boulders near the Housatonic—a place vividly evoked in *Sabbath's Theater* (like Sabbath and Drenka, they were almost spotted in flagrante by a helicopter scouring the area for marijuana farms)—and, in a pinch, a spot in the woods midway between their houses. Such outdoor emergencies were relatively rare, though, since Bloom was less and less in Connecticut; Roth estimated he and Inga met at his house or studio, all told, "over a thousand times." They also liked to meet socially: Roth was fond of Inga's husband—the man designed the remodeling of Roth's studio in the late seventies—and the two couples often entertained each other. During the decade that Roth lived half of each year in London, Inga would visit him and Claire for a few days en route to seeing relatives in Oslo (she so admired the decor of Bloom's guest bedroom that, on her return to the States, she went straight to the Laura Ashley store in Westport).

Inga was as much a kind of co-conspirator as she was a lover to Roth, who urged her not to skimp on details when telling him about her other affairs with, say, the wealthy alcoholic businessman whom she blew in his limousine. Often she'd marvel aloud at the disparity between her private shenanigans and public image as a supercompetent professional and homemaker—a duality, or multiplicity, Roth relished in both their lives: "the kick of having a multiple self who behaves various ways in numerous lives and of possessing an impressively lavish endowment of self-abandonment." Later Inga would refer to her and Roth's "mutual addiction to sex," an idea Roth would have rejected as psychobabble, though other perceptive friends were apt to describe their affinity in precisely that way. "They were both secret junkies," said one. "Philip's a secret junkie. . . . Because the nature of eroticism is a share under the table; it's not visible to others. And that's very important to him." Another friend—who used to attend AA meetings with Inga—said that Roth, though hardly an alcoholic, consummately behaved like an addict in the way he compartmentalized everyday life, the better to get away with transgressive behavior. More and more, however, in his life and certainly his work, he became almost disarmingly candid about things. He hooted at Bloom's coy reference to "the dark part of [her] sexual nature" that she'd discovered vis-à-vis Hilly Elkins: "I enjoyed, through my long, adulterous liaison with [Inga], the *bright* side of a stupendous sexual nature."

Roth's own endowment of self-abandonment arguably exceeded even Inga's, though she took pains to seem a worthy peer in that respect. She pretended to be pleased when he'd press on her a semen-encrusted napkin or some such fetish, and she became more and more adept at looking entranced whenever he'd suddenly, apropos de rien, begin masturbating in front of her. "This is a man led by the penis," her therapist observed when she mentioned this compulsion of his. Roth later pointed out that Inga had often assured him that she loved to watch men masturbate, the way they gradually lost control before coming; indeed her remarks on the subject were given almost verbatim to Drenka.

During his London years, Roth would call Inga long-distance and expect her to listen while he masturbated. Such calls were inconvenient, given the time difference. "Here I am," Inga remembered, "and here's this guy on the line there and I have patients and the doctors around and he wants me to listen. And then as soon as he has come, ejaculated, he bangs the receiver and that's it." She paused. "And then sometimes he calls back and there's a conversation: 'How are you?' . . ."

■   ■   ■   ■

IT WAS ROTH WHO suggested to Bloom that they live together in London for six months out of each year, beginning in September 1977, when she was returning to start rehearsals for Ibsen's *Rosmersholm* at the Haymarket. Roth would follow a couple of weeks later, once he'd gotten maximum seasonal use out of the recently completed, 18-by-55-foot Franklin Library Memorial Pool—so named because it was paid for with proceeds from Roth's signing six thousand books, at two bucks a copy, for the Franklin Library First Editions Book Club. Roth had phoned Updike to inquire whether the feat was really possible: "Just," Updike replied.

According to Bloom's memoir, Roth was willing to live with her in London on the condition that her daughter live elsewhere, until Bloom frantically persuaded him to give "some form of family life" a try—marveling the while at what would prove an all-too-characteristic "mixture of kindness and cruelty" on his part. Roth later insisted, however, that the subject of Anna's cohabitation "had never arisen" up to then, and as for his alleged "cruelty": "If there was any cruelty directed toward Anna, it was Bloom's, as Anna well understood and as the disastrous consequences I saw played out between mother and daughter in London confirmed. It will not do to shift the 'cruelty' onto me, who at this time barely knew Bloom's adolescent daughter and had no particular interest in her one way or another." Bloom's willingness to sacrifice her daughter (consciously or unconsciously) in favor of her own interests had hardly begun with Roth, who pointed out that the girl was all of nine when Bloom left her father for one of his closest friends. Hilly Elkins is perhaps best remembered as the producer of the risqué 1969 revue *Oh! Calcutta!*—the same year he began his liaison with Bloom. "Strangely, Hilly had some of the same features as [my father] Eddie—certainly the same weak mouth. Still more bizarre, they even shared the same birthday." Be that as it may, the main point of Elkins appeared to be his show-business pull, which helped his wife's career even as he stole, by Roth's account, "tens of thousands of her dollars, if not more, while she looked on and let him do it." Naturally Anna Steiger despised Elkins, and Bloom admitted she and the girl had seen little of each other during this turbulent but productive era: "Those years did a lot of damage to us as mother and daughter, and yet they were the years when I played the roles I so wanted." Bloom also pointed out, not unreasonably, that a child tends to resent the mother far more than the father for "going off like that." In the event, once she got rid of Elkins, he became "the unmentionable" to mother and daughter alike.

In later years Bloom would often concede that Roth "had tried at first to be kind and understanding of [her] daughter," as she told Charlie Rose in 1996; but the situation was fraught, to put it mildly, given the damage inflicted by her "brief and ridiculous" marriage to Elkins. In 1977 Anna was a seventeen-year-old singing student at the Guildhall School, and Roth's vague impression at the time was that she mostly lived with her grandmother while Claire "came and went as an actress." He had every reason to imagine that relations between mother and daughter were "loving and cordial," he said, though in fact certain passages in Bloom's letters might have given him pause. On Anna's sixteenth birthday, so Claire had written him, the mother was forced to "cower" in her room rather than mingle with the girl's guests, and a few months later she described "a dreadful scene" involving "AWFUL" insults because Anna had wanted to stay in London, alone, while Claire departed yet again for New York.

"We moved to London and at first it was all peaceful," she wrote in *Doll's House*, a state of affairs that Roth emended as "family hell." For three days after his arrival, so he recalled, Anna was missing; that first day he was entertaining the playwright Tom Stoppard (an Anglo Czech who was also interested in the plight of dissidents), when Bloom's sister-in-law phoned to say they couldn't locate Anna anywhere and were notifying the police. Then, on the third day, Anna appeared and casually announced she'd been staying with a friend. That evening the three sat down for their first family meal. The mood, as Roth later noted, was "tense":

> Anna sat stewing at her place. Eating mechanically without looking up, while Bloom, trying far too hard, as she would continue doing incessantly from the day I arrived to the day I left, asked the girl sweet, motherly questions of no consequence that remained unanswered and appeared only to feed Anna's scorn. And then the fight broke out. I couldn't say now over exactly what, but mother and daughter were up from the table

and into the living room, where, first, they were merely screaming at each other, then punches were being thrown and blows being struck—and then Anna screamed at her mother, "Kike bitch!"

I rushed into the living room and separated the two of them. "You can't use that language around here, ever," I told Anna, "and you cannot strike your mother. Both are forbidden." I'm tempted to say that from this moment forward Anna never gave up on the idea of me as the enemy, if it hadn't been that I was the enemy even before I arrived.

Though reticent about her other differences with Roth—content, that is, to stand by the accounts given in her book—Bloom was roused to dismiss the above scene as categorically false. "The idea that Anna 'punched' me, her mother, or threatened me in any way whatsoever, or used anti semitic slurs is pure and utter nonsense," she wrote in a 2013 email. Anna Steiger was even more strident in her denial. Roth, she wrote, "NEVER, EVER physically restrained me as in any case I am not physical when angry and more to the point, he is an immense physical coward. . . . As for the anti-semitic slurs that's most strange for him to invent. However, it is an invention." Roth was unsurprised by their denials ("It's too shaming to acknowledge") and stony in his insistence that the scene transpired precisely as he described it for his biographer, and barely fictionalized it in *I Married a Communist*: "The 'kike' part was indelible because it was partially for my benefit and aimed at me," he explained in 2015. "As for the 'bitch' part, that was a part of her repertoire."

The next day, his fourth in London, Roth went looking for a flat of his own in the same neighborhood. He declined simply to return to the States—because his homes in New York and Connecticut were already occupied, and because he was still devoted to Bloom and determined to make things work. He visited an American lawyer, Bob Gurland, who advised him that taking an apartment in London would have "disastrous" tax consequences. Also, when he mentioned his plan to Bloom, she "dropped to her knees," he said, and begged him to stay. So he stayed. "I'm not going to be defeated by this kid," he remembered thinking.

They hired a carpenter who converted the entire third floor into a separate apartment for Anna: a kitchenette was added, and the little spare room Roth had used as a study became a dining/sitting room. Meanwhile the girl's presence on Fawcett Street was relatively scarce—she was at school all day and tended to spend weekends visiting friends and attending concerts—and, after that one rebuke their first night together, Roth was careful not to argue with her. "She is turning out to be rather cooperative, and even some fun, now that the initial period of adjustment seems to have ended," he wrote hopefully to Conarroe.

"Anna is nuts," he wrote Riki Wagman. "A great pain in the ass who has spent the last two weeks trying to sabotage Claire's opening. . . . I just take off for my study (studio that is) in the morning and at home don't have much to do with her other than to ask her to turn down the punk rock on the record player every night. There will be problems there, and I feel sorry for the girl. She is fatter than ever and so confused and self-defeating. . . . But for the last month I've just tried to keep Claire and her apart." The three of them still had dinner together from time to time, and their "obsessive discussions" (as Bloom herself described them) were entirely focused on Anna's life and interests as a Guildhall student. Roth was appalled by the "abject woman" Bloom became in her daughter's presence—so unlike the witty, intelligent, self-possessed celebrity he'd come to know during the first year of their affair.

One morning in March—what would generally be described as the "most shocking part" of *Doll's House*—a grim-faced Roth "thrust a letter" into Bloom's hand. By then he'd learned that if he wanted to impart his thoughts on any remotely controversial matter, it was best to commit them to paper, since conversation was hampered by Bloom's tendency to scream and run away, sobbing, or assume a kind of wary crouch and cry, "Don't go for me," which Roth took to mean she feared some form of bodily harm. The letter, dated March 14, 1978, was only summarized very briefly in *Doll's House*; its main contents are given here:

> Though of course I am prepared to live with you and Anna until June 1st, when we leave for Conn., I think it would be a mistake to try to repeat this living arrangement again next year. The dynamics of your relationship with Anna make me tremendously uncomfortable, in large part because I know how very uncomfortable they make you. As the saying goes, you are either at each other's throats or at each other's feet, and it is emotionally exhausting for the both of you. . . . I think it is very clear to you that when we live alone—either in the country, or when Anna has

been away on a trip—there is a richness to our lives that simply withers away when we have to deal with the daily problems that are a consequence of the impasse which you and Anna have reached.

Roth proposed two alternatives: either Bloom would come live with him year-round in the States, in which case he'd gladly pay her way to visit Anna and her mother every month, or else Anna would go live in the Guildhall music hostel, Henry Wood House:

> I have telephoned them to inquire about living arrangements (not for Anna, of course, but only generally, as an interested parent). There are single rooms for £18 a week; the rate may go up some next year in Sept. . . . She would be near the school, she would never have to worry for companionship—and she will actually discover (I will bet you a hundred pounds tonight on this) that she likes it better herself. You will stop being the central problem in her life; we will stop being people who exclude her, and become people she can rely upon to help her as she moves on in school and towards her career—in brief, the whole childish side of her life will begin to dissolve. As it simply will not, so long as she is at home with her mother and a man who is not her father, but is really willing to be a friend. Of course she is going to resist this and be angry immediately at the idea. But so too does she reject the idea of a diet. . . .
>
> Lastly. The sooner the better. It is not after all hell one is consigning Anna to. I am only suggesting that she live like eighty per cent of the university and college students in the world. There are reasons for dormitories and university residence halls, and you know every last one of them. Children are too old to live at home but not old enough to rent houses or flats of their own or parents don't have money to pay for houses or flats.

Bloom would impute sinister motives to Roth's epistolary gambit—without, again, bothering to spell out the details, or else baldly misrepresenting them ("No explanation," she told Charlie Rose of the letter; "he just said he can't go on living like that"). It was not so much about "hatred," she wrote in her memoir, as "control. . . . Philip made character assessments the way surgeons make incisions. . . . If I was willing to jettison my own daughter in this manner, what could I ever deny him?" Nevertheless she came to the "shameful" decision that would invariably cause her, later, to choke up during media interviews: "Anna was asked to move out," she concluded the episode in *Doll's House*. "She was eighteen."

"So somber, so tragic, so tellingly concise," Roth observed, "as if she were writing, 'Anna was asked to move out. She was two.'" He then directed the reader to proceed seven paragraphs further in *Doll's House* to "the anticlimax of anticlimaxes": "Anna moved back home"—as she did, he claimed, within five months of moving to Henry Wood House, where in any case she'd spent only a few days per week before returning to Fawcett Street more or less permanently for many years. ("It wasn't that I sacrificed my daughter," Bloom rallies a little to her own defense while chatting with Charlie Rose. "Frankly my daughter in a year [sic] came back to the house.")* As Roth would tell friends during the difficult times ahead, "Maggie sent Anna to me."

---

* Not only was Anna Steiger enduringly furious about her hostel digs in the "insalubrious" neighborhood of Peckham, but she moreover indignantly denied that she moved back to Fawcett Street except for a few brief years and incidental visits: "I moved from [Henry Wood House] and into an apartment which I rented with another friend for a couple of years," she wrote on November 5, 2015. "I must have been about 21/22 when I moved back home"; she noted, however, that her career soon got under way and she was often touring, and she also claimed to have moved into her own apartment at age twenty-five, never again living full-time on Fawcett Street.

I shared this email with Roth, who replied the same day: "I repeat: from 1976[77], when I moved to London, until Anna did indeed . . . buy an apartment several blocks away from Fawcett St in the late 80s, the bulk of Anna's living and sleeping took place on the third floor of Fawcett St. As Claire makes very clear in her book, she, Claire, could not bear life any other way."

Thirty-One

I N 1974, ROTH SAID THAT HIS NOVELS TENDED TO BE "spawned by the interplay between my previous fiction, recent undigested personal history, the circumstances of my immediate, everyday life, and the books I've been reading and teaching." *The Professor of Desire*, composed in desperation after almost three years of foundering, was the quintessence of such a patchwork. His second Kepesh novel absorbed all his latest preoccupations about teaching, Kafka, Czechoslovakia, sexual libertinism, and so on, though it began as a vague notion to write some kind of sequel to *The Breast* about what becomes of Kepesh after he leaves the hospital and appears on the Johnny Carson show, say, or donates his "transformed carcass" to science. In the end it was more conducive to the use of Roth's real-life materials to write a prequel—who was David Kepesh *before* he became a breast?—and indeed he considered *The Life I Formerly Led* as a title. Roth's main preoccupation, and hence that of the book, was the failure of his love affair with Barbara Sproul, and on completion he admitted that the Kepesh of *Professor* bore little more than nominal resemblance to the hero of *The Breast*.

His new publisher, Roger Straus, read the manuscript over Easter weekend 1977 at his home in Purchase, New York, and commended the author for successfully weaving his "philosophical concepts" into the everyday life of his protagonist; what Straus arguably liked best about the book, however, was that it constituted a "highly salable" return to form for an author whose bawdy humor, in the context of a realistic story, was most likely to bring home the bacon. Meanwhile the prestige of Farrar, Straus and Giroux was made known to Roth via the modesty of his advance—$25,000 for *world* (versus North American only) rights—though Straus planned to "publish it very aggressively" and fix various problems Roth had been having with foreign publishers: "And we did a hell of a job for him I might add," Straus claimed the following year. "I switched his publishing house in Germany, I cleaned up his affairs in Italy, etc. etc." As for their personal rapport, Roth liked kibitzing for an hour or so with the flamboyant Straus over their annual lunch, which usually coincided with the completion of Roth's latest book. Also he was more amused than repelled by the great publishing house's squalid headquarters—the broken chairs, cracked linoleum floors, lightbulbs with strings attached—a chaotic jumble of cubicles crammed into almost every square inch of the fourth floor at 19 Union Square West.

What the Kepesh novels have most in common is, as Roth put it, "the great and maddening" subject of desire—a quandary embodied in *Professor* by the two Swedish girls Kepesh cavorts with while traveling around Europe: the shameless adventurer Birgitta and the tenderly submissive Elisabeth, who together requite the hero's almost every erotic and domestic need. "Either the furnace or the hearth!" he exults. "Ah, this must be what is meant by the possibilities of youth." Roth's detractors were apt to point out that such a dichotomy amounted to the same old stereotypes that dominate his other female casts, though in this case he also proposes a synthesis in the Sproul character, Claire Ovington: "As physically alluring to me as Helen"—Kepesh's disastrous first wife (one of the "bitchy, castrating women who attract and destroy" Roth's men, as Dickstein would have it)—"but there the resemblance ends. Poise and confidence and determination, but, in Claire, all of it marshaled in behalf of something more than high sybaritic adventure." The main rub for Kepesh, with his Swedish pair, was that Elisabeth couldn't bear sharing his love with the more exciting Birgitta; for a while, though, he has the best of both in Claire—only to learn, alas, that the furnace reduces love to ashes in any case, and one is inevitably left with the boredom of the hearth.

Roth was determined to work Czechoslovakia into the novel—though he worried about "faking it"—and found a rather blunt wedge in "Kafka's own erotic blockage" as portrayed metaphorically, Kepesh thinks, in *The Castle* ("a book engaged at every level with not reaching a climax"); also he likens his own loss of libido, his body's "cold indifference" to the "well-being of the spirit," to the repressive workings of the Czech regime. Perhaps the best feature of such thematic window dressing is a dream sequence in which Kepesh meets Kafka's whore: "Was he regularly able to have an erection?" he asks her. "Could he usually reach orgasm? I find the diaries inconclusive." (Roth's real-life inquiries on that point appear to have been just as earnest. "Roth surprised me by asking if I thought Kafka had been impotent," Klíma records in his memoir.) The ancient whore "gravely" assures Kepesh that, yes, "[s]he blew him."

Elsewhere, too, the novel is redeemed by the piquancy of its set pieces, whether or not they relate to a coherent whole. It's unclear why Roth opens with a long digression about Herbie Bratasky—social director of the Catskills resort owned by Kepesh's parents during his childhood—except to hook the reader with some easy laughs over Herbie's singular brand of virtuosity: "It turns out that not only can he simulate the panoply of sounds—ranging from the faintest springtime sough to the twenty-one-gun salute—with which mankind emits its gases, but he can also 'do diarrhea.'" And then there's the philandering Baumgarten, who tells an anecdote about tying up a girl, at her urging, with dental floss. Once she's securely bound, he races back to his apartment to fetch cocaine, only to find on his return that he can't remember which building is hers amid the Stuy Town–like complex where she lives; in the weeks following, he anxiously scans the tabloids for news of a floss-trussed skeleton, but then bumps into her outside a movie theater. "Far out!" she greets him. ("I'm glad you liked the dental floss," Roth wrote Updike. "It came to me while the dental assistant was pressing her breasts into my upper arm and cleaning the debris from between my teeth.") Such a miscellany of high- and lowbrow humor enabled Roth to place excerpts in periodicals as diverse as *American Poetry Review* and *Penthouse*.

The New York Times Book Review also ran a prepublication excerpt on its front page, followed a few weeks later by a laudatory notice, also on the cover, by Roth's old Iowa colleague Vance Bourjaily ("a thoughtful, even gentle, stylistically elegant novel about the paradox of male desire")—all of which would prove a false augury for the book's larger reception, at least in Manhattan. Once again, the main issue was Roth's apparent inability, as Robert Towers wrote in *The New York Review of Books*, "to create young women (as opposed to Jewish mothers) who convey the sense of an existence independent of the protagonist's need for sex or suffering or both." The same point was made more assertively by John Leonard, who implied in the daily *Times* that it was a moral as well as aesthetic failing on Roth's part that his women tended to be "cannibals and sponges and rocking chairs. . . . It is as if Thomas Mann had made a career of rewriting *Death in Venice*," Leonard concluded. "Being a grown-up, Mann, like Chekhov, did more." A warm friendship would not ensue between Roth and the critic.

"Your out-of-town reviews are about 3–1 favorable (lots of boring stuff about your 'comeback')," Aaron Asher consoled his friend, and in fact the book would prove one of Roth's most commercially successful: FSG sold about fifty thousand in hardback, and Bantam bought the paperback rights for $600,000 ("HIS BEST AND MOST EROTIC NOVEL SINCE **PORTNOY'S COMPLAINT**" the cover blurb promised).

■ ■ ■ ■

IN ADVANCE OF his arrival in London in the fall of 1977, Roth had inquired among friends for leads on a serviceable studio ("One big quiet room with a bowl for me to piss in would do fine"); as luck would have it, Alison Lurie had just moved out of an ideal ten-by-fifteen room on the second floor of a house at 5 Stanley Gardens in Notting Hill. There was a kitchenette with a mini-fridge and stove, french doors overlooking a neat little garden, and soon Roth installed the usual configuration of desk, typing table (with black IBM Selectric), and Eames chair to replicate his studios in New York and Connecticut.

Except for occasional domestic travail, Roth's days fell into a pleasant routine. After breakfast on Fawcett Street, he'd hail a cab to the Royal Automobile Club on Pall Mall (Bloom's uncle had put him up for membership), where he'd take a swim and sometimes get a massage from a courteous fellow named Frank, who'd escort him to the showers afterward, wait outside with warm towels, then put him to bed in his own little cubbyhole in a dark paneled room. (The RAC was also useful as an address for furtive personal mail.) In fine weather Roth would walk three miles through Hyde Park to his studio, work until one thirty or so, then adjourn to a little French restaurant, Monsieur Thompson's, where he'd usually have a salad and a slice of pâté. Around six or seven he'd leave off work and walk two or three miles home again ("I was fit as a fucking fiddle"), where his "difficulties would begin."

His work, at least, was going better than ever. That summer Mark Shechner, for Asher's benefit, had presciently aired his thoughts on *The Professor of Desire*: "Not least of the problems with it is that Phil gives these guys his sexual drives and conflicts but none of his talent or cre-ative accomplishment, as though he is only interested in his conflicts but not in those qualities that make him interesting to us: his imaginative resourcefulness." Evidently Roth had gotten the message. "Let 'em know what I know," he wrote Nina Schneider two months later, as he began work on what would become the first volume of his Zuckerman Trilogy. "Well, okay, if that's what the suckers want." Of course he'd previously conceived a writerly alter ego in *My Life as a Man*—though the hero's everyday, nonvocational conflicts were foremost—one of the many abor-tive drafts of which had featured an obsessively diligent, Malamud-like writer named S. P. Harshbarger, a slightly more irascible (versus austerely ironical) version of E. I. Lonoff. In this early draft, however, titled *Shop Talk*, Harshbarger serves mostly as a sounding board for a long, tire-some rant from his would-be protégé, Abner Abravanel, about (yes) the latter's ex-wife who tricked him into marriage with phony urine. "Why don't you write all this down?" Harshbarger suggests at last, a little wea-rily, whereupon Abravanel restates an old dilemma: "Who wants to read about another man being victimized by another woman? I mean the lit-erature on the subject is threatening to swamp us." "What subject?" says Hope Harshbarger, the great man's deceptively meek wife. "Misogyny?" Returning to Harshbarger/Lonoff seven years later, in 1977, Roth saw the possibility of an antithesis to the hedonistic, noncreative Kepesh: "Indeed," he wrote Miss Martin, "my subject is a man who can only write, do nothing more, is *without* desire for anything else. New subject."

In *Shop Talk* as well as *The Ghost Writer*, another important subject was suggested by Roth's memory of the fetching young woman he'd spotted on the floor of Malamud's study, in 1969, sorting manuscripts; such a figure is named Amy in both fictions, but in the latter case Zuckerman imagines the girl to be a fraught historical personage—Anne Frank. For over a decade Roth had been trying to find the right narrative context for this "Jewish saint." He'd read her diary many times, and made a spe-cial trip to Amsterdam to tour the Anne Frank House and walk around Frank's old school and the park where she'd played as a child. (He told David Plante that he'd "excused himself politely" from his first tour of the Achterhuis, then gone back to his hotel and thrown up.) When he returned to work on *My Life as a Man*, in 1972, he tried to incorporate a section from an earlier draft titled "The Continual Hazard of My Life or

My Love Affair with Ann [sic] Frank," in which Zuckerman/Tarnopol goes from Israel to London, where he meets a woman who (like Roth's old Chicago girlfriend Pat McEnerney) cannot be penetrated because of vaginismus; after a long night's ordeal, she confesses to him that she's Anne Frank, and the hero—skittishly on the lam from a Maggie-like wife—assumes she's crazy and leaves her. The episode was included in a late draft read by Dick Stern, who told Roth on the steps of the Metropolitan Museum "that having your hero come to Europe and fall in love with Anne Frank would be like finding a real, bloody leg in a frame in a new painting exhibition."

Stern was among the most enduring and perceptive ("always right") in a rotating group of friends whom Roth trusted to critique his work over the years. Roth was a fanatic reviser who typically went through four or five drafts of a given novel ("first drafts are terrible"), turning sentences around and around as he went; finally he'd hand over the penultimate (or so) draft to five or six readers who, as he put it, "I know are on my side, but who will speak candidly." Starting with *Goodbye, Columbus*, Roth relied on the judgment of Stern and Solotaroff, followed by Lurie, Conarroe, and various others who came and went over the years. "What they give me is not only their criticism," Roth said in 1977, "but along the way they *describe* the book to me, and that is really the best of it—hearing words *unlike* those with which you have been describing the book to yourself as you went along, finding out how it registers upon an intelligence that's not your own." In 1981, Stern wrote about their critiquing session for *Zuckerman Unbound*—the way Roth had listened and scribbled notes on a yellow pad (in later years he used a tape recorder), imperturbably murmuring "More" no matter how brutal the commentary: "Speech, debate, excitement, analysis, invention, the yellow pad fills. Fifty, sixty, a hundred murderous minutes. 'Don't stop. Keep going. . . .'" For the same novel Roth had also consulted Joanna Clark, who bluntly informed him it wasn't good enough to publish. Far from taking offense ("Nobody minds swallowing his medicine, if it is prescribed by a real doctor"), Roth went back to his typewriter and considered: "What have they said, individually and collectively? What have they told me about this book that I didn't know and I didn't see?" In the case of *Zuckerman Unbound*, Stern was astonished by how vastly transformed—and superior—the final product was to the draft he'd critiqued only a few months earlier.

Roth expected candor from his friends, and he emphatically returned the favor. In the old days his frankness could leave an author in tatters, and gradually Roth learned to evade the issue, honorably, by suggesting that a given manuscript wasn't "right" for him—or else he'd go to the trouble of composing a detailed, devastating critique and then append, punctiliously, his usual disclaimer: "Which may simply mean that I am not your book's ideal reader." For a time, indeed, Roth believed as a general rule "it would mitigate things if [he] went into great detail," but often found this had the opposite effect. After an exhaustive demolition of Nina Schneider's novel, *The Woman Who Lived in a Prologue*, the wounded author invoked Cynthia Ozick's relative enthusiasm, whereupon Roth felt obliged to explain himself further: "What Cynthia finds 'tough, wise, sane' seems to me an unrealized, self-conscious intention to be those things; I find attitudinizing where she senses these qualities. The dialogue particularly struck me as self-conscious and mannered, and tending at time towards the cute." As it happened the novel was published five years later and hailed in the *Times* as "astonishingly intelligent"—but when Nina died, in 2007, her novel was out of print and largely forgotten.

During Roth's first sojourn on Fawcett Street, the man who stayed in his New York apartment was a former Jesuit seminarian named Jack Miles—a nice approximation of the "monk or nun" Roth had sought as "ideal" tenants for his homes (Conarroe was in Connecticut). Miles was an editor at Doubleday at the time, though he'd come to the job via a circuitous path, attending universities in Rome and Jerusalem before receiving his doctorate in Near Eastern languages from Harvard. In 1974, Miles had been living in a Missoula trailer park, teaching at the University of Montana, when he wrote a letter to Roth praising his essay "Imagining Jews" as "one of the most remarkable pieces of literary criticism I have read in years." Not only did Roth answer the letter, he invited its author to come visit him in Connecticut, and the following summer Miles took him up on it. At the time Roth had no reason to think this obscure assistant professor of religious studies would go on to win a 1996 Pulitzer for *God: A Biography*, though he immediately twigged that Miles was "as smart as anybody" he knew. For his part Miles was surprised, during that first visit, by how readily Roth spoke about highly personal matters—he was still heartbroken over Sproul and in certain moods could speak of little else—though Roth rarely again discussed anything but his own work with Miles, who became one of his foremost reader-critics. Miles was among the happy few who received drafts of almost every novel, and he was also canvassed on such subjects as circumcision (for *The Counterlife*) and Jainism (for *American Pastoral*). Once, Miles visited Roth in Connecticut while Stern was also a guest, and Miles was struck by Stern's friendly interest in his personal affairs: "I realized that Dick had a kind of curiosity about people that Philip didn't have," he recalled; indeed, he came to regard Roth the way Dr. Watson regards Sherlock Holmes—as blithely indifferent to and even rather ignorant about much of the world and its people, but keenly focused on what he wants to know.

When it came to writing the Anne Frank section of *The Ghost Writer*, Roth had an intriguing proposition for his lodger on East Eighty-first. Both would read the diary and write each other their thoughts as they went along—"separate from the other, and not in response to each other. That way there'll be two different points of view and thereafter *two* dialogues. All the better! So I won't open your letter until after I have mailed mine, and you don't open mine until after you have mailed yours." A few days later Roth wrote that he considered Frank a "genius" insofar as she'd managed to portray herself "with such artful artlessness, as a civilized European child"—that is, as a basically secular bourgeois, hardly a product of the shtetl or ghetto, which enabled non-Jews to sympathize all the more. Miles, in turn, produced page upon page of erudite analysis, though perhaps his primary contribution was simple reassurance—Roth's choice of Frank as a subject, he wrote, was "inspired. . . . It is a choice no one would think of beforehand and of which everyone, afterwards, will say, 'Of course.'" Roth, who'd been miserably picking his way between pitfalls of sentimentality and tastelessness, was grateful:

I feel like a blasphemer, and have had dreams of disapproving fathers on and off for weeks. One I. Howe appears, as does my own father, and of all people Richard Nixon, who I try to suck up to, but who will not have me. This is true. But, you see, I am robbing them of their saint, and I know it. But your letter helps ENORMOUSLY, because now I have a co-conspirator, willing to see Anne as a girl, and one of us. She is enchanting and I too am half in love with her, as I know I would be with a daughter. Daughters must be irresistible, given that girls are generally.

Roth's main breakthrough was to consider Frank not as a saint but as a loving daughter and, above all, a *writer*, hence the eventual title of his book. Updike, for one, would notice the delicate progress of the "father/writer theme," and pleasurably reflect that the name Amy Bellette (whom Zuckerman imagines, falsely, to be Anne Frank) means "I love belles lettres."

■ ■ ■ ■

THE BEST PART OF living in London, for Roth, was that nobody approached him in restaurants to ask whether he'd ordered liver; nobody bothered him at all. "I'm not under fucking house arrest anymore in a city!" he exulted, at a time when he'd stopped putting his photograph on jackets and allowed only a few "carefully supervised" interviews (as Roger Straus noted a little ruefully). Of course he couldn't escape the glare of the local tabloids altogether, especially given the fame of his consort: MISS BLOOM HAS NO COMPLAINTS read the inevitable *Daily Mail* headline, which identified Roth as the wealthy author of an "onanistic best-seller." Roth clipped the item for Conarroe with the gloss "Merry Christmas from the onanist and the whore."

Roth rediscovered the joy of going to the theater, which he'd lost entirely in the States. He prepared for Royal Shakespeare productions by rereading a given play the afternoon of its performance, so he could have it "right in [his] head" while he watched. Bloom seemed to know everyone in this world, and he got to meet actresses such as Judi Dench and Maggie Smith, to attend a glamorous party *chez* Olivier (he tried to draw out his host, to no avail: "Do some of your imitations!"), to invite Bloom's mentor John Gielgud for lunch, and so on. He also struck up an amusing friendship with the young playwright David Hare, who remembered the rather fatherly interest Roth showed in his writing and bachelorhood, both encompassed by the Rothian maxim "Never let her sleep in your bed. Make sure *you're* the person who can leave." (Hare never perceived such an outlook as misogynistic, so much as a matter of ironclad priority: Work comes first, even before sex.) Best of all were dinners at the Hampstead home of his old friend Al Alvarez, whose second wife was a Canadian psychologist, Anne, whom Roth adored. On either side of their house on Flask Walk were two illustrious neighbors and frequent guests, the pianist Alfred Brendel and the novelist David Cornwell, a.k.a. John le Carré, whose *A Perfect Spy* (1986) Roth would come to view as the best British novel of the postwar era.

"Only Colette is her equal as a student of the ardors of an independent woman," Roth later wrote of Edna O'Brien, whose friendship with him began—for him if not for her—when he and Bloom came to dinner at her London flat in May 1978: "She is a great charmer," he wrote Conarroe afterward, "a wonderful story teller, and a generous woman—and loves her wine." The impression Roth had made on O'Brien was more equivocal: "There he sat, lean, watchful and scorchingly handsome," she reminisced in 2013. "In those days I was a gushing and eager cook. Suddenly, coming out of his reverie, he said, 'Do you do the soup and the soufflés in between writing your books?' I smarted somewhat. It was in an Irish accent and a not very convincing Irish accent." In fact she was "incensed" at being patronized thus, while "working like a horse, pouring Champagne, stoking a fire," and so forth, but she bore herself with decorum. Subsequently Roth read her novel *Night* and rang her up: "Hey," he said, with gratified surprise, "you're a good writer!" "So I am," she thinly replied.

Around this time Roth also got his first glimpse of the dazzling Lizzie Spender, at the home of her famous father, Stephen, where she appeared on the arm of Parviz C. Radji, the Shah of Iran's last ambassador to London. "Fascists, beauties, Spanish War Veteran poets," Roth noted. "Too much." The suave Radji was impressed enough by Roth and Bloom to invite them, a month later, to a dinner he was giving for former prime minister Edward Heath, whereupon Radji received "the following post-Valentine's Day *billet-doux*," as he recorded in his diary, describing its author, Roth, as a "[s]anctimonious little shit":

Dear Parviz:

Inasmuch as you are the official representative of a regime whose methods of putting down political opposition and suppressing freedom of expression I find wholly repugnant, I am unable to accept your invitation for dinner at the Iranian Embassy on March 14 in honor of Edward Heath. . . .

■ ■ ■ ■

"I'VE DONE SOME OF my best work since I've been with Philip," Bloom would tell *People* magazine in 1983. "I've had a chance to rub ideas against someone so intelligent. I'll ask: 'Why does this character do this?' He'll have ten answers where I have only two." Roth was fascinated by Bloom's profession and her own considerable gift; with intelligent direction, he said, she would "give you just what you asked for, even better than what you asked for"—as she had most memorably perhaps with Chaplin, whose tendency to feed actors their every gesture and inflection was ideal for Bloom (and almost drove Brando to murder). In Roth she had a companion with excellent directorial instincts, and one who knew her weaknesses and strengths. One of Bloom's signature roles, as Nora in *A Doll's House*, was well suited because the character combined her "two halves," as she put it: "the frivolous, silly, childish woman, and the stern woman"; Roth, however, was apt to point out that her most salient quality by far was "fragility," and hence her performance as Nora "is brilliant so long as she is Torvald's obedient wife, but lacks conviction in the final scene when she is proclaiming her independence."

Roth had arrived in London just in time to watch rehearsals of another Ibsen play, *Rosmersholm*—a potential fiasco for Bloom, given that her scenery-chewing costar (Raymond Massey) provoked the worst of her meekness, whereas the director was an "asshole," said Roth, who watched the disaster unfold with nary a comment. "What she felt her own way towards was, as a result, too refined, too ethereal, or so I felt when I saw it open out of town on Monday," he wrote Stern. "I made millions of notes and kept her up all night and then I went back down on Thursday to see it, and she had added the bite and the authority and kept the refinement and thrown out the etherealness and added some small erotic quotient—and God it bears writing." For the rest of the play's run, Roth attended as many as fifteen performances to make sure Bloom "didn't slide back into fleeing from Massey," and while reviews were generally tepid, she herself was applauded for a subtly "heroic" turn as Rebecca ("a beautiful portrait in water-colour").

On the whole Roth was "astonished" at how badly Bloom's career had stalled by then, though it helped explain why she constantly lunched with her mother and was so terrified of losing Anna's affection ("She feared the vacuum"). "I will never leave her," he told David Plante. "If I left her, she would kill herself. She may kill herself while with me, but that I could face, because I know I do everything I can to support her." Plante had become a friend after Roth returned for his second year in London, around the time Plante published a remembrance of the writer Jean Rhys in *The Paris Review*; Roth wrote him a fan letter and invited him to lunch at Monsieur Thompson's. Plante—an American novelist living in London with Nikos Stangos, a Thames & Hudson editor—was the first openly gay man Roth had ever befriended. Indeed, he was full of questions for Plante on that score, while Plante observed (à la Conarroe) that Roth himself was a man "completely devoid of femininity" (when Plante proposed to publish an assemblage of diary excerpts about Roth, his subject suggested the title "Straight Man"). Still, Roth and Plante began meeting for lunch so often that a rumor circulated that they were lovers; in fact they were collaborating on a television adaptation of Plante's Rhys memoir, another of Roth's efforts in behalf of Bloom's career that would come to naught.

"With *Brideshead*," Bloom wrote of her comeback role as Lady Marchmain in the television adaptation of Waugh's novel, "I had the sense not to allow my vanity to overpower my reason." According to Roth, however, vanity had all but pummeled reason through the ropes amid his steady reassurance that it was okay for Bloom to play a mother. "I don't want to play Diana Quick's mother," she clarified, referring to the actress who lived around the corner (with Albert Finney) and was only fifteen years younger than she. Eventually Roth prevailed, and during the months of filming at the majestic Castle Howard, in Yorkshire, he would occasionally come up for weekends and advise Bloom, as if they were nice Jewish tourists, "not to feel the curtain fabric" and ask about price. With respect to her performance, he invoked the advice Chekhov had given his actress-wife Olga Knipper—that she should find "a certain smile" for her character: "Imitate Antonia," he said, meaning Pinter's wife, Lady Antonia Fraser, who was known to keep a vague upper-class smile afloat. During the long, eleven-episode *Brideshead* shoot, Bloom took a month off to play Gertrude in a BBC-TV production of *Hamlet*, and her fears that she'd "never work again" were further belied when she was cast as Hera in *Clash of the Titans*.

And yet, quite like a Jean Rhys heroine, she had a terror of ending up old and penniless, and privately (at least) she credited Roth with helping put her finances in order—no small matter, given her misplaced trust in various agents, accountants, and producers since the age of seventeen, leading at last to the predations of Hilly Elkins. Later Roth remembered how she'd "forlornly" presented him with two IOUs from Elkins "totaling some $25,000," which she admitted were probably worthless; Roth turned them over to his lawyer, Helene Kaplan, who promptly recovered the debt. "He gave me very little money," Bloom told radio host Leonard Lopate in 1996, echoing a major theme of her book, which passes quietly over such incidental munificence as the $100,000 Roth gave her outright to restore her solvency, as well as the $400,000 he deposited in a twelve-year Clifford Trust that paid her roughly $28,500 a year in interest. The accountant at Wertheim and Company who helped Roth set up the trust, Jerry Kransdorf, phoned Roth after *Doll's House* was published and said he "was having fierce arguments at dinner parties" with people who gleefully denounced Roth as a cheapskate.

Soon after he arrived in London, Roth was alone on Fawcett Street one night, watching TV, when a commercial came on: An actor was playing Fagin, complete with a false nose and Yiddish accent; when the curtain fell, he went to his dressing room, removed the nose and other makeup, and revealed himself to be a Waspy Englishman. "Meanwhile," Roth recalled, "he was removing a cigarillo from a pack (the sponsor) and extolling its virtues. 'It's mild, it's tasty, it's relaxing,' he said, and then, with a glint in his eye and with Fagin's sleazy accent, he added, 'And it's *cheap.*' I was so surprised that I telephoned my friend Al Alvarez in Hampstead and told him what I'd just seen. Al, who is Jewish, laughed and said 'You'll get used to it.'"

Toward the beginning of *Doll's House*, Bloom describes herself as "profoundly Jewish. . . . Unlike many Jewish actresses of my generation, I never made any attempt to hide my origins or to change my name." This came as news to Roth, since he remembered how hard it was "to induce her simply to mention that she was Jewish" in the opening pages of *Limelight and After*: "To one who knew her social biases as intimately

Left to right, facing camera: David Ben-Gurion, Roth, and Margaret and Leslie Fiedler, during a June 1963 symposium on Jewish cultural issues in Israel. "Remember, this isn't yours," Ben-Gurion whispers to a young Nathan Zuckerman in The Counterlife, *when the two shake hands for a photographer, "—it's for your parents, to give them a reason to be proud of you." Roth's parents kept a framed photo of their much maligned son with the founder of Israel on a side table for the rest of their days.*

RIGHT: *Lucy Warner, model for Karen Oakes in* My Life as a Man, *who (à la Karen) said to Roth when she broke off their affair: "I can't save you, Philip. I'm only twenty-two."*
(Courtesy of Lucy Warner Kuemmerle)

BELOW: *Roth with the painter Julius Goldstein during his first visit to Yaddo, in 1964.*
(Courtesy of Philip Roth Estate)

Roth in his Kips Bay apartment.

ABOVE: *Roth was photographed beside a portrait of Kafka for* Life *magazine. The accompanying feature, by Albert Goldman, was titled "'Portnoy's Complaint' by Philip Roth Looms as a Wild Blue Shocker and the American Novel of the Sixties."*
(COPYRIGHT © BOB PETERSON)

The theater critic Robert Brustein (left) said Roth was like a "loony" little brother to him and his wife, Norma. "To Bob and Norma," Roth inscribed their copy of Portnoy, *"who encourage me in this madness."*
(COURTESY OF BARBARA C. SPROUL)

Alan Lelchuk (left) was Roth's best friend for a time. The younger man's first novel,
American Mischief—*for which Roth served as a rigorous midwife—led to a
dicey confrontation between the two friends and Norman Mailer.*

ABOVE: *Roth and Barbara Sproul in Woodstock, New York.*
(COURTESY OF BARBARA C. SPROUL)

LEFT: *Roth withdrew from the public eye after Portnoy, though he and Sproul liked to host friends at Broadview, their rented house in remote Woodstock. From left: Martin Garbus, Alan Lelchuk, Roth, Frances FitzGerald, Ruth Garbus.*
(COURTESY OF BARBARA C. SPROUL)

Roth and his friend Mel Tumin. "Mine became another life that Mel took it upon himself to assist and oversee as secretary of health, education, and welfare," Roth said in his eulogy.

(Courtesy of Barbara C. Sproul)

Sandy Roth (right), sweetly bemused by his zany little brother.

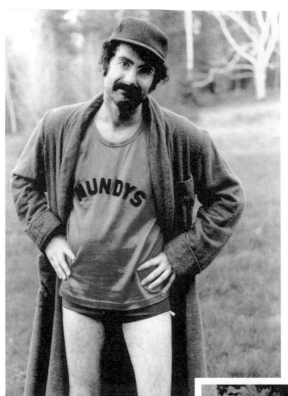

Roth in his Ruppert Mundys jersey, deeply into the spirit of The Great American Novel.
(COURTESY OF BARBARA C. SPROUL)

Herman, Bess, and their famous son enjoy a round of croquet.
(COURTESY OF BARBARA C. SPROUL)

ABOVE: *The artist Philip Guston and Roth, in Woodstock, "hiding themselves away from almost everything but their work and each other," as Roth put it.*

(COURTESY OF BARBARA C. SPROUL)

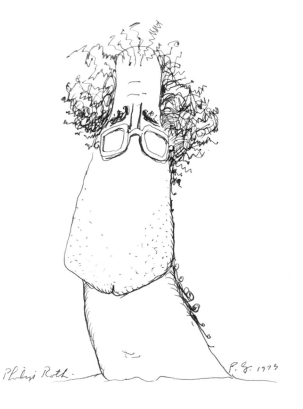

Philip Roth.   P. G. 1973

LEFT: *Guston's phallic caricature of his friend.*

(COURTESY OF THE GUSTON FOUNDATION)

Roth's beloved eighteenth-century farmhouse in Warren, Connecticut, where he moved in 1972.

(Courtesy of Philip Roth Estate)

Roth in the Stone Room of his Connecticut house.

Roth and Francine du Plessix Gray, his neighbor and fellow writer, in happier days.

(COURTESY OF BARBARA C. SPROUL)

Roth in Prague, 1973.

(COURTESY OF BARBARA C. SPROUL).

With Czechoslovak dissidents in Prague. From left: Stanislav Budín,
Rita Klímová, Ludvík Vaculík, Roth.

Roth and Sproul at his big fortieth birthday party in New York, 1973. "It was a little bit
of This Is Your Life," *said Sproul, who'd invited everyone from Roth's family*
to his college mentors, fellow writers, and Czech friends.

as I did," he noted, "her astonishing disclosure of her proud, unqualified Jewishness . . . [seems] the most dishonest sentence in her book." In the early days of their courtship, Bloom had looked "disbelieving and mystified," Roth said, whenever he spoke with pleasure about growing up in a Jewish neighborhood. Her own experience living among lower-middle-class American Jews—namely, the family of a paternal aunt in Florida, where she, her brother, and mother were evacuated during the war—was "disastrous," as she explained with relative restraint in *Limelight and After*: "Forty years have passed, but I am still reluctant to hurt people who were kind to us in their way." Almost fifty-five years had passed when Bloom wrote *Doll's House*, and by then she felt no such compunction, depicting her Florida relatives as typically crass American Jews.

While on a Lufthansa flight, in 1986, Bloom wrote Roth that she was en route to "the city of [her] ancestors"—Frankfurt—before admitting her people were probably from the "Polish Mess, like everyone else," and making light of her own "marvelous snobbism—to want to claim descent from *German* Jews." This was a relatively benign form of ambivalence, to be sure, and Roth himself was careful to point out that Bloom's distaste did not extend to Jews of distinction and refinement, such as their friends Harold Pinter, Mike Nichols, and Jonathan Miller. "The offensive ones," he wrote, "the abominations who stoked her anti-Semitism (or what might more precisely be called her selective Judeophobia), were Jews gathered in a group . . . like my undistinguished family and their ilk." Such ilk included the boisterous, cigar-smoking Mel Tumin, whose wife remarked that they saw a lot less of their friend Philip during the Bloom era ("We were too Jewish for her taste"), but more immediate offenders were indeed Roth's "undistinguished" parents, who proudly kept a portrait of Bloom on their living room side table, and whom Roth would overhear Bloom describe as "the dreaded parents" while chatting long-distance with Anna. "I wish my father were alive to read that declaration of Bloom's Jewish allegiance" in *Doll's House*, said Roth. "He would have come up with just the right pungent Yiddish phrase to register its preposterousness."

· · · ·

AFTER SUCH A promising start, Roth's progress on *The Ghost Writer* was blocked for "two dreadful months" toward the end of 1978, until he discovered the key to its completion. Amy Bellette was not, as he'd suggested in previous drafts, the real Anne Frank; such a delusion was a "grandiose dream of salvation" contrived by Zuckerman in response to the "assault upon his conscience" by Jews such as his father and the sanctimonious Judge Wapter—that is to say, how could they accuse him of anti-Semitism if he ended up marrying *Anne Frank*? Once Roth grasped the essential connection between his two main narrative threads, the final draft seemed to write itself, a phenomenon he often experienced with his best books, when "everything you read and everything you do or hear or say seems somehow to feed directly into the next day's work."

Roth proudly announced to friends that his entire novel, in two parts, would appear in *The New Yorker*—thus joining a handful of classics the magazine had deemed important enough over the years to publish in toto, including *Hiroshima, Eichmann in Jerusalem, Silent Spring,* and *In Cold Blood*. Roth had been absent from the magazine's pages ever since "Novotny's Pain," in 1962; indeed it was Roth's old editor there, Rachel MacKenzie, who'd urged her successor to pursue Roth for a new submission. Veronica Geng (like MacKenzie) was herself a writer of some renown, best known for her Perelman-esque "casuals" such as "Love Trouble Is My Business," which addresses the daunting challenge of how to work the words "Mr. Reagan" and "read Proust" into the same sentence via a whole detective yarn wherein *every* sentence contains these words. ("Then she touched me, with the practiced efficiency of a protocol officer steering some terribly junior diplomat through a receiving line to meet Mr. Reagan—and funny, but I got the idea she wasn't suggesting we curl up and read Proust.") As an editor she was known for her incisive but peremptory brand of frankness ("I never read Bible parodies" said the entirety of her rejection letter to Ian Frazier)—in other words, an editor after Roth's heart. "Veronica couldn't just spot the haywire sentence in a paragraph where a writer's vigilance had faltered," he wrote in an undelivered eulogy, "—she could spot the syllable. . . . Sentimental diction and platitudinous thinking and cultural righteousness revolted her at the biological level." After their first happy meeting at the Algonquin to discuss *The Ghost Writer*, Geng became one of the elect who read every one of Roth's novels in draft—a person who understood that great writers are great precisely because "they love continuing to work at something," as she once pointed out, perhaps thinking specifically of Roth.

And this was entirely relevant to *The Ghost Writer*. Pinned over Lonoff's desk is a famous passage from Henry James's "The Middle Years," whose writer-hero, Dencombe, is a "fingerer of style" doomed to eternal dissatisfaction with his books: "We work in the dark—we do what we can—we give what we have. Our doubt is our passion and our passion is our task. The rest is the madness of art." With *The Ghost Writer*, Roth revisited the careful elegance of James, both on the level of line-by-line prose and larger formal intricacy—a fastidiousness at the heart of Zuckerman's desire to become the "spiritual son" of Lonoff, a man whose life is wholly devoted to "turning sentences around," and who embodies a purity of purpose for which Roth and his fictional surrogates would strive but never quite attain in its quintessential form, to wit: Lonoff refuses all public honors, gives no interviews, and bans his own likeness ("a ridiculous irrelevancy") from his book jackets. At one point he mentions the nonallure of Cambridge academic society:

"I'd rather talk to the horse."
　"You have a horse?" [Zuckerman asks]
　"No."
　I loved him! Yes, nothing less than love for this man with no illusions: love for the bluntness, the scrupulosity, the severity, the estrangement; love for the relentless winnowing out of the babyish, preening, insatiable self; love for the artistic mulishness and the suspicion of nearly everything else; and love for the buried charm, of which he'd just given me a glimpse.

The rejection of the world in favor of the "transcendent calling" also relates to what was perhaps, again, the most prominent theme in Roth's work: the I against the They, the necessary revolt against one's community in order to capture it in art. "It is about Kikes," Nathan's father bleakly declares of his latest story. "Kikes and their love of money." The story in question, "Higher Education," was somewhat based on Roth family lore: Herman's indomitable cousin Fritzi Kuvin, whose husband died young, had made every sacrifice to put her two sons, Sandy and Seymour, through medical school. Zuckerman barely alters a similar but ignominious chapter from his own family history in "Higher Education," another reason for his father's wounded feelings: the title refers to the purpose of a trust left by Zuckerman's great aunt, Meema Chaya, to educate her daughter Essie's two fatherless sons; Essie wants to put the boys through medical school after college, but her raffish brother, Sidney, who stands to inherit the balance, manages to persuade a judge ("a *goy*") that "higher education" means *college*, not medical school, and thus Essie is reduced to the drudgery of selling shingles and siding door to door (like Roth's Aunt Honey). When Zuckerman refuses to disavow the story, his father submits it to the inspection of Newark's third-most admired Jew (after Mayor Ellenstein and Rabbi Prinz), Judge Leopold Wapter, whose "TEN QUESTIONS FOR NATHAN ZUCKERMAN" reprise some of the most galling charges made against Roth in his own career: Would Nathan have written such a story in Nazi Germany, Wapter wonders, challenging him to find anything in it "that would not warm the heart of a Julius Streicher or a Joseph Goebbels." Wapter's postscript urges young Nathan to see *The Diary of Anne Frank* on Broadway—more fodder still for Zuckerman's fantasy of settling their collective hash, and perhaps reconciling with his father in the bargain, by marrying *the* Anne Frank, a Jewish saint (and fellow writer).

In the end, though, Nathan chooses his spiritual father, Lonoff, and the life of lonely sacrifice he represents, rather the way Amy Bellette/ Anne Frank realizes she cannot return from the dead to be reunited with the darling father who survived her, Pim, because *her* writing has made her "the incarnation of the millions of unlived years robbed from the murdered Jews"—or so Nathan imagines until the next morning, when the sleeve of Amy's coat falls back and he marks the absence of a tattooed serial number on her forearm: "No scar; no book; no Pim. No, the loving father who must be relinquished for the sake of his child's art was not hers; he was mine."

The Ghost Writer appeared in the June 25 and July 2, 1979, issues of *The New Yorker*, two months before book publication, and Roth was especially pleased his novel would reach many readers "without first having to be strained through the sieve of its reviews." Amid the usual noisome quibbles, though, the reception was largely and rightly positive: "*The Ghost Writer* is his best novel yet," Peter Prescott announced in *Newsweek*, and the hitherto captious Robert Towers hailed Roth as "a superbly endowed storyteller" on the front-page of the *Times Book Review*. Roth, meanwhile, was trying not to notice. Recalling Flaubert's wisdom about the likely fate of one's art—"The crowd tramples on us"—he hoped to preserve his post-Howe detachment, but alas he had to *skim* the reviews, at least, because he didn't trust anyone else to cull quotes for advertisements. Thus he learned his novel was a "critical success" for the most part: "That means that the assholes failed to understand the book," he wrote Alvarez, "half of them missed the fact that Anne Frank is Zuckerman's invention and had her down for a hard fact of the story, etc. But dey love de humanistic stuff, Al. Sure fire stuff, dis humanism."

Lest this seem excessively testy: Lehmann-Haupt had returned as Roth's daily *Times* reviewer ("I may quit until he dies," Roth had written Updike)—this after a six-year respite that was likely the result of Roth's incidental broadside in his 1974 essay, "Imagining Jews," published in *The New York Review of Books*: "Bold, challenging"—he wrote of Lehmann-Haupt's apparent endorsement of confessional fiction ("I want the novelist to bare his soul")—"and inevitably to be flatly contradicted by the *Times* daily reviewer when he caught hold of the pendulum of received opinion as it swung the other way in the ensuing years, toward disguise, artifice, fantasy, montage, and complicated irony. . . . Well, mindlessness marches on." As Roth surely hoped he would, Lehmann-Haupt defended his acumen with an aggrieved letter to the editor, whereupon Roth *really* pounced—replying that such an untalented reviewer was "an insult to the community of American writers": "And the insult is not by Mr. Lehmann-Haupt, who can only do the best he can, but by the editors of the *New York Times*, who most assuredly would not send a reporter to Saigon, or the Stock Exchange, or even to Shea Stadium if he had so little feel for his subject and his task." In poker-faced earnest, Roth proposed that a properly qualified critic might be found via an application process à la the Guggenheim Fellowships.

In his review of *The Ghost Writer*, Lehmann-Haupt seemed eager to prove there were no hard feelings: "Almost as if to celebrate the 20th birthday of his first book, *Goodbye, Columbus*, Philip Roth has given us a beautifully intricate novel that fulfills the promise of those early stories," he innocently enthused, doubtless unaware that he'd sorely insulted Roth by referring to the (heretofore unfulfilled) "promise" of his juvenilia. And whatever nice things the critic went on to say, Roth's eyes were likely to fix on the subhead—"Women Fare Badly"—which referred to a subsequent observation that "women in the novel, except for the fantasy figure of Anne Frank, are treated with the utmost condescension." That would seem to mean Hope Lonoff, since there are only two major female characters in the book, and in fact Lehmann-Haupt quotes the narrator's supposedly denigrating remark that Hope is reduced to a "handmaiden in the House of Art," which scarcely does justice to her assertiveness (flinging a wineglass against the wall, etc.), or her desperate wish to flee such confinement once and for all.

Still, in Roth's eyes, Lehmann-Haupt was a relatively harmless booby next to the "semi-lunatic wise-guy" John Leonard, who edited the *Book Review* and also had pilloried Roth's previous novel for the daily edition; indeed, one likely reason Lehmann-Haupt returned to the parlous Roth Beat was that Leonard had elected to critique *The Ghost Writer* at greater and even more disparaging length in the *New York Review*. "The *chutzpa* of it," he wrote, "appropriating the Ophelia of the death camps for his dark, libidinal purposes, his angry punch line. . . . He just can't help himself." After this gross misrepresentation of how Roth actually handled the delicate subject of Anne Frank, Leonard gave a long, slyly deflating plot summary ("Nothing much happens . . ."), which included a swipe at Lonoff's Durante routine ("I don't believe [it] for a minute")— one of Roth's own favorite bits.* That year's Pulitzer committee was perhaps following Leonard's lead when they came to the rare decision to overrule the unanimous recommendation of their fiction jury—*The Ghost Writer*—and give the prize instead to Mailer's *The Executioner's Song*. Conarroe was visiting his friend in London when they got the news: "We wuz robbed" was the entirety of Roth's response.

■　■　■　■

ROTH TRIED TO KEEP prizes and honorary degrees in perspective; unlike Lonoff, however, he was hardly averse to such recognition. Eventually he'd receive degrees from Harvard, Columbia, Brown, Penn, and several others (but not the University of Chicago, he wistfully noted), though the first and perhaps most satisfactory of these came in 1979 from his alma mater, Bucknell—a near thing, according to his old classmate

---

* Roth sent the pertinent issue of *The New Yorker* to Durante, who at the time had only a few months to live. His wife replied with "a nice note," assuring Roth that she'd read the passages aloud to him.

Jane Brown Maas, who'd acceded to the board of trustees and nominated Roth herself. The board was split, inauspiciously, between those who considered Roth anti-Semitic and those who "didn't want him because he was Jewish"; fortunately, both the current and former university presidents, Dennis O'Brien and Charles Watts, were strongly in favor.

Over the years Roth had visited Mildred Martin every so often, in the spring, staying in the spare room of her old house on South Front Street, and so he did again when he and Bloom arrived for that year's commencement on June 2. "As I get older," Miss Martin had written Roth a month before, "fewer and fewer occasions arouse my joy, but this one does." Retired since 1972, she was occasionally sought out by journalists as the mentor of one of America's greatest—and filthiest—writers: "Never, *never* have I heard him talk that way," she insisted, again and again in so many words, and this was true. "I was a good boy for you," Roth told her in 1992, laughing. "The thing is, Mildred"—he'd finally given himself permission to use her Christian name—"you don't know about the Mr. Hyde part of any of us." But whereas Miss Martin was at pains to defend Roth's endearing personal comportment, she didn't mince words when it came to his work, a "great deal" of which she found distasteful: "I just couldn't finish *Portnoy's Complaint*," she plainly admitted to one interviewer. "I got halfway through and I thought, 'I don't have to read this.'" Five years later she upbraided Roth personally—hardly for the first or last time—over *My Life as a Man*: "I hope you have said enough about sex to have got it out of your system as the never-ending problem."

On the day of Roth's first honorary degree, Miss Martin accompanied him down the aisle ("as though we were going to be married in our academic gowns"), while Bloom, for her part, declined to join him on the dais ("No no, this is Philip's occasion"), disappearing into the crowd with a babushka knotted under her chin. She "captivated the entire campus," said Jane Maas, and Roth had a "truly marvelous time" showing her around—to the window where Betty Powell had fled the wrathful Mrs. Purnell; to the Maurers' cozy old hovel, where he'd spent so many happy hours listening to E. E. Cummings records and watching the Army–McCarthy hearings; to the Vaughan Lit Building, soon to be renamed in honor of another beloved professor, C. Willard Smith, who was very frail but rejuvenated by the radiance of Claire Bloom, with whom he animatedly discussed Shakespeare *chez* Wheatcroft. "I felt as though I'd brought him a gift," Roth wrote a few months later, after Willard had died, "something I had long wanted to do for all that he taught me in and out of class." One of the last books Willard finished was *The Ghost Writer*, for which he awarded the author an A.

Thirty-Two

I N THE SPRING OF 1981—AFTER A YEAR CONSUMED BY Roth's struggles over his second Zuckerman novel—he was asked to revise the David Magarshack translation of Chekhov's *The Cherry Orchard* for a production at the Chichester Festival in Sussex, where Bloom was cast as Madame Ranevskaya. Roth gave the festival good value for its nominal honorarium (about five hundred dollars, he recalled). Not only did he produce a modernized, smoothly colloquial script, but he also attended six weeks of rehearsals in London and put together a binder of some fifty typed pages of notes: "Her childhood, her innocence," he wrote of Madame Ranevskaya. "What happened to it is the mystery puzzling her throughout the play, particularly when she isn't speaking. I see her touching everything, going about picking things up that once were hers." Reviews were mixed, though most agreed with *The Telegraph* that Bloom's "fey performance" was "a devastating portrayal of a silly, shallow woman, destructive to all that she touches."

Roth and Bloom were staying in Chichester for the run of the play, but drove up to London for a few days on Sunday, May 17. Before leaving, Roth had phoned his parents, as he did every Sunday, and was relieved to find his mother in good spirits. After a mostly healthy life, she'd been feeling tired and breathless lately, but was trying to walk a little farther each day along their street in Elizabeth; Philip told her he was looking forward to walking a full mile with her when she came to Connecticut that summer, and she laughed and promised to do her best. Then, around midnight, Herman called: while they were having dinner with friends that night, Bess had had a heart attack; it was bad, he said, and Philip immediately booked a morning flight on the Concorde. He was packed and getting back into bed, when Herman called again and admitted that Bess was dead and had been dead when he'd called the first time; he hadn't wanted to shock his son. When Philip arrived in Elizabeth the next day, as he wrote in *Patrimony*, he found Sandy consoling their "devastated" father.

> "She ordered New England clam chowder," [Herman] told me as I kneeled beside him, still in my coat and holding his hand, "and I ordered Manhattan. When it came she said, 'I don't want this soup.' I said, 'Take mine—we'll switch,' but she was gone. Just slumped forward. Didn't even fall. Made no trouble for anyone. The way she always did everything."

Philip wrote a eulogy for the next day's funeral, but was too emotional when the time came and gave it to the rabbi to read: "Life," he wrote, "to be worth something, requires that out of the contradictions, despite the obstructions, order must be made anew every morning."

> Because she intended to live a worthy life, every morning and every day she went about the job of making order: order for a hard-working, exacting, ambitious husband; order for two temperamental, reflective, ambitious sons; order for sisters with difficult lives, for nieces and nephews with family problems, for grandsons to whom she dispensed not mere grandmothering but mothering as well. . . . [S]he proceeded with meticulous precision that we more readily associate with cutting diamonds than with performing the relentless daily chores of ordinary family life. But the daily chores of ordinary family life were just that to her—precious jewels to be cut to perfection and given to those she loved.

After the burial they returned to Herman's apartment; Sandy and Philip were occupied with greeting mourners at the door and hadn't noticed their father missing until Aunt Milly came rushing out of the bedroom. "You better go in there and do something, darling," she whispered into Philip's ear. "Your father's throwing everything out." Sure enough, Herman was busily emptying the closet and dresser drawers of his late wife's clothing. "What good is this stuff anymore?" he said to his son, proposing to give everything to Jewish relief. Philip insisted he stop for now and go talk to his guests—struck the while by how weirdly composed his father seemed: "he was simply doing what he had done all his life: the next difficult job."

As one may imagine, such a man had become a trial to live with—more of a trial—after he'd retired, in 1966, from managing fifty-two employees at the now thriving Maple Shade office of Metropolitan Life. Bess had been happy living in their garden apartment near her sisters Milly and Honey, but suddenly she had an obsessive, increasingly melancholic husband at home with her day and night. ("It's like that joke," said Milly's daughter, Anne, who heard plenty about Aunt Bess's tribulations: "'I married you, but not for lunch.'") For a while he tried volunteering at the Red Cross, the Veterans Hospital in East Orange, and even a friend's hardware store; mostly, though, he stayed home bossing his wife around—telling her, for instance, how to make the bed more efficiently, without having to walk around it so many times, which wasn't the sort of thing Bess needed help with. During a weekend visit to Connecticut, the summer before her death, she suddenly announced to Philip that she was considering divorce. "He doesn't listen to what I say," she wept. "He interrupts me all the time to talk about something else. When we're out, that's the worst. Then he won't let me speak at all. If I start to, he just shuts me up."

But of course Herman worshipped his wife—whom he invoked, always, as "my Bess"—and seemed scarcely aware that he was driving her crazy and quite possibly to the grave. On the lovely May day that she died, they'd walked three long city blocks to the drugstore; as Bess reported to Milly afterward, she was so exhausted she didn't think she could make the return trip, but after a little rest on a bench Herman rousted her to her feet and on they went. This might have been on his mind the next day, when Philip heard him crying in the bathroom: "Mommy, Mommy, where are you, Mommy?" Philip gave his father five milligrams of Valium and a glass of warm milk before bed, then held his hand until he fell asleep.

■　■　■　■

ROTH ONCE REFLECTED that there was usually about a ten-year gap between his life and his writing (versus, he said, less than twenty-four hours for Updike), and almost ten years exactly would pass between the time he started a novel, in 1979, tentatively titled *Fiasco* or *A Star Is Born*, and wrote the following, in 1969, to Tom Rogers: "All I can report so far about becoming a celebrity is that it is silly in the extreme and is only useful as it is a possible subject for future fictions." The main genesis of Roth's trilogy about "the unreckoned consequences of a life in art" had derived from his observations of literary life in Czechoslovakia, "where nothing goes and everything matters," juxtaposed with that of the States, "where everything goes and nothing matters." Thus an early draft of *Zuckerman Unbound* was divided neatly into two parts. The first was a tabulation of morbidities suffered by Zuckerman as a result of writing *Carnovsky* and so becoming the world's most famous sex freak, and the second entails his flight abroad with his mother, whom a crazed fan has threatened to kidnap. While in Prague, Zuckerman attends an orgy at a film director's palazzo, where he encounters the elderly would-be translator of *Carnovsky*, Kapper, who explains, "In this small country the writers have a great burden to bear: they make not only art, they must make general decency and the public conscience." Bloom read this draft and declared it "brilliant," but Roth ("she gets paid to say things like that") decided the thematic implications were "too obvious" and put aside the entirety of his Czech material for the trilogy's epilogue, *The Prague Orgy*, to be published four years later: "In order for Prague to have the impact upon the reader that it originally had on me," he said, "I had to write a 697-page introduction."

The Promethean import of *Zuckerman Unbound* relates, ironically, to the title hero's determination to "let the repellent in" (as Roth liked to say) by writing about his perverse alter ego, Carnovsky, and hence freeing himself and his readers from a degree of civilization's constraints. However, by sabotaging his own "dignified, high-minded gravity"—as his worldly agent, Andre, puts it—Zuckerman becomes all the more alienated from what Flaubert had wistfully called *le vrai*: "*Ils sont dans le vrai*" ("They are in the truth"), Flaubert had remarked, watching a young mother prosaically tending her children. Zuckerman is isolated foremost from the loved ones for whom he'd once aspired to be virtuous: "Cold-hearted betrayer of the most intimate confessions, cutthroat caricaturist of your own loving parents, graphic reporter of encounters with women to whom you have been deeply bound by trust, by sex, by love—no, the virtue racket ill becomes you." As for the *vrai* writ large—the philistine public—far from being grateful for the fruits of Zuckerman's insight, they mistake "impersonation for confession" and charge him with the sins of his hero. Utterly alone, and creatively impotent, Zuckerman is reduced to watching nonstop TV ("There was little else he could concentrate on"), at one point savoring the absurdity of listening to three therapists analyze "his castration complex" on channel 5.

Perhaps the most formidable personification of the *vrai* is a former quiz-show whiz, Alvin Pepler, a fellow Newarker who follows Zuckerman around New York maniacally reciting song titles in the precise order they appeared on the Hit Parade.* Pepler—whom Roth described to a friend as "the first of the father's avengers"—also believes that *Carnovsky* is a true confession, but goes one better, furiously accusing the author of appropriating the hero's "hang-ups" from Pepler's own life. To prove his point, he mails Zuckerman the handkerchief he'd borrowed the day before (while eating Zuckerman's sandwich), which is now redolent of a telltale "acrid odor." "Jerk Off Artist Kills Bard Of Jerking Off," Zuckerman imagines the headlines screaming; "Zuckerman Killed By Onanist's Hand." The next "avenger" is Zuckerman's younger brother, Henry, who assures Nathan that their dying father wasn't referring to Nixon or Lyndon Johnson with his last word on earth: "You *are* a bastard," Henry weeps. "A heartless conscienceless bastard. . . . Jewish morality, Jewish endurance, Jewish wisdom, Jewish families—everything is grist for your fun-machine." After Henry assures him that it was, in fact, Nathan's book that killed their father, Zuckerman becomes unbound in every sense. Pausing in a limo outside his childhood home in the now dangerous, riot-devastated Weequahic section, he reflects: "You are no longer any man's son, you are no longer some good woman's husband, you are no longer your brother's brother, and you don't come from anywhere anymore, either."

After the craftsmanly *Ghost Writer*, critics were a little disappointed by *Zuckerman Unbound*—a slender yet diffuse novel that was "reasonably funny, reasonably sad, reasonably interesting, and, occasionally, just plain reasonable," as Broyard wrote in his representative *New York Times*

---

* Pepler was inspired by Herb Stempel, the man who blew the whistle on quiz-show fraud in 1956, after he was forced to take a dive against the handsome, Waspy Charles Van Doren on the game show *Twenty-One*. In 1966, Roth began yet another ur-*Portnoy* novel, *The Big Money*, based on hours of research he'd done on the quiz-show scandals at the New York Public Library. The manuscript petered out after seventy-five pages, but Stempel/Pepler continued to evolve in Roth's imagination until he turned up in *Zuckerman Unbound*.

review. As ever, Roth affected not to pay attention to the newspaper of record, while being so enraptured by Edward Rothstein's long, thoughtful analysis in *The New York Review of Books* ("the most intelligent I've gotten in twenty-two years") that he pressed Aaron Asher to invite the young man to dinner so Roth could meet him in person. Rothstein's review—"The Revenge of the Vrai"—conceded that *Zuckerman Unbound* seemed "impoverished" on a superficial reading, especially in comparison to its predecessor, but was in fact "disturbing and challenging. . . . It asks that something be *made* of it, that it be understood, treated with more care than Nathan's *Carnovsky* is by the reading public. *Zuckerman Unbound* is almost the story of a book being misread—by its author as well as by its readers—chaotically mixing the real with the imagined."

And life would go on imitating art with a vengeance. In *The Observer*, Martin Amis derisively described Roth's latest as "an autobiographical novel about what it is like to write autobiographical novels," whereas the *Times* sent a culture reporter, Michiko Kakutani—soon to become its most indefatigable book critic—to interview him about this burning issue ("Is Roth Really Writing about Roth?"): "Those who convert literature into gossip don't get what reading's all about," Roth explained, ticking off the various ways his life differed from Zuckerman's (he didn't have a younger brother; his father was still alive; nobody ever tried to kidnap his mother, etc.). As for the subject of "self-travesty" in general, Roth's favorite analogy would always be Jack Benny, who was rumored to be a very generous man, though he found it funnier to play a miser on the radio.

■ ■ ■ ■

ON FEBRUARY 23, 1981—following certain financial disagreements with Roger Straus—Aaron Asher departed Farrar, Straus and Giroux to become executive editor at Harper & Row, where he'd been hired by his former employer's son, Roger Straus III, who'd dutifully sought his father's blessing: "I'd be delighted," said the latter, "help yourself." Two days after Asher's departure, the *Daily News* ran a story about the "great speculation" in publishing circles as to whether the legendary editor's authors—"most notably Philip Roth and Brian Moore"—would follow him; Asher himself seemed sanguine. "Yes," he replied, when asked about the two notables, "—and that's plural."

Where Roth was concerned, after all, Asher was not only a superb editor but one of his closest friends, and their scribbled exchanges on Roth's manuscripts often read like so much wacky banter: Querying the phrase "Since my discharge" in *The Ghost Writer*, Asher noted that it put him in mind of "a leaky cock," to which Roth scribbled back, "You must have your reasons. Stet." One of the first books Asher bought at Harper was Bloom's *Limelight and After*, which he shepherded along with courtly tact ("I'm at work on your text, dear Claire, not that it needs much"). Indeed, he and Roth were en rapport in almost every literary and political aspect, and while in London it was Asher's "intelligence and conversation" that Roth missed most.

Ten months after Asher's departure from FSG, Roth asked his opinion (as ever) of "Zuckerman III"—what would become *The Anatomy Lesson*—whereupon Asher decided it was time to lay his cards on the table: "I'll put in writing my offer of $100,000+ for it," he wrote. Since he knew Roth planned to publish his trilogy, once it was finished, as a single book—*Zuckerman Bound*—and was therefore reluctant to change publishers in the midst of things, Asher sought to reassure him: "Trilogy-shmilogy," he wrote, promising that Harper would match FSG's design of the first two volumes and "surpass them in sales." "This is a legal document," he concluded. "Happy 1982."

Five months passed, until Roth sent another draft of his work in progress to Asher, meanwhile assuring Straus that this was simply a matter of old friendship: "He understands this, I understand this, and I want you to understand it too. New York is a city world-famous for scuttle-butt and I don't want any false and malicious scuttle-butt drifting back to you." In fact, Asher wouldn't *fully* understand until seven months later, when Roth definitely informed him, at last, that he'd decided to stay with FSG—and still he requested yet another reading of his work in progress, but not if it gave Asher false hope that Roth would follow him to Harper & Row.

Asher's response was remarkably magnanimous. He wrote Roth that he'd begun to get the message over the past couple of years, and so had become reticent about "wooing" him further. But now that Roth's decision was final, Asher wished to speak frankly: "Roger is an amoral shit who has done and continues to do me injury. That a dear friend who also happens to be among the very best of writers chooses to stay with him doesn't exactly cheer me. Of course I understand your reasons: the trilogy, the earlier books (including foreign rights), . . . your desire for stability." Asher couldn't help wondering, though, whether Roth was feeling sensitive (not for the first time) about being perceived as greedy, or perhaps he coveted the vaunted "prestige" of FSG? If so, Asher assured him that the "New York chatterers" would simply assume he'd "followed a respected editor" who also happened to be a friend. Be that as it may: Roth's decision to stay with Roger—a man "not all that widely loved or respected in the trade," Asher allowed himself to say—was "something of an embarrassment to me." The next day Asher decided such a tack was unseemly, and wrote a final note emphasizing that Roth's conduct in the matter had been "exemplary, and, in fact, I owe you an apology for the distraction *my* move has caused *you.*" He forbore to mention that Roth had taken an awfully long time coming to the point—this while Asher gladly continued to exert his skills on Roth's (and Bloom's) behalf—but at least Roth hadn't asked a third party to lower the boom, as he had with Joe Fox.

Another factor in Roth's decision was his fondness for Asher's replacement, David Rieff, the brilliant son of a former Penn colleague, Philip Rieff, as well as the celebrated intellectual Susan Sontag, with whom Roth had conducted a "very brief friendship" that would later puzzle him. Sontag enjoyed considerable sway over Roger Straus, and her son had been hired as a senior editor right out of college; some people thought he was sensitive on that point, and hence given to a kind of pretentious flamboyance. With characteristic asperity Kazin noted in his diary that "little David Rieff, Susie Sunday's cupid bow son" was among those present *chez* Roth for Thanksgiving 1986: "But oh my, little Rieff," he wrote, "so knowing, so full of literary insideness like his phony ma." That said, even Asher considered him "very bright and very competent," though he was known to neglect authors who ranked low on the greasy pole; he let *Seven Thousand Days in Siberia*, by Karlo Stajner, languish in limbo so long that his colleagues dubbed it "Seven Thousand Days on David's Desk."

But Roth would always rank high, and therefore got the best of Rieff—tactful, attentive, humorous, shrewd—though the two were, at least superficially, very different people. "Look, David," Roth said, trying to explain a formulation in his prose: "remember when you were thirteen and you thought everybody was Jewish?" Rieff burst out laughing: "Philip, when I was thirteen I thought the whole world was gay and Hispanic, and I was right." Roth saw his point: Years ago he'd been on a panel with the bisexual Sontag, and her young son, David, was there and very much a part of her world (albeit straight himself). No wonder, then, that Rieff was—as Roth put it—"about brains and intelligence how a rich kid was about money. He was surrounded by it, and he couldn't tolerate anything else." In that respect they were perfectly attuned.

Around this time, Roth sought additional help from a woman he would come to call his "secret weapon," Roslyn Schloss. "I am willing to suggest that she has had more of an influence on the quality of Philip's prose than anybody at all," said Conarroe,* who'd worked with Schloss at the Modern Language Association and considered her "the best copy editor who ever lived." On Conarroe's recommendation Roth phoned her in the spring of 1983, when long galleys of *The Anatomy Lesson* were ready, and said he'd like to try out her services for a reasonable fee. He was staying at the Wyndham Hotel in New York—his invariable address in the city after he gave up his apartment on East Eighty-first Street— where Schloss showed up with her dictionaries and mechanical pencils ("I looked like some kind of call girl," she remembered, "only with dictionaries and mechanical pencils"); they ended up spending hours together, minutely discussing each correction, the kind of conversation Roth relished. Henceforth Schloss worked on every one of Roth's books, and was perhaps better acquainted with this preeminent aspect of his obsessiveness than anybody. Once, while visiting Balzac's cottage in the Sixteenth Arrondissement, Schloss scanned the heavily scored manuscripts lining the walls and thought, "They ain't seen nothing." Roth especially loved going to town on his galleys, since seeing his work in print for the first time was seeing it afresh: "Suddenly, lapses of thought, excesses of description, errors of style and even conception can become clear to you," he said, "just because of the change in format." And the more Roth loved a given novel, the more he and Schloss were apt to scrutinize multiple galleys, as in the case of *Sabbath's Theater*. "A five-bladed fan suspended on a long stem from the ceiling at the foot of the bed,"

---

* "She would have made me drop that 'at all,'" he added.

he'd written, which she emended to "A five-bladed ceiling fan hanging from a long stem above the foot of the bed": *Yes*, Roth scribbled in the margin—again and again. After a particularly feverish session back and forth one night, via fax, Roth signed off gratefully at last with his signature Flair pen: "And he said yes and yes and he said Yes! / Goodnight!"

■ ■ ■ ■

WHILE LIVING IN the States from (usually) June to October, Roth liked more and more to stay put in Connecticut, where he could pursue his favorite activities sans distraction: writing, reading, swimming, walking—but mostly writing. Bloom, who was with him roughly half the time, would summon him from his studio to dinner with an old, raucously clanging bell, until Roth got a second, incoming-call-accepting phone line to which only she and the odd other had the number. For recreation the two would sit in a little screened geodesic dome on the lawn, where they could commune with nature while reading. "I say *ssh* a lot," said Roth.

Some were bemused by the extent to which Bloom acquiesced to her hausfrau role, not to say the extent to which Roth encouraged and slightly ridiculed this. Though he often cooked for himself when necessary, Roth was happy to let his illustrious companion handle almost every aspect of dinner otherwise, from cooking to serving hors d'oeuvres to guests (while they chatted with Roth) to cleaning up afterward. When a detail was muffed, Roth was likely to observe "It's hard to get good help these days" or words to that effect. Jonathan Brent, who was interviewing Roth for the *Chicago Tribune*, spent a night in Connecticut during the summer of 1983; he was startled when Bloom appeared the next morning in a pinafore and apron to serve him breakfast. "I can't believe that the most beautiful woman in the world just made breakfast for me," he remarked to Roth, who sighed, "It gets tired." What Roth meant, in part, was the playacting side of Bloom's domestic ministrations. "She had a child's fantasy of life," he said.

Where they particularly differed, in Warren as in London, was on the subject of social life. Roth was becoming such a recluse that he rejoiced over the energy crisis of the late seventies, because there was very little gas: "We don't go *anywhere*," he exulted to Alvarez. "AND NOBODY

COMES HERE." As for Bloom, she was a city person who loved parties, and life in the woods was becoming, for her, a serious bummer. One of their parlor games, as a couple, was improvising dialogue whenever Roth needed to write a realistic scene between a man and a woman; in this respect, he thought, they came closest to being a latter-day Chekhov and Knipper. One day, while working on *The Ghost Writer*, he asked Bloom to describe what it was like living in the country with a writer. As she wrote in *Doll's House*, her response was used "almost verbatim" in the novel: "'We don't go anywhere! We don't do anything! We don't see anyone!' And so it went: wearing the mask of Hope Lanoff [sic], the writer's wife, I savored each moment."

Under the circumstances Roth could hardly begrudge Bloom's "precious" friendship with Francine du Plessix Gray, reassuring himself that she kept their neighbor basically in perspective. In his 1985 diary, he recorded her critique of Gray's new novel, *October Blood*, as the "work of 'a lunatic,'" and in fact Bloom often referred to the woman as Loony on returning from one of their walks, during which Gray was wont to educate her on some fine point in Ibsen's (or whoever's) work. "Francine has a wonderful way of saying stupid things with great authority," said Conarroe, who remembered walking home with Roth ("just about to explode") after a night of listening to Gray extol, say, the perspicacity of talk-show host Phil Donahue. Some observed that Roth was becoming more and more brazenly abrasive toward Gray, who, as their mutual friend Inga Larsen remarked, "was like a little child wanting to have his attention."

Back in London, meanwhile, a truce of sorts seemed to obtain, for a time, between Roth and Anna Steiger. When he was told that Anna was insecure about her writing, Roth sent her a letter "teeming with typographical errors and ungrammatical English," as Bloom remembered, and even Anna admitted that the two had had a similar sense of humor and "saw eye to eye" on "many subjects"; she also conceded that he was "very interested" in her singing and perceptive in his feedback. Indeed, many attest to Roth's heartfelt admiration for Steiger's talent. He insisted that a celebrated countertenor, Russell Oberlin, come to Guildhall to hear her perform, and Oberlin never forgot how intently both Roth and Bloom (who coached Anna about movement) watched and listened. Roth made a point of attending all her recitals, and sent flowers when she appeared at Wigmore Hall as the winner of the Richard Tauber Prize.

But in most respects their family life was still a strain. "The more I tried to make up to Anna for my past mistakes," Bloom wrote in *Doll's House*, "the more Philip resented the attention I paid her." "I was invisible," said Roth. "When I spoke at dinner Anna pointedly didn't listen, and regardless of what I may have said, Bloom didn't bother to listen either and instead, barely able to tolerate my interference, turned the conversation instantly back to Anna, flummoxed and in a panic should Anna feel insufficiently regarded." After dinner Bloom would disappear to the third floor, where she and her daughter would either listen to opera or "watch television while nestling together under the covers of Anna's bed," according to Roth, who "read alone and went to bed alone" and was either asleep or feigning sleep by the time Bloom ("still warm from snuggling Anna's body") came to bed.

While in London, at least, Roth looked forward to going out for dinner, since he was thereby spared the tensions of Fawcett Street; all too often, though, he'd arrive at the restaurant to find Anna—secretly invited by her mother—waiting for them. The same occurred when he and Bloom checked in at the Hotel de l'Université in Paris for a much anticipated visit with Milan Kundera. At dinner Kundera brought along the impressive young intellectual Alain Finkielkraut, with whom Roth would, in time, form a friendship; that first night, however, was consumed with talk about the French-speaking Anna's musical career, while the monoglot Roth sat stewing. Afterward Bloom proposed they fix her up with Finkielkraut.

Little wonder Roth spent longer and longer intervals at his Notting Hill studio, where the mini-fridge was stocked entirely with Stolichnaya vodka. Many nights he'd linger as late as eight o'clock or so, reading in his Eames chair and tippling; it was the only period in his life when he became a rather heavy drinker.

■ ■ ■ ■

ONE OF ROTH'S BEST friends in Connecticut was his physician, C. H. (Camille Henry) Huvelle, a peppy Princeton graduate who was chief of staff at nearby Charlotte Hungerford Hospital in Torrington.

Each June, on coming home for the summer, Roth would get his yearly physical from Huvelle, who was apt to declare him "fit as a fiddle"—a man in his forties, after all, who was still at his college weight. When Roth was examined in 1982, however, Huvelle found an abnormality on his EKG: The T-waves were "flipped," he said, which might be a fluke; Roth returned the next day for two more tests—one at rest, the other after running around the block—and the ominous result was confirmed. Huvelle referred him to a cardiologist at Waterbury Hospital, Victor Hurst, whereupon a thallium stress test and X-rays indicated a deadly occlusion of the left anterior descending (LAD) artery and an 80 percent occlusion of the posterior descending artery. At age forty-nine, in short, Roth was suffering from "significant" coronary artery disease—all the more disconcerting a year after his mother had died from a massive heart attack. To be sure, heart disease was rife among the Finkels, but Roth thought his own reckoning might have been delayed another ten years or so, were it not for his fateful move to Fawcett Street. In 2012— miraculously still alive, thirty years later—Roth noted: "I believe now that the strain and stress generated by my life in that household was not an insignificant cause of the sudden onset of heart disease in a healthy, vigorous, slender, temperate, well-exercised nonsmoker not yet fifty."

Dr. Hurst decided that a bypass operation was too risky, given the location of Roth's occlusions, and treated him instead with various medications, including the beta-blocker Corgard. Roth was also enjoined to alter his diet: no more red meat, chicken with skin, dairy products of any kind, eggs, salt, and so on. "Work on book as though death is imminent," Roth scribbled in his diary. "Winded walking up a rise. Will I die?" The only nondoctors he told were Bloom, Inga Larsen, his brother, the Alvarezes, and his then executors, Conarroe and Miles, whom he directed to look after Claire if he died, and to see that his trilogy was published in one volume "twelve to sixteen months after the hardcover publication of *The Anatomy Lesson*."

Another stress test, almost two months later, suggested the medications were working beyond all hope—though the beta-blocker had a most unfortunate side effect: "I couldn't accept the impotence as a permanent condition," Roth remembered. He implored the cardiologist to let him have bypass surgery and damn the risk, but the man could not condone it; Roth thought Dr. Huvelle "might understand better," but that worldly man, too, insisted that his friend's heart was the more important organ. A different beta-blocker, Lopressor, also caused impotence, and finally Roth determined to contain his disease with a regimen of diet and exercise and whatever medications were helpful but not positively lethal to his potency, which would remain a little compromised going forward: "I could override it in exciting situations," said Roth, "and I was in an exciting situation"—meaning (mostly) Inga.

Then, on May 13, 1983—almost two years to the day after Bess Roth's fatal heart attack—Bloom's mother, Alice, also succumbed to heart disease, in the back parlor of her antique shop on Walton Street, where she'd lived with her dog. "Visit C's mother," Roth had noted a few months before. "Frail from chest infection. She's sure she is dying— and she looks it. Gray." Roth was fond of the old woman: Alice, like her daughter, was curious about his experience as an American Jew, and they'd chat about suchlike matters when he happened to be in the neighborhood or when she came for dinner two or three times a month. He was at his studio when Bloom phoned him with the news, and went directly to Walton Street to join Bloom and her sister-in-law, Sheila, sitting with the body. "It took courage on his part to do this," Bloom wrote in *Doll's House*, "taking into account his inordinate fear of the dead." Alice Bloom, in fact, was his "first corpse"—duly noted in his diary—but the most macabre part was yet to come. As he remembered, "Bloom seemed strangely lighthearted while Sheila, who was ordinarily so accessible, seemed unusually constrained." Roth watched, bemused, as Bloom "stroked her mother's hair, kissed her face, fondled her hands," chatting the while, and occasionally shook one of her own hands in the air as though it were hurting her. Presently Sheila took Roth aside and explained that a man from Kenyon's funeral home had come to remove the body, and Bloom had struck him while he stood in the doorway, causing the startled man to depart.

"The following day," Roth wrote, "Bloom awakened early and hurried over to her mother's house with her embroidery." He returned to Walton Street that afternoon and found Bloom still chatting with her mother's body while she worked on her needlepoint. A man from Kenyon's stopped by to suggest that they allow one of their people to give the dead woman "an injection" if they planned to keep her at home any longer. It was dark when the embalmer arrived, carrying two large suitcases, and

Roth suggested that Bloom go home and let him deal with it. "At the request of Kenyon's embalmer," he remembered, "I helped carry Alice's body from the sofa to the middle of the floor of the darkened room on which he had laid a sheet. . . .

> He lifted Alice by the legs and I took her by the shoulders, and as we moved her I balanced her head up against my legs so that it didn't roll backward. I noticed her jewelry then and realized that if Kenyon's embalmer was preparing Alice for her funeral and cremation, the jewelry should be removed and given to Bloom. He took her ring off easily and handed it to me and then I held her head up off the floor while he unscrewed her earrings.

Once Alice had been removed, at last, to the funeral home, her daughter promptly paid her another visit. Roth stopped by on his way home from Notting Hill and found Bloom laughing and chatting as ever. "I am appalled," he recorded in handwritten notes from the time.

> How far is this going to go? . . . I think, "I'll never be able to make love to this woman again. She is killing sex forever, playing with this dead body." . . . [After returning home that evening, Bloom] Rushes right into the kitchen and in her coat without washing her hands or face begins to prepare the dinner. I cannot take anymore. "Claire, you must wash. You are grossly offending my sensibilities. I cannot take anymore of this. . . . This has become entirely morose and macabre. Your mother is a dead person. She is not a doll to play with. You must stop!"

According to Roth's notes, Bloom apologized and went upstairs to wash up, later explaining that she'd ill advisedly taken two Miltowns, a powerful sedative.

Given the whole ordeal,* Roth took a dim view of Bloom's reference in *Doll's House* to his "inordinate fear of the dead," retorting that he

---

* Roth first polished his notes about Alice's death and its aftermath for use in *Patrimony*—this while he was still married to Bloom—but on second thought held off until *Sabbath's Theater*, where the episode appears (largely unaltered) in at least a nominally fictional context.

didn't even have "an ordinary fear of the dead." This, however, was hardly true at the time. Alice's corpse was his first because he'd been "afraid" (as he admitted in notes) to view his own mother's at the funeral parlor. "Alice lying there dead from my disease," he wrote at the time. "That is the disease named on the death certificate—the same one that appears on my doctor's bills: ischaemic heart disease [i.e., coronary artery disease]. . . . I keep thinking now that my death will be soon."

B LOOM'S SPIRITS IMPROVED WHEN HER CAREER WAS
going well, so Roth continued to help where he could. After the
brief resurgence of *Brideshead Revisited*, she was in a rut again, finding
that if "she refused to do the crap," as Roth reported to Conarroe, she
didn't work at all. Casting about for more prestigious vehicles, Roth hit
on Eugenia Ginzburg's *Journey into the Whirlwind*, about the author's
long imprisonment in Stalin's gulags. He wrote a pilot script for what he
hoped would be a BBC miniseries, but when he sought permission from
Ginzburg's son, Vasily Aksyanov, the man said there was already Hollywood interest and turned him down.

Meanwhile a TV adaptation of *The Ghost Writer* had been commis-
sioned by director Tristram Powell (son of Anthony, the English novelist), and this he showed to the appalled Roth, who offered to write
it himself. "I had to," he told Stern, "or the whole thing would have
fallen through because of the fucked-up asinine job that was done by
the screenwriter, who had to be paid off, though I would gladly have
murdered him for nothing." As it happened, Powell wrote a subsequent
draft ("winnowing out stuff I wouldn't have the heart to cut myself"),
which Roth polished into final form. He also arranged for Bloom to play
the part of Hope Lonoff, putting her through the usual hectic rehearsal
paces in Connecticut, and also asking his friend Polly Hanson—the genteel Yankee who ran the office at Yaddo—to make a tape of her voice so
Bloom would have a better idea of a proper New England accent.

"I was now to be educated in the mildly agonizing art of giving your
work over to others to realize as they see fit," Roth wrote in a promotional piece for *TV Guide* ("How Could They Capture My Hero's Obsession with Anne Frank?"), which appeared a few days before the show
aired to open the third season of PBS's *American Playhouse* on January 17,

1984. In this case the "agonizing" part mostly had to do with the performance of Mark Linn-Baker as the young Nathan Zuckerman: Roth was always dissatisfied with screen portrayals of his own alter egos, as they were never "forceful" enough; for *The Ghost Writer* he'd spent two days observing the shoot in Vermont, fuming over the "cute, coy, girlish smile" that Linn-Baker flashed, as Roth saw it, after almost every utterance. Later he complained to Powell that an otherwise creditable production had been all but ruined by the actor's effeminacy ("When Lonoff says his work is full of 'turbulence,' it's a joke—how could it be?"), and got a bit of his own back in his *TV Guide* piece, pointedly noting that Nathan "must never be played *engagingly*, like some college-educated Henry Aldrich advertising boyish innocence." No less than Updike, however, singled out Linn-Baker's performance in a collegial note he wrote Roth the day after the broadcast: "I thought the young man who played Zuckerman conveyed wonderfully the deceptive baby fat of the young writer, all awkwardness and peach fuzz on the outside, all glitter and hunger within."

A few months earlier—the day, in fact, Roth had viewed a rough cut of *The Ghost Writer* at BBC headquarters in White City—he met the woman who would become his main sexual partner in London for the next few years. (Using his heart condition as a pretext, Roth had told Bloom that their relationship would have to be chaste from now on, which left him with the problem of how to conceal his morning erections: "Like a shot," he said, "I'd speed to the bathroom to pee . . . my hands all I had for a fig leaf.") Emma Smallwood,* herself a BBC employee, was preparing a program on American Jews when she first phoned Roth on Fawcett Street; "enchanted" by her lovely posh accent, Roth asked her to meet him for lunch in Covent Garden. The person attached to the accent proved to be a slender, pretty thirty-year-old with dark red hair, and Roth was struck not only by her beauty but her quietly ironical wit; after lunch he insisted she share a cab with him all the way to White City. A second lunch ensued, whereupon they learned that respective trips to New York would shortly coincide, and while in the city Emma came to his room at the Wyndham.

---

* A pseudonym.

"The rest was a devastating love affair," Roth remembered, "—devastating because she was married and had a small child and a husband she could no longer stand and I was living with Claire and Anna, equally unhappily." Emma lived near Roth's studio, and would often stop by on her way home from work; after sex on the rug or in the Eames chair, she'd sit in his lap and chat about the day's events while he listened and played with her hair and ears. ("Pause while we cry," he said in the telling of it.) Sometimes she'd bring along her two-year-old, and the little girl would also sit in Roth's lap and bang away at his typewriter. But mostly Emma came alone, and liltingly answered his many questions ("I learned everything about England from [Emma]") while he basked in the radiance of her fluency. "After her secretive visits to my studio I would feverishly try to remember and write down the most elegantly succulent of her locutions," he said, explaining how he came to create the hyperarticulate heroines of *The Counterlife* and *Deception*: "I was so possessed by memory that those lovely compound sentences just came pouring out of me in an act of mimicry and homage." When Bloom wondered about the model for the winsome Maria Freshfield in the first novel, Roth claimed she was based on Janet Hobhouse—a persuasive decoy, given the latter's accent and such details as the "deus ex machina" that had, in fact, derived from that pre-Bloom affair.

Around this time, too, he met a woman who was briefly a lover and a lifelong friend thereafter. As he mentioned to Miss Martin, he'd been reading a "remarkable biography" of Isak Dinesen ("Not horrifying at all, but hypnotic") by Judith Thurman, to whom he conveyed his admiration in a separate letter; the following month, March, he was coming to New York to deliver *The Anatomy Lesson* and celebrate his fiftieth birthday,* and perhaps Thurman would like to meet him at the Wyndham for a drink? Thurman, thrilled, replied that she happened to be "a longtime fan" (while wondering whether he was actually "Philip Roth the Indian chief, or Philip Roth the candlestick maker"). In the midst of divorcing her first husband, she wanted to make the most of this meeting with one of her favorite writers, and so consulted her Chinese therapist ("a very wise woman") as to the best way to proceed. "Ask him what his

---

* After completing his trilogy, Roth had to get his oldest Selectric repaired, and thus learned from the IBM technician that he'd worn off the "I" on the little golf ball.

sexual fantasies are," the woman advised. "*My* fantasies . . . ?" said Roth, delighted by the gambit.

"He values complicity very highly," said Thurman. "You laugh in the same places. You're well matched, there's this sort of game and no one lets go of the rope, so the tension is sort of constant." Thurman pointed out that her rapport with Roth was "hardwired," even down to a genealogical level: "We're these avian Jews from Kiev," she said, noting their spindly frames—though kindred features, and natures, in their case, never quite translated into sexual chemistry. Roth was inhibited by the beta-blocker during their first meeting at the Wyndham, and while they eventually slept together now and then, "it never really worked," said Roth, "so it dwindled off into a friendship." Thurman, for her part, would not have said "dwindled"; she found that being Roth's close friend was "preferable to being one of his women."

Not least among the benefits, for Roth, was gaining another superlative reader—as he learned when Thurman critiqued his latest manuscript. Colette's future biographer told him how Jenny would likely react to Zuckerman's gift of a thousand dollars ("What's this for?"), before blowing it on sexy expensive clothing; Roth duly altered the scene in question. She moreover congratulated him on this "admirable" line from Zuckerman (*qua* the pornographer Appel), which she called a "little bildungsroman in miniature": "'I can tell people a thousand times that I'm a serious person, but it's hard for them to take at face value when the prosecution holds up *Lickety Split* and on the cover is a white girl sucking a big black cock and simultaneously fucking a broom.'" Thurman was "a girl after my own heart," Roth replied, and promptly instructed his lawyer, Helene Kaplan, to revise his will so that Thurman was named his official biographer: "As my biographer-to-be . . . ," he'd occasionally remind her over the years.

■ ■ ■ ■

IN 1983, after six years of working on his trilogy, Roth found himself "mentally exhausted" and decided to take his first summer off since his trip to Europe in 1958. On the one hand he felt sick of writing and pondered (or pretended to ponder) other ways to fill his remaining years, while on the other he suspected he was just getting started: "As if it's all been apprentice work in some strange way," he told a *Washington Post* interviewer. "I feel I'm in charge now, in tune with my talent."

Amid such idleness he reminded George Plimpton that, twenty years ago, he (Roth) had promised to do a *Paris Review* interview at age fifty, and the time had come. Plimpton's response was immediate: "One of the reasons we have kept the magazine chugging along is so that we could get to your goddam fiftieth birthday and get that interview done!" Indeed, Roth already had an interviewer in mind. Recently he'd read a short monograph about his work by a young critic and lecturer at the University of York, Hermione Lee, who announced on the first page: "Now that he is no longer the *enfant terrible* of American-Jewish fiction, but a highly respected novelist in his middle years, it is possible to take stock of Philip Roth's achievement—of the range and quality of his work, and of his status as a 'contemporary writer.'" Roth, unused to such well-considered tenderness, wrote the author a warm note (one of the very few he'd ever write to an academic) and proposed they meet for lunch at Thompson's. As he notified Plimpton, Roth "liked her enormously," and vice versa. "There's nobody else in my life who makes me laugh so much," she said of Roth twenty-five years later, long after she'd become "Lipschitz" to him (because her father was Jewish), another first-stringer among his stable of manuscript readers.

Roth knew his *Paris Review* interview would become a touchstone for readers interested in his work and person, and approached the task with due squeamishness. Early that summer he and Lee had talked for three days at the Royal Automobile Club, and afterward she sent him the tapes and a transcript. Roth replied: "(1) I couldn't stand most of what I said, (2) the transcription wasn't always accurate"; he asked Lee to point out the interesting parts, once she received the corrected transcript, since he himself found "the sound of my own voice and what the voice is saying Yet Again boring in the fucking extreme." Lee rose to the occasion by "ruthlessly" pruning the interview from 182 to 32 pages, while striving "to keep the feel of a conversation"; Roth, in turn, acknowledged her hard work ("you've found the best of it"), while noting a little doubtfully that the whole thing would need to be "sharpened." Then he went silent for six months. When his revised copy materialized at last, it had been sharpened almost beyond recognition: "I seem to remember that I had to fight a bit to keep my questions as I had asked them," said Lee.

Roth used the interview to address some of the more galling aspects of his reputation—the most galling by far being that he was a confessional writer and hard on women. When Lee asked (or when Roth made her ask) about the relationship between the death of Zuckerman's parents and the death of his own, Roth offered to give her Herman's phone number in Elizabeth. As for the second issue: while editing their original transcript, Lee had done Roth a great favor by deleting "a shameless and unprovoked attack on a bunch of feminist midgets," as she wrote him at the time. This prompted Roth to take an opposite approach, affecting gentle mystification on the whole point: "What is it?" he asked, when Lee wondered what he made of the "feminist attack" on him:

Q: The force of the attack would be, in part, that the female characters are unsympathetically treated, for instance that Lucy Nelson in *When She Was Good* is hostilely presented.

A: Don't elevate that by calling it a "feminist" attack. That's just stupid reading.

Which led nicely, as intended, to a long explication of Lucy's more sympathetic qualities. While Roth almost certainly confected the whole exchange, or most of it, Lee could be a rigorous foil when the spirit moved her. "I think he thinks I'm more a fully paid-up conventional feminist than I think I am," she remarked in 2007, and certainly her 1982 monograph about Roth is uncommonly nuanced on the subject, conceding four (versus the usual two or three) basic female types in his fiction: "overprotective mothers," "monstrously unmanning wives," "consoling, tender, sensible girlfriends," and "recklessly libidinous sexual objects." Once, after she'd been a little too persistent in a "feminist" line of questioning during a radio interview with Roth, he phoned her at home in Yorkshire as she was about to leave for dinner with friends; his harangue went on so long that she finally had to tell her friends to go ahead without her.

"On the pendulum of self-exposure that oscillates between aggressively exhibitionistic Mailerism and sequestered Salingerism," Roth wrote in *The Facts*, "I'd say that I occupy a midway position, trying in the public arena to resist gratuitous prying or preening without making too holy a fetish of secrecy and seclusion." So important to Roth was his completed Zuckerman Trilogy, however, that he erred a little on the side of Mailerism this time, consenting to more vulgar forms of publicity than *The Paris Review*. "What happened to us?" he said to his friend Betsy Pochoda, while she accompanied him in an elevator to the studio of Irving Penn, who was shooting him for the cover of *Vanity Fair*. "We used to be so pure." "You're not getting such good reviews lately," Penn baited him, fishing for something "interesting" in Roth's face; at one point he directed his assistant to turn Roth's collar up. Afterward, back in the elevator, Roth remarked to Pochoda, "You're in charge of making sure that the shot with my collar up does not appear." He drew the line at a *Playboy* interview and also canceled a feature article in *People* ("temporary madness") before reconsidering at his publisher's request. "Portnoy's Creator Would Like It Known," read the *People* subhead, "His Books Are Novels, Not Confessionals"; Roth "stiffens visibly" when asked about personal matters, noted the *People* reporter, who then enumerated a few ("his unhappy early marriage," etc.) that Roth had chosen not to discuss.

■　■　■　■

THE ANATOMY LESSON had given Roth fits, and its fairly brutal reception was even more demoralizing after he'd done his little-all to flog it. By publication day, in early November, he'd seen enough: "I'll be glad to be getting out of here," he wrote Tumin. "I don't mind having to write the fucking books, but I'll be God damned if I'm going to stand here being insulted." One friend and steady reader had assured him that he liked *The Anatomy Lesson*, and when Roth heard that this same friend had belittled the book behind his back, he treated him to a particularly blistering phone call, then took a full three years to apologize: "Say whatever the hell you want to say about my books," he finally wrote the man, "—it's not Czechoslovakia."

"Best of luck," a well-wisher had remarked to Roth, "and I hope you get Michiko Kakutani instead of Chris Lehmann-Haupt." Kakutani would go on to review many Roth books for *The New York Times*, but for now he was back in the hands of the reliably ambivalent Lehmann-Haupt, who began his review by applauding Roth's "rich, satisfyingly complex conclusion to his Zuckerman trilogy" but was behooved, at last, to condemn the hero's "endless self-absorption and scab-picking." The latter view would prove all but unanimous. Zeroing in on the Howe/Appel subplot, *Commentary* enlisted a stalwart hit man, Joseph Epstein, to bash the novel as "a *roman* of clay. . . . A character who is having love affairs with four women and wishes to get his own back at a literary critic—this is not . . . exactly a figure of universal significance." Even Updike, in *The New Yorker*, was unable to sustain a somewhat strained enthusiasm for Roth's ever increasing "expertness" in handling "by now highly polished themes," admitting that *The Anatomy Lesson* was "the least successful" of the trilogy: "Zuckerman's babyish reduction of all women to mere suppliers eclipses much of Roth's engaging characterization of the mistresses, who are each set before us never to appear again." This, coming from Updike, had to hurt.

In *The Anatomy Lesson*, Roth described a phenomenon with which he would become even more intimately familiar in the years ahead: "The job was to give pain its due while at the same time rendering accurately the devastation it wreaks upon reason, dignity, pride, maturity, independence—upon all of one's human credentials." That Zuckerman supports his aching neck with a thesaurus his father gave him as a boy ("From Dad—you have my every confidence") would suggest the pain is "felt at a distance from its source," as the book's epigraph from the *Textbook of Orthopedic Medicine* would have it, and never mind the hero's impotence as a writer ever since his father, on his deathbed, called him a bastard. But then, such an explanation is too pat for a writer of Zuckerman's subtlety, and he wonders whether he's actually being tortured by the terrible, life-denying requirements of his vocation per se. Martin Amis's quip about Roth's morbid reflexiveness—reduced to writing an "autobiographical novel about what it's like to write autobiographical novels"—applies far more to *The Anatomy Lesson* than its predecessor. Zuckerman wishes he could write about someone who really suffers, like his Polish lover, Jaga—"the world of massive historical pain instead of this pain in the neck"—but realizes he could hardly be a writer at all without the subject of his own "semi-comical" suffering, such as it is. "My life as cud, that's what I'm running out on," he tells a doctor friend, explaining why he wants to go to medical school both as relief and atonement. "Swallow as experience, then up from the gut for a second go as art. . . . too much inward-dwelling, Bob, too much burrowing back."

But why atone for what he'd coughed up from his gut? "If he agreed with the Appels and their admonitions, he wouldn't have written those books in the first place." Zuckerman likes to believe he's squeezed the Nice Jewish Boy out of himself drop by drop, while at bottom he's almost as apt to appease his detractors as revolt against them (a dialectic that also defined his high-minded, impious creator): "Zuckerman is all *too* conscious of what he's up to, as M.D. and as porno king," Roth explained to Updike: "willed extremism at either end of the moral spectrum. My theme, son." Disgusted, on one level, by his penitent journey to Chicago and (maybe) medical school, Zuckerman adopts the identity of his sternest critic and turns him into the zany, debauched publisher of *Lickety Split* ("Je m'appelle Appel"), whose aria of obscenity ends only when he cracks his jaw against a gravestone. (Roth was thinking of another reproachful elder, Rabbi Rackman, who'd demanded of the Anti-Defamation League, "What is being done to silence this man?" "And that's why I broke Zuckerman's jaw," said Roth. "I did it for the rabbi.") Gagged at last, Zuckerman gets outside of himself long enough to focus on the suffering of others—a woman at the hospital, for instance, whose face is half-eaten by cancer:

> There was a hole in her cheek the size of a quarter. Through it Zuckerman could see her tongue as it nervously skittered about inside her mouth. The jawbone itself was partially exposed, an inch of it as white and clean as enamel tile. The rest, up to the eye socket, was a chunk of raw flesh, something off the butcher's floor to cut up for the cat. He tried not to inhale the smell. . . . *This is life. With real teeth in it.*

Roth liked this ending so much that he again discarded/tabled a previous ending, set in Prague, which he'd always envisaged as the proper conclusion to Zuckerman's education in "the unforeseen consequences of art." The first three books had examined the writer's life in a land where "everything goes and nothing matters," a phrase Roth invoked in *The Paris Review* as having defined every aspect of his own career. Asked about his influence on "the culture," Roth replied it was roughly what it would have been if he'd followed his original plan to be a lawyer: "In an enormous commercial society that demands complete freedom of expression, the culture is a maw." He moreover insisted that he was content to have it so, rather than embrace the alternative evoked in *The Prague Orgy*—his novella-length epilogue, published in *Zuckerman Bound*, that was meant to serve as "a lamp that shined backwards": from Czechoslovakia, where writers who aspire to cultural relevance are grievously punished—banned, jailed, exiled, forced into menial jobs—while, in the West, Zuckerman is "profusely" and "bizarrely" rewarded for writing a dirty book.

Thus Zuckerman's "dwarf drama" is put into final perspective—a matter made even more explicit in the screen version of *The Prague Orgy* that Roth was soon to write, wherein the Klíma/Kundera composite, Bolotka, mocks Zuckerman for his sheepish wish to make amends: "So why are you here? To play a 'worthwhile' role? To do a little, tiny penance for being spared the twentieth century?" At the museum where he works as a janitor, Bolotka leads the American into a storage room and invites him to swap clothing. "Now *I* will be the free man with a troubled conscience," Bolotka giddily declares, once Zuckerman is wearing the man's overalls. Meanwhile the regime rewards only such hacks as the culture minister, Novak, who's aghast to learn that his favorite American book, Betsy MacDonald's *The Egg and I*, has been all but forgotten in the decadent West. Again the vast disparity between the two worlds lends itself to cinematic treatment: Zuckerman returns to the "dense, enormous" freedom of New York—shown with a helicopter shot along the Hudson—while in voice-over "NOVAK describes small, imprisoned Czechoslovakia," where only philistines like himself may thrive: *"people who know how to submit decently to their historical misfortune! These* are the people to whom we owe the survival of our beloved land, and not to alienated, degenerate, egomaniacal artistes!"*

When *Zuckerman Bound* was published in May 1985, Roth prepared to lie low in Connecticut and thus avoid the "ritual slaughter" of the reviews, while allowing himself to hope that the "thematic architecture"

---

* Roth adapted *The Prague Orgy* as another vehicle for Bloom, who was to play Eva, the exiled Czech actress. Christopher Morahan (*The Jewel in the Crown*) was slated to direct in Vienna, but the small budget couldn't be reconciled with such crucial effects as the climactic helicopter shot. Roth was rightly proud of his screenplay, and included it in his Library of America edition. An English-language Czech adaptation of the novella, written and directed by Irena Pavlásková, was released in 2019.

of the novels would become more apparent once they were published in a single volume—a hope amply rewarded by Harold Bloom's definitive front-page rave in the *Times Book Review*: "*Zuckerman Bound* merits something reasonably close to the highest level of esthetic praise for tragicomedy, partly because as a formal totality it becomes much more than the sum of its parts," the Yale mandarin wrote. "Roth has earned a permanent place in American literature by a comic genius that need never be doubted again, wherever it chooses to take him next." Roth was becoming harder for the cultural maw to devour.

∎ ∎ ∎ ∎

EVER SINCE FINISHING his trilogy and epilogue, Roth had felt a growing desire to "sink [his] teeth into something new and BIG," though months passed while he did little more than stare at his Selectric. When Bloom was invited to perform at the Jerusalem Festival in late May 1984, Roth was eager for a change of scenery, even if it meant playing Stage Door Johnny again. Ever the dutiful student, he asked a knowledgeable friend to recommend books about modern Israel and Zionism generally.

They stayed at Mishkenot Sha'ananim ("Peaceful Dwellings"), a row of guesthouses provided by the city for visiting academics and artists, just outside the walls of Old Jerusalem. It was Roth's first trip to Israel since the summer of 1963, and he looked up old friends such as Amos Elon, the prominent left-wing journalist who wrote for *Haaretz* and *The New York Review of Books*. Through Elon he met luminaries like Shimon Peres, soon to be prime minister, whom Roth liked but was advised, by Elon, not to trust ("I don't have to trust or not trust anyone," Roth wrote Malamud, "—I just mostly listen"). Roth also gave an interview to the *Mishkenot Sha'ananim Newsletter*, as a courtesy to his hosts, though he'd declined to meet with other members of the Israeli press. "He has been called the Woody Allen of words and the Meyer Lansky of Jewish culture," Idith Zertal introduced him to newsletter readers. "He is said to be ready to sell his heritage for a few laughs. . . . This man, whose most intimate habits, whose darkest fancies, are supposedly familiar to millions of people, has become one of the most private public figures in the United States." Zertal seemed determined to make the most of things, though her peculiar truculence seemed almost to have a mellowing effect on Roth. "That goy?" she said, when Roth mentioned Updike in passing.

"I mean Updike, the American writer," he replied. "He's one of my contemporaries and I'm very interested in what he does too."

Roth detected a kind of "pressure" in Jerusalem that he hadn't felt since
Prague, and was eager to learn more. Equipped with "a list a yard long
of people to look up," he returned a few months later with David Plante,
whom he introduced as Claire Bloom at a pompous party. Privately he
told his friend ("just between you and your diary") that he needed to
know what a gentile like Plante made of things: Roth had started a novel
with a (provisionally) gentile character, and he wanted this character to
meet a few narrow-minded Israeli "fanatics" on the right, the ones who
wanted to annex the West Bank through violent means, if necessary,
versus the "fair minded, intelligent, humanist, cultured" liberals whom
Roth already knew in sufficient number.

The next day Roth informed Plante that they'd have to pay extra for
a taxi because of the danger involved in driving to Ofra, a West Bank
settlement whose Arab residents had been known to stone cars and the
Jews inside them. Roth had arranged to meet Israel Harel, a settlement
leader who glibly insisted the occupiers enjoyed good relations with the
local Arabs. "All Philip said in reaction, again and again," Plante noted,
"was, 'Ah-hun, ah-hun.'" Afterward Harel and an American woman
showed the two writers around the settlement: the kindergarten, print
shop, and a group of older students sitting around a table. Referring
to the West Bank as Judea and Samaria—lands rightfully belonging to
Israel, according to the Bible—a brash young man asked Roth what *he*
thought of the settlements. Roth smiled: "I have to tell you that everything that has to do with this country is peripheral to my real interests.
I'm here because I'm curious." A couple of days later, he met an even
more invaluable "treasure," the right-wing lawyer Elyakim Haetzni, who
packed a revolver while driving Roth around the Arab city of Hebron
and the huge Jewish settlement of Kiryat Abba; Haetzni's colorful pon-
tifications would be reproduced at length in *The Counterlife*, where he
appears as the aptly named Lippman. That night Roth and Plante had
dinner *chez* Amos Elon. A staunch advocate of Palestinian statehood
and total withdrawal from the occupied territories, Elon became furious
when Plante remarked that he'd been "impressed" by Harel: "He told
me it was as if I had been impressed by Himmler," Plante wrote in his
diary. "Israel Harel was a criminal. He was the chairman of a movement

that shot off the kneecaps of Arab leaders, threw bombs into bus loads of innocent Arab children, wanted to dispossess Arabs of their land and homes." Plante got the impression Elon's anger was really directed at Roth, whom he sternly lectured, alone, in a separate room after dinner.

Israel had changed since the wars of 1967 and 1973. "It wasn't Israel as California anymore," said Roth. "It was Israel as the Middle East, and all that people could talk about was politics." At the heart of the debate were the compromises of nationalism—the violence and injustice involved in countering enemies on all sides, and within, which seemed essential to the maintenance of the Jewish state even as it bristled against the Jewish conscience, not to say the world's, what with its readiness to condemn Jewish moral imperfection. "I was getting it from all sides in Israel," said Roth, "which was the best thing that could have happened."

When he returned to Israel yet again in February 1985, he spent much of his time with the novelist Aharon Appelfeld—a small, bald, round-faced man with "the playfully thoughtful air of a benign wizard," as Roth put it; the two had met at a London literary party a few years before, and liked each other immediately. Appelfeld's harrowing childhood in the midst of the Holocaust, Roth liked to say, could scarcely have been more at odds with his own sheltered idyll in Weequahic. Appelfeld's mother had been murdered by the Romanian army in 1941, when Aharon was eight, and eventually the boy escaped from a concentration camp in Transnistria and spent three years on the run—hiding in the woods, working as a shepherd, all the while concealing his Jewishness; finally he joined the Soviet army as a cook, and subsequently immigrated to Palestine. Roth would spend hours discussing "the sum of all these Jewish *antinomies*" with the author of *Badenheim 1939*, either at a pleasant café where Appelfeld went each day to write, the Ticho House, or during long walks all over Jerusalem.

Once again Roth had found a place where "everything matters," and suddenly "the bits and pieces of crap" he'd managed to write over the past year began, he said, "to flash signals and to arrange themselves in little constellations and I think I may be on the brink of an idea that won't bore me." He began to think of Israel and England as counterimages—the West Bank and Gloucestershire, Jerusalem and London—with opposing notions of Jewish assertiveness and self-hatred. Appelfeld had much to say about the latter, "an ancient Jewish ailment which in modern times has taken on various guises," as he remarked in a *New York Times* interview with Roth: "I grew up with the feeling that anything Jewish was blemished. From my earliest childhood my gaze was directed at the beauty of non-Jews. They were blond and tall and behaved naturally." Roundly accused of self-hatred for much of his career, Roth had witnessed the phenomenon at close range in London—embodied most vividly by his "Good Fairy," as Idith Zertal had described Bloom during the couple's first and last trip to Israel together. Exposed to an alarming mass of Jews at a bus station in Jerusalem, Bloom had been moved to comment on their "hideous faces." As Roth remembered: "'If we were in Italy, if we were in Greece,' she told me, 'the people are beautiful there!' I promised then to take her to the swarming bus stations of Naples and Genoa and Athens and Salonika, where she could gaze undisturbed upon all the undisgusting faces jamming those Italian and Greek buses." The "nasty, hateful scene" ended with Bloom in tears: "Don't you see—it's a sickness," she sobbed.

Hitherto Roth had been somewhat stymied in his attempts to write about England, since, as he put it, he didn't hate anything there: "a writer *has* to be driven crazy to help him to *see*." Now, almost everywhere he looked, he saw evidence of English anti-Semitism. He'd almost forgotten an incident several years ago, during his trip abroad with Ann Mudge, when a dowager at the Connaught had been so affronted by the sight of a lovely blonde woman dining with a Jew that she'd loudly complained about the "stink" while glaring in Roth's direction. He was reminded of this, dining with Bloom, when he heard a woman regale her companion (and indirectly Roth) about "a disgusting little Jew" who'd sold her a ring and "naturally" cheated her; she kept repeating the words "little Jew" until (over Bloom's mortified protests) Roth approached her table and called her a scumbag. In the hope of provoking such people all the more, he grew a beard that augmented his already conspicuously Semitic features*—and sure enough, as he remarked to Julian Mitchell, when he went to the loo at the Royal Automobile Club nowadays, he

---

* Thus he made a Hitchcockian cameo in *The Counterlife* (at Zuckerman's funeral) as a "bearded man of about fifty, a tall, thin man wearing gold-rimmed bifocals and a grey hat, looking from the conservative cut of his clothes as though he might be a broker—or perhaps even a rabbi."

sensed the scrutiny of fellow members who looked to see whether he was circumcised ("this may have been a joke," said Mitchell, "but I don't think it was").

Back in 1970, Roth had written Mitchell that his agonies over what would eventually become *My Life as a Man* had forced him into "being 'experimental,' which is only to say that I don't know where I am, and am so sick of fiction, and every fifty pages see through the fictional disguises, and so drop what I'm doing and start out a new way . . . and so I've decided that that's my book, those fifty pages of transparency piled atop one another. A grim business." The process had resolved itself in his using only the two notional beginnings—"Salad Days" and "Courting Disaster"—before getting on with his hero's "True Story"; now, in the early stages of *The Counterlife*, he found himself again writing a series of "false starts" that suddenly began to cohere like filings to a magnet. "I wrote one section and then I thought, 'What if the opposite happened?'"—and one such opposite was a chance to kill off Zuckerman: a nice way to silence critics who said he always wrote about his own experience ("Now I only hope I don't kick off before the book comes out," he told the *Times*, "—otherwise the wisdom will be that I based Zuckerman's funeral on my own"). When Susan Sontag later congratulated him on the "meta-narrative" of *The Counterlife*, Roth assured her he had no such aesthetic theory in mind, but rather was simply receptive to "the authority of dreams, in which characters who appear to be the same, are at least called XYZ in one dream after another, turn up dead and then alive and then turn out to be 'oneself,' etc." He was, in short, *trusting his confusion*—a directive that would stand him in good stead as his work continued to evolve in startling ways.

■ ■ ■ ■

IN AUGUST 1982, shortly after his own diagnosis of heart disease, Roth had visited Malamud while the man was recuperating from a stroke and bypass surgery: "Real to me now," Roth wrote in his notes. "Looks weak and vulnerable. Listing a little to one side." However diminished, Malamud impressed Roth with his determination to get on with his work, though he could hardly read at the time. "You have written wonderful books and you have been a kind, brave, and generous colleague—even when vexed," Roth wrote him afterward, with seeming contrition.

What had vexed Malamud foremost was Roth's essay "Imagining Jews," in the September 29, 1974, issue of *The New York Review of Books*, which had compared Roth's own work with that of his eminent Jewish rivals, Bellow and Malamud—the Hart, Schaffner, and Marx of American letters, as Bellow wryly dubbed the three of them. Roth admired Malamud and felt the usual filial stirrings (albeit faintly at times), but Bellow was his idol and would later become a good friend as well, a preference grounded in both personal and aesthetic affinity. Back in 1966, during his WNET interview with Jerre Mangione, Roth had commended Bellow for "knock[ing] off the reverence and piety" so common among Jewish writers of the time—and later, in 1999, a taped discussion between Bellow and Roth made it clear whose piety they found especially grating. "And Malamud," Roth remarked, "the great appeal Malamud had was he had the gentle, broken Jews."

BELLOW: Shtetl schtick adapted to the U.S.A.
ROTH: That's right, with all the sentimental baggage that comes with
    it. . . . And [Irving] Howe, who I loathed. . . .
BELLOW: He was a jerk.
ROTH: He was a big liar, and he's Saint Irving.

Roth's remarks capture something of the spirit that went into "Imagining Jews"; conceived as a rebuttal to Howe's exhaustive attack on Roth's work and *Portnoy* in particular, the essay took a long and sometimes invidious excursion through the oeuvres of Hart and Schaffner. Roth noted that, in Bellow's work, "almost invariably his heroes are Jewish in vivid and emphatic ways when they are actors in dramas of conscience"—e.g., the protagonist of *The Victim*, Asa Leventhal, who feels a morbid sense of responsibility for the parasitic Allbee. In *Henderson the Rain King*, however, the "hoggish and greedy hero" is a kind of anti-Jew who expresses his voracious appetites with the simple phrase "I want!" "In a Bellow novel," said Roth, "only a goy can talk like that and get away with it."

Roth then argued that the same tendencies are so schematic in Malamud's work that it amounts to a kind of "moral allegory" in which "the Jew is innocent, passive, virtuous," whereas the gentile is "corrupt, violent, and lustful." Roth cited *The Assistant* as a typical product of Malamud's "essentially folkloric and didactic" imagination—thus the suffering but decent Jewish grocer, Morris Bober, helps his Italian assistant, Frank Alpine, find redemption despite the man's many transgressions. Such remarks were liable to vex Malamud, to be sure, but he would take sterner exception to what Roth had to say about his novel *The Fixer* ("I have never admired your work more," Roth had written him in 1966, after reading galleys, "and I have admired it plenty"). Based on an actual episode in czarist Russia, the innocent, passive Jew in this case is Bok, who is jailed and tortured on suspicion of murdering a Christian boy during Passover; Malamud's Jew suffers so luridly (if virtuously) that Roth likened the novel to the work of the Marquis de Sade and "the pseudonymous author of *The Story of O*."

Having compared Bellow and Malamud to the latter's disadvantage, Roth went on to suggest that he himself had transcended, with *Portnoy*, the outworn notion of the Jew as an "alienated, hypersensitive Victim." Roth's sense of his own place in the scheme of things was the same as Zuckerman's in *The Ghost Writer*: "when I came upon Babel's description of the Jewish writer as a man with autumn in his heart and spectacles on his nose, I had been inspired to add, 'and blood in his penis,' and had then recorded the words like a challenge—a flaming Dedalian formula to ignite *my* soul's smithy." Unlike Bellow, and certainly unlike Malamud, Roth didn't feel obliged to make his lustful hero a goy, even though his portrait of a "Jew as sexual defiler" had brought the likes of Howe and Podhoretz roaring out of the woodwork, and never mind Marie Syrkin, who'd lumped him with Goebbels and Streicher. "Had she not been constrained by limitations of space," Roth wrote of the angry Zionist's letter to *Commentary*, "Syrkin might eventually have had me in the dock with the entire roster of Nuremberg defenders."

"I was highly entertained by your piece in the *New York Review*," wrote Bellow, who'd once groused about a general perception of himself as "a Bad Guy Jew" versus Malamud's "Good Guy Jew." "I didn't quite agree—that's too much to expect—but I shall slowly think over what you said." Roth was gratified and said so; meanwhile he warned Malamud about the piece: "I don't know what you'll make of my approach, but hope that in the long run (not to mention the short) it will add to our consciousness of what we've been writing and are yet to write." In a controversial tribute he would publish a few weeks after Malamud's death,

Roth characterized his colleague's subsequent note as having consisted of a single "terse and colloquial" sentence: What Roth had written in "Imagining Jews," said Malamud, "is your problem, not mine."

In fact, Malamud had considered saying more, and had carefully set aside previous drafts of his letter for posterity. "I wish I could say Roth is looking after his friend Malamud but I can't," the first draft began. Striking out a too-magnanimous bit about Roth's "brilliance of polemic," Malamud noted "errors of omission and commission, oversimplification, and distortion," concluding: "As they say, 'who needs enemies' if they have such friends." In another draft, he tried to be more definite about Roth's errors, pointing out that certain details of torture in *The Fixer*, for instance, came from research on the real-life case of Menahem Mendel Beilis: "If I make the scene of their torture violent I do so as an artist. To say I do it as a pornographer or sadist diminishes you in the eyes of anyone who reads and understands the book." On final reflection, however, the scrupulous man decided he didn't owe Roth such a measured response, hence the note he actually mailed: "When a man who can read, so badly misinterprets another writer's work and motives in justification of his own, he has a problem. I now seriously doubt that you can discuss me or my work with complete honesty. That's your problem."

Not a further word passed between the two for almost four years—until a night in London, when the Malamuds came to Fawcett Street for a conciliatory dinner. As Roth wrote in his posthumous tribute, he gave Ann Malamud a welcoming buss at the door, then "plunged" toward her husband with outstretched hand: "In our eagerness to be the first to forgive—or perhaps to be forgiven—we wound up overshooting the handshake and kissing on the lips, rather like the poor baker Lieb and the even less fortunate Kobotsky at the conclusion of 'The Loan.'"*

Their final meeting, on July 10, 1985, was less successful. Roth and Bloom drove up to Bennington for lunch, and Roth found his friend "a frail and very sick old man, his tenacity used up." Still, Malamud had managed to start a new novel, and after lunch he offered to read a few chapters aloud to his guests. "Listening to what he read," Roth wrote,

---

* In Malamud's story, Kobotsky comes to his old friend Lieb after a long estrangement and begs a loan of two hundred dollars for his wife's gravestone. Lieb's wife forbids it, but the two men are nonetheless reconciled with a kiss before parting forever.

"was like being led into a dark hole to see by torchlight the first Malamud story ever scratched upon a cave wall." When the reading was over, Roth ventured to say that it seemed to open slowly, and wondered where the story was heading. "What's next isn't the point," said Malamud, quietly furious. Afterward Roth asked Bloom whether he'd been too harsh, and Bloom assured him he had; Roth could only answer, as ever, that he was compelled to be honest when a fellow writer asked his opinion.

Malamud died of a heart attack eight months later, and Roth promptly phoned the editor of *The New York Times Book Review*, Mitchel Levitas, asking if he could write a commemorative piece. Given a tight deadline, Roth reread five of Malamud's books in a week, then produced a sometimes touching but starkly candid eulogy tracing their friendship from that not very auspicious meeting in Oregon (when Malamud had walked into the closet) to that final dreary lunch in Bennington. "Was much moved by your piece on Malamud in the *Times*," Bellow wrote. "You saw him at first as an insurance agent." (This referred to Roth's impression of the prosaic man on meeting him in Oregon.) "I privately thought of him as a CPA. But I have a secret weakness for the hidden dimensions of agents and CPAs." Meanwhile, in his diary, Alfred Kazin noted something a little gleeful and nasty about the piece—that it reflected Roth's "bouncy sense of his own success, his constant keeping of the score on other novelists (especially Joosh [Jewish] ones), turned Malamud the sage father etc. into the ragged failure."

Certainly that was the widow's opinion. "Bern would have found your article humiliating," she explained to Roth, since he'd asked; "if you cannot understand that, it is pointless for me to explain why. I must add that I am one of many who reacted with anger." With perhaps understandable chagrin, Roth asked her whether she believed he'd deliberately set out to humiliate her husband, "or whether you think I did it out of blind stupidity, wholly unaware of what I was saying. Does either really make sense to you?" He pointed out that "numerous" intelligent and sensitive people (Bellow, after all) "expressed a rather different reaction."

Some twenty-five years later, Roth wrote a heartfelt endorsement of Malamud's Library of America edition: "To me, as a young writer of the next generation starting out in the 1950s—and trying to lay claim to my own Jewish material—his fiction, along with Bellow's, meant the world." To that other writer who meant the world, however, Roth complained not only that Malamud had been too pious, but also that he'd "surrounded himself by real dopes" like a certain *Times* reviewer: "Now it's one thing if you entertain him for opportunistic reasons—get him a girl, get him a blowjob, get him a dinner—maybe he'll give you a good review. But to entertain him for the pleasure of having Christopher Lehmann-Haupt in your house?"

Thirty-Four

I N THE SUMMER OF 1983, WHILE NERVOUSLY AWAITING publication of *The Anatomy Lesson*, Roth met Ross Miller at their friend Philip Grausman's house in Litchfield County. The thirty-seven-year-old Miller was an English professor at the University of Connecticut in Storrs—a little over an hour's drive from Warren—and a year after their first meeting, he wrote Roth a letter praising *The Anatomy Lesson*, which he'd found "emotionally real"; he proceeded to explain what the book was about ("self-reconstruction") and assured the author that he valued it enormously. Starved for kind words of whatever sort about the maligned conclusion to his Zuckerman Trilogy, Roth promptly invited Miller to Warren so they could get better acquainted.

Roth learned that Ross was the son of Arthur Miller's older brother, Kermit, a decorated veteran of World War II who'd dropped out of college to work in his father's carpet business—this while Arthur distanced himself from the family, finished college, became a world-famous playwright and his parents' hero. Some say Kermit was the model for Victor Franz, the angry brother in Arthur's *The Price*, whose sacrifice on his family's behalf had made his brother's "whole life possible," as Victor saw it, and "strangled" his own. "Kermit was the second banana to Arthur," said Roth, "and then Ross picked up all his resentment against Arthur. Tremendous resentment." Ross, for his part, claimed it was Arthur who "carried the sibling rivalry right to his grave," whereas his honorable war-hero father was "contemptuous" of Arthur, "a fabricator" who once told Bellow (said Ross) an outlandish story about how Kermit had invented the electric car.

Roth's friendship with Ross was sealed when he canvassed the younger man's opinion of an early draft of *The Counterlife*. Ross scribbled "a pile of notes on every page," then phoned Roth and said, "I have bad news.

There's a good book in here somewhere." The two subsequently met in Roth's studio and talked for some thirteen hours; as Miller liked to say ever after, "I'd never talked to anybody this long and intense and didn't get laid." ("The funniest thing I ever heard him say," said Roth, who added: "I don't think it's true.") "His intelligence is precise and he knows how to elicit precision from an interlocutor or adversary," Roth wrote of Miller in one of his recommendation letters. "He is a writer and a teacher of enormous seriousness—and, for the record, a most loyal and devoted friend." Indeed, Miller became Roth's steadiest companion amid the increasing loneliness of Connecticut. Both men were unhappy with their mates, and found solace in long literary dinners at the Hopkins Inn, on Lake Waramaug, or in watching baseball and chatting about women.

■ ■ ■ ■

ROTH HAD ANOTHER marathon session over *The Counterlife* with his editor, David Rieff, who came to the Wyndham Hotel one afternoon in February 1986 and listened to Roth read the fourth draft aloud to him, word for word, for almost nine hours. Whenever Rieff heard something that was slightly off ("ambiguous, cheap, whatever," said Roth) he would speak up; otherwise he kept silent, and never once, it seemed to Roth, made an idle remark. It was a profound and delightful experience for both men, and later Roth was struck by how strong Rieff's influence had been on his thinking, from start to finish, while he wrote the book: "There's something there in the sustained intellectual energy that derives from my sense of your appetite for that kind of stuff. So I am grateful, maybe even more than you can know."

For once Roth was wholly satisfied with his work ("I gave it my all"), though he dreaded the usual misreadings. Of course he knew he'd be labeled "experimental" and "postmodern" and so forth—both disparagingly and not—and was already impatient toward such reduction. *The Counterlife* proposed alternative possibilities, and its discrete episodes were not linked in a causal way, but otherwise the book was a scrupulously realistic meditation ("no phantasmagoria, no surrealism") on what makes for a meaningful life, touching on all of Roth's great concerns. "These flesh-and-blood talkers coming apart in your hands, turning into rack and mist, letters of the alphabet!" Cynthia Ozick, an early reader, enthused. "What an imagining, what art, what schemings, what wizardry, what a piece of work!"

Lehmann-Haupt described the novel as "experimental" in his first sentence, and wondered how the reader could take seriously, say, the crazy anti-Semitic ravings of Maria Freshfield's sister—since, after all, she and other characters were merely whimsical figments of Roth's imagination, and the opposite could happen in some other chapter. "Apparently not yet recovered from the shock of having his earlier novels, especially *Portnoy's Complaint*, taken literally by the American reading public, Mr. Roth is determined to prove in as many ways as possible that autobiographical fiction, no matter how seemingly personal, is not the same thing as confession." ("To my father at eighty-five," the novel's dedication reads, establishing yet again that Roth's father, unlike Zuckerman's, is still alive.) More happily, William Gass (with some atonement, perhaps, for his caustic treatment of *The Great American Novel*) called the book "magnificent" and "a triumph" in the Sunday *Times*.

"Radical change is the law of life," Roth had written in his notes for *The Counterlife*, which he considered "very much a work by a middle-aged writer" given that "ideas of renewal and the possibility of change are a kind of leitmotif of middle age." Zuckerman's brother, Henry, an ostensibly well-adjusted dentist and family man, finds himself in such a dismal rut that he plumps for life-threatening bypass surgery rather than suffer the impotence caused by a beta-blocker and thus deprive himself of his assistant Wendy's blow jobs. Nathan, to whom Henry confides his dilemma, is rueful but only too comprehending when his brother does in fact die for the sake of a little "juicy pleasure": "It was your drop of theatrical existence, your disorder, your escapade, your risk, your little daily insurrection against all your overwhelming virtues—debauching Wendy for twenty minutes a day, then home at night for the temporal satisfactions of ordinary family life." Or so Nathan imagines at least one version of his dull-seeming brother's life—an "irresponsible exaggeration," as Henry himself considers it, when he raids his brother's study in a subsequent chapter, "Gloucestershire," and finds a manuscript much like the novel we're reading. In "Gloucestershire," Nathan is the one who dies from a risky bypass ("*He*, not me, would never accept the limits," the indignant Henry reflects, "—*he*, not me, was the fool who died for a fuck"), whereupon Henry attends his funeral and endures a eulogy praising the "exploitative aspects of *Carnovsky*," the book that made such a mockery of Jewish virtue and destroyed their family. Afterward, while rifling his brother's manuscripts, Henry discovers various drafts of that same eulogy—"all of it, text and corrections, in no one's hand but Nathan's" (a task one can easily imagine Roth undertaking on his own posthumous behalf)—as well as the present novel's second chapter, "Judea," in which Henry, to his horror, finds himself "brought back from the dead for a second drubbing."

"We are all writing fictitious versions of our lives all the time," said Roth, "contradictory but mutually entangling stories that, however subtly or grossly falsified, constitute our hold on reality and are the closest thing we have to the truth." Nathan Zuckerman—who once overheard the staid Lonoff mimicking Jimmy Durante for a fetching young mistress—knows that everyday life has a way of outstripping even the grossest falsifications. Thus, in "Judea," his brother Henry survives his bypass operation and heads to Israel, where he recovers his potency, in every sense, with a momentous epiphany: "I am nothing, I have never been *anything*, the way that I am this Jew." Reinventing himself as a pistol-packing settler on the West Bank, Henry abandons the self-absorbed pettiness of his old life—his willingness to risk death for a blow job—and joins the great history-changing project of his leader, Mordecai Lippman.

Israel then is the embodiment of Roth's theme of reversal and change—a nation of Jews tending to aggression and vengeance—and hence the Israel chapters, with their emphasis on politics and history, are regarded by some as a milestone in Roth's work. "It was as if he regained the world as a subject," said Solotaroff. "He started going back to the past with a purpose beyond 'Let's see what it was like when I was thirty.'" Of course the process was well under way with *The Prague Orgy*, though Updike, for one, thought both works were a little too mechanically polemical—"The conversations deteriorate into blocks of *talk*, one babbled essay after another"—a defect that would if anything become more pronounced until, finally, in certain parts of the American Trilogy, rival viewpoints are more seamlessly subsumed into the narrative. Meanwhile, in *The Counterlife*, Roth occasionally sacrificed plausibility for the sake of getting his ideas across—as when an Israeli security goon, a self-described "grease monkey," indulges in erudite historical analysis and literary allusion ("Who's the little Jew with a cigar in T. S. Eliot's wonderful poem?") while lecturing Nathan on "the universal loathing of the Jewish id, and the goy's half-hidden, justifiable fear of wild, belated Jewish justice."

Back in Christendom, Nathan falls in love with his dream shiksa, Maria Freshfield, but the idyll ends when he can't help sweeping her up in a blanket indictment of her family's—and England's—ineradicable anti-Semitism. In the crypt of a Gloucestershire church, Maria's older sister elaborates the nature of her mother's sordid misgivings where his union with Maria is concerned: "I don't think she really likes the idea of her languid, helpless Maria submitting to anal domination by a Jew." Just as Henry discovers his brother's fictionalized versions of his life, so Maria reads the manuscript of "Christendom" and is repelled by its monstrous distortion of what she'd once told Nathan was her mother's "touch of anti-Semitism." Aghast at such a hateful narrative, Maria decides to quit the marriage and indeed the novel itself.

And on this "coyly Pirandelloian" (Updike) point, Lehmann-Haupt was hardly alone in throwing up his hands. "A character in a book within a book deciding to take no further part in the narrative?" wrote Julian Barnes in the *London Review of Books*. "Not far from here lies preciosity, and perhaps there is a thinning of our interest as overt fictionality stomps on imagined life." But again, as Roth would have it, truth is what our imaginations make and remake of it, and whatever odious thing Nathan sees fit to make of Maria's family, in the context of art, is a valid extension of the England he comes to know. As for Maria herself, he (Roth) congratulated himself on having created "the most intelligent woman in American literature since Isabel Archer"—an accomplishment not at all vitiated by Nathan's conclusion, "There is no you, Maria, any more than there's a me."

Give or take the odd quibble, the overall response to *The Counterlife* was positive bordering on ecstatic, and for a while Roth allowed himself to enjoy it ("a favorable review in *Commentary*!"). Soon, however, the clouds began to regather, as he decided that what his former detractors had *really* liked about the book was its relative good manners. "'The deballing of Zuckerman is complete,' as the bearded fellow says," he wrote Rieff.* "That's what their fucking approval is all about. They can shove it."

Nevertheless he was glad to get the prizes that followed, as they were his first in twenty-eight years and seemed to augur (contra Howe et al.) a promising change in the cultural climate. "You don't appear to be worried because my book fails to propose a remedy for what is troublesomely Jewish in these lives," he said, accepting that year's National Jewish Book Award while noting Chekhov's formulation that it isn't the writer's part "to offer a solution to a problem but, rather, to provide a proper *presentation* of the problem." As for that year's National Book Critics Circle Award in fiction, it came down to a "heated discussion" over the merits of two finalists: *The Counterlife* and *The Bonfire of the Vanities*. "Why, that's lak choosin' between a flea and a louse," said the Kentucky-born Elizabeth Hardwick (or so Joel Conarroe, her fellow judge, remembered). Roth prevailed ten votes to six, and, when notified, left a return message on Conarroe's machine regretting that he'd have to miss the "Circle Jerk Prize" because he'd be in Israel again but would send a tape recording of his acceptance speech. On the appointed evening, then, Roth's disembodied voice assured the audience once more that he wrote fiction, not confession: "The butcher, imagination, wastes no times with niceties: it clubs the fact over the head, quickly it slits the throat, and then with its bare hands, it pulls forth the guts. . . . By the time the imagination is finished with a fact, believe me, it bears no resemblance to a fact."

■ ■ ■ ■

IN LATE APRIL 1986, Roth went with his friend Gaia Servadio to hear Primo Levi give a talk at the Italian Cultural Institute in Belgrave Square; Roth considered Levi's *Survival in Auschwitz*† "a masterpiece for ten different reasons" and had long wanted to meet the author. Levi, in turn, had read only one of Roth's books—*Lamento di Portnoy*—and therefore warily implored their mutual friend, Servadio, to come along as a translator and buffer. Both Servadio and Levi wrote for *La Stampa*,

---

* "The bearded fellow" meaning the Roth-like figure in the novel, who makes this remark to Henry at Nathan's funeral.

† Originally published in Italian as *Se questo è un uomo* (*If This Is a Man*).

Levi's hometown newspaper in Turin, and Levi also knew Servadio's father, a fellow chemist whose mother had died at Auschwitz. As it happened, he and Roth got along famously: "Meeting with you was for me a supererogatory and unhoped for pleasure," Levi wrote him afterward, "although hampered by language friction and by a noisy environment."

A few months later, Roth traveled to Turin to interview Levi for *The New York Times*, since the latter's *Monkey's Wrench* was about to be published in the States. Roth asked his host to show him around the paint factory where he'd been employed as a research chemist—a vocation, Roth thought, reflected in certain aspects of *Survival in Auschwitz*, which showed how a man could be "broken down and, like a substance decomposing in a chemical reaction, lose his characteristic properties," as Roth remarked during their interview. "Nothing belongs to us anymore," Levi had written; "they have taken away our clothes, our shoes, even our hair; if we speak, they will not listen to us, and if they listen, they will not understand. They will even take away our name: and if we want to keep it, we will have to find in ourselves the strength to do so, to manage somehow so that behind the name something of us, of us as we were, still remains." Toward the end of a three-day visit, *La Stampa* sent a photographer to capture the two writers chatting happily in Levi's study; in another room of the house, Levi's aged mother lay incapacitated, unwilling to let anybody but her son feed and care for her. Apart from that, Levi seemed content; he and Roth shared an emotional embrace on parting. "I don't know which of us is the younger brother and which is the older brother," said Levi. As Roth would later reflect, "I felt the great good fortune of one who believes himself to have made a most extraordinary new friend for life."

Roth himself was about to begin a long spell of misery. In November he abruptly returned to London, canceling all further *Counterlife* publicity in New York. He'd thrown out his back a few weeks before, and now was taking the opioid Percodan every three or four hours, along with a cocktail of other medications including the muscle relaxant Robaxin. Alone in Connecticut, he couldn't function otherwise; Sandy came from Chicago for a week or so to cook and care for him, but afterward Philip quickly deteriorated. "Halcion," he wrote in his diary on October 9, referring to the sleeping pill he'd been given because of drug-related insomnia. "Hallucinations. Panic. Bad drug trip." For a while he stopped taking the pill, though one night he was shaking and sweating so badly that he begged his neighbors the Grays to let him spend the night—a kindness for which he remained grateful even in the midst of later bitterness ("You're welcome to be a boy again at any time in any room of the house," Francine wrote him afterward). Finally, at the Wyndham in New York, Roth became so angst-ridden that Rieff had to keep him company until morning. "Throw the pills down the toilet," Dr. Kleinschmidt advised, and Roth did as he was told, returning to London in an agony of panic and pain.

Within a few weeks he "felt something happen to [his] knee" while frog kicking in the Royal Automobile Club swimming pool, and soon he could walk only short distances—a dire situation: in the absence of beta-blockers, he was all the more dependent on exercise to keep his heart healthy. Meanwhile his companions on Fawcett Street took a dim view of his frailty. When he'd yelp with pain while managing the one step down into the kitchen, Bloom would exhort him with bluff English expressions like "Just get on with it!"—which at least were meant to encourage; once, while wretchedly recovering from food poisoning, he'd heard Anna call from the landing outside his bedroom door, *"Is he still in there pissing and moaning?"* "You're in a POW camp," Roth remembered telling himself, "and you have to take care of yourself."

He was visiting his father, in March 1987, when he went to see an orthopedist at the Hospital for Special Surgery in New York; the man informed him that his knee pain was due to a medial meniscus tear that could be fixed with arthroscopic surgery taking less than an hour. Ecstatic at the prospect of relief—the man promised he'd be "back to exercising in a couple of weeks"—Roth promptly scheduled the procedure, arranging to recuperate for a few days in a spare room at the Ashers' on West Eighty-sixth. The operation, however, was not a success. On discovering that Roth's meniscus was, in fact, wholly intact, the surgeon decided to shave a bit of frayed cartilage on his femoral condyle (a procedure the *Times* would debunk as "a sham" in a front-page article fifteen years later). When it was over, Roth's knee was so swollen he could hardly pull his trousers back on, and the pain was more excruciating than ever. Within a week he was barely able to walk, even with crutches, and once again he was prescribed Halcion—which "should be shunned like cyanide" by anyone prone to depression, as Styron would write in 1993, the year the pill was banned in England because of adverse effects known as "Halcion madness."

In *Doll's House*, Bloom remembered her first ominous glimpse of Roth on his return in late March—"grim and pale" in a wheelchair at Heathrow; for his part Roth remembered that she was angry with him for impugning her caretaking capacity by having his surgery in New York and relying on Linda and Aaron Asher afterward. Her first response to his suffering, as he saw it, was elaborate apathy: "As best I can understand," he later wrote, "it was a way of *denying* that I was in physical trouble." During a small dinner party they gave shortly after his return, Roth was in so much pain he had to excuse himself early in the evening and lie down upstairs with an ice bag on his knee; for hours he listened to Bloom chatting with their guests downstairs, but not once did she come up to check on him. "My career is over," she cried, when he begged her to spend June with him in Connecticut. "I'll have to spend the rest of my life caring for you."

On April 11, 1987, a couple of weeks after his return to London, Roth was contacted by the *Times*: Primo Levi had just killed himself; did he have any comment? Roth was horrified. Though Levi had confessed a measure of dejection over his stroke-paralyzed mother, he'd otherwise seemed nothing but "vivacious" and "sound" only a few months before. Apparently, though, he'd begun to despair after prostate surgery left him at least temporarily incontinent, and meanwhile he'd revisited his Auschwitz nightmare in the book he finished shortly before his death, *The Drowned and the Saved*. Servadio remembered Roth was weeping and distraught when he came to her house in Pimlico that day, and for a long time afterward he fought with his own thoughts of suicide.

The last was among the most common symptoms of Halcion madness, along with a fear of being alone, both of which overwhelmed Roth when he returned that summer to Connecticut—where, as Bloom wrote, he "disintegrated before my eyes into a disoriented, terrified infant." He clung to her, trembling, while they walked around the fields, and paddled around the pool with frantic slapping motions, begging her not to make him stay in the water. Conarroe visited in July and was struck by Bloom's self-involvement ("It was all about her") in the face of Roth's desperation. "All hell broke loose late yesterday afternoon," he wrote in his diary on July 20:

P[hilip] has been increasingly despondent, probably in part because C[laire] is leaving for L.A. on Tuesday. When I walk over to the house at 6:30 they were in front, having come from the pool. C went in and P was left standing outside, looking dazed. When I asked if he was OK he broke into sobs and said he couldn't take it any more. We went into the kitchen & when she came down he asked her to stay. The next half-hour or so involved a terrible discussion, C in tears, P speaking quietly, trying to convince her that he was doing the best he can & needs patience from her—just as she asked it from him. C in tears, is terrified about not being able to go home—"I'll have nothing to look forward to." It all ended with rhetoric, C weepily saying she hoped she'd get sick and [be] taken care of. . . .

He spoke about his desire for oblivion—throwing himself out of the car, walking into Bantam Lake—and his utter sense of helplessness. Says if he goes back to London he'll have a breakdown in his studio. Can't stand the idea of the dinners with Anna. Expressed hurt that C, in London, & here, seems utterly insensitive to his situation. Sees himself as moving toward a breakdown with no place to turn—used the image of being in a maze & wherever he turns tears his flesh on nails. . . .

Actually Bloom vacillated between a panicky concern for her own welfare and "over-emotional" (her term) impulses to help—such as her impetuous idea to sell the house on Fawcett Street and look for an apartment with no stairs for Roth to climb. Sensing he'd disapprove of such an "excessive" response to what one hoped was a temporary setback, she hadn't told him, and indeed he was furious when he overheard her, in Connecticut, discussing the matter with a real estate agent over the phone. "I felt unfairly misunderstood and just started screaming," she remembered, running into the fields and refusing to come back inside. Finally, after they'd both calmed down a bit, Roth suggested they invite a friend of his, Bernard Avishai, to come stay for a week. "I am convinced that Bernie saved Philip's life," Bloom wrote.

Avishai had been twenty-five when he first met Roth, in 1974, around the time Avishai started writing about Israeli affairs for *The New York Review of Books*. When Bob Silvers asked him if there was anyone he wanted to meet in New York, Avishai named Roth ("half in jest") and Silvers sent him forthwith to East Eighty-first Street; Roth gave the young man breakfast and listened to his life story—a grim tale about a mentally ill mother who died when Avishai was sixteen, a father who committed suicide five years later, etc. "Philip was tremendously empathic," said Avishai. "I kept trying to steer the conversation to Jewish history, and he kept steering the conversation back to me." Roth became a kind of older brother to Avishai, who shared his taste for Jewish shtick. "You do a courtesy flush?" Roth would call in a Yiddish accent when Avishai flushed the toilet, and the two also liked sharing titles for Jewish country and western songs: "I Balanced Your Books but You're Breaking My Heart," "The Second Time She Said Shalom I Knew She Meant Goodbye."

When Avishai arrived in Connecticut, he was scarcely prepared for the "frightening" degree of Roth's deterioration. When the two were alone together, Roth confided that he was in unbearable pain and thinking incessantly of suicide, and Avishai asked him what pills he was taking. Roth mentioned a few, adding Halcion almost as an afterthought, whereupon Avishai phoned an MIT psychopharmacologist who'd helped him with his own benzodiazepine problem. The man directed Roth to stop taking the drug immediately, though cold-turkey withdrawal wasn't easy ("the ordeal verges on being beyond description in its nearly unalleviated anguish," Styron wrote); he told Roth to take a small dose of Valium the first night, a smaller dose the second, and none the third. Meanwhile Avishai would spend all three nights with Roth in a spare room with twin beds. "My first reaction was distrust," Bloom wrote of the situation in *Doll's House*. "I didn't know Bernie well at the time, and was extremely protective of Philip." "Malarkey," Roth retorted. "Her unmistakable first reaction was anger, jealousy, and fear at believing herself to have been displaced by Bernie because of her inadequacies." That was pretty much the way Avishai remembered it, too, though he thought it "natural" for Bloom to feel hurt. At any rate he mostly managed to stay awake with Roth for three long nights, while Roth "learned the meaning of 'climbing the walls,'" as he later remarked.

"I've had a helluva summer, the worst I can remember," Roth wrote Kazin the day of Avishai's departure, July 28. "I'm only just beginning to feel better, and tonight is the first night in four months that I've sat at my desk writing letters. I haven't written a word of anything else." The next day he and Bloom departed for a two-week visit with the Styrons on Martha's Vineyard, where Roth began to feel a bit more like himself

again. At a dinner party attended by Roth and other friends, Bob Brustein mentioned that Styron had recently sent him an old photograph
of their children, Alexandra Styron (then age four) and Daniel Brustein (six), tied up back to back in chairs by Styron's older son, Tommy;
a TV repairman came to Brustein's house, and the photo was missing
after the man departed. Soon Brustein was visited by a couple of detectives who wanted to know if he enjoyed abusing children, and Brustein
had to get the twenty-two-year-old Alexandra on the phone to attest
to his innocence. *"Innocent?!"* Roth erupted. "Ohhh no . . ." He began
cross-examining Brustein about his sex life ("the funniest thirty or forty
minutes I've ever been involved in," Brustein recalled), amid howling
laughter from all the guests but one: "I look at Claire," said Joanna Clark,
"and she is turning paler and paler and paler." Suddenly Bloom rushed
outside, where she could be seen pacing about until Roth ended his spiel
and joined her; the two stood remonstrating outside the window.

The next day they joined the Clarks for lunch in Menemsha. As
Blair and Philip walked ahead, discussing politics, Joanna overheard an
exchange between Bloom and the Clarks' fourteen-year-old son, Ian,
trailing a little behind: "So what's wrong with Philip's knee?" the boy
politely inquired. "The doctors say it's nothing," Bloom replied. "That's
what's wrong with Philip. There's always *something* wrong. He always
complains . . ."

■   ■   ■   ■

THAT FALL a specialist in New York recommended an exercise program for Roth's knee, and gradually he could walk again without too
much pain. That left the problem of living in London. After ten years
he was beginning to feel like a stranger in both places, London and
New York, and figured it was only a matter of time before such discon-
nection affected his work. Roth had "little or nothing to say" about a
country whose inner workings he knew only vaguely; in *The Counterlife*
he'd managed to evoke an aspect of English life that vexed him—anti-
Semitism—but this "tiny slice" had to be amalgamated with aspects of
Israel and America. "I knew that I wasn't likely to be able to pull another
rabbit out of that hat however much longer I remained in London," he
said, "and that if I did stay on there I would soon find myself without a

strong enough hold on any subject, English or American, to activate my writing energy."

Also, he was getting "awfully bored (bored more than anything)"—as he wrote his principal nemesis, Harold Pinter—with having to defend Reagan's "Amerika" from the "half-baked" attacks of liberal English friends. Roth chafed at their glee whenever his home country was a victim of terror, or struggled to prop up some right-wing regime, and was adamant in his defense of Reagan's bombing raid against Libya on April 14, 1986. "You're going to love being a Yank here post-Libya," Roth warned his friend Julius Goldstein, who was moving to Sussex after marrying an English writer, Joan Aiken. "You'll forget all about being a Yid—they've got a new reason to hate you that supersedes the other." Pinter, who'd been relatively apolitical when Roth first met him, became obsessed with American foreign policy toward Nicaragua in particular, and would invariably bait Roth while in his cups. A story was widely circulated that the two had argued so violently at a party that Alfred Brendel, seated nearby, was fearful lest they come to blows and land on the great pianist's hands—though Brendel himself emended the record, pointing out that while Pinter was certainly wont to lose control ("as he got more excited his vocabulary shrunk even more"), Roth only became more calmly sarcastic. "I am still meditating about Harold Pinter's out-bursts," Stephen Spender wrote Roth, after such an argument had all but spoiled Spender's birthday luncheon. "He is very like his writing, I think, in producing effects which make one think one is not understand-ing what he is saying and he is not understanding what one is saying."*

Most Sundays, toward the end of that problematic decade in London, Roth would commiserate over breakfast with another unhappy Amer-ican Jew, the artist R. B. Kitaj, at Tootsie's, an American-style diner on Fulham Road. Roth had met Kitaj (pronounced Kit-EYE) through

---

* Roth remained fond of Pinter, whom he wrote magnanimously when the sickly man won the Nobel, in 2005, at a time when Roth himself was considered a great favorite for the prize: "You are a wonderful playwright and deserve the prize no less than Piran-dello or Ibsen or O'Neill. I didn't like seeing you with a cane and hearing you with less than your full voice on TV here, but it filled me with happiness, nonetheless, and, while watching you being interviewed outside your house, I felt very proud, as though we were related by blood."

David Plante; the small bearded artist was one of the great draftsmen of his time, and would fax Roth dashed-off sketches of the decorous Anita Brookner, say, giving blow jobs. Roth was full of curiosity about Kitaj's youth as a sailor on a merchant ship, brothel-hopping at various ports, experiences Roth would bestow on Mickey Sabbath. Theirs was the kind of nonrivalrous camaraderie Roth had enjoyed with Philip Guston, who'd died in 1980; Kitaj and Roth, too, were of like eminence in their respective fields, and both relished the kitschier aspects of American culture. They also shared a morbid awareness of English anti-Semitism, and Kitaj would invoke his friend as a witness when critics savaged his last major exhibition at the Tate, in 1994: "There are *many* people," Kitaj wrote, "including Isaiah Berlin and Philip Roth, who have confirmed an ongoing, low-octane English anti-Semitism in polite and not-so-polite London circles." When Kitaj's beloved wife, Sandra, died of a brain aneurysm around this time, he blamed the English press and returned to America with their son. "Roth is a good listener and he and I talked often on the phone when Sandra died," he wrote in his diary on December 21, 2003, four years before killing himself after he'd received a diagnosis of Parkinson's disease.

Roth's life in London had been "sustained," he said, by his affair with Emma Smallwood; otherwise he would have begun living year-round in Connecticut sometime in the early eighties, letting Bloom visit whenever she felt like it. Neither he nor Emma could quite remember, later, why it ended in 1986 or thereabouts, except that both seemed to realize it had "nowhere to go": Emma wasn't willing to leave her unhappy home (mainly because of her daughter), and neither was Roth (for whatever reason).* They met only once more, for tea at the Ritz, during Roth's last-ever trip to London in 1990—a conversation Roth re-created in *Deception* as having taken place over the phone. Emma was rather cold on that occasion, complaining that her friends had recognized her as Maria in *The Counterlife*. (Roth: "I said 'How?' And she said, 'That's the way I talk. How do you *do* that?'" Roth chuckled: "That's the Nobel Prize.") As the

---

* "Little does Claire know how much she owed to [Emma]," Roth remarked in 2007. When the BBC was casting its 1985 production of *Shadowlands*, Emma recommended Bloom for the part of C. S. Lewis's wife, Joy Davidman, and later wrote a newspaper review applauding Bloom's "strong performance." Bloom won a BAFTA for the role.

mistress in *Deception* complains, "I object greatly to this taking people's lives and putting them into fiction. And then being a famous author who resents critics for saying that he doesn't make things up."

In September 1987, a couple of weeks after their visit with the Styrons on Martha's Vineyard, Roth and Bloom began living in a small suite at the Essex House on Central Park South. ("Philip Roth is coming back to New York," the *Post*'s Page Six reported, noting that his most recent novel "finds a horde of anti-Semites among the British upper crust.") Bloom "went crazy" when he'd first broached the idea with her, and later, at the Essex, made little effort to dissemble her gloom. Once again Roth promised to put ten thousand dollars aside in a "travel fund," to be replenished as needed, so she could visit Anna as often as she liked. But neither would budge on the essential point: Bloom was unwilling to live in Connecticut, and Roth was unwilling to live in London. Almost every morning at the Essex House she'd wake up crying, while Roth would go for a swim next door at the New York Athletic Club (as a guest of Bloom's friend Gore Vidal) and phone Sandy in Chicago: "She's crying again," he'd sigh, "and I don't know what to do with her. . . ." Bloom's therapist had advised her to leave Roth, who phoned the woman from the Essex one day and said, "I'm sitting here looking out the window"— i.e., at a view of Central Park—"and I don't see what's so awful." But a visiting friend wrote in his diary that the "impersonal hotel room" was a "depressing arrangement": "Claire, in dark glasses, was in a crabby mood. They were bickering over what movie to see that night."

■　■　■　■

THE ROMANIAN WRITER Norman Manea—who would become one of Roth's closest friends—first made contact with Roth at the beginning of 1987, when he was spending a year in West Berlin as a fellow at the Deutscher Akademischer Austauschdienst (German Academic Exchange Service, or DAAD). Manea spoke very little English at the time, so his letter to Roth was translated (from German) by a British colleague at DAAD. Manea reminded the editor of Writers from the Other Europe that the series was devoid of Romanians, and that recently their friend Aharon Appelfeld had sent Roth a couple of Manea's stories—the only two translated into English. Manea added that his present circumstances, as a writer and a Jew, were such that returning to Ceauşescu's

Romania wasn't really an option: "What does an unknown writer of fifty, who writes in this exotic language nobody knows, do?"

Manea and Appelfeld had in common a bleak childhood, which in Manea's case had become an almost equally bleak adulthood. Like Appelfeld he'd been deported as a boy, in 1941, to a Transnistria concentration camp, and later wrote fiction about how the trauma of the Holocaust was revived by life in a totalitarian state—a life that had become all but untenable after 1981, when Manea protested Romanian anti-Semitism and called for stronger moral stands on the parts of his fellow writers. "At 55," Roth would write of his friend in 1992, "Norman Manea is a plumpish, balding, melancholy man in dark-rimmed spectacles—mild, reserved, anxious, at times a bit timid. He does not strike even himself, I believe, as the ideal writer to have been pitted against perhaps the most vicious dictatorship of the last 40 years." Because Manea refused to bow to his country's cretinous leader—with "his ridiculous, self-awarded, ever more pompous titles," Manea wrote, "his endless speeches full of past platitudes with their perennial hoarse bathos"—he was not only forbidden to publish, but also forced to surrender his typewriter every night "to some central headquarters," as Roth recalled while telling his favorite Norman story: "He went to visit an older friend of his, a wise man, and told him the situation. The wise man said to him: 'Look, Norman: how many readers does a writer really need, when you think about it? . . . Six. You need six. You have six readers, that's fine. You, unfortunately, have only four.'"

In 1987, Roth wasn't sure what to do with Manea's two translated stories, though he encouraged the desperate man to come see him if he managed to visit the States. As luck would have it, Manea's DAAD grant was followed by a Fulbright that brought him to Catholic University in Washington, D.C., and Manea promptly arranged to visit Roth at the Essex House. "We have hands!" said Roth, when Manea warned him, over the phone, that his English was poor and maybe he should come another time. "It was uncomfortable for me to face this great Jewish American cowboy," he explained. "I was like a little beggar from Eastern Europe." Still, they managed to have a few laughs right from the start. Manea was unsure whether to live in Paris or remain in America, and Roth was determined it should be the latter; he took Manea for a walk among the milling hordes of Broadway, on the Upper West Side, leading him to Fairway Market so he could see for himself the superabundant fruits and vegetables piled outside. When Manea returned to Washington (where he was taking an English class "with old Chinese ladies and beautiful young Brazilian girls"), Roth phoned him almost daily to see how he was making out.

Manea's wife, Cella, had been chief of the art and paper restoration division of the Bucharest National Library and Museum, and, after Norman's Fulbright expired, Cella found work at an art conservation company in New York and the couple moved into a "very shabby" hotel on Eighth Avenue. Meanwhile Roth got in touch with his friend Leon Botstein, the president of Bard College, who promptly made Manea an international fellow for that academic year, inaugurating a happy career at the college that would continue the rest of his life. In 1990, Roth agreed to serve as a nominator for the MacArthur "genius" fellowships, scribbling on a letter of thanks from the program director, "Norman eligible?" "I can think of no writer of the first rank in such dire need of moral encouragement and financial support as is Norman Manea," he wrote the MacArthur committee, which awarded Manea an annual sum of $50,000 for five years. Roth also put him up for a Guggenheim, and arranged for him to meet Joel Conarroe, by then the president of the foundation, over dinner one night. Manea hadn't known what a MacArthur was, and was just as puzzled about Guggenheims, and certainly had no insight into the president's private life. "At a certain point," he recalled, "the discussion reached the problem of homosexuals. . . . I said I don't have any problem with this. I don't look at what other people do in their room and their bed. . . . Was this my exam for the Guggenheim? Perhaps not the essential one, a marginal one, but I passed it." Loaded with grant money, Manea still couldn't afford the one-bedroom apartment in a nice doorman building on West Seventieth Street that Roth wanted him to buy, so Roth contributed $20,000 and also wrote a letter to the co-op board.

In 1994, Roth accompanied Manea to the Federal Building in downtown Manhattan, and insisted on sitting next to him in the roped-off area where hundreds of happy immigrants, along with Manea, took the oath of citizenship. Afterward Roth and Manea had a celebratory lunch at an Italian restaurant in Greenwich Village, where Manea told "convoluted and ironic stories" about his desperate life in Romania. "I kept laughing and saying, 'Norman, go home and write that down,'" said Roth, "meanwhile remembering the day back at my hotel when he had so little English at his disposal and so much doubt and trepidation and no idea at all of the success he would make of life in America."

Thirty-Five

In August 1986, Gaia Servadio and her young son, Orlando, visited Roth in Connecticut.* Bloom was in England, but the three of them had a splendid visit; Roth had finished *The Counterlife* and was perfectly free to show his guests the pastoral beauty of Litchfield County. There was a little awkwardness when Roth kept trying to coax Servadio to bed, while she just as persistently (if politely) declined. As she remembered: "Claire told me very confidentially—as a close friend— that Philip could not make love to anybody because of his heart." Roth certainly didn't behave like a man troubled with impotence, and Servadio was (by her own admission) "cavalier" in those days about sleeping with whomsoever she liked, but she was too fond of Philip to embarrass him that way. At any rate, theirs was a fun-loving friendship, and Roth took it breezily in stride. "You fuck everybody!" he'd always joke with her afterward. "You never fucked me!"

A few months earlier—on May 1—he'd found himself sitting beside the actress Ava Gardner at a dinner party for Leonard Bernstein at the American embassy in London. "I never thought it would happen but I've finally come to envy Mickey Rooney," he wrote Bellow the next day, referring to Gardner's first husband. When Roth had mentioned to her that he was from New Jersey, she said, "I was married to a guy

---

* Roth sent a driver to collect them at JFK, since he was attending a concert of Beethoven quartets that evening at the Yale Chamber Music Festival in nearby Norfolk. "Welcome Gaia and Orlando!" read the note awaiting them at his home in Warren. "There is dinner for you in the refrigerator. On the top shelf in the blue casserole is soup to be warmed up. There's some parmesan cheese in a little envelope, grated, on top of the soup. Add. . . . The new super duper TV requires a technological genius to turn on and off. The Rabbi has the secret and will reveal it to you when he returns from the concert, which should be about eleven thirty tonight. . . . [Signed] Rabbi Philip Milton Roth."

from New Jersey"—meaning her third husband, Frank Sinatra. A friend of Roth, Alan Yentob, was seated on the other side of him, and attests that the sixty-three-year-old Gardner was still stunning: "Philip was just *at* her the whole time," he remembered, and Roth agreed the two had hit it off. Toward the end of the evening she scribbled her address and phone number on the back of her place card, and soon he passed a very pleasant afternoon at 34 Ennismore Gardens. Roth was already back in Connecticut when the drunken actress phoned Fawcett Street around three in the morning: "Where is he?" she demanded. "Your friend Ava Gardner called last night," Bloom coldly informed him, whereupon Roth assured her that Ava was just a friendly acquaintance ("deny deny deny") and decided on the spot to end things. He never saw Gardner again, and was saddened by her death, from pneumonia, only three and a half years later.

As Bloom would report in *Doll's House*, a far more damning episode "came to light" a few years later, when Anna Steiger and her friend Felicity*—a fellow singer and schoolmate—decided it was time to tell Bloom about advances he'd made toward Felicity on two occasions: in 1981 and "more explicitly" in 1988. The first advance allegedly went as follows: one early morning after sleeping over on Fawcett Street, Felicity was about to leave for rehearsals when Roth "suddenly appeared and attempted to French kiss her," according to Steiger; Felicity pushed him away and departed. Presented with the substance of that earlier charge, Roth called the story "preposterous" and offered his alibi in the form of a "bit of erotic trivia": "I for one have never found the 'French kiss' pleasurable. To go searching around the cavern of a woman's mouth with a jutting, insinuating tongue was never my idea of fun, not even as an adolescent and certainly not as a man, even one who willingly admits a profound fondness for cunnilingus." For what it's worth, a number of Roth's old lovers were happy to corroborate the point.

Roth also claimed that his relations with Felicity remained "affable" until 1988; indeed, Felicity was the one who fielded the phone call notifying Roth of his National Book Critics Circle Award for *The Counterlife*, ebulliently greeting him with the news when he came home that night

---

* A pseudonym.

("Anna remained unmoved and silent in her chair," he noted). That was on January 12, 1988; Bloom left for a movie shoot in Africa the next day, whereas Roth would leave for Israel on January 16; meanwhile Felicity was staying in Anna's old rooms on the top floor (Anna lived elsewhere by then), and for a few days she and Roth had the house to themselves.

On the second night, as Roth remembered, he came home from dinner around ten thirty and found Felicity in the first-floor living room. They began to talk. At some point Felicity mentioned that she'd had a passionate love affair with a famous opera basso, a married man with children, during a recent production in which he sang a leading role and she was in the chorus. "How she got from telling me about the circumstances of her growing up to speaking about her erotic adventures I no longer remember," Roth wrote. "Did I at some point ask her about them? I might well have, it's not impossible, but I actually think the subject arose spontaneously in the course of her talking freely to me about herself for the first time in all the years we'd known each other." As Felicity told her friend Anna, however, Roth's "line of questioning" could hardly have been more pointed ("Do you have many lovers? Are you seeing anyone?"); he'd also inquired about Steiger's love life, which Felicity declined to discuss.

The matter was on Roth's mind the following night, when he came home late from a jolly dinner *chez* Alvarez and encountered Felicity, in her nightgown, descending toward him on the second-floor landing. "Now, maybe she was going for a glass of buttermilk in the kitchen at midnight," he said, "but it certainly didn't look that way, particularly after last night's conversation." The tipsy Roth made to embrace the young woman, putting a hand on her waist; she recoiled and began shouting that he "was crazy and a monster to do this to [Claire] and that she was going back upstairs to pack her bag and leave"—so he recalled, along with his reply: "I apologize for misreading the situation. I seem to have taken a liberty. I thought an invitation was being extended." He was getting ready for bed when he heard the downstairs door slam—or, as he subsequently remembered in a 2015 email, he heard the door slam early the next morning, "before [he] even rose for breakfast." Afterward Felicity left an angry message on Bloom's machine: she wanted to return and collect the rest of her things, but not while Roth was there. "If I remember correctly," he wrote, "I left for work but put a note on her bed which said something like, 'This is pure sexual hysteria.'"

Anna Steiger said her friend was "incredibly upset" when she showed up at Anna's apartment, where she told a somewhat different story. His pass on the stairs, she said, hadn't bothered her all that much; she'd "simply declined and withdrew," reminding him that she was a guest in Claire's home and so on. The next morning she'd hoped to leave without seeing him, but an antic Roth was "awake and already in high gear," as Steiger put it (paraphrasing her friend). "Morning [Felicity]!" he said, scampering after her on the stairs. "Come on, how long is it since I made a pass at you? Ten years? What were you then, twelve?* What's the point of having a pretty girl in the house if you don't fuck her?" This—*not* the relatively innocuous business on the stairs—was what rattled and angered the young woman, hence her indignant message on the answering machine. Again, Roth claimed she was already gone by the time he got up that morning, and certainly a side of him would have hesitated to add insult to injury that way. But another side of Roth was the Mickey Sabbath who aspired "[t]o affront and affront and affront till there was no one on earth unaffronted"—indeed, his impulse to mock a certain kind of bourgeois piety was among his most pronounced traits, both as a writer and a man.

As for Felicity's considered view of the incident, she permitted Steiger to quote her directly: "When the woman in question is the close friend of his stepdaughter and wife,† the motive for making such a pass would indicate something more complex than simply responding to an 'inviting smile from an attractive woman.' . . . Its destructiveness seems clear; all the options were compromising." Certainly Bloom thought so: in *Doll's House*, she finds "intricate, subtle layers of intent" on the part of her former mate, a "Machiavellian strategist" whose moment of lechery on the staircase was part of "an ambitious and foolproof plan"—scrutinized at length in all its byzantine nuance—to punish the three women.

---

* An allusion to the first alleged incident in 1981. Assuming Felicity was roughly the same age as Steiger, her Guildhall schoolmate, she would have been about twenty-one in 1981.

† Not yet stepdaughter and wife: Roth and Bloom would finally, bewilderingly, marry on April 29, 1990.

"What, aside from a great nation's decision to go to war, can carry such an amplitude of meaning?" Roth replied, and offered an alternative motive—the same motive, indeed, that he ventured to impute to Richard Burton, Laurence Olivier, and Yul Brynner for committing adultery with the younger Bloom: desire. "This is what people are," Roth wrote. "This is what people do. Adultery does not correspond with anyone's holiest wishes for what the world should be. Yet there it is. . . . Hate me for what I am, not for what I'm not."

It bears adding that Roth was rarely penitent with respect to Felicity. The note he left on her bed was more brutal mockery: he was amused, he wrote, by her "performance of virtue defiled," as were the friends for whom he'd played her angry phone message, and if Claire wasn't equally amused, when he played it for *her*, he'd "eat his hat"; he signed off "Kisses, Philip." After he returned from Israel, he called her up on the pretext of discussing Claire's mail, which Felicity was supposed to forward, and lightly inquired whether she planned to tell Claire what had happened; it was up to her, he said, since he could "play it either way." And finally, later, on the odd occasion that he answered the phone when she called for Claire, he'd greet her with "Hi, little home wrecker," or simply "Felicity who?"

■ ■ ■ ■

ROTH'S NOMINAL REASON for returning to Israel that January was to interview Appelfeld, whose newly translated *The Immortal Bartfuss* was about to be published in America; as luck would have it, Roth's arrival also coincided with the war crimes trial of John Demjanjuk, a Ukrainian auto worker from Cleveland whom some had identified as a notoriously sadistic guard at Treblinka, "Ivan the Terrible." Roth saw in the newspaper that the trial was open to the public and took to attending each morning, listening to the harrowing testimony—translated from Polish, Yiddish, Russian, and Hebrew—and carefully watching Demjanjuk's face. "You're a liar!" the defendant bellowed at one point, and Roth turned to Avishai and said, "That's the tell." An innocent man, he said, would not so theatrically call a death-camp survivor a liar.

Meanwhile the Palestinian uprising known as the First Intifada had just erupted in the occupied West Bank and Gaza. Avishai was friends with the future prime minister Ehud Olmert, then a backbencher for the right-wing Likud party, and he arranged for Roth and Olmert to meet over lunch at the Knesset. Roth deplored the Israeli policy of violence against the rioters, many of them children, and wondered how Israelis hoped to cling to territories with such large and unruly Arab populations. Olmert countered by blaming the revolt in part on the failure of "inauthentic" American Jews to come over as settlers. "Are you crazy?" said Roth. "American Jews aren't coming." Olmert seemed surprised and asked why. "Because they have lives of their own! There *is* a Zion, and it's called America." As Avishai remembered, the lunch "quickly degenerated into raised voices and hurried departures," though years later a more pacifist Olmert admitted the argument had changed his thinking on the issue: "If a good Jew like Roth felt this way," he said, "then what could be expected of the others?"

A more heated argument ensued over dinner with the Tumins, at Lahiere's restaurant in Princeton, a few days after Roth's return to the States. Mel was passionately concerned with Jewish survival, and he infuriated Roth by loudly defending Israel's vicious reprisals against the Palestinians. Roth scribbled notes (some of them illegible) immediately afterward:

> . . . *Beatings?* [Mel:] Bad but another country would do even worse.
> I say the Palestinians should consider themselves lucky.
> [Mel:] "Right! Compare to Syria, compare to Jordan!"
> . . . The Israel myth. "Better" than other states. (Syria and Jordan) Better than France? Holland? Canada? Australia? Why can't it just be the same . . . a democracy like any other . . .
> Auschwitz—therefore justified.
> Mel: they ought to all get out before the catastrophe occurs. Come and resettle in America. . . . We can't afford to lose Jews again.

Mel's notion of a kind of patriotic, reverse Zionism ("Come and resettle in America")—the opposite of Olmert's solution—would stick in Roth's mind, all the more as he became aware of his own considerable ambivalence. In Israel he'd befriended Emma Playfair, an English lawyer for the Palestinian human-rights organization Al-Haq, and when she came to New York he arranged a dinner for her to meet various literary people. "I never heard my friends before engage in such anti-Israeli hatred as they displayed that night in Emma's presence," he remembered. "She was the catalyst, though she was by no means a hater herself. I practiced old dependable detached observation, though I was boiling within." One friend gloatingly observed that Israel had been "revealed," while another wondered, "Who needs a European country in the region anyway?"—as if to challenge, à la Arafat, Israel's very right to exist. To make matters worse, these "bourgeois-bohemians" (Roth) ended up sticking him with a four-hundred-dollar check. "What is going to happen in Israel?" he wrote Updike in March. "READ MY NEXT NOVEL AND FIND OUT."

■　■　■

HERMAN ROTH HAD spent much of that first summer after his wife's death (1981) lurking around Philip's house in Connecticut, at loose ends; when he could muster the energy, he'd go outside and rake leaves. One day he linked arms with a visitor, David Plante, and led him down to the pool. "Are you married, Dave?" he asked. Plante said he wasn't, and offered condolences about Bess. "A wonderful woman," said Herman, "a really wonderful woman, Dave," and his face crumpled with tears.

That winter he shared a condo in Bal Harbour, just north of Miami Beach, with a fellow widower and old Bradley Beach co-lodger, Bill Weber. His remarkable rejuvenation was due in part, Roth thought, to Weber's being "a fairly good stand-in for my mother—a good-natured, even-tempered, untroublesome partner whose faults and failings he could correct unceasingly." As for Herman's son, he was now an eminent novelist in midjourney, barely perturbed anymore by his father's *hocking* and gaucherie; on the contrary he loved hanging around with Herman and other "lucky survivors" gathered in Florida ("Either you're dead or you're there"), laughing at their jokes and returning their tenderness. "Spent an evening in the lobby of Meyer Lansky's hotel, The Singapore, with the last of Newark's Jewish population," he wrote a friend. "Old men I'd known as young men when I was a little boy. Strange to think of the anger it once took to free myself from their embrace. Now you could knock them over with a feather."

Roth reported to Mildred Martin that Herman had become "a great lively favorite with the widows" in Florida ("It's inspiring and admirable"), and after that first winter Herman was pretty much his old self again: railing at Reagan, phoning nephews and nieces and grandchildren with advice, writing letters to newspapers, and "monitoring the caloric intake" of his new girlfriend, Lillian Beloff, a plumpish, stoical widow eighteen years his junior. ("Always tell them you're ten years older than you are," Herman advised, "so if you say you're ninety, they say 'You look great!'—whereas, if you tell them you're eighty, they're like, 'Eh, he *looks* eighty.'") Herman had met Lillian while he was sitting at his back window one day and caught her pulling into Dr. Horowitz's parking space. "Hey!" he called. "You're in Dr. Horowitz's slot!" Then: "You're a good-looking woman. What's your name?" As it happened, Herman knew all about her: her late husband's father ("You were married to So-and-so, weren't you?") had run a stationery store on Central Avenue in downtown Newark; she worked at an auto supply place run by an old boyhood pal of Philip, Lenny Lonoff, whose family used to live right across the street from the Roths in Weequahic, etc. "She was dumbstruck," said Philip.

So it went for the next five or six years. Herman and Lillian had just arrived in West Palm Beach for the winter months of 1987–88, when he awoke one morning to find that the right side of his face "had gone slack and lifeless as though the bone had been filleted," Roth wrote in *Patrimony*. At first Herman thought he'd had a stroke—his "worst fear" given what he remembered of his own father's paralysis and slow death—but a subsequent MRI revealed a massive tumor that would prove to consist of cartilaginous material ("a little like your fingernail"), which, though not malignant, would in time become large enough to kill him.

Meanwhile—because the MRI alone couldn't determine the nature of the tumor—Herman endured a painful biopsy, in June 1988, that entailed getting a hole punched in his upper palate so the doctor could extract a sample of tumor tissue. During the two-hour drive to Connecticut afterward, Philip stopped at a restaurant and got a bag full of ice cubes, and by the time they got home Herman's shirt was soaked from the ice he'd sucked with his aching, half-paralyzed mouth. Father and son entered the house through the kitchen door and Bloom, standing there at the stove, "threw her hands up to her face in horror, began to scream, and ran out of the house," as Roth remembered. He steered his bewildered father upstairs and got him settled into the guest bedroom, then went looking for Bloom—whom he found, at last, "cowering beside the woods about a third of a mile from the house. . . . I said something like, 'He's sick. He's been in the hospital. He's dying. He's eighty-six and he's in hell. What do you expect him to look like? . . . Do you think I liked handling your mother's corpse?'"

Roth elided the episode in *Patrimony*, where he was careful to emphasize Bloom's good works—the way she'd prepared a big pot of vegetable soup for Herman and cut flowers for his room. The next day Herman felt well enough, at first, to sit down for lunch with Philip, Claire, and their visitors—Sandy's son Seth and his wife, Ruth—but Herman kept leaving the table at intervals; when it occurred to Philip, over coffee, that his father hadn't returned in a while, he went looking for him. "I smelled the shit halfway up the stairs to the second floor," he wrote in *Patrimony*. The anesthetic had painfully constipated his father, who'd tried and tried to defecate at various service stations on the way home from the hospital; now Roth found him standing naked in an upstairs bathroom, dripping wet from the shower. "I beshat myself," he said forlornly. While undressing, Herman had "managed to spread the shit over everything," and Philip helped him back into the shower and then wrapped him up in a clean bathrobe and put him to bed. Many readers of *Patrimony* would protest Roth's inclusion of the whole mortifying episode, but caring for his father so intimately, scrubbing up the ubiquitous shit (on his toothbrush, in his hair), had been a kind of holy experience—"one of the most extraordinary and wonderful things that's ever happened to me," he wrote Updike at the time. Afterward, Roth took Bloom aside and explained what had happened. "With undisguised loathing," he later recounted, "she said, 'Why can't he learn to control himself?'"

Roth didn't plan to publish *Patrimony* until after Herman's death, and never told his father he'd been taking notes as long ago as Bess's funeral. ("What kind of people are we?" Plante remarked back then. "We don't even stop taking notes at a funeral.") As Roth explained in 1993, "I imagined that somewhere down the line, it would be useful to know what it was like to watch someone you love die." He finished a partial "final draft" in January 1989; then, after his father's death nine months later, he wrote the last chapter, ending with an elegiac dream he'd had the previous summer, in which he stood on a Newark pier some fifty years ago, watching a "defunct warship driving blindly into shore"—a "plaintive metaphor" for his father that his "wide-awake mind" would never have condoned: "Rather, it was sleep that, in its wisdom, kindly delivered up to me this childishly simple vision so rich with truth and crystallized my own pain so aptly in the figure of a small, fatherless evacuee on the Newark docks, as stunned and bereft as the entire nation had once been at the passing of a heroic president."

■ ■ ■ ■

ROTH WROTE no fiction for almost two years after finishing *The Counterlife*, and sometimes wondered whether he'd ever write fiction again. In the midst of his pain problems and Halcion depression, the best he could do in the way of narrative was to "retrace the steps" of his own life—beginning with a few sketches about Bucknell and other early memories. "I'm tired of the make-up and the false whiskers and the wig," he wrote, "tired of putting the stuff on and taking it off and putting it on again. Autobiography is another kind of mask, of course, but it's a change." By the spring of 1987 he'd managed to produce fifty or sixty pages, and one day, in his usual funk, he began reading them aloud to Avishai—then, after an hour or so, he suddenly snapped the folder shut: "Oh well, this is boring."

But it served a purpose. While reading to Avishai, his low spirits lifted ever so slightly when he came to a line addressed to Maggie's corpse—"You're dead and I didn't have to do it"—which he repeated at least three times with dawning gratification. "I think what may lay behind the writing is the desire to make peace with a lot of old turmoil," he wrote Miss Martin.

> Also, an obsessive preoccupation with mortality. I've lived two-thirds of my life, maybe even more. I've done a lot of work. I've written and published what I think is not only my best book [*Counterlife*], but perhaps the best book I'll ever be able to write. Claire and I are clearly together for the rest of our lives. I've had no children and won't. My father is 85 and can't live much longer, despite his relatively good health. My mother is irrevocably gone, by which I mean that I don't really talk to her ghost any more, though I do miss her and love her, perhaps somewhat the way I did as a boy. Time is real, and so is one's history.

That prediction about his "best book" was arguably mistaken, and certainly the one about Bloom—indeed, he would do well to make peace with "old turmoil" given the fresh kind that lay ahead.

Still, when he'd finished what he alternately titled *A Countertale, Portrait of the Artist as a Young American, Raw Life: The Education of Philip Roth*—to name a few—he sensed the whole performance was flat and even a little disingenuous. "Protecting virtually everyone except Maggie and yourself," he wrote in his notes, "and even yourself." Then: "Assault your own book!" Roth's skepticism about his objectivity had been helped along by an early reader, Paul Fussell, who wryly suggested he change the subtitle from "A Novelist's Autobiography" to "An Autobiographer's Novel"—hence what most readers would agree was the best (or most artful) part of the finished book: Zuckerman's damning critique at the end, beginning with the advice, "Don't publish—you are far better off writing about me than 'accurately' reporting your own life." Roth, on the one hand, called Zuckerman his Charlie McCarthy, and pointed out that "the dummy is always smarter than the ventriloquist"; certainly the dummy was right to wonder, in this case, how the idyllic childhood portrayed in *The Facts* could have possibly "nurtured the author of *Portnoy's Complaint*." On the other hand, Roth would also claim—in the same interview where he called Zuckerman his Charlie McCarthy—that his alter ego is "wrong. . . . I think the book is pretty candid. I've come as close to the truth as I can."

For readers, the book's relative credibility was among the least of its problems. "Philip Roth sent me *The Facts*," Kazin wrote in his diary on September 25, 1988, "the latest issue in the plentiful long-standing journal of PR's every moment, love, emotion and visit to the analyst. After portraying himself under different names in some seven thousand novels, and after finding a counter-life, counter-Roth, counter-weight in the thinly imagined Nathan Zuckerman . . . he now gives us the 'facts.'" The next day he wrote Roth directly, turning the same withering assessment into an exquisitely backhanded compliment: He was in "awe," he said, since the book made him realize "that only a brilliant novelist can recycle his own story in so many ways. . . . Anybody but such a novelist would have had the world howling 'Enough already!'"—as Kazin himself was howling—"but I notice from the reviews that even the usual dummkopfen fall into fascinated discussion of the roles and counter-roles that you provide."

Not all the *dummköpfen*, by a long shot. "Despite Roth's constant disclaimers that his novels are not his life, the material here is familiar to the point of exhaustion," wrote Rhoda Koenig in *New York* magazine. "Obviously, there is still a great sympathy for Roth and a great appetite for his works. I, for one, however, am tired of hearing that old organ grind." Roth had forbidden himself the contrivance of scenes and dialogue in a book that purported to consist purely of facts, and Updike (under the cloak of "Briefly Noted" anonymity afforded by *The New Yorker*) was hardly alone in lamenting the "simultaneously dry and watered-down" prose that resulted. Along with other reviewers, however, he applauded (and seemed in accord with) Nathan's disparaging letter at the end, even while Nathan himself was reluctant to let his creator off the hook so easily: Zuckerman's letter, said Zuckerman, was "a self-defensive trick to have it both ways."

■ ■ ■ ■

ON FEBRUARY 26, 1988, Roth asked his friend Conarroe to come have a look at an apartment he and Bloom were thinking about buying on West Seventy-seventh Street, across from the Museum of Natural History. Conarroe was not impressed, noting in his diary the "skinny living room, small closed-in kitchen . . . mean little room for Claire's study, AND I heard noise from overhead." To Roth, though, its spartan quality was more a virtue than not, and $600,000 a small price to pay for a one-bedroom that wasn't big enough, he hoped, to accommodate Anna Steiger. Meanwhile he also paid $250,000 for a south-facing apartment a few blocks away on West Seventy-ninth, arranging to knock down the wall between its compact bedroom and living room, and so turning the place into a larger, well-lit studio with a small walk-in kitchen; here, too, for a long time, a bed was omitted with Steiger in mind. "I'm home, I'm home," Roth said to himself excitedly, when they finally moved in that October. "Everything delighted him," wrote Hermione Lee, who came to interview Roth for *The Independent*: "the glamorous city skyline from the apartment window, the all-night Puerto Rican food and flower shops, the hundred-and-one television channels, the New York news stories that everyone was always discussing, the badinage in every shop you went into, the busy vociferous *Jewishness* of New York."

Roth hadn't taught since moving to London more than a decade ago, but he refused to live again in New York "like a crazy man locked up in a room by himself," and let it be known that he wanted a job. After receiving offers from Rutgers and Bard, he ran into the chancellor of the CUNY system, Joe Murphy, at a Yaddo fund-raiser; it so happened Murphy had graduated from Weequahic half a year behind Roth. "I played on his feelings for our old alma mater and its hapless football teams," Roth wrote a friend. "That did it." In fact, Roth was tentatively willing to accept a CUNY job for the same salary offered by Rutgers and Bard ($65,000), provided Murphy agree to the following: Roth, with the title "Distinguished Professor," would teach two courses of his own devising, select his own eighteen or fewer students per course, and be forever exempt from meetings or public appearances of any kind ("I just want to teach"). All this granted, Murphy took Roth on a tour of a few CUNY colleges, and Roth settled on Hunter, in the East Sixties, where Barbara Sproul taught religion.

One of Roth's courses was titled The Literature of Extreme Situations, and its reading list included Borowski's *This Way for the Gas, Ladies and Gentlemen*, Céline's *Journey to the End of the Night*, Genet's *Thief's Journal*, and *Into That Darkness*, Gitta Sereny's terrifying account of the extermination camps at Treblinka and Sobibór, via her interviews with their commandant, Franz Stangl, a man ultimately responsible for the deaths of almost a million people. Roth's students balked at the last: "Why do you give us this to read?" they asked, in effect, and he shrugged: "Because it happened." One of the final exam questions featured a quote from Borowski:

"[The S. S. men] explain that it is not much farther and they pat on the back a little old man who runs over to a ditch, rapidly pulls down his trousers, and wobbling in a funny way squats down. An S. S. Man calls to him and points to the people disappearing round the bend. The little old man nods quickly, pulls up his trousers and, wobbling in a funny way, runs at a trot to catch up.

"You snicker, amused at the sight of a man in such a big hurry to get to the gas chamber."

. . . How can Borowski snicker at such a sight, let alone admit to it? Can you describe and make sense of Borowski's reaction to what he sees and endures at Auschwitz? . . . (250–500 words)

His other course, The Consciousness Industry, was as much for his own benefit as for his students'. While in London Roth had lost touch with American life, and thought it might be useful to scrutinize, each week, a representative American magazine "to determine its cultural and political perspective and to study the means by which it claims the attention of its specific audience." Roth started at the bottom, with *People*, and worked his way up to the *Harvard Business Review*, trying each week to invite a guest who worked at a given magazine—among them, Veronica Geng from *The New Yorker*, James Atlas from the *New York Times Book Review*, and Walter Isaacson from *Time*. Avishai came on behalf of the *Harvard Business Review*, and remembered how unabashedly fascinated Roth was by the subject of writing for a business community: "He liked the idea that he could get a little window into the world that his father lived with," Avishai remembered. "He had enough humility to just listen and learn." Roth also found it a salutary exercise to observe his friends— some of whom excited profoundly mixed emotions—doing what they do best.

For Roth it was a nice change teaching at "a tough urban school" like Hunter, which cost very little and was open to anyone with a diploma from a New York high school. "My students are all truckdrivers and lesbians and dey don't take to strangers," he wrote Riki Wagman. "And dey pack a wallop." These were fellow adults, for the most part, whose lives outside the classroom tended to be complicated. One of his more endearing students, Karen, lived in a rough neighborhood and worked as a stripper; she gave Roth a couple of short stories, and he agreed to meet with her privately (and chastely) to discuss her work. "I like her enormously and admire the sassy bravado with which she approaches just about everything," he wrote in a recommendation letter for the Columbia MFA program (she was accepted). "She's also vulnerable and extremely decent." In 1989, the young woman was showing signs of severe bipolar disorder, and twenty years later, when she got back in touch with Roth, she was living on Medicare at a low-income housing project. By then she'd finished a novel about her "long, uphill battle with mental illness," wherein Roth appeared as a character who, she feared, failed to do justice to the actual human being. "You were so kind to me," she wrote Roth, reminding him of the time he'd phoned her at the hospital after a breakdown. "And it is hard to make kindness interesting."*

∎ ∎ ∎ ∎

DURING THE SUMMER OF 1986, after eleven years as an FSG author, Roth was friendly enough with his publisher, Roger Straus, to join him and his wife, Dorothea, along with Carlos and Sylvia Fuentes, for a few days in Spain. In Madrid they stayed at the Ritz, near the Prado Museum, where Roth spent most of his free time before he and Bloom rented a car and toured Toledo, Córdoba, Seville, Granada, and Barcelona. "Roger's way of seeing a town is to drive through in his limo a little slower than he would ordinarily," said Roth. A couple of years later, Straus wrote a laudatory letter to Roth's prospective co-op board on West Seventy-seventh, pointing out that he was a "well-known author" with many awards and honorary degrees, as well as (perhaps more important) "a very successful author in monetary terms." The latter was—thanks to Roger—a rather shaky claim: after more than a decade of middling advances every other year, Roth found himself so strapped he had to sell two of his most valuable possessions—the Kafka manuscript and the Persian rug that used to adorn his living room on East Eighty-first—in order to afford the modest apartment and the studio on the Upper West Side.

His fortunes were about to change. Andrew Wylie was an agent who made a point of courting prestigious authors, whose proper market value could be assessed only via their backlists: "Shakespeare is more important than Danielle Steele," he said, "in large part because his work is

---

* Roth found Karen's manuscript "rough but strong" and sent it to an agent friend, who declined to represent her. "I have chosen a new path for myself," she wrote Roth three years later. "If you are not completely driven, writing is all but impossible." She was going back to school to become a psychotherapist, and meanwhile worked part-time as a counselor for homeless children. In 2017, I googled Karen (not her real name) and found her website as a "pre-licensed" therapist.

more lasting. So you have to negotiate with an eye toward capturing that long-term value." The year before, in 1988, he'd added Salman Rushdie to a list of clients that would eventually include the likes of Bellow, Mailer, and Sontag. David Rieff was about to retire from Farrar, Straus and Giroux and become (largely at Wylie's behest) a full-time writer, and, during a celebratory lunch with Roth, he revealed that Roger Straus had given Roth (*and* Rieff's mother) a very, very bad deal over the years. Roth's total advance for *The Counterlife*, for instance, was a seemingly munificent (by FSG standards) $450,000: "Get that Caribbean vacation in now," Roth had written Straus in 1985, while working on what was shaping up to be his masterpiece, "'cause you ain't goin' nowhere next year." What Roth didn't understand—because, as he admitted, he "didn't look at the fine print"—was that Straus was paying for *world* rights, which meant Roth's foreign sales reverted to FSG ("He'd say, 'Hey, we got $20,000 from Gallimard,'" Roth recalled, citing his French publisher, "and I'd say 'Great!' because I thought there was some kind of split or something"); moreover the $450,000 quietly included $200,000 for the paperback rights, which Straus had relinquished for the full term of Roth's copyright. Finally, Roger was an old-school shmoozer who treated the foreign market as so many friends and colleagues who shared his miserly perspective, and besides he'd already covered his ass with a lowball advance: "In the same way that he wouldn't be pushed by Philip to pay what the market value was," Wylie explained, "so too Roger would not demand of Gallimard or Hanser or Mondadori that *they* pay the market value with Philip." Wylie estimated that with a proper agent—who could "pull these deals apart and handle the foreign rights and push in each territory"—Roth stood to increase his revenue by about 500 percent.

A few days after that revelatory lunch, Roth attended a retirement party for Rieff where he met (perhaps by design) Wylie. "I discovered what it was like to be a pretty girl at a party," said Roth. "Every time I turned around, there was this guy." Roth was flattered, and impressed, and at a subsequent lunch he explained to Wylie that he was about to finish two books more or less simultaneously: a new novel, *Deception*, and a memoir, *Patrimony*, that was finished except for the last chapter; meanwhile he'd begun a draft of what would become *Operation Shylock*. Roth hadn't accepted an advance for unfinished work since *Letting Go*, in 1960, but when Wylie announced he could get Roth two million dollars for the three books, Roth said he'd think about it. But he remained skeptical. "Look," he said, over a second lunch, "this is my livelihood. This is my future. Do not make promises you can't keep." The conversation continued back at Wylie's office, and when the agent neither backed away from his original figure, nor inflated it even more, Roth decided he was "the real thing."

And yet he hated leaving FSG. He liked the "continuity" ("You break these people in when they work for you: the copy editor, the design lady . . ."), and besides, he was fond of Roger—they'd had some laughs and traveled together in Spain, etc. "I *begged* him," Roth remembered. "'Roger, make me an offer that won't make me look silly for turning down this enormous amount of money.'" But the genial Straus refused to budge, and Wylie began canvassing other publishers. The restive Asher had changed jobs again, from Harper & Row to Grove Weidenfeld, where he managed to muster $1.2 million; finally, though, Wylie sold the three books, sight unseen, to Michael Korda at Simon & Schuster for $1.8 million. On August 16, 1989, the deal was announced in the *Times* ("Roth Changes Houses"), for which Straus affected a kind of worldly insouciance. Reminded that he'd been willing to pay Tom Wolfe (via a paperback deal with Bantam) between five and seven million for his next novel, Straus replied: "I had lunch with Andrew Wylie. He said he could get between $3 million and $5 million for [Roth's] three books but that I could have them for $1.5 million. I said that's ridiculous. I told him we paid Philip about $160,000 a book for world rights and they just about break even." It was true Wolfe commanded a more promiscuous readership—*The Bonfire of the Vanities* had sold about 750,000 copies in hardcover, roughly the same as another FSG best seller that same year, Scott Turow's *Presumed Innocent*—but then, for that very reason, Straus might have used some of his windfall to compensate Roth for his relative prestige. "You were so wise not to ask for this information until you had closed with S&S," Straus grimly noted, providing Wylie with sales figures for Roth's hardcover FSG titles: *The Ghost Writer* and *The Counterlife* had sold 35,697 and 40,806 copies, respectively, but *The Anatomy Lesson* had sold only 18,718 and *The Facts* a dismal 13,439.

The following spring, Simon & Schuster published the first of Roth's three books, *Deception*, with a rather lurid jacket illustration—a naked couple embracing in bed—and the *Times* ran a second piece about the two feuding houses, "Roth's Publishers: The Spurned and the Spender." "This is not a subject that interests me," said Roth, taking the high road, whereas his agent was a little more forthcoming: Likening Roth's relationship with FSG to "a marriage in a rut," Wylie added, "The covers of his books [at FSG] conveyed the impression that they were difficult and literary"—whereupon he pointed to a poster for *Deception*: "As you can see, the Simon & Schuster approach is as night to day." Roger—the Spurned—was informed by the *Times* of his "somber image" vis-à-vis Roth's racy new publisher: "Those are just self-serving remarks to cover over the greed and avarice of Mr. Wylie and Mr. Roth," Straus replied, and for good measure dismissed *Deception* as "a bad book, by no means Mr. Roth's finest hour." Roth, speaking privately, thought it "ill suited" Roger—an heir to the Macy and Guggenheim fortunes, married to a woman with Rheingold brewery millions; born, in short, with "eighty-four silver spoons up his ass"—to accuse Roth, redundantly yet, of "greed and avarice."

According to the *Daily News*, "A spy swears she heard Straus remark 'Oh s——!'" when Roth won the National Book Award for *Sabbath's Theater* in 1995, and "the best part" of winning the Pulitzer three years later, for Roth, was his reunion with Roger Straus. Heading up the marble steps of Columbia's auditorium, Roth turned and spotted his old publisher behind him. He waited with a smile: "Then I extend my hand and shake his vigorously and I just keep shaking it and don't let go until he finally says, 'Congratulations.'" Truth be known, Roth had a soft spot for Roger until the very end, and made a point of attending his memorial ("people told stories about how cheap he was"). As for Andrew Wylie, Roth would forever consider him "the perfect agent and a good friend": "I am enormously fond of him," he wrote Wylie's co-op board, in 1992, "have absolute trust in him, and would be even more delighted to be writing this letter if he were moving into my building rather than yours!"

■ ■ ■ ■

WHILE PROMOTING *The Counterlife*, in 1987, an exasperated Roth had offered to bare his chest to an interviewer in order to prove that Zuckerman's quintuple bypass wasn't based on real life. "No good to me at all," he said two years later, when he himself had had a quintuple bypass. "I've already used it."

Ever since his first diagnosis of coronary artery disease seven years before, Roth had worried about a sudden heart attack. He exercised obsessively ("part soldier, part monk," said Bloom) and strictly adhered to a heart-healthy diet, which Bloom was happy to provide (Dick Stern remembered her serving, with wine, "vegetable caviar and cheeseless cheese served on weightless wafers"). During this time, Bloom wrote, Roth became more irritable than ever ("usually with me"), whereas Roth, in turn, was uncomfortably aware of her incipient panic even in moments of minor tumult. For that reason he told her nothing, at first, about an episode in early August 1989 when he was barely able to catch his breath after swimming a single lap in the pool; he clung to the side, heart and head pounding, before seeking the privacy of his studio to phone his friend and physician, C. H. Huvelle. As luck would have it, Roth was scheduled to get his annual coronary checkup at Waterbury Hospital the next day; until then, Huvelle advised him to take it easy and be sure to report the incident to his cardiologist. Huvelle said it was probably just a panic reaction to that day's visit with Herman, whose condition was vividly deteriorating.

Roth's doctor at Waterbury, Peter Monoson, discussed the results of his EKG with Roth's cardiologist at New York Hospital, Charles Smithen, who directed Roth to meet him as soon as possible in the emergency room. During the two-hour trip to New York, according to Bloom, Roth insisted on driving and told her "very calmly" to phone Sandy in Chicago and ask him to come to New York, and also to inform his close friends. As Roth recalled, "She was, as usual, unequal to the stress of the occasion and was hardly what you could describe as supportive. She was mute and timid." Dr. Smithen was waiting with a wheelchair and motioned for Roth to slow down and have a seat; after X-rays, the patient was wheeled to the ICU and put to bed, where he read Bellow's new novella, *The Bellarosa Connection*, with an oxygen prong in his nose. After "a flurry of activity around [his] bed" that night, Roth was informed in the morning that he would have immediate bypass surgery rather than the previously scheduled angioplasty.

Sandy, who'd endured the same five- or six-hour ordeal a few years before, had already arrived when the surgeon, Dr. Krieger, emerged to say the operation was a success and they were free to visit Philip in the ICU. Except for his ghastly scars—an eight-inch incision, from his clavicle to the base of his ribs, was freshly wired shut, and the interior length of his right leg, where they'd harvested arteries, looked like "the old Pan American highway"—he seemed weary but not terribly worse for wear. "Which of my friends is most frightened it's going to happen to him?" he asked Bloom. One or two of those friends must have spread the word, since the hospital's public affairs office soon received inquiring calls from the *Post* and *Daily News*. Roth had mainly hoped to shield his father, whom he'd phoned on arrival at the ICU: "I said, 'Dad, someone has backed out of a job at Yale on a weekend and there's a seminar and they asked me to come down.' And he said, 'How much they gonna give you?' And I said, 'Ten thousand bucks.' He said, 'That's not bad for a weekend.'" Worried the shock of finding out from the newspaper would kill him, Philip phoned again and told him what had happened. He said he was fine, but Herman was in tears: "I shoulda been there," he said. "I shoulda been there."

Servadio and her son had arrived in New York a few days before, and were wondering why they hadn't heard from Philip and Claire, when Sandy phoned and told them about the surgery; he also mentioned that Claire was "in an incredible state"—weeping and barely able to speak. A story Philip would never tire of telling—as it seemed, for him, to put the whole relationship in a nutshell—was included in his novel *Everyman*, wherein the title character's third wife becomes a "hazard" in times of emergency: "She certainly didn't inspire confidence on the morning of the [bypass] surgery, when she followed beside the gurney weeping and wringing her hands and finally, uncontrollably, cried out, 'What about me?'" Sandy worried about leaving his brother in her care, and related his concerns to the cardiologist, who refused to release Philip from the hospital until he agreed to hire two nurses, one for day and one for night, to look after him at home.

Roth became especially close to his day nurse, "a warm, competent, cheery young woman," he wrote, who "had twice to shout at Bloom in our own house to get her to bring her anxieties under control around me." As in *Everyman*, his nurse's "high-spirited devotion" would lead to an affair once Roth had "recovered his sexual prowess"—a rapport Bloom evidently suspected. Roth's physical therapist, Lori Monson, arrived one day to give him electrical stimulation for postoperative muscle spasms and was struck by the "attractive young woman" reading beside his bed. As she recalled, "The vibe was pretty intense" when Bloom came home and noticed not one but *two* young women in the bedroom. On her way out, Monson paused to collect a shopping bag she'd left by the door, and Bloom erupted *"Are you taking my things?!"*

■   ■   ■   ■

THE END CAME, for Herman, when his tumor began to interfere with his breathing and swallowing ("It would be better," his doctor said, "if he didn't eat"). Around three in the morning on the day of his death, October 25, 1989,* Herman's night nurse in New Jersey phoned Philip and said her patient was in crisis; Philip told her to call an ambulance and have Herman taken to nearby St. Elizabeth Hospital, where Philip would meet them in the emergency room. Herman was unconscious by the time he arrived, and Philip had to decide on the spot whether to keep him alive on a respirator ("easily the most wrenching decision of my life"); he declined, and spent the next eight hours watching Herman die. As he wrote in *Patrimony*, his father "fought for every breath with an awesome eruption, a final display, of his lifelong obstinate tenacity. It was something to see." When it was over, around noon, Roth chose not to notify the hospital staff; he went on sitting there, holding his father's hand. About an hour later Sandy arrived, saw he was too late, and burst into tears.

Because Herman was a semiobservant Jew, the son of Orthodox Jews, his sons arranged for his burial the next day. As with his mother, Philip

---

* The same day Roth assigned the following paper to his literature class at Hunter: "In his 'Letter to His Father' Kafka writes (page 87), 'My writing is all about you; all I did there, after all, was to bemoan what I could not bemoan upon your breast. It was an intentionally long-drawn-out leave-taking from you, yet, although it was enforced by you, it did take its course in the direction determined by me.'

"Kafka is pointing here to a relationship between his life and his art. On the basis of the fiction of his you have read and what you now know of his life, can you describe this relationship?"

was too emotional to read his eulogy, and asked Claire to do it ("which she did willingly and quite beautifully"). After a passage from *The Facts* about Herman's near fatal case of peritonitis in 1944, and his tearful reconciliation with his brother Bernie shortly before Bernie's death in 1981, Philip added a note:

> The last one *left*, the last one *gone*. Morris. Charlie. Milton. Ed. Betty. Berny [sic]. Herman. I don't think a day of his life went by when he did not utter one of their names.
>
> He was a solid man. He was an honest man. His sense of loyalty was monumental. . . . He loved his loved ones as doggedly as he did *everything*. But he was a fighter as well and fighters don't endure on love alone. He knew how to hate, and who to hate, and was not shy about letting you know the score. He simply did not understand what it meant to *quit* or to back away or to give in.

Afterward Sandy and Philip and the other mourners shoveled dirt over the coffin, then gathered at Herman's apartment. "I told Claire last night that I'm going to take an ad in the New York Review," Philip wrote Kazin a week later: "'Unemployed son, 56 years of experience, excellent credentials, seeks new position.'"

Every year for the rest of his life, Roth visited his parents' graves on their wedding anniversary, February 20, at Gomel Chesed, a run-down old cemetery in Elizabeth where various Finkel relatives are buried. "The visits are emotional but deeply satisfying," he wrote.

> Generally, after standing beside each of these graves for a while, thinking my family thoughts, I walk around the cemetery, invariably reading the gravestones I pass (any number of the names I use in my books are taken from the gravestones there). In all I spend an hour or so alone in the cemetery—I've never in my twenty-one years come upon another mourner there—before I leave to drive back to New York.

"Good. You lived," Everyman's mother tells him when he visits her grave; very like his creator, Everyman "put no stock in an afterlife and knew without a doubt that God was a fiction and this was the only life he'd have," but nonetheless spoke to his dead parents and heard their replies. Philip Roth, moreover, liked to pray when he was happy, as he confided to his friend Jack Miles, the former Jesuit seminarian: "I used to do this frequently at Yaddo, during the years when I was recovering from everything, and I have embraced trees and knelt on the ground in the rural isolation of Connecticut. Keep it under your hat."

CHAPTER

Thirty-Six

EIGHT DAYS AFTER THE AYATOLLAH KHOMEINI ISSUED his fatwa against Salman Rushdie on February 15, 1989, the BBC announced that the author had "broken his silence" and would review *The Facts* in *The Observer* because, as Rushdie remarked in the newspaper three days later, Roth's "responses to being so vilified" by his own people had been "very moving, even helpful, to this similarly beleaguered writer." Roth responded with a quote that was published on the front page: The "tiny turbulence" he'd experienced in 1959, with the publication of his first book, was hardly comparable to the "international crisis" precipitated by *The Satanic Verses*, nor was Roth ever remotely so menaced as Rushdie: "If, however, this brave and enormously talented writer has, in his duress, been able to find some strength in reading about my own apprenticeship in the unforeseen consequences of art, I'm both touched and pleased."

A month or two later, at Bloom's invitation, Rushdie came to Fawcett Street for dinner, along with his then wife, Marianne Wiggins, and, Roth recalled, "about six secret service guys," who stationed themselves around the house and on the street outside. Privately Roth considered Rushdie "a great writer" and, as a human being, "an interesting shit." They'd met once before, at a party given by Roth's former English agent, Deborah Rogers; Roth had just returned from his trip to Israel in November 1984, and enthused *chez* Rogers about all the lanky Ethiopian Jews he'd seen as a result of the Israeli rescue mission, Operation Moses. "Did they put them in concentration camps?" Rushdie asked, and Roth told him to go fuck himself. "The next time I saw him he was in my living room," Roth laughed. "I was going to call the Iranian Embassy"— his voice became urgently sotto voce—"'I won't tell you my name, but *he's here. . . .*'"

A year after the fatwa, Roth played another small role in world politics when he visited Prague, post–Velvet Revolution, to interview Ivan Klíma for *The New York Review of Books*. "It was thrilling to be in unoccupied democratic Prague," he wrote, almost fifteen years after he'd been harried out of the country by secret police. During his 1990 visit—his last—he remembered a walk he took around Wenceslas Square, where crowds had chanted their ecstatic approval for the revolution. Roth was especially heartened by the sight of pedestrians pausing near a loudspeaker outside the headquarters of Václav Havel's Civic Forum party, whence was played, on continuous loop, the dull squawking rhetoric of the ousted general secretary of the Czech Communist party, Miloš Jakeš: "Watching people walk back out into the street grinning," said Roth, "I thought that this must be the highest purpose of laughter, its sacramental reason for being—to bury wickedness in ridicule." A potently literate people at the worst of times—all the more given the unwatchable diet of state television over the past twenty-one years—Czechs now jammed the bookstores to snap up previously banned works, beginning, of course, with Kafka. The first banned *American* book to be published in a free Czechoslovakia, however, was *Portnoy's Complaint*—this as a rebuke to Soviet-era prudery and also as a fond tribute to its author, the editor of the Writers from the Other Europe series who'd championed the work of dissidents behind the Iron Curtain. Four years later, Roth became the first recipient of the Karel Čapek Prize, an award reserved for Czechs (Havel would not receive his until 2008), with only two foreign exceptions, Roth and Günter Grass. Finally, in 2001, Roth was the first-ever recipient (and only American) of the Franz Kafka Prize, which—not unlike the Nobel—recognizes an author's oeuvre for its "humanistic character and contribution to cultural, national, language and religious tolerance, its existential, timeless character, its generally human validity and its ability to hand over a testimony about our times." Such a recognition, said Roth, "beat Stockholm any day."

There was, however, one unfortunate result of that trip to Prague in 1990.

Fifteen years before, Milan Kundera had accepted an invitation to teach at the University of Rennes, in France, and was subsequently stripped of his citizenship by the Czech government. During a visit to London, he and Roth had walked around the city while Roth did his best to commiserate: how awful, he said, that Kundera had lost almost everything when he left his native country—his money, home, parents, language. . . . Kundera shook his head and finally stopped and said, a little impatiently, "Philip! No! I lost *sixteen girls!*"

Within a few years, though, things began to look up: *The Unbearable Lightness of Being* was published in 1984, in French and English translations, and was an international best seller; during a *New York Times* interview with Roth that year, Kundera admitted he was nothing but relieved to be free of Czechoslovakia's "eternal political discussions and their stereotyped and sterile content. . . . I understand Hannah Arendt very well when she says: 'It's easier to act than to think under tyranny.'" One may imagine how such sentiments went over with writers still suffering under that tyranny, whose books, far from being celebrated, were hardly known in the West. "There appears to be a controversy over what might be called [Kundera's] 'internationalism,'" Roth remarked to Klíma during their interview in 1990, shortly after the post-Soviet publication of Klíma's *Love and Garbage*. Roth had meant to defend Kundera from the charge that he'd "betrayed" his country by writing "for" the French or "for" the Americans, characterizing his recent novels as "a strong, innovative response to an inescapable challenge." Klíma's original reaction was so caustic Roth implored him to recast it in milder terms ("I had no intention of censoring the conversation—Ivan had had enough censorship"); what Klíma said instead, for print, was that Kundera's alleged "internationalism" was "only one of the many reproaches" addressed to him, noting the "bitter struggle" that had continued for Klíma and others in Czechoslovakia while Kundera became rich and famous in France.

Kundera was furious: for years now he'd weathered scathing abuse from less fortunate countrymen such as Klíma, and now Roth, his friend, had effectively invited the man to attack him again in the *New York Review*. He might have wondered, too, whether his decision to withdraw his books from Roth's reprint series, in 1985, had something to do with things, and never mind Roth's relative disdain for Kundera's best-known book ("The Unbearable etc is everything Milan hates," Roth wrote Updike: "sentimentality, pornography, and easy politics"). Roth caught wind of his friend's anger, and tried to explain: "If you think I was stupid and misguided, so be it—I can be stupid too. But don't be harsh and accuse me of disloyalty. That isn't fair and it isn't true. I can only tell you that Ivan Klíma's answer would not have been quite so moderate had I not argued with him too."

But it was no use. Kundera refused to speak to Roth or answer his letters. Finally, after more than a decade of silence, Roth wrote again and begged his friend to let the breach heal before it was too late; Kundera agreed, but by then neither man traveled anymore and it was understood they'd never meet again. "I have completely forgotten [how] to speak English," Kundera replied in a final note, when Roth asked him to be interviewed for a documentary about Roth. "Do not be angry with me, dear Philip, and count on my faithful friendship."

■ ■ ■ ■

"CLAIRE IS MAKING a heroic, heroinely adjustment to living in America," Roth wrote Nina Schneider on September 24, 1988. "It wasn't easy at the start but she's resilient and, as we all know, a trooper." So Roth would have the world believe. At least twice a year, though, without telling Bloom or anyone else, he'd drive sixty-odd miles to the Jersey Shore and order the bluefish platter for $7.95 at his favorite dockside restaurant, Ollie Klein's in Belmar, then wander the boardwalk for a couple of hours wondering what the hell he'd gotten himself into. "Look at those hideous faces!" Bloom observed, familiarly, of an old Jewish couple in Central Park, a remark she repeated to Conarroe while dining at a Chinese restaurant, Shun Lee, near Lincoln Center ("I don't think she was talking about Episcopalians"). Once, while eating out with both men, she kept decorously whispering the word "Jew"—as ever in public—despite Roth's assuring her that the word needn't be whispered on the Upper West Side; by way of proving this, he yelled, *"JEW JEW JEW JEW!"* once they were out on the street. Rankled by the paucity of Christmas cards from Roth's friends that year, she cried, "What's the matter with these Jews!"—whereupon Roth went for a long walk, "wondering how [he] could continue living with this woman." At a stationery store on Fifty-seventh he bought three Christmas cards and signed them Menachem Begin, Albert Einstein, and Franz Kafka. He left them on the hall table, where she found them the next morning and woke him up with her laughter.

"Phil and Claire in crisis, according to Francine on the phone," Conarroe wrote in his diary on August 18, 1988. The next day he recorded "a difficult phone conversation with Claire," and decided he'd better take a bus to Connecticut and see what he could do. As Roth recalled of the episode, Bloom had begun crying almost as soon as she'd arrived at JFK that summer and continued, on and off, for two days. "Eventually I had to ask her—not that I didn't know the answer—'What is it? Why are you crying?' She wanted to be in London, she told me. She wanted to be with her daughter." This time Roth told her to *go* then; he'd leave the house while she packed her things, and return once she was gone for good. After he departed, Bloom ran "screaming" half a mile to some neighbors—Inga Larsen and her husband, in fact—who drove her to the Grays; Francine located Roth by phone at the Huvelles and asked if they could bring Claire over. Roth said either *Absolutely not*—as he claimed in a 1997 interview—or *Yes* ("influenced by the moderate, conciliatory Huvelles," he later wrote); in any case Bloom came over, and, according to Roth, fell to her knees: "Clutching at my trousers, she said, 'I beg you! I beseech you! I implore you! Don't leave me, please!' . . . 'Get up,' I told her, 'stand up,' but she wouldn't until C. H. and I lifted her to her feet." "Claire thought she was being evicted, but that got cleared up," Conarroe wrote on August 21. "Easy bus ride back to N.Y."

Roth tried again to leave her the following summer—though it might have been a bit later: "Some weeks after [Herman's] funeral I had a series of nightmares about my dead father," he wrote in 2011, whereas in 1997, only eight years after the fact, Roth said the nightmares (and hence the contretemps described below) occurred *before* Herman's death.* Why does it matter? Because it was either before or after Roth's quintuple bypass surgery, in mid-August, that (as he recalled) Bloom "began to pummel [him] on the chest with her fists, shouting 'Stop it! Stop it! Stop it!'" while he thrashed and cried out in his sleep. Roth told a pretty consistent version of the story on various occasions, but only once did he claim that Bloom pummeled a chest that had recently been "sawed open with a bone saw." Anyway the chest was pummeled, and a disgusted Roth spent the rest of the night at Conarroe's apartment in the Village. After he'd been gone a few days, Bloom delivered a message via Conarroe that she wanted Roth to meet with her psychoanalyst. According to

---

* For example, Roth had the "defunct warship" dream, as he wrote in *Patrimony*, "at the end of July," or about three months before Herman's death.

Roth, this woman explained to him, "Women don't like weak men. If you're sick just dial 911, and they'll take care of you." Enraged,* Roth returned to West Seventy-seventh and left a note on Bloom's pillow— "Next time find a strong man"—then proceeded to Connecticut, where he stayed away for three weeks, determined never to return. "And still I went back," he later wrote. "Shameful. The most shameful thing I've ever done. She cried, she begged, I jumped. I am a part of the history of ugly marriages that people have not had the fortitude to leave." Though of course they weren't actually married yet.

There was also the problem of his most recent fiction, or whatever it was. After finishing *The Facts*—and tabling all he could write of *Patrimony* while Herman was still alive—Roth had felt "altogether stymied" in his work, what with living in a hotel and shuttling back and forth to New Jersey to care for his father. Finally, toward the end of 1988, he began a novel that he provisionally titled *Ears* because it was written almost entirely in dialogue (this in opposition to his previous rule whereby "all conversations should be summarized except the brilliant ones"): "I've gotten down to basics," he told a friend: "'I want to fuck you, shiksa.' 'Suck my cock.'"

The novel was an even more explicit tribute to the euphonious delectability of Emma Smallwood, whose appearance as Maria in *The Counterlife* had caused a stir in Roth's house. "You love Maria more than you love me," Bloom had remarked, to which Roth had replied (in roughly the same words as "Philip" in *Deception*), "Of course I love Maria, she doesn't exist—if you didn't exist I'd love you too." In the past he'd freely discussed his works in progress with Bloom—his "first reader," he liked to say—but now he was tight-lipped to the point of furtiveness. One day Bloom rushed over to his studio on West Seventy-ninth to share a piece of good news she'd received in the mail, but Roth was so "cold, alarmed, and unwelcoming" that she abruptly and rather crossly departed.

Twenty years before, while in London with Mudge, Roth had read his friend Julian Mitchell's *The Undiscovered Country*—a novel partly narrated by a character named Julian who resembles the author. For Roth, this planted an idea about "raising the moral stakes" by making

---

* Bloom's analyst "died of cancer two years later," Roth remembered. "I was delighted. I was thinking, 'Did you dial 911? Did they take care of you?'"

oneself, "Philip," a "miscreant" in one's own book— as it happened, the same approach adopted by some of his favorite later discoveries: Genet, Gombrowicz, and above all Céline, whose rabid anti-Semitism on the page was apt to make a reader forget that in real life he was also Dr. Destouches, humanely tending the wretched of Paris. Likewise Roth almost invariably made himself seem worse than he was. "Why not?" he wrote; "literature is not a moral beauty contest." But of course—as Zuckerman points out in *The Facts*—Roth also liked to have it both ways, and was wont to remind the reader, in so many words, that "the most cunning form of disguise is to wear a mask that bears the image of one's own face."

"Rightly or wrongly," he later wrote, "there was something hazardous, I thought, in assigning the adulterer my own name and identity, and right off the bat Bloom proved me correct." On September 25, 1989, Plante recorded in his diary that Roth had given him a typescript of *Deception*, which Plante stayed up reading that night; the next day he phoned Roth and said he "was very worried about Claire's reaction." Roth said he planned to let her read it over the weekend, and, if pressed, he'd simply repeat his previous alibi about Janet Hobhouse serving as the model for the English mistress; in any case he'd insist it was mostly invented. "Even if it is invented," said Plante, "won't Claire be humiliated by everyone's assuming it's the truth?" "She knows what it is to live with a writer," Roth blithely replied. The following week Plante called again to ask whether Bloom had read the book. "No," said Roth.

But one morning, at last, he presented her with the typescript and left for his studio. Bloom would retrospectively give a garbled account of the novel, as if it were a vague compound of both *The Counterlife* and *Deception*. "Oh well," she remembered thinking while reading the typescript, "he doesn't like my family"—this apropos of the "self-hating, Anglo-Jewish family" with whom the hero lives in England, presumably Bloom's faint recollection of Maria's anti-Semitic family in *The Counterlife*, though of course the Freshfields are Christian. Bloom also mentioned the various "Eastern European seductresses" who come to Philip's studio for sex, though the Philip of *Deception* only *listens* to these women, reserving his carnal energy for the one woman based on Emma. At any rate Bloom claimed to take the aforesaid in stride, but was outraged by Roth's portrayal of "his remarkably uninteresting, middle-aged wife"—

named Claire!—who is forever sobbing over his adultery with younger women. Roth himself would presently admit she was "perfectly right" to object to the use of her name. He hadn't named the mistress, after all. ("Of course the English mistress has a name," he playfully wrote Tom and Jacquie Rogers, "but do you think I'm going to blab it all over my book?")

Meanwhile, that day at his studio, Roth phoned his worldly friend Judith Thurman and explained his predicament; she told him to meet her at Fifth Avenue and Fifty-seventh, where Tiffany was on one corner and Bulgari on the other. At the latter Thurman directed him to buy a three-thousand-dollar serpent ring with an emerald head and diamond tail, and this he did without a moment's protest.

One of the first things he noticed, on returning to West Seventy-seventh, was his now vomit-stained typescript;* then Bloom emerged "like a wraith" ("I felt like Macbeth," said Roth) and began straightaway berating him—though not, to his mild surprise, about the mistress(es) per se:† "How dare you represent me as a bourgeois wife! How dare you represent me as a middle-class woman who would be concerned with adultery!" Roth thought back to the time she "nearly went out of her mind" on finding the maid's note—"Christa called"—but let it go; he promptly agreed to remove her name from the book. She was still inconsolable, so he slipped away and put the little Bulgari box under her pillow in the bedroom. She resumed berating him when he came back, and finally he said, "Why don't you go into the bedroom and see what's under the pillow?" A few minutes passed, then she returned smiling with the ring on her finger: "Who cares about that book, anyway?"

It was a momentary lull. In subsequent months she furiously buttonholed friends, and demanded the book's dedicatee, Rieff, meet her for lunch. *Why didn't you stop it?* she asked. When Rieff passed this along

---

* "I can't be sure," he remarked years later, "but I would imagine that the vomit-stained manuscript of *Deception* resides with the rest of my archive in the Manuscript Division of the Library of Congress in Washington, D.C."

† "Well, I hope it was fiction," Bloom told Leonard Lopate, in 1996, re the adultery depicted in *Deception*. "You never know what anybody else gets up to, but as far as I know it was fiction, but maybe it was not. . . . You know, he's a novelist . . . he has an imagination, which is why he's America's greatest writer."

to Roth, he laughed and said, "I can't even stop myself"—reminiscent of what "Philip" says to his lachrymose (but now anonymous) mate in *Deception*:

> "I write for a simple and ridiculous pathological reason—because I cannot stop myself! I write what I write the way I write it, and if and when it should ever happen, I will publish what I publish however I want to publish and I'm not going to start worrying at this late date what people misunderstand or get wrong!"
>
> "Or get right."

■　■　■　■

WITH *DECEPTION*, Simon & Schuster pulled out the stops to recoup its investment in Roth. The gleefully hyperbolic publicity campaign included a description of the novel as his "most original, poignant and provocative," and naturally predicted it would have the same generation-defining impact as *Portnoy's Complaint*. The cover of the February 1990 *Esquire*, where an excerpt appeared, featured a tousle-haired doxy wearing a negligee with one shoulder strap loose. "A famous writer has a mistress," the caption read. "They meet in a room with no bed. They have sex. They tell lies. They play games with each other. Then he exposes it all in a book." Will Blythe's introduction commented on the "fine carpets, paintings," and "monastic silence" of Roth's Manhattan apartment, and quoted Roth on the subjects of what feminists would think of his novel ("They'll probably hate it, but fuck 'em") and how the magazine might go about pitching his excerpt: "'Philip Roth calls his forthcoming novel *Deception*. But who can say how far the deception really goes? Is it actually a novel? Or is *that* the greatest deception?'" Such impolitic remarks had been made with the understanding that Roth would have a chance to vet the introduction in advance, and, when *Esquire* neglected to honor this agreement, Wylie grimly wrote the magazine's editor, Lee Eisenberg, that Roth was "outraged" and would "not allow his work to appear in *Esquire* again."

"His chinless head, nearly bald now, sniffs atop the slender neck with all the indignant sternness of a tortoise testing unfriendly air," Stephen Schiff generously evoked his subject for a *Vanity Fair* profile with which Roth had resignedly cooperated when his new publisher insisted. Schiff briskly dismissed the nominal occasion for the piece—Roth's novel—as follows: "Precious, often tedious, and practically devoid of forward momentum . . . lightweight, almost vapid. And because it grazes themes Roth has already excavated to the depths, it gives off a stale air." That done, he went on to quote an "old friend" who claimed Roth liked to behave rudely to "girls" at New York parties (Roth pointed out that he hadn't been to a party with "girls"—in New York anyway—since sometime in the sixties), and, more accurately, that Bloom was rumored to be "upset about the way he's purloined his private life for *Deception*." ("There aren't enough good things for me to say about them," Roth remarked of *Vanity Fair*, which went on to publish an excerpt from *Doll's House* about his 1993 stay at Silver Hill psychiatric hospital.)

Christopher Lehmann-Haupt's valedictory appraisal of Roth's work was a fittingly representative performance—fair-minded, full of padding quotes, and finally damning amid faint praise. Roth's readers, he concluded, "must surely be growing impatient for the author to stop analyzing his imagination and start exercising it, if he hasn't dissected it beyond repair by now." Fay Weldon was kinder in *The New York Times Book Review*, noting that *Deception* had been published the same week as Thomas Pynchon's more sprawling *Vineland*, and that she was happy to find herself "as exhilarated by one as by the other." Between *Vineland* and the "neat-and-steely" *Deception*, she wrote, "range the works of all other writers in the English language." She did, however, ding the author for being "rather old-fashioned about women" ("To flattery, to the power of the penis, the woman can only succumb"), and there was something of this, too, in Hermione Lee's review for *The New Republic*. Lee had mostly approved of the novel as art, but was a little dismayed by Roth's increasingly "reactionary" bent—the way he (or "Philip") takes the usual potshots at "feminist objections to his exploitation of women, the xenophobia and the parochialism of suburban Britain, the anti-Semitism of the fashionable English left," and permits little in the way of opposition. "'I wouldn't dare,'" his mistress says, when challenged to disagree. "Anyone who disagrees is stupid," Lee glossed—a provocation Roth would rebut in his next novel, characterized by a cacophony of disagreement on all sides.

Unlike his publisher, Roth was scarcely inclined to profess that *Deception* was his "most original" novel, but as a formal achievement he was mostly satisfied with it, and as ever he dismissed fiction-vs.-autobiography speculation as idle gossip. Perhaps his favorite endorsement came from Jonathan Brent's father, Stuart, a legendary Chicago bookseller (whom Roth had known for many years and described as a cross between a "Chicago intellectual and Persian rug dealer"): "*Deception* is a love story that is not a love story, and therein lies the deception. Its real subject is not the wiles of illicit love affairs, but those of the serious novelist, whose material becomes real only as it becomes art. The result is not so much a comedy of manners as a play of magic mirrors—a conjuring performance which I believe you will find to be an utter delight." Fair enough. In one of the novel's few scenes that Roth (probably) made up out of whole cloth, Philip's Czech friend Ivan—based on the director Jiří Weiss, whose much younger wife had left him after they immigrated to the States—accuses Philip of sleeping with his wife, and scoffs at his denials: "Even *this* you banally fictionalize. . . . Maybe you should have been a wonderful actor instead of a terrible novelist who will never understand the power of a narrative that *remains* latent." This made-up scene about Ivan later enables Philip (in perhaps the only other scene that might be indisputably described as pure fiction) to argue convincingly vis-à-vis his jealous wife that everything else is made up too.

For the most part, though, it suited Roth's imp of the perverse ("what it adds up to, honey, is *homo ludens!*") to be almost scrupulously accurate, in the novel, about even the most damning details of his actual life: "Three," Philip specifies, when his mistress asks how many affairs he's had with students—the same number that Roth (the real one) gave his biographer. "'What was he like?'" asks Philip, pretending to be his own biographer. "'A tall, thin man with a cheap watch,'" she replies. And that, too, was true.*

■   ■   ■   ■

---

* "Suppose I were to die and a biographer were to go through my notes and come upon your name," Philip says to his mistress in *Deception*. "He asks, 'Did you know him?' Would you talk?"

"Depends how intelligent he was. If it were someone really serious, yes, I might talk to him."

Emma Smallwood did not respond to my request for an interview.

"Once you've reached a certain age and you've been married, and you don't want children, what on earth is the point?" Bloom told *People* magazine in 1983. "Marriage gets vulgar after the second time." For more than ten years, Bloom had all but sneered at those who wondered why she and Roth weren't married ("We don't need it"), but later, once they moved to America, she became quite adamant to the contrary. Suddenly, according to Roth, she claimed to feel "embarrassed and humiliated," and wept bitter tears to prove it. In 2014—explaining why he'd married the two women he married, and didn't marry more suitable partners such as Ann Mudge and Barbara Sproul—Roth said: "It was not for lack of love that I did not marry any of those women I did not marry who would have married me. I did not marry them because none was a finagler, a cheat, or a manipulator made tenacious by panic who would have her man no matter what."

On January 1, 1990, Bloom wrote Roth a letter asking him to marry her, then went away to London to appear in Ibsen's *When We Dead Awaken*; a meditative three weeks passed before she received Roth's epistolary consent ("Dearest Actress, I love you. Will you marry me?")—a moment, Bloom wrote in *Doll's House,* of "radiant happiness."

"I'm going to have to marry her now," Roth sighed to Thurman on the way to Bulgari. In her New Year's Day letter, Bloom did her best to soften the blow, explaining simply that "it [was] time" after almost fifteen years together, and assuring him that she had no desire to take his money. As for their *Deception* controversy, she advanced the novel claim that what had *really* rankled was not "the silliness over the girls" but rather his mean comments about her "beloved country" ("*STOP* telling everyone how you hate London"). Finally there was the matter of her "wonderful" daughter: "*For God's sake* cut the crap," she wrote, entreating Roth to wish Anna a happy thirtieth birthday on February 13; it was time for everybody to be friends.

Perhaps the crucial factor in Roth's decision was the hope that Anna would be "out of [his] hair" for good; if he married Bloom, his thinking went, she'd feel more secure about staying in the States while her adult daughter pursued a singing career abroad. Also he was feeling "reborn" after bypass surgery—"a smashing success," as Dr. Huvelle assured him: "Now you have a perfectly sound, strong heart and a fine, brand-new blood supply." Buoyant after years of mortal foreboding, Roth even became sanguine about his moribund attachment with Bloom. "If she believed marriage would help, as she emphatically told me she did, if she thought it would make her happier and solidify her future and bring our union back to life—why not? What's to lose? Apparently while routing the five grafts to my coronary arteries, the surgeon had unwittingly extracted what was left of my common sense." In hindsight, of course, it occurred to Roth that he should have left Bloom, at long last, once his health had been restored; indeed, he was on the brink of leaving her when he was first diagnosed with coronary artery disease, in 1982, whereupon he began to worry about "being in the world alone." By 1990 he'd gotten used to the idea of having a helpmate, however fallible, in his life—someone "to take care of me when I'm old," as he remarked to friends who inquired about the dire step he was about to take.

Nor was that his only pragmatic thought: hardly a day passed that he didn't rue the way Maggie had absconded with more than half his earnings as a young man, and now that he was older—and more and more fretful about future productivity—he "did not wish again to turn to the court to adjudicate a marital property dispute and decide where [his] money went." In her book, Bloom referred to their prenuptial agreement as an "ominous" condition of Roth's willingness to marry, "glaring in its absence of any provision" for her in case of divorce. Moreover she seemed to imply, via remarks to *New York* magazine in 1996, that Roth had meant to leave her nothing in the way of an inheritance ("basically it comes down to the fact that Philip didn't want me to have anything because he felt I would leave it to my daughter")—a distortion not even supported by *Doll's House*, wherein she noted that Roth bequeathed her "a lifetime tenancy in the New York apartment" (which he himself had purchased in toto), "plus a generous sum of money" were he to predecease her during the marriage. The actual agreement—which her own lawyer, Benjamin J. Rosin (whose fees were paid by Roth), had approved—simply ensured that neither party would make a claim on the other's assets in the event of divorce. Nor was Bloom facing destitution in any case: Her London town house was worth almost three-quarters of a million 1990 dollars, and her total assets were estimated around $1.16 million—less than Roth's $5.46 million, but still. "So committed was I at this point to becoming Philip's wife," she wrote of signing the prenup (and initialing each page after careful perusal), "I accepted the insult offered, and chose to ignore it."

On April 29, 1990, Roth's old friend and divorce lawyer, Shirley Fingerhood—by then a New York Supreme Court justice—married him and Bloom at Barbara Epstein's apartment on West Sixty-seventh Street. Roth's memory of the occasion was mercifully dim in later years, though he did remember that the many attendees included the Ashers, Tumins, Maneas, Ross Miller, Sandy, "and unfortunately," he said, "me." The de facto best man was Avishai, who signed the marriage certificate and, on a moment's notice, gave a "beautiful toast" (Bloom) about how nice it was to marry one's best friend. Afterward the happy couple went home and read in bed. A week later Roth rang up Plante in London and told him all about it. "I believe now in fidelity," he laughed. "Fidelity is terrific"—a pronouncement belied somewhat, at the wedding, when he leered at Inga's cleavage in passing.

■ ■ ■ ■

THE PREVIOUS YEAR Bellow had married his fifth wife, Janis Freedman, a graduate student and his secretary at the Committee on Social Thought. Freedman, forty-three years his junior, was a great reader of Philip Roth, whom she made a point of welcoming into their lives. On June 9, 1990, the newlywed Roth and Bloom were invited to a surprise seventy-fifth birthday party for Bellow at Le Petit Chef, near the Bellows' summer home in Jacksonville, Vermont. One of the female guests observed that the occasion was mostly attended by "a lot of shaky old men with very young wives"—not unlike the guest of honor—but Roth loved the "Chekhovian" ambience of old Russian Jews "popping up to make speeches," or announcing "I chav a song!"

For Updike's benefit, Roth summed up the dynamic of his long and somewhat unrequited love for Bellow thus: "I still treat him like the maitre he is, acting in the process a little like the boy I is." Roth had few illusions about Bellow's ambivalence toward his work, though he'd gotten the misguided impression that Bellow at least liked *Goodbye, Columbus*, given the rave he'd written for *Commentary* ("The Roth review got some of its teeth drawn . . ."). In 2000, well after his friendship with Roth had finally flowered, Bellow admitted in *The New Yorker* that he "didn't get much of a kick out of *Portnoy's Complaint*" ("I was amused, but it wasn't pure joy")—if anything an understatement: his then girl-friend, Maggie Staats, had tried reading Roth's best seller on an airplane, but Bellow forbade it until she agreed to wrap the jacket in brown paper. That same year (1969), with his usual eager filial piety, Roth had written the great man, "You may not think it's done me much good, but nonetheless, reading you all these years has been of tremendous importance to my work"—and seven years later, when Bellow won the Nobel, Roth was among the first to send a telegram: "There IS justice in the world." Bellow's colleagues at the Committee, however, would joke ever after in October: "Stay away from Saul today. They're announcing the Nobel Prize and he can't win it a second time."

Roth's relations with Bellow suffered a grievous setback in 1979, when Roth thinly fictionalized him as Felix Abravanel in *The Ghost Writer*. "I thought it disgusting," Bellow said of the whole book, which included Lonoff's observation of his more famous peer: "Beautiful wives, beautiful mistresses, alimony the size of the national debt . . . it's no picnic up there in the egosphere."* In the years following, it suited Bellow to disparage Roth publicly—"What has Roth got?" he quipped to Dick Cavett in 1981—then charmingly apologize afterward, quite in keeping with Mark Harris's characterization of him as a "drumlin woodchuck," who (as Robert Frost wrote) "shrewdly pretends / That he and the world are friends." "I asked Aaron [Asher] to tell you that the Good Intentions Paving Company had fucked up again," Bellow wrote Roth two years after Cavett, when his rebuke of the Zuckerman books was quoted in *People*: "Why write three novels that examine one's career as a novelist? Things are bad out there. The knife is at our throats. One can't write books so attentive to one's own trouble." Bellow assured Roth he'd also told "the crooked little slut"—viz., Roth's *People* profiler—what a

---

* Roth tried to cover his tracks by claiming that Abravanel resembled *himself* more than Bellow, beginning with physical appearance: "The rug dealer's thinning dark hair, the guarded appraising black eyes, and a tropical bird's curving bill"—which of course rather nicely described Bellow, too, at least the way he looked in the fifties, when the novel is set. Still, Roth said that if Abravanel had made an appearance in the TV adaptation, he himself would have been the right man to play him.

good writer Roth was; that said, he belittled Roth further by suggesting that Roth had bought the whole "Freudian explanation" that a "writer is motivated by his desire for fame, money and sexual opportunities," whereas Bellow himself had never taken such motives seriously. "If my three books are about a writer motivated by his desire for fame, money, and sexual opportunities," Roth replied, betraying rare impatience with his wily maître, "I'll eat the foot in your mouth. What is surprising to Zuckerman is that he too writes for all THE GREAT REASONS, but what he *gets* is fame, money, and sexual opportunities. . . . I'm a big boy now with very little hair and I really do understand these things." Having gotten that off his chest, Roth reverted to his usual magnanimity and assured Bellow of his "admiration and affection."

As for Bellow's often vexed relations with women (especially wives), Roth was nothing but sympathetic. Both were bewildered by charges of misogyny, since it seemed to them the problem was opposite—that is, an all but helpless *susceptibility*, sexual and otherwise, hence a mutual tendency to stay in touch with old girlfriends, give them money, and basically remain interested in their lives. When Bellow visited London in April 1986, his fourth wife, Alexandra, had just "thrown [him] out" and he was, as he put it, "in the dumps"; moreover he disliked his hotel. Roth got him a nice room at the Royal Automobile Club and fixed him up with a flirtatious Edna O'Brien at a dinner party. "Philip," she rang him up the next day, "did the Nobel Prize winner ask for my phone number?" "No, I'm afraid he didn't." Pause. "Good, I didn't want him to."

∎ ∎ ∎ ∎

BELLOW WAS ROTH'S HERO—all the more so over time—though all good writers were heroic after a fashion and Roth was never shy about showing them a seemly regard. "Contact with writers I admire or toward whom I feel a kinship," he told Joyce Carol Oates, "is precisely my way *out* of isolation and furnishes me with whatever sense of community I have." His long if sporadic friendship with Don DeLillo, for instance, began the summer of 1988, when Roth read his colleague's new novel and was moved to write one of his typical fan letters: "The only thing comparable to *Libra* would have been the Warren Commission Report written by Dreiser, Dos Passos, and William Burroughs." He proposed they meet for an afternoon walk, which became something of a semi-annual ritual (though Roth found DeLillo almost disconcertingly silent and couldn't help wondering what the man really thought of him).

Roth also had a hand in discovering Louise Erdrich: as an occasional manuscript reader for his friend William Whitworth at *The Atlantic*, Roth selected Erdrich's "Saint Marie" as an "*Atlantic* First" for the March 1984 issue. The story was excerpted from her first novel, *Love Medicine*, which Roth touted to friends as the work of a "Native American Flannery O'Connor"; he wrote as much to the "astounded" author herself, who, with her husband and his two adopted children, met Roth for a jolly lunch in Connecticut the following year. Erdrich's first novel went on to win the American Academy of Arts and Letters' Sue Kaufman Prize for First Fiction, but, throughout her thirty-three-year friendship with Roth, he never mentioned that he was the one who'd put her up for it (as the Academy archive shows), among other favors.

He also did whatever he could for Douglas Hobbie, who was fated to have a far less illustrious career than Erdrich. "The sure-footedness of this rookie is dazzling," Roth wrote in praise of Hobbie's first novel, *Boomfell*, in 1991, "—I enjoyed *everything*, the ductile idiom, the narrative nimbleness, the ironizing fugue of countervoices, the poker-faced comedy, and, most enjoyable of all, Hobbie's skeptical-mordant-tender scrutiny of desire bamboozled and lust recklessly and grievously pursued." Thus plucked (he hoped) from the abyss of first-novel oblivion, the forty-something Hobbie abjectly replied to Roth that his endorsement had "felt like confirmation of a sort (religious connotation intended)." Soon the two men were meeting regularly in Warren and Conway, Massachusetts, where Hobbie lived about two hours to the north, or else midway in Great Barrington, and meanwhile Roth saw to it that *Boomfell* received that year's Rosenthal Award from the Academy.

The friendship lasted six years, until a day in May 1997 when Roth wrote Hobbie a regretful note: "I read the first fifty pages of your manuscript last night"—Hobbie's third novel, *This Time Last Year*—"and I'm going to stop there because I don't think the book is for me. With the exception of a few strong pages—34–35 and 37–38—I found myself out of sympathy with virtually every sentence I read." Hobbie was flabbergasted at such "cavalier" treatment from a friend: "There are several different fucking voices in the fucking novel and there's plenty of fucking good writing," he protested. Roth mildly replied that he'd read those first fifty pages very carefully, and, to prove it, he mailed the marked-up typescript to the author, who remembered such marginal scrawls as "Douglas, what happened?!"

As for Janet Hobhouse, Roth had liked her first book about Gertrude Stein but didn't think much of her novels and never hesitated to say so. Still, they remained friends and occasionally met for lunch in London, where Hobhouse returned after her divorce in 1980. They'd been a bit out of touch when Hobhouse got cancer in the mideighties, whereupon Roth phoned her at the hospital—a conversation he included almost verbatim in *Deception*:

> "I think we must be friends again now, old friends. Anyway, I'm not completely out of the woods, so you can still be a little nice to me."
>
> "And when you *are* completely out of the woods?"
>
> "Then you can return to normal."

They fell out of touch again after Hobhouse's rather miraculous recovery, but a few years later her cancer returned and this time Roth was among her most faithful friends. He accompanied her to chemotherapy sessions, and one day spent almost three hours with her at an East Side restaurant, Petaluma, awaiting the results of a test that would determine whether her tumor had shrunk. Roth promised to "fuck her silly" if the news was good, and she asked him to put it in writing; finally, at three o'clock, she phoned her doctor and learned the worst: the tumor hadn't shrunk, and therefore she was probably doomed. She and Roth spent the rest of the afternoon walking around the park, then he took her home.

About a month later, on February 1, 1991, Hobhouse died suddenly of a chemo-induced thrombosis. She was forty-two. At the funeral Roth thought of Hobhouse's various qualities—her "verbal slyness and quickness," her depth, her youth—and began to sob. She'd died broke, and her only family in America was her dead mother, a suicide, who was buried in Cornwall Cemetery about five miles from Roth's house in Warren. Roth bought his old lover a plot there ($750) and also paid the gravedigger ($450). He was alone in Connecticut that winter, and every few days he'd visit the cemetery and kneel on Janet's grave, imagining her young and beautiful again, looking up at him and laughing: "*Now* you love me."

C H A P T E R

Thirty-Seven

*P*ATRIMONY, PUBLISHED AT THE BEGINNING OF 1991, was received with almost universal acclaim. Readers seemed grateful that Roth had dispensed, for now, with what his new *Times* reviewer, Michiko Kakutani, called his "defensive mirror games"—this in favor of a sustained and (for some) surprising expression of deep filial tenderness. "I just saw Aharon Appelfeld at lunch," Avishai wrote his friend from Israel. "We agree that if this is not your best book, it is at least your best you." Roth claimed to be mystified: "I don't know what's happened," he told his friend Alain Finkielkraut. "I'm loved! What did I do wrong?"

Not everyone loved him, of course. Faithful detractors such as *Commentary* and an old foe, Rhoda Koenig (in *New York*), took bitter exception to the passage about his father's loss of bowel control. Noting that Roth had promised his father—in the book!—not to tell anyone, Koenig snapped, "Sure, Dad, no one but the Book-of-the-Month Club." She also had hard things to say about Roth's (admiring) description of his father's penis, and so forth. Roth, for his part, conceded that Herman "might not have liked some things" but he was, after all, dead: "So we needn't speculate." Still, most agreed with Kakutani that *Patrimony* was a "beautifully rendered portrait of a father and a son," and the book earned Roth another National Book Critics Circle Award and made a few best-seller lists. Even the hitherto caustic John Leonard saw fit to commend the author, albeit a trifle condescendingly: "Philip, at last, is all grown up."*

"I'm not known for making speeches," Roth said, accepting the Medal of Honor from the National Arts Club on February 28, 1991. "Making

---

* "Death is good for some people," said Roth (quoting Bellow) of Leonard's death in 2008.

speeches, ladies and gentlemen, is the thing I like least to do in life."
And yet Roth was, in fact, an exceptional reader of his own work, and
such speeches as he'd given over the years—his 1960 National Book
Award speech, for example, which led to "Writing American Fiction"
at that year's *Esquire* symposium—had been rather successful, or anyway
memorable. Given, too, that he'd recently published a beloved best seller,
Roth decided it was time to let his wife's booking agency, Royce Carlton,
make good on its promise that he could earn five to ten thousand dollars
per appearance for hour-long *Patrimony* readings at various colleges. A
further incentive—at least for reading at his own alma mater—was the
esteem his latest book had won from Miss Martin, certainly relative to
its predecessor. "I'm just an old woman who grew up in Central Illi-
nois," she'd written Roth, "and I've never understood such involutions
and complications as make up *Deception*." Thus, for her sole delectation,
Roth composed "The Mildred Martin Guide to DECEPTION," but the
central problem remained: "why so much use of *fuck*? You are at no loss
of words. This one gets monotonous. . . . anyway no more *Deceptions*. /
Forgive me, / Mildred."

"Nationally Renowned Poet [sic] to Do Reading at Bucknell,"
announced the nearby Williamsport *Sun-Gazette* of Roth's April 1
appearance at Bucknell Hall, where the poetry library and lounge had
recently been renamed in honor of his mentor. In his reading script, Roth
had carefully scribbled "who's sitting right there" (reminding himself to
point at her), above the line where he declared the evening was "dedicated to [his] teacher and friend, Professor Mildred Martin." His reading
was a radical abridgment of *Patrimony*—from the discovery of Herman's
tumor all the way to the end—and Roth left nothing to chance, prac-
ticing for weeks on end and constantly adding little directions with his
red Flair pen: "beat / beat / beat" he scribbled above the phrase "could
not stop," as in "Eating was [Lillian's] only revenge, and like the tumor,
it was something he *could not stop*, no matter how he railed against it";
every so often, too, he noted in margins exactly how much time should
have elapsed. His labor paid off: the readings, performed at some twenty
venues over the next two years, were a hit—but none so much as that
first reading before a standing-room-only crowd plus Miss Martin in the
front row. *"You made it! You made it!"* Roth excitedly muttered to himself

afterward, wandering the streets of Lewisburg. He would always consider it one of the great nights of his life.

■ ■ ■ ■

IN RECENT YEARS, Roth's affair with Inga Larsen had tapered off with the worsening of her alcoholism, which she'd mostly managed to conceal from him. On January 6, 1991, Inga entered a twenty-eight-day recovery program in Minnesota; a day or two before leaving, she phoned Roth and told him she was an alcoholic. "After beeing [sic] reassured that it did not involve you in any way," she rather pointedly reminded him twenty-one months later, "you were very supportive of me." Later Roth put her in touch with his AA friend Joanna Clark, and the two attended meetings together.

Once Inga got sober, her affair with Roth flourished—became less about hijinks and more of a bona fide romance. Her nightly AA meetings provided the perfect cover for trysts: after dinner with her family, she'd stay at a meeting just long enough to steep herself in cigarette smoke, then head to Roth's house for two or three carefree hours. Bloom's occasional visits to the country were brightened as a result. As Roth observed, "Adultery makes numerous bad marriages bearable and holds them together and in some cases can make the adulterer a far more decent husband or wife than . . . the domestic situation warrants. (See *Madame Bovary* for a pitiless critique of this phenomenon.)" Certainly everyone agreed that Roth behaved like a model husband on the occasion of Bloom's sixty-second birthday (February 15, 1993), putting their friends up at a local inn and hosting a celebratory dinner at their favorite restaurant, the West Street Grill in Litchfield, where Roth gave a loving toast that moved his wife to tears. C. H. Huvelle assured him afterward that the evening had been "a smash hit" ("it was particularly kind of you to seat [Inga's] mother at your side"), and reminded him that they were getting ready for "the next Big One": Roth's sixtieth birthday party, *chez* Huvelle, the following month. Inga and her husband were cohosts, and while setting up for the party she came tottering in with a flamboyant bouquet of sixty roses. Huvelle—the only person (other than Sandy, Thurman, and Ross Miller) who knew about her affair with Philip—took Inga aside and admonished her to make the roses a gift from her mother and oldest daughter instead, as she did.

Joel Conarroe stood before the twenty-two guests as emcee, reading aloud letters from absent friends, including a telegram from the goyish Updike that, in fact, Conarroe had composed himself: "Masel gov, you alte cocker. Much nachos on this glorious yuntuva to you and your mishpocha. Zei gesunt." Inga's husband and Francine Gray gave heartfelt toasts, and Bloom read some love sonnets from Shakespeare. Then Roth rose, and—trying not to grimace from a fearful spell of back pain—gave a speech that Plante described in his diary as "funny and tender." Finally the guests were entertained by a wonderful young magician Roth had discovered at the Pump Room in Chicago.

"Can I quit now?" Roth wrote Miss Martin after finishing his latest novel, *Operation Shylock*, which had caused the author "more misery than all the other books combined." Almost every morning for three years he'd flipped through the cards of his alphabet frieze—the capital A, the small a; the capital B, the small b—reciting such incantations as "Words, words, words" and "I'm free, I'm nineteen, I'm unpublished, I can write what I want." Also he reminded himself with an emphatic, all-caps memo: "DO *NOT JUDGE* IT / DO *NOT* TRY TO *UNDERSTAND* IT. / DO *NOT CENSOR* IT." The result of such persistent hectoring, he hoped, would be his masterpiece, and no less than the canonizing sage of Yale, Harold Bloom, seemed to bear him out: "The largest praise is that *Operation Shylock* for me matches *Gravity's Rainbow*," Bloom wrote him, after reading an all-but-final draft in August 1992. "They are the two American fictions of the last generation or so that, for me, share canonical place with Merrill and Ashbery among the poets." Cynthia Ozick went even further, proclaiming Roth to be a "divine manifestation" before whom she went down "on [her] knees": "In the Ultimate Library, they'll put you somewhere between Dostoyevsky and Mark Twain."

For *Shylock*, Roth plunged almost giddily into the publicity campaign prescribed by his deep-pocketed publisher, all the more since he genuinely believed the book deserved a big sale and that it would make Roger Straus look bad. Moreover his imp of the perverse had dictated that he pretend this time, even to Simon & Schuster, that the novel's account of his becoming a Mossad agent (etc.) was, indeed, a true "Confession" as per the book's subtitle: "You know from our conversations—and, of course, from the book itself—that I believe Operation Shylock to be as accurate a report as I could write of my experiences in Israel in 1988," he wrote his editor, Michael Korda.

> On the other hand, the Mossad has requested, for reasons of its own, that I publish the book as fiction. I think you know by now all my reasons for deciding to do as they wish. I hope that you and Simon and Schuster will do everything to facilitate my decision. The almighty Israeli intelligence service is not an agency that either you or I would want to treat capriciously.

Simon & Schuster seemed a little befuddled by things: the book was duly classified as fiction when the first wave of review copies went out in January, then changed to nonfiction when Roth kept publicly declaring it had really happened. *Library Journal* reviewed it as fiction, but added a disclaimer: "Roth reported in *The New York Times*, March 9, 1993, that all events depicted in this book are in fact true but that the Mossad insisted that he bill it as fiction.—Ed." In the *Times* Roth had pleasantly complained, hardly for the first time, that people were forever convinced he'd been writing about himself in *Portnoy* and the Zuckerman novels: "And now when I tell the truth, they all insist that I made it up. I tell them, 'Well, how can I make it up since you've always said I am incapable of making anything up?' I can't win!" He even agreed to cooperate with a BBC documentary, his first TV appearance since his WNET interview in 1966: "he has broken his long silence to set at least some of the record straight about his life, his books, and the links between the two." The documentary featured commentary from the likes of Bellow and Kazin, while a poker-faced Roth more or less accurately discussed his life, and finally repeated the claim that his "Mossad supervisor" had forced him to label his latest work as fiction. Kazin—in the privacy of his diary, at least—took a dim view of such shenanigans, dourly recording his wife's observation at the breakfast table: "Can you imagine Kafka selling himself like this?"

Since people liked to read Roth's novels as autobiography, Roth believed his fiction was an essential part of his life story: "AGAINST ITSELF / The Autobiography of an Antithesis," he'd intended to title his final (since he earnestly wished to retire) magnum opus, a multivalent self-portrait that would bring together his last four books in a single volume: "Part One / *The Facts*, a Novelist's Autobiography / Part Two / *Deception*, a Novel / Part Three / *Patrimony*, a True Story / Part Four / *Operation Shylock*, a Confession." Such a concerted muddle was not an idle conceit to Roth. In 1998, an obscure writer named Richard Elman—sometimes confused with the great Joyce biographer, Richard Ellmann, a friend of Roth—would admit in his book *Namedropping* that he'd once met "a certain well-known screen actress" who, to his surprise, had agreed to go home with him and have wild, all-night sex. "Oh come on," she said the next morning, when he wondered why she kept calling him Phil, "I'd recognize you anywhere, Phil Roth. I loved every minute of *Portnoy*." Reading this, the real Phil Roth realized that a couple of strange actresses he'd once seen on *The Tonight Show*—tittering about what a "sexual madman" he was—may well have been talking about Elman or some Elman-like person; the same possibility had occurred to him re any number of tabloid stories from the *Portnoy* era ("*Barbra Streisand has no complaints*"). The idea of a doppelganger leading a life "that has nothing to do with your life" moved Roth to conceive of the other "Philip Roth" in *Shylock*, whom he dubbed Moishe Pipik—Moses Bellybutton—after the imp invoked by his aunts and uncles whenever he said or did something endearingly ridiculous as a boy: "the little guy who wants to be a big shot, the kid who pisses in his pants, the comical shadow alongside whom we had all grown up."

"It's Zuckerman," Roth thinks, in the novel, when his (fictional) cousin Apter first informs him of his double's presence in Israel, "it's Kepesh, it's Tarnopol and Portnoy—it's all of them in one, broken free of print and mockingly reconstituted as a single satirical facsimile of me." What Pipik purports to be, vis-à-vis the "real" Roth, is "THE YOU THAT IS NOT WORDS": to wit, a private detective from Chicago, also named Philip Roth, who is dying from cancer but determined to enact his concept of "Diasporism"—a plan to avert a second Holocaust in the Middle East by returning European Jews to their original home-lands; once the population of Israel is thereby halved, Pipik explains, "then the state can be reduced to its 1948 borders, the army can be demo-bilized, and those Jews who have lived in an Islamic cultural matrix for centuries can continue to do so, independently, autonomously, but in peace and harmony with their Arab neighbors." This strikes the real Roth as "the final solution of the Jewish problem for Yasser Arafat," and indeed he finds a receptive audience for Diasporism in his old university friend, George Ziad, a Palestinian who's filled with rage against the Israeli occupiers. Roth, pretending to be his own double, explains to Ziad that he "got the idea" for Diasporism from Irving Berlin: "God gave Moses the Ten Commandments and then He gave to Irving Berlin 'Easter Parade' and 'White Christmas.' The two holidays that celebrate the divinity of Christ—the divinity that's the very heart of the Jewish rejection of Christianity—and what does Irving Berlin brilliantly do? He de-Christs them both! . . . *He turns their religion into schlock.* But nicely!" Despite his perverse performance for Ziad, the real Roth is only too aware that it would take more than Irving Berlin to rid Christianity of its Jew hatred: "Diasporism is a plot for a Marx Brothers movie," he says; never mind how Diasporist evacuees would be received in "bigoted, backwater, pope-ridden Poland"—or Germany, Romania, Ukraine, et al.—Roth wants "to see with [his] very own eyes the welcoming committee of English Goyim waiting on the platform with their champagne. 'They're here! More Jews! Jolly good!'"

That Jews may not meet with ecstatic receptions from their Christian countrymen is a problem Pipik claims to address with an organization designed to purge the world of anti-Semitism: Anti-Semites Anonymous. One of Pipik's "workout tapes" for one of their meetings, however, is titled "Did the Six Million Really Die?": a long rant (almost six pages of fine print) blaming the partial extinction of European Jews on "the breakdown of the German supply system at the end of the war" and outbreaks of scurvy and typhus in the camps—this versus the Jew-perpetuated hoax (as Pipik would have it) of "Holocaustomania." "Man, how can you *not* be anti-Semitic?" he concludes. "When you see them they're all on the fucking telephone, manipulating. For better jobs. Or helping their friends." Thus Roth comes to suggest that his closest double is not a sinister anti-Semite like Pipik, but the immortal villain evoked by the greatest writer in English—the "hook-nosed moneylender," Shylock, the archetypal Jew throughout the ages in Europe: "the Jew expelled in 1290 by the English, the Jew banished in 1492 by the Spanish, the Jew terrorized by Poles, butchered by Russians, incinerated by Germans, spurned by the British and the Americans while the furnaces roared at Treblinka."

Stationed at the entrance of the Treblinka gas chamber was a notorious guard, Ivan the Terrible—beating his victims with pipes, gutting them with a sword—who may or may not be the "hardworking, churchgoing family man" from Cleveland, John Demjanjuk, ostensibly Ivan's polar opposite. Roth and Pipik, too, seem to have little in common except name and physical resemblance ("he looked like the after to my before in the plastic surgeon's advertisement"), and Roth wonders whether Pipik got the idea for appropriating his identity from watching this man's trial. Meanwhile Roth—of all people—knows that a single human being can accommodate drastic contradictions, and hence can easily imagine that the harmless-looking oaf seated in the dock may well be the same man who tortured multitudes at Treblinka:

> What a job! A sensational blowout every day! One continuous party! Blood! Vodka! Women! Death! Power! And the screams! . . . A year, a year and a half of that is just enough to satisfy a man forever; after that a man need never complain that life had passed him by; after that anyone could be content with a routine, regular nine-to-five job where no blood ever really flowed except, on rare occasions, as a result of an accident on the factory floor.

And hence, too, the duality at the heart of modern Israel: throughout the novel the historical suffering of the Jewish people is balanced against Israel's brutality toward the Palestinians, the whole seething conflict coming to a head at last, it seems, with the Intifada. And Roth's own ambivalence is reflected in the stridency of voices on every side. So determined is he, indeed, to let every conceivable side of the argument be heard at lovingly nuanced length that he overindulges an old tendency described by Kazin as "the aria bit": monologues that go on and on until merely recreational readers are apt to collect their things and head for the exits. Since Ziad and others are given abundant opportunity to vilify Israel, countervailing voices are perforce given equal time: that of the wheelchair-bound martyr Leon Klinghoffer, for instance—murdered by the PLO aboard the cruise ship *Achille Lauro*—whose laughably dull diary fills four fine-print pages, often beginning with a gloss on the weather. No wonder even some of Roth's most incisive admirers tend to be a little reluctant to revisit *Shylock* as elective reading. "I can see it's a dazzling piece of work," said Hermione Lee, "but I feel like Keats sitting down to read *King Lear* again." She laughed. "*Must* I again?"

Roth was in San Francisco (for a *Patrimony* reading) when Bloom rushed to their hotel room to show him an early *Time* review that seemed to augur great things: "Roth has not riffed with quite this comic abandon since *Portnoy's Complaint*. And the social and historical range of *Operation Shylock* is broader than anything the author has attempted before." By the time Roth returned east, however, a slew of more damning reviews had followed, including what would prove the first of many brickbats wielded by Kakutani of the *Times*: The comedy and sociopolitical commentary of Roth's novel, she wrote, were "subsumed" and "overshadowed" (both) "by the author's tiresome games with mirrors."

An even nastier shock lay ahead. There was a time when Updike had hesitated to review his "American contemporaries" because, as he explained to Aaron Asher (in the course of declining to review *The Professor of Desire*), "Envy pulls one way, and friendship (in many cases, including this) another." But soon enough he let go of this scruple. Bellow was thinking of Updike's canny disparagements when he referred to "the fastidious goy critics on guard for the Protestant establishment and the genteel tradition," whereas Roth, less thin-skinned, had remarked in print that Updike's mixed review of *The Anatomy Lesson* was "first class," and he'd also professed to be satisfied with the man's even pricklier assessment of *The Counterlife*. As for Roth's view of Updike's work, he could scarcely have been more generous; though disinclined to write much in the way of formal criticism, he made a point of dropping Updike a letter of considered praise for almost every new novel, not least the recent *Rabbit at Rest*: "You're the master of Joyce's great modern trick," he wrote, "—what Lewis, O'Hara, and Dreiser didn't dare to do: join the social position and vernacular of a Leopold-Rabbit to the perceiving mentality of a Joyce-Updike." Quite properly this struck Updike as "a lovely act of readership," and left him feeling all the more chastened for his less charitable (and more public) treatment of Roth: "what a niggle-mouthed slyly hedging *critic* I am in comparison."

Alas, there was nothing sly or hedging about Updike's abuse of *Shylock* in the March 15, 1993, *New Yorker*. "Some readers may feel there has been too much Philip Roth in the writer's recent books," he announced at the outset. "Such readers should be warned: there are *two* Philip Roths in his new novel." It went downhill from there. "It's hard to wrap your mind around this paragon," Updike wrote of "Philip I"—that is, the author's persona in the novel—whose supporting cast appears to be in a competition to praise him, from Pipik's "slavish flattery" to Ziad's, Jinx Possesski's, and Smilesburger's remarks about his independence, leadership, and literary achievement respectively. "Somewhere after Philip I sleeps with Jinx, the novel stops pretending to coherence and becomes a dumping ground, it seems, for everything in Roth's copious file on Jewishness." Picking one's way over this landfill was, for Updike, an "exhausting" affair: Roth's characters talk and talk "until their mouths bleed," and there are too many of them ("they keep dropping out of sight, and when they reappear they don't talk the same"). Casting about for a positive note to end on, Updike commended his colleague's "artistic energy" withal, suggesting the novel was de rigueur for "anyone who cares about (1) Israel and its repercussions; (2) the development of the postmodern novel; (3) Philip Roth."

Quite apart from Updike, there was plenty to dismay Roth about the reception of *Shylock*. Though Harold Bloom had compared him with Aristophanes in *The New York Review of Books*, and the novel would go on to win Roth the first of his three PEN/Faulkner Awards, sales were fairly dismal in spite of the hype and Simon & Schuster abruptly stopped advertising. Worse still was the apathy of his key constituency: Jews, American *and* Israeli, outraged or delighted. "Will Roth be impaled on incensed Jewishness once more?" D. M. Thomas wondered in his front-page review for the Sunday *Times*. Given Roth's "merciless probing" of Israeli brutality, Thomas wrote, Roth "would be smart to have a double undertake his promotional tour." Indeed, Roth's own great expectations for his book had included a Rushdie-style scandal—at least in the Middle East—but no. Reviewing *Shylock* for the *Jerusalem Post*, S. T. Meravi noted, benignly enough, that the novel had been largely ignored: "The man hasn't lost any of his estimable skill; he's just lost an estimable readership. Which may be the ultimate comment on the Israel-Diaspora question." Now *that* was depressing.

■   ■   ■

ROTH'S MARRIAGE also had a morale-lowering effect, though things had gone surprisingly well at first. "My ordinary, everyday life with Claire, especially in the country, fills me with a satisfaction I've never known before," he wrote DeLillo on January 16, 1991. "It unnerves me a little that I can be made happy by the life I used to be impatient with. In the old days everything outside of writing bored the shit out of me. Now it's the writing that bores the shit out of me, and the walks, the eating, the sleeping, the comradery [sic] that thrills me." The couple had made a point of keeping their marriage certificate magnetized to the fridge in New York, and would entertain friends with spontaneous improvisations of bantering cockneys or whooping Indians; meanwhile Roth insisted on pouring her cereal (or whatever) while announcing in a "Jew voice" (Avishai), "You don't lift a finger! You're a *Roth* now."

"He's very uxorious and tremendously involved with Claire's career," David Rieff had told *Vanity Fair*, and so he was. Back in the early eighties, when Bloom's acting jobs had dried up again, Roth pushed her to do one-woman shows featuring the great speeches of Shakespeare's heroines. She was, after all, one of the preeminent Shakespearean actresses of her time, having played Cordelia to Gielgud's Lear, Lady Anne to Olivier's Richard III, and Ophelia to Paul Scofield's Hamlet. After grueling rehearsal sessions in Roth's studio, they tried out the show at Berkshire Community College in Pittsfield, Massachusetts, where Roth conferred with the playwright William Gibson (*The Miracle Worker*) about proper stage lighting, microphone levels, and so on. Leon Botstein conducted music for one such performance, and likened Roth's engagement to that of a "stage parent" ("You felt you would be subject to his ire if something went wrong"). Later Bloom expanded her repertoire to include characters such as Mrs. Dalloway and Jane Eyre, and Roth always took it upon himself to come up with pithy titles—e.g., "The Triumph of the Bereft Woman: Charlotte Brontë's JANE EYRE." ("Why? Why?" he wondered in a 2013 email. "I must have been nuts. / The ex-idiot, PR.")

Roth was especially doting to Bloom *qua* actress, and especially in the presence of their friends. "I have to go backstage now and see my little *tchotchkala*," he'd sweetly announce after one of her performances. Indeed, the more insightful of their friends detected a quality of play-acting to the whole relationship ("everything was perfect, but could shatter if someone made a false move"). Because of the couple's well-choreographed rapport, some were shocked by the rupture that lay ahead, while others had always viewed the match as essentially artificial (whether or not they knew of its more dire shortcomings)—that is, as a meeting of great artists in the abstract, modeled on Chekhov and Olga Knipper, a paradigm Roth cherished. But a 1991 note in his slanted lefty handwriting indicates a man struggling to grasp the person he's married: "[Claire] has many wonderful, endearing and admirable qualities," he began, then considered the various men in her life: "Sadists and bullies. Burton, Steiger, Elkins. Finally only a criminal [Elkins] could protect her (Fear led her to seek protection from sadists or bullies who seemed 'strong.' . . .) At bottom is *fear* . . . Fear of Anna. . . ."

The last was most germane to the health of their marriage. "The [Felicity] event was the coup de grâce, of course," said Anna Steiger of the sexual advance Roth had made toward her friend in 1988. "After that it was only avoid avoid avoid." She'd tried begging off on the wedding, claiming another engagement, but relented after a series of tearful phone calls. Neither on that occasion nor any other, however, did she bother to dissemble a baleful contempt for her latest stepfather—though of course, to their mutual chagrin, they could hardly help crossing paths. While in New York, Steiger stayed at the Cosmopolitan Club on East Sixty-sixth, but "camped out" (as Roth put it) during the day at her mother's apartment, making phone calls from Roth's study while he worked at his studio and sometimes, as he'd find on his return, lying between the sheets of his bed. Nor had Bloom become any more independent—as Roth had fondly hoped—now that an ocean divided her from her daughter; on the contrary she'd taken to phoning Anna in Europe sometimes three or four times a day. As for Steiger's visits to Connecticut, they were infrequent but unbearable to all concerned. She was bored by the country, and her mother "would work feverishly" (Roth) to keep her diverted and out of her husband's way. Given the terrible tension, Roth was "flabbergasted" when a real estate agent phoned one day, in the women's absence, to report on a nearby house the two were thinking about buying. For Anna.

Inga bore the brunt of Roth's rage and desperation, as he was forever phoning her at the office to vent. "The way I see it is: you are powerless over the Claire-Anna relationship," she wrote him. "For Claire, Anna is her addiction. Since addiction is an illness it cannot be resolved with reasoning." Citing the AA slogan "Take what you like and leave the rest," she advised him to identify what was definitely unacceptable and come to some kind of workable arrangement. Thus Roth's letter to Bloom dated January 18, 1993, which she characterized in *Doll's House* (without quoting it) as "a totally unwarranted attack on [her] daughter." "We have a very precious marriage," the attack began.

> I love you dearly and I love dearly our life together. I know that what I am writing is going to cause you pain and I don't want to cause you pain. But in the interest of preserving what's most precious to me—your life with me and mine with you—I have to tell you candidly about something that distresses and pains *me* with a stress that won't seem to go away.

Roth proposed a few "guidelines" for Anna's visits, asking that she not use his study anymore ("I think my room and my desk should be respected as mine"), and suggesting he stay in Connecticut whenever she was in New York. As for Steiger's occasional trips to the country, Roth hoped they could be limited henceforth to a single week per year: "What begins as a pleasant time ends as a difficult, edgy, and, for me, hollowly isolating time." He concluded:

> Claire, it's no accident that we got married in America, where we were able at long last *to live alone and intimately as two.* For us, living alone and intimately as two middle-aged adults had been long, long overdue. . . . I refuse to have my life corroded with resentments spawned by my sense of being encroached on by or entailed with, even temporarily, a relationship that is not of my making . . . a relationship to which I am superfluous anyway and always have been because, in my judgment, it does not really admit of another human presence. . . .
>
> Love, love, and love, / Philip

In *Doll's House*, Bloom conceded it had been "many years" since she'd received one of Roth's "written injunctions," but at the time she reacted as if it were a matter of menacing routine: *"No more letters!"* she screeched, throwing the envelope to the floor. Roth departed for his studio and tried vainly to work, then phoned Joanna Clark ("one of my wisest friends") and asked if he could come meet her for lunch in Princeton. At Lahiere's, Clark recalled, Roth broke down and wept: "What can I do, Joanna?

What can I do?" Bloom was also crying when he came home that night. She'd taken his letter to her analyst, who categorically agreed with Roth. "*Good*," Roth thought with sublime relief, lying on the floor because of his aching back. "*Good*." Then Bloom said: "But can't she come one last time?" Roth felt chest pains and gasped, "Call Chuck" (Smithen, his cardiologist), who advised him to lie still for ten minutes and try to calm down. Meanwhile Bloom decided, as she wrote in *Doll's House*, that "the only way to deal with his petty belligerence was to humor him and take no notice."

Pain was the final factor in Roth's breakdown. While on his *Patrimony* tour that winter and spring of 1993, he'd worn a back brace at the lectern and afterward, backstage, would gulp a couple of shots of vodka to get himself through the rest of the evening (he refused to take painkillers or sedatives because of the Halcion episode). Finally, on May 22, he drove two hours to western Massachusetts to receive an honorary degree from Amherst College; after sitting through an almost three-hour ceremony he thought he would faint with pain, and while driving home he pulled over and phoned Inga, begging her to go to his house and wait for him there, as she did. For the past few weeks Bloom had been in London with her daughter.

Home at last—with no further reading dates and only a vague idea of what (if anything) he wanted to write next—Roth planned a summer of rest and recuperation: swimming, hiking, reading, sleeping. "Then Claire came," he remembered, "and she just began to cry. And she said, 'I can't stand it here. I hate it here. . . . I miss my daughter.'" This went on for three days or so, during which Roth "tanked"—overcome again by a constant, uncontrollable terror of being alone. Almost every morning the spectral, trembling man would descend the stairs, and his wife would take one look at him and burst into tears. "Just put your arms around me," he remembered telling her. "And tell me, 'I'm here, sweetheart, and everything's going to be okay.' And she'd do it, after I told her, like an actress." Roth particularly remembered a day in July when he pretty much threw in the towel. Bloom had asked him to help her rehearse some passages from *Cymbeline** that she was considering for her one-

---

* Or *The Winter's Tale* or *A Midsummer Night's Dream*. Roth—hardly at his retentive best that summer—mentioned one or the other at various times.

woman show, and ("nearly out of my wits with pain") Roth followed her into his studio and listened, uncomprehending, for however long it went on. "Very good," he intoned when it was over, whereupon she informed him that Anna would be coming to New York for six weeks* in the fall to study with a brilliant new teacher, Ruth Falcon, a great opportunity. Roth sat pondering the six weeks of ghastly pain and panic he'd have to endure alone (mostly) in the country, and a phrase occurred to him that would become like a mantra in the days ahead: "My life is a problem I cannot solve."

In *Doll's House*, Bloom mentioned a journal she began keeping that summer, the better to fathom her husband's "emotional swings"; on July 18, she accurately recorded that he seemed "afraid of being alone with [her]." Desperate for friends who wouldn't automatically fidget or weep in his presence, Roth had asked Ross Miller and the Maneas to keep him company for a while. Norman arrived with his wife, Cella, and remembered finding his friend "weak as a child of twelve years old": "Norman, I am lost," Roth whispered. "I am totally lost." As for Bloom, she seemed even more "unsettled, ravaged" (said Manea) than her husband, until her hysteria erupted in a curious way. "We three, and Ross, were sitting outside talking," Roth wrote in a 2010 diary entry, "when Claire, prompted by nothing that could be seen, began to run crazily around the fields, her arms raised in the air and wailing uncontrollably." ("Claire began to run around screaming, yes," Manea confirmed.) Roth and the Maneas sat watching in silence, while Miller went off after her, trying to catch her and calm her down.

None of this would have surprised Philip's brother. According to his third wife, Dorene Marcus, Sandy liked to remark of any actress who struck him as unstable (Judy Davis, say), "She's like Claire." When he arrived in Connecticut that July, he quickly sized up the situation and decided he needed to get his brother out of there.

The two had become close again once their first wives had died. After the kindhearted Trudy—who, again, despised Maggie and considered

---

* "Six weeks" according to a 1997 interview with Roth; in *Doll's House*, Bloom quotes Roth's baleful reference to a three-month stay.

her brother-in-law "selfish"—succumbed to ovarian cancer in 1970, Philip went to stay awhile with Sandy in West Englewood, New Jersey. The widowed Sandy struck his brother as "lonely and lost," so Philip and Barbara Sproul made a point of inviting him and his boys for gemütlich weekends (touch football, etc.) in the country. In 1976, Sandy moved to Chicago to become a creative director at Ogilvy & Mather, and within a decade he'd remarried, divorced, and, at age fifty-six, retired from advertising. Philip remembered a day in the mideighties when Sandy visited him at the Wyndham and announced ("look[ing] a little like the cat who ate the canary") that he was taking acting lessons and intended to become an actor. Instead, he became a full-time painter—more or less for the fun of it, as he was always careful to stress: "I'm a journeyman who paints pretty well," he told a journalist, "but no better than pretty well." Philip was always a little bemused that his brother—who obsessively filled hundreds of nine-by-twelve sketch pads with skillful drawings over the course of his lifetime, whiling away afternoons at a mall or museum just to sketch people—chose, for his painting, big abstract acrylic canvases rather in the style of de Kooning. These however were good enough to rate a one-man show at SoHo's Jack Gallery in 1988: "It's Sandy's paintings, not my books, that are autobiographical," Philip told *Time* on that occasion, "—and embarrassing to all of us."

"He only took pride in him, and that was lovely," Sproul observed of Sandy's attitude toward his little brother's "big, big talent" versus his own "middling ability," as he put it. Usually the two kept loosely in touch, chatting on the phone every few weeks, but Sandy never failed his brother in a crisis. In the past, when Philip needed help while he was alone in Connecticut, Sandy had dropped everything to care for him, and he did so again in July 1993 after a disturbing phone call. That first night in the country Sandy was awoken by the sound of his brother sobbing in the next room (at Philip's request, Bloom was sleeping in "a far guest room"); Sandy lay beside him and Philip asked to be held. In her journal Bloom wrote that she felt like "an unwanted appendage," and when Sandy asked her how she was coping with things, she admitted that she felt "helpless" and sometimes "almost hate[d]" Philip, who suddenly appeared in the doorway. Years later, reading of how Bloom had suspected he'd "engineered" the scene, Roth wrote: "Even when I am disabled both physically and emotionally and might seem to most observers unlikely to be able to engineer anything, I remain capable, in her estimation, of wielding my power over her and of 'manipulat[ing]' and 'frighten[ing]' her."

After less than a week, Sandy had seen enough: "You can't stay here," he told Philip, "*she* wants to be the sick one. You're coming to Chicago with me." The next day, as Sandy was about to lead his fragile brother away, Bloom called them "two of the cruelest people in the world"—or, as Philip remembered it (giving the words to Eve Frame in *I Married a Communist*), "You are the worst people I have ever known!" Afterward she repented of her harshness to a visitor (Inga), who replied, "Not one of your best moments."

■　■　■　■

SANDY LIVED IN A residential tower on Lake Shore Drive, and Philip immediately felt better there. That first night they went to dinner with Sandy's companion, Dorene (the couple wouldn't marry until 2001), who, unlike Sandy's second wife, knew Philip's work and found him delightful. Philip became lively and talkative, and even ate with decent appetite for the first time in weeks—but he slept poorly, and was depressed again when he woke up. Dick Stern paid a visit, and while they strolled around the downstairs gardens, Roth clung to his friend and said, "Are you sure you love me? Am I all right?"

Ross Miller happened to be in Chicago, and one day while they walked to lunch Roth decided it was time to kill himself. He stopped on the sidewalk and told Miller to go ahead without him. Surmising the worst—that Roth planned to jump from the top of his brother's building—Miller said (in effect) that if Roth was planning to do what Miller suspected, he'd have to do it in front of him. "It was a stunning confrontation and it frightened me," said Roth, who was persuaded instead to phone a psychiatrist he'd occasionally consulted over the years, Bill Frosch. A few minutes later Frosch called back: he'd found a place for Roth at Silver Hill Hospital in New Canaan, Connecticut, where a friend of his named Bloch* was medical director. The next day, August 3,

---

* I borrow Bloom's pseudonym for this man from *Doll's House*.

Sandy flew back east with his brother, then drove him an hour north to Silver Hill, and hugged him goodbye outside Bloch's office.

"How did I get from Chancellor Avenue School to here?" Roth wondered that first night in the Intensive Care Room; what had become of that brash lad who'd skipped two terms and dazzled the mothers of Weequahic as a caped Columbus? Anxious to escape, Roth complained about his room to Bloch, who walked him over to a separate, all-women's residence and offered him a big white room under the eaves. This, Roth thought, was more like it: "a haven." Avishai, an early visitor, remembered the contented smile that came over Roth's face ("as if he were the happiest little boy in the world") every time the nurse knocked on his door—"*Mr. Roth?*"—and made sure he was all right.

Aaron Asher brought him a radio with a CD player and a collection of classical music, mostly Bach, to listen to while he soaked in a hot bath to relieve his aching back. Indeed, it was Roth's physical misery that received the most urgent attention: a doctor prescribed an anti-inflammatory (Voltaren) that wouldn't hurt his stomach, and made sure he got at least four weekly sessions of physical therapy—this along with psychiatric group meetings (both coed and men-only), a "coping strategies" session after lunch, and an elective "practicum" (swimming in Roth's case). Twice weekly he met one-on-one with Bloch, who spared him the "Freudian shit," as Roth was happy to note; mainly it was a matter of finding the right mix of medications—Klonopin for anxiety, Prozac for depression, and a bit of lithium as an activator.

Perhaps the most therapeutic aspect of Silver Hill, for Roth, was an almost cozy sense of communal malaise. At the end of the day, he liked chatting on the porch with four or five women patients, who discussed their terrible marriages and whatnot, every so often sighing, "It's hopeless." Nobody looked at him funny; they nodded with serene comprehension when he spoke of his wish for oblivion—a wish mitigated somewhat by visits from Inga, who always brought a little gift (sweater, socks, a toilet kit) and, after a jolly dinner, would return to Roth's room and do her best to bring him to climax despite lurking nurses and anorgasmic Prozac. "You know, you say terrible things about your wife," one of the women patients remarked, "but I see you having dinner with her and you seem to enjoy each other." Roth smiled: "That wasn't my wife."

Bloom was in London, and he grew angrier with her almost by the hour. Inga, for one, couldn't help feeling sorry for the poor woman—a friend, after all. By then Bloom could do no right in Roth's eyes. At one point she'd suggested they go to a spa together, and ever after Roth would grumble, "*A spa?! What the fuck does she think a* spa's *gonna do . . . ?*" That first Friday at Silver Hill he got a call from his wife, who'd just returned to New York and proposed a visit; Roth ("angry, remote") vetoed the idea, refusing to see her except in the presence of Dr. Bloch, who wasn't on duty until Sunday. Roth hung up, then called back and asked her to bring him a few changes of underwear ("So maybe I am his wife after all," she wrote in her journal).

Bloom would always claim to be flummoxed by her husband's sudden disaffection, wistfully surmising with interviewers like Charlie Rose that it was due to "some kind of a breakdown." When Bloch asked her, before Roth arrived for their three-way meeting on August 8, whether she understood why he was so mad at her, she answered (doubtless in all sincerity) that she "hadn't the faintest idea." According to *Doll's House* and Roth's own account, he spent two hours ("hardly pausing for breath") coldly trying to enlighten her. Among other grievances, he mentioned her tendency to panic during his illnesses; she replied that she'd "taken good care of him" during his knee operation, bypass, and two breakdowns. "I am sorry to disillusion you on that point," he said. "You were no help to me whatever." Finally he came to the crux: if Anna still planned to study in New York for six weeks (or three months, as the case may be), Roth wanted to terminate the marriage. "Look at her!" he said to Bloch, when she bolted from the room. "She's always running away."

After a few more unsatisfactory meetings at Silver Hill, Bloom flew to Toronto and on to Salzburg, where her daughter had a singing engagement. Mother and daughter then traveled to a movie shoot in Dublin, where Dr. Bloch got hold of Bloom almost the moment she checked into her hotel. His patient had requested the sole use of their New York apartment for six months after his discharge; he didn't want to be alone in the country (nor with Bloom in either place), and proposed to give her five thousand dollars a month to stay at the Wyndham or find a furnished apartment. Next Inga called, begging Bloom to accede to Roth's wishes lest he end up killing himself while alone in Connecticut. "I think Philip is using [Inga] to manipulate me," Bloom wrote in her journal, "but I have to take what she says on good faith—maybe Philip is in danger."

Roth, meanwhile, was released from Silver Hill on August 20, and at first seemed fine. Judith Thurman stayed with him in Connecticut for a week, joining him for swims and long walks, while Roth spent mornings in his studio going over a few sketchy pages of what would become *Sabbath's Theater*. He awoke without dread, and was even his old antic self at a dinner party *chez* Inga, where he regaled guests with the lighter side of life at Silver Hill. A little more than two weeks passed before he "went nuts" again: By then Joanna Clark was keeping him company, and one night she stood watching while he wandered outside and began screaming "WHERE IS SHE? WHERE *IS* SHE . . . ?!" "You have to go back to the hospital," Clark told him when he came back inside, and so he did.

When Roth returned to Silver Hill on September 8, he asked for Bloch's assurance that he wouldn't put Roth in the locked ward, but Bloch regretfully did so anyway. "That's when I talked to myself," Roth remembered, "and I said, 'You are gonna do everything they tell you to do, and you are gonna get out of here whole. But the party's over. You're getting rid of this woman.'" On a list of twelve "Goals after Discharge," Roth wrote "YOU BET" next to the ninth: "Change the environment you are returning to, to less stressful." When Thurman came to visit, Roth asked her to see Bloom in New York and calmly repeat his proposal for separate living quarters during the first six months following his discharge. What he didn't know—until Bloom's letter to him dated October 25—was that Bloom was then in the midst of selling her London town house ("Who in her right mind would do such a thing at such a moment?" he wondered), which might help to explain her extreme reaction to Thurman's turn as emissary. For a few minutes the women sipped tea and chatted, then Thurman repeated Roth's request; Bloom sat primly twitching for a moment, then ("literally like zero to sixty") burst into tears and began screaming, *What about me? What about me?* "I sort of backed out toward the door," Thurman recalled.

A few days later Roth enlisted yet another woman friend, Janet Malcolm, to phone his wife and plead his case. Bloom responded with a faxed letter, gently imploring Roth simply to tell her what he wanted in his own words; she would love him in any case, she wrote, but she was in a miserable predicament and needed "protection." "*My* dearest friend of seventeen years," Roth replied, quoting the same endearment she'd used for him, "the most loving thing you can do right now is to give me the time and the space that I require to put this terrible suicidal depression behind me and to find my [way] back to my life. . . .

> I am not ready to resume our domestic life now—I need time and psychiatric help to prepare me for that. In the meantime you of course need protection. That is why I gave you my offer [i.e., $5,000 a month], which I hope you will accept so that I can come down to New York in October and begin my recovery.
>   I too find it difficult not to be able to talk to you on the telephone but I'm not at all sure that I feel strong enough yet.

Relieved by the sweet if rather passive-aggressive implication that Roth would be ready, possibly, at some point, to resume their life together, Bloom replied that she would start looking for an apartment immediately. Six months didn't seem so long, she wrote, when there was something "so wonderful" to look forward to.

By the time she arrived at Silver Hill, however, on the eve of Roth's departure (he'd shown immediate improvement on learning of her acquiescence), Bloom had changed her mind. The two were in his room about to go down for dinner, when Bloom sat opposite him and announced that she intended to stay "home" on West Seventy-seventh—or so Roth remembered; in *Doll's House* and (more convincingly) in a letter she wrote around this time, Bloom claimed to have simply, wretchedly begged to be allowed to come back in *two* months rather than six. In either case Roth was struck dumb with anger. After glaring at her for "at least fifteen minutes," said Bloom, they went to dinner and ate in silence. Then, back in his room, Roth sternly forbade her to renege on their agreement, and perhaps also said something about her poisoning him (according to Bloom) or at any rate his life. "At this she made a grotesque face," Roth noted, "—as a child might make at Halloween to scare her little friends—wiggled her fingers at the sides of her ears, and began to scream." (Many years later, Thurman made "the same Halloween face" for Roth while trying to describe how Bloom had reacted to her proposal about the six-month separation.) In *Doll's House*, Bloom recounted how she'd fled the room and cried out for someone to help Philip, whereupon she was sedated by the nurse on duty; since Bloom had said something about wanting to die, the nurse (after a quick phone conference with Bloch) gave her pajamas and took her to the locked ward—the first visitor in Silver Hill history, or so Roth claimed, to be retained as a patient overnight ("Only Hans Castorp in *The Magic Mountain* has a similar experience"). As for Roth, the nurse found him sitting calmly in his room; his blood pressure was extremely high, but it was better the next day—Yom Kippur—and he departed as planned. Inga's husband drove him back to Warren, where Roth packed his things and went on to New York.

CHAPTER

Thirty-Eight

O PENING THE DOOR TO HIS EMPTY APARTMENT ON West Seventy-seventh, Roth was struck by the sight of sunlight gleaming on his highly polished parquet floor—so like the parlor floor of his childhood apartment on Summit Avenue. "You're gonna be all right," he thought. An hour or so later, he was back in his studio working on *Sabbath's Theater.*

He also wrote an encouraging note to his wife. He was glad to know, he said, that she'd had a nice long chat with Dr. Bloch the morning after their contretemps: "He really is the person to listen to. I am living proof!" After her night at Silver Hill, Bloom took a room at the Cosmopolitan Club, and in gratitude Roth asked her to join him for dinner, with the caveat that he tired easily and would have to leave early. The meeting, for Bloom, was "strained and miserable." Roth brought Conarroe along as a buffer, and made a point of directing most of his conversation to him. Still, when bemoaning her fate to friends, Bloom would generally insist it was Roth's welfare that foremost concerned her. "Please keep telling me he's all right!" she said to Alfred Kazin's wife, Judith Dunford, who endeavored to reassure her. "How *dare* you constantly stress to me how happy he is!" Bloom reproached the woman.

Meanwhile she was pointedly magnanimous in her notes to Roth; after taking a room at the Wyndham, she assured him that it didn't matter where she lived, but rather whom she loved. Again with Conarroe in tow, Roth attended her program ("Women in Love") of the Shakespeare speeches they'd rehearsed together that summer, and shared a cab with Bloom after the three had endured a "reasonably pleasant" dinner. "Never better," said Roth, when Bloom asked him how he felt; watching him cross the street to his apartment building, she reflected that he'd chosen the life of "a bitter, lonely, aging ascetic with no human ties."

Roth—who liked to say "Art is life too"—responded coldly to this observation: "As for my 'human ties,' I will not list them but merely say that Bloom's description of me, here as everywhere, is drawn from an imagination distorted by melodramatic hyperbole, not to mention psychological cliché, and hardly from one whose investigation is grounded in any serious fidelity to observed reality."

Roth sent Bloom a bouquet of tulips after her Shakespeare show, followed a day later by a brief agreement drawn up by his new matrimonial lawyer, William Beslow, that confirmed the basic terms of their temporary separation—mainly that Bloom must obtain Roth's consent to visit their apartment and collect personal items, whereas Roth in turn was obliged to pay Bloom five thousand dollars on the first day of each month. In *Doll's House* Bloom described the legal papers as a "body blow," to which she responded with an angry message on Roth's answering machine. Roth listened to the message, took notes, then called back and affected to be puzzled. The fact was, Beslow had warned him that he might render the prenup null and void if he paid Bloom a monthly allowance, unless she agreed in writing beforehand that her acceptance of the money did not alter the terms of their agreement. Roth tried to explain this in so many words, but was interrupted by his furious wife: "I am not signing any agreement! How *dare* you. . . ." In the background Roth heard familiar voices—Anna and her friend Felicity, he surmised. "That's how I understood that Bloom was at once out of control and showing off for the girls how very tough she could be with me." When he tried a second time to explain, she resumed berating him, and he hung up on her.*

Vexed, Roth went directly to his lawyer and explained what had happened. "This isn't working," said Beslow: Bloom could not have her five-thousand-dollar allowance if she refused to sign, simple as that, so he advised Roth to go ahead and serve her with divorce papers—that is, in New York; while Roth could get a no-fault divorce in Connecticut without Bloom's assent, the prenup was more likely to be overturned

---

* In *Doll's House*, Bloom claimed that Roth himself had begun "ranting," both against her and Francine Gray, whom he suspected of sending him a nasty anonymous letter. Roth remembered this October 23 phone call differently, and the undated letter he imputed to Gray (see below) was almost assuredly sent at least three weeks later.

there. Meanwhile Bloom was consulting her own lawyer, Sidney Liebowitz, who looked over the temporary separation agreement and saw nothing amiss; he advised her to sign it so she could start collecting her money. When she inquired whether she should just divorce Roth, the man sagely replied that that was precisely what Roth wanted, as it would preclude any hope of a settlement under the terms of the prenup.

Instead of divorcing him, then, Bloom wrote him a testy but mollifying letter. Naturally she'd been "shocked and dismayed" to receive legal papers "out of the blue," she wrote, since Roth had mentioned nothing of the sort over dinner the other night. Be that as it may, there was no chance of her violating an oral agreement "made in the best of faith," and moreover (as he well knew) she was soon to leave for London and thence to Cambridge, Massachusetts, for three months (to appear in a production of *The Cherry Orchard*), and had arranged to rent her own small Manhattan apartment for the sixth and final month of their separation, March. A few days later she phoned Roth to reiterate her willingness to sign; he "listened and politely hung up," as he recalled. Soon after, the Wyndham concierge rang Bloom in her room and said that a man named Frederick was waiting downstairs with a message he could deliver only in person—i.e., divorce papers, charging her with "the cruel and inhuman treatment" of her husband, Philip Roth.

■ ■ ■ ■

IN *DOLL'S HOUSE*, Bloom suggested that Inga Larsen's decision to divorce her husband of twenty-five years was due to her total commitment to her "new relationship" with Roth (an affair of some eighteen years' duration). In truth, Roth was perfectly happy with things as they were, though he certainly encouraged Inga to follow her own inclination, now that her children were grown, to release herself from a moribund marriage. "You can do it, Fallika," he liked to say,* and later Inga wrote to thank him—even after their decidedly acrimonious breakup—for helping her change her life for the better.

"I moved out and Erda [Inga] moved in," Bloom wrote in *Doll's House*—with less than perfect accuracy, or so Roth claimed. He

---

* "Fallika" was Roth's main term of endearment for Inga ("a tribute to her erotic magic").

acknowledged that Inga had stayed in the back bedroom of his Connecticut studio for "two weeks, if that long," during the summer of 1994,
amid leaving her husband and furnishing her new condo in a nearby
town (Roth had given her $20,000 toward the down payment). How-
ever, Roth's cleaning woman and friend, Kathy Meetz, remembered that
Inga had actually stayed in "Heartbreak Hotel" (as they called Roth's
studio, since Ross Miller had also camped there after his recent divorce)
the entire summer; Meetz had seen the two eating breakfast together,
but suspected nothing since she considered them simply old friends and
neighbors. According to Roth, the couple had mutually decided to keep
things secret awhile: "There would be time enough later for us to go
about in public together, without our having precipitously revealed that
we had been lovers all along." Whatever their relative furtiveness in the
meantime, Inga insisted she moved into Roth's studio as early as spring
1994, and moved out only when her condo was ready in late August;
after that, she said, "We lived like a couple and I cooked dinner every
night" at her place. Finally, once her divorce went through in October,
she tended to spend weekends with Roth at his apartment in New York.

Even then he was busily incorporating aspects of Inga's personality
into characters such as Sabbath's alcoholic second wife, Roseanna, and
especially his immortal mistress, Drenka Balich. "Every book has a million sources," said Roth, "but Drenka had only one." For Inga's benefit
he frankly described his heroine as an all but exact portrait, calling the
novel "a love poem" to her. And Sabbath, too, was a fairly exact version of *his* real-life model, or at least certain salient traits—"the nearest
I've come in all my fiction to drawing a realistic self-portrait," as Roth
freely admitted. Sabbath and Drenka build their "church" on "the rock
of sexual excess," and Drenka lovingly calls Sabbath her "secret American boyfriend," which was Inga's way of greeting Roth during a sylvan
rendezvous. In matters of sex, she was his "sidekicker"—one of her many
malapropisms that delighted Roth, who gave them to Drenka as well.

Roseanna was a more dubious tribute, to put it mildly. "'You're as
sick as your secrets,'" she parrots to Sabbath. "It was not the first time
that he was hearing this pointless, shallow, idiotic maxim. 'Wrong,' he
told her . . . 'you're as adventurous as your secrets, as abhorrent as your
secrets, as lonely as your secrets, as alluring as your secrets, as courageous
as your secrets, as vacuous as your secrets, as lost as your secrets.'" The

"deadliest" side to Inga's sobriety, as Roth would have it, was her tendency to impart AA wisdom and to examine her own feelings a mite too conspicuously. Inga herself was aware of these aversions, but her impulse to be supportive tended to override any misgivings. "As you said: we create our own reality," she reminded him. "Of course I have learned this from AA but it really has helped me so I am sharing it with you, even risking your cynicism [sic]." Roth's other great AA friend, Joanna Clark, was likewise apt to recite her favorite recovery slogans for Roth—"Yesterday's history, tomorrow's a mystery"; "No pain, no gain"—because she liked to make him laugh, *not* because she expected him to find them enlightening ("Do they all have to *rhyme*, Joanna?"). To his gratification she declared Roseanna, his consummate AA bore, "hilarious."

Ted Solotaroff, however, dismissed the character as little more than "a sitting duck for Sabbath's caricaturing disgust," a pitfall Roth had meant to skirt with evidence of Roseanna's poignant inner life in the form of diary entries and letters from her incestuous father. The latter (including a suicide note) were reproduced almost verbatim from letters written by Inga's own father. She'd given Roth permission to cull these materials as he saw fit, but in bitter retrospect decided "he was ruthlessly using [her] vulnerability." She might have found it galling, too, that Sabbath mocks his wife's sorrow just as readily as he mocks her more comic foibles. After reading her mournful diary, for instance, Sabbath composes a satirical reply in the voice of her dead father (without attempting to disguise his own handwriting): "Dear little Roseanna! / Of course you are in a mental hospital. I warned you again and again about separating yourself from me. . . . But why don't you judge me for a change by *my* pain, by *my* holy feelings? How you cling to your grievance! As though in a world of persecution you alone have a grievance."

Roth himself, of course, was hardly a slouch when it came to clinging to a grievance—the one against Francine du Plessix Gray, for instance, which would fester until the end. As far as Gray herself knew, everything had been fine between them until his breach with Bloom. When he first entered Silver Hill, Gray had written him a loving note wishing him a "speedy and serene" recovery, and even pleaded with Bloom (at Inga's and Thurman's urging) to agree to Roth's request for a six-month separation lest he end up killing himself. All this despite blatant signals from Roth that he found her, Gray, distasteful. When she was elected to the Academy of Arts and Letters, in 1992, she'd complained to him about the simultaneous election of a notable (but inferior in Gray's eyes) short story writer. Irritated that one of his least favorite writers (Gray) had gotten into the Academy, and moreover was already complaining ("she hadn't had time to take a crap") about a fellow inductee, Roth phoned the Academy's director and mentioned that he'd be attending that year's ceremonial luncheon, as Douglas Hobbie's chaperone, and wanted to be seated next to the story writer who'd offended Gray. His wish was granted.

The first sign that Gray returned his animus, and then some, came that Yom Kippur day when he departed Silver Hill for good. Before heading to New York, Roth had stopped for lunch at Inga's house—an occasion interrupted by a phone call from Gray: "We're organizing a support group for Claire," she said, inviting Inga to her pool that afternoon. That such a group, or at least its leader, was apt to have an anti-Roth agenda soon became manifest. Writing on October 19 to decline Bloom's invitation to her one-woman show in Litchfield, Roth explained that he wished to avoid the Grays: "They have been outspokenly malicious in slandering me since the first day I came out of the hospital, and I don't believe that I could control my contempt for them in their presence." By then he had a hunch about the identity of the "friend" who'd let slip to gossip columnist Charlotte Hays of the New York *Daily News*— for an October 15 item in "Charlotte's Web" ("For Roth, it's goodbye, Claire")—that he'd recently left his wife homeless.

These were minor matters next to a scurrilous, anonymous note Roth received around Thanksgiving 1993; on a single sheet of paper, the author had printed in red ballpoint pen: "EVERYBODY KNOWS / YOU'RE SEEING / JUDITH THURMAN." The European 7s on the envelope put him immediately in mind of Gray; he imagined she'd written and mailed the note in a fury, à la *The Human Stain*'s Delphine Roux, who rashly accuses Coleman Silk as follows: "Everyone knows you're / sexually exploiting an / abused, illiterate / woman half your / age." In both cases the charge was essentially false: Roth and Thurman had had no sexual contact for many years; indeed she was then engaged to another man, whom she married a few months later. Roth asked Inga to send him samples of Gray's handwriting from her files—Gray had been a patient—and Inga obliged. "Some ten days ago," Roth's old friend Marty

Garbus wrote Gray on December 1, "you sent an anonymous letter to Mr. Roth that is not only offensive, harassing and denigrating to Mr. Roth, but also deeply embarrassing to Ms. Thurman." Garbus threatened a lawsuit, and Gray lost no time enlisting a lawyer friend of her own, James Goodale, to deny the accusation and threaten a countersuit.

Roth let four and a half years pass, until he won the 1998 Pulitzer for *American Pastoral* and received a congratulatory note from an old high school classmate, Nona Fried, who happened to be a professional handwriting analyst. Roth promptly sent her samples of Gray's handwriting and, in his cover note, insisted she charge her usual fee: "Dear Porfiry Petrovich"—the magistrate who pursues Raskolnikov in *Crime and Punishment*—"Do your stuff." Three days later Fried mailed her report: "Based on the documents submitted, it is my professional opinion that the hand that penned all the known standards as Francine du Plessix Gray is one and the same hand that penned the questioned anonymous note and envelope."

■   ■   ■   ■

ROTH CLAIMED THAT Bloom had asked him whether she could "at least" have his studio on West Seventy-ninth, but he refused; already he was thinking about selling his main apartment and moving to Connecticut more or less full-time, keeping his studio (which had doubled in value) as a pied-à-terre. Bloom complained to their mutual friend Aaron Asher, who phoned Roth and implored him not to be so "selfish"; Roth angrily replied that Bloom had a perfectly nice place in London, where she preferred to live anyway, and besides it was none of Asher's business. The two didn't speak again for almost six years.

The prenuptial agreement, said Bloom's lawyer, was "unconscionable"—or so she quoted him in *Doll's House*, though her lawyer in 1990 had suggested only minor changes, which Roth had readily approved; still, Bloom claimed penury to friends and demanded a settlement outside the terms of the prenup. Roth, furious, wanted to take her to court, but his lawyer advised against it. Two of the three New York judges, he said, were "feminists"; if Roth got one of the latter, they'd charge him ten thousand bucks a week in support and endlessly delay his case, while the tabloids had a field day. The lawyer therefore suggested they offer Bloom a settlement of $100,000 plus legal fees ($17,000); Roth subsequently consulted his regular lawyer, Helene Kaplan, who assured him he was getting off easy.

Bloom accepted the sum "against [her] lawyer's strong advice," though it was hardly enough to cover a "dank little apartment" (as their friend Dick Stern described it) on East Ninety-fourth and Third Avenue. Eager to get on with her life, and still hoping she and Roth could be friends (or even a couple again, once he came to his senses), she told him she was ready to set up her new apartment and wondered when she might expect the belongings—"furniture, china, and linens"—she'd left behind on West Seventy-seventh and exhaustively listed. Roth responded by faxing her a list of his own, demanding she return the Bulgari snake ring, the $28,500 per annum provided by his twelve-year Clifford Trust, other lavish cash gifts, plus $150 per hour for the "five or six hundred hours" he'd spent rehearsing with her. On it went. Finally Roth proposed to fine her sixty-two billion dollars—a billion for every year of her life—for failing to honor their prenup. At first the mockery of the exercise was "entirely lost" on Bloom and her daughter, but after the ninth or tenth page they saw the joke and commenced laughing.

"She's behaved abominably about money and I've had to pay her off to get rid of her," Roth wrote his old friend Charlotte Maurer. "She's hysterical, irrational, deceitful, and, above and beyond everything else, A BLAMELESS VICTIM RESPONSIBLE FOR NOTHING. The last finally got me down." Roth wrote this on March 20, 1994, three days after shelling out the "distributive award" of $100,000 plus legal fees, on the condition that Bloom sign a new separation agreement relinquishing all further claims "from the beginning of the world to the date of this Agreement." In May, Roth composed the following directive: "To my executors and those planning my burial: It is my strong wish that Claire Bloom be barred from my funeral and from any memorial services arranged for me. All possible measures should be taken to enforce this."

■ ■ ■ ■

EARLIER THAT YEAR Roth had begun dating a thirty-one-year-old psychiatrist, Julia Golier, who taught at Mount Sinai Hospital on the Upper East Side and treated Vietnam veterans for PTSD at the VA hospital in the Bronx. Golier was tall and pretty, and moreover Roth was attracted to her "calm, rational" manner ("in that way very like Barbara and Ann, very unlike Claire and Maggie"). She also had a penchant for drollery, and over the years would send Roth clippings that fell under the rubric "As Joke Goes Awry"—like the one about the man who swallowed his friend's tropical fish and choked to death. That March of 1994, Francine du Plessix Gray published *Rage and Fire*, a biography of Louise Colet that advanced the novel thesis that Colet was a genius and Flaubert a chauvinist pig who crushed her spirit.* In *The New York Times*, Michiko Kakutani found the book shrill and ludicrous, whereas Golier made a copy of the "EVERYBODY KNOWS" letter and crossed out all but the first two words, emending it to read "EVERYBODY KNOWS YOU WROTE 'RAGE AND FIRE'"—which she then mailed to Gray from the Bronx.

As was his wont with much younger girlfriends, Roth couldn't resist playing Pygmalion—a benevolent role, for the most part. In the early days of their courtship he took Golier to see Satyajit Ray's *Apu Trilogy* at Lincoln Plaza on the Upper West Side, and for the rest of his life he and Golier referred to each other as Apu. He was also a little appalled by her sketchy apartment on First Avenue, which he would later give to the all-but-destitute Amy Bellette in *Exit Ghost*; when Golier decided to move, a year or so after they met, he successfully urged her to pick a place on Ninety-first and Park, then accompanied her on a furniture shopping expedition.

Roth's own living arrangements were in flux. He'd decided "there were too many traces of Claire" in his otherwise beloved house in Connecticut, and hired a local architect to design a smaller one-story that he

---

* Roth couldn't resist taking a dig at the book—and hence at Gray and Bloom—in *Sabbath's Theater*. While composing his own obituary, Sabbath ponders the mysterious disappearance of his Bloom-like first wife, the actress Nikki Kantarakis, and imagines a Francine-like mythographer coming along to set the record straight (as she sees it): "'The pig Flaubert murdered Louise Colet,' said Countess du Plissitas, the aristocrat's feminist, in a telephone interview today. Countess du Plissitas is best known for fictionalizing biography. She is currently fictionalizing the biography of Miss Kantarakis. 'The pig Fitzgerald murdered Zelda,' the countess continued, 'the pig Hughes murdered Sylvia Plath, and the pig Sabbath murdered Nikki. It's all there, all the different ways he murdered her, in *Nikki: The Destruction of an Actress by a Pig*." All this would prove unfortunately prophetic given the imminence of *Leaving a Doll's House*, which Roth would always suspect (mistakenly, I think) of being at least partially ghostwritten by Francine du Plessix Gray.

planned to build on a ten-acre parcel of his property (which included his swimming pool, the one thing he couldn't bear parting with) just south of his old house. Roth had already planted several dozen white pines and built a split-rail fence for privacy, and the excavator was due to cut a new road through the woods, when Golier spent her first weekend in the country as Roth's guest. "But why are you doing this?" she sensibly inquired. "Your house is so beautiful." He saw her point. In the end the new house never materialized except in miniature, as an architect's model, which Roth kept as a kind of centerpiece in his attic (where he also stored the vast foreign editions of his work).

By then his long affair with Inga had spectacularly imploded. As their mutual friend Thurman pointed out, the couple had thrived on trans-gression and subterfuge, but in a more conventional arrangement their basic incompatibilities came to the fore—or, as Roth put it, "She's a great adulteress, but not a great mate." The same was arguably true of Roth. "No more women," he promised a friend, post-Bloom. "Been at it for 45 years. Enough's enough. . . . Solitude is best." By this he meant, of course, that he'd never again permit any *one* woman to lay claim to him, which was somewhat at odds with Inga's own program. "I became a needy and helpless child pathologically bound to you," she wrote him after their final rupture. "That woman full of vigor and joy of life and fearless[ness] that you loved just evaporated."

Things blew up at Inga's breakfast table on New Year's Day, 1995. For a long time the couple had been planning a summer trip to Norway (coinciding with the publication of *Sabbath's Theater*, so Roth could avoid the reviews), where she looked forward to showing him her child-hood haunts. Meanwhile, though, she'd become increasingly uncom-fortable with Roth's insistence that they keep their affair a secret; she wanted to inform her children, at least, as to whom she was traveling with. Rattled by the prospect of more gossip, Roth told her he wouldn't go if she told her children, whereupon she became "wild with rage," as he recalled: "*'I want to tell my children! I want them to know where I am! I want them to know who I'm with!'*" Roth sat there for "ten or fifteen minutes," he said, then excused himself and left, while she followed him outside screaming. Inga told it differently. According to her, Roth was in an irritable mood that morning; while eating in fraught silence he suddenly announced, "Inga, why don't you put the caps on the toothpaste?!" After a few more crabby remarks in that vein, he did his exercises in her bedroom and finally stomped off with a farewell threat to cancel their plans for Norway.

"Inga, we should cool it," Roth said, when she phoned him ten days later to find out where they stood. It was then—her marriage and love affair both in ruins—that Inga suffered a breakdown, and on January 13 a psychiatrist diagnosed her as suicidal and referred her to the Institute of Living in Hartford. Only allowed to receive incoming calls, she asked her AA sponsor to get in touch with Judith Thurman, to inform Roth of her hospitalization and ask him to call her. For five days she remained "glued to the pay phone" waiting for his twice-daily calls, morning and night, until the eve of her departure, when two therapists explained that her attachment to Roth was dangerously self-destructive. "I hardly had time to say hello," Roth said of his final phone call to Hartford the next day, "before she was furiously and not entirely coherently berating me for having destroyed her life and telling me that I should never try to be in touch with her again or she would tell the world about me."

On January 22, Roth sent his cleaning woman, Kathy Meetz—who worked for both of them—over to Inga's condo with her belongings, neatly packed (each individual lipstick in bubble wrap), with a polite note to "Mrs. Larsen" explaining that she'd left them behind in his "attic," when in fact they'd mostly come from his New York apartment. Three days later, he received an angry fax: "Mr. Misogynist! / May you rot in hell! It gives me pleasure to know that one day indeed you will . . . when your depression returns. . . . You are the most ruthless man on this planet." She considered the matter further, then faxed him two days later on January 27:

> In my desperate attempt to rescue you I have deeply hurt my family and myself, a wound I may never be able to heal.
>
> You are pathetic in you [sic] rapid aging and decline, full of chronic pain and physically revolting with a double chin and pot belly and almost impotent.
>
> STAY AWAY FROM ME!!!!!! I MIGHT TALK WHEN YOUR BOOK IS PUBLISHED!!!!

Roth waited a month for the considerable smoke to clear, then wrote Inga that he hoped they could eventually be friends again. She replied on March 11, from Madrid, that she agreed and "harbor[ed] no ill-will," albeit admitting she sometimes wondered whether he'd wanted her to die like Drenka in the book: "This letter is for you, my once lover and American boy friend," she concluded. "Not the novelist Philip Roth! I hope you respect that. Be well maybe we can meet in the summer." It was still spring, though, when she paid him a final visit. As Roth remembered, she appeared at his studio "wearing over her seductive form the tightest jeans and lowest-cut blouse she owned . . . and when her attempts at seduction were, perhaps for the first time in her life, rebuffed, that most certainly was the end of everything." But nothing in the letter she wrote him afterward (dated April 9) suggested a thwarted seduction; rather she wistfully acknowledged the end of their affair, and chided Roth ("I feel so bored") for having boasted about "other women" in his life: "Do you need to flatter your ego in front of me? . . . you might surely find another woman in your life again but none like me."

■ ■ ■ ■

ROTH'S LONG AND HAPPY friendship with Mia Farrow went back to a near encounter at a party *chez* Styron, in Roxbury, during the summer of 1992, around the time the Woody Allen scandal broke. When Farrow arrived, Roth remembered, all the women in the room rushed to console her "like they were sucked down a tube." Bloom, who'd met Farrow briefly on the set of *Crimes and Misdemeanors* (Bloom had played Martin Landau's wife), insisted they have her over for dinner sometime, and Roth agreed. He was all the more sympathetic given that he'd despised Woody Allen even before the man was accused of sexual assault; in *Operation Shylock,* Pipik describes the director as a "little dork asshole"—an insult that a libel lawyer, vetting the novel, found gratuitous: "Has the author an axe to grind concerning Woody Allen? On what does he premise this language?" At the time it was mostly an aesthetic grievance. Updike had written Roth a polite note about the movie (because Bloom was in it), especially commending a scene, near the end, where a blind rabbi poignantly dances with his daughter at her wedding. Roth replied:

You have to be Jewish to hate Crimes and Misdemeanors openly, I guess. It is really the bottom of Jewish kitsch and the desecration of the memory of Primo Levi has sent me into a fury that won't quite subside.* When the rabbi came out dancing at the end, I shouted aloud in the theater, "Blind isn't enough!" . . . Claire learned to loathe Allen during the making of the film, not because she had nothing to do, but because he bore so little resemblance to a human being. The man, if that is the word, is a fake from top to bottom. Can you imagine, John?—he has even ruined shiksas for me.

The dinner with Farrow finally transpired a few months later, coinciding with a rare visit to Connecticut from Bloom's daughter. Farrow was also a Litchfield County resident, and on the snowy night in question she rendezvoused with Roth at a liquor store in Warren and followed him back to his house. "The dynamics were strange," she remembered of Roth's ménage. Anna Steiger was dour as ever, while Bloom dashed about nervously from kitchen to dining room; Roth, whose back was killing him, retired to a couch in the living room. At one point Steiger followed her mother into the kitchen, and Roth and their guest were left alone. They looked at each other and smiled. At length the evening ended, and Farrow followed Roth back to the liquor store, where he was sorely tempted to ditch his car and run away with her.

They were both cheerfully single two and a half years later, when they met again at another Styron party—this time for the visiting Czech president, Václav Havel. "That little smile that passed between us erupted like a baby atomic bomb," said Roth. The former ambassador to Czechoslovakia, Bill Luers, was also at the party with his wife, Wendy, who wanted to talk about NATO; Roth and Farrow excused themselves from that conversation and flirted. Roth grabbed a big cross around her neck and led her over to Havel: "Mr. President, do I have to put up with this?" Finally they disappeared awhile, and when Farrow returned, alone, Luers asked if Roth was okay. "He seemed fine as soon

---

* In the movie, the Woody Allen character is making a documentary about a humanistic philosopher and Holocaust survivor, Louis Levy, who appears to have been somewhat modeled on Primo Levi. Despite the essential optimism of his teachings, Levy ends up killing himself.

as he got his tongue out of my throat," she breezily replied.* The couple's canoodling, in Roth's car, had been inhibited somewhat by the ubiquity of Czech secret police and Connecticut state troopers, and the two made a date to see each other later.

The ensuing affair, such as it was, largely consisted of hilarious walks along the Housatonic, and lingered as a friendship that would strengthen in later years. As Farrow endeavored to describe it, "There were bursts of romance here or there, through the years, but the way good friends would have a friendship that has sexuality as a component." "Was I ever married to you?" the brain-cancer-stricken Amy Bellette asks Zuckerman in *Exit Ghost*—a remark derived from a bantering routine between Roth and Farrow: "Wasn't I once married to you," Roth would begin, "between Sinatra and Andre Previn?"

Banter was always a trickier business with Roth's actual spouse, and so it went during a meeting in March 1995, shortly before their divorce was finalized. As she noted in *Doll's House*, Bloom had often frustrated her lawyer by balking at his advice to take a more aggressive approach, lest she jeopardize her "valued friendship" with the man whose "subterfuge, treachery, and darkness"—as she otherwise characterized him—she would only just survive. But then, he was still capable of magnanimity despite his outrage over her refusal to abide by the prenup; while working on *The Cherry Orchard* the previous spring, Bloom had entreated him to send her the sheaf of notes he'd made during rehearsals of the same play at the Chichester Festival in 1981. "I had every good reason to tell her to go fuck herself," Roth said in 2013. "But I didn't want her (still! Still! Fucking idiot that I am!) to give anything less than her best performance so I sent them to her in Cambridge."

And finally Roth rewarded Bloom's patient hope that his "illness" (as she considered it) would pass—or so it seemed, when he wrote her on March 7, 1995, asking if they could still be friends. Bloom replied that she'd like nothing better, and Roth proposed meeting for coffee later that month at a restaurant, Sarabeth's, near her apartment on East Ninety-fourth. Meanwhile he'd consulted his psychiatrist, Bill Frosch, about how best to handle things. Frosch's advice was twofold: meet her

---

* A detail that, if true, slightly belies Roth's professed aversion to French kissing.

in a public place, where she was less likely to get emotional, and let her know in advance that he had a subsequent appointment so there was no chance of morbid lingering (thus he scheduled Bloom at four, followed hard upon by dinner with a friend, Alice Gordon, at five fifteen). Bloom treated herself to a facial and a manicure, and wore a particularly nice outfit for the occasion—only to be stymied by a barrage of "completely impersonal" shtick from Roth (his own way of dealing with nerves). "Oh, perversion," he replied, smiling, when she pensively inquired why he wanted to be friends. "Let down and deeply disappointed," Bloom concluded, "I left the restaurant; I swore I would never again go through such an ordeal."

Roth was bewildered by her account of this meeting. "Both of us lighthearted," he wrote in his diary the next day. "Warm. The damage we did each other! She seems perky, game—intelligent, pretty. The nervous energy but not mad. A first day [date?]. Part after hour and a quarter. Kiss goodbye. Sad—but okay. What it took!" He couldn't help wondering, in 2011, whether he'd deceived himself—but no: he found Bloom's warm reply to the note he'd sent her afterward, which seemed to confirm that she'd found the Sarabeth's meeting as "wonderful" as he, and certainly her vivacity at the time bore this out. As he later speculated, "Maybe it was the irrepressible joy of knowing she was about to stiff me"—i.e., by writing *Leaving a Doll's House*.

As it happened, her hopes for the meeting were perhaps unreasonably high. As she later confessed to Charlie Rose, she'd continued to believe that the time would come when "he's going to wake up and say 'Oh my god, what have I done?' . . . Didn't happen." Certainly she was a little stung by Roth's glibness, not to say his careful scheduling; several weeks later, on May 10, she proposed to Roth that they meet again, pointing out that a true friendship, going forward, would entail "honesty on both sides"; she also noted her preference for having an evening drink versus an afternoon "tea" (this because of regular working hours on her "wretched 'Soap,'" she explained*). Roth promptly replied that he looked forward to "coffee-hour [n.b.] number two" when he returned

---

* For eighteen months Bloom portrayed the villainous Orlena Grimaldi on *As the World Turns*. "I'm just a mother now," she told David Plante, "but if I stay on long enough they've promised me a lover."

to New York in the fall, adding "I hope you regain your equilibrium quickly" (she'd complained of feeling blue because of their imminent divorce) "and by the time we next meet I hope to find you once again as charmingly spirited as you were at Sarabeth's earlier this spring." Bloom, in turn, wished him a "relatively carefree" summer—a wish that apparently came true. Writing Andrew Wylie, Roth mentioned bumping into a Litchfield acquaintance who'd given him a long stare and remarked "You look different. You look good. Did you get a face-lift?" "No," Roth replied, "I got a divorce."

Their autumn coffee klatch never materialized, but meanwhile the two serendipitously met again on June 5—four days before their divorce was final—and Bloom could hardly have been sweeter. Roth had arrived late to Alfred Kazin's eightieth birthday celebration at the CUNY Graduate Center auditorium, and Kazin's wife, Judith, had beckoned him over to the only available seat: beside herself and Bloom. At the reception afterward, a smiling Bloom told her estranged husband that she needed advice (he thought she'd said "advice about money," but wasn't entirely sure), and Roth apologetically demurred. "She didn't dispute me in any way," he recalled, "but continued to be kittenishly cordial." "He granted me an hour's audience," Bloom had grimly reported to Dick Stern about their previous meeting at Sarabeth's. "No, we're not friends."

Roth would soon learn just how dangerous an enemy he'd made. Bloom explained to friends that his niggardly settlement had left her in desperate straits—and then, too, she just felt in need of "catharsis"—and hence proposed to write a "kiss-and-dis" (in the words of *People* magazine) memoir, which she promptly sold to Little, Brown along with lucrative serial rights to *Vanity Fair.* One factor that might have helped settle the matter was Roth's unflattering portrayal of Sabbath's "fragile, volatile" first wife, the actress Nikki Kantarakis, "whose pervasive sense of crisis he'd mistaken for a deep spirit and whom he had Chekhovianly nicknamed 'A-Crisis-a-Day.'" What seems to have made the deepest impression was Roth's exhaustive transcription of the events allegedly surrounding Alice Bloom's death: "I remember thinking by the third day," Sabbath reflects of the way his first wife had continued to caress and chat with her mother's corpse, "'If this goes on any longer, I'll never fuck this woman again—I won't be able to lie with her in the same bed.'"

"He found me repellent," Bloom told Stern the following spring

(1996). "My mother's death was the coup de grâce." When Stern wondered why she was writing a second autobiography "as if the other book didn't exist," she explained that nobody had read *Limelight and After*; she was more sanguine about this one. And when journalists asked, later, why she'd written such a "brutally candid" book, Bloom liked to quote Roth's own words: "Philip always said," she told *People*, "'Be private in your life and shameless in your work.'"

PART FIVE

AMERICAN
MASTER

1995–2006

*Roth with Newark historian Charles Cummings (left)
and Mayor Sharpe James (right), during Philip Roth
Day in Newark, October 23, 2005.*

(COURTESY OF PHILIP ROTH ESTATE)

Thirty-Nine

W ITH *Sabbath's Theater* Roth had "let the repellent in" with a vengeance, and during this era some thought he was becoming rather Sabbath-like in real life. When his German publisher neglected to seek his approval before proposing a different title for a paperback edition of *The Facts*,* Roth threatened to "come after them with a GUN": "Why can't a jew [sic] have his own title in Germany in 1994?" he faxed Wylie. "Can't we ever be forgiven? Fuckers." The publisher responded to Roth's complaint in German ("Ich habe nun unseren Umschlaghersteller . . ."), which made him angrier still: "How do I know what the fuck they're talking about? It's written in that fucking language they so taught the world to love between 1939 and 1945. Tell them to go fuck themselves and write in fucking English so we know what the fuck they're talking about." He moreover demanded an apology "IN FUCKING ENGLISH," then proposed ("ON THIRD FUCKING THOUGHT") that Wylie find him a different German publisher—in Switzerland. Wylie decorously suggested they let a scolding note suffice, and thereupon informed the publisher that neither he nor Roth were able to read German, etc. Roth approved the note with a single provision: "SEND IT TO THEM IN FUCKING YIDDISH."

He was almost as cranky toward his American publisher, Simon & Schuster, who hadn't sent copies of *Operation Shylock* to the PEN/Faulkner judges, nor did they commend his winning the award with so much as a postcard. Simon & Schuster, in turn, was perhaps chagrined over the bath they'd taken on Roth's three-book contract; in the event, Wylie declined their offer for *Sabbath* and showed the novel elsewhere. Nan

---

* The alternative title is unclear in the correspondence I read.

Talese of Doubleday professed to admire Roth's "all-out, life-embracing acceptance of Sabbath," but, she added, "it is the marketplace we must contend with and I fear that most readers are not going to find SAB-BATH good company." A few days later the book was sold to Roth's very first book publisher, Houghton Mifflin, for $300,000—half of what Simon & Schuster had paid for each of his three preceding books, a sacrifice Roth was happy to make: "Imagine," he wrote Solotaroff, "I proposed a jacket design [at Houghton] and wasn't met by a barrage of objections from my marketing betters (who always turn out to know shit)." Better still, he wasn't expected to do publicity. He was dismayed when the editor who bought the novel, John Sterling, left Houghton within a couple of months, but eventually became friends with the man's replacement, Wendy Strothman, despite her coming from the "feminist" (Roth) Beacon Press and regarding Mickey Sabbath with distaste.

Roth usually considered *Sabbath* his own favorite among his novels—certainly the one he had the most fun writing, as he mined a misanthropic vein that had flourished amid his travails with Bloom. "The misanthropy is genuine," he later remarked. "And a misanthrope can be a very funny fellow, so I learned." While choosing a burial plot, the suicidal Sabbath notes the recurrence of the word "Beloved" and imagines a suitable grave-stone for himself: "Morris Sabbath / 'Mickey' / Beloved Whoremonger, Seducer / Sodomist, Abuser of Women, / Destroyer of Morals, Ensnarer of Youth, / Uxoricide, / Suicide / 1929–1994." Such a man might have demanded sixty-two billion dollars in restitution from a recalcitrant wife, or mocked a young woman (despite her being the best friend of his future stepdaughter) for waxing indignant at his sexual advances—a man whose anger "takes the form of amusement, mischief, satire, hijinks, mimicry, impersonation, self-mockery, self-caricature, self-sabotage, and sheer playfulness," as Roth explained both Sabbath and himself. Martin Amis was one of the many who noted that Roth was "a divided self"—torn, like Portnoy, between altruism and perversity—but *Sabbath* "is the first time that Mr. Hyde has been given the floor." "I have chosen to make art of my vices rather than what I take to be my virtues," Roth said to Jack Miles, and nowhere is this desideratum more gloriously realized than in Sabbath, whose main regret is that he is not "loathsome, degenerate, and gross" *enough*. Thus he enlists his "sidekicker," Drenka, to filch her teenage niece's soiled underwear and press them to his lips, and likewise tries to abscond with panties belonging to his old friend Norman Cowan's daughter, until the girl's mother, whom Sabbath has tried to seduce, discovers them in his jacket along with a bag of crack.

Such lewdness would pall were it not inextricably linked with, and driven by, a profound sense of loss. For fifty years Sabbath has been haunted by nothingness—"Every third thought shall be my grave" reads the book's epigraph, from *The Tempest*—ever since the death of his brother Morty, "the kindest older brother in the world," who was shot down over the Philippines at age twenty. "The death of Morty sets the gold standard for grief," said Roth, who saw his best friend from Weequahic, Marty Weich, burst into tears when he remembered, fifty years later, his brother's death and their devastated parents. For Sabbath (if not for Dr. Weich), indulging in the repellent is the best, the only, revenge. "What a pathetic, outmoded old crank you are, Mickey Sabbath," says Cowan, a theater producer of uncommon eloquence (the better to serve as another of Roth's dialectical mouthpieces). "The discredited male polemic's last gasp. . . . [Y]ou persist in quarreling with society as though Eisenhower is president!" When Cowan pronounces his friend's isolation "horrifying," Sabbath, undaunted, replies: "I don't think you ever gave isolation a real shot. It's the best preparation I know of for death."

And death is at the heart of the "two best scenes" Roth ever wrote, as he saw it: Sabbath's visit to his hundred-year-old cousin, Fish, and his farewell to Drenka on her deathbed. Roth often spoke of his "freedom" while writing *Sabbath*—a sense he could do no wrong, slipping in and out of Sabbath's thoughts, the first and third person, dancing along a high wire between pathos and hilarity. Whispers of the novel's comic tone persist in the late scene with Fish, but the overall mood has become somber: Sabbath is solicitous toward the old man, sweetly in awe of his lonely perseverance, even as he (Sabbath) contrives to steal a carton of Morty's belongings that has found its way into Fish's possession:

> They were back together on the sofa holding hands. And he has no idea who I am. No problem stealing the carton. . . .
>
> "I think, when I think of dying," Fish happened to be saying, "I think I wish I was never born. I wish I was never born. That's right."

"Why?"

"Cause death, death is a terrible thing. . . ."

Just *how* terrible Sabbath realizes when he opens the carton, afterward, on what would have been Morty's seventieth birthday, and finds everything that materially remains of his brother's brief span on earth—photos, his track letter, the flag that had been draped over his coffin when his burned and mutilated body was returned from the Philippines. Sabbath's suffering at that moment is "the passionate, the violent stuff, the worst, invented to torment one species alone, the remembering animal, the animal with the long memory. And prompted merely by lifting out of the carton and holding in his hand what Yetta Sabbath had stored there of her older son's."

While Drenka lies dying of ovarian cancer—amid drainage bags full of her waste, her torso emaciated and her legs bloated with edema—the couple tenderly remember her malapropisms ("I pledge a legion to the flag"; "nuts and bulbs") and the joy of pissing on each other in their little woodland stream. Some think Roth's foot slips a little here, and elsewhere, while treading the novel's narrow, "preposterone"-fueled path ("To his left," as Amis put it, "the Scylla of schlock; to his right, the Charybdis of pornography"). "The pissing-on-me-on-you-on-the-grave has an elaborate sentimentality which made me (an old lady) cringe a little," Joanna Clark wrote, with her usual frankness. But for Roth, as for Sabbath, the violation of taboos in the company of one's beloved is the very essence of tenderness—an invigorating *épater* to a cruel and uncomprehending world. In the end, a bereft Sabbath seems about to fulfill his death wish when Drenka's son, a loutish state trooper, catches him pissing on Drenka's grave; rather than shooting or beating him to death, however, the man drives Sabbath into the woods and kicks him out of the squad car, "with no one to kill him except himself. . . . And he couldn't do it. He could not fucking die. How could he leave? How could he go? Everything he hated was here."

Understandably, Roth was warier than ever of what critics would say of his latest, filthiest, most beloved of books. He had particular reason "to live in fear of Ms. Kakutani's original mind," as he wrote Bellow, since one of the scores he'd endeavored to settle in *Sabbath* was with the young *Times* reviewer who, he thought, had tarred his previous novel with a pretty broad brush. Sabbath, who hates the Japanese for killing his brother, affects to fumble the Michiko Kakutani–like name of Dean Kimiko Kakizaki, who fires him in the wake of a phone-sex scandal with one of his students: "Kakizomi. Kazikomi. Who could remember their fucking names. Who wanted to." MICKEY SABBATH, YOU'RE NO PORT-NOY, read the headline of Kakutani's review: "Whereas Portnoy's attacks of conscience coupled with his rage to revolt gave that novel an exuberant comic energy, Sabbath's plodding pursuit of defiance lends *Sabbath's Theater* a static and claustrophobic air, resulting in a novel that's sour instead of manic, nasty instead of funny, lugubrious instead of liberating."

But this was not representative of the novel's mostly euphoric reception, including a rave in *The New York Review of Books* from Roth's favorite critic, Frank Kermode, who declared *Sabbath* "among the most remarkable novels in recent years. With his Rabelaisian range and fluency, his deep resources of obscenity, his sense that suffering and dying can be seen as unacceptable though inevitable aberrations from some huge possible happiness, Roth is equipped for his great subject—one that was treated in their own rather different ways by the authors of Genesis and *Paradise Lost*." Kermode made the point that both Sabbath and King Lear (the latter a kindred soul whom Sabbath portrays on stage and subway) deplore moral hypocrisy and its attendant forms of justice—the beadle lashing the whore, says Lear, whom he "hotly lust'st to use": "It is this justice that Sabbath rages against," wrote Kermode; "and so, with all his characteristic ironies and reservations, does the author of this splendidly wicked book."

∎ ∎ ∎ ∎

WHILE WRITING *SABBATH*, Roth refined his work routine with two crucial acquisitions: a stand-up desk, which spared his back a little and behooved him to walk around when he got stuck, and a word processor, which he found wonderfully conducive to revision and "a bit more company than the typewriter"—which is not to say he was tempted by the nascent internet. Almost ten years would pass before Roth bought a second computer for that purpose (and even longer before he bothered with email), and for the rest of his life he did most of his actual writing on the first, a Dell 466/L with a quaintly minuscule eight megabytes of RAM. "You've got a word processor!" Updike congratulated him.

"Welcome to this wonderful world. You'll be able to double your output, delighting your friends and confounding your foes."

He would need every advantage for his next project—a nice riposte to Kermode's rather waggish qualm that Roth had all but exhausted the possibilities of literate obscenity ("further outrage now seems close to impossible"). By early fall 1995, Roth was already forty thousand words into his new novel and hadn't used the word "fuck" once—a polarity harking back to Philip Rahv's "redskin" and "paleface" dialectic in American letters, not to say Roth's own divided nature. Roth, an urban Jewish redskin "to the candy store and the borscht belt born," had been semicivilized by the academy into a cultural amalgam he dubbed "redface": "To my mind," Roth had written in 1973, "being a redface accounts as much as anything for the self-conscious and deliberate zigzag that my own career has taken, each book veering sharply away from the one before, as though the author were mortified at having written it as he did and preferred to put as much light as possible between that *kind* of book and himself." One sign that he'd exhausted the pleasure of Sabbath's company was his visceral reaction to the sight of *Sabbath's Theater* on the bedside table of Julia Golier's sweet Catholic mother: "I felt so ashamed," said Roth.

The wholesome hero of Roth's present book, Seymour "Swede" Levov, had gestated in his imagination for more than twenty years. When Alan Lelchuk informed him, in 1973, that a prominent critic's daughter had been part of the radical antiwar movement, Roth remarked on "what a novel that might make, to trace the journey of [the critic's family] through the decade." For Roth, it was imperative that his own novel's radical terrorist (a word that didn't exist in his vocabulary back then) be a *daughter* rather than a son. Because women protesters in those days weren't in danger of being drafted and killed, they possessed a kind of ineffable "purity to their rage" that fascinated Roth. And while he was intrigued by the critic's daughter, his main model for Merry Levov was Kathy Boudin, the daughter of an activist left-wing lawyer whose clients had included Fidel Castro. Roth had met Leonard Boudin at one of the Schneiders' parties in the sixties, and on March 6, 1970, across the street from the Schneiders, four Weather Underground members had blown up a town house (at 18 West Eleventh Street) while making bombs. Kathy Boudin and a friend staggered away from the rubble and disappeared, while the decapitated torso of Diana Oughton wasn't found until four days later.

"LEBOW was not given to daydreaming about what he didn't have"—reads the first line of the draft Roth began in 1974, shortly after finishing *My Life as a Man*—"most likely because for most of his life he had had everything he most wanted." In this ur-version, tentatively titled *How the Other Half Lives*, Lebow is a decent but "dull and boring" Everyman, versus the more complicated paragon that is Swede Levov; otherwise, the core episodes of *American Pastoral* are mostly in place. By page three of the typescript, Lebow's daughter Merry is already a stuttering eleven-year-old in love with her father: "Daddy, kiss me the way you k-k-kiss umumumother," she says, after an outing on the beach, and Lebow angrily replies "N-n-no"—then, mortified, kisses her. "I thought, 'What if he does it?'" Roth said of that linchpin moment, remembering a similar episode between himself and Maggie's daughter. Also in *Other Half* (one page later!), Merry—"like some poor innocent in a fairy story who had been tricked into drinking a terrible potion"—becomes a stout, ungainly sixteen-year-old, mocked at school as "Ho Chi Lebow" because of her fanatical rage over the Vietnam War; on page six she blows up the Princeton Faculty Club bathroom, killing a janitor, and her father is left to wonder—forever—whether his wholly uncharacteristic lapse, when Merry was eleven, turned her into a terrorist.

Roth started over in the first person ("Who *is* the other half? . . . I am a parent, a husband, a manufacturer, an American, and a Jew"), and toyed mysteriously with incorporating some aspect of his Anne Frank obsession, trying such titles as *A Businessman's Sorrow (Anne Frank in America)* and *The Diary of Anne Frank's Contemporary*. Here, too, as in *Pastoral*, Merry the daughter emerges from the radical underground, years after the bombing, as an emaciated, veil-wearing Jain who works at a dog and cat hospital. But Roth couldn't imagine the world of her father—a "moderate, kindly, decent" cipher—beyond these few crucial scenes. For the next two decades, between each book, he'd pore over the seventy or so pages of false starts and wrack his brain; but it was only after spending two years with Mickey Sabbath that a worthy antithesis occurred to him: "*American Pastoral* got going when the Viet Nam book became the Swede Levov book," Roth wrote for the Franklin Library. "Whatever abundance of life this book may possess, arises from a head-on collision between those two words—'The Swede'—and my imagination." The nickname was derived from Seymour "Swede" Masin, a member of the Weequahic class of 1938—a legendary athlete considered, like Roth's hero, "the household Apollo of the Weequahic Jews." Taking only Masin's nickname and athletic prowess, Roth imagined the rest of Swede Levov's life—the gentile wife (a former Miss New Jersey), successful glove-making business, dream house in a rural exurb, troubled but beloved daughter, and a terrible portion of the national tragedy.

More and more, Roth insisted on transcending the merely personal—the "dwarf drama" of one alter ego after another—the better to explore "the world of massive historical pain instead of this pain in the neck," as Zuckerman puts it in *The Anatomy Lesson*. "Updike and Bellow hold their flashlights out into the world," Roth said in 1982, "reveal the real world as it is *now*. I dig a hole and shine my flashlight into the hole." *The Prague Orgy* gave a glimpse of the historical pain coveted by Zuckerman and his creator, whereas the canvases of *The Counterlife* and *Operation Shylock* were nothing if not sprawling—albeit dominated, still, by the "mirror games" (Kakutani) involving a Roth-like protagonist. Meanwhile he envied Updike's all-but-seamless incorporation of elaborate research, especially in the Rabbit novels—the way he became an expert on various nonliterary lives: "His hero is a Toyota salesman," Roth marveled of *Rabbit Is Rich*. "Updike knows everything about being a Toyota salesman. . . . I'm going to give up writing." Roth was actually a scrupulous post hoc researcher: Once he'd completed a draft or two, unconstrained by facts, he'd make sure the basic verisimilitude was sound. For *The Anatomy Lesson* he spent a few days shadowing an oncologist at St. Francis Hospital in Waterbury, and, as mentioned, he traveled to Amsterdam during the seventies and toured the Anne Frank House, along with her school and the streets she would have known. As Roth explained his method, "You're not 'inspired' by these people, it's quite the opposite: you write the thing and *then* you look for validation somewhere."

In November 1974, while casting about for some way to flesh out his hero's identity as a "manufacturer," Roth met the father of a Woodstock friend (the book publisher Peter Mayer), who invited Roth to tour his glove-making factory in Brooklyn. Roth had a "terrific visit" and became fascinated with every aspect of the business. Someone put him in touch with the manager of a leather tannery in Gloversville, New York—the heart of the (dying) glove-making industry—where Roth reveled in the "stink and dyes and water rushing everywhere"; afterward his host introduced him to a retired, old-time leather cutter, who made a pair of gloves for Roth, from scratch, that he cherished the rest of his life. "The more I learned about gloves in Gloversville," Roth wrote about the origins of his novel, "the more I realized it represented something to me that was important to this book. *It was about an era, about something else that's gone.*" Roth would always take pride in the fictional use to which he finally put his research, twenty years after that first trip to Gloversville. "I'll tell you what we're gonna do," Swede tells the baby-faced Rita Cohen, Merry's underground accomplice, who pretends to be a Wharton student writing her thesis on the Newark leather industry. "We're going to make you a pair of gloves and you're going to watch them being made from start to finish." After a virtuosic narrative seminar on the craft and milieu of glove making—the Swede momentarily distracted from his ceaseless misery—Rita Cohen reveals her true identity (*"Boom!"* Roth exclaimed, clapping his hands at the perfection of it): "She wants her Audrey Hepburn scrapbook," says Rita of the lost Merry.

What was mainly "gone" after the sixties, for Roth, was the Newark of his childhood—a vanished Atlantis he eulogized in *American Pastoral*. During the eighties, when visiting his father, Roth would detour through Weequahic and gape at the desolation—wondering, of course, what to make of it in his fiction. "Newark was Prague," he said. "Newark was the West Bank . . . a place that had a great historical fall." A key aspect of Newark's decline was the racial strife between black and white—particularly white Jews—given the gross disparity of economic opportunity; throughout the fifties and sixties, blacks came to occupy what had once been immigrant slums, while Jews deserted the city en masse for the suburbs. The Newark-born poet Amiri Baraka called the violence of 1967—in which he was charged but acquitted of weapons possession and inciting to riot—a "historical inevitability." This, after all, was a city where 52 percent of the population was black, whereas the police force was 90 percent white and only a single elected official was black. The fuse was lit on July 12, 1967, when white policemen beat a black cabdriver, John W. Smith, for allegedly resisting arrest after a minor traffic violation. Residents of a high-rise housing project, Hayes Homes, witnessed the police dragging Smith into the station, and black

Newarkers went on a rampage, looting and setting fires. Some businesses were spared, at first, when signs were hung like the signs that Levov's devoted black forelady, Vicky, hangs in the windows of Newark Maid: "Most of this factory's employees are NEGROES." As in the novel, however, white snipers soon made a point of shooting out windows where such signs were displayed. By the time the riots subsided, 1,058 businesses were damaged, and much of the city's public housing was in ruins. Jewish-owned businesses had been targets for particular violence, and some considered the riots a pogrom; within two years the once thriving community of Newark Jews had dwindled to a tenth of its original size. Finally, in 1975, *Harper's* magazine ranked American cities on the basis of census data in twenty-four categories: "The city of Newark stands without serious challenge as the worst of all."

Beginning with *American Pastoral*, Roth's right-hand man for local research was a librarian and Newark city historian, Charles Cummings. Roth adored Cummings—a "square, gay, and good-hearted" fellow, who never once failed him in any of his myriad requests. "You wouldn't be interviewing me if it weren't for Charles Cummings," Roth remarked to his biographer, referring to the hundreds of little flourishes he owed to Cummings's assiduity, such as the tunic and "NP"-emblazoned saddlecloth that Newark police and their horses wore during the war era of *The Plot Against America*. One winter day in 1995, Roth and Cummings spent hours looking for just the right building on which to model the Levov glove factory—"a smoke-darkened brick pile fifty years old and four stories high on Central Avenue and 2nd Street" that, once found, Cummings photographed from ten different angles.

Perhaps the most pleasant aspect of Roth's research, however, was by way of providing the exhaustive background for Dawn Levov's participation in the 1949 Miss America pageant. Roth had befriended the actor Ron Silver (narrator for a number of Roth's audiobooks, including *Portnoy* and, later, *American Pastoral*), who gave him the phone number of a girlfriend, Tawny Godin Little, Miss America 1976. Little put Roth in touch with the more age-appropriate Miss America 1951, Yolande Betbeze Fox, who agreed to visit Roth at his New York apartment and bring her pageant scrapbook. Roth was smitten: Fox, an opera singer, was funny, smart, and still stunning in her midsixties; the first Miss America to balk at posing in a bathing suit, she later devoted herself to progressive causes and studied philosophy at the New School. "In 1950," she smiled, when Roth kissed her goodbye on the cheek, "you wouldn't have stood a chance."

■ ■ ■ ■

BY THE TIME ROTH WON his second National Book Award, for *Sabbath's Theater*, winners were no longer announced in advance, and Roth had sensibly assumed his chances were slim. The chairman of the fiction jury, Thomas McGuane, admitted that his wife had thrown Roth's novel "across the room after the first 60 pages," while another judge, Erica Jong, said *Sabbath* "won *despite* its subject matter, which people on the committee universally found repellent, but which it transcends to become a meditation on mortality like no other." Amid a buzz of adverse comment, Roth was a no-show for the November 15 ceremony at the Plaza, and Wylie explained that his client had bronchial flu. In fact a death threat of sorts had been forwarded by William Pritchard of Amherst College, whose admiring review of *Sabbath* for the Sunday *New York Times* had provoked an anonymous letter addressed to him at the "Department of Sycophancy and English":

> Only a cheap little asskissing two-bit fucking "English professor" would have stooped to calling this Jew bastard's latest pile of dog shit "his richest and most rewarding." Or did the slimy kike's fascination with jerking himself off all his life give you the cozy feeling that you had found a fellow marathon masturbator to suck off in print? . . . Fags like you should be destroyed with concentrated AK-47 fire. That remedy would restore American higher education to what it once was. Or help to.*

After consulting the FBI, Roth asked Conarroe to attend the ceremony and, if necessary, deliver a brief acceptance speech on his behalf: "'I have written a wicked book,'" Roth had written, quoting Melville on the subject of *Moby-Dick*, "'and feel spotless as a lamb.'"

---

* A note with similar wording is received by one of Zuckerman's reviewers in *Exit Ghost*, whereas Zuckerman himself receives a couple of opprobrious postcards (both featuring Pope John Paul II) addressed to "Jew Bastard"—also similar to postcards Roth himself had received around this time.

An even more menacing development was news of a "'healing' session between [Inga] and Claire," as Joanna Clark reported to Roth in a November 2, 1995, note. Neither Clark nor Roth had any notion of the enormity of what lay ahead, though Clark deplored "the culture of victimhood, the great American Oprahdom" that, as she saw it, informed these women's sensibilities. Bloom would later tell Charlie Rose that she'd been "nearly finished" with her memoir when she learned the truth (or "The Truth," as she titled her final chapter) about Roth's affair with their mutual friend and neighbor. Inga doesn't recall Bloom using a tape recorder or taking notes while they chatted that day at Inga's town house, and later, when Bloom faxed her the relevant pages, Inga let them pass even though she hardly recognized herself in the "calm, undemanding" ("STAY AWAY FROM ME!!!!!!") Erda. Roth, needless to say, would also find the portrait somewhat out of focus: "Telling this story (if that is the story [Inga] told) she was able to confess to Claire of an affair lasting a year or two which she was drawn into like Florence Nightingale because I was in need, rather than to admit to the mischievous, audacious affair of 15"—actually more like eighteen—"years duration which provided the model for Drenka's affair with Sabbath."

A measure of Roth's self-involvement, and/or a kind of selective naiveté, was his inability to grasp at the time that Bloom meant to do him harm. ("Who would want to hurt Amasa Delano?" he'd mock himself many years later, paraphrasing Melville's "Benito Cereno": "Who would murder Amasa Delano?" wonders Amasa Delano, unwittingly menaced by mutinous slaves aboard the *San Dominick*.) Mia Farrow remembered that he still kept a picture of Bloom in his studio, and often spoke tenderly of the way he'd tried and tried, always, to coax this terribly insecure person into giving her best performance. He laughed when Manea worriedly related a rumor that Bloom was writing about their relationship: "Norman, she cannot write," said Roth, who assumed such a book would be a sequel to *Limelight and After*—perhaps about "the interesting nature of a marriage between an actress and a writer," he surmised, "which was not without precedent (Chekhov and Olga Knipper)." After all: How could such a book be scurrilous? What about the money he'd given her? The teleplays he'd written? The endless rehearsing and other career assistance? What about that genial meeting at Sarabeth's, and the friendly notes that followed?

Roth spent almost the entire summer of 1996 in Connecticut, working on *American Pastoral*, with Golier and occasionally Ross Miller his only weekend visitors. Neither friend was apt to hear the Manhattan gossip about the galleys of *Leaving a Doll's House* that were already circulating. Still, it appears Roth at least got the gist of David Streitfeld's piece in *The Washington Post* on August 30: *Doll's House*, Streitfeld revealed, "is in large part about Philip Roth: master novelist and master manipulator, a deeply troubled fellow who likes to make his loved ones part of his madness." When Streitfeld described the book's contents to him, Conarroe assayed a loyal and politic response: "Claire is a wonderful person and a great actress, but not necessarily a totally accurate observer. I hope anyone who reads this book will read it not only with a grain of salt, but a whole tablespoonful." One of the book's dedicatees, however, assured Streitfeld that her friend Claire was all but incapable of even the mildest exaggeration: "She's an amazingly accurate reporter," said Francine du Plessix Gray.

On September 3, Roth sent a terse memo to his closest friends, giving out his new telephone numbers in New York and Connecticut: "THESE NUMBERS ARE UNLISTED. PLEASE DO NOT GIVE THEM TO ANYONE." He also castigated Conarroe for talking to Streitfeld, though of course his friend had only meant to be helpful; nevertheless Roth had repeatedly asked him and others *not* to cooperate with the media in any form, especially during his breakup with Bloom.

Though Roth clearly had at least secondhand knowledge of the Streitfeld piece, he later claimed he hadn't twigged to the true nature of Bloom's memoir until September 17, when he was in New York to see his physical therapist, Lori Monson. As he was leaving, she remarked, "I wouldn't look at the *Times* today if I were you." Puzzled, he walked to the City Athletic Club ("Jewish guys," Roth glossed) on Fifty-fourth and Sixth to take a swim, relaxing afterward in the sauna. Two men were expostulating outside the door—"*Is he gonna let her get away with this shit?*"—when Roth came out to say hello. "What you gonna do about her?" one man asked. "Who's 'her'?" "You know what I'm talking about!" Roth didn't, though he declined to pursue the matter then and there. He said goodbye and proceeded up Central Park West toward his apartment on Seventy-seventh. Along the way, at last, he got the picture. Coming toward him was his and Bloom's old friend Barbara Epstein;

expecting the usual hug and hello, Roth was startled when the woman hurried past him without a word. At this point he thought to buy the *Times*. CLAIRE BLOOM LOOKS BACK IN ANGER AT PHILIP ROTH, read the headline of an article, by Dinitia Smith, about Bloom's forthcoming memoir. Roth's blurry scan of the first few sentences picked out key phrases: "self-centered misogynist . . . the gossip is considerable. . . ."

He stopped there and dumped the newspaper into the trash; then he went to his apartment, packed a few clothes, got his car out of the garage, and drove an hour and a half to the Jersey Shore—stopping en route to visit his parents' graves and pull himself together. "I thought: 'This whole life has been dedicated to serious matters. . . . And that I should wind up in the fucking *New York Times* saying "misogynist" and who knows what else is in there. And also there's the book to come . . .'" Roth took a room at a bed-and-breakfast in Spring Lake (a few miles south of his childhood haunts in Bradley Beach), and, after a day or so, left messages for Sandy, Wylie, and Golier (the last, under the circumstances, was frantic with worry by then), letting them know he'd gone away for a bit and was fine. For the next four days he did nothing but "walk and dive, walk and dive," eating his meals on the dock at Ollie Klein's in Belmar. At night he listened to the ocean a block away from his room. "I lay on the bed and I thought 'They can't touch you. They can't touch you.' In one day I was over it. I was centered." Which is to say, he was soon ready to collect his things in New York and hole up in Connecticut for a long while, working and seeing nobody but Julia and Ross; in a larger sense, he never got over it.

■ ■ ■ ■

IN HER PREFACE TO *Leaving a Doll's House*, Bloom described her marriage to Roth as "the most important relationship of [her] life" (not to be confused with her greatest love, who, she noted on page 93, was Richard Burton*). As Bloom recognized when she first saw Chekhov's

---

* "When her adulterous lover of forty or fifty years back, Richard Burton, died," said Roth, "she astonished me by her performance. She went around in long dark skirts acting, quite ethereally, like the widow herself, especially at mealtime, when she was quite beyond my reach. I tolerated it for about two days and then pointed out to her that she wasn't the widow."

Three Sisters, at age twelve, certain women are apt to spend their lives in pursuit of a "lost father," no matter how "tyrannical" such a figure tends to be. Ultimately, like Nora Helmer in *A Doll's House*, Bloom would be free of the final and most darkly formidable of the many father figures in her life, but the journey was painful, protracted, and *very* repetitive. "You have already had Portnoy's complaint," Gore Vidal advised her back in 1975, referring to her recent divorce from a man who'd exploited her sexually and otherwise, Hilly Elkins. "Do not involve herself with Portnoy." In lucidly rueful retrospect, Bloom realized her friend had been right— a conclusion she might have reached in the beginning, on the basis of Roth's novels, which "provided all one needed to know" about the kind of philandering, "Machiavellian" fiasco the author proved to be. Such, anyway, was *Leaving a Doll's House*.

Most of the reviewers were sympathetic to the story Bloom told. The word "harrowing" recurred a lot. Marion Winik wrote, in the *Los Angeles Times* ("Mrs. Portnoy's Complaint"), that there was "nothing funny" about the "mess" that is Philip Roth—who, it so happened, was Winik's "favorite living writer," though she was hardly surprised by his human failings: "Tall, moody, self-absorbed intellectuals with their sardonic insights have long been a disappointment to me in the romance department." Perhaps the most wholehearted affirmation came from Patricia Bosworth in the *Times Book Review*. Naturally she found the book "harrowing," though she commended Bloom's effort to be "fair to Mr. Roth, perhaps too fair. And too often she portrays herself as a victim, which is exasperating; she obviously is very strong; otherwise, she would not have survived."

Daphne Merkin, however, writing in *The New Yorker*, wondered at Bloom's lack of "any sense of moral accountability. . . . In her own eyes, she remains forever a passive being fatally attracted to men who issue demonic commands she has no choice but to obey."* As for Bloom's alleged fairness despite her victimhood, Merkin noted that Roth and others had proved

---

* When a radio interviewer mentioned that Merkin and others had objected to her "victim consciousness," Bloom allowed herself to be waspish: "Daphne Merkin had already written a most appalling piece, that I had remembered, which was an essay in her fantasy sexual life, and it was to be spanked. I ask you. I think she knows a little more about being a victim than I do."

quite useful to her career: "One can discern, through the pious gloss Bloom puts on the events of her life, the shrewd maneuverings of a stage brat"—a sentiment Zoë Heller echoed more bluntly in the *London Review of Books*: "beneath the guise of a bashed butterfly, a scorpion."

And yet, in his feature article for *New York* magazine (cover caption: "A Hell of a Marriage"), Peter J. Smith pointed out that Bloom's "most striking" traits were "her obvious kindness, sincerity, and eagerness to please. . . . [T]his blistering and ultimately very sad account exposes the artist as a spectacularly troubled and manipulative man, prone to recurring somatic and mental illness; someone who, in the words of one of Bloom's friends, 'is basically impossible, and should not have relationships.'" As evidence of her vaunted fairness, Bloom pronounced the prepublication *Times* piece "vile" because it gave a false impression of her book's harshness, when in fact she'd tried very hard to emphasize "that there were good times as well as bad, that it was a long and splendid relationship that in the end was marred." Smith added: "Later an acquaintance of Bloom's suggests that she was 'having you on,' claiming that Bloom, when informed about the *Times*'s early and unusual coverage, was 'chortling.'"

The nadir was a spot about Bloom on the prime-time *Dateline NBC*. Roth was alerted by his Silver Hill psychiatrist, Dr. Bloch, who phoned to warn him that he'd just escorted a film crew off the grounds when they asked his permission to shoot "Roth's room"; the crew was now filming from a nearby road. This was followed by a letter from Dennis Murphy:

> I'm an NBC News reporter with the network's *Dateline* program and over the weekend, in London, Claire gave us a taped interview, which we expect to air in a couple of weeks. Had there been an 11th chapter, Smilesburger's whisperers couldn't have done a better job in the *loshon hora* ["evil tongue," i.e., derogatory speech] department.
>
> Claire believes that you will never respond to her book or the accompanying publicity and though you are one who clearly knows how to be silent, patient and unprovoked in the most unsettling circumstances, I hope she's wrong?
>
> Would you consider a videotaped interview? . . .
>
> "He'd do it to me," Claire tells us.
>
> Would you?

Roth didn't reply, though he belatedly retained a lawyer, Russell Brooks of Milbank Tweed, who read *Doll's House* on his behalf ("for the sake of my health and sanity," said Roth, "I didn't want to"), and wrote a letter to Bloom, dated November 5, observing that her book was defamatory and demanding a retraction, absent which Roth had "authorized us to take whatever legal action is necessary." Six days later, during her WNYC radio interview with Leonard Lopate, Bloom spoke with unwonted tenderness of her "marvelous marriage" to Roth, with whom she'd had "the best relationship of her life." On the thirteenth Brooks sent a tape of this interview to an NBC lawyer, David Sternlicht, advising him to compare it with their own interview, "and then consider whether NBC News can rely on Ms. Bloom's statements to Dateline to be accurate." Roth's former lover and Penn student, Laurie Geisler Donovan, was now a senior vice president and general counsel for the network; as she regretfully informed Roth over the phone, they'd discussed aborting the segment but decided it was too late to fill the November 15 slot.

"I was the victim of a dreadful accident," Bloom announces at the beginning of her *Dateline* spot. "What caused it, I don't know. It's like being hit by a truck." Flashing lights, a blaring car horn. "I despise what he did to me. I despise the person who did it." An announcer explains: "It's her thermonuclear dish-all about her ex-husband, Philip Roth, that has smart circles buzzing. . . . [Roth] is such a towering intellect, he could be the Michael Jordan of the American literary scene." The actual interview builds with like subtlety to "the most shocking story" in Bloom's book, when Roth handed her a letter demanding that her daughter move out. "No, sorry, got to stop there," Bloom says, after a faltering attempt to discuss "the worst moment of [her] life": "Can't do this." ("He might see it differently," she breezily remarked of the Anna episode on WNYC. "That's what happened, but he might have his own reasons that he would give you, I'm sure.") "You've hit him with a haymaker," the *Dateline* interviewer congratulates her at last.

BLOOM [*girlishly covering her mouth*]: What's a "haymaker"?
INTERVIEWER: It's a full roundhouse punch that puts you back on your bum.

BLOOM: Oh, great! . . . That's exactly the way I feel. He hit me with a
haymaker; I fought back.

The day after the show, which Roth never watched, he went to the Cornwall Bridge general store to pick up his daily paper, and the store's owner,
Ed Baird, took him aside: "I didn't believe those things they said about
you, Phil. I know you, and I didn't believe a word."

Meanwhile Milbank Tweed had compiled a "Preliminary List of Possibly Defamatory Statements," seventy-two in all, which, if false, were
libelous. A few of these were highlighted in Brooks's November 5 letter
to Bloom:

- Mr. Roth is misogynic [sic] and has an innately hostile disposition
  toward women. These statements are patently false. . . .
- Mr. Roth demanded that you oust your daughter Anna from her
  family home in London to live in a student hostel in a poor and dangerous neighborhood ["one of the least salubrious," Bloom had writ-
  ten] of London. In fact, your daughter left home to live in the London
  residence facility of her London college—the Guild Hall School of
  Music, and, when she did not like it, returned home several months
  later and lived on the top floor of the home with a friend.
- Mr. Roth made improper sexual advances to [Felicity]. This statement
  is utterly false.
- Mr. Roth suffered from a disease identified as "bipolar disorder." This
  false and damaging statement appeared on page 178 of the galley
  proofs that you circulated to reviewers. . . .

If Bloom did not make a public retraction, Brooks concluded, Roth
intended to recover damages against her "in an amount not less than $10
million." ("He said, 'How much do you want to sue her for, ten mill or
twenty mill?'" Roth recalled. "And I said 'Ten mill.' Taking the high road.")

In fact Bloom's book never precisely described Roth as "misogynic,"* and
then, too, "utterly false" is a stretch vis-à-vis whatever transpired between

---

* Or even some form of the actual word "misogynist"—unless I missed it in my two or
three readings—though it was the invariable characterization that occurred to journalists
in describing the tenor of her perception of Roth.

Roth and Felicity; but he fastened on Bloom's explicit claim, in the galleys, that his struggle with "Halcion madness," in 1987, "was the first manifestation of the symptoms that were later identified as bipolar disorder." In 2008, Roth asked Bill Frosch, a psychiatrist he'd consulted for almost twenty years, to comment in writing on the validity of a bipolar diagnosis, and Frosch flatly denied that Roth had ever met DSM criteria for the illness: "I feel that I can say this with some confidence," he wrote: "1. I know you well; and 2. I served on the American Psychiatric Association Task Force for DSM III, which still serves as the basis of the current diagnostic classification." Two other psychiatrists, both familiar with Roth's occasional bouts of unipolar depression, also denied he'd ever exhibited signs of mania. "It's not an expression I would use, and I have no idea," Bloom backpedaled during her November 11 interview (a few days after Brooks's letter), when Lopate mentioned her reference to manic depression. He then asked about Roth's Halcion madness. "That's not being a manic-depressive," said Bloom; "that's being affected by dreadful drugs."

In a 2013 email, Bloom claimed that she'd had "very good grounds" for her assertion of Roth's supposed bipolar illness, "but it was agreed that these grounds were too feeble." The very good (if too feeble) grounds were characterized as "a reliable source" in a rebuttal composed by Little, Brown's general counsel, Carol Fein Ross, on November 12, 1996; nevertheless, Bloom had agreed to delete the reference. As for the rest of her allegedly defamatory statements, they were expressions of her "heartfelt" and "constitutionally protected opinions" and therefore not actionable, Ross concluded, on a deploring note:

> [We] are disappointed that a writer of such exceptional talent and prominence would attempt to stifle someone else's expression of opinion. . . .
>
> It is regrettable that Mr. Roth is dismayed over the publication of Ms. Bloom's book, as she had no intention of causing him harm. . . . Mr. Roth is a public figure who often writes about relationships, and, as such, there is public interest in information about relationships he has had. Because we have every confidence in Ms. Bloom's work and do not believe it to be defamatory, we see no need for a public retraction.

As Roth remembered, "I had been virtually assured victory in the U.K."—where libel laws are more stringent—"and Russell thought we had a pretty solid case in the U.S." Roth had retained a firm of London solicitors, Harbottle & Lewis, and was briefly tempted to proceed, but first consulted friends whose judgment he trusted: Wylie, Miles, and Dr. Bloch. They all advised against it, and for the same reasons that doubtless would have dissuaded Roth in any case: "I did not want interminable conferences with lawyers and exhausting courtroom appearances and sleepless nights of arguing the case in my head to displace everything else in my life, beginning with my work, nor did I relish encountering the media coverage incited by a suit between the two of us." Roth envisaged an ordeal akin to that of the ravaged litigants of *Jarndyce v. Jarndyce* in *Bleak House*: "Suffer any wrong that can be done you," Dickens wrote of his chancery court, "rather than come here!" Besides, Roth liked to think Bloom's book would go away soon enough, and meanwhile he could get on with his next two novels, *I Married a Communist* and *The Human Stain* (both about false accusation). "You know what Chekhov said when someone said to him 'This too shall pass'?" Roth asked his biographer. "'*Nothing* passes.' Put *that* in the fucking book."

■　■　■　■

FOR FIVE OR SIX MONTHS, Roth never ventured far from his Connecticut home, nor did he accept phone calls from New York. Golier found him "pretty distraught" and did her best to cheer him. The better to underline the point that Bloom's book was but a passing blip in an otherwise happy and accomplished life, she pasted three or four sheets of paper together and devised an elaborate timeline, past and future, on which the all but invisible pinprick of *Doll's House* was followed by honors and prizes galore ("I was not wrong," she said). The "worst moment" that fall—for Golier—was returning to Grand Central after an especially arduous weekend of bucking Roth up ("Nobody cares! It's going to be gone in ten seconds!"), and running smack into rows and rows of *New York* magazine with Roth and Bloom on the cover: "A Hell of a Marriage."

Above all, perhaps, Roth was hurt by what seemed an almost universal willingness to accept Bloom's account at face value. His friend Jack Miles noticed this too, and protested Patricia Bosworth's review of Bloom's book in the Sunday *Times* with a letter reminding its readers that "there are two sides to any divorce story. . . . In sum, what badly needs saying about this season's *succès de scandal* is that no one knows how much of it is true. I can only regret that your reviewer didn't say just that much and that little." Certainly Roth would have liked to rebut the charge that he caddishly discarded "one woman after another"; among the women who'd discarded *him*, rather than vice versa, and remained friends all the same, was Barbara Sproul, who'd bumped into Bloom at a party shortly before Bloom's divorce from Roth. "She went on about him being 'unreasonable,'" Sproul remembered, "and I said I found him to be eminently reasonable." Later Bloom's complaint seemed all the richer in light of her "disgusting" book ("the day you get carted off to the bin doesn't seem to be anyone's fucking business except the most intimate of friends"), and Sproul lost no time writing Roth a letter:

> I wanted you to hear it from somewhere other than your own inner voice: it ain't so, and I am glad to say it. You are good and kind and generous and true and if you have any flaw, surface cynicism notwithstanding, it is that you are hopeful and faithful enough to think others are as well. If you have failed here it is only in the sense that your love—of Maggie first, and then of Claire—wasn't enough to make them find what was truly worthwhile in themselves. . . .
>
> I would gladly write a public piece about you, but it seems to me quite irrelevant what "other people" think. . . . I'd also be delighted to write Claire personally with an "how could you" letter—just so she'd know there were limits some people at least still respected. . . .
>
> I am so sorry someone wants to hurt you; you deserve so much better.

As the months passed, Roth wrestled with the question of Bloom's motive for such a terrible attack; given a human tendency to underestimate his own failings, he focused mostly on her "continuing desire to win Anna's favor." That her efforts in that direction were unavailing was made uncomfortably public on Mothering Sunday, March 9, 1997, when the BBC presented *Stars and Mas*—an anodyne tribute whose TV listing betrayed at least one anomalous bit: "Spice Girl Emma Bunton and boxer Lennox Lewis talk about their close relationships with their mothers. Bob Marley's mother Cedella Booker speaks of her devotion to her son, while actress Claire Bloom reveals a more complex relationship with her daughter." The complexity is evident from the get-go, as Anna describes her mother (seated beside her) as "very childish for her age," then tells about the time she had to force Bloom into telling the truth about her imminent divorce from Anna's father: "I thought then that she was a weaker character than me already, at about five." Soon they get onto the subject of Roth's shocking demand that Anna move out:

> BLOOM: I don't believe in holding on to the past. Because it's too pain-ful. I believe in trying to let it go. [*Anna scowls at her fingertips.*] You believe in holding on to it.
>
> STEIGER: No, I don't. I just don't believe in ignoring it, that's all. Because I don't believe it really has been aired as an issue, or con-fronted or faced. Or really discussed properly.
>
> BLOOM: . . . Anna did come back; we lived together in the house for another I don't know how many years. So it wasn't a final break of any kind. I didn't say 'Go away and never come back.' And she was eighteen; she was not a baby. She would have gone on with her life. I couldn't face losing my relationship with Philip, that was so precious to me. [*Bloom keeps nervously glancing at Anna to see how she's taking things.*]
>
> STEIGER: I just feel there's a lot of whitewash going on here. And bull-shit frankly.
>
> BLOOM: I'm the one who brought it up in the public field, so how can it be whitewash?
>
> STEIGER: I don't know. All I know is what I hear I don't like. Some-how it makes me angry and I don't see it in the same way or have the same perspective on it at all.

Finally Bloom is alone on camera, weeping over the loss of "her treacher-ous Machiavelli" (as Roth put it): "I remember the good times with grat-itude and love," she admits. For *I Married a Communist*, Roth worked directly from this videotape while writing the scene in which the washed-up Eve Frame appears with her daughter, Sylphid, on a TV show called *The Apple and the Tree*: "Sylphid doesn't display a split second's worth of affection for this pathetic woman struggling to hang on," Murray Rin-gold observes. "Not a speck of generosity, let alone understanding."

About six years later, quite by chance, Roth and Bloom crossed paths for the last time. One night he was strolling along Columbus Avenue with a girlfriend, Susan Rogers;* they'd paused to look in the window of a ladies shoe shop, and when they turned around to head south toward Roth's apartment, there was Bloom and a friend, the flutist Eugenia Zukerman, about fifty yards away. "I decided to give Claire the kind of look you give somebody to whom you loaned your car, thirty years earlier, when you were in college, and who had banged it up and who now you were seeing for the first time since then," Roth remembered. He did his best to muster that look, but he and Rogers burst into laughter as soon as Bloom passed. Later a mutual friend told Roth that Bloom had described him as "shaking with rage." She "reported that I was 'trembling so' that she believed 'they would have to call an ambulance and have [me] hospitalized.'"

---

* Daughter of his old Chicago friends Tom and Jacquie Rogers.

CHAPTER

Forty

STOMPING ALONG THE HOUSATONIC, ROTH FOUND HIM-
self "swamped with anger" and knew he had to "write [his] way out
of it" lest his head explode. "I kept thinking, 'What is this like? What
is happening to me is not innately interesting to anybody else. But what
would be of interest? . . . That postwar Communist scare with the accusation: Communist, Communist. And now it's misogynist, misogynist.
You can't elude it. If you're stamped with it, you're stamped with it.'"
Roth had no desire to write about an innocent, and so conceived his
hero, Ira Ringold, as a furtive Communist "full of flaws," just as Roth
himself was guilty of conducting a florid sex life behind Bloom's back;
but Eve Frame isn't content with the mere truth, and her book accuses
Ringold of being a Soviet spy besides, whereas Bloom rendered Roth as
a "Machiavellian strategist" and all-around head case. "I wanted to get
the valences correct," said Roth.

The main model for Ira's brother, Murray, was Roth's freshman homeroom teacher, Dr. Robert ("Doc") Lowenstein. During a 1955 House
Un-American Activities Committee hearing in Newark, Lowenstein—
then serving as executive vice president of the Newark Teachers
Union—invoked the Fifth Amendment rather than discuss his former
membership in the Communist party. "How can you be paid by the tax-
payers' money when you are obligated by your damnable Communist
oath to teach the Soviet line?" Representative Clyde Doyle berated him.
Lowenstein lost his job for six years, until he was vindicated and rein-
stated after two appeals to the New Jersey Supreme Court; when he was
first fired, though, the *Newark Evening News* printed angry letters from
readers demanding the resignation of four Board of Education members
who'd dared to defend Lowenstein. Philip Roth, a year out of Bucknell,
answered with a letter of his own, pointing out that "in Russia dissent-

ers are asked to resign, and now in Newark dissenters are being asked to resign."

Bob Lowenstein was an eighty-nine-year-old retiree living in West Orange when Roth sent a driver to pick him up and take him out to Connecticut so Roth could canvass his views on the way Newark was portrayed, before and after the riots, in a late draft of *American Pastoral.* The two cemented their friendship a year later, when Roth paid several visits to West Orange to discuss Lowenstein's experiences as an ostracized teacher in the McCarthy era. Roth also had long talks with another old mentor, Irv Cohen, Cousin Florence's husband—"a loudmouth Jew" who was tall and lanky like Abe Lincoln, the man Ira Ringold (as "Iron Rinn") becomes famous for portraying. When Sandy read his brother's novel, he immediately recognized the model for Eve Frame's doomed, angry husband: "I could hear Irv's voice loud and clear."

■   ■   ■   ■

ROTH WAS ALSO CONSIDERING a *non*fictional corrective to Bloom's book—namely a biography of himself, written by his best friend at the time, Ross Miller. Indeed, the men had bonded over their mutual marital woes: Miller had witnessed firsthand such curious episodes as Bloom's wailing sprint around the fields *chez* Roth, while Roth had given his friend shelter in his studio when Miller was "emboldened" by Roth's example to leave his own wife. On April 2, 1995, Miller wrote Roth thanking him for his generosity and remarking on how he'd been inspired by Roth's "toughness"; Roth, in turn, never forgot the way Miller had stopped him from leaping off a tall building in Chicago. "Ross became a friend," Conarroe summed it up, "at a time when Philip needed a friend."*

It was true Roth didn't think much of Miller as a writer—his prose, said Roth, was "no jeweled and nuanced thing"—especially after helping to edit Miller's two published books, *American Apocalypse* (1990) and *Here's the Deal* (1996). The first, about the Great Chicago Fire, was respectfully reviewed in *The New York Times* by Thomas Hine, who found it on the loose and "repetitious" side, but "overall a very thought-

---

* Miller did not respond to my repeated requests for an interview.

ful work that is particularly valuable in these times." Wylie had agreed (via Roth) to represent Miller's second book, which he managed to sell to a major trade publisher, Knopf, though the book's most exhaustive reviewer, Cheryl Kent in the *Chicago Tribune*, doubted it would attract any interest outside her city—this despite a promising subject, with all sorts of universal implications: Block 37, an urban renewal project that had proposed the construction of a $350 million office-retail complex along the dilapidated block between Marshall Field's on State Street and the Richard J. Daley Center on Dearborn, only to be canceled in 1990 for lack of funding. "Miller has given us an undisciplined book that, sadly, tells us little about Block 37 or the way cities are shaped," wrote Kent, an architecture and urban planning critic, lamenting Miller's failure to "broaden the story by referring to other cities, other blocks, other building projects."

"I won't tell him," said Roth, smiling, when Douglas Hobbie opined that their mutual friend was a "shitty writer." The fact was, Roth was relatively isolated at the time and didn't know where else to turn; nor did he want to wait too long to counteract the damage done by *Doll's House*. "I thought: 'Someone's gotta correct this story, or this is gonna *be* the story.' And if I had dropped dead that year, that *would* have been the story." Another worry was that a less sympathetic biographer would come along and, without Roth's blessing, rely on Bloom's "serious and libelous distortions of reality and her numerous significant omissions as a starting point." By anointing Miller as his only authorized biographer, Roth hoped to discourage the less pure-hearted until a more or less accurate account could be published.

Miller himself was, at first, taken aback by the idea: Didn't their friendship present a conflict of interest? This qualm—massive in its obviousness—would not deter Roth until later; at the time he was simply a little surprised by how "uncertain and overwhelmed" his friend suddenly seemed, so unlike the glib, confident fellow Roth had come to know. At any rate, a month before *Doll's House* was published,* Roth pressed on Miller a list of interviewees to whom he ought to give priority because of their old age: "With all of these people," Roth noted,

---

* And two days before Dinitia Smith's *Times* piece of September 17, 1996—which suggests, again, that Roth already had a pretty good idea of what to expect from Bloom's book.

"I would arrange the introduction, and make it clear that you are the authorized biographer, and that it's my wish that they speak to no one else, if even approached." The list included Kleinschmidt, the Schneiders ("Claire couldn't stand the Schneiders . . . because they were bourgeois Jews"), his cousin Florence, and a couple of other elderly cousins living in Florida, Milton Roth and Gladys Kaplan. He coached Miller, too, on the line of questioning he should ("'should' is in quotation marks," said Roth) adopt with people who'd known him when: How was it that Roth ("with his background from Leslie Street in Newark") became a *writer* of all things? "Same thing with anybody in my family," Roth urged his friend to inquire—"'How did this guy become a writer?'"—as though Roth himself was burning to know the answer.

Meanwhile the two friends conducted a number of taped interviews between themselves, and Roth spoke freely about the kind of book he wanted Miller to write. Maxine Groffsky was "key" to understanding his early years as a writer and a man, said Roth, assuring Miller she had "no hostility" and would readily consent to an interview. Such interviews, he stressed—inside knowledge—would likely determine how much money Miller got for the book proposal Wylie would submit to publishers. Of course the Bloom issue was paramount, and it was crucial, Roth thought, that Miller persuade her to sit for an interview before *I Married a Communist* was published: "Her anti-Semitism you can leave out," Roth advised. "I'm going to get her in the other book." Indeed, he hoped Miller's biography would finally address the whole nonsalacious, Chekhov-and-Knipper side of things: "What *really* went on between this actress and this writer? He's a serious artist and she's a serious artist." But whenever Roth began exploring the more high-minded possibilities, he'd remember the main thesis of Bloom's own book, and become furious all over again. "I mean, the book of hers is cuckoo," he said during their November 13 session. "It's so fucking *cuckoo*, Ross!" Eleven days later he elaborated:

I've always had women lawyers. This whole mad fucking misogynistic bullshit! And Shirley [Fingerhood] was my *companion* through this. . . . Helene's [Kaplan] been my lawyer for twenty years. My advisers have been women. Who brought me to *The New Yorker*? Veronica [Geng]. The whole thing is crazy, Ross. . . . No one has more professional contacts with women, no writer, than I do. My first agent was Candida Donadio. . . . So all those key relations: lawyer, agent, editor—my first editor in New York was Rachel MacKenzie. . . . And of course I had a lifelong friendship with Mildred Martin. Of all the teachers I had at Bucknell, the lifelong friendship I had was with a [*shouting*] WOMAN!"

As for the ticklish subject of his sex life: Roth suggested (another word belonging in quotes) that Miller steer clear of the whole Inga Larsen can of worms, and concentrate instead on "philosophical" aspects—indeed, he insisted Miller needed to write a discrete essay, prior to the biography, about the "meaning" of sex in Roth's life, devoid of any concrete "instances," which could wait until the biography per se:

> It wasn't just "Fucked this one fucked that one fucked this one" [he told Miller] . . . if you're writing the biography of Henry Miller, or Norman Mailer, or any man who hasn't kept his sex hidden—or D. H. Lawrence, for God's sake. Or Colette! Why shouldn't I be treated as seriously as Colette on this? She gave a blow job to this guy in the railway station. Who gives a fuck about that? [*Roth ticked off other examples of Colette's sexual vagaries*] . . . That's just titillation. . . . That doesn't tell me anything. What did hand jobs *mean* to her? Why did she like that? It has a meaning!

The proposal that Miller finally gave Roth and Wylie, however, stinted on "meaning" if not on the sex itself—"as though he were writing my biography for serialization in *Hustler* magazine," said Roth, who described the proposal's main thrust as "The Story of My Penis." Though Miller hadn't managed to interview Groffsky (and never would), he'd included lurid details about her dalliance with the young Roth, as well as a colorful recounting of, say, his and Mudge's trip to England in the summer of 1968: "He was 'living by his dick' again, picking up 'Hong Kong' prostitutes on Curzon Street, doing just what he wanted—and upon his return to New York in August was ready again to 'take his life between his teeth' and move on."

Roth hardly knew where to begin. Calling Miller onto the carpet in Wylie's office, he pointed out that his *dick* hadn't written more than twenty books! And had it occurred to Miller that his proposal would be circulated among New York publishers, and would all but certainly land in the hands of Maxine Groffsky, now a prominent literary agent? "What do you think the *New York Post* is going to do with this document when they get their hands on it? What do you think Maxine is going to do when she sees it? What do you think *I* think when I see it?" Also, for the first and last time ever, Roth got angry at Wylie for even considering such a proposal.

"Oddly enough, they remained friends," said Julia Golier, who remembered that Miller was, withal, a little bitter about things. The proposal had taken time and trouble—he'd interviewed the Schneiders and Julius Goldstein, never mind his sessions with Roth himself—and Roth's peremptory dismissal wasn't fair. In fact, for Miller's sake, Roth had paused long enough to consult his trusted lawyer, Helene Kaplan, who, he later reflected, "foresaw everything." She reminded him that *American Pastoral* had, by then, elevated Roth to "a new plateau of extraordinary accomplishment and acclaim," hence a corrective biography could arguably wait, and also warned him that such a project might end up straining relations with Miller and Wylie, whose friendships, he'd often told her, were essential.

Her advice had (almost) the desired effect—that is to say, seven years would pass before Roth saw fit to give Miller another crack at it.

■ ■ ■ ■

THE HARDCOVER JACKET of *American Pastoral* featured an old photograph—burning along the top edge—of happy young people gathered outside a general store sipping Cokes; one of those youngsters was Hermine Pepinger Hartley, who wondered in the *Star-Ledger* how Roth had gotten hold of the 1938 photo and why he was using it to sell a book "about the turmoil of another generation." In the spring of 1996, Roth had been touring Mendham, New Jersey, with the state historian, John Cunningham—who thought the area perfect for the idyllic setting of "Old Rimrock," where Levov buys his dream house—when Roth spotted the photo on the wall of the general store in tiny Brookside, and asked the owner whether he could borrow it: an image of American innocence. Then he sat down, as ever, with his favorite graphic designer, Milton Glaser, and the two swapped ideas until they decided to set the photograph on fire, so to speak, suggesting the bombed general store in the book. Roth—who "tried to keep a strong hand in controlling and choosing book jacket design" (even for foreign editions)—directed Glaser to wash out the word "Brookside" from the photo, and arrange the back-flap copy as follows:

ACCLAIM FOR PHILIP ROTH IN THE 1990s:
1991 • *Patrimony,* winner of the National Book Critics Circle Award
1993 • *Operation Shylock,* winner of the PEN/Faulkner Award
1995 • *Sabbath's Theater,* winner of the National Book Award

A person in the Houghton publicity department wrote a letter to book-sellers to run in the front matter of the bound galleys: "Roth is the scourge of banality and middle-class rectitude," it read in part, "but *American Pastoral* is a virtual ode to decency and middle-class convention. (As Mr. Roth put it to me recently, in an ironic comment on his own literary reputation, 'This is the book that gives decency a good name.') No sex, no jokes, no withering satire—why read it?" Roth considered this vulgar if well-meaning gambit an "abomination"; not only did he veto the letter, but on December 4, 1996, he faxed Wylie a message of measured outrage, asking him to inform the publisher that he wouldn't be signing their contract ("I WILL REIMBURSE TO THEM ALL COSTS WHICH HAVE BEEN INCURRED UNTIL NOW"). Houghton smoothed things over with an apology, and invited Roth to write his own galley letter that would appear over the editorial director's name: After a concise plot summary, Roth's letter assured the reader that the present novel represented "the high point of an already illustrious career. I urge you to sit down as soon as you can to read the masterpiece of an American master." The last six words became the main slogan of the ad campaign, and Roth made sure a slew of public figures received copies, including Hillary Rodham Clinton, John Kenneth Galbraith, and Ruth Bader Ginsburg.

Roth was, in short, understandably proud of his book, which could hardly have come at a better time. "I was able to take the period in America that had the greatest impact on me," he explained to David Plante's writing class at Columbia, "and produce a narrative that encompassed everything I knew about it." He also expected the novel would silence those critics—Updike foremost among them—who'd become exasperated with reflexive fiction about the life of a Roth-like author. "You've never written a better novel," Aaron Asher wrote him, after remarking on the oddness of having to pay money for a Roth book (they were still estranged). "Come to think of it, who in our time has? About America it goes deeper than all the Rabbits put together."

Even Michiko Kakutani seemed to agree, congratulating Roth in the *Times* for doing away at last with "narcissistic pyrotechnics" and daring to tackle "the very subjects he once spurned as unmanageable" (an allusion to "Writing American Fiction," Roth's 1960 essay about how hard it is to "make *credible* much of American reality"—generally misread as an injunction against even trying). "The resulting book is one of Mr. Roth's most powerful novels ever, a big, rough-hewn work built on a grand design, a book that is as moving, generous and ambitious as his last novel, *Sabbath's Theater*, was sour, solipsistic and narrow."

Actually the stern Kakutani qualified her praise: Roth "*nearly*" (italics added) did away with his usual solipsism, given that his old alter ego, Nathan Zuckerman, was once again the narrator—though Roth himself had decided he'd "exhausted all the possibilities" of Zuckerman with *The Counterlife*, even while that same novel had suggested yet another possibility: Zuckerman as "mediating intelligence" rather than a major actor in the story. To emphasize this function, in *American Pastoral*, Roth reduced his surrogate to little more than a "recording device" by rendering him impotent as a result of prostate surgery. (Sandy had suffered the same fate a few years before.) For this and other reasons, Zuckerman has largely withdrawn from the world when the legendary Swede, an old Weequahic acquaintance, invites him to lunch, putatively to ask for advice about a tribute to his late father he's trying to write. But instead Levov rambles on about how well his three sons have turned out—with such persistent tedium, indeed, Zuckerman begins to question his sanity—and only later does Zuckerman learn that Levov's daughter from a previous marriage, Merry, was the "Rimrock Bomber," and therefore surmises that *this* was the real subject Swede had wanted help writing about, but lost his nerve.

Zuckerman's frame narrative takes about eighty pages—until Zuckerman begins "to contemplate the very thing that must have baffled the Swede till the moment he died: how had he become history's plaything?" Dancing at his high school reunion to the "honeysweet strains of 'Dream,'" by Johnny Mercer, Zuckerman begins to imagine Swede's tragedy and abruptly vanishes from the narrative—the action dissolving to a seaside vacation in Deal, New Jersey, where Swede will impulsively kiss the eleven-year-old Merry (the first scene of Roth's 1974 ur-version)—an oblique homage to the mysterious first-person-plural narrator of *Madame Bovary,* who vanishes from the book after its opening pages, never to return ("the finesse is beautiful, I think"). Zuckerman lingers, however, as the "mediating intelligence"—that is, he lends his consciousness to Levov in rather the same way Joyce and Updike endow the prosaic brains of Leopold Bloom and Rabbit Angstrom with, occasionally, the nicety of genius. Levov, for his part, lacks "a drop of wit or irony to interfere with his golden gift for responsibility," and so assumes that people who wish to seem good, loyal, and intelligent are in fact good, loyal, and intelligent. However, we are reminded that this is Zuckerman's *imagining* of Swede's story—versus whatever dull thing Swede himself would make of it—when an aperçu like this is planted in his head: "Marcia [Umanoff] *was* all talk—always had been: senseless, ostentatious talk, words with the whole purpose of scandalously exhibiting themselves, uncompromising, quarrelsome words expressing little more than Marcia's intellectual vanity and her odd belief that all her posturing added up to an independent mind."

Just as Roth, regarding his two marriages, sometimes liked to think he'd more or less accidentally stumbled into disastrous attachments with unstable women ("a man's fate is the joke that his life plays on his character"), so Roth couldn't abide the idea that Levov and his other tragic heroes are being "punished" for their human flaws; rather they're random victims of history, and hence Roth's notion to title his American Trilogy "Blindsided." In *American Pastoral,* the whole Job-like arc (including the ambiguous restitution implied by the three good sons Swede will sire with a second wife) is presaged by Zuckerman's memory of his favorite childhood book, *The Kid from Tomkinsville,* by John R. Tunis:

> Tunis concludes like this: "Dusk descended upon a mass of players, on a huge crowd pouring onto the field, on a couple of men carrying an inert form through the mob on a stretcher.* . . . There was a clap of thunder. Rain descended upon the Polo Grounds." Descended, descended, a clap of thunder, and thus ends the boys' Book of Job.

---

* The "inert form" being the Kid himself, of course, whose heroic catch sends the Dodgers to the World Series but leaves him "writhing in agony."

I was ten and I had never read anything like it. The cruelty of life. The injustice of it. I could not believe it.

Such inscrutable cruelty and injustice will lead Zuckerman to think of his book about the Swede as *The Kid from Keer Avenue*. And the more Swede tries to make sense of senseless tragedy ("Daddy, kiss me the way you k-k-kiss umumumother"), the more remorseful he feels.

One of the very few critics Roth respected, Louis Menand, suggested in *The New Yorker* that what Swede is "blindsided by is the culture of liberal permissiveness," and for this reason Menand predicted some readers would construe the novel as "a kind of recantation" by the author of *Portnoy's Complaint*, "a swerve to the cultural right." Lo and behold, Roth's old nemesis Norman Podhoretz applauded "a born-again Philip Roth. . . . Here, for once, it was the ordinary Jews of his childhood who were celebrated—for their decency, their sense of responsibility, their seriousness about their work, their patriotism—and here, for once, those who rejected and despised such virtues were shown to be either pathologically nihilistic or smug, self-righteous, and unimaginative." But Roth himself wasn't having any of it—or rather he was having it various ways, reflecting his own thoughtful ambivalence about things. Levov is nothing if not a decent, tolerant man, but he's hardly the embodiment of a "permissive" culture; his behavior toward Merry is sweet but unyielding: throughout his sixty-seven (numbered as such) conversations about letting her go to New York alone, he sternly imposes conditions, such as staying with their friends the Umanoffs; when she disobeys, he places her "under house arrest," while helpfully suggesting she "[b]ring the war home" by organizing the movement in Old Rimrock. Whereupon she blows up the general store.

After reviewing catalogue blurbs for *I Married a Communist*, Roth had a qualm: "I would like you to excise one of the quotations, the one from the *Chronicle* about how much I love America. I have mixed feelings." On the one hand, of course, Roth deeply loved America, and he articulated some of his reasons via Swede's outrage over his daughter's rebellion:

Stuttering, sputtering little bitch! Who the fuck did she think she was? . . .

How could she "hate" this country when she had no *conception* of this country? How could a child of his be so blind as to revile the "rotten system" that had given her own family every opportunity to succeed? To revile her "capitalist" parents. . . . There wasn't much difference, *and she knew it*, between hating America and hating them.

On the other hand, Roth himself had despised the war in Vietnam; he also despised the sort of sanctimonious bigotry—on the right *or* the left—that flourishes in America at the expense of enlightened tolerance. Some such idea was behind his decision (at Judith Thurman's urging) to give the Levovs an exciting sex life—that is, to refute the convention that such people tend to be uptight, repressed; as Roth put it, "I wanted to free them from the Flaubertian anti-bourgeois fantasy that these college-educated assholes have." The assholes in this case were the assholes on the left; hitherto Roth had said plenty about the assholes on the right, when in fact he had vitriol enough for both sides. "You're nothing but a shitty little capitalist who exploits the brown and yellow people of the world and lives in luxury behind the nigger-proof security gates of his mansion," Rita Cohen taunts Levov, who produces (yet again) an insight of Rothian percipience: "The *unreality* of being in the hands of this child! . . . What was the whole sick enterprise other than angry, infantile egoism thinly disguised as identification with the oppressed?" One imagines Podhoretz bolting up from his seat to applaud, though Roth would not relish his good opinion; besides, as any reader of *Patrimony* already knew, Roth had plenty of love for decent, hardworking people who lead "ordinary" lives. Indeed, the final two sentences of *American Pastoral*—though naturally meant "to cut both ways," as Roth wrote Solotaroff—serve rather as a refutation of Tolstoy: "Ivan Ilych's life had been most simple and most ordinary and therefore most terrible." To which Roth replied (only a little tongue-in-cheek), "What's so 'terrible' about this guy? He's a successful civil servant! He enjoys his draperies and his furniture and daughter, whatever. . . . Tolstoy's nuts. What does he expect people to be?" Thus, too, the Levovs: "And what is wrong with their life? What on earth is less reprehensible than the life of the Levovs?"

Roth's exquisitely nuanced rendering of "massive historical pain" in the person of Swede Levov, along with the tragic heroes to follow in his American Trilogy, would propel him into a category of his own as a novelist. "Roth is Niagara," his admiring peer Cynthia Ozick wrote of

American Pastoral. "They should stop fiddling in Stockholm already and make the telephone call."

■ ■ ■

IT WAS BOB LOWENSTEIN who first informed Roth that "Swede" Masin's real name was the same as Levov's: Seymour. That was news to Roth, who'd chosen the name because it alliterated with Swede; he'd had no desire to further risk a libel suit by borrowing Masin's nickname *and* first name. Not only that, said Lowenstein, but a decade ago he'd bumped into Masin at a reunion, and the man looked a lot like Mayor Lindsay—the same way Levov is described in the novel.

Six weeks after *American Pastoral* was published, *The New Yorker* ran a "Talk of the Town" piece about Masin, a seventy-eight-year-old former liquor salesman who, it turned out, had already discovered he'd been "Rothed" (as the magazine's Tad Friend put it). "Here was this big writer writing about me," said Masin. "But I'd never met him, never spoken to him, and only read one of his books, *Portnoy's Complaint*—it didn't thrill me. Some people said to me, 'You should sue!' Please. Roth portrayed me as a decent, good guy, which I think is unusual for him to do." Indeed, Masin was repeatedly struck by his resemblance to the other Swede ("almost everything in the book I would have done if I'd been in those situations"), though he found the sex scenes in poor taste: "it was *me* having this sex. Just not necessary."

Roth was disgusted by the *New Yorker* piece ("the tabloid-mentality is now standard and everywhere," he wrote Lowenstein), though he was delighted, a year later, to receive a note from Masin, who addressed him as "Phil" ("Pardon my Famillarity [sic] . . . I feel a sort of closeness to you through the 'Book'") and asked him to autograph his copy of the novel. Better still was meeting the Swede in person, on May 3, 1999, when Masin attended a Roth tribute at the New Jersey Performing Arts Center in Newark; after the program, Masin and his daughter introduced themselves to Roth in the lobby. The daughter quipped that she had nothing in common with Merry, the Rimrock Bomber, though her father pointed out yet another strange parallel between himself and the other Swede: the first Mrs. Masin, like Dawn Levov, had been a gentile beauty queen who'd competed in a Miss Essex County pageant. Whereupon Roth left the Weequahic sports legend to ponder one of his favorite

Flaubertian maxims: "'Everything one invents is true, you may be perfectly sure of that. Poetry is as precise as geometry.'"*

Roth's three previous books (as he'd been careful to note on his jacket copy) had each received different major awards, but the Pulitzer continued to elude him. The favorite to win in 1998, most agreed, was DeLillo's *Underworld*, a novel every bit as ambitious as Roth's in its socio-historical scope. "Baked ziti," DeLillo wrote Roth. "There is baked ziti in my book too. . . . Riots. You think I don't have riots? Bombs. I have bombs. . . . Decayed old neighborhoods. You have Newark, I have the Bronx." What DeLillo didn't have was a close friend—Joel Conarroe—on the Pulitzer jury, though in fairness the other two fiction judges, Gail Caldwell and Darcy O'Brien, also favored Roth's novel: Caldwell had described it as "infuriatingly gorgeous" in her *Boston Globe* review, whereas O'Brien (who would die six weeks before the prize was announced) wrote his fellow judges that "everything else, no, everything, shrinks beside" *American Pastoral*. At any rate, the judges were no longer allowed to indicate a preference among the three finalists they recommended to the board—Roth, DeLillo, and Robert Stone for *Bear and His Daughter*—and Roth had hardly forgotten what happened in 1980, when the board overruled *The Ghost Writer* even though it was explicitly named as the jury's favorite.

"You told me that would never happen because of politics," said Jack Wheatcroft, his old Bucknell friend, when Roth was announced as the winner on April 14, 1998. That afternoon Roth had been "cruising the aisles of Litchfield's Stop & Shop" and came home to find some twenty-five messages on his machine.† Jeffrey Posternak called from Wylie's office to offer their prompt congratulations and let Roth know that CNN, CBS, and the Associated Press were "all eager for interviews." "I'm a reporter for the Mountain Lakes *Pulpit*," said Conarroe, "which is a weekly paper, and we'd like to do an interview with you at your convenience about growing up in New Jersey and in Quahog—Queequeg?—

---

* Masin soon developed Alzheimer's disease and died in 2006. Two years later, on the seventy-fifth anniversary of Weequahic High School, he was inducted into the inaugural class of the Weequahic Alumni Hall of Fame, along with Roth and Lowenstein.

† Roth preserved his answering-machine tape from that day, which he included among materials he gave to his biographer.

whatever that is." Michael Herr: "What a thrill it must be to share the dais with Michiko Kakutani" (who'd won for criticism). "Everyone thought Anita Brookner was gonna get it." Other well-wishers included DeLillo ("Put some brandy in your Jell-O tonight"), Bellow ("I thought I would lay my bouquet"), Styron ("Richly deserved, as I said about fifteen years ago when you got euchred out of it"), Lowenstein ("Mazel tov!"), and an emotional Sylvia Tumin ("Big hugs, big kisses . . . *love* you"), whose husband, Mel, had died four years before and been movingly eulogized by Roth. But none was as emotional as Sandy, who burst into tears the moment his brother called him back.

C H A P T E R

Forty-One

B Y THE MIDNINETIES, ROTH'S FRIEND AND FAVORITE editor, Veronica Geng, had fallen on hard times. For years she'd worked at *The New Yorker* on a per-diem basis, but when Tina Brown took over as editor, in 1992, Geng decided she wanted the security of a salaried position; Brown (who considered Geng "too high-maintenance and flighty," according to Hendrik Hertzberg) would agree only to raise her per-diem, and Geng quit in a huff. Since then she'd published her occasional casuals in *The New York Review of Books* instead of *The New Yorker*, and made ends meet by editing writers such as Roth on a free-lance basis. She was living alone in a tiny apartment on the Upper East Side, in 1996, when she blacked out and collapsed; afterward, at New York Hospital, she was found to have a malignant, grapefruit-sized brain tumor on her right temporal lobe. She was fifty-five and had no health insurance.

Roth put up five thousand dollars for her medical expenses, and promptly arranged for her friends Barbara Epstein, Saul Steinberg, Roy Blount Jr., and James Hamilton to do likewise. Following her brain surgery, Geng stayed with a friend in Great Barrington, and, during Roth's visits, wore a "dress" improvised from her hospital gown—one detail of many (her lurid surgical scar was another) that Roth would give to the similarly afflicted Amy Bellette in *Exit Ghost*. When Geng's relations with her friend in the Berkshires became strained, Roth let her stay in his writing studio on West Seventy-ninth Street; with the help of nurses (hired by Roth) she lived there awhile, contentedly enough, until she had a seizure one night and was taken by ambulance to Sloan-Kettering. By then she was too weak to walk, and Roth would wheel her outside the hospital so she could smoke. On December 22, 1997, he noted in his diary that Geng had had trouble breathing during his visit, and two days later she died. On the cold, drizzly day she was buried at Green-Wood Cemetery in Brooklyn ("VERONICA GENG / BEAUTIFUL SOUL-FUL / HILARIOUS / JAN. 10, 1941 – DEC. 24, 1997"), Roth brought things to an abrupt end when he turned on his heel and walked away; he and other mourners repaired to Patrissy's Restaurant in Little Italy, and Roth picked up the tab ($540.05).

During this era he also performed good works in behalf of Emmanuel Dongala, a Congolese chemist and novelist Roth had befriended through the Huvelles, who'd served as Dongala's foster parents when he'd come to the States, almost thirty years before, to attend Oberlin College. In 1994, when Roth was awarded the Karel Čapek Prize, he'd asked Dongala, a PEN delegate, to read his English acceptance speech (Klíma read the Czech version) in Prague. Three years later Dongala was dean of Marien Ngouabi University, in Brazzaville, when civil war broke out; as he wrote the Huvelles on August 10, 1997, the city center and university had been looted and almost entirely destroyed: "You see 15-year-old kids with Kalashnikovs roaming around and stopping you in the many roadblocks and these kids have the right of life or death on you. . . . It is very surrealistic, me reading *American Pastoral* while mortars are pounding away, the family frightened and hiding in the house. My best to Philip when you talk to him next."

The Huvelles gave Roth the details and asked for his help getting Dongala and his family out of the country. Since a prerequisite for a visa was some promise of employment, Roth phoned his friend Leon Botstein, who promptly arranged an appointment for Dongala as a chemistry professor at Bard's affiliate in Great Barrington, Simon's Rock. Roth and the Huvelles were waiting at JFK when Dongala ("with a touch of malaria") arrived in March 1998; meanwhile his twenty-year-old brother-in-law had been randomly murdered by a militia squad, and his wife, Pauline, was still hiding in the bush with their three teenage daughters. With the help of an aide in Senator Kennedy's office, Roth managed to get visas a week later for Pauline and two of the daughters, but the United States consulate refused a visa for the oldest daughter, Assita—this by way of assurance, it seemed, that the other Dongalas wouldn't seek permanent asylum. On April 4, 1998, Roth summarized the family's predicament in a letter to President Clinton: "After experiencing some nine months of warfare, terror, and near-starvation," he wrote of Assita, "a traumatized eighteen-year-old girl has been separated from her immediate family for reasons that are unfathomable to me."

He still hadn't received a reply on April 20, when Styron took him to lunch at the West Street Grill in Litchfield to celebrate his Pulitzer. Toward the end of their meal, Styron mentioned he was leaving for Washington, D.C., in a few hours for a White House dinner in honor of National Poetry Month. "Wait right here," Roth said, and drove twenty minutes back to his house in Warren, retrieved a copy of his letter to the president, and drove back to the restaurant. "Put this in Bill Clinton's hands," he told Styron, "and tell him to read it." Three days later Roth received a fax from Susan Beveridge at the White House ("This office handles the President's casework and would be happy to assist"), and a month later Assita Dongala was reunited with her family in Great Barrington. As a housewarming gift, Roth gave the Dongalas one of his extra TV sets, and (as he had with Norman Manea) took the girls to a huge supermarket where they could marvel at "the ample displays of food in row after row. Tubs of frozen turkeys, mountains of oranges, etc."—the bounty of America. Roth paid their tuition at an intensive English institute, and, within a year, the two younger daughters were on the honor roll at the local high school.

A few years earlier, Roth had tried using his leverage with the MacArthur Foundation to get a lucrative "genius" grant for Alfred Kazin, who'd retired in 1985 after a nearly fifty-year career at CUNY and was now trying to subsist on his credentials as one of the country's preeminent literary critics. Just as Bellow's fifth wife, Janis, had boosted Roth as a worthy friend to her husband, so Kazin's fourth wife, Judith Dunford, had made it possible for Roth and Kazin to coexist more or less peaceably. In 1983, the Kazins bought a house in nearby Roxbury, and two or three times a year the couple would dine with Roth and Bloom, or else the two men would meet à deux at the Hopkins Inn. As Roth remembered, "Alfred began an evening by asking how you were and three minutes later, having barely been able to endure your reply, he began his lecture on the French Revolution or the poetry of Hart Crane or Lincoln's prose style." For the MacArthur Foundation, Roth described Kazin as "one of the treasures of American culture" and was furious when Kazin was passed over. "He is an old man, ill, without financial resources," Roth wrote the foundation. "I was stupified [sic] by the people you chose over him last year. Please do not turn to me again for assistance."

In early 1998, Kazin learned that his prostate cancer had spread to his bones, and Roth recommended the same hospice nurses he'd hired to take care of Geng in his apartment. The nurses were excellent but expensive: thirty-five dollars an hour, day and night. As Dunford observed, "It was one of those terrible American situations where you think maybe I should hope that he dies a little faster." Happily or not, it didn't last long—Kazin died on his eighty-third birthday, June 5—and meanwhile Dunford received a thousand dollars from Roth ("Please accept this as tuition for all I've learned from Alfred"), who also tried, again, to muster support from Barbara Epstein and other friends. After her husband's death, Dunford asked Roth to help her find an editor for an anthology of Kazin's work, and took his advice ("wisely," said Roth, "because he did a brilliant job") to approach Solotaroff; Roth also persuaded Wylie to handle Kazin's literary estate, even though, as Dunford put it, "if they made back their postage cost, I'd be surprised." Indeed, the posthumous anthology, *Alfred Kazin's America* (a title Roth suggested), was largely ignored—a sad commentary on the thankless labors of American belletrists; Roth pressed all but one or two of his twelve copies on friends and visitors.

In 2011, Kazin's journals were published by Yale University Press, and Roth learned how deeply one of his idols had loathed him. "Philip Roth, the male shrew" was a favorite epithet, referring (a little ironically, Roth thought) to the younger man's tendency to monopolize conversations in a noisy, pompous way, so that Kazin was "always glad to see him depart in all his prosperity and self-satisfaction." Roth brooded about things for a couple of years, and finally wrote the widow: "I fail to understand Alfred's profound distaste for me in his journals. I don't really care"—though plainly he did—"but I do find it peculiar. What did I ever do to him? That generation of Jewish intellectuals and their touchy fucking grievances."

■ ■ ■ ■

"HEMINGWAY SAID, 'Life is a cheap thing beside a man's work,'" Roth had written Riki Wagman in 1972. "It may be the smartest thing

Hemingway ever said." By the late nineties, Roth's life had shrunk (or expanded, as he would have it) almost entirely around his writing. Less and less did he see the point of visiting New York, except for a couple of days a month "to get a haircut and eat some good Chinese food"—but work was all that really mattered, and he always worked better in the country. "When you're in New York, in the apartment, and you're stuck, what can you do? Put your shoes on, go downstairs, walk to Zabar's and back? Walk in Central Park? This is better than Central Park; I own my own Central Park."

The apartment on West Seventy-seventh had always been cursed, as far as Roth was concerned, and he couldn't wait to get rid of it. The tenants above him (writer Nancy Friday and her husband, *Time* editor Norman Pearlstine) had a greenhouse on their terrace, and a decade of daily watering had rendered Roth's apartment all but uninhabitable. First the pictures on his walls—the Roth caricatures by David Levine, the Guston cartoon of a Roth-like writer stabbing a Howe-like critic, etc.—became stained and cockled from leaks, and he had to pay Cella Manea to restore them; toward the end, all the furniture and rugs had to be removed, and the apartment was vacant except for buckets to catch water. On March 9, 1998, Roth finally managed to sell the place—for $600,000, exactly what he'd paid for it a decade before—whereupon he notified Wylie via fax: "AS FAR AS ANYONE IS CONCERNED, I NO LONGER HAVE ANY CONNECTION TO NYC"—that is to say, his pied-à-terre on Seventy-ninth was *not* for public consumption.

Wherever he happened to be, Roth didn't want to be bothered. He demanded the removal of his entry from *International Who's Who* when they repeated the mistake of publishing his home address (albeit with a crucial typo that rendered it pretty much untraceable), and he posted two little signs near his desk: "Stay Put" and "No Optional Striving." Occasionally he'd complain of loneliness, but, almost in the same breath, remind himself (and perhaps his cleaning person or caretaker, if they happened to be around) that he'd only get in trouble with women if he ventured out. Sometimes, to be sure, on bleak winter days when he was snowed in, Roth would pull on his boots in the morning and feel about "three minutes" of melancholy; then he'd remember Bloom and think, "But there's *no friction*." And he'd smile. "My schedule is absolutely my own," he explained to David Remnick of *The New Yorker*. "Usually, I write all day, but if I want to go back to the studio in the evening, after dinner, I don't have to sit in the living room because someone else has been alone all day. I don't have to sit there and be entertaining or amusing. I go back and I work for two or three more hours." Around this time Roth heard that a developer wanted to buy ninety-three acres across the road and build a subdivision; foreseeing the ruin of his rural utopia ("a school bus, the whole works"), Roth immediately phoned his local lawyer and told him to find out a price for the land—two million, it turned out—and pay it. "Don't *hondel* [bargain]," said Roth. "Just give him the money."

"Beware the utopia of isolation," Murray Ringold warns Zuckerman toward the end of *I Married a Communist*. "Beware the utopia of the shack in the woods, the oasis defense against rage and grief. An impregnable solitude." For a while, Roth sought to assuage his own solitude by getting back in touch with the friends of his youth. Back in 1985, Marty Weich had arranged a reunion at his Manhattan apartment for Roth and the rest of the boys: Bob Heyman, Stu Lehman, and Bernie Swerdlow. Later, when Roth had returned to the States for good, he and Weich made a point of meeting twice a year at Barney Greengrass on the Upper West Side ("redolent of the smoked fish delis of our childhood"), and Roth was gratified to find his former best friend little changed. Every morning, after dropping his son at school, Weich would drive all the way out to New Jersey to visit his senile mother ("Stand up straight!" she'd greet him), then race back to Manhattan so he could start meeting patients around eleven. In his spare time he was writing a musical.

The others had led conventionally successful lives, for the most part. Heyman was an endodontist whose thriving Fifth Avenue practice attracted patients such as Lauren Bacall and Willie Mays, while Stu Lehman (still married to his college sweetheart) was an oral and maxillofacial surgeon. Howie Silver, another dentist, hadn't been part of the tight circle who used to gather for parties in Heyman's basement, but he'd also graduated with the class of 1950 and was an enthusiastic, good-natured addition to these later meetings. A more exotic creature (still) was Bernie Swerdlow, whose boyhood colitis and satyriasis Roth had given to Melvin Weiner and Smolka, respectively, in *Portnoy*. At Weich's apartment in 1985, Swerdlow had mentioned a memoir he was writing and asked Roth if he wanted to be his coauthor. "Everybody wants to write a book about themselves," said Roth.

Actually he might have made something interesting of Swerdlow's later adventures. A psychiatrist like Weich, Swerdlow had wangled his way into the University of Amsterdam medical school, whither he'd dragged his first wife (one of the few shiksas at Weequahic) until the marriage broke up amid their grinding poverty abroad ("the boys took up a collection," Heyman recalled, "and gave money to Bernie to see him through"). Swerdlow returned to the States, single, and set up a lively practice on the Jersey Shore—but invariably sex and drugs got him into trouble, until he'd flee the wreckage and hang his shingle in some other part of the country: California at one point, and finally Winter Park, Florida, where he (the author of *Whiplash and Related Headaches*) started his own headache clinic. At a high school reunion, as Lowenstein reported to Roth, Swerdlow had shown up, late, "with a girl twice his height and half the age of his daughter. . . . He claims he is flat broke, cleaned out by wife #5—I may be off there, but not by much."

Whatever his raffishness, Swerdlow was a sentimental soul who treasured his old friendships—he kept a memorabilia-filled "Weequahic Room" at his home in Winter Park—serving as the "spark plug" for what became periodic gatherings with Roth et al. He also tended to guide the discussions in predictable ways, until Howie Silver hosted a reunion at his house in Deal, New Jersey, and insisted they take things to a higher plane—that is, by drawing little slips of paper with heavy prompts ("What level of happiness are you experiencing?") out of a brandy snifter. "Screw that," said Heyman. "Let's talk about jerking off. Or almost getting laid in the old days." That would have suited Roth, who also hosted a meeting in Connecticut on October 27, 1996, less than two weeks after the publication of *Leaving a Doll's House*. "Don't mention Claire's name!" Sandy hissed into their guests' ears, intercepting each man on arrival.

It was Swerdlow who insisted—with Roth's tacit blessing—that wives be barred from the proceedings. "I have a lifestyle and a philosophy that, literally, have diverged from my friends," Swerdlow wrote Lowenstein in 1988, complaining that one of "the boys" was "married to a hypochondriac, hysterical, paranoid woman," and who the hell needed such people cramping his style? Then, too, by the late nineties, wives might have reminded Swerdlow that he himself was fated to die alone. "To sleep at night," he wrote Roth in 1998, "I hug my pillow and fantasize a loving woman. Of all the things I accomplished and did not accomplish in my life I regret not having had a long lasting relationship." Diabetes killed him a few months later, whereupon the reunions came to end—not least, for Roth, because the others wanted to bring wives now that Bernie wasn't around to object.

■　■　■　■

FOR A FEW YEARS Roth's isolation was mitigated by Julia Golier's company on weekends. Friday evenings she'd take a train to Wingdale, New York—stopping opposite a deserted asylum, the Harlem Valley Psychiatric Center—where she was met by an elderly Warren neighbor, Mr. Beecher, who'd drive her the half hour to Roth's house. A dinner of broiled fish, corn, and tomatoes was usually waiting. During her visits Golier would plug away at grant applications on her laptop while Roth worked in his studio, followed by an afternoon swim, another fish dinner, and maybe a few games of cards.

Roth looked forward to celebrating Thanksgiving *dans le vrai*—that is, with Golier's big Catholic family in Montvale, New Jersey. Golier's mother, Mary Lou, had tried reading *Portnoy* when it was first published, but had to quit about halfway in. "If I ever thought I would have a daughter who would be in touch with him, I don't know what I would have done," she said. But right away she was disarmed. Roth arrived with flowers, effusively praised the food, and made a point of accepting pumpkin pie despite his rigid diet. "It was a little bit of Bucknell again," he said, remembering the time Golier's father had asked him to say grace: "'I'm not a religious man,'" Roth quoted the Swede, "'but when I look around this table, I know that something is shining down on me.'"

By the time she was thirty-five or so, Golier wanted to marry and start a family—with Roth, preferably, who "thought very seriously" about it but finally declined, given his advanced age and "crushingly unsuccessful" marital history. The end was terrible for both of them ("I cried for a week," said Golier), but a loving friendship endured. In the years before Golier's marriage, in 2002, Roth often called to commiserate about her grueling ordeal of dating strange men, and meanwhile they continued to meet for dinners, movies, and concerts, even taking trips together; eventually Roth named her the co-executor of his estate.*

Once Golier was gone, as Roth put it, "exercise took the place of companionship." He went on long walks, even in freezing weather, and looked forward to his thrice-weekly meetings with a personal trainer, who helped him regain the strength he'd lost during his long siege of back pain in the early nineties. He also hired a caretaker and long-distance driver, Peter Carberry. Once, while cleaning out the attic, Roth directed Carberry to take one of his old IBM Selectrics to the dump, but Carberry suggested Roth autograph it and let Carberry try selling it on eBay, splitting the proceeds. Roth signed it above the keys with a Sharpie and gave it to Carberry on the condition he put the money aside for his daughter's education.†

Roth's retainers also included Kathy Meetz, his cleaner since 1990, who usually arrived around nine, when he was finishing his stretching routine before heading out to his studio. A bit of cordial banter was de rigueur. Once, Meetz mentioned that Francine Gray had interviewed her for a job. If hired, Meetz wondered, would she have to wear a uniform like Gray's cook? Roth urged her to do some spying for him *chez* Gray, then affected to have second thoughts ("She's too provincial for you"). In some such context he also remarked how nice it would be "to sit on a riverbank and watch all the dead bodies of [my] enemies floating by."

Roth was a kindly but demanding employer, who often left monitory notes for Meetz: "THERE IS LOTS OF DUST EVERYWHERE,"

---

* She and Wylie quietly superseded Conarroe and Miles in that capacity.

† In July 2019, Roth's beloved Olivetti was bought at an estate auction ($17,500) by Steve Sobaroff, a Los Angeles police commissioner who also owns typewriters once belonging to Hemingway, Cheever, and the Unabomber.

he wrote on returning from a weekend in New York. "Dust *all* surfaces, including base of lamps, rungs of chairs, etc. . . . There is a very fine dust there [floor] that has to be mopped up. But don't use anything on the floors with a strong smell." Meetz cherished one note, from 1997, that tallied the usual delinquencies before ending "OTHERWISE THE HOUSE IS *SPLENDID!*" She was keenly aware that Roth's life, post-Golier, had become almost morbidly lonely, and once encouraged him to inquire about a sign he'd seen—"Kittens for Sale"—over the reception-ist's desk at an ophthalmologist's office in Torrington. As Roth recalled, he picked out two "enchanting orange things" from a litter of six, and over the weekend did little more than watch them play. On Monday he asked Meetz to return them. As Zuckerman remarks to his friend Larry Hollis, who presses two orange kittens on the solitary writer in *Exit Ghost*, "They're too delightful."

■ ■ ■

OTHER THAN HIS TRAINER, Roth's only occasional companion in Litchfield County was C. H. Huvelle—"the loving, accepting, complic-itous grown-up," as Thurman described him, a "father figure" seventeen years older than Roth. Back when Huvelle was his regular physician, Roth used to envy the doting daily esteem he elicited from patients in his waiting room. "Nobody smiles at *me* when I walk into my studio in the morning," Roth told him. "Nobody eagerly looks up and reveren-tially says to *me*, 'Good morning, Writer, good morning, Dr. Roth.'" Huvelle retired in 1983—a year after he first detected Roth's coronary artery disease—because cataracts and retinal detachments had left him nearly blind. "I will be delighted to continue my professional services to you (and to Claire),"* he wrote Roth at the time, "as long as I know that Victor"—Hurst, Roth's cardiologist then—"is in the firehouse ready to respond if I pull the alarm."

During the summer of 1993, a month or so before he went to Silver Hill, Roth conceived the idea of writing a biographical essay about his

---

* As Bloom noted in *Doll's House*, once she and Roth became estranged, Huvelle politely informed her that his "primary allegiance" was to Roth.

friend—something of a pretext, he wrote, "to keep myself from drowning by putting myself at the service of this wonderfully reasonable and amiable man and just being in his company a few times a week." On these mornings, Roth would walk the cheerful streets of Litchfield until it was time to sit with Huvelle in his backyard arbor and discuss the man's days in the army, in medical school, and so forth; finally Roth would turn off his tape recorder and return to his own woes: "C. H., what should I do about Claire? I don't know what to do. She's not with me when I need her, and when she is with me, she's no use. I'm going under. . . ." *Dr. Huvelle: A Biographical Sketch* was written in the weeks after Silver Hill, while Roth was still picking around the threads of *Sabbath's Theater*; in October he took the manuscript to a Litchfield County print shop and ordered seventy-five copies of a thirty-four-page booklet, which began with a telling anecdote from Huvelle's childhood, when he'd ignored his father's admonition to stop sucking a penny and ended up swallowing it: "He had to defecate in a potty until the penny appeared. When it came out, the boy cleaned it and saved it. . . . The seeds of independence." Roth placed copies with the Litchfield Historical Society, the local library, and his archive at the Library of Congress, giving the rest to the Huvelles and their friends.

"Philip called," Conarroe wrote in his diary on June 22, 2000. "C. H. died. Said he couldn't go into detail or he'd cry." He saved the main detail for his novel *The Dying Animal*: like Kepesh's friend George O'Hearn, the barely conscious Huvelle had friends and family come to his bedside, one by one, and say goodbye; when his wife, Bab, appeared, "he began rather frantically to undo the buttons on her blouse," Roth remembered ("Wonder who he thought I was," the wife of the more goatish O'Hearn remarks afterward). For Huvelle's funeral at the Litchfield Congregational Church—where Lyman Beecher, the stern Calvinist father of Harriet Beecher Stowe, used to preach—Roth read a few passages from his biographical essay, ending with a quote from the subject: " 'If I die tonight, I've had a damn good life.' " Roth was told the minister winced; at any rate the man avoided Roth at the reception afterward.

∎ ∎ ∎ ∎

AFTER THE BLOOM FIASCO, said Bernie Avishai, "Philip desperately needed men in his life who he thought were on his side and he could count on to take care of him in certain ways that he increasingly thought women couldn't." One such man was Jonathan Brent, who'd met Roth in 1983 when he interviewed him for the *Chicago Tribune*. Brent was then teaching at Northwestern and running its university press; he told Roth about a journal he was starting, *Formations*, specializing in Eastern European literature, and Roth took it upon himself to solicit donations of a few hundred dollars apiece from a diverse roster of writers, including Updike, Mario Puzo, Toni Morrison, and Leon Uris. "He's a brilliant fellow and a good man," Roth said of Brent many years later, "and I wish we hadn't lost touch."

They lost touch roughly ten years after Brent's move, in 1991, to Yale University Press—hitherto a time of increasingly close friendship between the two, post-Bloom, when they'd meet for dinner every other month or so (sometimes with Ross Miller in tow) at a midway point between Warren and New Haven, Heritage Village in Southbury, a genteel retirement community that happened to have a good restaurant.* Brent was going through a bad patch in his marriage: for years he'd been frustrated in his writing projects (a novel and a book about Stalin) because of onerous family obligations; indeed he'd felt thwarted for most of his adult life, since he'd married right out of college and now had two children to support besides. Characteristically Roth advised him to strike out on his own and focus on his writing; he even managed to cajole Brent into consulting a divorce lawyer, but when it came to a point the younger man couldn't go through with it. He loved his wife and children too much, and besides he felt "afraid of Philip emotionally"— that is, Roth's interest in him seemed a little "voyeuristic," and also, on some level, he sensed Roth wanted him to get a divorce so he'd become

---

* Roth knew the place because his uncle Bernie had ended up there. As he mentioned to Brent, Roth sometimes went to a local bar to cruise well-heeled, middle-aged women. One night he got friendly with one such woman over drinks, and they made another date; she said she'd love to read a book of his in the meantime, and Roth suggested his latest, *Sabbath's Theater*. When she didn't show up for their next date, Roth gave her a call: "You are *never* to call me again," she said, and hung up.

more dependent on Roth ("Philip wants me to do this for *him*, not for myself," he thought). On June 29, 2000, Roth registered his irritation about Brent's change of heart with a little note to himself: " 'It would be a meaningful and beautiful experience for her.' Where did he get this language? From her? Needs the compensating sentimentality for the aggression against the wife. Now the divorce is off."

The friendship might have survived if Roth had confined his irritation to notes, but instead he worked things out by lampooning Brent in *The Dying Animal* as Kepesh's timid, self-righteous son, Kenny, who stays in a bad marriage despite his father's well-meaning advice: "As for conjugal sex, a heinous duty he stoically performs, that is beyond even his fortitude now. Arguments abound, irritable bowel syndrome abounds, placations abound, threats abound, as do counter-threats. But when I ask, 'Then why not leave?' he tells me that leaving would destroy his family." Lest there be any uncertainty on the point, Roth freely admitted to Brent that he'd used him as Kenny in the book (with the usual caveat that fiction is fiction, etc.), whereupon "at some stupid moment" Brent confided things to his wife, whose reaction may be imagined.

Afterward, relations with Roth were "very tepid at best," though Brent couldn't help feeling a little relieved. "He needed more emotionally from me than I could deliver," he said, some fourteen years later. "I don't know how else to put this: He needs somebody who can truly love him—that's why he's lost. Because he lives in kind of an empty world. Not intellectually empty; not artistically empty; but in some deep psychic way. And it's an emptiness that he has cultivated very carefully. Because he can control that world. But it leaves him empty and I think he's in great need of real love that he can't find." Other friends have groped their way toward similar observations. "I think there's something in his makeup he's missing," said Julius Goldstein in 1996. "I don't know who his close friends are, really." And when Roth marveled—deploringly—over the long duration of Alain Finkielkraut's marriage, it occurred to Finkielkraut that he and Roth didn't really understand each other and perhaps never would: "He doesn't know much about my life—my private life, my books . . . I guess I am useful, but why?" Finkielkraut paused, then said to his interviewer: "You should ask him."

∎ ∎ ∎

IN 1998, Roth's blood pressure shot up and couldn't be controlled with the usual medication; after a month of testing, an occlusion was found in his renal artery and the first of Roth's many stents was inserted. Soon he got another stent in his left carotid artery, and in 2000 his cardiac surgeon, Jeffrey Moses, inserted a stent in Roth's LAD artery—during which he discovered that, at some point, an obstructed graft had caused a silent heart attack on the posterior wall, permanently damaging the muscle. As Roth pointed out, Ross Miller—by then Roth's health care proxy and vice versa—"never failed" him throughout these ordeals and the many to come.

"I've had a bumper year," Roth wrote his friend on October 24, 2000, enclosing a check for ten thousand dollars. "I want you to share in the general prosperity." By then the two had become all but inseparable. Jack Miles remembered sitting in Roth's studio while Roth and Miller chatted on the phone—about nothing, really; the Mets maybe—and noting Roth's perfect laughing ease: "They'd spoken earlier in the day and they would speak again later in the day," said Miles. "It was like a marriage, I thought." After years of friction with Bloom and others, it was bliss talking with a like-minded chum about "boys stuff"—baseball and books, yes, but especially women—minus the kind of inhibition that marred his camaraderie with long-married friends like Finkielkraut and Michael Herr. As Zuckerman reflects in *The Human Stain*, "the male friendship is incomplete" if one can't speak openly about sex: "Most men never find such a friend. . . . But when it does happen, when two men find themselves in agreement about this essential part of being a man, unafraid of being judged, shamed, envied, or outdone, confident of not having the confidence betrayed, their human connection can be very strong and an unexpected intimacy results." Such a friend, for a while, was Ross Miller.

Another of Miller's assets (as Roth saw it) was that he was undaunted by Roth's fame because he himself, after all, was the nephew of Arthur Miller—that is, he was "inured" to fame, as opposed to being (as others saw it) galled by it, and pathologically envious of those who possessed it. At the height of their friendship, anyway, Miller seemed mostly requited by his status as boon companion to one of the world's greatest writers. "Don't think I'm second banana," he startled Hermione Lee, when she came to visit Roth in the hospital. Indeed, Miller considered himself to be Roth's intellectual equal (he said as much)—resembling, in this respect, the manqué Gersbach in *Herzog*: "Did Valentine Gersbach ever admit ignorance of any matter? He was a regular Goethe. He finished all your sentences, rephrased all your thoughts, explained everything." Conarroe, for one, never forgot the time he bumped into Miller during the intermission of a Dame Edna show, whereupon Miller proceeded to give a lecture on the nuances of camp to him, a gay professor. As for Miller's own attempts at humor, they were mostly aimed to please an audience of one—Roth—who was easily tickled by a bawdy bon mot, man to man, though not so much when Miller, say, conspicuously feigned sleep at Roth's table, during a public ceremony, while a boring dinner speaker went on too long praising Roth. "It's my third bad marriage," said Roth, in 2012, of the friendship. "I should have been put in jail when I was twenty, and locked up until I was seventy. That way I couldn't have done any harm. I don't mean harm to the community, I mean harm to myself."

■　■　■　■

MILLER WAS ALWAYS at his best, Roth thought, during their annual summer "pilgrimage" to the Bellows in Vermont. The two friends plus the Maneas would take rooms at the White House Inn in nearby Wilmington, and, for three or four days, devote themselves to amusing Bellow, who, again, had managed in the fullness of time to become well-disposed toward Roth, and who'd always had a soft spot for "lesser lights" like Miller—a point made by at least two of his biographers, James Atlas and Zachary Leader: "According to [Anthony] Hecht," noted the latter, "'Saul was always a sucker for flattery, and Jack'"—Ludwig, model for the treacherous Gersbach—"'would lay it on with a trowel.'"

Some of Janis Bellow's "happiest memories" were of these visits in the late nineties, when her husband was in his eighties but still lively enough to enjoy all-day excursions such as a boat trip along the Connecticut River. He and Roth would sit at a table together, their heads almost touching, and occasionally Bellow would throw his head back and laugh, which suggested they were off the subject of books and into more personal territory. ("Saul, how could you marry *five women?*" "I don't ask myself those questions any longer.")

It was Roth who, twelve years earlier, had suggested to James Atlas that he write a biography of Bellow. He and Atlas had become friends in 1977, when Roth read the twenty-eight-year-old Atlas's first biography and wrote one of his nicely considered fan letters:

> I've just finished reading your book on Delmore Schwartz and am still under its spell. It's an agonizing story, but you present it with such tact and clarity that finally—though I know it doesn't lessen his agony any— it at least comforts the reader knowing that someone has contemplated that life in its entirety and given its due. It is a beautiful act of sympathy and understanding.

Atlas was overwhelmed—Roth was one of his idols—and for the next few days he wrote a long, rather tortured letter of gratitude ("thousands of words"), until his wife, Anna Fels, advised him simply to say, in effect, "Thank you. Your letter meant a lot to me." Sensing he'd found another ideal reader, Roth invited the young man to Warren and gave him a draft of *The Ghost Writer*. Their subsequent discussion, he wrote Atlas, proved to be "of enormous value": "you are someone after my own heart, you know, because you do your homework, and it was clear you had done it for me with my manuscript."

A decade later Atlas was at sea. After five years of fitful labor, he'd decided to abort his biography of Edmund Wilson because of a "toxic response to his character" ("I warned you about that," said Roth), and also he'd left his job at *The New York Times*. Over lunch at the Russian Tea Room (so Atlas recorded in his journal), Roth "launched into a stunningly eloquent analysis of the decisions I'd made," meanwhile assuring Atlas that he'd soon find another project to his liking—namely Bellow, "a natural choice" for Atlas. "I had grown up in Chicago; my parents were from the same Northwest Side Jewish milieu that Bellow had rendered so vividly in a succession of books"; also, Bellow had been a great friend of Delmore Schwartz (model for Von Humboldt Fleisher in *Humboldt's Gift*) and naturally partook of the same cultural ethos. In 1992, Roth helped things along by recommending Atlas for a Guggenheim, and, on getting word from Conarroe (then the foundation's president), Roth phoned Atlas one Sunday morning with the good news ("so I don't learn like other normal people do; I learn from Philip Roth"). At times, though, Roth could be a cagey benefactor. The two were neighbors on West Seventy-seventh and would occasionally bump into each other—encounters that tended to make Atlas a little fretful. Once Roth invited him up to his apartment and left him alone in a room where Atlas spied, on a chair, a letter from Bellow; "You've probably already Xeroxed it," Roth said on returning, but didn't show it to him or discuss its contents. "As for Atlas's biography of Bellow," Roth wrote Ted Hoagland around this time, "I reserve judgment."

Roth decided his wariness was well founded when Atlas published a selection of journal entries about Bellow in the June 26, 1995, issue of *The New Yorker*. Titled "The Shadow in the Garden"—a phrase Bellow had used to describe Atlas, after the shadow cast by a gravestone—the entries revealed Atlas's growing disaffection with his subject, not to say envy ("why him and not me?") over the relative glamor of Bellow's life and achievement. "My greatest fear is that we'll have a falling out someday," Atlas wrote. "The person with whom I used to experience a huge paternal transference doesn't exist as powerfully for me anymore; I feel independent of him, but also sad. There is no Dad. Certainly not this difficult, prickly character."

After Atlas's *New Yorker* piece, Roth assumed a chill civility in his rare communications with his former friend. On June 21, 1997, he wrote Atlas a request to see, as agreed, any direct quotations from their earlier interview that Atlas planned to use in the finished book; Atlas replied that he was still in the process of cutting, and wouldn't know what he was definitely using until the fall. When Roth hadn't heard further by the following March, he wrote a brief reminder to Atlas, who replied as follows: "Relax. My book isn't done yet; it's been delayed. . . . Do you think I'm going to 'cheat' and smuggle in quotes from you without your approval? That's not how I do things. When I'm ready to seek your permission, I'll seek it. I want to do this book right." That tore it. Roth wrote Wylie (their mutual agent) that he found the note "egregiously rude," and now wanted to deny Atlas "use of any and all material" from their interview. In the end Roth relented on his threat,* but was unmoved by

---

* Roth made only small changes to his mostly innocuous quotes—deleting, for example, the word "pussy" from this summation of the third Mrs. Bellow: "Literature student, nice Chicago family, rich pussy."

Atlas's apology a few months later ("I'm sorry I snapped at you") and duly skeptical when Atlas ventured a diffident hope that Roth would find the published book "generous, fair, and interesting."

Roth found the book a "belittling distortion" of his literary and personal hero, blinded to its merits by what he described as "the banality of all that righteous, boring pseudo-p[s]ychiatric moralizing." Atlas himself would come to regret the scolding tone he sometimes took toward his subject, who once quipped that he'd married his second wife, Sondra, to "get into her pants": "It was a remarkably adolescent way of looking at the challenge of seduction for a man of almost forty," Atlas wrote; "if he was joking—a generous interpretation—the crudeness of his language was significant. Sondra was (to put it less bluntly than Bellow did) a sexual object; as such, she didn't require fidelity." Perhaps, but hardly the sort of thing that was apt to sit well with Roth, who was at least as fond of ribaldry as his beloved Bellow; nor did Roth agree with Atlas's judgment that the writer Vivian Gornick was "justifiably" offended by the way Bellow (*and* Roth) "depicted women in his novels." For his part, Atlas would remain rightly proud of his book's "scope and structure and literary insights," but he was aware, too, that something had misfired. He admitted to growing "impatient," over the years, with Bellow's evasions, vacillations, and general crabbiness ("I want to get on with my story, live *my* life," Atlas wrote in *The New Yorker*), and such irritation found its way into his book and at least one letter to Roth, whose vehement displeasure was conveyed to Atlas by a mutual friend.

And yet Atlas could scarcely have known the half of it. "You sounded in good spirits on the phone today," Roth wrote Bellow on September 14, 2000, about a month before publication of *Bellow: A Biography*. "You're taking this Atlas shit like a champ." By then Roth had spent more than two years working on a plan to neutralize the damage of Atlas's book (a book he'd taken no little part in encouraging): viz., a corrective interview with Bellow, covering his magisterial oeuvre from *Augie March* to the present day, that would be "four times longer" than any of the other interviews in Roth's forthcoming collection, *Shop Talk*—"the last, best word on this great man," as Roth would have it. After rereading each novel he proposed to send a list of questions for Bellow to answer at his leisure, and meanwhile Roth convened a reading group of three "smart Yeshiva bochers" to help enrich his insights: Miller, Manea, and

Ed Rothstein, the *Times* cultural reporter whose stellar review of *Zuckerman Unbound* ("The Revenge of the Vrai") Roth hadn't forgotten.* Manea soon dropped out for linguistic reasons, but the others met once a month at Roth's New York studio for "wonderful semi-fierce discussions" about a given Bellow novel, followed by a good Chinese meal. "Book talk, smart guys, chattering over dinner, going home," said Roth. "No friction."

But the fading Bellow was distracted by work on his final novel, *Ravelstein*, and it might have been clear to anyone but Roth that his *Shop Talk* interview was a lot more important to him than to Bellow, who took months to compose a single answer, when he bothered at all. "Yours, not Atlas's, should be the last word on what you've done," Roth hectored him on June 6, 1999, almost a year after proposing the project, and finally Roth decided to take matters even more firmly in hand. For a few days in early December, he informed Bellow, Roth would stay at the Charles Hotel in Cambridge, and spend "four or five hours a day"—two sessions a day, morning and afternoon—interviewing Bellow at his home in Brookline; afterward they'd prepare a transcript and Bellow could formulate his final answers based on that. Time was of the essence, Roth insisted, since David Remnick was eager to publish their interview in *The New Yorker* to coincide with (and, Roth hoped, to undermine) Atlas's biography.

Each morning Roth would join Bellow in his upstairs study at ten o'clock, and by noon Bellow "had had it"; the two men and Janis would adjourn to a nearby Thai restaurant, then Roth would work at his hotel in the afternoon and return *chez* Bellow for an early dinner and nightcap. As for the interviews themselves, Roth did most of the talking while Bellow listened and laughed and occasionally put up a kind of droll, token resistance to being led around by the nose, as though he were trying to fend off an overzealous encyclopedia salesman.

---

* Rothstein was doubly qualified because his youthful Bellow-worship had led him to study at the Committee on Social Thought, where he'd hoped to ingratiate himself with the great man. "Get in line: wives, children, students, writers, editors, lovers, biographers," Rothstein wrote of Bellow's aloofness, not unlike Abravanel's in *The Ghost Writer*: "a moat so oceanic that you could not even see the great turreted and buttressed thing it had been dug to protect."

ROTH: Whenever you go to Chicago in your books it's exuberant, whenever you come to New York you're depressed.

BELLOW: I never realized that.

ROTH: . . . You can't even imagine being lost in Chicago until *The Dean's December.*

BELLOW: I can't really see that I am so utterly place-dependent. . . .

ROTH [*after an exhaustive explanation*]: . . . You know?

BELLOW: With certain reservations, I do know.

"You're gonna finally understand yourself when this is over," Roth quipped at one point, while Bellow (perhaps in an effort to detach himself further from the ordeal) began referring to Roth in the third person: "Roth likes *Henderson*, and I am grateful to him for that. . . . Again Roth puts it better than I could have done." "I want you to understand that I'm not James Atlas," Roth reminded his weary elder, who replied, "I know that."

"Saul failing badly," Conarroe observed in his diary on July 12, 2000, but Roth persevered. With Atlas's book imminent, he was all the more determined to finish the job, going over their sketchy interview transcript and marking in red, for Bellow's benefit, whatever seemed most pertinent to a given set of questions. On July 15, he tried putting his foot down:

If you give me *two hours a day*, a morning hour and an afternoon hour, you should be able to do a question a week, which means that by the end of August the job will be done. If it is, we can then get it to Remnick for publication in *The New Yorker* in October. It would be the perfect response from you, and the only one necessary. **This is your job: DO IT.**

Otherwise, please:

1. Don't look at the Atlas book. . . .

2. Change your phone number NOW, and give the new number only to intimates. . . .

4. Say nothing about the book to anyone outside the very inner circle. NOT A WORD. NOTHING. DON'T SHOW THE WOUND TO A SOUL. THIS IS THE DISCIPLINE REQUIRED.

But it was no use, and finally Roth poured the collective insights of the last couple of years into a long essay, "Re-Reading Saul Bellow," which appeared in the October 9, 2000, issue of *The New Yorker*. "Remnick must know that he struck it rich, this time," a grateful Bellow wrote Roth, "—no Eng. Lit. Prof. would be capable of doing what you've done with my books."* Fair enough: with adulatory élan Roth explicated the better qualities of Bellow's mature novels, singling out *Herzog* as his "grandest creation" because it best exemplified "the nearly impossible undertaking that marks Bellow's work as strongly as it does the novels of Robert Musil and Thomas Mann: the struggle not only to infuse fiction with mind but to make mentalness itself central to the hero's dilemma— to think . . . about the *problem* of thinking." Finally, when Bellow died in April 2005, Roth saw to it that *The New Yorker* published Bellow's entire written response to Roth's interview question about the origin of *Augie March*—"without any editorial correction or alteration," oddly enough, since Bellow's incipient dementia was awkwardly highlighted by the way he circled back three times to the same basic (if charming) story, to wit: while spending a Guggenheim year in Paris, Bellow had been mired in writing a lugubrious philosophical novel set in a hospital, until one day he happened to think of a childhood friend who used to shout "I got a scheme!"—after which Bellow jettisoned the hospital novel and wrote an exuberant "speculative biography" of his lost chum, *The Adventures of Augie March*. And so a great writer was fledged.

■ ■ ■

"THIS IS HOW I whiled away the last fifteen months," Roth wrote the Bellows on December 10, 1997, enclosing the penultimate draft of *I*

---

* After a long and rather bitter absence from *The New Yorker* ("This woman sees the world through the lens of CELEBRITY," Roth had remarked of editor Tina Brown, "and that's the death of *everything*"), Roth had been welcomed back by Brown's successor, Remnick, who'd made a point of commissioning an excerpt from *I Married a Communist* for his first edited issue (August 3, 1998). "Even if this madness ends in a week," he'd written Roth, "I'll have published something—someone—supreme." The magazine's meticulous copy editor Mary Norris (later known as the Comma Queen), remembered going over Roth's "immaculate" manuscript and managing to find "a small inconsistency in a passage quoted from a children's history book." "Who is this woman?" Roth asked the fiction editor, Bill Buford. "And will she come live with me?"

Married a Communist. Bellow read the long book in three weeks, and was as stylish in aspersion as Roth (vis-à-vis Bellow) was in praise. Lamenting the "absence of distance" between Roth and his characters—a sin Bellow confessed to having committed in *Herzog* (where, however, he "hoped the comic effects might protect [him]")—he wondered how Roth could bear such a "cast-iron klutz" as Ira Ringold, and what about the other principals in his cast? "Eve is simply a pitiful woman and Sylphid is a pampered, wicked fat girl with a bison hump." Bellow ended his critique with the hope that Roth wouldn't "cast [him] off forever," and Roth replied with a vigorous defense of his novel followed by the usual gracious valediction: "You've been in my bloodstream since I read *Augie March*. It's going to take more than mere candor for me to cast you out for half an hour, let alone 'forever.'"

Truth be known, Roth was rather proud of the distance he'd achieved between his fictional world of midcentury Communist hysteria and his own latter-day personal woes, though he realized others might disagree on a legal (versus aesthetic) basis. For Milbank Tweed's consideration, he composed "a detailed anatomy of the relationship between major characters in the book and the real-life counterparts who, to a greater or lesser degree, serve as inspiration." Eve Frame, of course, was "modeled on the personality of Claire Bloom," though Roth had "substantially altered" the facts. It was true that Frame's second husband, Miles "Jumbo" Freedman, was a lot like Bloom's second husband, Hillard "Hilly" Elkins. Both, said Roth, were theatrical producers who might be described as "short and unattractive" and had perpetuated their wives' careers while stealing their money; in this case lawyers persuaded Roth to change Freedman into Frame's *third* husband, now a real estate speculator (but still a "sex clown"). Carlton Pennington therefore became Frame's second husband, based on the man who'd written a suavely bitchy blurb for *Doll's House*: "she even makes—inadvertently—her last husband, Philip Roth, into something he himself has failed to do—not for want of trying—interesting at last." Thus Roth was spurred, he confessed, to the task of making Gore Vidal "interesting" as the secretly gay, anti-Semitic Pennington, a silent-movie actor who manages to sire Sylphid and becomes more and more grotesque after his career tanks: "Drunk every night, on the prowl, a bitter ex-somebody ranting and raving about the Jews who run

Hollywood who ruined his career." Roth figured this character was sufficiently camouflaged as written.*

Sylphid was "modeled closely" on Anna Steiger, Roth informed his lawyers, though privately he considered the fictional version "much more appealing" than the real thing. For instance, at one of her mother's soirées, the wittily cynical Sylphid goes out of her way to put the young Zuckerman at ease by "helping [him] gradually to understand that there wasn't as much at stake as all the pomp suggested": "What's most laughable about that lunatic is her grandiosity," she remarks of one guest, the writer Katrina Van Tassel Grant, confiding to Nathan that her mother had secretly nicknamed the woman Loony. For Milbank Tweed, Roth explained the resemblance between Grant and Francine Gray as follows: "Both women are depicted as tall, thin, and blond-haired. Each has two private school-educated sons, each is a bad writer, and each is a calculating, incessant liar. There are no significant similarities beyond these."

Roth expected his novel to stir up a lot of gossip, the ubiquity of which was, after all, one of its major themes: "Gossip as gospel, the national faith. McCarthyism is the beginning not just of serious politics but of serious *everything* as entertainment to amuse the mass audience." Nowhere was the tendency more pronounced, Roth thought, than in so-called cultural journalism—"maniacally dedicated, as all gossip is, to knowing who is doing dirty to whom." As if to gratify his worst expectations, the *Times* ran a piece titled "Writers as Plunderers," by none other than Dinitia Smith, who decried the recent spate of "tell-all books" by such as Mia Farrow, Lillian Ross, and Roth, the last of whom "has made a career of taking elements from his life for his fiction," and whose new novel was regarded by some as "simply payback" (Smith also noted that *The Ghost Writer* had been "about" Malamud). As for the *Times* review of *I Married a Communist*—by Michiko Kakutani, Roth's fellow Pulitzer winner that year—it, too, disparaged the novel as "hogtied to a narrow,

---

* According to Roth and others, Vidal—who described himself as "homosexualist" (that is, a person who engages in homosexual acts but isn't confined to an orientation per se, the legitimacy of which Vidal staunchly disputed)—had asked Bloom to marry him. Also, Roth was far from alone in regarding Vidal as anti-Semitic.

personal agenda," the targets of which "are not transformed . . . into plausible or compelling fiction."

Among the more favorable reviews was one by historian Arthur Schlesinger Jr. in the *New York Observer*; Roth was especially pleased by the caption beneath a photo of himself, which he quoted in a letter to his editor, Wendy Strothman: "'PR, who understands how politics may serve as mask and outlet for extra-political resentments and obsessions.' . . . PR understands how book reviews may serve as mask and outlet for resentments and obsessions too." He was, at any rate, further consoled by a long, appreciative notice in the *New York Review* by Robert Stone, who applauded *Communist* as "a bitter, often funny, always engrossing story that wonderfully evokes a time and a place in our common past."

As a preemptive strike against old lefty friends who were apt to find Ira Ringold an unflattering reflection of their own susceptibilities, Roth incorporated the same verbatim sentiment into various letters: "if gullibility (that is, unforgivable naiveté about the horrors of the Soviet Union's totalitarian thuggery) wasn't the major idiocy of the American left, I don't know what was." Besides, he believed that Ira's own gullibility was particularized/extenuated by his hardscrabble childhood, richly evoked, which left him "an easy mark for the utopian vision," as Zuckerman reflects. Roth was especially proud of the canary funeral, a virtuosic set piece that "was most thrilling to write," he said, and that he'd "stake [his] longevity on." As with Swede's tour of the glove factory, the funeral was based on meticulous research (an actual event in Newark history), but what pleased Roth, as ever, was its potency as fiction: while the elaborate obsequies for an Italian cobbler's canary, Jimmy, leave most of the crowd in stitches, little Ira isn't "in on the joke" and weeps inconsolably, thereafter dubbed "Boo-hoo Ringold. The Jewboy who cried at the canary funeral." Thus the nature of Ira's alienation is picturesquely defined. He will forever identify with the weak and helpless thing—a tendency shared by his creator ("Don't step on the underdog")—hence his attraction to the likes of Eve Frame and the Communist party. Nor will the memory of his childhood humiliations ever go away, and beneath the polished façade of Iron Rinn, the Lincoln-impersonating radio celebrity, remains an unstable lout who once beat a man to death with a shovel.

Roth understood "how politics may serve as mask and outlet for extra-political resentments" regardless of ideology. As Murray Ringold explains to Zuckerman, the HUAC committee member most responsible for getting him fired from his teaching job was Bryden Grant—Katrina's odious husband—the same person who nominally cowrote ("as told to") the book that destroyed the career of Murray's brother, *I Married a Communist*. Murray traces the Grants' undying spite to a seemingly trivial episode at a party on West Eleventh Street, when Ira referred to the right-wing Bryden as "a pal of Wernher von Braun's": "The whole squabble took three minutes," says Murray, "but according to Ira, three minutes that sealed his fate and mine." Similarly, Roth would forever believe that a Katrina Grant–like figure was at least the partial ghostwriter of *Doll's House*, since he couldn't imagine Bloom coming up with certain characterizations any more than Eve Frame would be apt to call her gullible husband "a Machiavellian Communist, a vicious man of enormous cunning"—though she was certainly apt to pander to her daughter in whatever terms: "I don't believe I've ever seen anything so heroic in my life as my young daughter, who loved nothing so much as to sit quietly all day playing her harp, arguing strenuously in defense of American democracy against this Communist madman and his Stalinist, totalitarian lies." Politics may also provide a mask for failings one can't otherwise bear to acknowledge. As Murray explains Eve's self-exculpatory reasoning, "I didn't lose my husband because of the horrible trap I'm in with my daughter. I didn't lose my husband because of all those kneeling 'I implore you's.' . . . It has to be grander than that—and I must be blameless. . . . I lost my husband to Communism."

At bottom the novel is a bildungsroman—a portrait of the artist as a young man taking wobbly steps toward maturity and a kind of bleak wisdom. As a teenager Zuckerman writes radio plays glorifying the "little guy," inspired by Norman Corwin's *On a Note of Triumph* and his friendship with the manly Communist Ira.* This phase of his educa-

---

* "I am of course moved and honored by your allusion to *On a Note of Triumph*," the eighty-eight-year-old Corwin wrote Roth, after reading *Communist*. If he'd twigged to the novel's insinuation that his lyrical radio classic was so much simple-minded propaganda, he gave no sign—but then a part of Roth, too, loved Corwin's work to the end.

tion ends with college, when an admired instructor at the University of Chicago, Leo Glucksman, denounces Nathan's Corwinesque melodrama, *The Stooge of Torquemada*, as "crude, primitive, simple-minded, propagandistic crap." Speaking to students, Roth described his narrator's process of apprenticeship as "the struggle to change oneself, then the struggle to change others, and then to change the system"—casting off mentors along the way, and "thus making way for the orphanhood that is total," as Zuckerman puts it, "which is manhood." Finally the ninety-year-old Murray declares, "You cannot change anything"—an insight born of his own long education.

"Early on," said Roth, "I discovered the story would be told by two people"—Murray and Nathan—"who sort of pass the ball back and forth." The two accounts are meant to be mutually illuminating: Nathan remembers the Ira he idolized as a boy—Iron Rinn, the idealistic radio celebrity—while Murray tells of his brother's childhood and later, terrible decline, until both realize they didn't know the same man. Murray and Nathan talk to (at?) each other while sitting in the dark outside Nathan's house in the Berkshires, and their disembodied voices seem an apt way of telling a story about the radio era; but the actual effect is a clumsy one, perhaps the main reason (among others) that *I Married a Communist* is easily the weakest of Roth's American Trilogy. In *The Human Stain*, we learn toward the end of the novel that Zuckerman's earlier account of Coleman Silk's youth was based on his conversation with the man's sister, Ernestine, after Silk's funeral—but meanwhile her memories have been crafted into proper narrative scenes, versus the endless, unlovely yammering in *Communist*. "So, you see, Ira repeated to Pamela that stuff I'd told him at the outset about Sylphid but that he'd refused to take seriously coming from me," Murray explains, tediously, of his implausible omniscience—that is, how he came to infer the substance of a conversation (one of many) he never witnessed. And whereas Swede Levov expresses himself with improbable eloquence for the valid reason that he's a figment of Zuckerman's imagination—something a good reader never quite forgets—Murray is simply a cardboard sage who happens to talk a lot like his creator: "For stupidity, you know, there is no cure," he says of Katrina Grant. "The woman is the very embodiment of moral ambition, and the perniciousness of it, and the folly of it"—this after hours and hours of late-night maundering. ("I better settle down," he remarks a hundred-plus pages earlier. "I'm ninety years old.")

Still, Roth was satisfied that he'd managed to capture the essence of his ex-wife, though he was surprised and a little disappointed that "not a single reviewer" remarked on Eve's anti-Semitism. Nor did Bloom dispute the characterization legally, perhaps because of the so-called "small penis rule" (mentioned by Dinitia Smith): that is, fiction writers can protect themselves from libel suits by ascribing a small penis (or its equivalent) to a given character, since the real-life model is unlikely to announce "That character with the very small penis, that's me!" Roth wasn't taking chances, though: when their mutual friend Gaia Servadio assured him he'd gotten Bloom "exactly" right in the book, Roth said, "Put it all in writing—and not your terrible handwriting; *type it,* and send it to me!" As for Bloom's own thoughts on the matter, they may be gleaned in part from a 2004 article in *The Independent*, "Claire Bloom: The Human Pain" (a pun on Roth's title, and perhaps a commentary on Bloom herself). "No!" she whispered, clutching at her collar, when an interviewer described Eve Frame to her as a "self-loathing, anti-Semitic Jewess, [who] fawns over shallow society figures, [and] endures physical attacks from her overweight and vengeful daughter." Bloom confessed she'd never read her ex-husband's novel ("Every time I saw a copy, I felt sick or faint"), adding ("As if thinking aloud") that she still woke up "absolutely terrified" from nightmares about him.

Forty-Two

O N CHRISTMAS DAY 1997, ROTH WAS WALKING ALONG Columbus Avenue when a young man across the street yelled, "*Are you America's greatest writer?*" "Living," Roth replied. The young man proved to be George Stephanopoulos, who mentioned that Chelsea Clinton was back from Stanford for the holidays and working on a paper about *American Pastoral.* The following summer Roth met the Clintons on Martha's Vineyard, where he was visiting the Styrons: "Is your friend all right?" the president inquired of Dongala, remembering Roth's letter of a few months before. Bill Clinton had just come from being exhaustively grilled about the Lewinsky affair for the edification of millions (the cigar, etc.), and looked "like shit," thought Roth, who offered to help Chelsea with any future papers she may write about his work. "She doesn't need any help," Hillary interjected.

Apparently Roth made a good impression, since the president picked his name from a list of nominees to receive the National Medal of Arts that November, along with the likes of Gregory Peck and Fats Domino. Roth's entourage for the festive event included Golier, Sandy, the Maneas, Ross Miller, and Conarroe. Beneath a big tent on the South Lawn of the White House, Bill Clinton said of Roth, "What James Joyce did for Dublin, what William Faulkner did for Yoknapatawpha County, Philip Roth has done for Newark." As Conarroe recalled, "Philip flinched ever so slightly" at the last sentence of the president's citation: "Who would have thought that the brash kid from Newark would someday become the grand old man of American literature?" "Not as old as you think, Mr. President," Roth murmured as he came to retrieve his medallion, and Clinton, laughing, returned to the lectern and said to the crowd, "Do you know what he told me? 'I'm not as old as you think.' So I told him, 'Don't worry, Philip, it's just a literary expression.'"

■ ■ ■ ■

"I WRITE FROM eight o'clock in the morning until one," said Bellow. "Then I go out and make my mistakes." One of Roth's pleasant afternoon errands was getting his mail at the Cornwall Bridge post office, and one day in June 1998 he encountered "a rather arresting-looking, tall, lanky young woman in her thirties, with reddish-brown hair, who smilingly introduced herself" as Sylvia.* She knew who *he* was, and asked if he'd autograph a book; she worked next door to the post office, as a telephone dispatcher for an electrical repair company. When Roth stopped by to sign her book the next day, she mentioned a second job at a dairy farm that sold raw milk. Roth was just starting *The Human Stain*, and had vaguely conceived a love interest for Coleman Silk that needed fleshing out: "Can I come out and watch you?" he asked, and on June 27 he sat on a bench in the milking row (as Coleman does in the novel) watching the skinny woman, in shorts and a T-shirt, gamely shoving the cows around.

One morning Kathy Meetz arrived for work and there was a young woman at the breakfast table with Roth. "They had a really nice rapport," she remembered. Roth was squeamish about vermin ("mice or quick little bugs"), and the sassy Sylvia would tease him about being chicken; once, when a bat got into the house, Roth cringed while she calmly caught it with a towel and let it go outside. The name of her fictional counterpart, Faunia, was inspired by her affinity with animals and wild things generally, especially hawks and crows, at which the woman would squawk and caw while walking around Roth's land. Once, she took him along to meet the love of her life, Princess (called Prince in Roth's novel), a tame crow at the local Audubon center. Roth admired her moxie, all the more as she revealed, gradually, what she was up against—"the futility," as he put it, "that had been on her tail since she fled her pussycrazy stepfather at 14." Despite the blue-collar trappings of her life, Sylvia had grown up in the affluent Westchester town of Pound Ridge. Her mother, a former model and fashion director at a department store, refused to believe her when she accused her stepfather, a manufacturing executive, of fondling her and finally trying to rape her. After running away from home, she

---

* A pseudonym.

drifted from state to state before marrying a local farmer; now divorced, she had two children—"a sad fucked up little boy and girl" whom Roth had met in passing one weekend, "when they were allowed up for an hour from Roxbury to visit their fallen mom."

As Roth would presently learn, she'd lost custody of her children because she was an alcoholic with multiple DUI convictions; in fact, she'd definitively lost custody when she was arrested for DUI *and* child endangerment, having driven to her ex-husband's house "drunk out of her mind" (according to her brother), with her three (not two) children in the car. For a long time Roth knew nothing of this; in his company she rarely had more than half a glass of wine with dinner, and usually avoided sleeping over. Indeed, it was Roth's impression that this "cultural primitive" possessed a profound if nascent sensibility. When she visited on Sunday nights, he'd usually be listening to chamber music, and she'd raptly turn in her chair and stare at the speakers; the next time he was in the city, Roth made a point of stopping by Tower Records to buy her a collection of twenty-five CDs. Like Faunia, too, she'd murmur, "That's the ticket" when he penetrated her during sex, and on New Year's Eve ("which we spent largely in bed, fucking everywhichway [sic] and drinking good wine") she became "strangely and childishly frightened" when he suggested it was time to go home. He let her sleep in a spare room, and only later discovered she didn't have a driver's license and was afraid of being intercepted by state troopers—out in force that night—during the twenty-minute drive back to Sharon.

"I don't think he has a real sense of what it means to be an addict," said Roth's worldly cleaner, Meetz. "I don't think he understands the depth of what that does to people." Roth was apt to concede his naiveté on that point and certain others: "I'm still from 385 Leslie Street," he liked to say, when it came to homosexuality, violence, and alcoholism. In other words he was inclined to believe Sylvia when she told him—"with a wry acceptance of the shitty world"—about all the men who'd beaten and abandoned her, including the son of her psychotherapist, no less, whose abuse was so hideous she'd fled to the Susan B. Anthony Project for battered women in Torrington. Some of this might have been true, though her brother had reason to be skeptical. "She suffered from alcohol dependence and major depression," he pointed out, "but she *always* refused therapy." Contrary to what she'd told Roth, she hadn't run away from home at age fourteen, given that she was at least nineteen when she accused her stepfather of trying to seduce her; it was true her mother had chosen to believe her husband's denials, but so too did her brother (a gay activist who, alone in his family, maintained decent relations with his sister over the years): "[Sylvia] always had to be the center of attention," he said.

Roth thought her ultimate downfall began when she was injured in a car wreck and had to get an operation on her cervical spine. Afterward she complained of terrible pain, and Roth sent her to his local internist, whom he sent a series of alarmed faxes that spring: "URGENT! MEDICAL EMERGENCY / Your patient and my friend [Sylvia] —— is in a medical emergency," Roth faxed him on March 17, 1999, when Roth was in New York recovering from surgery on his carotid artery. Sylvia had told him over the phone that she was depressed and wanted to die, and he knew she'd lost some twenty-five pounds since her operation. He talked her into eating "half a container of yogurt, two spears of asparagus, and a glass of orange juice," he informed the doctor. *"That was her first food in two days."* The next day Roth faxed the man again, urging him to send an ambulance, and on April 4 he tried one more time: "[Sylvia's] case continues to spiral rapidly out of control. I learned just this evening, Sunday, that she was carried out of her house on Saturday by a neighbor and taken to Sharon Hospital with seizures. The diagnosis was drug withdrawal." That last detail might have suggested why the doctor was reluctant to get involved, but in any event Roth was disgusted and stopped seeing him as a result.

Roth went directly to check on her when he returned to Connecticut, and found her "staggering around her house and speaking with a slurred voice." During the six or seven hours they subsequently spent at the Sharon Hospital emergency room, a social worker interviewed them and Roth learned, at last, that Sylvia had been mixing painkillers with large quantities of alcohol. Sharon "didn't have the resources to deal with a patient like her," and Roth was told to take her to Charlotte Hungerford Hospital in Torrington, where, after another long wait—he pacing the floor while she glowered at him from a wheelchair—she was admitted to the psychiatric ward. Roth returned the next afternoon and entreated her "to get off the booze if not the painkillers," but she was furious and refused to speak to him. "She was like a surly child," he recalled.

"She was nothing like the witty, straight-shooting, and stoical woman I'd known." The psychiatrist in charge told him they couldn't keep her against her will ("and frankly they didn't think they could do anything for her anyway"), and Roth ended up driving her home in silence.

In the past Sylvia had refused to accept money from Roth, except for five hundred dollars she'd "borrowed" at Christmas to buy presents for her children. As her situation grew more desperate, though, Roth was determined to keep her afloat, though they'd stopped sleeping together and rarely spoke. When she lost both her jobs after neck surgery, Roth stopped by the electrical repair company and arranged to keep paying premiums for her COBRA insurance. He also arranged for a South Carolina lawyer to send her anonymous monthly stipends—two thousand dollars for March and April, one thousand for May, five hundred thereafter—because he knew she had relatives in the state and wanted her to think the money came from one of them. Meanwhile, too, he had Meetz deliver a weekly box of groceries to her latest digs, a cabin near Kent Falls, where she usually refused to open the door; Meetz would leave the box on her steps.

Roth heard rumors she was living with a shady laborer named Nick, and toward the end of May he paid her a visit and insisted she tell him the truth. "What I heard is very distressing," he wrote Ross Miller, "and I want to pass the information on to you so that you have a record, in case something violent does occur." Roth had met this Nick fellow, who once came to do work at his house; "Charlton Heston"—then president of the National Rifle Association—"Is My President" read the bumper sticker on his truck. Sylvia claimed the man had been beating her—even while she was wearing a cervical collar after surgery—and now he was "on the warpath" and might come after Roth. "The imagination's logic," Roth mused (alluding to a favorite Flaubertian maxim), since he'd already conjured the man as Les Farley in *The Human Stain*, and so surmised that he, Roth, might be in real danger. Wylie referred him to Rushdie's American security firm, whose consultant advised him just to leave town for a while until things cooled off.

Sylvia's brother had known Nick, the gun-nut boyfriend, and didn't think he was abusive ("though it probably wasn't a healthy relationship" since the two shared a fondness for liquor and drugs). "Philip Roth seems a nice man," he said. "He was trying to be helpful, and he found [Sylvia's] story compelling. If you're someone like [Sylvia], the one thing you want is someone who'll listen to you." By October 1999, anyway, she seemed to be over the worst of her troubles, and one day she left Roth a loaf of bread from Stroble's Bakery in Kent, along with a little note:

> . . . I will be forever grateful for all you have done for me.
>
> I hope, or should I say, my wish is that some day, I can thank you in person.
>
> Peace, Love, & Crows, [S.] :)

Her optimism was premature. On November 2, she was arrested for drunk driving again, this time without a license. A few weeks later she phoned Roth and said she was penniless ("Can't afford to buy shampoo"). He asked what had happened to her monthly check ($500), and she said the abusive boyfriend had cashed it and given her all of fifty bucks. "I'm going to pack it in," she said in a tearful voice.

At Roth's request, Meetz got in touch with the woman's mother in Pound Ridge, explaining that Sylvia was in a bad way and might die without some kind of intervention. "I can't do anything for her," said the mother, who shed a bit more light on things. In 1982, the nineteen-year-old Sylvia had married a young man in Florida (a Jew named Philip, it so happened) and had a son; needing help with the baby, the young couple soon moved to the environs of Pound Ridge, whereupon Sylvia "dropped off the planet" (as her brother put it), leaving the baby with her husband (also nineteen), until Sylvia's parents gained emergency custody and raised the boy as their own. There was also at least one other child (in addition to the three in Roxbury) who'd lived "fifteen or sixteen days" until her death from SIDS—or so Sylvia always told it, though her brother believed she'd fallen asleep drunk and rolled on top of the baby. Sylvia's present woes, anyway, were taken out of Roth's hands when she was duly convicted of her latest DUI (the fourth) and sent to the women's state prison in Niantic for six months.

■ ■ ■ ■

ON APRIL 17, 1999—while the smoke cleared after his latest angioplasty and recent trips to the ER with Sylvia—Roth reported to Solotaroff that he was 250 pages into *The Human Stain*, which was the only thing he wanted to think about: "I work up here day and night, it's bliss, pure bliss, what I should have been doing all my life and would have been doing if only it hadn't been for stupid p—k [sic]." During a 2004 interview, Ross Miller asked Roth whether he'd ever worked so close to his present experience as he had while evoking Sylvia on the page as Faunia Farley; Roth replied that he'd paid particular attention to her "matter-of-fact irony" (as when she told him about the time she'd cleaned up after a gunshot suicide, an experience he promptly gave to Faunia) and "vocal style," which he'd worked into Faunia's "crow monologue and dance-for-me monologue." "I don't know where she comes from, really," he said of Faunia during a 2003 interview with David Remnick; he mentioned there were a lot of crows on his property and so he thought, more or less randomly, "Why can't she too be interested in crows?"

Back when he'd been finishing *I Married a Communist*, it had occurred to Roth that he was writing a trilogy about postwar America, and soon he began casting about for another era that had affected him in some vital way—hitting on the present moment ("Treat '98 as though it were '48; treat '98 as if it were '68"), when Bill Clinton was being "tarred and feathered." "In 1998," he told the *Times* two years later, "you had the illusion that you were suddenly able to know this huge, unknowable country, to catch a glimpse of its moral core. What was being enacted on the public stage seemed to have the concentrated power of a great work of literature. The work I'm thinking of is *The Scarlet Letter*." Given his own pillorying in the wake of *Doll's House* (not to say his somewhat reckless conduct of late), Roth felt vaguely implicated in the president's humiliations and made the following notes about his novel in progress:

Very upset and can't understand it . . .
   Sexual hysteria . . .
   Turning men into contrite boys
   Hysterical fear of the dick
   . . . The Great Purity Binge
   My subject from the beginning.
   The Pure vs. the Impure
   . . . Feminism as the new righteousness . . .
   Women are blameless.

When an interviewer for *Le Figaro* later asked Roth whether his novel was a "polemic" against American political correctness, Roth said "it's not polemical at all. It's *representational*." The beginning of Coleman Silk's disgrace, for example—the accusation of racism ("spooks") that eventually leads to the even more damning accusation that he's "sexually exploiting an abused, illiterate woman half [his] age"—was closely based on an episode in the life of Roth's friend Mel Tumin. During the fall of 1976, two students had failed to appear for the first four weeks of Tumin's Sociology 332D precept at Princeton:* "Does anyone know these people?" he'd finally asked his fourteen students. "Do they exist or are they spooks?" As Tumin (and Silk, in so many words) would explain amid the inquisition that followed, "I was referring to their possibly ectoplasmic character. I had no idea what color they might be." It turned out the two students were African American women, whom Tumin advised at midterm to drop out, since they were both getting Fs in his course: "It was better, he felt, for me to 'drop out' than to 'flunk out,'" one of the young women wrote in her statement. "After all, he said, I would be able to get back in (the University) as I was black and also a woman, and black women being rarities at Princeton, *always* got back in." Both women had elected to remain in Tumin's class, and one claimed to have attended "religiously" after the professor's warning; meanwhile she learned from a classmate that Tumin had referred to her, on separate occasions, as a "spook" and a "wretch"—the latter insult arising as follows: Tumin had assigned the two women a fifteen-page paper summarizing the readings and lectures they'd missed, for which they took reserved books out of the library and deliberately held on to them until the end of the semester. "We took that into consideration," one of them said, impertinently, when Tumin asked whether they were aware that their classmates had also needed the books to study for final exams. Hence "wretches."

Lois Hinckley, an assistant professor on the board of advisers, reported that one of the two students had three Fs that semester, but should be allowed to remain at Princeton because of her "real effort"—in Tumin's class especially—"to reform: going to class and lecture, doing the work,

---

* A "precept," at Princeton, is a small weekly discussion group in which readings and topics of a particular course are explored in greater depth.

studying hard for the exam and, more important, a genuine change in her attitude, which was not, I gather, matched by any change on the professor's side." This student made Tumin's "discriminatory behavior" the basis of her appeal. A piquant irony in all this (albeit not as piquant as the one Roth would contrive for his novel) may be inferred by Tumin's 1994 obituary headline in *The New York Times*: "Melvin M. Tumin, 75, Specialist in Race Relations." In the novel, Herb Keble, a black colleague who owes his career to Coleman Silk, tells him, "I can't be with you on this"—the same words used by a black colleague who was similarly beholden to Tumin. In a letter to the deans overseeing the inquiry (one of whom was Neil Rudenstine, later president of Harvard), Tumin addressed certain misconceptions and moreover pointed out that his two truant students never did produce their makeup work, much less attend classes "religiously"—et cetera: "Must I go on? This is sickening." At length Tumin was exonerated—six months after referring to the ectoplasmic characters of students he'd never seen—whereupon he wrote a "gratified" letter to the deans, deploring, however, "the ease with which any faculty member can apparently be made subject of an inquiry on the basis of flimsy allegations by a desperate student."

Roth had long wanted to use the incident in his fiction, but figured it was a little too typical and needed another turn of the screw: "And then it dawned on me that the guy should be black, a pale-skinned black," he remembered in 2011—at least a little inspired here, again, by Tumin, who was sometimes reputed to be black because he was (as Roth described Silk) "one of those crimped-haired Jews of a light yellowish skin pigmentation." Roth gave a late draft of his novel to a black acquaintance from Newark, the social activist Barbara Bell Coleman, and over lunch she said most of his details about the young Coleman's family life seemed accurate. She did mention a light-skinned cousin of hers whose soft hair—"blow hair"—she'd envied as a child, and Roth put that expression into his novel. As for Steena Paulsson, the statuesque white girl Coleman brings home to meet his family, Roth was thinking of a poet with whom he'd had a fling at Yaddo some thirty years before, Freya Manfred, who remained a friend and later gave him details over the phone about her tiny Scandinavian hometown in Minnesota. Afterward she read *The Human Stain* and recognized her remarks almost verbatim ("It's unusual, Fergus Falls, because it has the Otter Tail Lake just to the east, and not far from our house it has the Otter Tail River"), and Roth apologized for taping her without her knowledge.

■ ■ ■ ■

ALONG WITH ROTH'S daily trips to the post office, other reasons for leaving his desk and relieving his loneliness included visits to David Plante's Columbia class that spring of 1999 and to Norman Manea's Bard class in the fall. Walking along the pathway outside Dodge Hall, Roth ran into a tall, fetching young woman with an Australian accent: "Hello," she said. "Are you Mr. Roth?" She offered to show him to Plante's class, and he got the impression she'd been waiting for him. After he seated himself with the other students around a large oval table, Roth glanced at his guide again—call her Margot—and noticed that she'd removed her sweater: "As well she should have," he said, "because she had lovely large breasts and I put them into *The Dying Animal*."

The main thing about their affair that would prove useful to his fiction, however, was the fierce jealousy it aroused—"for the first time in my life," said Roth—all the fiercer given his strong suspicion that the twenty-six-year-old had better things to do, at least sexually. While living in London, Roth had befriended the Australian comedian Barry Humphries ("Come to London," he wrote Dick Stern in 1979, "and I will take you to the theater to see a brilliant female impersonator named Barry Humphries who's not queer"), and that fall he took Margot to the Dame Edna show on Broadway; afterward he introduced her to the comedian backstage, and the next day Humphries gave his fellow Aussie a call and took her out to dinner. "You are a bad boy, Barry," the bedeviled Roth scolded him. "It was like taking out my niece," Humphries laughed ("which," said Roth, "didn't convince me of anything either way"). Nor did it help Roth's jealousy that the young woman proved vastly talented as a writer. He recommended her novel to Wylie, who promptly made a six-figure deal for British and North American rights.

"I'm sure that she was wildly ambitious," said one of Roth's subsequent girlfriends, who heard a lot more about Margot than she would have ideally liked. "He asks her out, she ends up in bed with him, he introduces her to his agent—" Here the woman burst into gleeful laughter: "Then she *leaves*." In *The Dying Animal*, Kepesh figures the young Consuela had only "experimented" with him, a much older man, "to see how overwhelming her breasts could be"—though in fact the real-life Margot was deeply fond of Roth. As he winningly admitted, however, she soon made it clear she didn't want to sleep with him anymore, and abruptly decided, at last, to get off a bus at Port Authority rather than spend another weekend in Connecticut with him. "That was the end," said Roth, who nonetheless remained interested in her literary career back in Australia, and even renewed a tender friendship, later, during her occasional visits to the States.

Nowadays Roth felt out of sympathy with academia, not least because of the "terrible xenophobia and philistinism that calls itself 'multiculturalism,'" as he had written Bob Brustein back in 1991. Eight years later, Roth visited an exhibit at the New York Public Library, "The Hallmarks of 20th Century American Literature," and "blew [his] stack." As he subsequently protested to Paul LeClerc, the president of the library (a job Roth had helped him get), it was nothing less than "an outrage" to feature the likes of Richard Wright, Ralph Ellison, and Edna St. Vincent Millay but make no mention whatever of Hemingway, Faulkner, or Robert Lowell. And multiculturalism was, for Roth, but one facet of a larger repugnancy: "You used to be able to sleep with the girls in the old days," he grumbled to Bellow. "And now of course it's impossible. You go to feminist prison; you serve twenty years to life. And it makes Joliet look like nothin' . . ." Mickey Sabbath—as an enduring protest against this state of affairs—considers leaving a bequest for a $500 annual college prize given to the female student who's "fucked more male faculty members than any other graduating senior during her undergraduate years."

Such was the Roth who came to Bard College, in the fall of 1999, for what would prove his final extensive teaching experience. As the subject of Manea's Contemporary Masters course, which met twelve times that semester to cover six of Roth's novels (*Portnoy's Complaint, The Ghost Writer, The Counterlife, Sabbath's Theater, American Pastoral,* and *I Married a Communist*), Roth would appear on Tuesdays to discuss salient themes and field questions from the fifteen or so students—this as a follow-up to Monday discussions headed by Manea, who later speculated (according to Roth) that his female students had been riled up by a certain "disagreeable feminist faculty member." In any case, Roth would call his friend every Monday evening to find out how things had gone with a particular novel; Manea seemed a little worried after the *Sabbath* session, but thought he'd "managed to tame the class" by reminding them, after all, that Drenka was every bit as nasty/interesting as Sabbath. ("A response to puritanical feminism," Roth had written in his teaching notes about the novel, which includes a scene where Sabbath looks over the classroom jottings of Deborah Cowan, the girl whose panties he steals: "Class criticized poem [Yeats's "Meru"] for its lack of a woman's perspective," she wrote. "Note unconscious gender privileging—*his* terror, *his* glory, *his* (phallic) monuments.") Manea may have stemmed the tide *Sabbath*-wise, but the water was lapping over the flood walls by the time his students read *I Married a Communist*. "I'm still doubtful," Roth said to Manea on the phone that Monday night, when the nervous Romanian ventured that things had seemed—well, turbulent but "okay."

Class was videotaped the next day—the final meeting—and open to the public, and before a full house Roth lost no time getting down to business. Manea had warned him, he said, that things had gotten a little heated (not for the first time) over "the portrayal of women" in his novel. "This is a woman who betrays her husband," he said of Eve Frame,

and I invented her. But I did not invent Linda Tripp.* Pamela Solomon [a friend of Sylphid] is a woman who has a dalliance with this man [Ira] who is impressive to her.

He's older, he has stature, he's heroic . . . and when things get hot for her she does what she can to save her skin. I invented Pamela Solomon but I didn't invent Monica Lewinsky. . . . I have to tell you that I accept any literary judgment having to do with the persuasiveness of the presentation, but I really cannot be told what I have a right to portray and what I don't have a right to portray. And I have no patience for it. . . .

The great thing about literature is, it doesn't matter if you like Emma Bovary or don't like her. Only one thing matters: Is she interesting? Do you like Raskolnikov? Or do you not like Raskolnikov? It's irrelevant. He's a murderer . . . it's kid stuff. How many of you were *engaged* by Raskolnikov, and how many of you weren't? . . . We don't have to have easy moralizing reactions to characters in literature. . . .

---

* Tripp was the civil servant who secretly taped her phone calls with Monica Lewinsky; Tripp subsequently shared these tapes—in which Lewinsky had discussed her and President Clinton's affair—with the independent counsel, Kenneth Starr.

There's something agitating, disturbing, questionable in the presentation of these women. Never in the presentation of the men. Sabbath is perfectly all right with you—this crazy cocksman. Fine. Ira? Violent, kills somebody? Fine. But there's something "wrong" in the presentation of Hope Lonoff, who doesn't want to leave this bad marriage she's in. Seems to be insufficiently forceful, assertive. . . . Isn't Sylphid assertive enough for you? Isn't Katrina Van Tassel Grant assertive enough? Plenty assertive. It's not so pretty.

A female student suggested it was more a matter of flat and round characters: Roth's male characters have an invariable roundness ("Sabbath can be the most corrupt—but we can sympathize with him because he's such a round character"), but in regard to Roth's women, "I'm not feeling, like, roundness from them, or complexity or sympathy." Roth asked her whether she considered Anne Frank/Amy Bellette to be flat, whereupon another young woman politely (but wrongly in terms of Roth's example) remarked that readers are "never inside" the heads of his female characters. "Aren't you interested in how men perceive women?" Roth asked her. "I'm interested in how women perceive men." A young man named Bernie, with a diffident tremor in his voice, attempted at length to clarify the matter. He was directing a play, he said, that "conformed to certain stereotypical conceptions of gender," and surely great art should "challenge" such types: "If perhaps you [Roth] could play with certain elements more, you know, by— . . ." "I don't buy any of this, Bernie," Roth said, genially enough. "You were very careful, you were excruciatingly careful in narrating this story which is a measure of how intimidating the atmosphere is. . . . I don't think this has to do with flat and round characters." Roth then produced a book, *On Trial: The Case of Sinyavsky and Daniel*, about the 1965 trial of two Soviet writers who were sent to a forced-labor camp for "slandering" the state in their work. Roth explained that Andrey Sinyavsky had written a satirical fable, *The Makepeace Experiment*, in which provincial Russians pretend, for instance, that toothpaste is caviar because their leader tells them so. "The judge didn't want to hear about satire or fantasy or hyperbole or playfulness or humor or the make-believe aspect of literature," said Roth; "all he wanted to know was: 'Why do you slander Lenin?'" Among the people in the Bard lecture hall that day was the writer Francine Prose, who noted that *On Trial* henceforth became her "favorite out-of-print book," given its invaluable lesson that "a fictional character is an individual and not a symbol of an entire gender or class or race, and one can criticize or satirize a society without being unpatriotic or seditious."

The book, however, didn't do Roth any favors that day. "I think we need to make an important distinction," said a not-so-diffident student named Lauren, "that we don't want to arrest you and put you on trial." Another young woman returned to the "question of roundness": "I think that it's important to maybe understand that for people our age, for women . . . most of the literature that we're exposed to and read growing up is about men." "I grew up in an extremely *Jewish* environment," Roth countered. "And when I read English literature there were no Jews in it—except in T. S. Eliot there were Jews to make fun of. . . . Do I have to read books with just Jews in them? What would I have read? Sholem Aleichem until the cows come home?" Amid a nervous ripple of laughter, Roth pressed on: flatness versus roundness, he said, is "a very elementary distinction," and perhaps now they could finally move on to what *is* present in his work rather than what may or may not be ("Isn't it *boring* after a while?").

But the class ended before other topics could be broached, and for the most part everyone seemed relieved. As for Roth, he'd maintained an air of good-humored civility throughout, but brooded and brooded afterward and seemed to grow increasingly bitter about things. Chatting with Bellow a couple weeks later, he said that young people's "aesthetic antennae have been cut" so that they only recognize the "political uses" of literature. Indeed he blamed the man-hating faculty "harpies" who corrupted such students, especially female students, and especially with respect to the work of Philip Roth, who wasn't about to lie down for these detractors. When he heard, in 2002, that Smith College had withdrawn permission for producers of *The Human Stain* to shoot on campus, allegedly because some of the dialogue was deemed offensive, Roth fired off a letter to President Carol Christ, wondering whether his novel (whence much of the dialogue was derived) had also been banned at Smith: "It's hard for me to believe that would be so, but I would appreciate it if you'd be kind enough to let me know if it is." And such matters continued to rankle twelve years later, when a teacher at St. Paul's Girls' School, in London, wrote Roth a friendly letter informing him that her students ("eight sharp and witty feminist critics") were reading *American Pastoral* in terms of "ideology, myth, intertextuality, gender and ambivalence." "I regret to tell you," Roth replied, "that the words 'ideology, myth, intertextuality, gender and ambivalence' make my flesh crawl."

■ ■ ■ ■

BY 2004, Roth's work appeared in thirty-one languages, and he informed a writer from *Time* that he was "not involved in the process of translation" except a little with his French translator, Josée Kamoun. Roth was "not involved" insofar as he spoke no language other than English; otherwise he was involved to the utmost degree. In the early days, to be sure, Roth had been remiss enough to allow his Italian publisher (then Bompiani) to translate his first book as *La ragazza di Tony*—i.e., *Tony's Girl*, which omitted the five short stories and renamed Neil Klugman in accordance with the revamped title. By 1981, Roth had a keener sense of his place in world literature, and when he learned at the last minute (from Kundera) that his French translator had misunderstood a Tolstoy reference at the end of *The Ghost Writer* ("It's like being married to Tolstoy," says Lonoff, about to pursue his fleeing wife), Roth wrote an irate letter to his august publisher, Claude Gallimard: "I now understand that this same translator is working on *Zuckerman Unbound*!"—and that wasn't the half of it: Only two of his books (*Goodbye, Columbus* and *Portnoy*) were available in French paperback editions, and if Gallimard would not agree to reprint most of Roth's backlist to coincide with his forthcoming Zuckerman Trilogy, he would have no choice but to seek another publisher. Gallimard replied that his translator, Henri Robillot, had been much acclaimed for his work on *Portnoy et son complexe* and other Roth titles: "I wish I could convince you, dear Philip Roth, that we feel a deep attachment to your books. According to me, publishing the *Grand Roman Americain* [*The Great American Novel*] should have been a living proof of that; because, in spite of its obvious qualities, the French public had a difficult approach to that book." Roth stayed with Gallimard.*

---

* In 2017, Gallimard published Roth in its canonical Bibliothèque de la Pléiade. Volume one, *Philip Roth: Romans et nouvelles 1959–1977*, omitted *Letting Go*, *When She Was Good*, *Our Gang*, and *The Great American Novel*.

In due course Roth put a system in place whereby his translators passed along their work (via Wylie's office) to handpicked authorities in various languages—including trusted friends such as Jacquie Rogers (French) and Aaron Asher's daughter Abigail (Italian)—who would make corrections and suggestions which Roth himself would then consider before preparing his own copious remarks. With Kamoun he had particular rapport, and for *The Dying Animal* he read the book aloud to her so she could get a better sense of the cadence and idioms of his first-person narrator. He also worked closely with his Swedish translator, Nancy Westman, who queried him as to a synonym for "base" apropos of Sabbath's remark, "I love your base qualities." After reviewing the manifold nuances of "base" according to *The Random House Dictionary of the English Language* (pressed on all his translators), Roth came to the point: "Sabbath is being playful with Nikki when he says he likes her base qualities, since she is almost singularly without any. Lighten up, sweetheart."

In 2000, Roth was described as "the biggest American export since David Hasselhoff" by *New York* magazine, which noted no fewer than three recent documentaries about the novelist in France, England, and Germany. Nowhere would Roth be more embraced than in France, thanks in part to critics such as *Le Monde*'s Josyane Savigneau, who insisted Roth was more than just the bawdy comic who'd written *Portnoy*. "This is only a guess," said Roth, when asked about his fame in France, "but I think they think that reading my books they're finding out something about America that they don't know and that they want to know." *American Pastoral* had established Roth as a major writer in France, and if anything *The Human Stain* would prove an even bigger success—a definitive indictment of the curious (to the French) puritanism that had led to the impeachment of a popular and admirable president. Even the hip left-wing magazine *Les Inrocks**** was clamoring for an interview, which Roth had refused at first ("I seem to have entered the post-interrogation period of my life"), until he was won over by its young literary editor, Marc Weitzmann, who began their interview in typically Gallic fashion. "My questions were very systematics [sic] and theoretic," he remembered, "until he stopped me and said 'I do not think

---

* Nickname for *Les Inrockuptibles*, itself a play on *Les Incorruptibles*, the French title of the American TV show *The Untouchables*.

that way'—to which I answered, 'Actually, neither do I'—I threw away my notes and started to ask the first thing I could think of and things got smoother."

Roth had a chance to bask in the adoration of the French en masse in October 1999, when he became only the third writer in nineteen years to be honored as the sole subject of the Book Festival of Aix-en-Provence, attended by more than twenty thousand people—another occasion he'd been inclined to forgo, until his Francophile friend Judith Thurman talked him into it. She acted as translator when Roth met with the festival director, Annie Terrier, to work out a format for the four-day program. Roth was especially eager to ameliorate what he considered French cultural condescension ("this stupid bullshit about 'McDonald's America'") and made sure the festival was as much about twentieth-century American art as it was about him and his work. Dan Talbot of Manhattan's Lincoln Plaza Cinema suggested five essential documentaries to screen (e.g., Frederick Wiseman's *Welfare*), and Leon Botstein helped arrange an American chamber music concert featuring the work of Barber, Copland, and others. Roth was especially pleased with the contribution of his librarian friend, Charles Cummings—a "first-class" photographic and historical exhibition of Newark—but Roth himself was the mastermind of it all, overseeing every detail and even providing a rather immodest but not inaccurate title: "The Roth Explosion."

He insisted on a quick flight aboard the Concorde because of his bad back, and his main companion and moral support, Julia Golier, remembered the rock-star greeting he received from a "gaggle of girls" in Aix (*"FEEL-up ROTH . . . FEEL-up ROTH"*), where the lampposts were festooned with enormous red banners bearing his likeness. "Now I know what it's like to be Chairman Mao," he said to the opening night audience. Roth's main duty was to preside over master classes about his work. While capacity crowds watched and listened, a portly gray-haired woman sat onstage taking notes for a few minutes at a time, then translating at lucid length whatever a panel of fifteen graduate students had said to Roth and vice versa. Roth would later describe his interlocutors as "young men and women educated to a crisp in the great French fryer of Continental literary education, with its bubbling Derridian rhetoric and dubious wordplay." Not unlike Norman Podhoretz, they'd concluded Roth was on the side of "tradition" because Levov (meaning "Love"? Or

"Lion" for Lev?) was a glove maker and gloves equaled tradition—etc. Roth spoke as carefully as he listened, with a kind of modest detachment toward his own work, as if he were just another (very) perceptive reader; decorously he suggested they think less about symbolic niceties and more about "the costs of a revolutionary period in American life . . . the inability to explain random events and catastrophes in a good man's life."

■ ■ ■ ■

AFTER THE ORDEAL of *I Married a Communist*, Roth expected even worse gossip mongering to taint the publication of *The Human Stain*. He'd been tempted to title his novel *Spooks*, but was dissuaded, he said, by the prospect of being reviewed in the Sunday *New York Times* by the Reverend Al Sharpton. "What's the most stupid possible reaction?" he wondered in his notes. "A big picture of Anatole Broyard in the NY Times 'Arts' section, next to a picture of PR. Roth steals AB's biography. That's the scoop on this book. He can never make anything up. Why did he want to put Anatole down? . . . Because Anatole gave him bad reviews. Roth is settling a score with Anatole." By then the former *Times* critic (who'd died in 1990) had become best known as a black man who'd ruthlessly cut ties with his family and "passed" as a white man with a white family in Connecticut. "*I* always suspected [him] of being a macaroon (one-eighth Jewish)," Roth wrote Updike, remembering his first meeting with Broyard on an Amagansett beach in 1959; in those days Broyard was considered a promising fiction writer, and Roth had admired an early story of his, "What the Cystoscope Said"; in hindsight, though, he decided Broyard's real talent had been "for elaborate mischief and deception." And cocksmanship: after Broyard had derided *Portnoy*, in *The New Republic*, as the kind of thing one hears "in midtown bars," Roth affected to concede that it was "probably true. . . . I guess one of the differences between [Broyard] and myself is that after all those nights in those great midtown bars I went home and wrote it down, while he, alas, went off to fuck another girl."

Publication of *The Human Stain* was heralded by a feature article— "Philip Roth Blows Up"—in *New York*, which respectfully proclaimed that "the unthinkable has occurred: Portnoy is a serious candidate for the Nobel Prize." Roth had refused to comment for the piece because he was "still irk[ed]" by the magazine's 1996 cover story, captioned "A Hell of a Marriage," but Harold Bloom and Bellow gladly attested to the greatness of his work in recent years. "It's almost a Shakespearean outburst of creativity," said Bloom, while Bellow professed an all but speechless awe: "I wish I understood it. I'm very impressed." Given the "very optimistic" first printing of 100,000, "the normally press-shy Roth" had agreed to cooperate with friendlier outlets, submitting to a long *New Yorker* profile and even the odd TV appearance.

As for coverage in the *Times*, it might have been worse: sure enough Broyard was invoked in both the daily and Sunday reviews, but no one accused Roth of settling scores. "The premise seems to have been inspired by the life story of Anatole Broyard," Kakutani wrote, adding that the basic story was a familiar one to Roth's readers: "Indeed, it closely parallels the story of Nathan Zuckerman, himself another dutiful, middle-class boy from New Jersey who rebelled against his family and found himself exiled, 'unbound' as it were, from his roots." Lorrie Moore, in the Sunday *Book Review*, made the debatable point that Roth ("usually fond of both sides of an argument") was content merely to ridicule the political correctness of a place like Athena College, "where prejudice may be trickily institutional and atmospheric, causing events like the 'spooks' utterance to be seized hold of and overinterpreted"; she concluded nonetheless that the novel was an "often very beautiful book."

Roth was warned away from reading a review in *The New Republic*, by James Wood, who found Silk's secret a little too easy and sentimentalizing, wishing instead Roth had let Silk *be*, in fact, a bigoted old Jew, or even a secret but self-hating black man: "Imagine the novelistic task of showing that an unpleasant old racist . . . had become the victim of political correctness, and *was* a rule-defying American individualist. Bigotry as the purest American individualism! That would be a novel to savor." As it was, said Wood, Roth had already written such a novel—*Sabbath's Theater*—"the story of an unsavory nihilist (sexist, racist, brutalist) whose battle-cry is 'fuck the laudable ideologies.'"

In a more muted way, the same battle cry may be heard in *The Human Stain*, given that ideologies of whatever sort tend to obscure the truth about human nature embodied by the stain on Monica Lewinsky's blue dress. "I myself dreamed of a mammoth banner," Zuckerman reflects, "draped dadaistically like a Christo wrapping from one end of the White House to the other and bearing the legend A HUMAN BEING LIVES HERE." In the first two novels of his American Trilogy, Roth had examined the "fantasy of purity" as imposed by the antiwar left and the anti-Communist right, and in his final book the puritanism is general—from the "Talibanism" of campus political correctness to the larger cynicism of the right's crusade to scapegoat Clinton and force his party out of power. Aptly, the brutalized Faunia speaks the eponymous phrase, "the human stain," while considering her beloved crow, Prince, violently rejected by other crows because he was raised by humans— by *people like us*, says Faunia, speaking "without revulsion or contempt or condemnation. Not even with sadness. . . . Impurity, cruelty, abuse, error, excrement, semen—there's no other way to be here. Nothing to do with disobedience."

Faunia loves her fellow misfit, Prince, a "crow that doesn't know how to be a crow"—a predicament shared by her human lover, a black man passing as a Jew. "Everyone knows you're sexually exploiting an abused, illiterate woman half your age," writes the sanctimonious department chair, Delphine Roux, who'd earlier accused Silk of racism and whose Delphic certainty will lead to rue (as the French might say). "Because we don't know, do we? . . . What underlies the anarchy of the train of events, the uncertainties, the mishaps, the disunity, the shocking irreg- ularities that define human affairs? *Nobody* knows, Professor Roux." The irony of mistaken judgment applies to Silk and his accuser equally: the latter begins as a kind of cartoon academic, an easy satirical target, but later is beautifully humanized into her own brand of lonely misfit— "isolated, estranged, confused about everything essential to a life, in a desperate state of bewildered longing and surrounded on all sides by admonishing forces defining her as the enemy." Among the things Roux fails to understand is that she herself is a bit of a racist, which suggests that her obsessive hostility toward Silk is rather the opposite of what it seems. Hence the bleak epiphany that follows her attempt to write a "subtly coded" personal ad, conveying a taste for swarthiness but not for negritude per se: "Mature man with backbone. Independent. Witty. Lively. . . . Mediterranean complexion. Green eyes preferred. . . . Gray- ing hair acceptable, even desirable." Coleman, in short, who incenses her (in part) by seeming to prefer an "illiterate woman" to an alluring cosmo- politan scholar such as herself.

The title of Roth's novel suggests another examination of the repel- lent, just as Coleman's flight from his race is a reworking of Roth's great theme going back to *Goodbye, Columbus*: the I against the They, a long-ing to live on one's own terms, free of the smothering community, amid, too, an abiding wistfulness to belong—to be a good son, a mensch, a libertine, a nihilist—all of the above. "She was marveling at discover-ing being one person in secret and another everywhere else, enjoying the kick of having a multiple self who behaves various ways in numer-ous lives and of possessing an impressively lavish endowment of self-abandonment": so Roth wrote of his lover Inga, and so he might have written about himself—or about Coleman Silk, whose dexterity in slip-ping among his multiple selves is foreshadowed by his career as a coun-terpunching boxer, "Silky Silk." As a boxer he makes his first foray into passing as white, but not until his arrival at Howard University does he fully grasp what awaits him, as a black man, in the wider world—at Woolworth's, for instance, where he and his roommate try to get a hot dog: "he was called a nigger. His first time. And they wouldn't give him the hot dog." Thus Silk decides to emancipate himself from both the "big they" and the "little they": "You can't let the big they impose its bigotry on you any more than you can let the little they become a we and impose its ethics on you. . . . The sliding relationship with everything. Not static but sliding. Self-knowledge but *concealed*. What is as powerful as that?"

In disgrace, at age seventy-one, Silk leaves his life behind for a second time—free to indulge the "Aschenbachian madness" of his affair with Faunia. Given his own Aschenbachian sprees of late, Roth had been all the more eager to bury himself in work on *The Human Stain*: "Nobody to disturb me," he told Finkielkraut. "Girls—when I need girls, they come! You see, Alain, when you get older you become smart." A reminder that he still had a thing or two to learn, perhaps, was Sylvia, who left prison in July 2000 and promptly got back in touch. "[Sylvia]—*record*," Roth jotted in his notes; afterward he typed a description of their brief exchange ("Call from [Sylvia] after getting out of Niantic prison," he wrote with a black Flair pen at top):

[Sylvia:] "Thank you. . . . For your undying whatever." Voice no longer confident. Empty. Lacking its cocky timbre. "You seem to have a way of paying for my insurance. It's a wonderful thing." . . .

"Well, [Sylvia], I wish you luck. Do you ever have any?"

Silence.

"I want to see you," she says.

"That's impossible. I'm afraid it's out of the question. Because I'm seriously involved with someone else [not true]. And that's the deal. And she's as possessive as I am, and that just cannot be. I'm sorry but that's the way it is."

Silence.

"Okay?"

"That's it?" she says.

"That's it . . . Okay . . . Good luck . . . Good luck, [Sylvia]."

Three months later, she called again. "Who's Faunia Farley?" she demanded ("not entirely coherent," Roth remembered). "A character in a novel," he replied. "You stole my life!" she said, threatening to sue him for "plagiarism." Indeed, she went so far as to phone his Connecticut lawyer, Perley Grimes, to whom she repeated the plagiarism charge and gave the name and number of a lawyer in Litchfield she'd allegedly hired. Neither Roth nor Grimes heard from her again, however; fourteen months later, while running errands in Cornwall Bridge, Roth heard that she'd been found dead in a Torrington motel room. "I foresaw her end," he told Miller, referring to Faunia's violent death at the hands of her crazed former husband. Roth, wondering whether foul play had been involved in Sylvia's case, "tried and failed" to get an autopsy report.

According to her brother, she'd died of heroin and alcohol poisoning (though she'd always insisted she never took illegal drugs). At some point she'd mentioned that her "mysterious benefactor" was a famous writer, and eventually her family figured out it was Roth. Sylvia's mother read *The Human Stain* and recognized her daughter in Faunia, though the details of her life were largely altered or mistaken: "It's supported by a story that itself is fiction," said her brother. "[Sylvia] created her own little world."

Her death coincided with perhaps the peak of Roth's literary reputation. In *Newsweek*, David Gates applauded his "magnificent Indian summer" as the author of the American Trilogy, and *The Human Stain* won a trifecta of major international awards: the PEN/Faulkner, the W. H. Smith in Britain, and the Prix Médicis Étranger for best foreign book in France, where the novel sold an astounding 300,000 copies—six times greater than its sale in the States.

CHAPTER

Forty-Three

IN 1960, WHEN TOM AND JACQUIE ROGERS CELEBRATED
Thanksgiving with the Roths in Iowa City, Jacquie was five months
pregnant with their second daughter, Susan. Twelve years later, the Rogerses stopped in Warren on their way to a summer rental in Maine, and,
amid hilarious rounds of croquet and darts, little Susie developed a crush
on Barbara Sproul; she liked Roth, too, and would always be an ideal
audience for his shtick. "*Now* I see why people have children," Roth said
to Tom, whose daughter was tittering away. "So somebody will laugh at
their jokes."

The years passed. In 1991, while Susan was finishing graduate work
at Columbia, she and her mother visited Roth and Bloom at their apartment on West Seventy-seventh; Susan remembered Roth as "kind of
wired" and "flirtatious" on that occasion—quite forward about pressing
the younger woman to meet him for dinner and so forth—even though
Susan was "very much identifying" as a lesbian at the time. Later, while
working as an editor for the *Journal of the History of Sexuality* at Bard, she
paid the odd visit to Roth in Connecticut for a chaste swim and dinner,
then moved to Tucson with her girlfriend in 1996.

When Rogers revisited her old family friend in Connecticut during
the fall of 2001, both were in a bad way. Rogers had left Tucson after
her girlfriend decided to get a sex-change operation and was now in
the midst of a tough, underpaid, and romantically complicated year of
teaching at Bard. As for Roth, he was beset by the three great calami-
ties that—in unison—invariably led to despair: "back pain, love trouble,
and an issue with writing," as Golier tabulated them. He'd been alone
for most of that summer, wracked with pain, and depressed over the lost
Margot and his failure to get another novel going since finishing *The
Dying Animal*. During Rogers's visit, he slipped on the step leading to his

studio porch and gashed his hand; Rogers ran back to the house for first-aid things and calmly bandaged him up. ("In his mind it was a turning point," she laughed. "He saw me as the one who could take care.") Roth was feeling better the next time she visited, and they became lovers after a jolly dinner at the Hopkins Inn.

"Why was I wasting my time all those years with straight women?" he said to her, while seeming to take a not-so-sneaking pride in having "converted" her to heterosexuality (in fact she'd always considered herself more or less bisexual). Mainly they had fun together, and she was disposed as ever to laugh at his jokes. "You are the easiest white girl to laugh that I ever knew," he'd say, paraphrasing Huck Finn. One winter night they sat in front of a fire collaborating on a map of Arizona that reflected Rogers's bittersweet memories of the place: the town of Far Right was at the head of Death Penalty River, amid the Broken Tits Wilderness Area, while Far from the Madding Crowd was well west of a cluster of villages labeled Madding Crowd, etc. Another thing about the strong-willed, athletic Rogers that appealed to Roth was—as he saw it—her waifish quality withal, which may explain why he was apt to assume a kind of loco parentis role. At Bard, Rogers had been hired through the efforts of an older woman, a dean, who'd fallen in love with her and wouldn't go quietly when Rogers tried to end the affair. As Roth recorded in one of several letters he mailed to himself as a record of possible harassment from the dean (this at the advice of his lawyer Russell Brooks), Rogers was visiting him in Warren when an "official-sounding" woman called his unlisted number and identified herself as "the Gallup poll calling for Susan Rogers"; afterward Rogers pointed out that the lovelorn dean had Roth's number on file because he'd taught at Bard. Privately (and correctly) Rogers doubted the woman was capable of any real malevolence, though she worried in earnest (correctly again) that the whole episode would wind up in Roth's fiction.

Above all, Roth enjoyed playing Pygmalion to the much younger woman—a Pygmalion with deep pockets, since she received a pauper's wage at Bard and was barely able to cover her bills. Roth's first gift of $10,000 was accompanied by a nice note ("There's no need to mention this"), and was soon followed by another check for $100,000 and a two-year-old Volvo that Roth picked out himself. A little less disinterested was his desire to help her dress better, as he thought she looked too butch to be seen on the arm of America's greatest living writer. It began with a snazzy jacket Roth spotted in the window of Derwin's, in Litchfield,* and evolved into shopping sprees at the chic Upper East Side consignment shops favored by Judith Thurman, who went around "whipping things off the rack" and handing them to Rogers in the dressing room. "It was fun," said Rogers. "There's a little too much on his side that he'd found a country bumpkin and he was polishing me up. That was a little offensive." "And her hair was *awful*," said Roth. "It was dyke hair. . . . I say, 'You could be a very pretty girl if you do something with your hair.' Why shouldn't I tell them that? They can say no. I don't twist their arm. So I pay a hundred bucks for her haircut. I'm rich, what do I care?" Actually it was $125, and never mind the ten or so trade magazines Roth bought at a kiosk near the City Athletic Club; after finding a style they both liked, Roth again consulted Thurman, who sent them to a posh stylist on East Fifty-ninth. "Philip went along the first time," Rogers recalled, "and ogled all the young beautiful women."

Indeed, if Roth had any qualm about dating Rogers, it had more to do with her age than her tonsorial/sartorial shortcomings—that is to say, she was too old. Reminded of their hilarious 2003 encounter with Claire Bloom on Columbus Avenue, Rogers consulted her journal (it happened on April 28) and read the following entry: "When we get back to the apartment, he said, 'Too bad [Margot] wasn't with me.' And I ask, 'Why? Because she's so beautiful?' 'No . . . because she's young. How old do you think you look?'" After Rogers returned that night to her room at the Athletic Club (Roth preferred sleeping alone and didn't have a spare bedroom in those days), he called to apologize. Again, the journal: "'I said a terrible thing to you. I meant that I wanted her to see me with someone really young.' 'I get it,' I said. 'And I am used to it.'"

■ ■ ■ ■

"I COULDN'T BEAR any longer writing about dickless Zuckerman," Roth remarked of his decision to resurrect Kepesh after he'd finished his American Trilogy. He considered the Kepesh novels—*The Breast* (1972), *The Professor of Desire* (1977), and *The Dying Animal* (2001)—as a trilogy

---

* Precisely described in *The Humbling* as "a tan close-fitting waist-length leather jacket with a shearling lining."

of sorts, too. "I wanted to portray a single man living three different erotic lives," he wrote Josyane Savigneau, "one grotesque, one conventional, and the last free, unencumbered, singularly pleasure-loving—Kepesh as an erotic hedonist, an aesthetician of fucking. Grotesque, conventional, hedonistic—I could as well be describing the erotic life of one man, one representative man over a lifetime, could I not?" Aboard the Concorde to Aix, Roth had reread one of his favorite novellas, Camus's *The Fall*, and was thus inspired to write *The Dying Animal* in the form of a confessional monologue addressed to a nameless interlocutor. As for the protagonist's main aesthetic concern—Consuela's gorgeously ample breasts—Roth was thinking of "a Dutch friend," he said, who'd also fixated on that feature of a much younger girlfriend; long after they'd parted, she came back to see him and break the news of her breast cancer.

Kakutani, for one, took a dim view of Roth's "flimsy and synthetic" novella—a particular disappointment to her after the lofty achievement of the American Trilogy, whose larger social canvas Roth had tried to insinuate, she thought, via Kepesh's "wholly unpersuasive" tendency to frame his life in terms of the transformative sixties. As an apologia for heedless libertinism, the book was bound to rub a lot of people the wrong way: A. O. Scott, in the Sunday *Times*, found the narrator a "garden-variety solipsist" with "a knack for pre-emptive self-forgiveness," whereas *The Economist* dismissed him simply as "a crashing bore." But the novella had formidable defenders. "What is rather unusual about it," David Lodge wrote in *The New York Review of Books*, "is the way it challenges the reader at every point to define and defend his own ethical position toward the issues raised by the story. It is a small, disturbing masterpiece." Michael Dirda agreed, in *The Washington Post*, ranking it among other classic "*récits*" of European fiction such as *The Fall* and Gide's *The Immoralist*: "Is Philip Roth now our finest living novelist?"

Certainly there was nothing contrived about the momentous view Kepesh—and his creator—takes of the sixties. Back in 1974, reflecting on the origins of *Portnoy*, Roth wrote: "I sometimes think of my generation of men as the first wave of determined D-day invaders, over whose bloody, wounded carcasses the flower children subsequently stepped ashore to advance triumphantly toward that libidinous Paris we had dreamed of liberating as we inched inland on our bellies, firing into the dark." Philip Larkin had lamented that the sexual revolution began "rather late" for him to benefit—also late for Roth, but not *too* late. In 1963 he fled his ghastly marriage for good, and endeavored to make up for lost time as a free man in Manhattan. His brother, Sandy, likewise awoke to the reality that he was trapped in a marriage to the sweet, decent, but sexually undesirable Trudy, while all sorts of unattached women were suddenly available to him ("he was driven mad by it," said Philip, who put some of his brother's madness into Portnoy). As Kepesh points out, his generation of men had spent their formative years as sexual thieves, and once they jumped the marital fence, they tried never to look back at the people they'd left behind. Roth cut loose a doting stepdaughter, Helen, while Kepesh accepts that his middle-aged son hates him. "The long white pageboy of important hair," Kenny describes his "pathetic old fool" of a father, "the turkey wattle half hidden behind the fancy foulard—when will you begin to rouge your cheeks, Herr von Aschenbach?"

Roth, of course, understood that sexual freedom is, as Kepesh observes, "a very risky game. A man wouldn't have two-thirds of the problems he has if he didn't venture off to get fucked. It's sex that disorders our normally ordered lives." Sex may lead to disorder in the form of, say, an unstable alcoholic paramour, or else—as Roth experienced with Margot and certain of her successors—to the ultimate disorder, love, and its concomitant loss of freedom and well-being. "I still can't say that anything I ever did sexually excited Consuela about me," Kepesh admits. "Which was largely why, from the evening we first went to bed eight years back, I never had a moment's peace, why, whether she realized it or not, I was all weakness and worry from then on." However: as a man gets older, and potency wanes, the sacrifice of sexual freedom would seem a less crucial matter. With that in mind, it's hard to imagine many readers biting their nails when Kepesh's hitherto silent auditor speaks up, portentously, on the last page of the book. "Think about it," s/he says, as Kepesh is tempted to go comfort Consuela in the hospital. "Think. Because if you go, you're finished." The end. Will Kepesh forfeit his long career as a roué for the homelier joys of monogamy? But never mind: one can enjoy *The Dying Animal* as a stylishly minor tour de force, without necessarily being impressed by every one of its moral perplexities. As the critic Lee Siegel put it, "It is like using exquisite Carrera marble to expertly carve the sculpture of a dildo."

. . . .

ROTH'S NEXT BOOK, *Shop Talk*, published four months later, mostly consisted of the interviews he'd conducted over the years with various European colleagues, including a number of Jewish writers whose sufferings under Nazism had led Roth to reflect on his very different life in America—survivors of the camps such as Levi, Appelfeld, and Klíma, writers "bound together by their post-Kafka sensibility," as Richard Bernstein wrote in one of the book's very few reviews. "They are the ones who lived the reality that was Kafka's nightmare—his conviction, as Mr. Klíma puts it, that 'a dependable world of dignity and justice is what is absurdly fantastic.'" A year later, during a *Partisan Review* symposium at Boston University ("Our Country, Our Culture"), Cynthia Ozick cited the neglect of Roth's most recent book as a grim bellwether: "A writer of Roth's stature—one of the shapers of the novel in our time—engaging with ten of the significant literary figures of the twentieth century! Fifty years ago, we can be sure, this would have been taken as an Event, as a cultural marker, as an occasion for heating up New York's literary stewpots as much as, or even more than, Franzen's explosive—and ephemeral—wistfulness" (a reference to the novelist Jonathan Franzen's controversial ambivalence toward Oprah's Book Club). Aside from Bernstein's review in the daily *Times*—even Kakutani excused herself this time—the only major notice was a "Books in Brief" mention in the Sunday *Times*, which described Roth *qua* interviewer as "a cross between Lionel Trilling and Barbara Walters."

Perhaps one reason for the general indifference was poor timing, given that *Shop Talk* was published the day after 9/11—the imminence of which had been eerily suggested in *The Dying Animal*: "Brilliance flaring across the time zones," Roth wrote of the millennial New Year's Eve celebration, "and none ignited by bin Laden." On the morning the Twin Towers fell, Roth had been at the City Athletic Club in Midtown; for a few minutes he watched the terrible footage with other members in the TV lounge, then went outside and gazed at the river of pedestrians milling uptown along Sixth Avenue. As on November 22, 1963, Roth spent the rest of the day walking around the city, "seeing what was to be seen" and commiserating with other New Yorkers. Rather than return to Connecticut the next day, as planned, Roth decided to stay put for the rest of the month, and expressed solidarity with a big American flag hung in his south-facing window; meanwhile he became "furious with people like Susan Sontag who were blaming America and blaming the victims—people who said the deed was a result of American policy in the Middle East rather than the result of the way these people were brought up and abused by their own countries."

His dismay was exacerbated by killing back pain, now accompanied by numbness in his right leg that made walking difficult and writing all but impossible—he had to stop every twenty minutes or so and lie on a floor mat. Because an unsympathetic colonel had called him a malingerer in 1956, Roth had let almost half a century pass before he sought serious treatment for his back. "I'm surprised you're still ambulatory," said a spinal surgeon at Lenox Hill Hospital, surveying the awful results of Roth's MRI: in addition to drastic degeneration at several levels of his lumbar spine, Roth learned for the first time that he'd been a lifelong sufferer of scoliosis. Surgery followed on March 26, 2002, but had to be stopped after the repair of a single disc (L5-S1) when Roth's blood pressure plummeted (caused, ironically, by the beta-blocker he'd taken to stabilize his heart pre-surgery).

Because of kidney damage caused by his previously occluded renal artery, Roth had low tolerance for certain drugs in high doses—including morphine, as he learned during a recovery that proved horrific for patient and caretakers alike. Roth, hallucinating, took a swing at a nurse who was trying to help him off the bed, and yelled terrible things at Susan Rogers, who'd canceled an entire week of her Bard classes prior to spring break so she could look after him ("nobody in my life knows that I'm involved [with Roth]," she remembered, "so this takes a lot of smoke and mirrors"). Finally she was so distraught that she phoned Roth's usual minder, Ross Miller, who was himself sick at the time: an old hand by then, Miller patiently explained that Roth was coming off painkillers and would be himself again, more or less, in five or six hours. Indeed, Roth was well enough to take a short walk with Rogers a few days later, but was irritated when she abruptly abandoned him to visit her hospitalized father (pancreatitis) and tend her ailing mother (shingles), which is how she spent her spring break.

．　．　．　．

IN DECEMBER 2000, Roth had been reading an advance copy of Arthur Schlesinger Jr.'s autobiography when he came across a "single, almost expendable sentence" about how the far-right wing of the Republican party had wanted to run Charles Lindbergh as their candidate for president in 1940. "What if they had?" Roth wrote in the margin. Over lunch he grilled Schlesinger about Lindbergh and the far right, as he'd begun to consider writing a novel with some such title as *Our Life under Lindbergh*—the first-person plural because he'd decided to feature his own family: "So on the one hand," he said, "the book is far out, in that it imagined Lindbergh as the president of the U.S., and on the other it's far *in*, to imagine my family as being victims."

"The book I'm working on gets bigger and bigger," he wrote his Gallimard editor on November 3, 2002. "Good! What else is there to do?" Roth absorbed himself in research about the book's various historical personages, especially Lindbergh himself, whom he was careful not "to caricature or revile" in the course of evoking his alternative presidency. As a figurehead of the noninterventionist America First Committee, Lindbergh had made his anti-Semitism explicit in a speech to an AFC rally on September 11, 1941, "Who Are the War Agitators?," which blamed "the Jewish race" for pushing the country toward war "for reasons which are not American." His good friend Henry Ford had encouraged such views, until even the AFC publicly disavowed Ford to avoid the taint of a more rabid anti-Semitism: "I know who caused the war," Ford had said in 1915: "German-Jewish bankers . . . a power that has no country and that can order the young men of all countries out to death." Such scapegoating was zealously promoted by "our nation's anti-Semitic propaganda minister"—as Roth called him—the radio priest, Father Charles Coughlin: "Jewish persecution only followed after Christians first were persecuted," Coughlin remarked of the Kristallnacht pogrom, and, five weeks later, on December 18, 1938, he incited followers in New York to march in protest against a law that would have enabled more European Jews to seek asylum in the United States. "Send Jews back where they came from in leaky boats!" the marchers chanted.

"Orwell imagined a huge change in the future with horrendous consequences for everyone," Roth wrote of his approach in *The Plot Against America*; "I tried to imagine a small change in the past with horrendous consequences for a relative few." Among the book's more persuasive elements are the insidious measures Lindbergh takes to target Jews—via the vaguely ("but only vaguely") hostile "Just Folks" program, for instance, which relocates Jews to predominantly gentile communities. Roth explained that he'd never previously written about his family as they really were—"good, hard-working, responsible"—because it was "boring. . . . What I discovered inadvertently was that if you put pressure on these decent people, then you've got a story." Roth was especially eager to rectify the public perception of his mother as Sophie Portnoy, and finally show her as the kind, competent person she was; however, his latest novel also required at least one defector in the family, and so Sandy became a rather unpleasant (and un-Sandy-like) Lindberghite.

The novel is dedicated to Susan Rogers ("To S. F. R."), whom Roth credited with the creation of the novel's "most tragic figure," Seldon Wishnow: "that nice, lonely little kid in your class whom you run away from when you're yourself a kid," said Roth, "because he demands to be befriended by you in ways that another child cannot stand." Whenever he got stuck writing about Seldon—whose family lives downstairs from the Roths, and whose parents are both dead by the end of the book—he would burst in on Rogers and insist she role-play Seldon with him in a given scene, thus: "Philip said something like 'I don't have to be nice to you just because your father hanged himself,'" Rogers remembered. "Something incredibly mean. And I burst into tears"—in part because her own father was sick with colon cancer at the time—"but I'm still *Seldon* in tears." Roth thought his companion's impression of the woebegone boy was "right on the money," whereas Rogers identified deeply with Seldon's "lostness," at least in terms of her relationship with Roth. "His view of who I am, even now," she said in 2014, "and who I actually am, has . . . There's not a one-for-one there." She laughed, bleakly. "The extent to which our relationship was lopsided, and seeing that pattern again and again in his relationships. . . . This wasn't equal in any way."

■ ■ ■ ■

THE PEREMPTORY SIDE of Roth's nature seemed to wax along with his eminence. "It's impossible to know Philip and know his history without knowing all the beached fish," said Kazin's widow, Judith Dunford, who'd washed up on that beach herself for a time, as had Judith Thurman ("I love him anyway"), who noted that Roth was decidedly prone to letting "old griefs and resentments fester," and hence his circle of friends tended to wane somewhat in these years. For almost five decades, Roth and Dick Stern—"Rawt" and "Shtoin," as they called each other—had engaged in high-minded and often hilarious discussions about literature, their own and the world's. That Stern seemed not to mind the chasm separating their respective reputations was due in part to his own good nature, as well as a firm awareness that Roth deeply respected Stern's work and was nearly as mystified by Stern's obscurity as was Stern himself. Over the years Roth's main engagement with the American Academy of Arts and Letters was to hector that august body to recognize Stern, who finally received the Academy's Medal of Merit for the Novel in 1985, twelve years after Roth first proposed him for it. His efforts to get Stern elected as an actual member were another matter. Not even the mighty triumvirate of Bellow, Malamud, and Roth—Hart, Schaffner, and Marx, after all—could do the trick in 1979. "Poor Dick," Roth wrote Bellow a decade later, suggesting they try again. "They really won't let him get a foot in the door."

"Things mount up in a friendship," said Stern, explaining his complicated falling-out with Roth in 2000. First there was Roth's thrashing of *Pacific Tremors*, Stern's final novel, which Stern suspected had bothered Roth for "extra-literary" reasons—such as its emphasis on the joys of grandfatherhood, which bristled against the whole weltanschauung of Roth's own recent novel, *The Dying Animal* (wherein, as Stern put it, "the only thing that counts is fucking"). Replying to Roth's sober but caustic critique of *Pacific Tremors*, Stern seemed to concede a few points with his usual equanimity, while getting in a few jujitsu jabs of his own: "the prose is not in the same league with the prose I wrote for most of my writing life (which was, even so, barer, quicker, less intense and striking than yours, and errs in those directions as yours perhaps errs in the direction of excess, beating a subject to death or boredom, and sometimes miscalculating the import of certain events and revelations)." Of course, the friendship would have easily survived such an exchange, but things had indeed mounted up over the years and Stern was not quite done getting his own back. Reviewing *Bellow: A Biography* in the December 11 issue of *The Nation*, Stern wrote that he'd assured his old friend Bellow—while still in the midst of reading Atlas's book—that he had little to worry about; then Stern read the latter part of Atlas and revised

Roth with his parents and Bess Roth's "other son," Joel Conarroe, in Warren, 1975.

(Copyright © Nancy Crampton)

ABOVE: *Mildred Martin with her famous former student and lifelong friend, who received an honorary degree (his first of many) from Bucknell in June 1979.*
(Courtesy of Philip Roth Estate)

LEFT: *Roth's minimalist but remarkably accurate self-portrait.*
(Courtesy of Philip Roth Estate)

ABOVE: *Roth with Veronica Geng, his friend and favorite editor.*
(COURTESY OF VERA KUNDERA)

RIGHT: *Roth and Milan Kundera. The Kunderas visited Connecticut— along with Geng—in the fall of 1980, while Roth was renovating his studio, hence the bulldozer.*
(COURTESY OF VERA KUNDERA)

LEFT: *When Roth decided that England was rife with anti-Semitism, he grew a beard to augment his already conspicuously Semitic features.*

(COURTESY OF PHILIP ROTH ESTATE)

BELOW: *In 1986, Roth traveled to Turin to interview Primo Levi, the author of* Survival at Auschwitz, *for The New York Times Book Review. The two felt an immediate bond. "I don't know which of us is the younger brother and which is the older brother," said Levi on parting.*

(COURTESY OF LA STAMPA)

Also for the Times, *Roth went to Jerusalem to interview the writer Aharon Appelfeld, whose harrowing childhood amid the Holocaust was in stark contrast to Roth's sheltered idyll in Weequahic.*

Sandy and Philip with their father, in Connecticut, 1983.

(Courtesy of Philip Roth Estate)

Philip with Herman and his companion, Lillian Beloff, in 1987, shortly after a massive cartilaginous brain tumor had caused one side of Herman's face to collapse.

(Courtesy of Philip Roth Estate)

ABOVE: *Roth and Julia Golier,*
whose sweet reasonableness (and
drollery) got him through the
fiasco of Leaving a Doll's House.
Golier remained a dear friend even
after their breakup, and eventually
Roth named her co-executor of his
estate.

(COURTESY OF JULIA GOLIER)

RIGHT: *Roth was a jolly*
(if wistful) guest at Golier's
wedding to Bill Bornmann
on March 9, 2002.

(COURTESY OF JULIA GOLIER)

A reunion, in Connecticut, with "the boys" from Weequahic High's class of 1950. From left: Stuart Lehman, Bernie Swerdlow, Howie Silver, Marty Weich, Roth, and Bob Heyman.

Roth with the Clintons, in 1998, after receiving the National Medal of the Arts at the White House.
(Courtesy of Philip Roth Estate)

ABOVE: *Roth strolls the Bard campus with his friends Emmanuel Dongala (left) and Norman Manea (right).*
(Courtesy of Philip Roth Estate)

RIGHT: *Lisa Halliday, whose romance with Roth would be evoked in* Asymmetry, *her 2018 novel.*
(Courtesy of Theo Collier)

81 Summit Avenue, in Weequahic, as it appears today (a half block away from Philip Roth Plaza). "This was the first childhood home of Philip Roth, one of America's greatest writers of the 20th and 21st centuries," reads the historical plaque.

Roth receives the National Humanities Medal from President Obama, 2011.
"You're not slowing down, are you?" Obama asked him. "Oh, Mr. President,"
Roth replied, "I'm slowing down, all right."

ABOVE: *Roth chats with Zadie Smith and Nathan Englander at the Center for Fiction in New York, 2011.*
(Courtesy of the Center for Fiction)

LEFT: *Roth doted on Julia Golier's twins, Amelia and William Bornmann, who became de facto grandchildren. Roth is shown here with Amelia in 2013.*
(Courtesy of Julia Golier)

ABOVE: *In Roth's final years, he often met Mia Farrow at his favorite Connecticut restaurant, the West Street Grill in Litchfield. The owners, Charlie Kafferman and James O'Shea (standing in back), were old friends.*
(Courtesy of Mia Farrow)

RIGHT: *Roth's eighty-fifth birthday, his last, was celebrated at his old friend Judith Thurman's house on the Upper East Side. Roth is holding a photo of Joe DiMaggio given to him by Don DeLillo, another guest; Mia Farrow is at Roth's right.*
(Courtesy of Joel Conarroe)

One of the last photos taken of Roth, on April 22, 2018, exactly a month before his death. He was delighted by Lisa Halliday's toddler daughter, Stella, shown here with her mother during a visit to Roth's Upper West Side apartment.

Roth's idiosyncratic gravestone at Bard College Cemetery—a boulder from his property in Connecticut, roughly inscribed (after the manner of Camus's gravestone) by his friend Russ Murdock, a stonemason.

his position somewhat: "I wrote Bellow telling him that although what counted—the portrait of a remarkable person becoming over decades even more remarkable—was intact, I believe that it was deformed by Atlas's querulous anger, if not by sanctimonious contempt, and that he and Janis would do well not to read it."* That said, Stern's main verdict was that Atlas had written a "fascinating and sometimes brilliant book."

Stern's mostly glowing notice of the Atlas book was pushing his luck, Rothwise, and yet all might have been well, still, if not for the following passage: "I've thought and talked about Bellow—and now this biography—with a few friends who know him," Stern wrote.

> One friend, a first-rate novelist, thinks Atlas not only misunderstands Bellow's radical independence but resents it. So he sees a politically correct Atlas piling up criticism along familiar—to Bellow critics—misogynist, conservative and racial lines. He thinks that Atlas is shocked by Bellow's anarchic "cocksmanship," and when I suggested that Bellow had a grand streak of bad boy, if not outlaw, in him, he found a different way to express his own view: "He's a transgressive monkey. And a great con man." He makes Bellow into a version of a favorite character of his own fiction, a brilliantly anarchic, half-crazed sexual adventurer.

Considering that blatant giveaway at the end, Roth's response was measured, really, albeit the more withering for that. He pointed out that Stern had mischaracterized his remarks in various ways, some more offensive than others. Roth hadn't, for example, said that Atlas was "shocked by Bellow's 'cocksmanship,'" but that Atlas was "envious of Saul's erotic freedom." He went on:

> It was, of course, Atlas and not Bellow . . . who I called "a little monkey" and "a con man." There's a certain mischief, is there not, in your getting that wrong? I'd like to chalk it up to a weak memory or to inattentiveness on your part, but you have made it difficult for me to be charitable by going out of your way to be sure that the identity of the "first-rate novel-

---

* Stern might have also wanted to deflect the Bellows from encountering such observations as this, on page 487 of Atlas: "it took [Bellow] years to forgive Richard Stern for his quip that Bellow had two hobbies: 'philosophy and fucking.'"

ist" and "friend" disparaging Bellow isn't too hard for a literate reader of *The Nation* to divine.

Stern later admitted to his wife, Alane Rollings, that his remarks in the Atlas review had indeed been mischievous, though at the time he seemed less than repentant. "Incidentally," he replied to Roth, "my 'tootsie' [Rollings], as you like to call her, wondered if I couldn't have disguised the 'friend' better by calling him 'a second-rate novelist'?"* Whereupon Roth didn't speak to him again for three years or more—a time when Stern cultivated a friendship with Sandy, in Chicago ("partly because he reminds me of Philip"); as for Roth himself, his ultimate view of the rift was magnanimous: "It was a stupid argument and I shouldn't have taken part in it."

While still in the outer darkness, Stern had written Jack Miles an email in which he reflected that their mutual friend had "a need to sep- arate from those he's 'devoured'"—i.e., used for his fiction in some more or less derogatory way—and Stern was relieved, at least, that such hadn't been his own fate (yet). Roth's old boon companion Alan Lelchuk was another matter, though Roth waited until things had cooled between them before lowering the boom. Critics had mostly savaged Lelchuk's first novel, *American Mischief*, and Roth, its midwife, was little other than consoling; he didn't mince words, however, when it came to the flaws he perceived as endemic to Lelchuk's work: "That superiority again," he wrote of a subsequent manuscript: "second-rate academics, so-called book reviews, pompous professors. All too easy. . . . Seriously, you had better watch out for the condescension in your heroes." And Roth's next critique betrayed an even more fraying patience: "Alan: NOTHING HAPPENS IN THIS BOOK, at least not in the first 100 pages. . . . And the sex is really the worst of all. It just means nothing, because NOTHING IS EVER AT STAKE FOR ANYONE. It's just cocks and cunts, boy: Porn!"

"I wrote about [Lelchuk] in a book," Roth admitted in 2012, "which

---

* Roth was certainly capable of the "tootsie" slur, but it wasn't a fair characterization of his attitude. As Stern himself admitted, when Roth first met the nineteen-year-old Rollings, in 1969, he'd been "totally open, welcoming, affectionate, approving" of her relationship with Stern. Roth and Rollings remained good friends, even after Stern's death in 2013.

he may or may not have read." Actually he wrote about Lelchuk in *two* books, and there was little confusion on his part as to whether Lelchuk had read them. "Correct me if I am wrong," Lelchuk had written him, after encountering the randy Baumgarten in *The Professor of Desire*, "but didn't we make an agreement or pact, some seven or eight years ago in a Yaddo study, that we would not write about each other's lives in fiction?" Kepesh, in the novel, considers Baumgarten "a parodied projection of myself," which was akin to how critics had come to view Lelchuk in relation to his mentor: "Lelchuk's enchantment with Philip Roth's aims and style is by now almost complete," wrote a *Kirkus* reviewer of Lelchuk's *Shrinking*, published the year after Roth's *Professor*. In the meantime Roth had hastened to reassure his friend about the composite Baumgarten: "There is no other colleague whose well-being and reputation I have ever concerned myself with more, and I don't think you have anything to worry about now, or ever, from me." The first part of this formulation was true enough, whereas the second was belied, six years later, by the Lelchukian Ivan Felt in *The Anatomy Lesson*—a "brash, presumptuous, overconfident, and ostentatious egotist," whose first novel "was as raw as Felt but, alas, only half as overbearing; Zuckerman's guess was that if he could get *all* that overbearing nature coursing through the prose, abandon his halfhearted objectivity and strange lingering respect for the great moral theme, Ivan Felt might yet become a real artist in the demonic, spiteful Céline line."

Over the next twenty years the friendship rotted and dropped off the vine. Then one day Betsy Pochoda phoned Roth about a vague rumor she'd heard that Lelchuk was writing a scabrous book about Roth's literary and sexual predations ("Everyone knows Philip wants to write books and screw women," said Pochoda; "more power to him"); the all-but-forgotten Lelchuk, it seemed, was even then shopping around for a publisher. "He doesn't need a publisher," Roth hooted, "he needs an English teacher." Roth would always insist he never bothered to read the roman à clef in question, *Ziff: A Life?* (2003), claiming total indifference—somewhat persuasively, in fact. Though naturally battered by the sustained character assassination of *Leaving a Doll's House*, a part of Roth really believed he had no right to object to his appearance in other people's work. He had an interesting exchange on this point, in 1998, with the German journalist Volker Hage:

HAGE: Have any friends of yours complained on finding themselves in
  your books?

ROTH: They're pleased as can be. Usually there's a line of people out
  there, saying "Do me, do me, do me next!"

HAGE: And how do you feel about being portrayed in a novel or in
  memoirs?

ROTH: Oh, I'm magnanimous.

Sometimes he was. Roth was portrayed unsympathetically in an early
draft of Alison Lurie's 1969 novel about Yaddo ("Illyria"), *Real People*,
and professed disappointment when she dropped the Roth-like character, Daniel Reck: "I couldn't care less about being maligned in literary works," he wrote her; "if I did I wouldn't have written my *own*
work. . . . The trouble was that the man, as you had conceived him, was
understood by the reader before he was even presented. . . . I am not just
a shit (when I am being one) but an interesting and intelligent shit. Reck
was dull and stupid, a malicious man without wit or intelligence." They
remained friends.

When Lelchuk worriedly offered to let him see the *Ziff* manuscript,
Roth replied with suave benignity that Lelchuk should just send a
bound galley when the time came. One can only guess what he would
have made of it. "One of the two or three most famous (serious) writers in the country," Lelchuk described Arthur Ziff, ex-"best pal" of the
washed-up narrator, Levitan, whom Ziff mercilessly lampoons in his
work ("a cartoonish distortion") but who now stands to get revenge as
Ziff's biographer. Hardly a work of demonic brilliance à la Céline, *Ziff*
nonetheless contains the odd aperçu: "Arthur Ziff was smart, shrewd,
self-protective, literary, and very clever. He also was vulnerable, blind,
narcissistic, missing in certain emotions, a man of rich paradoxes." *Ziff*
struck the critic Mark Shechner as a kind of latter-day *Henry IV*, "with
Ziff/Roth as Prince Hal and Levitan/Lelchuk as Falstaff. One moment
they are prowling the streets of Cambridge together, hot young men on
the make, and the next Prince Hal has grown up to be King Henry and
is no longer returning Falstaff's calls."

"As for the Gentileness of you and Joel [Conarroe] as Philipian survivors, that's intriguing," the estranged Stern wrote Miles in 2001. "I
think I prefer your 'diplomacy,' your loyalty, your intelligence and devo-

tion as criteria for executorship." Conarroe, in particular, had been a steadfast and essentially subordinate friend to Roth. During the seventies he'd acted as a good-natured procurer for Roth's Penn classes, then gladly promoted the work of both Roth *and* Roth's friends ("What's my next assignment, boss?" he wrote Roth, after making sure a friend's book was nominated for a major literary award in 1986) as a perennial member of prize juries. Conarroe accepted his role with stoic bemusement: "The conversation the other night," he wrote in an August 2000 diary entry, "—and I felt subtly put down 3 or 4 times—about Lieberman, Romania, Saint Simon's memoirs—made me feel remarkably superficial, what with my love of newspapers, magazines, tv shows, current books. One becomes an audience in Philip's blazing presence, occasionally throwing in a word or two but mostly without much presence."

Conarroe had trod safely for almost four decades—until suddenly, in 2003, his foot slipped on the tightrope between Roth and Roth's various bêtes noires. One of these was the poet Amiri Baraka, who'd been inducted into the Academy the same year Roth had received his Gold Medal (2001). A year later, Baraka was involved in a controversy over his poem "Somebody Blew Up America," which suggested Israel had known in advance about the 9/11 attacks:

> . . . *Who told 4000 Israeli workers at the Twin Towers*
> *To stay home that day*
> *Why did Sharon stay away?*
> *Who? Who? Who? . . .*

Apoplectic, Roth fired off a note to the Academy secretary: "'Who made the credit cards' is still my favorite line," he wrote her. "Which is yours?

> Who murdered the English language
> ~~Who the worst poet in America~~
> Who, who, who
> And who the idiot who nominated this jerk. Please let me know.

As Roth was shortly informed, Baraka had been proposed for membership by Francine du Plessix Gray ("She gets everything right").

It so happened the theme of "Somebody Blew Up America" was a well-worn aspect of Baraka's work. As an Anti-Defamation League report pointed out, his 1967 poem "Black People!" had suggested that merchandise in Jewish-owned stores such as Klein's and Hahne's could be had with the magic words, "Up against the wall, mother fucker, this is a stick up!" Lest one think this is so much abstract satire, Baraka (formerly known as LeRoi Jones, whose play *Dutchman* Roth had savaged in a 1964 issue of the *New York Review*) had been arrested during the 1967 Newark riots for carrying an illegal weapon and inciting to riot.* "A whole business is going down the drain because of that son of a bitch LeRoi Jones," says the Swede's obstreperous father in *American Pastoral*, "that Peek-A-Boo-Boopy-Do, whatever the hell he calls himself in that goddamn hat." Later Baraka was careful to make a distinction between Judaism and Zionism ("It is Zionists who control Israel and have the most influence now in the Jewish bourgeoisie"), though, to be sure, he wasn't advocating the robbery of Zionists per se in "Black People!"

Baraka was appointed Poet Laureate of New Jersey in 2002, a position the legislature proposed to abolish a few months later, in light of the outrage over "Somebody Blew Up America." Conarroe, as president of PEN America, had co-signed a protest letter written largely at the behest of K. Anthony Appiah, chairman of the PEN Freedom to Write Committee, advising the legislature that they stood to violate the First Amendment: "We are troubled by any controversy that focuses on a few short passages extracted from a much longer piece of literature and fails to acknowledge fully the context of the passages within the work or the context of the work within the traditions and conventions of the art." When other PEN members proposed to publish the same letter in *The New York Review of Books*, Conarroe balked; after talking things over with Roth, he explained his misgivings to PEN: "I'm bothered by the phrase 'a few short passages,' as if there's very little here, after all, to object to, and also by the idea of calling the diatribe a piece of 'literature,' which it's not, and to referring to the tradition and conventions of 'the art,' as if this unspeakable outburst had anything to do with art. Is 'Protocols of Zion' a work of art?" The next day Conarroe conclusively refused to sign a public letter in the *New York Review*.

---

* He was ultimately acquitted, as I mention on page 589.

Within a week, Roth somehow got word that his friend's signature had, in fact, been on the original letter to the legislature supporting "a ranting, demagogic, anti-Semitic liar," as Roth considered Baraka, "and a ridiculously untalented poet to boot"; furious that Conarroe had failed to mention his previous defense "of this cocksucker," he left a ranting message on Conarroe's answering machine, followed by a FedEx letter accusing him of deception: "My friends don't lie to me on serious issues nor do they deliberately withhold information that is vital to understanding their predicament when they ask for my assistance." "You seem to be angry about a lot of things (and people) these days," replied Conarroe, whose sweetness did, after all, have a limit. "Did I lie and say I hadn't signed? Bullshit. I called on an old friend for advice because . . . I thought the letter to be published in NYRB was to be a different letter, one that would newly state PEN's position, and not the one sent to NJ, and that I would be able to make changes that would reflect my own second thoughts." Such was Roth's lingering pique, however, that he had Wylie (or rather an employee in Wylie's office) return Conarroe's letter unopened.

When Conarroe made no further effort to explain, the better angel of Roth's nature finally asserted itself. Two months later he wrote Conarroe that he was to receive an honorary degree from Penn in May: "I'd like you to be there. It doesn't make any sense if you're not. Can we excise the month of March—or was it February?—from our long history as friends?" Conarroe replied that he certainly wouldn't miss "the canonization of [his] old Penn pal," and the following year he put up $50,000 of his own money to sponsor volume 1 of the Library of America Philip Roth edition.

■ ■ ■ ■

ANDREW WYLIE MADE a point of hiring Harvard graduates, and one of these, Lisa Halliday, caught Roth's eye when he visited the Midtown office in the spring of 2002. Soon enough the two found themselves in an elevator together (Halliday later told him she'd timed her departure to coincide with his), and Roth asked her to lunch at the Bagel Baron on West Fifty-seventh Street, where the young woman, an aspiring writer, produced "not just perfect sentences," he recalled, but "perfect paragraph after perfect paragraph" in the course of answering his questions about her (surprisingly working-class) origins. "Are you game?" Roth inquired as they were leaving, and she gave him a playful nod. Lori Monson, his physical therapist, was in the same building as Wylie, and subsequently Roth asked Halliday to pick up some paperwork for him there and bring it to his apartment on the Upper West Side. "Very smooth," Halliday remembered.

As it happened, Halliday lived just two blocks away from Roth—on West Eightieth, between Amsterdam and Broadway—and during the larky affair that followed, Roth's apartment became a kind of second home to her (he tended to see Susan Rogers more in the country); either she or Roth would pick up dinner at Zabar's, eat it *chez* Roth, go to bed, then watch baseball (Halliday, from the Boston suburbs, was a big Red Sox fan). Roth remembered with special pleasure ("charming, charming, charming") the time Halliday breezily pantomimed, atop his bed, a famous scene from Chaplin's *Modern Times*. During one of their rare excursions outside Roth's apartment—for a concert at Carnegie Hall—they were accosted by a street photographer: "No," Roth replied to the man's overture, "we'll pay you *not* to have it taken."

Around this time Roth also made the acquaintance of the actress Nicole Kidman, who'd been cast as Faunia Farley in *The Human Stain*. She and Roth had a divorce lawyer in common, Bill Beslow, who mentioned to Roth that she wanted to chat about Faunia over the phone. Roth advised her to go to a battered women's shelter and talk to the most intelligent woman there, then suggested they discuss things further over dinner in New York. Roth's "one and only hangout" in the city then was Russian Samovar, on West Fifty-second Street, where he was always ebulliently greeted by the owner, Roman Kaplan. "Hello, beautiful," said Kaplan, when Kidman arrived on Roth's arm, and the waitresses skittered across the street to buy disposable cameras at Rexall's.* The night was a success: Roth and Kidman "hit it off," he remembered, and on the sidewalk afterward pedestrians erupted, *"Nicole! . . . Nicole!"*

The Human Stain was shot mostly in Montreal, but in May the production moved to Williams College in the Berkshires, within easy driving distance of Warren, and over Memorial Day weekend Roth paid a visit to the set. "I hate to say this in front of Nicole," he said, after watching

---

* A photo from that night—Kaplan, Kidman, Roth—is easily found online.

a concert scene with Kidman and Anthony Hopkins (as Coleman Silk); Kidman bit her nails while Roth "paused for effect" (according to a *Times* reporter who wrote about Roth's visit). Finally he went on: "But what she did was terrific. You could see what was happening inside her head when all she did was go to touch this guy and then decide against it."

Until he'd met Kidman, Roth had shown little interest in the production. "You'll have only one problem with me," he told producer Tom Rosenberg of Lakeshore Entertainment, when they first met for lunch at the West Street Grill. "If the check doesn't clear." For his part Rosenberg was nervous about doing justice to what he considered "the great American novel"; the day he received the screenplay he could hardly bring himself to open the envelope, but was soon reassured that Nicholas Meyer (*The Seven-Per-Cent Solution*) had pulled it off. As for Roth, he considered the script "horrendously bad" and could barely force himself to sit through a rough-cut screening for his sole benefit. *"Oh no!"* he'd cry out in the projection room, or *"Good god!"* Afterward he had lunch with Rosenberg and the director, Robert Benton (*Kramer vs. Kramer*). "What were you guys *thinking* about?" he said to the stunned pair, who tried to explain that important stuff from his novel had to be jettisoned for the sake of filmic economy. Roth insisted they put in "the most important scene" in the book—when Coleman tells Faunia he's black—which, Roth tartly remarked, may mean cutting a few seconds from one of their jogging scenes (meant to indicate "male bonding" between Silk and Zuckerman). When they agreed to shoot the extra scene, Roth phoned Kidman and coached her on how to say the key line ("You think you're telling me something I don't know?"): "Just throw it away! His life's secret!" Roth never saw the final movie, but Kidman informed him they'd cut her line and rendered the scene nonsensical.*

Roth claimed his friendship with Kidman had petered out after a few phone calls, but a reliable source said there was at least one more abortive

---

* In his *New York Times* review, A. O. Scott pretty much nailed it when he described *The Human Stain* as "an honorable B+ term paper of a movie: sober, scrupulous and earnestly respectful of its literary source." He particularly questioned the casting of Wentworth Miller as the young Coleman, since the actor resembled neither his older self (Hopkins) nor the other Silks, putting Scott in mind of Steve Martin as the adopted son of black sharecroppers in *The Jerk*.

date. Roth, who'd excitedly hired a limo for the evening, arrived at Kidman's hotel and was taken aback when she came down to the lobby with a puzzled look, dressed in jeans. Apologetically she explained that she thought their date was for the next night, and offered to join him in the hotel bar for a glass of wine or something. Roth, however, was furious and left in a huff. Later a friend of his met Kidman and mentioned Roth. "Tell him to grow up," the actress replied.

THE BENEFIT OF ROTH'S PREVIOUS BACK SURGERY, IN March 2002, began to wear off a year or so later, and soon he was in terrible pain again. Making matters worse, as always, was his inability to get another novel started after he'd finished *The Plot Against America* in early 2004. His "physical predicament," he said, "was not conducive to the spontaneous overflow of powerful feelings and emotion recollected in tranquility"—or, as he told Ross Miller during a taped interview that summer, "I'm in a fucking rut in my life. Everything."

These days Roth often spoke in a slurred mumble because he was taking four to six Vicodin a day, along with Klonopin to steady his nerves and Ambien to help him sleep; the last had the unfortunate effect of causing random words and images to scroll along the inside of his eyelids. Looking back, Susan Rogers wondered "how much of his self-involvement, his unawareness, a lot of what he'd say or do that was mean, was part of his medical situation." To be sure, she'd sometimes encourage Roth to take a Vicodin to lift his spirits, since the alternative was a melancholy man in agonizing pain. But there were drawbacks as well to the playful, euphoric Roth, who sustained himself with drugs during a jolly trip to the Jersey Shore with Rogers: "How did *you* get here?" he kept asking her over dinner one night. "I guess someone had to be here. It might as well be you." The point of the shtick, hardly lost on Rogers, was that theirs was a more or less random connection, versus a romantic one vis-à-vis Margot and her ilk. "He thought he was being funny," said Rogers; "it just made me feel like crap."

Getting off such high doses of opioids was problematic, even for so iron-willed a person as Roth. Once, he tried quitting his medications cold turkey; since he couldn't bear being alone during such an ordeal, he persuaded Rogers to stay in Connecticut and keep him company for a weekend. "Nothing was okay," she recalled, "nothing was right: He felt abandoned, despairing." She'd start to put her arms around the trembling man but he didn't want to be touched, nor spoken to when she tried verbal reassurance. Rogers wanted to phone for an ambulance, but he'd insisted everything had to remain a secret. When she could leave, at last, she drove to a friend's house and collapsed sobbing.

One night, with Ross Miller, the couple attended a swank party on the Upper East Side, but Roth was taken ill and went home early. Miller walked with the barefoot (because of her heels) Rogers back to her room at the Athletic Club, and while they wended their way around the park she vented her frustrations as a caretaker. Miller, after all, was the only person she could talk to; none of her friends knew anything about the affair, and surely Miller of all people (so she figured) could relate to her predicament. Afterward Rogers received a note from Roth: "Ross tells me you're not 'cut out' for this," it began, proposing they take a long and perhaps permanent break from each other.

According to Rogers's journal, Roth got back in touch two months later—on May 8, 2004—and could hardly have been more charming. He invited her to come to Warren for dinner in a couple of weeks, when he'd give her back the clothing she'd left at his house. ("So on the one hand he's being flirtatious," she mused, "and on the other he's sending me back my clothes. A strange call.") She felt very nervous on arrival— she remembered her legs shaking—even before she spotted the weary apparition hobbling toward her from his studio. Roth wrapped his arms around her and began to sob: "Every time I came out to the house," he said, in effect, "I would walk around and say 'Susie's dead. Susie's not here, she must be dead.'"

For a few unsettling months they were a couple again, though Rogers was looking forward to spending six weeks in Antarctica, beginning in December, on a quirky, prestigious National Science Foundation grant for writers and artists (Roth and Leon Botstein had put her up for it). Since Roth didn't do email, they agreed Miller would be the conduit for both her personal, Roth-specific letters as well as her "Dear Family and Friends" bulletins. Roth received a few of the latter—via Conarroe—but nothing otherwise, and came to suspect Rogers was distracted by another affair, especially after Conarroe sent him an article from a gay magazine "suggesting that Antarctica was the lesbian capital of the world," as Roth put it, "kind of a continental Provincetown with penguins."

When Rogers returned, at the end of January 2005, Roth was in the grip of a monthlong flu and decidedly poor company, at least where Rogers was concerned. He didn't wait up for her late-night arrival in the city, and the next morning (after she'd slept in the adjacent apartment, which Roth had recently bought to combine with his one-bedroom unit) she reported to her host's sickbed and made desultory, one-sided conversation for less than an hour before catching a train back to Bard ("I was awful," she admitted, laughing). A few days later he called her: "What's the hardest part about being back?" he asked, and she replied, "The fact that it's impossible to talk to you." "Yeah," he said, and hung up.

After a month of silence, Rogers wrote him a semicontrite letter. She was "stunned" and "deeply sad" that things were ending this way, though she had to admit she'd never quite been able to believe Roth loved her: "Too often I felt that your need for me came before the love and with that need came a searing hatred—not necessarily of me, but of relying on anyone—as well as a deep gratefulness. I felt both and this clouded my understanding. . . . If there is anger on your part I hope it subsides with time and that some day we'll be able to move toward a friendship." There was, in fact, plenty of anger. Roth wondered how she could have doubted his love after he'd dedicated his book to her and "kissed [her] in plain view of everyone" at the National Book Awards because he wanted the world to know about them.

> None of that felt to you like love. You didn't know I loved you when I said I wanted to give you a hundred thousand dollars to get you out of your tight financial straits? You didn't know I loved you when I watched you trying on clothes at Assets and at Searles? You didn't know I loved you when I got you a car? You didn't know I loved you when I offered you the money to pay off the mortgage to your house? . . . Did you not even know that I loved you when I said that I loved you?
>
> Don't bother to answer. You never knew. You never "quite got it."

Nor were sorrows coming single spies for Roth. Now that Rogers was out of the picture, he thought it time to deepen his dalliance with Halliday—who, however, was even then falling in love with a nice young man in Europe, Theo, whom she'd freely discussed with Roth in the past, since he'd always given her the impression that such compartmentalization was only seemly. Then, early that summer, she sold a long story ("Stump Louie") to *The Paris Review*, and naturally lost no time reporting the news to Roth, who seemed not altogether pleasantly surprised. "This Theo," he said, over dinner a night or two later. "Is this a romantic relationship?" "Yes," she replied, wondering at his unwonted dismay. That fall she made arrangements to leave the Wylie Agency so she could devote herself to writing, and, soon after, she received a letter from a law office in Massachusetts, not far from where her grandfather lived. An anonymous benefactor wanted to pay her a monthly stipend of two thousand dollars, the letter said, provided she agree to remain in New York and not get married and so on. "This is you, right?" she asked Roth over the phone. At first he denied it, but finally said, "Okay, it's me." Politely but firmly she refused the money, and Roth, furious, stopped speaking to her for as long as it took (nearly a year) to admit she'd been right.

■ ■ ■ ■

HIS WRITING CAREER, at least, was better than ever. Two weeks before publication on October 5, 2004, *The Plot Against America* was already "barreling up the best-seller list," according to Frank Rich, who noted in the *Times* that the great novelist's latest was "sandwiched between Clay Aiken's memoir and *The South Beach Diet*" on Amazon's Top 25. One reason the larger public had "pick[ed] up the scent," Rich thought, was that Roth's dystopian account of a Lindbergh presidency was in fact an exigent allegory for the latter-day debacle of George W. Bush's misrule: "The other war, which politicians of all stripes want to pretend is a war on a tactic (terrorism) and not about religion, is, as everyone else seems to know, being fought against a bastardized form of Islam. Not unlike Jews in the 1930's, the innocent American practitioners of that creed are aliens to many in the heartland of just folks."

Four days before, also in the *Times*, Roth (who privately asserted that Bush was "the devil") had preemptively disavowed such a reading. His only aim, he wrote, was to reconstruct the Lindbergh era with the utmost verisimilitude; however:

Kafka's books played a strong role in the imagination of the Czech writers who were opposing the Russians' puppet government in Communist Czechoslovakia in the 1960's and 1970's, a phenomenon that alarmed the government and caused it to prohibit the sale and discussion of his books and to remove them from the library shelves. . . . [Bush] has merely reaffirmed for me the maxim that informed the writing of all these books and that makes our lives as Americans as precarious as anyone else's: all the assurances are provisional, even here in a 200-year-old democracy.

Roth, in short, denied the validity of an allegorical reading at the very moment he seemed to invite it.

Reviewing Roth's "terrific political novel" for the Sunday *Times*, Paul Berman likewise found Kafkaesque parallels in the "sinister, vivid, dreamlike, preposterous and, at the same time, creepily plausible" world that Roth evoked with such punctilious adherence to the trappings of the era—"as if, in constructing an imaginary fascist America under President Lindbergh, Roth has erected a giant and enigmatic symbol, whose meaning he will not define." Hardly for the first time, the *Book Review* verdict was contra Kakutani, who found the book "provocative but lumpy" given the awkward juxtaposition of the "psychologically vivid" Roth family with a "political landscape that remains cartoony in the extreme." Some readers, however, found the real-life political personages in the novel vivid enough in their own right—uncomfortably so in the case of Lindbergh's vice president, Senator Burton K. Wheeler of Montana, whom Roth portrayed as an actual fascist who declares martial law after Lindbergh's disappearance, rounding up prominent Jews as warmongering enemies of the state. Roth insisted he hadn't made Wheeler et al. "behave implausibly" at any point—explaining the historical underpinnings of his story and its characters in a twenty-seven-page "Postscript"—but the executive director of the Wheeler Center at Montana State University, Gordon G. Brittan Jr., disagreed; appalled by Roth's account, he pointed out in a letter to Arthur Schlesinger that Wheeler's America First sympathies were based on his pacifist Quaker roots, and certainly had nothing to do with anti-Semitism or a fondness for Hitler. The great historian begged to differ, referring in his reply to a dinner party held at the home of Rexford Tugwell, a member of FDR's "brain trust," on February 1, 1935 ("described on pp 141–2 of my third volume in the Age of Roosevelt"), when Wheeler emphatically favored "German domination of all Europe, our domination of the Americas, and Japanese domination of the Far East," and ominously predicted, "We shall soon be shooting up people here, like Hitler does." "I think the Tugwell dinner vindicates Philip Roth's portrait of Senator Wheeler," Schlesinger concluded.

As for the violent anti-Semitism unleashed by a Lindbergh presidency, Roth was right to imagine America's "first large-scale pogrom" as taking place in Detroit, where Henry Ford had stoked Jew hatred for decades with the help of Father Coughlin and "the dean of anti-Semites," Reverend Gerald L. K. Smith ("Christian character is the true basis of real Americanism"), whose headquarters were congenially located there. And well before the city's thirty thousand Jews flee across the Detroit River to Canada, Roth has scrupulously—over the course of 250 pages—depicted the insidious process whereby his "outgoing, hospitable" family become terrorized exiles in their own country. "Don't invent, just remember," Roth told himself whenever he got stuck—that is, *pretend* to remember what might have happened in the context of what did. "Compare Lincoln to Lindbergh? Boy oh boy," the fictional Herman Roth moans on the Washington Mall, whereupon a dapper stranger refers other sightseers to the "loudmouth Jew" in their midst, while an elderly woman declares, "I'd give anything to slap his face." "It was the most beautiful panorama I'd ever seen," the narrator ("Philip") muses of the mall, "a patriotic paradise, the American Garden of Eden spread before us, and we stood huddled together there, the family expelled."

The widespread persecution of Jews, under Lindbergh, is assisted by not only good men who do nothing but Jews who actively collude. A likely model for the odious Lindberghite Rabbi Lionel Bengelsdorf was the leader of Newark's Temple B'nai Jeshurun congregation, Solomon Foster,* who believed, even after Kristallnacht, that American Jews should refrain from public protest over perceived discrimination in their own country: "It is untrue, unwise and unnecessary to suggest that the Jewish people in the United States require special safeguards to

---

* An affinity is suggested, in the novel, when Foster presides over Bengelsdorf's wedding.

our economic and political rights." Opposing such views was Joachim Prinz of B'nai Abraham, whose daughter, Lucie, wrote Roth an appreciative note about her father's heroic cameo in *Plot*. Roth replied, "Your father seemed to me the right person to resist Rabbi Bengelsdorf in my book because I think it's just what he would have done in reality." It was Prinz, after all, who'd predicted the Holocaust in his Rosh Hashanah eve sermon of 1939: because the iniquity of the Nazi regime hadn't been recognized in time, he said, the casualties of war would likely include millions of Jews. "But how will this cruel fate that has befallen [German Jews] in their own land be alleviated by our great country going to war with their tormentors?" Bengelsdorf declaims to a pre-election Lindbergh rally at Madison Square Garden. "If anything, the predicament of *all* of Germany's Jews would only worsen immeasurably—worsen, I fear, tragically." As the fictional cousin Alvin remarks to Herman Roth, Bengelsdorf thus ensures a Lindbergh victory, by giving the goyim "permission" to vote for an anti-Semite who will keep them out of war.

Lindbergh's innocuous-sounding "Just Folks" program "encouraging America's religious and national minorities to become further incorporated into the larger society"—while mostly focusing on a single minority, Jews—also had its basis in real history, namely the long-held jingoistic grievance that Jews undermine the American "melting pot" by forming insular settlements and stubbornly clinging to "foreign" customs and observances. "The Jews of America can participate fully in the national life of their country," says Bengelsdorf, who directs the Office of American Absorption in New Jersey. "They need no longer dwell apart, a pariah community separated from the rest." (This while dining, *chez* Roth, in the pariah community of Weequahic.) "And this is not merely a dream of mine; it is the dream of President Lindbergh." Sandy Roth is won over to Lindbergh's dream when he's sent to live with a gentile farming clan in Kentucky, whither the Wishnows will also be sent under the auspices of "Just Folks," until Seldon's mother is savagely murdered by a mob of rioting Klansmen.*

---

* Roth didn't know that Mrs. Wishnow was going to die until he approached the end of the book. To deepen the impact, he subsequently added an earlier scene in which she patiently talks little Philip through the ordeal of having locked himself in the Wishnows' bathroom, and comforts the sobbing child afterward.

"The child's eye degeneralizes the general," Roth wrote in his notes, while wrestling with the challenge of dramatizing history on an intimate scale. "The way he focuses on details, it's genuine, it connects the tragic to the trivial. History in the living room." Originally Roth had tried writing the "far *in*" sections of the novel from his own seven-year-old perspective, but needed the richer diction of an adult voice—thus the narrator became an adult looking back on harrowing early experiences, with little reference to his subsequent adulthood or much historical perspective, period, beyond 1942.* Roth's solution resulted in a tone that Paul Berman described as "marvelously ruminative and sorrowful—the tone of a saddened older man recalling his own childhood." Moreover it was Roth's intention that the reader should not be distracted from so momentous a tale by a conspicuous prose style ("relax the language," he wrote in his notes), and hence the story ends with little Philip reflecting quite plainly on his tragic roommate, Seldon ("shattered by the malicious indignities of Lindbergh's America"), whose predecessor was another victim, Alvin, with his mangled stump: "There was no stump for me to care for this time. The boy himself was the stump, and until he was taken to live with his mother's married sister in Brooklyn ten months later, I was the prosthesis." Of course, in its strict avoidance of irony, operatic ridicule/denunciation, or other uproarious extremes of the Rothian register, the novel has a flatness that verges at times on banality. "At his best he is now a novelist of authentically tragic scope," wrote J. M. Coetzee, having noted such a deficiency in *The New York Review of Books*; "at his very best he reaches Shakespearean heights. By the standard set by *Sabbath's Theater*, *The Plot Against America* is not a major work."

But what diminished the novel somewhat as art—a schematic but compelling plot; stylized characters; unembellished prose—arguably made it all the more palatable to the general public. With some astonishment, Dwight Garner of the *Times Book Review* noted its appearance at number 6 on the Fiction best-seller list for the week of October 17—the first Roth novel to appear ("SAY IT AIN'T SO") since *The Counterlife*

---

* With occasional exceptions: Little Philip, a stamp collector, notes that Booker T. Washington is the first Negro to appear on an American stamp, and wonders whether a Jew will ever enjoy such a distinction. "In fact, another twenty-six years had to pass," the narrator remarks, "and it took Einstein to do it."

fluttered briefly around the list's nether region (*Patrimony* did the same as Nonfiction in 1991). The following week Roth's book was number 2—behind Stephen King's *Dark Tower*—and it was still number 10 as late as December. *Plot* went on to win the W. H. Smith Award for best book in the United Kingdom (making Roth the first writer to win the prize twice), as well as the Society of American Historians' James Fenimore Cooper Prize for the outstanding historical novel on an American theme.

Garner also reported that Roth was "poking his head out of his shell a bit more" these days: Though he refused to go on book tours, Roth was happy to sit in a New York studio and do radio interviews, albeit a bit less happy ("you feel like a goofball") appearing on TV; he seemed uneasy when Katie Couric of *Today* persisted in wondering why he wrote so many books: "I write them because I don't know how else to spend the day," he replied at last, sincerely enough. A *Newsday* journalist seemed rather surprised to find Roth "a very nice man" in person, cooperative and polite, though a certain line of inquiry would always get his hackles up. When a *Guardian* interviewer referred to *Plot* as his "great Jewish history," Roth's rebuke was swift: "It's my most *American* book," he said. "You would never tell Ralph Ellison that *Invisible Man* is his most Negro book, would you?" When the cowed man remarked that Roth was "extremely difficult" to interview, Roth laughed. "I wasn't put on this earth to make your life easy."

Roth's stipulations were clear: interview questions were "to be restricted to professional life, books published, literature and other writers, background (family, education, Newark). No questions on marriages, divorces, personal finances, current politics." With regard to that last verboten subject, Roth insisted he was "just a citizen like anybody else" and so disinclined to impose his irrelevant opinions on the public. And yet, in the wake of his American Trilogy and *The Plot Against America*, Roth was beginning to strike readers as a leading authority on our political life—what with his keen ear for the rhetoric of demagoguery, his insight into the way the electorate is manipulated by simple messages and hoked-up threats to national security. Finally, twelve years after *Plot*, with the election of Donald J. Trump, Roth would seem a bona fide prophet. Both his fictional Lindbergh and the forty-fifth president, after all, had stoked nativist bigotry while expressing admiration for murderous dictators, to whom each man seemed vaguely or not so vaguely beholden via some sinister form of *kompromat*.

Roth's everyday politics were roughly that of the *New York Times* editorial page, but in figuring out the intricate "geometry" (as Flaubert would have it) of a given novel, Roth attained a brand of "wisdom" as he saw it: "There's a knowledge that the writing produces that is not your knowledge," he said. "It's produced by the demands of the narrative." As a reality-TV celebrity rose to become the Republican nominee, then the president, pundits were increasingly apt to cite *Plot* as the book that "best explain[s] or illuminate[s] the political situation," as the French intellectual Bernard-Henri Lévy, for one, noted in the *Times* a few weeks prior to Trump's inauguration. Meanwhile Roth's old dismay over the presidencies of Nixon and Bush (much less Eisenhower) began to seem quaint: "neither was anything like as humanly impoverished as Trump is," he told *The New Yorker*: "ignorant of government, of history, of science, of philosophy, of art, incapable of expressing or recognizing subtlety or nuance, destitute of all decency, and wielding a vocabulary of seventy-seven words that is better called Jerkish than English." For the rest of his life, Roth never missed a chance to publicize his revulsion on the subject. "I'm eagerly awaiting my White House tweet," he liked to say.

∎ ∎ ∎ ∎

NOW THAT ROTH'S STATUS as our greatest living novelist was all but proverbial (amid the usual robust dissent), the editors of the canonical Library of America decided it was time for a definitive edition of Roth's work—making him only the third living writer to enjoy that distinction, after Eudora Welty in 1998 and Bellow in 2003; Welty and Bellow, however, had been ninety and eighty-eight respectively, and Welty had since died and Bellow was soon to die. Roth, at seventy-two, was "still reinventing himself," as the *Times* put it, and was energetic enough to collaborate actively with the project. "It's like being able to talk to Henry James about *The Portrait of a Lady*," said publisher Max Rudin.* James, in fact, was the only writer with more volumes in the series—fourteen

---

* Roth occasionally visited the LOA's offices. "Don't I recognize you from one of our book jackets?" asked one of the more puckish editors, bumping into Roth in the men's room. "Yes," Roth replied, "I'm Louisa May Alcott."

to Roth's ultimate ten—and, with James's New York Edition in mind, Rudin asked Roth whether he'd be willing to write special prefaces for each volume. Roth declined, and when Rudin suggested that Nathan Zuckerman write them instead, Roth didn't deign to reply.

Roth's first choice to edit his Library of America edition was his fastidious copy editor, Roslyn Schloss; the LOA, however, preferred an academic for the job, so Roth proposed Ross Miller, who certainly knew Roth's work inside and out, and was often impressive in discussion, though his previous labors in this line weren't altogether reassuring. Roth had been dissatisfied with the moralistic tone of his publisher's reading guide for *The Dying Animal* ("What do you think of the age difference between Consuela and the Monster?" he paraphrased a typical question), and asked Miller to write it instead. "These are *awful*!" he said of Miller's questions, which, as Rogers recalled, were on the pretentious "lit-scholar" side. ("I wouldn't myself know how to begin to answer half these questions, nor would I even try," Roth complained about his paperback publisher's *Sabbath's Theater* guide. "They smell of the unworldly classroom. Existential odyssey. Homer, Dante, Virgil. Spare poor Sabbath the highbrowism.") After loudly denouncing Miller's work during a long walk with Rogers, Roth returned to his studio and wrote the thing himself. "Why is Kepesh's description of Consuela's vulva so detailed?" he asked the reader, and also wondered why "emancipated manhood" (as Kepesh would have it) lacks social status: "If Kepesh were gay or female, would that alter your response to the book?"

For the Library of America, a volume editor's duties entail writing an appendix of Notes on the Texts, as well as a ten-thousand-word Chronology of the author's life. The latter, in Roth's case, was composed by Roth himself, originally for a special tribute issue of the Swiss magazine *Du*, though the "Chronik von Leben und Werk" was credited to Ross Miller—in both its German and LOA/English versions—so Roth could avoid the appearance of a self-serving motive. He also took it upon himself to update the Chronology in subsequent volumes, and wrote almost every word of his jacket copy ("It wasn't that Ross couldn't do it; I could do it better").

He also might have thought he could take a strong hand in writing his own biography, especially with his best friend at least nominally at the helm. When approached in 2000 (via Conarroe) by another would-be biographer, Roth had replied that he wouldn't want one "even if it was Boswell"; Ross Miller, however, was another matter. As Roth would later sheepishly explain, he thought Miller had "mature[d] a good deal" in the seven years since he'd written that ribald book proposal Roth had so vehemently rejected. As ever, too, Roth worried he might die at any time, in which case Bloom's version of his character would stand forever. Miller, of all people, knew the other side of the story.

On May 4, 2004, Roth's publisher issued a press release alerting the world to Houghton's acquisition of *two* books by Ross Miller: a "full-scale biography of Philip Roth" and *Free at Last: Why the Jews Discovered America*, about "the historical circumstances of the Jewish immigration to the U. S." Miller's book proposal for the biography, this time, had been in the more sober form of his *Du* chronology (that is to say, Roth's *Du* chronology). Lisa Halliday was still at the Wylie Agency when the deal was struck for a biography, and while preparing some of its paperwork she felt a distinct sense of foreboding: "I just thought, 'There's only so much you can control.'" That summer Miller gave an extended interview to the *St. Petersburg Times*, likening his book about Roth to Boswell's *Life of Johnson*, with two key differences: (1) "Boswell had to wait till Johnson died," and (2) "I'm not in this biography. I will not appear in this book." The second point seemed plausible given that Miller's friendship with his subject was strictly "intellectual," or so he claimed ("We don't go bowling together. . . . [I]t's all business")—that, indeed, he was more of an "editor" to the novelist: "You have a great heavyweight fighter and they need a trainer, or a great pianist and they need a coach. That's really the sort of relationship. This is a fragile thing we have. We're on a tightrope."

Finally, on the fraught topic of Roth and the Nobel Prize, Miller had this to say: "He's been on the short list of two or three at least a few times. It's inevitable. . . . His feeling is, let's get it over with." Roth's "furious" response to Miller, as he recalled, went something like this: "Why did you say that? It isn't so! . . . If I had the minutest chance you can be sure you killed whatever minute chance I had of getting it. Luckily I don't give a shit. But why do you say things that aren't true?" "No mas," Miller replied.

∎ ∎ ∎ ∎

WHEN ROTH RECEIVED an honorary degree from Harvard in 2003, he, Miller, and Rogers took the Bellows out to dinner at the Ritz-Carlton; Saul seemed frail and depressed that night, so Roth and Miller sat on either side of him, trying to cheer him up. Bellow's final novel, *Ravelstein* (2000)—a roman à clef about his friendship with fellow Committee member Allan Bloom—had seemed weak to Roth, but he forbore to write a frank critique and simply said he was "out of sympathy" with the hero and therefore an unfit reader. Four years later, the only novel Bellow wanted to read was *The Plot Against America*—"Where's the book?" he'd call to Janis, who knew which one he meant—opening at any page and reading as if for the first time. "I've been thinking about Lindbergh," he said to Roth very near the end. "He always moves away from my unclean presence." Roth cherished these rare glimpses of lucidity. Janis always knew when Roth was on the phone, because she'd hear her husband laughing in his old way—throwing his head back—after Roth had treated him to some "delicious" joke. And Roth kept calling even after Bellow was too confused to know who he was; once Bellow responded with a voice "so old, so dead," that Roth burst into tears. "Do you want to speak to your sister?" Bellow said (meaning Janis) the last time Roth called.

When Bellow died on April 5, 2005, Roth was in the midst of a grinding siege of back pain (he'd scheduled another surgery for the following month). Still, he managed the flight to Boston, with Wylie, then a three-hour drive from Bellow's house in Brookline to his burial site in Brattleboro, Vermont. Bellow had wanted to be buried with traditional Jewish rites, so the service was in Hebrew, with no eulogies, and later the mourners took turns shoveling dirt into the grave. By then Roth was almost crazed with pain, and had to walk back and forth to a bench some fifty feet from the grave site—"like a kind of brooding Hamlet," Bellow's son Greg observed in his memoir, *Saul Bellow's Heart*, "[Roth] wandered the edges of the funeral in deep thought." Greg also mentioned that his own final graveside words were quoted in Roth's *Everyman*—" 'Sleep easy, Pop' "—but declined to include what followed: "any note of tenderness, grief, love, or loss was terrifyingly absent from his voice."

Shortly after the funeral, Roth reported to Solotaroff that Bellow's middle son, Adam, "was the most visibly wracked, perhaps because his feelings about Saul are the most twisted"; within a few months, however, he decided that both older sons (he liked the youngest, Daniel) were "shallow shits." Adam had lost his good opinion by writing a *New York Times* op-ed about his neglectful father ("Missing: My Father") for what would have been Saul's ninetieth birthday: "We had no family occasions," Adam wrote. "He just sat up there like Wotan on his mountain, in Vermont, or in his aerie overlooking Lake Michigan, and I made pilgrimages by bus or car or plane." "I wonder if this is the first of a series to be published in your paper by the neglected children of divorce," Roth wrote in a rebuttal he never sent.

> If this is the case, you will have millions of submissions from aggrieved adults like Mr. Bellow to choose from, and I assume that after you have finished with the children of dead Nobel Prize winners you will lend space on your Op Ed page to the similarly neglected fifty- and sixty-year-old children of dead taxi drivers, dead plumbers, dead prize fighters, dead neurosurgeons, dead military personnel, etc.
>
> They too have a right for their lamentations to be gullibly taken at face value once the imperfect parent is unable to challenge the justness of possible simplifications, fabrications, and self-serving distortions of the truth.

This was mild next to what Roth thought about Greg's book, *Saul Bellow's Heart*, published in 2013: "The unworldliness, the lack of imagination, the terrible prose, the monomania, the vindictive spirit seasoned with self-congratulatory expressions of forgiveness and love," he wrote a friend, "—none of this makes this book easy reading. I think the book is an example of what is beautifully called 'pissing on the grave.'" Roth had always referred to Greg as Schmucko, and in the margins of Greg's memoir he scribbled a running commentary of "Oy" and suchlike glosses, until he wrote "I quit" on page 35; but he didn't quit: "He was being ironic, schmuck," Roth riposted on page 211, next to where Greg interprets his father's invariable "Hunky dory"—when asked about his health during that last year of life—to mean he "was too far gone to realize how frail he was." "You wicked bastards!" Everyman rails against his disaffected sons, Randy and Lonny. "You sulky fuckers! You condemning little shits!"

Preoccupied with filial resentment and thoughts of the grave, Roth began a new novel the day after Bellow's funeral. *The Life and Death of a Male Body** was to be "a story about a man's mortality from the perch of the operating room, that is, the history of his diseases"—a man who shared his creator's aversion to the metaphysical. A few months before, when Max Rudin's second child was born sixteen weeks premature, Roth had phoned every few days to ask how the boy was doing. At one point Rudin hesitated to share some piece of good news, because he didn't want "to jinx anything," and Roth shot back, "Nothing you say will make any difference." Rudin always remembered the moment as a nice instance of the staunch "Jewish rationalism" that informed Roth's everyday thinking and thus *Everyman*.

The sprawling, intricately layered *Plot* had exhausted something in Roth; he no longer had the "mental stamina" for big novels, and, like Bellow toward the end of his career, would henceforth content himself with the taut architecture of novellas. The fewer the motifs, or "props," of a narrative, the more potently they resonate for readers, and in *Everyman* Roth was particularly inspired by the jewelry shop owned by the hero's father (who calls it Everyman's so that gentile customers won't be put off by his Jewish name). One day, by way of research, Roth walked along Broadway until he came to a shop with a Dominican owner who was happy to break out his jewelry loupe and show Roth the intricacies of clocks and watches, carats—accoutrements that dovetail beautifully in the final passage of *Everyman* ("I felt very happy that day," said Roth), where the dying man remembers bodysurfing as a boy:

> Daylight, he thought, penetrating everywhere, day after summer day of that daylight blazing off a living sea, an optical treasure so vast and valuable that he could have been peering through the jeweler's loupe engraved with his father's initials at the perfect, priceless planet itself—at his home, the billion-, the trillion-, the quadrillion-carat planet Earth! . . . Cardiac arrest. He was no more, freed from being, entering into nowhere without even knowing it. Just as he'd feared from the start.

---

* Or, as he called it privately, his "geezer book."

C H A P T E R

Forty-Five

A FTER HIS FINAL BREAK WITH SUSAN ROGERS IN EARLY
2005—a time when he was feeling especially enfeebled and
gloomy—Roth suspected he was "too old to seriously consider attracting
the women who attracted him." One woman friend, who was "only" (as
Roth would have it) about twenty years younger than he, never forgot
the dispirited way he suggested she come live with him in Connecticut.
"It will be nice to have some companionship," he said. "One could go
her own way when one needed to, and there might be little visits to my
bed every now and then." The woman found it a chilly proposition, and
politely declined.

David Plante was then infatuated with one of his more gifted Columbia students—a young man who'd begun to publish in prestigious magazines and would soon finish an acclaimed novel. Plante thought he'd put
the fellow "in his place" by inviting him to dinner with Philip Roth, who
in turn might be able to shed light on whether or not the young man was
gay. As it happened their guest arrived with a former girlfriend, Brigit,*
who struck Roth as quite pretty, albeit in a nebulous "virginal mode"
that particular night. Roth, of course, was in pain—it was March 23,
2005, less than two months before his second major back surgery—but
receptive enough, with the help of Vicodin, to retain a basic dossier on
the woman: a twenty-nine-year-old graduate of an Ivy League college,
she'd grown up in privileged circumstances on the Upper West Side; her
Jewish father worked on Wall Street, and her gentile mother had been a

---

* A pseudonym. I've tweaked a few details of her background. Brigit declined to be interviewed for this book.

gifted artist before dying of cancer a few years back. The young woman was still starkly burdened with grief. "This would be a good place to commit suicide," she said to Roth, standing beside a grimy, alley-view window in Plante's apartment. "Let's do it," he replied.

Six months later Roth was pain-free; remembering the young woman, he asked Plante to arrange a dinner for the three of them at Russian Samovar. When Plante arrived, he spotted Roth and Brigit in a back booth, leaning toward each other, and walked around the block a few times. "Leave after dessert," Roth murmured to him at some point, and afterward Roth and Brigit sat talking for another two or three hours. "I can't let you go," he said on the sidewalk, and joined her in a taxi back to her Village apartment. "In the taxi," Roth remembered, "she grew a little shy of me and she began to talk self-consciously about all the things there were to learn and I said, 'Don't worry—I'll teach you.'" When the taxi pulled up to the curb, Roth stayed put ("Don't fuck it up," he thought; "don't go for her"), and promised to call her soon.

■ ■ ■

OCTOBER WAS the happiest month for Roth. His dinner with Brigit at Russian Samovar was on October 4, and, less than three weeks later, Philip Roth Day was celebrated in Newark: a historical plaque was unveiled at 81 Summit Avenue ("This was the first childhood home of Philip Roth, one of America's greatest writers of the 20th and 21st centuries"*), and the corner of Summit and Keer was named Philip Roth Plaza. The next morning, around seven thirty ("I had no finesse whatever"), Roth rang up Brigit and gave her "a full and gleeful report of the goings-on." He was in love. A month later he hired a limo and took her along for a shopping spree in SoHo. "Imagine a scene that Mann never wrote where Aschenbach buys clothes for Tadzio," he said, still delighting in the memory years later. At Assets he bought her a leather jacket and skirt, then at Barbara Bui he picked out a little black dress and asked her to try it on: "She was just delicious," he said, and she agreed it was nice but worried about the stupendous price tag. Roth handed her his credit

---

* The inscription was written by Roth himself.

card and went outside to wait in the car. "You know what the salesgirl said to me?" Brigit said afterward. "'You got the black dress *too?*'"* On December 7, the couple attended the annual *New Yorker* holiday party at Pastis—their first public outing. "Philip Roth made an appearance with a twenty-something young lady," *Gawker* reported. "Mr. Roth and his lady were the subject of much conversation."

The only cloud was her imminent departure—on January 1, 2006— for a five-month theater fellowship in Colorado. She and Roth spent their last weekends together in Connecticut, dancing on Saturday nights to the big-band music of Roth's youth, and one night, Faunia-like, Brigit performed a charming striptease in Roth's bedroom. "Who needs any more than this?" she exulted one snowy, twilit evening. The most memorable night of all was New Year's Eve: in front of a fire they drank Champagne and consumed a pot of caviar, then Roth sat opposite her in his Eames chair and asked her to tell him the story of her adult life, from college graduation to the present day. For the next three hours—midnight came and went; nobody noticed—she held forth, vividly, hardly pausing except to collect herself when she came to the terrible saga of her mother's illness and death. Her departure the next day was wrenching.

Except for Brigit's visits, the place in Connecticut had become too cold and lonely during winter months, and Roth was in the process of turning his New York apartment into a more permanent haven. Rather than soundproof the walls with cork à la Proust, Roth bought up the surrounding apartments: The first, below him, had been owned by a burly doting father who crashed around playing with his children every night; next Roth bought the apartments on either side of him, 12D and 12F, renting out the first to a temperate lodger, and renovating the second as an extension to his studio—an elaborate project that would take the full five months of Brigit's absence, during which he stayed at Plante's apartment on Claremont Avenue, near Columbia, while Plante was away in Europe on sabbatical.

The day after her arrival in Colorado, Brigit sent Roth some paint samples she'd picked out for the spare bedroom—that is, her room—in Roth's soon to be renovated New York apartment, as well as samples for

---

* Roth kept his Barbara Bui receipt as a sentimental souvenir. The little black dress cost $1,490, and the total came to $2,563.

the downstairs parlor in Warren, which was to be her office. The two spoke on the phone at least once a day, never briefly, and arranged to meet three times during Brigit's fellowship. For three days in early April, Roth booked a suite at the Peninsula in Chicago, showing Brigit around Hyde Park haunts from another halcyon period of his life. A rather grim memento mori, however, was the decrepitude of his brother, Sandy: in the eight or so months since Philip had seen him last, osteoporosis had bent Sandy almost double, and never mind the heart disease that would kill him in three more years. Meanwhile his wife, Dorene, was a little bemused by her seventy-three-year-old brother-in-law's romance, and not simply for the obvious reasons. "He saw none of her spoiled-brat qualities," she remembered. "She seemed like somebody who was poised to have a very man-filled life." Another tactical blunder on Roth's part, arguably, was arranging a dinner with Janis Bellow when the couple stayed at the Charles Hotel in Cambridge, or so Ross Miller opined during a taped interview with Dick Stern: "How crazy are you to put up Janis as a model?"—that is, of a devoted caretaker for a much much older man who, in her case, had recently died after a long decline into dementia. Roth, incensed when he heard Miller's comment on tape, insisted that Janis was just his "dear lovely friend" and he was hardly "selling" her to Brigit. Even so loyal a person as Judith Thurman, though, saw parallels in the Bellow union that might have appealed to Roth: "But [Brigit] didn't have that temperament," she added. "She was very ambitious. She didn't want to be a handmaiden."

For the time being, anyway, Brigit hardly had to worry about the caretaking side of things. Ribaldry inspired the otherwise proper young woman: she rhapsodized about their sex games in her letters, and for Roth's seventy-third birthday she composed a breathtakingly filthy parody of "Mr. Sandman"—"Mr. Hard-on," whom the singer begs to bring her something more tangible than a dream. Little wonder Roth kissed Plante on the lips when the two met again at Broadway and 116th, while students streamed around them through the campus gate. The whole thing was reminiscent of a favorite Roth joke: an old man goes into a confession booth in Ireland and says, "I'm eighty-three and I'm sleeping with a twenty-eight-year-old!" "Do I detect a Jewish accent?" the priest replies. "Why are you telling me this?" "I'm telling everybody!"

■ ■ ■ ■

BACK IN 1996, during Miller's first foray as biographer, he interviewed three people in addition to Roth: the Schneiders and Julius Goldstein. After signing his Houghton contract, in 2004, more than a year passed before he interviewed a fourth, Aaron Asher, on September 27, 2005, and another four months before he got around to Bob Lowenstein, who was a weary, bewildered ninety-eight by then.* When Roth's faithful librarian friend Charles Cummings died on December 21, 2005 (almost two months to the day after he'd jubilantly accompanied Roth on Philip Roth Day, an event he helped organize),† Roth complained to Julia Golier that Miller wasn't interviewing his more elderly family and friends—or hardly anyone else, for that matter—and now they were dying off; Golier earnestly offered to do it herself, though by then she had her hands full with motherhood and professional obligations.

When Roth learned that his and Bloom's old friend Barbara Epstein was dying of lung cancer, he could stand on the sidelines no longer. For almost ten years now, he'd been eager to confirm some gossip that Veronica Geng had heard from Epstein and shared with Roth—namely, that Francine du Plessix Gray had "practically dictated" *Leaving a Doll's House* to Bloom. At Roth's exasperated urging, Miller finally wrote Epstein on February 6, 2006, requesting an interview, and that same day Epstein faxed Roth a note on *New York Review* stationery: "Would you like me to talk to him? I'll do what you say." Miller, however, would later tell Dick Stern that Epstein had been disinclined to cooperate because she knew he was "close friends" with Roth, and then, too, Miller's own

---

* During the long if intermittent span (c. 1996–1997 and 2004–2009) that Miller worked on his biography, he appears to have interviewed a total of eleven people other than Roth himself: the Schneiders, Goldstein, Asher, Lowenstein, Bob Brustein, Florence Cohen, Sandy, Dick Stern, Joanna Clark, and Sylvia Tumin.

† A bust of Cummings was subsequently erected on the grounds of the Essex County Courthouse, with a quotation from Roth's memorial tribute engraved on the pedestal: "We doubt that Charles knew or would believe that he has earned heroic stature by the seemingly workaday labors of librarian and city historian, but we want to declare that he achieved nothing less, and that he will be remembered for nothing less." In Roth's original tribute the last sentence continued thus: "and not just by one who loved him as I did."

scruples were affronted: "[Philip] figured, 'Well, Ross, he's writing the biography, but we're such good friends, well, he can settle my scores for me.' . . . I'm supposed to get Barbara Epstein to talk to me about this"—i.e., the Francine rumor—"and she's dying. And the cruelty of it! . . . He sends me twenty questions to ask her, and they're all questions that make him look good."

Actually, some of the questions—Miller was expected to pretend they were of his own devising—were a little sly. Roth wondered whether Claire's descriptions of him in *Doll's House* were consistent with Epstein's own impressions during the years of their friendship ("Was there a Jekyll and Hyde division at the core of him?"), and waited stealthily until question 6 before pouncing on the Francine rumor:

> I ["Miller"] have read that book [*Doll's House*] as well as Claire's first book, *Limelight and After*, and it does strike me, as I think it would anybody with any sensitivity to language and literature who took the time to make the comparison, that the two books do indeed appear not only to have been written, sentence by sentence, by two different people* but to have been conceived by people of utterly divergent moral natures. This leads me to believe that what you told Veronica was indeed the case. Am I correct?

Perhaps because she hadn't heard further from Miller, Epstein changed her mind and declined an interview the following month (March); three months later she was dead.

By the time of the Epstein debacle, Roth "had already begun losing faith in Ross' capacity to do the job"; nevertheless he gave him a lavish sixtieth birthday party that same month (February 26). Fifteen or so guests—including Wylie, David Remnick, Jack Miles, and Brigit (along with Roth's official photographer, Nancy Crampton, the better to record for posterity this unwarranted act of generosity)—occupied the second floor of Roth's favorite Italian restaurant, Patsy's, a "decidedly

---

* In a way that's true, since *Doll's House* was written without Roth's considerable help. But again, there's no compelling evidence to suggest that Gray took a hand in writing Bloom's second memoir, though she did refer Bloom to a literary agency (Janklow & Nesbit) and doubtless offered a lot in the way of moral support.

unchic" place conceived "before the discovery of arugula."* After Roth gave a toast, the birthday boy rose and reminisced about Aunt Marilyn (Monroe). "This surprised me," said Roth, "because Ross made fun of his Uncle Arthur for never failing to bring up Marilyn's name when his monologue was losing hold on the crowd and he needed a hook."

Three months later, an explicit rift occurred over Miller's duties as editor of the Library of America Roth edition. "The initial delight is wonderful," Roth had said about his canonization as the only living author in the series. "But after a while, it's just another edition of a book." At other times, however, Roth conceded his considerable pleasure in the honor, and made a point of inserting it into press releases and the like. Max Rudin admitted that having a living author in the series—much less one so vigilant as Roth—was apt to keep him and his colleagues "on [their] toes"; and yet, in an uncharacteristic lapse (such was his faith in Miller perhaps), Roth hadn't bothered to check galley proofs for the first two volumes. As volume 3 was going to press, the LOA's Brian McCarthy volunteered a proof of Miller's Notes on the Texts, whereupon Roth was "astonished" to discover his friend had produced only nine pages for an 869-page book—nor were Miller's notes altogether accurate or clear, as Roth saw it, and there was no "logical reason why he had footnoted some things and not footnoted others." The only living author in the Library of America demanded they halt the presses while he peruse the volume from beginning to end, and when he did he "blew [his] stack."

The next morning Roth bombarded his friend with faxes: "this is unacceptable!" read one of Roth's many glosses. "You don't connect the footnote to the *context*. What is going on with you?" A lyrical passage from *The Great American Novel* about Spaulding's first cork-centered baseball, for example, was meant to "echo Melville's style." Finally he phoned Miller so he could berate him more directly, and Miller protested that he'd been specifically enjoined not to write "interpretive" notes. "I'm afraid I cannot talk to you about this," Roth faxed him afterward.

> I am too fucking angry. Nothing I sent you in my morning note had to do with being "interpretive." It had to do with being accurate and to the

---

* This is the "Italian restaurant in the West Forties" (actually on West Fifty-sixth) where Zuckerman lunches with the Swede in *American Pastoral*.

point of what was being footnoted. . . . Is it "interpretive" to point out that Danny Kaye was Jewish and that Tony Martin was Jewish in the notes about each?* Reread the first paragraph of the book and tell me if pointing that out is "interpretive" or if it isn't at the very heart of the job you are supposed to be doing. This has become ludicrous.

Miller's work as a Library of America editor led Roth to air more general grievances. "It pains me to have to write this letter but things are not going as I expected with your projects and I don't want them to get worse," his grand remonstrance began.

> You said you hadn't contacted Bob Silvers because you wanted Barbara [Epstein] "to feel flattered at being asked first." . . . [Y]ou were going to contact Bob precisely *because* Barbara has consistently *refused* to see you. I reminded you of this at the time and all you did was shrug off what was nothing less than a baldfaced lie. To *me*! . . . I remind you: this is my life's work that I have put into your hands, fifty years of work—so what are you *lying* for . . . *Why, why, why?*

Then there was Miller's recent trip to Chicago to interview Roth's only, rapidly fading brother. Afterward Miller told Roth the interview hadn't gone well because of Sandy's deteriorating mental state; but meanwhile Sandy had mentioned that he and Miller met at a museum cafeteria for all of thirty minutes before Miller bolted, sticking Sandy with the check. "Sandy said he was waiting for you to call him back the next day because he couldn't believe that was the interview. But you never did call him back. *What are you doing? . . . Nobody can be interviewed like that, and nobody is ever going to be interviewed for this biography like that in the future.*" At length Roth concluded: "This is excruciatingly awful for me to have to write as it must be for you to have to read, and I'm stopping here."

Max Rudin agreed that Miller "did a very sloppy job" as LOA editor, but in fairness pointed out that they'd agreed at the outset to "go lightly on the notes." Within two weeks, however, the in-house staff

---

* In the first paragraph of *The Professor of Desire*, the social director of the Kepesh family's Catskills resort, Herbie Bratasky, is advertised as being "a second Danny Kaye" and "another Tony Martin."

had reviewed volume 3 and expanded the notes from nine to twenty-seven pages, elucidating such matters as "Lake District," Jane Austen's *Persuasion*, and "objective correlative"; *The Great American Novel*, especially, with all its "quotations, allusions, and literary burlesques and parodies," needed amplification. After the staff's heroic efforts to appease him, Roth wrote Brian McCarthy a note apologizing for his occasional irritability in the past: "I had no idea until very recently that there was a serious editorial problem quite separate from the work done by you and your office." At the bottom of this fax, somebody drew a doghouse with "ROSS" over the door.

The outcome, at any rate, was arguably a boon to all concerned: henceforth the notes were prepared in-house before going to Roth ("They were solid and perfect," he wrote Rudin of volume 6, "—I made not a single correction or suggestion"), and finally, pro forma, to Miller, who was "pretty disengaged" (Rudin) but still nominally the editor. And of course Roth, as ever, went on updating the Chronology and writing almost every syllable of the jacket copy. To the back flap of volume 6, for instance, he wished to add that two of the greatest literary critics in the English-speaking world, Harold Bloom and Frank Kermode, had both proposed *Sabbath's Theater* "as the finest American novel of the last quarter of the twentieth century": "To accommodate this new line it may be necessary to shorten Ross's biographical note," Roth wrote, suggesting a particular sentence to delete ("[Miller's] criticism has appeared . . ."); it was duly deleted.

■ ■ ■ ■

FOR *EVERYMAN*, published that spring of 2006, Roth wanted the jacket to resemble a tombstone. ("This book is about death!" he said. "You'll love it!") A number of Roth's old friends assumed the novel was a "threnody" (Tom Rogers) inspired by the author's own grinding decline, a notion on which Roth was determined to put the kibosh, what with his reconstructed spine and twenty-nine-year-old girlfriend. "I've neither been languishing in 'loneliness and isolation' or sidetracked by 'the scourges of [my] illnesses,'" he scolded Brustein. "My model wasn't my life. My model was Tolstoy." Lest readers miss the point, Roth's author photo showed a grimly muscular septuagenarian in a short-sleeved shirt.

In her Sunday *New York Times* review, Nadine Gordimer raved about

Roth's celebration of "the splendid ingenuity of the body" via "the joy of loving sexual intercourse," lavishly concluding, "Philip Roth is a magnificent victor in attempting to disprove Georg Lukacs' dictum of the impossible aim of the writer to encompass all of life." Michiko Kakutani, however, fixed on the drearier aspects of Roth's novella. With dour tautology she described the novel as "a laundry list of complaints about the human condition" and (same sentence) "an existential litany of grievances, regrets and disappointments"; *Everyman*, indeed, was "sketchy," "labored," "contrived," and "etiolated" yet: "a cobbled-together production of a writer coasting wearily along on automatic pilot."

While there's a fair amount of joyful sexual intercourse in the book, *Everyman* is certainly more concerned with the morbid; Daniel Mendelsohn wryly observed in *The New York Review of Books* that the hero seems "to have enjoyed bizarrely poor health," given the many complaints he suffers en route to his eventual demise: a hernia, peritonitis, various heart ailments, and so on—in other words, Roth's own precisely documented medical history, minus the back surgeries. The pain of our all-too-finite span on this "perfect, priceless planet" is suggested from the start, when Everyman's older brother, Howie, remarks at Everyman's funeral that the dead man had removed their father's Hamilton watch just prior to the surgery that killed him; a page later we go back to forty-eight hours earlier, in the hospital, where Everyman tries distracting himself from mortal thoughts by remembering his first-ever operation (hernia) at age ten. So the novel proceeds: from illness to illness, interspersed with scenes of the hero's dotage, when the ravages and wrong turnings are everywhere evident. What struck Kakutani as "peculiarly abstract" and "oddly sketchy" (both) about Everyman's life was not just his anonymity per se, but also the rather generic nature of his virtues and flaws. Roth, in fact, hadn't noticed he'd neglected to assign a name to his character until he read his first draft and decided the accident was fortunate: "Let him be defined by his relationship to others." Thus his daughter, Nancy— the product of a loving second marriage—adores him, whereas his older children, Randy and Lonny, share their mother's (his first wife's) animus for the man she'd described, in court, as "a well-known philanderer." An average man, in short, whose average flaws leave him all but entirely alone in the world. "Without even Howie!" he laments near the end, having distanced himself, out of envy, from his more successful brother.

"Terrible and so human, as envy is," Roth wrote in his notes. "The lust for Merete"—Everyman's third wife—"that destroys his highly compatible marriage. Terrible and so human, as lust is. *Lust and envy isolate him.* But they are human things and so they befall him."

Roth's challenge was to make his eponymous hero, if average, then average in a relatively nuanced way. "EVERYTHING A MORALITY PLAY IS *NOT* IS WHAT MY BOOK *IS*," he noted. "UNLIKE EVERYMAN"—i.e., the medieval morality play—"IT IS *NOT* TOLD FROM THE CHRISTIAN PER-SPECTIVE, IT IS *NOT* PEOPLED BY CHARACTERS WHO ARE PERSONIFIED VIRTUES AND VICES, IT IS *NOT* DIDACTIC IN TONE. . . . THE TENSION BETWEEN THE TITLE AND THE CONTENT IS WHAT INTERESTS ME." Per-haps the main reason Everyman, as a character, seems interesting is his categorical refusal to accept the "lie" of religion, no matter how bleakly in need of such comfort he becomes. "But there's no remaking reality," he tells his thirteen-year-old daughter when she painfully rips a tendon in her hip and faces the end of her track career. "Just take it as it comes. Hold your ground and take it as it comes. There's no other way." And Roth (who liked to say "'Redemptive' isn't a word I use very much except at the grocery store") is merciless in portraying the "massacre" of old age, as the body deteriorates and there's less and less to fill one's days, and (at least in Everyman's case) almost nothing to look forward to. When even his painting avocation begins to pall, he has little to do but walk in the morning and swim in the afternoon; meanwhile the damage of his failed marriages, and the essential hollowness of his old professional friend-ships, leave him with nobody in his life but Nancy: "True, he had chosen to live alone, but not unbearably alone."

"This is a novel with, literally, Nothing to offer," David Gates wrote in *Newsweek*, "—except moving scenes with lovingly presented people, a beautifully shaped narrative and the resolution with which it faces the unfaceable." With *Everyman* Roth became the only writer to win the PEN/Faulkner three times, for three very different novels that showed the vast distance he'd traveled in only thirteen years of his (ultimately) fifty-five-year career—from the ludic reality games of *Operation Shylock* to the somber dissection of American puritanism in *The Human Stain*, and finally to the stark, unhappy *Everyman*, with its craftsmanly set pieces about jewelry and grave digging that pique the reader's imagina-tion without a whit of cliché—such as Roth found in yet another deplorable reading guide: "'Existential facts,'" he wrote his publisher. "Why not just [say] 'the facts of illness and aging and death.' Existential is a bullshit word to be avoided at all costs."

． ． ． ．

ONE OF ROTH'S FIRST meetings with Brigit, after she returned from Colorado in May 2006, was for breakfast at Nice Matin, near Roth's apartment on West Seventy-ninth (still under construction) and Brigit's family home on Riverside Drive. Roth had stayed up most of the night rewriting Miller's LOA notes and grinding them through his fax machine. *Would somebody bring my toast?!*" he yelled, smacking the table, and Brigit started, appalled. It was the kind of thing her boorish father would do, and she let Roth know she didn't like it.

By then it was clear she wasn't the same woman who used to sing "Mr. Hard-on." After her first night back with Roth, *chez* Plante, she left early the next morning to visit a friend in Brooklyn. A few days later Roth expected her for dinner at seven; he bought the food and laid it out, but she hadn't come by eight, and he sat watching a ball game, fuming. Finally she appeared; she'd been at a party, she explained, and had to wait for some old friends to show. "Sternly," Roth recalled, "meaning my words, I asked her, 'Do you want to get out of this? Do you want this to be over?' Very sheepishly she said, 'No.' (I thought, when she spoke, that she didn't have the courage, quite then, to say, 'Yes.') The meal that followed was eaten in silence."

Brigit was the first woman Roth had ever wanted to marry, but, given his own nearness to death, he thought it only fair to offer her a child— a prospect, in this case, that thrilled him too. Still, he knew the risks of siring a child at his age—Bellow's late-life daughter, with Janis, had turned out to have a degree of autism—and on March 8, 2006, he'd consulted a geneticist at New York–Presbyterian Hospital, Dr. Wendy Chung.* She canvassed Roth's family medical history and advised him that advanced paternal age could indeed result in autism, Marfan syndrome, and certain forms of dwarfism, but she couldn't make a proper determination until she had Brigit's information as well. Three months

---

* While sitting in the waiting room, Roth scribbled notes on the back of an envelope about the furniture, posters, and so forth, which he later found occasion to use in *The Humbling*.

later, then, after Brigit's return, Roth mentioned his visit with Dr. Chung and asked the young woman to make an appointment so they could complete the evaluation. "You are so responsible," she said, after a fraught silence, then began to cry.

She never made the appointment. "I don't feel in the mood for this tonight," she said in Connecticut, during sex, and Roth obligingly withdrew and went to sleep. At breakfast the next morning she announced that she wanted to end the affair. "The hours that followed were horrendous," Roth remembered. "As never before in my life with women (in my life with anyone), I begged and pleaded and I berated her for listening to her friends and her family, who knew nothing about what there was between us." Finally she seemed to relent, but a few days later mentioned she'd be spending the entire summer at her family house on Cape Cod, where she was directing a production of *Macbeth*. Roth had naturally hoped they'd spend the summer in Connecticut, but finally gave her one of his Volvo station wagons and off she went.

Roth arranged to visit her for a few days in early August, but a week or so before, while swimming, he felt a wrench in his back and knew he was in for a long siege of pain. At the Hyannis Port airport he hobbled from his gate, grimacing, and caught a glimpse of Brigit waiting for him beyond the glass partition: he knew at once she wasn't happy to see him. The visit was the expected bust. He'd booked a room at an inn near Brigit's house, but the days were boiling hot and the pool was always packed with children; Brigit was busy with rehearsals all day, and Roth sat alone in his room, unable even to walk. One night she made dinner for them, but he was in so much pain he lay on the floor trying not to scream: "Not even the Vicodin helped. This was the last thing I wanted her to see."

Back in New York, Roth's pain management doctor suggested a denervation of two arthritic facet joints in Roth's lower left vertebrae (a procedure using radio frequency to kill the nerves causing pain); he scheduled Roth's operation for the first week of September. Meanwhile Brigit returned from Cape Cod and came to Roth's refurbished New York apartment for dinner; "terrifically excited to see her," he mentioned something he wanted to do with her the next night, and Brigit produced a piece of paper on which she'd carefully plotted her booked-up social week, culminating in East Hampton for the weekend. Finally she agreed to return in time to pick him up from the hospital. Within forty-eight hours of his denervation, as the local anesthetic wore off, Roth was in worse pain than ever. His doctor explained that "the nerve was dying back," and a little more time would have to pass before things got better.

That week Brigit was sleeping in Roth's spare room, and one night she came back from dinner with her sister and father and sat on the edge of Roth's bed. "I just had the most wonderful time," she said, and began to tell him something funny her father had said. "I'm not interested in what your father says," he cut her off. The father had recently bought her a nice apartment in Brooklyn Heights—in exchange, Roth suspected, for ditching the elderly boyfriend—and now the father, as Roth put it, was "suddenly wonderful." "What did my father ever do to you?" said Brigit. "You're the one who says things about him." "*You're* the one who says things about him!" Roth rejoined, and Brigit fled weeping to her room. At an utter loss, Roth phoned Julia and told her the story of his summer. "Get rid of her," she said ("Good old Julia; she's so smart"), so the next day Roth told Brigit he saw no sense in going on this way, and that was that.

For the rest of his life, Roth would often imagine that a woman on the street was Brigit and quicken his steps to make sure. Only once did he see her again, roughly nine months after their breakup, when she passed him on West Seventy-ninth near his apartment. At the time he was on his way to meet his friend Claudia Roth Pierpont, who wrote in her diary that he looked "devastated" afterward: "She gave him a weak hello and he didn't answer at all," Pierpont noted.

Two years later Roth was cleaning out his studio and found Brigit's college yearbook, which he'd borrowed as research for *Exit Ghost*, along with two nude portraits she'd taken of herself for a college photography course. He returned them to her Brooklyn address with a note asking whether she'd like to meet "for a sociable cup of coffee" at Nice Matin some afternoon. Months later she replied with a tersely civil note: She'd decided this was "not the right time" for them to meet, though maybe later she'd be in touch. He never saw or heard from her again.

PART SIX

NEMESES

2006–2018

Roth at the White House, 2011.

R OTH'S OLD FRIENDS BEGAN TO DIE. THERE WERE
Bellow and Charles Cummings, of course, but the ball had gotten
rolling back in 2003, when Roth was "shocked" to open the newspaper
one morning and see that George Plimpton, his beloved early champion,
was gone. Just a week before, Plimpton had phoned to ask whether Roth
would make the introductory remarks at that year's *Paris Review* Revel
(no), and, a few years before, he'd presided over the English Speaking Union ceremony where Roth had won its Ambassador Award for *I
Married a Communist*. Mostly, though, Plimpton was a jaunty personage whom Roth had adored from afar over the decades, and he made
a point of attending the memorial at St. John the Divine on November
18. While standing in a side corridor he bumped into an old enemy,
Norman Mailer, hobbling along on two canes: "Sometimes I have to go
into a telephone kiosk to pee, Phil," Mailer announced. "You just can't
wait at my age." "I know," said Roth. "It's the same with me." "Well,"
Mailer quipped, "you always were precocious!" And the two shared a
hearty laugh. "It was the first time in our lives that we had both laughed
together," Mailer recalled. "I attribute this to George's spell."

Roth also saw Styron at the memorial ("He looked old and sedated"),
their first meeting since the summer of 2001, when Styron had introduced Roth as the recipient of that year's MacDowell Medal at the
Peterborough, New Hampshire, arts colony. Surveying their forty-year
friendship in his remarks, Styron remembered his feelings of "brotherly
accord" with Roth from the beginning, in Italy, when his friend was
"warding off his assaults from crazed and vindictive rabbis"—a bond that
grew stronger a few years later, after Styron was attacked by black intellectuals over his Pulitzer-winning *Confessions of Nat Turner*. Still smart-
ing from the ordeal five years later, Styron commiserated at length with

Roth over Irving Howe's "swinish and outrageous" attack in *Commentary*: "I would only suggest that the crashing silence surrounding Howe's 'reconsideration' of you means that, if many people read it at all, which I doubt, the unfair and hectoring tone which Howe adopted so bored people—as it did me—or turned them off, that they simply lost interest." He signed off, "Yours in the slime we sometimes find ourselves up to our asses in—Bill."

But arguably the bedrock of the friendship was their mutual delight in raunchy humor. "I adore your mustache and have had a single incredible fantasy," Styron wrote in 1971, when Roth had cultivated his Groucho look while getting into the spirit of *The Great American Novel*: "suppose I was a girl and you were going down on me with that mustache. What would it be like? Please destroy this letter." The friends' correspondence continued in this vein almost to the end. Twenty years later, Styron sent Roth an advertisement ("you might try this out on your VCR") for an "AMAZING MICRO VIDEO!" that took the viewer inside "a hot, wet pussy!": "Imagine witnessing massive ejaculations from loaded dicks—they'll be shooting right at you!"

In January 1986, when Styron had been admitted to Yale–New Haven Psychiatric Hospital for suicidal depression, Roth phoned him every other evening and also encouraged friends to keep in touch ("I think he likes to know that people are pulling for him," he wrote Conarroe). Though never quite the same, Styron recovered and wrote a celebrated account of his illness, *Darkness Visible*. In 2000, he was hospitalized again and given a series of shock treatments, but this time the pain remained, and Styron spent his last years in a highly medicated haze of declining health. Roth, for his part, stayed away. "Bill's suffering is over," Mia Farrow informed him on November 1, 2006, and also let him know that Styron's widow, Rose, deeply resented Roth's neglect in recent years. On January 22, he wrote her a long letter describing his own late-life woes—the long sieges of back pain, surgeries, and low spirits:

> This stuff has been at the heart of my life for the last two years—and longer than that. . . . [A]t the end of each day I had little left in the way of energy or good cheer. I saw very few people, took numerous drugs, and was almost entirely engaged with getting myself through the painful days while trying to stay productive.

> I also wish I had seen Bill. Of course I should have called you and I could and should have written him. But, lost in my own medical maze, I lost track of his condition.

All true enough, though of course it didn't account for the deliriously happy and healthy ten months or so when he was seeing Brigit, during which he was certainly well enough to visit Styron—if, perhaps, the latter hadn't been such a frightful reminder of his own mortality.

In the end, Rose Styron rather reluctantly—at Farrow's urging—decided to let bygones be bygones, and not only invited Roth to attend the memorial at St. Bartholomew's on Park Avenue, but seated him in the first two rows with the family. Among the more than eight hundred mourners, at least one continued to view Roth as persona non grata—Bill Clinton, who gave him a look of stern warning when he started to approach. The former president had, Roth surmised, read certain passages in *The Human Stain* where the Lewinsky scandal is discussed in luridly scurrilous terms. "I was just trying to capture what people at the time were saying, Bill," Roth wanted to say, but didn't.

■ ■ ■ ■

AFTER ROTH'S AFFAIR with Brigit ended, his friends feared for his life. One day he and Plante were walking along Riverside, when Roth spotted Brigit's childhood home and began walking into traffic "in a trance"; Plante yanked him back from a passing car in the nick of time. He relied on Conarroe and another devoted friend, Ben Taylor, a writer and New School professor, to take turns sleeping over at his apartment on what amounted to a suicide watch. "Last night was grim," Conarroe emailed Taylor on October 8, 2006, "—long crying jags, with arias alternating between denouncing the 'selfish little b****' [sic] and lamentations over the loss of 'my darling beautiful girl.' . . . He uses the S word more and more, and is worried about his sanity. I'm all twisted inside, he kept repeating."

Roth tried hard to pull himself together. He resumed seeing a psychiatrist, Richard Friedman, who'd helped him in the past with pain-related depression, and meanwhile he was "desperately analytical" (according to Taylor) with friends, to whom he'd talk and talk about his malaise. Almost any well-meaning person would do as an auditor. Roslyn Schloss, who'd always enjoyed an amiable working relationship with Roth, had rarely if ever seen him socially—until now, when he jumped at the chance to have dinner with her and her husband, two more people willing to listen while he articulated his pain. When Lori Monson (working on his back) mentioned that she and her husband were staying at a Connecticut inn for Thanksgiving, Roth insisted they stay at his house instead; he himself was keeping away, he freely admitted, because the place was haunted by memories of Brigit. Finally, gradually, as his facet-joint nerves died away, Roth became somewhat free of physical pain and better able to cope on his own.

Finding another young woman also helped. After finishing *Exit Ghost* in November, Roth remembered a perky Texan who'd assisted his research on the Kinkaid School in Houston (George W. Bush's alma mater, and also that of Roth's heroine, Jamie Logan). Back in May 2006, Roth had originally consulted another Kinkaid graduate, Alice Gordon, who helped him find the thirty-three-year-old Kaysie Wimberly,* who could better evoke the milieu as her fictional coeval Jamie would have known it. Kaysie googled Roth and saw that he was "a really big deal," so she did her best to help, bringing her yearbook and talking about "the country clubs, the society scene, and which club—blah blah blah— that kind of stuff," as she recalled. Six months later, Roth invited her to dinner at Hearth, in the East Village, where he brought the Houston pages from *Exit Ghost*. ("I actually corrected some of it in the first draft," said Kaysie. "The kids drove Broncos, I said it was the cool car for guys to drive; and he wrote something in the book that sounded like all these Kinkaid kids were driving around drunk in their Broncos, and I said, 'That's actually not accurate. . . . Kinkaid kids are pretty responsible for the most part.'") Roth used a car service for dates, and would always "book the next thing" as he dropped Kaysie at her apartment: "Well, I have tickets to . . ." They went to a chamber music concert at the Metropolitan Museum, a flamenco night at City Center, and while at Carnegie Hall the actress Debra Winger (who'd read the part of Faunia for an audio version of *The Human Stain*) came up to chat with Roth and

---

* A pseudonym.

his friend ("I thought, Wow! I'm cruising around town getting to do all these fun things with Philip"). Finally, as he was booking the next thing, Kaysie asked him if he had an email account; when Roth admitted he didn't, she told him to get one, and for almost three years she was his only correspondent.

It was hardly a grand passion, but the two found each other refreshing and had a good time together. Roth called Kaysie by her childhood nickname, Little Feather (she was part Cherokee), and Kaysie called Roth Figgy for the homemade fig newtons he liked to buy at a shop on Columbus. Roth could play Pygmalion with a person who actually relished his constant correction. "There's a word you use a lot," he calmly instructed her over dinner one night. "'Awesome.' You just need to drop it. The Sistine Chapel is 'awesome' in all its splendor, but this meal we're having isn't awesome." Kaysie would nod solemnly, taking it in—all part of the School of Roth, as she called it. As for her staunch religious faith (when Roth first went to the bathroom in her apartment, he was startled by the word "BELIEVE" scrawled across the mirror in big red letters), he found it more endearing than not, and was content to leave it alone.

Kaysie was a petite blonde ("a cross between Reese Witherspoon and Meg Ryan," Roth accurately described her) who still looked like the Kinkaid cheerleader she'd been, and Roth was powerfully attracted; then, too, she was another daughterly-waif type who was game ("against the odds of her background," Judith Thurman emphasized; "that's important") and would never have any particular qualm about the amorous turn their friendship took after a month or two of dating. Roth's almost seventy-four-year-old body, however, was covered by some pretty lurid scars,* and so, prior to disrobing that first time, he'd always prepare his bedmates (lest "they run naked into the street") with a ditty he remembered from the Bucknell production of *Knickerbocker Holiday*:

When lovely Venus lies beside
Her lord and master Mars

---

* An eight-inch scar from his clavicle to the base of his ribs from the quintuple bypass, a scar along the interior of his right leg from same, three scars all the way up his back, a scar on his side where doctors removed a bone to replace disc material in his spine, a scar where they entered to ream out his carotid artery, his old appendectomy scar, hernia scar, etc.

They mutually profit
By their scars.

Even in his last years, no longer a sexual being, Roth would sing these lines and chuckle: "Isn't it charming? And it gets them. It gets them." Certainly it got Kaysie, who sent Roth a card shortly after they began sleeping together: "You / are / fetching, / my / love / xxx / xxx / xxx / xx [heart]"

Mostly, though, they just cuddled; also Roth liked to read to her from Howard Pease, whose sea adventures had enchanted him as a boy. As for the various award ceremonies they attended just in 2007—the PEN/Faulkner, the PEN/Bellow, Italy's Grinzane-Masters (held at Columbia University)—she usually found herself the youngest person there, and more than a little out of her depth ("kinda like the ditsy blonde"), though she was so chic and pretty and artless that Roth himself was proud to be seen with her. Which is not to say there wasn't the odd misgiving: "She knows nothing," he confided to Pierpont, who recorded in her diary, "He was telling her something and she asked in a tiny voice, 'What's fascism?' He had to explain the whole 2nd World War. . . . He says it made him feel so lonely."

■ ■ ■ ■

FOR SOME SIX MONTHS AFTER their falling-out in May 2006, Roth and Ross Miller didn't speak to each other, and Roth saw no evidence that Miller was making progress on his biography. At Roth's request, Andrew Wylie wrote Miller a note on December 1, reminding him that he'd agreed to devote himself to the biography if he hadn't finished (as he hadn't) his book about the Jews, *Free at Last*, by Labor Day 2006; also they'd discussed his preparing a sample chapter of the biography to shop around to Roth's European publishers. Miller replied that his progress had been interrupted somewhat because of Roth's "behavior" during the past year; he was, however, "diligently" at work on the material Wylie required.

Wylie passed this missive along to Roth, who indignantly prepared a long memo on which Wylie was to base his reply. He pointed out that he'd FedExed a letter to Miller in late August 2006, expressing his readiness to resume work on the biography; Miller had signed for the letter but hadn't otherwise acknowledged it. Then, about two weeks ago, in

November, Roth had phoned Miller and mentioned in the course of "a friendly conversation" that he'd finished *Exit Ghost*; Miller "showed no interest in reading the novel" and said nothing about needing Roth's assistance on the biography. Meanwhile Roth's old friends were dying off, and others were in "declining health": Solotaroff, Dick Stern, Tom Rogers, Sandy, and the last surviving witnesses to his family's pre-Sandy years, his eighty-five-year-old cousin Florence Cohen and his even older cousins Gladys Kaplan and Milton Roth. "Has Philip's 'behavior' prevented you from interviewing any or all of these people?" Roth wrote in Wylie's name.

Harry Maurer—whom Roth and Betty Powell had babysat fifty-plus years ago for their Bucknell friends Bob and Charlotte—was the author of three books, including *Sex: An Oral History*, and Roth made a deal with him. For $250 a head, plus expenses, Maurer was to conduct extensive interviews with Roth's old friends—indeed, the older the better. For each interviewee, Roth provided Maurer with a long list of personalized questions, and his cover letter explained to his friends that he was in the midst of compiling "an audio archive" for an "autobiographical project." "Would you have expected him to achieve success on the scale he has?" Roth directed Maurer to ask Jack Wheatcroft, as well as various others in so many words ("just how surprised are you by the career he has made?"). Manea and Thurman were prompted to speculate on Roth's seemingly boundless appetite for hard work, solitude, and other noble privations ("How did he do it?"), while Joanna Clark was urged to reflect on her friend's productivity "at a time when most writers of his age begin to lose their writing energy."

Hermione Lee and Al Alvarez, in England, were interviewed by Lisa Halliday, who was now living part-time with her boyfriend, Theo, an employee in the London office of the Wylie Agency. She'd been back in New York on October 13, 2006, when she thought she spotted Roth—then at the nadir of his post-Brigit bereavement—sitting by the river, possibly near his lost love's childhood playground in Riverside Park. Halliday put a bright yellow note in his mailbox ("like a singing canary," said Roth): "I wonder how you are. (You—or your doppelganger—looked thoughtfully sad, staring at New Jersey.) I think of you often (obviously) and hope you're well. / Love, Lisa." Roth promptly got in touch and told her right off the bat (re the clandestine financial arrangement she'd refused several months earlier), "I'm sorry. You were right and I was wrong." Whereupon the two resumed seeing each other, quite platonically, whenever Halliday was back at her old apartment on West Eightieth. And the following summer, 2007, she rented an apartment in Paris, so she was able to interview Alain Finkielkraut too.

■ ■ ■ ■

BACK IN JUNE 1998—the day after he'd visited his new friend and incipient Faunia model, Sylvia, at the dairy farm—Roth was casting about for some way to use the interesting scene he'd just witnessed: "Lonoff gets dropped from the syllabi," he wrote in a notebook: "AB [Amy Bellette] living on the dairy farm." Eight years later he was ready to incorporate the first part of this idea into his final novel featuring Nathan Zuckerman as hero (versus peripheral narrator, as in the American Trilogy), coming full circle from his earlier appearance in *The Ghost Writer.* "This is how I will live," the young Nathan vows in the latter, admiring the snowy purity of Lonoff's isolated farmhouse in the Berkshires. *Exit Ghost* opens almost fifty years later: the reclusive Zuckerman has not set foot in New York in eleven years, and Lonoff has been dead since 1961, all but forgotten despite his terrible lifelong pains to perfect his art.

"From these bare bones of a plot," Michiko Kakutani wrote, "Mr. Roth has created a melancholy, if occasionally funny, meditation on aging, mortality, loneliness and the losses that come with the passage of time—very much the same themes he examined in his sketchy 2006 novel, *Everyman,* and his equally slight 2001 novel, *The Dying Animal.*" Words like "sketchy" and "slight" were part of the Kakutani boilerplate for Roth's later novels, but this time the same words occurred to other critics, too. Christopher Hitchens called *Exit Ghost* "very slight," and, after venturing to describe the plot, wrote, "Am I by any chance boring you? I promise that I have done my best to put a light skip into this summary of a weary trudge. Roth's own method of alleviation we can see coming a mile off: The female half of the want-ad couple"—that is, Jamie Logan and her husband, who place an ad in the *New York Review* offering a one-year swap of their Upper West Side apartment for a place in the country—"will turn out to be a fox, offering the ghost of a chance that Zuckerman's flaccid and piss-soaked member can be revived."

This, alas, proves not to be in the cards for the cancer-stricken Zuckerman, though the "beautiful, privileged, intelligent, self-possessed, languid-looking" Jamie is a stirring reminder of what he's lost in his later life as a backwoods celibate, and he can't resist teasing out the abstract possibilities in his intermittent playlet, *He and She*. James Wood pointed to a parallel scene in *The Ghost Writer* where Zuckerman overhears his revered mentor, Lonoff, singing like "the great Durante" for his young mistress: "If only I could invent as presumptuously as real life!" he reflects, then proceeds to transform Amy Bellette into Anne Frank, whom Nathan imagines himself marrying and thereby silencing his critics for good. "In the earlier novel," Wood observed, "fiction yearns to keep pace with the scandal and presumptuousness and fictionality of life; in the later novel, life yearns for the scandalous freedom and fantasy of fiction." In *Exit Ghost*, Zuckerman is unable to transcend the "bitter helplessness" of his impotence in life or in art (though Roth liked to point out that, when he began the novel, he himself could hardly have been fitter: "While Zuckerman was sinking I was exuberantly bouncing about, on the streets and in bed, with a most sublime creature").

Zuckerman returns to the world too late, and comes to rue his retreat even more when his old friend, the consummate worldling, dies: "Suddenly George Plimpton stood for all that I had squandered by removing myself as forcefully as I had and retreating onto Lonoff's mountain, to seek asylum there from the great variety of life." Thus Zuckerman spells out his point, at last, after a rhapsodic, almost six-page eulogy in which the dialectic between him and Plimpton is explored in its every nook and cranny. Whereas Plimpton came from a background of almost pristine privilege, and was all the more blithe for that—"the urbane, witty gentleman of easy intelligence and aristocratic bearing"—Zuckerman himself had "never imagined getting anywhere without the unstinting persistence in which my hardworking family had diligently schooled me." On and on it goes, the eulogy, devolving more and more into mawkishness: "George threw spirals as accurate as any a pass receiver could hope for in *any* league. . . ."

"Well, he knows he's writing shit now," Ross Miller chuckled during his interview with Brustein in 2008, particularly referring to the Plimpton screed: "It just lies there like a lox. This sort of a thing he never would have done before" (that is, when he still had the benefit of a proper "trainer" or "coach"). Listening to his old friend level him in these interviews, Roth decided he'd gotten at least one thing right in *Exit Ghost*—the ambitious literary biographer, Richard Kliman (pronounced "climbin'"), who has a salacious theory about his subject, Lonoff, to which he means to attach any number of other misdeeds: namely that Lonoff had an incestuous affair with his half sister, a scandal somewhat inspired by the alleged incest of Hawthorne and Henry Roth, the author of *Call It Sleep*. "Lonoff was in hiding, not just as a man but as a writer," Kliman glibly explains to an appalled Zuckerman. "The hiding was the catalyst for his genius. The wound and the bow." "Somebody has to protect Manny from this man," says Amy Bellette. "Any biography he writes will be the resentment of an inferior person writ large."

But who will protect Zuckerman? Or Philip Roth, for that matter? In interviews for *Exit Ghost*, Roth gave mixed signals as to how much the reader should infer about his own feelings toward the genre to which Kliman and Ross Miller aspire. He quipped in *The Observer* that, *Exit Ghost* and *Portnoy* notwithstanding, he counted himself "a friend of both" biography *and* masturbation; six weeks later, though, he remarked in a radio interview, "Biography gives a new dimension of terror to dying." Meanwhile the editors of *The New York Times Book Review*, already piqued by his invidious Kliman portrait, learned that Roth had hired Harry Maurer, an oral historian, to conduct interviews for a "personal project." In a piece that ran a month after publication of *Exit Ghost*, Ross Miller denied any kinship with Kliman and characterized his rapport with Roth as "the 'candor' of intellectual 'equals.'" Be that as it may—the *Times* pressed—was it possible Roth would stop cooperating with him? "The doomsday scenario, you mean?" said Miller. "I don't really know. I just think that we're pretty far along for that to happen."

Forty-Seven

W HEN DICK STERN WAS ASKED BY THE NOBEL PRIZE Committee, in 1983, to suggest candidates for its literature prize, he pointed out that the two he'd suggested when previously asked, almost twenty years before, had both gone on to win: Saul Bellow and Samuel Beckett. Now he urged the committee to consider four English-language writers "who may have been disregarded because of certain sorts of popularity": Philip Larkin, Harold Pinter, J. F. Powers, and Philip Roth—the last "a true craftsman with a streak of authentic comic genius." Given the Swedish Academy's aversion to comic genius, not to say "certain sorts of popularity," only one of Stern's candidates would ultimately be honored this time. Ten years later, in 1993, Harold Bloom named Roth in *The Washington Post* as the most deserving living candidate for the Nobel, and in the book Bloom published the following year, *The Western Canon*, he listed six Roth novels (the most of any living writer) as worthy of permanent interest—this, mind, *before* the publication of *Sabbath's Theater* and *American Pastoral*, which became Bloom's preeminent Roth novels thereafter.

Roth was the perennial American favorite for the prize during the twenty-three-year dry spell that followed the 1993 selection of Toni Morrison, and his chances seemed vastly improved after the magisterial, high-minded American Trilogy. Certainly his friends rallied to the cause. In 2003, Joel Conarroe, the president of PEN America, enumerated the major prizes Roth had won for just the five novels he'd written since the age of sixty; quite aware that Roth was mostly known in Sweden as the author of *Portnoy*, and never mind the even more lurid *Sabbath*, Conarroe also reminded the academy that Roth was altruistic, what with his editorship of the Writers from the Other Europe series—"but it is clearly for his own extraordinary fiction," he concluded, "and not for good international citizenship, as it were, that he is worthy of the one major award he has not yet been given. There is no living writer more deserving of a Nobel Prize for Literature." Five years later, writing on behalf of the British Academy, Hermione Lee tried a kind of decorous shaming: "It is a matter of amazement to many cultural commentators, readers, scholars and critics, not only within the United States but worldwide, that he has not yet been awarded the Nobel Prize for literature." Naturally she also mentioned Writers from the Other Europe, to no avail.

That was the year (2008) the permanent secretary of the Swedish Academy, Horace Engdahl, let it be known the fix was in for European, or anyway non-American, writers. The United States is "too isolated, too insular," he said, noting that only 3 percent of books published in the States each year were works in translation, versus 27 percent in France and 28 percent in Spain. "Europe," he said, "still is the center of the literary world." Roth was reminded of Engdahl's remarks the following year, when, as the first-ever recipient of the PEN/Bellow Award for Achievement in American Fiction, he sat on the 2009 jury considering "a superabundant pool of superior American talent" before deciding to give the award to Cormac McCarthy. "[W]e would contend," Roth said at the time, "that American novelists must surely be among the best in the world." Privately Roth was always dismissive on the subject of the Nobel, which he liked to call a "narcissistic extravaganza." So would he pull a Sartre and turn it down? "No, I wouldn't do anything out of the ordinary," he said on October 13, 2012, two days after the prize had gone to Mo Yan of China. "I would accept it. But it's not gonna happen."

∎ ∎ ∎

ON APRIL 11, 2008, in honor of Roth's seventy-fifth birthday, a tribute was held at Columbia's inauspiciously named Miller Theatre. While Roth sat in the front row, six feet away, two panels of writers and critics discussed his work. The first, moderated by Judith Thurman, was a relatively young group of writers including Charles D'Ambrosio, Nathan Englander, and Jonathan Lethem, who all mentioned their formative discovery of Roth's work on their parents' bookshelves. As a boy, Englander's identification with Roth was reinforced by the way his mother used to call him to table: "Dinner's ready, Portnoy!"

The second panel, moderated by Conarroe, comprised an older generation, each of whom was asked to discuss a favorite Roth novel for about five minutes. After Claudia Roth Pierpont and Ben Taylor gave loving appreciations of *Sabbath* and *Shylock*, respectively, Hermione Lee spoke with daunting poise about *The Ghost Writer*; meanwhile Ross Miller either peered at his notes or gazed wanly into the darkness. He was next.

"It seems like we planned this, Hermione," he began, noting that he intended to discuss *The Counterlife*, which, after all, "completes this first five-book exploration of the life of Nathan Zuckerman, the subject which is the, probably, an unprecedented series of books on the vocation of a writer. . . .

> So *The Counterlife* plays with, engages certain conceits or ideas that this career as a writer has generated in Zuckerman, that is, not only do writers, novelists, impersonate other people . . . but *we're* impersonating other people, that is, civilians, everyone here. We do various impersonations, and the exploration of this is titanically treated in *The Counterlife* with a series of, of, of episodes that have a certain logical connection but there's really no necessity for it.

On it went. "I was shocked by his performance," Roth said of Miller, who sidled up to him afterward and murmured, "I wasn't much impressed by the other three."

"Well, now he's surrounded with sycophants," said Miller, three months later, during what would prove his final interview (with Brustein) as a biographer. "The irony is that they're either homosexual men—of course he's homophobic—or these silly women. They're serious women, but they're silly in their presentation of self. They're low impact: he likes that." Two years later, Roth himself would listen to these interviews, one after another, all nine of them,[*] pausing to make notes along the way. "I don't even think Gitta Sereny's moral assessment of Albert Speer is as bleak as Ross's of me," he observed at one point.

Roth especially regretted exposing his only surviving family members to Miller's "mean, insatiably vilifying spirit"—his cousin Florence, for instance, who would die of cancer soon after Miller finally interviewed

---

[*] Nine versus eleven, since Miller's interviews with Joanna Clark and Sylvia Tumin went missing, though both women confirmed that some such interview had taken place.

her on March 4, 2007. At one point she regaled him with a memory of how she used to phone Philip from Sandy's New York apartment, alerting him that his parents had just left and would soon be home, where Philip was entertaining Maxine or some other young woman. "This is really a trip down *mammary* lane," Miller quipped for the eighty-five-year-old woman, followed by an outburst that must have startled her: "There is a predatory side to both Sandy and Philip. They look at women—I'm not gonna write about this—but they *are* misogynist. They talk about women in that way."

Miller also tried to entice Roth's sickly, adoring brother into confirming certain grim assumptions. "I always refer to it as the broken wing syndrome," Sandy mildly replied, after Miller noted how a number of Philip's girlfriends had had fathers who killed themselves. "I have a broken wing and I go for broken wings." "But you don't *break* wings," said Miller, and Sandy, after a shocked pause, replied, "Doesn't even enter my thinking." Miller riffed on the theme more explicitly with Stern, citing Roth's scheme to get Brigit pregnant so he could "capture her," the better to have a young woman taking care of him in his dotage—a young woman, moreover, who'd previously cared for a dying mother and therefore had the "Janis [Bellow] credential."

Stern mulled this disturbing conversation for more than two weeks before phoning Roth on December 31, 2006: Ross, he said, had interrupted him repeatedly, ranting away for some "85 percent" of the interview; ominous, too, Stern thought, was Ross's remark that he wouldn't publish his book until Roth was dead. "I conclude from this that Ross is in a hostilely rivalrous relationship with me," Roth noted after hanging up, "because of his work for Volume Three of the LOA series being criticized and rejected by me." In the months ahead, Roth continued to get reports that his biographer had gone rogue—"This man is not your friend," his cousin Florence informed him—until, after the Columbia tribute, Thurman got an earful from Miller. According to an alarmed memo Roth prepared on May 29, 2008, for his executors, Golier and Wylie, Miller had boasted to Thurman that he'd actually "coauthored" Roth's novels, beginning with *The Counterlife*, as opposed to reading them in rough draft and helpfully discussing them afterward. Also he'd confidently diagnosed Roth as manic-depressive; Thurman had argued with Miller that she'd certainly seen Roth depressed, but hardly *manic*—

if the happy relief that follows recovery from a major depression is mania, well, then most of her friends were manic-depressive. Hearing of this, Roth was reminded of the Little, Brown lawyer's mention of a "reliable source" for the reference to his alleged "bipolar disorder" in galleys for *Leaving a Doll's House.**

On November 14, 2009, Barbara Sproul wrote Roth a puzzled note: "Months ago some fellow from the University of Connecticut saying he was your biographer contacted me and then didn't follow up (sent me an email and then blocked the response, called to make a date and when I couldn't make that one didn't call again); I don't know if you still want him to talk to me or not." Whether this was vacillation or fecklessness on Miller's part is hard to say; around this time, anyway, he and his subject mutually decided to end things, and, in keeping with their (confidential) agreement, Miller returned four boxes of research to Roth.

Roth transferred Miller's interviews to CD format, then proceeded to listen carefully to every interview, hitting pause every five minutes or so and typing his exhaustive response to "the errors and lies recorded in those five minutes before proceeding to listen to the next five minutes." When he was done, months later, he had amassed hundreds of pages of commentary he decided to title "Notes on a Slander-Monger": "You are, of course, free to quote or paraphrase (or challenge) as you like," he wrote Miller's successor on March 28, 2013. "I think it's bigger than *Moby Dick* though written more in the spirit of *The Confidence Man.*"

■　■　■　■

ROTH WAS A GREAT ADMIRER of Sherwood Anderson, and always figured if Winesburg, Ohio, had had a college, it would have been the same kind of place ("just steeped in Christian values") as Bucknell in the fifties. Remembering, not altogether accurately perhaps, how appalled he'd been by Ann Sides's sudden fellatio in the cemetery†—such a young woman must be a child of divorce, he'd suspected at the time—Roth conceived a novel, *Indignation*, in which a bright young man attends Winesburg College during the Korean War, becomes smitten with an

---

* "The thing he was angriest about, with Claire's book, was that she said he was a manic-depressive," Miller remarked to Brustein. "Of course he *is* a manic-depressive."

† See page 78.

emancipated, troubled young woman, and dooms himself with a series of slight rebellions.

The trick, said Roth, was working out Marcus Messner's fate—death in the war—so that it seemed inevitable. "A tragedy in the original sense of the word," he wrote in his notes. "The Greek sense. . . . He runs away and that's how he gets caught." Like the young Roth, Marcus is eager to escape his crazily paranoid (i.e., weirdly prescient) father, a kosher butcher, who begins "hounding [him] day and night about [his] where-abouts": "You are a boy with a magnificent future before you—how do I know you're not going to places where you can get yourself killed?" Marcus finds sanctuary at Winesburg, where he hopes to become vale-dictorian while studying law—a profession "as far as you could get from spending your working life in a stinking apron covered with blood," the pursuit of which leads him to the bloodbath in Korea. His "angel of death" is a handsome Jewish boy, Sonny Cottler, who arranges for one of his fraternity brothers to attend chapel in Marcus's place—a chain of events the narrator evokes with a string of wistful "If only"s: "If only Cottler hadn't befriended him! If only he hadn't let Cottler hire Ziegler to proxy for him at chapel!"—and so on, every step inevitable given the hero's peculiar brand of hubris, a determined atheism: "If only he'd gone to chapel himself! . . . But he couldn't! Couldn't believe like a child in some stupid god! Couldn't listen to their ass-kissing hymns! . . . The dis-grace of religion, the immaturity and ignorance and shame of it all!" Nor does Marcus see any choice in his most fatal transgression: saying "Fuck you" (twice) to Dean Caudwell, who had demanded he write a letter of apology to the college president.

Roth's detractors were hard on *Indignation*, which Malcolm Jones denounced as "terrible" in *Newsweek*—"the work of the late-late Roth, the Roth of bitter, bitten-off miniatures like *Everyman* and *Exit Ghost*: curt, tetchy, unhumorous." That last adjective is surprising, since the tone of the novel is nothing if not droll. Seeing Olivia Hutton for the first time in the library, Marcus, loath to commit even the slightest error, forbears to masturbate: "The strong desire to rush off to the bathroom was quelled by my fear that if I did so, I might get caught by a librarian or a teacher or even by an honorable student, be expelled from school, and wind up a rifleman in Korea" (as he will in any case, partly because he allows Olivia to do the masturbatory honors while he lies abed in the hospital). The book's centerpiece—a long dispute between the dean and Marcus, who marshals the anti-Christian arguments of Bertrand Russell—was justly described by Frank Kermode as "impassioned, educated, silly, and very funny," while David Gates applauded the "ruthlessly economical and relentlessly deathbound" *craft* of the book. As in Waugh's early farces, Roth dispenses with exposition wherever possible to suggest things happening abruptly *to* Marcus, without (quite) his volition. One paragraph relates his happy, semi-independent freshman year at Robert Treat, in Newark, whereupon the next paragraph lands him bang in Winesburg, where in short order he'll fatefully take out Olivia, whose name we're told before we quite grasp that she's the same girl in the library a page earlier.

Praising the novel in the *London Review of Books*, Kermode remarked on the overall hostile trend toward Roth's later work: "He ought to be past caring, but it isn't always easy, given the man's temperament, to overlook the meanness of spirit that characterizes the attacks, determined as they are to 'get' him." This time they succeeded: Roth loved the first and last of his four "Nemeses" novellas, but he would always believe "something went haywire" with *Indignation*—not as haywire, to be sure, as his next novel, but haywire nonetheless.

■   ■   ■

AFTER ROTH'S FALLING-OUT with Aaron Asher in 1994—when Asher had admonished Roth not to be so "selfish" and let Bloom "at least" have his studio on West Seventy-ninth—Roth claimed it was he who made amends within "six months" or "about a year." Actually it was more like six years. Asher's friendly note about the strangeness of having to pay money for *American Pastoral* was followed three years later with a similar note about *The Human Stain* ("it definitively puts you right up there among the immortals"), ending thus: "This book makes me realize how much I miss our friendship"; Roth scribbled "Call Aaron" on the back of the envelope. Later that year Asher was found to have bladder cancer, and Roth promptly offered to help defray his medical expenses; then, four years later, Asher was diagnosed with Alzheimer's. "This is the greatest living writer in America," he kept telling his twelve-year-old granddaughter, Susanna, who'd walked him over to Roth's apartment one day to hear the author read from *Everyman*.

Asher succumbed to cancer on March 16, 2008, before Alzheimer's could entirely wipe out his mind. Almost three years later, Roth would complain to the Kunderas that his friends were dying in droves ("and most are irreplaceable, like Aaron"). When Roth had visited three or four days before Asher's death, they reminisced awhile about their fifty-year friendship, then Roth embraced him and said goodbye; Asher began to cry and said, "I love you," and Roth said he loved him too.*

Ted Solotaroff died five months later of emphysema. He'd come a long way from the tetchy, down-at-heels grad student who'd inspired the hapless Paul Herz of *Letting Go*; along with his successful career as an editor-critic, Solotaroff had finally married an heiress, Virginia Heiserman, his fourth wife (number two had been Shirley Fingerhood, Roth's divorce lawyer), with whom he shared a spacious apartment near Columbia, a house in the Hamptons, and even a pied-à-terre in Paris. Over the years he'd been one of Roth's most stalwart readers, one of a handful recruited to hold forth at "The Roth Explosion" in Aix, and also handpicked by Roth to edit, brilliantly, *Alfred Kazin's America*. "His distinctive voice will always be—in his own apt phrase—one of the few good voices in my head," Roth wrote in a subsequent tribute.

Roth and Updike had been estranged for almost a decade when Roth was "shocked and saddened" to learn of his great rival's death, from lung cancer, on January 27, 2009. Eight months later, the absence was still "incomprehensible" to Roth: "He was *the* indestructible writer with *the* indestructible fluency," he wrote Ted Hoagland. "He was an ace, maybe *the* ace. '*The*' suits him fine, in nearly every regard." Indeed, what Roth had always envied most about Updike was his "fucking fluency"—the "gush of prose" that flowed through the man's fingers at the rate of three pages a day, every day, for more than half a century, resulting in forty-five books of stories, poetry, and essays, and twenty-eight novels: seventy-three books!† Roth's own thirty-one came at a relative trickle of a page a day, usually, and he was "delighted to accept" that much. Given their kindred obsessions—and very different temperaments withal—it was

---

* Roth faxed the obituary editor at *The New York Times*, Bill McDonald, alerting him to Asher's death and giving career highlights, as well as contact information for himself and Linda Asher.

† *Not* including posthumous publications.

probably for the best they contented themselves with an amiable, occasional correspondence, meeting in person (Roth figured) maybe half a dozen times. One evening, in 1991, Roth and Bloom had gone to dinner at John and Martha Updike's mansion on the Atlantic in Beverly, Massachusetts, where John was pleased to conduct his colleague on a tour of his working annex—the four little offices where he wrote fiction, criticism, poetry, and miscellanea, respectively. That night at dinner the couples got to talking about a scene in Updike's memoir, *Self-Consciousness*, where he masturbates one of Mary Updike's friends in the backseat of a car while his first wife drives them home from the ski basin. "Martha was very upset that John had included the scene in the book," Roth recalled in a letter to Updike's biographer, "John was boyishly silent while she spoke and I ventured to say that he included it in the book for the same reason that he had done it—he was indulging 'the imp of the perverse'" ("Just like me," Roth told Stern).

A testament to Roth's essential magnanimity—especially among peers—was the initiative he took to invite Updike to lunch, in Cambridge, two years after the man's "very mean-spirited" review of *Operation Shylock*. Thanking him for it afterward, Updike promised never to review another Roth novel; chagrined by his tendency to go from "high homage" to "nagging complaint," he was determined now to be simply a "contented consumer." And so it went. Updike professed to love the "in-your-face (literally) sex" of *Sabbath's Theater* and was all the more "agog" when his colleague began to "lengthen [his] stride and intensify [his] focus" with *American Pastoral*.

When *Leaving a Doll's House* was published, however, Updike's imp of the perverse got the better of him. "A good woman wronged, that was my impression," he waggishly wrote a colleague. "And to think that my friendly little review"—of *Shylock*—"broke it up. Well you never . . ." The word "wronged" popped up again in Updike's long essay "On Literary Biography," which appeared in the February 4, 1999, issue of *The New York Review of Books*: "Claire Bloom, as the wronged ex-wife of Philip Roth, shows him to have been, as their marriage rapidly unraveled, neurasthenic to the point of hospitalization, adulterous, callously selfish, and financially vindictive." Roth's letter to the editor was swift and quasi-equable: "Allow me to imagine a slight revision of this sentence," he wrote:

"Claire Bloom, presenting herself as the wronged ex-wife of Philip Roth, alleges him to have been neurasthenic to the point of hospitalization, adulterous, callously selfish, and financially vindictive." Written thus, the sentence would have had the neutral tone that Mr. Updike is careful to maintain elsewhere in this essay on literary biography when he is addressing Paul Theroux's characterization of V. S. Naipaul and Joyce Maynard's characterization of J. D. Salinger. Would that he had maintained that neutral tone in my case as well.

Updike's reply followed: "Mr. Roth's imagined revisions sound fine to me, but my own wording conveys, I think, the same sense of one-sided allegations." That both his essay and reply were, as Roth later put it, "not only ungenerous but cruelly obtuse" seemed also to occur to Updike, who emended the key sentence as Roth had specified when the essay was reprinted as a chapbook by the University of South Carolina Press: "See page 28," he inscribed Roth's copy. "With apologies and best wishes, John."* But it was too little, too late: "Who's gonna see this fucking monograph from the USC press?" Roth said in 2012. "So I just never talked to him again."

In a long interview for *The Telegraph*, three months before he died, Updike gave "a cryptic smile" when asked whether he and Roth were friends. "Guardedly," he said, allowing that a sense of rivalry complicated matters, and concluding, "But he's been very good to have around as far as goading me to become a better writer." Which of course was Roth's view as well, and he went further when asked to comment for Updike's obituary in the *Times*: "John Updike is our time's greatest man of letters, as brilliant a literary critic and essayist as he was a novelist and short story writer. He is and always will be no less a national treasure than his 19th-century precursor, Nathaniel Hawthorne."

Finally, Roth's brother died on May 6, 2009. In recent years the two had grown closer still, in part because Sandy's third wife, Dorene Marcus, was a smart, good-natured lawyer who read books—indeed,

---

* Updike couldn't resist tweaking the language one last time—whether more or less offensively, the reader may judge—when his essay appeared again in *Due Considerations* (2007): "Claire Bloom, the ex-wife [no "wronged"] of Philip Roth, *portrays him as having been* [italics added], as their marriage rapidly unraveled, neurasthenic . . ."

had been reading her brother-in-law's work since her twenties, and now was delighted by the eerie similarities and differences between the two men. On the day she first met Sandy's celebrated sibling, she woke up and heard what "sounded like one person talking" in the living room— echoing what Stern had said about his impulse to visit Sandy, while estranged from Philip, because he loved to hear his absent friend's voice.*

Philip had been horrified by his brother's decline. He'd immediately arranged to get a prostate exam, in 1991, around the time Sandy had had his own cancerous prostate removed, resulting in impotence and frequent incontinence. (Philip interviewed him at length about the various embarrassments, passing them along to Zuckerman.) By then he'd come to regard Sandy as almost his "biological twin," all the more since the brothers had gotten bypass operations five years apart: their age difference. In 1997, thirteen years after Sandy's first bypass, he and Marcus were in New Jersey, visiting his son Jonathan, when Sandy began to experience chest pains and shortness of breath; Philip phoned his own surgeon at New York Hospital, Karl Krieger, and arranged for his brother to be transported by ambulance for emergency surgery. Meanwhile, Philip readied his apartment for Sandy's convalescence: filling the refrigerator with food, making up the bed with clean sheets, and arranging a fresh box of tissues and a water pitcher on the bedside table. Sandy, arriving, hobbled straight to bed and stretched out, smiling at the bedside table: "Just like Bessie," he sighed happily.

In his final two years Sandy could hardly walk to the bathroom. His spine had crumbled quite as badly as his brother's, and he lost six inches of height; meanwhile his heart failure made it hard to breathe or think. His wife's "saddest memory" was when she'd asked the lifelong draftsman to draw a clock, and he bunched all the numbers up on one side. Toward the end, too, he became more and more paranoid, suspecting she and the caregivers were conspiring to kill him. "Old age has been monstrous with him," Philip wrote their cousin Joan. As with Bellow, Philip saved up jokes to tell his brother on the phone, and could occasionally get a laugh. Sandy's own last joke came when the night nurse—"a very effu-

---

* Julia Golier remembered how, at the White House in 1998, Hillary Clinton had mistakenly congratulated Sandy for his brother's arts medal. "When corrected," said Golier, "she very smoothly moved to Philip without acknowledging the understandable error."

sive young man," Marcus remembered—tried to coax the invalid into drinking a little water: "Sandy," he said, "you are the apple of my eye!" "More like applesauce," Sandy feebly replied.

Philip delivered the eulogy at Sandy's funeral in Skokie, and hardly a day passed afterward that he didn't think about his kindly older brother and how much more alone in the world he was now. Of his annual visit to his parents' graves in 2011, he wrote Jack Miles: "It was the second time I've been there since my brother died in 2009 and I was overwhelmed by my sense of being the last of our little family left standing and by the fact that it is a matter of time now—and perhaps not that much—before I am gone and with me the memory of our family life together."

■ ■ ■ ■

DEATH, THEN, was much on Roth's mind when he began *The Humbling*, whose premise was based on a story Claire Bloom had told him about the actor Ralph Richardson. "The magic is gone," said the latter, after a bad night onstage when he found he couldn't act anymore. "He'd lost his magic," Roth's novel begins; as with its predecessor, the main exercise was to make the actor-hero's fate seem inevitable—"surprising, but inevitable," said Roth, "—just as suicides are?"

The Humbling is an enervated performance, and it's hard not to read Simon Axler's maundering about the loss of his gift ("You can get very good at getting by on what you get by on when you don't have anything else") as the author's lament for his own dying light—as if he's only too conscious of writing a bad novel about not being able to write anymore. Roth liked to describe creative fluency in terms of freedom— "He's free as a bird," he said of Updike's work in the *Rabbit* novels—and so with the stymied Axler, who tells his agent, "You're either free or you aren't. You're either free and it's genuine, it's real, it's alive, or it's nothing. I'm not free anymore." As for Roth's efforts to make acting a plausible, detailed correlative for writing—or at least an occupation somewhat understood from the inside—they seem perfunctory at best. He mentions, say, the old exercise of pretending to sip from a teacup ("There was always a sly voice inside me saying, 'There is no teacup'"), but it's a long way from Sabbath's puppetry or the glove factory in *American Pastoral*. Among Dick Stern's papers is a draft of his messy, unsent first response to Roth's novel, in which he gropes for a tactful way to tell Roth that he, like many a much lauded contemporary, was wearily going through the motions now, and maybe the time had come to quit: "I think you are updiking (and trolloping and bellowing and xing [sic] a la almost every active old writer), writing too quickly, even frantically [crossed out], too much for yourself, and not writing the little masterpieces you can still write. . . . Maybe you can't anymore. (I stopped because I spotted the repetitions and didn't have the strength to invent new ways or even carry out fictional impulses as I used to. . . .)."

Beginning with Axler himself, the characters are abstractions, and not very coherent abstractions; they make the cast of *Everyman*—the allegorical morality play, not the novel—seem marvels of roundness. Axler shares his creator's terror that life will be empty without his art, alone in the sticks with nothing to distract him from loneliness: "It's sometimes astonishing," he says, "sitting here month after month, season after season, to think that it's all going on without you. Just as it will when you die." But Axler has nothing of Roth's humor or charm, and one can't fathom why such a gloomy codger would attract (never mind sexually) the "vibrant" lesbian Pegeen—"solid, fit, brimming with energy," predatory and dildo wielding, yet utterly unremarkable otherwise: "She's not at all beautiful. She's not that intelligent." Indeed, she's little more than an agent of doom, about as nuanced as a safe falling out of the sky.

Michiko Kakutani reviewed the "slight, disposable work" with Kazuo Ishiguro's *Nocturnes: Five Stories of Music and Nightfall*, but at least she wasn't making an invidious comparison. The future Nobel laureate's stories were "psychologically obtuse, clumsily plotted and implausibly contrived," whereas Roth was still flogging away at "the same preoccupations sketched out in the flimsy *Everyman*." Kathryn Harrison's "witty takedown" of Roth in the *Times Book Review* earned her a "highbrow/brilliant" mention on *New York* magazine's "Approval Matrix." "Wow," she remarked of Pegeen's whipping up a batch of spaghetti carbonara for Axler prior to jumping into bed with him (her first heterosexual coupling since college). "That must happen to a lot of depressed people."

Roth conceded that *The Humbling* was easily "the weakest" of his later books, though he affected to be pleased with certain "audacious things" in it; the green dildo was surely among them: "The green cock plunged in and out of the abundant naked body," he wrote of Pegeen's stern treatment of Tracy, a drunk woman she and Axler pick up for a threesome. "This was not soft porn." "Bad sex award shortlist pits Philip Roth against stiff competition," punned *The Guardian*, when Roth was in the running for the *Literary Review*'s annual Bad Sex in Fiction Award—the only award he might have won for *The Humbling*, were it not for the even worse sex in Jonathan Littell's *The Kindly Ones*.*

Pegeen's model, Susan Rogers, had been in touch with Roth a couple of times since their ugly breakup in early 2005—namely when her mother, Jacquie, died that August, and again when her father died in April 2007. "The trouble with fiction, as our friend Phil pointed out long ago," Tom Rogers had written Stern six months before his death, "is that reality is more fantastic than anything we can imagine and make real to ourselves." Whether that meant he knew about his daughter's affair with Roth is uncertain. Once, Jacquie had predicted that Susan would run away with a young man named John, the son of her closest friend. "Worse things could happen," said Susan, and her father remarked, "Yes, like you run off with Phil."

The one and only time Susan ever felt grateful that her parents were dead was after reading *The Humbling*. "'Oh goody,'" she remembered thinking, when a new Roth book landed on her doorstep; that night she crawled into bed around ten, expecting to read for maybe half an hour before dropping off. She finished at one in the morning, fighting an urge to vomit. It was all there: Pegeen's parents are "good friends" of the protagonist; Pegeen's previous lover undergoes a sex change; Pegeen wangles a job in the east by sleeping with a college dean, who, once jilted, says to Axler, "Be forewarned, Mr. Famous: she's desirable, she's audacious, and she's utterly ruthless, utterly cold-hearted, incomparably selfish, and completely amoral." "I never stalked you," the real-life dean intoned over the phone, without referring to *The Humbling* per se. She didn't have to. "Yes," Rogers replied, "and I never made spaghetti carbonara."

Rogers let a year or so pass before agreeing to meet Roth for dinner at the West Street Grill. "You know, your book really hurt me," she said, and began to cry. Roth was looking "dumbstruck" when a stranger came over and introduced himself: "We met at a dinner party ten years ago," the man said, and Roth brightened: "Oh! You're the lawyer!" Oblivious

---

* The previous year, shortly before his death, Updike was given "a lifetime achievement prize" after four consecutive nominations for the Bad Sex Award.

to Roth's weeping companion, the man kept jumping up from his chair and coming back over to talk, and Roth did nothing to discourage him. Later Roth was pleased to mention that he and Rogers were back in touch. "She asked why was everyone in the book depicted as 'so mean.' I told her I didn't see it that way—and a friendship resumed." "Of all the books that would have to deal with me and my life," said Rogers, "it's his worst fucking novel." And yet she put it behind her, more or less; on the whole Roth was easier to take now that there was no question of a romantic attachment, and a friendship did in fact persist until the end.

Back in 1984, David Plante had observed what a relief it was to be "less and less obsessed" with sex, and Roth said, "I'll be obsessed when I'm eighty exactly as I was when I was eighteen." He didn't quite make it. The seventy-four-year-old wasn't entirely impotent with Kaysie Wimberly—his final lover—but he was mostly content to cuddle and read. "I've got a sweet Texas girl," he wrote Al Alvarez, "but she's only on lone [sic], until she can find someone who will give her babies." One potential baby-giver wondered about all the Roth novels on her shelf, and the ingenuous young woman admitted she'd had a fling with the author. The fellow was appalled: it just so happened, he said, that Roth once hit on a friend of his at an Upper West Side farmers' market! ("The guy's got a *terrible* reputation," Kaysie laughed in 2012.) He insisted she stop seeing such a notorious reprobate, even as a friend, and Kaysie did as she was told. Regretfully she wrote a farewell note to her "precious Philip," assuring him of her love and admiration. Roth replied: "A long time ago I told you you had a soul. You do. I don't mean it in the religious sense but in the poetic sense. You're gracious and kind and just as lovely as I thought."

No desperate melancholy ensued, as with Brigit's departure, but it was still a blow, and again his friends Ben Taylor and Joel Conarroe took turns keeping an eye on him ("Pretty grim evening with Philip," the latter reported, describing their friend as "terribly discouraged about being, at his age, alone"). Meanwhile Roth dedicated *Indignation* to "K.W.," and when *The Wall Street Journal* inquired about the dedicatee's identity, Roth replied, "That's a mystery. I'm not telling."

For a year or so, he absorbed himself in his work. Then, at a Christmas party given by the painter Caio Fonseca, he met the estranged wife of novelist Richard Price, Judy Hudson, who soon dropped him a note to the effect that she'd "adore" having a drink with him. Roth suggested they make it dinner instead, and thereafter playfully made a habit of saying "adore" when a less hyperbolic word would do. Hudson was a vivacious, slender woman, and the two enjoyed each other's company; by now, however, Roth was apt to shrink from the physical. ("I am well though I could use a new left hip, a new left shoulder, and a new libido," he wrote the Kunderas. "They're all wearing out.") "You kidding?" he'd say, when she'd suggest a degree of intimacy, even if it was simply kissing or holding hands—though he was still capable of romantic gestures after a fashion: a virtuosic whistler, Roth would sometimes phone Hudson and whistle a tune from beginning to end, then hang up; also he'd emerge from the bath with a towel around his waist, buffed and scented, and do a kind of Theda Bara dance with a second towel as a scarf.

That summer of 2009, as Roth was finishing *Nemesis*, Hudson joined him most weekends in Warren—the latest companion to marvel at his discipline, the ironclad sameness of his days. Every morning, after breakfast, he'd do his exercise/stretch routine, then work until late afternoon (breaking briefly and laconically for lunch), swim with Hudson for an hour or so, work until dinner, then read; finally the two would retire to separate bedrooms. By September it was clear they "didn't have the kind of connection that could go any further," as Roth put it, "and so we mutually agreed to part."

Also he'd begun (or resumed) seeing a tall, striking blonde, Mona,* almost twenty years younger than Hudson. The two had met at Updike's memorial on March 19, 2009—Roth's seventy-sixth birthday; he and some friends (Conarroe, Taylor, Thurman, one or two others) were adjourning to Russian Samovar for dinner, and Roth coaxed Mona into joining them. A couple of dates followed, but they lost touch during the summer, when Roth stayed in the country and buried himself in work; back in New York that fall, he began seeing the woman more seriously. "I didn't know that my sex life was over," he said three years later; certainly he found Mona desirable in an objective way, but not even Viagra availed him during a necking session, and the two decided to remain affectionate friends. "You sure you don't want to reconsider?" she asked

---

* A pseudonym.

him during a walk in the country. "Honey, it isn't you," said Roth. "It's my time."

As he advanced into old age, Roth's peers were all the more inclined to view him as one of the greatest and most devoted fiction writers the country has ever produced. In 2007, the young novelist Nicole Krauss had thought to let Roth know, in writing, what "a peculiar, sustaining solace" his work had offered her over the years:

> Something to do with your lifelong examination of the writing mind, its needs and paradoxes, its incompatibility with so much else, and also its fierce pleasures. . . .
>
> But I hope you will forgive me for also adding that I have often been struck by a sharp loneliness when reminded of the fact that you won't always be there, writing up in Connecticut. . . . I suppose it isn't any longer just your words, but their consolidated shape—the idea of you—which has brought me such comfort all these years, and I expect I won't know quite what to do without its reassurance.

A few weeks later, the two met for coffee at Nice Matin, and Krauss asked Roth whether he'd been writing that day. Alas, no, since he'd recently finished *Indignation* and had yet to feel the first ill-starred stirrings of *The Humbling*. "It's terrible," he said. "I'm a complete amateur. . . . On my way here I found myself wondering, 'What is a novel?'" That afternoon he wrote a list of "commandments" for Krauss to hang above her desk, including "IT'S NOT GOING TO GET BETTER, RESIGN YOURSELF TO THIS."

■ ■ ■ ■

"I'M AT THE POINT where I think it's shit and wish I'd never written it," Roth had written Paul Theroux, while bracing for publication of *The Humbling*, his penultimate novel. Anxious to redeem himself, he sat down with a legal pad and made a list of historical events, especially menacing ones, that he'd lived through and understood. There was the war, of course, but he'd pretty much covered that in *Sabbath's Theater*, whereas anti-Semitism had given him *The Plot Against America*. After some thought he circled the word "polio," and began making notes. *"What happened?"* he scribbled at the top of a typed page: "This happened in Newark in 1944, the year nineteen thousand cases of infantile paralysis—or poliomyelitis—were reported nationwide, constituting the worst outbreak in America in nearly thirty years." In fact, only a single childhood friend of Roth had gotten the disease—a boy named Jerry, who lived around the corner—but that was enough to cause panic among the parents of Weequahic. Bess forbade her sons to swim in the public pool or eat *chazerai* at Syd's and the like, while reminding them again and again to check themselves for symptoms such as headache, stiff neck, and nausea.

Desperate to avoid another dread verdict of "sketchy," "slight," and/or "pallid," Roth did whatever he could to enrich his narrative. He phoned his cousin Sandy Kuvin, an eminent infectious diseases doctor, and asked him to explain in detail how polio is transmitted and how it was treated in the years before the Salk vaccine. And what of the social ramifications? His friend Mia Farrow had contracted polio when she was nine, and on returning to school (she told Roth) the meaner kids had treated her as a pariah: *Eww! Here she comes! Don't touch me! She'll give you polio!*—whereupon she'd run after them with an outstretched finger. One day at the St. Bart's pool, on Fifty-first and Park, Roth saw a man roughly his own age remove a brace from his leg while changing, and Roth asked him whether he'd had polio; the man said yes, and they sat talking for a while. Finally Roth approached his old friend Stu Lehman and asked whether they could discuss a subject everyone had tactfully avoided when they were young: the experience of losing his mother as a boy, and, like Bucky Cantor in *Nemesis*, being raised by his grandparents.

Late that spring of 2009, Roth submitted the tenth draft of his novel to the publisher, but when he examined the copyedited manuscript, it wouldn't do: "In places the cadences seem off and the writing automatic and the diction less than alive," he wrote Andrea Schulz, his new editor at Houghton. He asked them to stop production while he went over it again. And again. Finally, in August, he relinquished "Draft 12A," wearily admitting he wasn't altogether happy but he didn't "know how to complicate it anymore." Then he became depressed. "I don't really have other interests," he told Alvarez in 2004. "My interest is in solving the problems presented by writing a book. That's what stops my brain spinning like a car wheel in the snow, obsessing about nothing."

A problem that had become all but insurmountable while writing *Nemesis*—indeed, the main reason he'd had to limit himself to the shorter form in the first place—was his "frayed" memory. He could no longer keep the whole story in his head, or even, sometimes, just the previous day's work. "For instance," he explained to a friend, "I know last night we had dinner together, but I don't remember anything we talked about." Still, the thought of having nothing more to write, nothing to do at all, was simply intolerable. "Give me subjects," he said to friends. "Let's think of catastrophes. . . ." The list making went on for a couple of months, but nothing seemed worth the wonderful agony of another book. Hoping "a dose of fictional juice" might help, Roth reread the masters who'd inspired him to become a writer some sixty years before: Dostoyevsky, Conrad, Turgenev, Faulkner, Hemingway. "Maybe it's over," he thought, and finally began rereading his own work from his latest book going backward, "casting a cold eye" and deciding, at last, à la the great heavyweight Joe Louis, "I did the best I could with what I had."

"Why am I so happy?" he wrote on October 14, 2010. "I haven't had any serious back pain for well over a year. And something more: for the first time in my adult life, I haven't written a word of fiction for over a year. Fourteen months now." Roth was free—not in the creative sense, but rather in the absence thereof. "The tyranny of writing and the tyranny of sex—overthrown," he wrote Miles. "Life hasn't been like this since I was ten and pre-pubescent." Nor was he entirely idle. The previous summer, while groping for fictional fodder, he'd begun to pore over letters and photographs he'd amassed during his almost forty years in Connecticut, which soon became "an exercise in recollection": The better to assist a new biographer,* he began writing a kind of ramshackle account of his life—"without worrying about sentences or repetitiousness or maundering. Much more pleasant. And useful."

∎ ∎ ∎ ∎

ROTH'S FINAL NOVEL was widely hailed as "a triumphant return to high form" (*Financial Times*)—a reception signaled by his friends' enthu-

---

* Hermione Lee had tentatively agreed to oblige, but first had to honor her commitments as president of Wolfson College, Oxford, and also finish her work in progress, a biography of Penelope Fitzgerald. She figured she could begin earnest work on a Roth book by 2014; meanwhile she wrote her old friend, "I will completely understand if, because of that [delay], you decide to approach someone else who can get going more quickly."

siastic (or at least relieved) early responses, the most prescient of which was Miles's: "Stop publishing. . . . In your depressed state, I wonder if you realize how great a book it is. It's a masterpiece, Philip. It's flawless. I don't know that it's your greatest book because, yes, others were more ambitious. What I do know is that you will never top this. You will never write a better book to have remembered as your envoi." Compared with *The Humbling*, certainly, *Nemesis* seems a minor masterpiece or anyway close enough, and most critics were nothing but charitably disposed. Leah Hager Cohen's front-page notice in *The New York Times Book Review* was almost giddily effusive. Admitting to an early distaste for Roth's books ("Oh: these are for *boys*"), she'd revisited them "with mounting, marveling pleasure" in preparation for the present assignment: "Before you stands a convert," she announced. "I come to swallow the leek." Michiko Kakutani, however, was acerbic as ever: once again she declared a late-Roth novel "pallid" and indulged in a last, damning tautology ("predictable" and "by the numbers"), while faintly praising Roth's "professionalism" and "granular period detail."

Roth let it be known he'd reread Camus's *The Plague* while working on his polio novel—this, he noted, "largely to *avoid* accidentally repeating any of his scenes or motifs"; J. M. Coetzee, in *The New York Review of Books*, pointed out that Camus, for his part, was familiar with Defoe's *A Journal of the Plague Year*, and all three were part of "a line of writers who have used the plague condition to explore the resolve of human beings and the durability of their institutions under attack by an invisible, inscrutable, and deadly force." Roth considered Dr. Rieux "the perfect narrator" for *The Plague*, though he professed to be puzzled as to why Camus had seen fit to conceal Rieux's identity until the end—and yet, such an approach would seem the most notable affinity between *Nemesis* and *The Plague*. Roth's first-person-plural narrator remains a mystery for some two-thirds of the story, a device Roth appropriated not from Camus but, again, from the beloved opening pages of *Madame Bovary*, in which the anonymous "we"—who remember Charles Bovary and his funny cap at school that first day—simply vanish after a few pages, never to return, the way Zuckerman vanishes after the first eighty or so pages of *American Pastoral*. In the case of *Nemesis*, the anonymous plural narrator serves mainly to suggest "a community that's in peril," as Roth would have it, and gradually transpires to be *one* of Bucky's playground charges (hence his curious tendency to refer to Bucky as "Mr. Cantor"), Arnie Mesnikoff, a boy who got polio that summer.

Roth needed to defer Arnie's story until the end, when he meets his former playground director and embittered fellow polio victim, Bucky, now a wizened middle-aged man and "maniac of the why"—akin to Rothian heroes going back to Gabe Wallach, of *Letting Go*, who morbidly prize their own virtue and poison their lives as a result. "We can be severe judges of ourselves when it is in no way warranted," the father of Bucky's fiancée warns him. "A misplaced sense of responsibility can be a debilitating thing." After standing his ground against the Italian toughs who come "spreadin' polio" by spitting on the sidewalk near his feet, Bucky becomes "an idolized, protective, heroic older brother" to the boys of Weequahic—a sacred trust he betrays, as he sees it, when he buckles to his fiancée's plea to escape the epidemic and work at a summer camp in the mountains. Bucky's moment of weakness leads swiftly to tragedy: three boys in his orbit promptly get polio, whereupon the entire camp is shut down. "Who brought polio here if not me?" Bucky decides, unable to forgive himself, never mind a malign deity who tortures children for sport.

"Chance is what I believed Mr. Cantor meant when he was decrying what he called God," Arnie reflects. *Nemesis* is another Roth novel that might have been titled *Blindsided*, about a hero who simply can't accept that sometimes *there is no why* (an idea that served Roth well when assessing his own culpability in respect to certain personal debacles). "He does not accept the absurdity of it," Roth wrote in his notes, "that's the tragedy because he has to pay the price. He transforms the tragic into guilt." Especially in the case of *Nemesis*, Roth was more interested in "psychological soundness" than "philosophical reverberations," and so was intrigued by a letter dated April 19, 2009 (around the time he was finishing his tenth draft), from an old Weequahic resident—a woman who hadn't learned until the age of eleven that, three years before her birth in 1948, her parents had lost two boys to polio a day apart. When she asked her mother whether the boys were in heaven, the woman replied that "they were just buried in the earth. . . . She never discussed the boys with me again. I knew that she was an unhappy person, and, as I got older, I realized that she wanted me to share her suffering and her view that the world was a terrible and frightening place." Roth used elements of the story in his subsequent drafts.

Correcting a reader's impression that his hero's nickname was in homage to another Weequahic playground director of the forties—Louis "Bucky" Harris—Roth pointed out that the much younger Cantor was given the name "because its associations to manliness were savagely ironic for a boy who winds up the way Bucky does." The tragedy echoes in the final pages—Roth's favorite passage—an exquisitely detailed flashback to the glory days of Bucky's youth: "Running with the javelin aloft, stretching his throwing arm back behind his body, bringing the throwing arm through to release the javelin high over his shoulder—and releasing it then like an explosion—he seemed to us invincible." "Invincible" was the last word of the novel, and an apt way to end Roth's thirty-one-book career.

■ ■ ■

SALES FOR *NEMESIS* were rather disappointing—it peaked, briefly, at number 16 on the *Times* best-seller list—but Roth claimed not to care as long as his usual fans bought it. Besides, one of his fondest jeremiads over the years was about the inevitable decline of "people who read serious books seriously and consistently"—Roth readers, in short. In a September 3, 1997, "Health Watch" column in the *Times*, Dr. Bradley Bute had urged people to "[t]ake the library out of the bathroom" because it encouraged prolonged straining at stool; "THE END OF ALL READING" Roth scribbled at top before sending to friends. By the time of Roth's retirement, given the more and more ubiquitous "gratifications of the screen," things had become far worse. Someday soon, said Roth, reading novels would be as "cultic" an activity as reading "Latin poetry."

He considered himself an anachronism—out of touch with America and crankily disinclined to keep up with the new gadgetry. His long-time copy editor, Roslyn Schloss, stuck with "the Philip M. Roth Fax Machine" for the benefit of a single client who refused to communicate via email (except with Kaysie), and he also went on using WordPerfect 5.1 (from 1989) until the bitter end. Eventually, rather grudgingly, he availed himself of the internet. In 2007, he bought an IBM laptop that he used strictly for that purpose—that is, for ordering his breakfast cereal from Fresh Direct, and books from Amazon and Alibris; finally, in 2010, he let a few more people know his email address. Certainly he was ready for more distractions, now that he'd stopped writing and even, for the most part, *reading* fiction. "Fiction has been the heart of my intellectual life since I was eighteen or nineteen years old," he explained to the Klímas, "—writing, reading, studying, and teaching it—and now, nearly sixty years later, I seem finally to have lost, not my love and respect for fiction, but my taste for it." He admitted as much publicly in a 2011 interview with the *Financial Times*, adding that he got pleasure nowadays from looking at "old newspapers": "I have to get *some* pleasure," he laughed.

His engagement with current events was enlivened somewhat by presidential elections, and during the 2008 primaries he threw his support to Barack Obama: "He's an attractive man, he's smart, he happens to be tremendously articulate. His position in the Democratic Party is more or less okay with me. And I think it would be important to American blacks if he became president." A little more than a year after Obama's inauguration, Roth was interviewed by an Italian journalist who wondered why he found the president "nasty, vacillating, and mired in the mechanics of power"—this according to an interview Roth had allegedly given one Tommaso Debenedetti of the right-wing *Libero*. "But I have never said anything of the kind!" Roth protested. "Obama, in my opinion, is fantastic." Afterward he asked Judith Thurman, who spoke Italian, to look into the matter. She discovered another interview with John Grisham, who was also quoted (falsely) as saying hard things about Obama, and eventually some seventy fraudulent Debenedetti interviews with American writers (as many as five with Roth alone) who putatively reviled the president.[*]

Roth's real-life fondness for Obama, at any rate, appeared to be reciprocated. On March 2, 2011, Roth was summoned back to the White House as one of eleven recipients of the National Humanities Medal, a roster including his old friends Bob Brustein and Joyce Carol Oates, as well as James Taylor, Sonny Rollins, and Van Cliburn. "How many young people have learned to *think*," Obama paused, deadpan, as he

---

[*] In 2012, Debenedetti created a fake Twitter account under Roth's name.

presented Roth's medal in the East Room, "by reading the exploits of Portnoy and his complaints?" Amid laughter ("that is something George Bush could never have pulled off," Conarroe punned), Roth headed to the podium, where Obama hung the medal around his neck and murmured, "You're not slowing down, are you?" "Oh, Mr. President," Roth replied, "I'm slowing down, all right."

■ ■ ■ ■

AN HONOR THAT WOULD prove less delightful befell Roth two months later, when he was named the fourth winner of the Man Booker International Prize, worth £60,000 and awarded biennially for a body of work that's published in English, whether originally or in translation; past winners included Chinua Achebe, in 2007, and Alice Munro two years later. The chair of the three-person jury, Rick Gekoski, said that Roth's work had "stimulated, provoked and amused an enormous, and still expanding, audience" for half a century, and "his imagination has not only recast our idea of Jewish identity, it has also reanimated fiction, and not just American fiction, generally."

That was on May 18, and so far so good. Seven hours after the award was announced, however, it became known that one of the judges, Carmen Callil, had bitterly withdrawn from the jury in protest over its selection of Roth. "He goes on and on and on about the same subject in almost every single book," she said. "It's as though he's sitting on your face and you can't breathe." The other two judges, Gekoski and novelist Justin Cartwright, reiterated that they felt "strongly and passionately" that Roth was the right choice, while *The Telegraph* deplored Callil's outburst with a May 19 editorial concluding that Roth "more than deserves the Booker judges' recognition."

The next day, Callil defended herself more temperately, if not coherently, with a piece in *The Guardian* ("Why I quit the Man Booker International panel"). Her main point was that her aversion to Roth was nothing personal. She'd hoped the prize would go, this time, to a work in translation, since it's important to "widen our understanding of other countries, other cultures," and besides the previous award had gone to the "truly great" North American writer, Munro; as for Roth, "He is clever, harsh, comic, but his reach is narrow. . . . Roth digs brilliantly into himself, but little else is there." Having described an author who'd never written the American Trilogy or certain other ambitious, non-narrow, non-solipsistic novels, Callil told a reporter that Roth's "best book, *American Pastoral*," was "wonderful about women"—the better not to seem bothered by Roth's alleged misogyny; meanwhile she claimed the whole "kerfuffle" was "an ad feminam attack from the boys." To be sure, Callil had reason to feel defensive, seeing as how she was a founder of the feminist Virago Press, English publisher of *Leaving a Doll's House*.

As Roth saw it (not altogether mistakenly), his reputation was still tainted by his ex-wife's second memoir. "Refused to answer impertinent question about Claire's book," he noted on September 10, 2010, when *CBS Sunday Morning* featured a spot on Roth, which included this exchange with interviewer Rita Braver:

> BRAVER: Your former wife, Claire Bloom, claimed that you don't even like women.
> ROTH [*very quietly; composed but seething*]: Let's forget that.
> BRAVER: You don't want to talk about her. That was a bad episode in your life.
> ROTH: No, I don't want to comment on libels.

A few years before, Norman Manea had served on the jury for the prestigious Neustadt International Prize for Literature, and mentioned to Roth that his fellow judges had rejected Roth "vehemently" because of his "treatment of women"—both in his fiction *and* according to Bloom. Indeed, Roth was hardly alone in suspecting that *Doll's House* was the main touchstone for the Swedish Academy, whose prize was intended for "the most outstanding work in an ideal direction." Given the manifold implications of that criterion—said another Bloom (Harold)—Roth's prospects for the Nobel were roughly nil: "He's not terribly politically correct, you know, and they are."

The same spring as the Callil controversy, Roth stumbled on galleys for a reference book to be published by Facts on File, *Critical Companion to Philip Roth*, whose editor, Ira Nadel, had included this sentence about "Erda" (Bloom's pseudonym for Inga) in his introductory biographical essay: "However, a familiar pattern emerged, characteristic of [Roth's] life with women: With intimacy increasing, his anxieties over being emotionally engulfed by a woman caused him to withdraw." Roth ended up paying $61,022.29 to his lawyers at Milbank Tweed, who forced Nadel to delete the sentence and rewrite the surrounding passage. Next Roth hired a research assistant to determine how widely the seepage from Bloom's book had spread throughout the academy; among the several scholarly articles citing *Doll's House* was one in *Philip Roth Studies* that described Bloom's "surprisingly compassionate yet devastating memoir" as an "indispensable" source on Roth's life.

The final straw, for Roth, was his discovery that the aforementioned Nadel had signed a contract with Oxford University Press to write "a full-scale biography" of Roth, at whose urging Wylie informed Nadel that he didn't have permission to quote from Roth's work, nor would Roth's friends and associates cooperate in any way: "I trust that you will make any prospective publisher aware of this, so as not to misrepresent your position." Another letter followed from Stacey Rappaport of Milbank Tweed, who admonished Nadel to "consider the credibility of any sources on which you choose to rely in writing such a biography," particularly the "false and defamatory" *Leaving a Doll's House*.

"I felt unfairly misunderstood and started screaming," Roth quoted his ex-wife's memoir for the epigraph to his 295-page rebuttal, "Notes for My Biographer," which he began that spring and finished ten months later. "Another writer my age awaiting a biography and awaiting death (which is worse?) might not care," Roth wrote of Bloom's book. "I do. I can no longer allow her falsifications to impinge on my personal and professional reputation. There are no mythical Erdas here." Roth wasn't concerned with the first nine chapters of *Doll's House*; he began with page 143—where, in 1975, he and Bloom bump into each other on Madison Avenue—and proceeded sequentially from there. Two pages later, Bloom begins to discuss Roth's first marriage to "Margaret Michaelson" [sic], the "shiksa to end all shiksas" who provided the model for the ghastly Maureen in *My Life as a Man*—a novel that Bloom examines as a kind of "medico-moral" (Roth) skeleton key to his relations with women, toward whom he harbors "a deep and irrepressible rage." Bloom's critique of the novel, said Roth, "is trifling as literary criticism and dubious as psychology, but as defamation it packs a punch and so requires scrutiny." Roth accused Bloom of indulging in what college lit students are taught to identify as the "biographical fallacy" and "hasty generalization." "Tarnopol's rage may be 'deep and irrepressible' but it is hardly invisible," Roth wrote. "And it has been provoked very specifically not by 'women,' as Bloom would have it, but by a wife, Maureen, who has deceived Tarnopol and viciously betrayed him."

Roth swiftly moved on to what he called the leitmotif of Bloom's book: "She is repeatedly being stripped of her will and overpowered and wronged by ruthless men—whether Hilly Elkins, her 'voyeuristic and sadistic' second husband, or her despised costar and lover Anthony Quinn, each with his abundant virility, or me with my 'razor-sharp wit.' In fact, the person she was most intimidated by was her teenage daughter." As Roth had proceeded with the long-shunned task of reading Bloom's second memoir, it occurred to him that it was nothing so much as an exhaustive exercise in mollifying Anna by shifting the blame for the "family debacle" away from her and entirely onto the "Machiavellian strategist"—the same man, that is, whom Bloom had often praised outside the indictment of *Doll's House*: "I remember the good times with gratitude and love," she tearfully admitted on *Stars and Mas*; her "marvelous marriage" to Roth, she told Leonard Lopate, was "the best relationship of her life."

Roth's greatest scorn was reserved for the final chapter about Erda/Inga, "The Truth," which, he said, should have been renamed "The Lie." Roth was incensed by the suggestion that Erda/Inga had to be "cruelly coerced" to leave her husband because of her "new relationship" with Roth, and Inga agreed: "I don't think it was a very good description of who I am at all," she remarked of the meekly submissive Erda—whose real-life counterpart was gleefully described by Roth as his "willing and gloriously happy accomplice in adultery for close to twenty years." In "Notes," Roth provided a droll counterversion of his long affair with Inga "as plainly, factually, and fully as [he] can tell it"—disguising real-life details with underlined substitutions ("Polish" for Norwegian, etc.)—but he concluded the story on a note of outrage: "As is so much else in Bloom's memoir, Erda and our 'several months' together, during which, according to Bloom, I mistreated her in the extreme and tormented her in order to make her do my bidding, are nothing less than a vile and actionable fantasy of the author."

Roth thought he'd found the "right tone" for his rejoinder and decided, as he recalled, "Fuck it. I'm gonna publish." A little reluctantly, Andrew

Wylie gave the manuscript to Houghton, which offered a middling advance that Roth was glad to accept. Meanwhile, in addition to the in-house lawyer's reading, Roth shelled out another $85,000 to Milbank Tweed to vet the book independently. Milbank worried about the anti-Semitic remarks Roth attributed to his former wife: "If Bloom asserts and proves that these quotations materially differ from her actual statements in a way that is damaging to her reputation you could be subject to potential liability." Also, while Milbank didn't foresee a problem with Roth's portrayal of Bloom's basic fragility, they hoped he was able to substantiate more serious allegations such as her conversing with and petting her dead mother, or running around fields "screaming like a lunatic character in an animated cartoon" (as Roth put it).

Roth was looking forward to the happy task of marshaling witnesses and documentation, but his friends were unanimously opposed to publication. Jack Miles and Nicole Krauss both wondered, and expected others to wonder, why Roth had stayed in such a relationship so long—a question Roth himself repeatedly posed in the book, finding no satisfactory answer. Both Hermione Lee and Jonathan Brent used the same phrase—"relentless self-justification"—to describe Roth's tone, and privately Brent deplored the way Roth had been "washing these little gemstones of memory, over and over and over again, so they come out as set pieces." Barbara Sproul, who loved him, was "saddened by the obsessiveness of it . . . that perpetual desire to be understood and to be justified"—still, still—and insisted on talking him out of it in person. As Roth recalled their conversation, she said, "'You're gonna do yourself more damage with this book than she did with hers.' I said, 'It's the truth!' And she said, 'You're gonna look like a bully.' . . . I said, 'I didn't start it!' And she just said, '*Don't do it.*'" After she left, it occurred to Roth that the only person who might have encouraged him was Ross Miller. "Let's just forget it," he told Wylie over the phone, deciding to use the manuscript in the sense implied by its title.

CHAPTER

Forty-Nine

Roth's heart condition steadily worsened. One night he had chest pains, and asked Lisa Halliday to accompany him to the hospital; after the usual wait, he was given a private room where a nurse helped fill out his paperwork. "Religion?" she asked, and Roth replied "Atheist." When she departed, Halliday wondered why they need to know a patient's religion. "Well," said Roth, "if you say you're Jewish and suddenly it's looking like it's getting close to the end, they'll send a rabbi around. And if you say you're Catholic, they'll send a priest around." "And if you say you're an atheist?" "They send Christopher Hitchens around."

His first leisurely summer in a long time, 2010, was marred by an extreme soreness of the tongue and gums that made it painful to eat; he'd lost nine pounds before a doctor told him he had "burning mouth disease," and suggested he dissolve a Klonopin on his tongue for three minutes, three times a day, then spit out the residue. Two days later— Labor Day—he and Ben Taylor were having lunch at the West Street Grill, and during the first course Taylor asked him to name the baseball player who'd been the model for Roy Hobbs in Malamud's *The Natural*.* Roth held a forefinger aloft—then collapsed. Taylor remembered the last sentence of *Death in Venice* ("And before nightfall a shocked and respectful world received the news of his decease") and called an ambulance. At the hospital Roth was stabilized with an IV and oxygen; his fainting spell was attributed to a combination of Klonopin and low

---

* In 1949, a first baseman for the Chicago Cubs, Eddie Waitkus, was shot by a deranged fan, like Hobbs in the novel; he survived and continued his career.

blood pressure. Meanwhile an echocardiogram showed that his coronary artery disease—diagnosed almost thirty years ago—had now progressed to "mild congestive heart failure," following the same course as Sandy's illness.

Soon Roth had a charming person to cook healthy meals for him. The reference had come from Kaysie, who'd hired a private chef, Catherine von Klitzing, to help her feed the enormous man (six foot seven, 280 pounds) she'd married shortly after breaking up with Roth; unfortunately the cook's first day on the job coincided with the final departure of Kaysie's husband. Roth came to dinner instead, and lavishly praised the meal; Kaysie replied that it had been prepared by a cook she no longer needed but whom Roth would do well to hire.

Roth would always have a weakness for vulnerable young women, and with Catherine he hit the jackpot. A recovering alcoholic prone to bouts of depression (a condition she'd inherited, she said, from a "bastard" of a father), she would sometimes become tearful for no discernible reason, and Roth was nothing but patient and concerned. He'd suggest she lie down for a while in the spare bedroom, or just go home "and take care of [her]self." That summer she stayed four days out of each week in Connecticut, where she lodged in Roth's studio; from nine to noon the pool was all hers, and Roth was careful never to intrude on her time. He still made his own breakfast, and took to greeting her through the kitchen screen door as she walked down to the pool each morning: "Slim!" he called her. "Why don't you come in and have some breakfast?" So, gradually, they became comfortable with each other.

■ ■ ■

AFTER LEARNING OF his congestive heart failure, Roth made a point of getting back in touch with dear people from his distant past. Dorothy Brand, his old friend from the Chancellor Avenue School, hadn't heard from Roth since 1957, when she moved to Chicago; at the time Roth had told her he was painting his Hyde Park apartment, and would get back to her as soon as he was done—then disappeared down the rabbit hole of ceaseless literary endeavor for the next fifty-odd years. "Are you the coauthor of *Let Freedom Ring*?" he abruptly inquired, phoning her in 2012. "I'm destroyed," he went on, when she seemed flummoxed. "That's the beginning of my writing career, and you don't remember . . . !" Suddenly it all came back to her—Prejudice and Tolerance; "The House I Live In"*—and the two "just picked up where [they] left off," chatting for half an hour or more. Roth followed with a letter, and they became pen pals.

Jane Brown Maas, his old costar (she'd played the title role) in the Bucknell production of *The Madwoman of Chaillot*, wrote Roth a fan letter about *The Plot Against America*, then went into the hospital for colon cancer surgery. Roth visited almost daily, and afterward made a point of meeting Maas for dinner once a month. (One night he brought two copies of *Madwoman* to Maas's apartment: "We read the play and couldn't make head nor tail of what it was all about," he recalled.) In late 2010, Maas was among those interviewed for a European documentary about Roth, and, while giving what she thought were candid-enough answers, was abruptly interrupted by her Italian interviewer: "He is not St. Philip, Jane! Does he have a dark side?" Maas soberly replied that he *does* have a dark side, and sometimes it comes out when he's in pain; however, while she was in the hospital with cancer, and told him over and over he didn't have to visit so often, he kept right on coming anyway.

As Roth kept telling their mutual friend Barbara Jakobson, one of the people he missed most was his sweet-natured companion from the sixties, Ann Mudge, who'd steadfastly refused to see him after her second marriage in 1983. "For a variety of reasons," she'd written Roth after an "awfully prickly" encounter *chez* Styron in 1974, "I seem to feel I must defend myself against you." Her prickliness was hardly unwarranted, given that she'd just read *My Life as a Man* with its portrayal of "Susan"— Tarnopol's feckless gentile girlfriend who can't have an orgasm and tries to kill herself with sleeping pills after he dumps her. Susan's real-life model, at any rate, managed to pull herself together quite nicely. Around the age of forty she completed her law degree, and, after a short-lived marriage, bought a house in Litchfield County. One night in 1981, she was dining with John Jakobson at the Hopkins Inn; returning from the men's room, he reported that Roth was there, too, with his father (it was the summer after Bess's death). Mudge went over to say hi, and Roth

---

* See page 49.

not only received her ebulliently but phoned the next day to invite her to dinner. "I stupidly said 'Yes,'" Mudge remembered, "and ended up going back to his house and that was the last one-night stand. Claire was due back from London the next day, and there was all this frantic *'We have to get the sheets washed!'* . . . And he called me up a couple days later in New York, and I said, 'Philip, I can't see you.'"

"I'm delighted for you," Roth wrote her two years later, when she married the advertising mogul Bill Backer, whose coups included the Coca-Cola "Hilltop" ad ("I'd Like to Buy the World a Coke") in 1971. "You never love an ex-wife more (and, as it turns out, you are that to me) than when she remarries." By the time Mudge finally relented and paid Roth a visit, in the spring of 2012, she was barely able to walk after various surgeries ("full of bolts and screws"), and he ditto. "She was a little old white-haired lady I wouldn't recognize in the street," said Roth, "until she sat down and began to speak, and then I began to see her face." Soon Roth was phoning her at least twice a week, usually after her even more decrepit husband had gone to sleep. "What are you wearing?" he'd greet her. "Where's your cane? I'll tell you where my cane is if you'll tell me where your cane is." Roth found his tender old friend "enchanting," and resumed his paternalistic advice-giving, nowadays about exercising in the pool and so on. "Annie dearest," he wrote her on April 25, 2013, "I was right about going back to college . . . and I am right about this" (proper water temperature). "The only thing I did wrong was failing to marry you and have a family, and that I couldn't do because by the time Mad Maggie and the State of New York were through with me I could as easily have married an aardvark as a woman, even one as lovely and loving as you."

"I can't save you, Philip," Lucy Warner had told him after their final tryst in the turbulent summer of 1962, when Roth had tried and failed to leave his first wife. "I'm only twenty-two years old." Four years later he called her, out of the blue, and offered to recommend her for an editorial-assistant opening at *The New York Review of Books*; as it happened she needed the job but had no relevant experience and wondered if she were suited. "I always had a higher opinion of you than you had of yourself," said Roth, who persuaded Barbara Epstein to hire her anyway. During the forty-six years that followed, before she and Roth got back in touch, Knopf published Warner's story collection, *Mirrors* (1969), which coincided with a bad patch in her life that led to her giving up as a writer; eventually she got married and became a reading teacher in public schools and homeless shelters. Neither to her husband, her therapist, nor any of her friends did she ever breathe a word of her bygone affair with Philip Roth—whom she'd seen (but not vice versa) only once, in 2006, while observing alternate-side-parking rules near her apartment on 116th and Riverside: There he was, walking along the opposite sidewalk with a *much* younger woman (Brigit). "Oh Philip," she thought, "I hope that's your niece."

In 2012, she was "shocked" to be contacted by Roth's biographer, having assumed Roth had forgotten her long ago. "For many of these intervening 50 years," she wrote him afterward, "I have been haunted by my abrupt and frightened leave-taking of you. . . . I remember you with enormous tenderness." Roth felt the same way, and promptly reassured her that she'd been quite right in Iowa City, and again in Connecticut, to leave the desperate, bewildered young man who'd begged her to run away with him: "I promise I won't ask you to run away with me again," he concluded in 2012. "In point of fact, I *can't* run. But I can walk to the corner and will for you if you give the word."

Their reunion was touching to both. Roth noticed that Lucy wore a cross around her neck these days, as she mostly consorted with the Episcopal nuns and monks she'd befriended during monastery retreats, whereas Lucy was struck by Roth's frailty, physical and otherwise. He was still recovering from his latest back surgery and taking powerful pain meds, and seemed a little "spacey" prior to embracing her on the sidewalk and saying "Of course, sweetheart," when she asked whether she could call him again. Their subsequent meetings took place mostly at Roth's apartment, where he would tell her (often while holding her hand) what had befallen him over the years—Maggie and Claire, his depressions, surgeries, drugs, and so on. Lucy became one of the helpers who took him to the hospital when needed, and he in turn reread her short stories and declared them "masterful," goading her to write at least "twenty sentences a day" instead of the sporadic few she'd managed since taking up fiction again a few years back. He also gave her a gift of ten thousand dollars for the upkeep of her childhood home in Maine, whither they still joked about running away: Roth would become "the first Jewish lobster man"—for five years or so, she said, until he ran off with someone else.

Not everyone was thrilled to hear from him again. Maxine Groffsky had returned from Paris in the midseventies, when she and Roth met for dinner—their first meeting in fifteen years or more. As he remembered it:

> She had lost none of her beauty and was very poised, but I remember having the feeling, rightly or wrongly, that she didn't approve of me and didn't like me. . . . I was surprised then, when afterward we were waiting outside for a taxi, that she suddenly turned her head and offered her mouth to be kissed. I didn't oblige her and mumbled something like "No, no." I remember this as making her angry and when I put her into a cab to take her home she barely said goodnight. Those are the bare bones that I can recall.

To others, Groffsky would occasionally vouchsafe—a little ruefully (at best)—that she was the model for Brenda Patimkin. In 1983, she married the chairman of Harper & Row, Winthrop Knowlton, and with Knowlton she bumped into Roth again, in 2008, while attending a concert at Carnegie Hall; she was perhaps startled when Roth ("somewhat swept away by the recollection of all she'd meant to me and the thought of the two of us now being in our seventies") gave her a big hug and whispered "You're still my girl" into her ear. "I'd love to see you and talk to you and listen to you before I die," he emailed her roughly four years later—an invitation she curtly declined with a one-line reply.

But he was most persistent with Brigit, the young woman who'd prompted "the last great outburst of everything" (as Roth wrote of Everyman's longing for the comely jogger who changes her route to avoid him). "We couldn't walk for five consecutive minutes along the shore of the Housatonic River without stopping in our tracks to excitedly talk," Roth reminded Brigit on December 17, 2010, more than four years after their final parting.

> Excitedly. Excitedly. Excitedly. You sang to me one night during one of our playful hour-long phone calls between [Colorado] and Connecticut,

you said, "Do you want to hear a lullaby?" And I said yes, and so you breathily sang a lullaby and I was wowed, as though you'd just sung from *Tosca*. I remember rolling onto my back on the bed and asking you (as though I didn't know), "Are you really as wonderful as this?"

"NO REPLY" he wrote with a Flair pen at the bottom of his file copy. On May 16, 2012, he tried again: "I insist on seeing you. Life offers few pleasures more thrilling and poignant than seeing someone you deeply loved years later, and not just fleetingly on the street. . . . I want to listen to you speak as I did all night long one New Year's Eve in Connecticut." "NO REPLY," he noted again, and a few months later he sent his "Old Flame" a Peninsula Hotel matchbox to remind her of their time in Chicago. "NO REPLY."

■ ▪ ▪ ■

MEMORIES OF BRIGIT (et al.) were part of a larger wistfulness, now that he was old, retired, and dependent on friends not only to stave off loneliness but to take him to the hospital and back. Remembering his pregnancy scare with Betty Powell, his long-dead Bucknell girlfriend, Roth said, "I would have married her. And just think. There would be a man or a woman on this earth, a person fifty-nine-years-old, who would be my son or daughter."

A degree of compensation—even the "love of his life," as some saw it—had come his way in November 2003, when Julia Golier gave birth to twins, Amelia and William. About ten days later, on December 9, Roth went to Julia's childhood home in Montvale, New Jersey, where "the loveliest picture" ever taken of him—according to Julia's mother—captured Roth gazing benevolently at the little girl's head cupped in his hand: "All you have to do is put a halo on him and you could call him St. Joseph." Roth spent the rest of the afternoon sitting on the floor beside the twins' blanket, and later, when the family moved back to Manhattan, he made a point of visiting once or twice a month, sometimes when only the Indian nanny was around.

He was their de facto grandfather—all the more once their actual grandfathers died. During play days at his pool, Roth would hold contests for craziest dive and the like, and afterward show the kids his favorite old musicals. "Amelia, go to sleep, sweetheart," he told the nine-year-old ("hanging on not just to the evening, but to life itself by a fine thread") while watching *My Fair Lady* after a "sun-blasted" day in the pool. "No, no, no, I can't," she moaned. "Why not?" "I have to see if he marries her." Talking with her mother, Amelia wondered whether it was proper to say "I love you" to Philip, and when it slipped out one day, she was mortified and he was elated. "Julia tells me that you and William have lots of spelling words to learn," he wrote her, after she'd made him a Valentine's heart. "Let me teach you one right now. B-E-A-U-T-I-F-U-L. That's what you are."

Roth and Amelia occasionally collaborated on stories, via email, under the pen name Phamelia. One of their early efforts, when the girl was eight, had to do with a family of monkeys who visit the Museum of Natural History while wearing human masks ("Their adventures there make the Marx Brothers look like Dostoyevsky," said Roth), and a year later Amelia proposed a story about an optimistic snail (Oppy) who goes for a walk (as it were) and encounters another snail named "Cry a baby CAB for short." Roth gamely took up the story from there: "Oppy said to Cry Baby, 'Don't cry, you silly snail. Life is beautiful. . . . You have suction on your belly so you can hold on to anything. You have a beautiful house that you carry around with you on your back so you can always be inside whenever it starts raining.'" Roth waited a few days for Amelia's installment (doubtless hoping she'd emulate the snailish quiddity of his descriptions), and finally wrote "Oppy? Where are you?" "I have writers block," Amelia replied, and that was that. Roth indulged his didactic bent, again, when the girl began a piece about wishing on a star for wealth and fame ("The white lights of Hollywood!"). "Wishing on a star has nothing to do with what brings you fame, money, and the admiration of others," Roth admonished. "GAINING FAME IS ALL ABOUT HARD WORK AND PERFECTING YOUR TALENT"—and he went on about how "boring" it is to be famous ("strangers come up to you while you are eating"). But this, apparently, was not what the girl had in mind, and again she fell silent.

. . . .

ROTH'S OCCASIONAL NONFICTION had tended to arise "mainly from a provocation," and so with Wikipedia's assertion that *The Human Stain* had been "allegedly inspired by the life of the writer Anatole Broyard." Jolted by this reminder of all the gossipy "babble" surrounding the publication of that novel—never mind the one preceding it, and never mind a certain scurrilous memoir preceding *that*—Roth demanded the offending misstatement be deleted and was advised by the "English Wikipedia Administrator" that he, Roth, was not in a position to make the call: "I understand your point that the author is the greatest authority on their [sic] own work," this administrator replied, "but we require secondary sources."

Such a source, then, was Roth's "Open Letter to Wikipedia," published September 6, 2012, on the *New Yorker* website. "Dear Wikipedia," it began—as if Roth's correspondent were a single, monolithic entity— "I am Philip Roth." After explaining the reason for what Remnick described as a "hilarious screed" (circa 2,655 words), Roth proceeded to give a rambling synopsis of *The Human Stain* vis-à-vis Mel Tumin's real-life "Spooks" episode, followed by a not very accurate account of Roth's vague acquaintance with Broyard, whom he'd met on the beach at Amagansett, in 1959, and only haphazardly encountered thereafter— most notably, he claimed, at the clothier Paul Stuart, sometime in the eighties: "Since Broyard was by this time the *Times*'s most intellectually stylish book reviewer, I told him that I would like to have him sit down in the chair beside me and allow me to buy him a pair of shoes, hoping thereby, I forthrightly admitted, to deepen his appreciation for my next book. It was a playful, amusing encounter, it lasted ten minutes at most, and was the only such encounter we ever had."

In 1989, however, while gravely ill with prostate cancer, Broyard had suggested a deeper kind of spiritual/aesthetic kinship with Roth: "He was my cynical big brother and my crazy little brother, too. . . . Like so many American readers, I felt that I had got gloriously drunk with Philip Roth, we had gone skinny-dipping together, and had suffered with the same kind of women." That last item was more than notional; back in the sixties, when Broyard was a writing teacher at the New School, he'd communicated with Roth (so to speak) by sending some of his comelier students to his colleague's nearby walkup on East Tenth, where, unbidden, but certainly welcome, they would announce via the intercom that "Mr. Broyard" had sent them, and were promptly buzzed upstairs. One of the women wrote Roth afterward:

If I were you I would find it very hard to resist telling about a visit like mine. Thats [sic] okay—it's like your share of the profits almost. What I wanted to ask was would you not get Broyard's name in it. I guess it could hurt him.

You were very nice to me and I feel I got off easily. Thank you.

"I should never have written that letter to Wikipedia," Roth admitted, a week after it appeared. "Stupidly I didn't realize it was going to let all of the cockroaches out of the woodwork." Most of his critics were merely amused (a few found the piece a little daft), but Broyard's daughter, Bliss, made it known via Facebook (and subsequently *Salon*) that her father's acquaintance with Roth "was more substantial" than Roth had described. Though perhaps unaware of their antics during the sixties, she mentioned an encounter at James Atlas's Thanksgiving Eve party, in 1988, that contradicted at least one point in Roth's Wikipedia piece— "I've never known, spoken to, or, to my knowledge, been in the company of a single member of Broyard's family"—and also suggested an abiding awareness on Roth's part re her father's main secret, to wit: after Broyard introduced his daughter to Roth, *chez* Atlas, Roth looked her over and said, "So lithe and pale. Like a ghost." "It was a brief encounter," Bliss reported twenty-four years later, "—one I'm not surprised that he might have forgotten—but I am sure you all can understand why I haven't."

Despite his rue over the reception of that first Wikipedia letter, Roth proceeded to pore over every other Roth-related entry and compose three more letters for inclusion in his tenth LOA volume (*Why Write? Collected Nonfiction 1960–2013*). His second letter countered the observation that "Jewish sons" such as Portnoy and Zuckerman "rebel by denouncing Judaism": "Far from denouncing Jews," Roth rejoined, "in *The Ghost Writer*, as a neophyte writer, Zuckerman is denounced *by* Jews," etc. "To begin with," Roth asserted in his third letter—citing a reference ("Wikipedia writes") to his "nervous breakdown" on the evidence of *Operation Shylock*—"there is no way to conclude anything with certainty about the flesh-and-blood author from something that is said about a character in a novel." And the last letter addressed another old and bothersome canard: "I knew nothing about [Swede Masin] when I was writing *American Pastoral* other than that he had been an outstanding all-around athlete."

Two months later, when Roth's retirement from writing fiction became widely known, *Tablet* magazine remembered that first Wikipedia letter as "just another piece of support for the tired wisdom that there are few things more dangerous (or tedious) than a retiree with a typewriter."

■   ■   ■

AND YET WORD of his retirement was a worldwide sensation. One woman wrote *The New York Times* that the news had reminded her of "a ten-block conversation" she'd once had with the indefatigable novelist. "By the end, he knew how old I was, my greatest failure, and how much I made an hour. He closed in on information that might be useful. He was working." Roth himself—who used to say he'd die if unable to write—mentioned on NPR what a relief it was not to feel compelled anymore to take notes after any vaguely significant conversation: "Now I just listen, and it's quite nice. I go home and go to sleep."

Some three years after writing his last page of fiction, Roth's admission that he'd quit had more or less slipped out during an interview for the October 9, 2012, issue of *Les Inrocks*—"Philip Roth arrête d'écrire," read a boxed banner on the cover—and a whole month passed before (as Roth wrote Hoagland) "some down-at-the-heels stringer somewhere must have gone to the barbershop in Paris to get a haircut and found the magazine." Actually it was *Salon* editor David Daley who noticed the item and hastily used Google to translate Roth's most pertinent remarks into awkward, as it were Gallic-inflected, English: "And after that"—i.e., Roth's rereading of his own books—"I decided that I was done with fiction. I do not want to read, to write more. I have dedicated my life to the novel: I studied, I taught, I wrote and I read. With the exclusion of almost everything else. Enough is enough! I no longer feel this fanaticism to write that I have experienced in my life."

Both the Associated Press and the *Times* pounced on Daley's item that same day—November 9—the latter reproducing the *Salon*/Google translation word for word, whereupon Roth gleefully paraphrased E. E. Cummings on the subject of President Warren Harding: "'The only man, woman, or child who could make six ["seven" in Cummings's poem] grammatical errors in a single declarative sentence.' Thus the paper of record." Four days later, *The Paris Review* website published a correct translation of the *Les Inrocks* interview, which established that Roth had stopped reading and writing *fiction* only ("I don't want to read *any more of it*, write *any more of it*" [italics added to indicate phrases omitted from the Google translation]), versus reading and writing altogether. Meanwhile Roth's admirers wondered whether it was really true, or whether, as Adam Gopnik would have it, Roth would succumb to the temptation of writing "one last Möbius strip of fictional-confessional construction, in which Zuckerman may be found creating a novelist, call him Isaac Kaplan, who, at the age of eighty, has decided to stop writing, only to find that this has increased, rather than limited, his fame." If so, it would be hard to improve on reality, as Roth's decision to retire was given front-page treatment by the *Times*: "Goodbye, Frustration: Pen Put Aside, Roth Talks." During a three-hour interview, Charles McGrath found Roth "cheerful, relaxed and at peace with himself"—all the more so, said Roth, since this was to be his final interview: "Free at last."

What followed was perhaps unique in American literary history. *New York* magazine canvassed thirty-three personages—twenty-eight men and five women, including Salman Rushdie, James Franco, Kathryn Schulz, and Neil LaBute—on various Roth-related issues. An impressive 77 percent voted him the greatest living American novelist; 24 percent named *Sabbath's Theater* his best book, 13 percent *The Counterlife*, and 10 percent each named *American Pastoral, The Ghost Writer, Goodbye, Columbus,* or *Portnoy's Complaint.* As for the still-burning question "Is Roth a misogynist?": 17 percent said yes, 30 percent no, and 52 percent "Well . . ." "I don't like the way he writes about women," said Nell Freudenberger, "and I don't like the way I sound complaining about it." Amid the vast coverage, too, was a survey of glowing tributes (via *Flavorwire*) from no fewer than three dozen prominent writers—or rather thirty-five who spoke more or less glowingly, whereas the poet and novelist Eileen Myles had this to say: "I'm happy he's still alive, and we won't have to keep hearing about his boring books. It's very generous of him to stop."

Give or take the odd barb, Roth seemed to enjoy the spectacle, likening himself to Tom Sawyer "listening to his own funeral proceedings." A similar parallel occurred to Daphne Merkin, who over the years had taken a somewhat acid interest in Roth's career: "Has there ever been a cannier promoter of his own work than Philip Roth, announcing his retirement?" she remarked in *The Daily Beast.* "Not Bellow, not Updike, certainly no female writer I can think of. It takes a certain kind of moxie—and egomania—both of which Roth has always had in spades." "Ah, Daphne sees right through me," Roth commented to a friend.

> Some six months ago, in the privacy of my apartment, telling a French journalist from an obscure French magazine . . . that I wasn't working on anything, hadn't been for several years, and didn't think I'd write fiction again—what a cagey (and, if I might add what Daphne is too shy to say, vulgar) act of self-promotion! Who other than Roth could have thought up a publicity gimmick like that? Not even Mailer! Not even Capote! Not even Tom Wolfe or Mike Tyson! . . . When it comes to naked self-promotion, I don't fuck around.

To be sure, Roth was more amenable to publicity now that he had time on his hands. Back in September 2009—as he was haplessly casting about for a new novel idea in the wake of *Nemesis*—an Italian journalist who'd become a friend, Livia Manera, met Roth for dinner to ask his advice about a proposed TV project on American writers who'd supported Obama. "When are you asking me?" said Roth, whose nonparticipation Manera had taken for granted. With Roth's eager approval, however, she promptly dropped the Obama project and decided to do a documentary exclusively on Roth (albeit one with no questions about Claire Bloom and the like). Directed by a Frenchman, William Karel, a fifty-two-minute version was filmed in the fall of 2010 and aired the following year on the French-German channel Arté as *Philip Roth, sans complexe* and *Philip Roth, ohne Beschwerden* ("without complaints"). Meanwhile Manera pitched it to Susan Lacy of PBS's *American Masters*—a platform Roth had quietly coveted going back to his BBC documentary in 1993— and Lacy was in favor, suggesting they expand it to ninety minutes by adding interviews with other writers: Pierpont, Krauss, Englander, and Franzen. Roth pointed out some errors in the first version and suggested bits of re-editing, declaring the final PBS version "much, much better"; he was even willing to appear via satellite at the Television Critics Association Press Tour in Pasadena, where he "stole the show" (*Los Angeles Times*) while promoting a program in which he himself proved to be "marvelous company," as the critic A. O. Scott wrote, "—expansive, funny, generous and candid."

Philip Roth: Unmasked was given a free weeklong screening at Film Forum, in SoHo, where a packed crowd sang "Happy Birthday" that first night (March 12, 2013, a week early) to Roth, who attended with an entourage including Manera and Conarroe, the latter in a thrift-store Weequahic High jacket ("because I'm a goy, Philip says it's a fake"). Roth had a wonderful time, shouting at himself onscreen and phoning Manera the next day: "We should have met twenty-five years ago," he said, after solemnly applauding her work. "It would have changed our lives."

■ ■ ■ ■

"I SAW AND HEARD something remarkable just a few hours ago," David Remnick wrote for the *New Yorker* website on March 20, 2013,

> something I'm not likely to forget until the mechanisms of remembering are shot and I'm tucked away for good. Philip Roth celebrated his eightieth birthday in the Billy Johnson Auditorium of the Newark Museum last night with the most astonishing literary performance I've ever witnessed. On his birthday night, and having sworn never again to give himself over to the "stringent exigencies of literature," he put on a farewell performance, a great burst of writing and sly self-display—a triumphal lope around the bases, like Ted Williams on his last day in a Red Sox uniform.

This triumph had been the brainchild of Professor Aimee Pozorski, the eager young president of the Philip Roth Society. During the summer of 2011, when Roth was renovating his house in Warren, Pozorski had volunteered to spend a weekend reshelving his vast library according to his careful system of alphabetized genres and relative priority. "How would you feel about a conference and a party in honor of your eightieth birthday?" she asked, once the job was completed to his satisfaction. Roth consented, and soon the project was enthusiastically adopted by Liz Del Tufo, president of the Newark Landmarks and Historic Preservation Committee, who was so persistent about touching base with Roth during the months of preparation that he took to answering her calls with the question, "Am I eighty yet?" The festivities would include a photographic exhibition of Roth's life, at the Newark Public Library, and the two curators, James Lewis and Rosemary Steinbaum, reported to Roth's apartment with some trepidation ("I had heard he was very private and could be prickly," said Lewis); but Roth was always happy to see them, and seemed to have a funny anecdote for almost every photo in his many boxes and albums. The curators took notes and finally emailed their rough captions to Roth, who "carefully rewrote them for his own voice," according to Steinbaum.

The Philip Roth Society's "Roth@80" conference was held at the Robert Treat Hotel, jammed with scholars from more than a dozen countries, including Brazil, France, Germany, Italy, Norway, Romania, and India (whence came Gurumurthy Neelakantan, who gave a seminar on how Roth challenges "notions of purity" inherent in the Brahmin caste system).* "That this scholarly organization is not necessarily an adoration society," Steven Kellman wrote in *Tablet*, "was apparent in several presentations that emphasized Roth's obsession with controlling every detail of his reputation, from cover to dust-jacket, from advertising to translation." Indeed, Roth took pains to ensure that his own select group of luminaries would be on hand to pay homage—the great Edna O'Brien, for instance, whom he insisted on personally reimbursing ($6,735) for her plane ticket and a week's stay at the Lotos Club on the Upper East Side. Joining O'Brien onstage at the Billy Johnson Auditorium—while the likes of Don DeLillo, Paul Auster, David Remnick, and Siri Hustvedt sat in the audience—was Jonathan Lethem, who "accepted the honor of batting lead-off in this highbrow's lineup."† Roth's favorite intellectuals, Alain Finkielkraut and Hermione Lee, discussed *Nemesis* and Shakespearean themes in Roth's work, respectively, while Claudia Roth Pierpont put the kibosh on accusations of misogyny ("There are no generalizations to be made about Roth's women, any more than about his men"). But O'Brien's tender, unsparing speech was per-

---

* Alan Lelchuk was invited to appear on a biography panel for the "Roth@80" conference; a fee of $135 was mentioned, and Lelchuk assumed this to be his meager honorarium. But no: as an earnest member of the Philip Roth Society regretfully informed him, Lelchuk himself was expected to pony up that amount. Lelchuk stayed home.

† "So he knew how to do even that, the hardest thing," Updike famously wrote of Ted Williams. "Quit." Williams's triumphant exit was an irresistible touchstone for Roth's, and the baseball/Williams motif was pervasive vis-à-vis Roth's 80th: "The evening felt almost as if Hank Aaron, Mickey Mantle, Willie Mays, and Duke Snider all showed up to toast Ted Williams," Kellman wrote.

haps the most memorable, as much for its content as for the bardic relish of its delivery. A little reluctantly she admitted that Roth and she had never been lovers, as naturally rumored, and imparted a few revealing (versus purely flattering) anecdotes. "So, friends," she concluded, "this is the tip of the iceberg, I can only give you a glimmer of the complexity of the man that is Philip Roth, feared and revered, plagiarized, envied, hermit and jester, lover and hater, by his own admission foolish and yet fiercely formidable, too adorable for words, a true friend and undoubtedly one of Yeats's Olympians."

Dressed in a black suit and shirt, Roth prompted a renewed burst of applause as he walked slowly onstage at the end of O'Brien's tribute, standing long enough to wave at friends and soak it in, then sitting at a table and opening a black binder. "Tempting as it is," he began, "I will not bury you tonight beneath a ton of stories about my happy childhood in the Weequahic section of this city or about my emotional affinity to nearly every commonplace, unpoetic thing that was the Newark of my day." Whereupon he launched into a loving litany of commonplace things, like the foil he used to pick from empty cigarette packs during the war, the books he'd carry home from Osborne Terrace Library in his bicycle basket ("Nobody needs to hear more about my bicycle basket"), the prizefights at Laurel Garden, the ball games at Ruppert Stadium (where "drunks slept the afternoon away, whimpering and snoring in the summer sun"). "I've described my last javelin throw and my last stamp album and my last glove factory and my last jewelry store and my last breast and my last butcher shop." Roth's recitation of things he wouldn't linger over now, or evoke in print ever again, led at last to a seven-page passage toward the end of *Sabbath's Theater* that, he said, "I like as well as any pages I've ever written"—Sabbath's welter of childhood memories while he looks for his family's graves at a Jersey Shore cemetery, until he places pebbles on the stones of his mother, his father, and his brother Morty: "Here I am." Roth allowed a beat of silence, closed the binder, and walked offstage amid a standing ovation. "It was a colossal dream for me," he thanked Del Tufo two days later, "a colossal, vibrant, mirth-filled, deeply touching dream. Because the meaning of life is that it stops, missing were my parents and my brother. But as I was waiting in the wings to come out to speak—while Edna lovingly roasted me—I invoked them and it didn't require too much encouragement for them to appear, full-blown."

And that wasn't all. Awaiting Roth in the museum's indoor courtyard were three members of the Weequahic marching band, their blasting fanfare followed by the three hundred or so guests singing "Happy Birthday." Roth cut into a book-shaped cake while Louise Erdrich gave an Ojibwe blessing, aptly dubbing him the Everlasting Man of Opposites.

■　■　■　■

ROTH WAS RICHLY HONORED during his final years. In 2012, he won Spain's Prince of Asturias Award (50,000 euros) for a writer "whose literary work represents a significant contribution to universal literature." At the October ceremony in Oviedo, the University of Chicago philosopher Martha Nussbaum agreed to read Roth's rather cranky acceptance speech, in which he affected a pleasant surprise that his work could "compete with the clichéd, super-simplified representation of America that befogs the perception of my country nearly everywhere."

The following spring he received the Literary Service Award from PEN America, appearing to fulfill Olga's bitter prediction in Roth's screenplay version of *The Prague Orgy*: "On top of all your millions of dollars and millions of girls, you will win the American Prize for Idealism about Literature"—this, in Zuckerman's case, for smuggling "from behind the Iron Curtain two hundred unpublished Yiddish stories written by the victim of a Nazi bullet," an endeavor that ultimately fails. Roth, however, had been quite successful in carrying out his clandestine Ad Hoc Fund subsidizing Czech dissidents in the seventies, not to say his editorship of Writers from the Other Europe.

As for his reputation in France, the cover of the September 21, 2011, issue of *Le Nouvel Observateur* said it all: "Philippe Roth: Le roi." Two years later he was named a Commandeur de la Légion d'honneur at the French consulate on Fifth Avenue, where they also laid a ceremonial brick for the first bookshop in Manhattan devoted entirely to French literature and translations. "He had a reputation as a literary troublemaker," Foreign Minister Laurent Fabius remarked of Roth to the chicly attired crowd of a hundred or so, "and at the time, nobody imagined such an award." "So quickly!" Roth sighed, when the medal clattered to the floor before Fabius could place it around his neck. Following brief remarks, France's most beloved American writer managed a phrase of the language he never came close to mastering: *"Je suis absolutement ravi.*" Afterward, he and his entourage—Julia Golier and her husband, Bill Bornmann, Amelia and William, Ben Taylor and Claudia Roth Pierpont—grabbed dinner at the Shake Shack on Columbus Avenue and returned to Roth's apartment. "The entertainment for the evening," said Roth, "requested by me, was Amelia singing, in her high, sweet, pure voice, the song she was to use for her audition the next day for a big school musical: 'Wouldn't It Be Loverly,' from *My Fair Lady*. Wonderful evening."

Perhaps the most momentous recognition was the honorary degree Roth received from the Jewish Theological Seminary on May 22, 2014—a kind of détente, at last, between Philip Roth and the Jewish cultural establishment. "Can you think of an American writer who took such a moral assault in the early years of his career?" Roth wondered aloud in 2004; even Mailer, he said, hadn't been so roundly denounced. Isaac Singer had wisely decided (so Roth thought) to publish an English translation of his novel *Shadows on the Hudson* posthumously, lest he be likewise reviled for suggesting American Jews are capable of gross vulgarity and sexual transgression. As for Roth: his Weequahic buddies Bob Heyman and Howie Silver had attended a lecture only a few years before at their temple in West Palm Beach, "Is PHILIP ROTH AN ANTI-SEMITE?"—so the signboard blared in big letters, for weeks, on the temple lawn facing a major thoroughfare.

Over the years Roth had received no fewer than four National Jewish Book Awards, and in 1998 the Jewish Book Council had given him its Lifetime Literary Achievement Award (Roth donated the honorarium to the Anti-Defamation League). "Roth has won," the *Forward* announced in 2012; "American Jews today are more the heirs of Portnoy than of his uptight community. . . . We can laugh today because we are no longer compelled to cry." Roth, more than anyone, was aware of his victory: "Now that writing's been over for close to four years," he wrote Conarroe in 2013, "virtually every night I go to sleep with a goofy smile on my face and in the dark am made positively gleeful by softly uttering aloud, 'I have recovered my life before I was embattled. The battles are over. I've come home. And I won.'"

But what the obsessive man still wanted, when he wasn't blissfully muttering in bed, was an *apology*: "This guy was brutally and unfairly attacked by people who have no right," he wanted some Jewish personage to say, publicly, and that's pretty much what his latest honorary degree amounted to. Thus the headline (again in the *Forward*) the day after: PHILIP ROTH, ONCE OUTCAST, JOINS JEWISH FOLD WITH JEWISH THEOLOGICAL SEMINARY HONOR. Roth had recognized the proffered degree as a "peace pipe" and promptly accepted; he'd also liked the cut of Chancellor Arnold Eisen's jib, and vice versa: Roth was "the greatest sociologist on American Jewish life, without doubt," said Eisen, himself an eminent sociologist. As Roth quipped to a friend, "All that's missing now is the Gloria Steinem Award from the National Organization for Women and the cherished Kakutani Prize."

The commencement took place on the seminary's tented quadrangle at Broadway and 122nd; a klezmer band played the processional march, and two young cantors, a man and a woman, sang "The Star-Spangled Banner" and "Hatikvah," the Israeli anthem. Roth was especially moved when all the parents were asked to stand: "I have about twelve honorary degrees," he said, "and I have never been at a commencement where parents were applauded for the success of their children. That had a special Jewish flavor." More than ever, in fact, what Roth missed amid an otherwise rapturously happy day was his mother and father ("what a present to have been able to deliver to them"). He would have dearly loved for them to witness the long standing ovation when he received his hood, the dozens of people lining up afterward to get their books signed (including a first edition of *Portnoy* brought by Ruth Calderon, a liberal member of the Knesset and fellow honoree). Roth had planned to skip the postceremonial luncheon, because his back was killing him, but he was having too good a time: "I just dosed myself," he said. "Nobody has ever been higher on opioids at the Jewish Seminary than me. It was really wonderful."

That left only one major award unwon; indeed, a large part of the fun by then—at least in Stockholm—seemed to be snubbing Roth. A gleeful rumor was spread that the poor fellow continued to make the two-hour trek from Connecticut to New York, every October, and sit in his agent's office forlornly awaiting the Call, whereupon the freshly printed publicity schedule would be activated at last: "There he would sit," Emma Brockes of *The Guardian* conjectured, "in a meeting room presumably prepared with refreshments, and at the end of the day, make the long, sad trip back to Connecticut."* Actually, on the appointed day, Roth was usually awoken by a morning phone call from his friend Bernie Avishai: "Mr. Rot," he'd say, in what he fancied was a Swedish accent, "ve are sorry to haf to inform you that, yet again, you did not vin the price."

"Can we please stop the nonsense and give Philip Roth a Nobel Prize for Literature before he dies?" Michael Bourne wrote in a 2011 "Open Letter to the Swedish Academy" that appeared in *The Millions*. The following year, *The Telegraph* urged the Swedes to give Roth the prize as a "retirement present," whereas Bloomberg News warned that they were in danger of rendering the whole thing "meaningless" if they continued to shaft Roth. In 2013, the day after Alice Munro was named the winner, *Tablet* magazine ran a series of pieces ("The Counter Prize") pretending that Roth's turn had come round at last. "How the King of Shmutz Won the World" was the title of one item by Josh Lambert, who commended the academy for finally proving they weren't, after all, "full of out-of-touch Swedish prigs." And speaking of shmutz: Alana Newhouse, the editor of *Tablet* (who occasionally met Roth for coffee), was on the phone with a plumber, trying to fix her parents' toilet, when she turned the wrong knob and "was covered essentially in shit water"; at that moment her cell phone indicated another call ("BLOCKED") that proved to be Roth. "This is hilarious," he said of her "Counter Prize" feature, and she sat there listening, befouled, while he went on about things.

In 2014, Roth guaranteed another snub when he made a brief remark ("I can't wait to be thrown the slow curve about the Nobel Prize," he said beforehand) in a long, eloquent interview for the Stockholm newspaper *Svenska Dagbladet*: "I wonder if I had called *Portnoy's Complaint* 'The Orgasm under Rapacious Capitalism,' if I would thereby have earned the favor of the Swedish Academy." Mischievously *The Guardian* began

---

* "You should know that not once in my life have I sat in the Wylie office or anywhere else waiting for the Nobel Prize committee to call," Roth indignantly disabused me. For one thing (he pointed out), the announcement is made at 6:00 a.m. EDT, so there's no question of waiting all day for the call. Back in the early 2000s, he admitted, when he was a more serious contender, Wylie *had* told him that, if he got the nod, he should report either to the agency or the Houghton office for a morning press conference; on the off chance he was still in Connecticut as late as October, one or two Wylie people would drive up early in the morning to coordinate a press response there.

to wonder who would take Roth's place, ten years hence, as the "white, male literary novelist" whose "excessive self-absorption, general snobbishness and high self-regard" would make him the perfect foil for the Swedes: "Step forward Jonathan Franzen! Your new role awaits!"

REACTIONS TO BOB DYLAN'S NOBEL PRIZE: *Shock, Elation and Concern for Philip Roth*, read a headline in *The Washington Post* on October 13, 2016. Giving it to Dylan—as *The New Yorker*'s Alexandra Schwartz tweeted—was "maybe the most effective trolling of Philip Roth the Swedes could ever have come up with" and effectively ended whatever fugitive hope remained for him: After all, twenty-three years had passed since the prize had gone to another American, Toni Morrison, who called Dylan "an impressive choice." Asked for his own thoughts, Roth said "It's okay, but next year I hope Peter, Paul and Mary get it."

C H A P T E R

Fifty

ROTH'S FAVORITE BOOKSELLER WAS ENRICO ADELMAN, a voluble Italian Jew who cherished a precise recollection of his first meeting with Roth—Mother's Day, 1989—when the great writer and his companion (Claire Bloom) paused at Adelman's book stand outside Zabar's. "Do you want it?" Roth asked Bloom, when she picked up a book by Simon Schama. "I'll buy it for you, mother." "You know," said Adelman, "you look a lot like Philip Roth." Roth extended his hand: "I am." After that, the bookman spotted his idol on Broadway from time to time, and would ask him to stop and sign a few copies of his work. Then Adelman "had a premonition" when *The Plot Against America* was about to be published, and ordered a thousand copies. "Didn't faze him in the least," he said of Roth, who gave him careful directions to his place in Connecticut, where they set up a signing table in the kitchen and got to work, breaking now and then to walk around the property. So it went with every book thereafter. "Because I like him," Roth explained of his kindness toward Adelman, who called Roth his "401K."

"Going out with Philip Roth in Manhattan is like going out with Louis XIV in Versailles," said Hermione Lee, an observation Roth amended: "Only as far down as West Sixty-ninth Street." "I know you!" a lively old man accosted Roth, who was walking along Upper Broadway with Claudia Roth Pierpont. In the midst of a nonstop ten-minute spiel, the old man volunteered that he was (1) a Korean War veteran and (2) Jewish. "Really?" Roth said of (2). "You coulda fooled me." They were suddenly interrupted by another passerby: "You're my husband's favorite novelist!" a woman said, then returned brandishing her cell phone: "My husband's on the phone!" Roth listened, smiling, while the husband explained he'd *love* to come to the corner but he was all tied up at work, etc. Meanwhile the Korean War veteran hung fire, eager to resume his monologue.

After his retirement, Roth claimed he wanted nothing better than "to fade forever from the public scene," but when it came to a point he found it rather hard to relinquish the spotlight. His front-page interview with the *Times*, published November 17, 2012, was supposed to be his "last," but within a few months he was chatting with NPR and the Television Critics Association, and a year later he couldn't resist "address[ing] those Nobel Prize idiots who said that American literature was 'provincial'" via his interview with *Svenska Dagbladet*, which the *Times* reprinted in full. Along with that bon mot about "The Orgasm under Rapacious Capitalism," Roth held forth about what had made his generation of American writers so exceptional, listing qualities the Swedish Academy (as Roth saw it) was likely to disdain:

> The American novelist's indifference to, if not contempt for, "critical" theory. Aesthetic freedom unhampered by all the high-and-mighty isms and their humorlessness. . . . Writing that is uncontaminated by political propaganda—or even political responsibility. . . . And surely the fact that writers don't mean a goddamn thing to nine-tenths of the population doesn't hurt. It's inebriating.

Roth then ticked off no fewer than seventy outstanding postwar American writers, in no particular order, except that Bellow came first. The list was nothing if not eclectic, including most of the obvious greats, several old and new friends, the odd curveball (Louis Auchincloss?), every type of stylist (Ann Beattie, John Barth, William Vollmann), and even a few bêtes noires like Gass (but not Baraka or du Plessix Gray).

For his reading at the 92nd Street Y on May 8, 2014, Roth said he'd wear a sign around his neck that said "Positively Last Appearance on Any Stage." It would have been a stellar exit. According to the *Huffington Post*, the excitement among the capacity crowd "felt more like a rock concert than a literary reading." Pierpont opened with a talk about the eminently round female characters in Roth's fiction, then Nicole Krauss introduced the main act, who seated himself at a table dramatically lit à la *Krapp's Last Tape*. Roth read a somber passage from *Sabbath* where the family learns of Morty's death, followed by the graveyard scene he'd read in Newark, and was furious when "all" the *Times* had to say about his valedictory performance was that he'd "kept things clean." "Content is meaningless to these culture journalists," he remarked, hardly for the first time. "Thirty-one books of a writing career and the truly indelible mark that I made is as a dirty writer."* "You can write this down," Roth said to a reporter before turning to greet fans at the 92Y. "This was absolutely the last appearance I will make on any public stage, anywhere."

A week later he appeared at the Edison Hotel in Manhattan to accept the inaugural Yaddo Artist Medal, and gave the usual witty, highly polished speech. Since he'd lately promised never to appear on a public stage again, his old friend Alison Lurie, who introduced him, wondered whether he'd show up—and naturally the *Times* made light of his short-lived retirement from the public eye, duly noting Lurie's quip about a possible no-show. "In over fifty years of making public appearances I have missed attending three public events," Roth bitterly responded to this latest snipe; as for the *Times*'s risibility over yet another "reading" (though in fact he'd promised never again to *appear*), "where is the contradiction or even the inconsistency? I was not giving a public reading, I was getting an award"—during which he'd delivered a speech about the opportunity Yaddo afforded artists who wished to retreat "from zany lovers, serpent-toothed children, dim-witted colleagues, unscrupulous rivals, illiterate students, dunning creditors, unmet deadlines, noisy upstairs neighbors, and cramped living quarters, in flight from a superabundance of trivialities, distractions, futilities, treacheries, and, not least, from the spreading miasma of everyday malice. . . ."

On May 17—the day after the *Times*'s jeering item about the déjà vu aspect of his Yaddo appearance (*The Wall Street Journal* also chimed in)—Robert McCrum wrote in *The Observer* that in a few days the BBC would air the "latest episode in Roth's long goodbye": a two-part interview in which he admitted to Alan Yentob, "Now that I don't write, I just want to chatter away." This time, however, Roth was prepared to "guarantee" that the BBC program was his "absolutely last appearance on any stage anywhere." "Every day I scan the headlines for a new one,"

---

* "The auditorium was filled with a general aura of entrancement"—the *Times* also reported, along with that remark about keeping things clean—"punctuated by laughter at lines like 'He had never found a goy yet who could talk fast enough for him.'"

Lisa Halliday wrote him. "'"No More Haircuts" Says Roth.' Or: 'Philip Roth Has Eaten His Last Everything Bagel.' Or: 'Roth: "The Struggle With Making the Bed is Over."'" Roth didn't mind such teasing from the well-meaning Halliday, but ("at the risk of being mistaken for just another paranoid artist like Vincent Van Gogh and Ezra Pound") he suggested that the media's gleefulness was a matter of Kierkegaardian leveling:

> [T]he dim afterglow of the barrage of indictment that began, in my case, with the *New Yorker* publication of "Defender of [the] Faith" and has never stopped, however silly the leveling (as in this case) or however savage (as with the indictments of the anti-Semite, the self-hating Jew, the pornographer, the misogynist, the Anna [Steiger] abuser and C[laire] B[loom]'s Machiavellian). . . . Why this media eagerness to find culpability in matters large and small? Is it PR who stabbed his beautiful young wife in the chest and who, with horrific results, later sponsored the freedom of a homicidal madman [Jack Henry Abbott]? Norman Mailer could only dream of such disapproval as I continue to arouse without lifting a finger. . . .

■ ■ ■ ■

AND THEN THERE WERE the movies they made out of his books. "Roth takes pride in the proposed filming and production of his work," Ira Nadel claimed in "Philip Roth and Film," "noting that film dramatically exposes his work to larger audiences." "Pure rubbish, from the first sentence to the last," Roth scribbled at the end of Nadel's paper with his red Flair pen. On the contrary—as he once remarked to Hanif Kureishi, a screenwriter (*My Beautiful Laundrette*) who also wrote fiction—Roth found verbal precision more lasting than the pictorial kind, and was forever annoyed when a TV or radio spot about him and his work opened with, say, a clip from *Goodbye, Columbus* (the movie), as if the one had anything to do with the other.

Still, an author could hope that just maybe, someday, a movie would do faint justice to its source. In the case of *The Dying Animal*, however, Roth was skeptical from the get-go, given that it was being adapted by the same team—screenwriter Nicholas Meyer and producer Tom Rosenberg of Lakeshore Entertainment—who had "ruined" *The Human Stain*.

And yet Roth was more proactive than ever, reading the whole novel aloud to Isabel Coixet, the Spanish director, who listened bemusedly (she told *The New York Times*) as he "faithfully reproduced 'all the noises the characters did,' even in the sex scenes, which he urged her to depict." Penélope Cruz was cast as Consuela, and when she phoned Roth for advice about the part, he suggested they have dinner together: "You can sit in Nicole's [Kidman] seat here in my apartment," he remembered telling her. "You can sit on the ottoman of the Eames chair." But he never heard from her again. As for the movie—renamed *Elegy* to avoid the stigma of "Dying" in the title—it was the expected disappointment and then some: "It's all wrong, this *Englishman*," Roth complained about the casting of Ben Kingsley; Kepesh, he said, is "an *American* talking about American college life in the sixties; he's not an Englishman!" Reminded that Kingsley/Kepesh, in the movie, briefly discusses the sixties on the Charlie Rose Show, Roth went red in the face: "Oh yeah, it gives him something to talk about on TV! No! He *lives* it, schmucko!"

"Whatever its limitations," Roth noted, in 2010, of *Goodbye, Columbus*, "it's still by far the best movie that's ever been made of my books"—this despite the casting of the "nebbishy" Richard Benjamin as Neil, another alter ego Roth thought should be played with "aggression" and "power." When Benjamin was cast *again* in *Portnoy*, Roth refused to see the (ghastly) movie when it was released in 1972, and Warner Brothers did nothing to dissuade him; that same year, however (and almost every year thereafter), Roth watched *The Godfather* and wistfully reflected that the young Al Pacino would have made a perfect Portnoy. He was guardedly pleased, then, when he met Pacino at a party in late 2009, and learned that the great (and forceful) actor had bought the rights to *The Humbling*. As Pacino described their encounter, "I remember saying to him that I was so excited by this book. . . . I said I found it so funny—and that wasn't such a wise thing to say." "Don't make the dildo into a joke," Roth sternly wrote him afterward: Kurosawa, he said, would make it into a dagger; Bergman would make it into a cross. "Rescue it from the easy *Seinfeld* jokes and allow it the erotic force of a weapon or of a religious object being blasphemously exploited." "You've written a beautiful dark piece and I probably misspoke when I said the word comedy," Pacino replied.

Roth's hopes mounted when he learned that Greta Gerwig—whom

he'd found "enchanting" in *Frances Ha* (she reminded him of Brigit)—had been cast as the capricious Pegeen, and no less than Oscar winner Barry Levinson (*Rain Man*) was hired to direct. Pacino's reassurances to Roth were belied, however, by the "zany ferocity" (*The New York Times*) he brought to the role of Axler, and meanwhile the dildos (plural) were decidedly played for laughs. "The Double Dog and the fisting mitt," says a fastidious housekeeper in the movie, "they're going in the washing." "No thoughts," said Roth, when asked for his thoughts.

After that, he seemed to cultivate a stoical detachment toward the movies. He no longer took an interest in the lead actresses and, when asked, refused to look at screenplays or offer other kinds of advice. He found the 2016 adaptation of *Indignation*, directed by James Schamus, to be every bit as respectable as *Goodbye, Columbus*: "It's quite watchable and at times, when they stick closely to the book, it's strong." One detected a slight, gentle waggery in his brief response to Tom Rosenberg—yes, of Lakeshore Entertainment—after watching the man's latest Roth production, *American Pastoral*: "Tom, I saw and enjoyed the movie. You're going to win all the prizes." The movie won no prizes, and Roth was privately appalled by the filmmakers' loss of nerve in the crucial early scene between the child Merry and Swede, who does *not* oblige his daughter with a kiss, and also by the movie's "false and meaningless" ending, wherein the daughter comes out of hiding to attend the Swede's funeral. But Roth's expectations were salubriously lowered by then, and he conceded that the main characters, at least, were nicely portrayed by Ewan McGregor (who also directed), Jennifer Connelly, and Dakota Fanning: "I did enjoy it for what it was," he said, "even if it's a sliver off the comet of the book."

∎ ∎ ∎ ∎

WHEN CYNTHIA OZICK FIRST got word of Roth's retirement, she (and many others) refused to believe it: "A writer who stops writing while still breathing has already declared herself posthumous." For Roth, of course, that was kind of the idea, and once the hubbub finally died down, it became something of a reality. Having knocked himself out for fifty-plus years, he found his life nowadays to be "full of quiet pleasure," divided between his "light-filled apartment" with its south-facing view of the Manhattan skyline, and "the splendor of my wooded, hilly corner of rural northwestern Connecticut."

Every day was pretty much the same. At ten o'clock he took a taxi to the St. Bart's pool, where he'd go through his aqua-jogging routine. His trainer, Luye Lui, adored him and vice versa: she called him Nails because he showed up even when "he could barely drag his walker," and he called her Slum Goddess of the Lower East Side (where she was born) after the Fugs song. Roth was home again for lunch, after which he'd strip down to his underwear and nap for an hour or so ("Take your clothes off and sleep in your underwear," his father had advised him; "you'll go to sleep much faster and have a deeper sleep"), then he'd resume poring over old files and writing little commentaries for his biographer—a task that kept him occupied until the end of 2013. Next he began examining hundreds of personal photographs with a magnifying glass and carefully labeling one after another—"an amazing trek backwards through all the many years of my life," he said, delighted to be looking one more time "at the faces of people who meant the world to me and were the world to me." He labeled his last photograph on January 26, 2014.

When Roth stopped writing, he pretty much stopped reading, too— and not just fiction, as he told the press. "Three things I don't do anymore," he liked to say: "fucking, writing, and reading." On November 21, 2010, he noncensoriously noted in his diary that he hadn't so much as looked inside a book for at least a month, and two years later he cheerfully admitted to Charles McGrath of the *Times* that his only reading these days was *iPhone for Dummies*. Eventually, though, he had to get back to it, because he went on living and the days only got longer: "I can't say I retain things as I once did," he wrote Ann Sides Bishop, "but while I'm at it it provides deep pleasure." One book led to another: while reading *FDR and the Jews*, he came across the name of Roosevelt's scandal-ruined strategist Sumner Welles ("great man, should have been president"), which led him to a biography of Welles by his son Benjamin, whence Roth learned that Welles had been named after a distant relative, Charles Sumner, the abolitionist senator who was caned by a South Carolina congressman, and this in turn sparked an interest in the Civil War and its antecedents, and so to Brenda Wineapple's *Ecstatic Nation* and his friend Sean Wilentz's "brimming, masterful" *The Rise of Amer-*

ican Democracy. To Wilentz he imparted a thought that, in his previous life, might have germinated into a novel: What if the Germans had lived with *two centuries* of Nazism the way the American South had lived with slavery? Surely the "beastliness" would continue to "blight their politics, and infiltrate their dreams" à la the "inexpungable" heartlessness of certain social attitudes in the South unto the present day.

One reason Roth, as a novelist, had kept such long writing hours was that he'd always been averse to serious reading in the daytime, which left him little alternative but to keep working; the retired Roth also preferred to do most of his reading while tucked into bed at night, but instead of writing during the day (as his next-door neighbor, and renter, would attest after his death) he watched lots of TV. Often this served an edifying purpose, as his reading would alert him to this or that speech by Roosevelt, Hitler, Mussolini, et al. that he watched via YouTube. But mostly he liked old baseball games: "This game broke my Dodger heart in 1952," he emailed Conarroe, including the YouTube link. "Watch Robinson bunt, watch Mantle swing. I've never recovered."* Roth also discovered that he himself had a considerable YouTube presence and would often send his more flattering clips to friends. Mia Farrow, for one, was "mystified and amused," noting that their mutual friend Styron would *never* have done that (albeit implying, too, a kind of endearing ingenuousness on Roth's part, versus simple egotism).

Roth's summer months in Connecticut were almost ideally monotonous. Sometimes he simply sat in his Eames chair listening to the rain ("Better to hear that than all the gossip") or watching, say, a "wild turkey perched on the stone wall outside of my studio honking like mad for her missing puffballs," which, he suspected, had been devoured by his "resident fox." Roth's mail was delivered to his house in the late afternoon if he failed to visit the post office beforehand, but nowadays he was loath to forgo the morning ritual of picking up his mail, buying a newspaper at the Cornwall Bridge general store, and proceeding on sunny days to a picnic table beside the Housatonic. It was nice, too, after forty-plus

---

* One of Roth's most cherished baseball memories was attending (with Solotaroff) Game One of the 1963 World Series, when his hero/lookalike Sandy Koufax struck out Mickey Mantle three times. "Great day for us Jewboys," he wrote me (including the YouTube link). "Jews 3–Oklahoma 0." I'm from Oklahoma, as was Mantle.

years, that his neighbors had mostly gotten used to his status as "the Jew porn writer"; the general store was now run by Ed Baird's son, Tom, who invariably greeted Roth with "How ya Mets doin'?"—even though Roth hadn't been a Mets fan since the late eighties or so—and this too was a cherished part of the ritual.

Except for his cook, Catherine von Klitzing, and a few visiting old friends, Roth saw almost nobody but incidental acquaintances. Most of his local friends were either dead (Styron, Huvelle, Kazin, Arthur Miller and his wife, Inge Morath) or permanently estranged (Ross Miller and the Grays). Roth was visiting his dying brother in Chicago on April 15, 2009, when he was slated to receive (along with the actor Campbell Scott and the chef Jacques Pépin) a Governor's Award for Excellence in Culture and Tourism, so he sent a proxy, Charlie Kafferman, co-owner of the West Street Grill, who always made a point of stopping at Roth's table to tell a few zingers and keep him company as needed.

Happily, around the time of his retirement, Roth revived his friendship with Mia Farrow, who took to joining him for dinner on Sunday evenings. One night she "caused a mini-uproar"—so the *Huffington Post* reported—by tweeting a photo of her and Roth with the caption "We're watching #sharknado": "Sites like Vulture and Gawker rightly jumped on the tweet almost immediately, if only because it was lolarious [sic] to imagine Roth watching a movie where Tara Reid and Ian Ziering fight tornado sharks." Privately Farrow admitted that they hadn't, in fact, been watching *Sharknado*, though she did try to persuade Roth that Twitter was fun and even worthwhile ("Margaret Atwood's on there"), but Roth wasn't having any. "So everybody's just *shouting*, right?" he said, indignant at the very thought of it.

Over the years Roth had been a sweetly attentive friend to Farrow. In 1999, when her eleven-year-old son, Seamus (later called Ronan), was bored in school, it was Roth who phoned his friend Bernie Rodgers, the dean of Simon's Rock, and persuaded him to make an "absolutely unprecedented" exception for the boy to attend college-level classes with students who were otherwise old enough for high school. Seamus flourished in Great Barrington but still wanted more of a challenge, so Roth devised a reading course for him, The American Novel and American History—various novels with supplemental nonfiction, such as *The Naked and the Dead* plus the LOA's *Reporting World War II* (two volumes) and *All the King's Men* plus T. Harry Williams's biography of Huey Long. "That should fill your spare hours for a while," Roth wrote the boy. "Good luck."

"He's probably the best listener in my life," Mia Farrow said of Roth, who once asked her why she kept looking out the window during their conversation. Far from seeming incredulous or dismissive when she frankly admitted a fear that Woody Allen would have her killed, Roth became an unfailing source of moral support—because he was fond of Farrow and had unwavering faith in her probity, and also because of his conviction, always firm, that Allen was a bad artist and a bad human being. "He seized upon the persona of the schlemiel as, in all senses, a profitable disguise," he said of Allen. "But inside this schlemiel there lives a crocodile."*

Farrow hardly viewed Roth as a misogynist, though she did admit his attitude toward women could be on the quaintly paternalistic side: "It comes out of the best part of the man: 'I want to help this person; I want to see them do their very best.' But it's according to his book." Roth's advice was always well meaning, and often welcome, except when it came in the form of unsolicited, Herman-like *hocking* about one's clothes, hair, or the like. Farrow hastened to point out that Roth had formidable women friends—Thurman, Pierpont, Lee, others—who were likely to be exempt from that sort of thing: "But unless you're in the elite that he can really look up to . . . I think the rest of womenkind falls into a different pool." Having been married to a domineering Italian who used to order her, say, to put on a sweater ("The other sleeve too! Button it up!"), Farrow was used to the phenomenon to put it mildly. "One more thing," Roth wrote her, after a 2013 *Vanity Fair* article revisited the Woody Allen scandal and threatened to disrupt her life again. "If anyone, friends not excluded, calls to talk to you about VF, don't let them. Interrupt and say, 'Sorry, can't talk—GRANDCHILDREN!' And immediately HANG UP THE PHONE WHOEVER IT MAY BE. Promise me that you will do this."

---

* Allen's alleged abuse of his daughter Dylan inspired the Sybil Van Buren episode in *The Humbling*. "No," said Farrow, when asked whether she'd minded; she pointed out that Roth always made it clear when he wanted to know something for the sake of his work.

. . . .

AS THEY GOT OLDER, Roth wearied a little of Joel Conarroe, who, he said, "can*not* be natural with me," though he knew Conarroe to be a witty man in less daunting company; also he was put off by Conarroe's increasing deafness. Thus the friendship was mostly conducted, in later years, via email, often during baseball games: "In order to win, you have to be able to hit," Roth emailed Conarroe on October 6, 2015, while watching the Yankees get eliminated from the play-offs. "Oh your prophetic soul!" his friend replied. "My grandmother could have done better than that."

Conarroe was aware of his own loss of status, at least relative to their friend Ben Taylor, who (said Conarroe) "seems to have assumed the role of favorite Bro." Roth and Taylor had first met at Conarroe's sixtieth birthday party in 1994, and, during the last decade or so of Roth's life, the younger man was without question Roth's most intimate male friend. The two met for dinner almost weekly. Roth delighted in finding Taylor always reading a book ("the only such person in the restaurant"), which he'd then discuss with humor and erudition, along with whatever else he was reading and teaching. "He is discrete [sic] and decorous almost to a fault," Roth noted, though of course discretion was no fault in Roth's eyes. "The only such person between the Battery and the Cloisters." When Janis Bellow mentioned she was looking for someone to edit a book of her late husband's letters, Roth promptly proposed Taylor; over breakfast at the Lotos Club, Taylor astutely held forth about Bellow's life and work for the benefit of Janis and their lawyer friend, Walter Pozen, while Roth sat beaming—proud of Taylor, he said, "like a father for a son," all the more when he read the final product three years later, and saw that Taylor had discharged his duties "brilliantly and meticulously."

Taylor was, indeed, like nothing so much as an unusually devoted son—forever at Roth's disposal, unlike his straight friends, who were often distracted by children and the like. "He did say 'I love you' to me once," Taylor said in 2014. "There's been other times when I thought he was going to say it, but he hung up on me."

. . . .

A LESS CLASSIFIABLE but no less steady companion, for a time, was Roth's cook, Catherine. "You're the best thing that's happened to me in years," he murmured into her ear at his eightieth birthday in Newark. Except for his slow daily walks and aqua-jogging at St. Bart's, Roth had become increasingly housebound, and New York would have been intolerably lonely without his cook's "lovely face" to look forward to in the late afternoon, when she arrived to make dinner and the next day's lunch. Also Roth was too infirm to spend summers alone in Connecticut, "And to have beautiful, sweet-tempered, ultracompetent" Catherine with him, he said, "sharing the plantation, is an unceasing source of joy."

Roth insisted on subsidizing her education, and arranged for her to take Barbara Sproul's Faith and Disbelief course at Hunter; he even read the assigned books with her—a daunting list including the likes of Kierkegaard, Buber, Teilhard de Chardin, Sartre, and Nietzsche. When she managed a B+ in the course, Roth exulted as though he (or she) had finally won the Nobel: "I don't know what life would have been like for her had she not been working for me now for three years. The bond of friendship between us is not improperly called love. She just makes me so damn happy!" Far from resting on this laurel, he promptly pushed her to enroll in German History 1848–1945 for the Fall 2014 semester, and packed two copies of the textbook so they could read it in tandem that summer in Connecticut. "I remember just panicking," said von Klitzing, whose interest in German history was, in fact, minimal, and who wanted more time to herself than Roth's reading program would likely allow. He was visibly downcast when she asked him to wait until fall.

German history wasn't the only thing Roth had gotten wrong about the young woman. Though he boasted to others about her atheism—he fancied her a proper Rothian skeptic—she had "a really big faith" that she kept to herself, lest he try talking her out of it, the way he tried talking her out of marriage and children. Whenever she arrived for work, he'd ask her to sit down and talk to him for half an hour or so, and once, while discussing Buber, he referred to theirs as the higher kind of "I and Thou" relationship. That would have been fine, if not for his occasionally calling her baby ("Look, I shaved for you, baby!"), or, while watching TV together in Connecticut, suddenly taking her hand and gazing at her searchingly. "What are you doing?" she asked. "I thought you wanted us to hold hands," he said vaguely, and she replied "No." Alarmed, she discussed such episodes with her AA sponsor, who reminded her that Roth was an octogenarian with a fentanyl patch, apt to have moments of confusion.

When Bernie Avishai visited Roth in the fall, he found him "deeply demoralized." Lame and weary, he had to cut their walk short, and while resting on a bench he confessed his loneliness and terror that he'd end up a total invalid like his brother. Catherine, meanwhile, was evasive whenever he tried to discuss German history, and finally admitted she'd dropped her courses that semester. Moreover she didn't want to return to Connecticut with him next summer. "So essentially you're quitting," said Roth. "I'm not firing you. You can't do the job." She stood up and began making dinner, while Roth turned around in his Eames chair and either stared out the darkened window or at the reflection of her in the kitchen behind him—she wasn't sure which. He was totally silent. At last she went to check on him, and his face was covered with tears.

■ ■ ■ ■

WHILE ROTH STRUGGLED against the steady encroachments of old age, his generation of friends went on sliding, he said, "like the warming glaciers into the oblivious sea." He'd been moved to mend relations with Dick Stern on February 1, 2004—his mother's 100th birthday: "This has to stop," he wrote, reminding Stern that he'd been a particular favorite of Bess. Afterward Roth went to Chicago to cement their reconciliation; Stern's wife, Alane, stayed upstairs while the two broke the ice, and when she came down they were laughing "as if no time had passed," and Roth bolted up to give her a big hug and kiss. On January 22, 2013, Roth phoned to chat about Obama's second inauguration, and Alane told him the doctors had diagnosed Stern with inoperable cancer. Two days later he died.

"He was an inspiring figure as a literature professor and an ace of great virtuosity as a novelist, short story writer, essayist and raconteur," Roth told *The New York Times* the day of Stern's death, resolved as ever to salvage the man's long-neglected literary reputation. He wrote an eloquent eulogy for Stern's memorial in Chicago, and later got in touch with Edwin Frank of New York Review Books, urging him (successfully) to publish a new edition of what Roth had always considered his friend's masterpiece, for which a modified version of Roth's eulogy served as the introduction: "*Other Men's Daughters* is to the sixties what *The Great Gatsby* was to the twenties, *The Grapes of Wrath* to the thirties, and *Rabbit Is Rich* to the seventies: a microscope exactly focused upon a thinly sliced specimen of what was once the present moment."

"I was thrilled that you were there," Roth wrote Stu and Bette Lehman after his eightieth birthday in Newark, "all of us back on native ground together, and still breathing." Naturally it pleased Roth that his Weequahic pals got to see what a fuss the world made over him, though his oldest friend, Marty Weich, had been too frail to attend. Having almost died from septicemia two years before, Weich was now a wizened, bewildered figure in a wheelchair—the embodiment of Roth's dictum "Old age isn't a battle; old age is a massacre." Propelled by a burly male nurse, Weich had managed a visit to Roth's apartment in October 2012; Roth brought out their high school yearbook, and the two men sat holding hands while Weich lowered his face within inches of each page muttering "Jesus Christ . . . Jesus Christ. . . ." Because of medical bills and other terrible setbacks, the Weichs were all but destitute; Roth wrote them a check for $25,000 and phoned Stu Lehman and Bob Heyman, who also agreed to help.

Lehman died of cancer in April 2014, having achieved a success in life very different from that of his world-famous friend. Happily married to his college sweetheart, with whom he had three children and many grandchildren, Lehman had divided his life among family, a successful oral surgery practice, and his boat—nice rewards after a childhood blighted by his mother's early death and his father's desertion. As for Weich—tall, handsome, smart, talented, athletic, polite, "every mother's dream of the Jewish prince"—he was kept afloat by Roth and others until he choked to death in 2016.

On December 5, 2015, Nela Wagman emailed Roth that her mother, Riki, was dying of pancreatic cancer. Roth had long ago lost interest in his friend's fiction. Her crazily transgressive early work, like Lelchuk's, had made Roth feel less alone as the author of *Portnoy*, but her stock had plummeted over the years, both in his eyes and the world's. "She writes the same book again and again," he said, "and always in screaming caps and italics . . . and everything exaggerated in the lamest way." He'd been all but entirely out of touch when her lovable, bearish husband, Howard, died in 2011, whereupon Roth showed up for the shiva; five years later, too, he visited Riki's deathbed and made one-sided conversation. "Riki, do you know who I am?" he asked her at last. She narrowed her eyes: "I know perfectly well who you are."

"It's the damn poignancy of everything that rocks me a little," Roth wrote Conarroe during this twilight era.

> I see something beautiful or just altogether ordinary and I say to myself, "Take a good, long look. Look at it as if you're never going to see it again. Because maybe you won't." Makes even one's familiar surroundings breathtaking, doesn't it? "Here I am," think I, "ambling happily into oblivion." The strategy I've been using on myself for decades now is that whenever death comes to mind in its most distressing form, I tell myself, quite simply, "I'm here and it's now." And those five little words do the trick. I'm here and it's now. So long as I am alive I'm immortal, am I not?

Sometimes those five little words did the trick, but often enough Roth was seized with angst—as when he realized that he was now older than Sandy ever got to be. "A great dynamism has gone out of my life," he said, his laughter subsiding after Ben Taylor had read aloud Sabbath's uproarious self-written obituary ("Did Nothing for Israel"). "And I feel the lack of it."

■ ■ ■ ■

ROTH WAS BUSILY putting his affairs in order. A spate of definitive editions were published in time for him to pore over proofs and translators' notes: the tenth and final LOA volume (the only one not "edited" by Ross Miller), *Why Write? Collected Nonfiction 1960–2013*; the first of four Pléiade volumes, *Romans et nouvelles 1959–1977*; and the first of three Meridiani volumes, *Romanzi 1959–1986*. The Pléiade was the prototype for all such canonical libraries, and Roth joined a handful of Americans—William Faulkner, Henry James, Jack London—and, with Mario Vargas Llosa, one of only two living non-French authors to be so enshrined. The inclusion of his work among the gorgeous, gold-embossed leather volumes ensured "that generations of foreign readers will study him with the reverence reserved for the so-called 'great books,'" said *The Washington Post*. "In a secular society that still tends to venerate literary achievement the way America worships athletics, the Pléiade *is*, in a sense, the Bible."

Roth's penultimate birthday was celebrated a day early, *chez* Thurman, on March 18, 2017: Along with Halliday, Krauss, Conarroe, Pierpont, Taylor, and the hostess, Roth raised a glass to Updike, whose eighty-fifth birthday it was; then, too, everyone roasted the recently inaugurated president. The next day, in an email, Roth described the occasion as "joyous," though two months later he candidly admitted he couldn't remember a thing about it. His short-term memory was shot, but in the moment Roth was as lucid as ever, and therefore appalled by the "nightmare now in America": "the man elected to be president of the United States is a malignant narcissist," he wrote a French journalist, "a pathological liar, a blustering ignoramus, vile, vengeful, and probably a bit demented. And I am minimizing his shortcomings." A few months later in the *Times* ("No Longer Writing, Philip Roth Still Has Plenty to Say"), he returned to the subject of this "massive fraud, the evil sum of his deficiencies, devoid of everything but the hollow ideology of a megalomaniac."

This was Roth's final interview—again with McGrath—published on January 16, 2018, four months before his death. Given his lifelong preoccupation with male sexual desire, Roth was expected to comment on the burgeoning #MeToo movement, a prospect that rattled him—all the more because he worried that Anna Steiger's friend Felicity would seize the moment to falsely accuse him of something more grievous than making a pass on the stairs (and whatever obnoxious ragging may have followed). "Help me with this," he wrote Avishai.

> I heed the cry of the women insulted and injured. I have nothing but sympathy for their pain and their need for justice. But I am also made anxious by the nature of the tribunal that is adjudicating these charges. I am made anxious, as a civil libertarian, because there doesn't seem to be a tribunal. What I see instead is publicized accusation instantly followed by peremptory punishment. I see the accused denied the right of habeas corpus, the right to face and examine his accuser, and the right to defend himself in anything resembling a genuine judicial setting, where careful distinctions might be able to be drawn as to the severity of the reported crime.

In the end Roth responded in rather nervously ornate language ("I have imagined"—i.e., in his work—"a small coterie of unsettled men possessed by just such inflammatory forces they must negotiate and contend with") to the effect that he was not "astonished" by the male misconduct that had recently come to light. Judging by the busy Comment section on the *Times* website, it was the least satisfactory answer in an otherwise well-received interview.

■ ■ ■ ■

THE BEST PART OF Roth's eighty-fourth birthday was a long visit from Halliday, who was five months pregnant. On their last day together, they went to see a matinee of *The Sense of an Ending*, based on the Julian Barnes novel; at the climax, the hero's daughter has just given birth but worries because the delivery room is silent ("Why isn't my baby crying?"). It turns out the baby is fine, but amid the suspense Halliday became tearful—her previous pregnancy had ended in miscarriage—and Roth took her hand and held it for the rest of the movie. "You will go on to have a baby," he'd told her after the miscarriage, "and you will love it. It's something I missed out on, but you won't."

Lisa's daughter, Stella Rose, was born on July 23, 2017, and six months later she and Theo and the baby came to New York for the publication of her first novel, *Asymmetry*—featuring a character named Ezra Blazer who is, essentially, a portrait of Roth's most benevolent self, which Halliday had a way of bringing out. The novel was a hit (it would appear on the *Times'* Ten Best list for 2018) and Roth loved it too, but above all he was enchanted by Stella: "a beautiful, smiling creature who seems never to cry and is curious about everything."* Several friends came to Roth's apartment to meet the baby, and on the last day Lucy Warner paid one of her periodic visits and stayed awhile: "So here we all were," said Roth, "past, present, and future, everybody jolly, everybody kissing everybody else—it was like the ending of *As You Like It*."

The previous summer—Roth's last—he'd spent half a day with his

---

* At Roth's funeral, a number of total strangers came up to Halliday and asked about her baby: "I've seen pictures of her," they explained, since Roth had proudly circulated photos as though Stella were his own granddaughter.

lawyer, revising his will and arranging other details relating to his funeral and estate: "and so," he wrote Joanna Clark afterward, "it seems I have entered a posthumous existence with everything in place for my demise." Too infirm to walk very far, he rode around his property in a golf cart, while at night he'd have "a deliberate memory session" in bed, trying to evoke as precisely as possible every person he'd ever known and every place he'd ever lived. Now and then it occurred to him that he'd never written about this or that person, place, or thing, and "out of ancient habit" he'd start to get up and write it down—then, with relief, he'd remember he wasn't "slavishly hearkening, day or night, to the demands of [his] talent anymore." "Getting into bed at night I smile and think, 'I lived another day,'" he told the *Times*. "And then it's astonishing again to awaken eight hours later and to see that it is morning of the next day and that I continue to be here. . . . I go to sleep smiling and I wake up smiling. I'm very pleased that I'm still alive."

■　■　■　■

IN AUGUST 2016, after a summer of fairly vigorous daily swimming, Roth had begun to feel breathless while climbing stairs, and thus learned he was due for a transcatheter aortic valve replacement, using (in Roth's case) cow tissue. On September 10 he left the hospital "feeling quite bouncy," but within nine days he was so exhausted he could hardly dress himself. For almost two months he was stranded in his apartment, tended by nurses, barely able to read: "I want to die I feel so rotten." At last a doctor found that blood clots had formed on the leaflets of his new valve, preventing proper function, so he was given a powerful blood thinner, Coumadin. "Boy, am I getting tired of my resilience," he said on February 3, 2017, finally able to return to the pool four times a week and force himself up and down the interior stairwell of his building.

A little over a year later, on April 29, 2018, Roth's pulse soared to 170. "I'm in the hospital of all places," he emailed Halliday, who was en route from Massachusetts to visit him in New York. "Was admitted last night to emergency room with bad bout of arrhythmia. Under control now and I'm resting quietly in hospital bed. Call me." Taylor had stayed with him at Lenox Hill Hospital overnight, and, when Halliday arrived, Roth told her he'd considered waiting until morning to go to the hospital but decided to call an ambulance right away because "You only have one life." At the direction of his cardiologist, Stanley Schneller, he was transferred to the cardiac ICU at New York–Presbyterian. Thirty-six years after his diagnosis of "significant" coronary artery disease, it looked as though Roth would cheat death again: within a few days Jeffrey Moses operated, replacing two blocked stents, and Schneller reported "a dramatic and immediate improvement in hemodynamic." Still, Roth was in ghastly pain. His anticoagulant had caused a spontaneous bleed in his pelvis, and any position in bed was torture. Finally, with the help of a physical therapist, he managed to stand and take a few steps on May 18, and again it looked as though he might go home.

But it soon became clear he was in end-stage heart failure. The attacks of arrhythmia returned, and his abdomen bloated with backed-up fluid. Doctors explained he could live perhaps another three to six months with the help of powerful IV diuretics, but when Roth realized he wouldn't be able to return to the country, swim, or even leave his bed, he decided to accept palliative care. He spoke briefly to his dearest friends. "I have been to see the great enemy," he told Ben, "and walked around him, and talked to him, and he is not to be feared. I promise." The day before his death, as he was drifting off, one of his Weequahic buddies, Howard Silver, called his cell phone. "Oh no!" said Silver, when Julia answered and explained the situation. "Tell him it's Howie! Shout it, so he can hear it!" She obliged, then told Silver that Philip had understood and smiled. Perhaps Roth was thinking along the lines of what another old classmate, Dorothy Brand, had written him not long before: "You've had a great family, good friends, a good life I hope, and incredible recognition for your talent and hard work. That's quite an accomplishment for a little boy from Chancellor Avenue School. Rabbi Kahan would be so proud of you."

When Roth kept waking up and realizing he was still alive—his wish to withdraw cardiac care had yet to be formalized, and he continued to receive medicine for arrhythmia—he became a little vexed. Golier, his health care agent, explained that certain "procedural issues" had to be observed. "Do you mean to tell me, Julia," he said in a slow, indignant voice, "that I have come to the end of my life only to find out that *absolutely nothing* is under my control?" One such procedure entailed consulting with his psychiatrist, Richard Friedman, whom Roth assured that he wasn't clinically depressed or even sad, but quite lucidly capable of a decision to end his life. Finally—on Tuesday afternoon, May 22—he was ready to receive terminal sedation, and said goodbye to Ben and Julia: "I loved your kiddos," he said to the latter. "They were the joy of my life." Then he thanked the nurses.

Julia, Ben, and Joel had visited the hospital every day and stayed at Roth's bedside whenever he was alone. Toward the end he was attended by a remarkable (all the more for a man reputed to have problems with women) number of former lovers. Barbara Sproul, Susan Rogers, and Judith Thurman came often, and a frail eighty-six-year-old Ann Mudge also managed a visit (with a helper), as did other friends: Andrew Wylie, Dorene Marcus, Bernie Avishai, Barbara Jakobson, Sean Wilentz, and the writer Mary Karr, who'd grown close to Roth in his last years. One by one they drifted into his room to say goodbye, while the sedated Roth—quite the way he'd described Herman in *Patrimony*—"fought for every breath with an awesome eruption, a final display, of his life-long obstinate tenacity. . . . Dying is work and he was a worker." The great rasping breaths became less and less frequent, and finally stopped around 10:30 that night, while his "ward" (as he'd wryly taken to calling her) Catherine held his hand and wept. Though she'd long ago quit as his cook, Roth had continued to pay for her education (she was due to receive her master's in social work degree the following month), and was, after all, the nearest thing she had to a father.

EPILOGUE

Roth's impressive *New York Times* obituary was above the fold on the front page, and he got even bigger star treatment in France: "Philip Roth: *Mort d'un géant*" read the headline in *Le Monde*. He would have been pleased, too, with his ninety-year-old colleague Cynthia Ozick's witty swat at the Swedish Academy in *The Wall Street Journal*: "How should those obtuse northland jurors, denizens of a frost-bitten society highly ranked for alcoholism and suicide, warm to the emotional temperature of the postwar Jewish Weequahic neighborhood of Newark, N. J., out of which the grandson of immigrants might emerge to become one of the most renowned American literary masters of his century?" The BBC agreed, hailing Roth as "arguably the best writer not to have won the Nobel Prize since Tolstoy."

The stark simplicity of a particular Nobel laureate's gravestone— Camus's, with its roughly carved name and years—was the kind of thing Roth wanted for himself. ("So it will just say your name on it?" Halliday asked. "No," said Roth. "It will say Camus's name on it.") Roth entrusted the job of finding and inscribing a proper gravestone to his caretaker in Connecticut, Russ Murdock, a stonemason. ("Hey!" Roth had yelled from his bedroom window one day, while Murdock was repairing one of his ancient stone walls. "I buried an ex-wife in that wall, just about where you're at. If you dig her up, you put that bitch right back where you found her!") Roth had wanted one of the moldy boulders strewn around his property, and after he left Warren that last time, Murdock found what struck him as the perfect specimen. Roth died before he could examine it firsthand, so Golier and Rogers visited the land and "went nuts" (Murdock) with enthusiasm.

One may find this singular marker at Bard College Cemetery, near the grave of Hannah Arendt. Roth had decided on this final resting place with his usual careful deliberation. Years before, while researching cemeteries for *Sabbath's Theater*, he'd considered buying a plot for himself near his parents at Gomel Chesed, but the waggish warden had advised him against it ("not enough legroom"); also he'd considered Cornwall Cemetery in Litchfield County (where he'd buried Janet Hobhouse), professing to admire its "quiet neighbors" and "nice setback." In the end, though, like Sabbath, Roth couldn't imagine spending eternity among so many decorous, laconic goyim, so finally he called Leon Botstein, the Bard president, and asked whether he and Manea were planning their burials at the campus cemetery. They were. "We will never separate," Manea had once told Roth, "because you are a sadist and I am a masochist."

The funeral took place on Memorial Day. Eighty or so mourners—a diverse group including bookseller Enrico Adelman, Jonathan Brent, Don DeLillo, Deborah Eisenberg, Nathan Englander, David Remnick, the actor Wallace Shawn, and Roth's devoted Manhattan cleaner, Estele Solano (whom he'd recently given $70,000 to help her buy an apartment in Jackson Heights)—boarded two chartered buses outside Riverside Chapel, on the Upper West Side, and took the two-hour trip to Annandale-on-Hudson. Naturally Roth had insisted on a secular service, though Botstein—who was hosting the reception afterward—considered it seemly to say Kaddish; Roth's old friend Marty Garbus, however, had an "imagined conversation" with Roth, who assured him he wanted nothing of the kind. Others agreed, and Botstein relented. Beneath a big tent in the wooded cemetery, Roth's loved ones read aloud from his work: Golier's fourteen-year-old son, William, read from *The Great American Novel* about the mystical perfection of the baseball diamond; his mother read the "great god of Loneliness" passage from *American Pastoral* ("Yes, alone we are, deeply alone, and always, in store for us, a layer of loneliness even deeper"); and finally, after several other readings, Mia Farrow intoned Roth's last word of fiction—"invincible"—and Golier's daughter, Amelia, with her violin teacher, Emily Kalish, played a Shostakovich duet. Each mourner then took a turn shoveling dirt into the grave, a haunting (and secular) aspect of the traditional Jewish funeral that Roth had allowed.

At the crowded and meticulously planned (by Roth) memorial at the New York Public Library, on September 25, Ben Taylor remarked in his eulogy that Roth "took a death-defying satisfaction in the vastness of what he'd wrought—a shelf of work augmenting the soul of the nation and built to outlast whatever unforeseeable chances and changes await us and our descendants." One was reminded of Roth's enduring relevance when, a month later, a man crazed with anti-Semitism ("all these Jews need to die"), and armed with an AR-15 and three handguns, slaughtered eleven worshippers during Shabbat services at the Tree of Life synagogue in Pittsburgh. The next day, amid added security, nine hundred people came to a previously scheduled reading of *The Plot Against America* at the 92nd Street Y. Michael Stuhlbarg was the first of nine actors to read ("Fear presides over these memories, a perpetual fear . . ."), while Jon Hamm waited his turn backstage: "When I read this book, I was like 'When was this written? The parallels are right there.'" He sipped his coffee. "I think Roth died from *grief.*"

■ ■ ■ ■

ROTH LAVISHLY ENDOWED an educational fund for Julia Golier's children and gave large individual bequests to his closest friends; he also donated $1.6 million to the Guggenheim Foundation to support writing fellowships. But the lion's share of his estate went to the Newark Public Library—an institution forever dear to his heart. On March 1, 1969, he'd published an indignant letter in the *Times* when the Newark City Council voted—eighteen months after the riots—to strike funding ($2.8 million) for the Newark Museum and Public Library: "It is strange (to put it politely) that now, when Newark is mostly black, the City Council (for fiscal reasons, we are told) has reached a decision that suggests that the books don't really belong to the public after all, and that what a library provides for the young is no longer essential to an education." What the library provides for at least half of its ten thousand weekly patrons, fifty years later, is a place where they can find help getting access to social services, or typing out job applications—a bastion for the poor, in short, more than ever, and hence still a target for budget cuts when times are bad (a third of its funding was cut during the 2008 recession).

Along with millions of dollars, Roth donated the four thousand books from his Connecticut house, to be kept in a special room designated the Philip Roth Personal Library Collection. Designed by the architect Ann Beha, the room will include a pair of Roth's writing desks, his reading chairs, and his beloved refectory table from the Stone Room, the better for readers to experience his books (marked up with his underlinings and marginal glosses in many cases) as he did. "We think the Newark Public Library can now become an important literary destination for students and scholars and even for tourists," said Rosemary Steinbaum, the library trustee who'd become Roth's friend while working on his eightieth birthday exhibition. In 2016, when Roth announced his gift, the library kicked off a fund drive to raise another three million dollars, an important part of which is the annual Philip Roth Lecture. The inaugural speaker was the novelist Zadie Smith,* another late-life friend of Roth, who discussed his influence on her—especially via *Portnoy's Complaint*—in a talk titled "The I Who Is Not Me": "I know that I stole Portnoy's liberties long ago. . . . He is part of the reason, when I write, that I do not try to create positive black role models for my black readers, and more generally have no interest in conjuring ideal humans for my readers to emulate." "It is a splendid, quietly subversive, gesture by Mr. Roth," *The Economist* noted of his library bequest; "a rich university would have paid handsomely for his books. It is also a reminder of how touchingly respectful of Newark, transformed though it has been by immigration, deindustrialization and riots, he always is."

■ ■ ■ ■

THE TRAUMA OF ROTH'S first marriage haunted him almost every day of his life. Toward the end, while putting himself to sleep with his nightly memory sessions, Roth came to the year 1964 and "a darkness invaded [his] mind": "I was trying not to remember Maggie in it," he realized. Shown long-lost photos of his 1959 wedding day, he became sick to his stomach. He was haunted, too, by the collateral damage. "I'd hate for you to see [Helen]," he said to Ross Miller, in 2004, of the woebegone stepdaughter he'd left behind. Roth took it for granted that, if Helen were still alive (which he doubted), her life was squalid and she'd be apt to say bitter things about him. "It breaks my heart to think of her," he went on, murmuring "Maggie picking up that bicycle pump—going after [Ronald]—I was in the wrong world—she was a criminal."

As it happened, Roth had been right when he wrote Solotaroff, in

---

* Subsequent speakers have included Robert Caro, Salman Rushdie, and Sean Wilentz.

1962, when Helen was a barely literate waif of eleven, "[She] changes daily under our eyes; she is blessed with deep self-preserving instincts and who knows, but they may get her through, and may even make of her something special." And lo, it came to pass: Helen reported, in 2013, that she was the mother of "two very accomplished adult children" and had been happily married for over thirty years to the cofounder of a multimillion-dollar company in the Bay Area. "I will always walk emotionally with a limp," she said, "but most people do. I insisted on surviving." One step in the process was distancing herself from her father, Burt, who was pleased to mention that the last time he'd seen her, in the late eighties, she'd just read a magazine excerpt from *The Facts* and was conspicuously disgruntled with her former stepfather. Told that Helen was alive and well, and moreover resented him for his "mean-spirited" and "distorted" portrayal of Maggie in *The Facts*, Roth replied: "Not even [Helen], who suffered terribly at her parents' hands, knows the depths of her mother's evil—and I know the meaning of the word—because she was only a child and a wayward adolescent when all this was happening to her and because, miraculously, she somehow saved herself"; her brother, Ronald, however, is "not so generous about his mother," Roth pointed out, "because his life was fucking blighted by her and, unlike [Helen], his life was shit forever after."

By Ronald's own account, this is true. "I've been a very arrogant asshole most of my life," he admitted, summing up. "A drunkard somewhat . . . bouncing around from job to job, moving all over the country, riding motorcycles now, fucking women I picked up." He laughed. "I imagine my life was more like Red"—his errant grandfather, the model for Whitey Nelson in *When She Was Good*—"than anybody else." Ronald candidly wonders whether he's a sociopath, unable to attach himself to others, a tendency he attributes (along with his misogyny: women, he said, "are lying, conniving little manipulators") to his mother's influence.*

---

* Ronald's speculation about his possible sociopathy reminds me of his mother's diary entry from April 7, 1958, quoted on page 145: "I really feel like one born without one of the senses but it's really that I have no conscience. I have the mind to reason what is right and wrong but I have no moral repugnance to keep me from anything but I have [a] huge amount of self pity where my wickedness keeps me from having the good things that life gives to good girls."

But Helen, over the years, steadily refused to feel bitterness toward Maggie, who, she liked to think, had done her best with a bad hand in life. When Helen first read about the urine ruse in *The Facts*, she considered it a "ridiculous" fabrication on Roth's part; twenty-five years later, however, when presented with evidence to the contrary, her defense collapsed immediately. "Aren't I lucky that I get to have these horrible fucking parents?" she said of Maggie and Burt. "I have a stepfather that wants nothing to do with me [because] I'm so inseparable from this crazy woman. I'm the one who lives without." Whatever her occasional resentment, Helen always kept a photograph of Roth on her dresser—a bespectacled young man with a protective arm around his shyly delighted stepdaughter—and was devastated to learn of his death. As for Ronald, he laughed at the very idea Roth would ever want to see him again. "He was good to me, and I'm doing this interview as a tribute to Philip," he told me. "I wish we were able to pick up the phone and call each other now and then, and I could ask him: 'What the fuck were you doing with my mother anyway?'"

■　■　■　■

On August 1, 2013, Roth wrote me one of his many apologias on these matters: "There's a wise observation in Erik Erikson's book *Young Man Luther* that I've never forgotten, for reasons that are all too obvious.

> "The crisis in a young man's life comes when he half-realizes that he is hopelessly overcommitted to what he is not." . . . Overcommitment for a writer is the name of the game. There's no other way to persevere up against the obstacle that writing fiction presents. Is. At least for someone like me. The intensity, the intensity—it kills you and it makes you all at once. . . . I didn't know how to disengage from whatever, mistakenly, when not disastrously as well, I took-take to be a responsibility. Alas, without that driving me I might never have become a writer of any worth let alone the chump, the patsy, the sucker, the walking bull's eye who married Maggie or who foolishly provided CB [Bloom] with everything she did nothing to deserve. Her financial losses, her never-satisfactory career, her fading reputation, her sickening household melodrama, the daily abasement before a bully of a daughter, her terror of life and fear of people, her delusions, her hatred of Jews and Connecticut and my parents,

the racing panic that substituted for thinking, her submissive friendship with that emaciated pointed stick of Literary Envy and Free-Floating Malice, Francine du Plissitas—none of it was any of my business anymore than were Maggie's jailbird father or her two helpless abandoned children or her dopey ex-husband, that poor bastard. That was her life, not mine—and yet, with just a snap of the fingers, a little fake urine pissed into an empty herring jar in a tenement hallway by a pregnant black woman for which Maggie paid two dollars (or was it three?), it became mine.

Roth never quite got over these mistakes; they went round and round and round in his head. Perhaps it was some little comfort knowing his second wife was similarly afflicted. "She loves him and she hates him," said David Plante, who miraculously managed to stay friends with both. "In public she'll say Richard Burton was the most important person in her life. It's Philip; she knows that." Francine du Plessix Gray adamantly shook her head at the word "hates": "I think it's much more *sorrow*." But Gaia Servadio insisted "hates" is the mot juste: "I forbid her to mention Philip," she said, "because every five words it's 'Philip. Bastard. . . . May he burn in hell.'" As for Bloom herself, she tends to wax pious, at least when speaking on the record: "I got many wonderful things from it," she said of her marriage to Roth, in a representative interview. "I heard about him saying recently he'd retired from writing. Very sad. He said: 'I've done the best with what I had.' I thought that was very touching."

By the time Roth died, it's possible she'd mastered the worst of her ambivalence and become the high-minded Commander of the Order of the British Empire (or CBE, an honor conferred in 2013) for whom the purest feelings alone remain. When Roth was in extremis, Marty Garbus took it upon himself to phone Bloom lest the media beat him to it. "She seemed to muffle a cry," he said of her reaction; during the long talk that followed, he suspected she wanted to ask whether Roth ever spoke lovingly of her. Afterward she inquired via email if Roth would have a Jewish funeral, and asked Garbus to include in his prayers a message that she loved him; she hoped Philip had found peace, what with his being "so afraid of dying." Meanwhile she appeared on BBC *Newsnight* looking mournful but well preserved. "You wrote with anger, Claire," presenter Emily Maitlis reminded her, and Bloom retorted that she "also wrote about our *love*, and people seem not to want to see that. . . . I remember him in the country, and we used to go for walks. I remember the joyful, wonderful times." Roth, however, tended to dwell on the other times. "Your job at my memorial is to make sure Claire doesn't show up," he instructed Russ Murdock, his faithful caretaker and stonemason.

. . . .

ROTH CONCLUDED HIS 2013 apologia thus: "High-powered people have a tendency to get carried away, to be sure, but twice in life, catastrophically, at the beginning and nearly approaching the end—as though I had learned NOTHING—I put the high-poweredness to the worst possible use. I didn't flee to Bora-Bora—not me! But then, 31 times I put it to a proper use, to the only use that was of any use to me and I (me?) to it, if that or anything here makes sense."

It makes sense. Roth's thirty-one books, his fifty-five years of intensity, leave an achievement that, as Jonathan Lethem put it, "encompasses and transcends modes of historical fiction, metafiction, memoir, the maximalist (or putters-in), the minimalist (or takers-out), the picaresque and counterfactual, etcetera and so forth—being the sort of writer who in his generosity half blots out the sky of possibility for those who come along after—to generate in his ambitious followers a sort of army of Counter-Roths." Indeed, how does one trace the influence of such a protean writer? Roth saw the problem. One day he told Plante he could parody the latter's writing, and instantly gave an example: "He sat on a train. The train started. His ankle was itchy. The train slowed down. He scratched his ankle. The train stopped." Then he challenged Plante to return the favor, but Plante was at a loss; Roth tried, but he couldn't do it either. "That may be a bad sign," he said.

And what about the protean man himself? In *Deception*, "Philip" imagines the predicament of Zuckerman's hapless biographer: "He's found a tremendous lack of objectivity in people's responses to Zuckerman. Everybody gives him a different story. . . . What interests him is the terrible ambiguity of the 'I,' the way a writer makes a myth of himself and particularly, *why*." Roth (the real one) thought a key phrase here would serve as a good title for his own biography—"THE TERRIBLE AMBIGUITY OF THE 'I,'" he typed it out for me, "The Life and Work of Philip Roth" —"given its applicability," he explained, "to the writer as imaginer and the characters whose being he imagines, men like Swede Levov, Ira Ringold, Coleman Silk, Mickey Sabbath, David Kepesh, Peter Tarnopol, even benighted Portnoy."

What Roth's farrago of alter egos (especially the ones who write) have in common is a nature divided along somewhat predictable lines: the isolato who lives to pursue his art; the impious libertine who endeavors to squeeze the Nice Jewish Boy out of himself "drop by drop"; and of course the Nice Jewish Boy per se, wishing mostly to be good and pining for *le vrai:* "There was nothing that could ever equal coming home through the snow in late afternoon from Chancellor Avenue School. That was the best life had to offer. Snow was childhood, protected, carefree, loved, obedient." Given the vastly different needs of his different selves, Roth's engagement with the world was bound to be incomplete, when it wasn't positively disastrous.

"Love!" he said, when an interviewer asked him about it; he pondered a moment, then burst into song à la Chaplin in *Limelight*:

. . . It's love, love, love, love, love, love, love, love, love, love, love, love, love. It's love, love, love, love, love, love, love, love, love, love, love, love, love. It's love, love, love, love, love, love, love, love, love, love, love, love, love. It's love, love, love, love, love, love, love, love, love. Love, love.

"You didn't figure on getting that, did you?" he said, and laughed.

ACKNOWLEDGMENTS

MY GREATEST DEBT BY FAR IS TO PHILIP ROTH, WHOSE cooperation was honorable and absolute. He gave me almost every particle of pertinent information, no matter how intimate, and let me make of it what I would (after telling me, often exhaustively, what I *ought* to make of it). Someday I may write at length about our interesting collaboration; suffice it to say, for now, that he was a person toward whom it was hard not to feel tenderly. He was all but incapable of dissembling his human essence. When he interviewed me for this job in the spring of 2012, at his apartment on the Upper West Side, he began as the imperious maestro—asking me to explain why "a gentile from Oklahoma should write [his] biography"—a persona that fell away within minutes, as he endearingly talked over me (unable to bear my imprecision) while I did my best to answer questions about, say, the Jewish American literary tradition vis-à-vis the work of Bellow, Malamud, and Roth. Soon he was inviting me to try on the top hat Bellow had worn in Stockholm, but his mood went abruptly black when the subject of his second wife came up—the look on his face! As if he'd only just now discovered her treachery, and was mortified anew, baffled and embittered forever. But finally his spirits were restored as we paged through a photo album devoted to his girlfriends over the years: an artifact attesting to the only passion that ever rivaled his writing. He doted on these women and vice versa; several of them came to his bedside while he lay dying, as did I.

Anyway, he gave me his blessing, and our association was sometimes complicated but rarely unhappy and never dull. That first summer I spent a week in Connecticut, interviewing him six hours a day in his studio. Now and then we had to take bathroom breaks, and we could hear each other's muffled streams through the door. One lovely sun-dappled afternoon I sat on his studio couch, listening to our greatest living novelist empty his bladder, and reflected that this was about as good as it gets for an American literary biographer.

The late James Atlas unwittingly got the ball rolling when he told me, over breakfast at Sarabeth's on Amsterdam Avenue, that Roth was between biographers at the moment. "What about you, Jim?" I said to the biographer of Bellow and Delmore Schwartz, and Atlas shook his head with wide-eyed alarm—the first hint I got of his complicated falling-out with Roth. (A week or so before Jim's sudden death on September 4, 2019, I showed him the relevant pages from this book, and he couldn't have been more good-humored and gracious about what was, after all, a painful episode in his life.) My colleague Steven Aronson also paved the way by mentioning to his and Roth's mutual friend, Barbara Jakobson, that I'd written a good biography of Cheever and was likely to do the same for Roth. Barbara was kind enough to pass this along.

Once I began work, a number of Roth's old friends went out of their way to be helpful. Joel Conarroe kept his vast trove of Rothiana—letters, printed-out emails, diaries, programs from award ceremonies, speeches, photos—in a big steamer trunk, with which he left me alone in his library for hours at a time; over the years that followed, he always made a point of sending me incidental nuggets that he thought might help the cause. Judith Thurman and Lisa Halliday read this book in draft and immeasurably improved it with their comments; their kindness in every other respect led to a friendship in both cases. I also became close to Roth's old Bucknell friend Charlotte Maurer, who devotedly searched her house for letters and back issues of *Et Cetera*; for a year or so we emailed almost weekly, until my last note was answered by her daughter, Charlo, who informed me that her ninety-one-year-old mother had died suddenly of late-detected cancer. Roth's longtime lover, "Inga Larsen"—model for the deathless Drenka—composed for my sole perusal a 100-plus-page remembrance of her affair with Roth and was remarkably affable and poised during the often ticklish (for me) interviews that followed. The children of Roth's first wife, Maggie—whom I call Helen and Ronald in this book—had little desire to revisit the desolation of their childhoods, but obliged me anyway out of love and gratitude for the man who, both agree, saved their lives. Barbara Sproul gave me abundant lunches in her New York apartment and always spoke of Roth with a nice blend of bluntness and love. Susan Rogers also chatted with me for hours on end, consulting her journal along the way for corroborating details. And special thanks to Roth's friends Jack Miles, Bernie Avishai, and the main helpmate of his later years, Ben Taylor, as well as Roth's co-executors, Julia Golier and Andrew Wylie, who were conscientious and fair-minded in reviewing my book on behalf of the estate.

Thanks to everyone on my list of interviewees (below), and especially to those who also sent letters, photographs, and other essential materials: Ann Mudge Backer, Ann Sides Bishop, Jason Epstein, Pamela Forcey, Martin Garbus, Vernon Gibberd, Philip Grausman, Bob Heyman, Ted Hoagland, Stuart Lehman, Gene Lichtenstein, Freya Manfred, Kathy Meetz, Claudia Roth Pierpont, David Plante, Max Rudin, Roslyn Schloss, Fredrica Wagman, and Jack Wheatcroft. Claire Bloom and her daughter, Anna Steiger, preferred not to be interviewed for this book, but were cordial and often forthcoming via email. Others who provided helpful materials or responded to my queries include Harold Bloom, Joanna Rostropowicz Clark, Robert A. Cohn, Richard Cook, Nancy Crampton, Blake Gilpin, A. R. Gurney, Kay Redfield Jamison, Michael Janeway, Cynthia Lichtenstein, William McPherson, Ben Moser, Lynn Nesbit, Dan Oren, Stathis Orphanos, Livia Manera Sambuy, Josyane Savigneau, Rabbi Arthur Steinberg, Michael Steiner, and Marc Weitzmann.

There are many librarians and other thoughtful people to thank, and I wish I had space to go into detail in certain heroic cases: Denise Anderson (University of Iowa); Andre Bernard (Guggenheim Foundation); Alice L. Birney (Library of Congress); Jane Ciabattari; Carolyn Cohen (B'nai B'rith); Kate Collins (Rubinstein Rare Book and Manuscript Library, Duke University); Dolores Colon and Moira Fitzgerald (Beinecke Library, Yale University); Tara C. Craig and Christopher M. Laico (Butler Library, Columbia University); Nicole C. Dittrich (Syracuse University); Susan Floyd and Richard B. Watson (Harry Ransom Center, University of Texas); Julia Gardner, Christine Colburn, Daniel Meyer, and Leah Richardson (Regenstein Library, University of Chicago); Jonathan Gourlay (MacDowell Colony); Rachel Howarth and Susan Pyzynski (Houghton Library, Harvard University); Sharon Hudak and John J. W. Plampin (University of Chicago Registrar's office); Oliver Urquhart Irvine, Sue Allison, Andy Appleyard, Andrew Gough, and Helen Melody (British Library); Sally Kent and Jean Rose (University of Reading); Declan Kiely and Carolyn Vega (Morgan Library); Breanne LaCamera (Columbia University Center for Oral History); Thomas Lannon, Kit Messick, Tal Nadan, Weatherly

Stephan, and William Stingone (Manuscripts and Archive Division, New York Public Library); Joshua McKeon (Berg Collection, New York Public Library); Nancy Malloy (American Academy of Arts and Letters); Sean D. Noel (Howard Gotlieb Archival Research Center, Boston University); Kevin Ray (Hoole Special Collections Library, University of Alabama); Trevor Sandgathe (Oregon State University Libraries); Sandra Stelts and Meredith Anne Weber (Penn State University); Gabriel Swift (Princeton University); and Candace Wait (Yaddo).

Thanks to Beth Schober, the wonderful proprietor of the Hopkins Inn, where I very contentedly lodged while visiting Roth in Warren, Connecticut. Also, I processed a lot of my research during a pleasant summer month in 2014, when I was the Kirby-Mewshaw Fellow in Writing at the Civitella Ranieri castle in Umbertide, Italy, and the same goes for the previous autumn as a Meymandi Fellow at the National Humanities Center in Durham, North Carolina.

Throughout I was guided by my brilliant editor at Norton, Matt Weiland. Thanks also to my incredibly scrupulous copy editor, Trent Duffy.

I can hardly say enough about my sage, sweet-natured agent, Shane Salerno, who has worked so hard to see that this book is launched properly into the world. I'm also grateful to my friend David McCormick for many past favors I'll never forget.

Loving gratitude, as ever, to my wife, Mary, and our wonderful daughter, Amelia, who let me go away to a castle in Italy and libraries all over the world because they love me and have, besides, their own stuff to do.

NOTES

DURING THE YEARS I WORKED ON THIS BIOGRAPHY, THE Manuscript Division of the Library of Congress—where the bulk of Philip Roth's papers are preserved—became a home away from home. Each day, during my visits, I'd begin by filling out another card, requesting my allotment of boxes, which a librarian would cart out to my table. At some point Roth informed me that he'd made a recent donation of papers that had yet to be catalogued, so the next time I visited Washington I asked a librarian whether I could venture into the main storage area and have a look at these new materials. The librarian escorted me back amid the vast columns of boxes until, after a few turns, we paused: "This is the Philip Roth stuff," he said, indicating a vista that put me in mind of the final, lingering crane shot in *Citizen Kane*—that is, if Kane were not a maniacally acquisitive tycoon but rather an obsessive novelist who'd written multiple drafts of his thirty-one published books and never mind all the *un*published books that had expired after five or ten or hundreds of unavailing pages.

In addition to this mother lode, Roth had his own "miles of files" (as he told the BBC) at home, and these he excavated during the early years of our collaboration. After examining the contents of a given file, Roth would type a little (or long) memo, attach it, and mail me the file in an envelope double-sealed with a thick strip of translucent brown tape (lest a bookish post-person notice the august name stamped on the envelope and let curiosity get the better of her). These materials are indicated in the notes below with the abbreviation PRPP—Philip Roth's personal papers—some of which will eventually be relinquished to the Library of Congress; it was Roth's wish that they remain sealed to the public until 2050.

When I quote one of Roth's memos to me, I give a citation below *only* in the following cases: (a) where the source is ambiguous and I want to emphasize that Roth himself is the source ("PR—memo"), or (b) where I quote from one of two unpublished Roth manuscripts, "Notes for My Biographer" and "Notes on a Slander-Monger"—the first a 295-page rebuttal of Claire Bloom's *Leaving a Doll's House*, and the second a longer, randomly paginated mélange of thoughts mostly provoked by Ross Miller's taped interviews with Roth's friends and family; Miller returned most of these tapes to Roth when they parted ways. It's possible neither "Notes for My Biographer" nor "Notes on a Slander-Monger" will ever see the light of day, even after a thirty-year embargo, but in any case I think it's important that the reader know when quotations are derived from such adversarial documents.

Other unattributed quotations come from interviews conducted by Blake Bailey, Ross Miller, Harry Maurer, Lisa Halliday, and Judith Thurman; I transcribed the interviews conducted by Miller et al. from audiocassettes and CDs provided to me by Roth.

INTERVIEWS

Blake Bailey's interviews: Enrico Adelman, 13 April 2013; Nelson W. Aldrich Jr., 20 November 2013; Al Alvarez, 7 July 2013; Anne Alvarez, 7 July 2013; Matthew Andresino, 30 March 2013; Don Aronson, 20 May 2014; Linda Asher, 1 May 2013; James Atlas, 29 April 2013; Bernard Avishai, 28 October 2013, 7 November 2013; Ann Mudge Backer, 16 August 2012, 27 August 2012, 15 October 2012; Marilyn Lerner Becker, 16 November 2012; Janis Freedman Bellow, 17 January 2015; Ann Sides Bishop, 21 February 2014; Anne Bolton Borchardt, 20 February 2014; Georges Borchardt, 20 February 2014; Leon Botstein, 14 September 2014; Alfred Brendel, 7 July 2013; Jonathan Brent, 31 March 2014, 3 April 2014; Robert Brustein, 30 May 2013, 12 October 2013; Amy Buxbaum, 21 May 2013; Peter Carberry, 25 February 2014; Martin Castelbaum, 3 October 2014, 15 October 2014; Susan Cheever, 21 September 2014; Nancy Chilton, 12 May 2014; Martha Clarke, 23 May 2013; Don Cole, 9 May 2013; Joel Conarroe, 31 July 2012, 7 December 2012; Elizabeth Del Tufo, 26 July 2012; Diane —— (Roth and Maggie's friend c. 1956–1957), 3 December 2012; Judith Dunford, 29 March 2013; Jason Epstein, 15 October 2013; Louise Erdrich, 26 May 2015; Shelly Estrin, 6 November 2013; Mia Farrow, 29 June 2015; Judy Feiffer, 20 September 2014; Jules Feiffer, 27 November 2012; Seymour Feldman, 18 December 2014; Sunya Lerner Felburg, 13 December 2012; Edward Finkel, 5 February 2016; Nancy Finkelstein, 5 August 2013; Frances FitzGerald, 17 February 2015; Pamela Forcey, 24 January 2015; Ralph Freedman, 21 August 2014; Betty Fussell, 18 April 2013; Martin Garbus, 10 December 2012; Harry Garvin, 11 October 2012; Arthur Geffen, 25 January 2013; Vernon Gibberd, 2 August 2013, 5 August 2013; Julia Golier, 17 April 2015; Mary Lou Golier, 3 April 2014; Alice Gordon, 16 July 2014; Philip Grausman, 17 May 2013; Francine du Plessix Gray, 22

March 2013; Eileen Lerner Greenberg, 10 June 2013; Martin Greenberg, 31 August 2014; Philip Greiss, 31 October 2015, 1 November 2015; Paul Groffsky, 5 March 2013; Herb Haber, 8 February 2013; Lisa Halliday, 15 October 2012, 14 October 2015; David Hare, 30 March 2015; Michael Herr, 16 February 2014, 22 February 2014; Robert Heyman, 3 July 2012, 24 September 2012; Edward Hoagland, 30 August 2014; Douglas Hobbie, 14 December 2012; Judy Hudson, 20 September 2014; Susan Jacoby, 17 August 2012; Barbara Jakobson, 13 October 2012, 9 December 2012, 14 September 2013; Joseph Josephson, 21 November 2012; Edmund Keeley, 4 April 2013; Penelope Kim, 25 April 2013; Ivan Klíma, 23 December 2013; Lucy Warner Kuemmerle, 10 October 2012, 6 March 2014; Sanford Kuvin, 3 September 2012; "Inga Larsen" (Roth's longtime lover), 8 November 2014, 9 November 2014; Paul LeClerc, 21 May 2015; Stuart Lehman, 18 June 2012; Alan Lelchuk, 28 October 2013; Gene Lichtenstein, 19 January 2015; Antonin Liehm, 11 June 2013; Louise —— (Roth's girlfriend c. 1975), 13 November 2013; William Luers, 27 September 2014; Alison Lurie, 24 May 2013; Jane Brown Maas, 11 October 2012; Norman Manea, 16 September 2013; Freya Manfred, 3 August 2013; Dorene Marcus, 2 February 2014; Alexandra Marshall, 28 August 2013; Jane Kome Mather, 22 February 2013; Charlotte Maurer, 16 January 2013, 20 January 2013; Kathy Meetz, 13 January 2014; Asher Milbauer, 20 September 2012; Jack Miles, 16 January 2014; "Burt Miller" (Maggie's first husband), 3 March 2013; "Ronald Miller" (Maggie's son), 1 February 2013, 6 February 2013; "Helen Miller" (Maggie's daughter), 27 July 2013, 17 August 2013, 24 August 2013, 7 September 2013, 22 November 2015; Julian Mitchell, 8 July 2015; Lori Monson, 16 July 2014; Honor Moore, 28 April 2013; Russ Murdock, 16 August 2018; Alana Newhouse, 7 March 2014; Russell Oberlin, 24 October 2013; Edna O'Brien, 22 March 2013; Cynthia Ozick, 1 August 2013; Claudia Roth Pierpont, 13 March 2015; Robert Pincus-Witten, 22 August 2013; David Plante, 18 September 2013; Elizabeth Pochoda, 26 September 2013, 4 October 2013; Christopher Prevatt, 9 May 2014; David Ray, 2 May 2013; David Rieff, 13 October 2012; Mary Elsie Robertson, 1 March 2013; Bernard Rodgers, 17 November 2015; Susan Fox Rogers, 26 September 2014, 14 October 2014, 20 October 2014, 24 October 2014; Alane Rollings, 2 April 2013; Joan Roth, 19 November 2012; Edward Rothstein, 7 November 2014; Max Rudin, 18 June 2012, 13 September 2013; Roslyn Schloss, 29 August 2015; Dr. Stanley Schneller, 16 July 2018; Gaia Servadio, 28 December 2012, 29 December 2012, 7 July 2013; Howard Silver, 13 November 2013; Dorothy Brand Slapcoff, 20 June 2013; Barbara Sproul, 8 December 2012, 21 March 2013, 14 September 2013; Ruth Green Stamler, 26 January 2015; Rose Styron,

20 October 2012; Tony Sylvester, 3 November 2014; Barry Targan, 9 February 2013; Benjamin Taylor, 6 November 2014, 13 October 2015; Judith Thurman, 14 July 2012; Sylvia Tumin, 20 July 2012; Anne Komisar Valentine, 28 September 2012, 3 October 2012; Peter Valentine, 28 September 2012; Catherine von Klitzing, 9 March 2014, 15 May 2015; Fredrica Wagman, 15 September 2013; Nela Wagman, 29 January 2014; Dan Wakefield, 19 October 2012; Martin Weich, 9 July 2012, 19 July 2012; Barbara Klein Weisman, 10 June 2013; Marc Weitzmann, 1 May 2014; Jack Wheatcroft, 16 December 2012, 17 December 2012; Diane Williams, 20 May 2015; "Kaysie Wimberly," 13 July 2012; Joan Wortis, 3 May 2013; Andrew Wylie, 14 October 2016; Alan Yentob, 8 July 2013.

Blake Bailey's interviews with Philip Roth: 6–12 July 2012, 11–14 October 2012, 7 December 2012, 10 December 2012; 29 April 2013, 15 September 2013; 25 May 2014; 13 March 2015, 14 May 2015, 14 October 2015; 17 October 2016; 18 May 2017.

Lisa Halliday's interviews: Al Alvarez, 19 July 2007; Alain Finkielkraut, 1 July 2007; Hermione Lee, 26 September 2007.

Harry Maurer's interviews: Joanna Rostropowicz Clark, 30 June 2007; Clive Cummis, 30 August 2007; Robert Heyman, 25 June 2007; Sandy Roth, 2 June 2007; Howard Stein, 4 June 2007; Richard Stern, 2–4 June 2007; Sylvia Tumin, 30 June 2007.

Ross Miller's interviews: Aaron Asher, 27 September 2005; Robert Brustein, 28 July 2008; Florence Roth Cohen, 4 March 2007; Julius Goldstein, 3 November 1996; Robert Lowenstein, 2 February 2006; Sandy Roth, 13 December 2006; Herman and Nina Schneider, 2 November 1996; Richard Stern, 14 December 2006.

Ross Miller's interviews with Philip Roth: 13 November 1996, 24 November 1996; 16 January 1997, n.d. [c. May–June 1997?]; 4 April 2004, 6 April 2004, 11 April 2004, 18 April 2004, 30 June 2004, 1 July 2004, 10 July 2004, 31 July 2004, 1–2 August 2004, 7 August 2004, 26 September 2004, 12 October 2004; 5–6 March 2005, 19 March 2005, 28 March 2005, 16 April 2005, 30 April 2005, 25 October 2005; 28 January 2006; 9 January 2007, 9 March 2007.

Judith Thurman's interviews (all conducted c. 1 April 1991, during a trip to Bucknell she took with Roth): Harry Garvin, Mildred Martin, Jack Wheatcroft.

Miscellaneous video interviews with Philip Roth: "Philip Roth: My True Story," BBC *Arena* documentary (1993), https://www.youtube.com/watch?v= 5G8Z2vrLpzA; "Philip Roth at 70: Interview with David Remnick" (2003), https://www.youtube.com/watch?v=lGbYxBxyUec; with Katie Couric on *Today* (2004), https://www.youtube.com/watch?v=4ColUyHplX8; with Tina Brown for *The Daily Beast*, 30 October 2009, https://www.thedailybeast.com/philip -roth-unbound-the-full-interview; with Rita Braver on *CBS Sunday Morning* (2010), https://www.youtube.com/watch?v=9Vz7oUhqTQk; with Christopher Sykes for *Web of Stories* (2011), https://www.webofstories.com/play/philip.roth/1; "Man Booker International Prize 2011 Winner Philip Roth Interviewed by Benjamin Taylor," https://www.youtube.com/watch?v=_QeIJ_xO7ns; *Philip Roth Unmasked*, PBS *American Masters* documentary (2013), https://www.pbs.org/ video/american-masters-watch-philip-roth-unmasked/; *Philip Roth Unleashed*, BBC *Imagine* documentary (2014), https://www.youtube.com/watch?time_ continue=1&v=Dh_tCH4ztRM (part 1) and https://www.youtube.com/watch? v=h5M1uTcBMrs (part 2).

I cite specific interviews, below, only when the source of a quotation is ambiguous, and the same goes for letters and other personal documents. Where the author and recipient of a given letter are named in the text, there is no further citation below. Unless otherwise indicated, cited letters are in the hands of the recipient. Roth's novels are cited only when their contents are quoted for biographical (versus critical) interest, and only when their titles aren't given in the text; page numbers for Roth's work are usually keyed to their Library of America editions.

This is problematic, however, in the case of Roth's tenth and final LOA volume, *Why Write? Collected Nonfiction 1960–2013*. Part One of the contents is headed "From *Reading Myself and Others*," but the text actually includes four interviews postdating that 1975 collection. Since those four interviews also appear in *Conversations with Philip Roth*, my citations are keyed to the latter volume, except in the case of Roth's 1984 *Paris Review* interview (keyed to *Why Write?*). Material that originally appeared in *Reading Myself and Others* but is omitted from *Why Write?* is keyed to the first volume.

Finally, when I cite a periodical, page numbers are given if available; where they don't appear, the reader may assume the original document is a clipping or (more likely) obtained from the internet.

FIRST PUBLICATION AND LIBRARY OF AMERICA EDITIONS OF PHILIP ROTH'S WORKS

Goodbye, Columbus and Five Short Stories (Boston: Houghton Mifflin, 1959); Library of America, 2005 (in *Philip Roth: Novels and Stories 1959–1962*).

Letting Go (New York: Random House, 1962); Library of America, 2005 (in *Philip Roth: Novels and Stories 1959–1962*).

When She Was Good (New York: Random House, 1967); Library of America, 2005 (in *Philip Roth: Novels 1967–1972*).

Portnoy's Complaint (New York: Random House, 1969); Library of America, 2005 (in *Philip Roth: Novels 1967–1972*).

Our Gang (New York: Random House, 1971); Library of America, 2005 (in *Philip Roth: Novels 1967–1972*).

The Breast (New York: Holt, Rinehart and Winston, 1972); Library of America, 2005 (in *Philip Roth: Novels 1967–1972*).

The Great American Novel (New York: Holt, Rinehart and Winston, 1973); Library of America, 2006 (in *Philip Roth: Novels 1973–1977*).

My Life as a Man (New York: Holt, Rinehart and Winston, 1974); Library of America, 2006 (in *Philip Roth: Novels 1973–1977*).

Reading Myself and Others (New York: Farrar, Straus and Giroux, 1975); Library of America, 2017 (partially reprinted in *Philip Roth: Why Write? Collected Nonfiction 1960–2013*).

The Professor of Desire (New York: Farrar, Straus and Giroux, 1977); Library of America, 2006 (in *Philip Roth: Novels 1973–1977*).

The Ghost Writer (New York: Farrar, Straus and Giroux, 1979); Library of America, 2007 (in *Philip Roth: Zuckerman Bound: A Trilogy and Epilogue 1979–1985*).

Zuckerman Unbound (New York: Farrar, Straus and Giroux, 1981); Library of America, 2007 (in *Philip Roth: Zuckerman Bound: A Trilogy and Epilogue 1979–1985*).

The Anatomy Lesson (New York: Farrar, Straus and Giroux, 1983); Library of America, 2007 (in *Philip Roth: Zuckerman Bound: A Trilogy and Epilogue 1979–1985*).

The Prague Orgy first published in *Zuckerman Bound: A Trilogy and Epilogue*

(New York: Farrar, Straus and Giroux, 1985); Library of America, 2007 (in *Philip Roth: Zuckerman Bound: A Trilogy and Epilogue 1979–1985*).

The Counterlife (New York: Farrar, Straus and Giroux, 1986); Library of America, 2008 (in *Philip Roth: Novels and Other Narratives 1986–1991*).

The Facts (New York: Farrar, Straus and Giroux, 1988); Library of America, 2008 (in *Philip Roth: Novels and Other Narratives 1986–1991*).

Deception (New York: Simon & Schuster, 1990); Library of America, 2008 (in *Philip Roth: Novels and Other Narratives 1986–1991*).

Patrimony (New York: Simon & Schuster, 1991). Library of America, 2008 (in *Philip Roth: Novels and Other Narratives 1986–1991*).

Operation Shylock (New York: Simon & Schuster, 1993); Library of America, 2010 (in *Philip Roth: Novels 1993–1995*).

Sabbath's Theater (Boston: Houghton Mifflin, 1995); Library of America, 2010 (in *Philip Roth: Novels 1993–1995*).

American Pastoral (New York: Houghton Mifflin, 1997); Library of America, 2011 (in *Philip Roth: The American Trilogy 1997–2000*).

I Married a Communist (New York: Houghton Mifflin, 1998); Library of America, 2011 (in *Philip Roth: The American Trilogy 1997–2000*).

The Human Stain (New York: Houghton Mifflin, 2000); Library of America, 2011 (in *Philip Roth: The American Trilogy 1997–2000*).

Shop Talk (New York: Houghton Mifflin, 2001); Library of America, 2017 (in *Philip Roth: Why Write? Collected Nonfiction 1960–2013*).

The Dying Animal (New York: Houghton Mifflin, 2001); Library of America, 2013 (in *Philip Roth: Novels 2001–2007*).

The Plot Against America (New York: Houghton Mifflin, 2004); Library of America, 2013 (in *Philip Roth: Novels 2001–2007*).

Everyman (New York: Houghton Mifflin, 2006); Library of America, 2013 (in *Philip Roth: Nemeses*).

Exit Ghost (New York: Houghton Mifflin, 2007); Library of America, 2013 (in *Philip Roth: Novels 2001–2007*).

Indignation (New York: Houghton Mifflin, 2008); Library of America, 2013 (in *Philip Roth: Nemeses*).

The Humbling (New York: Houghton Mifflin, 2009); Library of America, 2013 (in *Philip Roth: Nemeses*).

Nemesis (New York: Houghton Mifflin, 2010); Library of America, 2013 (in *Philip Roth: Nemeses*).

ABBREVIATIONS USED IN THE NOTES

AL	*The Anatomy Lesson*
AP	*American Pastoral*
BB	Blake Bailey
BCS	Barbara C. Sproul
BL	The British Library
BU	Howard Gotlieb Archival Research Center, Mugar Memorial Library, Boston University
CB	Claire Bloom
CPR	*Conversations with Philip Roth*, edited by George J. Searle (Jackson: University Press of Mississippi, 1992)
CU–B	Butler Library, Columbia University
CU–COHC	Columbia University Center for Oral History Collection
DP	David Plante's diary (in Berg Collection, New York Public Library)
F	*The Facts*
FSG	Farrar, Straus and Giroux
GC	*Goodbye, Columbus*
HM	Harry Maurer
HU–HL	Houghton Library, Harvard University
JC	Joel Conarroe
JT	Judith Thurman
JU	John Updike
LA	*Limelight and After*, by Claire Bloom (New York: Harper & Row, 1982)
LC	Library of Congress
LDH	*Leaving a Doll's House*, by Claire Bloom (New York: Little Brown 1996)
LH	Lisa Halliday
LOA	Library of America
MLAM	*My Life as a Man*
Morgan	The Pierpont Morgan Library, New York
MR	Margaret Roth
NFMB	"Notes for My Biographer" (unpublished typescript by PR)
NSM	"Notes on a Slander-Monger" (unpublished typescript by PR)
NYPL–Berg	Henry W. and Albert A. Berg Collection of English and American Literature, New York Public Library
NYPL–M&A	Manuscripts and Archives Division, New York Public Library

P	*Patrimony*
PAA	*The Plot Against America*
PO	*The Prague Orgy*
PR	Philip Roth
PR@80	*Philip Roth at 80: A Celebration (*New York: Library of America, 2014)
PR–LC	Philip Roth Papers, Library of Congress
PR—memo	Roth's unspecified/untitled memoranda to his biographer(s)
PRPP	Philip Roth's personal papers
PUL	Princeton University library
Ransom	Harry Ransom Humanities Research Center, University of Texas
RGS	Richard G. Stern
RM	Ross Miller
RMO	*Reading Myself and Others*
RSB	Robert S. Baker
RU	*Roth Unbound: A Writer and His Books*, by Claudia Roth Pierpont (New York: Farrar, Straus and Giroux, 2013)
RWS	Roger W. Straus Jr.
SR	Sandy Roth
TR–PSU	Thomas Rogers Papers, Pennsylvania State University libraries
TS	Ted Solotaroff
UC	Regenstein Library, University of Chicago
UR	Jonathan Cape Archive, University of Reading library
WW	*Why Write? Collected Nonfiction 1960–2013*

PROLOGUE

1 **"Now you just step up here"**: PR—memo.
2 **"Mr. Roth is a writer"**: Frank Kermode to David G. Brewster, 31 Jan. 1997, LC.
3 **"If we has asked for the single best writer"**: A. O. Scott, "In Search of the Best," *New York Times*, 21 May 2006.
3 **"the truest picture"**: *Proceedings of the American Academy of Arts and Letters: Second Series* (New York: The American Academy of Arts and Letters, 2002).
4 **"not just the speed of his mind"**: Janet Hobhouse, *The Furies* (New York: New York Review Books, 2004), 196.
4 **"My reputation as a 'recluse'"**: PR to Jack Miles, 19 Apr. 2012.
6 **"a pertinent little misunderstanding"**: PR's remarks on receiving the National Book Foundation's Medal for Distinguished Contribution to American Letters on 20 November 2002. A revised version of this speech appears as "I Have Fallen in Love with American Names" in *WW*, 331–35.

6 **"The child in me is delighted"**: James Atlas, *Bellow* (New York: Random House, 2000), 457.

6 **"It's actually quite ugly, isn't it?"**: BB int. LH, 14 Oct. 2015.

CHAPTER ONE

9 **"You could be in a shtetl"**: DP.

9 **"singing show tunes"**: *F*, 403.

9 **"Pole, Yid, and hound"**: Anna Reid, *Borderland: A Journey Through the History of Ukraine* (Boulder, Col.: Westview, 1999), 144.

10 **"Often the relations between"**: Irving Howe, *World of Our Fathers* (New York: Harcourt Brace Jovanovich, 1976), 10.

11 **"Yid, Yid, Yid!"**: Joseph Roth, *The Radetzky March* (New York: Overlook, 2002), 94.

11 **Sender's sister Fannie:** Herman Roth to Sunya Felburg, 30 Nov. 1984.

12 **Uri Zvi Greenberg:** Jewish Virtual Library; https://www.jewishvirtuallibrary.org/uri-zvi-greenberg.

13 **"What's interesting"**: PR to Sunya Felburg, n.d. [c. Mar. 2013].

15 **"his shrunken face disclosed itself"**: *F*, 316.

15 **"gentle" grandfather:** RM int. PR, 9 Jan. 2007.

15 **grandson described as a "mansion"**: BB int. Edward Finkel, 15 Feb. 2016.

17 **"miserable and nasty" people:** Email from Anne Valentine to BB, 12 Jan. 2016.

18 **"All right, boys, here we go!"**: BB int. PR, 6 July 2012.

19 **"Bernie, you don't have enough larceny"**: Bernard Disner to PR, 1 Feb. 1991, PRPP.

19 **"every boy [he] knew had been born"**: *PAA*, 160.

19 **"cheap high-class building plots"**: Robert Weiner, "Forgosh Speaks at NJPAC about Newark's Jews," *Jewish Historical Society of New Jersey*, Spring 2016.

19 **"I think we could get it now"**: Scott Raab, "Philip Roth Goes Home Again," *Esquire*, Oct. 2010.

20 **"was as safe and peaceful"**: *F*, 330.

21 **"the boredom, the righteousness, the bigotry"**: *AL*, 378.

CHAPTER TWO

22 **"I *told* you I should have it!"**: HM int. SR, 25 June 2007.

23 **"It soon became apparent"**: Hans J. Kleinschmidt, "The Angry Act: The Role of Aggression in Creativity," *American Imago* 24, no. 1 (Spring 1967), 124.

24 **"New York's last Freudian"**: Adam Gopnik, "Man Goes to See a Doctor," *The New Yorker*, 24–31 Aug. 1998, 114. Kleinschmidt appears as "Max Grosskurth."

24 **"compulsive masturbation"**: Kleinschmidt, "Angry Act," 126.

25 **"superior to these people"**: RM int. PR, 28 Jan. 2006.

26 **"Lafayette, we are here!"**: Colin DeVries, "Philip Roth Gets France's Highest Honor; French Will Open Public Bookstore in Embassy Building," New York *Daily News*, 2 Oct. 2013.

26 **"I was clever and liked school"**: Roth's typed draft for his entry in the 1965 edition of *Midcentury Authors* was among his papers at the Library of Congress—a verbose (for Roth) self-accounting in which he confesses his cleverness as a schoolboy but also winningly implies he wasn't much of a reader. I have no idea how much of this made its way into the published volume, but it's interesting to note that his next

typed entry, for the 1970 edition (also among his papers), omits anything of the personal—this in the wake of his harrowing *Portnoy* fame.

27 **"the Joseph Conrad of children's literature"**: PR's remarks at his seventy-fifth birthday tribute at Columbia University on 11 April 2008, PRPP.

27 **"not junk but popular novels"**: *F*, 399.

28 **Jewish mothers' "forced feedings"**: Isaac Rosenfeld, "Adam and Eve on Delancey Street," *Commentary*, Oct. 1949.

29 **"In a predominantly gentile environment"**: *F*, 341.

29 **"a little too comme il faut"**: *RU*, 67.

30 *"You call this handwriting?"*: RM int. PR, 9 Jan. 2007.

30 **"The idea that you don't have to work"**: Lynn Darling, "His Father's Son," *Newsday*, 28 Jan. 1991.

31 **waiting list was "hundreds long"**: George Finneman to PR, 21 Mar. 1991, PRPP.

31 **"Polonius-like advice-giving"**: PR to Dorothy Brand Slapcoff, 13 Jan. 2011.

31 **"the man in the middle"**: PR's acceptance remarks for the New Jersey Historical Society Award, 5 Oct. 1992, PRPP.

32 **"This action says more about the relation of non-observant Jews"**: Alfred Kazin, "Roth's Remarkable 'Patrimony': A Comic and Heartbreaking Saga," *Litchfield County Times*, 18 Jan. 1991.

33 **"We are the Flaschner Family"**: *Flaschner Family History* (1951), 72.

34 **"disappear right up his ass"**: PR's eulogy for SR, 11 May 2009, PRPP.

CHAPTER THREE

37 **"The Jews have *drei veltn*"**: Quoted in Irving Howe, *World of Our Fathers* (New York: Harcourt Brace Jovanovich, 1976), 393.

38 **"of powerful forces, unknown"**: PR's remarks (undelivered) on the occasion of Philip Roth Day in Newark, 23 Oct. 2005, PRPP.

39 *"Turn your light out!"*: RM int. PR, Jan. 28, 2006.

39 **"terrifying symbol"**: PR, "My Life as an American," *Observer*, 19 Oct. 1998.

40 **"Philip was an all-American boy"**: Maureen Dowd, "Roth's Real Father Likes His Books," *New York Times*, 26 Oct. 1983.

40 **"that validated our own spotless credentials"**: *F*, 332.

42 **hanged "more than once"**: Ibid., 402.

42 **"learned to be funny"**: *CPR*, 30.

42 **"drawn to the rhetoric and postures of ridicule"**: Curt Suplee, "Philip Roth, at Ease at Mid-Journey, *Washington Post*, 30 Oct. 1983.

43 **"as if he hadn't had enough of a kid brother"**: PR's eulogy for SR, 11 May 2009, PRPP.

45 **"longest, saddest day"**: *PR@80*, 52.

45 **"passed with lumbering solemnity"**: *P*, 728.

45 **"So they've given up"**: Norman Corwin, *On a Note of Triumph* (New York: Simon & Schuster, 1945), 9.

46 **the incursion of *"lumpen* kids"**: *F*, 324.

46 **"a nice and regular guy"**: *RU*, 20.

46 **"a slightly mysterious German accent"**: *F*, 324.

46 **"a lawyer for the underdog"**: Ibid., 326.

48 **CHILDREN SHUN DAR CONTEST**: Undated, unpaginated *Newark Star-Ledger* clipping provided by PR himself, who also gave me other related clippings and corre-

spondence, including Sable's letter of 3 November 2010, politely disabusing Roth of his role in the affair.

49 **"the smartest girl in the class"**: PR to Hermione Lee, 29 Feb. 2012, PRPP.

CHAPTER FOUR

50 **"at breakneck speed"**: *F*, 401.

52 **"ten or fifteen of the enemy"**: Ibid., 327.

53 **"wise guy talk and sex talk"**: William Gordon, "Prodigal Son Returns: Literary Lion Philip Roth Misses a Step on Library Lions," *Newark Star-Ledger*, 3 Nov. 1991.

53 **"one of us taking the black guy"**: *PR@80*, 56.

54 **"stupefied, finished"**: PR to BB, 9 Oct. 2012.

54 The boy expected a **"right hook"**: Swerdlow to Lowenstein, n.d. [c. 1998], PRPP.

55 **"I am using the book"**: Undated, unpaginated *Newark Star-Ledger* clipping (c. 1969) provided by PR.

55 **"*Eat up!*"**: BB int. Stuart Lehman, 18 June 2012.

56 **"He's a wise guy"**: BB int. Robert Heyman, 3 July 2012.

56 **"something like the folk narrative"**: *CPR*, 82.

56 **"Phil, the feeling there"**: *F*, 333.

57 **"a figure of considerable pathos"**: *CPR*, 82.

58 **"Philip, nobody understood him"**: PR to TS, 1 Aug. [1977?], NYPL–M&A.

58 **"She's not really Jewish"**: RM int. Florence Cohen, 4 Mar. 2007.

58 **"looks old enough to be your mother"**: *P*, 633.

58 **"were as stunned as if they'd heard"**: *F*, 317.

59 his **"other wife"**: BB int. Don Aronson, 20 May 2014.

59 a piquant new moniker: BB int. Nancy Chilton, 12 May 2014.

61 **"Don't give me that Commie crap!"**: RM int. PR, 18 Apr. 2004.

61 **"Okay, Pop," said Florence. "Irv is here"**: BB int. PR, 8 July 2012.

62 **"second- and third-hand Buicks"**: HM int. SR, 2 June 2007.

63 **"fifteen minutes *by the clock*"**: BB int. Dorothy Brand Slapcoff, 20 June 2013.

63 **"intelligent but unimpressive"**: Arnold H. Lubasch, "Philip Roth Shakes Weequahic High," *New York Times*, 28 Feb. 1969.

63 **"a terribly nice woman"**: BB int. PR, 6 July 2012.

64 **"That's a girl, Ethel, you can do it"**: NSM.

CHAPTER FIVE

66 **"*Watch the rack*"**: HM int. Robert Heyman, 25 June 2007.

66 **"through the ruthless intimacy"**: A revised version of this speech appears as "I Have Fallen in Love with American Names" in *WW*, 331–35.

67 **"*This is it!*"**: *RU*, 22.

67 **"I spent many Sunday afternoons there"**: Bruce Bahrenburg, "Newark Boyhood Fiction Material," *Newark News*, 7 Dec. 1958.

68 **"You're not going to Missouri"**: *F*, 339.

69 **"What took place here"**: Mervyn Rothstein, "To Newark, with Love. Philip Roth," *New York Times*, 29 Mar. 1991.

69 **"to prevent him from marrying a worldly woman"**: *P*, 632.

70 **"key moment"**: Bernard Avishai, *Promiscuous: "Portnoy's Complaint" and Our Doomed Pursuit of Happiness* (New Haven: Yale University Press, 2012), 16.

70 **"poignant abyss"**: *P*, 679.

70   "**The father desires in his son**": Irving Howe, "The Lost Young Intellectual," in *Mid-Century: An Anthology of Jewish Life and Culture in Our Times*, ed. Harold U. Ribalow (New York: Beechhurst Press, 1955), 156.

73   "**a complex of values**": "Jewishness and the Younger Intellectuals: A Symposium," *Commentary*, Apr. 1961, 350.

73   "**I felt like a Houyhnhnm**": *CPR*, 114.

74   "**an honorary WASP**": *F*, 347.

74   "**pushiest of pushy Jews**": Ibid., 344.

76   "**Material which depends on filth**": Anne Schoonmaker, lead editorial, *Et Cetera*, March 1952, 5.

76   "**One of our friends, a sociology major**": "Transit Lines," *Et Cetera*, Mid-Year 1952–53, 7.

76   "**two-page miscellany of putatively witty reportage**": *F*, 355.

76   "**the philistine majority**": Ibid., 356.

76   "**the poor benighted egghead**": PR to JC, 2 Dec. 1987.

77   "**Thank you, Philip!**": BB int. PR, 7 July 2012.

78   "**They think we're crazy**": BB int. Jane Brown Maas, 11 Oct. 2012.

81   "**Stop *mooning*!**": RM int. PR, 11 Apr. 2004.

81   "**a goy drunk**": RM int. PR, 28 Jan. 2006.

CHAPTER SIX

83   "**She scared nine-tenths**": "The Passing of an Era," *Bucknell World*, July 1995, 6.

83   "**from its beginnings to the present**": *F*, 360.

84   "**life of reading books and writing about them**": Ibid., 361.

84   "**She herself had no more animus**": PR's remarks on the occasion of Mildred Martin's receiving the Bucknell Order of Merit, 2 Sept. 1981, PRPP.

86   "**Swiftberg**": *RU*, 27.

87   "**this is *not* in the Bucknell spirit**": RM int. PR, 12 Oct. 2004.

87   "**nearly in tears**": *F*, 359.

88   "**Don't you *know* me?**": BB int. Martin Castelbaum, 5 Oct. 2014.

88   "**Get out of there, you hussy!**": *F*, 365.

88   "**There never was and there won't be a response**": Andrew Larson, "Roth to Receive Taylor Medal at Commencement," *The Bucknellian*, 16 May 2008, 7.

91   "**the color of an Irish setter**": *RU*, 329.

91   not "**conventional**": PR to Stuart Lehman, 23 Jan. 1955.

92   "**E. E. Cummings reading to students**": *GC*, 84.

CHAPTER SEVEN

93   "**Byronic dream**": *CPR*, 142.

94   "**Alongside him I'm John Wayne**": TS, *First Loves* (New York: Seven Stories, 2003), 205.

94   "**like some highly evolved, utopian**": *F*, 396.

94   "**Chicago Maxwell Perkins**": PR to Bob and Charlotte Maurer, 8 Apr. 1955, PR–LC.

95   "**he'd rather we didn't write**": PR to Robert Heyman, 22 Oct. 1954.

95   "**the course isn't as pompous**": PR to Maurers, 8 Apr. 1955.

96   "**sleepwalking . . . toward a decent retirement**": George Starbuck, "Wonkiness," in *An Unsentimental Education: Writers and Chicago*, ed. Molly McQuade (Chicago: University of Chicago Press, 1995), 173.

96   **"not a scholar or a critic"**: TS, *First Loves*, 193.

96   **"Jamesian superciliousness and pomposity"**: PR to Heyman, 22 Oct. 1954.

97   **"he's always lecturing in terms of 'we'"**: PR to Lehman, 23 Jan. 1955.

97   **"Suddenly people began to disappear"**: PR, "The Day It Snowed," *Chicago Review* 8, no. 4 (Fall 1954), 34–44.

98   **"It's good, Roth"**: RM int. PR, 24 Nov. 1996.

98   **"I'd rather see you entering a brothel!"**: PR—memo.

98   **"It took hundreds of years"**: PR, "The Contest for Aaron Gold," *Epoch* 7, no. 1 (Fall 1955), 37–50.

99   **"I feel skyrocketed into fame"**: PR to Bob and Charlotte Maurer, 11 July 1956, PR–LC.

99   **"lost to all their people"**: Charles McGrath, "Zuckerman's Alter Brain," *New York Times*, 7 May 2000.

100   **"sweet spontaneous sensibility"**: PR to Bob and Charlotte Maurer, 15 Feb. 1956, PR–LC.

100   **"almost anxious"**: PR to Bob and Charlotte Maurer, 25 Aug. 1955, PR–LC.

101   **"I mean, for christ [sic] sake"**: Ibid.

CHAPTER EIGHT

103   **"Willa Cather I'm not"**: PR to Bob and Charlotte Maurer, 11 Mar. 1955, PR–LC.

103   **"the slaphappy Congress"**: PR to Stuart Lehman, 23 Jan. 1955.

105   **"brutally boring"**: PR to Bob and Charlotte Maurer, 3 Jan. 1956, PR–LC.

106   **"You should be damn proud"**: PR to Bob and Charlotte Maurer, 15 Feb. 1956, PR–LC.

106   **"about an old Jew"**: PR to Maurers, 3 Jan. 1956.

107   **"I've got to begin to work"**: PR to Robert Heyman, 9 Feb. 1956.

107   **"the power of a voice"**: CPR, 213.

107   **"kind of high-faluting"**: PR to Maurers, 3 Jan. 1956.

107   **"he has managed brilliantly"**: *WW*, 299.

107   **"apologists, nostalgists, publicists"**: CPR, 128.

108   **"the day they appeared"**: *WW*, 278.

108   **"As for Augie March"**: PR to Bob and Charlotte Maurer, 26 Nov. 1956, PR–LC.

108   **"In the next two years"**: Saul Bellow, "I Got a Scheme!," *New Yorker*, 25 Apr. 2005, 75.

109   **"I've never been so in control"**: PR to Bob and Charlotte Maurer, 20 Mar. 1956, PR–LC.

109   **"'To have a baby you gotta get laid'"**: GC, 110.

110   **"I'm out"**: BB int. Matthew Andresino, 30 Mar. 2013.

111   **"I was learning how things"**: PR, "Juice or Gravy?," *New York Times Book Review*, 18 Sept. 1994; appears in slightly revised form in *WW*, 313–21.

111   **"It's what we use"**: PR, "Novotny's Pain," *New Yorker*, 27 Oct. 1962, 55.

111   **"injury existed prior to service"**: PR to Bob and Charlotte Maurer, 21 Feb. 1957, PR–LC.

111   **"very kind, in his gnome-like way"**: PR to Bob and Charlotte Maurer, 29 Aug. 1956, PR–-LC.

112   **"I was flabbergasted"**: Ibid.

CHAPTER NINE

116   **"With that act of jailing"**: NFMB, 10.

116   **"Then go back to period of college"**: PR gave me MR's journal and the abortive

beginnings to her novel(s) in progress contained therein. The story of how this intriguing artifact came into PR's possession is told at the end of chapter 19.

118 **"by force"**: Email from PR to BB, 19 July 2012.

118 **"I divorced my first husband"**: MR's plaintiff affidavit, 27 Nov. 1963, PRPP.

122 **"messy, usual, uninteresting-to-others"**: PR to Bob and Charlotte Maurer, 9 Jan. 1957, PR–LC.

122 **"John Whateverthehellhisnameis"**: PR to Bob and Charlotte Maurer, 10 May 1957, PR–LC.

122 **"want to be [Betty's] friend"**: PR to Bob and Charlotte Maurer, 15 Oct. 1957, PR–LC.

122 **"the relation between accident-proneness"**: "Dr. Elizabeth van Laer, 47, Dies; Professor of Psychology at L. I. U.," *New York Times*, 26 Sept. 1979.

123 **"about a Jewish guy who marries a Gentile girl"**: PR to Bob and Charlotte Maurer, 17 Oct. 1956, PR–LC.

124 **"friend from the goose district"**: Tom Rogers's notes on PR (courtesy of Susan Rogers).

124 **"On the first day of a course"**: TS, *First Loves* (New York: Seven Stories, 2003), 192.

125 **"symbolic religious interpretations"**: TS, "The Journey of Philip Roth," *Atlantic Monthly*, Apr. 1969, 64.

125 **"exhausted Hemingway stuff"**: TS, *First Loves*, 197.

126 **"like a social worker"**: Ibid., 198.

CHAPTER TEN

128 **"left [Roth] where he found [him]"**: PR to RGS, 3 June 1968, RGS Papers, UC.

129 **"[T]he most distasteful article"**: "Correspondence: Eisenhower and God," *New Republic*, 24 June 1957, 3.

129 **"Miss [Audrey] Hepburn"**: PR, "Nymphs and Satyrs," *New Republic*, 14 Oct. 1957, 21.

130 **" 'But Jake has this wound—' "**: PR, "Photography Does Not a Movie Make," *New Republic*, 30 Sept. 1957, 22.

130 **"from the gleeful ooze"**: PR, "Coronation on Channel Two," *New Republic*, 22 Sept. 1957, 21.

130 **the magazine's "butchers"**: PR to Bob and Charlotte Maurer, 8 Feb. 1958, PR–LC.

131 **"a quiet, easygoing, plainish girl"**: *F*, 388.

132 **"just in case Harvard falls through"**: PR to Bob and Charlotte Maurer, 27 Jan. 1957, PR–LC.

133 **"Just now I put down Portrait of A Lady"**: PR to Bob and Charlotte Maurer, 15 Oct. 1957, PR–LC.

133 **"wanted to leave [their] narrow backgrounds"**: PR to Raymond Rosenthal, 27 Sept. 1974, PR–LC.

134 **"Thirty-nine Japs had lined up"**: PR, "Expect the Vandals," in *The Esquire Reader*, ed. Arnold Gingrich, L. Rust Hills, and Gene Lichtenstein (New York: Dial, 1960), 74–110.

135 **"I laughed all the way to the bank"**: TS, *First Loves* (New York: Seven Stories, 2003), 209.

135 **"Those guineas'll take anything"**: PR to Bob and Charlotte Maurer, 2 Oct. 1956, PR–LC.

136 **"Professor, I know that if you're writing"**: *MLAM*, 437. PR confirmed that this anecdote appeared in his novel pretty much as he remembered it. "That was my introduction to night school," he remarked. "You might say to life."

136 **"a powerful moral document"**: PR to Bob and Charlotte Maurer, 13 Sept. [1957], PR–LC.

136 **"exciting and crucial"**: PR to Maurers, 8 Feb. 1958.

136 **adventures "in Jewish suburbia"**: From PR's eulogy for RGS, which, in revised form, would serve as the introduction to a reprint of RGS's novel *Other Men's Daughters* (New York: NYRB Classics, 2017).

137 **"a discrepancy between Philip"**: From RGS's interview with Denis Bisson, who produced a French documentary about PR in 1997; PR provided me with audiotapes.

137 **"literary antecedents"**: *CPR*, 6.

139 **"positively the best thing I've done"**: PR to Bob and Charlotte Maurer, 10 Apr. 1958, PR–LC.

139 **"adapting [Yiddishkeit] to modernism"**: TS, *First Loves*, 206.

140 **"I'm just going to go up"**: Zachary Leader, *The Life of Saul Bellow: To Fame and Fortune 1915–1964* (New York: Alfred A. Knopf, 2015), 593.

141 **"Well," she said, "if *that's* what you like—!"**: *F*, 383.

141 **"a disastrous Cupid role"**: RGS, *Sistermony* (New York: Donald I. Fine, 1995), 101.

141 **"very distraught"**: BB int. David Ray, 2 May 2013.

142 **"Maggie saw a lot of people"**: PR to Maurers, 10 Apr. 1958.

142 **"worldly and glamorous and gracious"**: PR's remarks on receiving the *Paris Review*'s Hadada Award, 6 Aug. 2009, PRPP.

143 **"six or seven" finalists**: Blair Fuller to PR, 16 Apr. 1958, PR–LC.

143 **"The *shmutz* is the story!"**: TS, *First Loves*, 209.

143 **"watched as she dropped her white nightdress"**: *GC*, 155.

144 **"the only editorial help"**: Bruce Weber, "The Gripes of Roth," *Northeast Magazine* (*Hartford Courant* supplement), 20 Nov. 1983, 14.

144 **"for just about everybody we knew in Hyde Park"**: PR, "The Armies of Hypocrisy" (unpublished ms., c. Oct. 1972), PRPP.

144 **"all of bohemian Chicago was there"**: RM int. PR, 24 Nov. 1996.

CHAPTER ELEVEN

146 **"a handsome young man of qualities"**: PR's remarks on receiving The *Paris Review*'s Hadada Award, 6 Aug. 2009, PRPP.

147 **"to do absolutely nothing"**: PR to Mildred Martin, 12 Aug. [1958], PRPP.

147 **"Every surface in the city"**: PR to TS, 31 July 1958, TS Papers, NYPL–M&A.

147 **"calmly alone"**: PR to Bob and Charlotte Maurer, 20 Oct. 1958, PR–LC.

148 **"I shall be twenty-five"**: PR to George Starbuck, 14 Mar. 1958, Houghton Mifflin Company Records, HU–HL.

148 **"knotty publishing problem"**: Houghton Mifflin memo from Paul Brooks to Lovell Thompson, 25 July 1958, Houghton Mifflin Company Records.

149 **"Maybe that was the idea"**: *F*, 386.

150 **"*I don't want a strange man*"**: BB int. Gene Lichtenstein, 19 Jan. 2015.

150 **"Why didn't you *warn* me?"**: Email from Cynthia Crawford Lichtenstein to BB, 16 Jan. 2015.

150 **"humor and seriousness"**: Rachel MacKenzie to PR, 20 Nov. 1957, *New Yorker* Records, NYPL–M&A.

150 **"the best thing I've done"**: PR to Bob and Charlotte Maurer, 20 Oct. 1958, PR–LC.

151 **"Let the goyim clean the floors!"**: *GC*, 133.

152 **"The stores along Coach House Road"**: Ibid., 187.

154 **"which is stupid on their part"**: PR to TS, 31 July 1958, TS Papers, NYPL–M&A.

154   **"page by page"**: PR to Maurers, 20 Oct. 1958.

154   **"George, in a way, determined my future"**: *CPR*, 282.

155   **"mesmerized each other"**: PR, Hadada speech, 6 Aug. 2009.

155   **"great anguish"**: PR to CB, 5 May 1995, CB/Theatre and Film Archive, BU.

155   **"awfully small, awfully over priced apartment"**: PR to TS, 23 Oct. 1958, TS Papers, NYPL–M&A.

156   **"all the girls [he] screwed in Europe"**: *F*, 386.

156   **"It isn't fair!"**: Ibid., 385.

CHAPTER TWELVE

157   **"such a lurid, pathological"**: Mervyn Rothstein, "From Philip Roth, 'The Facts' as He Remembers Them," *New York Times*, 6 Sept. 1988.

160   **"prove [him]self otherwise"**: *F*, 387.

160   **"Well, Philip has time for his writing"**: BB int. David Ray, 2 May 2013.

161   **"leave it on [his] parents' doorstep"**: PR to Shirley Fingerhood, n.d. [c. Dec. 1963], PRPP.

161   **"a scientific experiment"**: Email from PR to Jeff Posternak, 13 Jan. 2015.

162   **"more precisely duplicated the autobiographical facts"**: *F*, 391.

164   **"That's the hook you get him on"**: BB int. BCS, 21 Mar. 2013.

164   **"Seven years ago this month"**: PR to Alison Lurie, 11 Feb. 1966, PRPP.

165   **"not an accident"**: PR's "Affidavit in Opposition," 25 Nov. 1964, PRPP.

CHAPTER THIRTEEN

167   **"We found Philip Roth's"**: PR's later editor at the magazine, Veronica Geng, sent him a copy of this letter; presumably it's also included among the vast *New Yorker* Records, NYPL–M&A.

167   **"adverse or not"**: Robert Henderson to PR, 9 Apr. 1959, *New Yorker* Records.

167   **"Your one story makes people"**: *WW*, 58.

168   **"any Jewish American novelist"**: Alfred Kazin, "To Be Jew or to Be Jewish in Philip Roth's Fiction," *Forward*, 9 Apr. 1993, 9.

168   **"Oh to be a liberal now"**: PR to Rachel MacKenzie, 10 Apr. 1959, *New Yorker* Records, NYPL–M&A.

169   **"What outcry?"**: *F*, 401.

169   **"I do not want to compound"**: *WW*, 59.

170   **"his name carries immense weight"**: PR to Connie (a Houghton Mifflin advertising contact), 4 June 1959, Houghton Mifflin Company Records, HU–HL.

170   **Reviews of *Goodbye, Columbus***: Alfred Kazin, *The Reporter*, 28 May 1959, 42; Saul Bellow, *Commentary*, Apr. 1959, 77; Leslie Fiedler, *Midstream*, Summer 1959, 96–99; Irving Howe, *New Republic*, 15 June 1959, 17; Jeremy Larner, *Partisan Review* 27, no. 4 (Fall 1960), 760.

171   **"I think he suspects me of wanting"**: PR to Bob and Charlotte Maurer, 7 Mar. 1958, PR–LC.

172   **"phenomenal for a book of stories"**: PR to RSB and Ida Baker, n.d. [c. 14 July 1959], RSB Papers, LC.

173   **"Jee-sus"**: PR to TS, 19 Nov. 1960, TS Papers, NYPL–M&A.

173   **"fulfilled the promise"**: Stephen E. Rubin, "A Conversation with Philip Roth," *Philadelphia Inquirer*, 2 Apr. 1978, 44.

174   **"Roth was way ahead"**: Notes from JT's interview with Arnold Eisen, c. May 2014.

CHAPTER FOURTEEN

176 **"what made me so curious"**: *F*, 420.

176 **"never had no desire"**: PR to RSB and Ida Baker, n.d. [c. 14 July 1959], RSB Papers, LC.

178 **"extraordinarily mundane and flat"**: Blair Fuller to PR, 5 Oct. 1988, PR–LC.

179 **"vulgar and ludicrous"**: *F*, 406.

179 **"Maggie does a good deal of reading"**: PR to TS, 25 Oct. 1959, TS Papers, NYPL–M&A.

180 **"flashy idea"**: PR to TS, 31 July 1958, TS Papers, NYPL–M&A.

181 **"What patience you need, what faith"**: PR to Bakers, c. 14 July 1959.

181 **"I'm flying"**: PR to Bob and Charlotte Maurer, 15 Sept. [1959], PR–LC.

181 **a first draft he was "crazy about"**: Ibid.

182 **"whose ships were about to sink"**: Hannah Arendt, *Eichmann in Jerusalem* (New York: Viking, 1963), 118.

183 **"quality of nervousness"**: PR to Robert A. Aurther, 27 Oct. 1959, PRPP.

183 **"a civil war"**: Fred Kaplan, "The Woman Who Saw Banality in Evil," *New York Times*, 24 May 2013.

184 **"marvelous" four-room apartment**: PR to George Starbuck, 5 Mar. 1960, Houghton Mifflin Company Records, HU–HL.

CHAPTER FIFTEEN

186 **"quietly high"**: PR to TS, 19 Feb. 1960, TS Papers, NYPL–M&A.

186 **"looking at the tarts"**: PR to RSB, 17 July 1960, RSB Papers, LC.

187 **"If you're gonna live there"**: BB int. PR, 9 July 2012.

188 **"Could you go out"**: BB int. PR, 12 July 2012.

189 **"*Testy*"**: George Starbuck's holograph notes on the logistics of getting PR to the National Book Awards ceremony, n.d. [c. 19 Mar. 1960], Houghton Mifflin Company Records, HU–HL.

190 **"What the hell's he doing with *her*?"**: RM int. Aaron Asher, 27 Sept. 2005.

190 **"one of those transatlantic murder birds"**: PR to RSB, 17 May 1960, RSB Papers.

190 **"National Book Award!"**: BB int. Edmund Keeley, 4 Apr. 2013.

190 **"they treated their questioners"**: "Words, Words," *New Yorker*, 2 Apr. 1960, 32.

190 **"I'm bustin' my buttons!"**: BB int. PR, 9 July 2012.

191 **"the largest turnout"**: Russell Thacher, "Dr. Gross Has Them Thinking," *Bergen Evening Record*, 2 Apr. 1960, 4.

191 **"large female semi-literate"**: Leslie Fiedler, "The 1960 National Book Awards," *New Leader*, undated clipping.

191 **"why [he] didn't want to say"**: PR's unpublished typescript about events surrounding the 1960 National Book Awards and the subsequent (October 1960) *Esquire* symposium is in PR–LC.

191 **"I burst onto the stage"**: PR's acceptance remarks for the PEN/Nabokov Award, 22 May 2006, PRPP.

192 **"Maybe we can get his back up"**: The fascinatingly devious notes taken by Mike Wallace's assistant, prior to Roth's 1960 appearance on his boss's television show, may be found among the Mike Wallace Papers at Syracuse University library.

193 **"a very sweet woman"**: PR's unpublished typescript about events surrounding the 1960 NBA and *Esquire*.

193 **"like Dick and Nicole Diver"**: PR to RSB, 17 July 1960.

194   **"Joycean trek":** William Styron, "Dear Dirty Dublin: My Joycean Trek with Philip Roth," *New York Times*, 9 June 1991.

194   **"We became friends from the start":** A. Alvarez, *Risky Business* (London: Bloomsbury, 2007), 31.

195   **"were full of cancer":** Herb Mitchell to MR, 5 July 1960, PR–LC.

195   **"I think that'll be good for everyone":** PR to TS, 26 May 1960, TS Papers.

196   **"perhaps the sorriest salary":** PR to Richard Gilman, 15 Oct. 1966, PR–LC.

CHAPTER SIXTEEN

197   **"prolonged and intense dissatisfaction":** Houghton Mifflin memo from George Starbuck to Paul Brooks, 22 June 1960, Houghton Mifflin Company Records, HU–HL.

197   **"screwed it up":** PR to Bob and Charlotte Maurer, 17 Mar. 1959, PR–LC.

197   **"a bunch of pricks":** Ibid.

197   **"the people are sweet":** PR to TS, 19 Nov. 1960, TS Papers, NYPL–M&A.

197   **"I think that the whole Philip Roth business":** Paul Brooks to Evan W. Thomas, 9 Nov. 1960, Houghton Mifflin Company Records.

198   **"propitious time":** Candida Donadio to Paul Brooks, 9 Sept. 1960, Houghton Mifflin Company Records.

199   **"rosy-cheeked town":** David Boroff, "The Muses Meet in Squaresville," *Mademoiselle*, Nov. 1961, 126.

200   **"The impact he makes":** PR to Gerald Freund, 20 Jan. 1967, PR–LC.

200   **"we're even a little leery":** PR to Bob and Charlotte Maurer, 18 Mar. 1961, PR–LC.

201   **"educating the students in the workings":** PR to Robert Lucid, 9 Dec. 1965, PR–LC.

201   **"The most brilliant scholars":** Boroff, "The Muses Meet," 146.

201   **"Not only do you have to read":** PR to TS, 11 Oct. 1960, TS Papers, NYPL–M&A.

201   **"Part of our function":** Boroff, "The Muses Meet," 145.

202   **"I know that I am a holy terror":** PR to RSB, 17 July 1960, RSB Papers, LC.

202   **"slow going":** PR to George Starbuck, 5 Mar. 1960, Houghton Mifflin Company Records.

202   **"under the wire":** PR to RSB, 13 Dec. 1960, RSB Papers.

203   **"Let the other fellow be alienated":** PR to Tom and Jacquie Rogers, 14 Oct. 1958, TR–PSU.

203   **"If anything we had unity":** PR's unpublished typescript about events surrounding the 1960 National Book Awards and the subsequent (October 1960) *Esquire* symposium is in PR–LC. The remarks given here largely derive from this typescript, which appears to have been written within weeks of the experience.

203   **"This is not for publication":** BB, *Cheever* (New York: Alfred A. Knopf, 2009), 283.

203   **"[In 1959] I first read a paragraph or two":** BB, *Cheever*, 588.

204   **"that is, the unmanageability":** PR to TS, 14 Jan. 1961, TS Papers.

204   **"edgy and mean and unstable":** PR to TS, 11 Oct. 1960.

204   **"Broadway's *amor-vincit-omnia* boys":** *WW*, 29.

206   **"Jewish dialect jokes, expertly recounted":** Ibid., 280.

206   **"Patiently, exactly, he laid out":** RSB, letter to the editor, *New York Times Book Review*, 18 May 1986.

206   **"I didn't talk about Bellow":** PR to Bob and Charlotte Maurer, 19 Nov. 1960, PR–LC.

206   **"Bellow gets Nobel Prize":** *Bernard Malamud: Novels and Stories of the 1940s and 50s*, ed. Philip Davis (New York: Library of America, 2013), 700.

207 **"I was not, in R. G.'s phrase"**: PR, "What Was Really Said?," *New York Times Book Review*, 11 Dec. 1960.

207 **"I love joy, especially sheer joy"**: PR replies re "Writing American Fiction," *Commentary*, Sept. 1961.

208 **"taking them to task"**: Robert Gutwillig, "Dim Views Through Fog," *New York Times Book Review*, 13 Nov. 1960.

208 **"Little did we know"**: *WW*, 157–58.

208 **"a generation of serious young writers"**: Tom Wolfe, "Stalking the Billion-Footed Beast: A Literary Manifesto for the New Social Novel," *Harper's*, Nov. 1989, 48–49.

209 **"the American Dickens"**: PR reply to Tom Wolfe, *Harper's*, Feb. 1990, 4.

209 **"Tom's strengths don't lie"**: Bob Frost, "Philip Roth," *West*, 7 Mar. 1993, 4.

CHAPTER SEVENTEEN

212 **"His torturing of Maggie"**: PR to TS, 8 Oct. 1961, TS Papers, NYPL–M&A.

212 **"after much expense and anguish"**: PR to RSB and Ida Baker, n.d. [c. summer 1961], RSB Papers, LC.

214 **"His father has made special use"**: PR to TS, 8 Oct. 1961.

215 **"Your IQ is higher than Philip's!"**: BB int. "Helen Miller," 24 Aug. 2013.

215 **"whopping I.Q."**: PR to Bob and Charlotte Maurer, 11 Jan. 1962, PR–LC.

216 **"sure I'd never put down another word"**: PR to RSB and Ida Baker, 14 Jan. 1962, RSB Papers.

217 **"gala week"**: PR to William Cole, 6 Dec. 1961, *Paris Review* Archives, Morgan.

220 **Book Award to Roth**: This yellowed clipping included neither the name of the newspaper nor the date.

220 **"were very well groomed"**: "Second Dialogue in Israel," *Congress Bi-Weekly* 30 (16 Sept. 1963), 63.

221 **"Why don't you leave us alone?"**: *WW*, 50.

221 **"alienated Jewish intellectual"**: "Rabbi Criticizes Jewish Writers," *New York Times*, 30 June 1963.

221 **"'Why do you write about Jewish thieves'"**: *WW*, 250.

221 **While privately "bemused"**: *F*, 405.

221 **"I find that I am suddenly living"**: *WW*, 41.

222 **"I accepted the job"**: PR to TS, 7 Mar. 1962, TS Papers.

222 **"sin of informing"**: *WW*, 61–63.

223 **"would you write the same stories"**: *F*, 407.

223 **"What's going on here?"**: David Remnick, "Into the Clear," *New Yorker*, 8 May 2000, 81.

223 **"I'll never write about Jews again"**: *F*, 408.

223 **the usual "inanities"**: PR to TS, 7 Apr. 1962, *Commentary* Magazine Archive, Ransom.

223 **"Roth attempts to defend himself"**: "From the Rabbi," *Progressive Synagogue Temple Topics* 17, no. 15 (30 Dec. 1963), PR–LC.

224 **"'Look, folks, no hands'"**: Letters re "Writing about Jews," *Commentary*, Apr. 1964.

CHAPTER EIGHTEEN

226 **"a sad book"**: PR to TS, 7 Apr. 1962, *Commentary* Magazine Archive, Ransom.

228 **"tall, commanding, humorless"**: Gopnik, "Man Goes to See a Doctor," *New Yorker*, 24–31 Aug. 1998, 114.

228   **"the interplay of narcissism"**: Kleinschmidt, "The Angry Act: The Role of Aggression in Creativity," *American Imago* 24, no. 1 (Spring 1967), 123.

231   **Reviews of *Letting Go***: Orville Prescott, *New York Times*, 15 June 1962; Arthur Mizener, *New York Times Book Review*, 17 June 1962; Bellow's *Encounter* review was reprinted as "Some Notes on Recent American Fiction," in *The Novel Today: Contemporary Writers on Modern Fiction*, ed. Malcolm Bradbury (Manchester, Eng.: Manchester University Press, 1977), 62–64; Granville Hicks, *Saturday Review*, 16 June 1962, 16.

233   **"There's a deep innocence in these people"**: *CPR*, 10.

235   **"Novels do not pussyfoot around"**: PR, "They Won't Make You Normal," in *In My Opinion: The* Seventeen *Book of Very Important Persons* (New York: Macmillan, 1966), 66 (originally published in the April 1963 issue of *Seventeen*).

235   **"so solemn and morally in earnest"**: PR's remarks on accepting the Yaddo Artist Medal, 14 May 2014, PRPP.

235   **"I tried to make them attend carefully"**: PR to Jerre Mangione, 13 Dec. 1964, PR–LC.

237   **"wild and wooly time"**: PR to RSB, 27 Jan. [1963], RSB Papers, LC.

237   **"Our menage is once more intact"**: MR to Nina Schneider, 19 Nov. 1962, PR–LC.

238   **"an evil streak"**: PR's affidavit in *Roth v. Roth*, 14 Nov. 1963, PRPP.

238   **"Where's a knife?"**: PR to RSB, 28 Dec. 1964, RSB Papers.

CHAPTER NINETEEN

242   **"She was less restrained"**: Betty Fussell, *My Kitchen Wars* (New York: North Point Press, 1999), 131–32.

242   **"I will go anywhere people"**: PR to Edmund Keeley, n.d. [24 May 1963], Edmund Keeley Papers, PUL.

242   **"someplace pleasant in Europe"**: PR to Bob and Charlotte Maurer, 13 May [1963], PR–LC.

243   **"Remember, this isn't yours"**: *The Counterlife*, 51.

243   **"the Negro problem"**: "Second Dialogue in Israel," *Congress Bi-Weekly* 30 (16 Sept. 1963), 30–31.

244   **"I am not a Jewish writer"**: Ibid., 35.

245   **"always aware of them looking down"**: DP.

249   **"a husband is responsible only for debts"**: Shirley Fingerhood to William C. Baggitt, 11 Jan. 1965, PRPP.

250   **"foul and filthy"**: PR to RSB, 2 Feb. 1964, RSB Papers, LC.

251   **"Tell me, Mr. Roth"**: PR—memo.

251   **"It kept me from killing my first wife"**: David Plante, *Worlds Apart* (London: Bloomsbury, 2015), 64.

252   **"made sure somebody would find her"**: BB int. Pamela Forcey, 24 Jan. 2015.

253   **"about as interesting"**: *MLAM*, 664.

CHAPTER TWENTY

254   **"He arrived just on time"**: Robert Brustein, "Philip Roth at 80: Tales Told out of Schul," *Huffington Post*, 30 May 2013.

255   **"Albert, your father and I"**: *CPR*, 29–30.

255   **"That guy just made a million dollars"**: Scott Raab, "Philip Roth Goes Home Again," *Esquire*, Oct. 2010.

255 "a little radio with an orange dial": *CPR*, 30.

255 "reckless narrative disclosure": *F*, 414.

257 "tended to cover with a patina": *WW*, 71.

257 "Like the York cycle of mystery plays": *CPR*, 15.

257 "in the business end of the theater": PR, "An Actor's Life for Me," *Playboy*, Jan. 1964, 86.

259 "nobody has ever written worse plays": "Man Booker International Prize 2011 Winner Philip Roth Interviewed by Benjamin Taylor, New York, May 2011"; https://www.youtube.com/watch?v=_QeIJ_xO7ns.

259 "Young, supple, gifted, intelligent": *The Journals of John Cheever*, ed. Robert Gottlieb (New York: Alfred A. Knopf, 1991), 190.

260 "That's Philip Roth": BB int. Ann Mudge, 16 Aug. 2012.

260 "intriguingly estranged from the very strata": *F*, 410.

261 "shoved a red hot poker": PR to Alison Lurie, 15 Sept. 1964, PRPP.

262 "You have to leave now!": BB int. Mudge, 16 Aug. 2012.

262 "next mean female novelist": BB int. Alison Lurie, 24 May 2013.

263 "When a Jew says *goy*": PR to Lurie, 15 Sept. 1964.

263 "after 200 pages and much sweat": PR to RSB, 2 Feb. 1964, RSB Papers, LC.

263 "like the work of a lunatic": PR to RSB, 28 Dec. 1964, RSB Papers.

263 "good habits of patience": PR to Charlotte Maurer, 13 July 1964, PR–LC.

263 "Philip, there will always be a bed": PR to Alison Lurie, 18 Oct. [1964], PR–LC.

263 "ideal guest": Elizabeth Ames to Granville Hicks, 26 Nov. 1965, Yaddo Papers, NYPL–M&A.

264 "You're only boring": BB int. "Helen Miller," 7 Sept. 2013.

265 "of course the drama and the harassment": PR to Alison Lurie, 4 Sept. 1964, PRPP.

265 a "collage" of quotes: PR to Alison Lurie, 4 Nov. 1964, PRPP.

265 "To put it bluntly": PR to Herman and Nina Schneider, 24 Sept. 1964, PR–LC.

CHAPTER TWENTY-ONE

266 "Let's split it": BB int. Russell Oberlin, 24 Oct. 2013.

266 "hatchet man in the theater": PR to Alison Lurie, 27 Jan. [1965], PR–LC.

267 "It is soap opera": PR, "Channel X: Two Plays on the Race Conflict," *New York Review of Books*, 28 May 1964.

267 "Sir, it is not my fault": LeRoi Jones's reply to PR, *New York Review of Books*, 9 July 1964.

268 "I hope to do for the fags": PR to Lurie, 27 Jan. [1965].

268 "a dirty little secret": Morris Belsnick, letter to the editor, *New York Review of Books*, 8 Apr. 1965.

270 "I seem to have made an enemy": PR to Alison Lurie, 19 Mar. 1965, PRPP.

271 chatting lucidly with elegant little hand gestures: Roth provided me with a videotape of this program, a faithful transcript of which appears in *CPR*.

272 "without cohabitation and without reasonable": Quoted in *MLAM*, 520.

273 "I go to parties": PR to RSB, 28 Dec. 1964, RSB Papers, LC.

273 "100 of America's wealthiest": Sherman L. Morrow, "The In Crowd and the Out Crowd," *New York Times Magazine*, 18 July 1965, 12.

274 "Do you want to come upstairs?": *RU*, 45.

275 an "old-fashioned" need: RM int. Julius Goldstein, 3 Nov. 1996.

275 Roth was "overwhelmed": PR to Julius Goldstein, 30 Aug. 1965, PR–LC.

276 **"Watch it!" Roth laughed:** BB int. Jules Feiffer, 27 Nov. 2012.

276 **"What century was that":** PR to Alison Lurie, n.d. [summer 1966], PR–LC.

277 **"Is Mr. Roth going to marry you":** BB int. Ann Mudge, 15 Oct. 2012.

277 **"It depends, Senator":** *F*, 422.

277 **"We don't want to go to this thing":** PR, "The Armies of Hypocrisy" (unpublished ms., c. Oct, 1972), PRPP.

CHAPTER TWENTY-TWO

281 **"Since Lucy is rendered monolithic":** Malamud to PR, 17 May 1967, Random House Records, CU–B.

281 **Reviews of *When She Was Good*:** Jean Stafford, *Vogue*, 17 Feb. 1967; Eliot Fremont-Smith, *New York Times*, 2 June 1967; Wilfrid Sheed, *New York Times Book Review*, 11 June 1967; Raymond Rosenthal, *New Leader*, 19 June 1967, 19.

282 **"Can't I have both, he asked":** PR to Alison Lurie, 19 May [1967], PRPP.

283 **"rain, fog, and damp":** PR to Julius Goldstein, 26 Aug. 1967, PR–LC.

283 **"How can you be in an administration":** Jules Feiffer, *Backing into Forward* (New York: Nan A. Talese/Doubleday, 2010), 359.

284 **"a kind of engaging, elongated leprechaun":** PR to Adam Begley, 1 Dec. 2011.

285 **"I'm a writer, and whatever":** Henry Raymont, "Shy Roth Emerges: New Book and Play," *New York Times*, 26 Oct. 1971, L48.

285 **"speaking up for masturbators":** JU to PR, 30 Mar. [1995], PR–LC.

285 **"longish monologue":** *WW*, 73.

286 **"I would say I was more strongly influenced":** *CPR*, 39.

286 **"a novel about yet another family-obsessed Jewish bachelor":** PR to "XX (President of the Czech Writers' Union)," n.d. [c. June 1975], PRPP.

287 **"hover over this little flame":** "Second Dialogue in Israel," *Congress Bi-Weekly* 30 (16 Sept. 1963), 73.

287 **"the fantastic obsessive care, care, care":** BBC transcript of Alfred Kazin interview for "Philip Roth: My True Story" (1993 *Arena* documentary), PRPP.

288 **"blocks of consciousness":** *CPR*, 35.

289 **"coming out of [his] ears":** TS, "The Journey of Philip Roth," *Atlantic Monthly*, Apr. 1969, 70.

289 **proposed to call "Cunt Crazy":** PR to William and Rose Styron, 2 Dec. 1967, PRPP.

290 **"one of the most important writers":** Tom Hedley to PR, 9 Apr. 1968, PR–LC.

290 **"for the first time":** PR to Alison Lurie, 25 June 1967, PRPP.

291 **"Since in my article I introduce":** Jeffrey Berman, "Revisiting Roth's Psychoanalysts," in *The Critical Companion to Philip Roth*, ed. Timothy Parrish (New York: Cambridge University Press, 2007), 99.

CHAPTER TWENTY-THREE

295 **"for a price of at least":** MR's plaintiff affidavit, 21 Feb. 1968, PRPP.

296 **"Paul's letter, written in his usual":** MR to Edmund and Mary Keeley, 19 May 1966, Edmund Keeley Papers, PUL.

297 **"depression and acute anxiety":** MR's affidavit of reply, 12 Mar. 1968, PRPP.

298 **" 'It's so cold out here' ":** Grace Glueck, "600 at Museum for Garden Fete," *New York Times*, 9 May 1968.

299 **"to say something self-incriminating":** *F*, 424.

299 **"Got the good news early, huh?":** Ibid., 426.

300   "dazed and shaken": Ibid., 423.

300   "Now we can run away together": PR—memo.

300   "a secondary, more personal irony": *F*, 431.

CHAPTER TWENTY-FOUR

303   "stand Kafka on his head": *CPR*, 34.

303   "probably astronomical and worth": Random House memo from Joe Fox to Bennett Cerf et al., 29 May 1968, Random House Records, CU–B.

303   "the most brilliant piece of radical humor": Quoted in *CPR*, 16.

304   "I have my personal life": BB int. Edward Hoagland, 30 Aug. 2014.

305   "the length and breadth of the British Isles": PR to Vernon Gibberd, 22 June 1968.

305   "I could take you back to Pittsburgh": *F*, 431. To protect Mudge's anonymity in *The Facts*, Roth substituted Cleveland for Pittsburgh.

305   "a delight, the food perfect": PR to Herman and Nina Schneider, 28 July 1968, PR–LC.

306   "in a pissy-smelling (cat piss)": Ibid.

306   "like an ad for the Mattachine Society": Quoted in *CPR*, 22.

306   "I've been a perfect crab": PR to Schneiders, 28 July 1968.

306   "[I] wondered what the hell": *F*, 432.

307   "Delighted to be back in this madhouse": PR to Julian Mitchell, 13 Oct. 1968, Julian Mitchell Archive, BL.

307   "You're never coming back, lamb chop": PR—memo.

308   "In his writing, his humor": Email from BCS to BB, 9 Dec. 2012.

308   "A mature woman wouldn't take your shit": PR to Alan Lelchuk, n.d. [16 July 1969], Alan Lelchuk Papers, BU.

309   "formal women's club": Alison Lurie to PR, 1 July 1969, PR–LC.

309   "the biggest book in history": Jason Epstein to PR, 3 July 1968, PR–LC.

309   "Roth kicked the nice Jewish boy bit": *CPR*, 15.

310   "A savior and scapegoat of the '60s": Ibid., 23.

311   Reviews of *Portnoy's Complaint*: *Time*, 21 Feb. 1969; Brendan Gill, *New Yorker*, 8 Mar. 1969, 118–20; Alfred Kazin, *New York Review of Books*, 27 Feb. 1969; Josh Greenfeld, *New York Times Book Review*, 23 Feb. 1969, 1; Christopher Lehmann-Haupt, *New York Times*, 18 Feb. 1969; Granville Hicks and Marya Mannes, *Saturday Review*, 22 Feb. 1969, 39.

312   "shameful, solitary addiction": *WW*, 82.

312   "the whole world of forbidden sexuality": Isaac Rosenfeld, "Adam and Eve on Delancey Street," *Commentary*, Oct. 1949.

314   "Whom do *you* suffer for, Alex P.?": Alfred Kazin, "The Earthly City of the Jews: Bellow, Malamud, and Roth," in *Alfred Kazin's America: Critical and Personal Writings*, ed. TS (New York: HarperCollins, 2003), 269.

314   outnumbered "10 to 1": Bennett Cerf to PR, 19 Mar. 1969, PR–LC.

314   "In both views the Jewish male": Marie Syrkin, "The Fun of Self-Abuse," *Midstream*, Apr. 1969, 64–68.

314   "This is the book for which all anti-Semites": Gershom Scholem's *Haaretz* review is quoted in Bernard Avishai, *Promiscuous: "Portnoy's Complaint" and Our Doomed Pursuit of Happiness* (New Haven: Yale University Press, 2012), 111–12.

315   "I said that history had obviously": *CPR*, 246.

315   "I haven't read a novel in thirty years": Jodi Kantor, "When Politics Catches Up with 'Portnoy,'" *New York Times*, 3 Aug. 2013.

CHAPTER TWENTY-FIVE

316 **"good boys and fine men"**: Herman Roth to PR, 25 Apr. [1969], PR–LC.

317 **"My Philip," she'd sigh**: Herman Roth to PR, 22 Mar. 1969, PR–LC.

317 **"You walk down the street"**: BB int. BCS, 8 Dec. 2012.

317 ***"Philip Roth! The enemy of the Jews!"***: *Philip Roth Unmasked*, PBS *American Masters*, 2013; https://www.pbs.org/video/american-masters-watch-philip-roth-unmasked/.

317 **"I am so sorry," said Roth**: BB int. Alison Lurie, 24 May 2013.

318 **"the Jewish Mafia"**: *Conversations with Truman Capote*, ed. Thomas Inge (Jackson: University Press of Mississippi, 1987), 158.

319 **"When Truman Capote later attacked"**: Quoted in Saul Bellow, "A Jewish Writer in America" (typescript found in RGS Papers, UC).

320 **"I hope that it is now understood"**: PR to Marc Jaffe, 6 May 1969, PRPP.

321 **"Barbra Streisand has no complaints"**: *WW*, 79.

321 **"a sex maniac and a millionaire"**: PR, "The Armies of Hypocrisy" (unpublished ms., c. Oct, 1972), PRPP.

321 **"a lusty young buck"**: From Michael King's biography of Frame, the pertinent galley pages of which were among some papers PR gave me.

322 **"blunt inquisitorial style"**: PR, "Armies of Hypocrisy."

322 **"Every day I had ten opportunities"**: PR to TS, 21 Apr. 1969, TS Papers, NYPL–M&A.

327 **"What the hell did you do this for?"**: PR—memo.

327 **"I'm *happy*," she said**: BB int. PR, 7 Dec. 2012.

327 **"I wish to hell I could live"**: PR to Tom Maschler, 30 Apr. 1969, UR.

328 **"beats the pneumatic drill"**: PR to Alan Lelchuk, 2 July [1969], Alan Lelchuk Papers, BU.

328 **"It was lovely and we both"**: From a reminiscence dated 4 Feb. 2008, written by BCS at PR's request, PRPP.

328 ***"It's Portnoy!"***: BB int. BCS, 8 Dec. 2012.

329 **"American abstract art is a lie"**: Charles McGrath, "Philip Guston and His Barbed-Pen Nixon Years," *New York Times*, 30 Oct. 2016.

329 **"terrible loneliness"**: From the transcript of an interview that Guston's daughter, Musa Mayer, conducted with PR, 3 Mar. 1987, PRPP.

330 **"This bed is so big"**: BB int. PR, 10 Dec. 2012.

330 **"I think [Roth] made it up,"**: Julia Felsenthal, "In *Scary Old Sex*, Writer Arlene Heyman Confronts a Timeless Taboo," vogue.com, 12 Mar. 2016; https://www.vogue.com/article/scary-old-sex-arlene-heyman-profile.

331 **"Some self-styled Lord Jim"**: PR to Norman Mailer, 30 Mar. 1970, Norman Mailer Papers, Ransom.

332 **"After declining to take a bow"**: "People," *Time*, 30 Mar. 1970, 42.

332 **"At least they called me"**: Norman Mailer to PR, 8 Apr. 1970, PR–LC.

332 **"ineffable, mysterious, strange"**: PR to Julian Mitchell, 5 Mar. 1970, Julian Mitchell Archive, BL.

332 **"He sleepy"**: BB int. PR, 25 May 2014.

332 **"like a large tear falling"**: *RMO*, 185.

332 **"because it makes fun of the President"**: PR to RSB, n.d. [c. Aug. 1970], RSB Papers, LC.

CHAPTER TWENTY-SIX

334 **"We weren't idealistic"**: James Walton, "Give Philip Roth the Nobel Prize as a Retirement Present," *Telegraph*, 13 Nov. 2012.

334 **"saints of the imagination"**: Josyane Savigneau, "Philip Roth: An Américain pas si tranquille," *Hors-Série Le Monde*, Feb.–Mar. 2013.

334 **"the last pre-television generation"**: PR's acceptance remarks for the MacDowell Medal, 19 Aug. 2001, PRPP.

335 **"We're hicks"**: *CPR*, 160.

335 **"radiated wonderful family feeling"**: JU to PR, 21 May [1981], PRPP.

335 **"to be all bad manners"**: From the transcript of an interview that Musa Mayer conducted with PR, 3 Mar. 1987, PRPP.

335 **"know-it-all *goy*"**: PR, "On the Air," *New American Review* 10 (Aug. 1970), 8.

336 **"The comic imagination"**: Geoffrey Wolff, "Beyond Portnoy," *Newsweek*, 3 Aug. 1970, 67.

336 **"What do you think I ought"**: Anatole Broyard, "Reading and Writing; Listener with a Voice," *New York Times*, 22 Feb. 1981.

337 **"Reading the morning *New York Times*"**: *CPR*, 87.

337 **"I can't square [it] with my personal belief"**: Ibid., 41.

337 **"*Bad taste?!*"**: From a reminiscence dated 4 Feb. 2008, written by BCS at PR's request, PRPP.

337 **"You always pull out Swift"**: *RU*, 72.

338 **"a first-rate contingency plan"**: *CPR*, 47.

338 **"more people are killed"**: Ibid., 53.

338 **"lonesome and wanted some students"**: PR to RSB, n.d. [c. Aug. 1970], RSB Papers, LC.

338 **"My education comes from"**: Scott Raab, "Philip Roth Goes Home Again," *Esquire*, Oct. 2010.

338 **"We students arrived early"**: Lisa Scottoline, "English Class with Mr. Roth," *New York Times*, 3 May 2014.

338 **"She was very observant"**: Email from PR to JC, 4 May 2014.

338 **"habitual moralizing, ingenious interpretation"**: Cynthia Haven, "The Novelist's Obsession Is with Language," 10 Jan. 2014; https://bookhaven.stanford.edu/2014/02/an-interview-with-philip-roth-the-novelists-obsession-is-with-language/.

339 **"How can you open your mouth"**: BB int. Fredrica Wagman, 15 Sept. 2013.

340 **"I felt at times you were going"**: Marc Rovner to PR, 16 Jan. 1974, PR–LC.

340 **"a very clear and wholly scrutable"**: PR to Marc Rovner, 25 Jan. 1974, PR–LC.

341 **"as it turned out, the role of"**: Email from JC to BB, 20 Oct. 2013.

341 **"skated their Christmas trees"**: JC's introduction on the occasion of PR's receiving the New Jersey Historical Society Award, 5 Oct. 1992, PRPP.

342 **"a card-carrying beast"**: PR—memo.

342 **"It would appear from *Playing House*"**: *RMO*, 210.

343 **"probably the best unpublished writer in America"**: PR to Fredrica Wagman, 1 Apr. [1972].

343 **"Only Philip"**: Fredrica Wagman to PR, n.d. [c. 1989], PR–LC.

343 **"Well! I just don't know how"**: BB int. Nela Wagman, 29 Jan. 2014.

345 **"I do not intend to read such garbage"**: Mrs. Walter Thompson to PR (care of Random House), 8 Oct. 1971, Random House Records, CU–B.

346 *"Our Gang* is a political satire": Dwight Macdonald, "Our Gang," *New York Times Book Review*, 7 Nov. 1971.

347 **"an old fashioned villain in the Tartuffian mold":** *CPR*, 45.

347 **"would have been laughed out of Hollywood":** Quoted in Hermione Lee, *Philip Roth* (London: Methuen, 1982), 55.

349 **"Novelist Philip Roth may well be hoping":** "One Man's Loss," *Newsweek*, 24 June 1974, 15.

349 **"I wish publicly to apologize":** *Our Gang*, 664.

350 **"as indecent as the language":** Ibid., 665.

350 **"I was raised to be a Quaker, not a quitter":** *RMO*, 62.

350 *"Go to Hell!":* Robert Brustein, *Making Scenes* (New York: Random House, 1981), 174.

CHAPTER TWENTY-SEVEN

351 **"the 'serious' values of official literary culture":** *CPR*, 72.

352 **"hot as a firecracker":** PR to Tom Maschler, 4 Feb. 1972, UR.

352 **"walking prick":** *RU*, 77.

352 **"inspired by dwelling within the room's contour":** *PR@80*, 13.

353 **"the best thing [he'd] ever done":** PR to Robert Brustein, 10 June [1972], Robert Brustein Archive, BU.

354 **"no later than October 15, 1972":** PR to Jason Epstein, 14 Apr. 1972, Random House Records, CU–B.

354 **"I want to put away any notion":** "The Letting Go of Random House by Philip Roth," *Book-of-the-Month Club Newsletter* 1, no. 3 (1972).

355 **"distant enough to give a feeling":** *Selected Letters of William Styron*, ed. Rose Styron with R. Blakeslee Gilpin (New York: Random House, 2012), 206.

356 **"Malamud has already been at it":** BB int. BCS, 14 Sept. 2013.

357 **"Philip wouldn't let go":** Alfred Kazin, diary entry, c. 30 Oct. 1987, Alfred Kazin Papers, NYPL–Berg.

357 **"it is only the prospect":** *Selected Letters of William Styron*, 634.

358 **"You just don't want me to write fiction":** BB int. PR, 11 Oct. 2012.

359 **"somewhat stunned":** PR to "XX (President of the Czech Writers' Union)," n.d. [c. June 1975], PRPP.

360 **"All those people are swine":** BB int. PR, 12 July 2012.

360 **"amid gales of laughter":** PR's acceptance remarks for the PEN Literary Service Award, 30 Apr. 2013, PRPP.

360 **"he licked her pan":** BB int. BCS, 21 Mar. 2013.

360 **"undermined the identity of the nation":** Milan Kundera, "The Tragedy of Central Europe," *New York Review of Books*, 26 Apr. 1984, 37.

361 **Reviews of *The Breast*:** Christopher Lehmann-Haupt, *New York Times*, 12 Sept. 1972; John Gardner, *New York Times Book Review*, 17 Sept. 1972; TS, *Esquire*, Oct. 1972, 178; Peter Prescott, *Newsweek*, 25 Sept. 1972.

363 *"In The Breast*, my approach to the outlandish":** *CPR*, 56.

364 **"I have a feeling":** PR to TS, n.d. [Aug. 1972], TS Papers, NYPL–M&A.

364 **"to read Kafka as though":** PR to Rust Hills, n.d. [c. Nov. 1973], PR–LC.

365 **"What have I in common with the Jews?":** Quoted in *WW*, 11.

365 **"I'll tell you the truth":** *CPR*, 207.

CHAPTER TWENTY-EIGHT

366 **"mean, pricky streak"**: *RMO*, 196.

366 **"since he was a writer whose animating principle"**: My account of PR's clash with Mailer derives mostly from PR's unpublished typescript "The Armies of Hypocrisy," PRPP, which, internal evidence suggests, was written within weeks or even days of the episode in question. Unless otherwise noted, all quotes are taken from this source.

368 **"in that it attributes a character"**: Eric Pace, "Mailer Finds Book Is No Advertisement for Himself," *New York Times*, 18 Oct. 1972.

369 **"nothing less than furious"**: Alan Lelchuk to Wilfrid Sheed, 9 June 1973, PR–LC.

369 **"fanaticism in the hatred of things Jewish"**: Quoted in *WW*, 101.

369 **"Whatever the final merits"**: "Portnoy Defended" (letter to the editor), *Commentary*, July 1969.

370 **"was at his core a dutiful immigrant son"**: Sam Tanenhaus, "A Midcentury Agitator, Boxing Left and Right," *New York Times Book Review*, 9 Nov. 2014.

370 **"young Jewish intellectual"**: Mark Shechner, *Up Society's Ass, Copper: Rereading Philip Roth* (Madison: University of Wisconsin Press, 2003), 47.

371 **"a mugging, pure and simple"**: Ibid., 9.

371 **"prissy" young man's disgust"**: Norman Podhoretz, "The Adventures of Philip Roth," *Commentary*, Oct. 1998.

371 **"He has largely lost his sense"**: Irving Howe, "The Lost Young Intellectual," in *Mid-Century: An Anthology of Jewish Life and Culture in Our Times*, ed. Harold U. Ribalow (New York: Beechhurst Press, 1955), 152.

372 **"give an inch of encouragement"**: Irving Howe, "The Suburbs of Babylon," *New Republic*, 15 June 1959, 17.

373 **"straight out of the Goebbels-Streicher script"**: Marie Syrkin, letter to the editor, *Commentary*, Mar. 1973.

376 **"We can be sure that in some Roth story"**: Mark Shechner, "Roth Against the Jews," 7 Nov. 1973; this thirty-seven-page typescript, which was eventually revised for publication in *Partisan Review*, was included among papers PR passed along to me.

376 **"You sententious bastard"**: *AL*, 369.

376 **"Much boom lowering"**: PR to James Atlas, 2 May 1983, James Atlas Papers, NYPL–Berg.

377 **"I wasn't trying to alienate"**: *RU*, 78.

377 **Reviews of *The Great American Novel***: Christopher Lehmann-Haupt, *New York Times*, 14 May 1973; William H. Gass, *New York Review of Books*, 31 May 1973.

378 **"Please advise Professor Gass"**: PR, letter to the editor, *New York Review of Books*, 19 July 1973.

378 **"a means to dramatize the *struggle*"**: *CPR*, 74.

379 **"Enough to make Flaubert spin"**: Ibid., 99.

379 **"alone in this world"**: PR to Andrew Wylie, n.d. [c. May 1992], PRPP.

380 **"the trivializing idiocies"**: PR, "Bruno Schulz," undated typescript, PRPP.

380 **"looked like an intellectual Ringo Starr"**: BB int. BCS, 21 Mar. 2013.

381 **"Why don't *you* leave?"**: BB int. PR, 12 July 2012.

382 **"I learned the value of humor"**: *WW*, 258.

382 **"Optimism is the opium"**: Milan Kundera, *The Joke*, trans. Michael Henry Heim (New York: Penguin, 1982), 26.

383 **"Or else," said Roth, "She was waiting for an offer"**: *RU*, 96.

386 **"What a book"**: PR to A. Alvarez, 27 July [1976], Alvarez Papers, BL.

386 **"the only writer in America other than myself"**: PR to Peter Godwin, 16 Feb. 2013, PRPP.

386 **"Tell, then, how you bought places"**: Tadeusz Borowski, *This Way for the Gas, Ladies and Gentlemen*, trans. Barbara Vedder (New York: Penguin, 1976), 22.

386 **"He shot my Jew, so I shot his"**: *PO*, 487.

387 **"Joanna," he said, "you're drunk"**: HM int. Joanna Clark, 30 June 2007.

388 **"But maybe that wasn't so bad"**: Michael Henry Heim, *The Man Between: Michael Henry Heim and a Life in Translation*, ed. Esther Allen and Sean Cotter (Rochester, N.Y.: Open Letter, 2014), 88.

CHAPTER TWENTY-NINE

389 **"novel about trying to write that novel"**: PR to CB, 4 Dec. 1975, CB/Theatre and Film Archive, BU.

390 **Reviews of *My Life as a Man***: Anatole Broyard, *New York Times*, 23 May 1974; Morris Dickstein, *New York Times Book Review*, 2 June 1974, 1.

391 **"I kept being virtuous"**: PR int. Saul Bellow, 2 Dec. 1999, PRPP.

393 **"distinct dis-interest"**: Joyce Carol Oates to PR, n.d. [c. 1974], PR–LC.

393 **"dealing with a woman"**: RM int. PR, 5 Mar. 2005.

393 **"killer of women"**: NSM.

394 **"crossed the line into deeply boring"**: BB int. BCS, 14 Sept. 2013.

395 **"I'm sad," he wrote a friend**: PR to A. Alvarez, 30 Oct. [1974], Alvarez Papers, BL.

395 **"Empty eyes, a pale face"**: James Atlas, journal, 4 Sept. 1987, James Atlas Papers, NYPL–Berg.

395 **"lovely and generous"**: BB int. Francine Gray, 22 Mar. 2013.

395 **"dumb lug"**: PR to Julius Goldstein, 23 June [1975], PR–LC.

396 **"holding operation"**: Reminiscences of RWS, n.d. [c. late 1978], CU–COHC.

396 **Reviews of *Reading Myself and Others***: Anatole Broyard, *New York Times*, 5 June 1975; Roger Sale, *New York Times Book Review*, 25 May 1975.

397 **"a typhoon"**: PR to A. Alvarez, 3 May 1975, Alvarez Papers.

397 **"A selling point for his damn building"**: Janet Hobhouse, *The Furies* (New York: New York Review Books, 2004), 194.

398 **"Where is that boredom"**: PR to Alvarez, 3 May 1975.

398 **"I don't want to be the thing"**: Hobhouse, *The Furies*, 201.

399 **"increasingly cruel and hopeless"**: PR to "Czech Fund Contributor," 19 Apr. 1975, Lillian Hellman Papers, Ransom.

399 **"Stalin-era methods"**: Dusko Doder, "Prague Presses Dissidents," *Washington Post*, June 15, 1975.

399 **"thereby having learned something"**: PR to "XX (President of the Czech Writers' Union)," n.d. [c. June 1975], PRPP.

399 **"Philip, they were trying"**: PR—memo.

399 **"muddy Poland"**: PR to A. Alvarez, 19 Apr. [1975], Alvarez Papers.

400 **"What is Roth doing here in Czechoslovakia?"**: PR—memo. This is how PR usually characterized Klíma's response re PR's purpose in Czechoslovakia—"He comes for the girls"—though in a contemporary letter to Julius Goldstein, PR gave a more succinct wording: "Sex."

400 **"harried and sad"**: PR to Goldstein, 23 June [1975].

400 **"I could have done without the slice of pineapple"**: PR to CB, 13 June 1976, CB/Theatre and Film Archive.

400 **"Which one of you guys wears the skirt?"**: BB int. PR, 13 Oct. 2012.

400 **"Get yourself a girl, Joel"**: Ibid.
401 **"Do I have to eat the mandible?"**: BB int. Louise ——, 13 Nov. 2013.
402 **"I am out of bed"**: PR to CB, 6 Jan. 1976, CB/Theatre and Film Archive.
403 **"I can be good for Philip"**: RM int. Herman and Nina Schneider, 2 Nov. 1996.

CHAPTER THIRTY

407 **"Her family name is not BLOOM"**: Hilda Myra Fell to Harper & Row, 6 Sept. 1982, PRPP.
408 **"And she did not merely survive that"**: NFMB, 23.
408 **"who had a bit of a martyr streak"**: *Stars and Mas*, BBC-TV, aired 9 Mar. 1997.
408 **"wasn't what we would call normal"**: Ibid.
408 **"twisting [her] hair in knots"**: *LA*, 15.
408 **"reduced his life to practically nothing"**: *CPR*, 159.
409 **"Wasn't she wonderful?"**: BB int. BCS, 21 Mar. 2013.
409 **"I'm sure he's a monster"**: Stephen Schiff, "Rothballs," *Vanity Fair*, Apr. 1990, 78.
410 **"dark, piercing eyes"**: CB to PR, 8 Dec. [1975], PRPP.
410 **"deep ambivalence"**: *LDH*, 148.
410 **"I thought I was with a peer"**: PR to Jack Miles, 8 Apr. 2012, PRPP.
411 **"What else is there to do?"**: PR to CB, n.d. [c. late Apr. 1976], CB/Theatre and Film Archive, BU.
411 **"I was happy and cheerful"**: *LDH*, 154.
411 **"I didn't come here to be insulted"**: PR—memo.
411 **"She was a natural writer"**: NFMB, 101.
412 **"He was very hard"**: David Dugas, "Claire Bloom Tells Story of Her Drive for Success," United Press International, 22 Mar. 1982.
412 **"I think it's the most intelligent book"**: PR to Robert Brustein, 8 Jan. 1981, Robert Brustein Archive, BU.
413 **"luxurious, slightly whorish"**: PR to JC, 23 Nov. 1977.
413 **"terrible (alas)"**: PR to Jack Wheatcroft, 31 Aug. [1976].
414 **"made the rounds"**: Memo from PR to Russell Brooks of Milbank, Tweed, Hadley & McCloy, n.d. [c. 1996], PRPP.
414 **"a frail, white-china faced woman"**: Kevin Kelly, "The Adolescence of Claire Bloom," *Boston Sunday Globe*, 26 Sept. 1976, B1.
414 **"I went into the kitchen"**: NFMB, 64.
415 **"falsified beyond recognition"**: Ibid., 255.
416 **"over a thousand times"**: Ibid., 257.
416 **"the kick of having a multiple self"**: Ibid., 263.
417 **"the dark part of [her] sexual nature"**: Ibid., 259.
417 **"This is a man led by the penis"**: BB int. "Inga Larsen," 9 Nov. 2014.
418 **"If there was any cruelty directed"**: NFMB, 54.
419 **"family hell"**: NFMB, 70.
421 **"Anna sat stewing at her place"**: Ibid., 67.
421 **"abject woman"**: Ibid., 72.
421 **"thrust a letter"**: *LDH*, 157.
421 **"Don't go for me"**: PR—memo.
423 **"So somber, so tragic"**: NFMB, 93.
423 **"Maggie sent Anna to me"**: Quoted in RGS to RM, 20 Feb. 2007, RGS Papers, UC.

CHAPTER THIRTY-ONE

424   **"spawned by the interplay"**: *CPR*, 99.

424   **"philosophical concepts"**: RWS to PR, 11 Apr. 1977, FSG Papers, NYPL–M&A.

424   **"And we did a hell of a job"**: Reminiscences of RWS, n.d. [c. late 1978], CU–COHC.

425   **"the great and maddening" subject**: *CPR*, 105.

425   **"faking it"**: PR to A. Alvarez, 30 Oct. [1974], Alvarez Papers, BL.

426   Reviews of *The Professor of Desire*: Vance Bourjaily, *New York Times Book Review*, 18 Sept. 1977, 1; Robert Towers, *New York Review of Books*, 27 Oct. 1977; John Leonard, *New York Times*, 16 Sept. 1977.

427   **"One big quiet room"**: PR to Julian Mitchell, 6 June [1977], Julian Mitchell Archive, BL.

429   **"that having your hero come to Europe"**: RGS to PR, n.d. [c. Jan. 1979], PR–LC.

429   **"always right"**: BB int. PR, 29 Apr. 2013.

429   **"I know are on my side"**: *RU*, 146.

429   **"What they give me is not only"**: *CPR*, 106.

429   **"Speech, debate, excitement"**: RGS, typescript draft for an inset piece published with a longer feature about PR in *Saturday Review*, June 1981, RGS Papers, UC.

430   **"Which may simply mean"**: As in PR to A. Alvarez, 2 May 1978, Alvarez Papers.

430   **"astonishingly intelligent"**: Quoted in Dennis Hevesi, "Nina Schneider, Author of Children's Science Books, Dies at 94," *New York Times*, 27 Sept. 2007.

430   **"monk or nun"**: PR to Tom Maschler, 31 May 1977, UR.

432   **"father/writer theme"**: JU to PR, 18 Jan. [1984], PR–LC.

432   **"I'm not under fucking house arrest"**: PR to Fredrica Wagman, 15 Oct. 1977.

433   **"There he sat, lean, watchful"**: *PR@80*, 43.

433   **"Fascists, beauties, Spanish War Veteran poets"**: PR to Jack Miles, 11 Jan. 1978.

433   **"[s]anctimonious little shit"**: Tariq Ali's column, *Time Out*, 11–17 Feb. 1983, 12; PR's 15 Feb. 1978 letter was originally published in Parviz C. Radji, *In the Service of the Peacock Throne: The Diaries of the Shah's Last Ambassador to London* (London: Hamish Hamilton, 1983), 152.

434   **"the frivolous, silly, childish woman"**: *LA*, 146.

434   **"didn't slide back into fleeing"**: NFMB, 109.

434   **"a beautiful portrait in water-colour"**: B. A. Young, "Rosmersholm," *Financial Times*, 20 Oct. 1977, 3.

435   **"I will never leave her"**: David Plante, *Worlds Apart* (London: Bloomsbury, 2015), 63.

435   **"completely devoid of femininity"**: *CPR*, 159.

435   **"I don't want to play Diana Quick's mother"**: NFMB, 139.

435   **"not to feel the curtain fabric"**: *LDH*, 161.

435   **"Imitate Antonia"**: NFMB, 139.

436   she'd **"forlornly" presented him**: Ibid., 60.

436   **"was having fierce arguments at dinner parties"**: PR—memo.

437   **"The offensive ones"**: NFMB, 128.

437   **"I wish my father were alive to read"**: Ibid., 188.

437   **"two dreadful months"**: PR to James Atlas, 14 Dec. 1978, James Atlas Papers, NYPL–Berg.

438   **"everything you read and everything you do"**: *CPR*, 107.

438   **"Then she touched me"**: Veronica Geng, "Love Trouble Is My Business," *New Yorker*, 1 Oct. 1984, 33.

438   **"I never read Bible parodies"**: Jennifer Senior, "Humor Came Her," *New York*, 17 May 1999.

438 **"they love continuing to work at something"**: Scot Nourok, "A Conversation with Veronica Geng," *The Writing Self* 5, no. 2 (Spring 1996), 7.

440 **"without first having to be strained"**: Helen May, "An Interview with Philip Roth," *New York Post*, 29 Sept. 1979, 15.

440 **Reviews of *The Ghost Writer***: Peter Prescott, *Newsweek*, 10 Sept. 1979, 72; Robert Towers, *New York Times Book Review*, 2 Sept. 1979, 1; Christopher Lehmann-Haupt, *New York Times*, 4 Sept. 1979, C10; John Leonard, *New York Review of Books*, 25 Oct. 1979.

441 **"Bold, challenging"**: *WW*, 81.

441 **"an insult to the community"**: PR, "Philip Roth Replies," *New York Review of Books*, 12 Dec. 1974.

442 **"semi-lunatic wise-guy"**: PR to Bernard Malamud, 12 Jan. 1984, Bernard Malamud Papers, Ransom.

442 **"a nice note"**: PR to Steve Berg, 20 July [1979], *Paris Review* Archives, Morgan.

443 **"didn't want him because he was Jewish"**: BB int. Jane Brown Maas, 11 Oct. 2012.

443 **"Never, *never* have I heard him talk"**: Deirdre Donahue, "Exploring the Pain of His Father's Loss," *USA Today*, undated clipping [c. 1991].

443 **"I was a good boy for you"**: Videotaped conversation between PR and Mildred Martin, c. June 1992, during one of PR's visits to Lewisburg.

443 **"I just couldn't finish *Portnoy's Complaint*"**: Gail Rippey, "Author Pays Tribute to Bucknell Professor," *Lewisburg Daily Item*, 2 Apr. 1991.

443 **"as though we were going to be married"**: PR—memo.

444 **"I felt as though I'd brought him a gift"**: PR to "A. V. and Webster," 23 Oct. 1979, PR–LC.

CHAPTER THIRTY-TWO

445 **"fey performance"**: Rosemary Say, "The Man from Whitehall," *Telegraph*, undated clipping [c. spring 1981], 16.

446 **"You better go in there"**: *P*, 597.

447 **"He doesn't listen to what I say"**: Ibid., 602.

447 **"Mommy, Mommy, where are you, Mommy?"**: Ibid., 609.

448 **"the unreckoned consequences"**: *WW*, 160.

448 **"where nothing goes and everything"**: PR, "The Book That I'm Writing," *New York Times*, 12 June 1983.

448 **"she gets paid to say things like that"**: PR to Mildred Martin, 25 July [1979], PRPP.

448 **"In order for Prague to have"**: Mervyn Rothstein, "The Unbounded Spirit of Philip Roth," *New York Times*, 1 Aug. 1985.

449 **"the first of the father's avengers"**: PR to James Atlas, 16 Mar. 1981, James Atlas Papers, NYPL–Berg.

449 **Reviews of *Zuckerman Unbound***: Anatole Broyard, *New York Times*, 9 May 1981; Edward Rothstein, *New York Review of Books*, 25 June 1981; Martin Amis's *Observer* review was reprinted in *The War Against Cliché* (New York: Vintage, 2001), 287–89.

450 **"the most intelligent I've gotten"**: PR to RWS, 4 June 1981, FSG Papers, NYPL–M&A.

450 **"Those who convert literature"**: Michiko Kakutani, "Is Roth Really Writing about Roth?," *New York Times*, 11 May 1981.

450 **"I'd be delighted"**: Boris Kachka, *Hothouse: The Art of Survival and the Survival of Art at America's Most Celebrated Publishing House, Farrar, Straus and Giroux* (New York: Simon & Schuster, 2013), 231.

450 **"great speculation"**: Stephen Rubin, "A New Executive Editor at Harper and Row," New York *Daily News*, 25 Feb. 1981.

452 **"very bright and very competent"**: Kachka, *Hothouse*, 236.

452 **"Look, David"**: BB int. David Rieff, 13 Oct. 2012.

454 **"I say *ssh* a lot"**: *CPR*, 132.

455 **"precious" friendship**: *LDH*, 165.

456 **"I was invisible"**: NFMB, 74.

457 **"fit as a fiddle"**: BB int. PR, 11 Oct. 2012.

457 **Huvelle "might understand better"**: NFMB, 153.

458 **"stroked her mother's hair"**: Ibid., 37.

CHAPTER THIRTY-THREE

461 **"winnowing out stuff"**: PR to James Atlas, 21 Mar. 1982, James Atlas Papers, NYPL–Berg.

461 **"I was now to be educated"**: PR, "How Could They Capture My Hero's Obsession with Anne Frank?," *TV Guide*, 14 Jan. 1984, 12.

462 **"cute, coy, girlish smile"**: PR to JT, 2 Apr. 1983.

464 **"What's this for?"**: JT to PR, 12 Mar. 1983, PRPP.

464 **"mentally exhausted"**: PR to Herman and Nina Schneider, 20 June 1983, PR–LC.

464 **"As if it's all been apprentice work"**: Curt Suplee, "Philip Roth, at Ease at Mid-Journey," *Washington Post*, 30 Oct. 1983, L1.

465 **"Now that he is no longer the *enfant terrible*"**: Hermione Lee, *Philip Roth* (London: Methuen, 1982), 9.

465 **"(1) I couldn't stand most"**: LH int. Hermione Lee, 26 Sept. 2007. During this taped interview, Lee read aloud parts of her letter from PR dated 4 June 1983; I'm quoting from the interview transcript, since I never obtained a copy of the letter in question.

465 **"ruthlessly" pruning**: Hermione Lee to PR, 7 Aug. 1983, PR–LC.

466 **"feminist attack"**: *WW*, 152.

467 **"You're not getting such good"**: BB int. Elizabeth Pochoda, 26 Sept. 2013.

467 **"temporary madness"**: PR to David Rieff, Oct. 28, 1983, FSG Papers, NYPL–M&A.

467 **"Portnoy's Creator Would Like It Known"**: Andrea Chambers, "Philip Roth," *People*, 19 Dec. 1983.

467 **"Say whatever the hell you want to say"**: PR to James Atlas, 12 Aug. 1986, James Atlas Papers.

467 **"Best of luck"**: Susan Jacoby to PR, 31 Aug. 1983, PR–LC.

467 **Reviews of *The Anatomy Lesson***: Christopher Lehmann-Haupt, *New York Times*, 19 Oct. 1983; Joseph Epstein, *Commentary*, Jan. 1984; JU's review in the 7 Nov. 1983 *New Yorker* was reprinted in *Odd Jobs* (New York: Alfred A. Knopf, 1991), 372.

468 **"The job was to give pain its due"**: *CPR*, 140.

469 **"And that's why I broke Zuckerman's jaw"**: *RU*, 137.

470 **"So why are you here?"**: *PO* screenplay (included in LOA edition), 570.

470 **"ritual slaughter"**: PR to Robert Brustein, 20 Apr. 1985, Robert Brustein Archive, BU.

470 **"thematic architecture"**: *CPR*, 197.

471 **"*Zuckerman Bound* merits something"**: Harold Bloom, "His Long Ordeal by Laughter," *New York Times Book Review*, 19 May 1985, 1, 42.

471 **"sink [his] teeth into something"**: PR to JT, 12 May 1983.

471 **"He has been called the Woody Allen of words"**: "Philip Roth Face to Face with Idith Zertal," *Mishkenot Sha'ananim Newsletter*, no. 1 (1984).

472 **"a list a yard long"**: PR to RGS, 19 Nov. 1984, RGS Papers, UC.

472 **"fair minded, intelligent, humanist, cultured"**: DP.

472 **"I have to tell you"**: Ibid.

473 **"It wasn't Israel as California"**: *RU*, 147.

473 **"the playfully thoughtful air"**: *WW*, 201.

473 **"the sum of all these Jewish *antinomies*"**: *Operation Shylock*, 181.

473 **"the bits and pieces of crap"**: PR to TS, 8 Dec. 1984, TS Papers, NYPL–M&A.

473 **"an ancient Jewish ailment"**: *WW*, 213.

474 **"'If we were in Italy'"**: NFMB, 187.

474 **"nasty, hateful scene"**: Email from PR to BB, 23 Jan. 2016.

474 **"a writer *has* to be driven crazy"**: *RU*, 150.

474 **"little Jew"**: Ibid., 152.

475 **"false starts"**: PR to JC, 5 Aug. 1984, PRPP.

475 **"I wrote one section and then I thought"**: *RU*, 145.

475 **"Now I only hope I don't kick off"**: Mervyn Rothstein, "Philip Roth and the World of 'What If,'" *New York Times*, 17 Dec. 1986.

476 **"Shtetl schtick adapted"**: PR int. Saul Bellow, 2 Dec. 1999, PRPP.

476 **"almost invariably his heroes"**: *WW*, 85.

477 **"a Bad Guy Jew"**: James Atlas, *Bellow* (New York: Random House, 2000), 329.

478 **"terse and colloquial"**: *WW*, 282.

478 **"I wish I could say Roth"**: Malamud's unsent replies to Roth re "Imagining Jews" are among his papers at Ransom.

478 **"When a man who can read"**: Malamud to PR, 11 Oct. 1974, Bernard Malamud Papers, Ransom.

478 **"a frail and very sick old man"**: *WW*, 283.

480 **"surrounded himself by real dopes"**: PR int. Bellow, Dec. 2, 1999.

CHAPTER THIRTY-FOUR

481 **"emotionally real"**: RM to PR, 12 June 1984, PR–LC.

481 **"whole life possible"**: Quoted in Martin Gottfried, *Arthur Miller: His Life and Work* (Cambridge: Da Capo Press, 2003), 394.

481 **"carried the sibling rivalry"**: RM int. Robert Brustein, 28 July 2008.

481 **Kermit had invented the electric car**: RM int. Aaron Asher, 27 Sept. 2005.

481 **"a pile of notes on every page"**: Christopher Goffard, "Philip Roth Unbound," *St. Petersburg Times*, 4 July 2004.

482 **"I'd never talked to anybody this long"**: RM int. RGS, 14 Dec. 2006.

482 **"I gave it my all"**: *CPR*, 205.

482 **"no phantasmagoria, no surrealism"**: RM int. PR, 9 Mar. 2007.

483 **Reviews of *The Counterlife***: Christopher Lehmann-Haupt, *New York Times*, 29 Dec. 1986; William Gass, *New York Times Book Review*, 4 Jan. 1987; JU's review in the 2 Mar. 1987 *New Yorker* was reprinted in *Odd Jobs* (New York: Alfred A. Knopf, 1991), 373–79; Julian Barnes, *London Review of Books*, 5 Mar. 1987.

483 **"very much a work by a middle-aged writer"**: *CPR*, 210.

484 **"We are all writing fictitious versions of our lives"**: Ibid., 253.

484 **"It was as if he regained the world"**: Jennifer Senior, "Philip Roth Blows Up," *New York*, 1 May 2000, 40.

485   "the most intelligent woman": PR to Susan Sontag, 31 Oct. 1986, Susan Sontag Papers, Charles E. Young Research Library, UCLA.

485   "a favorable review in *Commentary*!": James Atlas, journal, 4 Sept. 1987, James Atlas Papers, NYPL–Berg.

486   "heated discussion": Edwin McDowell, "Roth and Rhodes Books Get Critics Circle Awards," *New York Times*, 12 Jan. 1988.

486   "Circle Jerk Prize": JC, journal, 12 Jan. 1988.

487   "broken down and, like a substance": *WW*, 193.

487   "I felt the great good fortune": PR's remarks on accepting the Grinzane Literary Masters Award, 17 Apr. 2007, PRPP.

488   "Throw the pills down the toilet": PR—memo.

488   "Just get on with it!": RM int. PR, n.d. [c. late spring 1997].

488   "*Is he still in there*": PR—memo.

488   "back to exercising": NFMB, 166.

488   "a sham": Ibid., 167. PR notes that the *Times* article in question appeared 11 July 2002.

488   "should be shunned like cyanide": William Styron, "Prozac Days, Halcion Nights," *Nation*, 4–11 Jan. 1993, 18.

489   "My career is over": NFMB, 165.

489   "vivacious" and "sound": *WW*, xii.

491   "the ordeal verges": Styron, "Prozac Days, Halcion Nights," 20.

492   "*Innocent?!*": HM int. Joanna Clark, 30 June 2007.

492   "little or nothing to say": NFMB, 182.

494   "There are *many* people": Quoted in R. B. Kitaj, *Confessions of an Old Jewish Painter*, ed. Eckhart J. Gillen (Munich: Schirmer/Mosel, 2017), 368.

495   "Philip Roth is coming back": "Page Six," *New York Post*, 29 Mar. 1988.

495   Bloom "went crazy": PR, holograph notes re CB, undated [c. 1991], PRPP.

495   "She's crying again": NSM.

495   "impersonal hotel room": James Atlas, journal, 4 Sept. 1987.

496   "At 55, Norman Manea is a plumpish, balding": PR, "I Couldn't Restrain Myself," *New York Times Book Review*, 21 June 1992, 3.

496   "his ridiculous, self-awarded": Quoted in JU, "Of Sickened Times," *New Yorker*, 16 Nov. 1992, 135.

496   "to some central headquarters": Steve Paulson int. PR, "To the Best of Our Knowledge," 20 Nov. 2007; PR provided me with a CD recording of this radio interview.

CHAPTER THIRTY-FIVE

501   "How she got from telling me": NFMB, 233.

501   Roth's "line of questioning": Email from Anna Steiger to BB, 6 Dec. 2015.

503   "performance of virtue defiled": Ibid.

504   "Are you crazy?": Daniel Treiman, "How Philip Roth Changed Ehud Olmert's Mind," Jewish Telegraphic Agency, 4 Dec. 2012.

504   lunch "quickly degenerated": Bernard Avishai, *Promiscuous: "Portnoy's Complaint" and Our Doomed Pursuit of Happiness* (New Haven: Yale University Press, 2012), 143–44.

505   "Are you married, Dave?": *CPR*, 151.

505   "a fairly good stand-in for my mother": *P*, 611.

505   "Either you're dead": PR to James Atlas, 12 Mar. 1983, James Atlas Papers, NYPL–Berg.

506   "monitoring the caloric intake": *F*, 320.

506   "Always tell them you're ten years older": Christopher Lydon int. PR, *Open Source*, 29 May 2006.

506   "threw her hands up": NFMB, 49.

507   "'Why can't he learn to control himself?'": Ibid., 54.

507   "What kind of people are we?": *CPR*, 150.

507   "I imagined that somewhere": "Philip Roth: My True Story," BBC *Arena* documentary, 1993; https://www.youtube.com/watch?v=5G8Z2vrLpzA.

507   "defunct warship driving blindly into shore": *P*, 729.

508   "retrace the steps": *F*, 310.

508   "I'm tired of the make-up": PR to Mildred Martin, 26 Nov. 1986, PRPP.

509   "the dummy is always smarter": *CPR*, 240.

510   Reviews of *The Facts*: Rhoda Koenig, *New York*, 19 Sept. 1988; JU's "Briefly Noted" *New Yorker* review was reprinted in *Odd Jobs* (New York: Alfred A. Knopf, 1991), 380.

510   "Everything delighted him": *CPR*, 263.

511   "I played on his feelings": PR to Edward Hoagland, 26 Mar. 1989.

511   "I just want to teach": PR to Joe Murphy, 27 Apr. 1988, PRPP.

513   "Shakespeare is more important": Craig Lambert, "Fifteen Percent of Immortality," *Harvard Magazine*, July–Aug. 2010, 46.

515   "I had lunch with Andrew Wylie": Edwin McDowell, "Roth Changes Houses," *New York Times*, 16 Aug. 1989.

516   "This is not a subject": Roger Cohen, "Roth's Publishers: The Spurned and the Spender," *New York Times*, 9 Apr. 1990.

516   "A spy swears she heard Straus remark": "Rush & Molloy," New York *Daily News*, 20 Nov. 1995, 17.

516   "No good to me at all": *CPR*, 263.

516   "part soldier, part monk": *LDH*, 174.

517   "vegetable caviar and cheeseless cheese": RGS, *Sistermony* (New York: Donald I. Fine, 1995), 99.

518   "the old Pan American highway": PR to JU, 20 Sept. 1989, JU Papers, HU–HL.

518   "Which of my friends is most frightened": DP.

518   "a warm, competent, cheery young woman": NFMB, 216.

519   "It would be better": *P*, 720.

519   "easily the most wrenching decision": PR to TS, 14 Dec. 1989, TS Papers, NYPL–M&A.

520   "which she did willingly and quite beautifully": NFMB, 53–54.

520   "Generally, after standing beside": Ibid., 43.

CHAPTER THIRTY-SIX

522   "responses to being so vilified": Salman Rushdie, "Beginning of a Novelist's Thralldom," *Observer*, 26 Feb. 1989, 47.

523   "Watching people walk back": *WW*, 223.

524   "beat Stockholm any day": PR to Peter Godwin, 16 Feb. 2013, PRPP.

524   "eternal political discussions": PR, "In Defense of Intimacy," *Sunday Times Magazine* (London), 20 May 1984, 51.

524   "There appears to be a controversy": *WW*, 227–28.

525   "Look at those hideous faces!": PR—memo.

526   "Eventually I had to ask her": NFMB, 161.

526   "Some weeks after [Herman's] funeral": Ibid., 163.

527 "Shameful. The most shameful thing": Ibid., 164.

527 "all conversations should be summarized": PR to Alison Lurie, 13 Feb. [1967], PRPP.

527 "I've gotten down to basics": James Atlas, journal, 22 Oct. 1989, James Atlas Papers, NYPL–Berg.

527 "You love Maria more": PR to Jacquie Rogers, 26 Jan. 1987, TR–PSU.

527 "cold, alarmed, and unwelcoming": *LDH*, 183.

527 "raising the moral stakes": PR to Julian Mitchell, 10 Nov. 2010, Julian Mitchell Archive, BL.

528 "literature is not a moral beauty contest": NFMB, 195.

529 "How dare you represent me": PR—memo.

529 *"Why didn't you stop it?"*: BB int. David Rieff, 13 Oct. 2012.

529 "vomit-stained manuscript of *Deception*": NFMB, 193.

530 "His chinless head": Stephen Schiff, "Rothballs," *Vanity Fair*, Apr. 1990, 71.

531 Reviews of *Deception*: Christopher Lehmann-Haupt, *New York Times*, 5 Mar. 1990; Fay Weldon, *New York Times Book Review*, 11 Mar. 1990; Hermione Lee, *New Republic*, 30 Apr. 1990, 39–42.

532 "Chicago intellectual and Persian rug dealer": Quoted in Mary Wisniewski, *Algren* (Chicago: Chicago Review Press, 2016), 127.

533 "reborn" after bypass surgery: NFMB, 207.

534 "being in the world alone": NSM.

534 "did not wish again to turn": NFMB, 202.

534 "basically it comes down": Peter J. Smith, "Cruel and Unusual," *New York*, 21 Oct. 1996, 31.

535 "a lot of shaky old men": James Atlas, *Bellow* (New York: Random House, 2000), 554.

535 "Chekhovian" ambience: PR to Saul Bellow, 11 June 1990, Saul Bellow Papers, UC.

536 "didn't get much of a kick": David Remnick, "Into the Clear," *New Yorker*, 8 May 2000, 85.

536 "Stay away from Saul today": Edward Rothstein, "Saul Bellow, Saul Bellow, Let Down Your Hair," *New York Times*, 9 Apr. 2005.

536 "I thought it disgusting": Atlas, *Bellow*, 489.

536 "Why write three novels": Andrea Chambers, "Philip Roth," *People*, 19 Dec. 1983.

537 "in the dumps": *Saul Bellow: Letters*, ed. Benjamin Taylor (New York: Penguin, 2010), 430.

537 "did the Nobel Prize winner": PR to RGS, 17 Apr. 1986, RGS Papers, UC.

538 "Native American Flannery O'Connor": PR to Edward Hoagland, 4 Nov. 1983.

539 *"Now* you love me": RM int. PR, 9 Jan. 2007.

CHAPTER THIRTY-SEVEN

540 Reviews of *Patrimony*: Michiko Kakutani, *New York Times*, 1 Jan. 1991; Neal Kozodoy, *Commentary*, May 1991, 52–54; Rhoda Koenig, *New York*, 21 Jan. 1991, 70; John Leonard, *New York Newsday*, 19 Mar. 1992.

540 "might not have liked some things": *CPR*, 272.

541 *"You made it! You made it!"*: DP.

542 "Adultery makes numerous bad marriages": NFMB, 281.

543 "I'm free, I'm nineteen": Quoted in RGS, *Sistermony* (New York: Donald I. Fine, 1995), 45.

544 **"And now when I tell":** Esther B. Fein, "Philip Roth Sees Double. And Maybe Triple, Too," *New York Times*, 9 Mar. 1993.

548 **Reviews of *Operation Shylock*:** Paul Gray, *Time*, 8 Mar. 1993, 69; Michiko Kakutani, *New York Times*, 4 Mar. 1993; JU, *New Yorker*, 15 Mar. 1993, 109–12; D. M. Thomas, *New York Times Book Review*, 7 Mar. 1993, 1; S. T. Meravi's review in the 23 July 1993 *Jerusalem Post* is quoted in Mark Shechner, *Up Society's Ass, Copper: Rereading Philip Roth* (Madison: University of Wisconsin Press, 2003), 210.

548 **"the fastidious goy critics":** James Atlas, *Bellow* (New York: Random House, 2000), 502.

548 **Updike's mixed review of *The Anatomy Lesson*:** CPR, 188.

548 **"a lovely act of readership":** JU to PR, 28 Aug. [1990], PR–LC.

550 **"He's very uxorious":** Stephen Schiff, "Rothballs," *Vanity Fair*, Apr. 1990, 78.

550 **"I have to go backstage now":** BB int. Judith Dunford, 29 Mar. 2013.

550 **"everything was perfect, but":** BB int. Jonathan Brent, 31 Mar. 2014.

552 *"No more letters!"*: RM int. PR, n.d. [c. late spring 1997].

554 **"My life is a problem":** NSM.

555 **"lonely and lost":** PR to Daniel Stern, 8 Feb. [1971?], Daniel Stern Papers, Ransom.

555 **"I'm a journeyman who paints":** Grant Pick, "Chicago Lives: Sanford Roth and the Art of Living," *Chicago Reader*, 30 Mar. 1995.

555 **"It's Sandy's paintings, not my books":** "People," *Time*, 14 Mar. 1988, 93.

555 **"Even when I am disabled":** NFMB, 219.

556 **"You can't stay here":** Ibid.

556 **"two of the cruelest people in the world":** *LDH*, 199.

556 **"Are you sure you love me?":** HM int. RGS, 2 June 2007.

557 **"It's hopeless":** NFMB, 276.

558 *"A spa?! What the fuck"*: BB int. "Inga Larsen," 9 Nov. 2014.

558 **"angry, remote":** *LDH*, 200.

558 **"Look at her!":** Ibid., 203.

559 **"went nuts":** RM int. PR, 19 Mar. 2005.

560 **"At this she made a grotesque face":** NFMB, 160.

CHAPTER THIRTY-EIGHT

562 **"Never better":** *LDH*, 215.

563 **"As for my 'human ties' ":** NFMB, 243.

563 **"I am not signing any agreement!":** Ibid., 246.

563 **"This isn't working," said Beslow:** RM int. PR, 19 Mar. 2005.

564 **"the cruel and inhuman treatment":** *LDH*, 220.

565 **"There would be time enough later":** NFMB, 264.

565 **"a love poem":** "Inga Larsen" to PR, 9 Apr. 1995, PRPP.

566 **"a sitting duck for Sabbath's":** PR to TS, 24 July 1995, TS Papers, NYPL–M&A.

567 **"We're organizing a support group":** PR to Hermione Lee, 14 June 2010, PRPP.

568 **Two of the three New York judges:** RM int. PR, 19 Mar. 2005.

569 **"against [her] lawyer's strong advice":** *LDH*, 226.

571 **"But why are you doing this?":** NSM.

571 **"No more women":** PR to Charlotte Maurer, 20 Mar. 1994, PR–LC.

572 **"I hardly had time to say hello":** NFMB, 270.

573 **"wearing over her seductive form":** Ibid., 272.

573 **"Has the author an axe":** Libel report for Jonathan Cape (PR's U.K. publisher) prepared by Michael Rubinstein, 8 Dec. 1992, PRPP.

574   **"Mr. President, do I have to"**: BB int. PR, 12 July 2012.

574   **"He seemed fine as soon"**: BB int. William Luers, 27 Sept. 2014.

576   **"completely impersonal" shtick**: *LDH*, 242.

576   **"Maybe it was the irrepressible joy"**: NFMB, 287.

577   **"He granted me an hour's audience"**: RGS journal, 12 Apr. 1996, RGS Papers, UC.

577   **felt in need of "catharsis"**: Rafael Garcia-Navarro, "Roth's Revenger Tragedy," *Spectator*, 16 Jan. 1999, 21.

578   **"brutally candid"**: Kim Hubbard, "Life with Portnoy," *People*, 28 Nov. 1996.

CHAPTER THIRTY-NINE

583   **"The death of Morty sets the gold standard"**: NFMB, 43.

584   **Reviews of *Sabbath's Theater***: Martin Amis's review in the *Sunday Times* (London) was reprinted in *The War Against Cliché* (New York: Vintage, 2001), 294–96; Michiko Kakutani, *New York Times*, 22 Aug. 1995; Frank Kermode, *New York Review of Books*, 16 Nov. 1995; William H. Pritchard, *New York Times Book Review*, 10 Sept. 1995.

585   **"a bit more company than the typewriter"**: PR to Edward Hoagland, 8 Sept. 1995.

586   **"to the candy store and the borscht belt born"**: *CPR*, 69.

586   **"I felt so ashamed"**: BB int. Jack Miles, 16 Jan. 2014.

586   **"purity to their rage"**: *RU*, 207.

588   **"Updike and Bellow hold their flashlights"**: *CPR*, 154.

588   **"His hero is a Toyota salesman"**: Ibid., 151.

589   **"The more I learned about gloves"**: PR's notes for Norman Manea's Contemporary Masters class at Bard, fall 1999, PRPP.

589   **a "historical inevitability"**: Ronald Smothers, "In Riots' Shadow, a City Stumbles On," *New York Times*, 17 July 1997, 1, B4.

590   **"The city of Newark stands"**: Quoted in John T. Cunningham, *Newark* (Newark: New Jersey Historical Society, 1988), 342.

590   **"a smoke-darkened brick pile fifty years old"**: *AP*, 15.

591   **"across the room after the first 60 pages"**: Celia McGee, "Drama at the Book Awards," *New York Observer*, 27 Nov. 1995, 27.

592   **"Norman, she cannot write"**: BB int. Norman Manea, 16 Sept. 2013.

593   **"I wouldn't look at the *Times*"**: BB int. PR, 9 July 2012.

594   **"self-centered misogynist"**: Dinitia Smith, "Claire Bloom Looks Back in Anger at Philip Roth," *New York Times*, 17 Sept. 1996.

595   **Reviews of *Leaving a Doll's House***: Marion Winik, *Los Angeles Times*, 13 Oct. 1996; Patricia Bosworth, *New York Times Book Review*, 13 Oct. 1996; Daphne Merkin, *New Yorker*, 4 Nov. 1996, 105; Zoë Heller, *London Review of Books*, 20 Feb. 1997.

596   **"her obvious kindness, sincerity"**: Peter J. Smith, "Cruel and Unusual," *New York*, 21 Oct. 1996, 28.

598   **"I didn't believe those things they said"**: PR—memo.

600   **"I did not want interminable conferences"**: NFMB, 1.

600   **"there are two sides to any divorce story"**: Jack Miles's letter appeared in *New York Times Book Review*, 10 Nov. 1996.

CHAPTER FORTY

604   **"How can you be paid"**: Max Wiener, "2 Teachers Defy Probe: Carlin Favors Dismissal; Lowenstein, Another in Balk," *Newark Evening News*, 19 May 1955, 1.

605   **"no jeweled and nuanced thing"**: PR to Jack Miles, 19 Apr. 2012.

605   **"overall a very thoughtful work"**: Thomas Hine, "Don't Blame Mrs. O'Leary," *New York Times Book Review*, 15 July 1990.

606   **"Miller has given us"**: Cheryl Kent, "What's the Deal? A Look at Chicago's Block 37 Misses the Chance to Explain How Big Cities Take Shape," *Chicago Tribune*, 28 Apr. 1996.

606   **"I won't tell him," said Roth**: BB int. Douglas Hobbie, 14 Dec. 2012.

606   **"serious and libelous distortions"**: NSM.

606   **"uncertain and overwhelmed"**: Ibid.

608   **"as though he were writing"**: Ibid.

609   **"What do you think the *New York Post*"**: PR to BB, 22 July 2013.

611   **Reviews of *American Pastoral***: Michiko Kakutani, *New York Times*, 15 Apr. 1997; Louis Menand, *New Yorker*, 19 May 1997, 88–94.

613   **"a born-again Philip Roth"**: Norman Podhoretz, "The Adventures of Philip Roth," *Commentary*, Oct. 1998.

613   **"I would like you to excise"**: PR to Chris Coffin, 4 Mar. 1998, PRPP.

614   **"Roth is Niagara"**: Cynthia Ozick to PR, 26 Jan. 1997, PR–LC.

615   **"Here was this big writer"**: Tad Friend, "Talk of the Town," *New Yorker*, 26 May 1997, 29.

616   **"infuriatingly gorgeous"**: Gail Caldwell, *Boston Globe*, 20 Apr. 1997.

CHAPTER FORTY-ONE

618   **"too high-maintenance and flighty"**: Jennifer Senior, "Humor Came Her," *New York*, 17 May 1999.

623   **"My schedule is absolutely"**: David Remnick, "Into the Clear," *New Yorker*, 8 May 2000, 89.

623   **"Stand up straight!"**: PR to RGS, 9 Apr. 1989, RGS Papers, UC.

624   **"Everybody wants to write a book"**: Bernie Swerdlow to Robert Lowenstein, 6 June 1988, PR–LC.

624   **"What level of happiness"**: BB int. Howard Silver, 13 Nov. 2013.

624   **"Don't mention Claire's name!"**: BB int. Robert Heyman, 3 July 2012.

631   **"Don't think I'm second banana"**: BB int. PR, 8 July 2012.

632   **"According to [Anthony] Hecht"**: Zachary Leader, *The Life of Saul Bellow: To Fame and Fortune, 1915–1964* (New York: Alfred A. Knopf, 2015), 467.

632   **"Saul, how could you marry *five women*?"**: BB int. PR, 10 July 2012.

633   **"toxic response to his character"**: James Atlas, *Bellow* (New York: Random House, 2000), ix.

633   **"I warned you about that"**: James Atlas, journal, 4 Sept. 1987, James Atlas Papers, NYPL–Berg.

633   **"I had grown up in Chicago"**: Atlas, *Bellow*, xi.

634   **"You've probably already Xeroxed it"**: James Atlas, "Notes on Roth, Sept. 9, 1989," James Atlas Papers.

635   **a "belittling distortion"**: Ibid.

635   **"scope and structure and literary insights"**: BB int. James Atlas, 29 Apr. 2013.

635   **"the last, best word"**: PR to Wendy Strothman, n.d. [c. 15 Sept. 1998], PR–LC.

635   **"smart Yeshiva bochers"**: PR int. Saul Bellow, 2 Dec. 1999, PRPP.

636   **"Get in line: wives, children"**: Edward Rothstein, "Saul Bellow, Saul Bellow, Let Down Your Hair," *New York Times*, 9 Apr. 2005.

638   **"without any editorial correction"**: PR quoted in Saul Bellow, "I Got a Scheme!," *New Yorker*, 25 Apr. 2005, 72.

638   **"This woman sees the world"**: PR to Charlotte Maurer, 5 Apr. 1993, PR–LC.

638   **"a small inconsistency in a passage"**: Mary Norris, "How I Proofread My Way to Philip Roth's Heart," *Guardian*, 10 May 2015.

639   **"a detailed anatomy"**: PR to Russell Brooks, 15 Jan. 1998, PRPP.

640   **"maniacally dedicated, as all gossip is"**: *Exit Ghost*, 586.

640   **recent spate of "tell-all books"**: Dinitia Smith, "Writers as Plunderers," *New York Times*, 24 Oct. 1998, B9, 11.

640   **Reviews of *I Married a Communist***: Michiko Kakutani, *New York Times*, 6 Oct. 1998; Arthur Schlesinger Jr., *New York Observer*, 12 Oct. 1998; Robert Stone, *New York Review of Books*, 5 Nov. 1998.

643   **"the struggle to change oneself"**: PR's notes for Norman Manea's Contemporary Masters class at Bard, 17 Nov. 1999, PRPP.

644   **"Put it all in writing"**: BB int. Gaia Servadio, 29 Dec. 2012.

644   **"No!" she whispered, clutching at her collar**: Charlotte O'Sullivan, "Claire Bloom: The Human Pain," *Independent*, 12 May 2004.

CHAPTER FORTY-TWO

645   **"Is your friend all right?"**: *RU*, 244.

645   **"She doesn't need any help"**: BB int. PR, 11 Oct. 2012.

645   **"What James Joyce did for Dublin"**: Jennifer Senior, "Philip Roth Blows Up," *New York*, 1 May 2000, 40.

645   **"Not as old as you think"**: PR to Lowenstein, 21 Nov. 1998, PR–LC.

646   **"I write from eight o'clock"**: James Atlas, *Bellow* (New York: Random House, 2000), 407.

647   **"which we spent largely in bed"**: Email from PR to BB, 3 Jan. 2014.

650   **"I'm going to pack it in"**: RM int. PR, 1 July 2004.

651   **"I don't know where she comes from"**: "Philip Roth at 70: Interview with David Remnick"; https://www.youtube.com/watch?v=lGbYxBxyUec.

651   **"Treat '98 as though it were '48"**: Ibid.

651   **"you had the illusion"**: Charles McGrath, "Zuckerman's Alter Brain," *New York Times*, 7 May 2000.

652   **"Does anyone know these people?"**: Melvin Tumin to Deans Lemonick and Rudenstine, 9 Apr. 1977, PRPP.

652   **"to reform: going to class"**: Lois V. Hinckley statement, 8 Feb. 1977, PRPP.

658   **"favorite out-of-print book"**: Francine Prose, "What's Your Favorite Out-of-Print Book?," *New York Times Book Review*, 10 Aug. 2014.

659   **"eight sharp and witty feminist critics"**: Emily Hardy to PR, 27 Jan. 2014, PR–LC.

659   **"not involved in the process of translation"**: PR to Grant Rosenberg, n.d. [c. 25 Oct. 2004].

660   **"the biggest American export"**: Senior, "Philip Roth Blows Up," 40.

660   **"This is only a guess"**: PR to Rosenberg, c. 25 Oct. 2004.

660   **"I seem to have entered the post-interrogation"**: PR to Marc Weitzmann, n.d., PR–LC.

661   **"young men and women educated to a crisp"**: David Remnick, "Into the Clear," *New Yorker*, 8 May 2000, 81.

663   **Reviews of *The Human Stain***: Michiko Kakutani, *New York Times*, 2 May 2000;

Lorrie Moore, *New York Times Book Review*, 7 May 2000, 1; James Wood, *New Republic*, 17–24 Apr. 2000, 70–78; David Gates, *Newsweek*, 15 May 2000, 70

665   **"Nobody to disturb me"**: LH int. Finkielkraut, 1 July 2007.

CHAPTER FORTY-THREE

667   *"Now* **I see why people"**: BB int. Susan Rogers, 26 Sept. 2014.

668   **"the Gallup poll calling"**: From notes Roth mailed to himself, 10 Sept. 2002, PRPP.

669   **"writing about dickless Zuckerman"**: PR to Saul Bellow, 14 Sept. 2000, Saul Bellow Papers, UC.

670   **Reviews of** *The Dying Animal*: Michiko Kakutani, *New York Times*, 8 May 2001; A. O. Scott, *New York Times Book Review*, 27 May 2001, 8; [unsigned], *The Economist*, 9 June 2001, 88; David Lodge, *New York Review of Books*, 5 July 2001; Michael Dirda, *Washington Post Book World*, 6–12 May 2001; Lee Siegel, *Los Angeles Times Book Review*, 6 May 2001.

670   **"I sometimes think of my generation"**: *CPR*, 84–85.

672   **Reviews of** *Shop Talk*: Richard Bernstein, *New York Times*, 26 Sept. 2001; Benjamin Anastas, *New York Times Book Review*, 28 Oct. 2001.

672   **"A writer of Roth's stature"**: "Our Country, Our Culture," *Partisan Review* 69, no. 4 (Fall 2002), 618.

673   **"furious with people like Susan Sontag"**: *RU*, 271.

673   **"I'm surprised you're still ambulatory"**: NFMB, 150.

674   **"single, almost expendable sentence"**: PR's remarks on accepting the James Fenimore Cooper Award from the Society of American Historians, 2 May 2005, PRPP.

674   blamed **"the Jewish race"**: *PAA*, 439.

674   **"I know who caused the war"**: Steven Watts, *The People's Tycoon: Henry Ford and the American Century* (New York: Random House, 2005), 383.

674   **"our nation's anti-Semitic propaganda minister"**: PR, "The Story Behind 'The Plot Against America,'" *New York Times*, 19 Sept. 2004.

674   **"Jewish persecution only followed"**: Maud Casey, "Radio Priest," *Salon*, 24 July 1996; https://www.salon.com/1996/07/24/sneakpeeks_118/.

674   **"Orwell imagined a huge change"**: PR, "The Story Behind 'The Plot Against America.'"

675   **"good, hard-working, responsible"**: A. Alvarez, "The Long Road Home," *Guardian*, 10 Sept. 2004.

675   **"most tragic figure"**: PR, "The Story Behind 'The Plot Against America.'"

679   **"He doesn't need a publisher"**: BB int. Elizabeth Pochoda, 4 Oct. 2013.

680   **"Have any friends of yours"**: Volker Hage int. PR, 26 July 1998, later collected in PR and Volker Hage, *A Writer at Work* (Cambridge, Eng.: Polity Press, 2011). PR gave me a prepublication typescript of this book.

680   **"with Ziff/Roth as Prince Hal"**: Mark Shechner, *Up Society's Ass, Copper: Rereading Philip Roth* (Madison: University of Wisconsin Press, 2003), 226.

681   **"Who murdered the English language"**: PR to Virginia Dajani of American Academy of Arts and Letters, n.d. [c. Oct. 2002].

683   **"Are you game?"**: NSM.

684   **"we'll pay you** *not*": BB int. LH, 15 Oct. 2012.

684   **"Hello, beautiful," said Kaplan**: BB int. PR, 12 July 2012.

684   **"I hate to say this in front of Nicole"**: Barbara Kantrowitz, "A Rare Screen Test for Philip Roth," *New York Times*, 11 Aug. 2002.

685   "an honorable B+": A. O. Scott, "Secrets of the Skin, and of the Heart," *New York Times*, 31 Oct. 2003.

CHAPTER FORTY-FOUR

688   "Ross tells me you're not": BB int. Susan Rogers, 20 Oct. 2014.

690   "barreling up the best-seller list": Frank Rich, "President Lindbergh in 2004," *New York Times*, 23 Sept. 2004.

691   "Kafka's books played a strong role": PR, "The Story Behind 'The Plot Against America,'" *New York Times*, 19 Sept. 2004.

691   Reviews of *The Plot Against America*: Paul Berman, *New York Times Book Review*, 3 Oct. 2004; Michiko Kakutani, *New York Times*, 21 Sept. 2004; J. M. Coetzee, *New York Review of Books*, 18 Nov. 2004.

692   "Don't invent, just remember": PR on *PBS NewsHour*, 27 Oct. 2004.

693   "It is untrue, unwise": William B. Helmreich, *The Jews of Newark and Metrowest* (New Brunswick, N.J.: Transaction Publishers, 1999), 218.

695   "a very nice man": John Freeman, "Veering Off History's Course," *Newsday*, 20 Sept. 2004, B2.

695   "It's my most *American* book": Martin Krasnik, "Philip Roth: 'It No Longer Feels a Great Injustice That I Have to Die,'" *Guardian*, 14 Dec. 2005.

695   interview questions were "to be restricted": PR to Jeff Posternak, 26 May 2011, LC.

695   "just a citizen like anybody else": Nelly Kaprielian, "In Which Philip Roth Announces His Retirement (in English)," *Paris Review* blog, 13 Nov. 2012; https://www.theparisreview.org/blog/2012/11/13/in-which-philip-roth-announces-his-retirement-in-english/.

696   "There's a knowledge that the writing": "Philip Roth at 70: Interview with David Remnick"; https://www.youtube.com/watch?v=lGbYxBxyUec.

696   "best explain[s] or illuminate[s]": Bernard-Henri Lévy, "By the Book," *New York Times Book Review*, 1 Jan. 2017.

696   "neither was anything like as humanly impoverished": JT, "Roth on Trump," *New Yorker*, 30 Jan. 2017.

696   "still reinventing himself": Charles McGrath, "Why Is This Man Smiling?," *New York Times*, 4 Sept. 2005, sec. 2, pp. 1, 16.

696   "It's like being able to talk to Henry James": "Making It into America's Library: A Conversation with Max Rudin, Publisher of Library of America," *Philip Roth Society Newsletter*, Spring 2005, 10–13.

696   "Don't I recognize you": BB int. Max Rudin, 13 Sept. 2013.

697   "I wouldn't myself know how to begin": PR to Marty Asher, 2 July 1996, PR–LC.

698   "even if it was Boswell": JC, journal, 25 July 2000.

698   "Boswell had to wait": Christopher Goffard, "Philip Roth Unbound," *St. Petersburg Times*, 4 July 2004.

699   "Where's the book?": *RU*, 284.

699   "I've been thinking about Lindbergh": PR to TS, 28 May 2005, TS Papers, NYPL–M&A.

699   "so old, so dead": Quoted in A. Alvarez, *Risky Business* (London: Bloomsbury, 2007), 40.

700   "shallow shits": PR to Edward Hoagland, 3 Feb. 2006.

700   "The unworldliness, the lack of imagination": Email from PR to Ben Taylor, 25 Dec. 2012.

701   "mental stamina": *RU*, 296.

CHAPTER FORTY-FIVE

702 **"too old to seriously consider"**: From an unpublished fragment, which PR described as "a tiny dress rehearsal for *Exit Ghost*," PRPP.

703 **"This would be a good place"**: BB int. David Plante, 18 Sept. 2013.

704 **"Philip Roth made an appearance"**: "Media Christmas Potpourri: Philip Roth on the Prowl, 'T+L Tonight, &c.," *Gawker*, 8 Dec. 2005.

705 **"I'm eighty-three"**: James Atlas, journal, 4 Sept. 1987, James Atlas papers, NYPL–Berg.

706 **"practically dictated"**: NSM.

707 **"had already begun losing faith"**: Ibid.

708 **"The initial delight is wonderful"**: Charles McGrath, "Why Is This Man Smiling?," *New York Times*, 4 Sept. 2005, sec. 2, p. 16.

708 **"on [their] toes"**: "Making It into America's Library: A Conversation with Max Rudin, Publisher of Library of America," *Philip Roth Society Newsletter*, Spring 2005, 10–13.

708 **Roth was "astonished"**: NSM.

710 **"quotations, allusions"**: Max Rudin to PR, 9 June 2006, LOA.

710 **Reviews of *Everyman*:** Nadine Gordimer, *New York Times Book Review*, 7 May 2006, 1; Michiko Kakutani, *New York Times*, 26 Apr. 2006; Daniel Mendelsohn, *New York Review of Books*, 8 June 2006; David Gates, *Newsweek*, 1 May 2006.

CHAPTER FORTY-SIX

719 **"Sometimes I have to go into a telephone kiosk"**: "Norman Mailer: The Art of Fiction No. 193," *Paris Review*, Summer 2007.

719 **"It was the first time in our lives"**: *George, Being George*, ed. Nelson W. Aldrich Jr. (New York: Random House, 2008), 385.

719 **"warding off his assaults"**: "Roth Accepts 42nd MacDowell Medal," *MacDowell Colony Newsletter* 30, no. 2 (Winter–Spring 2002), 5.

720 **"Bill's suffering is over"**: PR—memo.

723 **"There's a word you use a lot"**: BB int. "Kaysie Wimberly," 13 July 2012.

726 **"I'm sorry. You were right"**: BB int. LH, 15 Oct. 2012.

726 **Reviews of *Exit Ghost*:** Michiko Kakutani, *New York Times*, 2 Oct. 2007; Christopher Hitchens, *Atlantic Monthly*, Oct. 2007; James Wood, *New Yorker*, 15 Oct. 2007.

728 **"a friend of both"**: Hermione Lee, "An Audience with Philip Roth," *Observer*, 6 Oct. 2007.

728 **"the 'candor' of intellectual 'equals'"**: Rachel Donadio, "Bio Engineering," *New York Times Book Review*, 4 Nov. 2007.

CHAPTER FORTY-SEVEN

730 **"too isolated, too insular"**: Carolyn Kellogg, "7 Reasons Why the Winner of the Nobel Prize in Literature Is a Belarusian You Don't Know," Los Angeles Times Jacket Copy, 8 Oct. 2015; https://www.latimes.com/books/jacketcopy/la-et-jc-7-reasons-nobel-prize-in-literature-unknown-20151008-story.html.

730 **"a superabundant pool"**: PR's citation for Cormac McCarthy, the 2009 winner of the PEN/Bellow Award, PRPP.

730 **"Dinner's ready, Portnoy!"**: Patricia Cohen, "Philip Roth, Provocateur, Is Celebrated at 75," *New York Times*, 12 Apr. 2008.

731   **"It seems like we planned this, Hermione"**: "Tribute to Philip Roth," C-SPAN, 11 Apr. 2008; https://www.c-span.org/video/?204924-1/tribute-philip-roth.

731   **"I was shocked by his performance"**: NSM.

731   **"I don't even think Gitta Sereny's moral assessment"**: Ibid.

732   **"This man is not your friend"**: Ibid.

734   **Reviews of *Indignation***: Malcolm Jones, *Newsweek*, 3 Nov. 2008, 75–76; Frank Kermode, *London Review of Books*, 23 Oct. 2008; David Gates, *New York Times Book Review*, 21 Sept. 2008.

735   **made amends within "six months" or "about a year"**: PR claimed the first in NSM, and the second during our interview on 12 Oct. 2013.

735   **"This is the greatest living writer"**: NSM.

736   **"His distinctive voice"**: PR's tribute to TS appeared in *New England Review* 30, no. 3 (2009), 24.

736   **"fucking fluency"**: PR to JU, 23 Dec. 1978, JU Papers, HU–HL.

736   **"delighted to accept"**: *RU*, 305.

737   **"Martha was very upset"**: PR to Adam Begley, 1 Dec. 2011.

737   **"A good woman wronged"**: Adam Begley, *Updike* (New York: HarperCollins, 2014), 279.

737   **"Allow me to imagine"**: PR, "Slight Revision," *New York Review of Books*, 4 Mar. 1999.

738   **"not only ungenerous but cruelly obtuse"**: PR to Begley, 1 Dec. 2011.

738   **"a cryptic smile"**: Mick Brown, "John Updike: Descent of Man," *Telegraph*, 26 Oct. 2008.

738   **"John Updike is our time's greatest man of letters"**: Christopher Lehmann-Haupt, "John Updike, a Lyrical Writer of the Middle-Class Man, Dies at 76," *New York Times*, 28 Jan. 2009.

739   **"biological twin"**: DP.

741   **Reviews of *The Humbling***: Michiko Kakutani, *New York Times*, 23 Oct. 2009; Kathryn Harrison, *New York Review of Books*, 15 Nov. 2009.

741   **"witty takedown"**: "Approval Matrix," *New York*, 30 Nov. 2009, 112.

742   **"We met at a dinner party"**: BB int. Susan Rogers, 24 Oct. 2014.

CHAPTER FORTY-EIGHT

744   **"I'll be obsessed when I'm eighty"**: *CPR*, 154.

744   **"That's a mystery"**: Jeffrey A. Trachtenberg, "Philip Roth Goes Back to College," *Wall Street Journal*, 12 Sept. 2008, W5.

747   **"know how to complicate it anymore"**: BB int. Claudia Roth Pierpont, 13 Mar. 2015.

747   **"I don't really have other interests"**: A. Alvarez, "The Long Road Home," *Guardian*, 10 Sept. 2004.

748   **"I know last night we had dinner"**: Livia Manera Sambuy, "You'll Never Write about Me Again," *Believer*, Jan.–Feb. 2015.

748   **"Give me subjects"**: BB int. Pierpont, 13 Mar. 2015.

748   **"a dose of fictional juice"**: Charles McGrath, "Goodbye, Frustration: Pen Put Aside, Roth Talks," *New York Times*, 17 Nov. 2012, 1.

748   **"an exercise in recollection"**: Tom Shone, "A Slim Volume Loosing Catastrophe," *These Violent Delights*, 25 Sept. 2010; http://tomshone.blogspot.com/2010/09/slim-volumes-loosing-catastrophe.html.

748 **"a triumphant return to high form"**: Jan Dalley, "Life after 'Nemesis,'" *Financial Times*, 24 June 2011.

749 **Reviews of *Nemesis***: Leah Hager Cohen, *New York Times Book Review*, 8 Oct. 2010, 1; Michiko Kakutani, *New York Times*, 4 Oct. 2010; J. M. Coetzee, *New York Review of Books*, 28 Oct. 2010.

749 **"largely to *avoid* accidentally"**: PR to Philip Glucksman, 16 Mar. 2012, PRPP.

749 **"the perfect narrator"**: PR to Jack Miles, 3 Oct. 2009, PR–LC.

750 **"maniac of the why"**: *RU*, 317.

750 **"psychological soundness"**: Ibid., 318.

750 **"they were just buried"**: Barbara Winard to PR, 19 Apr. 2009, PRPP.

751 **"because its associations to manliness"**: PR to Linda Forgosh, 27 Oct. 2010, PR–LC.

751 **"people who read serious books"**: David Remnick, "Into the Clear," *New Yorker*, 8 May 2000, 86.

751 **"gratifications of the screen"**: Josyane Savigneau, "Philip Roth: An Américain pas si tranquille," *Hors-Série Le Monde*, Feb.–Mar. 2013.

752 **"I have to get *some* pleasure"**: Dalley, "Life after 'Nemesis.'"

752 **"nasty, vacillating, and mired"**: JT, "Counterfeit Roth," *New Yorker*, 5 Apr. 2010.

752 **"How many young people"**: *Philip Roth Unleashed*, Part One, BBC *Imagine* documentary, 2014; https://www.youtube.com/watch?time_continue=1&v=Dh_tCH4ztRM.

753 **"stimulated, provoked and amused"**: Alison Flood, "Philip Roth Protest Had Nothing to Do with Feminism, Says Virago Founder," *Guardian*, 20 May 2011.

753 **"He goes on and on"**: Macy Halford, "Philip Roth and the Booker Judge," newyorker.com, 18 May 2011.

753 **"more than deserves the Booker"**: Toby Young, "Carmen Callil's Complaint Against Philip Roth," *Telegraph*, 19 May 2011.

754 **"Your former wife, Claire Bloom"**: *CBS Sunday Morning*, 2010; https://www.youtube.com/watch?v=9Vz7oUhqTQk.

754 **"He's not terribly politically correct"**: Jennifer Senior, "Roth Blows Up," *New York*, 1 May 2000.

755 **"surprisingly compassionate"**: Peter L. Rudnytsky, "True Confessions in *Operation Shylock*," *Philip Roth Studies* 3, no. 1 (Spring 2007), 27.

755 **"a deep and irrepressible rage"**: *LDH*, 145.

CHAPTER FORTY-NINE

759 **"mild congestive heart failure"**: PR to Hermione Lee, 4 Sept. 2011, PRPP.

759 **"Are you the coauthor"**: BB int. Dorothy Brand Slapcoff, 20 June 2013.

760 **"He is not St. Philip, Jane!"**: BB int. Jane Brown Maas, 11 Oct. 2012.

761 **"She was a little old white-haired lady"**: *RU*, 324.

761 **"I always had a higher opinion"**: BB int. Lucy Warner Kuemmerle, 10 Oct. 2012.

763 **"She had lost none of her beauty"**: Email from PR to BB, 4 Feb. 2016.

763 **"You're still my girl"**: PR to Barbara Solomon, 25 Apr. 2011, PR–LC.

764 **"I would have married her"**: Jane Maas, "St. Philip: Sixty-two Years with Philip Roth," *Bucknell Magazine*, Fall 2013.

764 **"love of his life"**: BB int. Susan Rogers, 24 Oct. 2014.

765 **"mainly from a provocation"**: *WW*, xi.

766 **"I understand your point"**: Ibid., 349.

766 **"hilarious screed"**: Remnick, "Philip Roth Says Enough," newyorker.com, 9 Nov. 2012.

766 **"He was my cynical big brother":** Quoted in Alan Cooper, *Philip Roth and the Jews* (Albany: SUNY Press, 1996), 4.

767 **"I should never have written":** PR to Hermione Lee, 14 Sept. 2012, PR–LC.

767 **"was more substantial":** Prachi Gupta, "Does Philip Roth Know What Inspired His Novel?," *Salon*, 19 Sept. 2012.

768 **"just another piece of support":** David Hadar, "Is Roth Really Done?," *Tablet*, 13 Nov. 2012.

768 **"Now I just listen":** PR's interview with *Weekend Edition* is from 23 Mar. 2013; https://www.npr.org/2013/03/23/174949848/at-80-philip-roth-reflects-on-life-literature-and-the-beauty-of-naps.

769 **"I don't want to read":** Nelly Kaprielian, "In Which Philip Roth Announces His Retirement (in English)," *Paris Review* blog, Nov. 13, 2012; https://www.theparisreview.org/blog/2012/11/13/in-which-philip-roth-announces-his-retirement-in-english/.

769 **"one last Möbius strip":** Adam Gopnik, "Happy Birthday," *New Yorker*, 18 Mar. 2013.

769 **"cheerful, relaxed and at peace":** Charles McGrath, "Goodbye, Frustration: Pen Put Aside, Roth Talks," *New York Times*, 17 Nov. 2012, 1.

769 **"I don't like the way":** "Literary Caucus: Salman Rushdie, James Franco, and 28 More Notables Assess Philip Roth's Career," *New York*, 4 Mar. 2013.

769 **"I'm happy he's still alive":** Emily Temple, "36 Famous Writers on Philip Roth's Retirement," *Flavorwire*, 30 Nov. 2012.

769 **"listening to his own funeral proceedings":** PR to Edward Hoagland, 21 Jan. 2013.

769 **"Has there ever been a cannier promoter":** "Writers Pick Their Favorite Philip Roth Novel," *Daily Beast*, 18 Dec. 2012.

770 **"Ah, Daphne sees right through":** PR to BB, 19 Dec. 2012.

770 **"When are you asking me?":** David Odegard, "The Roth I Know: A Q&A with the Director of 'Philip Roth: Unmasked,'" *Word and Film*, 26 Mar. 2013.

770 where he **"stole the show":** David L. Ulin, "Philip Roth in Pasadena (Sort of) Talks Career and Retirement," latimes.com, Jan. 15, 2013.

770 **"marvelous company":** A. O. Scott, "Looking Past the Alter Egos to the Novelist," *New York Times*, 12 Mar. 2013.

771 **"because I'm a goy":** Robert Wiener, "Book World Comes to Newark to Honor Roth on His 80th," *New Jersey Jewish News*, 26 Mar. 2013.

771 **"We should have met":** Livia Manera Sambuy, "You'll Never Write about Me Again," *Believer*, Jan.–Feb. 2015.

771 **"How would you feel":** Amy Ellis Nutt, "Jersey's Literary Lion Philip Roth Still Roars at 80," *Star-Ledger*, 20 Mar. 2013.

772 **"I had heard he was very private":** Ibid.

772 **"That this scholarly organization":** Steven G. Kellman, "Four Score and Philip Roth: A Dispatch from the Author's 80th Birthday," *Tablet*, 22 Mar. 2013.

772 **"accepted the honor of batting lead-off":** *PR@80*, 12.

772 **"There are no generalizations to be made":** Ibid., 31.

773 **"this is the tip of the iceberg":** Ibid., 49.

773 **"Tempting as it is":** Ibid., 51.

774 **"On top of all your millions of dollars":** *PO*, 576.

774 **"He had a reputation as a literary troublemaker":** Mike Vilensky, "High Honors for Author Philip Roth: Writer Receives France's Insignia of Commander of the Legion of Honor," *Wall Street Journal*, 1 Oct. 2013.

774   *"Je suis absolutement ravi"*: Colin DeVries, "Philip Roth Gets France's Highest Honor; French Will Open Public Bookstore in Embassy Building," New York *Daily News*, Page Views, 2 Oct. 2013.

775   **"Is Philip Roth an Anti-Semite?"**: Email from PR to Steve Zipperstein, 18 May 2014.

775   **"Roth has won"**: Jay Michaelson, "When He Was Good," *Forward*, 7 Dec. 2012.

776   **"the greatest sociologist"**: "Sacred and Profane: Philip Roth, Onetime 'Enfant Terrible,' Gets Seminary Honor," *Jewish Exponent*, 27 May 2014.

776   **"There he would sit"**: Emma Brockes, "The Real Scandal of Patrick Modiano's Nobel Win Is That Philip Roth Is a Huge Loser—Again," *Guardian*, 9 Oct. 2014.

777   **"retirement present"**: James Walton, "Give Philip Roth the Nobel Prize as a Retirement Present," *Telegraph*, 13 Nov. 2012.

777   **the whole thing "meaningless"**: Hephzibah Anderson, "Bookies Tout Murakami as Nobels Flirt with Literary Irrelevance," Bloomberg News, 9 Oct. 2012.

777   **"I wonder if I had called"**: PR's *Svenska Dagbladet* interview later appeared as "My Life as a Writer," *New York Times Book Review*, 16 Mar. 2014.

778   **"Step forward Jonathan Franzen!"**: Brockes, "The Real Scandal."

778   **"an impressive choice"**: "Philip Roth Emails Bob Dylan about His Nobel Win in a New Amy Rigby Song," *Slate*, 1 Dec. 2016.

778   **"It's okay, but next year I hope Peter, Paul and Mary get it"**: David Remnick, "Postscript: Philip Roth," *New Yorker*, 4–11 June 2018.

CHAPTER FIFTY

779   **"Going out with Philip Roth"**: Hermione Lee, "An Audience with Philip Roth," *Observer*, 6 Oct. 2007.

779   **"I know you!"**: BB int. Claudia Roth Pierpont, 13 Mar. 2015.

780   **"to fade forever from the public scene"**: PR to Edna O'Brien, 3 May 2013, PRPP.

780   **"The American novelist's indifference to"**: "My Life as a Writer," *New York Times Book Review*, 16 Mar. 2014.

780   **"Positively Last Appearance"**: PR to Steve Isenberg, 15 June 2013, PRPP.

780   **"felt more like a rock concert"**: Anne Margaret Daniel, "Philip Roth Reads One Last Time," *Huffington Post*, 14 May 2014.

781   **"You can write this down"**: Jennifer Schuessler, "Philip Roth Says He Has Given His Last Public Reading," *New York Times*, 9 May 2014.

782   **"Roth takes pride"**: Nadel's essay was faxed to Roth as an unpublished typescript; it later appeared in *Roth and Celebrity* (Lanham, Md.: Lexington Books, 2012).

783   **he "faithfully reproduced 'all the noises'"**: Nicholas Rapold, "Eternal Regard for a Self-Obsessed Id," *New York Times*, 12 Oct. 2014.

783   **"I remember saying"**: Pacino's interview, dated 10 Dec. 2014, is posted at https://www.youtube.com/watch?v=Y8x-7Lihpf4.

784   **"A writer who stops writing"**: "Philip Roth Tells French Publication He's Done Writing Books," Associated Press, 9 Nov. 2012.

784   **"full of quiet pleasure"**: PR to Catherine Camus, 23 Jan. 2014, PRPP.

784   **"light-filled apartment"**: PR to Edna O'Brien, 8 Apr. 2014, PRPP.

785   **"he could barely drag his walker"**: Luye Lui's undelivered eulogy for PR.

785   **"Three things I don't do anymore"**: BB int. Freya Manfred, 3 Aug. 2013.

786   **"wild turkey perched on the stone wall"**: PR to Susan Jacoby, 15 June 2013.

787   **"caused a mini-uproar"**: Christopher Rosen, "Mia Farrow's 'Sharknado' Tweet with Photo of Philip Roth Was a Joke," *Huffington Post*, 12 July 2013.

787 **"absolutely unprecedented"**: BB int. Bernard Rodgers, 17 Nov. 2015.

791 **"He was an inspiring figure"**: Bruce Weber, "Richard G. Stern, Writers' Writer, Dies at 84," *New York Times*, 24 Jan. 2013.

793 **"I know perfectly well who you are"**: Email from PR to BB, 28 Jan. 2016.

793 **"that generations of foreign readers"**: James McAuley, "Philip Roth Is France's Newest Literary Superstar. Why?," *Washington Post*, 27 Oct. 2017.

794 **"nightmare now in America"**: PR to Josyane Savigneau, 2 Sept. 2017, PRPP.

795 **"You will go on to have a baby"**: Email from LH to BB, 19 Apr. 2017.

797 **"I have been to see the great enemy"**: Ben Taylor's remarks at PR's memorial, 25 Sept. 2018.

797 **"Do you mean to tell me, Julia"**: Email from Julia Golier to BB, 27 Oct. 2019.

EPILOGUE

799 **"How should those obtuse"**: Cynthia Ozick, "In Praise of Zest and Laughter," *Wall Street Journal*, 26 May 2018.

799 **"I buried an ex-wife"**: Email from Russ Murdock to BB, 16 Aug. 2018.

800 **"not enough legroom"**: *RU*, 190.

800 **"quiet neighbors" and "nice setback"**: JT's eulogy at PR's memorial, 25 Sept. 2018.

801 **"I think Roth died from *grief*"**: Paige Williams, "Reading Philip Roth after the Pittsburgh Massacre," *New Yorker*, 12 Nov. 2018.

801 **"It is strange (to put it politely)"**: *RMO*, 177.

802 **"We think the Newark Public Library"**: Charles McGrath, "A Scene Right Out of Philip Roth: His Books Come Home to Newark's Library," *New York Times*, 25 Oct. 2016.

802 **"It is a splendid"**: "America Across the River," *The Economist*, 5 Nov. 2016.

805 **"I got many wonderful things"**: Jane Graham, "The Loves and Lives of Claire Bloom," www.bigissue.com, 29 Jan. 2013.

805 **"so afraid of dying"**: Email from CB to Martin Garbus, 24 May 2018.

805 **"You wrote with anger, Claire"**: CB's appearance on *BBC Newsnight*, 23 May 2018; https://www.bbc.co.uk/programmes/p0682t0y.

806 **"encompasses and transcends modes"**: *PR@80*, 12.

806 **"He sat on a train"**: David Plante, *Worlds Apart* (London: Bloomsbury, 2015), 108.

807 **"There was nothing that could ever equal"**: *AL*, 421.

807 **"It's love, love, love, love, love, love"**: Christopher Sykes int. PR, c. Jan. 2011, *Web of Stories*; https://www.webofstories.com/play/philip.roth/163;jsessionid=D0BACA0FCA9249DA3AFFE99EA679C00C.

INDEX

Page numbers in *italics* refer to photographs.